THE
EXPERIENCE OF LITERATURE

THE
EXPERIENCE
OF LITERATURE

A READER WITH COMMENTARIES

LIONEL TRILLING

Doubleday & Company, Inc.
Garden City, New York
1967

COPYRIGHT ACKNOWLEDGMENTS

CITY LIGHTS BOOKS
for Allen Ginsberg, "A Supermarket in California" from *HOWL and Other Poems,* copyright 1956, 1959 by Allen Ginsberg; and "To Aunt Rose" from *KADDISH and Other Poems,* copyright 1961 by Allen Ginsberg. Reprinted by permission of City Lights Books.

COLLINS-KNOWLTON-WING, INC.
for Robert Graves, "Warning to Children" and "To Juan at the Winter Solstice" from *Collected Poems of Robert Graves,* Doubleday and Company. Reprinted by permission of Collins-Knowlton-Wing, Inc., copyright © 1955 by International Authors, N.V.

CORRIGAN, ROBERT W.
for *The Three Sisters* by Anton Chekhov from *Six Plays of Chekhov,* Holt, Rinehart and Winston, edited and translated by Robert W. Corrigan, copyright © 1962 by Robert W. Corrigan. All rights reserved: no public or private performance of the plays, professional or amateur, may be given, no film, radio or television use or public reading, without authorization from Literary Discoveries, Inc., 604 Mission Street, San Francisco 5, Calif.

J. M. DENT & SONS LTD.
for Joseph Conrad, "The Secret Sharer," reprinted by permission of J. M. Dent & Sons Ltd. and the Trustees of the Joseph Conrad Estate.
for Dylan Thomas, "The Force that through the Green Fuse," "Do Not Go Gentle into that Good Night," "In My Craft or Sullen Art," and "Fern Hill" from *The Collected Poems of Dylan Thomas,* copyright 1953 by Dylan Thomas, published by New Directions, reprinted in Canada by the permission of J. M. Dent & Sons Ltd. and the Literary Executors of the Dylan Thomas Estate.

DODD, MEAD & COMPANY, INC.
for George Bernard Shaw, *The Doctor's Dilemma,* copyright 1911, 1913, 1930, 1941 by George Bernard Shaw. Copyright 1957 by The Public Trustee as Executor of the Estate of George Bernard Shaw. Reprinted by permission of Dodd, Mead & Co., Inc. and The Public Trustee (and The Society of Authors for reprinting in Canada).

DOUBLEDAY & COMPANY, INC.
for Theodore Roethke, "Frau Bauman, Frau Schmidt, and Frau Schwartze," copyright 1952 by Theodore Roethke. From the book *Words for the Wind* by Theodore Roethke. Reprinted by permission of Doubleday & Company, Inc. And for Theodore Roethke, "The Far Field," copyright © 1963 by Beatrice Roethke as Administratrix of the Estate of Theodore Roethke; and "Light Listened," copyright © 1964 by Beatrice Roethke as Administratrix of the Estate of Theodore Roethke, from the book *The Far Field* by Theodore Roethke. Reprinted by permission of Doubleday & Company, Inc.
for Rudyard Kipling, "Recessional" and "Danny Deever" from *Rudyard Kipling's Verse: Definitive Edition.* Reprinted by permission of Mrs. George Bambridge and Doubleday & Company, Inc.
for W. Somerset Maugham, "The Treasure," copyright 1934 by W. Somerset Maugham from the book *The Mixture As Before* by W. Somerset Maugham. Reprinted by permission of Doubleday & Company, Inc.

DOWNER, ALAN S.
for the notes on William Shakespeare's *King Lear* from *Shakespeare, Five Plays,* Holt, Rinehart and Winston, edited and notes by Alan S. Downer, copyright 1951 by Alan S. Downer and reprinted with his permission.

INTRODUCTION

THE INTRODUCTION to a book that deals with literature in general might naturally propose the question of why we read literature, of what use it is in our lives. The question is as engaging as it is natural—it has the allure of all questions that cannot be answered, not really answered. For a satisfactory explanation of why we read literature, a truly adequate account of the purposes it serves, must amount to nothing less than a description of the whole nature of man.

Partial answers can of course be given. The practitioner of one or another of the so-called behavioral sciences—the psychologist, the psychoanalyst, the sociologist—will tell us that we read literature because we want to escape from a harsh or dull reality to a pleasant or interesting fantasy, or to justify unlicensed hidden impulses, or to gain a measure of relief from or control over these impulses. The humanistic educator tells us that certain good things happen if we read literature, and he makes this the ground for saying we *should* do so—because we will be rewarded by an increased awareness, a heightened sensibility, a finer moral perception.

All this is true and worth saying. And the list of reasons could go on to be much longer, for literature serves all kinds of purposes, varying with different cultures, with different groups in the same culture, with individuals in the same group, with the age and emotional circumstance of individuals. Yet in the end the sum of all reasons that might be adduced does not really give us an entire explanation. Just so we do not understand why people engage in a sport when we have enumerated the benefits their activity is commonly said to bring. That it keeps one fit, that it distracts the mind from its troubles, that it affords an opportunity for the harmless release of aggressive and competitive impulses, that it gratifies pride—none of these, nor all of them together, come anywhere near suggesting why the skier is drawn to the slopes, the fisherman to the stream, the tennis-player to the court. In each case the attraction is finally gratuitous, lying beyond the reach of explanation. The same is to be said of artistic creation. If we were to ask, say, a poet why he engages in his enterprise and if he were to consent to answer (as perhaps he would not, finding the question absurd), he might grant that the love of fame or the hope of money or the wish to advance a certain view of life had some part in what he did, but the only answer that would seem to him to make sense was that he wrote poetry because he was a poet.

And to the question of why we read literature we must give a cognate answer, which is no answer: because we are human. Especially when we have it in mind that in every stage of culture, down to the simplest that we know, men make and experience what in our culture is called literature, that no aboriginal tribe, not the most primitive, is without its stories and poems to which a considerable value is assigned, we must recognize that the making and the experience of literature is what the zoologists call a species-characteristic trait of mankind.

But if this is so, another question at once proposes itself. If literature is that natural why need it be taught and studied? It is a question that is often put with some asperity, out of the sense that the processes of teaching and study, whether they go on in the classroom or in writing and reading literary scholarship and criticism, have the effect of interfering with the simple act of reading, that they make abstract and all too self-conscious what should of its nature be spontaneous and immediate. If the experience of literature is in fact what I have called it, a species-characteristic trait of mankind, then surely the pedagogical or scholarly or critical discourse that goes on about it is not necessary.

The objection has its cogency. And a teacher of literature may be quite as disposed to make it as anyone else; there are moments when it seems to him—when it seems to me—that all the discourse that goes on in the classroom and in essays and books is beside the point, that all this secondary activity is obtruding itself upon the primary activity of reading literature, and getting in its way. But although it is true that discourse about literature can on occasion become excessive and have the effect of dulling and obscuring what it is intended to illuminate, it is also true that talking about literature is as natural as producing and reading it. The literary experience is communal—it asks to be shared in discourse. In any developed culture the urge to say things about what we have read and to take account of what others say about it is no less natural than the creation and enjoyment of the art. The Florentines of the fifteenth century were not exactly a people given to abstractness or pedantic intellectuality, yet when they wanted to honor their most famous local poet fifty years after his death, they thought that the most appropriate way to do this was to institute a series of public discourses on his great poem, and the person they invited to lecture on Dante's *Divine Comedy* was not a university professor—at that time Florence did not have what we would call a university—but Boccaccio.

We find a pleasure that seems instinctual not only in the emotions that are aroused by what we read but also in communicating them to each other, in trying to understand why we feel as we do, in testing our emotions by those that others tell us that they have, in discovering what we might possibly feel beyond what we do feel. And discourse leads to dialectic: we disagree with others in observation and response and in the general principles that we and they have been led to formulate. This activity, in itself interesting and pleasant, increases the interest and pleasure of our private experience.

This will explain why in this anthology, following each of the plays and stories and certain of the poems, I have provided commentaries in the form of brief essays. They have one purpose only—to make it more likely that the act of reading will be an experience, having in mind what the word implies of an activity of consciousness and response. They try to suggest that the work of literature is an object that may be freely touched and handled, picked up, turned over, looked at from this angle or that, and, at least in some sense, possessed.

No special theory of literature or method of criticism informs what I have written. In some of the commentaries the emphasis falls on formal and technical matters—such as imagery, tone, point of view, versification, diction, and so on—that the reader ought to be aware of. Others deal with literary conventions that, whether because they are old or because they are new, the reader might not be familiar with. I have felt free to discuss the overt or implicit meanings of a work and to pursue (and sometimes to question) its moral or social or religious ideas. Where I have thought it useful to refer to critical theories or standards of taste of the past, I have done so. Although my concern is always with the work itself and not with the biographical or historical circumstances in which it was written, if a circumstance of biography or history seems to be to the point, I have adduced it. In short, I have availed myself of any of the elements of literary discourse that I have thought relevant to the work and likely to make it more accessible or interesting to the reader.

The commentaries could hardly say all there is to be said about the works to which they address themselves; and I have tried to have them say no more than might suggest to the reader how he could come into a more active connection with what he has read. It will be seen, I think, that they do not impose themselves as anything like doctrine, or limit in any way the reader's autonomy of response: they will not have failed of their purpose—on the contrary!—if they arouse the reader to disagreement.

Literature is a continuous enterprise and in choosing the works to be included in this anthology I have included on an equal footing both the traditional and the new. I have preferred those works that I thought would prove memorable to the reader by reason of their momentousness or their force of dramatic or intellectual energy. That a work has already proved memorable to many is always a special recommendation: not all the works I have chosen are "great" but I have made preponderant those to which the adjective might be applied.

The examples of each genre are arranged chronologically, although there are a few violations of this order for particular indicated reasons. The plays and stories have been drawn from several literatures, with due regard to the accuracy of the translations in which they appear. Because the adequate translation of poems is a virtually hopeless enterprise, the poems included are all English and American. Although the selection of poems for further reading is large, it does not pretend to be canonical, and this is especially to be said of the selection of contemporary poets. It is perhaps here that I should remark that I have thought it best that the poets of our own time who are included in this section of the anthology should be read without footnotes.

New York, N.Y.   L.T.
January, 1967

CONTENTS

PART 3: POETRY

PART 4: POETRY FOR FURTHER READING

PART

1 DRAMA

OEDIPUS REX

SOPHOCLES

496–406 B.C.

PERSONS REPRESENTED

OEDIPUS

A PRIEST

KREON

TEIRESIAS

IOKASTE

MESSENGER

SHEPHERD OF LAÏOS

SECOND MESSENGER

CHORUS OF THEBAN ELDERS

SCENE

Before the palace of Oedipus, King of Thebes. A central door and two lateral doors open onto a platform which runs the length of the façade. On the platform, right and left, are altars; and three steps lead down into the "orchêstra," or chorus-ground. At the beginning of the action these steps are crowded by suppliants who have brought branches and chaplets of olive leaves and who sit in various attitudes of despair. OEDIPUS *enters.*

3

OEDIPUS.   My children, generations of the living
In the line of Kadmos,[1] nursed at his ancient hearth:
Why have you strewn yourselves before these altars
In supplication, with your boughs and garlands?
The breath of incense rises from the city
With a sound of prayer and lamentation.

                         Children,
I would not have you speak through messengers,
And therefore I have come myself to hear you—
I, Oedipus, who bear the famous name.

[*To a* PRIEST.] You, there, since you are eldest in the company,
Speak for them all, tell me what preys upon you,
Whether you come in dread, or crave some blessing:
Tell me, and never doubt that I will help you
In every way I can; I should be heartless
Were I not moved to find you suppliant here.
    PRIEST.   Great Oedipus, O powerful king of Thebes!
You see how all the ages of our people
Cling to your altar steps: here are boys
Who can barely stand alone, and here are priests
By weight of age, as I am a priest of God,
And young men chosen from those yet unmarried;
As for the others, all that multitude,
They wait with olive chaplets[2] in the squares,
At the two shrines of Pallas,[3] and where Apollo[4]
Speaks in the glowing embers.

                        Your own eyes
Must tell you: Thebes is tossed on a murdering sea
And can not lift her head from the death surge.
A rust consumes the buds and fruits of the earth;
The herds are sick; children die unborn,
And labor is vain. The god of plague and pyre
Raids like detestable lightning through the city,
And all the house of Kadmos is laid waste,

---

[1] Legendary founder of Thebes. This text of the play uses a transliteration of proper names that often differs from common usage. More frequently seen spellings are Cadmus, Creon, Tiresias, Jocasta (or Iocasta), Laius, Menoeceus, Phoebus, Athena, Bacchus, Dionysus, Polydorus, Cithaeron, Parnassus, Polybus, Phocis, Lycia, Cyllene, Polyneices, Eteocles.

[2] Wreaths of olive branches to be worn on the head; the olive symbolized peace.

[3] Pallas Athenê, goddess of war, handicraft, and wisdom and patron goddess of Athens.

[4] God of light and healing, among other things; one of the principal Greek gods. Apollo was thought to speak through the oracle at Delphi, where a priestess muttered incomprehensibly and was interpreted by priests or seers.

All emptied, and all darkened: Death alone
Battens upon the misery of Thebes.

You are not one of the immortal gods, we know;
Yet we have come to you to make our prayer
As to the man surest in mortal ways
And wisest in the ways of God. You saved us
From the Sphinx,[5] that flinty singer, and the tribute
We paid to her so long; yet you were never
Better informed than we, nor could we teach you:
A god's touch, it seems, enabled you to help us.

Therefore, O mighty power, we turn to you:
Find us our safety, find us a remedy,
Whether by counsel of the gods or of men.
A king of wisdom tested in the past
Can act in a time of troubles, and act well.
Noblest of men, restore
Life to your city! Think how all men call you
Liberator for your boldness long ago;
Ah, when your years of kingship are remembered,
Let them not say *We rose, but later fell*—
Keep the State from going down in the storm!
Once, years ago, with happy augury,
You brought us fortune; be the same again!
No man questions your power to rule the land:
But rule over men, not over a dead city!
Ships are only hulls, high walls are nothing,
When no life moves in the empty passageways.

    OEDIPUS.   Poor children! You may be sure I know
All that you longed for in your coming here.
I know that you are deathly sick; and yet,
Sick as you are, not one is as sick as I.
Each of you suffers in himself alone
His anguish, not another's; but my spirit
Groans for the city, for myself, for you.

I was not sleeping, you are not waking me.
No, I have been in tears for a long while
And in my restless thought walked many ways.
In all my search I found one remedy,
And I have adopted it: I have sent Kreon,

---

[5] A monster that, according to legend, had plagued Thebes, singing the riddle, "What is it that walks on four legs in the morning, on two at midday, and on three in the evening?" Those who could not answer were devoured, but Oedipus, when asked, promptly replied, "Man, for he crawls in infancy, walks erect in maturity, and uses a staff in old age." This was the correct answer, and the Sphinx, on receiving it, destroyed herself. Kreon, who acted as regent of Thebes after the death of her king, Laïos, then offered Oedipus the throne and the hand of Iokaste, Laïos' widow and Kreon's sister.

Son of Menoikeus, brother of the Queen,
To Delphi, Apollo's place of revelation,
To learn there, if he can,
What act or pledge of mine may save the city.
I have counted the days, and now, this very day,
I am troubled, for he has overstayed his time.
What is he doing? He has been gone too long.
Yet whenever he comes back, I should do ill
Not to take any action the god orders.

  PRIEST. It is a timely promise. At this instant
They tell me Kreon is here.

  OEDIPUS.   O Lord Apollo!
May his news be fair as his face is radiant!

  PRIEST. Good news, I gather: he is crowned with bay,[6]
The chaplet is thick with berries.

  OEDIPUS.   We shall soon know;
He is near enough to hear us now. [*Enter* KREON]
        O Prince:
Brother: son of Menoikeus:
What answer do you bring us from the God?

  KREON. A strong one. I can tell you, great afflictions
Will turn out well, if they are taken well.

  OEDIPUS. What was the oracle? These vague words
Leave me still hanging between hope and fear.

  KREON. Is it your pleasure to hear me with all these
Gathered around us? I am prepared to speak,
But should we not go in?

  OEDIPUS.   Speak to them all.
It is for them I suffer, more than for myself.

  KREON. Then I will tell you what I heard at Delphi.
In plain words
The god commands us to expel from the land of Thebes
An old defilement we are sheltering.
It is a deathly thing, beyond cure;
We must not let it feed upon us longer

  OEDIPUS. What defilement? How shall we rid ourselves of it?

  KREON. By exile or death, blood for blood. It was
Murder that brought the plague-wind on the city.

  OEDIPUS. Murder of whom? Surely the god has named him?

  KREON. My lord: Laïos once ruled this land,
Before you came to govern us.

  OEDIPUS.   I know;
I learned of him from others; I never saw him.

  KREON. He was murdered; and Apollo commands us now
To take revenge upon whoever killed him.

  OEDIPUS. Upon whom? Where are they? Where shall we find a clue
To solve that crime, after so many years?

  [6] Laurel, an emblem of victory or excellence.

KREON.   Here in this land, he said. Search reveals
Things that escape an inattentive man.
    OEDIPUS.   Tell me: Was Laïos murdered in his house,
Or in the fields, or in some foreign country?
    KREON.   He said he planned to make a pilgrimage.
He did not come home again.
    OEDIPUS.   And was there no one,
No witness, no companion, to tell what happened?
    KREON.   They were all killed but one, and he got away
So frightened that he could remember one thing only.
    OEDIPUS.   What was that one thing? One may be the key
To everything, if we resolve to use it.
    KREON.   He said that a band of highwaymen attacked them,
Outnumbered them, and overwhelmed the King.
    OEDIPUS.   Strange, that a highwayman should be so daring—
Unless some faction here bribed him to do it.
    KREON.   We thought of that. But after Laïos' death
New troubles arose and we had no avenger.
    OEDIPUS.   What troubles could prevent your hunting down the killers?
    KREON.   The riddling Sphinx's song
Made us deaf to all mysteries but her own.
    OEDIPUS.   Then once more I must bring what is dark to light.
It is most fitting that Apollo shows,
As you do, this compunction for the dead.
You shall see how I stand by you, as I should,
Avenging this country and the god as well,
And not as though it were for some distant friend,
But for my own sake, to be rid of evil.
Whoever killed King Laïos might—who knows?—
Lay violent hands even on me—and soon.
I act for the murdered king in my own interest.

Come, then, my children: leave the altar steps,
Lift up your olive boughs!
                    One of you go
And summon the people of Kadmos to gather here.
I will do all that I can; you may tell them that. [*Exit a* PAGE.]
So, with the help of God,
We shall be saved—or else indeed we are lost.
    PRIEST.   Let us rise, children. It was for this we came,
And now the King has promised it.
Phoibos[7] has sent us an oracle; may he descend
Himself to save us and drive out the plague.
[*Exeunt* OEDIPUS *and* KREON *into the palace by the central door. The* PRIEST
and the SUPPLIANTS *disperse right and left. After a short pause the* CHORUS
                    enters the orchêstra.]

    [7] Phoibus Apollo.

CHORUS.   What is God[9] singing in his profound   [STROPHE I]
Delphi of gold and shadow?
What oracle for Thebes, the sunwhipped[10] city?

Fear unjoints me, the roots of my heart tremble.

Now I remember, O Healer, your power and wonder:
Will you send doom like a sudden cloud, or weave it
Like nightfall of the past?

Speak to me, tell me, O
Child of golden Hope, immortal Voice.

Let me pray to Athenê, the immortal daughter of Zeus,   [ANTISTROPHE I]
And to Artemis her sister
Who keeps her famous throne in the market ring,[11]

And to Apollo, archer from distant heaven—[12]

O gods, descend! Like three streams leap against
The fires of our grief, the fires of darkness;
Be swift to bring us rest!

As in the old time from the brilliant house
Of air you stepped to save us, come again!

Now our afflictions have no end,   [STROPHE 2]
Now all our stricken host lies down
And no man fights off death with his mind;

The noble plowland bears no grain,
And groaning mothers can not bear—

See, how our lives like birds take wing,
Like sparks that fly when a fire soars,
To the shore of the god of evening.[13]

The plague burns on, it is pitiless,   [ANTISTROPHE 2]
Though pallid children laden with death
Lie unwept in the stony ways,

And old gray women by every path
Flock to the strand about the altars

---

[8] This is an ode chanted by the Chorus, who remain on stage hereafter and comment, always in chanted odes, on the action of the play. When the Chorus participates in the actual dialogue, only its leader (Choragos) speaks, but he speaks for the entire group.

[9] Apollo, worship of whom sometimes approached monotheism.

[10] Whipped by Apollo, who was sometimes identified with the Sun-god.

[11] Artemis was the goddess of hunting; she was usually associated with forests and hills, where wild animals predominate, but was sometimes thought of as a city goddess.

[12] Apollo was also the god of archery.

[13] Death.

There to strike their breasts and cry
Worship of Phoibos in wailing prayers:
Be kind, God's golden child!

There are no swords in this attack by fire,   [STROPHE 3]
No shields, but we are ringed with cries.

Send the besieger plunging from our homes
Into the vast sea-room of the Atlantic
Or into the waves that foam eastward of Thrace—[14]

For the day ravages what the night spares—

Destroy our enemy, lord of the thunder!
Let him be riven by lightning from heaven!

Phoibos Apollo, stretch the sun's bowstring,   [ANTISTROPHE 3]
That golden cord, until it sing for us,
Flashing arrows in heaven!
                    Artemis, Huntress,
Race with flaring lights upon our mountains!

O scarlet god, O golden-banded brow,
O Theban Bacchos[15] in a storm of Maenads,[16] [*Enter* OEDIPUS, *center.*]
Whirl upon Death, that all the Undying hate!
Come with blinding torches, come in joy!

SCENE I

OEDIPUS.   Is this your prayer? It may be answered. Come,
Listen to me, act as the crisis demands,
And you shall have relief from all these evils.

Until now I was a stranger to this tale,
As I had been a stranger to the crime.
Could I track down the murderer without a clue?
But now, friends,
As one who became a citizen after the murder,
I make this proclamation to all Thebans:

If any man knows by whose hand Laïos, son of Labdakos,
Met his death, I direct that man to tell me everything,
No matter what he fears for having so long withheld it.
Let it stand as promised that no further trouble
Will come to him, but he may leave the land in safety.

Moreover: If anyone knows the murderer to be foreign,
Let him not keep silent: he shall have his reward from me.

---

[14] The eastern half of the Balkan Peninsula.
[15] Dionysos; god of wine who is frequently represented with a scarlet face.
[16] Female attendants of Dionysos who were inspired to ecstatic frenzy by the god.

However, if he does conceal it; if any man
Fearing for his friend or for himself disobeys this edict,
Hear what I propose to do:

I solemnly forbid the people of this country,
Where power and throne are mine, ever to receive that man
Or speak to him, no matter who he is, or let him
Join in sacrifice, lustration, or in prayer.
I decree that he be driven from every house,
Being, as he is, corruption itself to us: the Delphic
Voice of Apollo has pronounced this revelation.
Thus I associate myself with the oracle
And take the side of the murdered king.

As for the criminal, I pray to God—
Whether it be a lurking thief, or one of a number—
I pray that that man's life be consumed in evil and wretchedness.
And as for me, this curse applies no less
If it should turn out that the culprit is my guest here,
Sharing my hearth.
                          You have heard the penalty.

I lay it on you now to attend to this
For my sake, for Apollo's, for the sick
Sterile city that heaven has abandoned.
Suppose the oracle had given you no command:
Should this defilement go uncleansed for ever?
You should have found the murderer: your king,
A noble king, had been destroyed!
                          Now I,
Having the power that he held before me,
Having his bed, begetting children there
Upon his wife, as he would have, had he lived—
Their son would have been my children's brother,
If Laïos had had luck in fatherhood!
(And now his bad fortune has struck him down)—
I say I take the son's part, just as though
I were his son, to press the fight for him
And see it won! I'll find the hand that brought
Death to Labdakos' and Polydoros' child,
Heir of Kadmos' and Agenor's line.
And as for those who fail me,
May the gods deny them the fruit of the earth,
Fruit of the womb, and may they rot utterly!
Let them be wretched as we are wretched, and worse!

For you, for loyal Thebans, and for all
Who finds my actions right, I pray the favor
Of justice, and of all the immortal gods.

    CHORAGOS.   Since I am under oath, my lord, I swear
I did not do the murder, I can not name

The murderer. Phoibos ordained the search;
Why did he not say who the culprit was?

    OEDIPUS.   An honest question. But no man in the world
Can make the gods do more than the gods will.

    CHORAGOS.   There is an alternative, I think—

    OEDIPUS.   Tell me.
Any or all, you must not fail to tell me.

    CHORAGOS.   A lord clairvoyant[17] to the lord Apollo,
As we all know, is the skilled Teiresias.
One might learn much about this from him, Oedipus.

    OEDIPUS.   I am not wasting time:
Kreon spoke of this, and I have sent for him—
Twice, in fact; it is strange that he is not here.

    CHORAGOS.   The other matter—that old report—seems useless.

    OEDIPUS.   What was that? I am interested in all reports.

    CHORAGOS.   The King was said to have been killed by highwaymen.

    OEDIPUS.   I know. But we have no witnesses to that.

    CHORAGOS.   If the killer can feel a particle of dread,
Your curse will bring him out of hiding!

    OEDIPUS.   No.
The man who dared that act will fear no curse.

                   [*Enter the blind seer* TEIRESIAS, *led by a* PAGE.]

    CHORAGOS.   But there is one man who may detect the criminal.
This is Teirsias, this is the holy prophet
In whom, alone of all men, truth was born.

    OEDIPUS.   Teiresias: seer: student of mysteries,
Of all that's taught and all that no man tells,
Secrets of Heaven and secrets of the earth:
Blind though you are, you know the city lies
Sick with plague; and from this plague, my lord,
We find that you alone can guard or save us.

Possibly you did not hear the messengers?
Apollo, when we sent to him,
Sent us back word that this great pestilence
Would lift, but only if we established clearly
The identity of those who murdered Laïos.
They must be killed or exiled.

                   Can you use
Birdflight[18] or any art of divination
To purify yourself, and Thebes, and me
From this contagion? We are in your hands.
There is no fairer duty
Than that of helping others in distress.

    TEIRESIAS.   How dreadful knowledge of the truth can be
When there's no help in truth! I knew this well,
But did not act on it: else I should not have come.

    [17] Seer or priest.
    [18] Augurs observed the flight and behavior of birds, which supposedly revealed the future or the forgotten or unknown past.

OEDIPUS.   What is troubling you? Why are your eyes so cold?

TEIRESIAS.   Let me go home. Bear your own fate, and I'll
Bear mine. It is better so: trust what I say.

OEDIPUS.   What you say is ungracious and unhelpful
To your native country. Do not refuse to speak.

TEIRESIAS.   When it comes to speech, your own is neither temperate
Nor opportune. I wish to be more prudent.

OEDIPUS.   In God's name, we all beg you—

TEIRESIAS.   You are all ignorant.
No; I will never tell you what I know.
Now it is my misery; then, it would be yours.

OEDIPUS.   What! You do know something, and will not tell us?
You would betray us and wreck the State?

TEIRESIAS.   I do not intend to torture myself, or you.
Why persist in asking? You will not persuade me.

OEDIPUS.   What a wicked old man you are! You'd try a stone's
Patience! Out with it! Have you no feeling at all?

TEIRESIAS.   You call me unfeeling. If you could only see
The nature of your own feelings . . .

OEDIPUS.   Why,
Who would not feel as I do? Who could endure
Your arrogance toward the city?

TEIRESIAS.   What does it matter?
Whether I speak or not, it is bound to come.

OEDIPUS.   Then, if 'it' is bound to come, you are bound to tell me.

TEIRESIAS.   No, I will not go on. Rage as you please.

OEDIPUS.   Rage? Why not!

                              And I'll tell you what I think:
You planned it, you had it done, you all but
Killed him with your own hands: if you had eyes,
I'd say the crime was yours, and yours alone.

TEIRESIAS.   So? I charge you, then,
Abide by the proclamation you have made:
From this day forth
Never speak again to these men or to me;
You yourself are the pollution of this country.

OEDIPUS.   You dare say that! Can you possibly think you have
Some way of going free, after such insolence?

TEIRESIAS.   I have gone free. It is the truth sustains me.

OEDIPUS.   Who taught you shamelessness? It was not your craft.

TEIRESIAS.   You did. You made me speak. I did not want to.

OEDIPUS.   Speak what? Let me hear it again more clearly.

TEIRESIAS.   Was it not clear before? Are you tempting me?

OEDIPUS.   I did not understand. Say it again.

TEIRESIAS.   I say that you are the murderer whom you seek.

OEDIPUS.   Now twice you have spat out infamy. You'll pay for it!

TEIRESIAS.   Would you care for more? Do you wish to be really angry?

OEDIPUS.   Say what you will. Whatever you say is worthless.

TEIRESIAS.   I say you live in hideous shame with those
Most dear to you. You can not see the evil.
        OEDIPUS.   Can you go on babbling like this for ever?
        TEIRESIAS.   I can, if there is power in truth.
        OEDIPUS.   There is:
But not for you, not for you,
You sightless, witless, senseless, mad old man!
        TEIRESIAS.   You are the madman. There is no one here
Who will not curse you soon, as you curse me.
        OEDIPUS.   You child of total night! I would not touch you;
Neither would any man who sees the sun.
        TEIRESIAS.   True: it is not from you my fate will come.
That lies within Apollo's competence,
As it is his concern.
        OEDIPUS.   Tell me, who made
These fine discoveries? Kreon? or someone else?
        TEIRESIAS.   Kreon is no threat. You weave your own doom.
        OEDIPUS.   Wealth, power, craft of statesmanship!
Kingly position, everywhere admired!
What savage envy is stored up against these,
If Kreon, whom I trusted, Kreon my friend,
For this great office which the city once
Put in my hands unsought—if for this power
Kreon desires in secret to destroy me!

He has bought this decrepit fortune-teller, this
Collector of dirty pennies, this prophet fraud—
Why, he is no more clairvoyant than I am!
                                Tell us:
Has your mystic mummery ever approached the truth?
When that hellcat the Sphinx was performing here,
What help were you to these people?
Her magic was not for the first man who came along:
It demanded a real exorcist. Your birds—
What good were they? or the gods, for the matter of that?
But I came by,
Oedipus, the simple man, who knows nothing—
I thought it out for myself, no birds helped me!
And this is the man you think you can destroy,
That you may be close to Kreon when he's king!
Well, you and your friend Kreon, it seems to me,
Will suffer most. If you were not an old man,
You would have paid already for your plot.
        CHORAGOS.   We can not see that his words or yours
Have been spoken except in anger, Oedipus,
And of anger we have no need. How to accomplish
The god's will best: that is what most concerns us.
        TEIRESIAS.   You are a king. But where argument's concerned
I am your man, as much a king as you.

I am not your servant, but Apollo's.
I have no need of Kreon's name.

Listen to me. You mock my blindness, do you?
But I say that you, with both your eyes, are blind:
You can not see the wretchedness of your life,
Nor in whose house you live, no, nor with whom.
Who are your father and mother? Can you tell me?
You do not even know the blind wrongs
That you have done them, on earth and in the world below.
But the double lash of your parents' curse will whip you
Out of this land some day, with only night
Upon your precious eyes.
Your cries then—where will they not be heard?
What fastness of Kithairon[19] will not echo them?
And that bridal-descant of yours—you'll know it then,
The song they sang when you came here to Thebes
And found your misguided berthing.
All this, and more, that you can not guess at now,
Will bring you to yourself among your children.

Be angry, then. Curse Kreon. Curse my words.
I tell you, no man that walks upon the earth
Shall be rooted out more horribly than you.
    OEDIPUS.   Am I to bear this from him?—Damnation
Take you! Out of this place! Out of my sight!
    TEIRESIAS.   I would not have come at all if you had not asked me.
    OEDIPUS.   Could I have told that you'd talk nonsense, that
You'd come here to make a fool of yourself, and of me?
    TEIRESIAS.   A fool? Your parents thought me sane enough.
    OEDIPUS.   My parents again!—Wait: who were my parents?
    TEIRESIAS.   This day will give you a father, and break your heart.
    OEDIPUS.   Your infantile riddles! Your damned abracadabra!
    TEIRESIAS.   You were a great man once at solving riddles.
    OEDIPUS.   Mock me with that if you like; you will find it true.
    TEIRESIAS.   It was true enough. It brought about your ruin.
    OEDIPUS.   But if it saved this town?
    TEIRESIAS [*To the* PAGE].   Boy, give me your hand.
    OEDIPUS.   Yes, boy; lead him away.

               —While you are here
We can do nothing. Go; leave us in peace.
    TEIRESIAS.   I will go when I have said what I have to say.
How can you hurt me? And I tell you again:
The man you have been looking for all this time,
The damned man, the murderer of Laïos,
That man is in Thebes. To your mind he is foreign-born,
But it will soon be shown that he is a Theban,
A revelation that will fail to please.

   [19] A mountain near Thebes.

A blind man,
Who has his eyes now; a penniless man, who is rich now;
And he will go tapping the strange earth with his staff.
To the children with whom he lives now he will be
Brother and father—the very same; to her
Who bore him, son and husband—the very same
Who came to his father's bed, wet with his father's blood.

Enough. Go think that over.
If later you find error in what I have said,
You may say that I have no skill in prophecy.

        [*Exit* TEIRESIAS, *led by his* PAGE. OEDIPUS *goes into the palace.*]

ODE I

    CHORUS.   The Delphic stone of prophecies[20]   [STROPHE 1]
Remembers ancient regicide
And a still bloody hand.
That killer's hour of flight has come.
He must be stronger than riderless
Coursers of untiring wind,
For the son of Zeus[21] armed with his father's thunder
Leaps in lightning after him;
And the Furies[22] hold his track, the sad Furies.

Holy Parnassos' peak of snow[23]   [ANTISTROPHE 1]
Flashes and blinds that secret man,
That all shall hunt him down:
Though he may roam the forest shade
Like a bull gone wild from pasture
To rage through glooms of stone.
Doom comes down on him; flight will not avail him;
For the world's heart calls him desolate,
And the immortal voices follow, for ever follow.

But now a wilder thing is heard   [STROPHE 2]
From the old man skilled at hearing Fate in the wing-beat of a bird.
Bewildered as a blown bird, my soul hovers and can not find
Foothold in this debate, or any reason or rest of mind.
But no man ever brought—none can bring

---

20 The shrine at Delphi contained a large ceremonial stone that was called, because Delphi was thought to be at the center of the earth, Earth's Navel.
    21 Apollo.
    22 Hideous female deities who pursued and drove mad those who had committed such heinous crimes as patricide.
    23 Parnassos was a mountain with two peaks, one of which was consecrated to Apollo and the Muses (goddesses of arts and sciences) and the other to Dionysos; the "peak of snow" would be the peak of Apollo and the Muses. Delphi was located on the southern slope of Parnassos.

Proof of strife between Thebes' royal house,
Labdakos' line,[24] and the son of Polybos;[25]
And never until now has any man brought word
Of Laïos' dark death staining Oedipus the King.

Divine Zeus and Apollo hold   [ANTISTROPHE 2]
Perfect intelligence alone of all tales ever told;
And well though this diviner[26] works, he works in his own night;
No man can judge that rough unknown or trust in second sight,
For wisdom changes hands among the wise.
Shall I believe my great lord criminal
At a raging word that a blind old man let fall?
I saw him, when the carrion woman[27] faced him of old,
Prove his heroic mind. These evil words are lies.

SCENE II

    KREON.   Men of Thebes:
I am told that heavy accusations
Have been brought against me by King Oedipus.

I am not the kind of man to bear this tamely.

If in these present difficulties
He holds me accountable for any harm to him
Through anything I have said or done—why, then,
I do not value life in this dishonor.

It is not as though this rumor touched upon
Some private indiscretion. The matter is grave.
The fact is that I am being called disloyal
To the State, to my fellow citizens, to my friends.
    CHORAGOS.   He may have spoken in anger, not from his mind.
    KREON.   But did you not hear him say I was the one
Who seduced the old prophet into lying?
    CHORAGOS.   The thing was said; I do not know how seriously.
    KREON.   But you were watching him! Were his eyes steady?
Did he look like a man in his right mind?
    CHORAGOS.   I do not know.
I can not judge the behavior of great men.
But here is the King himself. [*Enter* OEDIPUS.]
    OEDIPUS.   So you dared come back.
Why? How brazen of you to come to my house,
You murderer!

    24 The family of Laïos.
    25 Polybos was thought to be Oedipus' father.
    26 Teiresias.
    27 The Sphinx.

Do you think I do not know
That you plotted to kill me, plotted to steal my throne?
Tell me, in God's name: am I coward, a fool,
That you should dream you could accomplish this?
A fool who could not see your slippery game?
A coward, not to fight back when I saw it?
You are the fool, Kreon, are you not? hoping
Without support or friends to get a throne?
Thrones may be won or bought: you could do neither.

KREON.   Now listen to me. You have talked; let me talk, too.
You can not judge unless you know the facts.

OEDIPUS.   You speak well: there is one fact; but I find it hard
To learn from the deadliest enemy I have.

KREON.   That above all I must dispute with you.

OEDIPUS.   That above all I will not hear you deny.

KREON.   If you think there is anything good in being stubborn
Against all reason, then I say you are wrong.

OEDIPUS.   If you think a man can sin against his own kind
And not be punished for it, I say you are mad.

KREON.   I agree. But tell me: what have I done to you?

OEDIPUS.   You advised me to send for that wizard, did you not?

KREON.   I did. I should do it again.

OEDIPUS.   Very well. Now tell me:
How long has it been since Laïos—

KREON.   What of Laïos?

OEDIPUS.   Since he vanished in that onset by the road?

KREON.   It was long ago, a long time.

OEDIPUS.   And this prophet,
Was he practicing here then?

KREON.   He was; and with honor, as now.

OEDIPUS.   Did he speak of me at that time?

KREON.   He never did;
At least, not when I was present.

OEDIPUS.   But . . . the enquiry?[28]
I suppose you held one?

KREON.   We did, but we learned nothing.

OEDIPUS.   Why did the prophet not speak against me then?

KREON.   I do not know; and I am the kind of man
Who holds his tongue when he has no facts to go on.

OEDIPUS.   There's one fact that you know, and you could tell it.

KREON.   What fact is that? If I know it, you shall have it.

OEDIPUS.   If he were not involved with you, he could not say
That it was I who murdered Laïos.

KREON.   If he says that, you are the one that knows it!—
But now it is my turn to question you.

OEDIPUS.   Put your questions. I am no murderer.

[28] Into Oedipus' background.

KREON.   First, then: you married my sister?
OEDIPUS.   I married your sister.
KREON.   And you rule the kingdom equally with her?
OEDIPUS.   Everything that she wants she has from me.
KREON.   And I am the third, equal to both of you?
OEDIPUS.   That is why I call you a bad friend.
KREON.   No. Reason it out, as I have done.
Think of this first: Would any sane man prefer
Power, with all a king's anxieties,
To that same power and the grace of sleep?
Certainly not I.
I have never longed for the king's power—only his rights.
Would any wise man differ from me in this?
As matters stand, I have my way in everything
With your consent, and no responsibilities.
If I were king, I should be a slave to policy.
How could I desire a sceptre more
Than what is now mine—untroubled influence?
No, I have not gone mad; I need no honors,
Except those with the perquisites I have now.
I am welcome everywhere; every man salutes me,
And those who want your favor seek my ear,
Since I know how to manage what they ask.
Should I exchange this ease for that anxiety?
Besides, no sober mind is treasonable.
I hate anarchy
And never would deal with any man who likes it.

Test what I have said. Go to the priestess
At Delphi, ask if I quoted her correctly.
And as for this other thing: if I am found
Guilty of treason with Teiresias,
Then sentence me to death. You have my word
It is a sentence I should cast my vote for—
But not without evidence!
                              You do wrong
When you take good men for bad, bad men for good.
A true friend thrown aside—why, life itself
Is not more precious!
                    In time you will know this well:
For time, and time alone, will show the just man,
Though scoundrels are discovered in a day.
CHORAGOS.   This is well said, and a prudent man would ponder it.
Judgments too quickly formed are dangerous.
OEDIPUS.   But is he not quick in his duplicity?
And shall I not be quick to parry him?
Would you have me stand still, hold my peace, and let
This man win everything, through my inaction?

KREON.   And you want—what is it, then? To banish me?

OEDIPUS.   No, not exile. It is your death I want,

So that all the world may see what treason means.

KREON.   You will persist, then? You will not believe me?

OEDIPUS.   How can I believe you?

KREON.   Then you are a fool.

OEDIPUS.   To save myself?

KREON.   In justice, think of me.

OEDIPUS.   You are evil incarnate.

KREON.   But suppose that you are wrong?

OEDIPUS.   Still I must rule.

KREON.   But not if you rule badly.

OEDIPUS.   O city, city!

KREON.   It is my city, too!

CHORAGOS.   Now, my lords, be still. I see the Queen,

Iokastè, coming from her palace chambers;

And it is time she came, for the sake of you both.

This dreadful quarrel can be resolved through her. [*Enter* IOKASTE.]

IOKASTE.   Poor foolish men, what wicked din is this?

With Thebes sick to death, is it not shameful

That you should rake some private quarrel up?

[*To* OEDIPUS.] Come into the house.

                                —And you, Kreon, go now:

Let us have no more of this tumult over nothing.

KREON.   Nothing? No, sister: what your husband plans for me

Is one of two great evils: exile or death.

OEDIPUS.   He is right.

                        Why, woman I have caught him squarely

Plotting against my life.

KREON.   No! Let me die

Accurst if ever I have wished you harm!

IOKASTE.   Ah, believe it, Oedipus!

In the name of the gods, respect this oath of his

For my sake, for the sake of these people here!

                                                        [STROPHE 1]

CHORAGOS.   Open your mind to her, my lord. Be ruled by her, I beg you!

OEDIPUS.   What would you have me do?

CHORAGOS.   Respect Kreon's word. He has never spoken like a fool,

And now he has sworn an oath.

OEDIPUS.   You know what you ask?

CHORAGOS.   I do.

OEDIPUS.   Speak on, then.

CHORAGOS.   A friend so sworn should not be baited so,

In blind malice, and without final proof.

OEDIPUS.   You are aware, I hope, that what you say

Means death for me, or exile at the least.

CHORAGOS.   No, I swear by Helios,[29] first in Heaven!   [STROPHE 2]
May I die friendless and accurst,
The worst of deaths, if ever I meant that!
 It is the withering fields
 That hurt my sick heart:
Must we bear all these ills,
 And now your bad blood as well?

 OEDIPUS.   Then let him go. And let me die, if I must,
Or be driven by him in shame from the land of Thebes.
It is your unhappiness, and not his talk,
That touches me.

    As for him—
Wherever he goes, hatred will follow him.
 KREON.   Ugly in yielding, as you were ugly in rage!
Natures like yours chiefly torment themselves.
OEDIPUS.   Can you not go? Can you not leave me?
 KREON.   I can.
You do not know me; but the city knows me,
And in its eyes I am just, if not in yours. [*Exit* KREON.]

           [ANTISTROPHE 1]
 CHORAGOS.   Lady Iokastè, did you not ask the King to go to his chambers?
 IOKASTE.   First tell me what has happened.
 CHORAGOS.   There was suspicion without evidence; yet it rankled
As even false charges will.
 IOKASTE.   On both sides?
 CHORAGOS.   On both.
 IOKASTE.   But what was said?
 CHORAGOS.   Oh let it rest, let it be done with!
Have we not suffered enough?
 OEDIPUS.   You see to what your decency has brought you:
You have made difficulties where my heart saw none.

           [ANTISTROPHE 2]
 CHORAGOS.   Oedipus, it is not once only I have told you—
You must know I should count myself unwise
To the point of madness, should I now forsake you—
  You, under whose hand,
   In the storm of another time,
  Our dear land sailed out free.
  But now stand fast at the helm!

 IOKASTE.   In God's name, Oedipus, inform your wife as well:
Why are you so set in this hard anger?
 OEDIPUS.   I will tell you, for none of these men deserves

 [29] The Sun-god.

My confidence as you do. It is Kreon's work,
His treachery, his plotting against me.

    IOKASTE.   Go on, if you can make this clear to me.

    OEDIPUS.   He charges me with the murder of Laïos.

    IOKASTE.   Has he some knowledge? Or does he speak from hearsay?

    OEDIPUS.   He would not commit himself to such a charge,
But he has brought in that damnable soothsayer
To tell his story.

    IOKASTE.   Set your mind at rest.
If it is a question of soothsayers, I tell you
That you will find no man whose craft gives knowledge
Of the unknowable.

                Here is my proof:
An oracle was reported to Laïos once
(I will not say from Phoibos himself, but from
His appointed ministers, at any rate)
That his doom would be death at the hands of his own son—
His son, born of his flesh and of mine!

Now, you remember the story: Laïos was killed
By marauding strangers where three highways meet;
But his child had not been three days in this world
Before the King had pierced the baby's ankles[30]
And left him to die on a lonely mountainside.

Thus, Apollo never caused that child
To kill his father, and it was not Laïos' fate
To die at the hands of his son, as he had feared.
This is what prophets and prophecies are worth!
Have no dread of them.
                It is God himself
Who can show us what he wills, in his own way.

    OEDIPUS.   How strange a shadowy memory crossed my mind,
Just now while you were speaking; it chilled my heart.

IOKASTE.   What do you mean? What memory do you speak of?

    OEDIPUS.   If I understand you, Laïos was killed
At a place where three roads meet.

    IOKASTE.   So it was said;
We have no later story.

    OEDIPUS.   Where did it happen?

    IOKASTE.   Phokis, it is called: at a place where the Theban Way
Divides into the roads toward Delphi and Daulia.

    OEDIPUS.   When?

    IOKASTE.   We had the news not long before you came
And proved the right to your succession here.

    OEDIPUS.   Ah, what net has God been weaving for me?

    IOKASTE.   Oedipus! Why does this trouble you?

[30] Perhaps to prevent his ghost from walking.

OEDIPUS.   Do not ask me yet.
First, tell me how Laïos looked, and tell me
How old he was.

    IOKASTE.   He was tall, his hair just touched
With white; his form was not unlike your own.

    OEDIPUS.   I think that I myself may be accurst
By my own ignorant edict.

    IOKASTE.   You speak strangely.
It makes me tremble to look at you, my King.

    OEDIPUS.   I am not sure that the blind man can not see.
But I should know better if you were to tell me—

    IOKASTE.   Anything—though I dread to hear you ask it.

    OEDIPUS.   Was the King lightly escorted, or did he ride
With a large company, as a ruler should?

    IOKASTE.   There were five men with him in all: one was a herald;
And a single chariot, which he was driving.

    OEDIPUS.   Alas, that makes it plain enough!

                               But who—
Who told you how it happened?

    IOKASTE.   A household servant,
The only one to escape.

    OEDIPUS.   And is he still
A servant of ours?

    IOKASTE.   No; for when he came back at last
And found you enthroned in the place of the dead king,
He came to me, touched my hand with his, and begged
That I would send him away to the frontier district
Where only the shepherds go—
As far away from the city as I could send him.
I granted his prayer; for although the man was a slave,
He had earned more than this favor at my hands.

    OEDIPUS.   Can he be called back quickly?

    IOKASTE.   Easily.
But why?

    OEDIPUS.   I have taken too much upon myself
Without enquiry; therefore I wish to consult him.

    IOKASTE.   Then he shall come.

                         But am I not one also
To whom you might confide these fears of yours?

    OEDIPUS.   That is your right; it will not be denied you,
Now least of all; for I have reached a pitch
Of wild foreboding. Is there anyone
To whom I should sooner speak?

Polybos of Corinth is my father.
My mother is a Dorian: Meropê.
I grew up chief among the men of Corinth
Until a strange thing happened—
Not worth my passion, it may be, but strange.

At a feast, a drunken man maundering in his cups
Cries out that I am not my father's son!
I contained myself that night, though I felt anger
And a sinking heart. The next day I visited
My father and mother, and questioned them. They stormed,
Calling it all the slanderous rant of a fool;
And this relieved me. Yet the suspicion
Remained always aching in my mind;
I knew there was talk; I could not rest;
And finally, saying nothing to my parents,
I went to the shrine at Delphi.

The god dismissed my question without reply;
He spoke of other things.
                              Some were clear,
Full of wretchedness, dreadful, unbearable:
As, that I should lie with my own mother, breed
Children from whom all men would turn their eyes;
And that I should be my father's murderer.

I heard all this, and fled. And from that day
Corinth to me was only in the stars
Descending in that quarter of the sky,
As I wandered farther and farther on my way
To a land where I should never see the evil
Sung by the oracle. And I came to this country
Where, so you say, King Laïos was killed.

I will tell you all that happened there, my lady.

There were three highways
Coming together at a place I passed;
And there a herald came towards me, and a chariot
Drawn by horses, with a man such as you describe
Seated in it. The groom leading the horses
Forced me off the road at his lord's command;
But as this charioteer lurched over towards me
I struck him in my rage. The old man saw me
And brought his double goad down upon my head
As I came abreast.
                        He was paid back, and more!
Swinging my club in this right hand I knocked him
Out of his car, and he rolled on the ground.
                                                    I killed him.
I killed them all.
Now if that stranger and Laïos were—kin,
Where is a man more miserable than I?
More hated by the gods? Citizen and alien alike
Must never shelter me or speak to me—
I must be shunned by all.

And I myself
Pronounced this malediction upon myself!

Think of it: I have touched you with these hands,
These hands that killed your husband. What defilement!

Am I all evil, then? It must be so,
Since I must flee from Thebes, yet never again
See my own countrymen, my own country,
For fear of joining my mother in marriage
And killing Polybos, my father.

                                      Ah,
If I was created so, born to this fate,
Who could deny the savagery of God?

O holy majesty of heavenly powers!
May I never see that day! Never!
Rather let me vanish from the race of men
Than know the abomination destined me!

    CHORAGOS.   We too, my lord, have felt dismay at this.
But there is hope: you have yet to hear the shepherd.

    OEDIPUS.   Indeed, I fear no other hope is left me.

    IOKASTE.   What do you hope from him when he comes?

    OEDIPUS.   This much:
If his account of the murder tallies with yours,
Then I am cleared.

    IOKASTE.   What was it that I said
Of such importance?

    OEDIPUS.   Why, 'marauders', you said,
Killed the King, according to this man's story.
If he maintains that still, if there were several,
Clearly the guilt is not mine: I was alone.
But if he says one man, singlehanded, did it,
Then the evidence all points to me.

    IOKASTE.   You may be sure that he said there were several;
And can he call back that story now? He can not.
The whole city heard it as plainly as I.
But suppose he alters some detail of it:
He can not ever show that Laïos' death
Fulfilled the oracle: for Apollo said
My child was doomed to kill him; and my child—
Poor baby!—it was my child that died first.

No. From now on, where oracles are concerned,
I would not waste a second thought on any.

    OEDIPUS.   You may be right.

                              But come: let someone go
For the shepherd at once. This matter must be settled.

    IOKASTE.   I will send for him.
I would not wish to cross you in anything,
And surely not in this.—Let us go in. [*Exeunt into the palace.*]

ODE II

CHORUS. Let me be reverent in the ways of right, [STROPHE 1]
Lowly the paths I journey on;
Let all my words and actions keep
The laws of the pure universe
From highest Heaven handed down.
For Heaven is their bright nurse,
Those generations of the realms of light;
Ah, never of mortal kind were they begot,
Nor are they slaves of memory, lost in sleep:
Their Father is greater than Time, and ages not.

The tyrant is a child of Pride [ANTISTROPHE 1]
Who drinks from his great sickening cup
Recklessness and vanity,
Until from his high crest headlong
He plummets to the dust of hope.
That strong man is not strong.
But let no fair ambition be denied;
May God protect the wrestler for the State
In government, in comely policy,
Who will fear God, and on His ordinance wait.

Haughtiness and the high hand of disdain [STROPHE 2]
Tempt and outrage God's holy law;
And any mortal who dares hold
No immortal Power in awe
Will be caught up in a net of pain:
The price for which his levity is sold.
Let each man take due earnings, then,
And keep his hands from holy things,
And from blasphemy stand apart—
Else the crackling blast of heaven
Blows on his head, and on his desperate heart.
Though fools will honor impious men,
In their cities no tragic poet sings.

Shall we lose faith in Delphi's obscurities, [ANTISTROPHE 2]
We who have heard the world's core
Discredited, and the sacred wood
Of Zeus at Elis praised no more?
The deeds and the strange prophecies
Must make a pattern yet to be understood.
Zeus, if indeed you are lord of all,
Throned in light over night and day,
Mirror this in your endless mind:
Our masters call the oracle

Words on the wind, and the Delphic vision blind!
Their hearts no longer know Apollo,
And reverence for the gods has died away.

SCENE III

Enter IOKASTE

IOKASTE.   Princes of Thebes, it has occurred to me
To visit the altars of the gods, bearing
These branches as a suppliant, and this incense.
Our King is not himself: his noble soul
Is overwrought with fantasies of dread,
Else he would consider
The new prophecies in the light of the old.
He will listen to any voice that speaks disaster,
And my advice goes for nothing. [*She approaches the altar, right.*]
                    To you, then, Apollo,
Lycéan lord,[31] since you are nearest, I turn in prayer.

Receive these offerings, and grant us deliverance
From defilement. Our hearts are heavy with fear
When we see our leader distracted, as helpless sailors
Are terrified by the confusion of their helmsman.   [*Enter* MESSENGER.]
    MESSENGER.   Friends, no doubt you can direct me:
Where shall I find the house of Oedipus
Or, better still, where is the King himself?
    CHORAGOS.   It is this very place, stranger; he is inside.
This is his wife and mother of his children.
    MESSENGER.   I wish her happiness in a happy house,
Blest in all the fulfillment of her marriage.
    IOKASTE.   I wish as much for you: your courtesy
Deserves a like good fortune. But now, tell me:
Why have you come? What have you to say to us?
    MESSENGER.   Good news, my lady, for your house and your husband.
    IOKASTE.   What news? Who sent you here?
    MESSENGER.   I am from Corinth.
The news I bring ought to mean joy for you,
Though it may be you will find some grief in it.
    IOKASTE.   What is it? How can it touch us in both ways?
    MESSENGER.   The word is that the people of the Isthmus[32]
Intend to call Oedipus to be their king.
    IOKASTE.   But old King Polybos—is he not reigning still?
    MESSENGER.   No. Death holds him in his sepulchre.
    IOKASTE.   What are you saying? Polybos is dead?
    MESSENGER.   If I am not telling the truth, may I die myself.
    IOKASTE [*to a* MAIDSERVANT].   Go in, go quickly; tell this to your master.

31 Apollo was thought to have been born at Lycéa.
32 Corinth was an isthmus.

O riddlers of God's will, where are you now!
This was the man whom Oedipus, long ago,
Feared so, fled so, in dread of destroying him—
But it was another fate by which he died. [*Enter* OEDIPUS, *center*]

OEDIPUS.   Dearest Iokastê, why have you sent for me?

IOKASTE.   Listen to what this man says, and then tell me
What has become of the solemn prophecies.

OEDIPUS.   Who is this man? What is his news for me?

IOKASTE.   He has come from Corinth to announce your father's death!

OEDIPUS.   Is it true, stranger? Tell me in your own words.

MESSENGER.   I can not say it more clearly: the King is dead.

OEDIPUS.   Was it by treason? Or by an attack of illness?

MESSENGER.   A little thing brings old men to their rest.

OEDIPUS.   It was sickness, then?

MESSENGER.   Yes, and his many years.

OEDIPUS.   Ah!
Why should a man respect the Pythian hearth,[33] or
Give heed to the birds that jangle above his head?
They prophesied that I should kill Polybos,
Kill my own father; but he is dead and buried,
And I am here—I never touched him, never,
Unless he died of grief for my departure,
And thus, in a sense, through me. No. Polybos
Has packed the oracles off with him underground.
They are empty words.

IOKASTE.   Had I not told you so?

OEDIPUS.   You had; it was my faint heart that betrayed me.

IOKASTE.   From now on never think of those things again.

OEDIPUS.   And yet—must I not fear my mother's bed?

IOKASTE.   Why should anyone in this world be afraid,
Since Fate rules us and nothing can be foreseen?
A man should live only for the present day.

Have no more fear of sleeping with your mother:
How many men, in dreams, have lain with their mothers!
No reasonable man is troubled by such things.

OEDIPUS.   That is true; only—
If only my mother were not still alive!
But she is alive. I can not help my dread.

IOKASTE.   Yet this news of your father's death is wonderful.

OEDIPUS.   Wonderful. But I fear the living woman.

MESSENGER.   Tell me, who is this woman that you fear?

OEDIPUS.   It is Meropê, man; the wife of King Polybos.

MESSENGER.   Meropê? Why should you be afraid of her?

OEDIPUS.   An oracle of the gods, a dreadful saying.

MESSENGER.   Can you tell me about it or are you sworn to silence?

OEDIPUS.   I can tell you, and I will.
Apollo said through his prophet that I was the man

[33] Delphi, where Apollo's medium was the Pythia.

Who should marry his own mother, shed his father's blood
With his own hands. And so, for all these years
I have kept clear of Corinth, and no harm has come—
Though it would have been sweet to see my parents again.

  MESSENGER. And is this the fear that drove you out of Corinth?

  OEDIPUS. Would you have me kill my father?

  MESSENGER.   As for that
You must be reassured by the news I gave you.

  OEDIPUS. If you could reassure me, I would reward you.

  MESSENGER. I had that in mind, I will confess: I thought
I could count on you when you returned to Corinth.

  OEDIPUS. No: I will never go near my parents again.

  MESSENGER. Ah, son, you still do not know what you are doing—

  OEDIPUS. What do you mean? In the name of God tell me!

  MESSENGER. —If these are your reasons for not going home.

  OEDIPUS. I tell you, I fear the oracle may come true.

  MESSENGER. And guilt may come upon you through your parents?

  OEDIPUS. That is the dread that is always in my heart.

  MESSENGER. Can you not see that all your fears are groundless?

  OEDIPUS. Groundless? Am I not my parents' son?

  MESSENGER. Polybos was not your father.

  OEDIPUS.   Not my father?

  MESSENGER. No more your father than the man speaking to you.

  OEDIPUS. But you are nothing to me!

  MESSENGER.   Neither was he.

  OEDIPUS. Then why did he call me son?

  MESSENGER   I will tell you:
Long ago he had you from my hands, as a gift.

  OEDIPUS. Then how could he love me so, if I was not his?

  MESSENGER. He had no children, and his heart turned to you.

  OEDIPUS. What of you? Did you buy me? Did you find me by chance?

  MESSENGER. I came upon you in the woody vales of Kithairon.

  OEDIPUS. And what were you doing there?

  MESSENGER.   Tending my flocks.

  OEDIPUS. A wandering shepherd?

  MESSENGER.   But your savior, son, that day.

  OEDIPUS. From what did you save me?

  MESSENGER.   Your ankles should tell you that.

  OEDIPUS. Ah, stranger, why do you speak of that childhood pain?

  MESSENGER. I pulled the skewer that pinned your feet together.

  OEDIPUS. I have had the mark as long as I can remember.

  MESSENGER. That was why you were given the name you bear.[34]

  OEDIPUS. God! Was it my father or my mother who did it?
Tell me!

  MESSENGER. I do not know. The man who gave you to me
Can tell you better than I.

  OEDIPUS. It was not you that found me, but another?

[34] *Oedipus* means "swell-foot."

MESSENGER. It was another shepherd gave you to me.

OEDIPUS. Who was he? Can you tell me who he was?

MESSENGER. I think he was said to be one of Laïos' people.

OEDIPUS. You mean the Laïos who was king here years ago?

MESSENGER. Yes; King Laïos; and the man was one of his herdsmen.

OEDIPUS. Is he still alive? Can I see him?

MESSENGER.   These men here
Know best about such things.

OEDIPUS.   Does anyone here
Know this shepherd that he is talking about?
Have you seen him in the fields, or in the town?
If you have, tell me. It is time things were made plain.

CHORAGOS. I think the man he means is that same shepherd
You have already asked to see. Iokastê perhaps
Could tell you something.

OEDIPUS.   Do you know anything
About him, Lady? Is he the man we have summoned?
Is that the man this shepherd means?

IOKASTE.   Why think of him?
Forget this herdsman. Forget it all.
This talk is a waste of time.

OEDIPUS.   How can you say that,
When the clues to my true birth are in my hands?

IOKASTE. For God's love, let us have no more questioning!
Is your life nothing to you?
My own is pain enough for me to bear.

OEDIPUS. You need not worry. Suppose my mother a slave,
And born of slaves: no baseness can touch you.

IOKASTE. Listen to me, I beg you: do not do this thing!

OEDIPUS. I will not listen; the truth must be made known.

IOKASTE. Everything that I say is for your own good!

OEDIPUS.   My own good
Snaps my patience, then; I want none of it.

IOKASTE. You are fatally wrong! May you never learn who you are!

OEDIPUS. Go, one of you, and bring the shepherd here.
Let us leave this woman to brag of her royal name.

IOKASTE. Ah, miserable!
That is the only word I have for you now.
That is the only word I can ever have. [*Exit into the palace.*]

CHORAGOS. Why has she left us, Oedipus? Why has she gone
In such a passion of sorrow? I fear this silence:
Something dreadful may come of it.

OEDIPUS.   Let it come!
However base my birth, I must know about it.
The Queen, like a woman, is perhaps ashamed
To think of my low origin. But I
Am a child of Luck; I can not be dishonored.
Luck is my mother; the passing months, my brothers,
Have seen me rich and poor.

If this is so,
How could I wish that I were someone else?
How could I not be glad to know my birth?

ODE III

CHORUS. If ever the coming time were known [STROPHE]
To my heart's pondering,
Kithairon, now by Heaven I see the torches
At the festival of the next full moon,[35]
And see the dance, and hear the choir sing
A grace to your gentle shade:
Mountain where Oedipus was found,
O mountain guard of a noble race!
May the god who heals us[36] lend his aid,
And let that glory come to pass
For our king's cradling-ground.

Of the nymphs that flower beyond the years,[37] [ANTISTROPHE]
Who bore you, royal child,
To Pan of the hills[38] or the timberline Apollo,[39]
Cold in delight where the upland clears,
Or Hermês for whom Kyllenê's heights are piled?[40]
Or flushed as evening cloud,
Great Dionysos, roamer of mountains,[41]
He—was it he who found you there,
And caught you up in his own proud
Arms from the sweet god-ravisher[42]
Who laughed by the Muses' fountains?

SCENE IV

OEDIPUS. Sirs: though I do not know the man,
I think I see him coming, this shepherd we want:
He is old, like our friend here, and the men

[35] Almost every god who was at all important had a festival day, most of which were
celebrated at the full moon.
[36] Apollo.
[37] Immortal nymphs; the Chorus is attempting to attribute immortality to Oedipus.
[38] Pan was god of pastures, forests, flocks, and herds.
[39] Apollo was also associated with the care of flocks and herds.
[40] Hermês, the messenger of the gods and also a god of flocks, roads, trading, etc., was
born on Mt. Kyllenê.
[41] Dionysos, the god of wine (hence "flushed") and also of vegetation, was honored
in ceremonies on Mt. Parnassos.
[42] The nymph who is conjectured to have borne Oedipus.

Bringing him seem to be servants of my house.
But you can tell, if you have ever seen him.

[*Enter* SHEPHERD *escorted by servants.*]

CHORAGOS.   I know him, he was Laïos' man. You can trust him.

OEDIPUS.   Tell me first, you from Corinth: is this the shepherd
We were discussing?

MESSENGER.   This is the very man.

OEDIPUS [*to* SHEPHERD].   Come here. No, look at me. You must answer
Everything I ask.—You belonged to Laïos?

SHEPHERD.   Yes: born his slave, brought up in his house.

OEDIPUS.   Tell me: what kind of work did you do for him?

SHEPHERD.   I was a shepherd of his, most of my life.

OEDIPUS.   Where mainly did you go for pasturage?

SHEPHERD.   Sometimes Kithairon, sometimes the hills near-by.

OEDIPUS.   Do you remember ever seeing this man out there?

SHEPHERD.   What would he be doing there? This man?

OEDIPUS.   This man standing here. Have you ever seen him before?

SHEPHERD.   No. At least, not to my recollection.

MESSENGER.   And that is not strange, my lord. But I'll refresh
His memory: he must remember when we two
Spent three whole seasons together, March to September,
On Kithairon or thereabouts. He had two flocks;
I had one. Each autumn I'd drive mine home
And he would go back with his to Laïos' sheepfold.—
Is this not true, just as I have described it?

SHEPHERD.   True, yes; but it was all so long ago.

MESSENGER.   Well, then: do you remember, back in those days,
That you gave me a baby boy to bring up as my own?

SHEPHERD.   What if I did? What are you trying to say?

MESSENGER.   King Oedipus was once that little child.

SHEPHERD.   Damn you, hold your tongue!

OEDIPUS.   No more of that!
It is your tongue needs watching, not this man's.

SHEPHERD.   My King, my Master, what is it I have done wrong?

OEDIPUS.   You have not answered his question about the boy.

SHEPHERD.   He does not know . . . He is only making trouble . . .

OEDIPUS.   Come, speak plainly, or it will go hard with you.

SHEPHERD.   In God's name, do not torture an old man!

OEDIPUS.   Come here, one of you; bind his arms behind him.

SHEPHERD.   Unhappy king! What more do you wish to learn?

OEDIPUS.   Did you give this man the child he speaks of?

SHEPHERD.   I did.
And I would to God I had died that very day.

OEDIPUS.   You will die now unless you speak the truth.

SHEPHERD.   Yet if I speak the truth, I am worse than dead.

OEDIPUS [*to* ATTENDANT].   He intends to draw it out, apparently—

SHEPHERD.   No! I have told you already that I gave him the boy.

OEDIPUS.   Where did you get him? From your house? From somewhere
else?

SHEPHERD.   Not from mine, no. A man gave him to me.

OEDIPUS.   Is that man here? Whose house did he belong to?

SHEPHERD.   For God's love, my King, do not ask me any more!

OEDIPUS.   You are a dead man if I have to ask you again.

SHEPHERD.   Then . . . Then the child was from the palace of Laïos.

OEDIPUS.   A slave child? or a child of his own line?

SHEPHERD.   Ah, I am on the brink of dreadful speech!

OEDIPUS.   And I of dreadful hearing. Yet I must hear.

SHEPHERD.   If you must be told, then . . .

            They said it was Laïos' child;
But it is your wife who can tell you about that.

OEDIPUS.   My wife!—Did she give it to you?

SHEPHERD.   My lord, she did.

OEDIPUS.   Do you know why?

SHEPHERD.   I was told to get rid of it.

OEDIPUS.   Oh heartless mother!

SHEPHERD.   But in dread of prophecies . . .

OEDIPUS.   Tell me.

SHEPHERD.   It was said that the boy would kill his own father.

OEDIPUS.   Then why did you give him over to this old man?

SHEPHERD.   I pitied the baby, my King,
And I thought that this man would take him far away
To his own country.

      He saved him—but for what a fate!
For if you are what this man says you are,
No man living is more wretched than Oedipus.

OEDIPUS.   Ah God!
It was true!

   All the prophecies!

         —Now,
O Light, may I look on you for the last time!
I, Oedipus,
Oedipus, damned in his birth, in his marriage damned,
Damned in the blood he shed with his own hand!

          [*He rushes into the palace.*]

ODE IV

CHORUS.   Alas for the seed of men.   [STROPHE I]

What measure shall I give these generations
That breathe on the void and are void
And exist and do not exist?

Who bears more weight of joy
Than mass of sunlight shifting in images,
Or who shall make his thought stay on
That down time drifts away?

Your splendor is all fallen.

O naked brow of wrath and tears,
O change of Oedipus!
I who saw your days call no man blest—
Your great days like ghósts góne.

That mind was a strong bow.   [ANTISTROPHE 1]

Deep, how deep you drew it then, hard archer,
At a dim fearful range,

And brought dear glory down!

You overcame the stranger—
The virgin with her hooking lion claws—[43]
And though death sang, stood like a tower
To make pale Thebes take heart.

Fortress against our sorrow!

True king, giver of laws,
Majestic Oedipus!
No prince in Thebes had ever such renown,
No prince won such grace of power.

And now of all men ever known   [STROPHE 2]
Most pitiful is this man's story:
His fortunes are most changed, his state
Fallen to a low slave's
Ground under bitter fate.

O Oedipus, most royal one!
The great door that expelled you to the light[44]
Gave at night—ah, gave night to your glory:
As to the father, to the fathering son.

All understood too late.

How could that queen whom Laïos won,
The garden that he harrowed at his height,[45]
Be silent when that act was done?

But all eyes fail before time's eye,   [ANTISTROPHE 2]
All actions come to justice there.
Though never willed, though far down the deep past,
Your bed, your dread sirings,
Are brought to book at last.[46]

[43] The Sphinx, who had the face of a woman, the body of a lion, and the wings of a bird.
[44] Iokaste's womb.
[45] Another reference to Iokaste's womb and, by implication, to Iokaste herself.
[46] An allusion to the fates of Oedipus' children ("dread sirings"). His sons, Polyneikês and Etioklês, killed each other in battle, and his daughter Antigonê died tragically; the circumstances of her death are related in another of Sophocles' plays. A second daughter, Ismenê, seems never to have attained any significance.

Child by Laïos doomed to die,
Then doomed to lose that fortunate little death,
Would God you never took breath in this air
That with my wailing lips I take to cry:

For I weep the world's outcast.

I was blind, and now I can tell why:
Asleep, for you had given ease of breath
To Thebes, while the false years went by.

ÉXODOS

Enter, from the palace, SECOND MESSENGER.

SECOND MESSENGER.   Elders of Thebes,[47] most honored in this land,
What horrors are yours to see and hear, what weight
Of sorrow to be endured, if, true to your birth,
You venerate the line of Labdakos!
I think neither Istros nor Phasis, those great rivers,
Could purify this place of all the evil
It shelters now, or soon must bring to light—
Evil not done unconsciously, but willed.

The greatest griefs are those we cause ourselves.
CHORAGOS.   Surely, friend, we have grief enough already;
What new sorrow do you mean?
SECOND MESSENGER.   The Queen is dead.
CHORAGOS.   O miserable Queen! But at whose hand?
SECOND MESSENGER.   Her own.
The full horror of what happened you can not know,
For you did not see it; but I, who did, will tell you
As clearly as I can how she met her death.

When she had left us,
In passionate silence, passing through the court,
She ran to her apartment in the house,
Her hair clutched by the fingers of both hands.
She closed the doors behind her; then, by that bed
Where long ago the fatal son was conceived—
That son who should bring about his father's death—
We heard her call upon Laïos, dead so many years,
And heard her wail for the double fruit of her marriage,
A husband by her husband, children by her child.

Exactly how she died I do not know:
For Oedipus burst in moaning and would not let us
Keep vigil to the end: it was by him
As he stormed about the room that our eyes were caught.

[47] The Chorus.

From one to another of us he went, begging a sword,
Hunting the wife who was not his wife, the mother
Whose womb had carried his own children and himself.
I do not know: it was none of us aided him,
But surely one of the gods was in control!
For with a dreadful cry
He hurled his weight, as though wrenched out of himself,
At the twin doors: the bolts gave, and he rushed in.
And there we saw her hanging, her body swaying
From the cruel cord she had noosed about her neck.
A great sob broke from him, heartbreaking to hear,
As he loosed the rope and lowered her to the ground.

I would blot out from my mind what happened next!
For the King ripped from her gown the golden brooches
That were her ornament, and raised them, and plunged them down
Straight into his own eyeballs, crying, 'No more,
No more shall you look on the misery about me,
The horrors of my own doing! Too long you have known
The faces of those whom I should never have seen,
Too long been blind to those for whom I was searching!
From this hour, go in darkness!' And as he spoke,
He struck at his eyes—not once, but many times;
And the blood spattered his beard,
Bursting from his ruined sockets like red hail.

So from the unhappiness of two this evil has sprung,
A curse on the man and woman alike. The old
Happiness of the house of Labdakos
Was happiness enough: where is it today?
It is all wailing and ruin, disgrace, death—all
The misery of mankind that has a name—
And it is wholly and for ever theirs.
          CHORAGOS.   Is he in agony still? Is there no rest for him?
          SECOND MESSENGER.   He is calling for someone to open the doors wide
So that all the children of Kadmos may look upon
His father's murderer, his mother's—no,
I can not say it!
                    And then he will leave Thebes,
Self-exiled, in order that the curse
Which he himself pronounced may depart from the house.
He is weak, and there is none to lead him,
So terrible is his suffering.
                    But you will see:
Look, the doors are opening; in a moment
You will see a thing that would crush a heart of stone.
          [*The central door is opened;* OEDIPUS, *blinded, is led in.*]
          CHORAGOS.   Dreadful indeed for men to see.
Never have my own eyes
Looked on a sight so full of fear.

Oedipus!
What madness came upon you, what daemon
Leaped on your life with heavier
Punishment than a mortal man can bear?
No: I can not even
Look at you, poor ruined one.
And I would speak, question, ponder,
If I were able. No.
You make me shudder.

OEDIPUS.   God.   God.
Is there a sorrow greater?
Where shall I find harbor in this world?
My voice is hurled far on a dark wind.
What has God done to me?

CHORAGOS.   Too terrible to think of, or to see.

OEDIPUS.   O cloud of night,   [STROPHE 1]
Never to be turned away: night coming on,
I can not tell how: night like a shroud!

My fair winds brought me here.

                        O God. Again
The pain of the spikes where I had sight,
The flooding pain
Of memory, never to be gouged out.

CHORAGOS.   This is not strange.
You suffer it all twice over, remorse in pain,
Pain in remorse.

OEDIPUS.   Ah dear friend   [ANTISTROPHE 1]
Are you faithful even yet, you alone?
Are you still standing near me, will you stay here,
Patient, to care for the blind?

                        The blind man!
Yet even blind I know who it is attends me,
By the voice's tone—
Though my new darkness hide the comforter.

CHORAGOS.   Oh fearful act!
What god was it drove you to rake black
Night across your eyes?

OEDIPUS.   Apollo. Apollo. Dear   [STROPHE 2]
Children, the god was Apollo.
He brought my sick, sick fate upon me.
But the blinding hand was my own!
How could I bear to see
When all my sight was horror everywhere?

CHORAGOS.   Everywhere; that is true.
OEDIPUS.   And now what is left?
Images? Love? A greeting even,
Sweet to the senses? Is there anything?
Ah, no, friends: lead me away.
Lead me away from Thebes.
                              Lead the great wreck
And hell of Oedipus, whom the gods hate.

CHORAGOS.   Your misery, you are not blind to that.
Would God you had never found it out!
OEDIPUS.   Death take the man who unbound   [ANTISTROPHE 2]
My feet on that hillside
And delivered me from death to life! What life?
If only I had died,
This weight of monstrous doom
Could not have dragged me and my darlings down.

CHORAGOS.   I would have wished the same.

OEDIPUS.   Oh never to have come here
With my father's blood upon me! Never
To have been the man they call his mother's husband!
Oh accurst! Oh child of evil,
To have entered that wretched bed—
                              the selfsame one!
More primal than sin itself, this fell to me.
CHORAGOS.   I do not know what words to offer you.
You were better dead than alive and blind.
OEDIPUS.   Do not counsel me any more. This punishment
That I have laid upon myself is just.
If I had eyes,
I do not know how I could bear the sight
Of my father, when I came to the house of Death,
Or my mother: for I have sinned against them both
So vilely that I could not make my peace
By strangling my own life.
                              Or do you think my children,
Born as they were born, would be sweet to my eyes?
Ah never, never! Nor this town with its high walls,
Nor the holy images of the gods.
                              For I,
Thrice miserable!—Oedipus, noblest of all the line
Of Kadmos, have condemned myself to enjoy
These things no more, by my own malediction
Expelling that man whom the gods declared
To be a defilement in the house of Laïos.
After exposing the rankness of my own guilt,
How could I look men frankly in the eyes?
No, I swear it,

If I could have stifled my hearing at its source,
I would have done it and made all this body
A tight cell of misery, blank to light and sound:
So I should have been safe in my dark mind
Beyond external evil.

                    Ah Kithairon!
Why did you shelter me? When I was cast upon you,
Why did I not die? Then I should never
Have shown the world my execrable birth.

Ah Polybos! Corinth, city that I believed
The ancient seat of my ancestors: how fair
I seemed, your child! And all the while this evil
Was cancerous within me!

                    For I am sick
In my own being, sick in my origin.

O three roads, dark ravine, woodland and way
Where three roads met: you, drinking my father's blood,
My own blood, spilled by my own hand: can you remember
The unspeakable things I did there, and the things
I went on from there to do?

                         O marriage, marriage!
The act that engendered me, and again the act
Performed by the son in the same bed—

                              Ah, the net
Of incest, mingling fathers, brothers, sons,
With brides, wives, mothers: the last evil
That can be known by men: no tongue can say
How evil!

            No. For the love of God, conceal me
Somewhere far from Thebes; or kill me; or hurl me
Into the sea, away from men's eyes for ever.
Come, lead me. You need not fear to touch me.
Of all men, I alone can bear this guilt. [*Enter* KREON.]
     CHORAGOS.   Kreon is here now. As to what you ask,
He may decide the course to take. He only
Is left to protect the city in your place.
     OEDIPUS.   Alas, how can I speak to him? What right have I
To beg his courtesy whom I have deeply wronged?
     KREON.[48]   I have not come to mock you, Oedipus,
Or to reproach you, either.
[*To* ATTENDANTS.]   —You, standing there:
If you have lost all respect for man's dignity,
At least respect the flame of Lord Helios:
Do not allow this pollution to show itself
Openly here, an affront to the earth

---

[48] Kreon acts as Regent of Thebes because Oedipus' sons are too young to rule.

And Heaven's rain and the light of day. No, take him
Into the house as quickly as you can.
For it is proper
That only the close kindred see his grief.

     OEDIPUS.   I pray you in God's name, since your courtesy
Ignores my dark expectation, visiting
With mercy this man of all men most execrable:
Give me what I ask—for your good, not for mine.

     KREON.   And what is it that you turn to me begging for?

     OEDIPUS.   Drive me out of this country as quickly as may be
To a place where no human voice can ever greet me.

     KREON.   I should have done that before now—only,
God's will had not been wholly revealed to me.

     OEDIPUS.   But his command is plain: the parricide
Must be destroyed. I am that evil man.

     KREON.   That is the sense of it, yes; but as things are,
We had best discover clearly what is to be done.

     OEDIPUS.   You would learn more about a man like me?

     KREON.   You are ready now to listen to the god.

     OEDIPUS.   I will listen. But it is to you
That I must turn for help. I beg you, hear me.

The woman in there—
Give her whatever funeral you think proper:
She is your sister.
           —But let me go, Kreon!
Let me purge my father's Thebes of the pollution
Of my living here, and go out to the wild hills,
To Kithairon, that has won such fame with me,
The tomb my mother and father appointed for me,
And let me die there, as they willed I should.
And yet I know
Death will not ever come to me through sickness
Or in any natural way: I have been preserved
For some unthinkable fate. But let that be.

As for my sons, you need not care for them.
They are men, they will find some way to live.
But my poor daughters, who have shared my table,
Who never before have been parted from their father—
Take care of them, Kreon; do this for me.
And will you let me touch them with my hands
A last time, and let us weep together?
Be kind, my lord,
Great prince, be kind!
          Could I but touch them,
They would be mine again, as when I had my eyes.
               [*Enter* ANTIGONE *and* ISMENE, *attended.*]

Ah, God!
Is it my dearest children I hear weeping?

Has Kreon pitied me and sent my daughters?

    KREON.   Yes, Oedipus: I knew that they were dear to you
In the old days, and know you must love them still.

    OEDIPUS.   May God bless you for this—and be a friendlier
Guardian to you than he has been to me!

Children, where are you?
Come quickly to my hands: they are your brother's—
Hands that have brought your father's once clear eyes
To this way of seeing—

                    Ah dearest ones,
I had neither sight nor knowledge then, your father
By the woman who was the source of his own life!
And I weep for you—having no strength to see you—,
I weep for you when I think of the bitterness
That men will visit upon you all your lives.
What homes, what festivals can you attend
Without being forced to depart again in tears?
And when you come to marriageable age,
Where is the man, my daughters, who would dare
Risk the bane that lies on all my children?
Is there any evil wanting? Your father killed
His father; sowed the womb of her who bore him;
Engendered you at the fount of his own existence!

That is what they will say of you.

                             Then, whom
Can you ever marry? There are no bridegrooms for you,
And your lives must wither away in sterile dreaming.

O Kreon, son of Menoikeus!
You are the only father my daughters have,
Since we, their parents, are both of us gone for ever.
They are your own blood: you will not let them
Fall into beggary and loneliness;
You will keep them from the miseries that are mine!
Take pity on them; see, they are only children,
Friendless except for you. Promise me this,
Great Prince, and give me your hand in token of it.

                                 [KREON *clasps his right hand.*]

Children:
I could say much, if you could understand me,
But as it is, I have only this prayer for you:
Live where you can, be as happy as you can—
Happier, please God, than God has made your father.

    KREON.   Enough. You have wept enough. Now go within.

    OEDIPUS.   I must; but it is hard.

    KREON.   Time eases all things.

    OEDIPUS.   You know my mind, then?

KREON. Say what you desire.

OEDIPUS. Send me from Thebes!

KREON. God grant that I may![49]

OEDIPUS. But since God hates me . . .

KREON. No, he will grant your wish.

OEDIPUS. You promise?

KREON. I can not speak beyond my knowledge.

OEDIPUS. Then lead me in.

KREON. Come now, and leave your children.

OEDIPUS. No! Do not take them from me!

KREON. Think no longer
That you are in command here, but rather think
How, when you were, you served your own destruction.

[*Exeunt into the house all but the* CHORUS; *the*
CHORAGOS *chants directly to the audience.*]

CHORAGOS. Men of Thebes: look upon Oedipus.

This is the king who solved the famous riddle
And towered up, most powerful of men.
No mortal eyes but looked on him with envy,
Yet in the end ruin swept over him.

Let every man in mankind's frailty
Consider his last day; and let none
Presume on his good fortune until he find
Life, at his death, a memory without pain.

COMMENTARY

The plot of *Oedipus Rex* is at once the most ingenious and the most terrible
that has ever been conceived. It can be thought of as a detective story in
which the detective, secure in his own virtue and in the consciousness that he
is doing his duty, undertakes to discover the identity of the person who has
committed a crime of great seriousness and is forced by the evidence he turns
up to recognize that the criminal is none other than himself. And more than
this is in store for him. As he pursues his investigations further, he learns that
the criminal act, because it was he who committed it, is immeasurably worse
than at first it had seemed.

Summarized even in this abstract way, the story of Oedipus is calculated to
disturb us in our deepest and most private emotions, for most of us live with
the sense of a guilty secret, although what the secret is about we do not know.
And of course the play haunts and disturbs us the more because of the peculiar
heinousness of what Oedipus has done. He has committed not merely terrible
crimes but terrible sins, violating not only the law of society but of the gods.
And even the idea of sin does not comprehend the horror of a man's having
killed his father and married his mother. These acts are, as we say, unthinkable;
the human mind can do nothing with them.

[49] Kreon refuses to act until he knows the will of the gods in this matter.

Our disturbance is not lessened but increased by the consideration that Oedipus did not commit his awful acts by intention. Of all the circumstances of the hero's fate, this is the one that most teases, baffles, and terrifies. It is reasonable to say—it has been said—that Oedipus is not accountable for what he did, that he had not really incurred guilt in killing his father and marrying his mother because he had not meant to do these things; on the contrary, once he had heard the awful prophecy, he had bent all his effort toward not doing them. This exculpation of Oedipus is based upon Aristotle's doctrine, set forth in his *Ethics,* to which assent is given by law and morality throughout the Western world, that for an act to have ethical significance, for good or bad, the person who commits it must have done so with consciousness and will. It is in these terms that Oedipus argues for his blamelessness in *Oedipus at Colonus,* the play that Sophocles wrote thirty years later. Worn out with suffering and on the point of death, the aged Oedipus, in a moment of bitterness and self-pity, says that he should not have been adjudged guilty because he had had no intention of wrong-doing. But in *Oedipus Rex* he makes no such claim to innocence. He does not justify himself; his mind is wholly given over to horror and self-loathing. We feel this response to be appropriate. The rationality of Aristotle's doctrine of intention seems quite inapplicable to the emotion evoked by Oedipus' situation, which occurs at a depth to which reason cannot penetrate. It is from the disclosure of this primitive depth that the play derives its terrible power, leading us to recognize that a man may incur guilt, and of an ultimate kind, even though a rational ethic might pronounce him innocent; we are brought to confront the possibility that reason can be superseded by darker modes of judgment. The security that a rational ethic had seemed to afford is taken from us.

An engaging question often raised about *Oedipus Rex* is whether or not it is a tragedy of fate. Much ingenuity has been expended to show that it is not. Some critics feel that the play becomes less interesting and impressive if it is taken as a tragedy of fate, for the protagonist then lacks the dignity that we associate with the possession of free will; he becomes, as we say, a puppet in the hands of destiny. Those who hold this position believe that they have an ally in Aristotle, who, in his *Poetics,* says that the protagonist of a tragedy should be a man worthy of respect and admiration but having some discernible weakness or fault of character to which his tragic disaster may be attributed. In some important sense, that is, he is to be thought responsible for what befalls him.

Aristotle's prescription would certainly seem to be satisfied by the character of Oedipus. He is admirable for many qualities. He is wise and courageous; it was he who, when everyone else stood helpless before the Sphinx that ravaged Thebes, answered her riddle and destroyed her, thus freeing the land of which he then became the ruler. As a king he is virtuous and conscientious. To be sure, he is called *tyrannos,* which, although it is not to be translated as "tyrant," means a king who rules by his own power, as distinguished from *basileus,* a king by legal right. Yet he is in no way arbitrary or repressive; he admits his wife to equal rule with him and allows her brother Kreon to stand almost on a parity with the royal couple. As husband and father he is dutiful and loving. He is not lacking in piety; although he speaks contemptuously to the great seer Teiresias, the protégé of Apollo, he holds the gods in due awe and is quick to undertake what Apollo's oracle at Delphi tells him should be done to rid the city of plague.

One fault, however, Oedipus does have, that of pride, and he is quick to anger when his pride is offended. His slaying of his unknown father Laïos at the crossroads had been the outcome of this trait. And it is his choleric pride, amounting to arrogance, that prevents him from heeding any word of caution when he is pursuing his search for the killer of Laïos, with the result that he is forced to confront the truth that he himself is the killer—and, of course, something more than that.

Yet no matter how fully we take account of Oedipus's fault of character, we have no ground for saying that the tragic disaster is brought about by this personal flaw and not by the predestination announced in the prophecy. That the fault detonates the disaster is of course true, but the explosives have been laid by what, in the nature of the prophecy about Oedipus, we can only call fate. The young hero's hot-blooded response to Laïos' insult and show of violence did indeed lead him to kill *a man*, and, what is worse, a king; but it was the fated ignorance of his parenthood and the unsought but destined occasion of the meeting between father and son that led him to kill *his father*. Any other proud and hot-blooded man who had done what Oedipus did would have committed an act that was to be deplored and condemned: for Oedipus alone the act was immitigable, and the more so because it led to an act yet more horrifying, his marriage to his mother.

If we take the line that Oedipus brought about his tragedy by refusing to heed the advice to be cautious in his search for Laïos' killer, we find ourselves in the position of supposing that all would have been well if he had prudently given up his investigation and settled to live in contented ignorance with his wife and children in plague-ridden Thebes. Of course we can suppose no such thing. Nor would we have any satisfaction if any such thing came about. To be sure, we are impelled to cry out a warning to the impetuous man not to call upon *that* witness, not to ask *that* question; we are fearful of the moment when the full dreadful knowledge will come to him of who he is and what he has done. But we do not want Oedipus to remain oblivious of the truth about himself. An Oedipus who prudently gave up his search would be an object of condescension, even of contempt: the Oedipus who presses on to the conclusion that destroys him compels our awed respect.

In short, then, whatever it may also be, the story of Oedipus must certainly be called a tragedy of fate. Yet to say this is, after all, not to say much. Something of what must be added if we are to account for the peculiar power of *Oedipus Rex* is suggested by a comparison of the story of the play with a well-known tale of similar purport. In the city of Ispahan, in Persia, a certain man's servant came to him and said, "I was in the market place and there I saw Death and he made a threatening gesture to me." The man said, "Let us flee," and he and his servant set out posthaste for Samarra. No sooner had they entered that city than they encountered Death, to whom the man said, "Why did you threaten my servant in the market place in Ispahan?" Death replied, "My gesture was not one of threat but of surprise, for I had an appointment to meet you in Samarra, and I was surprised to learn, from seeing your servant, that you were still in Ispahan." In its barest outline, the story of Oedipus is no different from this—a man, fleeing his fate, encounters it. But the wry little parable of fatalism evokes no other response than an ironic shrug; the mind does not engage it, there is really nothing in the tale for the mind to engage. The implied generalization, that all men must submit to what is ordained for them, that some fulfil their fate by the very intention of evading it, may win from us a certain assent but not much interest. We respond very differently when a man such as Oedipus fulfils his fate by seeking to evade it—a man whose pride, courage, and intellect suggest an ideal of mankind, and whose particular destiny it is to experience on so great a scale the peculiarly human pain of remorse and self-reproach. The man who flees from Ispahan to Samarra is indeed without dignity, a mere puppet in the hands of destiny; the joke is on him, fate has made a fool of him. But Oedipus, who is unable to save himself by intelligence and right intention and who is subject to an order of things which does not proceed by human rules and is not susceptible to human understanding, is enhanced in stature by his doom.

Aristotle's *Poetics* is chiefly devoted to a discussion of tragedy, and it is obvious that among all the Athenian achievements in this genre the author gives his highest admiration to *Oedipus Rex.* One cannot resist the speculation that he held the play in especial regard because it so deeply challenges and so successfully baffles the rational intellect, of which he was the great exemplar, and that he loved this play because it proposed the existence of forces inscrutable to human reason. If his spirit was as large as his mind, he may well have found pleasure in contemplating an order that did not yield its secrets to the demands of rational intellect.

Oedipus at Colonus, the play that Sophocles wrote in the year of his death at the age of ninety, also speaks of an order that baffles reason. Oedipus is now very old; he has been wandering the earth, an outcast, attended only by his two daughters. Although he is feeble and foredone, his quickness to anger has not diminished, and now his rage is directed toward his two sons because they have permitted him to continue in the exile to which he had doomed himself. He is bitter at his fate and he insists on his blamelessness—he is not, it is plain, an endearing person. Yet word has gone out that the city will be blessed which gives this accursed outcast his last resting place and buries him with honor. And when death comes to him at Colonus, a suburb of Athens, it is not death as ordinary men know it, but apotheosis: by divine agency he is carried off from earth to live as a demigod. This end is not granted Oedipus in compensation for his suffering but in recognition of some power of his nature that approaches the divine. We are left to ponder how it is that this cursed man became a blessing and why this guilty man should have been so supremely rewarded.

The Tragedy of KING LEAR

WILLIAM SHAKESPEARE
1564–1616

CHARACTERS

LEAR, *King of Britain*

KING OF FRANCE

DUKE OF BURGUNDY

DUKE OF CORNWALL

DUKE OF ALBANY

EARL OF KENT

EARL OF GLOUCESTER

EDGAR, *son to* GLOUCESTER

EDMUND, *bastard son to*
  GLOUCESTER

CURAN, *a courtier*

OLD MAN, *tenant to* GLOUCESTER

DOCTOR

FOOL

OSWALD, *steward to* GONERIL

A CAPTAIN *employed by* EDMUND

GENTLEMAN *attendant on* CORDELIA

A HERALD

SERVANTS *to* CORNWALL

GONERIL

REGAN } *daughters to* LEAR

CORDELIA

Knights of Lear's Train, Captains, Messengers, Soldiers,
and Attendants

SCENE: *Britain.*

King Lear's palace.

[*Enter* KENT, GLOUCESTER, *and* EDMUND.]

KENT. I thought the King had more affected[1] the Duke of Albany than Cornwall.

GLOUCESTER. It did always seem so to us; but now, in the division of the kingdom, it appears not which of the Dukes he values most; for equalities[2] are so weigh'd,[3] that curiosity[4] in neither can make choice of[5] either's moiety.[6]

KENT. Is not this your son, my lord?

GLOUCESTER. His breeding, sir, hath been at my charge. I have so often blushed to acknowledge him, that now I am brazed[7] to 't.

KENT. I cannot conceive[8] you.

GLOUCESTER. Sir, this young fellow's mother could; whereupon she grew round-wombed, and had, indeed, sir, a son for her cradle ere she had a husband for her bed. Do you smell a fault?

KENT. I cannot wish the fault undone, the issue of it being so proper.

GLOUCESTER. But I have a son, sir, by order of law, some year older than this, who yet is no dearer in my account. Though this knave came something saucily into the world before he was sent for, yet was his mother fair; there was good sport at his making, and the whoreson[9] must be acknowledged. Do you know this noble gentleman, Edmund?

EDMUND. No, my lord.

GLOUCESTER. My Lord of Kent. Remember him hereafter as my honourable friend.

EDMUND. My services to your lordship.

KENT. I must love you, and sue to know you better.

EDMUND. Sir, I shall study deserving.

GLOUCESTER. He hath been out nine years, and away he shall again. The King is coming.

[*Sennet.*[10] *Enter one bearing a coronet, then* KING LEAR, *then the* DUKES OF ALBANY *and* CORNWALL, *next* GONERIL, REGAN, CORDELIA, *with followers.*]

LEAR. Attend the lords of France and Burgundy, Gloucester.

GLOUCESTER. I shall, my liege. [*Exeunt* GLOUCESTER *and* EDMUND.]

LEAR. Meantime we shall express our darker[11] purpose.
Give me the map there. Know that we have divided
In three our kingdom; and 't is our fast intent
To shake all cares and business from our age,
Conferring them on younger strengths, while we
Unburden'd crawl toward death. Our son of Cornwall,
And you, our no less loving son of Albany,

---

[1] affected—favored. [*The footnotes used are those of the editor of this edition of the play, Alan S. Downer. L.T.*]   [2] equalities—shares.   [3] weigh'd—balanced.   [4] curiosity—close examination.   [5] of—between.   [6] moiety—share.   [7] brazed—hardened.   [8] conceive—understand.   [9] whoreson—bastard.   [10] Sennet—trumpet fanfare.   [11] darker—hitherto secret.

We have this hour a constant will to publish
Our daughters' several[12] dowers, that future strife
May be prevented now. The Princes, France and Burgundy,
Great rivals in our youngest daughter's love,
Long in our court have made their amorous sojourn,
And here are to be answer'd. Tell me, my daughters,—
Since now we will divest us both of rule,
Interest[13] of territory, cares of state,—
Which of you shall we say doth love us most,
That we our largest bounty may extend
Where nature[14] doth with merit[15] challenge?[16] Goneril,
Our eldest-born, speak first.

    GONERIL.   Sir, I do love you more than words can wield[17] the matter;
Dearer than eye-sight, space, and liberty:
Beyond what can be valued, rich or rare;
No less than life, with grace, health, beauty, honour;
As much as child e'er lov'd, or father found;
A love that makes breath poor, and speech unable:
Beyond all manner of so much[18] I love you.

    CORDELIA [aside].   What shall Cordelia speak? Love and be silent.

    LEAR.   Of all these bounds, even from this line to this,
With shadowy forest and with champains[19] rich'd,
With plenteous rivers and wide-skirted meads,
We make thee lady. To thine and Albany's issues
Be this perpetual. What says our second daughter,
Our dearest Regan, wife of Cornwall? Speak.

    REGAN.   I am made of that self[20] metal as my sister,
And prize me at her worth.[21] In my true heart
I find she names my very deed of love;
Only she comes too short, that I profess
Myself an enemy to all other joys
Which the most precious square[22] of sense possesses;
And find I am alone felicitate[23]
In your Highness' love.

    CORDELIA [aside].   Then poor Cordelia!
And yet not so; since, I am sure, my love's
More ponderous[24] than my tongue.

    LEAR.   To thee and thine hereditary ever
Remain this ample third of our fair kingdom;
No less in space, validity,[25] and pleasure,

---

12 several—separate.   13 Interest—possession.   14 nature—natural affection.   15 with merit—plus individual merit.   16 challenge—make a claim.   17 wield—express.   18 of so much—of these things.   19 champains—fields.   20 self—same.   21 prize me at her worth—appraise myself her equal.   22 square—criterion.   23 felicitate—made happy.   24 more ponderous—weightier.   25 validity—value.

Than that conferr'd on Goneril. Now, our joy,
Although our last and least, to whose young love
The vines of France and milk of Burgundy
Strive to be interess'd,[26] what can you say to draw
A third more opulent than your sisters? Speak.

    CORDELIA.   Nothing, my lord.

    LEAR.   Nothing!

    CORDELIA.   Nothing.

    LEAR.   Nothing will come of nothing. Speak again.

    CORDELIA.   Unhappy that I am, I cannot heave
My heart into my mouth. I love your Majesty
According to my bond;[27] nor more nor less.

    LEAR.   How, how, Cordelia! Mend your speech a little,
Lest you may mar your fortune.

    CORDELIA.   Good my lord,
You have begot me, bred me, lov'd me: I
Return those duties back as are right fit;
Obey you, love you, and most honour you.
Why have my sisters husbands, if they say
They love you all? Haply,[28] when I shall wed,
That lord whose hand must take my plight[29] shall carry
Half my love with him, half my care and duty.
Sure, I shall never marry like my sisters
To love my father all.

    LEAR.   But goes thy heart with this?

    CORDELIA.   Ay, my good lord.

    LEAR.   So young, and so untender?

    CORDELIA.   So young, my lord, and true.

    LEAR.   Let it be so; thy truth, then, be thy dower!
For, by the sacred radiance of the sun,
The mysteries of Hecate,[30] and the night;
By all the operation of the orbs[31]
From whom we do exist, and cease to be;
Here I disclaim all my paternal care,
Propinquity[32] and property of blood,
And as a stranger to my heart and me
Hold thee, from this, for ever. The barbarous Scythian,[33]
Or he that makes his generation messes[34]

To gorge his appetite, shall to my bosom
Be as well neighbour'd, piti'd, and reliev'd,
As thou my sometime daughter.

    KENT.   Good my liege,—

    LEAR.   Peace, Kent!
Come not between the dragon[35] and his wrath.

---

[26] be interess'd—enter a claim.   [27] bond—bounden duty.   [28] Haply—It may happen.
[29] plight—troth.   [30] Hecate—goddess of witchcraft.   [31] orbs—stars.   [32] Propinquity
—relationship.   [33] Scythian—South Russian, regarded as extremely savage.   [34] makes
his generation messes—makes food of his children.   [35] dragon—traditional symbol of
British kings.

I lov'd her most, and thought to set my rest[36]
On her kind nursery. [*To* CORDELIA.] Hence, and avoid[37] my sight!—
So be my grave my peace, as here I give
Her father's heart from her! Call France.—Who stirs?
Call Burgundy. Cornwall and Albany,
With my two daughters' dowers digest[38] this third;
Let pride, which she calls plainness, marry her.
I do invest you jointly in my power,
Pre-eminence,[39] and all the large effects[40]
That troop with majesty. Ourself, by monthly course,
With reservation of an hundred knights,
By you to be sustain'd, shall our abode
Make with you by due turn. Only we still retain
The name, and all th' additions[41] to a king;
The sway, revénue, execution of the rest,
Beloved sons, be yours; which to confirm,
This coronet part betwixt you.

     KENT.   Royal Lear,
Whom I have ever honour'd as my king,
Lov'd as my father, as my master follow'd,
As my great patron thought on in my prayers,—

     LEAR.   The bow is bent and drawn; make from the shaft.[42]

     KENT.   Let it fall rather, though the fork[43] invade
The region of my heart: be Kent unmannerly
When Lear is mad. What wouldst thou do, old man?
Think'st thou that duty shall have dread to speak
When power to flattery bows? To plainness honour's bound,
When majesty falls to folly. Reserve thy state;
And, in thy best consideration, check
This hideous rashness. Answer my life my judgement,
Thy youngest daughter does not love thee least;
Nor are those empty-hearted whose low sounds
Reverb[44] no hollowness.

     LEAR.   Kent, on thy life, no more.

     KENT.   My life I never held but as a pawn[45]
To wage[46] against thine enemies, nor fear to lose it,
Thy safety being the motive.

     LEAR.   Out of my sight!

     KENT.   See better, Lear; and let me still remain
The true blank[47] of thine eye.

     LEAR.   Now, by Apollo,—

     KENT.   Now, by Apollo, king,
Thou swear'st thy gods in vain.

---

[36] set my rest—rely completely.   [37] avoid—leave.   [38] digest—incorporate.   [39] Pre-eminence—authority.   [40] large effects—show of power.   [41] additions—titles. [42] shaft—arrow.   [43] fork—barb.   [44] Reverb—echo.   [45] pawn—pledge.   [46] wage—stake.   [47] blank—target.

LEAR.   O, vassal! miscreant!

[*Laying his hand on his sword.*]

ALBANY.   }
CORNWALL.   } Dear sir, forbear.

KENT.   Kill thy physician, and thy fee bestow
Upon the foul disease. Revoke thy doom;
Or, whilst I can vent clamour from my throat,
I'll tell thee thou dost evil.

LEAR.   Hear me, recreant!
On thine allegiance, hear me!
That thou hast sought to make us break our vows,
Which we durst never yet, and with strain'd pride
To come betwixt our sentence and our power,
Which nor our nature nor our place can bear,
Our potency made good,[48] take thy reward.
Five days we do allot thee, for provision
To shield thee from diseases of the world;
And on the sixth to turn thy hated back
Upon our kingdom. If, on the tenth day following,
Thy banish'd trunk be found in our dominions,
The moment is thy death. Away! By Jupiter,[49]
This shall not be revok'd.

KENT.   Fare thee well, king! Sith[50] thus thou wilt appear,
Freedom lives hence, and banishment is here.
[*To* CORDELIA.] The gods to their dear shelter take thee, maid,
That justly think'st, and hast most rightly said!
[*To* REGAN *and* GONERIL.] And your large speeches may your deeds approve,[51]
That good effects[52] may spring from words of love.
Thus Kent, O princes, bids you all adieu;
He'll shape his old course[53] in a country new. [*Exit.*]

[*Flourish.[54] Enter* GLOUCESTER, *with* FRANCE *and* BURGUNDY, *Attendants.*]

GLOUCESTER.   Here's France[55] and Burgundy,[56] my noble lord.

LEAR.   My Lord of Burgundy,
We first address toward you, who with this king
Hath rivall'd for our daughter. What, in the least,
Will you require[57] in present[58] dower with her,
Or cease your quest of love?

BURGUNDY.   Most royal Majesty.
I crave no more than hath your Highness offer'd,
Nor will you tender[59] less.

LEAR.   Right noble Burgundy,
When she was dear to us, we did hold her so;
But now her price is fal'n. Sir, there she stands:

---

[48] our potency made good—my royal will having been asserted.   [49] Jupiter—chief of the Roman gods. The classic pantheon is used in this play to fit a pagan, not necessarily Roman, society.   [50] Sith—since.   [51] approve—confirm.   [52] effects—actions.   [53] old course—i.e., as a faithful, plain-spoken subject.   [54] Flourish—trumpet fanfare.   [55] France—the king of France.   [56] Burgundy—the duke of Burgundy.   [57] require—request.   [58] present—immediate.   [59] tender—offer.

If aught within that little-seeming substance,
Or all of it, with our displeasure piec'd,[60]
And nothing more, may fitly like your Grace,
She's there, and she is yours.

    BURGUNDY.   I know no answer.

    LEAR.   Will you, with those infirmities she owes,[61]
Unfriended, new-adopted to our hate,
Dower'd with our curse, and stranger'd with our oath,
Take her, or leave her?

    BURGUNDY.   Pardon me, royal sir;
Election[62] makes not up in such conditions.

    LEAR.   Then leave her, sir; for, by the power that made me,
I tell you all her wealth. [*To* FRANCE.] For you, great king,
I would not from your love make such a stray,
To match you where I hate; therefore beseech you
T' avert your liking a more worthier way
Than on a wretch whom Nature is asham'd
Almost t' acknowledge hers.

    FRANCE.   This is most strange,
That she, that even but now was your best object,[63]
The argument of your praise, balm of your age,
Most best, most dearest, should in this trice[64] of time
Commit a thing so monstrous, to dismantle
So many folds of favour. Sure, her offence
Must be of such unnatural degree,
That monsters[65] it, or your fore-vouch'd[66] affection
Fall'n into taint;[67] which to believe of her,
Must be a faith that reason without miracle
Should never plant in me.

    CORDELIA.   I yet beseech your Majesty,—
If for I want that glib and oily art,
To speak and purpose not; since what I well intend,
I'll do 't before I speak,—that you make known
It is no vicious blot,[68] murder, or foulness,
No unchaste action, or dishonoured step,
That hath depriv'd me of your grace and favour;
But even for want[69] of that for which I am richer,
A still-soliciting[70] eye, and such a tongue
That I am glad I have not, though not to have it
Hath lost me in your liking.

    LEAR.   Better thou
Hadst not been born than not to have pleas'd me better.

    FRANCE.   It is but this,—a tardiness[71] in nature
Which often leaves the history unspoke

---

[60] piec'd—added.   [61] owes—possesses.   [62] Election—choice.   [63] best object—favorite.   [64] trice—moment.   [65] monsters—makes monstrous.   [66] fore-vouch'd—previously declared.   [67] into taint—decay.   [68] vicious blot—immoral act.   [69] want—lack.   [70] still-soliciting—always asking favors.   [71] tardiness—reticence.

That it intends to do? My Lord of Burgundy,
What say you to the lady? Love is not love
When it is mingled with regards[72] that stands
Aloof from th' entire point.[73] Will you have her?
She is herself a dowry.

      BURGUNDY.   Royal Lear,
Give but that portion which yourself propos'd,
And here I take Cordelia by the hand,
Duchess of Burgundy.

      LEAR.   Nothing. I have sworn; I am firm.

      BURGUNDY.   I am sorry, then, you have so lost a father
That you must lose a husband.

      CORDELIA.   Peace be with Burgundy!
Since that respects of fortune[74] are his love,
I shall not be his wife.

      FRANCE.   Fairest Cordelia, that art most rich being poor,
Most choice forsaken, and most lov'd despis'd!
Thee and thy virtues here I seize upon,
Be it lawful I take up what's cast away.
Gods, gods! 't is strange that from their cold'st neglect
My love should kindle to inflam'd[75] respect.
Thy dowerless daughter, king, thrown to my chance,
Is queen of us, of ours, and our fair France.
Not all the dukes of waterish Burgundy
Shall buy this unpriz'd precious maid of me.
Bid them farewell, Cordelia, though unkind;
Thou losest here, a better where[76] to find.

      LEAR.   Thou hast her, France. Let her be thine; for we
Have no such daughter, nor shall ever see
That face of hers again.—[To CORDELIA.] Therefore be gone
Without our grace, our love, our benison.[77]
Come, noble Burgundy. [Flourish. Exeunt LEAR and BURGUNDY.]

      FRANCE.   Bid farewell to your sisters.

      CORDELIA.   The jewels of our father, with wash'd eyes
Cordelia leaves you. I know you what you are;
And like a sister am most loath to call
Your faults as they are named. Use well our father,
To your professed[78] bosoms I commit him;
But yet, alas, stood I within his grace,
I would prefer him to a better place.
So, farewell to you both.

      REGAN.   Prescribe not us our duties.

      GONERIL.   Let your study
Be to content your lord, who hath receiv'd you

---

[72] regards—considerations.   [73] entire point—love.   [74] respects of fortune—considerations of my dowry.   [75] inflam'd—passionate.   [76] where—place.   [77] benison—blessing.   [78] professed—professing (love).

At fortune's alms.[79] You have obedience scanted,[80]
And well are worth[81] the want[82] that you have wanted.[83]

    CORDELIA.   Time shall unfold what plighted[84] cunning hides;
Who covers faults, at last shame them derides.
Well may you prosper!

    FRANCE.   Come, my fair Cordelia. [*Exeunt* FRANCE *and* CORDELIA.]

    GONERIL.   Sister, it is not little I have to say of what most nearly appertains to us both. I think our father will hence tonight.

    REGAN.   That's most certain, and with you; next month with us.

    GONERIL.   You see how full of changes his age is; the observation we have made of it hath not been little. He always loved our sister most; and with what poor judgement he hath now cast her off appears too gross.[85]

    REGAN.   'T is the infirmity of his age; yet he hath ever but slenderly known himself.

    GONERIL.   The best and soundest of his time[86] hath been but rash; then must we look to receive from his age not alone the imperfections of long-engrafted condition,[87] but therewithal the unruly waywardness that infirm and choleric years bring with them.

    REGAN.   Such unconstant starts[88] are we like to have from him as this of Kent's banishment.

    GONERIL.   There is further compliment of leave-taking between France and him. Pray you, let's hit[89] together; if our father carry authority with such disposition as he bears, this last surrender of his will but offend[90] us.

    REGAN.   We shall further think on 't.

    GONERIL.   We must do something, and i' th' heat.[91] [*Exeunt.*]

ACT I · 2

The Earl of Gloucester's castle.

[*Enter* EDMUND *with a letter.*]

    EDMUND.   Thou, Nature, art my goddess; to thy law
My services are bound. Wherefore should I
Stand in the plague[1] of custom, and permit
The curiosity[2] of nations to deprive me,
For that I am some twelve or fourteen moonshines
Lag[3] of a brother? Why bastard? Wherefore base?
When my dimensions are as well compact,
My mind as generous, and my shape as true,
As honest madam's issue? Why brand they us

---

79 at fortune's alms—as charity from fortune.   80 scanted—fallen short in.   81 worth—deserve.   82 want—lack of love (from your husband.   83 wanted—as you have shown lack of love for your father.   84 plighted—folded.   85 gross—obvious.   86 of his time—periods of his life.   87 long-engrafted condition—natural temperament.   88 starts—whims.   89 hit—agree.   90 offend—give trouble.   91 i' th' heat—while the iron is hot.
1 plague—vexation.   2 curiosity—absurd law.   3 Lag—behind.

With base? with baseness? bastardy? base, base?
Who, in the lusty stealth of nature, take
More composition[4] and fierce quality[5]
Than doth, within a dull, stale, tired bed,
Go to th' creating a whole tribe of fops,
Got[6] 'tween asleep and wake? Well then,
Legitimate Edgar, I must have your land.
Our father's love is to the bastard Edmund
As to th' legitimate. Fine word, "legitimate"!
Well, my legitimate, if this letter speed[7]
And my invention thrive, Edmund the base
Shall top th' legitimate. I grow; I prosper.
Now, gods, stand up for bastards!

[*Enter* GLOUCESTER.]

GLOUCESTER.   Kent banish'd thus! and France in choler[8] parted!
And the King gone to-night! subscrib'd[9] his power!
Confin'd to exhibition![10] All this done
Upon the gad![11] Edmund, how now! what news?

EDMUND.   So please your lordship, none. [*Putting up the letter.*]

GLOUCESTER.   Why so earnestly seek you to put up that letter?

EDMUND.   I know no news, my lord.

GLOUCESTER.   What paper were you reading?

EDMUND.   Nothing, my lord.

GLOUCESTER.   No? What needed, then, that terrible dispatch of it into
your pocket? The quality of nothing hath not such need to hide itself. Let's see.
Come, if it be nothing, I shall not need spectacles.

EDMUND.   I beseech you, sir, pardon me. It is a letter from my brother,
that I have not all o'erread; and for so much as I have perused, I find it not fit
for your o'erlooking.

GLOUCESTER.   Give me the letter, sir.

EDMUND.   I shall offend, either to detain or give it. The contents, as in
part I understand them, are to blame.[12]

GLOUCESTER.   Let's see, let's see.

EDMUND.   I hope, for my brother's justification, he wrote this but as an
essay[13] or taste of my virtue.

GLOUCESTER [*reads*].

This policy[14] and reverence of age makes the world bitter to the best of our
times;[15] keeps our fortunes from us till our oldness cannot relish them. I begin to
find an idle and fond[16] bondage in the oppression of aged tyranny; who sways, not
as it hath power, but as it is suffered.[17] Come to me, that of this I may speak more.
If our father would sleep till I waked him, you should enjoy half his revénue for
ever, and live the beloved of your brother,

> EDGAR.

---

[4] composition—strength.   [5] fierce quality—energy.   [6] Got—conceived.   [7] speed—
prosper.   [8] choler—anger.   [9] subscrib'd—signed away.   [10] exhibition—a pension.
[11] gad—spur of the moment.   [12] to blame—blameworthy.   [13] essay—test.   [14] policy and reverence—strategy of requiring reverence for.   [15] our times—our youth.
[16] fond—foolish.   [17] suffered—submitted to.

Hum—conspiracy!—"Sleep till I wake him, you should enjoy half his revénue!" My son Edgar! Had he a hand to write this? a heart and brain to breed it in?—When came this to you? Who brought it?

EDMUND. It was not brought me, my lord; there's the cunning of it. I found it thrown in at the casement of my closet.[18]

GLOUCESTER. You know the character[19] to be your brother's?

EDMUND. If the matter were good, my lord, I durst swear it were his; but, in respect of that, I would fain think it were not.

GLOUCESTER. It is his.

EDMUND. It is his hand, my lord; but I hope his heart is not in the contents.

GLOUCESTER. Hath he never heretofore sounded you in this business?

EDMUND. Never, my lord; but I have heard him oft maintain it to be fit that, sons at perfect age, and fathers declined, the father should be as ward to the son, and the son manage his revénue.

GLOUCESTER. O villain, villain! His very opinion in the letter! Abhorred villain! Unnatural, detested, brutish villain! worse than brutish! Go, sirrah, seek him; I'll apprehend him. Abominable villain! Where is he?

EDMUND. I do not well know, my lord. It it shall please you to suspend your indignation against my brother till you can derive from him better testimony of his intent, you should run a certain course;[20] where, if you violently proceed against him, mistaking his purpose, it would make a great gap in your own honour, and shake in pieces the heart of his obedience. I dare pawn down my life for him, that he hath wrote this to feel my affection to your honour, and to no further pretence of danger.

GLOUCESTER. Think you so?

EDMUND. If your honour judge it meet, I will place you where you shall hear us confer of this, and by an auricular assurance[21] have your satisfaction; and that without any further delay than this very evening.

GLOUCESTER. He cannot be such a monster—

EDMUND. Nor is not, sure.

GLOUCESTER. To his father, that so tenderly and entirely loves him. Heaven and earth! Edmund, seek him out; wind me into him,[22] I pray you. Frame the business after your own wisdom. I would unstate[23] myself, to be in a due resolution.[24]

EDMUND. I will seek him, sir, presently;[25] convey[26] the business as I shall find means, and acquaint you withal.[27]

GLOUCESTER. These late eclipses in the sun and moon portend no good to us. Though the wisdom of nature can reason[28] it thus and thus, yet nature finds itself scourged by the sequent[29] effects. Love cools, friendship falls off, brothers divide: in cities, mutinies; in countries, discord; in palaces, treason; and the bond cracked 'twixt son and father. This villain of mine comes under the prediction; there's son against father: the King falls from bias of nature; there's father against child. We have seen the best of our time; machinations,

---

[18] closet—private room.   [19] character—handwriting.   [20] certain course—proceed more surely.   [21] auricular assurance—hearing the evidence.   [22] wind me into him—gain his confidence.   [23] unstate—give up my earldom.   [24] in a due resolution—freed of doubts.   [25] presently—immediately.   [26] convey—conduct.   [27] withal—with the results.   [28] reason—explain.   [29] sequent—consequent.

hollowness, treachery, and all ruinous disorders, follow us disquietly to our graves. Find out this villain, Edmund; it shall lose thee nothing; do it carefully. And the noble and true-hearted Kent banished! his offence, honesty! 'T is strange. [*Exit.*]

EDMUND. This is the excellent foppery[30] of the world, that, when we are sick in fortune,—often the surfeit[31] of our own behaviour,—we make guilty of our disasters the sun, the moon, and the stars, as if we were villains on necessity, fools by heavenly compulsion, knaves, and treachers by spherical predominance,[32] drunkards, liars, and adulterers by an enforced obedience of planetary influence, and all that we are evil in, by a divine thrusting on. An admirable evasion of whoremaster man, to lay his goatish[33] disposition on the charge of a star! My father compounded with my mother under the dragon's tail and my nativity was under *Ursa major;*[34] so that it follows, I am rough and lecherous. Fut, I should have been that I am, had the maidenliest star in the firmament twinkled on my bastardizing. Edgar—

[*Enter* EDGAR.]

and pat he comes like the catastrophe[35] of the old comedy. My cue is villainous melancholy, with a sigh like Tom o' Bedlam.[36]—O, these eclipses do portend these divisions! *fa, sol, la, mi.*

EDGAR. How now, brother Edmund! what serious contemplation are you in?

EDMUND. I am thinking, brother, of a prediction I read this other day, what should follow these eclipses.

EDGAR. Do you busy yourself with that?

EDMUND. I promise you, the effects he writ of succeed[37] unhappily; as of unnaturalness between the child and the parent; death, dearth,[38] dissolutions of ancient amities; divisions in state, menaces and maledictions against king and nobles; needless diffidences, banishment of friends, dissipation of cohorts, nuptial breaches, and I know not what.

EDGAR. How long have you been a sectary astronomical?[39]

EDMUND. Come, come; when saw you my father last?

EDGAR. Why, the night gone by.

EDMUND. Spake you with him?

EDGAR. Ay, two hours together.

EDMUND. Parted you in good terms? Found you no displeasure in him by word nor countenance?

EDGAR. None at all.

EDMUND. Bethink yourself wherein you may have offended him; and at my entreaty forbear his presence until some little time hath qualified[40] the heat of his displeasure, which at this instant so rageth in him, that with the mischief of[41] your person it would scarce allay.

EDGAR. Some villain hath done me wrong.

EDMUND. That's my fear. I pray you, have a continent forbearance[42] till

---

[30] foppery—folly.   [31] surfeit—overeating, i.e., because of our own overindulgence. [32] spherical predominance—influence of the planets.   [33] goatish—lustful.   [34] *Ursa major*—the constellation of the Great Bear.   [35] catastrophe—final event.   [36] Tom o' Bedlam—lunatic beggar.   [37] succeed—follow.   [38] dearth—famine.   [39] sectary astronomical—believer in astrology.   [40] qualified—modified.   [41] Mischief of—injury to. [42] continent forbearance—self-control.

the speed of his rage goes slower; and, as I say, retire with me to my lodging, from whence I will fitly bring you to hear my lord speak. Pray ye, go; there's my key. If you do stir abroad, go armed.

EDGAR.   Armed, brother!

EDMUND.   Brother, I advise you to the best; I am no honest man if there be any good meaning towards you. I have told you what I have seen and heard; but faintly, nothing like the image and horror of it. Pray you, away.

EDGAR.   Shall I hear from you anon?[43]

EDMUND.   I do serve you in this business. [*Exit* EDGAR.]

A credulous father, and a brother noble,
Whose nature is so far from doing harms
That he suspects none; on whose foolish honesty
My practices[44] ride easy. I see the business.
Let me, if not by birth, have lands by wit:
All with me's meet[45] that I can fashion fit. [*Exit.*]

ACT I · 3

The Duke of Albany's palace.

[*Enter* GONERIL, *and* OSWALD, *her Steward.*]

GONERIL.   Did my father strike my gentleman for chiding of his Fool?

OSWALD.   Ay, madam.

GONERIL.   By day and night he wrongs me; every hour
He flashes into one gross crime or other
That sets us all at odds. I'll not endure it.
His knights grow riotous, and himself upbraids us
On every trifle. When he returns from hunting,
I will not speak with him; say I am sick.
If you come slack of former services,
You shall do well; the fault of it I'll answer.

OSWALD.   He's coming, madam; I hear him. [*Horns within.*]

GONERIL.   Put on what weary negligence you please,
You and your fellows; I'd have it come to question,[1]
If he distaste[2] it, let him to our sister,
Whose mind and mine, I know, in that are one,
Not to be over-rul'd. Idle old man,
That still would manage those authorities
That he hath given away! Now, by my life,
Old fools are babes again, and must be us'd
With checks[3] as[4] flatteries, when they are seen abus'd.[5]
Remember what I have said.

OSWALD.   Well, madam.

---

[43] anon—soon.   [44] practices—plots.   [45] meet—proper.
[1] question—open discussion.   [2] distaste—dislike.   [3] checks—rebukes.   [4] as—as well as.   [5] abus'd—misled.

GONERIL.   And let his knights have colder looks among you;
What grows of it, no matter. Advise your fellow so.
I would breed from hence occasions,[6] and I shall,
That I may speak. I'll write straight to my sister,
To hold my very course. Prepare for dinner. [*Exeunt.*]

ACT I · 4

A hall in the same.

[*Enter* KENT *disguised.*]
KENT.   If but as well I other accents borrow,
That can my speech defuse,[1] my good intent
May carry through itself to that full issue
For which I raz'd[2] my likeness. Now, banish'd Kent,
If thou canst serve where thou dost stand condemn'd,
So may it come, thy master, whom thou lov'st,
Shall find thee full of labours.
            [*Horns within. Enter* LEAR, KNIGHTS, *and Attendants.*]
LEAR.   Let me not stay a jot for dinner; go get it ready.
[*Exit an Attendant.*] How now! what art thou?
KENT.   A man, sir.
LEAR.   What dost thou profess? What wouldst thou with us?
KENT.   I do profess to be no less than I seem; to serve him truly that will put me in trust; to love him that is honest; to converse with him that is wise and says little; to fear judgement; to fight when I cannot choose; and to eat no fish.[3]
LEAR.   What art thou?
KENT.   A very honest-hearted fellow, and as poor as the King.
LEAR.   If thou be as poor for a subject as he is for a king, thou art poor enough. What wouldst thou?
KENT.   Service.
LEAR.   Who wouldst thou serve?
KENT.   You.
LEAR.   Dost thou know me, fellow?
KENT.   No, sir; but you have that in your countenance which I would fain call master.
LEAR.   What's that?
KENT.   Authority.
LEAR.   What services canst thou do?
KENT.   I can keep honest counsel, ride, run, mar a curious tale in telling it, and deliver a plain message bluntly. That which ordinary men are fit for, I am qualified in; and the best of me is diligence.

---

[6] occasions—opportunities.
[1] defuse—disguise.   [2] raz'd—shaved off (my beard).   [3] eat no fish—be a Protestant.

LEAR.   How old art thou?

KENT.   Not so young, sir, to love a woman for singing, nor so old to dote on her for anything. I have years on my back forty-eight.

LEAR.   Follow me; thou shalt serve me. If I like thee no worse after dinner, I will not part from thee yet. Dinner, ho, dinner! Where's my knave? my Fool? Go you, and call my Fool hither. [*Exit an Attendant.*]

[*Enter the Steward,* OSWALD.]

You, you, sirrah, where's my daughter?

OSWALD.   So please you,— [*Exit.*]

LEAR.   What says the fellow there? Call the clotpoll[4] back. [*Exit a* KNIGHT.] Where's my Fool, ho? I think the world's asleep.

[*Enter* KNIGHT.]

How now! where's that mongrel?

KNIGHT.   He says, my lord, your daughter is not well.

LEAR.   Why came not the slave back to me when I called him?

KNIGHT.   Sir, he answered me in the roundest[5] manner, he would not.

LEAR.   'A[6] would not!

KNIGHT.   My lord, I know not what the matter is; but, to my judgement, your Highness is not entertain'd with that ceremonious affection as you were wont. There's a great abatement of kindness appears as well in the general dependants as in the Duke himself also and your daughter.

LEAR.   Ha! say'st thou so?

KNIGHT.   I beseech you, pardon me, my lord, if I be mistaken; for my duty cannot be silent when I think your Highness wronged.

LEAR.   Thou but rememb'rest me of mine own conception.[7] I have perceived a most faint neglect of late, which I have rather blamed as mine own jealous curiosity[8] than as a very pretence and purpose of unkindness. I will look further into 't. But where's my Fool? I have not seen him this two days.

KNIGHT.   Since my young lady's going into France, sir, the Fool hath much pined away.

LEAR.   No more of that; I have noted it well. Go you, and tell my daughter I would speak with her. [*Exit an Attendant.*] Go you, call hither my Fool. [*Exit an Attendant.*]

[*Enter* OSWALD.]

O, you sir, you sir, come you hither. Who am I, sir?

OSWALD.   My lady's father.

LEAR.   "My lady's father"! My lord's knave! You whoreson dog! you slave! you cur!

OSWALD.   I am none of these, my lord; I beseech your pardon.

LEAR.   Do you bandy[9] looks with me, you rascal? [*Striking him.*]

OSWALD.   I'll not be strucken, my lord.

KENT.   Nor tripped neither, you base football player. [*Tripping up his heels.*]

LEAR.   I thank thee, fellow. Thou serv'st me, and I'll love thee.

KENT.   Come, sir, arise, away! I'll teach you differences.[10] Away, away!

---

4 clotpoll—blockhead.   5 roundest—most direct.   6 'A—he.   7 conception—idea, thought.   8 curiosity—watchfulness.   9 bandy—exchange.   10 differences—distinctions (of rank).

If you will measure your lubber's length again, tarry; but away! go to.[11] Have you wisdom? So. [*Pushes* OSWALD *out.*]

LEAR. Now, my friendly knave, I thank thee. There's earnest[12] of thy service. [*Giving* KENT *money.*]

[*Enter* FOOL.]

FOOL. Let me hire him too; here's my coxcomb.[13] [*Offering* KENT *his cap.*]

LEAR. How now, my pretty knave! how dost thou?

FOOL. Sirrah, you were best take my coxcomb.

KENT. Why, Fool?

FOOL. Why? For taking one's part that's out of favour. Nay, an thou canst not smile as the wind sits,[14] thou 'lt catch cold shortly. There, take my coxcomb. Why, this fellow hath banished two on[15] 's daughters, and did the third a blessing against his will; if thou follow him, thou must needs wear my coxcomb.—How now, nuncle![16] Would I had two coxcombs and two daughters!

LEAR. Why, my boy?

FOOL. If I gave them all my living, I'd keep my coxcombs myself. There's mine; beg another of thy daughters.

LEAR. Take heed, sirrah; the whip.

FOOL. Truth's a dog must to kennel; he must be whipped out, when Lady the brach[17] may stand by the fire and stink.

LEAR. A pestilent gall[18] to me!

FOOL. Sirrah, I'll teach thee a speech.

LEAR. Do.

FOOL. Mark it, nuncle:

> Have more than thou showest,
> Speak less than thou knowest,
> Lend less than thou owest,[19]
> Ride more than thou goest,
> Learn more than thou trowest,[20]
> Set[21] less than thou throwest;
> Leave thy drink and thy whore,
> And keep in-a-door,
> And thou shalt have more
> Than two tens to a score.

KENT. This is nothing, Fool.

FOOL. Then 'tis like the breath of an unfee'd lawyer; you gave me nothing for 't. Can you make no use of nothing, nuncle?

LEAR. Why, no, boy; nothing can be made out of nothing.

FOOL. [*To* KENT] Prithee, tell him so much the rent[22] of his land comes to. He will not believe a Fool.

LEAR. A bitter fool!

FOOL. Dost thou know the difference, my boy, between a bitter fool and a sweet fool?

LEAR. No, lad; teach me.

---

[11] go to—an exclamation of impatience. [12] earnest—advance money. [13] coxcomb—fool's cap, the badge of the fool's profession. [14] smile as the wind sits—agree with those in power. [15] on—of. [16] nuncle—uncle. [17] brach—favorite bitch. [18] pestilent gall—always rubbing a sore spot. [19] owest—own. [20] trowest—believe. [21] Set—wager. [22] rent—income.

FOOL.

> That lord that counsell'd thee
> To give away thy land,
> Come place him here by me,
> Do thou for him stand:
> The sweet and bitter fool
> Will presently appear;
> The one in motley[23] here,
> The other found out there.

LEAR. Dost thou call me fool, boy?

FOOL. All thy other titles thou hast given away; that thou wast born with.

KENT. This is not altogether fool, my lord.

FOOL. No, faith, lords and great men will not let me; if I had a monopoly[24] out, they would have part[25] on 't. And ladies, too, they will not let me have all the fool to myself; they'll be snatching. Nuncle, give me an egg, and I'll give thee two crowns.

LEAR. What two crowns shall they be?

FOOL. Why, after I have cut the egg i' th' middle, and eat up the meat, the two crowns of the egg. When thou clovest thy crown i' th' middle, and gav'st away both parts, thou bor'st thine ass[26] on thy back o'er the dirt. Thou hadst little wit in thy bald crown, when thou gav'st thy golden one away. If I speak like myself[27] in this, let him be whipped that first finds it so.

> Fools had ne'er less grace[28] in a year;
> For wise men are grown foppish,
> And know not how their wits to wear,
> Their manners are so apish.[29]

LEAR. When were you wont to be so full of songs, sirrah?

FOOL. I have used it, nuncle, ever since thou mad'st thy daughters thy mother, for when thou gav'st them the rod, and puttest down thine own breeches,

> Then they for sudden joy did weep,
> And I for sorrow sung,
> That such a king should play bo-peep[30]
> And go the fools among.

Prithee, nuncle, keep a schoolmaster that can teach thy Fool to lie. I would fain learn to lie.

LEAR. An[31] you lie, sirrah, we'll have you whipped.

FOOL. I marvel what kin thou and thy daughters are. They'll have me whipped for speaking true, thou 'lt have me whipped for lying; and sometimes I am whipp'd for holding my peace. I had rather be any kind o' thing than a Fool; and yet I would not be thee, nuncle; thou hast pared thy wit o' both sides, and left nothing i' the middle. Here comes one o' the parings.

---

[23] motley—the professional fool's parti-colored costume. [24] monopoly—the right to be sole dealer (in folly). [25] part—their share. [26] thine ass—like the countryman who carried his donkey when the roads were bad. [27] like myself—foolishly. [28] grave— favor. [29] apish—i.e., imitating fools. [30] bo-peep—hide and seek. [31] An—if.

LEAR.　How now, daughter! what makes that frontlet[32] on? Methinks you are too much of late i' th' frown.

FOOL.　Thou wast a pretty fellow when thou hadst no need to care for her frowning; now thou art an O[33] without a figure. I am better than thou art now; I am a Fool, thou art nothing. [*To* GONERIL.] Yes, forsooth, I will hold my tongue; so your face bids me, though you say nothing.

> Mum, mum,
> He that keeps nor crust nor crumb,
> Weary of all, shall want some.

[*Pointing to* LEAR.] That's a sheal'd peascod.[34]

GONERIL.　Not only, sir, this your all-licens'd[35] Fool,
But other of your insolent retinue
Do hourly carp and quarrel, breaking forth
In rank and not-to-be-endured riots. Sir,
I had thought, by making this well known unto you,
To have found a safe redress; but now grow fearful,
By what yourself, too, late have spoke and done,
That you protect this course, and put it on[36]
By your allowance;[37] which if you should, the fault
Would not scape censure, nor the redresses sleep,
Which, in the tender[38] of a wholesome weal,[39]
Might in their working do you that offence,
Which else were shame, that then necessity
Will call discreet proceeding.

FOOL.　For, you know, nuncle,
"The hedge-sparrow fed the cuckoo[40] so long,
That it had it head bit off by it young."[41]
So, out went the candle, and we were left darkling.[42]

LEAR.　Are you our daughter?

GONERIL.　Come, sir,
I would you would make use of that good wisdom,
Whereof I know you are fraught,[43] and put away
These dispositions,[44] which of late transport you
From what you rightly are.

FOOL.　May not an ass know when the cart draws the horse?
"Whoop,[45] Jug! I love thee."

LEAR.　Doth any here know me? This is not Lear.
Doth Lear walk thus? speak thus? Where are his eyes?
Either his notion[46] weakens, or his discernings
Are lethargied—Ha! waking?[47] 'T is not so.
Who is it that can tell me who I am?

FOOL.　Lear's shadow.

---

[32] frontlet—frown.　　[33] O—zero.　　[34] sheal'd peascod—shelled peapod (nothing). [35] all-licens'd—privileged to say and do as he pleases.　　[36] put it on—encourage it. [37] allowance—approval.　　[38] tender—care for.　　[39] weal—commonwealth.　　[40] cuckoo —i.e., the cuckoo's young.　　[41] young—ungrateful nestling.　　[42] darkling—in the dark. [43] fraught—furnished with.　　[44] dispositions—moods.　　[45] "Whoop, etc."—nonsense. [46] notion—understanding.　　[47] waking—am I awake?

LEAR. I would learn that; for, by the marks of sovereignty, knowledge, and reason, I should be false persuaded I had daughters.

FOOL. Which they will make an obedient father.

LEAR. Your name, fair gentlewoman?

GONERIL. This admiration,[48] sir, is much o' th' savour
Of other your new pranks. I do beseech you
To understand my purposes aright.
As you are old and reverend, you should be wise.
Here do you keep a hundred knights and squires;
Men so disorder'd, so debosh'd[49] and bold,
That this our court, infected with their manners,
Shows like a riotous inn. Epicurism[50] and lust
Makes it more like a tavern or a brothel
Than a grac'd palace. The shame itself doth speak
For instant remedy. Be then desir'd
By her, that else will take the thing she begs,
A little to disquantity[51] your train;
And the remainders, that shall still depend,
To be such men as may besort[52] your age,
Which know themselves and you.

LEAR.   Darkness and devils!
Saddle my horses; call my train together!
Degenerate bastard! I'll not trouble thee;
Yet have I left a daughter.

GONERIL. You strike my people; and your disorder'd rabble
Make servants of their betters.

[*Enter* ALBANY]

LEAR. Woe, that too late repents!—O, sir, are you come?
Is it your will? Speak, sir.—Prepare my horses.—
Ingratitude, thou marble-hearted fiend,
More hideous when thou show'st thee in a child
Than the sea-monster!

ALBANY.   Pray, sir, be patient.[53]

LEAR. [*To* GONERIL]. Detested kite![54] thou liest.
My train are men of choice and rarest parts,
That all particulars of duty know,
And in the most exact regard[55] support
The worships[56] of their name. O most small fault,
How ugly didst thou in Cordelia show!
Which, like an engine,[57] wrench'd my frame of nature
From the fix'd place; drew from my heart all love,
And added to the gall.[58] O Lear, Lear, Lear!
Beat at this gate, that let thy folly in [*striking his head*],
And thy dear judgement out! Go, go, my people.

ALBANY. My lord, I am guiltless as I am ignorant
Of what hath moved you.

---

[48] admiration—pretended surprise. [49] debosh'd—debauched. [50] Epicurism—gluttony.
[51] disquantity—reduce. [52] besort—befit. [53] patient—calm. [54] Detested kite—detestable scavenger. [55] regard—detail. [56] worships—honor. [57] engine—machine.
[58] gall—bitterness.

LEAR.   It may be so, my lord.
Hear, Nature! hear, dear goddess, hear!
Suspend thy purpose, if thou didst intend
To make this creature fruitful!
Into her womb convey sterility!
Dry up in her the organs of increase,[59]
And from her derogate[60] body never spring
A babe to honour her! If she must teem,[61]
Create her child of spleen,[62] that it may live
And be a thwart[63] disnatur'd[64] torment to her!
Let it stamp wrinkles in her brow of youth,
With cadent[65] tears fret[66] channels in her cheeks,
Turn all her mother's pains and benefits
To laughter and contempt, that she may feel
How sharper than a serpent's tooth it is
To have a thankless child!—Away, away! [*Exit.*]
    ALBANY.   Now, gods that we adore, whereof comes this?
    GONERIL.   Never afflict yourself to know the cause;
But let his disposition[67] have that scope
That dotage gives it.
                     [*Re-enter* LEAR.]
    LEAR.   What, fifty of my followers at a clap!
Within a fortnight!
    ALBANY.   What's the matter, sir?
    LEAR.   I'll tell thee. [*To* GONERIL.] Life and death! I am asham'd
That thou hast power to shake my manhood thus;
That these hot tears, which break from me perforce,
Should make thee worth them. Blasts[68] and fogs upon thee!
The untented[69] woundings of a father's curse
Pierce every sense about thee! Old fond eyes,
Beweep this cause again, I'll pluck ye out,
And cast you, with the waters that you loose,
To temper clay. Ha! it 't come to this?
Let it be so: I have another daughter,
Who, I am sure, is kind and comfortable.
When she shall hear this of thee, with her nails
She'll flay thy wolvish visage. Thou shalt find
That I'll resume the shape which thou dost think
I have cast off for ever. Thou shalt, I warrant thee.
            [*Exeunt* LEAR, KENT, *and Attendants.*]
    GONERIL.   Do you mark that, my lord?
    ALBANY.   I cannot be so partial,[70] Goneril,
To the great love I bear you,—
    GONERIL.   Pray you, content.—What, Oswald, ho!
[*To the* FOOL.]   You, sir, more knave than fool, after your master.

---

[59] increase—fertility.   [60] derogate—blighted.   [61] teem—conceive.   [62] spleen—malice.   [63] thwart—perverse.   [64] disnatur'd—unnatural.   [65] cadent—falling. [66] fret—wear away.   [67] disposition—mood.   [68] Blasts—pestilence.   [69] untented—too deep to be probed.   [70] partial . . . To—influenced by.

FOOL.   Nuncle Lear, nuncle Lear! tarry and take the Fool with thee.

> A fox, when one has caught her,
> And such a daughter,
> Should sure to the slaughter,
> If my cap would buy a halter.
> So the Fool follows after. [*Exit.*]

GONERIL.   This man hath had good counsel,—a hundred knights!
'T is politic and safe to let him keep
At point[71] a hundred knights; yes, that, on every dream,
Each buzz, each fancy, each complaint, dislike,
He may enguard his dotage with their powers,
And hold our lives in mercy.[72] Oswald, I say!
ALBANY.   Well, you may fear too far.
GONERIL.   Safer than trust too far.
Let me still take away the harms I fear,
Not fear still to be taken.[73] I know his heart.
What he hath utter'd I have writ my sister.
If she sustain him and his hundred knights,
When I have show'd the unfitness,—
                         [*Enter* OSWALD.]
GONERIL.   How now, Oswald!
What, have you writ that letter to my sister?
OSWALD.   Ay, madam.
GONERIL.   Take you some company, and away to horse:
Inform her full of my particular[74] fear;
And thereto add such reasons of your own
As may compact it more. Get you gone;
And hasten your return. [*Exit* OSWALD.] No, no, my lord,
This milky gentleness and course of yours
Though I condemn not, yet, under pardon,
You are much more at task[75] for want of wisdom
Than prais'd for harmful mildness.
ALBANY.   How far your eyes may pierce I cannot tell.
Striving to better, oft we mar what's well.
GONERIL.   Nay, then—
ALBANY.   Well, well; the event. [*Exeunt.*]

ACT I · 5

[*Enter* LEAR, KENT, *and* FOOL.]

LEAR.   Go you before to Gloucester with these letters. Acquaint my
daughter no further with anything you know than comes from her demand out
of the letter. If your diligence be not speedy, I shall be there afore you.

---

[71] at point—full armed.   [72] in mercy—at his mercy.   [73] taken—i.e., by some harm.
[74] particular—own.   [75] at task—to be criticized.

KENT. I will not sleep my lord, till I have delivered your letter. [*Exit.*]

FOOL. If a man's brains were in 's heels, were 't not in danger of kibes?[1]

LEAR. Ay, boy.

FOOL. Then, I prithee, be merry; thy wit shall ne'er go slip-shod.[2]

LEAR. Ha, ha, ha!

FOOL. Shalt see thy other daughter will use thee kindly;[3] for though she's as like this as a crab[4] 's like an apple, yet I can tell what I can tell.

LEAR. What canst tell, boy?

FOOL. She will taste as like this as a crab does to a crab. Thou canst tell why one's nose stands i' th' middle on 's face?

LEAR. No.

FOOL. Why, to keep one's eyes of[5] either side 's nose, that what a man cannot smell out, he may spy into.

LEAR. I did her wrong—

FOOL. Canst tell how an oyster makes his shell?

LEAR. No.

FOOL. Nor I neither; but I can tell why a snail has a house.

LEAR. Why?

FOOL. Why, to put 's head in; not to give it away to his daughters, and leave his horns without a case.

LEAR. I will forget my nature. So kind a father! Be my horses ready?

FOOL. Thy asses are gone about 'em. The reason why the seven stars are no moe[6] than seven is a pretty reason.

LEAR. Because they are not eight?

FOOL. Yes, indeed: Thou wouldst make a good Fool.

LEAR. To take 't again perforce! Monster ingratitude!

FOOL. If thou wert my Fool, nuncle, I'd have thee beaten for being old before thy time.

LEAR. How's that?

FOOL. Thou shouldst not have been old till thou hadst been wise.

LEAR. O, let me not be mad, not mad, sweet heaven!
Keep me in temper;[7] I would not be mad!

[*Enter* GENTLEMAN.]

How now! are the horses ready?

GENTLEMAN. Ready, my lord.

LEAR. Come, boy.

FOOL. She that's a maid now, and laughs at my departure,
Shall not be a maid long, unless things be cut shorter. [*Exeunt.*]

ACT II · 1

The Earl of Gloucester's castle.

[*Enter* EDMUND *and* CURAN, *meeting*]

EDMUND. Save thee, Curan.

CURAN. And you, sir. I have been with your father, and given him notice

---

[1] kibes—chilblains.   [2] slip-shod—in slippers (to protect you from chilblains).   [3] kindly —charitably; also, according to her nature.   [4] crab—crab apple.   [5] of—on.   [6] moe —more.   [7] temper—sanity.

that the Duke of Cornwall and Regan his duchess will be here with him this night.

EDMUND. How comes that?

CURAN. Nay, I know not. You have heard of the news abroad; I mean the whispered ones, for they are yet but ear-kissing[1] arguments?

EDMUND. Not I. Pray you, what are they?

CURAN. Have you heard of no likely wars toward[2] 'twixt the Dukes of Cornwall and Albany?

EDMUND. Not a word.

CURAN. You may, then, in time. Fare you well, sir. [*Exit.*]

EDMUND. The Duke be here to-night? The better! best!
This weaves itself perforce into my business.
My father hath set guard to take my brother;
And I have one thing, of a queasy question,[3]
Which I must act. Briefness and fortune, work!
Brother, a word; descend. Brother, I say!

[*Enter* EDGAR.]

My father watches; O sir, fly this place;
Intelligence[4] is given where you are hid;
You have now the good advantage of the night.
Have you not spoken 'gainst the Duke of Cornwall?
He's coming hither, now, i' th' night, i' th' haste,
And Regan with him. Have you nothing said
Upon his party 'gainst the Duke of Albany?
Advise yourself.[5]

EDGAR. I am sure on 't, not a word.

EDMUND. I hear my father coming: pardon me;
In cunning[6] I must draw my sword upon you.
Draw; seem to defend yourself; now quit[7] you well.
Yield! Come before my father. Light, ho, here!
Fly, brother. Torches, torches! So, farewell.

[*Exit* EDGAR]

Some blood drawn on me would beget opinion [*Wounds his arm.*]
Of my more fierce endeavour. I have seen drunkards
Do more than this in sport. Father! father!
Stop, stop! No help?

[*Enter* GLOUCESTER, *and Servants with torches.*]

GLOUCESTER. Now, Edmund, where's the villain?

EDMUND. Here stood he in the dark, his sharp sword out,
Mumbling of wicked charms, conjuring the moon
To stand 's auspicious mistress,[8]—

GLOUCESTER. But where is he?

EDMUND. Look, sir, I bleed.

GLOUCESTER. Where is the villain, Edmund?

EDMUND. Fled this way, sir. When by no means he could—

---

[1] ear-kissing—whispered. [2] toward—imminent. [3] of a queasy question—requiring delicate handling. [4] Intelligence—information. [5] Advise yourself—consider. [6] cunning—pretense. [7] quit—acquit. [8] 's auspicious mistress—be favorable to him.

GLOUCESTER. Pursue him, ho! Go after. [*Exeunt some Servants.*] "By no means" what?

EDMUND.   Persuade me to the murder of your lordship;
But that I told him, the revenging gods
'Gainst parricides did all their thunders bend;
Spoke, with how manifold and strong a bond
The child was bound to the father; sir, in fine,[9]
Seeing how loathly opposite I stood
To his unnatural purpose, in fell[10] motion,
With his prepared sword he charges home
My unprovided body, lanc'd mine arm;
But when he saw my best alarum'd spirits,
Bold in the quarrel's right, rous'd to the encounter,
Or whether gasted[11] by the noise I made,
Full suddenly he fled.

GLOUCESTER.   Let him fly far.
Not in this land shall he remain uncaught;
And found,—dispatch.[12] The noble Duke my master,
My worthy arch[13] and patron, comes to-night.
By his authority I will proclaim it,
That he which finds him shall deserve our thanks,
Bringing the murderous coward to the stake;
He that conceals him, death.

EDMUND.   When I dissuaded him from his intent,
And found him pight[14] to do it, with curst[15] speech
I threaten'd to discover[16] him; he replied,
"Thou unpossessing bastard! dost thou think,
If I would stand against thee, would the reposal
Of any trust, virtue, or worth in thee
Make thy words faith'd?[17] No! what I should deny,—
As this I would; ay, though thou didst produce
My very character,—I'd turn it all
To thy suggestion, plot, and damned practice;
And thou must make a dullard of the world
If they not thought the profits of my death
Were very pregnant[18] and potential[19] spurs
To make thee seek it."

GLOUCESTER.   O strong and fasten'd[20] villain!
Would he deny his letter? I never got him. [*Tucket[21] within.*]
Hark, the Duke's trumpets! I know not why he comes.
All ports[22] I'll bar, the villain shall not scape;
The Duke must grant me that. Besides, his picture
I will send far and near, that all the kingdom
May have due note of him; and of my land,

[9] in fine—briefly.   [10] fell—fierce.   [11] gasted—panic-stricken.   [12] dispatch—kill him.
[13] arch—chief.   [14] pight—determined.   [15] curst—angry.   [16] discover—reveal.
[17] faith'd—believed.   [18] pregnant—ready.   [19] potential—powerful.   [20] fasten'd—hardened.   [21] Tucket—trumpet signal.   [22] ports—seaports.

Loyal and natural boy, I'll work the means
To make thee capable.[23]

                [*Enter* CORNWALL, REGAN, *and Attendants.*]

CORNWALL.   How now, my noble friend! since I came hither,
Which I can call but now, I have heard strange news.

REGAN.   If it be true, all vengeance comes too short
Which can pursue the offender. How dost, my lord?

GLOUCESTER.   O, madam, my old heart is crack'd, is crack'd!

REGAN.   What, did my father's godson seek your life?
He whom my father nam'd? your Edgar?

GLOUCESTER.   O, lady, lady, shame would have it hid!

REGAN.   Was he not companion with the riotous knights
That tends upon my father?

GLOUCESTER.   I know not, madam. 'T is too bad, too bad.

EDMUND.   Yes, madam, he was of that consórt.[24]

REGAN.   No marvel, then, though he were ill affected:[25]
'T is they have put him on[26] the old man's death,
To have th' expense[27] and waste of his revénues.
I have this present evening from my sister
Been well inform'd of them; and with such cautions,
That if they come to sojourn at my house,
I'll not be there.

CORNWALL.   Nor I, assure thee, Regan.
Edmund, I hear that you have shown your father
A child-like[28] office.

EDMUND.   'T was my duty, sir.

GLOUCESTER.   He did bewray[29] his practice; and receiv'd
This hurt you see, striving to apprehend him.

CORNWALL.   Is he pursued?

GLOUCESTER.   Ay, my good lord.

CORNWALL.   If he be taken, he shall never more
Be fear'd of doing harm. Make your own purpose,
How in my strength[30] you please. For you, Edmund,
Whose virtue and obedience doth this instant
So much command itself, you shall be ours.
Natures of such deep trust we shall much need;
You we first seize on.

EDMUND.   I shall serve you, sir,
Truly, however else.

GLOUCESTER.   For him I thank your Grace.

CORNWALL.   You know not why we came to visit you,—

REGAN.   Thus out of season, threading[31] dark-ey'd night?
Occasions, noble Gloucester, of some poise,[32]
Wherein we must have use of your advice.
Our father he hath writ, so hath our sister,

---

[23] capable—i.e., legitimate.   [24] consórt—gang.   [25] ill affected—disloyal.   [26] put him on—incited him to.   [27] expense—spending.   [28] child-like—dutiful.   [29] bewray—reveal.   [30] strength—authority.   [31] threading—traveling through.   [32] poise—importance.

Of differences, which I best thought it fit
To answer from[33] our home; the several messengers
From hence attend[34] dispatch. Our good old friend,
Lay comforts to your bosom; and bestow
Your needful counsel to our business,
Which craves the instant use.

   GLOUCESTER.   I serve you, madam.
Your Graces are right welcome. [*Exeunt. Flourish.*]

ACT II · 2

Before Gloucester's castle.

[*Enter* KENT *and the Steward* OSWALD, *meeting.*]

OSWALD. Good dawning to thee, friend. Art of this house?

KENT. Ay.

OSWALD. Where may we set our horses?

KENT. I' th' mire.

OSWALD. Prithee, if you lov'st me, tell me.

KENT. I love thee not.

OSWALD. Why, then, I care not for thee.

KENT. If I had thee in Lipsbury pinfold,[1] I would make thee care for me.

OSWALD. Why dost thou use me thus? I know thee not.

KENT. Fellow, I know thee.

OSWALD. What dost thou know me for?

KENT. A knave; a rascal; an eater of broken meats;[2] a base, proud, shallow, beggarly, three-suited, hundred-pound, filthy, worsted-stocking knave; a lily-livered, action-taking[3] knave; a whoreson, glass-gazing, super-serviceable, finical rogue; one-trunk-inheriting[4] slave; one that wouldst be a bawd, in way of good service, and art nothing but the composition[5] of a knave, beggar, coward, pandar, and the son and heir of a mongrel bitch; one whom I will beat into clamorous whining, if thou deni'st the least syllable of thy addition.

OSWALD. Why, what a monstrous fellow art thou, thus to rail on one that is neither known of thee nor knows thee!

KENT. What a brazen-faced varlet art thou, to deny thou knowest me! Is it two days since I tripped up thy heels, and beat thee before the King? Draw, you rogue; for, though it be night, yet the moon shines. I'll make a sop o' th' moonshine[6] of you, you whoreson cullionly[7] barber-monger![8] Draw! [*Drawing his sword.*]

OSWALD. Away! I have nothing to do with thee.

KENT. Draw, you rascal! You come with letters against the King; and take Vanity the puppet's part against the royalty of her father. Draw, you rogue, or I'll so carbonado[9] your shanks,—draw, you rascal! Come your ways.

---

33 from—away from. 34 attend—await.
1 Lipsbury pinfold—between my jaws (?). 2 broken meats—left-overs, food for the lower servants. 3 action-taking—going to law instead of fighting for his rights. 4 one-trunk-inheriting—one trunk will hold all his possessions. 5 composition—combination.
6 sop o' th' moonshine—mess (?). 7 cullionly—vile. 8 barber-monger—fop.
9 carbonado—slice (into steaks).

OSWALD.   Help, ho! murder! help!

KENT.   Strike, you slave! Stand, rogue, stand! You neat slave, strike.
[*Beating him.*]

OSWALD.   Help, ho! murder! murder!

[*Enter* EDMUND *with his rapier drawn,* CORNWALL, REGAN, GLOUCESTER, *and
Servants.*]

EDMUND.   How now! What's the matter?

KENT.   With you, goodman boy, an you please: come, I'll flesh[10] ye; come
on, young master.

GLOUCESTER.   Weapons! arms! What's the matter here?

CORNWALL.   Keep peace, upon your lives!
He dies that strikes again. What is the matter?

REGAN.   The messengers from our sister and the King.

CORNWALL.   What is your difference? Speak.

OSWALD.   I am scarce in breath, my lord.

KENT.   No marvel, you have so bestirred your valour. You cowardly rascal.
Nature disclaims in thee. A tailor made thee.

CORNWALL.   Thou art a strange fellow: a tailor make a man?

KENT.   A tailor, sir. A stone-cutter[11] or a painter could not have made him
so ill, though they had been but two hours at the trade.

CORNWALL.   Speak yet, how grew your quarrel?

OSWALD.   This ancient ruffian, sir, whose life I have spared at suit of his
grey beard,—

KENT.   Thou whoreson zed![12] thou unnecessary letter! My lord, if you
will give me leave, I will tread this unbolted[13] villain into mortar, and daub the
wall of a jakes[14] with him.
Spare my grey beard, you wagtail?

CORNWALL.   Peace, sirrah!
You beastly knave, know you no reverence?

KENT.   Yes, sir; but anger hath a privilege.

CORNWALL.   Why art thou angry?

KENT.   That such a slave as this should wear a sword,
Who wears no honesty. Such smiling rogues as these,
Like rats, oft bite the holy cords[15] a-twain
Which are too intrinse t' unloose; smooth[16] every passion
That in the natures of their lords rebel;
Bring oil to fire, snow to their colder moods;
Renege, affirm, and turn their halcyon[17] beaks
With every gale and vary of their masters,
Knowing nought, like dogs, but following.
A plague upon your epileptic visage!
Smile you my speeches, as I were a fool?
Goose, an I had you upon Sarum[18] Plain,
I'd drive ye cackling home to Camelot.[19]

CORNWALL.   What, art thou mad, old fellow?

GLOUCESTER.   How fell you out? Say that.

---

[10] flesh—initiate you to fighting.   [11] stone-cutter—sculptor.   [12] zed—the letter Z.
[13] unbolted—coarse.   [14] jakes—privy.   [15] holy cords—bonds of natural affection.
[16] smooth—encourage.   [17] halcyon—the king-fisher, supposed to be a natural weathervane.   [18] Sarum—Salisbury.   [19] Camelot—site of King Arthur's court.

KENT.   No contraries hold more antipathy
Than I and such a knave.
　　　CORNWALL.   Why dost thou call him knave? What is his fault?
　　　KENT.   His countenance likes[20] me not.
　　　CORNWALL.   No more, perchance, does mine, nor his, nor hers.
　　　KENT.   Sir, 't is my occupation to be plain;
I have seen better faces in my time
Than stands on any shoulder that I see
Before me at this instant.
　　　CORNWALL.　　　　　This is some fellow
Who, having been prais'd for bluntness, doth affect
A saucy roughness, and constrains[21] the garb
Quite from his nature. He cannot flatter, he;
An honest mind and plain, he must speak truth!
An they will take it, so; if not, he's plain.
These kind of knaves I know, which in this plainness
Harbour more craft and more corrupter ends
Than twenty silly ducking óbservants[22]
That stretch their duties nicely.[23]
　　　KENT.   Sir, in good sooth, in sincere verity,
Under th' allowance of your great aspéct,
Whose influence, like the wreath of radiant fire
On flickering Phoebus' front,[24]—
　　　CORNWALL.　　　　　What mean'st by this?
　　　KENT.   To go out of my dialect, which you discommend so much. I know,
sir, I am no flatterer. He that beguiled you in a plain accent was a plain knave;
which for my part I will not be, though I should win your displeasure to entreat
me to 't.
　　　CORNWALL.   What was th' offence you gave him?
　　　OSWALD.   I never gave him any.
It pleas'd the King his master very late
To strike at me, upon his misconstruction;[25]
When he, conjunct, and flattering his displeasure,
Tripp'd me behind; being down, insulted, rail'd,
And put upon him such a deal of man
That worthied him,[26] got praises of the King
For him attempting who was self-subdued;[27]
And, in the fleshment[28] of this dread exploit,
Drew on me here again.
　　　KENT.　　　　　None of these rogues and cowards
But Ajax[29] is their fool.[30]
　　　CORNWALL.　　　　　Fetch forth the stocks!
You stubborn ancient knave, you reverend braggart,
We'll teach you—
　　　KENT.   Sir, I am too old to learn.

[20] likes—pleases.　　　[21] constrains—puts on.　　　[22] óbservants—obsequious parasites.
[23] nicely—punctiliously.　　[24] Phoebus' front—sun's forehead.　　[25] upon his misconstruction—because of a misunderstanding.　　[26] worthied him—won him favor.　　[27] was self-
subdued—made no resistance.　　[28] fleshment—excitement.　　[29] Ajax—the famous Greek
braggart warrior.　　[30] their fool—inferior to them.

Call not your stocks for me; I serve the King,
On whose employment I was sent to you.
You shall do small respects, show too bold malice
Against the grace and person of my master,
Stocking his messenger.

  CORNWALL. Fetch forth the stocks! As I have life and honour,
There shall he sit till noon.

  REGAN. Till noon! Till night, my lord; and all night too.

  KENT. Why, madam, if I were your father's dog,
You should not use me so.

  REGAN.   Sir, being his knave, I will.
         [*Stocks brought out.*]

  CORNWALL. This is a fellow of the self-same colour
Our sister speaks of. Come, bring away the stocks!

  GLOUCESTER. Let me beseech your Grace not to do so.
His fault is much, and the good King his master
Will check[31] him for 't. Your purpos'd low correction
Is such as basest and contemned'st wretches
For pilferings and most common trespasses
Are punish'd with. The King must take it ill
That he, so slightly valued in his messenger,
Should have him thus restrained.

  CORNWALL.   I'll answer that.

  REGAN. My sister may receive it much more worse
To have her gentleman abus'd, assaulted,
For following her affairs. Put in his legs. [KENT *is put in the stocks.*]
Come, my good lord, away. [*Exeunt all but* GLOUCESTER *and* KENT.]

  GLOUCESTER. I am sorry for thee, friend; 't is the Duke's pleasure,
Whose disposition, all the world well knows,
Will not be rubb'd nor stopp'd. I'll entreat for thee.

  KENT. Pray, do not, sir. I have watch'd[32] and travell'd hard;
Some time I shall sleep out, the rest I'll whistle.
A good man's fortune may grow out at heels.
Give you good morrow!

  GLOUCESTER. The Duke's to blame in this; 't will be ill took. [*Exit.*]

  KENT. Good King, that must approve the common saw,[33]
Thou out of heaven's benediction com'st
To the warm sun!
Approach, thou beacon[34] to this under globe,
That by thy comfortable beams I may
Peruse this letter! Nothing almost sees miracles
But misery. I know 't is from Cordelia,
Who hath most fortunately been inform'd
Of my obscured[35] course; [*Reads.*] "—and shall find time
From this enormous state[36]—seeking to give
Losses their remedies."—All weary and o'erwatch'd,

---

[31] check—rebuke. [32] watch'd—gone without sleep. [33] saw—saying. [34] beacon—
rising sun. [35] obscured—in disguise. [36] this enormous state—these evil times.

Take vantage,[37] heavy eyes, not to behold
This shameful lodging.
Fortune, good-night! Smile once more; turn thy wheel![38] [*Sleeps.*]

ACT II · 3

Near Gloucester's castle.

[*Enter* EDGAR.]
EDGAR.   I heard myself proclaim'd;
And by the happy hollow of a tree
Escap'd the hunt. No port is free; no place
That guard and most unusual vigilance
Does not attend my taking.[1] Whiles I may scape
I will preserve myself, and am bethought
To take the basest and most poorest shape
That ever penury,[2] in contempt[3] of man,
Brought near to beast. My face I'll grime with filth,
Blanket my loins, elf[4] all my hairs in knots,
And with presented[5] nakedness out-face
The winds and persecutions of the sky.
The country gives me proof and precedent[6]
Of Bedlam[7] beggars, who, with roaring voices,
Strike in their numb'd and mortified bare arms
Pins, wooden pricks, nails, sprigs of rosemary;
And with this horrible object, from low farms,
Poor pelting[8] villages, sheep-cotes, and mills,
Sometimes with lunatic bans,[9] sometimes with prayers,
Enforce their charity. "Poor Turlygod![10] poor Tom!"
There's something yet. Edgar I nothing[11] am. [*Exit.*]

ACT II · 4

Gloucester's castle. Kent in the stocks.

[*Enter* LEAR, FOOL, *and* GENTLEMAN.]
LEAR.   'T is strange that they should so depart from home,
And not send back my messenger.

---

[37] vantage—advantage of drowsiness.   [38] wheel—i.e., the wheel, turned by the goddess
Fortune, on which all men were bound to rise and fall.
[1] attend my taking—await my capture.   [2] penury—poverty.   [3] in contempt—to show
the worthlessness.   [4] elf—mat.   [5] presented—exposed.   [6] proof and precedent—
examples.   [7] Bedlam—from Bethlehem Hospital for lunatics.   [8] pelting—insignificant.
[9] bans—curses.   [10] "Poor Turlygod!"—the bedlam's cry.   [11] nothing—as good as dead.

GENTLEMAN. As I learn'd,
The night before there was no purpose in them
Of this remove.

KENT. Hail to thee, noble master!

LEAR. Ha!
Mak'st thou this shame thy pastime?

KENT. No, my lord.

FOOL. Ha, ha! he wears cruel garters. Horses are tied by the heads, dogs
and bears by the neck, monkeys by the loins, and men by the legs. When a
man's over-lusty at legs,[1] then he wears wooden nether-stocks.[2]

LEAR. What's he that hath so much thy place[3] mistook
To set thee here?

KENT. It is both he and she;
Your son and daughter.

LEAR. No.

KENT. Yes.

LEAR. No, I say.

KENT. I say, yea.

LEAR. No, no, they would not.

KENT. Yes, they have.

LEAR. By Jupiter, I swear, no.

KENT. By Juno,[4] I swear, ay.

LEAR. They durst not do 't;
They could not, would not do 't. 'T is worse than murder,
To do upon respect[5] such violent outrage.
Resolve[6] me, with all modest[7] haste, which way
Thou mightst deserve, or they impose, this usage,
Coming from us.

KENT. My lord, when at their home
I did commend[8] your Highness' letters to them,
Ere I was risen from the place that show'd
My duty kneeling, came there a reeking post,
Stew'd in his haste, half breathless, panting forth
From Goneril his mistress salutations;
Deliver'd letters, spite of intermission,[9]
Which presently, they read. On whose contents,
They summon'd up their meiny,[10] straight took horse;
Commanded me to follow, and attend
The leisure of their answer; gave me cold looks:
And meeting here the other messenger,
Whose welcome, I perceiv'd, had poison'd mine,—
Being the very fellow which of late
Display'd[11] so saucily against your Highness,—
Having more man than wit about me, drew:
He rais'd the house with loud and coward cries.

---

[1] over-lusty at legs—a vagabond.   [2] nether-stocks—stockings.   [3] place—position.
[4] Juno—queen of the gods.   [5] upon respect—against the respect due a king.   [6] Resolve—inform.   [7] modest—moderate.   [8] commend—deliver.   [9] spite of intermission—in spite of interrupting me.   [10] meiny—attendants.   [11] Display'd—acted.

Your son and daughter found this trespass worth[12]
The shame which here it suffers.

    FOOL.   Winter's[13] not gone yet, if the wild geese fly that way.

> Fathers that wear rags
>   Do make their children blind;
> But fathers that bear bags[14]
>   Shall see their children kind.
> Fortune, that arrant whore,
>   Ne'er turns the key[15] to the poor.

But, for all this, thou shalt have as many dolours[16] for thy daughters as thou canst tell[17] in a year.

    LEAR.   O, how this mother[18] swells up toward my heart!
Hysterica passio, down, thou climbing sorrow,
Thy element[19]'s below!—Where is this daughter?

    KENT.   With the Earl, sir; here within.

    LEAR.   Follow me not; stay here. [*Exit.*]

    GENTLEMAN.   Made you no more offence but what you speak of?

    KENT.   None.
How chance the King comes with so small a number?

    FOOL.   An thou hadst been set i' th' stocks for that question, thou hadst well deserv'd it.

    KENT.   Why, Fool?

    FOOL.   We'll set thee to school to an ant, to teach thee there's no labouring i' th' winter. All that follow their noses are led by their eyes but blind men; and there's not a nose among twenty but can smell him that's stinking. Let go thy hold when a great wheel runs down a hill, lest it break thy neck with following; but the great one that goes upward, let him draw thee after. When a wise man gives thee better counsel, give me mine again; I would have none but knaves follow it, since a fool gives it.

> That sir which serves and seeks for gain,
>   And follows but for form,
> Will pack[20] when it begins to rain,
>   And leave thee in the storm.
> But I will tarry; the Fool will stay,
>   And let the wise man fly.
> The knave turns fool that runs away;
>   The Fool no knave, perdy.[21]

                  [*Enter* LEAR *and* GLOUCESTER.]

    KENT.   Where learn'd you this, Fool?

    FOOL.   Not i' th' stocks, fool.

    LEAR.   Deny to speak with me! They are sick? They are weary?
They have travell'd all the night? Mere fetches,[22]
The images[23] of revolt and flying off.
Fetch me a better answer.

---

[12] worth—deserving of.   [13] Winter's—trouble's.   [14] bags—moneybags.   [15] turns the key—admits.   [16] dolours—griefs, with a pun on "dollars."   [17] tell—count.
[18] mother—hysteria (*hysterica passio*).   [19] element—proper place.   [20] pack—desert.
[21] perdy—by God.   [22] fetches—pretexts.   [23] images—signs.

GLOUCESTER.   My dear lord,
You know the fiery quality of the Duke;
How unremovable and fix'd he is
In his own course.

LEAR.   Vengeance! plague! death! confusion!
Fiery! What quality? Why, Gloucester, Gloucester,
I'd speak with the Duke of Cornwall and his wife.

GLOUCESTER.   Well, my good lord, I have inform'd them so.

LEAR.   Inform'd them! Dost thou understand me, man?

GLOUCESTER.   Ay, my good lord.

LEAR.   The King would speak with Cornwall; the dear father
Would with his daughter speak, commands her service.
Are they inform'd of this? My breath and blood!
Fiery? The fiery duke? Tell the hot duke that—
No, but not yet; may be he is not well.
Infirmity doth still neglect all office[24]
Whereto our health is bound; we are not ourselves
When nature, being oppress'd, commands the mind
To suffer with the body. I'll forbear;
And am fallen out[25] with my more headier will,[26]
To take the indispos'd and sickly fit
For the sound man.—Death on my state! wherefore [*looking on* KENT]
Should he sit here? This act persuades me
That this remotion[27] of the Duke and her
Is practice only. Give me my servant forth.[28]
Go tell the Duke and 's wife I'd speak with them,
Now, presently. Bid them come forth and hear me,
Or at their chamber-door I'll beat the drum
Till it cry sleep to death.[29]

GLOUCESTER.   I would have all well betwixt you. [*Exit.*]

LEAR.   O me, my heart, my rising heart! But, down!

FOOL.   Cry to it, nuncle, as the cockney did to the eels when she put 'em
i' th' paste[30] alive; she knapped 'em o' th' coxcombs[31] with a stick, and cried,
"Down, wantons, down!" 'T was her brother that, in pure kindness to his horse,
buttered his hay.

[*Enter* CORNWALL, REGAN, GLOUCESTER, *and Servants.*]

LEAR.   Good morrow to you both.

CORNWALL.   Hail to your Grace!

[KENT *here set at liberty.*]

REGAN.   I am glad to see your Highness.

LEAR.   Regan, I think you are; I know what reason
I have to think so. If thou shouldst not be glad,
I would divorce me from thy mother's tomb,
Sepúlchring an adultress. [*To* KENT.] O, are you free?
Some other time for that. Beloved Regan,

---

24 office—duty.   25 fallen out—angry.   26 more headier will—hastiness.   27 remotion—keeping away from me.   28 Give me my servant forth—release my servant.
29 cry sleep to death—make sleep impossible.   30 paste—pastry crust.   31 knapped
'em o' th' coxcombs—rapped them on the heads.

Thy sister's naught.[32] O Regan, she hath tied
Sharp-tooth'd unkindness, like a vulture, here. [*Points to his heart.*]
I can scarce speak to thee; thou 'lt not believe
With how deprav'd a quality—O Regan!

REGAN.   I pray you, sir, take patience. I have hope
You less know how to value her desert
Than she to scant[33] her duty.

LEAR.   Say, how is that?

REGAN.   I cannot think my sister in the least
Would fail her obligation. If, sir, perchance
She have restrain'd the riots of your followers,
'T is on such ground, and to such wholesome end,
As clears her from all blame.

LEAR.   My curses on her!

REGAN.   O, sir, you are old;
Nature in you stands on the very verge
Of her confine.[34] You should be rul'd and led
By some discretion that discerns your state[35]
Better than you yourself. Therefore, I pray you,
That to our sister you do make return;
Say you have wrong'd her, sir.

LEAR.   Ask her forgiveness?
Do you but mark how this becomes the house:[36]
"Dear daughter, I confess that I am old; [*Kneeling.*]
Age is unnecessary.[37] On my knees I beg,
That you'll vouchsafe me raiment, bed, and food."

REGAN.   Good sir, no more; these are unsightly tricks.
Return you to my sister.

LEAR [*rising*].   Never, Regan:
She hath abated me of half my train;
Look'd black upon me; struck me with her tongue,
Most serpent-like, upon the very heart.
All the stor'd vengeances of heaven fall
On her ingrateful top![38] Strike her young bones,
You taking[39] airs, with lameness!

CORNWALL.   Fie, sir, fie!

LEAR.   You nimble lightnings, dart your blinding flames
Into her scornful eyes! Infect her beauty,
You fen-suck'd fogs, drawn by the powerful sun,
To fall[40] and blast her pride!

REGAN.   O the blest gods! so will you wish on me,
When the rash mood is on.

LEAR.   No, Regan, thou shalt never have my curse.
Thy tender-hefted[41] nature shall not give
Thee o'er to harshness. Her eyes are fierce; but thine

---

[32] naught—wicked.   [33] scant—fall short in.   [34] confine—boundary.   [35] state—condition of mind.   [36] the house—royal family.   [37] Age is unnecessary—the old are useless.   [38] top—head.   [39] taking—infectious.   [40] fall—humble.   [41] tender-hefted—moved by tenderness.

Do comfort and not burn. 'T is not in thee
To grudge my pleasures, to cut off my train,
To bandy hasty words, to scant my sizes,[42]
And in conclusion to oppose the bolt[43]
Against my coming in. Thou better know'st
The offices[44] of nature, bond of childhood,
Effects of courtesy, dues of gratitude.
Thy half o' th' kingdom hast thou not forgot,
Wherein I thee endow'd.

  REGAN.   Good sir, to the purpose. [*Tucket within.*]
  LEAR.   Who put my man i' th' stocks?
           [*Enter* OSWALD.]
  CORNWALL.   What trumpet's that?
  REGAN.   I know 't; my sister's. This approves her letter,
That she would soon be here. [*To* OSWALD.] Is your lady come?
  LEAR.   This is a slave whose easy-borrowed pride[45]
Dwells in the fickle grace of her he follows.
Out, varlet,[46] from my sight!
  CORNWALL.   What means your Grace?
           [*Enter* GONERIL.]
  LEAR.   Who stock'd my servant? Regan, I have good hope
Thou didst not know on 't. Who comes here? O heavens,
If you do love old men, if your sweet sway
Allow[47] obedience, if you yourselves are old,
Make it your cause; send down, and take my part!
[*To* GONERIL.] Art not asham'd to look upon this beard?
O Regan, wilt thou take her by the hand?
  GONERIL.   Why not by the hand, sir? How have I offended?
All's not offence that indiscretion finds
And dotage terms so.
  LEAR.   O sides, you are too tough;
Will you yet hold? How came my man i' th' stocks?
  CORNWALL.   I set him there, sir; but his own disorders
Deserv'd much less advancement.
  LEAR.   You! did you?
  REGAN.   I pray you, father, being weak, seem so.
If, till the expiration of your month,
You will return and sojourn with my sister,
Dismissing half your train, come then to me.
I am now from home, and out of[48] that provision
Which shall be needful for your entertainment.
  LEAR.   Return to her, and fifty men dismiss'd!
No, rather I abjure all roofs, and choose
To wage against the enmity o' the air;
To be a comrade with the wolf and owl,—
Necessity's sharp pinch. Return with her?

---

[42] sizes—allowances.   [43] oppose the bolt—bar the door.   [44] offices—duties.   [45] easy-borrowed pride—vanity.   [46] varlet—low fellow.   [47] Allow—approve.   [48] out of—lack.

Why, the hot-blooded France, that dowerless took
Our youngest born, I could as well be brought
To knee his throne, and, squire-like, pension beg
To keep base life afoot. Return with her?
Persuade me rather to be slave and sumpter[49]
To this detested groom. [*Pointing at* OSWALD.]
    GONERIL.   At your choice, sir.
    LEAR.   I prithee, daughter, do not make me mad;
I will not trouble thee, my child; farewell!
We'll no more meet, no more see one another
But yet thou art my flesh, my blood, my daughter;
Or rather a disease that's in my flesh,
Which I must needs call mine; thou art a boil,
A plague-sore, an embossed[50] carbuncle,
In my corrupted blood. But I'll not chide thee;
Let shame come when it will, I do not call it.
I do not bid the thunder-bearer[51] shoot,
Nor tell tales of thee to high-judging[52] Jove.
Mend when thou canst; be better at thy leisure.
I can be patient; I can stay with Regan,
I and my hundred knights.
    REGAN.   Not altogether so;
I look'd not for you yet, nor am provided
For your fit welcome. Give ear, sir, to my sister;
For those that mingle reason with your passion[53]
Must be content to think you old, and so—
But she knows what she does.
    LEAR.   Is this well spoken?
    REGAN.   I dare avouch it, sir. What, fifty followers!
Is it not well?[54] What should you need of more?
Yea, or so many, sith that both charge[55] and danger
Speak 'gainst so great a number? How, in one house,
Should many people, under two commands,
Hold amity? 'T is hard; almost impossible.
    GONERIL.   Why might not you, my lord, receive attendance
From those that she calls servants or from mine?
    REGAN.   Why not, my lord? If then they chanc'd to slack[56] ye,
We could control them. If you will come to me,—
For now I spy a danger—I entreat you
To bring but five and twenty; to no more
Will I give place or notice.
    LEAR.   I gave you all.
    REGAN.   And in good time you gave it.
    LEAR.   Made you my guardians, my depositaries;

---

[49] sumpter—pack horse.   [50] embossed—swollen.   [51] thunder-bearer—Jupiter.
[52] high-judging—almighty.   [53] mingle reason with your passion—consider your anger from a reasonable point of view.   [54] well—enough.   [55] charge—expense.   [56] slack —neglect.

But kept a reservation[57] to be followed
With such a number. What, must I come to you
With five and twenty, Regan? Said you so?

REGAN.   And speak 't again, my lord; no more with me.

LEAR.   Those wicked creatures yet do look well-favour'd[58]
When others are more wicked; not being the worst
Stands in some rank of praise. [*To* GONERIL.] I'll go with thee.
Thy fifty yet doth double five and twenty,
And thou art twice her love.

GONERIL.   Hear me, my lord:
What need you five and twenty, ten, or five,
To follow[59] in a house where twice so many
Have a command to tend you?

REGAN.   What need one?

LEAR.   O, reason not the need! Our basest beggars
Are in the poorest thing superfluous.[60]
Allow not nature more than nature needs,
Man's life is cheap as beast's. Thou art a lady;
If only to go warm were gorgeous,
Why, nature needs not what thou gorgeous wear'st,
Which scarcely keeps thee warm. But, for true need,—
You heavens, give me that patience, patience I need!
You see me here, you gods, a poor old man,
As full of grief as age; wretched in both!
If it be you that stirs these daughters' hearts
Against their father, fool[61] me not so much
To bear it tamely; touch me with noble anger,
And let not women's weapons, water-drops,
Stain my man's cheeks! No, you unnatural hags,
I will have such revenges on you both
That all the world shall—I will do such things,—
What they are, yet I know not; but they shall be
The terrors of the earth. You think I'll weep:
No, I'll not weep.
I have full cause of weeping; but this heart [*Storm and tempest.*]
Shall break into a hundred thousand flaws,[62]
Or ere[63] I'll weep. O, Fool! I shall go mad!

                    [*Exeunt* LEAR, GLOUCESTER, KENT, *and* FOOL.]

CORNWALL.   Let us withdraw, 't will be a storm.

REGAN.   This house is little: the old man and 's people
Cannot be well bestow'd.

GONERIL.   'T is his own blame; hath put himself from rest,
And must needs taste his folly.

REGAN.   For his particular,[64] I'll receive him gladly,
But not one follower.

---

[57] reservation—condition.   [58] well-favour'd—handsome.   [59] follow—attend you.
[60] are . . . superfluous—have more than is absolutely necessary.   [61] fool—degrade.
[62] flaws—bits.   [63] Or ere—before.   [64] particular—himself alone.

GONERIL.   So am I purpos'd.
Where is my Lord of Gloucester?

[*Enter* GLOUCESTER.]

CORNWALL.   Followed the old man forth. He is return'd.

GLOUCESTER.   The King is in high rage.

CORNWALL.   Whither is he going?

GLOUCESTER.   He calls to horse; but will I know not whither.

CORNWALL.   'T is best to give him way; he leads himself.

GONERIL.   My lord, entreat him by no means to stay.

GLOUCESTER.   Alack, the night comes on, and the bleak winds
Do sorely ruffle;[65] for many miles about
There's scarce a bush.

REGAN.   O, sir, to wilful men,
The injuries that they themselves procure
Must be their schoolmasters. Shut up your doors.
He is attended with a desperate train;
And what they may incense[66] him to, being apt
To have his ear abus'd,[67] wisdom bids fear.

CORNWALL.   Shut up your doors, my lord; 't is a wild night:
My Regan counsels well: come out o' th' storm. [*Exeunt.*]

ACT III · 1

A heath.

[*Storm still. Enter* KENT *and a* GENTLEMAN, *meeting.*]

KENT.   Who's there, besides foul weather?

GENTLEMAN.   One minded like the weather, most unquietly.

KENT.   I know you. Where's the King?

GENTLEMAN.   Contending with the fretful elements;
Bids the wind blow the earth into the sea,
Or swell the curled waters 'bove the main,[1]
That things might change or cease; tears his white hair,
Which the impetuous blasts, with eyeless[2] rage,
Catch in their fury, and make nothing of;
Strives in his little world of man to out-scorn
The to-and-fro-conflicting wind and rain.
This night, wherein the cub-drawn[3] bear would couch,[4]
The lion and the belly-pinched wolf
Keep their fur dry, unbonneted he runs,
And bids what will take all.

KENT.   But who is with him?

---

[65] ruffle—rage.   [66] incense—instigate.   [67] abus'd—deceived.
[1] main—land.   [2] eyeless—blind.   [3] cub-drawn—sucked dry.   [4] couch—take shelter.

GENTLEMAN.   None but the Fool; who labours to outjest
His heart-struck injuries.

KENT.   Sir, I do know you;
And dare, upon the warrant of my note,
Commend a dear[5] thing to you. There is division,
Although as yet the face of it be cover'd
With mutual cunning, 'twixt Albany and Cornwall;
Who have—as who have not, that their great stars
Thron'd and set high?—servants, who seem no less,
Which are to France the spies and speculations[6]
Intelligent[7] of our state; what hath been seen,
Either in snuffs[8] and packings[9] of the Dukes,
Or the hard rein which both of them have borne
Against the old kind king, or something deeper,
Whereof perchance these are but furnishings[10]
But, true it is, from France there comes a power[11]
Into this scattered[12] kingdom; who already,
Wise in our negligence, have secret feet
In some of our best ports, and are at point[13]
To show their open banner. Now to you:
If on my credit you dare build so far
To make your speed to Dover, you shall find
Some that will thank you, making just[14] report
Of how unnatural and bemadding sorrow
The King hath cause to plain.
I am a gentleman of blood and breeding;
And, from some knowledge and assurance, offer
This office to you.

GENTLEMAN.   I will talk further with you.

KENT.   No, do not.
For confirmation that I am much more
Than my out-wall,[15] open this purse, and take
What it contains. If you shall see Cordelia,—
As fear not but you shall,—show her this ring;
And she will tell you who your fellow is
That yet you do not know. Fie on this storm!
I will go seek the King.

GENTLEMAN.   Give me your hand. Have you no more to say?

KENT.   Few words, but, to effect,[16] more than all yet;
That, when we have found the King,—in which your pain[17]
That way, I'll this,—he that first lights on him
Holla the other. [*Exeunt severally.*]

---

5 dear—important.   6 speculations—informers.   7 Intelligent—giving information.
8 snuffs—resentment.   9 packings—plottings.   10 furnishings—excuses.   11 power
—army.   12 scattered—divided.   13 at point—ready.   14 just—accurate.   15 out-
wall—appearance., i.e., in servant's livery.   16 to effect—in importance.   17 pain—
best efforts.

Another part of the heath. Storm still.

[*Enter* LEAR *and* FOOL.]

LEAR. Blow, winds, and crack your cheeks! Rage! Blow!
You cataracts and hurricanoes, spout
Till you have drench'd our steeples, drown'd the cocks![1]
You sulph'rous and thought-executing[2] fires,
Vaunt-couriers[3] to oak-cleaving thunderbolts,
Singe my white head! And thou, all-shaking thunder,
Smite flat the thick rotundity o' th' world!
Crack nature's moulds, all germens[4] spill[5] at once,
That makes ingrateful man!

FOOL. O nuncle, court holy-water[6] in a dry house is better than this rainwater out o' door. Good nuncle, in, and ask thy daughter's blessing. Here's a
night pities neither wise man nor fool.

LEAR. Rumble thy bellyful! Spit, fire! Spout, rain!
Nor rain, wind, thunder, fire, are my daughters.
I tax[7] not you, you elements, with unkindness,
I never gave you kingdom, call'd you children;
You owe me no subscription:[8] then let fall
Your horrible pleasure. Here I stand, your slave,
A poor, infirm, weak, and despis'd old man;
But yet I call you servile ministers,[9]
That will with two pernicious daughters join
Your high-engender'd[10] battles 'gainst a head
So old and white as this. Oh! Oh! 't is foul!

FOOL. He that has a house to put 's head in has a good head-piece.

> The cod-piece that will house
>   Before the head has any,
> The head and he shall louse;
>   So beggars marry many.
> The man that makes his toe
>   What he his heart should make
> Shall of a corn cry woe,
>   And turn his sleep to wake.

For there was never yet fair woman but she made mouths[11] in a glass.

[*Enter* KENT.]

LEAR. No, I will be the pattern of all patience; I will say nothing.
KENT. Who's there?
FOOL. Marry, here's grace and a cod-piece; that's a wise man and a fool.
KENT. Alas, sir, are you here? Things that love night

---

[1] cocks—weathervanes.   [2] thought-executing—killing as quick as thought.   [3] Vaunt-
couriers—forerunners.   [4] germens—seeds of life.   [5] spill—destroy.   [6] court holy-
water—flattery.   [7] tax—accuse.   [8] subscription—obedience.   [9] ministers—agents.
[10] high-engender'd—begotten on high.   [11] made mouths—grimaces.

Love not such nights as these; the wrathful skies
Gallow[12] the very wanderers of the dark,
And make them keep their caves. Since I was man,
Such sheets of fire, such bursts of horrid thunder,
Such groans of roaring wind and rain, I never
Remember to have heard: man's nature cannot carry[13]
Th' affliction nor the fear.

    LEAR.   Let the great gods,
That keep this dreadful pudder[14] o'er our heads,
Find out their enemies now. Tremble, thou wretch,
That hast within thee undivulged crimes,
Unwhipp'd of justice; hide thee, thou bloody hand;
Thou perjur'd, and thou simular[15] man of virtue
That art incestuous; caitiff, to pieces shake,
That under covert and convenient seeming[16]
Has practis'd on man's life; close pent-up guilts,
Rive[17] your concealing continents, and cry
These dreadful summoners grace.[18] I am a man
More sinn'd against than sinning.

    KENT.   Alack, bare-headed!
Gracious my lord, hard by here is a hovel;
Some friendship will it lend you 'gainst the tempest.
Repose you there; whilst I to this hard house—
More harder than the stone whereof 't is rais'd;
Which even but now, demanding after[19] you,
Deni'd[20] me to come in—return, and force
Their scanted courtesy.

    LEAR.   My wits begin to turn.
Come on, my boy. How dost, my boy? Art cold?
I am cold myself. Where is this straw, my fellow?
The art of our necessities[21] is strange,
That can make vile things precious. Come, your hovel.
Poor Fool and knave, I have one part in my heart
That's sorry yet for thee.

    FOOL [*singing*].

        He that has and a little tiny wit,—
           With heigh-ho, the wind and the rain,—
        Must make content with his fortunes fit,
           For the rain it raineth every day.

    LEAR.   True, boy. Come, bring us to this hovel. [*Exeunt* LEAR *and* KENT.]

    FOOL.   This is a brave night to cool a courtezan.
I'll speak a prophecy[22] ere I go:

---

[12] Gallow—terrify.   [13] carry—endure.   [14] pudder—turmoil.   [15] simular—hypocritical.   [16] convenient seeming—mask of conventional virtue.   [17] Rive—break out of.
[18] grace—for mercy.   [19] demanding after—inquiring for.   [20] Deni'd—forbade.   [21] art of our necessities—skill created by need.   [22] prophecy—what follows is a familiar Elizabethan "gag": the Fool solemnly prophesies a number of absurd truisms.

When priests are more in word than matter;
When brewers mar their malt with water;
When nobles are their tailors' tutors;
No heretics burn'd, but wenches' suitors;
When every case in law is right;
No squire in debt, nor no poor knight;
When slanders do not live in tongues;
Nor cutpurses come not to throngs;
When usurers tell their gold i' th' field;
And bawds and whores do churches build;
Then shall the realm of Albion
Come to great confusion.
Then comes the time, who lives to see 't,
That going shall be us'd with feet.

This prophecy Merlin shall make; for I live before his time. [*Exit.*]

ACT III · 3

Gloucester's castle.

[*Enter* GLOUCESTER *and* EDMUND.]

GLOUCESTER. Alack, alack, Edmund, I like not this unnatural dealing. When I desired their leave that I might pity him, they took from me the use of mine own house; charged me, on pain of their perpetual displeasure, neither to speak of him, entreat for him, nor any way sustain[1] him.

EDMUND. Most savage and unnatural!

GLOUCESTER. Go to; say you nothing. There is division between the Dukes, and a worse matter than that. I have received a letter this night; 't is dangerous to be spoken; I have locked the letter in my closet. These injuries the King now bears will be revenged home;[2] there is part of a power already footed;[3] we must incline to the King. I will seek him, and privily relieve him. Go you and maintain talk with the Duke, that my charity be not of him perceived. If he ask for me, I am ill, and gone to bed. If I die for it, as no less is threatened me, the King my old master must be relieved. There is some strange thing toward, Edmund; pray you, be careful. [*Exit.*]

EDMUND. This courtesy, forbid[4] thee, shall the Duke
Instantly know; and of that letter too.
This seems a fair deserving,[5] and must draw me
That which my father loses; no less than all.
The younger rises when the old doth fall. [*Exit.*]

---

[1] sustain—succour.   [2] home—to the utmost.   [3] footed—landed.   [4] forbid—forbidden to.   [5] deserving—action which will deserve reward.

The heath. Before a hovel.

[*Enter* LEAR, KENT, *and* FOOL.]

KENT.   Here is the place, my lord; good my lord, enter.
The tryanny of the open night's too rough
For nature to endure. [*Storm still.*]
    LEAR.   Let me alone.
    KENT.   Good my lord, enter here.
    LEAR.   Wilt break my heart?
    KENT.   I had rather break mine own. Good my lord, enter.
    LEAR.   Thou think'st 't is much that this contentious storm
Invades us to the skin; so 't is to thee;
But where the greater malady is fix'd,
The lesser is scarce felt. Thou 'dst shun a bear;
But if thy flight lay toward the roaring sea,
Thou 'dst meet the bear i' th' mouth. When the mind's free,[1]
The body's delicate;[2] the tempest in my mind
Doth from my senses take all feeling else
Save what beats there. Filial ingratitude!
Is it not as this mouth should tear this hand
For lifting food to 't? But I will punish home:
No, I will weep no more. In such a night
To shut me out! Pour on; I will endure.
In such a night as this! O Regan, Goneril!
Your old kind father, whose frank heart gave all,—
O, that way madness lies; let me shun that;
No more of that.
    KENT.   Good my lord, enter here.
    LEAR.   Prithee, go in thyself; seek thine own ease.
This tempest will not give me leave to ponder
On things would hurt me more. But I'll go in.
[*To the* FOOL.] In, boy; go first. You houseless poverty,[3]—
Nay, get thee in. I'll pray, and then I'll sleep. [*Exit* FOOL.]
Poor naked wretches, wheresoe'er you are,
That bide the pelting of this pitiless storm,
How shall your houseless heads and unfed sides,
Your loop'd and window'd raggedness,[4] defend you
From seasons such as these? O, I have ta'en
Too little care of this! Take physic,[5] pomp;
Expose thyself to feel what wretches feel,
That thou mayst shake the superflux[6] to them,
And show the heavens more just.
    EDGAR [*within*].   Fathom and half, fathom and half! Poor Tom!

---

[1] free—untroubled.   [2] delicate—sensitive.   [3] houseless poverty—homeless paupers.
[4] loop'd and window'd raggedness—ragged clothing full of holes.   [5] physic—medicine.
[6] shake the superflux—give in charity what is superfluous.

[The FOOL *runs out from the hovel.]*

FOOL.   Come not in here, nuncle, here's a spirit. Help me, help me!

KENT.   Give me thy hand. Who's there?

FOOL.   A spirit, a spirit! He says his name's poor Tom.

KENT.   What art thou dost grumble there i' th' straw? Come forth.

[Enter EDGAR, *disguised as a madman.]*

EDGAR.   Away! the foul fiend follows me! "Through the sharp hawthorn blow the winds." Hum! go to thy cold bed, and warm thee.

LEAR.   Did'st thou give all to thy two daughters, and art thou come to this?

EDGAR.   Who gives anything to poor Tom? whom the foul fiend hath led through fire and through flame, and through ford and whirlpool, o'er bog and quagmire; that hath laid knives under his pillow, and halters in his pew;[7] set ratsbane[8] by his porridge; made him proud of heart, to ride on a bay trotting-horse over four-inched[9] bridges, to course[10] his own shadow for a traitor. Bless thy five wits! Tom's a-cold,—O, do de, do de, do de. Bless thee from whirl-winds, star-blasting, and taking![11] Do poor Tom some charity, whom the foul fiend vexes. There could I have[12] him now, and there, and there again, and there. *[Storm still.]*

LEAR.   What, his daughters brought him to this pass?
Couldst thou save nothing? Wouldst thou give 'em all?

FOOL.   Nay, he reserved a blanket, else we had been all shamed.

LEAR.   Now, all the plagues that in the pendulous air
Hang fated o'er men's faults light on thy daughters!

KENT.   He hath no daughters, sir.

LEAR.   Death, traitor! nothing could have súbdu'd nature
To such a lowness but his únkind daughters.
Is it the fashion, that discarded fathers
Should have thus little mercy on their flesh?
Judicious punishment! 'T was this flesh begot
Those pelican[13] daughters.

EDGAR.   Pillicock[14] sat on Pillicock-hill.
Alow, alow, loo, loo!

FOOL.   This cold night will turn us all to fools and madmen.

EDGAR.   Take heed o' th' foul fiend. Obey thy parents; keep thy word justly; swear not; commit not with man's sworn spouse; set not thy sweet heart on proud array. Tom's a-cold.

LEAR.   What hast thou been?

EDGAR.   A serving-man, proud in heart and mind; that curled my hair; wore gloves in my cap; served the lust of my mistress' heart, and did the act of darkness with her; swore as many oaths as I spake words, and broke them in the sweet face of heaven: one that slept in the contriving of lust, and waked to do it. Wine loved I deeply, dice dearly, and in woman out-paramoured the Turk:[15] false of heart, light of ear, bloody of hand; hog in sloth, fox in stealth, wolf in greediness, dog in madness, lion in prey. Let not the creaking of shoes nor the rustling of silks betray[16] thy poor heart to woman. Keep thy foot out of

---

[7] pew—balcony.   [8] ratsbane—poison.   [9] four-inched—narrow.   [10] course—chase.
[11] taking—infection.   [12] have—catch.   [13] pelican—who feed on their mother's blood.
[14] Pillicock, etc.—"pelican" reminds Poor Tom of an old nursery rhyme.   [15] Turk—Sultan.   [16] betray—tempt you to give.

brothels, thy hand out of plackets,[17] thy pen from lenders' books, and defy the foul fiend. [*Sings.*] "Still through the hawthorn blows the cold wind." Says suum, mun, nonny. Dolphin my boy, boy, sessa! let him trot by. [*Storm still.*]

LEAR. Why, thou wert better in thy grave than to answer with thy un-covered body this extremity of the skies. Is man no more than this? Consider him well. Thou ow'st the worm no silk, the beast no hide, the sheep no wool, the cat[18] no perfume. Ha! here's three on's are sophisticated! Thou art the thing itself; unaccommodated man is no more but such a poor, bare, forked[19] animal as thou art. Off, off, you lendings![20] come, unbutton here.

[*Tearing off his clothes.*]

[*Enter* GLOUCESTER, *with a torch.*]

FOOL. Prithee, nuncle, be contented; 't is a naughty night to swim in. Now a little fire in a wild field were like an old leper's heart; a small spark, all the rest on 's body cold. Look, here comes a walking fire.

EDGAR. This is the foul fiend Flibbertigibbet; he begins at curfew, and walks till the first cock;[21] he gives the web and the pin,[22] squints the eye, and makes the hare-lip; mildews the white wheat, and hurts the poor creature of earth.

> Swithold footed thrice the 'old;[23]
> He met the night-mare, and her ninefold;[24]
> Bid her alight,
> And her troth plight,
> And, aroint[25] thee, witch, aroint thee!

KENT. How fares your Grace?

LEAR. What's he?

KENT. Who's there? What is 't you seek?

GLOUCESTER. What are you there? Your names?

EDGAR. Poor Tom, that eats the swimming frog, the toad, the tadpole, the wall-newt,[26] and the water; that in the fury of his heart, when the foul fiend rages, eats cow-dung for salads; swallows the old rat and the ditchdog; drinks the green mantle of the standing pool; who is whipp'd from tithing[27] to tithing, and stocked, punished, and imprisoned; who hath had three suits to his back, six shirts to his body,

> Horse to ride, and weapon to wear;
> But mice and rats, and such small deer,[28]
> Have been Tom's food for seven long year.

Beware my follower. Peace, Smulkin; peace, thou fiend!

GLOUCESTER. What, hath your Grace no better company?

EDGAR. The prince of darkness is a gentleman. Modo he's call'd, and Mahu.

---

[17] plackets—openings in petticoats.   [18] cat—civet-cat.   [19] forked—two-legged.
[20] lendings—clothes.   [21] cock—cockcrow (midnight).   [22] web and the pin—cataract of the eye.   [23] 'old—wold, i.e., field.   [24] ninefold—nine colts.   [25] aroint—go away.
[26] wall-newt—lizard.   [27] tithing—district.   [28] deer—game.

GLOUCESTER.   Our flesh and blood, my lord, is grown so vile
That it doth hate what gets it.

EDGAR.   Poor Tom's a-cold.

GLOUCESTER.   Go in with me; my duty cannot suffer
T' obey in all your daughters' hard commands.
Though their injunction be to bar my doors
And let this tyrannous night take hold upon you,
Yet have I ventur'd to come seek you out,
And bring you where both fire and food is ready.

LEAR.   First let me talk with this philosopher.[29]
What is the cause of thunder?

KENT.   Good my lord, take his offer; go into the house.

LEAR.   I'll talk a word with this same learned Theban.
What is your study?

EDGAR.   How to prevent the fiend, and to kill vermin.

LEAR.   Let me ask you one word in private.

KENT.   Importune him once more to go, my lord;
His wits begin to unsettle.

GLOUCESTER.   Canst thou blame him? [*Storm still.*]
His daughters seek his death. Ah, that good Kent!
He said it would be thus, poor banish'd man!
Thou say'st the King grows mad; I'll tell thee, friend,
I am almost mad myself. I had a son,
Now outlaw'd from my blood; 'a sought my life,
But lately, very late. I lov'd him, friend,
No father his son dearer; true to tell thee,
The grief hath craz'd my wits. What a night's this!
I do beseech your Grace,—

LEAR.   O, cry you mercy, sir.
Noble philosopher, your company.

EDGAR.   Tom's a-cold.

GLOUCESTER.   In, fellow, there, into the hovel; keep thee warm.

LEAR.   Come, let's in all.

KENT.   This way, my lord.

LEAR.   With him;
I will keep still with my philosopher.

KENT.   Good my lord, soothe him; let him take the fellow.

GLOUCESTER.   Take him you on.

KENT.   Sirrah, come on; go along with us.

LEAR.   Come, good Athenian.

GLOUCESTER.   No words, no words: hush.

EDGAR.

Child[30] Rowland to the dark tower came;
His word was still, Fie, foh, and fum,
I smell the blood of a British man.

[*Exeunt.*]

---

[29] philosopher—scientist.   [30] child—candidate for knighthood.

Gloucester's castle.

[*Enter* CORNWALL *and* EDMUND.]

CORNWALL.   I will have my revenge ere I depart his house.

EDMUND.   How, my lord, I may be censured that nature[1] thus gives way to loyalty, something fears me to think of.

CORNWALL.   I now perceive, it was not altogether your brother's evil disposition made him seek his death; but a provoking merit,[2] set a-work by a reproveable badness in himself.

EDMUND.   How malicious is my fortune, that I must repent to be just! This is the letter he spoke of, which approves[3] him an intelligent party[4] to the advantages of France. O heavens! that this treason were not, or not I the detector!

CORNWALL.   Go with me to the Duchess.

EDMUND.   If the matter of this paper be certain, you have mighty business in hand.

CORNWALL.   True or false, it hath made thee Earl of Gloucester. Seek out where thy father is, that he may be ready for our apprehension.[5]

EDMUND [*aside*].   If I find him comforting the King, it will stuff his suspicion more fully.—I will perséver in my course of loyalty, though the conflict be sore between that and my blood.

CORNWALL.   I will lay trust upon thee; and thou shalt find a dearer father in my love. [*Exeunt.*]

A building attached to Gloucester's castle.

[*Enter* KENT *and* GLOUCESTER.]

GLOUCESTER.   Here is better than the open air; take it thankfully. I will piece out the comfort with what addition I can. I will not be long from you.

KENT.   All the power of his wits have given way to his impatience.[1] The gods reward your kindness! [*Exit* GLOUCESTER.]

[*Enter* LEAR, EDGAR, *and* FOOL.]

EDGAR.   Fraretto calls me; and tells me Nero[2] is an angler in the lake of darkness.[3] Pray, innocent, and beware the foul fiend.

FOOL.   Prithee, nuncle, tell me whether a madman be a gentleman or a yeoman?

LEAR.   A king, a king!

FOOL.   No, he's a yeoman[4] that has a gentleman to his son; for he's a mad

---

[1] nature—natural affection.   [2] provoking merit—a good quality that impelled him.
[3] approves—reveals.   [4] intelligent party—spy.   [5] apprehension—arrest.
[1] impatience—suffering.   [2] Nero—the debauched emperor of Rome.   [3] darkness—i.e., hell.   [4] yeoman—property-holder.

yeoman that sees his son a gentleman before him.

LEAR.   To have a thousand with red burning spits
Come hissing in upon 'em,—

EDGAR.   The foul fiend bites my back.

FOOL.   He's mad that trusts in the tameness of a wolf, a horse's health, a boy's love, or a whore's oath.

LEAR.   It shall be done; I will arraign them straight.[5]
[*To* EDGAR.] Come, sit thou here, most learned justicer;
[*To the* FOOL.] Thou, sapient sir, sit here. Now, you she foxes!

EDGAR.   Look, where he stands and glares!
Wantest thou eyes[6] at trial, madam?

> Come o'er the bourn,[7] Bessy, to me,—

FOOL [*sings*].

> Her boat hath a leak,
> And she must not speak
> Why she dares not come over to thee.

EDGAR.   The foul fiend haunts poor Tom in the voice of a nightingale. Hoppedance cries in Tom's belly for two white herring. Croak not, black angel; I have no food for thee.

KENT.   How do you, sir? Stand you not so amaz'd:[8]
Will you lie down and rest upon the cushion?

LEAR.   I'll see their trial first. Bring in their evidence.
[*To* EDGAR.] Thou robed man of justice, take thy place;
[*To the* FOOL.] And thou, his yoke-fellow of equity,
Bench by his side. [*To* KENT.] You are o' th' commission,[9]
Sit you too.

EDGAR.   Let us deal justly.

> Sleepest or wakest thou, jolly shepherd?
> Thy sheep be in the corn;
> And for one blast of thy minikin[10] mouth,
> Thy sheep shall take no harm.

Purr! the cat is grey.

LEAR.   Arraign her first; 't is Goneril. I here take my oath before this honourable assembly, she kicked the poor king her father.

FOOL.   Come hither, mistress. Is your name Goneril?

LEAR.   She cannot deny it.

FOOL.   Cry you mercy, I took you for a joint-stool.[11]

LEAR.   And here's another, whose warp'd looks proclaim
What store[12] her heart is made on. Stop her there!
Arms, arms, sword, fire! Corruption in the place!
False justicer, why hast thou let her scape?

EDGAR.   Bless thy five wits!

---

[5] straight—at once.   [6] wantest thou eyes—do you wish spectators.   [7] bourn—brook.
[8] amaz'd—astonished.   [9] commission—commissioned as a justice.   [10] minikin—dainty.
[11] joint-stool—wooden stool.   [12] store—material.

KENT.   O pity! Sir, where is the patience[13] now
That you so oft have boasted to retain?

EDGAR [aside].   My tears begin to take his part so much,
They'll mar my counterfeiting.

LEAR.   The little dogs and all,
Tray, Blanch, and Sweetheart, see, they bark at me.

EDGAR.   Tom will throw his head at them. Avaunt, you curs!

> Be thy mouth or black or white,
> Tooth that poisons if it bite;
> Mastiff, greyhound, mongrel grim,
> Hound or spaniel, brach or lym,[14]
> Or bobtail tike or trundle-tail,[15]
> Tom will make him weep and wail;
> For, with throwing thus my head,
> Dogs leapt the hatch,[16] and all fled.

Do de, de, de. Sessa! Come, march to wakes[17] and fairs and market-towns. Poor
Tom, thy horn is dry.

LEAR.   Then let them anatomize[18] Regan; see what breeds about her
heart. Is there any cause in nature that make these hard hearts? [To EDGAR.]
You, sir, I entertain for one of my hundred; only I do not like the fashion of
your garments. You will say they are Persian attire, but let them be changed.

[Enter GLOUCESTER.]

KENT.   Now, good my lord, lie here and rest a while.

LEAR.   Make no noise, make no noise; draw the curtains; so, so, so. We'll
go to supper i' th' morning; so, so, so.

FOOL.   And I'll go to bed at noon.

GLOUCESTER.   Come hither, friend; where is the King my master?

KENT.   Here, sir; but trouble him not, his wits are gone.

GLOUCESTER.   Good friend, I prithee, take him in thy arms;
I have o'erheard a plot of death upon him.
There is a litter ready; lay him in 't,
And drive toward Dover, friend, where thou shalt meet
Both welcome and protection. Take up thy master.
If thou shouldst dally[19] half an hour, his life,
With thine, and all that offer to defend him,
Stand in assured loss. Take up, take up;
And follow me, that will to some provision
Give thee quick conduct.

KENT.   Oppressed nature sleeps.
This rest might yet have balm'd[20] thy broken sinews,
Which, if convenience will not allow,
Stand in hard cure.[21] [To the FOOL.] Come, help to bear thy master;
Thou must not stay behind.

GLOUCESTER.   Come, come, away. [Exeunt all but EDGAR.]

---

13 patience—self-control.   14 brach or lym—bitch or bloodhound.   15 trundle-tail—
drooping tail.   16 hatch—lower half of a divided door.   17 wakes—merrymakings.
18 anatomize—dissect.   19 dally—delay.   20 balm'd—soothed.   21 stand in hard cure
—will hardly be cured.

EDGAR.   When we our betters see bearing our woes,
We scarcely think our miseries our foes.
Who alone suffers,[22] suffers most i' th' mind,
Leaving free things and happy shows behind;
But then the mind much sufferance doth o'erskip,
When grief hath mates, and bearing fellowship.
How light and portable my pain seems now,
When that which makes me bend makes the King bow,
He childed as I fathered! Tom, away!
Mark the high noises;[23] and thyself bewray
When false opinion, whose wrong thoughts defile thee,
In thy just proof repeals and reconciles thee.
What will hap more to-night, safe scape the King!
Lurk, lurk.[24] [*Exit.*]

ACT III · 7

Gloucester's castle.

[*Enter* CORNWALL, REGAN, GONERIL, EDMUND, *and Servants.*]
    CORNWALL [*to* GONERIL].   Post speedily to my lord your husband; show
him this letter. The army of France is landed.—Seek out the traitor Gloucester.
                                                  [*Exeunt some of the Servants.*]
    REGAN.   Hang him instantly.
    GONERIL.   Pluck out his eyes.
    CORNWALL.   Leave him to my displeasure.—Edmund, keep you our sister
company; the revenges we are bound to take upon your traitorous father are not
fit for your beholding. ·Advise the Duke, where you are going, to a most festi-
nate[1] preparation; we are bound to the like. Our posts shall be swift and intel-
ligent betwixt us. Farewell, dear sister; farewell, my lord of Gloucester. [*Enter
OSWALD.*] How now! where's the King?
    OSWALD.   My Lord of Gloucester hath convey'd him hence.
Some five or six and thirty of his knights,
Hot questrists[2] after him, met him at gate,
Who, with some other of the lords dependants,
Are gone with him towards Dover, where they boast
To have well-armed friends.
    CORNWALL.   Get horses for your mistress.
    GONERIL.   Farewell, sweet lord, and sister.
    CORNWALL.   Edmund, farewell. [*Exeunt* GONERIL, EDMUND, *and* OSWALD.]
                                        Go seek the traitor Gloucester,
Pinion him like a thief, bring him before us. [*Exeunt other Servants.*]
Though well we may not pass upon his life

---

[22] alone suffers—suffers by himself.   [23] high noises—discord among the great.
[24] Lurk, lurk—remain in hiding.
[1] festinate—speediest possible.   [2] questrists—searchers.

Without the form of justice, yet our power
Shall do a courtesy to our wrath, which men
May blame, but not control.

[*Enter* GLOUCESTER *brought in by two or three Servants.*]

Who's there? The traitor?

REGAN.   Ingrateful fox! 't is he.

CORNWALL.   Bind fast his corky[3] arms.

GLOUCESTER.   What means your Graces? Good my friends, consider
You are my guests. Do me no foul play, friends.

CORNWALL.   Bind him, I say. [*Servants bind him.*]

REGAN.   Hard, hard. O filthy traitor!

GLOUCESTER.   Unmerciful lady as you are, I'm none.

CORNWALL.   To this chair bind him. Villain, thou shalt find—

[REGAN *plucks his beard.*]

GLOUCESTER.   By the kind gods, 't is most ignobly done
To pluck me by the beard.

REGAN.   So white, and such a traitor!

GLOUCESTER.   Naughty lady,
These hairs, which thou dost ravish from my chin,
Will quicken,[4] and accuse thee. I am your host:
With robber's hands my hospitable favours
You should not ruffle[5] thus. What will you do?

CORNWALL.   Come, sir, what letters had you late from France?

REGAN.   Be simple-answer'd, for we know the truth.

CORNWALL.   And what confederacy have you with the traitors
Late footed in the kingdom?

REGAN.   To whose hands you have sent the lunatic king?
Speak.

GLOUCESTER.   I have a letter guessingly set down,
Which came from one that's of a neutral heart,
And not from one oppos'd.

CORNWALL.   Cunning.

REGAN.   And false.

CORNWALL.   Where hast thou sent the King?

GLOUCESTER.   To Dover.

REGAN.   Wherefore to Dover? Wast thou not charg'd at peril—

CORNWALL.   Wherefore to Dover? Let him answer that.

GLOUCESTER.   I am tied to th' stake, and I must stand the course.[6]

REGAN.   Wherefore to Dover?

GLOUCESTER.   Because I would not see thy cruel nails
Pluck out his poor old eyes; nor thy fierce sister
In his anointed flesh stick boarish fangs.
The sea, with such a storm as his bare head
In hell-black night endur'd, would have buoy'd[7] up
And quench'd the stelled fires;[8]
Yet, poor old heart, he holp[9] the heavens to rain.

---

[3] corky—withered.   [4] quicken—come to life.   [5] ruffle—violate.   [6] course—attack.
[7] buoy'd—swelled up.   [8] stelled fires—light of the stars.   [9] holp—helped.

If wolves had at thy gate howl'd that stern time,
Thou shouldst have said, "Good porter, turn the key."
All cruels else subscrib'd:[10] but I shall see
The winged vengeance overtake such children.

CORNWALL.   See 't shalt thou never. Fellows, hold the chair.
Upon these eyes of thine I'll set my foot.

GLOUCESTER.   He that will think to live till he be old,
Give me some help!—O cruel! O ye gods!

REGAN.   One side will mock another; th' other too.

CORNWALL.   If you see vengeance,—

FIRST SERVANT.   Hold your hand, my lord!
I have serv'd you ever since I was a child;
But better service have I never done you
Than now to bid you hold.

REGAN.   How now, you dog!

FIRST SERVANT.   If you did wear a beard upon your chin,
I'd shake it on this quarrel. What do you mean?

CORNWALL.   My villain![11] [*They draw and fight.*]

FIRST SERVANT.   Nay, then, come on, and take the chance of anger.

REGAN.   Give me thy sword. A peasant stand up thus?
               [*She takes a sword, and runs at him behind.*]

FIRST SERVANT.   Oh, I am slain! My lord, you have one eye left
To see some mischief on him. Oh! [*Dies.*]

CORNWALL.   Lest it see more, prevent it. Out, vile jelly!
Where is thy lustre now?

GLOUCESTER.   All dark and comfortless. Where's my son Edmund?
Edmund, enkindle all the sparks of nature,
To quit[12] this horrid act.

REGAN.   Out, treacherous villain!
Thou call'st on him that hates thee. It was he
That made the overture[13] of thy treason to us,
Who is too good to pity thee.

GLOUCESTER.   O my follies! then Edgar was abus'd[14]
Kind gods, forgive me that, and prosper him!

REGAN.   Go thrust him out at gates, and let him smell
His way to Dover.

               [*Exit one with* GLOUCESTER.]
               How is 't, my lord? How look you?

CORNWALL.   I have received a hurt; follow me, lady.
Turn out that eyeless villain; throw this slave
Upon the dunghill. Regan, I bleed apace;
Untimely comes this hurt. Give me your arm. [*Exit* CORNWALL, *led by* REGAN.]

SECOND SERVANT.   I'll never care what wickedness I do,
If this man come to good.

THIRD SERVANT.   If she live long,

---

[10] cruels else subscribed—other cruel animals submitted.   [11] villain—servant.   [12] quit —requite.   [13] overture—disclosure.   [14] abus'd—wronged.

And in the end meet the old course[15] of death,
Women will all turn monsters.

    SECOND SERVANT.   Let's follow the old earl, and get the Bedlam
To lead him where he would: his roguish madness
Allows itself to anything.

    THIRD SERVANT.   Go thou: I'll fetch some flax and whites of eggs
To apply to his bleeding face. Now, Heaven help him! [*Exeunt severally.*]

ACT IV · 1

The open country near Gloucester's castle.

[*Enter* EDGAR.]

    EDGAR.   Yet better thus, and known to be contemn'd,[1]
Than, still contemn'd and flatter'd, to be worst.
The lowest and most dejected thing of fortune
Stands still in esperance,[2] lives not in fear.
The lamentable change is from the best;
The worst returns[3] to laughter. Welcome, then,
Thou unsubstantial air that I embrace!
The wretch that thou hast blown unto the worst
Owes nothing to thy blasts.

                [*Enter* GLOUCESTER, *led by an* OLD MAN.]
                     But who comes here?
My father, poorly led? World, world, O world!
But that thy strange mutations make us hate thee,
Life would not yield to age.[4]

    OLD MAN.   O, my good lord, I have been your tenant, and your father's
tenant, these four-score years.

    GLOUCESTER.   Away, get thee away! Good friend, be gone;
Thy comforts can do me no good at all;
Thee they may hurt.

    OLD MAN.   Alack, sir, you cannot see your way.

    GLOUCESTER.   I have no way, and therefore want no eyes;
I stumbled when I saw. Full oft 't is seen,
Our means secure[5] us, and our mere defects
Prove our commodities.[6] Ah! dear son Edgar,
The food[7] of thy abused father's wrath!
Might I but live to see thee in my touch,
I'd say I had eyes again!

    OLD MAN.   How now! Who's there?

    EDGAR [*aside*].   O gods! Who is 't can say, "I am at the worst"?
I am worse than e'er I was.

---

[15] old course—natural death in old age.
[1] contemn'd—despised.   [2] esperance—hope.   [3] returns—can only change to.   [4] yield
to age—consent to live.   [5] secure—make careless.   [6] commodities—advantages.
[7] food—object.

OLD MAN.   'T is poor mad Tom.

EDGAR [aside].   And worse I may be yet; the worst is not
So long as we can say, "This is the worst."

OLD MAN.   Fellow, where goest?

GLOUCESTER.   Is it a beggar-man?

OLD MAN.   Madman and beggar too.

GLOUCESTER.   He has some reason, else he could not beg.
I' th' last night's storm I such a fellow saw,
Which made me think a man a worm. My son
Came then into my mind, and yet my mind
Was then scarce friends with him. I have heard more since.
As flies to wanton[8] boys, are we to the gods,
They kill us for their sport.

EDGAR [aside].   How should this be?
Bad is the trade that must play fool to sorrow,[9]
Ang'ring itself and others.—Bless thee, master!

GLOUCESTER.   Is that the naked fellow?

OLD MAN.   Ay, my lord.

GLOUCESTER.   Then, prithee, get thee gone. If, for my sake,
Thou wilt o'ertake us, hence a mile or twain
I' th' way toward Dover, do it for ancient love;
And bring some covering for this naked soul,
Who I'll entreat to lead me.

OLD MAN.   Alack, sir, he is mad.

GLOUCESTER.   'T is the time's plague,[10] when madmen lead the blind.
Do as I bid thee, or rather do thy pleasure;
Above the rest, be gone.

OLD MAN.   I'll bring him the best 'parel that I have,
Come on 't what will. [Exit.]

GLOUCESTER.   Sirrah, naked fellow,—

EDGAR.   Poor Tom's a-cold. [Aside.] I cannot daub[11] it further—

GLOUCESTER.   Come hither, fellow.

EDGAR [aside].   And yet I must.—Bless thy sweet eyes, they bleed.

GLOUCESTER.   Know'st thou the way to Dover?

EDGAR.   Both stile and gate, horse-way and foot-path. Poor Tom hath been
scared out of his wits. Bless thee, good man's son, from the foul fiend! Five
fiends have been in poor Tom at once; of lust, as Obdicut; Hobbididence,
prince of dumbness; Mahu, of stealing; Modo, of murder; Flibbertigibbet, of
mopping and mowing,[12] who since possesses chambermaids and waiting-women.
So, bless thee, master!

GLOUCESTER.   Here, take this purse, thou whom the heavens' plagues
Have humbled to all strokes:[13] that I am wretched
Makes thee the happier; heavens, deal so still!
Let the superfluous and lust-dieted man,
That slaves[14] your ordinance,[15] that will not see

---

[8] wanton—playful.   [9] sorrow—to one in sorrowful plight.   [10] time's plague—a symbol
of these bad times.   [11] daub—pretend.   [12] mopping and mowing—face making.
[13] to all strokes—to be able to endure all misfortunes.   [14] slaves—subordinates to his
desires.   [15] ordinance—commands.

Because he does not feel, feel your power quickly;
So distribution should undo excess,
And each man have enough. Dost thou know Dover?

    EDGAR.   Ay, master.

    GLOUCESTER.   There is a cliff, whose high and bending head
Looks fearfully in the confined deep.
Bring me but to the very brim of it,
And I'll repair the misery thou dost bear
With something rich about me. From that place
I shall no leading need.

    EDGAR.   Give my thy arm;
Poor Tom shall lead thee. [*Exeunt.*]

ACT IV · 2

Before the Duke of Albany's palace.

[*Enter* GONERIL, EDMUND, *and* OSWALD.]

    GONERIL.   Welcome, my lord! I marvel our mild husband
Not met us on the way.—Now, where's your master?

    OSWALD.   Madam, within; but never man so chang'd.
I told him of the army that was landed;
He smil'd at it: I told him you were coming;
His answer was, "The worse:" of Gloucester's treachery,
And of the loyal service of his son,
When I inform'd him, then he call'd me sot,[1]
And told me I had turn'd the wrong side out.
What most he should dislike seems pleasant to him;
What like, offensive.

    GONERIL [*To* EDMUND].   Then shall you go no further.
It is the cowish[2] terror of his spirit,
That dares not undertake; he'll not feel wrongs
Which tie[3] him to an answer. Our wishes on the way
May prove effects.[4] Back, Edmund, to my brother;
Hasten his musters and conduct his powers.
I must change arms at home, and give the distaff[5]
Into my husband's hands. This trusty servant
Shall pass between us. Ere long you are like to hear,
If you dare venture in your own behalf,
A mistress's command. Wear this; spare speech;
Decline your head. This kiss, if it durst speak,
Would stretch thy spirits up into the air.
Conceive,[6] and fare thee well.

---

[1] sot—fool.   [2] cowish—cowardly.   [3] tie—force.   [4] prove effects—be fulfilled.
[5] distaff—spinning staff, i.e., symbol of woman's place.   [6] Conceive—understand my
meaning.

EDMUND.   Your's in the ranks of death. [*Exit.*]

GONERIL.   My most dear Gloucester!
O, the difference of man and man!
To thee a woman's services are due;
My Fool usurps my body.

OSWALD.   Madam, here comes my lord. [*Exit.*]
                              [*Enter the* DUKE OF ALBANY.]

GONERIL.   I have been worth the whistle.

ALBANY.   O Goneril!
You are not worth the dust which the rude wind
Blows in your face. I fear your disposition.
That nature which contemns its origin
Cannot be border'd certain[7] in itself.
She that herself will sliver and disbranch
From her material sap,[8] perforce must wither
And come to deadly use.[9]

GONERIL.   No more; the text is foolish.

ALBANY.   Wisdom and goodness to the vile seem vile;
Filths savour but themselves. What have you done?
Tigers, not daughters, what have you perform'd?
A father, and a gracious aged man,
Whose reverence even the head-lugg'd[10] bear would lick,
Most barbarous, most degenerate! have you madded.
Could my good brother suffer you to do it?
A man, a prince, by him so benefited!
If that the heavens do not their visible spirits
Send quickly down to tame[11] these vile offences,
It will come,
Humanity must perforce prey on itself,
Like monsters of the deep.

GONERIL.   Milk-liver'd man!
That bear'st a cheek for blows, a head for wrongs,
Who hast not in thy brows an eye discerning
Thine honour from thy suffering, that not know'st
Fools do those villains pity who are punish'd
Ere they have done their mischief; where's thy drum?
France spreads his banners in our noiseless[12] land,
With plumed helm thy state begins to threat;
Whiles thou, a moral fool, sits still, and criest,
"Alack, why does he so?"

ALBANY.   See thyself, devil!
Proper[13] deformity seems not in the fiend
So horrid as in woman.

---

[7] be border'd certain—have sure boundaries of conduct.   [8] sap—i.e., trunk.   [9] deadly
use—destruction.   [10] head-lugg'd—led by a leash.   [11] tame—put a stop to.   [12] noiseless—passive.   [13] Proper—natural to a fiend.

GONERIL.   O vain fool!

ALBANY.   Thou changed and self-cover'd[14] thing, for shame!
Be-monster not thy feature. Were 't my fitness
To let these hands obey my blood,
They are apt enough to dislocate and tear
Thy flesh and bones; howe'er thou art a fiend,
A woman's shape doth shield thee.

GONERIL.   Marry, your manhood—Mew!

[*Enter a* MESSENGER.]

ALBANY.   What news?

MESSENGER.   O, my good lord, the Duke of Cornwall's dead;
Slain by his servant, going to put out
The other eye of Gloucester.

ALBANY.   Gloucester's eyes!

MESSENGER.   A servant that he bred, thrill'd with remorse,
Oppos'd against the act, bending his sword
To his great master; who, thereat enrag'd,
Flew on him, and amongst them fell'd him dead;
But not without that harmful stroke, which since
Hath pluck'd him after.

ALBANY.   This shows you are above,
You justicers, that these our nether[15] crimes
So speedily can venge! But, O poor Gloucester!
Lost he his other eye?

MESSENGER.   Both, both, my lord.
This letter, madam, craves a speedy answer:
'T is from your sister.

GONERIL [*aside*].   One way I like this well;
But being widow, and my Gloucester with her,
May all the building in my fancy[16] pluck[17]
Upon my hateful life: another way,
The news is not so tart. I'll read, and answer. [*Exit.*]

ALBANY.   Where was his son when they did take his eyes?

MESSENGER.   Come with my lady hither.

ALBANY.   He is not here.

MESSENGER.   No, my good lord; I met him back again.

ALBANY.   Knows he the wickedness?

MESSENGER.   Ay, my good lord; 't was he inform'd against him;
And quit the house on purpose, that their punishment
Might have the freer course.

ALBANY.   Gloucester, I live
To thank thee for the love thou show'dst the King,
And to revenge thine eyes. Come hither, friend;
Tell me what more thou know'st. [*Exeunt.*]

---

[14] self-cover'd—disguising your real nature.   [15] nether—in this world.   [16] building in
my fancy—castle in the air.   [17] pluck—pull down.

The French camp near Dover.

[*Enter* KENT *and a* GENTLEMAN.]

KENT. Why the King of France is so suddenly gone back, know you no reason?

GENTLEMAN. Something he left imperfect in the state, which since his coming forth is thought of; which imports[1] to the kingdom so much fear and danger that his personal return was most required and necessary.

KENT. Who hath he left behind him General?

GENTLEMAN. The Marshal of France, Monsieur La Far.

KENT. Did your letters pierce the Queen to any demonstration of grief?

GENTLEMAN. Ay, sir; she took them, read them in my presence;
And now and then an ample tear trill'd down
Her delicate cheek. It seem'd she was a queen
Over her passion,[2] who, most rebel-like,
Sought to be king o'er her.

KENT. O, then it mov'd her.

GENTLEMAN. Not to a rage; patience and sorrow strove
Who should express her goodliest.[3] You have seen
Sunshine and rain at once: her smiles and tears
Were like a better way; those happy smilets
That play'd on her ripe lip seem'd not to know
What guests were in her eyes, which, parted thence,
As pearls from diamonds dropp'd. In brief,
Sorrow would be a rarity[4] most beloved,
If all could so become it.

KENT. Made she no verbal question?

GENTLEMAN. Faith, once or twice she heav'd the name of "father"
Pantingly forth, as if it press'd her heart;
Cried, "Sisters! sisters! Shame of ladies! sisters!
Kent! father! sisters! What, i' th' storm? i' th' night?
Let pity not be believ'd!" There she shook
The holy water from her heavenly eyes;
And clamour-moisten'd, then away she started
To deal with grief alone.

KENT. It is the stars,
The stars above us, govern our conditions;
Else one self mate and make[5] could not beget
Such different issues.[6] You spoke not with her since?

GENTLEMAN. No.

KENT. Was this before the King return'd?

GENTLEMAN. No, since.

---

[1] imports—threatens. [2] passion—sorrow. [3] express her goodliest—give her the more beautiful expression. [4] rarity—something precious. [5] self mate and make—same husband and wife. [6] issues—children.

KENT.   Well, sir, the poor distressed Lear's i' th' town;
Who sometime, in his better tune, remembers
What we are come about, and by no means
Will yield to see his daughter.
    GENTLEMAN.   Why, good sir?
    KENT.   A sovereign shame so elbows[7] him. His own unkindness,
That stripp'd her from his benediction, turn'd her
To foreign casualties,[8] gave her dear rights
To his dog-hearted daughters,—these things sting
His mind so venomously, that burning shame
Detains him from Cordelia.
    GENTLEMAN.   Alack, poor gentleman!
    KENT.   Of Albany's and Cornwall's powers you heard not?
    GENT.   'T is so, they are afoot.
    KENT.   Well, sir, I'll bring you to our master Lear,
And leave you to attend him. Some dear cause
Will in concealment wrap me up a while;
When I am known aright, you shall not grieve
Lending[9] me this acquaintance. I pray you, go
Along with me. [*Exeunt.*]

ACT IV · 4

The same. A tent.

[*Enter, with drum and colours,*[1] CORDELIA, DOCTOR, *and Soldiers.*]
    CORDELIA.   Alack, 't is he! Why, he was met even now
As mad as the vex'd sea, singing aloud,
Crown'd with rank fumiter[2] and furrow-weeds,
With hardocks, hemlock, nettles, cuckoo-flowers,
Darnel, and all the idle weeds that grow
In our sustaining corn.[3] A century[4] send forth;
Search every acre in the high-grown field,
And bring him to our eye. [*Exit an Officer.*]
    What can[5] man's wisdom[6]
In the restoring his bereaved sense?
He that helps him take all my outward worth.
    DOCTOR.   There is means, madam.
Our foster-nurse of nature is repose,
The which he lacks; that to provoke in him,
Are many simples[7] operative, whose power
Will close the eye of anguish.

---

[7] elbows—stands at his side.   [8] casualties—accidents.   [9] Lending—affording.
[1] drum and colours—drummers and colour-bearers.   [2] fumiter, etc.—the names of wild
flowers and weeds.   [3] sustaining corn—wheat that supports life.   [4] century—a company of soldiers.   [5] What can—what power is in.   [6] man's wisdom—science.
[7] simples—medicinal herbs.

CORDELIA.   All blest secrets,
All you unpublish'd virtues of the earth,
Spring with my tears! be aidant and remediate[8]
In the good man's distress! Seek, seek for him,
Lest his ungovern'd rage dissolve the life
That wants the means[9] to lead it.

                                        [*Enter* MESSENGER.]
MESSENGER.   News, madam!
The British powers are marching hitherward.

    CORDELIA.   'T is known before; our preparation stands
In expectation of them. O dear father,
It is thy business that I go about;
Therefore great France
My mourning and important[10] tears hath pitied.
No blown[11] ambition doth our arms incite,
But love, dear love, and our ag'd father's right.
Soon may I hear and see him! [*Exeunt.*]

ACT IV · 5

Gloucester's castle.

                    [*Enter* REGAN *and* OSWALD.]
    REGAN.   But are my brother's powers set forth?
    OSWALD.   Ay, madam.
    REGAN.   Himself in person there?
    OSWALD.   Madam, with much ado.[1]
Your sister is the better soldier.
    REGAN.   Lord Edmund spake not with your lord at home?
    OSWALD.   No, madam.
    REGAN.   What might import my sister's letter to him?
    OSWALD.   I know not, lady.
    REGAN.   Faith, he is posted[2] hence on serious matter.
It was great ignorance, Gloucester's eyes being out,
To let him live; where he arrives he moves
All hearts against us. Edmund, I think, is gone,
In pity of his misery, to dispatch
His nighted[3] life; moreover, to descry
The strength o' the enemy.
    OSWALD.   I must needs after him, madam, with my letter.
    REGAN.   Our troops set forth to-morrow, stay with us;
The ways are dangerous.

---

[8] aidant and remediate—helpful remedies.   [9] means—sense.   [10] important—importunate.   [11] blown—inflated.
[1] ado—effort.   [2] posted—ridden.   [3] nighted—blinded.

OSWALD.   I may not, madam:
My lady charg'd my duty in this business.
    REGAN.   Why should she write to Edmund? Might not you
Transport her purposes by word? Belike
Some thing—I know not what. I'll love thee much,
Let me unseal the letter.
    OSWALD.   Madam, I had rather—
    REGAN.   I know your lady does not love her husband;
I am sure of that; and at her late being here
She gave strange eliads⁴ and most speaking looks
To noble Edmund. I know you are of her bosom.⁵
    OSWALD.   I, madam?
    REGAN.   I speak in understanding; y' are, I know 't.
Therefore I do advise you, take this note:⁶
My lord is dead; Edmund and I have talk'd;
And more convenient is he for my hand
Than for your lady's. You may gather more.
If you do find him, pray you, give him this;
And when your mistress hears thus much from you,
I pray, desire her call her wisdom to her:
So, fare you well.
If you do chance to hear of that blind traitor,
Preferment⁷ falls on him that cuts him off.
    OSWALD.   Would I could meet him, madam! I would show
What party I do follow.
    REGAN.   Fare thee well. [*Exeunt.*]

ACT IV · 6

The country near Dover.

[*Enter* GLOUCESTER, *and* EDGAR *dressed like a peasant.*]
    GLOUCESTER.   When shall we come to th' top of that same hill?
    EDGAR.   You do climb up it now; look, how we labour.
    GLOUCESTER.   Methinks the ground is even.
    EDGAR.   Horrible steep.
Hark, do you hear the sea?
    GLOUCESTER.   No, truly.
    EDGAR.   Why, then, your other senses grow imperfect
By your eyes' anguish.
    GLOUCESTER.   So may it be, indeed.
Methinks thy voice is alter'd, and thou speak'st
In better phrase and matter than thou didst.

---

⁴ eliads—languishing looks.   ⁵ of her bosom—in her confidence.   ⁶ take this note—
consider this.   ⁷ Preferment—promotion.

EDGAR.   You're much deceiv'd. In nothing am I chang'd
But in my garments.

GLOUCESTER.   Methinks you're better spoken.

EDGAR.   Come on, sir; here's the place; stand still. How fearful
And dizzy 't is, to cast one's eyes so low!
The crows and choughs[1] that wing the midway air
Show scarce so gross[2] as beetles. Half way down
Hangs one that gathers sampire,[3] dreadful trade!
Methinks he seems no bigger than his head.
The fishermen, that walk upon the beach,
Appear like mice; and yond tall anchoring bark,
Diminish'd to her cock,[4] her cock, a buoy
Almost too small for sight. The murmuring surge,
That on th' unnumber'd idle pebbles chafes,
Cannot be heard so high. I'll look no more,
Lest my brain turn, and the deficient sight[5]
Topple down headlong.

GLOUCESTER.   Set me where you stand.

EDGAR.   Give me your hand; you are now within a foot
Of th' éxtreme verge. For all beneath the moon
Would I not leap upright.

GLOUCESTER.   Let go my hand.
Here, friend, 's another purse; in it a jewel
Well worth a poor man's taking. Fairies and gods
Prosper it with thee! Go thou further off;
Bid me farewell, and let me hear thee going.

EDGAR.   Now fare you well, good sir.

GLOUCESTER.   With all my heart.

EDGAR.   Why I do trifle with his despair
Is done to cure it.

GLOUCESTER [kneeling].   O you mighty gods!
This world I do renounce, and in your sights
Shake patiently my great affliction off.
If I could bear it longer, and not fall
To quarrel with your great opposeless wills,
My snuff[6] and loathed part of nature should
Burn itself out. If Edgar live, O bless him!
Now, fellow, fare thee well.

EDGAR.   Gone, sir; farewell!
—And yet I know not how conceit[7] may rob
The treasury of life, when life itself
Yields to the theft.

     [GLOUCESTER throws himself forward and falls on the stage floor.]
                    Had he been where he thought,
By this had thought been past. Alive or dead?—

---

[1] choughs—jackdaws.   [2] gross—big.   [3] sampire—aromatic plant, used as seasoning.
[4] cock—cockboat.   [5] deficient sight—failing sight.   [6] snuff—useless remnant.   [7] conceit—imagination.

Ho, you sir! friend! Hear you, sir! speak!—
Thus might he pass[8] indeed; yet he revives.—
What are you, sir?

GLOUCESTER. Away, and let me die.

EDGAR. Hadst thou been aught but gossamer,[9] feathers, air,
So many fathom down precipitating,
Thou'dst shiver'd like an egg: but thou dost breathe;
Hast heavy substance; bleed'st not; speak'st; art sound.
Ten masts at each[10] make not the altitude
Which thou hast perpendicularly fell.
Thy life's a miracle. Speak yet again.

GLOUCESTER. But have I fall'n, or no?

EDGAR. From the dread summit of this chalky bourn.[11]
Look up a-height; the shrill-gorg'd[12] lark so far
Cannot be seen or heard. Do but look up.

GLOUCESTER. Alack, I have no eyes.
Is wretchedness depriv'd that benefit,
To end itself by death? 'T was yet some comfort,
When misery could beguile[13] the tyrant's rage,
And frustrate his proud will.

EDGAR.   Give me your arm.
Up: so; How is 't? Feel your legs? You stand.

GLOUCESTER. Too well, too well.

EDGAR.   This is above all strangeness.
Upon the crown o' th' cliff, what thing was that
Which parted from you?

GLOUCESTER.   A poor unfortunate beggar.

EDGAR. As I stood here below, methought his eyes
Were two full moons; he had a thousand noses,
Horns whelk'd[14] and waved like the enridged sea.
It was some fiend; therefore, thou happy father,[15]
Think that the clearest gods, who make them honours
Of men's impossibilities,[16] have preserv'd thee.

GLOUCESTER. I do remember now. Henceforth I'll bear
Affliction till it do cry out itself,
"Enough, enough," and die. That thing you speak of,
I took it for a man; often would it say,
"The fiend, the fiend:" He led me to that place.

EDGAR. Bear free and patient thoughts.

[Enter LEAR, mad.]

                               But who comes here?
The safer sense[17] will ne'er accommodate[18]
His master thus.

LEAR. No, they cannot touch me for coining; I am the King himself.

EDGAR. O thou side-piercing sight!

---

[8] pass—die.   [9] gossamer—spider's webbing.   [10] at each—laid end to end.   [11] bourn
—boundary.   [12] gorg'd—throated.   [13] beguile—elude.   [14] whelk'd—twisted.
[15] father—old man.   [16] men's impossibilities—by doing things impossible to man.
[17] safer sense—sane mind.   [18] accommodate—dress up.

LEAR. Nature's above art in that respect. There's your press-money. That fellow handles his bow like a crow-keeper; draw me a clothier's yard.[19] Look, look, a mouse! Peace, peace; this piece of toasted cheese will do 't. There's my gauntlet; I'll prove it on a giant. Bring up the brown bills.[20] O, well flown, bird! I' th' clout,[21] i' th' clout! Hewgh! Give the word.[22]

EDGAR. Sweet marjoram.

LEAR. Pass.

GLOUCESTER. I know that voice.

LEAR. Ha! Goneril, with a white beard! They flattered me like a dog, and told me I had white hairs in my beard ere the black ones were there. To say "ay" and "no" to everything I said! "Ay" and "no" too was no good divinity.[23] When the rain came to wet me once, and the wind to make me chatter; when the thunder would not peace at my bidding; there I found 'em, there I smelt 'em out. Go to, they are not men o' their words: they told me I was everything; 't is a lie, I am not agueproof.

GLOUCESTER. The trick of that voice I do well remember.
Is 't not the King?

LEAR.   Ay, every inch a king!
When I do stare, see how the subject quakes.
I pardon that man's life. What was thy cause?[24]
Adultery?
Thou shalt not die. Die for adultery! No:
The wren goes to 't, and the small gilded fly
Does lecher in my sight.
Let copulation thrive; for Gloucester's bastard son
Was kinder to his father than my daughters
Got 'tween the lawful sheets.
To 't, luxury,[25] pell-mell! for I lack soldiers.
Behold yond simp'ring dame,
Whose face between her forks[26] presageth snow,[27]
That minces virtue, and does shake the head
To hear of pleasure's name,—
The fitchew,[28] nor the soiled horse, goes to 't
With a more riotous appetite.
Down from the waist they are Centaurs,[29]
Though women all above;
But to the girdle do the gods inherit,
Beneath is all the fiends';
There's hell, there's darkness, there's the sulphurous pit,
Burning, scalding, stench, consumption; fie, fie, fie! pah, pah!
Give me an ounce of civet, good apothecary, to sweeten my imagination.
There's money for thee.

GLOUCESTER. O, let me kiss that hand!

LEAR. Let me wipe it first; it smells of mortality.

---

[19] clothier's yard—the length of an arrow. [20] brown bills—halberds. [21] clout—bull's-eye. [22] word—password. [23] no good divinity—false doctrine. [24] cause—offense. [25] luxury—lasciviousness. [26] forks—part of the headdress. [27] snow—chastity. [28] fitchew—pole-cat. [29] Centaurs—mythical beasts, half-man, half-horse.

GLOUCESTER.   O ruin'd piece of nature! This great world
Shall so wear out to nought. Dost thou know me?

LEAR.   I remember thine eyes well enough. Dost thou squiny[30] at me? No,
do thy worst, blind Cupid; I'll not love. Read thou this challenge; mark but the
penning of it.

GLOUCESTER.   Were all thy letters suns, I could not see one.

EDGAR [aside].   I would not take[31] this from report. It is;
And my heart breaks at it.

LEAR.   Read.

GLOUCESTER.   What, with the case[32] of eyes?

LEAR.   O, ho, are you there with me? No eyes in your head, nor no money
in your purse? Your eyes are in a heavy case, your purse in a light; yet you see
how this world goes.

GLOUCESTER.   I see it feelingly.

LEAR.   What, art mad? A man may see how this world goes with no eyes.
Look with thine ears; see how yond justice rails upon yond simple thief. Hark,
in thine ear: change places, and, handy-dandy,[33] which is the justice, which
is the thief? Thou hast seen a farmer's dog bark at a beggar?

GLOUCESTER.   Ay, sir.

LEAR.   And the creature run from the cur? There thou mightst behold
the great image of authority: a dog's obeyed in office.
Thou rascal beadle, hold thy bloody hand!
Why dost thou lash that whore? Strip thine own back;
Thou hotly lusts to use her in that kind[34]
For which thou whip'st her. The usurer hangs the cozener.[35]
Through tatter'd clothes small vices do appear;
Robes and furr'd gowns hides all. Plate sins with gold,
And the strong lance of justice hurtless breaks;
Arm it[36] in rags, a pigmy's straw does pierce it.
None does offend, none, I say, none; I'll able[37] 'em.
Take that of me, my friend, who have the power
To seal th' accuser's lips. Get thee glass eyes,
And, like a scurvy politician, seem
To see the things thou dost not. Now, now, now, now.
Pull off my boots; harder, harder: so.

EDGAR.   O, matter and impertinency[38] mix'd;
Reason in madness!

LEAR.   If thou wilt weep my fortune, take my eyes.
I know thee well enough; thy name is Gloucester.
Thou must be patient; we came crying hither.
Thou know'st, the first time that we smell the air,
We wawl and cry. I will preach to thee; mark.

GLOUCESTER.   Alack, alack the day!

LEAR.   When we are born, we cry that we are come
To this great stage of fools.—This a good block.[39]

---

30 squiny—squint.   31 take—believe.   32 case—sockets.   33 handy-dandy—formula
in a child's game.   34 kind—manner.   35 cozener—petty cheat.   36 it—sin.
37 able—license.   38 impertinency—incoherent talk.   39 block—well-fashioned hat.

It were a delicate stratagem, to shoe
A troop of horse with felt, I'll put 't in proof;[40]
And when I have stol'n upon these son-in-laws,
Then, kill, kill, kill, kill, kill, kill!

[Enter a GENTLEMAN *with Attendants.]*

GENTLEMAN.   O, here he is! Lay hand upon him. Sir,
Your most dear daughter—

LEAR.   No rescue? What, a prisoner? I am even
The natural fool[41] of fortune. Use me well;
You shall have ransom. Let me have a surgeon;
I am cut to th' brains.

GENTLEMAN.   You shall have anything.

LEAR.   No seconds?[42] All myself?
Why, this would make a man a man of salt,
To use his eyes for garden water-pots,
Ay, and laying autumn's dust.

GENTLEMAN.   Good sir,—

LEAR.   I will die bravely, like a smug bride groom. What!
I will be jovial. Come, come; I am a king,
My masters, know you that?

GENTLEMAN.   You are a royal one, and we obey you.

LEAR.   Then there's life in 't. Come, an you get it, you shall get it by
running. Sa, sa, sa, sa. *[Exit running; Attendants follow.]*

GENTLEMAN.   A sight most pitiful in the meanest wretch,
Past speaking of in a king! Thou hast one daughter
Who redeems Nature from the general curse
Which twain have brought her to.

EDGAR.   Hail, gentle sir.

GENTLEMAN.   Sir, speed you: what's your will?

EDGAR.   Do you hear aught, sir, of a battle toward?[43]

GENTLEMAN.   Most sure and vulgar;[44] every one hears that,
That can distinguish sound.

EDGAR.   But, by your favour,
How near's the other army?

GENTLEMAN.   Near and on speedy foot; the main descry
Stands on the hourly thought.

EDGAR.   I thank you, sir; that's all.

GENTLEMAN.   Though that the Queen on special cause is here,
Her army is mov'd on. *[Exit.]*

EDGAR.   I thank you, sir.

GLOUCESTER.   You ever-gentle gods, take my breath from me;
Let not my worser spirit tempt me again
To die before you please!

EDGAR.   Well pray you, father.

GLOUCESTER.   Now, good sir, what are you?

EDGAR.   A most poor man, made tame[45] to fortune's blows;

---

[40] in proof—to trial.   [41] natural fool—born to the sport of.   [42] No seconds—no one
to aid me.   [43] toward—imminent.   [44] vulgar—commonly known.   [45] tame—submissive.

Who, by the art of known and feeling sorrows,
Am pregnant[46] to good pity. Give me your hand,
I'll lead you to some biding.[47]
    GLOUCESTER.   Hearty thanks;
The bounty and the benison of Heaven
To boot, and boot!

                          [Enter OSWALD.*]*
    OSWALD.   A próclaim'd prize! Most happy![48]
That eyeless head of thine was first fram'd flesh
To raise my fortunes. Thou old unhappy traitor,
Briefly thyself remember;[49] the sword is out
That must destroy thee.
    GLOUCESTER.   Now let thy friendly hand
Put strength enough to 't. [EDGAR *interposes.*]
    OSWALD.   Wherefore, bold peasant,
Dar'st thou support a publish'd traitor? Hence;
Lest that th' infection of his fortune take
Like hold on thee. Let go his arm.
    EDGAR.   'Chill[50] not let go, zir, without vurther 'casion.
    OSWALD.   Let go, slave, or thou diest!
    EDGAR.   Good gentleman, go your gait, and let poor volk pass. An 'chud ha'
bin zwaggered out of my life, 't would not ha' bin zo long as 't is by a vort-
night. Nay, come not near th' old man; keep out, 'che vor[51] ye, or Ise try
whether your costard[52] or my ballow[53] be the harder. 'Chill be plain with you.
    OSWALD.   Out, dunghill!
    EDGAR.   'Chill pick your teeth, zir. Come, no matter vor your foins.[54]

                  [They fight, and EDGAR *knocks him down.*]
    OSWALD.   Slave, thou hast slain me. Villain, take my purse.
If ever thou wilt thrive, bury my body;
And give the letters which thou find'st about me
To Edmund Earl of Gloucester; seek him out
Upon the English party. O, untimely death!
Death! [*Dies.*]
    EDGAR.   I know thee well; a serviceable villain,
As duteous to the vices of thy mistress
As badness would desire.
    GLOUCESTER.   What, is he dead?
    EDGAR.   Sit you down, father; rest you.
Let's see these pockets; the letters that he speaks of
May be my friends. He's dead; I am only sorry
He had no other death's-man.[55] Let us see.
Leave, gentle wax; and, manners, blame us not.
To know our enemies' minds, we'd rip their hearts;
Their papers, is more lawful. [*Reads the letter.*]

---

[46] pregnant—susceptible.   [47] biding—refuge.   [48] happy—opportune.   [49] thyself remember—prepare thy conscience for death.   [50] 'Chill—I will (Edgar assumes a peasant
dialect).   [51] vor—warn.   [52] costard—head.   [53] ballow—cudgel.   [54] foins—thrusts.
[55] death's-man—executioner.

Let our reciprocal vows be remembered. You have many opportunities to cut him off; if your will want not, time and place will be fruitfully offered. There is nothing done, if he return the conqueror; then am I the prisoner, and his bed my jail; from the loathed warmth whereof deliver me, and supply the place for your labour.

Your—wife, so I would say—

Affectionate servant,

GONERIL.

O indistinguish'd[56] space of woman's will!
A plot upon her virtuous husband's life;
And the exchange my brother! Here, in the sands,
Thee I'll rake up,[57] the post unsanctified
Of murderous lechers; and in the mature time
With this ungracious paper strike the sight
Of the death-practis'd[58] duke. For him 't is well
That of thy death and business I can tell.

    GLOUCESTER.   The King is mad; how stiff is my vile sense
That I stand up and have ingenious[59] feeling
Of my huge sorrows! Better I were distract;
So should my thoughts be sever'd from my griefs, [*Drum afar off.*]
And woes by wrong imaginations lose
The knowledge of themselves.

    EDGAR.   Give me your hand.
Far off, methinks, I hear the beaten drum.
Come, father, I'll bestow you with a friend. [*Exeunt.*]

ACT IV · 7

A tent in the French camp.

[*Enter* CORDELIA, KENT, *and* DOCTOR, *and Gentleman.*]
    CORDELIA.   O thou good Kent, how shall I live and work
To match thy goodness? My life will be too short,
And every measure fail me.

    KENT.   To be acknowledg'd, madam, is o'erpaid.
All my reports go with[1] the modest truth;
Nor more nor clipp'd, but so.

    CORDELIA.   Be better suited;[2]
These weeds are memories of those worser hours.
I prithee, put them off.

    KENT.   Pardon, dear madam;
Yet to be known shortens[3] my made intent.

---

[56] indistinguish'd—infinite.   [57] rake up—bury.   [58] death-practis'd—whose death is plotted.   [59] ingenious—acute.
[1] go with—correspond to.   [2] suited—clothed.   [3] shortens—cuts short.

My boon I make it, that you know me not
Till time and I think meet.

    CORDELIA.   Then be 't so, my good lord. [*To the* DOCTOR.] How does the
King?

    DOCTOR.   Madam, sleeps still.

    CORDELIA.   O you kind gods,
Cure this great breach in his abused nature!
Th' untun'd and jarring senses, O, wind up
Of this child-changed father!

    DOCTOR.   So please your Majesty
That we may wake the King? He hath slept long.

    CORDELIA.   Be govern'd by your knowledge, and proceed
I' th' sway of your own will.

                    [*Enter* LEAR *in a chair carried by Servants.*]
                Is he array'd?

    DOCTOR.   Ay, madam; in the heaviness of sleep
We put fresh garments on him.

    GENTLEMAN.   Good madam, be by, when we do awake him;
I doubt not of his temperance.[4] [*Music.*]

    CORDELIA.   Very well.

    DOCTOR.   Please you, draw near.—Louder the music there!

    CORDELIA.   O my dear father! Restoration hang
Thy medicine on my lips; and let this kiss
Repair those violent harms that my two sisters
Have in thy reverence made!

    KENT.   Kind and dear princess!

    CORDELIA.   Had you not been their father, these white flakes[5]
Did challenge pity of them. Was this a face
To be oppos'd against the warring winds?
To stand against the deep dread-bolted thunder?
In the most terrible and nimble stroke
Of quick, cross lightning? to watch—poor pérdu![6]—
With this thin helm? Mine enemy's dog,
Though he had bit me, should have stood that night
Against my fire; and wast thou fain,[7] poor father,
To hovel thee with swine and rogues forlorn
In short and musty straw? Alack, alack!
'T is wonder that thy life and wits at once
Had not concluded all. He wakes; speak to him.

    DOCTOR.   Madam, do you; 't is fittest.

    CORDELIA.   How does my royal lord? How fares your Majesty?

    LEAR.   You do me wrong to take me out o' th' grave.
Thou art a soul in bliss;[8] but I am bound
Upon a wheel of fire, that mine own tears
Do scald like molten lead.

---

[4] temperance—sanity.   [5] flakes—hairs.   [6] pérdu—isolated sentry.   [7] fain—glad.
[8] bliss—Heaven.

CORDELIA.   Sir, do you know me?

LEAR.   You are a spirit, I know; when did you die?

CORDELIA.   Still, still, far wide![9]

DOCTOR.   He's scarce awake; let him alone a while.

LEAR.   Where have I been? Where am I? Fair daylight?
I am mightily abus'd. I should even die with pity,
To see another thus. I know not what to say.
I will not swear these are my hands. Let's see;
I feel this pin prick. Would I were assur'd
Of my condition!

CORDELIA.   O, look upon me, sir.
And hold your hand in benediction o'er me.
No, sir, you must not kneel.

LEAR.   Pray, do not mock me.
I am a very foolish fond old man.
Fourscore and upward, not an hour more nor less;
And, to deal plainly,
I fear I am not in my perfect mind.
Methinks I should know you, and know this man;
Yet I am doubtful; for I am mainly[10] ignorant
What place this is, and all the skill I have
Remembers not these garments; nor I know not
Where I did lodge last night. Do not laugh at me;
For, as I am a man, I think this lady
To be my child Cordelia.

CORDELIA.   And so I am, I am.

LEAR.   Be your tears wet? Yes, faith. I pray, weep not.
If you have poison for me, I will drink it.
I know you do not love me; for your sisters
Have, as I do remember, done me wrong:
You have some cause, they have not.

CORDELIA.   No cause, no cause.

LEAR.   Am I in France?

KENT.   In your own kingdom, sir.

LEAR.   Do not abuse me.

DOCTOR.   Be comforted, good madam; the great rage,
You see, is kill'd in him: and yet it is danger
To make him even o'er[11] the time he has lost.
Desire him to go in; trouble him no more
Till further settling.

CORDELIA.   Will 't please your Highness walk?

LEAR.   You must bear with me.
Pray you now, forget and forgive; I am old and foolish.

[*Exeunt all but* KENT *and* GENTLEMAN.]

GENTLEMAN.   Holds it true, sir, that the Duke of Cornwall was so slain?

KENT.   Most certain, sir.

GENTLEMAN.   Who is conductor of his people?

---

[9] wide—astray (in his wits).   [10] mainly—completely.   [11] even o'er—recall past events.

KENT. As 't is said, the bastard son of Gloucester.

GENTLEMAN. They say Edgar, his banished son, is with the Earl of Kent in Germany.

KENT. Report is changeable.[12] 'T is time to look about; the powers of the kingdom approach apace.

GENTLEMAN. The arbitrement[13] is like to be bloody. Fare you well, sir.

[Exit.]

KENT. My point[14] and period will be thoroughly wrought,
Or well or ill, as this day's battle's fought. [Exit.]

ACT V · 1

The British camp, near Dover.

[*Enter, with drum and colours,* EDMUND, REGAN, *Gentlemen, and Soldiers.*]

EDMUND. Know of the Duke if his last purpose hold,
Or whether since he is advis'd by aught
To change the course. He's full of alteration
And self-reproving; bring his constant pleasure.[1]

[*To a Gentleman, who goes out.*]

REGAN. Our sister's man is certainly miscarried.[2]

EDMUND. 'T is to be doubted,[3] madam.

REGAN.   Now, sweet lord,
You know the goodness I intend upon you.
Tell me—but truly—but then speak the truth,
Do you not love my sister?

EDMUND.   In honour'd love.

REGAN. But have you never found my brother's way
To the forfended[4] place?

EDMUND.   That thought abuses you.

REGAN. I am doubtful that you have been conjunct
And bosom'd[5] with her,—as far as we call hers.[6]

EDMUND. No, by mine honour, madam.

REGAN. I never shall endure her. Dear my lord,
Be not familiar with her.

EDMUND.   Fear me not.
She and the Duke her husband!

[*Enter, with drum and colours,* ALBANY, GONERIL, *and Soldiers.*]

GONERIL [*aside*]. I had rather lose the battle than that sister
Should loosen him and me.

ALBANY. Our very loving sister, well be-met.
Sir, this I heard: the King is come to his daughter,

---

12 Report is changeable—rumors are not reliable.   13 arbitrement—decision.   14 point —full stop.
1 constant pleasure—final determination.   2 miscarried—come to harm.   3 doubted— feared.   4 forfended—forbidden.   5 conjunct and bosom'd—intimate.   6 as far as we call hers—in every way.

With others whom the rigour of our state[7]
Forc'd to cry out. Where I could not be honest,
I never yet was valiant. For this business,
It toucheth us, as France invades our land,
Not bolds[8] the King, with others, whom, I fear,
Most just and heavy causes make oppose.[9]

EDMUND.   Sir, you speak nobly.

REGAN.   Why is this reason'd?

GONERIL.   Combine together 'gainst the enemy;
For these domestic and particular broils
Are not the question here.

ALBANY.   Let's then determine
With the ancient[10] of war on our proceeding.

EDMUND.   I shall attend you presently at your tent.

REGAN.   Sister, you'll go with us?

GONERIL.   No.

REGAN.   'T is most convenient; pray you, go with us.

GONERIL [aside].   O, ho, I know the riddle. I will go.

[Exeunt both the armies.]

[As they are going out, enter EDGAR disguised.]

EDGAR.   If e'er your Grace had speech with man so poor,
Hear me one word. [ALBANY remains.]

ALBANY.   I'll overtake you.—Speak.

EDGAR.   Before you fight the battle, ope this letter.
If you have victory, let the trumpet sound
For him that brought it. Wretched though I seem,
I can produce a champion that will prove
What is avouched there. If you miscarry,
Your business of the world hath so an end,
And machination ceases. Fortune love you!

ALBANY.   Stay till I have read the letter.

EDGAR.   I was forbid it.
When time shall serve, let but the herald cry,
And I'll appear again. [Exit.]

ALBANY.   Why, fare thee well; I will o'erlook thy paper.

[Re-enter EDMUND.]

EDMUND.   The enemy's in view; draw up your powers.
Here is the guess of their true strength and forces
By diligent discovery;[11] but your haste
Is now urg'd on you.

ALBANY.   We will greet the time. [Exit.]

EDMUND.   To both these sisters have I sworn my love;
Each jealous[12] of the other, as the stung
Are of the adder. Which of them shall I take?
Both? one? or neither? Neither can be enjoy'd,
If both remain alive. To take the widow

---

[7] rigour of our state—our harsh government.   [8] Not bolds—not as it encourages.
[9] make oppose—make them oppose us.   [10] ancient—veteran leaders.   [11] discovery—
scouting.   [12] jealous—suspicious.

Exasperates, makes mad her sister Goneril;
And hardly shall I carry out my side,
Her husband being alive. Now then we'll use
His countenance for the battle; which being done,
Let her that would be rid of him devise
His speedy taking off. As for the mercy
Which he intends to Lear and to Cordelia,
The battle done, and they within our power,
Shall never see his pardon; for my state
Stands on[13] me to defend, not to debate. [*Exit.*]

ACT V · 2

A field between the two camps.

[*Alarum*[1] *within. Enter, with drum and colours,* LEAR, CORDELIA, *and Soldiers,
marching over the stage; and exeunt.*]
     [*Enter* EDGAR *and* GLOUCESTER.]
EDGAR.   Here, father, take the shadow of this tree
For your good host; pray that the right may thrive.
If ever I return to you again,
I'll bring you comfort.
     GLOUCESTER.   Grace go with you, sir! [*Exit* EDGAR.]
          [*Alarum and retreat sounded within. Re-enter* EDGAR.]
EDGAR.   Away, old man; give me thy hand; away!
King Lear hath lost, he and his daughter ta'en.
Give me thy hand; come on.
     GLOUCESTER.   No further, sir; a man may rot even here.
     EDGAR.   What, in ill thoughts again? Men must endure
Their going hence, even as their coming hither;
Ripeness is all. Come on.
     GLOUCESTER.   And that's true too. [*Exeunt.*]

ACT V · 3

The British camp near Dover.

[*Enter in conquest, with drum and colours,* EDMUND; LEAR *and* CORDELIA *as
prisoners;* CAPTAIN, *Soldiers, etc.*]
     EDMUND.   Some officers take them away. Good guard,
Until their greater pleasures first be known
That are to censure[1] them.

---

13 Stands on—requires.
1 Alarum—summons to battle.
1 censure—judge.

CORDELIA.   We are not the first
Who, with best meaning, have incurr'd the worst.
For thee, oppressed king, am I cast down;
Myself could else out-frown false Fortune's frown.
Shall we not see these daughters and these sisters?
        LEAR.   No, no, no, no! Come, let's away to prison;
We two alone will sing like birds i' th' cage.
When thou dost ask me blessing, I'll kneel down
And ask of thee forgiveness. So we'll live,
And pray, and sing, and tell old tales, and laugh
At gilded butterflies, and hear poor rogues
Talk of court news; and we'll talk with them too,
Who loses and who wins; who's in, who's out;
And take upon's² the mystery of things
As if we were God's spies;³ and we'll wear out,
In a wall'd prison, packs and sects of great ones,
That ebb and flow by the moon.
        EDMUND.   Take them away.
        LEAR.   Upon such sacrifices, my Cordelia,
The gods themselves throw incense. Have I caught thee?
He that parts us shall bring a brand from heaven,
And fire us⁴ hence like foxes. Wipe thine eyes;
The good-years⁵ shall devour them, flesh and fell,
Ere they shall make us weep. We'll see 'em starve first.
Come. [Exeunt LEAR and CORDELIA, guarded.]
        EDMUND.   Come hither, captain; hark.
Take thou this note; [Giving a paper.] go follow them to prison.
One step I have advanc'd thee; if thou dost
As this instructs thee, thou dost make thy way
To noble fortunes. Know thou this, that men
Are as the time is; to be tender-minded
Does not become a sword. Thy great employment
Will not bear question; either say thou 'lt do 't,
Or thrive by other means.
        CAPTAIN.   I'll do 't, my lord.
        EDMUND.   About it; and write happy when thou hast done.
Mark, I say, instantly; and carry⁶ it so
As I have set it down.
        CAPTAIN.   I cannot draw a cart, nor eat dried oats;
If it be man's work, I'll do 't. [Exit.]
        [Flourish. Enter ALBANY, GONERIL, REGAN, another CAPTAIN, and Soldiers.]
        ALBANY.   Sir, you have show'd to-day your valiant strain,
And fortune led you well. You have the captives
Who were the opposites⁷ of this day's strife;
I do require them of you, so to use them

---

² take upon's—pretend to understand.   ³ God's spies—angels.   ⁴ fire us—drive us out
by fire.   ⁵ good-years—pestilence.   ⁶ carry—execute.   ⁷ opposites—opponents.

As we shall find their merits and our safety
May equally determine.

EDMUND.   Sir, I thought it fit
To send the old and miserable king
To some retention and appointed guard;
Whose age has charms in it, whose title more,
To pluck the common bosom[8] on his side,
And turn our impress'd lances[9] in our eyes
Which do command them. With him I sent the Queen,
My reason all the same; and they are ready
To-morrow, or at further space, t' appear
Where you shall hold your session. At this time
We sweat and bleed: the friend hath lost his friend;
And the best quarrels, in the heat, are curs'd
By those that feel their sharpness:
The question of Cordelia and her father
Requires a fitter place.

ALBANY.   Sir, by your patience,
I hold you but a subject[10] of this war,
Not as a brother.

REGAN.   That's as we list to grace him.
Methinks our pleasure might have been demanded,
Ere you had spoke so far. He led our powers,
Bore the commission of my place and person;
The which immediacy[11] may well stand up,
And call itself your brother.

GONERIL.   Not so hot.
In his own grace he doth exalt himself,
More than in your addition.

REGAN.   In my rights,
By me invested, he compeers[12] the best.

ALBANY.   That were the most, if he should husband you.

REGAN.   Jesters do oft prove prophets.

GONERIL.   Holla, holla!
That eye that told you so look'd but a-squint.

REGAN.   Lady, I am not well; else I should answer
From a full-flowing[13] stomach. General,
Take thou my soldiers, prisoners, patrimony;
Dispose of them, of me; the walls are thine.
Witness the world, that I create thee here
My lord and master.

GONERIL.   Mean you to enjoy him then?

ALBANY.   The let-alone[14] lies not in your good will.

EDMUND.   Nor in thine, lad.

ALBANY.   Half-blooded[15] fellow, yes.

---

[8] common bosom—the affections of the people.   [9] impress'd lances—weapons of our soldiers.   [10] subject—subordinate officer.   [11] The which immediacy—he, as my immediate representative.   [12] compeers—equals.   [13] full-flowing—angry.   [14] let-alone—prohibition.   [15] Half-blooded—bastard.

REGAN [*to* EDMUND].   Let the drum strike, and prove my title thine.

ALBANY.   Stay yet; hear reason. Edmund, I arrest thee
On capital treason; and, in thine attaint,[16]
This gilded serpent. [*Pointing to* GONERIL.] For your claim, fair sister,
I bar it in the interest of my wife.
'T is she is sub-contracted to this lord,
And I, her husband, contradict your bans.
If you will marry, make your loves to me,
My lady is bespoke.

GONERIL.   An interlude![17]

ALBANY.   Thou art armed, Gloucester; let the trumpet sound.
If none appear to prove upon thy person
Thy heinous, manifest, and many treasons,
There is my pledge [*Throwing down a glove.*]

I'll prove it on thy heart,
Ere I taste bread, thou art in nothing less
Than I have here proclaim'd thee.

REGAN.   Sick, O sick!

GONERIL [*aside*].   If not, I'll ne'er trust medicine.

EDMUND.   There's my exchange. [*Throwing down a glove.*]
What in the world he is
That names me traitor, villain-like he lies.
Call by the trumpet;—he that dares approach,
On him, on you, who not? I will maintain
My truth and honour firmly.

ALBANY.   A herald, ho!

EDMUND.   A herald, ho, a herald!

ALBANY.   Trust to thy single virtue;[18] for thy soldiers,
All levied in my name, have in my name
Took their discharge.

REGAN.   My sickness grows upon me.

ALBANY.   She is not well; convey her to my tent. [*Exit* REGAN, *led.*]
[*Enter a* HERALD.]
Come hither, herald,—Let the trumpet sound—
And read out this.

CAPTAIN.   Sound, trumpet! [*A trumpet sounds.*]

HERALD.   [*Reads.*]

> If any man of quality or degree within the lists of the
> army will maintain upon Edmund, supposed Earl of Glouces-
> ter, that he is a manifold traitor, let him appear by the third
> sound of the trumpet. He is bold in his defence.

EDMUND.   Sound! [*First trumpet.*]

HERALD.   Again! [*Second trumpet.*]

HERALD.   Again! [*Third trumpet.*]
[*Trumpet answers within.*]
[*Enter* EDGAR, *at the third sound, armed with a trumpet before him.*]

---

[16] in thine attaint—accused with you.   [17] An interlude—what a farce.   [18] virtue—strength.

ALBANY.   Ask him his purposes, why he appears
Upon this call o' th' trumpet.

HERALD.   What are you?
Your name, your quality? and why you answer
This present summons?

EDGAR.   Know, my name is lost,
By treason's tooth bare-gnawn and canker-bit;[19]
Yet am I noble as the adversary
I come to cope.

ALBANY.   Which is that adversary?

EDGAR.   What's he that speaks for Edmund Earl of Gloucester?

EDMUND.   Himself; what say'st thou to him?

EDGAR.   Draw thy sword,
That, if my speech offend a noble heart,
Thy arm may do thee justice; here is mine.
Behold, it is the privilege of mine honours,
My oath, and my profession. I protest,
Maugre[20] thy strength, youth, place, and eminence,
Despite thy victor-sword and fire-new fortune,
Thy valour, and thy heart, thou art a traitor;
False to thy gods, thy brother, and thy father;
Conspirant 'gainst this high illustrious prince;
And from th' extremest upward of thy head
To the descent and dust beneath thy foot,
A most toad-spotted traitor. Say thou "No,"
This sword, this arm, and my best spirits are bent
To prove upon thy heart, whereto I speak,
Thou liest.

EDMUND.   In wisdom I should ask thy name;
But, since thy outside looks so fair and warlike,
And that thy tongue some 'say[21] of breeding breathes,
What safe and nicely I might well delay,
By rule of knighthood, I disdain and spurn.
Back do I toss these treasons to thy head,
With the hell-hated lie o'erwhelm thy heart,
Which, for they yet glance by and scarcely bruise,
This sword of mine shall give them instant way,
Where they shall rest for ever. Trumpets, speak!

            [*Alarums. They fight.* EDMUND *falls.*]

ALBANY.   Save him, save him!

GONERIL.   This is mere practice,[22] Gloucester.
By the law of arms thou wast not bound to answer
An unknown opposite: thou art not vanquish'd,
But cozen'd and beguil'd.

ALBANY.   Shut your mouth, dame,
Or with this paper shall I stop it. Hold, sir.—

[19] canker-bit—worm eaten.   [20] Maugre—despite.   [21] 'say—trace.   [22] practice—trickery.

Thou worse than any name, read thine own evil.
No tearing, lady; I perceive you know it.

    GONERIL.   Say, if I do, the laws are mine, not thine,
Who can arraign me for 't?

    ALBANY.   Most monstrous! oh!—
Know'st thou this paper?

    GONERIL.   Ask me not what I know. [*Exit.*]

    ALBANY.   Go after her; she's desperate; govern[23] her.

    EDMUND.   What you have charg'd me with, that have I done;
And more, much more; the time will bring it out.
'T is past, and so am I. But what art thou
That has this fortune on me? If thou 'rt noble,
I do forgive thee.

    EDGAR.   Let's exchange charity.
I am no less in blood than thou art, Edmund;
If more, the more thou 'st wrong'd me.
My name is Edgar, and thy father's son.
The gods are just, and of our pleasant vices
Make instruments to plague us.
The dark and vicious place where thee he got
Cost him his eyes.

    EDMUND.   Thou 'st spoken right, 't is true.
The wheel is come full circle; I am here.

    ALBANY.   Methought thy very gait did prophesy
A royal nobleness. I must embrace thee.
Let sorrow split my heart, if ever I
Did hate thee or thy father!

    EDGAR.   Worthy prince, I know 't.

    ALBANY.   Where have you hid yourself?
How have you known the miseries of your father?

    EDGAR.   By nursing them, my lord. List a brief tale;
And when 't is told, oh, that my heart would burst!
The bloody proclamation to escape,
That follow'd me so near,—oh, our lives' sweetness!
That we the pain of death would hourly die
Rather than die at once!—taught me to shift
Into a madman's rags, t' assume a semblance
That very dogs disdain'd; and in this habit
Met I my father with his bleeding rings,
Their precious stones new lost; became his guide,
Led him, begg'd for him, sav'd him from despair;
Never,—O fault!—reveal'd myself unto him,
Until some half-hour past, when I was arm'd.
Not sure, though hoping, of this good success,
I ask'd his blessing, and from first to last
Told him my pilgrimage; but his flaw'd heart,
Alack, too weak the conflict to support!

[23] govern—restrain.

'Twixt two extremes of passion, joy and grief,
Burst smilingly.

    EDMUND.   This speech of yours hath mov'd me,
And shall perchance do good. But speak you on;
You look as you had something more to say.

    ALBANY.   If there be more, more woeful, hold it in;
For I am almost ready to dissolve,
Hearing of this.

    EDGAR.   This would have seem'd a period[24]
To such as love not sorrow; but another,
To amplify too much, would make much more,
And top extremity.[25]
Whilst I was big in clamour came there in a man,
Who, having seen me in my worst estate,
Shunn'd my abhorr'd society; but then, finding
Who 't was that so endur'd, with his strong arms
He fasten'd on my neck, and bellow'd out
As he'd burst heaven: threw him on my father;
Told the most piteous tale of Lear and him
That ever ear received; which in recounting,
His grief grew puissant,[26] and the strings of life
Began to crack. Twice then the trumpets sounded,
And there I left him tranc'd.[27]

    ALBANY.   But who was this?

    EDGAR.   Kent, sir, the banish'd Kent; who in disguise
Follow'd his enemy[28] king, and did him service
Improper for[29] a slave.

               [*Enter a* GENTLEMAN *with a bloody knife.*]

    GENTLEMAN.   Help, help, O, help.

    EDGAR.   What kind of help?

    ALBANY.   Speak, man.

    EDGAR.   What means this bloody knife?

    GENTLEMAN.   'T is hot, it smokes;
It came from the heart of—O, she's dead!

    ALBANY.   Who dead? Speak, man.

    GENTLEMAN.   Your lady, sir, your lady; and her sister
By her is poison'd; she confesses it.

    EDMUND.   I was contracted to them both. All three
Now marry in an instant.

    EDGAR.   Here comes Kent.

                   [*Enter* KENT.]

    ALBANY.   Produce the bodies, be they alive or dead.
This judgement of the heavens, that makes us tremble,
Touches us not with pity. [*Exit* GENTLEMAN.]

                   —O, is this he?
The time will not allow the compliment[30]

---

[24] period—end.   [25] top extremity—pass all limits.   [26] puissant—powerful.   [27] tranc'd
—unconscious.   [28] enemy—who had declared him an enemy.   [29] Improper for—
more than would be demanded of.   [30] compliment—ceremony.

Which very manners urges.

KENT.   I am come
To bid my king and master aye good-night.
Is he not here?

ALBANY.   Great thing of us forgot!
Speak, Edmund, where's the King? and where's Cordelia?

[*The bodies of* GONERIL *and* REGAN *are brought in.*]

See'st thou this object, Kent?

KENT.   Alack, why thus?

EDMUND.   Yet Edmund was belov'd!
The one the other poison'd for my sake,
And after slew herself.

ALBANY.   Even so. Cover their faces.

EDMUND.   I pant for life. Some good I mean to do,
Despite of mine own nature. Quickly send,
Be brief in it, to the castle; for my writ
Is on the life of Lear and on Cordelia.
Nay, send in time.

ALBANY.   Run, run, O, run!

EDGAR.   To whom, my lord? Who has the office? Send
Thy token of reprieve.

EDMUND.   Well thought on. Take my sword,
Give it the captain.

EDGAR.   Haste thee, for thy life. [*Exit* GENTLEMAN.]

EDMUND.   He hath commission from thy wife and me
To hang Cordelia in the prison, and
To lay the blame upon her own despair,
That she fordid[31] herself.

ALBANY.   The gods defend her! Bear him hence a while.

[EDMUND *is borne off.*]

[*Enter* LEAR *with* CORDELIA *in his arms,* GENTLEMAN *following.*]

LEAR.   Howl, howl, howl! O, you are men of stones!
Had I your tongues and eyes, I'd use them so
That heaven's vault should crack. She's gone for ever!
I know when one is dead, and when one lives;
She's dead as earth. Lend me a looking-glass;
If that her breath will mist or stain the stone,[32]
Why, then she lives.

KENT.   Is this the promis'd end?[33]

EDGAR.   Or image of that horror?

ALBANY.   Fall, and cease!

LEAR.   This feather stirs; she lives! If it be so,
It is a chance which does redeem all sorrows
That ever I have felt.

KENT [*kneeling*].   O my good master!

LEAR.   Prithee, away.

---

[31] fordid—destroyed.   [32] stone—glass, mirror.   [33] promis'd end—Day of Judgement.

EDGAR.   'T is noble Kent, your friend.

LEAR.   A plague upon you, murderous traitors all!
I might have sav'd her; now she's gone for ever!
Cordelia, Cordelia! stay a little. Ha!
What is 't thou say'st? Her voice was ever soft,
Gentle, and low; an excellent thing in woman.
I kill'd the slave that was a-hanging thee.

GENTLEMAN.   'T is true, my lords, he did.

LEAR.   Did I not, fellow?
I have seen the day, with my good biting falchion[34]
I would have made them skip. I am old now,
And these same crosses[35] spoil me. Who are you?
Mine eyes are not o' th' best. I'll tell you straight.

KENT.   If Fortune brag of two she lov'd and hated,[36]
One of them we behold.

LEAR.   This is a dull sight. Are you not Kent?

KENT.   The same,
Your servant Kent. Where is your servant Caius?

LEAR.   He's a good fellow, I can tell you that;
He'll strike and quickly too. He's dead and rotten.

KENT.   No, my good lord; I am the very man,—

LEAR.   I'll see that straight.

KENT.   —That, from your first of difference[37] and decay,
Have follow'd your sad steps.

LEAR.   You're welcome hither.

KENT.   Nor no man else; all's cheerless, dark, and deadly.
Your eldest daughters have fordone themselves,
And desperately are dead.

LEAR.   Ay, so I think.

ALBANY.   He knows not what he says; and vain is it
That we present us to him.

[*Enter a* MESSENGER.]

EDGAR.   Very bootless.

MESSENGER.   Edmund is dead, my lord.

ALBANY.   That's but a trifle here,—
You lords and noble friends, know our intent.
What comfort to this great decay[38] may come
Shall be appli'd. For us, we will resign,
During the life of this old majesty,
To him our absolute power; [*To* EDGAR *and* KENT.] you, to your rights,
With boot, and such addition as your honours
Have more than merited. All friends shall taste
The wages of their virtue, and all foes
The cup of their deservings. O, see, see!

LEAR.   And my poor fool[39] is hang'd! No, no, no life!
Why should a dog, a horse, a rat, have life,

---

[34] falchion—sword.   [35] crosses—sufferings.   [36] lov'd and hated—i.e., at the same time.   [37] first of difference—beginning of the change in your fortunes.   [38] decay—fallen man.   [39] poor fool—i.e., Cordelia.

And thou no breath at all? Thou 'lt come no more,
Never, never, never, never, never!
Pray you, undo this button. Thank you, sir.
Do you see this? Look on her, look, her lips,
Look there, look there! [*Dies.*]

  EDGAR.   He faints! My lord, my lord!

  KENT. Break, heart; I prithee, break!

  EDGAR.   Look up, my lord.

  KENT. Vex not his ghost; O, let him pass! He hates him
That would upon the rack[40] of this tough world
Stretch him out longer.

  EDGAR.   He is gone, indeed.

  KENT. The wonder is he hath endur'd so long;
He but usurp'd his life.

  ALBANY. Bear them from hence. Our present business
Is general woe. [*To* KENT *and* EDGAR.] Friends of my soul, you twain
Rule in this realm, and the gor'd[41] state sustain.

  KENT. I have a journey, sir, shortly to go:
My master calls me, I must not say no.

  EDGAR. The weight of this sad time we must obey;
Speak what we feel, not what we ought to say.
The oldest hath borne most; we that are young
Shall never see so much, nor live so long. [*Exeunt, with a dead march.*]

COMMENTARY

Of the supreme achievements of the creative mind with which *King Lear* is usually compared, it is perhaps the only one that seems to issue in hopelessness. Our conception of greatness in art inclines to set special store by the tragic vision, and our highest admiration most readily goes to those works that have some large element of darkness and dread. But when we bring to mind the masterpieces of art, and not only of literary art, with which *King Lear* is commonly ranked—the *Iliad, Oedipus Rex, The Divine Comedy,* Michelangelo's *Last Judgment,* Bach's *B-Minor Mass,* Beethoven's *Fifth Symphony*—we perceive that in all of them the dark elements are countered by strong affirmative emotions and attitudes. If in any of these works hope is not fully ascendant, it at least holds in balance the elements that might make for despair.

We do not necessarily feel this of *King Lear.* Here is a pre-eminently great work in which the positive expectations of life are considerably outweighed by the horrifying circumstances that are put before us. It is true that at the end of the play the evil-doers have been destroyed, the good are in control of the kingdom, and order and justice are soon to be restored. But the concluding scene speaks less of peace, let alone of hope, than of an ultimate weariness. Again and again in the course of the play the goodness and meaningfulness of life have been brought into question, and now, as life is about to resume its normal course, it

---

[40] rack—instrument of torture. [41] gor'd—wounded.

can show little of the energy that might dispel the doubts that have been raised. In his last speech Kent refuses Albany's invitation to share the rule of the realm, giving as his reason that his death, which he desires, is near at hand. And Edgar's concluding words seem so charged with fatigue that they can scarcely get themselves uttered:

> The weight of this sad time we must obey;
> Speak what we feel, not what we ought to say.
> The oldest hath borne most; we that are young
> Shall never see so much, nor live so long.

No other of Shakespeare's tragedies ends on anything like the note of exhaustion sounded by these gray monosyllables. The closing speeches of *Hamlet*, *Macbeth*, and *Antony and Cleopatra* move to a music that summons the future into being.

Perhaps nothing can better suggest the uniquely despairing quality of *King Lear* than Keats's sonnet "On Sitting Down to Read *King Lear* Once Again." The young poet confronts with anxiety the experience he has freely chosen to undergo. He speaks of the play as "the fierce dispute / Between damnation and impassion'd clay." It is not a dispute from which he can stand apart, a passive listener; he must be involved in it, and with a painful intensity—he must, as he says, "burn through" it. This burning-through is not only painful but dangerous, and Keats is impelled to address a prayer to Shakespeare and the "clouds of Albion," asking their protection in the ordeal to which he is about to submit himself:

> Let me not wander in a barren dream,
> But when I am consumed in the fire,
> Give me new Phoenix wings to fly at my desire.

Keats's fear lest his experience leave him "barren" suggests how far *King Lear* may be from conforming to Aristotle's belief that tragedy fulfils a hygienic or therapeutic function. By inducing in the spectator emotions that are kept under strict control by its circumstantial or formal elements, a tragic play is said to bring about the discharge of such distress as habitually besets the mind and to establish an emotional equilibrium that sustains the vital energies. But Keats, from his previous readings of *King Lear*, anticipates that this particular tragedy may have exactly the opposite effect upon him.

His anxiety is not hard to understand; we share his apprehension of the destructive power the play might exert, for it seems to have the avowed intention of *assaulting* us. The storm in Act III, which is described as being more violent than any storm in memory, figures in the minds of many readers as the epitome or emblem of a play that batters and overwhelms us. One incident, the blinding of Gloucester, is so painful to read, let alone see on the stage, that doubts of its propriety as art have been expressed even by critics who are reluctant to admit that Shakespeare can ever be at fault. The murder of Cordelia in the face of our reasonable expectation that she will be rescued seems so gratuitous a blow to our hopes that the famous Shakespeare critic, A. C. Bradley, has actually defended, although not with entire seriousness, the eighteenth-century version of *King Lear* that revised the ending into a happy one.

One way in which the play manifests its intention of assault is by its refusal of artistic economy in favor of redundancy and excess. Thus, in representing filial disloyalty it is not content with the instance of Lear's two elder daughters but adds, what is no part of the traditional story upon which the play is based, Edmund's betrayal of Gloucester. One aged man wandering the world in misery is not enough: there must be two. As Lear's plight is paralleled by Gloucester's, so the overthrow of his mind is reiterated by the madness Edgar assumes, and this antiphony of significant irrationality is pointed up by the wild joking of the Fool. No play has ever had so many villains. Four of the leading characters, Edmund, Goneril, Regan, and Cornwall, are evil almost beyond belief, and they are appropriately served by the contemptible Oswald and the brutal captain who murders Cordelia. It has become almost a commonplace of critical analysis of *King Lear* to remark on its plethora of references to animals—133 references to 64 different animals—as if to press upon us a vision of humanity descending to brutishness.

The question of the governance of the world is often touched on in the play and always with the effect of reminding us either of its harshness or of its mysteriousness. The characters frequently appeal to or speak about "the gods," but from the things they say of them it is impossible to conclude what the divine disposition can be. Little ground is left for believing the gods beneficent. Gloucester calls them "ever-gentle" but in circumstances that lead us to take that epithet (and Gloucester's subsequent reference to "the bounty and the benison of Heaven") as ironical, the irony being intended not by Gloucester himself but by the play. Edgar says that the gods are "just," but the instance of the divine justice he cites, his father's having lost his sight in punishment for the "darkness" of the illicit sexual episode in which he begot Edmund, disgusts us with its agents and alienates us from the person who remarks it. The characterization of the gods that we are likely to remember best speaks of their affinity with the devils who are so often mentioned in the play:

> As flies to wanton boys, are we to the gods,
> They kill us for their sport.

"Nature" is frequently referred to in *King Lear* as a governing principle, but we can never be sure what nature means. It is invoked by Edmund as his "goddess," a deity who will provide the "law" that justifies his machinations. Lear calls it to witness the wrongs that have been done him, but to no avail. If nature is sometimes portrayed as normative and beneficent, it is also shown to be indifferent or hostile. The assaulting storm, after all, is a phenomenon of nature. If nature may at one moment represent a principle of order, duty, and innocence, at another it is the principle of those animals, almost always regarded with aversion, which haunt the play.

That *King Lear* raises very dark thoughts indeed is denied by no one. The question debated by critics is whether the play in its whole and final effect is one of unrelieved pessimism or whether from the darkness some new light is born, possibly the brighter for the blackness from which it shines. One party to the debate takes its stand on the Aristotelean paradox of tragedy, that from dire events emerges some sensation of peace or reconciliation, some new readiness to accept life's pain, and not in passive acquiescence but in augmented strength of soul, and even with something like hope. To which the opposing party rejoins that, whatever tragedy is supposed to do and whatever in general it may do, this particular tragedy does not conform to type.

In the end the party of hope is forced to rely upon specious reasoning. It argues that the experience of Lear and Gloucester comprises not only their terrible sufferings but also the spiritual changes they undergo as a result of their agony. These changes are said to amount to regeneration—at the end of the play Lear and Gloucester are better men than they were at the beginning, they have been redeemed through suffering. A universal order that permits this redemption to take place is to be regarded as hopeful, as making no occasion for pessimism. In his introduction to *King Lear* in the Cambridge *New Shakespeare*, G. I. Duthie formulates the position thus: "The gods are merciful. If, after all their agony, Lear and Gloucester died uneducated, unregenerate, then we should indeed have to speak of pessimism. But both, as they die, are wise and redeemed. 'Nothing is here for tears'—unless we weep for the means that conduces to the end, for the dreadful cost of the salutary outcome. We must do so; and the conclusion of the play has indeed a sober colouring. Yet the unassailable fact remains that the gods, in benignity, permit Lear and Gloucester to die in a state of spiritual health. Their sufferings are redemptive. There is no ultimate ground for pessimism here."

One must wonder what special meaning this writer assigns to "merciful" and what sort of "benignity" it is that "permits" the two old men to die in the state of "spiritual health" they have so grimly won. In the *Book of Job* one of Job's friends advances the idea that suffering, because it can serve to discipline and enlighten man's spirit, is to be understood as an instance of God's benevolence; but Job will have none of this facile defence of the divine order, and the Voice that speaks out of the whirlwind, God's own voice, says that Job is right to reject his friend's view as a mere rationalization. Some three thousand years later Mr. Duthie proposes the same view. It is perhaps possible to find comfort in the idea that the world is a school in which the soul is "educated" or a sanitorium in which it may regain "spiritual health"; yet we must inevitably remark that the authorities who govern these two institutions charge quite exorbitant fees for their redemptive services. Mr. Duthie himself speaks of the "dreadful cost of the salutary outcome" over which we might understandably shed tears. A cost dreadful indeed: so very dreadful that tears scarcely seem adequate to it, rather some awful cry, such as Lear's "Howl, howl, howl." Or, if tears at all, then those that Lear wept on his "wheel of fire," that "do scald like molten lead."[1]

As against arguments of the kind that Mr. Duthie advances, the opposite position accords more closely with our usual human experience of the play. The formulation which in our time has commanded most attention is that of the

---

[1] It is oddly tactless of Mr. Duthie to quote the famous "Nothing is here for tears" from Milton's *Samson Agonistes*. The line refers to Samson's death. Samson has died in a moment of triumph, performing an act that serves his God and his people. Having sinned against the divine gift of his superhuman strength, he had been betrayed by his Philistine wife, who cut off his long hair, in which lay his power, and delivered him to his Philistine enemies. After a period of humiliation, suffering, and repentance as a slave of the Philistines, Samson finds his strength returning as his hair grows again. On a religious festival of his heathen masters, he brings down the roof of the temple in which the Philistine nobility is gathered, knowing that he too must perish. He dies not only as a man redeemed but as a victorious hero, the savior of his people. It is indeed true that nothing is *here* for tears, but how different is his situation from that of King Lear!

Polish critic Jan Kott in his influential book, *Shakespeare Our Contemporary*. Professor Kott says that *King Lear* has never been dealt with in a direct and unembarrassed way, that "the cruelty of Shakespeare's world" has never been fully confronted. He finds the clue to this failure in the lack of appreciation of the mode of the *grotesque* which is salient in the play. The mode of the grotesque, he says, is crueller than the tragic mode, and the critics have ignored the extent of its presence in *King Lear*, occupied as they have been with finding justification for their belief that the play makes the traditional "affirmation" of tragedy, such justification as may be found in the idea that "suffering ennobled Lear and restored his tragic greatness." And he undertakes to demonstrate the affinity of *King Lear* with the so-called theatre of the absurd, that strong and often impressive tendency of contemporary drama to represent, by the grotesque or by "black" comedy, the metaphysical pointlessness of human life.

Professor Kott does not do justice to the awareness of the pessimistic force of *King Lear* that has in fact prevailed; as for the element of the grotesque in the play, its importance was demonstrated in elaborate detail in a well-known essay by G. Wilson Knight as long ago as 1930.[2] Yet perhaps no critic has been so uncompromising as Professor Kott in insisting on the pessimism of *King Lear*. Indeed, pessimism scarcely describes what he tells us Shakespeare is propounding, which is nothing less than nihilism, the view that there is no meaning to be discovered in the universe, and, in consequence, but little in human existence.

Professor Kott reminds us that the basic assumption of traditional tragedy was that the universe, or, as he calls it, the absolute, was informed by a transcendent reason variously thought of as the gods, or God, or Nature, or History understood as a process. Because this transcendent reason was inscrutable, never available to human understanding, man was likely to be out of step with it and, in consequence, all too susceptible to defeat and suffering. But the downfall of the tragic hero was the means by which tragedy affirmed the existence of a transcendent reason. Such affirmation is no longer possible—in our time the assumption that a transcendent reason exists has lost virtually all its old force. Reason may be thought of as an attribute of man but not as an attribute of the universe; and man's suffering, which once could be supposed to have meaning because of its relation to the universal reason, can now be thought only grotesque. "In the world of the grotesque," Professor Kott says, "downfall cannot be justified by, or blamed on, the absolute. The absolute is not endowed with any ultimate reasons; it is stronger, and that is all. The absolute is absurd." It is in the light of this modern conception of absurdity that *King Lear* must be understood—only thus, Professor Kott says, can we comprehend the full extent of the cruelty of its world, a cruelty that it is not possible to explain because it is wholly without meaning.

There can be no doubt that *King Lear* gives us ground for thinking the universe absurd. Again and again it proposes the idea of some ineluctable contradiction between the universe and man. Man's existence proceeds in circumstances so painful that we may well think of them as arranged by a hostile power which is the more terrible because no purpose can be ascribed to its enmity nor any order discerned in its behavior. Again this irrational animus there is no defence—all that men can do is endure. And the despair that King Lear embodies

2 "*King Lear* and the Comedy of the Grotesque," in *The Wheel of Fire*.

is concentrated in the line in which Edgar says what it is that they must endure, their "going hence, even as their coming hither"—it is surely a despairing imagination that proposes the bitterness of dying in terms of the bitterness of being born. The phrase that follows, "Ripeness is all," does not qualify the sentiment, for "ripeness" here does not mean richness or fulness of life but readiness for death, the only escape from absurdity.

But the incompatibility between rational man and an absurd universe is only one of the two explanations of human suffering suggested in *King Lear*. The other holds man himself accountable for his pain, either through his self-deception or through the cruelty of other members of the race. The play makes no hard and fast distinction between the two explanations. Nevertheless we can scarcely doubt that it requires us to see that the immediate cause of any man's suffering is his fellow man: the cruel will of nonhuman powers is put into execution by evil men. The intensity of the suffering is such and the bitterness over man's destiny of suffering is such that they can find adequate expression only by crying out to heaven. But at the quiet heart of the whirling speculations about the universe or the absolute there lies the idea of human justice and human mercy. When it is said that Lear is "regenerated" and "redeemed," the change that is being remarked upon in the aged king is his new consciousness of man's inhumanity to man, of the general failure of justice: his mind becomes obsessed with justice, he is filled with disgust at those human traits that stand in the way of its being done—greed, lust, pride, and the hypocrisy that masks them. And with the new consciousness of justice goes a new sense of the need for *caritas*, which is not "charity" in our usual modern sense, but "caring," the solicitude of loving-kindness:

> Poor naked wretches, wheresoe'er you are,
> That bide the pelting of this pitiless storm,
> How shall your houseless heads and unfed sides,
> Your loop'd and window'd raggedness, defend you
> From seasons such as these? O, I have ta'en
> Too little care of this! Take physic, pomp;
> Expose thyself to feel what wretches feel,
> That thou mayst shake the superflux to them,
> And show the heavens more just.

Although Lear does touch upon the cruelty of the universe, this is far less the object of his new consciousness than the failure of man's governance of himself, his falling short of what is required of him in doing justice and in loving mercy.

If we speak of a "failure" and a "falling short," we suggest not merely a thing to be desired, but also a standard or norm. I have said that we never know just how to understand the word "nature" as it is used in *King Lear*. But we cannot fail to recognize that among its several meanings is that of a normative principle. And one element of the human norm it implies, one term of the definition of man, is a certain degree of moral virtue, or at least the propensity for conduct which, if it departs from virtue, does not do so beyond a certain point. The play offers abundant evidence that human beings are capable of going well beyond that point. Yet the supposition that man's nature is to be defined in moral terms is not thereby denied.

Our commitment to the idea of the normative virtue of man is apparent in our language, as in our use of the word "humanity" to mean kindness or at least compunction in dealing with other members of the race, or with animals. Burns's famous lines, "Man's inhumanity to man / Makes countless thousands mourn," which everyone understands, would be nonsense were we not to take normative virtue for granted, for what could it possibly mean to speak of human beings acting in an inhuman fashion unless the *idea* of being human implied a degree of goodness, whatever the *actuality* of being human may mean? Bradley has remarked on the frequency with which the idea of monstrosity appears in *King Lear*; the play, he says, is replete with "beings, actions, states of mind, which appear not only abnormal but absolutely contrary to nature." In the degree to which people are good, they are felt to be natural, Kent and Cordelia being obvious cases in point: we are aware of their naturalness as a positive quality of their being, expressing itself in their manner and mode of speech. But Goneril and Regan are said by Lear to be "unnatural hags." Cornwall's blinding of Gloucester is an unnatural act, and an especially moving moment of the play represents the natural response to the monstrosity of this deed: one of Cornwall's servants cannot endure it and, knowing that he risks his life, draws his sword to prevent it. To Shakespeare's contemporary audience, this action must have been even more momentous than it is to us, for to the Elizabethans the idea of a servant confronting his master with a show of force would have been shocking, even unnatural. The Elizabethan judgment is underscored by Cornwall's crying out amazed, "My villain!" (using the word in its old sense of farm servant), and by Regan's exclamation, "A peasant stand up thus!" To the feudal lord and lady it was as much a shattering of the natural order for their servant to defy them as Lear felt it to be when his daughters rejected him. Shakespeare quite shared the opinion of his time; he believed that the deference given to superiors was in the order of nature. But in this instance his sympathy is given to the peasant who flares into hopeless rebellion at the hideous deed, who, though he break the "natural" bonds of society, does so because he recognizes a claim yet *more* natural, that of his humanity, of justice and mercy.

An awareness of the Elizabethan feeling about the naturalness of the social order will lead us to a more accurate judgment of the act out of which all the horrors and misfortunes arose, Lear's division of his kingdom. To this no Elizabethan, and surely not Shakespeare himself, would have responded with indifference. Again and again in his plays, Shakespeare speaks in praise of unity, of the organic interrelation of the parts of a polity. To divide a kingdom, to treat a realm as if it were not a living organism, was worse than imprudent, it was unnatural. It may have been unavoidable in view of Lear's failing strength and the lack of a male heir, but still it went against nature; its consequences could only be bad.

In short, *King Lear* raises moral, social, and even political considerations that mark out an area in which human life is not wholly determined by non-human forces, in which the absurdity of the universe is not wholly decisive. Although this area is not coextensive with man's existence, it is of very large extent. One hesitates to speak of it as an area of freedom, if only because any one individual is so little likely to be free within it. Yet it is the precinct in which mankind as a whole, with due regard to the well-being of its individual members, has the possibility of freedom. To be aware of this possibility will scarcely dispel all the dark thoughts that the play induces. But it does qualify the view that human suffering is to be referred only to an absurd dispensation.

Some large part of the human condition is, however, imposed upon man and makes a fate that is as grotesque as it is inescapable. Lear must grow old, his powers of body and mind must wane and fail. Nothing can save him from this destined end. Yet this in itself is not the root of his suffering as the play represents it. What maddens the old man is the loss of what might sustain him in his decline, the honor and dignity he had assumed to be his inalienable right. To grow old is a hard destiny. But to grow old in honor and dignity is not unendurable, while to grow old shorn of respect is a nightmare, the very essence of the grotesque. Respect is sometimes regarded as a sort of social fiction because it is expressed through signs and outward forms, such as the manner and tone in which the respected person is addressed, or the appurtenances of life that are bestowed upon him. Lear himself defines the symbolic nature of respect in his great reply to Regan's statement that he has no "need" of his train of knights:

> O, reason not the need! Our basest beggars
> Are in the poorest thing superfluous.
> Allow not nature more than nature needs,
> Man's life is cheap as beast's. Thou art a lady;
> If only to go warm were gorgeous,
> Why, nature needs not what thou gorgeous wear'st,
> Which scarcely keeps thee warm.

He says in effect that man creates his own needs—and that these are even more imperative than those of biology. The meanings and "values" that social man invents for himself are presented as of transcendent importance not only in this speech of Lear's but throughout the play, most notably in all that Kent and Cordelia say to the old man and all they do for him, in the one short time when they have him in their loving charge, to assure him that he has been restored to his kingliness and to the respect that befits it.

Of all that is implied by the play's intense awareness of that area of life in which human conceptions and conduct are prepotent, Professor Kott takes no account in his effort to demonstrate the nihilism of *King Lear*. "The theme of *King Lear*," he says, "is the decay and fall of the world." And so in part it is, but in part only—the full theme of *King Lear* is the decay and fall of the world as a consequence of a decay and fall of the human soul. It is indeed true that the vitality of the meanings and values created by man depends to some extent on a belief in a transcendent reason, and that to doubt the existence of such reason puts all in doubt. This would seem to be the animating idea of the theatre of the absurd in which Professor Kott finds such strong affinities with *King Lear*. But the dramatist of the theatre of the absurd takes for granted a metaphysical negation which has the effect of destroying the old human meanings and of making human life grotesque, whereas such a causal sequence was not conceived by Shakespeare. He took for granted a rational and moralized universe but proposed the idea that this universal order might be reduced to chaos by human evil.

Speaking in praise of *King Lear*, the English novelist Iris Murdoch said, "Only the very greatest art invigorates without consoling. . . ." That *King Lear* does not console is plain enough. If we ask how, in the face of its dire report of life, this play can be said to invigorate, the answer is that it does us the honor of supposing that we will make every possible effort of mind to withstand the force of its despair and to understand the complexity of what it tells us about the nature of human existence: it draws us into more activity than we had thought ourselves capable of.

THE

WILD

DUCK

HENRIK IBSEN

1828–1906

CHARACTERS

HAAKON WERLE, wholesale merchant and millowner
GREGERS WERLE, his son
OLD EKDAL
HJALMAR EKDAL, his son, a photographer
GINA EKDAL, Hjalmar's wife
HEDVIG, their daughter, aged fourteen
MRS. SØRBY, housekeeper for the elder Werle
RELLING, a doctor
MOLVIK, a former divinity student
GRAABERG, a bookkeeper
PETTERSEN, manservant to the elder Werle
JENSEN, a hired waiter
A FAT MAN
A BALD-HEADED MAN
A NEARSIGHTED MAN
SIX OTHER MEN, dinner guests at Werle's
OTHER HIRED SERVANTS

The first act takes place in WERLE's *house; the following four acts in* HJALMAR EKDAL's *studio.*

ACT I

At WERLE's *house. A richly and comfortably furnished study, with book-cases and upholstered furniture, a writing table, with papers and reports, in the middle of the floor, and green-shaded lamps softly illuminating the room. In the rear wall, open folding doors with curtains drawn back disclose a large, fashionable room, brightly lit by lamps and candelabra. In the right foreground of the study, a small private door leads to the offices. In the left foreground, a fireplace filled with glowing coals, and further back a double door to the dining room.*

WERLE's *manservant,* PETTERSEN, *in livery, and* JENSEN, *a hired waiter, in black, are straightening up the study. In the larger room two or three other hired waiters are moving about, putting things in order and lighting more candles. In from the dining room come laughter and the hum of many voices in conversation; a knife clinks upon a glass; silence; a toast is made; cries of "Bravo," and the hum of conversation resumes.*

PETTERSEN [*lighting a lamp by the fireplace and putting on the shade*]. Ah, you hear that, Jensen. Now the old boy's up on his feet, proposing a long toast to Mrs. Sørby.

JENSEN [*moving an armchair forward*]. Is it really true what people say, that there's something between them?

PETTERSEN. Lord knows.

JENSEN. I've heard he was a real goat in his day.

PETTERSEN. Could be.

JENSEN. But they say it's his son he's throwing this party for.

PETTERSEN. Yes. His son came home yesterday.

JENSEN. I never knew before that old Werle had any son.

PETTERSEN. Oh yes, he's got a son. But he spends all his time up at the works in Hoidal. He hasn't been in town all the years I've served in this house.

A HIRED WAITER [*in the door to the other room*]. Say, Pettersen, there's an old guy here who—

PETTERSEN [*muttering*]. What the hell—somebody coming now!

[*Old* EKDAL *appears from the right through the inner room. He is dressed in a shabby overcoat with a high collar, woolen gloves, and in his hand, a cane and a fur cap; under his arm is a bundle wrapped in brown paper. He has a dirty, reddish-brown wig and a little gray moustache.*]

PETTERSEN [*going toward him*]. Good Lord, what do *you* want in here?

EKDAL [*at the door*]. Just have to get into the office, Pettersen.

PETTERSEN. The office closed an hour ago, and—

EKDAL. Heard that one at the door, boy. But Graaberg's still in there. Be nice, Pettersen, and let me slip in that way. [*Pointing toward the private entrance.*] I've gone that way before.

PETTERSEN. All right, go ahead, then. [*Opens the door.*] But don't forget now—take the other way out; we have guests.

EKDAL. Got you—hmm! Thanks, Pettersen, good old pal! Thanks. [*To himself.*] Bonehead! [*He goes into the office;* PETTERSEN *shuts the door after him.*]

JENSEN. Is *he* on the office staff too?

PETTERSEN. No, he's just someone who does copying on the outside when it's needed. Still, in his time he was well up in the world, old Ekdal.

JENSEN. Yes, he looks like he's been a little of everything.

PETTERSEN. Oh yes. He was a lieutenant once, if you can imagine.

JENSEN. Good Lord—him a lieutenant!

PETTERSEN. So help me, he was. But then he went into the lumber business or something. They say he must have pulled some kind of dirty deal on the old man once, for the two of them were running the Hoidal works together then. Oh, I know good old Ekdal, all right. We've drunk many a schnapps and bottle of beer together over at Eriksen's.

JENSEN. He can't have much money for standing drinks.

PETTERSEN. My Lord, Jensen, you can bet it's me that stands the drinks. I always say a person ought to act refined toward quality that's come down in life.

JENSEN. Did he go bankrupt, then?

PETTERSEN. No, worse than that. He was sent to jail.

JENSEN. To jail!

PETTERSEN. Or maybe it was the penitentiary. [*Laughter from the dining room.*] Hist! They're leaving the table.

[*The dining room door is opened by a pair of servants inside.* MRS. SØRBY, *in conversation with two gentlemen, comes out. A moment later the rest of the guests follow, among them* WERLE. *Last of all come* HJALMAR EKDAL *and* GREGERS WERLE.]

MRS. SØRBY [*to the servant, in passing*]. Pettersen, will you have coffee served in the music room?

PETTERSEN. Yes, Mrs. Sørby.

[*She and the two gentlemen go into the inner room and exit to the right.* PETTERSEN *and* JENSEN *leave in the same way.*]

A FAT GUEST [*to a balding man*]. Phew! That dinner—that was a steep bit of work!

THE BALD-HEADED GUEST. Oh, with a little good will a man can do wonders in three hours.

THE FAT GUEST. Yes, but afterward, my dear fellow, afterward.

A THIRD GUEST. I hear we can sample coffee and liqueur in the music room.

THE FAT GUEST. Fine! Then perhaps Mrs. Sørby will play us a piece.

THE BALD-HEADED GUEST [*in an undertone*]. Just so Mrs. Sørby doesn't play us to pieces.

THE FAT GUEST. Oh, now really, Berta wouldn't punish her old friends, would she? [*They laugh and enter the inner room.*]

WERLE [*in a low, depressed tone*]. I don't think anyone noticed it, Gregers.

GREGERS. What?

WERLE. Didn't you notice it either?

GREGERS. What should I have noticed?

WERLE. We were thirteen at the table.

GREGERS. Really? Were we thirteen?

WERLE [*with a glance at* HJALMAR EKDAL]. Yes—our usual number is twelve. [*To the others.*] Be so kind, gentlemen. [*He and those remaining, excepting* HJALMAR *and* GREGERS, *go out to the rear and right.*]

HJALMAR [*who has heard the conversation*]. You shouldn't have sent me the invitation, Gregers.

GREGERS. What! The party's supposed to be for *me*. And then I'm not supposed to have my best and only friend—

HJALMAR. But I don't think your father likes it. Ordinarily I never come to this house.

GREGERS. So I hear. But I had to see you and talk with you, for I'm sure to be leaving soon again. Yes, we two old classmates, we've certainly drifted a long way apart. You know, we haven't seen each other now in sixteen—seventeen years.

HJALMAR. Has it been so long?

GREGERS. Yes, all of that. Well, how have you been? You look well. You're almost becoming stout.

HJALMAR. Hm, stout is hardly the word, though I probably look more of a man than I did then.

GREGERS. Yes, you do. The outer man hasn't suffered.

HJALMAR [*in a gloomier tone*]. Ah, but the inner man! Believe me, he has a different look. You know, of course, what misery we've been through, I and my family, since the last time the two of us met.

GREGERS [*dropping his voice*]. How's it going for your father now?

HJALMAR. Oh, Gregers, let's not talk about that. My poor, unhappy father naturally lives at home with me. He's got no one else in the whole world to turn to. But this all is so terribly hard for me to talk about, you know. Tell me, instead, how you've found life up at the mill.

GREGERS. Marvelously solitary, that's what—with a good chance to mull over a great many things. Come on, let's be comfortable. [*He sits in an armchair by the fire and urges* HJALMAR *down into another by its side.*]

HJALMAR [*emotionally*]. In any case, I'm grateful that you asked me here, Gregers, because it proves you no longer have anything against me.

GREGERS [*astonished*]. How could you think that I had anything against you?

HJALMAR. In those first years you did.

GREGERS. Which first years?

HJALMAR. Right after that awful misfortune. And it was only natural you should. It was just by a hair that your own father escaped being dragged into this—oh, this ugly business.

GREGERS. And that's why I had it in for you? Whoever gave you that idea?

HJALMAR. I know you did, Gregers; it was your father himself who told me.

GREGERS [*startled*]. Father! I see. Hm—is that why I never heard from you—not a single word?

HJALMAR. Yes.

GREGERS. Not even when you went out and became a photographer.

HJALMAR. Your father said it wasn't worth writing you—about anything.

GREGERS [*looking fixedly ahead*]. No, no, maybe he was right there—But tell me, Hjalmar—do you find yourself reasonably content with things as they are?

HJALMAR [*with a small sigh*]. Oh, I suppose I do. What else can I say? At first, you can imagine, it was all rather strange for me. They were such completely different expectations that I came into. But then everything was so different. That immense, shattering misfortune for Father—the shame and the scandal, Gregers—

GREGERS [*shaken*]. Yes, yes. Of course.

HJALMAR. I couldn't dream of going on with my studies; there wasn't a penny to spare. On the contrary, debts instead—mainly to your father, I think—

GREGERS. Hm—

HJALMAR. Anyway, I thought it was best to make a clean break—and cut all the old connections. It was your father especially who advised me to; and since he'd already been so helpful to me—

GREGERS. He had?

HJALMAR. Yes, you knew that, didn't you? Where could *I* get the money to learn photography and fit out a studio and establish myself? I can tell you, that all adds up.

GREGERS. And all that Father paid for?

HJALMAR. Yes, Gregers, didn't you know? I understood him to say that he'd written you about it.

GREGERS. Not a word saying *he* was the one. Maybe he forgot. We've never exchanged anything but business letters. So that was Father, too—!

HJALMAR. That's right. He never wanted people to know, but he was the one. And he was also the one who put me in a position to get married. Or perhaps—didn't you know that either?

GREGERS. No, not at all. [*Takes him by the arm.*] But Hjalmar, I can't tell you how all this delights me—and disturbs me. Perhaps I've been unfair to my father—in certain ways. Yes, for all this does show good-heartedness, doesn't it? It's almost a kind of conscience—

HJALMAR. Conscience?

GREGERS. Yes, or whatever you want to call it. No, I can't tell you how glad I am to hear this about my father. So you're married, then, Hjalmar. That's further than I'll ever go. Well, I hope you're happy as a married man?

HJALMAR. Oh, absolutely. She's as capable and fine a wife as any man could wish for. And she's not entirely without culture, either.

GREGERS [*a bit surprised*]. No, I'm sure she's not.

HJALMAR. No. Life is a teacher, you see. Associating with me every day—and then there are one or two gifted people who visit us regularly. I can tell you, you wouldn't recognize Gina now.

GREGERS. Gina?

HJALMAR. Yes, Gregers, had you forgotten her name is Gina?

GREGERS. Whose name is Gina? I haven't the faintest idea—

HJALMAR. But don't you remember, she was here in this very house a while—in service?

GREGERS [*looking at him*]. You mean Gina Hansen—?

HJALMAR. Yes, of course, Gina Hansen.

GREGERS. Who was housekeeper for us that last year of Mother's illness?

HJALMAR. Exactly. But my dear Gregers, I know for sure that your father wrote you about my marriage.

GREGERS [who has gotten up]. Yes, of course he did. But not that— [walks about the floor]. Yes, wait a minute—it may well be, now that I think of it. My father's letters are always so brief. [Sits on chair arm.] Listen, tell me, Hjalmar—this is interesting—how did you come to know Gina?—your wife, I mean.

HJALMAR. Oh, it was all very simple. Gina didn't stay long here in the house; there was so much confusion—your mother's sickness and all. Gina couldn't stand it, so she just up and left. That was the year before your mother died—or maybe it was the same year.

GREGERS. It was the same year. And I was up at the works at the time. But what then?

HJALMAR. Well, then Gina lived at home with her mother, a Mrs. Hansen, a very capable, hardworking woman who ran a little restaurant. She also had a room for rent, a very pleasant, comfortable room.

GREGERS. And you were lucky enough to find it?

HJALMAR. Yes. Actually it was your father who suggested it to me. And it was there, you see—there that I really got to know Gina.

GREGERS. And then your engagement followed?

HJALMAR. Yes. Young people fall in love so easily—hm—

GREGERS [getting up and pacing about a little]. Tell me—when you became engaged—was it then that my father got you to—I mean, was it then that you started in learning photography?

HJALMAR. That's right. I wanted to get on and set up a home as soon as possible, and both your father and I decided that this photography idea was the most feasible one. And Gina thought so too. Yes, and you see, there was another inducement, a lucky break, in that Gina had already taken up retouching.

GREGERS. That worked out wonderfully all around.

HJALMAR [pleased, getting up]. Yes, isn't that so? Don't you think it's worked out wonderfully all around?

GREGERS. Yes, I must say. My father has almost been a kind of providence to you.

HJALMAR [with feeling]. He didn't abandon his old friend's son in a time of need. You see, he does have a heart.

MRS. SØRBY [entering with WERLE on her arm]. No more nonsense, my dear Mr. Werle. You mustn't stay in there any longer, staring at all those lights; it's doing you no good.

WERLE [freeing his arm from hers and passing his hand over his eyes]. Yes, I guess you're right about that.

[PETTERSEN and JENSEN enter with trays.]

MRS. SØRBY [to the guests in the other room]. Gentlemen, please—if anyone wants a glass of punch, he must take the trouble to come in here.

THE FAT GUEST [comes over to MRS. SØRBY]. But really, is it true you've abolished our precious smoking privilege?

MRS. SØRBY. Yes. Here in Mr. Werle's sanctum, it's forbidden.

THE BALD-HEADED GUEST.   When did you pass these drastic amendments to the cigar laws, Mrs. Sørby?

MRS. SØRBY.   After the last dinner—when there were certain persons here who let themselves exceed all limits.

THE BALD-HEADED GUEST.   And my dear Berta, one isn't permitted to exceed the limits, even a little bit?

MRS. SØRBY.   Not in any instance, Mr. Balle.

[*Most of the guests have gathered in the study; the waiters are proffering glasses of punch.*]

WERLE [*to* HJALMAR, *over by a table*].   What is it you're poring over, Ekdal?

HJALMAR.   It's only an album, Mr. Werle.

THE BALD-HEADED GUEST [*who is wandering about*].   Ah, photographs! Yes, of course, that's just the thing for you.

THE FAT GUEST [*seated in an armchair*].   Haven't you brought along some of your own?

HJALMAR.   No, I haven't.

THE FAT GUEST.   You really should have. It's so good for the digestion to sit and look at pictures.

THE BALD-HEADED GUEST.   And then it always adds a morsel to the entertainment, you know.

A NEARSIGHTED GUEST.   And all contributions are gratefully received.

MRS. SØRBY.   These gentlemen mean that if one's invited for dinner, one must also work for the food, Mr. Ekdal.

THE FAT GUEST.   Where the larder's superior, *that* is pure joy.

THE BALD-HEADED GUEST.   My Lord, it's all in the struggle for existence—

MRS. SØRBY.   How right you are! [*They continue laughing and joking.*]

GREGERS [*quietly*].   You should talk with them, Hjalmar.

HJALMAR [*with a shrug*].   What could I talk about?

THE FAT GUEST.   Don't you think, Mr. Werle, that Tokay compares favorably as a healthful drink for the stomach?

WERLE [*by the fireplace*].   The Tokay you had today I can vouch for in any case; it's one of the very, very finest years. But you recognized that well enough.

THE FAT GUEST.   Yes, it had a remarkably delicate flavor.

HJALMAR [*tentatively*].   Is there some difference between the years?

THE FAT GUEST [*laughing*].   Oh, that's rich!

WERLE [*smiling*].   It certainly doesn't pay to offer you a noble wine.

THE BALD-HEADED GUEST.   Tokay wines are like photographs, Mr. Ekdal—sunshine is of the essence. Isn't that true?

HJALMAR.   Oh yes, light is very important.

MRS. SØRBY.   Exactly the same as with court officials—who push for their place in the sun too, I hear.

THE BALD-HEADED GUEST.   Ouch! That was a tired quip.

THE NEARSIGHTED GUEST.   The lady's performing—

THE FAT GUEST.   And at our expense. [*Frowning.*] Mrs. Sørby, Mrs. Sørby!

MRS. SØRBY.   Yes, but it certainly is true now that the years can vary enormously. The old vintages are the finest.

THE NEARSIGHTED GUEST. Do you count me among the old ones?

MRS. SØRBY. Oh, far from it.

THE BALD-HEADED GUEST. Ha, you see! But what about *me*, Mrs. Sørby—?

THE FAT GUEST. Yes, and me! What years would you put us among?

MRS. SØRBY. I would put you all among the sweet years, gentlemen. [*She sips a glass of punch; the guests laugh and banter with her.*]

WERLE. Mrs. Sørby always finds a way out—when she wants to. Pass your glasses, gentlemen. Pettersen, take care of them. Gregers, I think we'll have a glass together. [GREGERS *does not stir.*] Won't you join us, Ekdal? I had no chance to remember you at the table.

[GRAABERG, *the bookkeeper, peers out from the door to the offices.*]

GRAABERG. Beg pardon, Mr. Werle, but I can't get out.

WERLE. What, are you locked in again?

GRAABERG. Yes, and Flakstad's left with the keys—

WERLE. Well, then, go through here.

GRAABERG. But there's someone else—

WERLE. All right, all right, both of you. Don't be shy.

[GRAABERG *and old* EKDAL *come out from the office.*]

WERLE [*involuntarily*]. Oh no!

[*The laughter and small talk die among the guests.* HJALMAR *starts at the sight of his father, sets down his glass, and turns away toward the fireplace.*]

EKDAL [*without looking up, but bowing slightly to each side and mumbling*]. Door locked. Door locked. Beg your pardon. [*He and* GRAABERG *exit in back to the right.*]

WERLE [*between his teeth*]. That damned Graaberg!

GREGERS [*with open mouth, staring at* HJALMAR]. But it couldn't have been—!

THE FAT GUEST. What's going on? Who was that?

GREGERS. Oh, no one. Only the bookkeeper and somebody else.

THE NEARSIGHTED GUEST [*to* HJALMAR]. Did *you* know him?

HJALMAR. I don't know—I didn't notice—

THE FAT GUEST [*getting up*]. What in thunder's wrong? [*He goes over to some others, who are talking.*]

MRS. SØRBY [*whispering to the waiter*]. Slip something to him outside, something really fine.

PETTERSEN [*nodding*]. I'll see to it. [*He goes out.*]

GREGERS [*in a shocked undertone*]. Then it really was him!

HJALMAR. Yes.

GREGERS. And yet you stood here and denied you knew him!

HJALMAR [*whispering fiercely*]. But how could I—!

GREGERS. Be recognized by your father?

HJALMAR [*painfully*]. Oh, if you were in my place, then—

[*The hushed conversations among the guests now mount into a forced joviality.*]

THE BALD-HEADED GUEST [*approaching* HJALMAR *and* GREGERS *amiably*]. Ah ha! You over here, polishing up old memories from your student years? Well? Won't you smoke, Mr. Ekdal? Have a light? Oh, that's right, we're not supposed to—

HJALMAR. Thanks, I couldn't—

THE FAT GUEST. Haven't you got a neat little poem to recite for us, Mr. Ekdal? In times past you did that so nicely.

HJALMAR. I'm afraid I can't remember any.

THE FAT GUEST. Oh, that's a shame. Well, Balle, what can we find to do?

[*The two men cross the floor into the other room and go out.*]

HJALMAR [*somberly*]. Gregers—I'm going! When a man's felt a terrible blow from fate—you understand. Say good night to your father for me.

GREGERS. Yes, of course. Are you going straight home?

HJALMAR. Yes, why?

GREGERS. Well, I may pay you a visit later.

HJALMAR. No, you mustn't. Not to my home. My house is a sad one, Gregers—especially after a brilliant occasion like this. We can always meet somewhere in town.

MRS. SØRBY [*who has approached; in a low voice*]. Are you going, Ekdal?

HJALMAR. Yes.

MRS. SØRBY. Greet Gina.

HJALMAR. Thank you.

MRS. SØRBY. And tell her I'll stop by to see her one day soon.

HJALMAR. Yes. Thanks. [*To* GREGERS.] Stay here. I'd rather disappear without any fuss. [*He strolls around the floor, then into the other room and out to the right.*]

MRS. SØRBY [*quietly to the waiter, who has returned*]. Well, did the old man get something to take home?

PETTERSEN. Sure. I slipped him a bottle of cognac.

MRS. SØRBY. Oh, you could have found something better.

PETTERSEN. Not at all, Mrs. Sørby. He knows nothing better than cognac.

THE FAT GUEST [*in the doorway, holding a score of music*]. How about the two of us playing something, Mrs. Sørby?

MRS. SØRBY. All right. Let's.

[*The guests shout approval.* MRS. SØRBY *and the others exit right, through the inner room.* GREGERS *remains standing by the fireplace.* WERLE *looks for something on the writing table, seeming to wish that* GREGERS *would leave; when he fails to stir,* WERLE *crosses toward the door.*]

GREGERS. Father, won't you wait a moment?

WERLE [*pausing*]. What is it?

GREGERS. I must have a word with you.

WERLE. Can't it wait till we're alone?

GREGERS. No, it can't, because it just might occur that we never are alone.

WERLE [*coming closer*]. What does *that* mean?

[*Distant piano music is heard from the music room during the following conversation.*]

GREGERS. How could anyone here let that family decay so pitifully?

WERLE. You're referring to the Ekdals, no doubt.

GREGERS. Yes, I mean the Ekdals. Lieutenant Ekdal was once so close to you.

WERLE. Yes, worse luck, he was all too close; and for that I've paid a price these many years. He's the one I can thank for putting something of a blot on my good name and reputation.

GREGERS [*quietly*]. Was *he* really the only guilty one?

WERLE. Who else do you mean!

GREGERS. You and he were both in on buying that big stand of timber—

WERLE. But it was Ekdal, wasn't it, who made the survey of the sections —that incompetent survey? He was the one who carried out all the illegal logging on state property. In fact, he was in charge of the whole operation up there. I had no idea of what Lieutenant Ekdal was getting into.

GREGERS. Lieutenant Ekdal himself had no idea of what he was getting into.

WERLE. Very likely. But the fact remains that he was convicted and I was acquitted.

GREGERS. Yes, I'm aware that no proof was found.

WERLE. Acquittal is acquittal. Why do you rake up this ugly old story that's given me gray hair before my time? Is this what you've been brooding about all those years up there? I can assure you, Gregers—here in town the whole business has been forgotten long ago—as far as I'm concerned.

GREGERS. But that miserable Ekdal family!

WERLE. Seriously, what would you have me do for these people? When Ekdal was let out, he was a broken man, beyond any help. There are people in this world who plunge to the bottom when they've hardly been winged, and they never come up again. Take my word for it, Gregers; I've done everything I could, short of absolutely compromising myself and arousing all kinds of suspicion and gossip—

GREGERS. Suspicion—? So that's it.

WERLE. I've gotten Ekdal copying jobs from the office, and I pay him much, much more than his work is worth—

GREGERS [*without looking at him*]. Hm. No doubt.

WERLE. You're laughing? Maybe you think what I'm saying isn't true? There's certainly nothing to show in my books; I don't record such payments.

GREGERS [*with a cold smile*]. No. I'm sure that certain payments are best left unrecorded.

WERLE [*surprised*]. What do you mean by *that?*

GREGERS [*plucking up his courage*]. Did you record what it cost you to have Hjalmar Ekdal study photography?

WERLE. I? Why should I?

GREGERS. I know now it was you who paid for that. And now I know, too, that it was you who set him up so comfortably in business.

WERLE. Well, and I suppose this still means that I've done nothing for the Ekdals! I can assure you, those people have already cost me enough expense.

GREGERS. Have you recorded any of the expenses?

WERLE. Why do you ask that?

GREGERS. Oh, there are reasons. Listen, tell me—the time when you developed such warmth for your old friend's son—wasn't that just when he was planning to marry?

WERLE. How the devil—how, after so many years, do you expect me—?

GREGERS. You wrote me a letter then—a business letter, naturally; and in a postscript it said, brief as could be, that Hjalmar Ekdal had gotten married to a Miss Hansen.

WERLE. Yes, that's right; that was her name.

GREGERS. But you never said that this Miss Hansen was Gina Hansen— our former housekeeper.

WERLE [*with a derisive, yet uneasy laugh*]. No, it just never occurred to me that you'd be so very interested in our former housekeeper.

GREGERS. I wasn't. But—[*dropping his voice*] there were others in the house who were quite interested in her.

WERLE. What do you mean by that? [*Storming at him.*] You're not referring to me!

GREGERS [*quietly but firmly*]. Yes, I'm referring to you.

WERLE. And you dare—! You have the insolence—! How could he, that ungrateful dog, that—photographer; how could he have the gall to make such insinuations?

GREGERS. Hjalmar hasn't breathed a word of it. I don't think he has the shadow of a doubt about all this.

WERLE. Then where did you get it from? Who could have said such a thing?

GREGERS. My poor, unhappy mother said it—the last time I saw her.

WERLE. Your mother! Yes, I might have guessed. She and you—you always stuck together. It was she who, right from the start, turned your mind against me.

GREGERS. No. It was everything she had to suffer and endure until she broke down and died so miserably.

WERLE. Oh, she had nothing to suffer and endure—no more, at least, than so many others. But you can't get anywhere with sick, high-strung people. I've certainly learned that. Now you're going around suspecting that sort of thing, digging up all manner of old rumors and slanders against your own father. Now listen, Gregers, I really think that at your age you could occupy yourself more usefully.

GREGERS. Yes, all in due time.

WERLE. Then your mind might be clearer than it seems to be now. What can it lead to, you up there at the works, slaving away year in and year out like a common clerk, never taking a penny over your month's salary. It's pure stupidity.

GREGERS. Yes, if only I were so sure of that.

WERLE. I understand you well enough. You want to be independent, without obligation to me. But here's the very opportunity for you to become independent, your own man in every way.

GREGERS. So? And by what means—?

WERLE. When I wrote you that it was essential you come to town now, immediately—hmm—

GREGERS. Yes. What is it you really want of me? I've been waiting all day to find out.

WERLE. I'm suggesting that you come into the firm as a partner.

GREGERS. I! In your firm? As a partner?

WERLE. Yes. It wouldn't mean we'd need to be together much. You could take over the offices here in town, and then I'd move up to the mill.

GREGERS. You *would*?

WERLE. Yes. You see, I can't take on work now the way I once could. I have to spare my eyes, Gregers; they're beginning to fail.

GREGERS. They've always been weak.

WERLE. Not like this. Besides—circumstances may make it desirable for me to live up there—at least for a while.

GREGERS. I never dreamed of anything like this.

WERLE. Listen, Gregers, there are so very many things that keep us apart, and yet, you know—we're father and son still. I think we should be able to reach some kind of understanding.

GREGERS. Just on the surface, is that what you mean?

WERLE. Well, at least that would be something. Think it over, Gregers. Don't you think it ought to be possible? Eh?

GREGERS [looking at him coldly]. There's something behind all this.

WERLE. How so?

GREGERS. It might be that somehow you're using me.

WERLE. In a relationship as close as ours, one can always be of use to the other.

GREGERS. Yes, so they say.

WERLE. I'd like to have you home with me now for a while. I'm a lonely man, Gregers; I've always felt lonely—all my life through, but particularly now when the years are beginning to press me. I need to have someone around—

GREGERS. You have Mrs. Sørby.

WERLE. Yes, I do—and she's become, you might say, almost indispensable. She's witty, even-tempered; she livens up the house—and that's what I need so badly.

GREGERS. Well, then, you've got everything the way you want it.

WERLE. Yes, but I'm afraid it can't go on. The world is quick to make inferences about a woman in her position. Yes, I was going to say, a man doesn't gain by it either.

GREGERS. Oh, when a man gives dinner parties like yours, he can certainly take a few risks.

WERLE. Yes, Gregers, but what about her? I'm afraid she won't put up with it much longer. And even if she did—even if, out of her feeling for me, she ignored the gossip and the backbiting and so on—do you still think, Gregers, you with your sharp sense of justice—

GREGERS [cutting him off]. Tell me short and sweet just one thing. Are you planning to marry her?

WERLE. And if I were planning such a thing—what then?

GREGERS. Yes, that's what I'm asking. What then?

WERLE. Would you be so irreconcilably set against it?

GREGERS. No, not at all. Not in any way.

WERLE. Well, I really didn't know whether, perhaps out of regard for your dead mother's memory—

GREGERS. I am not high-strung.

WERLE. Well, you may or may not be, but in any case you've taken a great load off my mind. I'm really very happy that I can count on your support in this.

GREGERS [staring intently at him]. Now I see how you want to use me.

WERLE. Use you! That's no way to talk!

GREGERS. Oh, let's not be squeamish in our choice of words. At least, not when it's man to man. [He laughs brusquely.] So that's it! That's why I—

damn it all!—had to make my personal appearance in town. On account of Mrs. Sørby, family life is in order in this house. Tableau of father with son! That's something new, all right!

WERLE. How dare you speak in that tone!

GREGERS. When has there ever been family life here? Never, as long as I can remember. But *now*, of course, there's need for a little of that. For who could deny what a fine impression it would make to hear that the son—on the wings of piety—came flying home to the aging father's wedding feast. What's left then of all the stories about what the poor dead woman suffered and endured? Not a scrap. Her own son ground them to dust.

WERLE. Gregers—I don't think there's a man in this world you hate as much as me.

GREGERS. I've seen you at too close quarters.

WERLE. You've seen me with your mother's eyes. [*Dropping his voice.*] But you should remember that those eyes were—clouded at times.

GREGERS [*faltering*]. I know what you mean. But who bears the guilt for Mother's fatal weakness? You, and all those—! The last of them was that female that Hjalmar Ekdal was fixed up with when you had no more—ugh!

WERLE [*shrugs*]. Word for word, as if I were hearing your mother.

GREGERS [*paying no attention to him*]. . . . and there he sits right now, he with his great, guileless, childlike mind plunged in deception—living under the same roof with that creature, not knowing that what he calls home is built on a lie. [*Coming a step closer.*] When I look back on all you've done, it's as if I looked out over a battlefield with broken human beings on every side.

WERLE. I almost think the gulf is too great between us.

GREGERS [*bows stiffly*]. So I've observed; therefore I'll take my hat and go.

WERLE. You're going? Out of this house?

GREGERS. Yes. Because now at least I can see a purpose to live for.

WERLE. What purpose is that?

GREGERS. You'd only laugh if you heard it.

WERLE. A lonely man doesn't laugh so easily, Gregers.

GREGERS [*pointing toward the inner room*]. Look—your gentleman friends are playing blindman's buff with Mrs. Sørby. Good night and goodbye.

[*He goes out at the right rear. Laughter and joking from the company, which moves into view in the inner room.*]

WERLE [*muttering contemptuously after* GREGERS]. Huh! Poor fool—and he says he's not high-strung!

ACT II

HJALMAR EKDAL's *studio. The room, which is fairly spacious, appears to be a loft. To the right is a sloping roof with great panes of glass, half hidden by a blue curtain. In the far right corner is the entrance; nearer on the same side, a door to the living room. Similarly, at the left there are two doors, and between these an iron stove. At the back is a wide double door, designed to slide back to the sides. The studio is simply but comfortably furnished and decorated.*

Between the right-hand doors, slightly away from the wall, stands a sofa beside a table and some chairs; on the table is a lighted lamp with a shade; by the stove an old armchair. Photographic apparatus and equipment of various sorts are set up here and there in the room. At the left of the double doors stands a bookcase containing a few books, small boxes and flasks of chemicals, various tools, implements, and other objects. Photographs and such small articles as brushes, paper, and the like lie on the table.

GINA EKDAL *sits on a chair by the table, sewing.* HEDVIG *sits on the sofa, hands shading her eyes, thumbs in her ears, reading a book.*

GINA [*having glanced over several times at* HEDVIG, *as if with anxiety*]. Hedvig! [HEDVIG *does not hear.*]

GINA [*louder*].   Hedvig!

HEDVIG [*removing her hands and looking up*].   Yes, Mother?

GINA.   Hedvig, dear, you mustn't sit and read anymore.

HEDVIG.   Oh, but Mother, can't I please read a little longer? Just a little!

GINA.   No, no—you must set the book down. Your father doesn't like it; he never reads in the evening.

HEDVIG [*closing the book*].   No, Daddy's no great one for reading.

GINA [*lays her sewing aside and takes a pencil and a small notebook from the table*].   Do you remember how much we spent for butter today?

HEDVIG.   It was one sixty-five.

GINA.   That's right. [*Making a note.*] It's awful how much butter gets used in this house. And then so much for smoked sausage, and for cheese—let me see—[*making more notes*] and so much for ham—hmm. [*Adds.*] Yes, that adds right up to—

HEDVIG.   And then there's the beer.

GINA.   Yes, of course. [*Makes another note.*] It mounts up—but it can't be helped.

HEDVIG.   Oh, but you and I had no hot food for dinner, 'cause Daddy was out.

GINA.   No, and that's to the good. What's more, I also took in eight crowns fifty for photographs.

HEDVIG.   No! Was it that much?

GINA.   Exactly eight crowns fifty.

[*Silence.* GINA *again picks up her sewing.* HEDVIG *takes paper and pencil and starts to draw, shading her eyes with her left hand.*]

HEDVIG.   Isn't it something to think that Daddy's at a big dinner party at old Mr. Werle's?

GINA.   You can't really say that he's at old Mr. Werle's. It was his son who sent him the invitation. [*After a pause.*] We have nothing to do with old Mr. Werle.

HEDVIG.   I can hardly wait for Daddy to come home. He promised he'd ask Mrs. Sørby about bringing me a treat.

GINA.   Yes, you can bet there are lots of treats to be had in *that* house.

HEDVIG [*again drawing*].   Besides, I'm a little hungry, too.

[*Old* EKDAL, *with a bundle of papers under his arm and another bundle in his coat pocket, comes in through the hall door.*]

GINA.   My, but you're late today, Grandfather.

EKDAL. They'd locked the office. Had to wait for Graaberg. And then I had to go through—uhh.

GINA. Did they give you something new to copy, Grandfather?

EKDAL. This whole pile. Just look.

GINA. That's fine.

HEDVIG. And you've got a bundle in your pocket, too.

EKDAL. Oh? Nonsense; that's nothing. [*Puts his cane away in the corner.*] Here's work for a good spell, Gina, this here. [*Pulls one of the double doors slightly open.*] Shh! [*Peers into the room a moment, then carefully closes the door again.*] He, he! They're sound asleep, the lot of them. And she's bedded down in the basket all on her own. He, he!

HEDVIG. Are you sure she won't be cold in the basket, Grandpa?

EKDAL. What a thought! Cold? In all that straw? [*Goes toward the farther door on the left.*] I'll find some matches in here, eh?

GINA. The matches are on the bureau.

[EKDAL *goes into his room.*]

HEDVIG. It's wonderful that Grandpa got all that copying to do.

GINA. Yes, poor old Father; he'll earn himself a little pocket money.

HEDVIG. And he also won't be able to sit the whole morning down in that horrid Mrs. Eriksen's café.

GINA. That too, yes. [*A short silence.*]

HEDVIG. Do you think they're still at the dinner table?

GINA. Lord only knows; it may well be.

HEDVIG. Just think, all the lovely food Daddy's eaten! I'm sure he'll be happy and content when he comes. Don't you think so, Mother?

GINA. Of course. Imagine if we could tell him now that we'd rented out the room.

HEDVIG. But that's not necessary tonight.

GINA. Oh, it could well come in handy, you know. It's no good to us as it is.

HEDVIG. No, I mean it's not necessary because tonight Daddy's feeling good. It's better we have news about the room some other time.

GINA [*looking over at her*]. Are you glad when you have something nice to tell your father when he comes home at night?

HEDVIG. Yes, for things here are pleasanter then.

GINA [*reflecting*]. Well, there's something to that.

[*Old* EKDAL *comes in again and starts out through the nearer door to the left.*]

GINA [*half turning in her chair*]. Does Grandfather want something from the kitchen?

EKDAL. I do, yes. Don't stir. [*He goes out.*]

GINA. He never fusses with the fire out there. [*After a moment.*] Hedvig, go see what he's doing.

[EKDAL *reenters with a small jug of steaming water.*]

HEDVIG. Are you after hot water, Grandpa?

EKDAL. Yes, I am. Need it for something. Have to write, and the ink is caked thick as porridge—hmm.

GINA. But you ought to have supper first, Grandfather. It's all set and waiting in there.

EKDAL.   Never mind about the supper, Gina. Terribly busy, I tell you. I don't want anybody coming into my room—nobody. Hmm. [*He goes into his room.* GINA *and* HEDVIG *exchange glances.*]

GINA [*lowering her voice*].   Where do you figure he's gotten money?

HEDVIG.   He must have got it from Graaberg.

GINA.   Not a chance. Graaberg always sends the pay to me.

HEDVIG.   Maybe he got a bottle somewhere on credit.

GINA.   Poor Grandpa, no one'll give him credit.

[HJALMAR EKDAL, *wearing an overcoat and a gray felt hat, enters from the right.*]

GINA [*dropping her sewing and getting up*].   Ah, Hjalmar, here you are!

HEDVIG [*jumping up at the same time*].   At last you're home, Daddy!

HJALMAR [*putting his hat down*].   Yes, most of them were leaving.

HEDVIG.   So early?

HJALMAR.   Yes, it was only a dinner party. [*Starts to remove his overcoat.*]

GINA.   Let me help you.

HEDVIG.   Me too.

[*They take off his coat;* GINA *hangs it up on the rear wall.*]

HEDVIG.   Were there many there, Daddy?

HJALMAR.   Oh no, not many. We were some twelve, fourteen people at the table.

GINA.   And you got to talk with every one of them?

HJALMAR.   Oh yes, a little, though Gregers rather monopolized me.

GINA.   Is Gregers as ugly as ever?

HJALMAR.   Well, he doesn't look any better. Isn't the old man home?

HEDVIG.   Yes, Grandpa's inside, writing.

HJALMAR.   Did he say anything?

GINA.   No, what should he say?

HJALMAR.   Didn't he mention anything of—I thought I heard that he'd been with Graaberg. I'll go in and have a word with him.

GINA.   No, no, don't bother.

HJALMAR.   Why not? Did he say he wouldn't see me?

GINA.   He doesn't want anyone in there this evening.

HEDVIG [*making signals*].   Uh—uh!

GINA [*not noticing*].   He's already been out here and gotten hot water.

HJALMAR.   Aha! Is he—?

GINA.   Yes, exactly.

HJALMAR.   Good Lord, my poor old white-haired father! Well, let him be, enjoying life's pleasures as he may.

[*Old* EKDAL *in a bathrobe, smoking a pipe, enters from his room.*]

EKDAL.   Home, eh? Thought it was your voice I heard.

HJALMAR.   I just arrived.

EKDAL.   You didn't see me at all, did you?

HJALMAR.   No, but they said you'd been through—so I thought I'd follow after.

EKDAL.   Hm, good of you, Hjalmar. Who were they, all those people?

HJALMAR.   Oh, different sorts. There was Flor—he's at the court—and Balle and Kaspersen and, uh—I forget his name, but people at court, all of them—

EKDAL [*nodding*].   Listen to that, Gina! He travels only in the best circles.

GINA.   Yes, it's real elegant in that house now.

HEDVIG.   Did the court people sing, Daddy? Or give readings?

HJALMAR.   No, they just babbled away. Of course they wanted *me* to recite for them, but I couldn't see that.

EKDAL.   You couldn't see that, eh?

GINA.   That you could easily have done.

HJALMAR.   Never. One mustn't be a doormat for every passing foot. [*Walking about the room.*] At least, that's not my way.

EKDAL.   No, no, that's not for Hjalmar.

HJALMAR.   I don't know why I should always provide the entertainment, when I'm out in society so rarely. Let the others make an effort. There those fellows go from one banquet to the next, eating and drinking day in and day out. So let them do their tricks in return for all the good food they get.

GINA.   But you didn't say that there?

HJALMAR [*humming*].   Um—um—um—they were told a thing or two.

EKDAL.   Right to the nobility!

HJALMAR.   I don't see why not. [*Casually.*] Later we had a little quibble about Tokay.

EKDAL.   Tokay, you mean? That's a fine wine, that.

HJALMAR [*coming to a halt*].   On occasion. But I must tell you that not all years are equally good. Everything depends strictly on how much sun the grapes have had.

GINA.   Really? Oh, Hjalmar, you know everything.

EKDAL.   And they could argue about that?

HJALMAR.   They tried to. But then they were informed that it's exactly the same with court officials. Among them as well, all years are not equally fine—it was said.

GINA.   The things you think of!

EKDAL.   He—he! So you served that up to them, eh?

HJALMAR.   Smack between the eyes they got it.

EKDAL.   Hear, Gina! He laid that one smack between the eyes of the nobility.

GINA.   Just think, smack between the eyes.

HJALMAR.   That's right. But I don't want a lot of talk about this. One doesn't speak of such things. Everything really went off in the most friendly spirit, naturally. They're all pleasant, genial people. How could I hurt their feelings? Never!

EKDAL.   But smack between the eyes—

HEDVIG [*ingratiatingly*].   How nice to see you in evening clothes, Daddy. You look so well in them.

HJALMAR.   Yes, don't you think so? And this one here really fits very well. It's almost as if it were made for me. A bit snug under the arms, maybe—help me, Hedvig. [*Takes off the coat.*] I'd rather wear my jacket. What did you do with my jacket, Gina?

GINA.   Here it is. [*Brings the jacket and helps him into it.*]

HJALMAR.   There! Now don't forget to give Molvik his coat back first thing in the morning.

GINA [*putting it away*].   I'll take care of it.

HJALMAR [*stretching*].   Ah, but this feels much more comfortable. This kind of free and easy dress suits my whole personality better. Don't you think so, Hedvig?

HEDVIG. Yes, Daddy.

HJALMAR. And when I pull my necktie out into a pair of flowing ends—so! Look! What then?

HEDVIG. Yes, it goes so well with your moustache and your long, curly hair.

HJALMAR. Curly? I wouldn't say it's that. I'd call it wavy.

HEDVIG. Yes, but it *is* so curly.

HJALMAR. No—wavy.

HEDVIG [*after a moment, tugs at his sleeve*]. Daddy!

HJALMAR. What is it?

HEDVIG. Oh, you know what.

HJALMAR. No, I don't. Honestly.

HEDVIG [*laughing fretfully*]. Come on, Daddy, don't tease me any longer.

HJALMAR. But what is it, then?

HEDVIG [*shaking him*]. Silly! Out with it, Daddy. You know—all the treats you promised me.

HJALMAR. Oh—no! How did I ever forget that?

HEDVIG. No, you can't fool me. Shame on you! Where have you hidden it?

HJALMAR. So help me if I didn't forget. But wait a minute! I've got something else for you, Hedvig. [*Goes over and rummages in his coat pockets.*]

HEDVIG [*jumping and clapping her hands*]. Oh, Mother, Mother!

GINA. You see, if you're only patient enough, then—

HJALMAR [*returning with a piece of paper*]. See, here we have it.

HEDVIG. That? But that's just a piece of paper.

HJALMAR. It's the bill of fare, the complete bill of fare. Here it says "menu"; that means "bill of fare."

HEDVIG. Don't you have anything else?

HJALMAR. I forgot to bring anything else, I tell you. But take my word for it: it's bad business, this doting on sugar candy. Now, if you'll sit down at the table and read the menu aloud, I'll describe for you just how each dish tasted. How's that, Hedvig?

HEDVIG [*swallowing her tears*]. Thanks. [*She sits, but does not read.* GINA *makes gestures at her, which* HJALMAR *notices.*]

HJALMAR [*pacing about the floor*]. What incredible things a family breadwinner is asked to remember; and if he forgets even the tiniest detail—immediately he's met with sour faces. Well he has to get used to that, too. [*Pauses at the stove beside* EKDAL.] Have you looked inside this evening, Father?

EKDAL. Oh, that you can be sure of. She's gone into the basket.

HJALMAR. No! Into the basket? Then she's begun to get used to it.

EKDAL. Yes. You see, it was just as I predicted. But now there are some little things to do—

HJALMAR. Some improvements, eh?

EKDAL. But they've got to be done, you know.

HJALMAR. All right, let's talk a bit about the improvements, Father. Come, we'll sit here on the sofa.

EKDAL. Very good. Umm—think I'll fill my pipe first. Needs cleaning, too. Hmm. [*He goes into his room.*]

GINA [*smiling at* HJALMAR].   Clean his pipe!

HJALMAR.   Ah, now, Gina, let him be. Poor old derelict. Yes, the improvements—it's best we get those off our hands tomorrow.

GINA.   Tomorrow you won't have time, Hjalmar—

HEDVIG [*interrupting*].   Oh yes, he will, Mother!

GINA.   Remember those prints that need retouching. They've been called for so many times already.

HJALMAR.   Oh yes, those prints again. They'll be finished in no time. Did any new orders come in?

GINA.   No such luck. For tomorrow, I have nothing except those two portrait sittings you know about.

HJALMAR.   Nothing else? Ah, well, if people won't even try, then naturally—

GINA.   But what else can I do? I've put ads in the papers time and again.

HJALMAR.   Yes, ads, ads—you see what a help they are. And of course nobody's been to look at the spare room either?

GINA.   No, not yet.

HJALMAR.   That was to be expected. If one doesn't keep wide awake—Gina, you've simply got to pull yourself together.

HEDVIG [*going to him*].   Let me bring you your flute, Daddy.

HJALMAR.   No, no flute. I want no pleasures in this world. [*Pacing about.*] Ah, yes, work—I'll be deep in work tomorrow; there'll be no lack of *that*. I'll sweat and slave as long as my strength holds out—

GINA.   But Hjalmar dear, I didn't mean it that way.

HEDVIG.   Can't I get you a bottle of beer, then?

HJALMAR.   Absolutely not. There's nothing I need. [*Stopping.*] Beer? Did you say beer?

HEDVIG [*vivaciously*].   Yes, Daddy, lovely cool beer.

HJALMAR.   Well—if you really insist, I suppose you could bring in a bottle.

GINA.   Yes, do that. Then we'll have it cozy.

[HEDVIG *runs toward the kitchen door.* HJALMAR *by the stove stops her, gazes at her, clasps her about the head and hugs her to him.*]

HJALMAR.   Hedvig! Hedvig!

HEDVIG [*with tears of joy*].   Oh, my dearest Daddy!

HJALMAR.   No, don't call me that. There I sat, helping myself at a rich man's table, gorging myself with all good things—! I could at least have remembered—

GINA [*sitting at the table*].   Oh, nonsense, Hjalmar.

HJALMAR.   Yes, I could! But you mustn't be too hard on me. You both know I love you anyway.

HEDVIG [*throwing her arms around him*].   And we love you too, so much!

HJALMAR.   And if I should seem unreasonable at times, then—good Lord—remember that I am a man assailed by a host of cares. Ah, yes! [*Drying his eyes.*] No beer at a time like this. Bring me my flute. [HEDVIG *runs to the bookcase and fetches it.*] Thank you. There—so. With flute in hand, and you two close by me—ah!

[HEDVIG *sits at the table by* GINA, HJALMAR *walks back and forth, then forcefully begins to play a Bohemian folk dance, but in a slow elegiac tempo with sentimental intonation. After a moment he breaks off the melody and extends his left hand to* GINA.]

HJALMAR [*with feeling*]. So what if we skimp and scrape along under this roof, Gina—it's still our home. And I'll say this: it's good to be here. [*He starts playing again; immediately there comes a knock on the hall door.*]

GINA [*getting up*]. Shh, Hjalmar. I think someone's there.

HJALMAR [*returning the flute to the bookcase*]. What, again! [GINA *goes over and opens the door.*]

GREGERS WERLE [*out in the hallway*]. Excuse me—

GINA [*drawing back slightly*]. Oh!

GREGERS. But doesn't Mr. Ekdal, the photographer, live here?

GINA. Yes, that's right.

HJALMAR [*going toward the door*]. Gregers! Is it really you? Well, come right in.

GREGERS [*entering*]. I said I was going to drop in on you.

HJALMAR. But tonight? Have you left the party?

GREGERS. Left both party and family home. Good evening, Mrs. Ekdal. I don't know whether you recognize me?

GINA. Oh yes. Young Mr. Werle is not so hard to recognize.

GREGERS. No. I look like my mother, and you remember her, no doubt.

HJALMAR. Did you say you'd left your home?

GREGERS. Yes, I've moved into a hotel.

HJALMAR. I see. Well, now that you've come, take off your things and sit down.

GREGERS. Thank you. [*Removes his overcoat. He is dressed now in a simple grey suit of somewhat rustic cut.*]

HJALMAR. Here, on the sofa. Make yourself at home.

[GREGERS *sits on the sofa,* HJALMAR *on a chair at the table.*]

GREGERS [*looking around*]. So this is where you work, then, Hjalmar. And you live here as well.

HJALMAR. This is the studio, as you can see—

GINA. There's more room in here, so we like it better.

HJALMAR. We had a better place before; but this apartment has one great advantage: it has such wonderful adjoining rooms—

GINA. And so we have a room on the other side of the hall that we can rent out.

GREGERS [*to* HJALMAR]. Ah, then you have lodgers, too.

HJALMAR. No, not yet. It's not that easy, you know. One has to keep wide awake. [*To* HEDVIG.] But how about that beer?

[HEDVIG *nods and goes into the kitchen.*]

GREGERS. So that's your daughter, then?

HJALMAR. Yes, that's Hedvig.

GREGERS. An only child?

HJALMAR. She's the only one, yes. She's the greatest joy of our lives, and —[*lowering his voice*] also our deepest sorrow, Gregers.

GREGERS. What do you mean?

HJALMAR. Yes. You see, there's the gravest imminent danger of her losing her sight.

GREGERS. Going blind!

HJALMAR. Yes. So far only the first signs are present, and things may go well for a while. All the same, the doctor has warned us. It will come inevitably.

GREGERS. What a dreadful misfortune! How did this happen?

HJALMAR [*sighing*]. Heredity, most likely.

GREGERS [*startled*]. Heredity?

GINA. Hjalmar's mother also had bad eyes.

HJALMAR. Yes, so my father says. I don't remember her.

GREGERS. Poor child. And how is she taking it?

HJALMAR. Oh, you can well imagine, we haven't the heart to tell her. She suspects nothing. She's carefree, gay, and singing like a tiny bird, she's fluttering into life's eternal night. [*Overcome.*] Oh, it's a brutal blow for me, Gregers.

[HEDVIG *brings in beer and glasses on a tray, which she sets down on the table.*]

HJALMAR [*stroking her head*]. Thanks. Thanks, Hedvig.

[HEDVIG *puts her arms around his neck and whispers in his ear.*]

HJALMAR. No, No bread and butter now. [*Looking over.*] Or maybe Gregers will have a piece?

GREGERS [*making a gesture of refusal*]. No. No, thanks.

HJALMAR [*his tone still mournful*]. Well, you can bring in a little anyway. If you have a crust, that would be fine. And please, put enough butter on, too.

[HEDVIG *nods contentedly and returns to the kitchen.*]

GREGERS [*after following her with his eyes*]. In every other respect she looks so strong and healthy.

GINA. Yes, thank God, she's got nothing else wrong with her.

GREGERS. She'll certainly look like you when she grows up, Mrs. Ekdal. How old is she now?

GINA. Hedvig is almost fourteen exactly; her birthday's the day after tomorrow.

GREGERS. Rather tall for her age.

GINA. Yes, she's shot right up this past year.

GREGERS. Nothing like the growth of a child to show us how old we're getting. How long is it you've been married now?

GINA. We've been married now for—yes, near fifteen years.

GREGERS. No, truly! Has it been that long?

GINA [*looking at him, becoming wary*]. Yes, no doubt about it.

HJALMAR. That's right. Fifteen years, short a few months. [*Changing the subject.*] They must have been long years for you, Gregers, up there at the works.

GREGERS. They were long while I was living them—but now I scarcely know what became of the time.

[Old EKDAL *enters from his room, without his pipe, but with his old military cap on his head; his walk a bit unsteady.*]

EKDAL. There, now, Hjalmar. Now we can settle down and talk about that—umm. What was it again?

HJALMAR [*going toward him*]. Father, someone is here. Gregers Werle. I don't know if you remember him.

EKDAL [*regarding* GREGERS, *who has gotten up*]. Werle? That's the son, isn't it? What does he want with me?

HJALMAR. Nothing; it's me he's come to see.

EKDAL. Well, then nothing's up, eh?

HJALMAB. No, of course not.

EKDAL [*swinging his arms*]. It's not that I'm scared of anything, you know, but—

GREGERS [*going over to him*]. I just want to greet you from your old hunting grounds, Lieutenant Ekdal.

EKDAL. Hunting grounds?

GREGERS. Yes, up there around the Hoidal works.

EKDAL. Oh, up there. Yes, I was well known there once.

GREGERS. In those days you were a tremendous hunter.

EKDAL. So I was. Still am, maybe. You're looking at my uniform. I ask nobody permission to wear it in here. As long as I don't walk in the streets with it— [HEDVIG *brings a plate of buttered bread, which she places on the table.*]

HJALMAR. Sit down, Father, and have a glass of beer. Help yourself, Gregers.

[EKDAL *stumbles, muttering, over to the sofa.* GREGERS *sits on the chair nearest him,* HJALMAR *on the other side of* GREGERS. GINA *sits near the table and sews;* HEDVIG *stands beside her father.*]

GREGERS. Do you remember, Lieutenant Ekdal, when Hjalmar and I would come up to visit you summers and at Christmas?

EKDAL. Did you? No, no, no, I don't recall. But I'll tell you something: I've been a first-rate hunter. Bear— I've shot them, too. Shot nine in all.

GREGERS [*looking sympathetically at him*]. And now you hunt no more.

EKDAL. Oh, I wouldn't say *that*, boy. Get some hunting in now and then. Yes, but not that kind there. The woods, you see—the woods, the woods— [*Drinks.*] How do the woods look up there?

GREGERS. Not so fine as in your time. They've been cut into heavily.

EKDAL. Cut into? [*More quietly, as if in fear.*] It's a dangerous business, that. It catches up with you. The woods take revenge.

HJALMAR [*filling his glass*]. Here, a little more, Father.

GREGERS. How can a man like you—such an outdoorsman—live in the middle of a stuffy city, cooped up in these four walls?

EKDAL [*half laughs and glances at* HJALMAR]. Oh, it's not so bad here. Not bad at all.

GREGERS. But all those other things, the very roots of your soul—that cool, sweeping breeze, that free life of the moors and forests, among the animals and birds—?

EKDAL [*smiling*]. Hjalmar, should we show him?

HJALMAR [*quickly and a bit embarrassed*]. No, no, Father, not tonight.

GREGERS. What's that he wants to show me?

HJALMAR. Oh, it's only a sort of—you can see it some other time.

GREGERS [*speaking again to* EKDAL]. Yes, my point was this, Lieutenant Ekdal, that now you might as well return with me to the works, for I'm sure to be leaving very soon. Without a doubt, you could get some copying to do up there; and here you've nothing in the world to stir your blood and make you happy.

EKDAL [*staring at him, astonished*]. I have nothing, nothing at all—!

GREGERS. Of course you have Hjalmar, but then again, he has his own.

And a man like you, who's always felt himself so drawn to whatever is free and wild—

EKDAL [*striking the table*].   Hjalmar, now he's *got* to see it!

HJALMAR.   But Father, is it worth it now? It's dark, you know—

EKDAL.   Nonsense! There's moonlight. [*Getting up.*] I say he's got to see it. Let me by. Come and help me, Hjalmar!

HEDVIG.   Oh yes, do that, Father!

HJALMAR [*getting up.*].   Well—all right.

GREGERS [*to* GINA].   What's this all about?

GINA.   Oh, you really mustn't expect anything special.

[EKDAL *and* HJALMAR *have gone to the back wall to push aside the two halves of the double door;* HEDVIG *helps her grandfather, while* GREGERS *remains standing by the sofa and* GINA *sits, imperturbably sewing. The doorway opens on an extensive, irregular loft room with many nooks and corners, and two separate chimney shafts ascending through it. Clear moonlight streams through skylights into certain parts of the large room; others lie in deep shadow.*]

EKDAL [*to* GREGERS].   All the way over here, please.

GREGERS [*going over to them*].   What *is* it, then?

EKDAL.   See for yourself—hmm.

HJALMAR [*somewhat self-conscious*].   All this belongs to Father, you understand.

GREGERS [*peering in at the doorway*].   So you keep poultry, Lieutenant Ekdal!

EKDAL.   I'll say we keep poultry! They're roosting now; but you just ought to see our poultry by daylight!

HEDVIG.   And then there's a—

EKDAL.   Shh, shh—don't say anything yet.

GREGERS.   And you've got pigeons too, I see.

EKDAL.   Oh yes, it might just be we've got some pigeons. They have their nesting boxes up there under the eaves; pigeons like to perch high, you know.

HJALMAR.   They're not ordinary pigeons, all of them.

EKDAL.   Ordinary! No, I should say not! We have tumblers, and we have a couple of pouters also. But look here! Can you see that hutch over there by the wall?

GREGERS.   Yes. What do you use that for?

EKDAL.   The rabbits sleep there at night, boy.

GREGERS.   Well, so you have rabbits too?

EKDAL.   Yes, what the devil do you think we have but rabbits! He asks if we have rabbits, Hjalmar! Hmm! But now listen, this is really something! This is it! Out of the way, Hedvig. Stand right here—that's it—and look straight down there. Do you see a basket there with straw in it?

GREGERS.   Yes, and there's a bird nesting in the basket.

EKDAL.   Hmm! "A bird"—

GREGERS.   Isn't it a duck?

EKDAL [*hurt*].   Yes, of course it's a duck.

HJALMAR.   But what *kind* of duck?

HEDVIG.   It's not just any old duck—

EKDAL.   Shh!

GREGERS.   And it's no exotic breed, either.

EKDAL.   No, Mr.—Werle, it's not any exotic breed—because it's a wild duck.

GREGERS.   No, is it really? A wild duck?

EKDAL.   Oh yes, that's what it is. That "bird" as you said—that's a wild duck. That's our wild duck, boy.

HEDVIG.   *My* wild duck—I own it.

GREGERS.   And it can survive up here indoors? And do well?

EKDAL.   You've got to understand, she's got a trough of water to splash around in.

HJALMAR.   Fresh water every other day.

GINA [*turning to* HJALMAR].   Hjalmar dear, it's freezing cold in here now.

EKDAL.   Hmm, let's close up, then. Doesn't pay to disturb their rest either. Lend a hand, Hedvig dear. [HJALMAR *and* HEDVIG *push the double doors together.*] Another time you can get a proper look at her. [*Sits in the armchair by the stove.*] Oh, they're most curious, the wild ducks, you know.

GREGERS.   But how did you capture it, Lieutenant Ekdal?

EKDAL.   Didn't capture it myself. There's a certain man here in town we can thank for it.

GREGERS [*starts slightly*].   That man—it wouldn't be my father?

EKDAL.   Exactly right—your father. Hmm.

HJALMAR.   It was odd you were able to guess that, Gregers.

GREGERS.   Well, you said before that you owed Father for so many different things, so I thought here too—

GINA.   But we didn't get the duck from Mr. Werle himself—

EKDAL.   We might just as well thank Haakon Werle for her anyhow, Gina. [*To* GREGERS.] He was out in his boat—follow me?—and he shot for her, but he sees so bad now, your father, that—hm—he only winged her.

GREGERS.   I see. She took some shot in her body.

HJALMAR.   Yes, some one, two—three pieces.

HEDVIG.   She got it under the wing, and so she couldn't fly.

GREGERS.   Ah, so she dived right for the bottom, eh?

EKDAL [*sleepily, with a thick voice*].   You can bet on that. They always do, the wild ducks—streak for the bottom, deep as they can get, boy—bite right into the weeds and sea moss—and all that devil's beard that grows down there. And then they never come up again.

GREGERS.   But Lieutenant Ekdal, *your* wild duck came up again.

EKDAL.   He had such a remarkably clever dog, your father. And that dog —he dove down and brought her up.

GREGERS [*turning to* HJALMAR].   And then you got her here.

HJALMAR.   Not directly. First she went home to your father's, but there she didn't do well, so Pettersen got his orders to put an end to her—

EKDAL [*half asleep*].   Hm—yes, Pettersen—that bonehead—

HJALMAR [*speaking more softly*].   That's the way we got her, you see. Father knows Pettersen a bit and when he heard all this about the wild duck, he arranged to have her handed over to us.

GREGERS.   And now she's absolutely thriving in that attic room.

HJALMAR.   Yes, it's incredible. She's gotten fat. I think she's been in there so long, too, that she's forgotten her old wild life, and that's what it all comes down to.

GREGERS. You're certainly right there, Hjalmar. Just don't let her ever catch sight of the sea and the sky— But I mustn't stay any longer, for I think your father's asleep.

HJALMAR. Oh, don't bother about that.

GREGERS. But incidentally—you said you had a room for rent, a free room?

HJALMAR. Yes. Why? Do you know someone, perhaps—?

GREGERS. Could I take that room?

HJALMAR. You?

GINA. No, not *you*, Mr. Werle—

GREGERS. Could I take the room? If so, I'll move in first thing in the morning.

HJALMAR. By all means, with the greatest pleasure—

GINA. No, but Mr. Werle, it's not at all the room for *you*.

HJALMAR. But Gina, how can you say that?

GINA. Oh, the room isn't large enough, or light enough, and—

GREGERS. That really doesn't matter, Mrs. Ekdal.

HJALMAR. I think it's a very pleasant room, and it's not badly furnished, either.

GINA. But remember those two who live right below.

GREGERS. What two are those?

GINA. Oh, one of them's been a private tutor—

HJALMAR. That's Molvik, from the university.

GINA. And then there's a doctor named Relling.

GREGERS. Relling? I know him somewhat. He practiced a while up in Hoidal.

GINA. They're a pretty wild pair, those fellows. They go out on the town evenings and then come home in the dead of night, and they're not always so—

GREGERS. One gets used to that soon enough. I'm hoping things will go for me the same as with the wild duck—

GINA. Well, I think you ought to sleep on it first, anyway.

GREGERS. You're not very anxious to have me in the house, Mrs. Ekdal.

GINA. Goodness, what makes you think that?

HJALMAR. Yes, Gina, this is really peculiar of you. [*To* GREGERS.] But tell me, do you expect to stay here in town till the first?

GREGERS [*putting on his overcoat*]. Yes, now I expect to stay on.

HJALMAR. But not at home with your father? What do you plan to do with yourself?

GREGERS. Yes, if I only knew that—then I'd be doing all right. But when one is cursed with being called Gregers—"Gregers"—and then "Werle" coming after—have you ever heard anything so disgusting?

HJALMAR. Oh, I don't agree at all.

GREGERS. Ugh! Phew! I feel I'd like to spit on any man with a name like that. But when one has to *live* with that curse of being called Gregers, as I do—

HJALMAR [*laughing*]. If you weren't Gregers Werle, who would you want to be?

GREGERS. If I could choose, above all else I'd like to be a clever dog.

GINA. A dog?

HEDVIG [*involuntarily*]. Oh no!

GREGERS.   Yes. A really fantastic, clever dog, the kind that goes to the bottom after wild ducks when they dive under and bite fast into the weeds down in the mire.

HJALMAR.   You know, Gregers—I can't follow a word you're saying.

GREGERS.   Never mind. There's really nothing very remarkable in it. But tomorrow morning, early, I'll be moving in. [*To* GINA.] I won't be any trouble to you; I do everything for myself. [*To* HJALMAR.] The rest we can talk over tomorrow. Good night, Mrs. Ekdal. [*Nods to* HEDVIG.] Good night.

GINA.   Good night, Mr. Werle.

HEDVIG.   Good night.

HJALMAR [*who has lit a lamp*].   Just a minute. I'd better light your way; it's quite dark on the stairs.

[GREGERS *and* HJALMAR *go out through the hall.*]

GINA [*gazing into space, her sewing in her lap*].   Wasn't that a queer business, his wanting to be a dog?

HEDVIG.   I'll tell you something, Mother—it seemed to me he meant something else by that.

GINA.   What else could he mean?

HEDVIG.   I don't know—but it was just as if he meant something else from what he said, all the time.

GINA.   Do you think so? It was strange, all right.

HJALMAR [*coming back*].   The light was still lit. [*Putting out the lamp and setting it down.*] Ah, at last one can get a bite to eat. [*Beginning on the bread and butter.*] Well, now you see, Gina—if you simply keep wide awake, then—

GINA.   What do you mean, wide awake?

HJALMAR.   Well, it was lucky, then, that we got the room rented out for a while at last. And think—to a person like Gregers—a good old friend.

GINA.   Yes. I don't know what to say. I don't.

HEDVIG.   Oh, Mother, you'll see. It'll be fun.

HJALMAR.   You really are peculiar. Before you were so eager to rent, and now you don't like it.

GINA.   Yes, Hjalmar, if it could only have been somebody else. What do you think the old man will say?

HJALMAR.   Old Werle? This doesn't concern him.

GINA.   But you can sure bet that something has come up between them, since the son is moving out. You know how those two get along together.

HJALMAR.   Yes, that may well be, but—

GINA.   And now maybe the old man thinks it's you that's behind—

HJALMAR.   He can think that as much as he likes! Old Werle has done a tremendous amount for me. God knows, I'm aware of that. But even so, I can't make myself eternally dependent on him.

GINA.   But Hjalmar dear, that can have its effect on Grandfather. He may now lose that miserable little income he gets from Graaberg.

HJALMAR.   I could almost say, so much the better! Isn't it rather humiliating for a man like me to see his gray-haired father go around like an outcast? But now time is gathering to a ripeness, I think. [*Takes another piece of bread and butter.*] Just as sure as I've got a mission in life, I'm going to carry it out!

HEDVIG.   Oh yes, Daddy! Do!

GINA. Shh! Don't wake him up.

HJALMAR [more quietly]. I *will* carry it out, I tell you. There will come a day when— And that's why it's good we got the room rented out, for now I'm more independently fixed. Any man *must* be that, who's got a mission in life. [Over by the armchair; emotionally.] Poor old white-haired Father—lean on your Hjalmar. He has broad shoulders—powerful shoulders, in any case. One fine day you'll wake up and— [To GINA.] You do believe that, don't you?

GINA [getting up]. Yes, of course I do. But first let's see about getting him to bed.

HJALMAR. Yes, let's do that.

[Gently they lift up the old man.]

ACT III

HJALMAR EKDAL's studio. It is morning. Daylight streams through the large window in the sloping roof; the curtain is drawn back.

HJALMAR is sitting at the table, busy retouching a photograph; many other pictures lie in front of him. After a moment GINA, wearing a hat and coat, enters by the hall door; she has a covered basket on her arm.

HJALMAR. Back so soon, Gina?

GINA. Oh yes. Got to keep moving. [She sets the basket on a chair and takes her coat off.]

HJALMAR. Did you look in on Gregers?

GINA. Um-hm, I certainly did. Looks real nice in there. The moment he came, he got his room in beautiful shape.

HJALMAR. Oh?

GINA. Yes. He wanted to do everything himself, he said. So he starts building a fire in the stove, and the next thing he's closed down the damper so the whole room is full of smoke. Phew! What a stink, enough to—

HJALMAR. Oh no!

GINA. But that's not the best part! So then he wants to put it out, so he empties his whole water pitcher into the stove and now the floor's swimming in the worst muck.

HJALMAR. That's a nuisance.

GINA. I got the janitor's wife to come and scrub up after him, the pig; but it'll be unfit to live in till afternoon.

HJALMAR. What's he doing with himself in the meantime?

GINA. Thought he'd take a little walk, he said.

HJALMAR. I was in to see him for a moment too—after you left.

GINA. I heard that. You asked him for lunch.

HJALMAR. Just the tiniest little midday snack, you understand. It's the very first day—we could hardly avoid it. You always have something in the house.

GINA. I'll see what I can find.

HJALMAR. But now don't make it too skimpy. Because Relling and Molvik are dropping in too, I think. I just met Relling on the stairs, you see, so of course I had to—

GINA. Oh? Must we have those two also?

HJALMAR. Good Lord, a couple of sandwiches more or less; what's the difference?

EKDAL [opening his door and looking in]. Say, listen, Hjalmar— [Noticing GINA.] Oh, well.

GINA. Is there something Grandfather wants?

EKDAL. Oh no. Let it be. Hmm. [Goes in again.]

GINA [picking up the basket]. Keep a sharp eye on him so he doesn't go out.

HJALMAR. Oh yes, I'll do that. Listen, Gina, a little herring salad would be awfully good—because Relling and Molvik were out on a binge last night.

GINA. Just so they don't come before I'm ready—

HJALMAR. Not a chance. Take your time.

GINA. That's fine, then—and meanwhile you can get a little work done.

HJALMAR. Can't you see how I'm working! I'm working for all I'm worth.

GINA. Because then you'll have those off your hands, you know. [She carries the basket out to the kitchen. HJALMAR sits for a while, tinting the photograph in a glum and listless manner.]

EKDAL [peeks in, peers about the studio, and whispers]. Are you busy, boy?

HJALMAR. Of course. I'm sitting here struggling with these pictures—

EKDAL. Oh well, don't bother. If you're so busy, then— Hm! [He reenters his room, leaving the door ajar.]

HJALMAR [continues for a moment in silence, then puts down the brush and goes over to the door]. Father, are you busy?

EKDAL [grumbling from within]. When you're busy—I'm busy too. Huh!

HJALMAR. Yes, of course. [Returns to his work.]

EKDAL [a moment later, coming in again]. Hm. Well, now, Hjalmar, I'm really not that busy.

HJALMAR. I thought you had copying to do.

EKDAL. Oh, the devil! Can't he, Graaberg, wait a day or two? I'm sure it's no matter of life or death.

HJALMAR. No, and you're no slave, either.

EKDAL. And then there was that other business inside—

HJALMAR. Yes, that's just it. Maybe you want to go in? Shall I open it up for you?

EKDAL. Wouldn't be a bad idea, really.

HJALMAR [getting up]. And then we'd have that off our hands.

EKDAL. Yes, exactly. And it has to be ready first thing tomorrow. But it is tomorrow, isn't it?

HJALMAR. It certainly is tomorrow.

[HJALMAR and EKDAL each push back one of the double doors. Within, morning sunlight shines through the skylights. A few doves fly back and forth; others perch, cooing, on the rafters. Chickens cackle now and then from back in the loft.]

HJALMAR. There, now you can get in, Father.

EKDAL [going in]. Aren't you coming along?

HJALMAR. Well, you know what—I almost think— [*Sees* GINA *in the kitchen doorway.*] I? No, I haven't the time; I've got to work. But that means our new mechanism—

[*He pulls a cord; inside a curtain descends, its lower portion composed of a strip of old sailcloth, the upper part being a piece of worn-out fishnetting. By this means, the floor of the loft is rendered invisible.*]

HJALMAR [*returning to the table*]. That's that. Now at last I can work in peace for a while.

GINA. Is he in there, romping around again?

HJALMAR. Isn't that better than having him run down to Mrs. Eriksen's? [*Sitting.*] Is there anything you want? You look so—

GINA. I only wanted to ask, do you think we can set the lunch table in here?

HJALMAR. Well, we haven't any portraits scheduled that early, have we?

GINA. No. I don't expect anybody except that couple who want to be taken together.

HJALMAR. Why the devil can't they be taken together some other day?

GINA. Now, Hjalmar dear, I've got them booked for during your midday nap.

HJALMAR. Well, that's fine, then. So we'll eat in here.

GINA. All right. But there's no hurry about setting the table, you can certainly use it a while longer.

HJALMAR. Oh, it's obvious I'm using the table as much as I can!

GINA. Because then you'll be free later on, you know.

[*She goes back into the kitchen. A short pause.*]

EKDAL [*at the door to the loft, behind the net*]. Hjalmar!

HJALMAR. Well?

EKDAL. 'Fraid we'll have to move the water trough after all.

HJALMAR. Yes, that's what I've been saying all along.

EKDAL. Hm—hm—hm. [*Disappears from the doorway.*]

[HJALMAR *works a bit, glances toward the loft, and half rises.* HEDVIG *enters from the kitchen.*]

HJALMAR [*hurriedly sitting again*]. What do you want?

HEDVIG. I was just coming in to you, Father.

HJALMAR [*after a moment*]. You seem to be kind of snooping around. Are you checking up, maybe?

HEDVIG. No, not at all.

HJALMAR. What's Mother doing out there now?

HEDVIG. Oh, she's half through the herring salad. [*Going over to the table.*] Don't you have some little thing I could help you with, Daddy?

HJALMAR. Oh no. It's better just to leave me alone with all this—so long as my strength holds out. Nothing to worry about, Hedvig—if only your father can keep his health—

HEDVIG. Oh, Daddy, no. That's horrid; you mustn't talk like that. [*She wanders about a little, stops by the loft doorway, and looks in.*]

HJALMAR. What's he trying to do now?

HEDVIG. It must be a new pathway up to the water trough.

HJALMAR. He can't possibly rig that up on his own! And I'm condemned to sit here—!

HEDVIG [*going to him*]. Let *me* take the brush, Daddy. I know I can.

HJALMAR. Oh, nonsense, you'll only ruin your eyes.

HEDVIG. No such thing. Give me the brush.

HJALMAR [*getting up*]. Well, it'll only be for a minute or two.

HEDVIG. Pooh! How could that hurt me? [*Takes the brush.*] There now. [*Sitting.*] And here's one to go by.

HJALMAR. But don't ruin your eyes! Hear me? I won't take the blame; you can take the blame yourself—you hear me?

HEDVIG [*at work retouching*]. Yes, yes, sure I will.

HJALMAR. You're wonderfully clever, Hedvig. Just for a couple of minutes now.

[*He slips around the edge of the curtain into the loft.* HEDVIG *sits at her work.* HJALMAR *and* EKDAL *are heard arguing inside.*]

HJALMAR [*appearing behind the net*]. Hedvig, just hand me the pliers from the shelf. And the chisel, please. [*Turning, over his shoulder.*] Yes, now you'll see, Father. Will you give me a chance to show you the way I mean! [HEDVIG *fetches the desired tools from the bookcase and passes them in to him.*] Ah, thanks. See, dear, it was a good thing I came. [*He vanishes from the doorway; sounds of carpentry and bantering are heard.* HEDVIG *remains, looking in at them. A moment later, a knock at the hall door; she fails to notice it.*]

GREGERS [*bareheaded, and without his overcoat, enters, hesitating slightly at the door*]. Hm—

HEDVIG [*turning and going toward him*]. Good morning. Please come in.

GREGERS. Thanks. [*Looking at the loft.*] You seem to have workmen in the house.

HEDVIG. No, that's only Father and Grandfather. I'll go tell them.

GREGERS. No, no, don't bother. I'd rather wait a bit. [*He sits on the sofa.*]

HEDVIG. It's so messy here— [*Starts to remove the photographs.*]

GREGERS. Oh, they can stay. Are those some pictures that have to be finished?

HEDVIG. Yes, it's a little job I'm helping Daddy with.

GREGERS. Please don't let me disturb you.

HEDVIG. All right. [*She gathers her materials around her and sets to work again;* GREGERS *meanwhile regards her in silence.*]

GREGERS. Did the wild duck sleep well last night?

HEDVIG. Yes, I'm sure she did, thanks.

GREGERS [*turning toward the loft*]. It looks so very different by daylight than it did by moonlight.

HEDVIG. Yes, it can change so completely. In the morning it looks different from in the afternoon; and when it rains it's different from when it's clear.

GREGERS. Have you noticed that?

HEDVIG. Sure. You can't help it.

GREGERS. And do you like it in there with the wild duck, too?

HEDVIG. Yes, whenever I can be there—

GREGERS. But of course you don't have much free time; you do go to school, don't you?

HEDVIG. No, not any more. Daddy's afraid I'll hurt my eyes.

GREGERS. Oh. Then he reads to you himself.

HEDVIG.   Daddy's promised to read to me, but he hasn't found time for that yet.

GREGERS.   But isn't there anyone else to help you a little?

HEDVIG.   Sure, there's Mr. Molvik, but he isn't always exactly, really—well—

GREGERS.   He gets drunk, eh?

HEDVIG.   He *certainly* does.

GREGERS.   Well, then you do have time to yourself. And inside—I'll bet in there it's just like a world of its own—am I right?

HEDVIG.   Oh, completely! And then there are so many wonderful things.

GREGERS.   Really?

HEDVIG.   Yes, big cupboards with books in them; and lots of the books have pictures.

GREGERS.   Ah!

HEDVIG.   And then there's an old cabinet with drawers and compartments, and a huge clock with figures that are supposed to come out. But the clock doesn't go any more.

GREGERS.   Even time doesn't exist in there—with the wild duck.

HEDVIG.   Yes. And then there's an old watercolor set and things like that. And then all the books.

GREGERS.   And of course you read the books?

HEDVIG.   Oh yes, whenever I can. But they're mostly in English, and I don't understand that. But then I look at the pictures. There's one just enormous book called *Harryson's History of London;* it must be a hundred years old, and it's got ever so many pictures in it. At the front there's a picture of Death with an hourglass and a girl. I think that's horrible. But then there are all the other pictures of churches and castles and streets and great ships sailing on the ocean.

GREGERS.   But tell me, where did all these rare things come from!

HEDVIG.   Oh, an old sea captain lived here once, and he brought them home. They called him "the flying Dutchman"—and that's the strangest thing, because he wasn't a Dutchman at all.

GREGERS.   No?

HEDVIG.   No. But then he didn't come back finally, and he left all these things behind.

GREGERS.   Listen, tell me—when you sit in there and look at pictures, don't you ever want to go out and see the real world all for yourself?

HEDVIG.   No, never! I'm going to stay at home always and help Daddy and Mother.

GREGERS.   You mean finishing photographs?

HEDVIG.   No, not just that. Most of all, I'd like to learn how to engrave pictures like those in the English books.

GREGERS.   Hm. What does your father say to that?

HEDVIG.   I don't think he likes it. Daddy's so funny about such things. Just think, he talks about me learning basket-making and wickerwork! But I don't see anything in *that*.

GREGERS.   Oh no, I don't either.

HEDVIG.   But Daddy's right when he says that if I'd learned how to make baskets, I could have made the new basket for the wild duck.

GREGERS.   You could have, yes—and that really was up to you.

HEDVIG.   Yes, because it's *my* wild duck.

GREGERS.   Yes, of course it is.

HEDVIG.   Uh-huh, I own it. But Daddy and Grandpa can borrow it as much as they want.

GREGERS.   Oh? What do they do with it?

HEDVIG.   Oh, they look after it and build things for it and so on.

GREGERS.   I can well imagine. The wild duck rules supreme in there, doesn't she?

HEDVIG.   Yes, she does, and that's because she's a real wild bird. And then it's so sad for her; the poor thing has no one to turn to.

GREGERS.   No family, like the rabbits—

HEDVIG.   No. Even the chickens have all the others that they were baby chicks with, but she's so completely apart from any of her own. So you see, everything is so really mysterious about the wild duck. There's no one who knows her, and no one who knows where she's come from, either.

GREGERS.   And actually, she's been in the depths of the sea.

HEDVIG [*glances at him, suppresses a smile, and asks*].   Why did you say "depths of the sea"?

GREGERS.   What else should I say?

HEDVIG.   You could have said "bottom of the sea"—or "the ocean's bottom"?

GREGERS.   But couldn't I just as well say "depths of the sea"?

HEDVIG.   Sure. But to me it sounds so strange when someone else says "depths of the sea."

GREGERS.   But why? Tell me why?

HEDVIG.   No, I won't. It's something so stupid.

GREGERS.   It couldn't be. Now tell me why you smiled.

HEDVIG.   That was because always, when all of a sudden—in a flash—I happen to think of that in there, it always seems to me that the whole room and everything in it is called "the depths of the sea"! But that's all so stupid.

GREGERS.   Don't you dare say that.

HEDVIG.   Oh yes, because it's only an attic.

GREGERS.   Are you so sure of that?

HEDVIG [*astonished*].   That it's an attic!

GREGERS.   Yes. Do you know that for certain?

[HEDVIG, *speechless, stares at him open-mouthed.* GINA *enters from the kitchen with a tablecloth.*]

GREGERS [*getting up*].   I'm afraid I've come too early for you.

GINA.   Oh, you can find yourself a spot; it's almost ready now. Clear the table, Hedvig.

[HEDVIG *puts away the materials; during the following dialogue, she and* GINA *set the table.* GREGERS *settles in the armchair and pages through an album.*]

GREGERS.   I hear you can retouch photographs, Mrs. Ekdal.

GINA [*with a side-glance*].   Um-hm, so I can.

GREGERS.   That's really very lucky.

GINA.   Why "lucky"?

GREGERS.   With Hjalmar a photographer, I mean.

HEDVIG.   Mother can take pictures, too.

GINA. Oh yes, I even got lessons in that.

GREGERS. So we might say it's you who runs the business.

GINA. Yes, when my husband hasn't the time himself—

GREGERS. He finds himself so taken up with his old father, I suppose.

GINA. Yes, and then a man like Hjalmar shouldn't have to go snapping pictures of every Tom, Dick and Harry.

GREGERS. I agree; but once he's chosen this line of work, then—

GINA. Mr. Werle, you must realize that my husband is not just any old photographer.

GREGERS. Well, naturally; but even so—

[*A shot is fired in the loft.*]

GREGERS [*jumping up*]. What's that!

HEDVIG. They go hunting.

GREGERS. What! [*Going to the loft doorway.*] Have you gone hunting, Hjalmar?

HJALMAR [*behind the net*]. Are you here? I didn't realize; I was so occupied—[*To* HEDVIG.] And you, you didn't tell us. [*Comes into the studio.*]

GREGERS. Do you go shooting in the loft?

HJALMAR [*producing a double-barreled pistol*]. Oh, only with this here.

GINA. Yes, some day you and Grandfather'll have an accident with that there gun.

HJALMAR [*annoyed*]. I believe I've remarked that this type of firearm is called a pistol.

GINA. I don't see that that makes it any better.

GREGERS. So you've turned out a "hunter" as well, Hjalmar?

HJALMAR. Just a little rabbit hunt, now and then. It's mainly for Father's sake, you understand.

GINA. Men are so funny, really; they've always got to have their little diversities.

HJALMAR [*angrily*]. That's right, yes—they always have to have their little diversions.

GINA. Yes, that's just what I was saying.

HJALMAR. Oh, well! [*To* GREGERS.] So that's it, and then we're very lucky in the way the loft is placed—nobody can hear us when we're shooting. [*Puts the pistol on the highest bookshelf.*] Don't touch the pistol, Hedvig! One barrel's still loaded, don't forget.

GREGERS [*peering through the netting*]. You've got a hunting rifle too, I see.

HJALMAR. Yes, that's Father's old rifle. It won't shoot any more; something's gone wrong with the lock. But it's a lot of fun to have anyway, because we can take it all apart and clean it and grease it and put it together again— Of course, it's mostly Father who fools around with that sort of thing.

HEDVIG [*crossing to* GREGERS]. Now you can really see the wild duck.

GREGERS. I was just now looking at her. She seems to drag one wing a little.

HJALMAR. Well, no wonder; she took a bad wound.

GREGERS. And then she limps a little. Isn't that so?

HJALMAR. Maybe just a tiny bit.

HEDVIG. Yes, that was the foot the dog bit her in.

HJALMAR. But she hasn't a thing wrong with her otherwise; and that's simply remarkable when you think that she's had a charge of shot in her and been held by the teeth of a dog—

GREGERS [*with a glance at* HEDVIG]. And been in the depths of the sea—so long.

HEDVIG [*smiling*]. Yes.

GINA [*arranging the table*]. Oh, that sacred duck—there's fuss enough made over her.

HJALMAR. Hm. Are you nearly ready?

GINA. Yes, right away. Hedvig, now you can come and help me.

[GINA *and* HEDVIG *exit into the kitchen.*]

HJALMAR [*in an undertone*]. I don't think it's so good that you stand there, watching my father. He doesn't like it. [GREGERS *comes away from the loft doorway.*] And it's better, too, that I close up before the others come. [*Shooing away the menagerie with his hands.*] Hssh! Hssh! Go 'way now! [*With this he raises the curtain and draws the double doors together.*] I invented these contraptions myself. It's really great fun to have such things around to take care of and fix when they get out of whack. And besides, it's absolutely necessary, you know; Gina doesn't go for rabbits and chickens out here in the studio.

GREGERS. Of course not. And I suppose it *is* your wife who manages here?

HJALMAR. My general rule is to delegate the routine matters to her, and that leaves me free to retire to the living room to think over more important things.

GREGERS. And what sort of things are these, Hjalmar?

HJALMAR. I've been wondering why you haven't asked me that before. Or maybe you haven't heard about my invention.

GREGERS. Invention? No.

HJALMAR. Oh? Then you haven't? Well, no, up there in that waste and wilderness—

GREGERS. Then you've really invented something!

HJALMAR. Not completely invented it yet, but I'm getting very close. You must realize that when I decided to dedicate my life to photography, it wasn't my idea to spend time taking pictures of a lot of nobodies.

GREGERS. Yes, that's what your wife was just now saying.

HJALMAR. I swore that if I devoted my powers to the craft, I would then exalt it to such heights that it would become both an art and a science. That's when I decided on this amazing invention.

GREGERS. And what does this invention consist of? What's its purpose?

HJALMAR. Yes, Gregers, you mustn't ask for details like that yet. It takes time, you know. And you mustn't think it's vanity that's driving me, either. I'm certainly not working for myself. Oh no, it's my life's work that stands before me day and night.

GREGERS. What life's work is that?

HJALMAR. Remember the silver-haired old man?

GREGERS. Your poor father. Yes, but actually what can you do for him?

HJALMAR. I can raise his self-respect from the dead—by restoring the Ekdal name to dignity and honor.

GREGERS. So that's your life's work.

HJALMAR. Yes. I am going to rescue that shipwrecked man. That's just what he suffered—shipwreck—when the storm broke over him. When all those harrowing investigations took place, he wasn't himself anymore. That pistol, there—the one we use to shoot rabbits with—it's played a part in the tragedy of the Ekdals.

GREGERS. Pistol! Oh?

HJALMAR. When he was sentenced and facing prison, he had that pistol in his hand—

GREGERS. You mean he—!

HJALMAR. Yes. But he didn't dare. He was a coward. That shows how broken and degraded he'd become by then. Can you picture it? He, a soldier, a man who'd shot nine bears and was directly descended from two lieutenant colonels—I mean, one after the other, of course. Can you picture it, Gregers?

GREGERS. Yes, I can picture it very well.

HJALMAR. Well, I can't. And then that pistol intruded on our family history once again. When he was under lock and key, dressed like a common prisoner—oh, those were agonizing times for me, you can imagine. I kept the shades of both my windows drawn. When I looked out, I saw the sun shining the same as ever. I couldn't understand it. I saw the people going along the street, laughing and talking of trivial things. I couldn't understand it. I felt all creation should be standing still, like during an eclipse.

GREGERS. I felt that way when my mother died.

HJALMAR. During one of those times Hjalmar Ekdal put a pistol to his own breast.

GREGERS. You were thinking of—

HJALMAR. Yes.

GREGERS. But you didn't shoot?

HJALMAR. No. In that critical moment I won a victory over myself. I stayed alive. But you can bet it takes courage to choose life in those circumstances.

GREGERS. Well, that depends on your point of view.

HJALMAR. Oh, absolutely. But it was all for the best, because now I've nearly finished my invention; and then Dr. Relling thinks, just as I do, that they'll let Father wear his uniform again. That's the only reward I'm after.

GREGERS. So it's really the uniform that he—?

HJALMAR. Yes, that's what he really hungers and craves for. You've no idea how that makes my heart ache. Every time we throw a little family party—like my birthday, or Gina's, or whatever—then the old man comes in, wearing that uniform from his happier days. But if there's even a knock at the door, he goes scuttering back in his room fast as the old legs will carry him. You see, he doesn't dare show himself to strangers. What a heartrending spectacle for a son!

GREGERS. Approximately when do you think the invention will be finished?

HJALMAR. Oh, good Lord, don't hold me to a timetable. An invention, that's something you can hardly dictate to. It depends a great deal on inspiration, on a sudden insight—and it's nearly impossible to say in advance when that will occur.

GREGERS.   But it *is* making progress?

HJALMAR.   Of course it's making progress. Every single day I think about my invention. I'm brimming with it. Every afternoon, right after lunch, I lock myself in the living room where I can meditate in peace. But it's no use driving me; it simply won't work. Relling says so too.

GREGERS.   And you don't think all those contraptions in the loft distract you and scatter your talents?

HJALMAR.   No, no, no, on the contrary. You mustn't say that. I can't always go around here, brooding over the same nerve-racking problems. I need some diversion to fill in the time. You see, inspiration, the moment of insight—when that comes, nothing can stop it.

GREGERS.   My dear Hjalmar, I suspect you've got a bit of the wild duck in you.

HJALMAR.   Of the wild duck? What do you mean?

GREGERS.   You've plunged to the bottom and clamped hold of the seaweed.

HJALMAR.   I suppose you mean that near-fatal shot that brought down Father—and me as well?

GREGERS.   Not quite that. I wouldn't say you're wounded; but you're wandering in a poisonous swamp, Hjalmar. You've got an insidious disease in your system, and so you've gone to the bottom to die in the dark.

HJALMAR.   Me? Die in the dark! You know what, Gregers—you'll really have to stop that talk.

GREGERS.   But never mind. I'm going to raise you up again. You know, I've found my purpose in life, too. I found it yesterday.

HJALMAR.   Yes, that may well be; but you can just leave me out of it. I can assure you that—apart from my quite understandable melancholy—I'm as well off as any man could wish to be.

GREGERS.   And your thinking so is part of the sickness.

HJALMAR.   Gregers, you're my old friend—please—don't talk any more about sickness and poison. I'm not used to that kind of conversation. In my house nobody talks to me about ugly things.

GREGERS.   That's not hard to believe.

HJALMAR.   Yes, because it isn't good for me. And there's no swamp air here, as you put it. In a poor photographer's house, life is cramped; I know that. My lot is a poor one—but, you know, I'm an inventor. And I'm the family breadwinner, too. *That's* what sustains me through all the pettiness. Ah, here they come with the lunch.

[GINA *and* HEDVIG *bring in bottles of beer, a decanter of brandy, glasses, and the like. At the same time,* RELLING *and* MOLVIK *enter from the hall.*
     Neither wears a hat or overcoat; MOLVIK *is dressed in black.*]

GINA [*setting things down on the table*].   Well, the two of them—right on time.

RELLING.   Molvik was positive he could smell that herring salad, and there was just no holding him back. 'Morning for the second time, Ekdal.

HJALMAR.   Gregers, I'd like you to meet Mr. Molvik. And Dr.—ah, but don't you know Relling?

GREGERS.   Yes, slightly.

RELLING.   Well, Mr. Werle junior. Yes, we've had a few run-ins together up at the Hoidal works. You've just moved in, haven't you?

GREGERS. I moved in this morning.

RELLING. And Molvik and I live downstairs; so you're not very far from a doctor and a priest, if you ever have need of such.

GREGERS. Thanks; that could happen. After all, we had thirteen at the table last night.

HJALMAR. Oh, don't start in on ugly subjects again!

RELLING. You don't have to worry, Hjalmar; Lord knows this doesn't involve you.

HJALMAR. I hope not, for my family's sake. But let's sit down and eat and drink and be merry.

GREGERS. Shouldn't we wait for your father?

HJALMAR. No, he'll have his lunch sent in to him later. Come now!

[*The men sit at the table, eating and drinking.* GINA *and* HEDVIG *go in and out, serving the food.*]

RELLING. Last night Molvik was tight as a tick, Mrs. Ekdal.

GINA. Oh? Last night again?

RELLING. Didn't you hear him when I finally brought him home?

GINA. No, can't say I did.

RELLING. That's lucky—because Molvik was revolting last night.

GINA. Is that so, Molvik?

MOLVIK. Let's draw a veil over last night's activities. They have no bearing on my better self.

RELLING [*to* GREGERS]. All of a sudden he's possessed by an impulse; and then I have to take him out on a bat. You see, Mr. Molvik is demonic.

GREGERS. Demonic?

RELLING. Molvik is demonic, yes.

GREGERS. Hm.

RELLING. And demonic natures aren't made to go through life on the straight and narrow; they've got to take detours every so often. Well—and you're still sticking it out there at that dark, hideous mill.

GREGERS. I've stuck it out till now.

RELLING. And did you ever collect on that "summons" you were going around with?

GREGERS. Summons? [*Understanding him.*] Oh, that.

HJALMAR. Were you serving summonses, Gregers?

GREGERS. Nonsense.

RELLING. Oh, but he was, definitely. He was going around to all the farms and cabins with copies of something he called "Summons to the Ideal."

GREGERS. I was young then.

RELLING. You're right, there. You were very young. And that summons to the ideal—it wasn't ever honored during my time up there.

GREGERS. Nor later, either.

RELLING. Well, I guess you've learned enough to cut down your expectations a bit.

GREGERS. Never—when I meet a man who's a real man.

HJALMAR. Yes, that seems quite reasonable to me. A little butter, Gina.

RELLING. And then a piece of pork for Molvik.

MOLVIK. Ugh, no pork!

[*There is a knock at the loft door.*]

HJALMAR. Open it, Hedvig; Father wants to get out.

[HEDVIG *goes to open the door a little; old* EKDAL *enters with a fresh rabbit skin. He closes the door after him.*]

EKDAL. Good morning, gentlemen. Good hunting today. Shot a big one.

HJALMAR. And you went ahead and skinned it without waiting for me!

EKDAL. Salted it, too. It's nice tender meat, this rabbit meat. And it's so sweet. Tastes like sugar. Enjoy your food, gentlemen! [*He goes into his room.*]

MOLVIK [*getting up*]. Pardon—I, I can't—got to go downstairs right—

RELLING. Drink soda water, man!

MOLVIK [*rushing out the hall door*]. Ugh—ugh!

RELLING [*to* HJALMAR]. Let's empty a glass to the old hunter.

HJALMAR [*clinking glasses with him*]. Yes, to the gallant sportsman on the brink of the grave.

RELLING. To the old, gray-haired— [*Drinks.*] Tell me something, is it gray hair he's got, or is it white?

HJALMAR. It's really a little of both. But as a matter of fact, he's scarcely got a hair on his head.

RELLING. Well, fake hair will take you through life, good as any. You know, Ekdal, you're really a very lucky man. You have your high mission in life to fight for—

HJALMAR. And I am fighting for it, too.

RELLING. And then you've got this clever wife of yours, padding around in her slippers and waggling her hips and keeping you neat and cozy.

HJALMAR. Yes, Gina—[*nodding at her*] you're a good companion for life's journey, you are.

GINA. Oh, don't sit there deprecating me.

RELLING. And what about your Hedvig, Ekdal?

HJALMAR [*stirred*]. My child, yes! My child above all. Hedvig, come here to me. [*Caresses her head.*] What day is tomorrow, dear?

HEDVIG [*shaking him*]. Oh, don't talk about it, Daddy!

HJALMAR. It's like a knife turning in my heart when I think how bare it's all going to be, just the tiniest celebration out in the loft—

HEDVIG. Oh, but that will be just wonderful!

RELLING. And wait till that marvelous invention comes to the world, Hedvig!

HJALMAR. Ah, yes—then you'll see! Hedvig, I've resolved to make your future secure. As long as you live, you'll live in style. I'll assure you of something, one way or another. That will be the poor inventor's sole reward.

HEDVIG [*whispering with her arms around his neck*]. Oh, you dear, dear Daddy!

RELLING [*to* GREGERS]. Well, now, isn't it good for a change to be sitting around a well-spread table in a happy family circle?

HJALMAR. Yes, I really prize these hours around the table.

GREGERS. I, for my part, don't thrive in marsh gas.

RELLING. Marsh gas?

HJALMAR. Oh, don't start that rubbish again!

GINA. Lord knows there isn't any marsh gas here, Mr. Werle; every blessed day I air the place out.

GREGERS [*leaving the table*]. You can't air out the stench I mean.

HJALMAR. Stench!

GINA. What about that, Hjalmar!

RELLING. Beg pardon—but it wouldn't be you who brought that stench in with you from the mines up there?

GREGERS. It's just like you to call what I'm bringing into this house a stench.

RELLING [crossing over to him]. Listen, Mr. Werle junior, I've got a strong suspicion that you're still going around with the uncut version of that "Summons to the Ideal" in your back pocket.

GREGERS. I've got it written in my heart.

RELLING. I don't care where the devil you've got it; I wouldn't advise you to play process-server here as long as I'm around.

GREGERS. And what if I do anyway?

RELLING. Then you'll go head first down the stairs, that's what.

HJALMAR [getting up]. Come, now, Relling!

GREGERS. Yes, just throw me out—

GINA [coming between them]. You can't do that, Relling. But I'll tell you this, Mr. Werle—that you, who made all that mess with your stove, have no right to come to me talking about smells.

[A knock at the hall door.]

HEDVIG. Mother, somebody's knocking.

GINA. I'll go—[She crosses and opens the door, gives a start, shudders and shrinks back.] Uff! Oh no!

[Old WERLE, in a fur coat, steps into the room.]

WERLE. Excuse me, but I think my son is living in this house.

GINA [catching her breath]. Yes.

HJALMAR [coming closer]. If Mr. Werle will be so good as to—

WERLE. Thanks, I'd just like to talk with my son.

GREGERS. Yes, why not? Here I am.

WERLE. I'd like to talk with you in your room.

GREGERS. In my room—fine—[Starts in.]

GINA. No. Good Lord, that's in no condition for—

WERLE. Well, out in the hall, then. This is just between us.

HJALMAR. You can talk here, Mr. Werle. Come into the living room, Relling.

[HJALMAR and RELLING go out to the right; GINA takes HEDVIG with her into the kitchen.]

GREGERS [after a brief interval]. Well, now it's just the two of us.

WERLE. You dropped a few remarks last night—And since you've now taken a room with the Ekdals, I must assume that you're planning something or other against me.

GREGERS. I'm planning to open Hjalmar Ekdal's eyes. He's going to see his situation just as it is—that's all.

WERLE. Is that the mission in life you talked about yesterday?

GREGERS. Yes. You haven't left me any other.

WERLE. Am I the one that spoiled your mind, Gregers?

GREGERS. You've spoiled my entire life. I'm not thinking of all that with Mother. But you're the one I can thank for my going around, whipped and driven by this guilt-ridden conscience.

WERLE. Ah, it's your conscience that's gone bad.

GREGERS. I should have taken a stand against you when the trap was laid for Lieutenant Ekdal. I should have warned him, for I had a pretty good idea what was coming off.

WERLE.   Yes, you really should have spoken up then.

GREGERS.   I didn't dare; I was so cowed and frightened. I was unspeakably afraid of you—both then and for a long time after.

WERLE.   That fright seems to be over now.

GREGERS.   It is, luckily. The harm done to old Ekdal, both by me and—others, can never be undone; but Hjalmar I can free from all the lies and evasions that are smothering him here.

WERLE.   You believe you'd be doing him good by that?

GREGERS.   That's what I believe.

WERLE.   Maybe you think Ekdal's the kind of man who'll thank you for that friendly service?

GREGERS.   Yes! He *is* that kind of man.

WERLE.   Hmm—we'll see.

GREGERS.   And besides—if I'm ever to go on living, I'll have to find a cure for my sick conscience.

WERLE.   It'll never be sound. Your conscience has been sickly from childhood. It's an inheritance from your mother, Gregers—the only inheritance she left you.

GREGERS [*with a wry half-smile*].   You've never been able to accept the fact, have you, that you calculated wrong when you thought she'd bring you a fortune?

WERLE.   Let's not get lost in irrelevancies. Then you're still intent on this goal of putting Ekdal on what you suppose is the right track?

GREGERS.   Yes, I'm intent on that.

WERLE.   Well, then I could have saved myself the walk up here. For there's no point in asking if you'll move back home with me?

GREGERS.   No.

WERLE.   And you won't come into the business either?

GREGERS.   No.

WERLE.   Very well. But since I'm now planning a second marriage, the estate, of course, will be divided between us.

GREGERS [*quickly*].   No, I don't want that.

WERLE.   You don't want it?

GREGERS.   No, I wouldn't dare, for the sake of my conscience.

WERLE [*after a pause*].   You going back to the works again?

GREGERS.   No. I consider that I've retired from your service.

WERLE.   But what are you going to do, then?

GREGERS.   Simply carry out my life's mission; nothing else.

WERLE.   Yes, but afterwards? What will you live on?

GREGERS.   I have some of my salary put aside.

WERLE.   Yes, that won't last long!

GREGERS.   I think it will last my time.

WERLE.   What do you mean by that?

GREGERS.   I'm not answering any more.

WERLE.   Good-bye then, Gregers.

GREGERS.   Good-bye.

[Old WERLE *goes out.*]

HJALMAR [*peering out*].   Has he gone?

GREGERS. Yes.

[HJALMAR *and* RELLING *come in.* GINA *and* HEDVIG *also return from the
kitchen.*]

RELLING. There's one lunch gone to the dogs.

GREGERS. Put your things on, Hjalmar; you've got to take a long walk
with me.

HJALMAR. Yes, gladly. What did your father want? Was it anything to
do with me?

GREGERS. Just come. We have some things to talk over. I'll go and get my
coat. [*He leaves by the hall door.*]

GINA. You mustn't go out with him, Hjalmar.

RELLING. No, don't go. Stay where you are.

HJALMAR [*getting his hat and overcoat*]. But why? When a childhood
friend feels a need to open his mind to me in private—

RELLING. But damn it all! Can't you see the man's mad, crazy, out of his
skull!

GINA. Yes, that's the truth, if you'd listen. His mother, off and on, had
those same conniption fits.

HJALMAR. That's just why he needs a friend's watchful eye on him. [*To*
GINA.] Be sure dinner's ready in plenty of time. See you later. [*Goes out the
hall door.*]

RELLING. It's really a shame that fellow didn't go straight to hell down
one of the Hoidal mines.

GINA. Mercy—why do you say that?

RELLING [*muttering*]. Oh, I've got my reasons.

GINA. Do you think Gregers Werle is really crazy?

RELLING. No, worse luck. He's no crazier than most people. But he's got
a disease in his system all the same.

GINA. What is it that's wrong with him?

RELLING. All right, I'll tell you, Mrs. Ekdal. He's suffering from an acute
case of moralistic fever.

GINA. Moralistic fever?

HEDVIG. Is that a kind of disease?

RELLING. Oh yes, it's a national disease, but it only breaks out now and
then. [*Nodding to* GINA.] Thanks for lunch. [*He goes out through the hall
door.*]

GINA [*walking restlessly around the room*]. Ugh, that Gregers Werle—
he was always a cold fish.

HEDVIG [*standing by the table, looking searchingly at her*]. This is all
so strange to me.

ACT IV

HJALMAR EKDAL's *studio. A photograph has just been taken; a portrait
camera covered with a cloth, a stand, a couple of chairs, a console table, among
other things, stand well out in the room. Late afternoon light; it is near sunset;
somewhat later it begins to grow dark.*

GINA *is standing in the hall doorway with a plate-holder and a wet photographic plate in her hand, talking with someone outside.*

GINA.   Yes, that's definite. When I promise something, I keep my word. On Monday the first dozen will be ready. Good-bye. Good-bye. [*Footsteps are heard descending the stairs.* GINA *closes the door, puts the plate into the holder, and slips both back into the covered camera.*]

HEDVIG [*coming in from the kitchen*].   Are they gone?

GINA [*tidying up*].   Yes, thank goodness, at last I'm rid of them.

HEDVIG.   But why do you suppose Daddy isn't home yet?

GINA.   Are you sure he's not below with Relling?

HEDVIG.   No, he's not there. I ran down the back stairs just now and asked.

GINA.   And his dinner's standing and getting cold, too.

HEDVIG.   Just imagine—Daddy's always sure to be on time for dinner.

GINA.   Oh, he'll be right along, you'll see.

HEDVIG.   Oh, I wish he would come! Everything's so funny around here.

GINA [*calling out*].   There he is!

[HJALMAR *comes in by the hall door.*]

HEDVIG [*running toward him*].   Daddy! Oh, we've waited ages for you!

GINA [*eyeing him*].   You've been out pretty long, Hjalmar.

HJALMAR [*without looking at her*].   I've been a while, yes. [*He takes off his overcoat.* GINA *and* HEDVIG *start to help him; he waves them away.*]

GINA.   Did you eat with Werle, maybe?

HJALMAR [*hanging his coat up*].   No.

GINA [*going toward the kitchen*].   I'll bring your dinner in, then.

HJALMAR.   No, the dinner can wait. I don't want to eat now.

HEDVIG [*coming closer*].   Don't you feel well, Daddy?

HJALMAR.   Well? Oh yes, well enough. We had an exhausting walk, Gregers and I.

GINA.   You shouldn't do that, Hjalmar; you're not used to it.

HJALMAR.   Hm. There are a lot of things a man's got to get used to in this world. [*Walking about the room a bit.*] Did anyone come while I was out?

GINA.   No one but that engaged couple.

HJALMAR.   No new orders?

GINA.   No, not today.

HEDVIG.   You'll see, there'll be some tomorrow, Daddy.

HJALMAR.   I certainly hope so, because tomorrow I'm going to throw myself into my work—completely.

HEDVIG.   Tomorrow! But don't you remember what day tomorrow is?

HJALMAR.   Oh yes, that's right. Well, the day after tomorrow, then. From now on, I'm doing everything myself; I just want to be left alone with all the work.

GINA.   But Hjalmar, what's the point of that? It'll only make your life miserable. Let me handle the photographing, and then you'll be free to work on the invention.

HEDVIG.   And free for the wild duck, Daddy—and for all the chickens and rabbits—

HJALMAR.   Don't talk to me about that rubbish! Starting tomorrow I shall never again set foot in that loft.

HEDVIG. Yes, but Daddy, you promised me tomorrow there'd be a celebration.

HJALMAR. Hm, that's true. Well, the day after, then. That infernal wild duck—I'd almost like to wring its neck!

HEDVIG [*crying out*]. The wild duck!

GINA. What an idea!

HEDVIG [*shaking him*]. Yes, but Daddy—it's my wild duck!

HJALMAR. That's why I won't do it. I haven't the heart—for your sake, Hedvig, I haven't the heart. But deep inside me I feel I ought to. I shouldn't tolerate under my roof a creature that's been in that man's hands.

GINA. My goodness, just because Grandfather got her from that worthless Pettersen—

HJALMAR [*pacing the floor*]. There are certain standards—what should I call them—ideal standards, let's say—certain claims on us that a man can't put aside without damaging his soul.

HEDVIG [*following him*]. But think—the wild duck—the poor wild duck!

HJALMAR [*stopping*]. You heard me say I'd spare it—for your sake. It won't be hurt, not a hair on its—well, anyway, I'll spare it. There are more important matters to settle. But Hedvig, now you better get out for your afternoon walk; it's already pretty dark for you.

HEDVIG. No, I don't want to go out now.

HJALMAR. Yes, go on. You seem to be blinking your eyes so. All these fumes in here aren't good for you; the air here under this roof is bad.

HEDVIG. All right, then, I'll run down the back stairs and take a little walk. My coat and hat? Oh, they're in my room. Daddy—promise you won't hurt the wild duck while I'm out.

HJALMAR. There won't be a feather ruffled on its head. [*Drawing her to him.*] You and I, Hedvig—we two! Now run along, dear.

[HEDVIG *nods to her parents and goes out through the kitchen.*]

HJALMAR [*walking around without looking up*]. Gina.

GINA. Yes?

HJALMAR. From tomorrow on—or let's say the day after tomorrow—I'd prefer to keep the household accounts myself.

GINA. You want to keep the household accounts, too?

HJALMAR. Yes, or budget the income, in any case.

GINA. Lord love us, there's nothing to that.

HJALMAR. One wouldn't think so. It seems to me you can make our money stretch remarkably far. [*Stopping and looking at her.*] How *is* that?

GINA. Hedvig and I, we don't need much.

HJALMAR. Is it true that Father gets such good pay for the copying he does for Werle?

GINA. I don't know how good it is. I don't know rates for such things.

HJALMAR. Well, what does he get, just roughly? Tell me!

GINA. It's never the same. I suppose it's roughly what he costs us, with a little pocket money thrown in.

HJALMAR. What he costs us! That's something you've never told me before!

GINA. No, I never could. You were always so happy thinking he got everything from you.

HJALMAR.   And instead it comes from Mr. Werle.

GINA.   Oh, but he's got plenty to spare, that one.

HJALMAR.   Let's have the lamp lit!

GINA [*lighting it*].   And then we can't know if it really is the old man; it could well be Graaberg—

HJALMAR.   Why try to put me off with Graaberg?

GINA.   No, I don't know. I just thought—

HJALMAR.   Hm!

GINA.   You know it wasn't me that got Grandfather the copying. It was Berta, that time she came here.

HJALMAR.   Your voice sounds so shaky.

GINA [*putting the shade on the lamp*].   It does?

HJALMAR.   And then your hands are trembling. Or aren't they?

GINA [*firmly*].   Say it straight out, Hjalmar. What is it he's gone and said about me?

HJALMAR.   Is it true—can it possibly be that—that there was some kind of involvement between you and Mr. Werle while you were in service there?

GINA.   That's not true. Not then, there wasn't. Werle was after me, all right. And his wife thought there was something to it, and she made a big fuss and bother, and she roasted me coming and going, she did—so I quit.

HJALMAR.   But then what!

GINA.   Yes, so then I went home. And Mother—well, she wasn't all you took her to be, Hjalmar; she ran on telling me one thing and another, because Werle was a widower by then.

HJALMAR.   Yes. And then!

GINA.   Well, you might as well know it all. He didn't give up till he had his way.

HJALMAR [*with a clap of his hands*].   And this is the mother of my child! How could you keep that hidden from me!

GINA.   Yes, I did the wrong thing; I really should have told you long ago.

HJALMAR.   Right at the start, you mean—so I could have known what sort you are.

GINA.   But would you have married me anyway?

HJALMAR.   How can you think that?

GINA.   No. But that's why I didn't dare say anything then. Because I'd come to be so terribly in love with you, as you know. And then how could I make myself utterly miserable—

HJALMAR [*walking about*].   And this is my Hedvig's mother! And then to know that everything I see around me—[*kicking at a table*] my whole home —I owe to a favored predecessor. Ah, that charmer Werle!

GINA.   Do you regret the fourteen, fifteen years we've lived together?

HJALMAR [*stopping in front of her*].   Tell me—don't you every day, every hour, regret this spider web of deception you've spun around me? Answer me that! Don't you really go around in a torment of remorse?

GINA.   Hjalmar dear, I've got so much to think about just with the housework and the day's routine—

HJALMAR.   Then you never turn a critical eye on your past!

GINA.   No. Good Lord, I'd almost forgotten that old affair.

HJALMAR.   Oh, this dull, unfeeling content! To me there's something outrageous about it. Just think—not one regret!

GINA.   But Hjalmar, tell me now—what would have happened to you if you hadn't found a wife like me?

HJALMAR.   Like you—!

GINA.   Yes, because I've always been a bit more hard-headed and resourceful than you. Well, of course I'm a couple of years older.

HJALMAR.   What would have happened to me?

GINA.   You were pretty bad off at the time you met me; you can't deny that.

HJALMAR.   "Pretty bad off" you call it. Oh, you have no idea what a man goes through when he's deep in misery and despair—especially a man of my fiery temperament.

GINA.   No, that may be. And I shouldn't say nothing about it, either, because you turned out such a good-hearted husband as soon as you got a house and home—and now we've made it so snug and cozy here, and pretty soon both Hedvig and I could begin spending a little on food and clothes.

HJALMAR.   In the swamp of deception, yes.

GINA.   Ugh, that disgusting creature, tracking his way through our house!

HJALMAR.   I also thought this home was a good place to be. That was a pipe dream. Now where can I find the buoyancy I need to carry my invention into reality? Maybe it'll die with me; and then it'll be your past, Gina, that killed it.

GINA [close to tears].   No, you mustn't ever say such things, Hjalmar. All my days I've only wanted to do what's best for you!

HJALMAR.   I wonder—what happens now to the breadwinner's dream? When I lay in there on the sofa pondering my invention, I had a hunch it would drain my last bit of strength. I sensed that the day I took the patent in my hand—that would be the day of—departure. And it was my dream that then you would go on as the departed inventor's prosperous widow.

GINA [drying her eyes].   No, don't say that, Hjalmar. Lord knows I never want to see the day I'm a widow.

HJALMAR.   Oh, what does it matter? Everything's over and done with now. Everything!

[GREGERS cautiously opens the hall door and looks in.]

GREGERS.   May I come in?

HJALMAR.   Yes, do.

GREGERS [advancing with a beaming countenance, hands outstretched as if to take theirs].   Now, you dear people—! [Looks from one to the other, then whispers to HJALMAR.] But isn't it done, then?

HJALMAR [resoundingly].   It's done.

GREGERS.   It is?

HJALMAR.   I've just known the bitterest hour of my life.

GREGERS.   But also the most exalted, I think.

HJALMAR.   Well, anyway, it's off our hands for the moment.

GINA.   God forgive you, Mr. Werle.

GREGERS [with great surprise].   But I don't understand this.

HJALMAR.   What don't you understand?

GREGERS. With this great rapport—the kind that forges a whole new way of life—a life, a companionship in truth with no more deception—

HJALMAR. Yes, I know, I know all that.

GREGERS. I was really positive that when I came through that door I'd be met by a transfigured light in both your faces. And what do I see instead but this gloomy, heavy, dismal—

GINA. How true. [*She removes the lampshade.*]

GREGERS. You don't want to understand me, Mrs. Ekdal. No, no, you'll need time— But you yourself, Hjalmar? You must have gained a sense of high purpose out of this great unburdening.

HJALMAR. Yes, naturally. That is—more or less.

GREGERS. Because there's nothing in the world that compares with showing mercy to a sinner and lifting her up in the arms of love.

HJALMAR. Do you think a man can recover so easily from the bitter cup I've just emptied!

GREGERS. Not an ordinary man, no. But a man like you—!

HJALMAR. Good Lord, yes, I know that. But you mustn't be driving me, Gregers. You see, these things take time.

GREGERS. You've *lots* of the wild duck in you, Hjalmar.

[RELLING *has entered through the hall door.*]

RELLING. Aha! The wild duck's flying again, eh?

HJALMAR. Yes, the wounded trophy of old Werle's hunt.

RELLING. Old Werle? Is it him you're talking about?

HJALMAR. Him and—all of us.

RELLING [*under his breath to* GREGERS]. The devil take you!

HJALMAR. What'd you say?

RELLING. I merely expressed my heartfelt desire that this quack would cut out for home. If he stays here, he's just the man to ruin you both.

GREGERS. They won't be ruined, Mr. Relling. Regarding Hjalmar, I'll say nothing. We know him. But she, too, surely, in the depths of her being, has something authentic, something sincere.

GINA [*near tears*]. Well, if I *was* that, why didn't you leave me alone?

RELLING [*to* GREGERS]. Would it be nosy to ask what you're really trying to do in this house?

GREGERS. I want to establish a true marriage.

RELLING. Then you don't think Ekdal's marriage is good enough as it is?

GREGERS. It's about as good a marriage as most, unfortunately. But it isn't yet a *true* marriage.

HJALMAR. You don't believe in ideals in life, Relling.

RELLING. Nonsense, sonny boy! Excuse me, Mr. Werle, but how many—in round numbers—how many "true marriages" have you seen in your time?

GREGERS. I believe I've hardly seen a single one.

RELLING. And I likewise.

GREGERS. But I've seen innumerable marriages of the opposite kind. And I've had a chance to see at close range what such a marriage can destroy in two people.

HJALMAR. A man's whole moral foundation can crumble under his feet; that's the dreadful thing.

RELLING. Well, I've never really exactly been married, so I'm no judge of these things. But I do know this, that the child is part of the marriage too. And you've got to leave the child in peace.

HJALMAR. Ah, Hedvig! My poor Hedvig!

RELLING. Yes, you'll please see that Hedvig's left out of it. You're both grown people; you're free, God knows, to slop up your private lives all you want. But I tell you, you've got to be careful with Hedvig, or else you might do her some serious harm.

HJALMAR. Harm!

RELLING. Yes, or she could do harm to herself—and possibly others as well.

GINA. But how can you know that, Relling?

HJALMAR. There's no immediate threat to her eyes, is there?

RELLING. This has nothing to do with her eyes. Hedvig's arrived at a difficult age. She's open to all kinds of erratic ideas.

GINA. You know—she is at that! She's begun to fool around something awful with the fire in the kitchen stove. She calls it playing house afire. I'm often scared she *will* set the house on fire.

RELLING. See what I mean? I knew it.

GREGERS [*to* RELLING]. But how do you explain something like that?

RELLING [*brusquely*]. Her voice is changing, junior.

HJALMAR. As long as the child has *me*! As long as I'm above the sod.

[*A knock is heard at the door.*]

GINA. Shh, Hjalmar, someone's in the hall. [*Calling out.*] Come on in!

[MRS. SØRBY, *wearing street clothes, enters.*]

MRS. SØRBY. Good evening!

GINA [*going toward her*]. Is it you, Berta!

MRS. SØRBY. Oh yes, it's me. But perhaps I came at an awkward time?

HJALMAR. Oh, not at all; a messenger from *that* house—

MRS. SØRBY [*to* GINA]. As a matter of fact, I'd hoped that I wouldn't find your menfolk in at this hour, so I ran over just to have a word with you and say good-bye.

GINA. Oh? Are you going away?

MRS. SØRBY. Yes, tomorrow, early—up to Hoidal. Mr. Werle left this afternoon. [*Casually to* GREGERS.] He sends his regards.

GINA. Just think!

HJALMAR. So Mr. Werle has left? And you're following him?

MRS. SØRBY. Yes, what do you say to that, Ekdal?

HJALMAR. I say watch out.

GREGERS. Let me explain. My father is marrying Mrs. Sørby.

HJALMAR. He's marrying her!

GINA. Oh, Berta, it's come at last!

RELLING [*his voice quavering slightly*]. This really can't be true.

MRS. SØRBY. Yes, my dear Relling, it's completely true.

RELLING. You want to marry again?

MRS. SØRBY. Yes, so it seems. Werle has gotten a special license, and we're going to have a very quiet wedding up at the works.

GREGERS. So I ought to wish you happiness, like a good stepson.

MRS. SØRBY. Thank you, if you really mean it. I'm hoping it will bring us happiness, both Werle and me.

RELLING. That's a reasonable hope. Mr. Werle never gets drunk—as far as *I* know; and he's certainly not given to beating up his wives the way the late horse doctor did.

MRS. SØRBY.   Oh, now let Sørby rest in peace. He did have some worthy traits, you know.

RELLING.   Old Werle's traits are worth rather more, I'll bet.

MRS. SØRBY.   At least he hasn't wasted the best that's in him. Any man who does *that* has to take the consequences.

RELLING.   Tonight I'm going out with Molvik.

MRS. SØRBY.   You shouldn't, Relling. Don't do it—for my sake.

RELLING.   What else is left? [*To* HJALMAR.] If you'd care to, you could come too.

GINA.   No, thanks. Hjalmar never goes dissipating.

HJALMAR [*in an angry undertone*].   Can't you keep quiet!

RELLING.   Good-bye, Mrs.—Werle. [*He goes out the hall door.*]

GREGERS [*to* MRS SØRBY].   It would seem that you and Dr. Relling know each other quite intimately.

MRS. SØRBY.   Yes, we've known each other for many years. At one time something might have developed between us.

GREGERS.   It was certainly lucky for you that it didn't.

MRS. SØRBY.   Yes, that's true enough. But I've always been wary of following my impulses. After all, a woman can't just throw herself away.

GREGERS.   Aren't you even a little bit afraid that I'll drop my father a hint about this old friendship?

MRS. SØRBY.   You can be sure I've told him myself.

GREGERS.   Oh?

MRS. SØRBY.   Your father knows every last scrap of gossip that holds any grain of truth about me. I told him all of those things; it was the first thing I did when he made his intentions clear.

GREGERS.   Then I think you're more frank than most people.

MRS. SØRBY.   I've always been frank. In the long run, it's the best thing for us women to be.

HJALMAR.   What do you say to that, Gina?

GINA.   Oh, women are all so different. Some live one way and some live another.

MRS. SØRBY.   Well, Gina, I do think it's wisest to handle things as I have. And Werle, for his part, hasn't held back anything either. Really, it's this that's brought us so close together. Now he can sit and talk to me as freely as a child. He's never had that chance before. He, a healthy, vigorous man, had to spend his whole youth and all his best years hearing nothing but sermons on his sins. And generally those sermons were aimed at the most imaginary failings—at least from what *I* could see.

GINA.   Yes, that's just as true as you say.

GREGERS.   If you women are going to explore this subject, I'd better leave.

MRS. SØRBY.   You can just as well stay, for that matter; I won't say another word. But I did want you to understand that I haven't done anything sly or in any way underhanded. I suppose it looks like I've had quite a nice piece of luck, and that's true enough, up to a point. But, anyway, what I mean is that I'll not be taking any more than I give. One thing I'll never do is desert him.

And I can be useful to him and care for him now better than anyone else after he's helpless.

HJALMAR.   After he's helpless?

GREGERS [to MRS. SØRBY].   All right, don't talk about that here.

MRS. SØRBY.   No need to hide it any longer, much as he'd like to. He's going blind.

HJALMAR [astounded].   He's going blind? But that's peculiar. Is he going blind too?

GINA.   Lots of people do.

MRS. SØRBY.   And you can imagine what that means for a businessman. Well, I'll try to make my eyes do for his as well as I can. But I mustn't stay any longer; I've so much to take care of now. Oh yes, I was supposed to tell you this, Ekdal—that if there's anything Werle can do for you, please just get in touch with Graaberg.

GREGERS.   That offer Hjalmar Ekdal will certainly decline.

MRS. SØRBY.   Come, now, I don't think that in the past he's—

GINA.   No, Berta, Hjalmar doesn't need to take anything from Mr. Werle now.

HJALMAR [slowly and ponderously].   Would you greet your future husband from me and say that I intend very shortly to call on his bookkeeper, Graaberg—

GREGERS.   What! Is that what you want?

HJALMAR.   To call on his bookkeeper Graaberg, as I said, to request an itemized account of what I owe his employer. I shall repay this debt of honor— [Laughs.] That's a good name for it, "debt of honor"! But never mind. I shall repay every penny of it, with five percent interest.

GINA.   But Hjalmar dear, God knows we don't have the money for that.

HJALMAR.   Will you tell your husband-to-be that I'm working away relentlessly at my invention. Would you tell him that what keeps by spirits up through this grueling ordeal is the desire to be quit of a painful burden of debt. That's why I'm making my invention. The entire proceeds will be devoted to shedding my monetary ties with your imminent partner.

MRS. SØRBY.   Something has really happened in this house.

HJALMAR.   Yes, it certainly has.

MRS. SØRBY.   Well, good-bye, then. I still have a little more to talk about with you, Gina, but that can keep till another time. Good-bye.

[HJALMAR and GREGERS silently nod; GINA accompanies MRS. SØRBY to the door.]

HJALMAR.   Not across the threshold, Gina!

[MRS. SØRBY leaves; GINA closes the door behind her.]

HJALMAR.   There, now, Gregers—now I've got that pressing debt off my hands.

GREGERS.   You will soon, anyway.

HJALMAR.   I believe my attitude could be called correct.

GREGERS.   You're the man I always thought you were.

HJALMAR.   In certain circumstances it's impossible not to feel the summons of the ideal. As the family provider, you know, I've got to writhe and groan beneath it. Believe you me, it's really no joke for a man without means to try and pay off a long-standing debt over which the dust of oblivion, so to speak, had fallen. But it's got to be, all the same; my human self demands its rights.

GREGERS [*laying one hand on his shoulder*]. Ah, Hjalmar—wasn't it a good thing I came?

HJALMAR. Yes.

GREGERS. Getting a clear picture of the whole situation—wasn't that a good thing?

HJALMAR [*a bit impatiently*]. Of course it was good. But there's one thing that irks my sense of justice.

GREGERS. What's that?

HJALMAR. It's the fact that—oh, I don't know if I dare speak so freely about your father.

GREGERS. Don't hold back on my account.

HJALMAR. Well, uh—you see, I find something so irritating in the idea that I'm not the one, he's the one who's going to have the true marriage.

GREGERS. How can you say such a thing!

HJALMAR. But it's true. Your father and Mrs. Sørby are entering a marriage based on complete trust, one that's wholehearted and open on both sides. They haven't bottled up any secrets from each other; there isn't any reticence between them; they've declared—if you'll permit me—a mutual forgiveness of sins.

GREGERS. All right. So what?

HJALMAR. Yes, but that's the whole thing, then. You said yourself that the reason for all these difficulties was the founding of a true marriage.

GREGERS. But that marriage is a very different sort, Hjalmar. You certainly wouldn't compare either you or her with those two—well, you know what I mean.

HJALMAR. Still, I can't get over the idea that there's something in all this that violates my sense of justice. It really seems as if there's no just order to the universe.

GINA. Good Lord, Hjalmar, you mustn't say such things.

GREGERS. Hm, let's not start on that question.

HJALMAR. But then, on the other hand, I can definitely make out what seems to be the meticulous hand of fate. He's going blind.

GINA. Oh, that's not for sure.

HJALMAR. That is indisputable. Anyway, we oughtn't to doubt it, because it's precisely this fact that reveals the just retribution. Years back he abused the blind faith of a fellow human being—

GREGERS. I'm afraid he's done that to many others.

HJALMAR. And now a pitiless, mysterious something comes and claims the old man's eyes in return.

GINA. What a horrible thing to say! It really frightens me.

HJALMAR. It's useful sometimes to go down deep into the night side of existence.

[HEDVIG, *in her hat and coat, comes in, happy and breathless, through the hall door.*]

GINA. Back so soon?

HEDVIG. Yes, I got tired of walking, and it was just as well, 'cause then I met someone down at the door.

HJALMAR.   That must have been Mrs. Sørby.

HEDVIG.   Yes.

HJALMAR [*pacing back and forth*].   I hope that's the last time you'll see her.

[*Silence.* HEDVIG *glances timidly from one to the other, as if trying to read their feelings.*]

HEDVIG [*coaxingly, as she approaches*].   Daddy.

HJALMAR.   Well—what is it, Hedvig?

HEDVIG.   Mrs. Sørby brought along something for me.

HJALMAR [*stopping*].   For you?

HEDVIG.   Yes. It's something meant for tomorrow.

GINA.   Berta's always brought some little gift for your birthday.

HJALMAR.   What is it?

HEDVIG.   No, you can't know that yet, because Mother has to bring it to me in bed first thing in the morning.

HJALMAR.   Oh, all this conspiracy that I'm left out of!

HEDVIG [*hurriedly*].   Oh, you can see it all right. It's a big letter. [*She takes the letter out of her coat pocket.*]

HJALMAR.   A letter, too?

HEDVIG.   Well, it's only the letter. I guess the rest will come later. But just think—a letter! I've never gotten a real letter before. And on the outside there, it says "Miss." [*She reads.*] "Miss Hedvig Ekdal." Just think—that's me.

HJALMAR.   Let me see the letter.

HEDVIG [*handing it over*].   See, there.

HJALMAR.   That's old Werle's writing.

GINA.   Are you positive, Hjalmar?

HJALMAR.   See for yourself.

GINA.   Oh, how would I know?

HJALMAR.   Hedvig, mind if I open the letter—and read it?

HEDVIG.   Sure. If you want to, go right ahead.

GINA.   No, not tonight, Hjalmar. It's meant for tomorrow.

HEDVIG [*softly*].   Oh, won't you let him read it! It's got to be something good, and then Daddy'll be happy and things will be pleasant again.

HJALMAR.   May I open it, then?

HEDVIG.   Yes, please do, Daddy. It'll be fun to find out what it is.

HJALMAR.   Good. [*He opens the envelope, takes out a sheet of paper, and reads it through with growing bewilderment.*] Now what's this all about?

GINA.   But what does it say?

HEDVIG.   Oh yes, Daddy—tell us!

HJALMAR.   Be quiet. [*He reads it through once more, turns pale, then speaks with evident restraint.*] This is a deed of gift, Hedvig.

HEDVIG.   Honestly? What am I getting?

HJALMAR.   Read for yourself.

[HEDVIG *goes over to the lamp and reads for a moment.*]

HJALMAR [*clenching his fists, in almost a whisper*].   The eyes! The eyes—and now that letter!

HEDVIG [*interrupting her reading*].   Yes, but I think the gift is for Grandfather.

HJALMAR [*taking the letter from her*].   Gina—do you understand this?

GINA.   I know nothing at all about it. Just tell me.

HJALMAR.   Mr. Werle writes Hedvig to say that her old grandfather needn't trouble himself any longer with copying work, but that henceforth he can draw one hundred crowns a month from the office—

GREGERS.   Aha!

HEDVIG.   One hundred crowns, Mother! I read that.

GINA.   That'll be nice for Grandfather.

HJALMAR.   One hundred crowns, as long as he needs it. That means till death, of course.

GINA.   Well, then he's provided for, poor dear.

HJALMAR.   But there's more. You didn't read far enough, Hedvig. Afterwards this gift passes over to you.

HEDVIG.   To me! All of it?

HJALMAR.   You're assured the same income for the rest of your life, he writes. Hear that, Gina?

GINA.   Yes, of course I heard.

HEDVIG.   Imagine me getting all that money! [*Shaking* HJALMAR.] Daddy, Daddy, aren't you glad?

HJALMAR [*disengaging himself*].   Glad! [*Walking about the room.*] Ah, what vistas—what perspectives it offers me. Hedvig is the one, she's the one he remembers so bountifully.

GINA.   Of course, because it's Hedvig's birthday.

HEDVIG.   And anyway, you'll have it, Daddy. You know that I'll give all the money to you and Mother.

HJALMAR.   To Mother, yes! There we have it.

GREGERS.   Hjalmar, this is a trap that's been set for you.

HJALMAR.   You think it could be another trap?

GREGERS.   When he was here this morning, he said, "Hjalmar Ekdal is not the man you think he is."

HJALMAR.   Not the man—!

GREGERS.   "You'll find that out," he said.

HJALMAR.   Find out if I could be bought off for a price, eh—!

HEDVIG.   But Mother, what's this all about?

GINA.   Go and take your things off.

[HEDVIG, *close to tears, goes out the kitchen door.*]

GREGERS.   Yes, Hjalmar—now we'll see who's right, he or I.

HJALMAR [*slowly tearing the paper in half and putting both pieces on the table*].   That is my answer.

GREGERS.   What I expected.

HJALMAR [*going over to* GINA, *who is standing by the stove, and speaking quietly*].   And now no more pretenses. If that thing between you and him was all over when you—came to be so terribly in love with me, as you put it—then why did he give us the means to get married?

GINA.   Maybe he thought he could come and go here.

HJALMAR.   Is that all? Wasn't he afraid of a certain possibility?

GINA.   I don't know what you mean.

HJALMAR.   I want to know if—your child has the right to live under my roof.

GINA [*draws herself up, her eyes flashing*].   And you can ask that?

HJALMAR. Just answer me this: does Hedvig belong to me—or—? Well!

GINA [regarding him with chill defiance]. I don't know.

HJALMAR [with a slight quaver]. You don't know!

GINA. How would I know that? A woman of my sort—

HJALMAR [softly, turning from her]. Then I have nothing more to do in this house.

GREGERS. You must think about this, Hjalmar.

HJALMAR [putting on his overcoat]. There's nothing to think about for a man like me.

GREGERS. Oh, there's so very much to think about. You three have got to stay together if you're ever going to win through to a self-sacrificial, forgiving spirit.

HJALMAR. I don't want that. Never, never! My hat! [Takes his hat.] My home is down in ruins around me. [Breaks into tears.] Gregers, I have no child!

HEDVIG [who has opened the kitchen door]. What are you saying! [Running toward him.] Daddy, Daddy!

GINA. Now look!

HJALMAR. Don't come near me, Hedvig! Keep away. I can't bear seeing you. Oh, the eyes! Good-bye. [Starts for the door.]

HEDVIG [clinging fast to him and shrieking]. Oh no! Oh no! Don't leave me.

GINA [crying out]. Watch the child, Hjalmar. Watch the child!

HJALMAR. I won't. I can't. I've got to get out—away from all this! [He tears himself loose from HEDVIG and goes out through the hall door.]

HEDVIG [with desperate eyes]. He's left us, Mother! He's left us! He'll never come back again!

GINA. Now don't cry, Hedvig. Daddy's coming back.

HEDVIG [throws herself, sobbing, on the sofa]. No, no, he'll never come home to us again.

GREGERS. Will you believe I've wanted everything for the best, Mrs. Ekdal?

GINA. Yes, I think I believe that—but God have mercy on you all the same.

HEDVIG [lying on the sofa]. I think I'll die from all this. What did I do to him? Mother, you've got to make him come home!

GINA. Yes, yes, yes, just be calm, and I'll step out and look for him. [Putting on her coat.] Maybe he's gone down to Relling's. But now don't you lie there, wailing away. Will you promise?

HEDVIG [sobbing convulsively]. Yes, I'll be all right—if only Daddy comes back.

GREGERS [to GINA, about to leave]. Wouldn't it be better, though, to let him fight through his painful battle first?

GINA. Oh, he can do that later. First of all, we've got to comfort the child. [She goes out the hall door.]

HEDVIG [sitting up and drying her tears]. Now you have to tell me what it's all about. Why does Daddy not want to see me any more?

GREGERS. That's something you mustn't ask until you're big and grown-up.

HEDVIG [catching her breath]. But I can't go on being so horribly unhappy till I'm big and grown-up. I bet I know what it is. Perhaps I'm really not Daddy's child.

GREGERS [*disturbed*].   How could that ever be?

HEDVIG.   Mother could have found me. And now maybe Daddy's found out. I've read about these things.

GREGERS.   Well, but if that was the—

HEDVIG.   Yes, I think he could love me even so. Or maybe more. The wild duck was sent us as a present too, and I'm terribly fond of it, all the same.

GREGERS [*divertingly*].   Of course, the wild duck, that's true. Let's talk a bit about the wild duck, Hedvig.

HEDVIG.   The poor wild duck. He can't bear to see her again, either. Imagine, he wanted to wring her neck!

GREGERS.   Oh, he certainly wouldn't do that.

HEDVIG.   No, but that's what he said. And I think it was awful for Daddy to say, because each night I make a prayer for the wild duck and ask that she be delivered from death and everything evil.

GREGERS [*looking at her*].   Do you always say your prayers at night?

HEDVIG.   Uh-huh.

GREGERS.   Who taught you that?

HEDVIG.   I taught myself, and that was once when Daddy was so sick and had leeches on his neck, and then he said he was in the jaws of death.

GREGERS.   Oh yes?

HEDVIG.   So I said a prayer for him when I went to bed. And I've kept it up ever since.

GREGERS.   And now you pray for the wild duck, too?

HEDVIG.   I thought it was best to put the wild duck in, because she was ailing so at the start.

GREGERS.   Do you say morning prayers, too?

HEDVIG.   No, not at all.

GREGERS.   Why not morning prayers as well?

HEDVIG.   In the morning it's light, and so there's nothing more to be afraid of.

GREGERS.   And the wild duck you love so much—your father wants to wring her neck.

HEDVIG.   No. He said it would be the best thing for him if he did, but for my sake he would spare her; and that was good of Daddy.

GREGERS [*coming closer*].   But what if you now, of your own free will, sacrificed the wild duck for *his* sake.

HEDVIG [*springing up*].   The wild duck!

GREGERS.   What if you, in a sacrificing spirit, gave up the dearest thing you own and know in the whole world?

HEDVIG.   Do you think that would help?

GREGERS.   Try it, Hedvig.

HEDVIG [*softly, with shining eyes*].   Yes, I'll try it.

GREGERS.   And the strength of mind, do you think you have it?

HEDVIG.   I'll ask Grandpa to shoot the wild duck for me.

GREGERS.   Yes, do that. But not a word to your mother about all this!

HEDVIG.   Why not?

GREGERS.   She doesn't understand us.

HEDVIG.   The wild duck? I'll try it tomorrow, early.

[GINA *comes in through the hall door.*]

HEDVIG [*going toward her*].   Did you find him, Mother?

GINA.   No. But I heard he'd looked in downstairs and gotten Relling along.

GREGERS.   Are you sure of that?

GINA.   Yes, I asked the janitor's wife. And Molvik was with them, she said.

GREGERS.   And this, right when his mind needs nothing so much as to wrestle in solitude—!

GINA [*taking off her coat*].   Oh, men are strange ones, they are. God knows where Relling has led him! I ran over to Mrs. Eriksen's café, but they weren't there.

HEDVIG [*struggling with her tears*].   Oh, what if he never comes back again!

GREGERS.   He *will* come back. I'll get a message to him tomorrow, and then you'll see just how quick he comes. Believe that, Hedvig, and sleep well. Good night. [*He goes out the hall door.*]

HEDVIG [*throwing herself, sobbing, into* GINA's *arms*].   Mother, Mother!

GINA [*pats her on the back and sighs*].   Ah, me, Relling was right. That's the way it goes when these crazy people come around, summoning up their ideals.

ACT V

HJALMAR EKDAL's *studio. A cold, gray morning light filters in; wet snow lies on the huge panes of the skylight.* GINA, *wearing a pinafore, comes in from the kitchen, carrying a feather duster and a cleaning cloth, and makes for the living room door. At the same moment* HEDVIG *rushes in from the hallway.*

GINA [*stopping*].   Well?

HEDVIG.   You know, Mother, I'm pretty sure he's down at Relling's—

GINA.   There, you see!

HEDVIG.   'Cause the janitor's wife said she heard Relling had two others with him when he came in last night.

GINA.   That's about what I thought.

HEDVIG.   But it's still no good if he won't come up to us.

GINA.   At least I can go down there and talk with him.

[EKDAL, *in dressing gown and slippers, smoking a pipe, appears in the doorway to his room.*]

EKDAL.   Say, Hjalmar— Isn't Hjalmar home?

GINA.   No, he's gone out, I guess.

EKDAL.   So early? In a raging blizzard like this? Oh, well, never mind; I'll take my morning walk alone, that's all.

[*He pulls the loft door ajar,* HEDVIG *helping him. He goes in; she closes up after him.*]

HEDVIG [*lowering her voice*].   Just think, Mother, when Grandpa finds out that Daddy's leaving us.

GINA. Go on, Grandpa won't hear anything of the kind. It was a real stroke of providence he wasn't here yesterday in all that racket.

HEDVIG. Yes, but—

[GREGERS *comes in the hall entrance.*]

GREGERS. Well? Had any reports on him?

GINA. He should be down at Relling's, they tell me.

GREGERS. With Relling! Did he really go out with those fellows?

GINA. Apparently.

GREGERS. Yes, but he who needed so much to be alone to pull himself together—!

GINA. Yes, just as you say.

[RELLING *enters from the hall.*]

HEDVIG [*going toward him*]. Is Daddy with you?

GINA [*simultaneously*]. Is he there?

RELLING. Yes, of course he is.

HEDVIG. And you never told us!

RELLING. Oh, I'm a beast. But first of all, I had that other beast to manage—you know, the demonic one, him—and then, next, I fell so sound asleep that—

GINA. What's Hjalmar been saying today?

RELLING. He's said absolutely nothing.

HEDVIG. Hasn't he talked at all?

RELLING. Not a blessed word.

GREGERS. No, no, I can well understand that.

GINA. But what's he doing, then?

RELLING. He's laid out on the sofa, snoring.

GINA. Oh? Yes, Hjalmar's great at snoring.

HEDVIG. He's asleep? Can he sleep?

RELLING. Well, so it seems.

GREGERS. It's conceivable—when all that strife of spirit has torn him.

GINA. And then he's never been used to roaming around the streets at night.

HEDVIG. Maybe it's a good thing that he's getting some sleep, Mother.

GINA. I think so too. But then it's just as well we don't rouse him too soon. Thanks a lot, Relling. Now I've got to clean and straighten up here a bit, and then— Come and help me, Hedvig.

[GINA *and* HEDVIG *disappear into the living room.*]

GREGERS [*turning to* RELLING]. Have you an explanation for the spiritual upheaval taking place within Hjalmar Ekdal?

RELLING. For the life of me, I can't remember any spiritual upheaval in him.

GREGERS. What! At a time of crisis like this, when his life has been recast? How can you believe that a rare personality like Hjalmar—?

RELLING. Pah! Personality—him! If he's ever had a tendency toward anything so abnormal as what you call personality, it was ripped up, root and vine, by the time he was grown, and that's a fact.

GREGERS. That's rather surprising—with all the loving care he had as a child.

RELLING. From those two warped, hysterical maiden aunts, you mean?

GREGERS. I want to tell you they were women who always lived up to the highest ideals—yes, now of course you'll start mocking me again.

RELLING. No, I'm hardly in a mood for that. Besides, I'm well informed here; he's regurgitated any amount of rhetoric about his "twin soul-mothers." I really don't believe he has much to thank them for. Ekdal's misfortune is that in his circle he's always been taken for a shining light—

GREGERS. And isn't he, perhaps, exactly that? In his heart's core, I mean?

RELLING. I've never noticed anything of the kind. His father thinks so—but that's nothing; the old lieutenant's been a fool all his life.

GREGERS. He has, all his life, been a man with a childlike awareness; and that's something you just don't understand.

RELLING. Oh, sure! But back when our dear, sweet Hjalmar became a student of sorts, right away he got taken up by his classmates as the great beacon of the future. Oh, he was good-looking, the lout—pink and white—just the way little moon-eyed girls like boys. And then he had that excitable manner and that heart-winning tremor in his voice, and he was so cute and clever at declaiming other people's poems and ideas—

GREGERS [indignantly]. Is it Hjalmar Ekdal you're speaking of that way?

RELLING. Yes, with your permission. That's an inside look at him, this idol you're groveling in front of.

GREGERS. I really didn't think I was utterly blind.

RELLING. Well, you're not far from it. Because you're a sick man, you are. You know that.

GREGERS. There you're right.

RELLING. Oh yes. Your case has complications. First there's this virulent moralistic fever; and then something worse—you keep going off in deliriums of hero worship; you always have to have something to admire that's outside of yourself.

GREGERS. Yes, I certainly have to look for it outside myself.

RELLING. But you're so woefully wrong about these great miraculous beings you think you see and hear around you. You've simply come back to a squatter's cabin with your summons to the ideal; there's nobody solvent here.

GREGERS. If you've got no higher estimate of Hjalmar Ekdal than this, how can you ever enjoy seeing him day after day?

RELLING. Good Lord, I *am* supposed to be some kind of doctor, I'm ashamed to say. Well, then I ought to look after the poor sick people I live with.

GREGERS. Oh, come! Is Hjalmar Ekdal sick, too?

RELLING. Most of the world is sick, I'm afraid.

GREGERS. And what's your prescription for Hjalmar?

RELLING. My standard one. I try to keep up the vital lie in him.

GREGERS. The vital—lie? I don't think I heard—

RELLING. Oh yes, I said the vital lie. The vital lie, don't you see—that's the animating principle of life.

GREGERS. May I ask what kind of lie has infected Hjalmar?

RELLING. No, thanks, I don't betray secrets like that to quacks. You'd just be able to damage him all the more for me. My method is tested, though. I've also used it on Molvik. I made him "demonic." That was my remedy for him.

GREGERS. Then he isn't demonic?

RELLING. What the devil does it mean to be demonic? That's just some hogwash I thought up to keep life going in him. If I hadn't done that, the poor innocent mutt would have given in years ago to self-contempt and despair. And then take the old lieutenant! But he really discovered his own cure himself.

GREGERS. Lieutenant Ekdal? How so?

RELLING. Well, what do you think of this bear hunter going into a dark loft to stalk rabbits? There isn't a happier sportsman in the world than the old man when he's prowling around in that junkyard. Those four or five dried-out Christmas trees he's got—to him they're like all the green forests of Hoidal; the hens and the rooster—they're the game birds up in the fir tops; and the rabbits hopping across the floor—they're the bears that call up his youth again, out in the mountain air.

GREGERS. Poor, unhappy old Ekdal, yes. He certainly had to pare down his early ideals.

RELLING. While I remember it, Mr. Werle junior—don't use that exotic word *ideals*. Not when we've got a fine native word—*lies*.

GREGERS. You're implying the two have something in common?

RELLING. Yes, about like typhus and typhoid fever.

GREGERS. Dr. Relling, I won't rest till I've gotten Hjalmar out of your clutches.

RELLING. So much the worse for him. Deprive the average man of his vital lie, and you've robbed him of happiness as well. [*To* HEDVIG, *entering from the living room.*] Well, little wild-duck mother, now I'll go down and see if Papa's still lying and pondering his marvelous invention. [*He goes out the hall door.*]

GREGERS [*approaching* HEDVIG]. I can see by your face that it isn't done.

HEDVIG. What? Oh, about the wild duck. No.

GREGERS. Your courage failed you when the time came to act, I suppose.

HEDVIG. No, it's not exactly that. But when I woke up this morning early and thought of what we talked about, then it seemed so strange to me.

GREGERS. Strange?

HEDVIG. Yes, I don't know— Last night, right at the time, there was something so beautiful about it, but after I'd slept and then thought it over, it didn't seem like so much.

GREGERS. Ah, no, you couldn't grow up here without some taint in you.

HEDVIG. I don't care about that; if only Daddy would come up, then—

GREGERS. Oh, if only your eyes were really open to what makes life worth living—if only you had the true, joyful, courageous spirit of self-sacrifice, *then* you'd see him coming up to you. But I still have faith in you. [*He goes out the hall door.*]

[HEDVIG *wanders across the room, then starts into the kitchen. At that moment a knock comes on the loft door,* HEDVIG *goes over and opens it a space;* EKDAL *slips out, and she slides it shut again.*]

EKDAL. Hm, a morning walk alone is no fun at all.

HEDVIG. Don't you want to go hunting, Grandpa?

EKDAL. The weather's no good for hunting. Awfully dark in there; you can hardly see ahead of you.

HEDVIG.   Don't you ever want to shoot at anything but rabbits?

EKDAL.   Aren't rabbits good enough, eh?

HEDVIG.   Yes, but the wild duck, say?

EKDAL.   Ha, ha! You're afraid I'll shoot the wild duck for you? Never in this world, dear. Never!

HEDVIG.   No, you couldn't do that. It must be hard to shoot wild ducks.

EKDAL.   Couldn't? I certainly could!

HEDVIG.   How would you go about it, Grandpa?—I don't mean with *my* wild duck, but with others.

EKDAL.   I'd be sure to shoot them in the breast, understand; that's the safest. And then they've got to be shot *against* the feathers, you see—not *with* the feathers.

HEDVIG.   They die then, Grandpa?

EKDAL.   Oh yes, they do indeed—if you shoot them right. Well, got to go in and clean up. Hm—you understand—hm. [*He goes into his room.*]

[HEDVIG *waits a moment, glances at the living room door, goes to the book-case, stands on tiptoe, takes down the double-barreled pistol from the shelf and looks at it.* GINA, *with duster and cloth, comes in from the living room.* HEDVIG *hastily sets down the pistol, unnoticed.*]

GINA.   Don't mess with your father's things, Hedvig.

HEDVIG [*leaving the bookcase*].   I was just straightening up a little.

GINA.   Go out in the kitchen instead and make sure the coffee's still hot; I'll take a tray along to him when I go down.

[HEDVIG *goes out;* GINA *begins to dust and clean up the studio. After a moment the hall door is cautiously opened, and* HJALMAR *peers in. He wears his overcoat, but no hat. He is unwashed, with tousled, unruly hair; his eyes are dull and inert.*]

GINA [*standing rooted with duster in hand, looking at him*].   Don't tell me, Hjalmar—are you back after all?

HJALMAR [*steps in and answers in a thick voice*].   I'm back—but only for one moment.

GINA.   Oh yes, I'm sure of that. But my goodness—what a sight you are!

HJALMAR.   Sight?

GINA.   And then your good winter coat! Well, it's done for.

HEDVIG [*at the kitchen door*].   Mother, should I— [*Seeing* HJALMAR, *giving a squeal of delight, and running toward him.*] Oh, Daddy, Daddy!

HJALMAR [*turning from her and waving her off*].   Get away! Get away! [*To* GINA.] Make her get away from me, will you!

GINA [*in an undertone*].   Go in the living room, Hedvig.

[HEDVIG *silently goes out.*]

HJALMAR [*with a busy air, pulling out the table drawer*].   I must have my books along. Where are my books?

GINA.   What books?

HJALMAR.   My scientific works, of course—the technical journals I use for my invention.

GINA [*looking over the bookshelves*].   Are these them, the ones without covers?

HJALMAR.   Yes, exactly.

GINA [*putting a stack of booklets on the table.*]   Could I get Hedvig to cut the pages for you?

HJALMAR.   Nobody has to cut pages for me. [*A short silence.*]

GINA.   Then it's definite that you're moving out, Hjalmar?

HJALMAR [*rummaging among the books*].   Yes, that would seem to me self-evident.

GINA.   I see.

HJALMAR.   How could I go on here and have my heart shattered every hour of the day!

GINA.   God forgive you for thinking so badly of me.

HJALMAR.   Show me proof—

GINA.   I think *you're* the one to show proof.

HJALMAR.   After your kind of past? There are certain standards—I'd like to call them ideal standards—

GINA.   But Grandfather? What'll happen to him, poor dear?

HJALMAR.   I know my duty; that helpless old soul leaves with me. I'm going downtown and make arrangements—hm—[*Hesitantly.*] Did anybody find my hat on the stairs?

GINA.   No. Have you lost your hat?

HJALMAR.   I had it on, naturally, when I came in last night; I'm positive of that. But today I couldn't find it.

GINA.   My Lord, where did you go with those two stumblebums?

HJALMAR.   Oh, don't bother me with petty questions. Do you think I'm in a mood to remember details?

GINA.   I just hope you didn't catch cold, Hjalmar. [*She goes out into the kitchen.*]

HJALMAR [*muttering to himself in exasperation, as he empties the table drawer*].   You're a sneak, Relling! A barbarian, that's what! Oh, snake in the grass! If I could just get someone to strangle you! [*He puts some old letters to one side, discovers the torn deed of the day before, picks it up and examines the pieces. He hurriedly puts them down as GINA enters.*]

GINA. [*setting a breakfast tray on the table*].   Here's a drop of something hot, if you care for it. And there's some bread and butter and a little salt meat.

HJALMAR [*glancing at the tray*].   Salt meat? Never under this roof! Of course I haven't enjoyed going without food for nearly twenty-four hours; but that doesn't matter— My notes! My unfinished memoirs! Where can I find my journal and my important papers? [*Opens the living room door, then draws back.*] There she is again!

GINA.   Well, goodness, the child has to be somewhere.

HJALMAR.   Come out. [*He stands aside, and HEDVIG, terrified comes into the studio.*]

HJALMAR [*with his hand on the doorknob, says to GINA*].   These last moments I'm spending in my former home, I'd like to be free from intruders— [*Goes into the living room.*]

HEDVIG [*rushing to her mother, her voice hushed and trembling*].   Does he mean me?

GINA.   Stay in the kitchen, Hedvig. Or, no—go into your own room instead. [*Speaking to HJALMAR as she goes in to him.*] Just a minute, Hjalmar. Don't muss up the bureau like that; I know where everything is. [HEDVIG *stands for a moment as if frozen by fright and bewilderment, biting her lips to keep the tears back; then she clenches her fists convulsively.*]

HEDVIG [*softly*].   The wild duck. [*She steals over and takes the pistol from the shelf, sets the loft door ajar, slips in and draws the door shut after her.* HJALMAR *and* GINA *start arguing in the living room.*]

HJALMAR [*re-enters with some notebooks and old loose papers, which he lays on the table*].   Oh, what good is that traveling bag! I've got a thousand things to take with me.

GINA [*following with the traveling bag*].   So leave everything else for the time being, and just take a shirt and a pair of shorts with you.

HJALMAR.   Phew! These agonizing preparations! [*Takes off his overcoat and throws it on the sofa.*]

GINA.   And there's your coffee getting cold, too.

HJALMAR.   Hm. [*Unthinkingly takes a sip and then another.*]

GINA.   The hardest thing for you will be to find another room like that, big enough for all the rabbits.

HJALMAR.   What! Do I have to take all the rabbits with me, too?

GINA.   Yes, Grandfather couldn't live without the rabbits, I'm sure.

HJALMAR.   He's simply got to get used to it. The joys of life *I* have to renounce are higher than rabbits.

GINA [*dusting the bookcase*].   Should I put your flute in the traveling bag?

HJALMAR.   No. No flute for me. But give me the pistol!

GINA.   You want your pistol along?

HJALMAR.   Yes. My loaded pistol.

GINA [*looking for it*].   It's gone. He must have taken it inside.

HJALMAR.   Is he in the loft?

GINA.   Of course he's in the loft.

HJALMAR.   Hm—lonely old man. [*He takes a piece of bread and butter, eats it, and finishes the cup of coffee.*]

GINA.   Now if we only hadn't rented the room, you could have moved in there.

HJALMAR.   I should stay on under the same roof as—! Never! Never!

GINA.   But couldn't you put up in the living room just for a day or two? You've got everything you need in there.

HJALMAR.   Never within these walls!

GINA.   Well, how about down with Relling and Molvik?

HJALMAR.   Don't mention those barbarians' names! I can almost lose my appetite just thinking about them. Oh no, I've got to go out in sleet and snow —tramp from house to house and seek shelter for Father and me.

GINA.   But you haven't any hat, Hjalmar! You've lost your hat.

HJALMAR.   Oh, those two vermin, wallowing in sin! The hat will have to be bought. [*Taking another piece of bread and butter.*] Someone's got to make arrangements. I certainly don't intend to risk my life. [*Looking for something on the tray.*]

GINA.   What are you looking for?

HJALMAR.   Butter.

GINA.   Butter's coming right up. [*Goes into the kitchen.*]

HJALMAR [*calling after her.*]   Oh, never mind; I can just as easily eat dry bread.

GINA [*bringing in a butter dish*]. Look. It's fresh today. [*She passes him another cup of coffee. He sits on the sofa, spreads more butter on the bread, eats and drinks a moment in silence.*]

HJALMAR. Could I—without being annoyed by anybody—anybody at all —put up in the living room just for a day or two?

GINA. Yes, of course you could, if you want to.

HJALMAR. Because I can't see any possibility of getting all Father's things out in one trip.

GINA. And then there's this, too, that you've first got to tell him you're not living with us any longer.

HJALMAR [*pushing the coffee cup away*]. That too, yes. All these intricate affairs to unravel. I've got to clear my thinking; I need a breathing spell; I can't shoulder all these burdens in one day.

GINA. No, and not when the weather's like it is out.

HJALMAR [*picking up* WERLE's *letter*]. I see this letter's still kicking around.

GINA. Yes, I haven't touched it.

HJALMAR. This trash is nothing to me—

GINA. Well, I'm not going to use it for anything.

HJALMAR. All the same, there's no point in throwing it around helter-skelter. In all the confusion of my moving, it could easily—

GINA. I'll take good care of it, Hjalmar.

HJALMAR. First and foremost, the deed of gift is Father's; it's really his affair whether or not he wants to use it.

GINA [*sighing*]. Yes, poor old Father—

HJALMAR. Just for safety's sake—where would I find some paste?

GINA [*going to the bookcase*]. Here's the pastepot.

HJALMAR. And then a brush.

GINA. Here's a brush, too. [*Bringing both.*]

HJALMAR [*taking a pair of scissors*]. A strip of paper down the back, that's all. [*Cutting and pasting.*] Far be it from me to take liberties with another's property—least of all, a penniless old man's. No, nor with—the other person's. There, now. Let it lie a while. And when it's dry, then take it away. I don't want to set eyes on that document again. Ever!

[GREGERS *enters from the hall.*]

GREGERS [*somewhat surprised*]. What? Are you lounging in here, Hjalmar?

HJALMAR [*springing up*]. I was overcome by fatigue.

GREGERS. Still, you've had breakfast, I see.

HJALMAR. The body makes its claims now and then too.

GREGERS. What have you decided to do?

HJALMAR. For a man like me there's only one way open. I'm in the process of assembling my most important things. But that takes time, don't you know.

GINA [*a bit impatient*]. Should I get the room ready for you, or should I pack your bag?

HJALMAR [*after a vexed glance at* GREGERS]. Pack—and get the room ready!

GINA [*taking the traveling bag*]. All right, then I'll put in the shirt and the rest. [*She goes into the living room, shutting the door behind her.*]

GREGERS [*after a short silence*]. I never dreamed that things would end like this. Is it really necessary for you to leave house and home?

HJALMAR [*pacing restlessly about*]. What would you have me do? I wasn't made to be unhappy, Gregers. I've got to have it snug and secure and peaceful around me.

GREGERS. But why can't you, then? Give it a try. Now I'd say you have solid ground to build on—so make a fresh start. And don't forget you have your invention to live for, too.

HJALMAR. Oh, don't talk about the invention. That seems such a long way off.

GREGERS. Oh?

HJALMAR. Good Lord, yes. What would you really have me invent? Other people have invented so much already. It gets more difficult every day—

GREGERS. And you've put so much work in it.

HJALMAR. It was that dissolute Relling who got me started.

GREGERS. Relling?

HJALMAR. Yes, he was the one who first made me aware that I had a real talent for inventing something in photography.

GREGERS. Aha—that was Relling!

HJALMAR. Oh, I was so blissfully happy as a result. Not so much from the invention itself, but because Hedvig believed in it—believed in it with all the power and force of a child's mind. Yes, in other words, fool that I am, I've gone around imagining that she believed in it.

GREGERS. You can't really think that Hedvig could lie to you!

HJALMAR. Now I can think anything. It's Hedvig that ruins it all. She's managed to blot the sun right out of my life.

GREGERS. Hedvig! You mean Hedvig? How could she ever do that?

HJALMAR [*without answering*]. How inexpressibly I loved that child! How inexpressibly happy I was whenever I came home to my poor rooms and she came flying to meet me with those sweet, fluttering eyes. I was so unspeakably fond of her—and so I dreamed and deluded myself into thinking that she, too, was fond of me beyond words.

GREGERS. Can you call *that* just a delusion?

HJALMAR. How can I tell? I can't get anything out of Gina; and besides, she has no feeling at all for the ideal phase of these complications. But with you, Gregers, I feel impelled to open my mind. There's this horrible doubt—maybe Hedvig never really, truly has loved me.

GREGERS. She may perhaps give you proof that she has. [*Listening.*] What's that? I thought I heard the wild duck cry.

HJALMAR. The duck's quacking. Father's in the loft.

GREGERS. Is he? [*His face radiates joy.*] I tell you, you may yet have proof that your poor, misjudged Hedvig loves you!

HJALMAR. Oh, what proof could she give me? I don't dare hope to be reassured from that quarter.

GREGERS. Hedvig's completely free of deceit.

HJALMAR. Oh, Gregers, that's just what I can't be sure of. Who knows what Gina and this Mrs. Sørby have whispered and gossiped about in all the times they've sat here? And Hedvig uses her ears, you know. Maybe the deed of gift wasn't such a surprise, after all. In fact, I seemed to get that impression.

GREGERS.   What is this spirit that's gotten into you?

HJALMAR.   I've had my eyes opened. Just wait—you'll see; the deed of gift is only the beginning. Mrs. Sørby has always cared a lot for Hedvig, and now she has the power to do what she wants for the child. They can take her away from me any time they like.

GREGERS.   You're the last person in the world Hedvig would leave.

HJALMAR.   Don't be too sure of that. If they stand beckoning her with all they have—? Oh, I who've loved her so inexpressibly! I who'd find my highest joy in taking her tenderly by the hand and leading her as one leads a child terrified of the dark through a huge, empty room! I can feel it now with such gnawing certainty; the poor photographer up in this attic has never meant much to her. She's merely been clever to keep on a good footing with him till the right time came.

GREGERS.   You really don't believe that, Hjalmar.

HJALMAR.   The worst thing is precisely that I don't know what to believe —that I'll never know. But can you honestly doubt that it's just what I'm saying? [*With a bitter laugh.*] Ah, you're just too idealistic, my dear Gregers! Suppose the others come with their hands full of riches and call out to the child: Leave him. Life waits for you here with us—

GREGERS [*quickly*].   Yes, then what?

HJALMAR.   If I asked her then: Hedvig, are you willing to give up life for me? [*Laughs derisively.*] Yes, thanks—you'd hear all right what answer I'd get!

[*A pistol shot is heard in the loft.*]

GREGERS [*with a shout of joy*].   Hjalmar!

HJALMAR.   Hear that. He's got to go hunting as well.

GINA [*coming in*].   Oh, Hjalmar, it sounds like Grandfather's shooting up the loft by himself.

HJALMAR.   I'll take a look—

GREGERS [*animated and exalted*].   Wait now! Do you know what that was?

HJALMAR.   Of course I know.

GREGERS.   No, you don't know. But *I* do. That was the proof!

HJALMAR.   What proof?

GREGERS.   That was a child's sacrifice. She's had your father shoot the wild duck.

HJALMAR.   Shoot the wild duck!

GINA.   No, really—!

HJALMAR.   What for?

GREGERS.   She wanted to sacrifice to you the best thing she had in the world, because she thought then you'd have to love her again.

HJALMAR [*stirred, gently*].   Ah, that child!

GINA.   Yes, the things she thinks of!

GREGERS.   She only wants your love again, Hjalmar; she felt she couldn't live without it.

GINA [*struggling with tears*].   There you are, Hjalmar.

HJALMAR. Gina, where's she gone?

GINA [*sniffling*].   Poor thing. I guess she's out in the kitchen.

HJALMAR [*going over and flinging the kitchen door open*].   Hedvig, come!
Come here to me! [*Looking about.*] No, she's not there.

GINA.   Then she's in her own little room.

HJALMAR [*out of sight*].   No, she's not there either. [*Coming back in.*]
She may have gone out.

GINA.   Yes, you didn't want her around anywhere in the house.

HJALMAR.   Oh, if only she comes home soon—so I can just let her
know—! Things will work out now, Gregers—for now I really believe we can
start life over again.

GREGERS [*quietly*].   I knew it; through the child everything rights itself.
[EKDAL *appears at the door to his room; he is in full uniform and is
absorbed in buckling his sword.*]

HJALMAR [*astonished*].   Father! Are you there?

GINA.   Were you out gunning in your room?

EKDAL [*approaching angrily*].   So you've been hunting alone, eh, Hjalmar?

HJALMAR [*baffled and anxious*].   Then it wasn't you who fired a shot in
the loft?

EKDAL.   Me, shoot? Hm!

GREGERS [*shouting to* HJALMAR].   She's shot the wild duck herself!

HJALMAR.   What is all this! [*Rushes to the loft doors, throws them open,
looks in and cries:*] Hedvig!

GINA [*running to the door*].   Lord, what now!

HJALMAR [*going in*].   She's lying on the floor!

GINA [*simultaneously*].   Hedvig! [*Going into the loft.*] No, no, no!

EKDAL.   Ha, ha! So she's a hunter, too.
[HJALMAR, GINA, *and* GREGERS *carry* HEDVIG *into the studio; her right hand
hangs down and her fingers curve tightly about the pistol.*]

HJALMAR [*distraught*].   The pistol's gone off. She's wounded herself. Call
for help! Help!

GINA [*running into the hall and calling downstairs*].   Relling! Relling! Dr.
Relling, come up as quick as you can!

EKDAL [*hushed*].   The woods take revenge.

HJALMAR [*on his knees by her*].   She's just coming to now. She's coming
to now—oh yes, yes.

GINA [*who has returned*].   Where is she wounded? I can't see anything—
[RELLING *hurries in, and right after him,* MOLVIK, *who is without vest or
tie, his dress coat open.*]

RELLING.   What's up here?

GINA.   They say Hedvig shot herself.

HJALMAR.   Come here and help.

RELLING.   Shot herself! [*He shoves the table to one side and begins to
examine her.*]

HJALMAR [*kneeling still, looking anxiously up at him*].   It can't be serious? Huh, Relling? She's hardly bleeding. It can't be serious?

RELLING.   How did this happen?

HJALMAR.   Oh, how do I know—

GINA.   She wanted to shoot the wild duck.

RELLING. The wild duck?

HJALMAR. The pistol must have gone off.

RELLING. Hm. I see.

EKDAL. The woods take revenge. But I'm not scared, even so. [*He goes into the loft, shutting the door after him.*]

HJALMAR. But Relling—why don't you say something?

RELLING. You can see for yourself that Hedvig is dead.

GINA [*breaking into tears*]. Oh, my child, my child!

GREGERS [*hoarsely*]. In the depths of the sea—

HJALMAR [*jumping up*]. No, no she *must* live! Oh, in God's name, Relling—just for a moment—just enough so I can tell her how inexpressibly I loved her all the time!

RELLING. It's reached the heart. Internal hemorrhage. She died on the spot.

HJALMAR. And I drove her from me like an animal! And she crept terrified into the loft and died out of love for me. [*Sobbing.*] Never to make it right again! Never to let her know—! [*Clenching his fists and crying to heaven.*] Oh, you up there—if you *do* exist. Why have you done this to me!

GINA. Hush, hush, you mustn't carry on like that. We just didn't deserve to keep her, I guess.

MOLVIK. The child isn't dead; she sleepeth.

RELLING. Rubbish!

HJALMAR [*becoming calm, going over to the sofa to stand, arms folded, looking at* HEDVIG]. There she lies, so stiff and still.

RELLING [*trying to remove the pistol*]. She holds it so tight, so tight.

GINA. No, no, Relling, don't break her grip. Let the gun be.

HJALMAR. She should have it with her.

GINA. Yes, let her. But the child shouldn't lie displayed out here. She ought to go into her own little room, she should. Give me a hand, Hjalmar.

[HJALMAR *and* GINA *lift* HEDVIG *between them.*]

HJALMAR [*as they carry her off*]. Oh, Gina, Gina, how can you bear it!

GINA. We must try to help each other. For now she belongs to us both, you know.

MOLVIK [*outstretching his arms and mumbling*]. Praise be to God. Dust to dust, dust to dust—

RELLING [*in a whisper*]. Shut up, you fool; you're drunk.

[HJALMAR *and* GINA *carry the body out through the kitchen door.* RELLING *closes it after them.* MOLVIK *steals out the hall door.*]

RELLING [*going over to* GREGERS]. Nobody's ever going to sell me the idea that this was an accident.

GREGERS [*who has stood in a convulsive fit of horror*]. Who can say how this awful thing happened?

RELLING. There are powder burns on her blouse. She must have aimed the pistol point-blank at her breast and fired.

GREGERS. Hedvig did not die in vain. Did you notice how grief freed the greatness in him?

RELLING. The grief of death brings out greatness in almost everyone. But how long do you think this glory will last with *him*?

GREGERS. I should think it would last and grow all his life.

RELLING. In less than a year little Hedvig will be nothing more to him than a pretty theme for recitations.

GREGERS. You dare say that about Hjalmar Ekdal!

RELLING. We'll be lectured on this when the first grass shows on her grave. Then you can hear him spewing out phrases about "the child torn too soon from her father's heart," and you'll have your chance to watch him souse himself in conceit and self-pity. Wait and see.

GREGERS. If you're right, and I'm wrong, then life isn't worth living.

RELLING. Oh, life would be good in spite of all, if we only could have some peace from these damned shysters who come badgering us poor people with their "summons to the ideal."

GREGERS [staring straight ahead]. In that case, I'm glad my destiny is what it is.

RELLING. Beg pardon—but what *is* your destiny?

GREGERS [about to leave]. To be the thirteenth man at the table.

RELLING. Oh, the hell you say.

COMMENTARY

In T. S. Eliot's *Murder in the Cathedral*, the Archbishop Becket utters a sentence which has become famous—"Human kind," he says, "cannot bear very much reality."[1] The sad dictum may serve to summarize the purport of *The Wild Duck*. And the play goes on to suggest that it is wicked for one person to seek to impose upon another a greater amount of reality than can comfortably be borne. That this should be the "message" of a play by Henrik Ibsen came as a great surprise—indeed, a shock—when *The Wild Duck* was first presented in 1884.

And even now it is likely to startle any reader or playgoer acquainted with the author's characteristic early work. For Ibsen was an outstanding figure in the movement of modern art and intellect that subjected all existing institutions, and the conventions of thought and feeling, to relentless scrutiny in the interests of truth; it was the stern judgment of this movement that society is a contrivance to mask or evade or distort reality. The effort to discriminate between what is real and what is illusory is of course not a new endeavor for literature. But in the modern epoch it has been undertaken with a new particularity and aggressiveness, and by none more than by Ibsen. He had made his reputation with four plays—*Pillars of Society, A Doll's House, Ghosts,* and *An Enemy of the People*—and in each of them he had pressed home the view that falsehood, whether in the form of social lies and hypocrisy or of self-deception, weakens the fabric of life and deprives human kind of its dignity. Expectably enough, his work had met with resistance by the larger part of his audience, that is to say, the more conventional part. But by the same token, the "advanced" minority, a growing force in European culture, received him as a master of truth. In his lifetime and for many years after his death, people spoke of "Ibsenism," by which they meant the radical questioning of all established

_____
[1] The sentence also appears in the first section of Eliot's "Burnt Norton."

and respectable modes of life and the unyielding opposition to sham and pretense. It can therefore be imagined with what bewilderment and dismay the Ibsenites received a play which said that truth may be dangerous to life, that not every man is worthy to tell it or receive it, and that the avoidance and concealment of the truth, or even a lie, may have a vital beneficence.

In speaking of the fate of Oedipus (see page 43), I remarked that although we feel apprehension as Oedipus approaches closer and closer to the knowledge that will destroy him, and although we may wish to warn him against continuing his investigation, we do not really want the dreadful truth to stay hidden from him. As I put it, "we do not want Oedipus to remain oblivious of the truth about himself. An Oedipus who prudently gave up his search would be an object of condescension, even of contempt . . ." This is of course pretty much the feeling on which Gregers Werle proceeds when he resolves to bestow on Hjalmar Ekdal the terrible gift of reality. Hjalmar does not know that his wife had once been secretly the mistress of the elder Werle and that he is not in point of biological fact the father of his daughter. Gregers discloses the true state of affairs because he wants Hjalmar to "face reality" in order to gain the dignity which is presumed to follow upon that disagreeable confrontation. Why, then, do we blame Gregers for making the revelation?

The answer is that Hjalmar is not Oedipus, as poor Hjalmar himself well knows until he is tempted to believe otherwise. Perhaps no moment in the play is more bitterly affecting than that in which, after the disclosure has been made, Hjalmar says, "Do you think a man can recover so easily from the bitter cup I've just emptied?" Gregers replies, "Not an ordinary man, no. But a man like you—!" And Hjalmar desperately and feebly tries to accept the moral heroism that has been ruthlessly thrust upon him: "Good Lord, yes, I know that. But you mustn't be driving me, Gregers. You see, these things take time."

It may indeed be true that people cannot bear very much reality, but some can bear even less than others. Hjalmar is one of those who can bear scarcely any at all. Yet it might be said that in his weakness there is a kind of strength. Whatever his announced claims for himself may be, in his heart of hearts he estimates himself fairly accurately. Until Gregers comes into his life with high talk of what the "summons to the ideal" ought to mean to "a man like you," Hjalmar knows that in order to get through life he needs all the help that illusion can give him, and he takes all the help he can get. It is plain enough that Hjalmar does not really believe he will vindicate the family honor and rehabilitate his old father by making a fortune as an inventor, but the double pose of righter of wrongs and of lonely man of genius sustains and comforts him. We can scarcely suppose that the truth about his wife and daughter had all these years lain very far from his consciousness; if he had wanted to grasp it, he could have reached out for it long ago. He had no such desire, and in consequence he is established in a small but cozy way of life, provided with an affectionate wife who cheerfully performs not only her own tasks but his, and an adoring daughter; he lives in such self-esteem as may arise from the uncontradicted assertion of his natural superiority. In the light of his wife's goodness of heart, it is not of the least importance that this simple woman was once another man's mistress; in the light of his daughter's boundless affection and trust, it is of no consequence that he had not actually engendered her; and Hjalmar had seen to it that what did not matter was never allowed to come into his consciousness. But once the explicit truth is forced upon him, it does its destructive work. We may feel that it should not have had the effect upon the poor man that it does have; we comment on the pettiness of his pride, on how accomplished he is in nursing his grievance. Yet if we consider the sexual ethos of his time, we recognize that only a saint or a philosopher could have received the revelation with magnanimous good sense. The fact that Hjalmar is neither saint nor philosopher does not decisively distinguish him from most men.

The device by which Ibsen suggests the possible beneficence of illusion is a charming one, and also deeply moving, even more in actual presentation on the stage than on the printed page—it is always an electrifying moment for the audience when the forest in the garret is first revealed to view. There is something strangely affecting in a fiction, a mere fancy, that stands before us as a palpable actuality, to be seen and and entered into; and the actuality of the forest is made more than palpable by its being inhabited by the beautiful and tragic wild duck. When first the sliding door is pushed back to reveal the moonlit scene, we have the sense that we have been permitted to look out through Keats's "magic casements, opening on the foam / Of perilous seas, in faery lands forlorn."

For the Ekdals, this fictive forest is a source not only of pleasure but of life itself. It calls forth their best emotions. Toward it, especially toward its most notable denizen, the wounded wild duck, Hedvig directs the natural grace of her spirit, and it is the means by which old Lieutenant Ekdal reconciles himself to his ruined old age. Even Hjalmar rises above his uneasy self-regard and surrenders to a childlike innocence when he comes under the spell of this avowed illusion, which so touchingly binds the family together. The little wilderness is a mere game which the Ekdals play, but into all the activities of human kind, even the most serious and practical, some element of the game is introduced; "make believe" and "as if" do not come to an end with childhood. And the "let's pretend" of play is the very essence of one of man's most characteristic and important activities, that of art.

Hjalmar's father, Lieutenant Ekdal, the simple-minded old hunter, who in his best days had been the mighty killer of actual bears, plays the forest game with the perfectly clear consciousness that it is a game, even though it is also, for him, life itself; and Hedvig plays it as a child, with an absolute commitment to it but with no real confusion of the fancy with reality. And when Hjalmar plays it, he too knows it for what it is. But there are illusions from which some people in The Wild Duck cannot detach themselves. Hjalmar must have some rôle which will conceal from his own perception and that of the world the fact that he is a man of no talent or distinction. In school he had been known as a great declaimer of poetry and therefore as a person of notable sensibility and high ideals, and it is partly the illusioned memory of Hjalmar as he was in the past that leads Gregers to intervene on behalf of his friend's moral dignity; Gregers accepts without question Hjalmar's claim to being a wronged man and an unfulfilled genius. Molvik, the former theological student, is a feckless drunkard but he takes heart from the rôle that Dr. Relling invents for him, that of a "demonic" character, a personality which manifests its power in the "wildness" of a supernal intoxication. As for Gregers himself, we can scarcely fail to see that his behavior as the uncompromising idealist is dictated not only by his grievance against his robust father but also by his desire to acquire a moral status that will mask the emptiness of his unloving heart.

People like these, living by illusions of personal distinction, did not always exist. Like the bereaved doctor of Chekhov's "Enemies" (pages 548 ff.) and Gabriel Conroy of Joyce's "The Dead" (pages 624 ff.), they are the creatures of modernity, especially of that aspect of modernity which Hegel, in his *Philosophy of History,* called the "secularization of spirituality." What Hegel meant by that phrase is suggested by the authority that Ibsen himself achieved and the means by which he achieved it. Where once the moral life of human kind had been chiefly in the keeping of the Church, it was now, by Ibsen's time, increasingly in the charge of playwrights, novelists, poets, and philosophers. Where once life had been relatively simple under the Church's guidance or direction, it was now complex in response to the questioning of writers. Where once it had been concerned with the fulfilment of the duties that were appropriate to one's station in life, it was now concerned with the fulness of a person's life as an individual, with its integrity and dignity, with the proud, vexed commitment to the ideal, that new moral and spiritual sanction which would have been quite incomprehensible a century or two earlier. Ibsen had done much to forward the "secularization of spirituality" and to advance the new self-consciousness, demanding that people be heroes of the spirit. *The Wild Duck* was written in a moment of brilliant self-doubt. This was perhaps induced by the disaffection from his disciples that any master may feel when he perceives how his own hard-won ideas are distorted by those who make easy use of them. But this turning of Ibsen upon himself cannot be attributed merely to his desire to discomfit his Ibsenite followers and to detach himself from the doctrinaire conception of what he had done. It came also, we feel sure, from a magnanimous mind's awareness of the difficulty of life and the impossibility of forcing upon it any single rule, even that of reality.

THE THREE
SISTERS

ANTON PAVLOVICH CHEKHOV

1860–1904

CHARACTERS

OLGA SERGEYEVNA PROZOROV

IRINA SERGEYEVNA PROZOROV

MARYA SERGEYEVNA PROZOROV (Masha)

BARON NIKOLAI LVOVICH TUSENBACH, *an army lieutenant*

IVAN ROMANICH CHEBUTYKIN, *an army doctor*

VASSILY VASSILYEVICH SOLYONY, *an army captain*

ANFISA, *the nurse, an old woman of eighty*

FERAPONT, *an old porter from the County Council*

LIEUTENANT-COLONEL ALEXANDER IGNATYEVICH
    VERSHININ, *battalion commander*

ANDREY SERGEYEVICH PROZOROV

FYODOR ILYICH KULYGIN, *a high school teacher and Masha's husband*

NATALYA IVANOVNA (Natasha), *fiancée and later Andrey's wife*

ALEXEY PETROVICH FEDOTIK, *an army second-lieutenant*

VLADIMIR KARLOVICH RODÉ, *an army second-lieutenant*

The action takes place in a provincial town.

ACT I

A drawing room in the Prozorovs' house: It is separated from a large ballroom at the back by a row of columns. It is midday; there is a cheerful sunshine outside. In the ballroom the table is being laid for lunch. OLGA, *wearing the regulation dark-blue dress of a secondary school teacher, is correcting her pupils' work, standing or walking about as she does so.* MASHA, *in a black dress, is sitting reading a book, her hat on her lap.* IRINA, *in white, stands lost in thought.*

OLGA. Father died just a year ago today, on the fifth of May—your birthday, Irina. I remember, it was very cold and it was snowing. It seemed to me I would never live through it; and you had fainted and were lying there quite still, just as if you were dead. And now—a year's gone by, and we talk about it so easily. You're dressed in white again, and your face is positively radiant . . . [*The clock strikes twelve.*] The clock struck twelve then, too. *A pause.* I remember, the band was playing as they carried father to the cemetery and they fired a salute. That was because he was the general in command of the brigade. And yet there weren't many people there. Of course, it was raining hard, and there was some snow, too.

IRINA. Why must we bring up all these memories?

[TUSENBACH, CHEBUTYKIN, *and* SOLYONY *appear behind the columns by the table in the ballroom.*]

OLGA. It's so warm today that we can keep the windows wide open, but the birches haven't any leaves yet. It was eleven years ago that father got his brigade and we left Moscow. I remember so well how everything was in bloom by now; it was warm and yet I remember everything there as though we'd left it only yesterday. Why, when I woke up this morning and saw the warm sun, saw that spring was here, my heart leapt with joy. I wanted so much to go home again. Go home to Moscow!

CHEBUTYKIN [*sarcastically to* SOLYONY]. A small chance of that!

TUSENBACH [*also to* SOLYONY]. Of course, it's nonsense.

[MASHA, *absorbed in her book, whistles part of a song softly.*]

OLGA. Stop whistling, Masha! How can you? [*A pause.*] I suppose being at school every day from morning till night gives me this constant headache. And my thoughts are as gloomy as those of an old woman. Honestly, I feel as if my strength and my youth were running out of me! Drop by drop; day by day; every day, for the last four years. . . . And one dream keeps growing stronger and stronger. . . .

IRINA. Go to Moscow! Sell the house, leave everything here, and go back to Moscow.

OLGA. Yes, to go back to Moscow! As soon as possible.

[CHEBUTYKIN *and* TUSENBACH *laugh.*]

IRINA. Andrey will probably be a professor soon, anyway he won't keep on living here. The only problem is poor Masha.

OLGA. Masha can come to Moscow every year and spend the whole summer with us.

[MASHA *whistles a song softly.*]

IRINA. Everything will take care of itself with God's help. [*Looking out of the window.*] How beautiful it is today! I don't know why I feel so joyful.

I woke up this morning and remembered it was my birthday, and suddenly I felt so happy. I thought of the time when we were children and mother was still alive. And then such wonderful thoughts came to me . . . such wonderful thoughts.

OLGA. You're all aglow today—lovelier than ever. And Masha is beautiful, too. Andrey could be good-looking, too, if he hadn't put on so much weight; it doesn't suit him. As for me, I've just aged and grown a lot thinner. I suppose it's because I get so angry with the girls at school. Anyway, today I'm free, I'm home, and my head doesn't ache, and I feel so much younger than I did yesterday. After all, I'm only twenty-eight, but . . . Oh well, I suppose everything that God wills must be right and good . . . and yet, it seems to me, if I had married and stayed at home it would have been better. [A pause.] I would have loved my husband, very much.

TUSENBACH [to SOLYONY]. Really, you talk such a lot of nonsense, I'm tired of listening to you. [Comes into the drawing room.] I forgot to tell you, Vershinin, our new battery commander, is coming to call today.

OLGA. Oh really, how nice.

IRINA. Is he old?

TUSENBACH. No, not very. Forty, forty-five at most. He seems like a good fellow. Not a fool, that's for sure. Only he talks a lot.

IRINA. Is he interesting?

TUSENBACH. Yes, so-so—only he has a wife, a mother-in-law, and two little girls. What's more, she's his second wife. He goes around calling on everybody and everywhere he goes he tells people that he has a wife and two little girls. He'll tell you the same thing. It seems his wife's half crazy. She wears her hair in long braids just like a girl, and she is always philosophizing, and frequently she attempts to commit suicide, apparently to annoy her husband. I'd have left a woman like that long ago, but he puts up with her and merely complains.

SOLYONY [entering the drawing room with CHEBUTYKIN]. With one hand I can lift only sixty pounds, but with two I can lift two hundred or even two hundred and forty pounds. From this I conclude that two men are not twice as strong as one, but three times, or even more. . . .

CHEBUTYKIN [reading a newspaper as he comes in]. For falling hair . . . two ounces of naphthalene to half a bottle of alcohol . . . dissolve and apply daily. [Writes it down in his notebook.] Must make a note of it! No I don't want it . . . [Scratches it out.] It doesn't matter.

IRINA. Ivan Romanich, dear Ivan Romanich!

CHEBUTYKIN. What is it, my child, what is it?

IRINA. Tell me, why is it I'm so happy today? It's just as if I were sailing along in a boat with big white sails, and above me the open, blue sky, and in the sky great white birds flying. Why is all this? Why?

CHEBUTYKIN [kissing both her hands tenderly]. My little white bird!

IRINA. You know when I woke up this morning, I suddenly felt I understood everything about the world, and I knew the way I ought to live. I know it all now, my dear Ivan Romanich. Man must work by the sweat of his brow whatever his class, for in that lies the whole meaning and purpose of his life; and his happiness and contentment, too. Oh, how good it must be to be a workman, getting up with the sun and digging ditches . . . or a farmer . . . or a teacher, teaching little children, or an engineer on a railroad. Goodness! It's better to be an ox or a horse and work, than the kind of young woman who wakes up at twelve, drinks her coffee in bed, and then takes two hours dressing . . . How dreadful! You know how you long for a cool drink when it's hot? Well, that's the way I long for work. And if I don't get up early from now on and really work, you can give me up as a friend, Ivan Romanich.

CHEBUTYKIN [*tenderly*].   I will, my dear, I will . . .

OLGA.   Father taught us to get up at seven o'clock and so Irina always wakes up at seven—but then she stays in bed till at least nine, thinking about something or other. And with such a serious expression on her face, too! [*Laughs.*]

IRINA.   You think it's strange when I look serious because you always think of me as a little girl. I'm twenty, you know!

TUSENBACH.   All this longing for work . . . My God! How well I can understand it! I have never worked in my life. I was born in Petersburg, that bleak and idle city—born into a family where work and worries were simply unknown. I remember a valet pulling off my boots for me when I came home from military school . . . I grumbled at the way he did it, and my mother looked on in admiration. She was quite surprised when other people looked at me in any other way. I was protected from work! But I doubt if they have succeeded in protecting me completely . . . yes, I doubt it very much! The time has come . . . a terrific storm is coming, in fact, it's almost here. It will blow away all the laziness, the indifference, the boredom, and the prejudice against work which is ruining our society. I'm going to work, and in twenty-five or thirty years everyone will be working. Every one of us!

CHEBUTYKIN.   I'm not going to work.

TUSENBACH.   You don't count.

SOLYONY [*to* TUSENBACH].   In twenty-five years you'll be dead, thank God. You'll probably die of a stroke in a year or two—or I'll lose my temper and put a bullet through your head, my friend. [*Takes a phial of perfume from his pocket and sprinkles his chest and hands.*]

CHEBUTYKIN [*laughing*].   Really, it's quite true; I haven't done any work since I left the University, no, not a bit. I haven't even read a book, only newspapers. [*Takes another newspaper out of his pocket.*] For instance, here . . . I know from the paper that there was a person called Dobrolyubov, but God only knows what he wrote about. I don't know anything. [*Someone knocks on the floor from downstairs.*] What's that . . . they're calling me downstairs, somebody must have come to see me. I'll be back in a moment . . . [*Going.*] I'm coming . . . [*Goes out hurriedly, stroking his beard.*]

IRINA.   He's up to one of his little games.

TUSENBACH.   Yes. He looked very solemn as he left. He's obviously going to give you a present.

IRINA.   Oh, I wish he wouldn't.

OLGA.   Yes, isn't it dreadful? He's always doing something silly.

MASHA.   "A green oak grows by a curving shore, And round that oak hangs a golden chain" . . . [*Gets up as she sings under her breath.*]

OLGA.   You're sad today, Masha.

[MASHA *puts on her hat singing.*]

OLGA.   Where are you going?

MASHA. Home.

IRINA. That's a strange way to act.

TUSENBACH. What! Leaving your sister's birthday party?

MASHA. What's the difference? I'll be back later. Good-bye, my darling. And once again, I wish you health. . . . I wish you happiness. In the old days when father was alive we used to have thirty or forty officers at our parties. What gay parties we had! And today . . . what have we got today? A man and a half, and the place is as quiet as a tomb. I'm going home. I'm depressed today, I'm sad, so don't listen to me. [*Laughs through her tears.*] We'll talk later on, but goodbye for now, my dear. I'll go somewhere or other . . .

IRINA [*displeased*]. Really, you are such a . . .

OLGA [*tearfully*]. I understand you, Masha.

SOLYONY. When a man philosophizes, you'll get philosophy . . . or sophistry; but if a woman or a couple of women start philosophizing, you might as well forget it!

MASHA. What do you mean by that? You're a horrible man!

SOLYONY. Nothing. "He had hardly time to catch his breath / before the bear was hugging him to death." [*A pause.*]

MASHA [*to* OLGA, *crossly*]. Do stop that crying!

[*Enter* ANFISA *and* FERAPONT, *the latter carrying a large cake.*]

ANFISA. Come along, my dear, come in. Your boots are clean. [*To* IRINA.] A cake from Mr. Protopopov, at the Council Office. From Mihail Ivanich . . .

IRINA. Thank you. Please tell him I'm very grateful. [*Takes the cake.*]

FERAPONT. What's that, Miss?

IRINA [*louder*]. Thank Mr. Protopopov.

OLGA. Nurse, will you give him a piece of cake? Go along, Ferapont, they'll give you some cake.

FERAPONT. What's that, Miss?

ANFISA. Come along with me, my dear, come along. [*Goes out with* FERAPONT.]

MASHA. I don't like that Protopopov, Mihail Potapich or Ivanich, or whatever it is. You shouldn't have invited him.

IRINA. I didn't invite him.

MASHA. Thank goodness.

[*Enter* CHEBUTYKIN, *followed by a maid carrying a silver samovar. Murmurs of astonishment and displeasure.*[1]]

OLGA [*covering her face with her hands*]. A samovar! But this is dreadful! [*Goes through to the ballroom and stands by the table.*]

IRINA. My dear Ivan Romanich, what are you thinking of?

TUSENBACH [*laughing*]. Didn't I tell you?

MASHA. Ivan Romanich, you ought to be ashamed of yourself!

CHEBUTYKIN. My dear, sweet girls, I've no one in the world but you. You're dearer to me than anything in the world! I'm nearly sixty, I'm an old man, a lonely, insignificant old man. The only thing that's worth anything in me is my love for you, and if it weren't for you, really I would have been dead long ago. [*To* IRINA.] My dear, my sweet little girl, I've known you ever since you were born—I used to carry you in my arms—I loved your mother. . . .

---

1 A samovar is a traditional wedding present.

IRINA. But why such an expensive present?

CHEBUTYKIN [*tearfully and crossly*]. Expensive present! Don't talk such nonsense! [*To the maid.*] Take the samovar to the other room. [*In a mocking tone, mimicking* IRINA.] Expensive presents! [*The maid takes the samovar to the ballroom.*]

ANFISA [*crosses the drawing room*]. Girls, a strange colonel has just arrived. He's taken off his coat and he's on his way up. Irinushka, do be nice to him, won't you. [*As she goes out.*] And it's time for lunch already . . . mercy on us . . .

TUSENBACH. It's Vershinin, I imagine.

[*Enter Vershinin.*]

TUSENBACH. Lieutenant-Colonel Vershinin!

VERSHININ [*to* MASHA *and* IRINA]. Allow me to introduce myself— Lieutenant-Colonel Vershinin. I'm very, very glad to be here at last. How you've changed!

IRINA. Please sit down. We're delighted to see you.

VERSHININ [*gayly*]. I'm so glad to see you, so glad! But there were three little girls. I don't remember their faces, but I knew your father, Colonel Prozorov, and I remember he had three little girls. Oh, yes, I saw them myself. I remember them quite well. How time flies! My, how it flies!

TUSENBACH. Alexander Ignatyevich comes from Moscow.

IRINA. From Moscow? You come from Moscow?

VERSHININ. Yes, from Moscow. Your father was a battery commander there, and I was an officer in his brigade. [*To* MASHA.] I seem to remember your face.

MASHA. I don't remember you.

IRINA. Olga, Olga! [*Calls towards the ballroom.*] Olga, come here! [OLGA *enters from the ballroom.*] It seems that Lieutenant-Colonel Vershinin comes from Moscow.

VERSHININ. You must be Olga Sergeyevna, the oldest. And you are Marya . . . and you are Irina, the youngest. . . .

OLGA. You're from Moscow?

VERSHININ. Yes, I studied in Moscow and entered the service there. I stayed there quite awhile, but then I was put in charge of a battery here—so I moved out here, you see. I don't really remember you, you know, I only remember that there were three sisters. I remember your father, though, I remember him very well. All I need to do is to close my eyes and I can see him standing there as if he were alive. I used to visit you in Moscow.

OLGA. I thought I remembered everybody, and yet . . .

VERSHININ. My Christian names are Alexander Ignatyevich.

IRINA. Alexander Ignatyevich, and you come from Moscow! Well, what a surprise!

OLGA. We're going to move there, you know.

IRINA. We're going in the fall. It's our home, we were born there . . . On old Basmanaya Street. [*Both laugh happily.*]

MASHA. Imagine, meeting someone from home so unexpectedly! [*Eagerly.*] I remember now. Do you remember, Olga, they used to talk of "the lovesick Major"? You were a Lieutenant then, weren't you, and you were in love with someone or other, and everyone used to tease you about it. They called you "Major" for some reason or other.

VERSHININ [*laughs*]. That's it, that's it . . . "The lovesick Major," that's what they called me.

MASHA. In those days you only had a moustache . . . Oh, dear, how much older you look! [*Tearfully.*] How much older!

VERSHININ. Yes, I was still a young man in the days when they called me "the lovesick Major." I was in love then. It's different now.

OLGA. You've aged, yes, but you're certainly not an old man.

VERSHININ. I'm going on forty-three. How long has it been since you left Moscow?

IRINA. Eleven years. Now what are you crying for, Masha, you silly? [*Tearfully.*] You'll make me cry, too.

MASHA. I'm not crying. What street did you live on?

VERSHININ. On old Basmanaya.

OLGA. We did, too.

VERSHININ. At one time I lived on Nyemstsky Street. I used to walk from there to the Krasny Barracks, and I remember there was such a gloomy looking bridge I had to cross. I used to hear the noise of the water rushing under it. I remember how lonely and sad I felt there. [*A pause.*] But what a magnificently wide river you have here! It's a marvelous river!

OLGA. Yes, but this is a cold place, and there are too many mosquitoes.

VERSHININ. Really? I should have said you had a splendid climate here, a real Russian climate. Forests, a river . . . birch trees, too. Charming, unpretentious birch trees—I love them more than any other tree. It's nice living here. But there's one thing I can't understand: the train station is fifteen miles away, and no one knows why.

SOLYONY. I know why. [*Everyone looks at him.*] Because if the station were nearer, it wouldn't be so far away, and since it's so far away it can't be nearer.

[*An awkward silence.*]

TUSENBACH. You like your little joke, Vassily Vassilyevich.

OLGA. I'm sure I remember you now. I know I do.

VERSHININ. I knew your mother.

CHEBUTYKIN. She was a fine woman, God bless her!

IRINA. Mother is buried in Moscow.

OLGA. At the convent of Novo-Dievichye.

MASHA. Would you believe it, I'm even beginning to forget what she looked like. I suppose people will not remember us either. . . . We'll be forgotten.

VERSHININ. Yes, we'll all be forgotten. Such is our fate and we can't do anything about it. And what seems so very important to us now will be forgotten, and seem trivial. [*A pause.*] It's strange to think that we can't possibly tell what will be regarded as great and important in the future and what will be thought of as small and insignificant. Didn't the great discoveries of Copernicus—or of Columbus—appear useless and unimportant at first?—while the nonsense written by some eccentric was regarded as a revelation of a great new truth? It may well be that in time the life we live today will be considered primitive and ugly and strange, and perhaps even evil . . .

TUSENBACH. Who knows? It's just as possible that future generations will think of our age as great and remember us with respect. After all, we've done away with hangings and public torture, and there haven't been any invasions, although a lot of people still suffer.

SOLYONY [*in a high-pitched voice as if calling to chickens*]. Cluck, cluck, cluck! There's nothing our good Baron loves as much as philosophizing.

TUSENBACH. Vassily Vassilyevich, will you let me alone? I'm getting sick of it.

SOLYONY [*as before*]. Cluck, cluck, cluck! . . .

TUSENBACH [*to* VERSHININ]. All the suffering we see around us—and there's a great deal—proves that our society has achieved a higher standard of morality than . . .

VERSHININ. Yes, yes, of course.

CHEBUTYKIN. Baron, you just said that our age will be called great; but people are small . . . [*Gets up.*] Look how small I am.

[*A violin is played off-stage.*]

MASHA. That's our brother, Andrey, playing the violin.

IRINA. He's our scholar . . . He'll probably be a professor. Father was a soldier, but his son has chosen an academic career.

OLGA. We've been teasing him today. He thinks he's in love.

IRINA. With a girl who lives here. She'll probably come later on.

MASHA. Heavens, how she dresses! It's not that her clothes are not pretty, but she has no taste. She'll put on some weird-looking bright yellow skirt with a cheap-looking fringe, and then a red blouse to go with it. And she has such a scrubbed look. Andrey's not in love with her—I can't believe it; he's not that vulgar. I think he's playing the fool, just to annoy us. I heard yesterday that she's going to marry Protopopov, the chairman of the local board. I think that's an excellent idea. [*Calls through the side door.*] Andrey, come here, will you? Just for a minute.

[*Enter* ANDREY.]

OLGA. This is my brother, Andrey Sergeyevich.

VERSHININ. Vershinin.

ANDREY. Prozorov [*wipes the perspiration from his face*]. I understand you've been appointed battery commander here?

OLGA. What do you think, dear? Alexander Ignatyevich comes from Moscow.

ANDREY. Do you, really? Congratulations! You'll get no peace from my sisters now.

VERSHININ. I'm afraid your sisters must be bored with me already.

IRINA. See what a lovely picture frame Andrey gave me for my birthday. [*Shows him the frame.*] He made it himself.

VERSHININ [*looks at the frame, not knowing what to say*]. Yes, it's . . . it's very nice. . . .

IRINA. And do you see that frame on the piano? He made that, too.

[*Andrey waves his hand impatiently and walks off.*]

OLGA. He's a scholar, and he plays the violin, and he makes all sorts of things, too. In fact, he can do almost anything. Andrey, please, don't go. He's got such a bad habit—always walking away. Come here!

[MASHA *and* IRINA *take him by the arms and lead him back, laughing.*]

MASHA.   Now you come here!

ANDREY.   Leave me alone, please!

MASHA.   What a silly! They used to call Alexander Ignatyevich "the love-sick major," and he didn't get annoyed.

VERSHININ.   Not at all.

MASHA.   I feel like calling you a "lovesick fiddler."

IRINA.   Or a "lovesick professor."

OLGA.   He's fallen in love! Our Andriusha's in love!

IRINA [*clapping her hands*].   Three cheers for Andriusha! Andriusha's in love!

CHEBUTYKIN.   "Nature created us for love alone." [*Laughs loudly, still holding his paper in his hand.*]

ANDREY.   That's enough, that's enough . . . [*Wipes his face.*] I didn't sleep all night, and I'm not feeling very well today. I read till four, and then I went to bed, but I couldn't sleep. I kept thinking about one thing and another . . . and it gets light so early; the sun just pours into my room. I'd like to translate a book from the English while I'm here during the summer.

VERSHININ.   You read English?

ANDREY.   Yes. My father—God bless him—inflicted education upon us. It sounds silly, I know, but I must confess that since he died I've begun to put on weight. It's almost as if I'd been relieved of the strain. I've gotten quite fat this past year. Yes, thanks to Father, my sisters and I know French, German, and English, and Irina here knows Italian, too. But what an effort it was!

MASHA.   Knowing three languages in a town like this is an unnecessary luxury. In fact, not even a luxury, just a useless encumbrance . . . like having a sixth finger. We know a lot that's just useless.

VERSHININ.   Really! [*Laughs.*] You know a lot that's useless! It seems to me that there's no place on earth, no matter how dull and depressing it may be, where intelligent and educated people aren't needed. Let's suppose that among the hundred thousand people living here, there are just three people like you—all the rest being uneducated and uncultured. Obviously, you can't hope to win out over the ignorance of the masses around you; in the course of your life, you'll have to give in little by little until you are lost in that crowd of one hundred thousand. Life will swallow you up, but not completely, for you'll have made some impression. After you've gone, perhaps there'll be six more people like you, then twelve, and so on, until finally most people will have become like you. Why, in two or three hundred years life on this earth will be wonderfully beautiful. Man longs for a life like that, and if he doesn't have it right now, he must imagine it, wait for it, dream about it, prepare for it; he must know more and see more than his father and his grandfather did. [*Laughs.*] And you complain because you know a lot that's useless.

MASHA [*takes off her hat*].   I'm staying for lunch.

IRINA [*with a sigh*].   Really, someone should have written all that down.

[ANDREY *has left the room unnoticed.*]

TUSENBACH.   You say that in time to come life will be wonderfully beautiful. That's probably true. But if we're to have a part in it right now, at a distance so to speak, we've got to prepare for it and work for it.

VERSHININ [*gets up*].   Yes . . . Why, look at all the flowers! [*Looks *around.*] And what a marvelous house! How I envy you! All my life I seem to have lived in a small apartment, with two chairs and a sofa and a stove which always smokes. It's the flowers that I've missed in my life, flowers like these! . . . [*Rubs his hands.*] But then, it's no use thinking about it.

TUSENBACH. Yes, we must work. I suppose you think I'm just a sentimental German. But believe me, I'm not—I'm Russian. I don't know a word of German, and my father was a member of the Orthodox Church.

[*A pause.*]

VERSHININ [*walks up and down the room*]. You know, I often wonder what it would be like if we could begin our lives over again—deliberately, I mean, consciously . . . as if the life we'd already lived were just a kind of rough draft, and we could begin all over again with the final copy. If that happened, I think the things we'd all want most would be not to repeat ourselves. We'd try at least to create a new environment, say a house like this one, for instance, with flowers and lots of light. . . . I have a wife, as you know, and two little girls; and my wife's not very well, and . . . Well, if I could begin my life all over again, I wouldn't marry. . . . No, no!

[*Enter* KULYGIN *in the uniform of a teacher.*]

KULYGIN [*approaches* IRINA]. Congratulations, my dear sister—from the bottom of my heart, congratulations on your birthday. I wish you the best of health and everything else a girl of your age ought to have! And allow me to give you this little book. [*Hands her a book.*] It's the history of our school covering the whole fifty years of its existence. I wrote it myself. It's not much, of course—I wrote it in my spare time when I had nothing better to do—but, nevertheless, I hope you'll read it. Good morning to you all! [*To* VERSHININ.] Allow me to introduce myself. Kulygin's the name; I'm a teacher at the high school here. [*To* IRINA.] You'll find a list in the book of all the pupils who have graduated from our school during the last fifty years. "*Feci quod potui, faciant meliora potentes.*" [*Kisses* MASHA.]

IRINA. But you gave me this book last Easter!

KULYGIN [*laughs*]. Did I really? In that case, give it back to me—or no, better give it to the Colonel. Please take it, Colonel. Maybe you'll read it sometime when you've nothing better to do?

VERSHININ. Thank you very much. [*Prepares to leave.*] I'm very happy to have made your acquaintance . . .

OLGA. You aren't going, are you? . . . Really, you mustn't.

IRINA. You must stay and have lunch with us! Please do.

OLGA. Please do.

VERSHININ [*bows*]. It looks like I've interrupted your birthday party. I didn't know. Forgive me for not congratulating you. [*Goes into the ballroom with* OLGA.]

KULYGIN. Today is Sunday, my friends, a day of rest; let us rest and enjoy it, each according to his age and position in life! We shall have to take up the carpets and put them away till the winter . . . And we mustn't forget to put some naphthalene on them or Persian powder . . . The Romans were a healthy people because they knew how to work *and* how to rest. They had "*mens sana in corpore sano.*" Their life had a definite shape, a form . . . The headmaster says that the most important thing about life is form. . . . A thing that loses its form is finished—that's just as true of our ordinary, everyday lives. [*Takes* MASHA *by the waist and laughs.*] Masha loves me. My wife loves me. Yes, and the curtains will have to be put away with the carpets, too . . . I'm happy today, very happy . . . Masha, we're invited to the headmaster's at four o'clock. A walk in the country has been arranged for the teachers and their families.

MASHA. I'm not going.

KULYGIN [*distressed*]. Masha, darling, why not?

MASHA. I'll tell you later . . . [*Crossly.*] All right, I'll come, only leave me alone now . . . [*Walks off.*]

KULYGIN. And after the walk we'll all spend the evening at the head-master's house. In spite of his poor health, that man certainly tries to be pleasant. A fine, thoroughly enlightened man! A remarkable person! After the meeting yesterday he said to me: "I'm tired, Fyodor Ilyich. I'm tired!" [*Looks at the clock, then at his watch.*] Your clock is seven minutes fast. Yes, "I'm tired," he said.

[*The sound of the violin is heard off-stage.*]

OLGA. Will you all come and sit down, please! Lunch is ready. There's pie.

KULYGIN. Ah, Olga, my dear! Last night I worked till eleven, and I felt tired, but today I'm so happy. [*Goes to the table in the ballroom.*] My dear Olga!

CHEBUTYKIN [*puts the newspaper in his pocket and combs his beard*]. A pie? Excellent!

MASHA [*sternly to* CHEBUTYKIN]. Remember, no drinking today. Do you hear? It's bad for you.

CHEBUTYKIN. Never mind. I stopped that long ago! I haven't had a drink for two years. [*Impatiently.*] Anyway, my dear, what difference does it make?

MASHA. All the same, there'll be no drinking. Don't you dare! [*Crossly, but taking care that her husband does not hear.*] Damn, I'll have to spend another boring evening at the headmaster's!

TUSENBACH. I wouldn't go if I were you . . . It's very simple.

CHEBUTYKIN. Don't go, my dear.

MASHA. Oh, yes. Don't go! What a miserable life! It's intolerable . . . [*Goes into the ballroom.*]

CHEBUTYKIN [*follows her*]. Well, well! . . .

SOLYONY [*as he passes* TUSENBACH *on the way to the ballroom*]. Cluck, cluck, cluck!

TUSENBACH. Stop it, Vassily Vassilyevich. I've had enough . . .

SOLYONY. Cluck, cluck, cluck! . . .

KULYGIN [*gayly*]. Your health, Colonel! I'm a schoolteacher . . . and a member of the family. I'm Masha's husband. She has a sweet nature, such a very sweet nature!

VERSHININ. I think I'll have a little of this dark vodka. [*Drinks.*] Your health! [*To* OLGA.] It feels so good to be with you all. I'm so happy.

[*Only* IRINA *and* TUSENBACH *remain in the drawing-room.*]

IRINA. Masha's in a bad mood today. You know, she got married when she was eighteen, and she thought her husband was the most brilliant man in the world. It's different now. He's the kindest of men, but not the most brilliant.

OLGA [*impatiently*]. Andrey, will you please come?

ANDREY [*off-stage*]. I'm coming. [*Enters and goes to the table.*]

TUSENBACH. What are you thinking about?

IRINA. Oh, not much. You know, I don't like Solyony, he frightens me. He says such stupid things.

TUSENBACH. He's a strange man. I'm sorry for him, even though he annoys me. In fact, I feel more sorry for him than annoyed. I think he's shy. When he's alone with me, he can be most intelligent and very friendly, but in company he's offensive and rude. Don't go yet, let them sit down first. I just want to be close to you for a moment. What are you thinking about? [*A pause.*] You're twenty . . . and I'm still not thirty. We've got years and years ahead of us, a whole lifetime, all full of my love for you! . . .

IRINA. Don't talk to me about love, Nikolai Lvovich.

TUSENBACH [*not listening*]. Oh, I long so passionately for life, to work and aspire, and all this longing is a part of my love for you, Irina. And because you are beautiful, life is beautiful for me, too! What are you thinking about?

IRINA. You say that life is beautiful. Maybe it is—but what if it only seems to be beautiful? Our lives, I mean the lives of us three sisters, haven't been beautiful. The truth is that life has been stifling us, like weeds in a garden. I'm sorry I'm crying . . . I shouldn't . . . [*Quickly dries her eyes and smiles.*] We must work! work! The reason we feel depressed and have such a gloomy view of life is that we've never known what it is to really work. We're the children of parents who despised work . . . [*Enter* NATALYA IVANOVNA. *She is wearing a pink dress with a green belt.*]

NATASHA. They've gone into lunch already. . . . I'm late . . . [*Glances at herself in a mirror, adjusts her dress.*] Is my hair all right . . . [*Catches sight of* IRINA.] My dear Irina Sergeyevna, congratulations! [*Gives her a vigorous and prolonged kiss.*] You've got so many guests . . . I feel quite shy . . . How do you do, Baron?

OLGA [*enters the drawing room*]. Oh, there you are, Natalya Ivanovna! How are you, my dear? [*They kiss each other.*]

NATASHA. Congratulations! There are so many people here, I am so afraid . . .

OLGA. It's all right, they're all old friends. [*Alarmed, dropping her voice.*] You've got a green belt on! My dear, that must be a mistake!

NATASHA. Why, is it a bad omen, or what?

OLGA. No, but it just doesn't go with your dress . . . it looks so strange. . . .

NATASHA [*tearfully*]. Really? But it isn't really green, it's just sort of a dull color . . . [*Follows* OLGA *to the ballroom.*]

[*All are now seated at the table; the drawing room is empty.*]

KULYGIN. Irina, you know, I do wish you'd find yourself a good husband. It's high time you got married.

CHEBUTYKIN. You ought to be getting married, too, Natalya Ivanovna.

KULYGIN. Natalya Ivanovna already has a husband picked out.

MASHA [*strikes her plate with her fork*]. Let's have a glass of vodka! Oh, life is sweet—what the hell. . . .

KULYGIN. Masha, black mark for conduct!

VERSHININ. I say, this wine's very good. What's it made of?

SOLYONY. Beetles!

IRINA. Ugh! Ugh! How disgusting!

OLGA. We're having turkey and apple pie for dinner tonight. Thank goodness, I'll be here all day today . . . tonight, too. You must all come this evening.

VERSHININ.   Am I invited, too?

IRINA.   Yes, please come.

NATASHA.   There are no formalities here.

CHEBUTYKIN.   "Nature created us for love alone . . ." [*Laughs.*]

ANDREY [*crossly*].   Will you stop it, please? Aren't you tired of it yet?

[FEDOTIK *and* RODÉ *come in with a large basket of flowers.*]

FEDOTIK.   Look, they're eating already!

RODÉ [*in a loud voice*].   Eating? So they are.

FEDOTIK.   Wait a minute. [*Takes a snapshot.*] One! Just one more! . . . [*Takes another snapshot.*] Two! That's all.

[*They pick up the basket and go into the ballroom where they are greeted uproariously.*]

RODÉ [*loudly*].   Congratulations, Irina Sergeyevna! I wish you the best of everything! Marvelous weather today, absolutely gorgeous. I've been out walking with the boys all morning long. You know I teach gym at the high school, don't you?

FEDOTIK.   You may move now, Irina Sergeyevna, that is, if you want to. [*Takes snapshot.*] My, you look attractive today. [*Takes a top out of his pocket.*] By the way, look at this top. It's got a wonderful hum.

IRINA.   How lovely!

MASHA.   "A green oak grows by a curving shore, And round that oak hangs a golden chain." . . . A green chain around that oak . . . [*Peevishly.*] Why do I keep on saying that? Those lines have been going through my head all day long!

KULYGIN.   Do you know, there are thirteen of us at the table?

RODÉ [*loudly*].   You don't really believe in those old superstitions, do you? [*Laughter.*]

KULYGIN.   When there are thirteen at the table, it means that someone's in love. Is it you, by any chance, Ivan Romanich?

CHEBUTYKIN.   Oh, I'm just an old sinner. . . . But what I can't make out is why Natalya Ivanovna looks so embarrassed.

[*Loud laughter.* NATASHA *runs out into the drawing room.* ANDREY *follows her.*]

ANDREY.   Please, Natasha, don't pay any attention to them! Stop . . . wait a moment. . . . Please!

NATASHA.   I feel so ashamed . . . I don't know what's the matter with me, and they're all laughing at me. I know it's bad manners to leave the table like that, but I just couldn't help it . . . I just couldn't. . . . [*Covers her face with her hands.*]

ANDREY.   My darling, please, please don't be upset. Believe me, they aren't trying to hurt you, they're just teasing. My dearest, darling, they're really very kind, really they are, and they love us both. Come over here to the window, they can't see us here . . . [*Looks round.*]

NATASHA.   You see, I'm not used to being with so many people.

ANDREY.   Oh, how young you are, Natasha, how wonderfully, beautifully young! My darling, my darling, don't be worried! Believe me, believe me . . . I'm so happy, so full of love, of joy . . . No, they won't see us! They can't see us! Why do I love you, when did I fall in love? . . . I don't understand anything. My precious, my sweet, my innocent girl, please—please marry me! I love you, I love you as I've never loved anybody . . . [*Kisses her.*]

[*Enter two officers who, seeing* NATASHA *and* ANDREY *kissing, stand and stare in amazement.*]

Curtain

ACT II

The scene is the same as in Act I. It is eight o'clock in the evening. The faint sound of an accordion is heard coming from the street. The stage is unlit. Enter NATALYA IVANOVNA *in a dressing gown carrying a candle. She crosses the stage and stops by the door leading to* ANDREY's *room.*

NATASHA. What are you doing, Andriusha? Reading? Oh, it's nothing. I only wanted you to know . . . [*Goes to another door, opens it, looks inside and shuts it again.*] No one's left a light. . . .

ANDREY [*enters with a book in his hand*]. What is it, Natasha?

NATASHA. I was just looking to see if anyone had left any lights burning. It's carnival week, and the servants are so excited about it . . . If you don't watch them anything can happen. Last night about midnight I happened to go into the dining room and—would you believe it?—there was a candle burning on the table. I haven't found out who lit it. [*Puts the candle down.*] What time is it?

ANDREY [*glances at his watch*]. Quarter past eight.

NATASHA. And Olga and Irina still out. They aren't back from work yet, poor things! Olga's still at some faculty meeting, and Irina's at the post office. [*Sighs.*] This morning I said to Irina: "Darling, please take care of yourself." But she won't listen. Did you say it was a quarter past eight? I'm afraid Bobik isn't well. Why does he get so cold? Yesterday he had a fever, but today he is cold all over. . . . I'm so worried!

ANDREY. It's all right, Natasha. The boy's all right.

NATASHA. Still, I think he ought to have a special diet. I'm so anxious about him. Oh, by the way, they tell me that some carnival party's supposed to be coming at nine. I'd rather they didn't come, Andriusha.

ANDREY. Well, I really don't know what I can do. They've been asked to come.

NATASHA. This morning the little angel woke up and looked at me, and suddenly he smiled. He recognized me. "Good morning, Bobik," I said, "good morning, my darling!" And he laughed. You know, babies understand everything; they understand us perfectly well. Anyway, Andriusha, I'll tell the servants not to let that carnival party in.

ANDREY [*irresolutely*]. Well . . . it's really for my sisters to decide, isn't it? It's their house, after all.

NATASHA. Yes, it's their house too. I'll tell them . . . They're so kind . . . [*Walks off.*] I've ordered pudding for supper. The doctor says you ought to eat nothing but pudding or you'll never get any thinner. [*Stops.*] Bobik feels so cold. I'm afraid his room is too cold for him. He ought to be in a warmer room, at least until spring comes. For instance, Irina's room would be a perfect room for a baby: it's dry, and it's sunny all day long. I must tell her. She could share Olga's room for awhile . . . Anyway, she's never at home during the day, she just sleeps here . . . [A pause.] Andriusha, why don't you say something?

ANDREY. I was thinking . . . Anyway, what's there to say . . .

NATASHA. Well . . . What was it I was going to tell you? Oh, yes! Ferapont from the Council Office wants to see you about something.

ANDREY [yawns]. Tell him to come in.

[NATASHA goes out; ANDREY, bending over the candle which she has left behind, begins to read his book. Enter FERAPONT in an old shabby overcoat, his collar turned up, his ears muffled in a scarf.]

ANDREY. Hello, old man! What is it?

FERAPONT. The chairman's sent you these reports and a letter or something. Here! [Hands him the book and the letter.]

ANDREY. Thanks. That's all. By the way, why have you come so late? It's after eight.

FERAPONT. What's that?

ANDREY [raising his voice]. I said, why have you come so late? It's after eight.

FERAPONT. Yes, yes. The sun was shining when I came, but they wouldn't let me see you. The master's busy, they said. Well, if you're busy, you're busy. I'm in no hurry. [Thinking that ANDREY has said something.] How's that?

ANDREY. Nothing. [Turns over the pages of the register.] Tomorrow's Friday, there's no meeting, but I'll go to the office just the same . . . do some work. I'm so bored at home! . . . [A pause.] Yes, old man, how things change, what a fraud life is! It's strange. Why, today I picked up this notebook, I was bored and didn't have anything to do . . . Imagine, my lecture notes from the University . . . My God! Just think—I'm secretary of the local council now, and Protopopov's chairman, and the most I can ever hope for is to become a member of the council myself! I—a member of the local council! I, who dream every night that I'm a professor at the University of Moscow, a distinguished scholar, the pride of all Russia!

FERAPONT. I'm sorry, I wouldn't know. I don't hear very well.

ANDREY. Do you think I'd be talking to you like this if you could? I've got to talk to someone, and my wife doesn't seem to understand me, and as for my sisters . . . for some reason they frighten me. I'm afraid they'll laugh at me and I couldn't stand it . . . I don't drink and I don't like going to taverns, but how I'd enjoy just sitting at Tyestov's again, or the Great Moscow Restaurant! Just for an hour. Yes, old man, I would indeed!

FERAPONT. The other day at the office a contractor was telling me about some businessmen who were eating pancakes in Moscow. One of them ate forty pancakes and died. It was either forty or fifty, I can't remember for sure.

ANDREY. You can sit in some huge restaurant in Moscow and not know a soul, and no one knows you; yet somehow you feel that you belong there. . . . But here you know everybody, and everybody knows you, and yet you don't feel you belong here, no, not at all. . . . You're a stranger and all alone.

FERAPONT. What's that? [Pause.] The same man told me—of course, he could have been lying—that there's a long rope stretched all the way across Moscow.

ANDREY. Whatever for?

FERAPONT. I'm sorry, I don't know, but that's what he said.

ANDREY. Nonsense! [*Reads the book.*] Have you ever been to Moscow?

FERAPONT [*after a pause*]. No. It wasn't God's wish. [*A pause.*] Shall I go now?

ANDREY. Yes, you may go. Good-bye [FERAPONT *goes out.*] Good-bye. [*Reading.*] Come in the morning, I'll have some letters for you . . . You can go now. [*A pause.*] He's gone. [*A bell rings.*] Yes, that's how it is . . . [*Stretches and slowly goes to his room.*]

[*Singing is heard off-stage; a nurse is putting a baby to sleep. Enter* MASHA *and* VERSHININ. *While they talk together a maid lights a lamp and candles in the ballroom.*]

MASHA. I don't know. [*A pause.*] I don't know. Habit's a very important thing of course. For example, after Father died, it took a long time to get used to the idea of not having any orderlies around to wait on us. But even apart from habit, I think I'm perfectly justified in saying—and of course, this may be different in other places, but in this town the officers are certainly the nicest and most generous and best mannered people.

VERSHININ. I'm thirsty. I'd like some tea.

MASHA [*glances at her watch*]. They'll bring it in soon. You see, I was married when I was eighteen. I was so afraid of my husband because he was a teacher, and I had just finished school myself. He seemed terribly brilliant then, very learned and important. But now, unfortunately, it's quite different.

VERSHININ. Yes . . . I see . . .

MASHA. Oh, I'm not speaking of my husband—I'm used to him now—but there are so many vulgar and unpleasant and ill-mannered people here. Rudeness upsets me, it hurts me, I actually suffer when I meet someone who lacks refinement and courtesy. When I'm with my husband's colleagues, I'm simply miserable.

VERSHININ. Yes, I understand. But it seems to me it's all the same whether they are civilian or military, they are equally dull, in this town at least. It's all the same! If you talk to one of the local intelligentsia—civilian or military, he'll generally tell you that he's just worn out. It's either his wife, or his house, or his estate, or his horse, or something . . . We Russians are peculiarly given to exalted ideas—but why is it we always fall so short in life? Why is it, why?

MASHA. Why?

VERSHININ. Yes, why does his wife wear him out, why is he worried to death by his children? And what about *him* exhausting his wife and children?

MASHA. You're really depressed today, aren't you?

VERSHININ. Perhaps. I've had nothing to eat since morning. One of the girls isn't feeling very well, and when the children are sick, I get too worried. My conscience torments me for having given them a mother like theirs. Oh, if only you could have seen her this morning! What a despicable woman! We began quarrelling at seven and at nine I finally walked out and slammed the door. [*A pause.*] I never talk about it. Strange, it's only to you I complain. [*Kisses her hand.*] Don't be angry with me. I've nobody, nobody but you . . . [*A pause.*]

MASHA. What a noise the wind's making in the stove! Just before Father died the wind howled in the chimney. There, just like that.

VERSHININ. Are you superstitious?

MASHA. Yes.

VERSHININ. How strange. [*Kisses her hand.*] You really are a wonderful creature, a marvelous woman! Wonderful, magnificent! It's dark here, but I can see your eyes shining.

MASHA [*moves to another chair*]. There's more light over here.

VERSHININ. I love you, I love you, I love you . . . I love your eyes, love the way you move . . . I see them in my dreams. A wonderful, marvelous woman!

MASHA [*laughing softly*]. When you talk to me like that, somehow I can't help laughing, although I'm frightened. Don't do it again, please. [*Half-audibly.*] No . . . go on. I don't mind . . . [*Covers her face with her hands.*] I don't mind . . . Someone's coming . . . talk about something else.

[*Enter* IRINA *and* TUSENBACH *through the ballroom.*]

TUSENBACH. I have a triple-barrelled name—Baron Tusenbach-Krone-Alschauer—but actually I'm a Russian. I was baptized in the Orthodox Church, just like yourself. There's nothing German about me, except maybe the obstinate way I keep on pestering you. Look how I bring you home every night.

IRINA. How tired I am!

TUSENBACH. And I'll keep bringing you home every night for the next twenty years—unless you send me away . . . [*Noticing* MASHA *and* VERSHININ, *with pleasure.*] Oh, it's you! How are you!

IRINA. Well, here I am, home at last! [*To* MASHA.] A woman came into the office just as I was leaving. She wanted to send a wire to her brother in Saratov to tell him her son had just died, but she couldn't remember the address. So she sent it without an address, just to Saratov. She was crying and I was rude to her, for no reason at all. "I've no time to waste," I told her. It was stupid of me. Are the carnival people coming tonight?

MASHA. Yes.

IRINA [*sits down*]. How nice it is to relax! I'm so tired!

TUSENBACH [*smiling*]. When you get home from work, you look so young and so unhappy, somehow. [*A pause.*]

IRINA. I'm tired. No, I don't like working at the post office, I don't like it at all.

MASHA. You've gotten so much thinner . . . [*Whistles.*] You look younger, too, and your face is beginning to look like a little boy's.

TUSENBACH. It's the way she does her hair.

IRINA. I must get another job. This one doesn't suit me. It lacks all the things I long for and dream of. It's work without poetry, without meaning. [*Someone knocks at the floor from below.*] There's the Doctor knocking. [*To* TUSENBACH.] Will you answer him? I can't . . . I'm too tired. [TUSENBACH *knocks on the floor.*]

IRINA. He'll be up in a minute. We've got to do something about all this. Andrey and the Doctor went to the club last night and lost again. They say Andrey lost two hundred roubles.

MASHA [*with indifference*]. Well, what are we to do?

IRINA. He lost two weeks ago, and he lost in December, too. I wish he'd just lose everything as soon as possible. Perhaps then we'd leave for Moscow. Oh dear, I dream of Moscow every night. Sometimes I feel as if I were going mad. [*Laughs.*] We're going back to Moscow in June. How many months are there till June? . . . February, March, April, May . . . almost half a year!

MASHA. We must be careful that Natasha doesn't find out about his gambling.

IRINA. I don't think she'd care.

[*Enter* CHEBUTYKIN. *He has been resting on his bed since dinner and has only just got up. He combs his beard, then sits down at the table and takes out a newspaper.*]

MASHA. Here he comes. Has he paid his rent yet?

IRINA [*laughs*]. No. Not a penny for the last eight months. He's probably forgotten.

MASHA [*laughs*]. Look, how solemnly he sits there!

[*They all laugh. A pause.*]

IRINA. Why are you so quiet, Alexander Ignatyevich?

VERSHININ. I don't know. I just want some tea. I'd give my life for a glass of tea! I haven't eaten anything since morning . . .

CHEBUTYKIN. Irina Sergeyevna!

IRINA. What is it?

CHEBUTYKIN. Please come here. "*Venez ici!*"[2] [IRINA *goes over to him and sits down at the table.*] I can't do without you. [IRINA *lays out the cards for a game of solitaire.*]

VERSHININ. Well, if we can't have any tea, let's philosophize a bit, anyway.

TUSENBACH. Yes, fine idea. What about?

VERSHININ. What about? Well . . . let's try to imagine what life will be like after we're dead, say in two or three hundred years.

TUSENBACH. All right, then. . . . After we're dead, people will fly in balloons, fashions will change, the sixth sense will be discovered, and for all I know, even developed and used . . . But life itself won't be very different; it will still be mysterious, always difficult, yet filled with happiness. And in a thousand years people will still sigh and complain "How hard life is!"—and yet they'll still be afraid of death and unwilling to die, just as they are now.

VERSHININ [*after a moment's thought*]. Well, you know . . . How shall I put it? I think everything is bound to change gradually—in fact, it's changing before our very eyes. In two or three hundred years, maybe it will take a thousand—how long doesn't really matter—life will be different. It will be happy. Of course, we won't be able to share it, we work and . . . yes, we suffer in order to create it. That's the purpose of our life, and you might say that's the only happiness we shall ever have.

[MASHA *laughs quietly.*]

TUSENBACH. Why are you laughing?

MASHA. I don't know. I've been laughing all day today.

VERSHININ [*to* TUSENBACH]. I went to the same school as you did but I never went on to the Academy. I read a great deal of course, but I never know what books I ought to choose, and I probably read the wrong things. And yet the longer I live the more I want to know. I'm getting older—my hair's getting gray, and yet how little I know, how little! All the same, I think I do know one

---

[2] Chebutykin repeats in French what he has just said. The use of French conveyed an aura of intimacy; servants and children couldn't understand it.

thing which is not only true but also most important. I'm certain of it. Oh, if only I could convince you that there's not going to be any happiness for us and our generation, that there mustn't be and won't be . . . we must work and work. Happiness, well, that's for those who come after us, our remote descendants. [*A pause.*] So even if I'll never be happy, at least my grandchildren will be.

[FEDOTIK *and* RODÉ *enter the ballroom; they sit down and sing quietly, one of them playing on a guitar.*]

TUSENBACH. So you think it's useless to even dream of happiness! But what if I *am* happy?

VERSHININ. You're not.

TUSENBACH [*flinging up his hands and laughing*]. Obviously, we don't understand each other. How can I convince you?

[MASHA *laughs quietly.*]

TUSENBACH [*holds up a finger to her*]. She'll laugh at the drop of a hat! [*To* VERSHININ.] And life won't be any different, no, not only a couple of hundred years from now, but a million. Life doesn't change, it always goes on the same; it follows its own laws, which don't concern us and which we can't discover anyway. Think of the birds flying South in the autumn, the cranes, for instance: they just fly on and on. It doesn't matter what they're thinking, whether their heads are filled with great ideas or small ones, they just keep flying, not knowing where or why. And they'll go on flying no matter how many philosophers they happen to have flying with them. Let them philosophize as much as they like, as long as they go on flying.

MASHA. Isn't there some meaning?

TUSENBACH. Meaning? . . . Look there, it's snowing. What's the meaning of that? [*A pause.*]

MASHA. But man has to have some faith, or at least he's got to seek it, otherwise his life will be empty, empty . . . How can you live and not know why the cranes fly, why children are born, why the stars shine in the sky! . . . You must either know why you live, or else . . . nothing matters . . . everything's just nonsense and waste . . . [*A pause.*]

VERSHININ. Yes, it's sad when one's youth has gone.

MASHA. "It's a bore to be alive in this world, friends," that's what Gogol says.

TUSENBACH. And I say: it's impossible to argue with you, friends! Let's drop the subject.

CHEBUTYKIN [*reads out of the paper*]. Balzac was married in Berditchev.[3]

[IRINA *sings softly to herself.*]

CHEBUTYKIN. I think I'll make a note of that. [*Writes.*] Balzac was married in Berditchev. [*Reads on.*]

IRINA [*playing patience, pensively.*] Balzac was married in Berditchev.

TUSENBACH. Well, the die is cast. Did you know that I'd sent in my resignation, Marya Sergeyevna?

MASHA. So I heard. But what good will come of it? Besides, I don't like civilians.

TUSENBACH. Never mind. What kind of a soldier am I anyway? I'm not

---

3 Honoré de Balzac (1799–1850), the great French novelist, in the last year of his life married Mme. Hanska, a Polish widow, after a long liaison that did not, however, interfere with his numerous other affairs.

even handsome. Anyway, what difference does it make? I'll work. For once in my life, I'd like to work so hard that when I came home I'd collapse on my bed exhausted and go to sleep at once. [*Goes to ballroom.*] Working men must sleep well!

FEDOTIK [*to* IRINA]. I bought you some crayons at Pyshikov's, on Moscow Street. And this little penknife, too . . .

IRINA. You still treat me as if I were a little girl. I wish you'd realize that I've grown up. [*Takes the crayons and the penknife, joyfully.*] Oh, they're wonderful!

FEDOTIK. Look, I bought myself a knife, too. You see, it's got another blade here, and there's another . . . this is for cleaning your ears, and this for cutting your nails, and this is for cleaning them . . .

RODÉ [*in a loud voice*]. Doctor, how old are you?

CHEBUTYKIN. I? Thirty-two. [*Laughter.*]

FEDOTIK. I'll show you another kind of solitaire. [*Sets out the cards.*]

[*The samovar is brought in, and* ANFISA *attends to it. Shortly afterwards* NATASHA *comes in and begins to fuss around the table.* SOLYONY *enters, bows to the company and sits down at the table.*]

VERSHININ. My, what a wind there is tonight!

MASHA. Yes. I'm tired of winter. I've almost forgotten what summer is like.

IRINA [*playing solitaire*]. I'm going to go out. We'll get to Moscow!

FEDOTIK. No, you're not. See, the eight has to go on the two of spades. [*Laughs.*] That means you won't go to Moscow.

CHEBUTYKIN [*reads the paper*]. Tsitsiker. A smallpox epidemic is raging. . . .

ANFISA [*goes up to* MASHA]. Masha dear, the tea's ready. [*To* VERSHININ.] Will you please come to the table, your excellency? Forgive me, your name's slipped my memory . . .

MASHA. Bring it here, Nanny. I don't feel like getting it.

IRINA. Nanny!

ANFISA. I'm comi-ing!

NATASHA [*to* SOLYONY]. You know, even little babies understand what we say, they can understand us completely! Why, this morning I said to Bobik, "Good morning, Bobik, good morning, my precious!"—and he looked up at me in his special way. You can say it's only a mother's imagination, but it isn't, I promise you. No, no! He is really a most unusual child!

SOLYONY. If that child were mine, I'd fry him in a pan and eat him. [*Picks up his glass, goes into the drawing room and sits down in a corner.*]

NATASHA [*covers her face with her hands*]. What a rude, disgusting man!

MASHA. People don't even notice whether it's summer or winter when they're happy. If I lived in Moscow I wouldn't care what the weather was like.

VERSHININ. The other day I was reading the diary of some French minister—he wrote it in prison. He was convicted for his involvement in the fraud of the Panama affair.[4] He writes with such enthusiasm and delight about the birds he can see through the prison window—the birds he never even

---

[4] A French Panama Canal company in 1879 made an unsuccessful attempt to construct a canal across the isthmus. A sensational financial scandal ensued. (Note that Chekhov is incorrect in attributing this scandal to a time preceding Balzac's marriage.)

noticed when he was a minister. Of course, now that he's released he doesn't notice them any more . . . Just as you won't notice Moscow when you live there. We're not happy and we can't be happy; we only want happiness.

TUSENBACH [*picks up a box from the table*]. Where's all the candy gone?

IRINA. Solyony's eaten it.

TUSENBACH. All of it?

ANFISA [*serving* VERSHININ *with tea*]. Here's a letter for you, sir.

VERSHININ. For me? [*Takes the letter.*] From my daughter. [*Reads it.*] Yes, of course . . . Forgive me, Marya Sergeyevna, I'll just slip out quietly. I won't have any tea. [*Gets up, agitated.*] Always the same thing . . .

MASHA. What is it? Can't you tell me?

VERSHININ [*in a low voice*]. My wife's tried to poison herself again. I've just got to go. I'll leave without them seeing me. How horrible all this is. [*Kisses* MASHA's *hand.*] My dear, good, my sweet . . . I'll leave quietly out this way . . . [*Goes out.*]

ANFISA. Where's he going now? And I've just poured his tea! What a strange man!

MASHA [*flaring up*]. Leave me alone! Why do you keep pestering me? Why don't you leave me in peace? [*Goes to the table, cup in hand.*] I'm sick and tired of you, you silly old woman!

ANFISA. Why . . . But I didn't mean to offend you, dear.

ANDREY'S VOICE [*off-stage*]. Anfisa!

ANFISA [*mimics him*]. Anfisa! Sitting there in his study . . . ! [*Goes out.*]

MASHA [*by the table in the ballroom, crossly*]. Let me sit down somewhere! [*Fumbles up the cards laid out on the table.*] You take up the whole table with your cards! Drink your tea!

IRINA. How cross you are, Masha!

MASHA. Well, if I'm cross, don't talk to me, then. Just don't bother me!

CHEBUTYKIN [*laughs*]. Don't bother her! . . . Be careful you don't bother her!

MASHA. You may be sixty, but you're always jabbering about nothing, just like a baby . . .

NATASHA [*sighs*]. Masha dear, must you talk that way? You know, with your good looks you'd be thought so charming, even by the best people—yes, I honestly mean it—if only you wouldn't talk that way. "*Je vous prie, pardonnez moi, Marie, mais vous avez des manières un peu grossières.*"[5]

TUSENBACH [*with suppressed laughter*]. Give me . . . will you please pass me . . . Isn't there some cognac?

NATASHA. "*Il paraît que mon Bobik déjà ne dort pas*"[6] . . . I think he's crying. He hasn't been feeling well today. I must go and take care of him . . . Excuse me. [*Goes out.*]

IRINA. Where has Alexander Ignatyevich gone?

MASHA. Home. His wife's done something crazy again.

TUSENBACH [*goes over to* SOLYONY *with a decanter of cognac*]. You always sit alone brooding about something or other—although there's no telling what

---

[5] (French) Excuse me please, Masha, but your manners are a bit gross. (It is an affectation with Natasha to say what she can in French, which she uses rather awkwardly.)

[6] (French) It seems that my Bobik is already awake.

about. Come, let's make up. Let's have a drink of cognac together. [*They drink.*] I suppose I'll have to play the piano all night tonight—a lot of trash . . . Oh, well!

SOLYONY. Why did you say "let's make up"? We haven't quarrelled.

TUSENBACH. You always make me feel that something is wrong between us. You're a strange character, that you must admit.

SOLYONY [*recites*]. "I am strange, who isn't strange? Be not wrath, Aleko!"

TUSENBACH. What's Aleko got to do with it? . . . [*A pause.*]

SOLYONY. When I'm alone with someone I'm all right, I'm just like everybody else. But when I'm in a group of people, I get depressed and shy, and . . . I talk all sorts of nonsense. All the same, I'm a damned sight more honest than a lot of people. And I can prove it, too.

TUSENBACH. You make me mad whenever you pester me when we're in company—but, you know for some reason I still like you . . . I'm going to get drunk tonight, I don't care what happens! Let's have another drink!

SOLYONY. Yes, let's [*A pause.*] I've never had anything against you personally, Baron. But I have the temperament of Lermontov.[7] [*In a low voice.*] I even look something like Lermontov, at least that's what they say . . . [*Takes a scent bottle from his pocket and sprinkles some scent on his hands.*]

TUSENBACH. I have sent in my resignation! I've had enough! I've been thinking about it for five years now, and finally I've made up my mind. I'm going to work.

SOLYONY [*recites*]. "Be not wrath, Aleko . . . Forget, forget your dreams!"

[*During the conversation* ANDREY *enters quietly with a book in his hand and sits down by the candle.*]

TUSENBACH. I'm going to work!

CHEBUTYKIN [*comes into the drawing room with* IRINA]. And the food was really Caucasian: onion soup, and then "*chehartma*"—that's a wonderful roast.

SOLYONY. "*Chereshma*" isn't meat at all; it's a plant, like an onion.

CHEBUTYKIN. No, no, my friend, "*chehartma*" isn't an onion, it's roast lamb.

SOLYONY. And I tell you "*chereshma*" is a kind of onion.

CHEBUTYKIN. Well, why should I argue with you about it? You've never been to the Caucasus and you've never eaten "*chehartma*."

SOLYONY. I haven't eaten it because I can't stand it. "*Chereshma*" smells just like garlic.

ANDREY [*imploringly*]. Stop it, my friends! Please stop it!

TUSENBACH. When's the carnival party coming?

IRINA. They said nine—that means any time now.

TUSENBACH [*embraces* ANDREY *and sings*]. "Oh, my porch, oh my beautiful new porch, my . . ."

ANDREY [*dances and sings*]. "With posts of maple wood . . ."

CHEBUTYKIN [*dances*]. "And fancy lattice-work . . ." [*Laughter.*]

TUSENBACH [*kisses* ANDREY]. Let's have a drink, what the hell! Andruisha,

---

[7] Mikhail Yurievich Lermontov (1814–1841) was a Russian poet and novelist who, in his work and his life, was the outstanding example of the influence of Byronic romanticism in Russian literature. As a poet, he was second only to Pushkin in his time, and he made an important contribution to the development of the Russian novel.

let's drink to eternal friendship. I'll go to Moscow with you when you go back to the University.

SOLYONY.   Which one? There are two universities in Moscow.

ANDREY.   There's only one.

SOLYONY.   I tell you there are two.

ANDREY.   All right, let's make it three. The more the better.

SOLYONY.   There are two universities in Moscow. [*Murmurs of protest and cries of "Hush!"*] There are two universities in Moscow, the old one and the new one. But if you don't want to listen to me, if what I say bothers you, I'll keep quiet. In fact, I'll leave . . . [*Goes out through one of the doors.*]

TUSENBACH.   Bravo, bravo! [*Laughs.*] My friends, let's get started. I'll play for you. What a funny fellow that Solyony is! . . . [*Sits down at the piano and plays a waltz.*]

MASHA [*dances alone*].   The Baron is drunk, the Baron is drunk, the Baron is drunk . . .

[*Enter* NATASHA.]

NATASHA [*to* CHEBUTYKIN].   Ivan Romanich! [*Speaks to him, then goes out quietly.* CHEBUTYKIN *touches* TUSENBACH *on the shoulder and whispers to him.*]

IRINA.   What is it?

CHEBUTYKIN.   It's time we were going.

TUSENBACH.   Yes, it's time we were going. Good night.

IRINA.   But wait . . . What about the carnival people?

ANDREY [*embarrassed*].   They're not coming. You see, my dear, Natasha says that Bobik isn't feeling very well, and well . . . Anyway, I don't know . . . and I couldn't care less . . .

IRINA [*shrugs her shoulders*].   Bobik's not feeling well! . . .

MASHA.   Forget it, so what! If they kick us out, well out we go! [*To* IRINA.] It isn't Bobik who's sick, it's her . . . Here! . . . [*Taps her forehead with her finger.*] Petty "hausfrau!"[8]

[ANDREY *goes to his room on the right.* CHEBUTYKIN *follows him. The guests say good-bye in the ballroom.*]

FEDOTIK.   What a pity! I'd counted on spending the evening, but of course, if the baby's sick . . . I'll bring him some toys tomorrow.

RODÉ [*in a loud voice*].   I had a nap after lunch today on purpose, I thought I'd be dancing all night. Why, it's only nine o'clock.

MASHA.   Let's go outside and talk about it. We can decide what to do then.

[*Voices are heard saying "Good-bye! God bless you!" and* TUSENBACH *is heard laughing gayly. Everyone goes out.* ANFISA *and a maid clear the table and put out the lights. The nurse sings to the baby off-stage. Enter* ANDREY, *wearing an overcoat and hat, followed by* CHEBUTYKIN. *They move quietly.*]

CHEBUTYKIN.   I've never had time to get married, somehow . . . because my life's just flashed by like lightning, and because I was always very much in love with your mother and she was married . . .

ANDREY.   One shouldn't marry. One shouldn't marry, it's so boring.

CHEBUTYKIN.   That may be, but what about the loneliness? You can talk

---

8 (German) Housewife. The German word, used in any language, has a special connotation of contempt for the frequently bourgeois outlook of housewives.

all you want, my boy, but loneliness is a horrible thing. Though, as a matter of fact . . . oh well, what difference does it make! . . .

ANDREY.   Let's get going.

CHEBUTYKIN.   What's the hurry? We've plenty of time.

ANDREY.   I'm afraid my wife'll stop me.

CHEBUTYKIN.   Ah!

ANDREY.   I won't gamble tonight, I'll just sit and watch. You know, I don't feel very well . . . What should I do for this shortness of breath, Ivan Romanich?

CHEBUTYKIN.   Don't ask me. I can't remember, my boy—I really don't know.

ANDREY.   Let's go through the kitchen.

[*They go out. A bell rings. The ring is repeated, then voices and laughter are heard.*]

IRINA [*coming in*].   Who is it?

ANFISA [*in a whisper*].   The carnival party.

[*The bell rings again.*]

IRINA.   Tell them there's no one at home, Nanny. They'll have to excuse us.

[ANFISA *goes out.* IRINA *walks up and down the room, lost in thought. She seems agitated. Enter* SOLYONY.]

SOLYONY [*puzzled*].   No one here . . . Where is everybody?

IRINA.   They've gone home.

SOLYONY.   That's strange! Are you alone?

IRINA.   Yes. [*A pause.*] Well . . . good night.

SOLYONY.   I know I behaved tactlessly before, I just lost control of myself. But you're not like the others, you're high-minded—you're pure, you can see the truth . . . You're the only one who understands me. I love you . . . I love you with a deep, with an infinite . . .

IRINA.   Go away, please. Good night!

SOLYONY.   I can't live without you. [*Follows her.*] Oh it's so wonderful just to look at you! [*With tears.*] Oh, my joy! Your glorious, marvelous, bewitching eyes—the most beautiful eyes in all the world . . .

IRINA [*coldly*].   Vassily Vassilyevich, stop it!

SOLYONY.   I've never spoken to you of my love before . . . it's as if I were living on a different planet . . . [*Rubs his forehead.*] Forget it! I can't make you love me. But there will be no successful rivals . . . I swear to you by all that's sacred that if there's anyone else, I'll kill him. Oh, how wonderful, how wonderful you are!

[*Enter* NATASHA *carrying a candle.*]

NATASHA [*pokes her head into one room, then into another, but passes the door leading to her husband's room*].   Andrey's reading. Might as well let him. Forgive me, Vassily Vassilyevich, I didn't know you were here. I'm afraid I'm not properly dressed.

SOLYONY.   I don't care. Good-bye. [*Goes out.*]

NATASHA.   You must be tired, my poor girl. [*Kisses* IRINA.] You should go to bed earlier.

IRINA.   Is Bobik asleep?

NATASHA.   Yes, but not very quietly. By the way, dear, I keep meaning to speak to you, but then there's always been something . . . either you're not here, or I'm too busy . . . Bobik's nursery is so cold and damp . . . And your room is just perfect for a baby. Darling, I'm sure you won't mind moving in with Olga.

IRINA [*not understanding her*].   Where?

[*The sound of bells is heard outside, as a troika is driven up to the house.*]

NATASHA.   You can share Olga's room—just for a little while—and Bobik can have your room. He is such a darling! This morning I said to him: "Bobik, you're my very own! My very own!" And he looked up at me with his sweet little eyes. [*The door bell rings.*] That must be Olga. How late she is! [*A maid comes up to* NATASHA *and whispers in her ear.*] Protopopov! What a strange man! Why, Protopopov's come to take me for a drive. In his troika. [*Laughs.*] How strange men are! . . . [*The door bell rings again.*] Somebody else's ringing. Shall I go out for a little bit? Just for a quarter of an hour? [*To the maid.*] Tell him I'll be right there. [*The door bell rings.*] There's the bell again. It must be Olga. [*Goes out.*]

[*The maid runs out;* IRINA *sits lost in thought. Enter* KULYGIN *and* OLGA, *followed by* VERSHININ.]

KULYGIN.   Well! What's going on here? You said you were going to have a party.

VERSHININ.   That's strange. I left not more than half an hour ago, and they were still expecting the party.

IRINA.   They've all gone.

KULYGIN.   Masha, too? Where did she go? And what's Protopopov doing outside in his troika? Who's he waiting for?

IRINA.   Don't ask me questions please. I'm tired.

KULYGIN.   You . . . spoiled child!

OLGA.   The faculty meeting just ended. I'm exhausted. The headmistress is sick and I had to take her place. My head aches, oh, my head, my head . . . [*Sits down.*] Andrey lost again last night—two hundred roubles. The whole town's talking about it.

KULYGIN.   Yes the meeting exhausted me, too. [*Sits down.*]

VERSHININ.   So now my wife's decided to frighten me. She tried to poison herself. But it's all right now, so I can relax . . . So we have to leave? Well, good night. Fyodor Ilyich, let's go somewhere together? I can't go home yet, I just can't . . . Come!

KULYGIN.   I'm tired. I don't think I'll come. [*Gets up.*] I'm tired. Has my wife gone home?

IRINA.   She must have.

KULYGIN [*kisses* IRINA's *hand*].   Good night. We'll rest all day tomorrow and the day after tomorrow, two whole days! Well, I . . . ahh . . . [*Going out.*] My, I'd like some tea! I was planning on spending the evening in pleasant company, but—"*o, fallacem hominum spem*"![9] Accusative of exclamation.

VERSHININ.   Well, it looks as if I'll have to go alone. [*Goes out with* KULYGIN, *whistling.*]

OLGA.   My headaches , oh, how my head aches . . . Andrey lost at cards . . . the whole town's talking . . . I'll go and lie down. [*Going out.*] Tomorrow

___

[9] (Latin) O fallacious hopes of man. (In the phrase that follows, Kulygin, mocking his own schoolteacher manner, gives a grammatical explanation of the Latin.)

I'm free. Goodness, how pleasant that will be. Tomorrow I'm free, and the day after tomorrow I'm free . . . Oh, my head aches, my head . . .

IRINA [*alone*]. They've all gone. There's no one left.

[*Someone is playing an accordion in the street. The nurse sings in the next room.*]

NATASHA [*crosses the ballroom, wearing a fur coat and cap. She is followed by the maid*]. I'll be back in half an hour. I'm just going for a short drive. [*Goes out.*]

IRINA [*alone, with intense dejection*]. Oh, to go to Moscow! To Moscow! Moscow!

Curtain.

ACT III

A bedroom shared by OLGA *and* IRINA. *To the left and to the right are beds, each screened off from the rest of the room. It is going on three o'clock in the morning. Off-stage a fire alarm is ringing for a fire which has been raging some time. No one in the house has gone to bed.* MASHA *lies on the couch, dressed, as usual, in black.* OLGA *and* ANFISA *enter.*

ANFISA. They're sitting there under the staircase. I keep telling them to come up here, but they just cry. "Where's our Daddy?" they say, "he's been burned in the fire." And then all those poor people out in the yard . . . half dressed . . . can you imagine thinking things like that!

OLGA [*takes a dress out of a wardrobe*]. Here, take this grey dress, Nurse . . . And this one . . . This blouse, too . . . And the skirt. Oh, Lord! what a dreadful night! It looks like all of Kirsanovsky Street's burned down . . . Take this . . . and this, too . . . [*Throws the clothes into* ANFISA's *arms.*] The poor Vershinins were frightened to death. Their house nearly burned down. They must spend the night here . . . we just can't let them go home. And poor Fedotik's lost everything, too, he's got nothing left. . . .

ANFISA. You'll have to call Ferapont, Olyushka, I can't carry all this.

OLGA [*rings*]. No one answers when I ring. [*Calls through the door.*] Is anyone there? Please, will someone come up! [*A window, red with the glow of the fire, can be seen through the open door. The sound of a passing fire engine is heard.*] How awful it is! And I am so tired! [*Enter* FERAPONT.] Take this downstairs . . . give it to the Kolotilin girls, they're under the staircase . . . and this, too . . .

FERAPONT. Yes, miss. Moscow burnt down in 1812 too . . . Mercy on us! . . . Yes, the French were surprised all right.[10]

OLGA. Get along with you, take these things downstairs.

FERAPONT. Yes, miss. [*Goes out.*]

[10] Napoleon occupied Moscow in September of 1812. On the night after his entry, the city was set on fire through carelessness. More than three-fourths of the houses burned, the citizens fled, and the city was plundered by the troops of both armies. The burning of Moscow became the signal, however, for the general rising of the peasants against the French. The event occupies an important place in Tolstoi's novel, *War and Peace.*

OLGA. Give them everything, Nurse dear. We don't need it, give it all away . . . I'm so tired, I can hardly stand up. We can't let the Vershinins go home. Let's see, the little girls can sleep in the drawing room, and Alexander Ignatyevich can go in with the Baron. Fedotik can too, or maybe he'd better sleep in the dining room. The Doctor's terribly drunk—you'd almost thing he'd done it on purpose; he's so frightfully drunk we can't let anyone go into his room. And Vershinin's wife will have to go into the drawing room, too.

ANFISA [wearily]. Don't send me away, Olyushka, darling! Don't send me away!

OLGA. What kind of nonsense is that, Nurse! No one's going to send you away.

ANFISA [leans her head against OLGA's breast]. Oh, dearest! I do work, you know, I try as hard as I can . . . I suppose now that I can't do as much, they'll tell me to go. But where can I go? Where? I'm eighty years old, almost eight-two!

OLGA. Here, dear, you sit down for a bit . . . You're tired, poor thing . . . [Makes her sit down.] You just rest. How pale you look.

[Enter NATASHA.]

NATASHA. They're saying we ought to form a society to help the victims of the fire. Well, why not? It's a fine idea! We must always try to help the poor whenever we can. Bobik and Sofotchka are sound asleep as though nothing had happened. But I wish we didn't have such a crowd of people in the house. No matter where you turn, you bump into them. You know the flu's in town . . . and I'm so afraid the children may get it.

OLGA [without listening to her]. You can see the fire from the window, but it's quiet when the drapes are closed.

NATASHA. Yes . . . Oh, my hair must be all over the place. [Stands in front of the mirror.] They say I've gotten fat, but it's not true! I haven't added a pound. Masha's asleep . . . she's so tired, poor dear . . . [Notices ANFISA, coldly.] How dare you sit down in my presence? Get up! Get out of here! [ANFISA goes out. A pause.] I can't understand why you keep that old woman around here.

OLGA [taken aback]. Forgive my saying it, but I don't know how you . . .

NATASHA. She's useless. She's just a peasant and belongs in the country. Why do you pamper her like this? I like order in my house, and there's no room for useless people. [Strokes OLGA's cheek.] Poor dear, you're so tired! Our head-mistress is tired! You know, when my Sofotchka grows up and goes to school, I'll be so afraid of you.

OLGA. I'm not going to be the headmistress.

NATASHA. You'll be elected, Olya. Why, it's all settled.

OLGA. I'll refuse. I couldn't do it . . . I haven't the strength for it. [Drinks water.] You were very rude to Nurse just now . . . You must forgive my saying it, but I just can't stand such inconsiderateness . . . I'm afraid I'm going to faint . . .

NATASHA [agitated]. Forgive me, Olya, forgive me. I didn't mean to upset you.

[MASHA gets up, picks up a pillow and goes out angrily.]

OLGA. Please try to understand . . . Perhaps we've been brought up in a strange way, but I just can't stand it. When people are treated like that, it depresses me. It makes me ill . . . It completely upsets me.

NATASHA.   Forgive me, dear, forgive me! . . . [*Kisses her.*]

OLGA.   Any cruel or tactless remark, even when it's not intentional, upsets me . . .

NATASHA.   I know I talk too much, I must be more careful—but you must admit, that she might just as well be out in the country.

OLGA.   She's been with us for thirty years.

NATASHA.   But she can't work any more, can she? Either I don't understand you, or you won't understand me. She can't work, she just sleeps and sits.

OLGA.   Well, let her sit.

NATASHA [*in surprise*].   What do you mean, let her sit? She *is* a servant, you know! [*Tearfully.*] I just don't understand you, Olya! I have a nurse for the children and a wet nurse and we have a maid and a cook. What do we need that old woman for? What for?

[*The alarm is sounded again.*]

OLGA.   I've grown ten years older tonight.

NATASHA.   We must come to some sort of understanding, Olya. You're working at the school, and I'm working at home. You're teaching and I run the house. And if I say anything about the servants, I know what I'm talking about . . . That old thief, that old hag must get out of here tomorrow! . . . [*Stamps her feet.*] Do you understand! How dare you annoy me? How dare you? [*Recovering her self-control.*] Really, if you don't move downstairs, we'll always be quarrelling. It's terrible!

[*Enter* KULYGIN.]

KULYGIN.   Where's Masha? It's time to go home. They say the fire's dying down. [*Stretches.*] Only one block burned, but at first it looked as if the whole town was going to be set on fire by the wind. [*Sits down.*] I'm so tired, Olya, my dear. You know, I've often thought that if I hadn't married Masha, I'd have married you, Olya. You're such a good person. I'm worn out. [*Listens.*]

OLGA.   What's that?

KULYGIN.   The Doctor's drunk just as if he'd done it on purpose. Drunk out of his mind . . . As if he'd done it on purpose. [*Gets up.*] I think he's coming up here . . . Hear him? Yes, here he comes. [*Laughs.*] What a man, really! . . . I'm going to hide. [*Goes to the wardrobe and stands between it and the wall.*] What a scoundrel!

OLGA.   He hasn't had a drink for two years, and suddenly now he gets drunk. [*Goes with* NATASHA *behind one of the screens.*]

[CHEBUTYKIN *enters; without staggering, as if he were sober, he crosses the room, stops, looks around, then goes to the washstand and begins to wash his hands.*]

CHEBUTYKIN, [*glumly*].   The devil take them all . . . the whole lot of them! They think I can cure anything just because I'm a doctor, but I don't know anything . . . nothing at all. I've forgotten everything I ever knew. I don't remember anything, absolutely nothing . . . [OLGA *and* NATASHA *come out from behind the screen and leave the room without his noticing.*] The hell with them! Last Wednesday I treated a woman at Zasyp. She died, and it's all my fault that she died. Yes . . . I knew something twenty-five years ago, but I don't remember anything now. Not a thing! Perhaps I'm not even a man at all, but just imagine that I've got hands and feet and a head. Perhaps I don't exist at all, and I only imagine that I walk and eat and sleep. [*Weeps.*] Oh, if only I didn't exist! [*Stops crying, glumly.*] God knows . . . The other day they were talking about Shakespeare and Voltaire at the club . . . I hadn't read them, never read a single line, but I pretended that I had. The others did the same thing. How small we all are! How disgusting! And then all of a sudden I remembered that woman I killed on Wednesday. Everything came back to me, and I felt such a disgust, so sick of myself that I went and got drunk . . .

[*Enter* IRINA, VERSHININ, *and* TUSENBACH. TUSENBACH *is wearing a fashionable new civilian suit.*]

IRINA.   Let's sit here. No one will come in here.

VERSHININ.   The whole town would have burned if it hadn't been for the soldiers. They're a fine bunch of men! [*Rubs his hands with pleasure.*] Excellent men! Yes, a splendid group!

KULYGIN [*approaches them*].   What time is it?

TUSENBACH.   It's after three. As a matter of fact, it's getting light.

IRINA.   Everyone's sitting in the dining room and no one seems to think of going. That Solyony is there, too . . . [*To* CHEBUTYKIN.] You should be in bed, Doctor.

CHEBUTYKIN.   I'm all right . . . Thanks . . . [*Combs his beard.*]

KULYGIN [*laughs*].   You're pretty far gone, Ivan Romanich! [*Slaps him on the shoulder.*] You're a fine one! "*In vino veritas*" as the Romans used to say.

TUSENBACH.   I've been asked to arrange a benefit concert for the victims of the fire.

IRINA.   But, who . . .

TUSENBACH.   It could be arranged if we tried. In my opinion, Marya Sergeyevna plays the piano beautifully.

KULYGIN.   Oh, yes, she does play very well.

IRINA.   But she's forgotten how. It's been at least three, maybe four, years since she's played.

TUSENBACH.   In this town nobody understands music, not a soul. But I, I do understand it—and believe me, Marya Sergeyevna plays magnificently, almost like a concert pianist.

KULYGIN.   You're right, Baron. I'm very fond of Masha. She's such a nice girl.

TUSENBACH.   Just imagine, being able to play so well, and to know all the time that there is no one to appreciate it—no one!

KULYGIN [*sighs*].   Yes . . . But would it be proper for her to take part in a concert? [*A pause.*] Of course, I know nothing about such matters. It may be quite all right. But you know, although our headmaster is a good man, a very fine man indeed, a most intelligent man, I know he has certain opinions . . . Of course, it's none of his business, but I'll ask him about it, just the same, if you like.

[CHEBUTYKIN *picks up a china clock and examines it.*]

VERSHININ.   I've gotten my clothes all dirty helping with the fire, I must look terrible. [*A pause.*] They were saying yesterday that our brigade might be transferred to somewhere a long ways away from here. Some said to Poland, and others thought it would be to Northern Siberia, near Cheeta.

TUSENBACH.   I heard that, too. The town will really be empty then.

IRINA. And we're going away, too!

CHEBUTYKIN [*drops the clock and breaks it*]. Smashed to smithereens!

[*A pause. Everyone looks upset and embarrassed.*]

KULYGIN [*picks up the pieces*]. Imagine breaking such a valuable thing! Ah, Ivan Romanich, Ivan Romanich! Black mark for conduct!

IRINA. It was mother's clock.

CHEBUTYKIN. Well, so it was. If it was your mother's clock, then it was your mother's. Perhaps I didn't break it but it just seems as though I did. Perhaps we only imagine that we exist, but we don't really exist at all. Perhaps I don't know anything, no one knows anything. [*Stops at the door.*] Why are you staring at me? Natasha's having a disgusting affair with Protopopov, and you don't see it. You sit here seeing nothing, and all the time Natasha's having a pleasant little affair with Protopopov . . . [*Sings.*] "Won't you accept this little present from me?" . . . Strange. [*Goes out.*]

VERSHININ. So . . . [*Laughs.*] How strange it all is, really! [*A pause.*] When the fire started, I ran home as fast as I could. When I got to the house, I saw that it was all right and out of danger, but my two little girls were standing in the doorway in their pajamas. Their mother was gone. People were rushing about, horses, dogs, and in the children's faces I saw terror and anxiety, the most helpless look, I don't know what! . . . When I saw their faces, my heart sank. My God, I thought, what will these children have to go through for the rest of their lives? I grabbed them and ran back here, and all the time I kept thinking one thing: What else will they have to live through? [*The alarm is sounded. A pause.*] When I got here, my wife was already here . . . shouting and angry. [*Enter* MASHA *carrying a pillow.*] And while my little girls were standing there in the doorway with nothing on but their pajamas, and the street was red with the fire and full of terrible noises, I suddenly realized that this is what it must have been like years ago, when armies used to make sudden raids, plundering and burning . . . Anyway, is there really any difference between things as they used to be and the way they are now? And you know, it won't be very long, say another two or three hundred years, before people will look at our way of life with horror and scorn, just as we look at the past now. Everything about our life will seem uncouth to them, boring and awkward and strange . . . Oh, what a great life that will be! What a life! [*Laughs.*] Forgive me I'm philosophizing again . . . but may I go on, please? I have a great desire to talk about the future. [*A pause.*] It looks like everyone's gone to sleep. As I was saying: How wonderful life will be then! Just imagine . . . Today there are only three people like you in this town, but in the future there will be more and more people like you. At last the time will come when everything will be just as you'd want it to be. People will begin to live their lives in your way, in fact, they may even make improvements, and a new group will emerge even better than you are . . . [*Laughs.*] I'm in a very strange mood today. I have such a tremendous longing for life . . . [*Sings.*] "To Love all ages are in fee, The passion's good for you and me" . . . [*Laughs.*]

MASHA [*sings*]. Tara-ta-tum . . .

VERSHININ. Tum-tum . . .

MASHA. Tara-tara-tara . . .

VERSHININ. Tum-tum, tum-tum . . . [*Laughs.*]

[*Enter* FEDOTIK.]

FEDOTIK [*dancing about*].   Burnt, burnt to the ground! Everything I had in the world—burnt!

[*All laugh.*]

IRINA.   What kind of joke is that? Is everything gone?

FEDOTIK [*laughs*].   Everything. Nothing's left. My guitar, my camera, all my letters, why even the little notebook I was going to give you has been burnt.

[*Enter* SOLYONY.]

IRINA.   No, please go away, Vassily Vassilyevich. You can't come in here.

SOLYONY.   Can't I? But why can the Baron come in here if I can't?

VERSHININ.   We've really got to go, all of us. How's the fire?

SOLYONY.   They say it's dying down. But I can't understand why the Baron can come in here, and I can't. [*Takes a scent bottle from his pocket and sprinkles himself with scent.*]

VERSHININ.   Tara-tara.

MASHA.   Tum-tum, tum-tum.

VERSHININ [*laughs; to* SOLYONY].   Let's go into the dining room.

SOLYONY.   Very well, but I'll make a note of it. "I hardly need to make my moral clear: That might be teasing geese, I fear!" [*Looks at* TUSENBACH]. Cluck, cluck, cluck! [*Goes out with* VERSHININ *and* FEDOTIK.]

IRINA.   That Solyony has filled the room with smoke . . . [*Puzzled.*] The Baron's asleep. Baron! Baron!

TUSENBACH [*waking out of his doze*].   I must be tired. The brickyard, and . . . No, I'm not talking in my sleep. I really am going to the brickyard and will start working there soon . . . I've talked to the manager. [*To* IRINA, *tenderly.*] You are so pale, so beautiful, so bewitching . . . It seems to me your paleness brightens the darkness around you like light, somehow . . . You're sad, you're dissatisfied with life . . . Oh, come away with me, we can work together!

MASHA.   Nikolai Lvovich, I wish you'd go away.

TUSENBACH [*laughs*].   Are you here? I didn't see you. [*Kisses* IRINA's *hand.*] Good-bye, I'm going. You know, as I look at you now, I keep thinking of the day—it seems like such a long time ago on your birthday—when you talked about the joy of work . . . You were so gay and confident then . . . And what a happy life I imagined for us! Where is it all now? [*Kisses her hand.*] There are tears in your eyes. Go to bed, it's getting light . . . it's almost morning . . . Oh, if only I could give my life for you!

MASHA.   Nikolai Lvovich, please leave! Really now . . .

TUSENBACH.   I'm going [*Goes out.*]

MASHA [*lies down*].   Are you asleep, Fyodor?

KULYGIN.   Eh?

MASHA.   Why don't you go home?

KULYGIN.   My darling Masha, my dear Masha . . .

IRINA.   She's tired. Let her rest awhile, Fedya.

KULYGIN.   I'll go in a minute. My wife, my dear, good wife! How I love you! . . . Only you!

MASHA [*crossly*].   "Amo, amas, amat, amamus, amatis, amant!"[11]

KULYGIN [*laughs*].   Really, what an amazing woman she is!—I've been

---

[11] Conjugation of the Latin verb *amare*, "to love."

married to you for seven years, but it seems as if we were married only yesterday. Honest, it does! You really are wonderful! Oh, I'm so happy, happy, happy!

MASHA.   And I'm so bored, bored, bored! [*Sits up.*] I can't get it out of my head . . . It's so annoying. It sticks in my head like a nail . . . I've just got to say something. It's about Andrey . . . He's actually mortgaged the house to the bank, and his wife's taken all the money—but the house doesn't belong to him, but to the four of us! He must know that, if he has any decency at all.

KULYGIN.   Why talk about it, Masha? Why think of it now? Andriusha owes money to everyone . . . Let him alone.

MASHA.   Anyway, it's revolting. [*Lies down.*]

KULYGIN.   At any rate, we aren't poor, Masha. I've got work, I teach at the high school, and I tutor in my spare time . . . I'm just a simple, honest man . . . "*Omnia mea mecum porto*,"[12] as they say.

MASHA.   I'm not asking for anything, I just don't like the injustice. [*A pause.*] Why don't you go home, Fyodor?

KULYGIN [*kisses her*].   You're tired. Just rest here for a while . . . I'll wait for you . . . Go to sleep. [*Goes to the door.*] I'm happy, happy, happy! [*Goes out.*]

IRINA.   As a matter of fact, Andrey has become awfully dull. He's getting old and since he's been living with that woman he's lost all his ambition! He used to work for his professorship and just yesterday he was buzzing about getting elected to the County Council. Imagine him a member, with Protopopov as chairman! The whole town's laughing at him, and he's the only one who doesn't know or see anything. Here everyone's rushing off to the fire and he just sits in his study playing his violin. He hasn't even noticed it. [*Agitated.*] Oh, it's awful, just awful, awful! I can't take it any more, I can't, I really can't! . . .

[*Enter* OLGA. *She starts arranging things on her bedside table.*]

IRINA [*sobs loudly*].   Turn me out! You must turn me out of here! I can't stand it any more!

OLGA [*alarmed*].   What is it? What is it, my darling?

IRINA [*sobbing*].   Where . . . Where has it all gone? Where is it? Oh, God! I've forgotten . . . I've forgotten everything . . . Everything's so confused . . . I don't remember the Italian for "window" or for "ceiling" . . . Every day I'm forgetting more and more, and life's slipping by, and it will never, never return . . . We'll never go to Moscow . . . I just know we'll never go . . .

OLGA.   Don't, dear, don't . . .

IRINA [*trying to control herself*].   I'm miserable. [*Pause.*] I've had enough, enough. I can't, I won't, I will not work! . . . First I worked at the post office, now I'm a secretary at the Council office, and I hate and despise it all. I'm nearly twenty-four, and all I've done is work, my brain's drying up. I know I'm getting thinner and uglier and older, and there's nothing, nothing I can look forward to, no satisfaction in life that I can hope for, none at all. Time is flying past . . . and I feel as if I'm moving from any hope of a genuine fine life, and I seem to be getting further and further away from real life, from a life that is beautiful. I feel that I am heading for some horrible disaster. I'm in

12 (Latin) I carry all my possessions with me. (The philosopher's proverbial scorn of material possessions.)

despair and I don't know why I go on living, why I haven't killed myself . . .

OLGA. Don't cry, my child, don't cry . . .

IRINA. I'm not crying—I'm not crying. I've stopped now, see? I'm not crying any more. I've stopped. I've stopped . . .

OLGA. Darling, let me tell you something . . . as your sister, as your friend . . . if you'll take my advice . . . you'll marry the Baron. [IRINA *weeps quietly*.] You do respect him don't you? You think highly of him . . . It's true, he's not handsome, but he's such an honest, decent man . . . After all, people don't marry for love, but to fulfill their duty. At least, I think so, and I'd marry even if I weren't in love. I'd marry anyone that proposed to me, as long as he was a decent man. I'd even marry an old man.

IRINA. I've been waiting all this time, expecting that we'd be moving to Moscow, and that there I'd meet the man I'm meant for. I've dreamt about him and I've loved him in my dreams . . . But it's all turned out to be nothing . . . nothing . . .

OLGA [*embracing her*]. My darling sister, I think I understand everything. When the Baron resigned his commission and came to see us dressed in his civilian clothes, I thought he looked so ugly that I actually started to cry . . . He asked me why I was crying . . . How could I tell him? But, if it were God's will that he should marry you, I'd be happy about it. That's a different thing, you know, quite different!

[NATASHA, *carrying a candle, comes out of the door on the right, crosses the stage and goes out through the door on the left without saying anything.*]

MASHA [*sits up*]. She walks around looking as if she'd set the town on fire herself.

OLGA. You're silly, Masha. You're the silliest person in our family. You must forgive me for saying it. [*A pause.*]

MASHA. My dear sisters, I've got something to confess to you. I have to tell someone, I need to . . . I'll confess it to the two of you, and then never again, never to anybody! NO! Right now. [*In a low voice.*] It's a secret, but you must know everything. I can't keep silent any longer. [*A pause.*] I'm in love, in love . . . I love that man . . . You just saw him . . . Oh, what's the use? . . . I love Vershinin . . .

OLGA [*goes behind her screen*]. Don't say it. I don't want to hear it.

MASHA. But, what am I to do? [*Holding her head.*] At first I thought him very strange, then I felt sorry for him and—and then I fell in love with him . . . love everything about him—his voice, his words, his troubles, his two little girls . . .

OLGA. I don't want to hear it. You can talk as much nonsense as you like, I'm not listening.

MASHA. Don't be silly, Olya! If I love him, well—that's my fate! That's my destiny. And he loves me. It's frightening, isn't it? Is it wrong? [*Takes* IRINA *by the hand and draws her to her.*] Oh, my darling! . . . How are we going to live through the rest of our lives? What's to become of us? When you read a novel, everything in its seems too trite and obvious. It's so understandable—but when you fall in love yourself, you suddenly discover that no one really knows anything, and you've got to make your own choices . . . My dear sisters, my dear sisters! . . . I've confessed to you, and now I'll be silent . . . Like Gogol's madman—silence . . . silence! . . .

[*Enter* ANDREY *followed by* FERAPONT.]

ANDREY [*crossly*].   What do you want? I don't understand.

FERAPONT [*stopping in the doorway, impatiently*].   I've told you ten times already, Andrey Sergeyevitch.

ANDREY.   In the first place, I'm not Andrey Sergeyevitch—you're to call me "Your Honor."

FERAPONT.   Your Honor, the firemen want to go through the garden to go to the river. They've been taking the long way round and it's been a terrible nuisance!

ANDREY.   All right. Tell them it's all right. [FERAPONT *goes out.*] Why do they keep on bothering me? Where's Olga? [OLGA *comes from behind the screen.*] I've come to get the key to the cupboard; I've lost mine. You know the one I mean, the little one . . .

[OLGA *silently hands him the key.* IRINA *goes behind the screen on her side of the room.*]

ANDREY.   What a wonderful fire! It's dying down though. Ferapont made me lose my temper, damn him! That was stupid of me . . . Telling him to call me "Your Honor"! . . . [*A pause.*] Why don't you say something, Olya? [*A pause.*] Let's stop this foolishness . . . There's no reason to sulk . . . You here, Masha? And Irina, too. Good! Let's have it out once and for all. What have you got against me? What is it?

OLGA.   Forget it for now, Andriusha. We'll talk about it tomorrow. [*Agitated.*] What a horrible night!

ANDREY [*in great embarrassment*].   Don't get upset. I'm asking you calmly, what have you got against me? Tell me frankly.

VERSHININ'S VOICE [*off-stage*].   Tum-tum-tum!

MASHA [*in a loud voice, getting up*].   *Tara-tara-tara!* [*To* OLGA.] Good-night, Olya, God bless you! [*Goes behind the screen and kisses* IRINA.] Sleep well . . . Good night, Andrey. I'd go away now, they're tired . . . talk about it tomorrow . . . [*Goes out.*]

OLGA.   Yes, really, Andriusha, let's wait until tomorrow . . . [*Goes behind the screen on her side of the room.*] It's time we were in bed.

ANDREY.   I only want to say one thing, then I'll go, as soon as . . . First of all, you've got something against my wife, against Natasha. I've noticed it from the day we got married. Natasha is a very fine woman, she's honest and straight-forward and . . . that's my opinion. I love and respect my wife. Do you under-stand? I respect her, and I expect others to respect her, too. I repeat; she's an honest, honorable person, and all your complaints against her—and I must say this—are all in your imagination, and nothing more . . . [*A pause.*] Second, you seem disappointed in me for not being a professor, because I've stopped studying. But I'm working, I'm a member of the Council, and I feel my work there is just as important as any academic work I might do. I'm a member of the Council, and if you want to know, I'm proud of it! [*A pause.*] Third . . . there's something else I must tell you . . . I know I mortgaged the house without asking your permission . . . That was wrong, I admit it, and I ask you to forgive me . . . I had to because of my debts . . . thirty-five thousand roubles, but I don't gamble any more, I gave that up long ago . . . The only thing I can say in my defense, is that all of you get an annuity, while I don't get anything . . . no salary, I mean . . . [*A pause.*]

KULYGIN [*calling through the door*]. Is Masha there? She's not? [*Alarmed.*] Where can she be then? That's strange . . . [*Goes away.*]

ANDREY. So you won't listen? Natasha, I tell you, is a fine, honest woman. [*Walks up and down the stage, then stops.*] When we got married I was sure we'd be happy, all of us . . . But . . . Oh, my God! . . . [*Weeps.*] My dear sisters, my dear, good sisters, don't believe what I've been saying, don't believe it . . . [*Goes out.*]

KULYGIN [*through the door, agitated*]. Where's Masha? Isn't Masha here? How strange. [*Goes away.*]

[*The alarm is heard again. The stage is empty.*]

IRINA [*speaking from behind the screen*]. Olya! Who's that knocking on the floor?

OLGA. It's the Doctor, Ivan Romanich. He's drunk.

IRINA. It's been one catastrophe after another all night. [*A pause.*] Olya! [*Peeps out from behind the screen.*] Have you heard? The brigade is leaving . . . they're being transferred to some place far away.

OLGA. That's only a rumor.

IRINA. Then we shall be alone . . . Olya!

OLGA. Well?

IRINA. Olya, darling, I respect the Baron . . . I think a great deal of him, he's a very good man . . . I'll marry him, Olya, I'll agree to marry him, if only we can go to Moscow! Let's go, please let's go! There's no place in the world like Moscow. Let's go, Olya! Let's go!

Curtain.

ACT IV

An old garden in front of the PROZOROVS' *house. A river is seen at the end of a long avenue of fir trees, and on the other side of the river a forest. To the right, a terrace with a table on which champagne bottles and glasses have been left. It is noon. Occasionally people from the street pass through the garden to get to the river. Five or six soldiers march through quickly.* CHEBUTYKIN, *in an affable mood which does not leave him throughout the act, is sitting in a chair in the garden waiting to be called. He is wearing his army cap and is holding a walking stick.* KULYGIN, *with a decoration round his neck and with his moustache shaved off,* TUSENBACH *and* IRINA *are standing on the terrace saying good-bye to* FEDOTIK *and* RODÉ, *who are coming down the steps. Both officers are in dress uniform.*

TUSENBACH [*embracing* FEDOTIK]. You're a fine fellow, Fedotik; we've been good friends! [*Embraces* RODÉ] Once more, then . . . Good-bye, my friends!

IRINA. Au revoir!

FEDOTIK. No, it's not au revoir—It's good-bye. We'll never meet again!

KULYGIN. Who knows? [*Wipes his eyes, smiling.*] There, I'm beginning to cry, too.

IRINA. We'll meet some day.

FEDOTIK. In ten or fifteen years maybe. But by then we'll hardly know each other . . . We'll just meet and say very coldly, "How are you?" [*Takes a picture.*] Stand still . . . Just one more, for the last time.

RODÉ [*embraces* TUSENBACH]. We probably won't meet again . . . [*Kisses* IRINA's *hand.*] Thank you for everything . . . everything!

FEDOTIK [*annoyed*]. Just wait a second!

TUSENBACH. I hope we do, and we will meet again if it's our fate. But write to us. Be sure to write.

RODÉ [*glancing around the garden*]. Good-bye, trees! [*Shouts.*] Halloo! [*A pause.*] Good-bye, echo!

KULYGIN. It wouldn't surprise me if you got married in Poland . . . You'll get some Polish wife, and she'll put her arms around you and say: "*Kohane*"![13] [*Laughs.*]

FEDOTIK [*glances at his watch*]. We leave in less than an hour. Solyony is the only one from the battery who's going on the barge. Everyone else is marching with the division. Three batteries are leaving today and the other three tomorrow—then the town will have peace and quiet.

TUSENBACH. Yes, and dreadful boredom, too.

RODÉ. By the way, where's Marya Sergeyevna?

KULYGIN. She's somewhere in the garden.

FEDOTIK. We must say good-bye to her.

RODÉ. Good-bye. I really must go, or I'll start crying. [*Quickly embraces* TUSENBACH *and* KULYGIN, *kisses* IRINA's *hand.*] We've had a wonderful time here . . .

FEDOTIK [*to* KULYGIN]. Here's a souvenir for you—a notebook and pencil . . . We'll go down to the river this way. [*They go off, glancing back.*]

RODÉ [*shouts*]. Halloo!

KULYGIN [*shouts*]. Good-bye!

[*At the back of the stage* FEDOTIK *and* RODÉ *meet* MASHA, *and say good-bye to her; she goes off with them.*]

IRINA. They've gone . . . [*Sits down on the bottom step of the terrace.*]

CHEBUTYKIN. They forgot to say good-bye to me.

IRINA. Well, what about you?

CHEBUTYKIN. That's true, I forgot, too. Oh well, I'll be seeing them again soon. I leave tomorrow. Yes . . . only one more day. And then, in a year I'll retire. I'll come back and spend the rest of my life with you. Just one more year and then I get my pension . . . [*Puts a newspaper in his pocket and takes out another.*] I'll come back here and lead a reformed life. I'll become a nice, quiet, respectable little man.

IRINA. Yes, it's about time you reformed, Ivan Romanich. You ought to lead a better kind of life.

CHEBUTYKIN. Yes . . . I think so, too. [*Sings quietly.*] "Tarara-boom-di-ay . . . I'm sitting on a tomb-di-ay" . . .

KULYGIN. You're incorrigible, Ivan Romanich! Absolutely incorrigible!

CHEBUTYKIN. Yes, if only you had taken me in hand. You'd have reformed me!

IRINA. Fyodor's shaved his moustache off. I can't bear to look at him.

KULYGIN. Why not?

---

[13] (Polish) Love!

CHEBUTYKIN.   If I could only tell you what your face looks like now—but I'd better not.

KULYGIN.   Well! It's the fashion now! The *"modus vivendi,"* you know. The headmaster shaved his moustache off, so when I became the principal, I shaved mine off, too. No one likes it, but I don't care. I'm content. Whether I've got a moustache or not, it's all the same to me. [*Sits down.*]

[ANDREY *passes across the back of the stage pushing a baby carriage with a child asleep in it.*]

IRINA.   Ivan Romanich, my dear friend, I'm terribly worried about something. You were in town last night—tell me what happened?

CHEBUTYKIN.   What happened? Nothing. Just a trifle. [*Reads his paper.*] It doesn't matter anyway.

KULYGIN.   They say that Solyony and the Baron met outside the theatre last night and . . .

TUSENBACH.   Stop it, please! What's the good? . . . [*Waves his hand at him deprecatingly and goes into the house.*]

KULYGIN.   It was outside the theatre . . . Solyony started insulting the Baron, and the Baron lost his temper and insulted him.

CHEBUTYKIN.   I don't know anything about it. It's all nonsense.

KULYGIN.   A teacher once wrote "nonsense" on one of his student's papers, and the student couldn't figure it out. He thought it was a Latin word. [*Laughs.*] Isn't that funny? They say that Solyony's in love with Irina and that he hates the Baron . . . Well, that's understandable. Irina's a very sweet girl. She's a lot like Masha, all wrapped up in her own thoughts. [*To* IRINA.] But you have a gentler disposition than Masha. And yet Masha has a very pleasant disposition, too. I love my Masha, I love her.

[*From the back of the stage comes a shout: "Halloo!"*]

IRINA [*starts*].   Everything seems to frighten me today. [*A pause.*] Well, all my things are ready. I'm sending the luggage off after lunch. The Baron and I are going to get married tomorrow, and then we're moving to the brickyard, and the next day I begin work at the school. So, God willing, our new life will begin. When I passed my exams, I felt so happy that I cried with a feeling of pure bliss . . . [*A pause.*] They will be coming for my things in a minute . . .

KULYGIN.   That's all very well, but it doesn't seem serious. Nothing but ideas and theories, nothing really serious. Anyway, I wish you the best of luck.

CHEBUTYKIN [*moved*].   My precious little girl, my dear child! You've gone on so far ahead of me, I'll never catch up with you now. I've been left behind like a bird that's too old and can't keep up with the rest of the flock. Fly away, my dear, fly away, and God bless you! [*A pause.*] It's a shame you've shaved your moustache off, Fyodor Ilyich.

KULYGIN.   Don't keep that up, please. [*Sighs.*] Well, the soldiers are leaving today, and then everything will be as it used to. I don't care what they say, Masha is a fine, loyal wife and I love her very much and I'm grateful for what God has given me. Fate treats people so differently. For instance, there's a clerk in the tax office called Kozyrev. We went to school together and he was expelled in his fifth year because he just couldn't understand the *"ut consecutivum."*[14] He's terribly poor now; and in bad health, too, and whenever I meet

---

14 (Latin) And consequently. (An allusion to the simple "cause and effect" reasoning frequently inculcated in schools.)

him, I say to him: "Hello, '*ut consecutivum!*' " "Yes," he says, "that's just the trouble—'*consecutivum*' " . . . and he begins to cough. And here I am—I've always been successful. I'm happy. Why, I've even been awarded the order of Saint Stanislav, second class—and now I'm teaching the students the same old "*ut consecutivum.*" Of course, I'm clever, cleverer than most people, but happiness doesn't consist of being clever . . .

[*In the house someone plays "The Maiden's Prayer" on the piano.*]

IRINA.   After tomorrow I won't have to listen to "The Maiden's Prayer." I won't have to meet Protopopov. . . . [*A pause.*] By the way, he's in the drawing room. He's here again today.

KULYGIN.   Hasn't the headmistress come yet?

IRINA.   No, we've sent for her. If you only knew how hard it's been for me to live here by myself, without Olya! Now that she's the headmistress and lives at school and is busy all day long and I'm here alone, I'm bored, I've nothing to do, and I hate the room I live in. So I've decided that if I'm not going to live in Moscow, then it just can't be helped. It's my fate and there's nothing to be done about it. It's God's will, everything that happens, there's no doubt about it. Nikolai Lvovich proposed to me . . . Well, I thought it over, and I just decided. He's a good man, it's really amazing how kind he is . . . And then suddenly I felt as though my soul had grown wings. I was more cheerful and I longed to work again. To work! . . . Except something happened yesterday, and now there's a mystery hanging over me . . .

CHEBUTYKIN.   Nonsense!

NATASHA [*speaking through the window*].   Our headmistress!

KULYGIN.   Our headmistress has come! Let's go in. [*Goes indoors with* IRINA.]

CHEBUTYKIN [*reads his paper and sings quietly to himself*].   "Tarara-boom-di-ay . . . I'm sitting on a tomb-di-ay . . ."

[MASHA *walks up to him;* ANDREY *passes across the back of the stage pushing the baby carriage.*]

MASHA.   You look comfortable . . .

CHEBUTYKIN.   Well, why not? Anything happening?

MASHA [*sits down*].   No, nothing. [*A pause.*] Tell me something. Were you in love with my mother?

CHEBUTYKIN.   Yes, very much in love.

MASHA.   Did she love you?

CHEBUTYKIN [*after a pause*].   I can't remember any more.

MASHA.   Is my man here? Our cook Marfa always used to call her policeman "my man." Is he here?

CHEBUTYKIN.   Not yet.

MASHA.   When you have to take your happiness in bits and snatches, and then you lose it, as I have, you can't help but get hardened and bitter. [*Points at her breast.*] I'm seething inside as if I'll boil over. [*Looking at* ANDREY, *who again crosses the stage with the carriage.*] And there's our Andrey . . . All our hopes are shattered. It's the same as when thousands of men raise a huge bell up into a tower. A lot of work and money is spent on it, and then suddenly it falls and gets smashed. Suddenly, for no reason at all. That is Andrey . . .

ANDREY.   When will they be quiet in the house? There is so much noise.

CHEBUTYKIN.   Soon. [*Looks at his watch.*] You know, this is a very old watch: it strikes . . . [*Winds his watch, which then strikes.*] The first, second and fifth batteries are going at one o'clock. [*A pause.*] And I am going tomorrow.

ANDREY.   For good?

CHEBUTYKIN.   I don't know. Perhaps I'll come back next year. Although, God knows . . . it doesn't matter one way or the other.

[*The sounds of a harp and a violin are heard.*]

ANDREY.   The town will be empty. Just as if life were snuffed out like a candle. [*A pause.*] Something happened yesterday at the theatre; everybody's talking about it. But I don't know anything about it.

CHEBUTYKIN.   It was nothing. Just a lot of nonsense. Solyony started bothering the Baron again, and the Baron lost his temper and insulted him, and so Solyony had to challenge him to a duel. [*Looks at his watch.*] It's about time to go . . . At half-past twelve, in the forest, on the other side of the river . . . Bang-bang! [*Laughs.*] Solyony thinks he's Lermontov. Why he even writes poetry. But, all kidding aside, this is his third duel.

MASHA.   Whose?

CHEBUTYKIN.   Solyony's.

MASHA.   What about the Baron?

CHEBUTYKIN.   Well, what about him? [*A pause.*]

MASHA.   My thoughts are all confused. Anyway you shouldn't let them fight. He might wound the Baron or even kill him.

CHEBUTYKIN.   The Baron's a fine man, but what does it really matter if there's one Baron more or less in the world? What difference does it make? [*The shouts of "Yoo-hoo!" and "Halloo!" are heard from beyond the garden.*] That's Skvortsov, the second, shouting from the boat. Let him wait.

ANDREY.   Frankly, I think it's downright immoral to fight a duel, or even to be present at one as a doctor.

CHEBUTYKIN.   It only seems that way . . . We don't really exist, nothing does, we only think so . . . And anyway, what difference does it make?

MASHA.   Talk, talk, talk, nothing but talk all day long! . . . [*Starts to go.*] To have to live in this terrible climate with the snow threatening to fall all the time, and then to have to listen to all this talk . . . [*Stops.*] I'm not going into the house, I can't stand going in there . . . Will you let me know when Vershinin comes? . . . [*Walks off along the avenue.*] Look, the birds are beginning to fly away already! [*Looks up.*] Swans or geese . . . Lovely birds, happy birds . . . [*Goes off.*]

ANDREY.   The house will seem awfully empty. The officers are leaving, you're going, my sister's getting married, and I'll be left alone in the house.

CHEBUTYKIN.   What about your wife?

[*Enter* FERAPONT *with some papers.*]

ANDREY.   My wife is my wife. She's a good, decent woman . . . and she's really very kind, but there's something about her that reduces her to the level of some petty, blind, hairy animal. Anyway, she's not a human being. I'm telling you this as a friend, the only person I can really talk to. I do love Natasha, but sometimes she seems so completely vulgar, that I don't know what to think, and then I can't understand why I love her—or, why I ever did love her . . .

CHEBUTYKIN [*gets up*].   Well, my boy, I'm leaving tomorrow and I might never see you again. So I'll give you a piece of advice. Put on your hat, take a walking stick, and go away . . . Go away, and don't ever look back. And the further you go, the better. [*Pause.*] But do as you like! What difference does it make?

[SOLYONY *passes across the back of the stage accompanied by two officers. Seeing* CHEBUTYKIN, *he turns towards him, while the officers walk on.*]

SOLYONY. It's time, Doctor. Twelve-thirty already. [*Shakes hands with* ANDREY.]

CHEBUTYKIN. Just a minute. Oh, I'm so sick of you all. [*To* ANDREY.] Andriusha, if anyone asks for me, tell them I'll be back. [*Sighs.*] Oh-ho-ho!

SOLYONY. "He had hardly time to catch his breath / Before the bear was hugging him to death." [*Walks off with him.*] What are you grumbling about, old man?

CHEBUTYKIN. Oh, well!

SOLYONY. How do you feel?

CHEBUTYKIN [*crossly*]. Fit as a fiddle.

SOLYONY. There's nothing to be so upset about, old man. I shan't go too far, I'll just touch his wings a little, like a snipe. [*Takes out a perfume bottle and sprinkles perfume over his hands.*] I've used up a whole bottle today, but my hands still smell . . . like a corpse. [*A pause.*] By the way . . . Do you remember that poem of Lermontov's "And he, rebellious, seeks a storm, / As if in storm there were tranquility" . . .

CHEBUTYKIN. Yes. "He had hardly time to catch his breath / Before the bear was hugging him to death." [*Goes out with* SOLYONY.]

[*Shouts of "Halloo! Yoo-hoo!" are heard.*]

FERAPONT. Will you sign these, please?

ANDREY [*with irritation*]. Let me alone. Let me alone, please. [*Goes off with the carriage.*]

FERAPONT. That's what papers are for—to be signed. [*Goes to back of stage.*]

[*Enter* IRINA *and* TUSENBACH, *wearing a straw hat.* KULYGIN *crosses the stage, calling: "Yoo-hoo! Masha! Yoo-hoo!"*]

TUSENBACH. He's probably the only person in town who's glad the officers are leaving.

IRINA. That's understandable, I guess. [*A pause.*] The town will be quite empty now.

TUSENBACH. Darling, I'll be back in just a minute.

IRINA. Where are you going?

TUSENBACH. I've got to go to town, and then . . . I want to see some of my comrades off.

IRINA. It's not true . . . Nikolai, why are you so absent-minded today? [*A pause.*] What happened last night at the theatre?

TUSENBACH [*with a gesture of impatience*]. I'll be back in an hour . . . back with you again. [*Kisses her hands.*] My beautiful one . . . [*Gazes into her eyes.*] I've loved you now for five years and still I can't get used to it. You seem more beautiful every day. What marvelous, lovely hair! What wonderful eyes! I'll take you away tomorrow. We'll work, we'll be rich and my dreams will come true. And you'll be happy! But—there's only one thing, only one— you don't love me!

IRINA. I can't help that! I'll be your wife, I'll be faithful and loyal to you, but I can't love you . . . We can't do anything about it. [*Weeps.*] I've never really loved anyone in my life. Oh, I've dreamt about being in love! I've been dreaming about it for years and years, day and night . . . but somehow my soul is like an expensive grand piano that someone has locked and the key's been lost. [*A pause.*] What's wrong?

TUSENBACH. I didn't sleep last night. Not that there's anything I'm afraid of. It's just that the thought of that lost key torments me and I can't sleep. Say something to me . . . [*A pause.*] Say something!

IRINA. What? What am I to say? What?

TUSENBACH. Anything.

IRINA. Don't, my dear, don't, please . . . [*A pause.*]

TUSENBACH. It's strange how little things—trifles sometimes become so important in our lives, for no reason at all. You laugh at them, just as you always have done, you still regard them as trifles, and yet you suddenly find they're controlling you, and you haven't the power to stop them. But let's not talk about that! Really, I feel fine. I feel as if I were seeing those pine trees and maples and birches for the first time in my life. They all seem to be look-ing at me, waiting for something. What beautiful trees—and when you think of it, how beautiful life ought to be when there are trees like these! [*Shouts of "Halloo!" are heard.*] I've got to go . . . Look at that tree, it's dead, but it goes on swaying in the wind with the others. And it seems to me that in the same way, if I die, I'll still have a part in life, one way or another. Good-bye, my darling . . . [*Kisses her hands.*] The papers you gave me are on my desk, under the calendar.

IRINA. I'm coming with you.

TUSENBACH [*alarmed*]. No, no! [*Goes off quickly, then stops in the avenue.*] Irina!

IRINA. What?

TUSENBACH [*not knowing what to say*]. I didn't have any coffee this morning. Will you tell them to make me some? [*Goes off quickly.*]

[IRINA *stands, lost in thought, then goes to the back of the stage and sits down on a swing. Enter* ANDREY *with the carriage;* FERAPONT *appears.*]

FERAPONT. Andrey Sergeyevich, the papers aren't mine, you know; they're official. I didn't invent them.

ANDREY. Oh, where has it gone?—What's become of my past when I was young and gay and clever, when I had beautiful dreams and was full of ideas, and the present and the future were bright with hope? Why do you become so dull, so ordinary, so uninteresting almost before we've begun to live? . . . This town's been here for two hundred years; a hundred thousand people live in it, but we're all the same! There's never been a scholar or an artist or a saint in this place, not one man remarkable enough to make you feel envy or want to imitate him. They only eat, drink and sleep . . . Then they die and others take their places, and they eat, drink and sleep, too—and as if for variety, just to avoid being bored to death, they gossip, drink vodka, gamble and cheat. The wives deceive their husbands, and the husbands lie to their wives, and pretend they don't see or hear anything . . . And it's this overwhelming vulgarity that crushes our children and destroys any talent they might have, so that they become miserable and more dead than alive, all alike and just like their parents . . . [*To* FERAPONT, *crossly.*] What do you want?

FERAPONT.   What? Here are the papers to sign.

ANDREY.   What a nuisance you are!

FERAPONT [*hands him the papers*].   The janitor at the tax office was saying that last winter they had two hundred degrees of frost in Petersburg.

ANDREY.   I hate my life as I am living it now, but oh! the sense of elation when I think of the future! Then I feel so light-hearted, have such a sense of release! I seem to see a bright light in the distance, light and freedom. I'll be free, and my children, too,—free from idleness, free from kvass, free from those meals of goose and cabbage, from after-dinner naps, and from all this degrading parasitism! . . .

FERAPONT.   And he said two thousand people were frozen to death and that everyone was frightened to death. It was either in Petersburg or in Moscow, I don't remember for sure.

ANDREY [*with sudden emotion, tenderly*].   My dear sisters, my wonderful sisters! [*Tearfully.*] Masha, my dear sister! . . .

NATASHA [*through the window*].   Who's talking so loudly out there? Is that you, Andryusha? You'll wake Sofotchka. "*Il ne faut pas faire du bruit, la Sophie est dormie déjà. Vous êtes un ours.*"[15] [*Getting angry.*] If you want to talk, give the carriage to someone else. Ferapont, take the carriage from the master.

FERAPONT.   Yes, Ma'am. [*Takes the carriage.*]

ANDREY [*embarrassed*].   I was talking quietly.

NATASHA [*in the window, caressing her small son*].   Bobik! Naughty Bobik! You naughty boy, you!

ANDREY [*glancing through the papers*].   All right, I'll go through these. You can take them back to the office later. [*Goes into the house, reading the papers.*]

[FERAPONT *wheels the carriage into the garden.*]

NATASHA [*in the window*].   What's Mommy's name, Bobik? You little angel! And who's that? Auntie Olya. Say: "Hello, Auntie Olya."

[*Two wandering musicians, a man and a girl, enter and play a violin and a harp.* VERSHININ, OLGA, *and* ANFISA *come out of the house and listen in silence for a few moments; then* IRINA *approaches them.*]

OLGA.   Our garden's like a city park; everybody goes through it. Nurse, give this to the musicians.

ANFISA [*giving them money*].   Get along with you and God bless you! Poor souls! [*The musicians bow and go away. To* IRINA.] How are you, Irinushka? [*Kisses her.*] Ah, my child, what a time I'm having! Living in a big apartment at the school with Olyushka—and no rent to pay, either! The Lord's been good to me in my old age. I've never lived so well in my life, old sinner that I am! A big apartment, and a whole room to myself with my own bed, and no rent to pay. When I wake up in the night, why then—Oh, Lord! Oh, Holy Mother of God! I'm the happiest person in the world!

VERSHININ [*glances at his watch*].   They'll be leaving soon, Olga Serge-yevna. It's time I left, too. [*A pause.*] I wish you all the happiness in the world . . . only the best . . . Where's Marya Sergeyevna?

IRINA.   She's somewhere in the garden. I'll go and look for her.

15 (French) You must not make any noise; Sophie is already asleep. You're a bear!

VERSHININ. Would you please? I've really got to hurry.

ANFISA. I'll come and help you. [*Calls out.*] Mashenka, yoo-hoo, yoo-hoo!

VERSHININ. Everything comes to an end. Well, here we are—and it's time to say "good-bye." [*Looks at his watch.*] There was a lunch for us at the city hall, and we drank champagne and the mayor made a speech. I ate and listened, but my heart was with all of you here . . . [*Glances round the garden.*] I've grown so . . . so accustomed to you.

OLGA. Do you think we'll ever meet again?

VERSHININ. Probably not! [*A pause.*] My wife and two little girls will be staying on for another month or so. Please, if anything happens, if they need anything . . .

OLGA. Yes, yes, of course. Don't worry about it. [*A pause.*] Tomorrow there won't be a single soldier left in town . . . Everything will be just a memory, and a new life will begin for us here . . . [*A pause.*] Nothing has turned out as we expected. I didn't want to be headmistress, but I've become one, which means that I shall never go to Moscow . . .

VERSHININ. Well . . . Thank you for everything. Forgive me if ever I've done anything wrong . . . I've talked a lot, far too much, I'm afraid . . . Forgive me for that, too.

OLGA [*wipes her eyes*]. Oh . . . why doesn't Masha come?

VERSHININ. What else can I say now it's time to say "good-bye"? What shall I philosophize about now? . . . [*Laughs.*] Yes, life is hard. It seems quite hopeless for most of us, just a blank . . . And yet you must admit that it is gradually getting easier and more hopeful, and there's no doubt about it that the time isn't far off when happiness will be everywhere. [*Looks at his watch.*] It's time for me to go . . . In the old days men were always at war, our life was filled with nothing but campaigns, invasions, retreats, victories . . . All that's out of date now, and in its place there's a great void which can't be filled. Humanity is passionately searching for something to fill that void, and, of course, it will find something some day. Oh! If only it would happen soon! [*A pause.*] If only we could make working people aware of culture and make our cultured people work . . . [*Looks at his watch.*] I really must go . . .

OLGA. Here she comes!

[*Enter* MASHA.]

VERSHININ. I've come to say good-bye . . .

[OLGA *walks off and stands a little to one side so they can say good-bye.*]

MASHA [*looking into his face*]. Good-bye! [*A long kiss.*]

OLGA. All right, that'll do.

[MASHA *sobs loudly.*]

VERSHININ. Write to me . . . Don't forget me! Let me go now . . . It's time. Olga Sergeyevna, please take her . . . I must go . . . I'm late as it is . . . [*Deeply moved, he kisses* OLGA's *hands, then embraces* MASHA *once more and goes out quickly.*]

OLGA. Please, Masha! Don't my dear, don't . . .

[*Enter* KULYGIN.]

KULYGIN [*embarrassed*]. Never mind, let her cry, let her . . . My good Masha, my dear, sweet Masha . . . You're my wife, and I'm happy in spite of everything . . . I'm not complaining, I won't blame you—Olga is my witness

. . . We'll start our life over again just like it used to be, and I won't say a word . . . Not a word . . .

MASHA [*suppressing her sobs*]. "A green oak grows by a curving shore, And round that oak hangs a golden chain." . . . "A golden chain round that oak." . . . Oh, I'm going mad . . . By a curving shore . . . a green oak . . .

OLGA. Quiet, Masha, calm yourself . . . Give her some water.

MASHA. I'm not crying any more . . .

KULYGIN. She's stopped crying . . . she's such a good girl.

[*The hollow sound of a gunshot is heard in the distance.*]

MASHA. "A green oak grows by a curving shore, And round that oak hangs a golden chain." A green cat . . . a green oak . . . I've got it all mixed up . . . [*Drinks water.*] My life's mixed up . . . I don't want anything now . . . I'll be quiet in a minute . . . It doesn't matter . . . What *is* "the curving shore"? Why does it keep coming into my head all the time? Why does it haunt me? My thoughts are all mixed up.

[*Enter* IRINA.]

OLGA. Calm down, Masha. That's right . . . good girl! . . . Let's go inside.

MASHA [*irritably*]. I'm not going in there! [*Sobs, but immediately checks herself.*] I am not going into that house ever again!

IRINA. Let's all just sit here for a minute, and not say anything. I'm leaving tomorrow, you know . . . [*A pause.*]

KULYGIN. Yesterday I took this beard away from one of the boys. I've got it here. [*Puts it on.*] Do I look just like the German teacher? . . . [*Laughs.*] I do, don't I? Those boys are funny.

MASHA. Yes, you do look like that German of yours.

OLGA [*laughs*]. Yes, he does.

[MASHA *cries.*]

IRINA. Stop it, Masha!

KULYGIN. Yes, a great deal like him, I think!

NATASHA [*to the maid*]. What? Oh, yes. Mr. Protopopov is going to watch Sofotchka, and Andrey Sergeyevich is going to take Bobik out in the carriage. Children are such a bother! . . . [*To* IRINA.] So you're really leaving tomorrow, Irina? What a shame! Why don't you stay another week? [*Seeing* KULYGIN, *shrieks; he laughs and takes off the false beard.*] Why look at you! How you frightened me! [*To* IRINA.] I've gotten so used to your being here . . . You mustn't think it's going to be easy for me after you're gone. I'll put Andrey and his old violin into your room: there he can saw away at it as much as he likes. And then we'll put Sofotchka into his study. She's such a darling child, really! Really a wonderful child! This morning she looked at me with her big eyes and said: "Mommie!"

KULYGIN. That's true, she is a beautiful child.

NATASHA. So tomorrow I'll be alone here. [*Sighs.*] First, I'll have these firs cut down, then that maple tree. It's so ugly in the evening . . . [*To* IRINA.] My dear, that sash doesn't suit you at all. It's such bad taste. You ought to get something bright and shiny . . . I'll tell them to put flowers everywhere, lots of flowers, and there'll be such a lovely scent . . . [*Sternly.*] What's this fork doing on the table? [*Going into the house, to the maid.*] Why was that fork left? [*Shouts.*] Answer me!

KULYGIN. She's started again!

[*A band plays a military march off-stage; all listen.*]

OLGA.   They're going.

[*Enter* CHEBUTYKIN.]

MASHA.   The soldiers are going. Well . . . happy journey to them! [*To her husband.*] We must go home . . . where are my hat and cape? . . .

KULYGIN.   I took them into the house. I'll get them.

OLGA.   Yes, we can go home now. It's time.

CHEBUTYKIN.   Olga Sergeyevna!

OLGA.   What is it? [*A pause.*] What?

CHEBUTYKIN.   Nothing . . . I don't know quite how to tell you . . . [*Whispers in her ear.*]

OLGA [*frightened*].   It can't be!

CHEBUTYKIN.   Yes . . . it's too bad . . . I'm so tired . . . worn out . . . I don't want to say another word . . . [*With annoyance.*] Anyway, nothing matters!

MASHA.   What happened?

OLGA [*puts her arms around* IRINA].   This is a terrible day! . . . I don't know how to tell you dear . . .

IRINA.   What is it? Tell me quickly, what is it? For God's sake! . . . [*Cries.*]

CHEBUTYKIN.   The Baron's just been killed in a duel.

IRINA [*cries quietly*].   I knew it, I knew it . . .

CHEBUTYKIN [*goes to the table and sits down*].   I'm tired . . . [*Takes a newspaper out of his pocket.*] Let them cry . . . [*Sings quietly to himself.*] "Tarara-boom-di-ay, I'm sitting on a tomb-di-ay" . . . What difference does it make?

[*The three sisters stand huddled together.*]

MASHA.   Oh, listen to the music! They're leaving us . . . one has already gone, gone for good . . . forever! And now we're left alone . . . to start our lives all over again. We must go on living . . . we must go on living . . .

IRINA [*puts her head on* OLGA's *breast*].   Some day people will know why such things happen, and what the purpose of all this suffering is . . . Then there won't be any more mysteries . . . Meanwhile we must go on living . . . we must work. To work! Tomorrow I'll go away alone and teach in a school somewhere; I'll give my life to people who need it . . . It's autumn now, it will be winter soon, and everything will be covered with snow . . . But I'll go on working . . . I will work . . .

OLGA [*puts her arms round both her sisters*].   How happy the music is . . . I almost feel as if I wanted to live! Oh, God! The years will pass, and we shall all be gone. We shall be forgotten . . . Our faces, our voices will be forgotten and people will even forget that there were once three of us here . . . But our sufferings will mean happiness for those who come after us . . . Then peace and happiness will reign on earth, and we shall be remembered kindly and blessed. No, my dear sisters, our lives aren't finished yet. We shall live! The band is playing and soon we shall know why we live, why we suffer . . . Oh, if we only knew, if only we knew!

[*The music grows fainter and fainter.* KULYGIN, *smiling cheerfully, brings out the hat and the cape.* ANDREY *enters pushing the carriage with Bobik in it.*]

CHEBUTYKIN [*sings quietly to himself*].   "Tarara-boom-di-ay . . . I'm sitting on a tomb-di-ay" [*Reads the paper.*] It doesn't matter. Nothing matters!

OLGA.   If only we knew, if only we knew! . . .

Curtain.

COMMENTARY

Three Sisters is surely one of the saddest works in all literature. It is also one of the most saddening. As it draws to a close, and for some time after Olga has uttered her hopeless desire to know whether life and its suffering have any meaning, we must make a conscious effort if we are not to be overcome by the depression that threatens our spirits. The frustration and hopelessness to which the persons of the drama fall prey seems to be not only their doom but ours as well. For between ourselves and those persons in *Three Sisters* with whom we sympathize there is remarkably little distance, certainly as compared, say, with the distance that separates us from Lear. Apart from the difference in nationality, nothing stands in the way of our saying that they are much like ourselves and our friends. They are decent, well-intentioned people, not extraordinary in their gifts but above the general run of mankind in intelligence and sensitivity, well enough educated to take pleasure in the arts and to aspire to freedom, the enjoyment of beauty, and the natural development of their personalities, all the benefits to which we give the name of "the good life."

And in fact, apart from their recognizability, these people are made especially easy for us to come close to because Chekhov, in representing them, takes full account of an element of human life that the tragic dramatists were not concerned with. Sophocles and Shakespeare represented life in terms of character and fate. Chekhov proposes the part that is played in our existence by environment. There is nothing that more readily fosters our intimacy with other people than an awareness of the actual and particular conditions in which they live their lives from day to day.

Character, in the sense in which we use it of the creations of the great tragic dramatists, means the way in which a person confronts the things that happen to him, a number of which may come about as a consequence of his characteristic behavior. Fate is the sum of the decisive things that happen to a person, whether as the result of his characteristic behavior, or fortuitously, or at the behest of some transcendent power. Environment signifies those material and social circumstances in which an individual leads his existence, in particular those that make for his well-being or lack of it and that seem to condition his character and fate.

Since all events take place under nameable conditions, environment is an integral element of all dramatic genres, including tragedy. In the story of Oedipus, for example, it is clearly of consequence that Oedipus is king of Thebes, not of Athens, and that he lives as befits a king and not, say, a merchant. But we are not asked to be aware of these circumstances except in a general way. Our imagination of Oedipus in his regal life does not include particularities such as the boring ceremonial a king must endure, the strain of being always in the public eye, his exasperated sense of the frivolity of the innumerable palace servants, whose gossip and petty intrigue are a perpetual nuisance . . . and so on.

The modern literary imagination almost always conceives environment as adverse, as comprising those material and social conditions of life which constrain and hamper the protagonist and thwart his ideal development and which, more than anything that might happen to him in a sudden dramatic way, make his destiny. The habit of thinking about a human life in relation to its environment is of relatively recent growth. It began, roughly speaking, in the eighteenth century. Since then it has achieved an importance that can scarcely be overestimated.

This sense of the influence of environment on character and fate has deeply changed the traditional way of thinking about morality and politics. It enables us to believe in an essential quality of humanity, about which predications can be made, usually to the effect that it is by nature good, and then to go on to judge whether a particular circumstance in which an individual is placed is appropriate or inappropriate to his essential humanity. It thus serves as a principle of explanation in the personal life, and as a ground of social action. Few people can hear the contemporary phrase "juvenile delinquent" without immediately thinking of the family and neighborhood circumstances—the environment—that fostered the undesirable behavior of the young person. And in our view of ourselves we have learned to give great significance to the conditions of our lives, those that made us what we are and those that keep us from being what we might wish to be.

The awareness of environment is, as I have said, salient in our response to *Three Sisters*. We are never permitted to forget that the people in Chekhov's play are required to live in a certain way—far from the metropolis, Moscow, in a dreary provincial city; possessing the tastes and desires of a certain social class yet lacking the money to fulfill their expectations of life; bored by and disaffected from their professions. Their desperate unhappiness is not the result of an event, of some catastrophic shock, but, rather, a condition of life itself, the slow relentless withdrawal of all that had once been promised of delight and satisfaction. To catastrophe we can sometimes respond by mustering up our energies of resistance or fortitude, but the unhappiness that Chekhov represents is that of people who, as the environment takes its toll of them, have fewer and fewer energies of resistance or endurance, let alone renovation. It is a state that few of us can fail in at least some degree to know from experience, and our knowledge of it makes us peculiarly responsive to the pathos of *Three Sisters*. We are not surprised to hear that when the manuscript of the play was read to the members of the Moscow Art Theatre who were to perform it, the company was so deeply moved that many wept as they listened.

Chekhov did not take their tears as a tribute. He told them that they had quite misconceived the nature of *Three Sisters,* which was, he said, a "gay comedy, almost a farce." This may well be the strangest comment on his own work that a writer ever made. And Chekhov did not make it casually or playfully, as a provocative paradox. He insisted on it. The famous head of the Moscow Theatre, Constantin Stanislavsky, who directed and championed Chekhov's plays, says in his memoirs that he can remember no opinion ever expressed by Chekhov that the author defended so passionately; he held it, Stanislavsky says, "until his dying day" and believed that his play had failed if it was understood otherwise. Yet he was never able to make clear what he meant by this strange idea. Another theatrical colleague, Vladimir Nemirovich Danchenko, who was even closer to Chekhov than Stanislavsky was, tells us that when the actors asked him for an explanation of such a view, he never could advance reasons to substantiate it.[1] To his friends in the theatre it was plain that Chekhov was not being perverse, that he truly believed that this saddest of plays was a comedy. But why he believed this they did not know.

And perhaps we cannot know. At the end of Plato's *Symposium,* when all the other guests at the great party have fallen asleep, Socrates sits drinking with the comic poet Aristophanes and the tragic poet Agathon, compelling them "to acknowledge that the genius of comedy was the same with that of tragedy, and that the true artist in tragedy was an artist in comedy also. To this they were constrained to assent, being drowsy and not quite following the argument."[2] How the argument ran was not reported and will never be known. And it may well be that Chekhov's reason for calling *Three Sisters* a comedy despite all its sadness will also never be known, even by inference.

But perhaps we today are in a better position to speculate about it than were the members of the Moscow Art Theatre. To the people of his own time, the new and striking thing about the plays of Chekhov was that they expressed so fully the pathos of personal aspiration frustrated by social and cultural circumstances. The latter part of the nineteenth century in Russia saw the rapid development of the class of intelligentsia, as it was called, people of sensibility and education, readily accessible to the influence of ideas and ideals, who could imagine and desire more in the way of fulness of life than they would ever achieve.[3] This discrepancy is common to similar groups in all nations, but what made it especially marked in Russia was the repressiveness of the Czarist government and the backwardness of the economy. A young Russian who undertook to live the life of intellect and art, or simply the good life in which intellect and art have their place, had fewer opportunities to do so than a young person elsewhere in Europe. His will, checked and baffled, lost its impetus and turned back upon itself in bitterness and self-recrimination. All Chekhov's plays are concerned with the defeat of delicate and generous minds, and the warmth of feeling that the Russian intelligentsia directed to Chekhov in his lifetime was in gratitude for his having made its plight so fully explicit and for having treated its pathos with so affectionate a tenderness. It is not too much to say that the intelligentsia of Chekhov's time received the pathos of his plays as a precious gift and cherished it dearly.

[1] I have derived this account of Chekhov's view of the play from *The Oxford Chekhov,* translated and edited by Ronald Hingley, Volume III, pp. 314–316.

[2] Jowett's translation.

[3] "Intelligentsia" is the form in which the Russian word *intelligentsiya* came into English (about 1914). Although it is now an accredited English word, it is used rather less frequently than it formerly was, having been somewhat displaced by "intellectuals." But "intelligentsia" has a special usefulness because it implies not so much the actual use of the intellect as the prestige of living by ideas and ideals and in relation to the arts. There is thus an overtone of irony in the use of the word which is perhaps intended to appear in the definition given by the *Oxford English Dictionary:* "The class of society to which culture, superior intelligence, and advanced political views are attributed."

The Russian intelligentsia was recruited from several social classes, but most of the characters of Chekhov's plays derive from the minor aristocracy or gentry, usually more or less impoverished.

But what was new at the turn of the century is now fairly old. Although the theme of the adverse social or cultural environment is still central to our thought, by the same token it is pretty much taken for granted. The personal frustration that Chekhov's characters suffered is now no longer assumed to be the inevitable fate of the members of the intelligentsia; today, at least in some countries, they can look forward to lives of considerable freedom and activity, even affluence and power. As a consequence, while we respond, and even deeply, to the pathos of Chekhov's plays, we are not likely to value it in the same degree that it was valued by the members of the Moscow Art Theatre.

This being so, it is easier for us than it was for his colleagues in the theatre to suppose that Chekhov himself did not want his audiences to feel only the sadness of *Three Sisters*, although it had of course been his purpose to evoke it and make it poignant and salient. He also had another and what might seem a contradictory intention: to lead his audience *away* from those very emotions in the play which they most cherished. When Chekhov said that *Three Sisters* was a comedy, even a farce, he was not talking to critics or theorists of literature but to actors, and he was trying to suggest what should be brought to the text by those who put it on the stage, a complexity of meaning which the text might not at first reveal. The meaning of a highly developed work of literature cannot ever be given in a formula, and Chekhov's plays resist formulation rather more than most. Chekhov did not undertake to solve life; he was averse to the propagation of ideas; his sole purpose, he said, was to represent life as it really is. But life cannot be seen without judgment of some kind, and throughout *Three Sisters,* as throughout his other great plays, Chekhov undertakes to influence our judgment in many ways, giving us ground for sympathy with one character, of antipathy to another, of contempt for yet another, of distaste for this or that circumstance of existence, controlling not only the direction of our feelings but their duration and intensity as well, so that contempt begins to give way suddenly to understanding, or admiration to irony. Much, then, of our sense of the meaning of *Three Sisters* when we see it performed depends upon the style of the performance—upon, that is, the ability of the actors to complicate its emotional communication.

Stanislavsky, we are told, had a tendency to produce all Chekhov's plays in a deliberate and dramatic style, which emphasized the moments of painful feeling and made the plays into what were called "heavy dramas." This method, which in effect invited the audience to self-pity before the hopelessness of life, was no doubt the loyal Stanislavsky's way of expressing his sense of Chekhov's seriousness and importance. But if *Three Sisters* is acted with the lightness and the rapid tempo of the comic style, or with some of the briskness of farce, the response of the audience is bound to be different. The play will not then offer an exactly cheerful view of things; it will still be saying that life is, in all conscience, hard and bitterly disappointing. But this will not be its sole judgment. The seeming contradiction between the sadness of the text and the vivacity of the style will suggest an inconclusiveness of judgment, inviting the audience not to the indulgence of self-pity but to a thoughtful, perhaps even an ironic detachment.

Whether or not we accept the play as a comedy, we cannot fail to see that there is comedy in it, and a performance in the comic style will give full recognition to its abundant humor of character. All the male characters, in one degree or another, provoke our laughter or at least our smiles—Vershinin by his compulsion to make visionary speeches about mankind's future happiness, Andrey by his fatness, Chebutykin by his avowed total ignorance of medicine, Solyony by his absurd social behavior, especially his belief that he resembles the great romantic poet Lermontov, Kulygin by his pedantry and silliness, even poor good Tusenbach by his confidence that he can solve the problems of existence by going to work for a brick company. It is an aspect of his gift that Chekhov is able to make us laugh at these people without allowing us to despise them. Our laughter is a skeptical comment on the facile belief that nothing but the circumstances of environment account for people's destinies, for what we laugh at is the self-deception, or the pretension, or the infirmity of purpose that in some large part explains their pain and defeat—and our own.

The three sisters themselves, however, appear in a light very different from that in which the male characters are placed. We cannot say of them, as we do of the men, that they have helped contrive their defeat; the situation of women being what it was when Chekhov was writing, there was virtually no way by which they might have triumphed over circumstances to avoid the waste of their lives. Each of the three girls had, to be sure, overestimated the chances of happiness, but what they had imagined and desired was not beyond reason. Such deceptions as they practice on themselves do not warp their personalities into comic eccentricity, as happens with all the men. In the sisters, we feel, life appears in its normality, rather beautiful: they are finely developed human beings of delicate and generous mind. And the end of the play finds each of them doomed to unfulfilment, bitterly grieving over her fate, despite the resolution to live out her life in courageous affirmation. That this final scene is intensely sad goes without saying. But it is an open question for the reader or the stage director whether the exaltation of fortitude and faith that the sisters muster up in the face of defeat is to be taken ironically, as a delusion which makes the sadness yet more intense, or whether it is to be understood as sounding a true note of affirmation. The answer to the question should perhaps be conditioned by the knowledge that the scene was written by a dying man.

Chekhov suffered from tuberculosis, at that time a disease not easily cured. A physician of considerable skill, although he had given up the practice of medicine, he was not likely to be under any illusion about his chances of recovery; he died four years after the production of *Three Sisters*, at the age of forty-five. His illness did not deprive him of all gratification. He worked, although against odds. His work was honored, and he was much loved. But he had to live in exile from Moscow, even from Russia; he was often in pain, physical activity became ever less possible; he was often separated from his young wife for long periods. It could not have been without thought of himself that he wrote such despairing speeches as the one in which Irina says, "Where has it all gone? Where is it? . . . life's slipping by, and it will never, never return. . . ."

Yet as we read Chekhov's letters of the last years of his illness, we find no despair in them, no bitterness, not even the sorrow we might expect to find. They are full of the often trivial details of travel, business, and work, of expressions of concern and affection for others, they address themselves to ordinary, unexceptional life, without tragic reverberations, even without drama. Perhaps an unwillingness to burden others with his darker thoughts in some part explains why Chekhov wrote as he did, but as one reads the letters along-side the plays, one feels that Chekhov was living life as the speeches at the end of *Three Sisters* suggest it must be lived: without the expectation of joy, yet in full attachment, and cherishing what may be cherished, even if that is nothing more than the idea of life itself. A man of affectionate disposition upon whom death had laid its hand would probably not be concerned with making a rational or prudential judgment upon life: more likely he would be moved to wonder if a transcendent judgment might not be made. And when Chekhov wrote that "it will be winter soon, and everything will be covered with snow," he may well have wished to suggest that in the cycle of the seasons the spring will follow and that, sad as we may be over what befalls ourselves and others, life itself is to be celebrated. Over the centuries the attributes and intentions of comedy have been numerous and various. But one of the oldest of them has been to say that, appearances to the contrary notwithstanding, all will be well, the life of the earth will renew itself.

THE

DOCTOR'S

DILEMMA

GEORGE BERNARD SHAW

1 8 5 6 – 1 9 5 0

ACT I

On the 15th June 1903, in the early forenoon, a medical student, surname REDPENNY, Christian name unknown and of no importance, sits at work in a doctor's consulting room. He devils for the doctor by answering his letters, acting as his domestic laboratory assistant, and making himself indispensable generally, in return for unspecified advantages involved by intimate intercourse with a leader of his profession, and amounting to an informal apprenticeship and a temporary affiliation. REDPENNY is not proud, and will do anything he is asked without reservation of his personal dignity if he is asked in a fellow-creaturely way. He is a wide-open-eyed, ready, credulous, friendly, hasty youth, with his hair and clothes in reluctant transition from the untidy boy to the tidy doctor.

REDPENNY is interrupted by the entrance of an old serving-woman who has never known the cares, the preoccupations, the responsibilities, jealousies, and anxieties of personal beauty. She has the complexion of a never-washed gypsy, incurable by any detergent; and she has, not a regular beard and moustaches, which could at least be trimmed and waxed into a masculine presentableness, but a whole crop of small beards and moustaches, mostly springing from moles all over her face. She carries a duster and toddles about meddlesomely, spying out

256

dust so diligently that whilst she is flicking off one speck she is already looking elsewhere for another. In conversation she has the same trick, hardly ever looking at the person she is addressing except when she is excited. She has only one manner, and that is the manner of an old family nurse to a child just after it has learnt to walk. She has used her ugliness to secure indulgences unattainable by Cleopatra or Fair Rosamund, and has the further great advantage over them that age increases her qualification instead of impairing it. Being an industrious, agreeable, and popular old soul, she is a walking sermon on the vanity of feminine prettiness. Just as REDPENNY *has no discovered Christian name, she has no discovered surname, and is known throughout the doctor's quarter between Cavendish Square and the Marylebone Road simply as* EMMY.*

The consulting room has two windows looking on Queen Anne Street. Between the two is a marble-topped console, with haunched gilt legs ending in sphinx claws. The huge pierglass which surmounts it is mostly disabled from reflection by elaborate painting on its surface of palms, ferns, lilies, tulips, and sunflowers. The adjoining wall contains the fireplace, with two arm-chairs before it. As we happen to face the corner we see nothing of the other two walls. On the right of the fireplace, or rather on the right of any person facing the fireplace, is the door. On its left is the writing-table at which* REDPENNY *sits. It is an untidy table with a microscope, several test tubes, and a spirit lamp standing up through its litter of papers. There is a couch in the middle of the room, at right angles to the console, and parallel to the fireplace. A chair stands between the couch and the window. Another in the corner. Another at the other end of the windowed wall. The windows have green Venetian blinds and rep curtains; and there is a gasalier; but it is a convert to electric lighting. The wall paper and carpets are mostly green, coeval with the gasalier and the Venetian blinds. The house, in fact, was so well furnished in the middle of the XIXth century that it stands unaltered to this day and is still quite presentable.*

EMMY [*Entering and immediately beginning to dust the couch*]. Theres[1] a lady bothering me to see the doctor.

REDPENNY [*distracted by the interruption*]. Well, she cant see the doctor. Look here: whats the use of telling you that the doctor cant take any new patients, when the moment a knock comes to the door, in you bounce to ask whether he can see somebody?

EMMY. Who asked you whether he could see somebody?

REDPENNY. You did.

EMMY. I said theres a lady bothering me to see the doctor. That isnt asking. Its telling.

REDPENNY. Well, is the lady bothering you a reason for you to come bothering me when I'm busy?

EMMY. Have you seen the papers?

REDPENNY. No.

EMMY. Not seen the birthday honors?

REDPENNY [*beginning to swear*]. What the—

EMMY. Now, now, ducky!

[1] Shaw, who enjoyed adopting radical positions, wanted to reform English spelling. He particularly disliked the apostrophe, where he thought it useless.

REDPENNY. What do you suppose I care about the birthday honors? Get out of this with your chattering. Dr Ridgeon will be down before I have these letters ready. Get out.

EMMY. Dr Ridgeon wont never be down any more, young man. [*She detects dust on the console and is down on it immediately.*]

REDPENNY [*jumping up and following her*]. What?

EMMY. He's been made a knight. Mind you dont go Dr Ridgeoning him in them letters. Sir Colenso Ridgeon is to be his name now.

REDPENNY. I'm jolly glad.

EMMY. I never was so taken aback. I always thought his great discoveries was fudge (let alone the mess of them) with his drops of blood and tubes full of Maltese fever and the like. Now he'll have a rare laugh at me.

REDPENNY. Serve you right! It was like your cheek to talk to him about science. [*He returns to his table and resumes his writing.*]

EMMY. Oh, I dont think much of science; and neither will you when youve lived as long with it as I have. Whats on my mind is answering the door. Old Sir Patrick Cullen has been here already and left first congratulations—hadnt time to come up on his way to the hospital, but was determined to be first—coming back, he said. All the rest will be here too: the knocker will be going all day. What I'm afraid of is that the doctor'll want a footman like all the rest, now that he's Sir Colenso. Mind: dont you go putting him up to it, ducky; for he'll never have any comfort with anybody but me to answer the door. I know who to let in and who to keep out. And that reminds me of the poor lady. I think he ought to see her. She's just the kind that puts him in a good temper. [*She dusts* RED-PENNY'*s papers.*]

REDPENNY. I tell you he cant see anybody. Do go away, Emmy. How can I work with you dusting all over me like this?

EMMY. I'm not hindering you working—if you call writing letters working. There goes the bell. [*She looks out of the window.*] A doctor's carriage. Thats more congratulations. [*She is going out when* SIR COLENSO RIDGEON *enters.*] Have you finished your two eggs, sonny?

RIDGEON. Yes.

EMMY. Have you put on your clean vest?

RIDGEON. Yes.

EMMY. Thats my ducky diamond! Now keep yourself tidy and dont go messing about and dirtying your hands: the people are coming to congratulate you. [*She goes out.*]

[SIR COLENSO RIDGEON *is a man of fifty who has never shaken off his youth. He has the off-handed manner and the little audacities of address which a shy and sensitive man acquires in breaking himself in to intercourse with all sorts and conditions of men. His face is a good deal lined; his movements are slower than, for instance,* REDPENNY'*s; and his flaxen hair has lost its lustre; but in figure and manner he is more the young man than the titled physician. Even the lines in his face are those of overwork and restless skepticism, perhaps partly of curiosity and appetite, rather than that of age. Just at present the announcement of his knighthood in the morning papers makes him self-conscious, and consequently specially off-hand with* REDPENNY.]

RIDGEON. Have you seen the papers? Youll have to alter the name in the letters if you havnt.

REDPENNY.   Emmy has just told me. I'm awfully glad. I—

RIDGEON.   Enough, young man, enough. You will soon get accustomed to it.

REDPENNY.   They ought to have done it years ago.

RIDGEON.   They would have; only they couldnt stand Emmy opening the door, I daresay.

EMMY [*at the door, announcing*].   Dr Shoemaker. [*She withdraws.*]

[*A middle-aged gentleman, well dressed, comes in with a friendly but pro-pitiatory air, not quite sure of his reception. His combination of soft manners and responsive kindliness, with a certain unseizable reserve and a familiar yet for-eign chiselling of feature, reveal the Jew: in this instance the handsome gentle-manly Jew, gone a little pigeon-breasted and stale after thirty, as handsome young Jews often do, but still decidedly good-looking.*]

THE GENTLEMAN.   Do you remember me? Schutzmacher. University College school and Belsize Avenue. Loony Schutzmacher, you know.

RIDGEON.   What! Loony! [*He shakes hands cordially.*] Why, man, I thought you were dead long ago. Sit down. [SCHUTZMACHER *sits on the couch:* RIDGEON *on the chair between it and the window.*] Where have you been these thirty years?

SCHUTZMACHER.   In general practice, until a few months ago. Ive retired.

RIDGEON.   Well done, Loony! I wish *I* could afford to retire. Was your practice in London?

SCHUTZMACHER.   No.

RIDGEON.   Fashionable coast practice, I suppose.

SCHUTZMACHER.   How could I afford to buy a fashionable practice? I hadnt a rap. I set up in a manufacturing town in the midlands in a little surgery at ten shillings a week.

RIDGEON.   And made your fortune?

SCHUTZMACHER.   Well, I'm pretty comfortable. I have a place in Hertford-shire besides our flat in town. If you ever want a quiet Saturday to Monday, I'll take you down in my motor at an hour's notice.

RIDGEON.   Just rolling in money! I wish you rich g.p.'s would teach me how to make some. Whats the secret of it?

SCHUTZMACHER.   Oh, in my case the secret was simple enough, though I suppose I should have got into trouble if it had attracted any notice. And I'm afraid youll think it rather infra dig.

RIDGEON.   Oh, I have an open mind. What was the secret?

SCHUTZMACHER.   Well, the secret was just two words.

RIDGEON.   Not Consultation Free, was it?

SCHUTZMACHER [*shocked*].   No, no. Really!

RIDGEON [*apologetic*].   Of course not. I was only joking.

SCHUTZMACHER.   My two words were simply Cure Guaranteed.

RIDGEON [*admiring*].   Cure Guaranteed!

SCHUTZMACHER.   Guaranteed. After all, thats what everybody wants from a doctor, isnt it?

RIDGEON.   My dear Loony, it was an inspiration. Was it on the brass plate?

SCHUTZMACHER.   There was no brass plate. It was a shop window: red, you know, with black lettering. Doctor Leo Schutzmacher, L.R.C.P., M.R.C.S. Advice and medicine sixpence. Cure Guaranteed.

RIDGEON.   And the guarantee proved sound nine times out of ten, eh?

SCHUTZMACHER [*rather hurt at so moderate an estimate*]. Oh, much oftener than that. You see, most people get well all right if they are careful and you give them a little sensible advice. And the medicine really did them good. Parrish's Chemical Food: phosphates, you know. One tablespoonful to a twelve-ounce bottle of water: nothing better, no matter what the case is.

RIDGEON. Redpenny: make a note of Parrish's Chemical Food.

SCHUTZMACHER. I take it myself, you know, when I feel run down. Goodbye. You dont mind my calling, do you? Just to congratulate you.

RIDGEON. Delighted, my dear Loony. Come to lunch on Saturday next week. Bring your motor and take me down to Hertford.

SCHUTZMACHER. I will. We shall be delighted. Thank you. Goodbye. [*He goes out with* RIDGEON, *who returns immediately.*]

REDPENNY. Old Paddy Cullen was here before you were up, to be the first to congratulate you.

RIDGEON. Indeed. Who taught you to speak of Sir Patrick Cullen as old Paddy Cullen, you young ruffian?

REDPENNY. You never call him anything else.

RIDGEON. Not now that I am Sir Colenso. Next thing, you fellows will be calling me old Colly Ridgeon.

REDPENNY. We do, at St Anne's.

RIDGEON. Yach! Thats what makes the medical student the most disgusting figure in modern civilization. No veneration, no manners—no—

EMMY [*at the door, announcing*]. Sir Patrick Cullen. [*She retires.*]

[SIR PATRICK CULLEN *is more than twenty years older than* RIDGEON, *not yet quite at the end of his tether, but near it and resigned to it. His name, his plain, downright, sometimes rather arid common sense, his large build and stature, the absence of those odd moments of ceremonial servility by which an old English doctor sometimes shows you what the status of the profession was in England in his youth, and an occasional turn of speech, are Irish; but he has lived all his life in England and is thoroughly acclimatized. His manner to* RIDGEON, *whom he likes, is whimsical and fatherly: to others he is a little gruff and uninviting, apt to substitute more or less expressive grunts for articulate speech, and generally indisposed, at his age, to make much social effort. He shakes* RIDGEON'S *hand and beams at him cordially and jocularly.*]

SIR PATRICK. Well, young chap. Is your hat too small for you, eh?

RIDGEON. Much too small. I owe it all to you.

SIR PATRICK. Blarney, my boy. Thank you all the same. [*He sits in one of the armchairs near the fireplace.* RIDGEON *sits on the couch.*] Ive come to talk to you a bit. [*To* REDPENNY.] Young man: get out.

REDPENNY. Certainly, Sir Patrick. [*He collects his paper and makes for the door.*]

SIR PATRICK. Thank you. Thats a good lad. [REDPENNY *vanishes.*] They all put up with me, these young chaps, because I'm an old man, a real old man, not like you. Youre only beginning to give yourself the airs of age. Did you ever see a boy cultivating a moustache? Well, a middle-aged doctor cultivating a grey head is much the same sort of spectacle.

RIDGEON. Good Lord! yes: I suppose so. And I thought that the days of my vanity were past. Tell me: at what age does a man leave off being a fool?

SIR PATRICK. Remember the Frenchman who asked his grandmother at what age we get free from the temptations of love. The old woman said she didnt know. [RIDGEON *laughs*.] Well, I make you the same answer. But the world's growing very interesting to me now, Colly.

RIDGEON.   You keep up your interest in science, do you?

SIR PATRICK.   Lord! yes. Modern science is a wonderful thing. Look at your great discovery! Look at all the great discoveries! Where are they leading to? Why, right back to my poor dear old father's ideas and discoveries. He's been dead now over forty years. Oh, it's very interesting.

RIDGEON.   Well, theres nothing like progress, is there?

SIR PATRICK.   Dont misunderstand me, my boy. I'm not belittling your discovery. Most discoveries are made regularly every fifteen years; and it's fully a hundred and fifty since yours was made last. Thats something to be proud of. But your discovery's not new. It's only inoculation. My father practised inoculation until it was made criminal in eighteen-forty. That broke the poor old man's heart, Colly: he died of it. And now it turns out that my father was right after all. Youve brought us back to inoculation.

RIDGEON.   I know nothing about smallpox. My line is tuberculosis and typhoid and plague. But of course the principle of all vaccines is the same.

SIR PATRICK.   Tuberculosis? M-m-m-m! Youve found out how to cure consumption, eh?

RIDGEON.   I believe so.

SIR PATRICK.   Ah yes. It's very interesting. What is it the old cardinal says in Browning's play? "I have known four and twenty leaders of revolt." Well, Ive known over thirty men that found out how to cure consumption. Why do people go on dying of it, Colly? Devilment, I suppose. There was my father's old friend George Boddington of Sutton Coldfield. He discovered the open-air cure in eighteen-forty. He was ruined and driven out of his practice for only opening the windows; and now we wont let a consumptive patient have as much as a roof over his head. Oh, it's very very interesting to an old man.

RIDGEON.   You old cynic, you dont believe a bit in my discovery.

SIR PATRICK.   No, no: I dont go quite so far as that, Colly. But still, you remember Jane Marsh?

RIDGEON.   Jane Marsh? No.

SIR PATRICK.   You dont!

RIDGEON.   No.

SIR PATRICK.   You mean to tell me that you dont remember the woman with the tuberculous ulcer on her arm?

RIDGEON [*enlightened*].   Oh, your washerwoman's daughter. Was her name Jane Marsh? I forgot.

SIR PATRICK.   Perhaps youve forgotten also that you undertook to cure her with Koch's tuberculin.

RIDGEON.   And instead of curing her, it rotted her arm right off. Yes: I remember. Poor Jane! However, she makes a good living out of that arm now by shewing it at medical lectures.

SIR PATRICK.   Still, that wasnt quite what you intended, was it?

RIDGEON.   I took my chance of it.

SIR PATRICK.   Jane did, you mean.

RIDGEON.   Well, it's always the patient who has to take the chance when an experiment is necessary. And we can find out nothing without experiment.

SIR PATRICK.   What did you find out from Jane's case?

RIDGEON.   I found out that the inoculation that ought to cure sometimes kills.

SIR PATRICK.   I could have told you that. Ive tried these modern inoculations a bit myself. Ive killed people with them; and Ive cured people with them; but I gave them up because I never could tell which I was going to do.

RIDGEON [taking a pamphlet from a drawer in the writing-table and handing it to him].   Read that the next time you have an hour to spare; and youll find out why.

SIR PATRICK [grumbling and fumbling for his spectacles].   Oh, bother your pamphlets. Whats the practice of it? [Looking at the pamphlet.] Opsonin? What the devil is opsonin?

RIDGEON.   Opsonin is what you butter the disease germs with to make your white blood corpuscles eat them. [He sits down again on the couch.]

SIR PATRICK.   Thats not new. Ive heard this notion that the white corpuscles—what is it that whats his name?—Metchnikoff[2]—calls them?

RIDGEON.   Phagocytes.

SIR PATRICK.   Aye, phagocytes: yes, yes, yes. Well, I heard this theory that the phagocytes eat up the disease germs years ago: long before you came into fashion. Besides, they dont always eat them.

RIDGEON.   They do when you butter them with opsonin.

SIR PATRICK.   Gammon.

RIDGEON.   No: it's not gammon. What it comes to in practice is this. The phagocytes wont eat the microbes unless the microbes are nicely buttered for them. Well, the patient manufactures the butter for himself all right; but my discovery is that the manufacture of that butter, which I call opsonin, goes on in the system by ups and downs—Nature being always rhythmical, you know—and that what the inoculation does is to stimulate the ups and downs, as the case may be. If we had inoculated Jane Marsh when her butter factory was on the up-grade, we should have cured her arm. But we got in on the down-grade and lost her arm for her. I call the up-grade the positive phase and the down-grade the negative phase. Everything depends on your inoculating at the right moment. Inoculate when the patient is in the negative phase and you kill: inoculate when the patient is in the positive phase and you cure.

SIR PATRICK.   And pray how are you to know whether the patient is in the positive or the negative phase?

RIDGEON.   Send a drop of the patient's blood to the laboratory at St Anne's; and in fifteen minutes I'll give you his opsonin index in figures. If the figure is one, inoculate and cure: if it's under point eight, inoculate and kill. Thats my discovery: the most important that has been made since Harvey discovered the circulation of the blood. My tuberculosis patients dont die now.

SIR PATRICK.   And mine do when my inoculation catches them in the negative phase, as you call it. Eh?

RIDGEON.   Precisely. To inject a vaccine into a patient without first testing his opsonin is as near murder as a respectable practitioner can get. If I wanted to kill a man I should kill him that way.

[2] Elie Metchnikoff (1845–1916), a Russian biologist, in 1908 was awarded the Nobel prize, jointly with Paul Ehrlich, for his work on immunity.

EMMY [*looking in*]. Will you see a lady that wants her husband's lungs cured?

RIDGEON [*impatiently*]. No. Havnt I told you I will see nobody? [*To* SIR PATRICK.] I live in a state of siege ever since it got about that I'm a magician who can cure consumption with a drop of serum. [*To* EMMY.] Dont come to me again about people who have no appointments. I tell you I can see nobody.

EMMY. Well, I'll tell her to wait a bit.

RIDGEON [*furious*]. Youll tell her I cant see her, and send her away: do you hear?

EMMY [*unmoved*]. Well, will you see Mr Cutler Walpole? He dont want a cure: he only wants to congratulate you.

RIDGEON. Of course. Shew him up. [*She turns to go.*] Stop. [*To* SIR PATRICK.] I want two minutes more with you between ourselves. [*To* EMMY.] Emmy: ask Mr. Walpole to wait just two minutes, while I finish a consultation.

EMMY. Oh, he'll wait all right. He's talking to the poor lady. [*She goes out.*]

SIR PATRICK. Well? what is it?

RIDGEON. Dont laugh at me. I want your advice.

SIR PATRICK. Professional advice?

RIDGEON. Yes. Theres something the matter with me. I dont know what it is.

SIR PATRICK. Neither do I. I suppose youve been sounded.

RIDGEON. Yes, of course. Theres nothing wrong with any of the organs: nothing special, anyhow. But I have a curious aching: I dont know where: I cant localize it. Sometimes I think it's my heart: sometimes I suspect my spine. It doesnt exactly hurt me; but it unsettles me completely. I feel that something is going to happen. And there are other symptoms. Scraps of tunes come into my head that seem to me very pretty, though theyre quite commonplace.

SIR PATRICK. Do you hear voices?

RIDGEON. No.

SIR PATRICK. I'm glad of that. When my patients tell me that theyve made a greater discovery than Harvey, and that they hear voices, I lock them up.

RIDGEON. You think I'm mad! Thats just the suspicion that has come across me once or twice. Tell me the truth: I can bear it.

SIR PATRICK. Youre sure there are no voices?

RIDGEON. Quite sure.

SIR PATRICK. Then it's only foolishness.

RIDGEON. Have you ever met anything like it before in your practice?

SIR PATRICK. Oh, yes: often. It's very common between the ages of seventeen and twenty-two. It sometimes comes on again at forty or thereabouts. Youre a bachelor, you see. It's not serious—if youre careful.

RIDGEON. About my food?

SIR PATRICK. No: about your behavior. Theres nothing wrong with your spine; and theres nothing wrong with your heart; but theres something wrong with your common sense. Youre not going to die; but you may be going to make a fool of yourself. So be careful.

RIDGEON. I see you dont believe in my discovery. Well, sometimes I dont believe in it myself. Thank you all the same. Shall we have Walpole up?

SIR PATRICK. Oh, have him up. [RIDGEON *rings.*] He's a clever operator, is

Walpole, though he's only one of your chloroform surgeons. In my early days, you made your man drunk; and the porters and students held him down; and you had to set your teeth and finish the job fast. Nowadays you work at ease; and the pain doesnt come until afterwards, when youve taken your cheque and rolled up your bag and left the house. I tell you, Colly, chloroform has done a lot of mischief. It's enabled every fool to be a surgeon.

RIDGEON [to EMMY, who answers the bell]. Shew Mr Walpole up.

EMMY. He's talking to the lady.

RIDGEON [exasperated]. Did I not tell you—

[EMMY goes out without heeding him. He gives it up, with a shrug, and plants himself with his back to the console, leaning resignedly against it.]

SIR PATRICK. I know your Cutler Walpoles and their like. Theyve found out that a man's body's full of bits and scraps of old organs he has no mortal use for. Thanks to chloroform, you can cut half a dozen of them out without leaving him any the worse, except for the illness and the guineas it costs him. I knew the Walpoles well fifteen years ago. The father used to snip off the ends of people's uvulas for fifty guineas, and paint throats with caustic every day for a year at two guineas a time. His brother-in-law extirpated tonsils for two hundred guineas until he took up women's cases at double the fees. Cutler himself worked hard at anatomy to find something fresh to operate on; and at last he got hold of something he calls the nuciform sac, which he's made quite the fashion. People pay him five hundred guineas to cut it out. They might as well get their hair cut for all the difference it makes; but I suppose they feel important after it. You cant go out to dinner now without your neighbor bragging to you of some useless operation or other.

EMMY [announcing]. Mr Cutler Walpole. [She goes out.]

[CUTLER WALPOLE is an energetic, unhesitating man of forty, with a cleanly modelled face, very decisive and symmetrical about the shortish, salient, rather pretty nose, and the three trimly turned corners made by his chin and jaws. In comparison with RIDGEON's delicate broken lines, and SIR PATRICK's softly rugged aged ones, his face looks machine-made and beeswaxed; but his scrutinizing, daring eyes give it life and force. He seems never at a loss, never in doubt: one feels that if he made a mistake he would make it thoroughly and firmly. He has neat, well-nourished hands, short arms, and is built for strength and compactness rather than for height. He is smartly dressed with a fancy waistcoat, a richly colored scarf secured by a handsome ring, ornaments on his watch chain, spats on his shoes, and a general air of the well-to-do sportsman about him. He goes straight across to RIDGEON and shakes hands with him.]

WALPOLE. My dear Ridgeon, best wishes! heartiest congratulations! You deserve it.

RIDGEON. Thank you.

WALPOLE. As a man, mind you. You deserve it as a man. The opsonin is simple rot, as any capable surgeon can tell you; but we're all delighted to see your personal qualities officially recognized. Sir Patrick: how are you? I sent you a paper lately about a little thing I invented: a new saw. For shoulder blades.

SIR PATRICK [meditatively]. Yes: I got it. It's a good saw: a useful, handy instrument.

WALPOLE [confidently]. I knew youd see its points.

SIR PATRICK. Yes: I remember that saw sixty-five years ago.

WALPOLE. What!

SIR PATRICK. It was called a cabinetmaker's jimmy then.

WALPOLE. Get out! Nonsense! Cabinetmaker be—

RIDGEON. Never mind him, Walpole. He's jealous.

WALPOLE. By the way, I hope I'm not disturbing you two in anything private.

RIDGEON. No, no. Sit down. I was only consulting him. I'm rather out of sorts. Overwork, I suppose.

WALPOLE [swiftly]. I know whats the matter with you. I can see it in your complexion. I can feel it in the grip of your hand.

RIDGEON. What is it?

WALPOLE. Blood-poisoning.

RIDGEON. Blood-poisoning! Impossible.

WALPOLE. I tell you, blood-poisoning. Ninety-five per cent of the human race suffer from chronic blood-poisoning, and die of it. It's as simple as A.B.C. Your nuciform sac is full of decaying matter—undigested food and waste products —rank ptomaines. Now you take my advice, Ridgeon. Let me cut it out for you. Youll be another man afterwards.

SIR PATRICK. Dont you like him as he is?

WALPOLE. No I dont. I dont like any man who hasnt a healthy circulation. I tell you this: in an intelligently governed country people wouldnt be allowed to go about with nuciform sacs, making themselves centres of infection. The operation ought to be compulsory: it's ten times more important than vaccination.

SIR PATRICK. Have you had your own sac removed, may I ask?

WALPOLE [triumphantly]. I havnt got one. Look at me! Ive no symptoms. I'm sound as a bell. About five per cent of the population havnt got any; and I'm one of the five per cent. I'll give you an instance. You know Mrs. Jack Foljambe: the smart Mrs. Foljambe? I operated at Easter on her sister-in-law, Lady Gorran, and found she had the biggest sac I ever saw: it held about two ounces. Well, Mrs Foljambe had the right spirit—the genuine hygienic instinct. She couldnt stand her sister-in-law being a clean, sound woman, and she simply a whited sepulchre. So she insisted on my operating on her, too. And by George, sir, she hadnt any sac at all. Not a trace! Not a rudiment! I was so taken aback—so interested, that I forgot to take the sponges out, and was stitching them up inside her when the nurse missed them. Somehow, I'd made sure she'd have an exceptionally large one. [He sits down on the couch, squaring his shoulders and shooting his hands out of his cuffs as he sets his knuckles akimbo.]

EMMY [looking in]. Sir Ralph Bloomfield Bonington.

[A long and expectant pause follows this announcement. All look to the door; but there is no Sir Ralph.]

RIDGEON [at last]. Where is he?

EMMY [looking back]. Drat him, I thought he was following me. He's stayed down to talk to that lady.

RIDGEON [exploding]. I told you to tell that lady—[EMMY vanishes.]

WALPOLE [jumping up again]. Oh, by the way, Ridgeon, that reminds me. I've been talking to that poor girl. It's her husband; and she thinks it's a case of consumption: the usual wrong diagnosis: these damned general practitioners ought never to be allowed to touch a patient except under the orders of a consultant. She's been describing his symptoms to me; and the case is as plain as a pikestaff: bad blood-poisoning. Now she's poor. She cant afford to have him operated on. Well, you send him to me: I'll do it for nothing. Theres room for him in my nursing home. I'll put him straight, and feed him up and make her happy. I like making people happy. [*He goes to the chair near the window.*]

EMMY [*looking in*].   Here he is.

[SIR RALPH BLOOMFIELD BONINGTON *wafts himself into the room. He is a tall man, with a head like a tall and slender egg. He has been in his time a slender man; but now, in his sixth decade, his waistcoat has filled out somewhat. His fair eyebrows arch goodnaturedly and uncritically. He has a most musical voice; his speech is a perpetual anthem; and he never tires of the sound of it. He radiates an enormous self-satisfaction, cheering, reassuring, healing by the mere incompatibility of disease or anxiety with his welcome presence. Even broken bones, it is said, have been known to unite at the sound of his voice; he is a born healer, as independent of mere treatment and skill as any Christian scientist. When he expands into oratory or scientific exposition, he is as energetic as Walpole; but it is with a bland, voluminous, atmospheric energy, which envelops its subject and its audience, and makes interruption or inattention impossible, and imposes veneration and credulity on all but the strongest minds. He is known in the medical world as B. B.; and the envy roused by his success in practice is softened by the conviction that he is, scientifically considered, a colossal humbug: the fact being that, though he knows just as much (and just as little) as his contemporaries, the qualifications that pass muster in common men reveal their weakness when hung on his egregious personality.*]

B. B.   Aha! Sir Colenso, Sir Colenso, eh? Welcome to the order of knighthood.

RIDGEON [*shaking hands*]   Thank you, B. B.

B. B.   What! Sir Patrick! And how are we today? a little chilly? a little stiff? but hale and still the cleverest of us all. [SIR PATRICK *grunts*.] What! Walpole! the absent-minded beggar: eh?

WALPOLE.   What does that mean?

B. B.   Have you forgotten the lovely opera singer I sent you to have that growth taken off her vocal cords?

WALPOLE [*springing to his feet*].   Great heavens, man, you dont mean to say you sent her for a throat operation!

B. B. [*archly*].   Aha! Ha ha! Aha! [*trilling like a lark as he shakes his finger at Walpole*]. You removed her nuciform sac. Well, well! force of habit! force of habit! Never mind, ne-e-e-ver mind. She got back her voice after it, and thinks you the greatest surgeon alive; and so you are, so you are, so you are.

WALPOLE [*in a tragic whisper, intensely serious*].   Blood-poisoning. I see. I see. [*He sits down again.*]

SIR PATRICK.   And how is a certain distinguished family getting on under your care, Sir Ralph?

B. B.   Our friend Ridgeon will be gratified to hear that I have tried his opsonin treatment on little Prince Henry with complete success.

RIDGEON [*startled and anxious*].   But how—

B. B. [*continuing*].   I suspected typhoid: the head gardener's boy had it; so I just called at St Anne's one day and got a tube of your very excellent serum. You were out, unfortunately.

RIDGEON.   I hope they explained to you carefully—

B. B. [*waving away the absurd suggestion*].   Lord bless you, my dear fellow, I didnt need any explanations. I'd left my wife in the carriage at the door; and I'd no time to be taught my business by your young chaps. I know all about it. Ive handled these anti-toxins ever since they first came out.

RIDGEON.   But theyre not anti-toxins; and theyre dangerous unless you use them at the right time.

B. B.   Of course they are. Everything is dangerous unless you take it at the right time. An apple at breakfast does you good: an apple at bedtime upsets you for a week. There are only two rules for anti-toxins. First, dont be afraid of them: second, inject them a quarter of an hour before meals, three times a day.

RIDGEON [*appalled*].   Great heavens, B. B., no, no, no.

B. B. [*sweeping on irresistibly*].   Yes, yes, yes, Colly. The proof of the pudding is in the eating, you know. It was an immense success. It acted like magic on the little prince. Up went his temperature; off to bed I packed him; and in a week he was all right again, and absolutely immune from typhoid for the rest of his life. The family were very nice about it: their gratitude was quite touching; but I said they owed it all to you, Ridgeon; and I am glad to think that your knighthood is the result.

RIDGEON.   I am deeply obliged to you. [*Overcome, he sits down on the chair near the couch.*]

B. B.   Not at all, not at all. Your own merit. Come! come! come! dont give way.

RIDGEON.   It's nothing. I was a little giddy just now. Overwork, I suppose.

WALPOLE.   Blood-poisoning.

B. B.   Overwork! Theres no such thing. I do the work of ten men. Am I giddy? No. NO. If youre not well, you have a disease. It may be a slight one; but it's a disease. And what is a disease? The lodgment in the system of a pathogenic germ, and the multiplication of that germ. What is the remedy? A very simple one. Find the germ and kill it.

SIR PATRICK.   Suppose theres no germ?

B. B.   Impossible, Sir Patrick: there must be a germ: else how could the patient be ill?

SIR PATRICK.   Can you shew me the germ of overwork?

B. B.   No; but why? Why? Because, my dear Sir Patrick, though the germ is there, it's invisible. Nature has given it no danger signal for us. These germs— these bacilli—are translucent bodies, like glass, like water. To make them visible you must stain them. Well, my dear Paddy, do what you will, some of them wont stain. They wont take cochineal: they wont take any methylene blue: they wont take gentian violet: they wont take any coloring matter. Consequently, though we know, as scientific men, that they exist, we cannot see them. But can you disprove their existence? Can you conceive the disease existing without them? Can you, for instance, shew me a case of diphtheria without the bacillus?

SIR PATRICK.   No; but I'll shew you the same bacillus, without the disease, in your own throat.

B. B.   No, not the same, Sir Patrick. It is an entirely different bacillus; only the two are, unfortunately, so exactly alike that you cannot see the difference. You must understand, my dear Sir Patrick, that every one of these interesting little creatures has an imitator. Just as men imitate each other, germs imitate each other. There is the genuine diphtheria bacillus discovered by Loeffler; and there is the pseudo-bacillus, exactly like it, which you could find, as you say, in my own throat.

SIR PATRICK.   And how do you tell one from the other?

B. B.   Well, obviously, if the bacillus is the genuine Loeffler, you have diphtheria; and if it's the pseudo-bacillus, youre quite well. Nothing simpler. Science is always simple and always profound. It is only the half-truths that are dangerous. Ignorant faddists pick up some superficial information about germs; and they write to the papers and try to discredit science. They dupe and mislead many honest and worthy people. But science has a perfect answer to them on every point.

> A little learning is a dangerous thing:
> Drink deep; or taste not the Pierian spring.

I mean no disrespect to your generation, Sir Patrick: some of you old stagers did marvels through sheer professional intuition and clinical experience; but when I think of the average men of your day, ignorantly bleeding and cupping and purging, and scattering germs over their patients from their clothes and instruments, and contrast all that with the scientific certainty and simplicity of my treatment of the little prince the other day, I cant help being proud of my own generation: the men who were trained on the germ theory, the veterans of the great struggle over Evolution in the seventies. We may have our faults; but at least we are men of science. That is why I am taking up your treatment, Ridgeon, and pushing it. It's scientific. [*He sits down on the chair near the couch.*]

EMMY [*at the door, announcing*].   Dr Blenkinsop.

[*DR BLENKINSOP is in very different case from the others. He is clearly not a prosperous man. He is flabby and shabby, cheaply fed and cheaply clothed. He has the lines made by a conscience between his eyes, and the lines made by continual money worries all over his face, cut all the deeper as he has seen better days, and hails his well-to-do colleagues as their contemporary and old hospital friend, though even in this he has to struggle with the diffidence of poverty and relegation to the poorer middle class.*]

RIDGEON.   How are you, Blenkinsop?

BLENKINSOP.   Ive come to offer my humble congratulations. Oh dear! all the great guns are before me.

B. B. [*patronizing, but charming*].   How d'ye do, Blenkinsop? How d'ye do?

BLENKINSOP   And Sir Patrick, too! [SIR PATRICK *grunts.*]

RIDGEON.   Youve met Walpole, of course?

WALPOLE.   How d'ye do?

BLENKINSOP.   It's the first time Ive had that honor. In my poor little practice there are no chances of meeting you great men. I know nobody but the St Anne's men of my own day. [*To* RIDGEON.] And so youre Sir Colenso. How does it feel?

RIDGEON.   Foolish at first. Dont take any notice of it.

BLENKINSOP.   I'm ashamed to say I havnt a notion what your great discovery is; but I congratulate you all the same for the sake of old times.

B. B. [*shocked*].   But, my dear Blenkinsop, you used to be rather keen on science.

BLENKINSOP.   Ah, I used to be a lot of things. I used to have two or three decent suits of clothes, and flannels to go up the river on Sundays. Look at me now: this is my best; and it must last til Christmas. What can I do? Ive never opened a book since I was qualified thirty years ago. I used to read the medical papers at first; but you know how soon a man drops that; besides, I cant afford them; and what are they after all but trade papers, full of advertisements? Ive forgotten all my science: whats the use of my pretending I havnt? But I have great experience: clinical experience; and bedside experience is the main thing, isnt it?

B. B.   No doubt; always provided, mind you, that you have a sound scientific theory to correlate your observations at the bedside. Mere experience by itself is nothing. If I take my dog to the bedside with me, he sees what I see. But he learns nothing from it. Why? Because he's not a scientific dog.

WALPOLE.   It amuses me to hear you physicians and general practitioners talking about clinical experience. What do you see at the bedside but the outside of the patient? Well: it isnt his outside thats wrong, except perhaps in skin cases. What you want is a daily familiarity with people's insides; and that you can only get at the operating table. I know what I'm talking about: Ive been a surgeon and a consultant for twenty years; and Ive never known a general practitioner right in his diagnosis yet. Bring them a perfectly simple case; and they diagnose cancer, and arthritis, and appendicitis, and every other itis, when any really experienced surgeon can see that it's a plain case of blood-poisoning.

BLENKINSOP.   Ah, it's easy for you gentlemen to talk; but what would you say if you had my practice? Except for the workmen's clubs, my patients are all clerks and shopmen. They darent be ill: they cant afford it. And when they break down, what can I do for them? You can send your people to St. Moritz or to Egypt, or recommend horse exercise or motoring or champagne jelly or complete change and rest for six months. *I* might as well order my people a slice of the moon. And the worst of it is, I'm too poor to keep well myself on the cooking I have to put up with. Ive such a wretched digestion; and I look it. How am I to inspire confidence? [*He sits down disconsolately on the couch.*]

RIDGEON [*restlessly*].   Dont, Blenkinsop: it's too painful. The most tragic thing in the world is a sick doctor.

WALPOLE.   Yes, by George: it's like a bald-headed man trying to sell a hair restorer. Thank God I'm a surgeon!

B. B. [*sunnily*].   I am never sick. Never had a day's illness in my life. Thats what enables me to sympathize with my patients.

WALPOLE [*interested*].   What! youre never ill!

B. B.   Never.

WALPOLE.   Thats interesting. I believe you have no nuciform sac. If you ever do feel at all queer, I should very much like to have a look.

B. B.   Thank you, my dear fellow; but I'm too busy just now.

RIDGEON.   I was just telling them when you came in, Blenkinsop, that I have worked myself out of sorts.

BLENKINSOP.   Well, it seems presumptuous of me to offer a prescription to a great man like you; but still I have great experience; and if I might recommend a pound of ripe greengages every day half an hour before lunch, I'm sure youd find a benefit. Theyre very cheap.

RIDGEON.   What do you say to that, B. B.?

B. B. [*encouragingly*]. Very sensible, Blenkinsop: very sensible indeed. I'm delighted to see that you disapprove of drugs.

SIR PATRICK [*grunts*]!

B. B. [*archly*]. Aha! Haha! Did I hear from the fireside armchair the bow-wow of the old school defending its drugs? Ah, believe me, Paddy, the world would be healthier if every chemist's shop in England were demolished. Look at the papers! full of scandalous advertisements of patent medicines! a huge commercial system of quackery and poison. Well, whose fault is it? Ours. I say, ours. We set the example. We spread the superstition. We taught the people to believe in bottles of doctor's stuff; and now they buy it at the stores instead of consulting a medical man.

WALPOLE. Quite true. Ive not prescribed a drug for the last fifteen years.

B. B. Drugs can only repress symptoms: they cannot eradicate disease. The true remedy for all diseases is Nature's remedy. Nature and Science are at one, Sir Patrick, believe me; though you were taught differently. Nature has provided, in the white corpuscles as you call them—in the phagocytes as we call them—a natural means of devouring and destroying all disease germs. There is at bottom only one genuinely scientific treatment for all diseases, and that is to stimulate the phagocytes. Stimulate the phagocytes. Drugs are a delusion. Find the germ of the disease; prepare from it a suitable anti-toxin; inject it three times a day quarter of an hour before meals; and what is the result? The phagocytes are stimulated; they devour the disease; and the patient recovers—unless, of course, he's too far gone. That, I take it, is the essence of Ridgeon's discovery.

SIR PATRICK [*dreamily*]. As I sit here, I seem to hear my poor old father talking again.

B. B. [*rising in incredulous amazement*]. Your father! But Lord bless my soul, Paddy, your father must have been an older man than you.

SIR PATRICK. Word for word almost, he said what you say. No more drugs. Nothing but inoculation.

B. B. [*almost contemptuously*]. Inoculation! Do you mean smallpox inoculation?

SIR PATRICK. Yes. In the privacy of our family circle, sir, my father used to declare his belief that smallpox inoculation was good, not only for smallpox, but for all fevers.

B. B. [*suddenly rising to the new idea with immense interest and excitement*]. What! Ridgeon: did you hear that? Sir Patrick: I am more struck by what you have just told me than I can well express. Your father, sir, anticipated a discovery of my own. Listen, Walpole. Blenkinsop: attend one moment. You will all be intensely interested in this. I was put on the track by accident. I had a typhoid case and a tetanus case side by side in the hospital: a beadle and a city missionary. Think of what that meant for them, poor fellows! Can a beadle be dignified with typhoid? Can a missionary be eloquent with lockjaw? No. NO. Well, I got some typhoid anti-toxin from Ridgeon and a tube of Muldooley's anti-tetanus serum. But the missionary jerked all my things off the table in one of his paroxysms; and in replacing them I put Ridgeon's tube where Muldooley's ought to have been. The consequence was that I inoculated the typhoid case for tetanus and the tetanus case for typhoid. [*The doctors look greatly concerned. B. B., undamped, smiles triumphantly.*] Well, they recovered. THEY RECOVERED. Except for a touch of St. Vitus's dance the missionary's as well today as ever; and the beadle's ten times the man he was.

BLENKINSOP. Ive known things like that happen. They cant be explained.

B. B. [*severely*]. Blenkinsop: there is nothing that cannot be explained by science. What did I do? Did I fold my hands helplessly and say that the case could not be explained? By no means. I sat down and used my brains. I thought the case out on scientific principles. I asked myself why didnt the missionary die of typhoid on top of tetanus, and the beadle of tetanus on top of typhoid? Theres a problem for you, Ridgeon. Think, Sir Patrick. Reflect, Blenkinsop. Look at it without prejudice, Walpole. What is the real work of the anti-toxin? Simply to stimulate the phagocytes. Very well. But so long as you stimulate the phagocytes, what does it matter which particular sort of serum you use for the purpose? Haha! Eh? Do you see? Do you grasp it? Ever since that Ive used all sorts of anti-toxins absolutely indiscriminately, with perfectly satisfactory results. I inoculated the little prince with your stuff, Ridgeon, because I wanted to give you a lift; but two years ago I tried the experiment of treating a scarlet fever case with a sample of hydrophobia serum from the Pasteur Institute, and it answered capitally. It stimulated the phagocytes; and the phagocytes did the rest. That is why Sir Patrick's father found that inoculation cured all fevers. It stimulated the phagocytes. [*He throws himself into his chair, exhausted with the triumph of his demonstration, and beams magnificently on them.*]

EMMY [*looking in*]. Mr Walpole: your motor's come for you; and it's frightening Sir Patrick's horses; so come along quick.

WALPOLE [*rising*]. Goodbye, Ridgeon.

RIDGEON. Goodbye; and many thanks.

B. B. You see my point, Walpole?

EMMY. He cant wait, Sir Ralph. The carriage will be into the area if he dont come.

WALPOLE. I'm coming. [*To B. B.*] Theres nothing in your point. Phagocytosis is pure rot: the cases are all blood-poisoning; and the knife is the real remedy. Bye-bye, Sir Paddy. Happy to have met you, Mr Blenkinsop. Now, Emmy. [*He goes out, followed by* EMMY.]

B. B. [*sadly*]. Walpole has no intellect. A mere surgeon. Wonderful operator; but, after all, what is operating? Only manual labor. Brain—BRAIN remains master of the situation. The nuciform sac is utter nonsense: theres no such organ. It's a mere accidental kink in the membrane occurring in perhaps two-and-a-half per cent of the population. Of course I'm glad for Walpole's sake that the operation is fashionable; for he's a dear good fellow; and after all, as I always tell people, the operation will do them no harm: indeed, Ive known the nervous shake-up and the fortnight in bed do people a lot of good after a hard London season; but still it's a shocking fraud. [*Rising.*] Well, I must be toddling. Goodbye, Paddy [SIR PATRICK *grunts.*] goodbye, goodbye. Goodbye, my dear Blenkinsop, goodbye! Goodbye, Ridgeon. Dont fret about your health: you know what to do: if your liver is sluggish, a little mercury never does any harm. If you feel restless, try bromide. If that doesnt answer, a stimulant, you know: a little phosphorus and strychnine. If you cant sleep, trional trional, trion—

SIR PATRICK [*dryly*]. But no drugs, Colly, remember that.

B. B. [*firmly*]. Certainly not. Quite right, Sir Patrick. As temporary expedients, of course; but as treatment, no, NO. Keep away from the chemist's shop, my dear Ridgeon, whatever you do.

RIDGEON [*going to the door with him*].   I will. And thank you for the knighthood. Goodbye.

B. B. [*stopping at the door, with the beam in his eye twinkling a little*]. By the way, who's your patient?

RIDGEON.   Who?

B. B.   Downstairs. Charming woman. Tuberculous husband.

RIDGEON.   Is she there still?

EMMY [*looking in*].   Come on, Sir Ralph: your wife's waiting in the carriage.

B. B. [*suddenly sobered*].   Oh! Goodbye. [*He goes out almost precipitately.*]

RIDGEON.   Emmy: is that woman there still? If so, tell her once for all that I cant and wont see her. Do you hear?

EMMY.   Oh, she aint in a hurry: she doesnt mind how long she waits. [*She goes out.*]

BLENKINSOP.   I must be off, too: every half-hour I spend away from my work costs me eighteenpence. Goodbye, Sir Patrick.

SIR PATRICK.   Goodbye. Goodbye.

RIDGEON.   Come to lunch with me some day this week.

BLENKINSOP.   I cant afford it, dear boy; and it would put me off my own food for a week. Thank you all the same.

RIDGEON [*uneasy at* BLENKINSOP'S *poverty*]. Can I do nothing for you?

BLENKINSOP.   Well, if you have an old frock-coat to spare? you see what would be an old one for you would be a new one for me; so remember me the next time you turn out your wardrobe. Goodbye. [*He hurries out.*]

RIDGEON [*looking after him*].   Poor chap. [*Turning to* SIR PATRICK.] So thats why they made me a knight! And thats the medical profession!

SIR PATRICK.   And a very good profession, too, my lad. When you know as much as I know of the ignorance and superstition of the patients, youll wonder that we're half as good as we are.

RIDGEON.   We're not a profession: we're a conspiracy.

SIR PATRICK.   All professions are conspiracies against the laity. And we cant all be geniuses like you. Every fool can get ill; but every fool cant be a good doctor: there are not enough good ones to go round. And for all you know, Bloomfield Bonington kills less people than you do.

RIDGEON.   Oh, very likely. But he really ought to know the difference between a vaccine and an anti-toxin. Stimulate the phagocytes! The vaccine doesnt affect the phagocytes at all. He's all wrong: hopelessly, dangerously wrong. To put a tube of serum into his hands is murder: simple murder.

EMMY [*returning*].   Now, Sir Patrick. How long more are you going to keep them horses standing in the draught?

SIR PATRICK.   Whats that to you, you old catamaran?

EMMY.   Come, come, now! none of your temper to me. And it's time for Colly to get to his work.

RIDGEON.   Behave yourself, Emmy. Get out.

EMMY.   Oh, I learnt how to behave myself before I learnt you to do it. I know what doctors are: sitting talking together about themselves when they ought to be with their poor patients. And I know what horses are, Sir Patrick. I was brought up in the country. Now be good; and come along.

SIR PATRICK [*rising*]. Very well, very well, very well. Goodbye, Colly. [*He pats* RIDGEON *on the shoulder and goes out, turning for a moment at the door to look meditatively at* EMMY *and say, with grave conviction:*] You are an ugly old devil, and no mistake.

EMMY [*highly indignant, calling after him*]. Youre no beauty yourself. [*To* RIDGEON, *much flustered.*] Theyve no manners: they think they can say what they like to me; and you set them on, you do. I'll teach them their places. Here now: are you going to see that poor thing or are you not?

RIDGEON. I tell you for the fiftieth time I wont see anybody. Send her away.

EMMY. Oh, I'm tired of being told to send her away. What good will that do her?

RIDGEON. Must I get angry with you, Emmy?

EMMY [*coaxing*]. Come now: just see her for a minute to please me: theres a good boy. She's given me half-a-crown. She thinks it's life and death to her husband for her to see you.

RIDGEON. Values her husband's life at half-a-crown!

EMMY. Well, it's all she can afford, poor lamb. Them others think nothing of half-a-sovereign just to talk about themselves to you, the sluts! Besides, she'll put you in a good temper for the day, because it's a good deed to see her; and she's the sort that gets around you.

RIDGEON. Well, she hasnt done so badly. For half-a-crown she's had a consultation with Sir Ralph Bloomfield Bonington and Cutler Walpole. Thats six guineas' worth to start with. I daresay she's consulted Blenkinsop too: thats another eighteenpence.

EMMY. Then youll see her for me, wont you?

RIDGEON. Oh, send her up and be hanged. [EMMY *trots out, satisfied.* RIDGEON *calls:*] Redpenny!

REDPENNY [*appearing at the door*]. What is it?

RIDGEON. Theres a patient coming up. If she hasnt gone in five minutes, come in with an urgent call from the hospital for me. You understand; she's to have a strong hint to go.

REDPENNY. Right O! [*He vanishes.*]

[RIDGEON *goes to the glass, and arranges his tie a little.*]

EMMY [*announcing*]. Mrs Doobidad [RIDGEON *leaves the glass and goes to the writing-table.*]

[*The Lady comes in.* EMMY *goes out and shuts the door.* RIDGEON, *who has put on an impenetrable and rather distant professional manner, turns to the lady, and invites her, by a gesture, to sit down on the couch.*

MRS DUBEDAT *is beyond all demur an arrestingly good-looking young woman. She has something of the grace and romance of a wild creature, with a good deal of the elegance and dignity of a fine lady.* RIDGEON, *who is extremely susceptible to the beauty of women, instinctively assumes the defensive at once, and hardens his manner still more. He has an impression that she is very well dressed; but she has a figure on which any dress would look well, and carries herself with the unaffected distinction of a woman who has never in her life suffered from those doubts and fears as to her social position which spoil the manners of most middling people. She is tall, slender, and strong; has dark hair, dressed so as to look like hair and not like a bird's nest or a pantaloon's wig (fashion wavering just then between these two models); has unexpected narrow, subtle, dark-fringed eyes that alter her expression disturbingly when she is excited and flashes them wide open; is softly impetuous in her speech and swift in her movements; and is just now in mortal anxiety. She carries a portfolio.]*

MRS DUBEDAT [*in low urgent tones*]. Doctor—

RIDGEON [*curtly*]. Wait. Before you begin, let me tell you at once that I can do nothing for you. My hands are full. I sent you that message by my old servant. You would not take that answer.

MRS DUBEDAT. How could I?

RIDGEON. You bribed her.

MRS DUBEDAT. I—

RIDGEON. That doesnt matter. She coaxed me to see you. Well, you must take it from me now that with all the good will in the world, I cannot undertake another case.

MRS DUBEDAT. Doctor: you must save my husband. You must. When I explain to you, you will see that you must. It is not an ordinary case, not like any other case. He is not like anybody else in the world: oh, believe me, he is not. I can prove it to you: [*Fingering her portfolio.*] I have brought some things to shew you. And you can save him: the papers say you can.

RIDGEON. Whats the matter? Tuberculosis?

MRS DUBEDAT. Yes. His left lung—

RIDGEON. Yes: you neednt tell me about that.

MRS DUBEDAT. You can cure him, if only you will. It is true that you can, isnt it? [*In great distress.*] Oh, tell me, please.

RIDGEON [*warningly*]. You are going to be quiet and self-possessed, arnt you?

MRS DUBEDAT. Yes. I beg your pardon. I know I shouldnt—[*Giving way again.*] Oh, please, say that you can; and then I shall be all right.

RIDGEON [*huffily*]. I am not a curemonger: if you want cures, you must go to the people who sell them. [*Recovering himself, ashamed of the tone of his own voice.*] But I have at the hospital ten tuberculosis patients whose lives I believe I can save.

MRS DUBEDAT. Thank God!

RIDGEON. Wait a moment. Try to think of those ten patients as ten shipwrecked men on a raft—a raft that is barely large enough to save them—that will not support one more. Another head bobs up through the waves at the side. Another man begs to be taken aboard. He implores the captain of the raft to save him. But the captain can only do that by pushing one of his ten off the raft and drowning him to make room for the new comer. That is what you are asking me to do.

MRS DUBEDAT. But how can that be? I dont understand. Surely—

RIDGEON. You must take my word for it that it is so. My laboratory, my staff, and myself are working at full pressure. We are doing our utmost. The treatment is a new one. It takes time, means, and skill; and there is not enough for another case. Our ten cases are already chosen cases. Do you understand what I mean by chosen?

MRS DUBEDAT. Chosen. No: I cant understand.

RIDGEON [*sternly*]. You must understand. Youve got to understand and to face it. In every single one of those ten cases I have had to consider, not only whether the man could be saved, but whether he was worth saving. There were fifty cases to choose from; and forty had to be condemned to death. Some of the forty had young wives and helpless children. If the hardness of their cases could have saved them they would have been saved ten times over. Ive no doubt your case is a hard one: I can see the tears in your eyes [*She hastily wipes her eyes.*]: I know that you have a torrent of entreaties ready for me the moment I stop speaking; but it's no use. You must go to another doctor.

MRS DUBEDAT. But can you give me the name of another doctor who understands your secret?

RIDGEON. I have no secret: I am not a quack.

MRS DUBEDAT. I beg your pardon: I didnt mean to say anything wrong. I dont understand how to speak to you. Oh pray dont be offended.

RIDGEON [*again a little ashamed*]. There! there! never mind. [*He relaxes and sits down.*] After all, I'm talking nonsense: I daresay I am a quack, a quack with a qualification. But my discovery is not patented.

MRS DUBEDAT. Then can any doctor cure my husband? Oh, why dont they do it? I have tried so many: I have spent so much. If only you would give me the name of another doctor.

RIDGEON. Every man in this street is a doctor. But outside myself and the handful of men I am training at St Anne's, there is nobody as yet who has mastered the opsonin treatment. And we are full up. I'm sorry; but that is all I can say. [*Rising.*] Good morning.

MRS DUBEDAT [*suddenly and desperately taking some drawings from her portfolio*]. Doctor: look at these. You understand drawings: you have good ones in your waiting room. Look at them. They are his work.

RIDGEON. It's no use my looking. [*He looks, all the same.*] Hallo! [*He takes one to the window and studies it.*] Yes: this is the real thing. Yes, yes. [*He looks at another and returns to her.*] These are very clever. Theyre unfinished, arnt they?

MRS DUBEDAT. He gets tired so soon. But you see, dont you, what a genius he is? You see that he is worth saving. Oh, doctor, I married him just to help him to begin: I had money enough to tide him over the hard years at the beginning—to enable him to follow his inspiration until his genius was recognized. And I was useful to him as a model: his drawings of me sold quite quickly.

RIDGEON. Have you got one?

MRS DUBEDAT [*producing another*]. Only this one. It was the first.

RIDGEON [*devouring it with his eyes*]. Thats a wonderful drawing. Why is it called Jennifer?

MRS DUBEDAT. My name is Jennifer.

RIDGEON. A strange name.

MRS DUBEDAT. Not in Cornwall. I am Cornish. It's only what you call Guinevere.

RIDGEON [*repeating the names with a certain pleasure in them*]. Guinevere. Jennifer. [*Looking again at the drawing.*] Yes: it's really a wonderful drawing. Excuse me; but may I ask is it for sale? I'll buy it.

MRS DUBEDAT. Oh, take it. It's my own: he gave it to me. Take it. Take them all. Take everything; ask anything; but save him. You can: you will: you must.

REDPENNY [*entering with every sign of alarm*].   Theyve just telephoned from the hospital that youre to come instantly—a patient on the point of death. The carriage is waiting.

RIDGEON [*intolerantly*].   Oh, nonsense: get out. [*Greatly annoyed.*] What do you mean by interrupting me like this?

REDPENNY.   But—

RIDGEON.   Chut! cant you see I'm engaged? Be off.

[REDPENNY, *bewildered, vanishes.*]

MRS DUBEDAT [*rising*].   Doctor: one instant only before you go—

RIDGEON.   Sit down. It's nothing.

MRS DUBEDAT.   But the patient. He said he was dying.

RIDGEON.   Oh, he's dead by this time. Never mind. Sit down.

MRS DUBEDAT [*sitting down and breaking down*].   Oh, you none of you care. You see people die every day.

RIDGEON [*petting her*].   Nonsense! it's nothing: I told him to come in and say that. I thought I should want to get rid of you.

MRS DUBEDAT [*shocked at the falsehood*].   Oh!

RIDGEON [*continuing*].   Dont look so bewildered: theres nobody dying.

MRS DUBEDAT.   My husband is.

RIDGEON [*pulling himself together*].   Ah, yes: I had forgotten your husband. Mrs Dubedat: you are asking me to do a very serious thing?

MRS DUBEDAT.   I am asking you to save the life of a great man.

RIDGEON.   You are asking me to kill another man for his sake; for as surely as I undertake another case, I shall have to hand back one of the old ones to the ordinary treatment. Well, I dont shrink from that. I have had to do it before; and I will do it again if you can convince me that his life is more important than the worst life I am now saving. But you must convince me first.

MRS DUBEDAT.   He made those drawings; and they are not the best—nothing like the best; only I did not bring the really best: so few people like them. He is twenty-three: his whole life is before him. Wont you let me bring him to you? wont you speak to him? wont you see for yourself?

RIDGEON.   Is he well enough to come to a dinner at the Star and Garter at Richmond?

MRS DUBEDAT.   Oh yes. Why?

RIDGEON.   I'll tell you. I am inviting all my old friends to a dinner to celebrate my knighthood—youve seen about it in the papers, havnt you?

MRS DUBEDAT.   Yes, oh yes. That was how I found out about you.

RIDGEON.   It will be a doctors' dinner; and it was to have been a bachelors' dinner. I'm a bachelor. Now if you will entertain for me, and bring your husband, he will meet me; and he will meet some of the most eminent men in my profession: Sir Patrick Cullen, Sir Ralph Bloomfield Bonington, Cutler Walpole, and others. I can put the case to them; and your husband will have to stand or fall by what we think of him. Will you come?

MRS DUBEDAT.   Yes, of course I will come. Oh, thank you, thank you. And may I bring some of his drawings—the really good ones?

RIDGEON.   Yes. I will let you know the date in the course of tomorrow. Leave me your address.

MRS DUBEDAT.   Thank you again and again. You have made me so happy:

I know you will admire me and like him. This is my address. [*She gives him her card.*]

RIDGEON.   Thank you. [*He rings.*]

MRS DUBEDAT [*embarrassed*].   May I—is there—should I—I mean—[*She blushes and stops in confusion.*]

RIDGEON.   Whats the matter?

MRS DUBEDAT.   Your fee for this consultation?

RIDGEON.   Oh, I forgot that. Shall we say a beautiful drawing of his favorite model for the whole treatment, including the cure?

MRS DUBEDAT.   You are very generous. Thank you. I know you will cure him. Goodbye.

RIDGEON.   I will. Goodbye. [*They shake hands.*] By the way, you know, dont you, that tuberculosis is catching. You take every precaution, I hope.

MRS DUBEDAT.   I am not likely to forget it. They treat us like lepers at the hotels.

EMMY [*at the door*].   Well, deary: have you got round him?

RIDGEON.   Yes. Attend to the door and hold your tongue.

EMMY.   Thats a good boy. [*She goes out with MRS DUBEDAT.*]

RIDGEON [*alone*].   Consultation free. Cure guaranteed. [*He heaves a great sigh.*]

ACT II

After dinner on the terrace at the Star and Garter, Richmond. Cloudless summer night; nothing disturbs the stillness except from time to time the long trajectory of a distant train and the measured clucking of oars coming up from the Thames in the valley below. The dinner is over; and three of the eight chairs are empty. SIR PATRICK, *with his back to the view, is at the head of the square table with* RIDGEON. *The two chairs opposite them are empty. On their right come, first, a vacant chair, and then one very fully occupied by* B. B., *who basks blissfully in the moonbeams. On their left,* SCHUTZMACHER *and* WALPOLE. *The entrance to the hotel is on their right, behind* B. B. *The five men are silently enjoying their coffee and cigarettes, full of food, and not altogether void of wine.* . . . MRS DUBEDAT, *wrapped for departure, comes in. They rise, except* SIR PATRICK; *but she takes one of the vacant places at the foot of the table, next* B. B.; *and they sit down again.*

MRS DUBEDAT [*as she enters*].   Louis will be here presently. He is shewing Dr Blenkinsop how to work the telephone. [*She sits.*] Oh, I am so sorry we have to go. It seems such a shame, this beautiful night. And we have enjoyed ourselves so much.

RIDGEON.   I dont believe another half-hour would do Mr Dubedat a bit of harm.

SIR PATRICK.   Come now, Colly, come! come! none of that. You take your man home, Mrs Dubedat; and get him to bed before eleven.

B. B.   Yes, yes. Bed before eleven. Quite right, quite right. Sorry to lose you, my dear lady; but Sir Patrick's orders are the laws of—er—of Tyre and Sidon.

WALPOLE. Let me take you home in my motor.

SIR PATRICK. No. You ought to be ashamed of yourself, Walpole. Your motor will take Mr and Mrs Dubedat to the station, and quite far enough too for an open carriage at night.

MRS DUBEDAT. Oh, I am sure the train is best.

RIDGEON. Well, Mrs Dubedat, we have had a most enjoyable evening.

WALPOLE. } Most enjoyable.

B. B. } Delightful. Charming. Unforgettable.

MRS DUBEDAT [*with a touch of shy anxiety*]. What did you think of Louis? Or am I wrong to ask?

RIDGEON. Wrong! Why, we are all charmed with him.

WALPOLE. Delighted.

B. B. Most happy to have met him. A privilege, a real privilege.

SIR PATRICK [*grunts*]!

MRS DUBEDAT [*quickly*]. Sir Patrick: are you uneasy about him?

SIR PATRICK [*discreetly*]. I admire his drawings greatly, maam.

MRS DUBEDAT. Yes; but I meant—

RIDGEON. You shall go away quite happy. He's worth saving. He must and shall be saved.

[MRS DUBEDAT *rises and gasps with delight, relief, and gratitude. They all rise except* SIR PATRICK *and* SCHUTZMACHER, *and come reassuringly to her.*]

B. B. Certainly, cer-tainly.

WALPOLE. Theres no real difficulty, if only you know what to do.

MRS DUBEDAT. Oh, how can I ever thank you! From this night I can begin to be happy at last. You dont know what I feel.

[*She sits down in tears. They crowd about her to console her.*]

B. B. My dear lady: come come! come come! [*very persuasively*] come come!

WALPOLE. Dont mind us. Have a good cry.

RIDGEON. No: dont cry. Your husband had better not know that weve been talking about him.

MRS DUBEDAT [*quickly pulling herself together*]. No, of course not. Please dont mind me. What a glorious thing it must be to be a doctor! [*They laugh.*] Dont laugh. You dont know what youve done for me. I never knew until now how deadly afraid I was—how I had come to dread the worst. I never dared let myself know. But now the relief has come: now I know.

[LOUIS DUBEDAT *comes from the hotel, in his overcoat, his throat wrapped in a shawl. He is a slim young man of 23, physically still a stripling, and pretty, though not effeminate. He has turquoise blue eyes, and a trick of looking you straight in the face with them, which, combined with a frank smile, is very engaging. Although he is all nerves, and very observant and quick of apprehension, he is not in the least shy. He is younger than* JENNIFER; *but he patronizes her as a matter of course. The doctors do not put him out in the least: neither* SIR PATRICK's *years nor* BLOOMFIELD BONINGTON's *majesty have the smallest apparent effect on him: he is as natural as a cat: he moves among men as most men move among things, though he is intentionally making himself agreeable to them on this occasion. Like all people who can be depended on to take care of themselves, he is welcome company; and his artist's power of appealing to the imagination gains him credit for all sorts of qualities and powers, whether he possesses them or not.*]

LOUIS [*pulling on his gloves behind* RIDGEON'S *chair*]. Now, Jinny-Gwinny: the motor has come round.

RIDGEON. Why do you let him spoil your beautiful name like that, Mrs Dubedat?

MRS DUBEDAT. Oh, on grand occasions I am Jennifer.

B. B. You are a bachelor: you do not understand these things, Ridgeon. Look at me. [*They look.*] I also have two names. In moments of domestic worry, I am simple Ralph. When the sun shines in the home, I am Beedle-Deedle-Dumkins. Such is married life! Mr Dubedat: may I ask you to do me a favor before you go. Will you sign your name to this menu card, under the sketch you have made of me?

WALPOLE. Yes; and mine too, if you will be so good.

LOUIS. Certainly. [*He sits down and signs the cards.*]

MRS DUBEDAT. Wont you sign Dr Schutzmacher's for him, Louis?

LOUIS. I dont think Dr Schutzmacher is pleased with his portrait. I'll tear it up. [*He reaches across the table for* SCHUTZMACHER'S *menu card, and is about to tear it.* SCHUTZMACHER *makes no sign.*]

RIDGEON. No, no: if Loony doesnt want it, I do.

LOUIS. I'll sign it for you with pleasure. [*He signs and hands it to* RIDGEON.] Ive just been making a little note of the river tonight: it will work up into something good. [*He shews a pocket sketch-book.*] I think I'll call it the Silver Danube.

B. B. Ah, charming, charming.

WALPOLE. Very sweet. Youre a nailer at pastel.

[LOUIS *coughs, first out of modesty, then from tuberculosis.*]

SIR PATRICK. Now then, Mr Dubedat: youve had enough of the night air. Take him home, maam.

MRS DUBEDAT. Yes. Come, Louis.

RIDGEON. Never fear. Never mind. I'll make that cough all right.

B. B. We will stimulate the phagocytes. [*With tender effusion, shaking her hand.*] Goodnight, Mrs Dubedat. Goodnight. Goodnight.

WALPOLE. If the phagocytes fail, come to me. I'll put you right.

LOUIS. Goodnight, Sir Patrick. Happy to have met you.

SIR PATRICK. 'Night [*half a grunt*].

MRS DUBEDAT. Goodnight, Sir Patrick.

SIR PATRICK. Cover yourself well up. Dont think your lungs are made of iron because theyre better than his. Goodnight.

MRS DUBEDAT. Thank you. Thank you. Nothing hurts me. Goodnight.

[LOUIS *goes out through the hotel without noticing* SCHUTZMACHER. MRS DUBEDAT *hesitates, then bows to him.* SCHUTZMACHER *rises and bows formally, German fashion. She goes out, attended by* RIDGEON. *The rest resume their seats, ruminating or smoking quietly.*]

B. B. [*harmoniously*]. Dee-lightful couple! Charming woman! Gifted lad! Remarkable talent! Graceful outlines! Perfect evening! Great success! Interesting case! Glorious night! Exquisite scenery! Capital dinner! Stimulating conversation! Restful outing! Good wine! Happy ending! Touching gratitude! Lucky Ridgeon—

RIDGEON [*returning*]. Whats that? Calling me, B. B.? [*He goes back to his seat next* SIR PATRICK.]

B. B.   No, no. Only congratulating you on a most successful evening! Enchanting woman! Thorough breeding! Gentle nature! Refined—

[BLENKINSOP *comes from the hotel and takes the empty chair next* RIDGEON.]

BLENKINSOP.   I'm so sorry to have left you like this, Ridgeon; but it was a telephone message from the police. Theyve found half a milkman at our level crossing with a prescription of mine in its pocket. Wheres Mr Dubedat?

RIDGEON.   Gone.

BLENKINSOP [*rising, very pale*].   Gone!

RIDGEON.   Just this moment—

BLENKINSOP.   Perhaps I could overtake him—[*he rushes into the hotel*].

WALPOLE [*calling after him*].   He's in the motor, man, miles off. You cant—[*giving it up*]. No use.

RIDGEON.   Theyre really very nice people. I confess I was afraid the husband would turn out an appalling bounder. But he's almost as charming in his way as she is in hers. And theres no mistake about his being a genius. It's something to have got a case really worth saving. Somebody else will have to go; but at all events it will be easy to find a worse man.

SIR PATRICK.   How do you know?

RIDGEON.   Come now, Sir Paddy, no growling. Have something more to drink.

SIR PATRICK.   No, thank you.

WALPOLE.   Do you see anything wrong with Dubedat, B. B.?

B. B.   Oh, a charming young fellow. Besides, after all, what could be wrong with him? Look at him. What could be wrong with him?

SIR PATRICK.   There are two things that can be wrong with any man. One of them is a cheque. The other is a woman. Until you know that a man's sound on these two points, you know nothing about him.

B. B.   Ah, cynic, cynic!

WALPOLE.   He's all right as to the cheque, for a while at all events. He talked to me quite frankly before dinner as to the pressure of money difficulties on an artist. He says he has no vices and is very economical, but that theres one extravagance he cant afford and yet cant resist; and that is dressing his wife prettily. So I said, bang plump out, "Let me lend you twenty pounds, and pay me when your ship comes home." He was really very nice about it. He took it like a man; and it was a pleasure to see how happy it made him, poor chap.

B. B. [*who has listened to* WALPOLE *with growing perturbation*].   But—but—but—when was this, may I ask?

WALPOLE.   When I joined you that time down by the river.

B. B.   But, my dear Walpole, he had just borrowed ten pounds from me.

WALPOLE.   What!

SIR PATRICK [*grunts*]!

B. B. [*indulgently*].   Well, well, it was really hardly borrowing; for he said heaven only knew when he could pay me. I couldnt refuse. It appears that Mrs Dubedat has taken a sort of fancy to me—

WALPOLE [*quickly*].   No: it was to me.

B. B.   Certainly not. Your name was never mentioned between us. He is so wrapped up in his work that he has to leave her a good deal alone; and the poor innocent young fellow—he has of course no idea of my position or how busy I am—actually wanted me to call occasionally and talk to her.

WALPOLE.   Exactly what he said to me!

B. B.   Pooh! Pooh pooh! Really, I must say. [*Much disturbed, he rises and goes up to the balustrade, contemplating the landscape vexedly.*]

WALPOLE.   Look here. Ridgeon! this is beginning to look serious.

[BLENKINSOP, *very anxious and wretched, but trying to look unconcerned, comes back.*]

RIDGEON.   Well, did you catch him?

BLENKINSOP.   No. Excuse my running away like that. [*He sits down at the foot of the table, next* BLOOMFIELD BONINGTON's *chair.*]

WALPOLE.   Anything the matter?

BLENKINSOP.   Oh no. A trifle—something ridiculous. It cant be helped. Never mind.

RIDGEON.   Was it anything about Dubedat?

BLENKINSOP [*almost breaking down*].   I ought to keep it to myself, I know I cant tell you, Ridgeon, how ashamed I am of dragging my miserable poverty to your dinner after all your kindness. It's not that you wont ask me again; but it's so humiliating. And I did so look forward to one evening in my dress clothes (theyre still presentable, you see) with all my troubles left behind, just like old times.

RIDGEON.   But what has happened?

BLENKINSOP.   Oh, nothing. It's too ridiculous. I had just scraped up four shillings for this little outing; and it cost me one-and-fourpence to get here. Well, Dubedat asked me to lend him half-a-crown to tip the chambermaid of the room his wife left her wraps in, and for the cloakroom. He said he only wanted it for five minutes, as she had his purse. So of course I lent it to him. And he's forgotten to pay me. Ive just twopence to get back with.

RIDGEON.   Oh, never mind that—

BLENKINSOP [*stopping him resolutely*].   No: I know what youre going to say; but I wont take it. Ive never borrowed a penny; and I never will. Ive nothing left but my friends; and I wont sell them. If none of you were to be able to meet me without being afraid that my civility was leading up to the loan of five shillings, there would be an end of everything for me. I'll take your old clothes, Colly, sooner than disgrace you by talking to you in the street in my own; but I wont borrow money. I'll train it as far as the twopence will take me; and I'll tramp the rest.

WALPOLE.   Youll do the whole distance in my motor. [*They are all greatly relieved; and Walpole hastens to get away from the painful subject by adding*] Did he get anything out of you, Mr Schutzmacher?

SCHUTZMACHER [*shakes his head in a most expressive negative*].

WALPOLE.   You didnt appreciate his drawing, I think.

SCHUTZMACHER.   Oh yes I did. I should have liked very much to have kept the sketch and got it autographed.

B. B.   But why didnt you?

SCHUTZMACHER.   Well, the fact is, when I joined Dubedat after his conversation with Mr Walpole, he said that the Jews were the only people who knew anything about art, and that though he had to put up with your Philistine twaddle, as he called it, it was what I said about the drawings that really pleased him. He also said that his wife was greatly struck with my knowledge, and that she always admired Jews. Then he asked me to advance him £50 on the security of the drawings.

B. B.		No, no. Positively! Seriously!
WALPOLE	*[all exclaiming together]*	What! Another fifty!
BLENKINSOP		Think of that!
SIR PATRICK		*[grunts]*!

SCHUTZMACHER. Of course I couldnt lend money to a stranger like that.

B. B. I envy you the power to say No, Mr Schutzmacher. Of course, I knew I oughtnt to lend money to a young fellow in that way; but I simply hadnt the nerve to refuse. I couldnt very well, you know, could I?

SCHUTZMACHER. I dont understand that. *I* felt that I couldnt very well lend it.

WALPOLE. What did he say?

SCHUTZMACHER. Well, he made a very uncalled-for remark about a Jew not understanding the feelings of a gentleman. I must say you Gentiles are very hard to please. You say we are no gentlemen when we lend money; and when we refuse to lend it you say just the same. I didnt mean to behave badly. As I told him, I might have lent it to him if he had been a Jew himself.

SIR PATRICK [*with a grunt*]. And what did he say to that?

SCHUTZMACHER. Oh, he began trying to persuade me that he was one of the chosen people—that his artistic faculty shewed it, and that his name was as foreign as my own. He said he didnt really want £50; that he was only joking; that all he wanted was a couple of sovereigns.

B. B. No, no, Mr Schutzmacher. You invented that last touch. Seriously, now?

SCHUTZMACHER. No. You cant improve on Nature in telling stories about gentlemen like Mr Dubedat.

BLENKINSOP. You certainly do stand by one another, you chosen people, Mr Schutzmacher.

SCHUTZMACHER. Not at all. Personally, I like Englishmen better than Jews, and always associate with them. Thats only natural, because, as I am a Jew, theres nothing interesting in a Jew to me, whereas there is always something interesting and foreign in an Englishman. But in money matters it's quite different. You see, when an Englishman borrows, all he knows or cares is that he wants money; and he'll sign anything to get it, without in the least understanding it, or intending to carry out the agreement if it turns out badly for him. In fact, he thinks you a cad if you ask him to carry it out under such circumstances. Just like the Merchant of Venice, you know. But if a Jew makes an agreement, he means to keep it and expects you to keep it. If he wants money for a time, he borrows it and knows he must pay it at the end of the time. If he knows he cant pay, he begs it as a gift.

RIDGEON. Come, Loony! do you mean to say that Jews are never rogues and thieves?

SCHUTZMACHER. Oh, not at all. But I was not talking of criminals. I was comparing honest Englishmen with honest Jews.

[*One of the hotel maids, a pretty, fair-haired woman of about 25, comes from the hotel, rather furtively. She accosts* RIDGEON.]

THE MAID. I beg your pardon, sir—

RIDGEON. Eh?

THE MAID. I beg your pardon, sir. It's not about the hotel. I'm not allowed to be on the terrace; and I should be discharged if I were seen speaking to you, unless you were kind enough to say you called me to ask whether the motor has come back from the station yet.

WALPOLE. Has it?

THE MAID. Yes, sir.

RIDGEON. Well, what do you want?

THE MAID. Would you mind, sir, giving me the address of the gentleman that was with you at dinner?

RIDGEON [sharply]. Yes, of course I should mind very much. You have no right to ask.

THE MAID. Yes, sir, I know it looks like that. But what am I to do?

SIR PATRICK. Whats the matter with you?

THE MAID. Nothing, sir. I want the address: thats all.

B. B. You mean the young gentleman?

THE MAID. Yes, sir: that went to catch the train with the woman he brought with him.

RIDGEON. The woman! Do you mean the lady who dined here? the gentleman's wife?

THE MAID. Dont believe them, sir. She cant be his wife. I'm his wife.

B. B. ⎤ ⎡ [in amazed remonstrance]. My good girl!

RIDGEON ⎥ ⎥ You his wife!

WALPOLE ⎦ ⎣ What! whats that? Oh, this is getting perfectly fascinating, Ridgeon.

THE MAID. I could run upstairs and get you my marriage lines in a minute, sir, if you doubt my word. He's Mr Louis Dubedat, isnt he?

RIDGEON. Yes.

THE MAID. Well, sir, you may believe me or not; but I'm the lawful Mrs Dubedat.

SIR PATRICK. And why arnt you living with your husband?

THE MAID. We couldnt afford it, sir. I had thirty pounds saved; and we spent it all on our honeymoon in three weeks, and a lot more that he borrowed. Then I had to go back into service, and he went to London to get work at his drawing; and he never wrote me a line or sent me an address. I never saw nor heard of him again until I caught sight of him from the window going off in the motor with that woman.

SIR PATRICK. Well, thats two wives to start with.

B. B. Now upon my soul I dont want to be uncharitable; but really I'm beginning to suspect that our young friend is rather careless.

SIR PATRICK. Beginning to think! How long will it take you, man, to find out that he's a damned young blackguard?

BLENKINSOP. Oh, thats severe, Sir Patrick, very severe. Of course it's bigamy; but still he's very young; and she's very pretty. Mr Walpole: may I spunge on you for another of those nice cigarets of yours? [He changes his seat for the one next Walpole.]

WALPOLE. Certainly. [He feels in his pockets.] Oh bother! Where—? [Suddenly remembering.] I say: I recollect now: I passed my cigaret case to Dubedat and he didnt return it. It was a gold one.

THE MAID. He didnt mean any harm: he never thinks about things like that, sir. I'll get it back for you, sir, if youll tell me where to find him.

RIDGEON. What am I to do? Shall I give her the address or not?

SIR PATRICK. Give her your own address; and then we'll see. [*To the maid.*] Youll have to be content with that for the present, my girl. [RIDGEON *gives her his card.*] Whats your name?

THE MAID. Minnie Tinwell, sir.

SIR PATRICK. Well, you write him a letter to care of this gentleman; and it will be sent on. Now be off with you.

THE MAID. Thank you, sir. I'm sure you wouldnt see me wronged. Thank you all, gentlemen; and excuse the liberty.

[*She goes into the hotel. They watch her in silence.*]

RIDGEON [*when she is gone*]. Do you realize, you chaps, that we have promised Mrs Dubedat to save this fellow's life?

BLENKINSOP. Whats the matter with him?

RIDGEON. Tuberculosis.

BLENKINSOP [*interested*]. And can you cure that?

RIDGEON. I believe so.

BLENKINSOP. Then I wish youd cure me. My right lung is touched, I'm sorry to say.

RIDGEON		What! your lung is going!
B. B.		My dear Blenkinsop, what do you tell me? [*Full of concern for Blenkinsop, he comes back from the balustrade.*]
	[*all together*]	
SIR PATRICK		Eh? Eh? whats that?
WALPOLE		Hullo! you mustnt neglect this, you know.

BLENKINSOP [*putting his fingers in his ears*]. No, no: it's no use. I know what youre going to say: Ive said it often to others. I cant afford to take care of myself; and theres an end of it. If a fortnight's holiday would save my life, I'd have to die. I shall get on as others have to get on. We cant all go to St Moritz or to Egypt, you know, Sir Ralph. Dont talk about it.

[*Embarrassed silence.*]

SIR PATRICK [*grunts and looks hard at Ridgeon*]!

SCHUTZMACHER [*looking at his watch and rising*]. I must go. It's been a very pleasant evening, Colly. You might let me have my portrait if you dont mind. I'll send Mr Dubedat that couple of sovereigns for it.

RIDGEON [*giving him the menu card*]. Oh dont do that, Loony. I dont think he'd like that.

SCHUTZMACHER. Well, of course I shant if you feel that way about it. But I dont think you understand Dubedat. However, perhaps thats because I'm a Jew. Goodnight, Dr Blenkinsop [*shaking hands*].

BLENKINSOP. Goodnight, sir—I mean—Goodnight.

SCHUTZMACHER [*waving his hand to the rest*]. Goodnight, everybody.

WALPOLE	
B. B.	
SIR PATRICK	Goodnight.
RIDGEON	

B. B. *repeats the salutation several times, in varied musical tones.* SCHUTZMACHER *goes out.*

SIR PATRICK.   It's time for us all to move. [*He rises and comes between* BLENKINSOP *and* WALPOLE. RIDGEON *also rises.*] Mr Walpole: take Blenkinsop home; he's had enough of the open air cure for tonight. Have you a thick overcoat to wear in the motor, Dr Blenkinsop?

BLENKINSOP.   Oh, theyll give me some brown paper in the hotel; and a few thicknesses of brown paper across the chest are better than any fur coat.

WALPOLE.   Well, come along. Goodnight, Colly. Youre coming with us, arnt you, B. B.?

B. B.   Yes: I'm coming. [WALPOLE *and* BLENKINSOP *go into the hotel.*] Goodnight, my dear Ridgeon [*shaking hands affectionately*]. Dont let us lose sight of your interesting patient and his very charming wife. We must not judge him too hastily, you know. [*With unction.*] Goooooooodnight, Paddy. Bless you, dear old chap. [SIR PATRICK *utters a formidable grunt.* B. B. *laughs and pats him indulgently on the shoulder.*] Goodnight. Goodnight. Goodnight. Goodnight. [*He goodnights himself into the hotel.*]

[*The others have meanwhile gone without ceremony.* RIDGEON *and* SIR PATRICK *are left alone together.* RIDGEON, *deep in thought, comes down to* SIR PATRICK.]

SIR PATRICK.   Well, Mr Savior of Lives: which is it to be? that honest decent man Blenkinsop, or that rotten blackguard of an artist, eh?

RIDGEON.   It's not an easy case to judge, is it? Blenkinsop's an honest decent man; but is he any use? Dubedat's a rotten blackguard; but he's a genuine source of pretty and pleasant and good things.

SIR PATRICK.   What will he be a source of for that poor innocent wife of his, when she finds him out?

RIDGEON.   Thats true. Her life will be a hell.

SIR PATRICK.   And tell me this. Suppose you had this choice put before you: either to go through life and find all the pictures bad but all the men and women good, or to go through life and find all the pictures good and all the men and women rotten. Which would you choose?

RIDGEON.   Thats a devilishly difficult question, Paddy. The pictures are so agreeable, and the good people so infernally disagreeable and mischievous, that I really cant undertake to say offhand which I should prefer to do without.

SIR PATRICK.   Come come! none of your cleverness with me: I'm too old for it. Blenkinsop isnt that sort of good man; and you know it.

RIDGEON.   It would be simpler if Blenkinsop could paint Dubedat's pictures.

SIR PATRICK.   It would be simpler still if Dubedat had some of Blenkinsop's honesty. The world isnt going to be made simple for you, my lad: you must take it as it is. Youve to hold the scales between Blenkinsop and Dubedat. Hold them fairly.

RIDGEON.   Well, I'll be as fair as I can. I'll put into one scale all the pounds Dubedat has borrowed, and into the other all the half-crowns that Blenkinsop hasnt borrowed.

SIR PATRICK.   And youll take out of Dubedat's scale all the faith he has destroyed and the honor he has lost, and youll put into Blenkinsop's scale all the faith he has justified and the honor he has created.

RIDGEON.   Come come, Paddy! none of your claptrap with me: I'm too sceptical for it. I'm not at all convinced that the world wouldnt be a better world if everybody behaved as Dubedat does than it is now that everybody behaves as Blenkinsop does.

SIR PATRICK.   Then why dont you behave as Dubedat does?

RIDGEON.   Ah, that beats me. Thats the experimental test. Still, it's a dilemma. It's a dilemma. You see, theres a complication we havnt mentioned.

SIR PATRICK.   Whats that?

RIDGEON.   Well, if I let Blenkinsop die, at least nobody can say I did it because I wanted to marry his widow.

SIR PATRICK.   Eh! Whats that?

RIDGEON.   Now if I let Dubedat die, I'll marry his widow.

SIR PATRICK.   Perhaps she wont have you, you know.

RIDGEON [with a self-assured shake of the head].   I've a pretty good flair for that sort of thing. I know when a woman is interested in me. She is.

SIR PATRICK.   Well, sometimes a man knows best; and sometimes he knows worst. Youd much better cure them both.

RIDGEON.   I cant. I'm at my limit. I can squeeze in one more case, but not two. I must choose.

SIR PATRICK.   Well, you must choose as if she didn't exist: thats clear.

RIDGEON.   Is that clear to you? Mind: it's not clear to me. She troubles my judgment.

SIR PATRICK.   To me, it's a plain choice between a man and a lot of pictures.

RIDGEON.   It's easier to replace a dead man than a good picture.

SIR PATRICK.   Colly: when you live in an age that runs to pictures and statues and plays and brass bands because its men and women are not good enough to comfort its poor aching soul, you should thank Providence that you belong to a profession which is a high and great profession because its business is to heal and mend men and women.

RIDGEON.   In short, as a member of a high and great profession, I'm to kill my patient.

SIR PATRICK.   Dont talk wicked nonsense. You cant kill him. But you can leave him in other hands.

RIDGEON.   In B. B.'s, for instance: eh? [Looking at him significantly.]

SIR PATRICK [demurely facing his look].   Sir Ralph Bloomfield Bonington is a very eminent physician.

RIDGEON.   He is.

SIR PATRICK.   I'm going for my hat.

[RIDGEON strikes the bell as SIR PATRICK makes for the hotel. A waiter comes.]

RIDGEON [to the waiter].   My bill, please.

WAITER.   Yes, sir.

[He goes for it.]

ACT III

In DUBEDAT's studio. Viewed from the large window the outer door is in the wall on the left at the near end. The door leading to the inner rooms is in the opposite wall, at the far end. The facing wall has neither window nor door. The plaster on all the walls is uncovered and undecorated, except by scrawlings of charcoal sketches and memoranda. There is a studio throne (a chair on a dais) a little to the left, opposite the inner door, and an easel to the right, opposite the *outer door, with a dilapidated chair at it. Near the easel and against the wall is a bare wooden table with bottles and jars of oil and medium, paint-smudged rags, tubes of color, brushes, charcoal, a small lay figure, a kettle and spirit-lamp, and other odds and ends. By the table is a sofa, littered with drawing blocks, sketchbooks, loose sheets of paper, newspapers, books, and more smudged rags. Next the outer door is an umbrella and hat stand, occupied partly by* LOUIS' *hats and cloak and muffler, and partly by odds and ends of costumes. There is an old piano stool on the near side of this door. In the corner near the inner door is a little tea-table. A lay figure, in a cardinal's robe and hat, with an hour-glass in one hand and a scythe slung on its back, smiles with inane malice at* LOUIS, *who, in a milk-man's smock much smudged with colors, is painting a piece of brocade which he has draped about his wife. She is sitting on the throne, not interested in the painting, and appealing to him very anxiously about another matter.*

MRS DUBEDAT.   Promise.

LOUIS [*putting on a touch of paint with notable skill and care and answering quite perfunctorily*].   I promise, my darling.

MRS DUBEDAT.   When you want money, you will always come to me.

LOUIS.   But it's so sordid, dearest. I hate money. I cant keep always bothering you for money, money, money. Thats what drives me sometimes to ask other people, though I hate doing it.

MRS DUBEDAT.   It is far better to ask me, dear. It gives people a wrong idea of you.

LOUIS.   But I want to spare your little fortune, and raise money on my own work. Dont be unhappy, love: I can easily earn enough to pay it all back. I shall have a one-man-show next season; and then there will be no more money troubles. [*Putting down his palette.*] There! I mustnt do any more on that until it's bone-dry; so you may come down.

MRS DUBEDAT [*throwing off the drapery as she steps down, and revealing a plain frock of tussore[3] silk*].   But you have promised, remember, seriously and faithfully, never to borrow again until you have first asked me.

LOUIS.   Seriously and faithfully. [*Embracing her.*] Ah, my love, how right you are! how much it means to me to have you by me to guard me against living too much in the skies. On my solemn oath, from this moment forth I will never borrow another penny.

MRS DUBEDAT [*delighted*].   Ah, thats right. Does his wicked worrying wife torment him and drag him down from the clouds. [*She kisses him.*] And now, dear, wont you finish those drawings for Maclean?

LOUIS.   Oh, they dont matter. Ive got nearly all the money from him in advance.

MRS DUBEDAT.   But, dearest, that is just the reason why you should finish them. He asked me the other day whether you really intended to finish them.

LOUIS.   Confound his impudence! What the devil does he take me for? Now that just destroys all my interest in the beastly job. Ive a good mind to throw up the commission, and pay him back his money.

MRS DUBEDAT.   We cant afford that, dear. You had better finish the draw-

---

[3] An oriental silkworm that produces a brownish silk.

ings and have done with them. I think it is a mistake to accept money in advance.

LOUIS.   But how are we to live?

MRS DUBEDAT.   Well, Louis, it is getting hard enough as it is, now that they are all refusing to pay except on delivery.

LOUIS.   Damn those fellows! they think of nothing and care for nothing but their wretched money.

MRS DUBEDAT.   Still, if they pay us, they ought to have what they pay for.

LOUIS [coaxing].   There now: thats enough lecturing for today. Ive promised to be good, havnt I?

MRS DUBEDAT [putting her arms round his neck].   You know that I hate lecturing, and that I dont for a moment misunderstand you, dear, dont you?

LOUIS [fondly].   I know. I know. Im a wretch; and youre an angel. Oh, if only I were strong enough to work steadily, I'd make my darling's house a temple, and her shrine a chapel more beautiful than was ever imagined. I cant pass the shops without wrestling with the temptation to go in and order all the really good things they have for you.

MRS DUBEDAT.   I want nothing but you, dear. [She gives him a caress, to which he responds so passionately that she disengages herself.] There! be good now: remember that the doctors are coming this morning. Isnt it extraordinarily kind of them, Louis, to insist on coming? all of them, to consult about you?

LOUIS [coolly].   Oh, I daresay they think it will be a feather in their cap to cure a rising artist. They wouldnt come if it didnt amuse them, anyhow. [Someone knocks at the door.] I say: it's not time yet, is it?

MRS DUBEDAT.   No, not quite yet.

LOUIS [opening the door and finding RIDGEON there].   Hello, Ridgeon. Delighted to see you. Come in.

MRS DUBEDAT [shaking hands].   It's so good of you to come, doctor.

LOUIS.   Excuse this place, wont you? It's only a studio, you know: theres no real convenience for living here. But we pig along somehow, thanks to Jennifer.

MRS DUBEDAT.   Now I'll run away. Perhaps later on, when youre finished with Louis, I may come in and hear the verdict. [RIDGEON bows rather constrainedly.] Would you rather I didnt?

RIDGEON.   Not at all. Not at all.

[MRS DUBEDAT looks at him, a little puzzled by his formal manners; then goes into the inner room.]

LOUIS [flippantly].   I say: dont look so grave. Theres nothing awful going to happen, is there?

RIDGEON.   No.

LOUIS.   Thats all right. Poor Jennifer has been looking forward to your visit more than you can imagine. She's taken quite a fancy to you, Ridgeon. The poor girl has nobody to talk to: I'm always painting. [Taking up a sketch.] Theres a little sketch I made of her yesterday.

RIDGEON.   She shewed it to me a fortnight ago when she first called on me.

LOUIS [quite unabashed].   Oh! did she? Good Lord! how time does fly! I could have sworn I'd only just finished it. It's hard for her here, seeing me piling up drawings and nothing coming in for them. Of course I shall sell them next year fast enough, after my one-man-show; but while the grass grows the steed starves. I hate to have her coming to me for money, and having none to give her. But what can I do?

RIDGEON.   I understood that Mrs Dubedat had some property of her own.

LOUIS.   Oh yes, a little; but how could a man with any decency of feeling touch that? Suppose I did, what would she have to live on if I died? I'm not insured: cant afford the premiums. [*Picking out another drawing.*] How do you like that?

RIDGEON [*putting it aside*].   I have not come here today to look at your drawings. I have more serious and pressing business with you.

LOUIS.   You want to sound my wretched lung. [*With impulsive candor.*] My dear Ridgeon: I'll be frank with you. Whats the matter in this house isnt lungs but bills. It doesnt matter about me; but Jennifer has actually to economize in the matter of food. Youve made us feel that we can treat you as a friend. Will you lend us a hundred and fifty pounds?

RIDGEON.   No.

LOUIS [*surprised*].   Why not?

RIDGEON.   I am not a rich man; and I want every penny I can spare and more for my researches.

LOUIS.   You mean youd want the money back again.

RIDGEON.   I presume people sometimes have that in view when they lend money.

LOUIS [*after a moment's reflection*].   Well, I can manage that for you. I'll give you a cheque—or see here: theres no reason why you shouldnt have your bit too: I'll give you a cheque for two hundred.

RIDGEON.   Why not cash the cheque at once without troubling me?

LOUIS.   Bless you! they wouldnt cash it: I'm overdrawn as it is. No: the way to work it is this. I'll postdate the cheque next October. In October Jennifer's dividends come in. Well, you present the cheque. It will be returned marked "refer to drawer" or some rubbish of that sort. Then you can take it to Jennifer, and hint that if the cheque isnt taken up at once I shall be put in prison. She'll pay you like a shot. Youll clear £50; and youll do me a real service; for I do want the money very badly, old chap, I assure you.

RIDGEON [*staring at him*].   You see no objection to the transaction; and you anticipate none from me!

LOUIS.   Well, what objection can there be? It's quite safe. I can convince you about the dividends.

RIDGEON.   I mean on the score of its being—shall I say dishonorable?

LOUIS.   Well, of course I shouldnt suggest it if I didnt want the money.

RIDGEON.   Indeed! Well, you will have to find some other means of getting it.

LOUIS.   Do you mean that you refuse?

RIDGEON.   Do I mean—! [*Letting his indignation loose.*] Of course I refuse, man. What do you take me for? How dare you make such a proposal to me?

LOUIS.   Why not?

RIDGEON.   Faugh! You would not understand me if I tried to explain. Now, once for all, I will not lend you a farthing. I should be glad to help your wife; but lending you money is no service to her.

LOUIS.   Oh well, if youre in earnest about helping her, I'll tell you what you might do. You might get your patients to buy some of my things, or to give me a few portrait commissions.

RIDGEON. My patients call me in as a physician, not as a commercial traveller.

[*A knock at the door.* LOUIS *goes unconcernedly to open it, pursuing the subject as he goes.*]

LOUIS. But you must have great influence with them. You must know such lots of things about them—private things that they wouldnt like to have known. They wouldnt dare to refuse you.

RIDGEON [*exploding*]. Well, upon my—

[LOUIS *opens the door, and admits* SIR PATRICK, SIR RALPH, *and* WALPOLE.]

RIDGEON [*proceeding furiously*]. Walpole: Ive been here hardly ten minutes; and already he's tried to borrow £150 from me. Then he proposed that I should get the money for him by blackmailing his wife; and youve just interrupted him in the act of suggesting that I should blackmail my patients into sitting to him for their portraits.

LOUIS. Well, Ridgeon, if that is what you call being an honorable man! I spoke to you in confidence.

SIR PATRICK. We're all going to speak to you in confidence, young man.

WALPOLE [*hanging his hat on the only peg left vacant on the hat-stand*]. We shall make ourselves at home for half an hour, Dubedat. Dont be alarmed; youre a most fascinating chap; and we love you.

LOUIS. Oh, all right, all right. Sit down—anywhere you can. Take this chair, Sir Patrick [*indicating the one on the throne*]. Up-z-z-z! [*helping him up:* SIR PATRICK *grunts and enthrones himself*]. Here you are, B. B. [SIR RALPH *glares at the familiarity; but* LOUIS, *quite undisturbed puts a big book and a sofa cushion on the dais, on* SIR PATRICK's *right; and* B. B. *sits down, under protest.*] Let me take your hat. [*He takes* B. B.'s *hat unceremoniously and substitutes it for the cardinal's hat on the head of the lay figure, thereby ingeniously destroying the dignity of the conclave. He then draws the piano stool from the wall and offers it to* WALPOLE.] You dont mind this, Walpole, do you? [WALPOLE *accepts the stool, and puts his hand into his pocket for his cigaret case. Missing it, he is reminded of his loss.*]

WALPOLE. By the way, I'll trouble you for my cigaret case, if you dont mind?

LOUIS. What cigaret case?

WALPOLE. The gold one I lent you at the Star and Garter.

LOUIS [*surprised*]. Was that yours?

WALPOLE. Yes.

LOUIS. I'm awfully sorry, old chap. I wondered whose it was. I'm sorry to say this is all thats left of it. [*He hitches up his smock; produces a card from his waistcoat pocket; and hands it to* WALPOLE.]

WALPOLE. A pawn ticket!

LOUIS [*reassuringly*]. It's quite safe: he cant sell it for a year, you know. I say, my dear Walpole, I am sorry. [*He places his hand ingenuously on* WALPOLE's *shoulder and looks frankly at him.*]

WALPOLE [*sinking on the stool with a gasp*]. Dont mention it. It adds to your fascination.

RIDGEON [*who has been standing near the easel*]. Before we go any further, you have a debt to pay, Mr Dubedat.

LOUIS. I have a precious lot of debts to pay, Ridgeon. I'll fetch you a chair. [*He makes for the inner door.*]

RIDGEON [*stopping him*]. You shall not leave the room until you pay it. It's a small one; and pay it you must and shall. I dont so much mind your borrowing £10 from one of my guests and £20 from the other—

WALPOLE. I walked into it, you know. I offered it.

RIDGEON. —they could afford it. But to clean poor Blenkinsop out of his last half-crown was damnable. I intended to give him that half-crown and to be in a position to pledge him my word that you paid it. I'll have that out of you, at all events.

B. B. Quite right, Ridgeon. Quite right. Come, young man! down with the dust. Pay up.

LOUIS. Oh, you neednt make such a fuss about it. Of course I'll pay it. I had no idea the poor fellow was hard up. I'm as shocked as any of you about it. [*Putting his hand into his pocket.*] Here you are. [*Finding his pocket empty.*] Oh, I say, I havnt any money on me just at present. Walpole: would you mind lending me half-a-crown just to settle this.

WALPOLE. Lend you half—[*his voice faints away*].

LOUIS. Well, if you dont, Blenkinsop wont get it; for I havnt a rap: you may search my pockets if you like.

WALPOLE. Thats conclusive. [*He produces half-a-crown.*]

LOUIS [*passing it to Ridgeon*]. There! I'm really glad thats settled: it was the only thing that was on my conscience. Now I hope youre all satisfied.

SIR PATRICK. Not quite, Mr Dubedat. Do you happen to know a young woman named Minnie Tinwell?

LOUIS. Minnie! I should think I do; and Minnie knows me too. She's a really nice good girl, considering her station. Whats become of her?

WALPOLE. It's no use bluffing, Dubedat. Weve seen Minnie's marriage-lines.

LOUIS [*coolly*]. Indeed? Have you seen Jennifer's?

RIDGEON [*rising in irrepressible rage*]. Do you dare insinuate that Mrs Dubedat is living with you without being married to you?

LOUIS. Why not?

B. B.		Why not!
SIR PATRICK	[*echoing him in various tones of scandalized amazement*]	Why not!
RIDGEON		Why not!
WALPOLE		Why not!

LOUIS. Yes, why not? Lots of people do it: just as good people as you. Why dont you learn to think, instead of bleating and baahing like a lot of sheep when you come up against anything youre not accustomed to? [*Contemplating their amazed faces with a chuckle.*] I say: I should like to draw the lot of you now: you do look jolly foolish. Especially you, Ridgeon. I had you that time, you know.

RIDGEON. How, pray?

LOUIS. Well, you set up to appreciate Jennifer, you know. And you despise me, dont you?

RIDGEON [*curtly*]. I loathe you. [*He sits down again on the sofa.*]

LOUIS. Just so. And yet you believe that Jennifer is a bad lot because you think I told you so.

RIDGEON. Were you lying?

LOUIS. No; but you were smelling out a scandal instead of keeping your mind clean and wholesome. I can just play with people like you. I only asked you had you seen Jennifer's marriage lines; and you concluded straight away that she hadnt got any. You dont know a lady when you see one.

B. B. [*majestically*].   What do you mean by that, may I ask?

LOUIS.   Now, I'm only an immoral artist; but if youd told me that Jennifer wasnt married, I'd have had the gentlemanly feeling and artistic instinct to say that she carried her marriage certificate in her face and in her character. But you are all moral men; and Jennifer is only an artist's wife—probably a model; and morality consists of suspecting other people of not being legally married. Arnt you ashamed of yourselves? Can one of you look me in the face after it?

WALPOLE.   It's very hard to look you in the face, Dubedat; you have such a dazzling cheek. What about Minnie Tinwell, eh?

LOUIS.   Minnie Tinwell is a young woman who has had three weeks of glorious happiness in her poor little life, which is more than most girls in her position get, I can tell you. Ask her whether she'd take it back if she could. She's got her name into history, that girl. My little sketches of her will be fought for by collectors at Christie's. She'll have a page in my biography. Pretty good, that, for a still-room[4] maid at a seaside hotel, I think. What have you fellows done for her to compare with that?

RIDGEON.   We havnt trapped her into a mock marriage and deserted her.

LOUIS.   No: you wouldnt have the pluck. But dont fuss yourselves. *I* didnt desert little Minnie. We spent all our money—

WALPOLE.   All her money. Thirty pounds.

LOUIS.   I said all our money: hers and mine too. Her thirty pounds didnt last three days. I had to borrow four times as much to spend on her. But I didnt grudge it; and she didnt grudge her few pounds either, the brave little lassie. When we were cleaned out, we'd had enough of it: you can hardly suppose that we were fit company for longer than that; I an artist, and she quite out of art and literature and refined living and everything else. There was no desertion, no misunderstanding, no police court or divorce court sensation for you moral chaps to lick your lips over at breakfast. We just said, Well, the money's gone: we've had a good time that can never be taken from us; so kiss; part good friends; and she back to service, and I back to my studio and my Jennifer, both the better and happier for our holiday.

WALPOLE.   Quite a little poem, by George!

B. B.   If you had been scientifically trained, Mr Dubedat, you would know how very seldom an actual case bears out a principle. In medical practice a man may die when, scientifically speaking, he ought to have lived. I have actually known a man die of a disease from which he was, scientifically speaking, immune. But that does not affect the fundamental truth of science. In just the same way, in moral cases, a man's behavior may be quite harmless and even beneficial, when he is morally behaving like a scoundrel. And he may do great harm when he is morally acting on the highest principles. But that does not affect the fundamental truth of morality.

SIR PATRICK.   And it doesnt affect the criminal law on the subject of bigamy.

LOUIS.   Oh bigamy! bigamy! bigamy! What a fascination anything connected with the police has for you all, you moralists! Ive proved to you that you

---

[4] In Great Britain, a room connected with the kitchen where liquors, preserves, and cakes are kept and tea, coffee, and other beverages are prepared.

were utterly wrong on the moral point: now I'm going to shew you that youre utterly wrong on the legal point; and I hope it will be a lesson to you not to be so jolly cocksure next time.

WALPOLE. Rot! You were married already when you married her; and that settles it.

LOUIS. Does it! Why cant you think? How do you know she wasnt married already too?

B. B.		[all		Walpole! Ridgeon!
RIDGEON		crying		This is beyond everything.
WALPOLE		out		Well, damn me!
SIR PATRICK		together]		You young rascal.

LOUIS [ignoring their outcry]. She was married to the steward of a liner. He cleared out and left her; and she thought, poor girl, that it was the law that if you hadnt heard of your husband for three years you might marry again. So as she was a thoroughly respectable girl and refused to have anything to say to me unless we were married I went through the ceremony to please her and to preserve her self-respect.

RIDGEON. Did you tell her you were already married?

LOUIS. Of course not. Dont you see that if she had known, she wouldnt have considered herself my wife? You dont seem to understand, somehow.

SIR PATRICK. You let her risk imprisonment in her ignorance of the law?

LOUIS. Well, I risked imprisonment for her sake; I could have been had up for it just as much as she. But when a man makes a sacrifice of that sort for a woman, he doesnt go and brag about it to her; at least, not if he's a gentleman.

WALPOLE. What are we to do with this daisy!

LOUIS [impatiently]. Oh, go and do whatever the devil you please. Put Minnie in prison. Put me in prison. Kill Jennifer with the disgrace of it all. And then, when youve done all the mischief you can, go to church and feel good about it. [He sits down pettishly on the old chair at the easel, and takes up a sketching block, on which he begins to draw.]

WALPOLE. He's got us.

SIR PATRICK [grimly]. He has.

B. B. But is he to be allowed to defy the criminal law of the land?

SIR PATRICK. The criminal law is no use to decent people. It only helps blackguards to blackmail their families. What are we family doctors doing half our time but conspiring with the family solicitor to keep some rascal out of jail and some family out of disgrace?

B. B. But at least it will punish him.

SIR PATRICK. Oh yes: it'll punish him. It'll punish not only him but everybody connected with him, innocent and guilty alike. It'll throw his board and lodging on our rates and taxes for a couple of years, and then turn him loose on us a more dangerous blackguard than ever. It'll put the girl in prison and ruin her: it'll lay his wife's life waste. You may put the criminal law out of your head once for all: it's only fit for fools and savages.

LOUIS. Would you mind turning your face a little more this way, Sir Patrick. [Sir Patrick turns indignantly and glares at him.] Oh, thats too much.

SIR PATRICK. Put down your foolish pencil, man; and think of your position. You can defy the laws made by men; but there are other laws to reckon with. Do you know that youre going to die?

LOUIS. We're all going to die, arnt we?

WALPOLE. We're not all going to die in six months.

LOUIS. How do you know?

[*This for* B. B. *is the last straw. He completely loses his temper and begins to walk excitedly about.*]

B. B. Upon my soul, I will not stand this. It is in questionable taste under any circumstances or in any company to harp on the subject of death; but it is a dastardly advantage to take of a medical man. [*Thundering at* DUBEDAT.] I will not allow it, do you hear?

LOUIS. Well, I didnt begin it: you chaps did. It's always the way with the inartistic professions: when theyre beaten in argument they fall back on intimidation. I never knew a lawyer yet who didnt threaten to put me in prison sooner or later. I never knew a parson who didnt threaten me with damnation. And now you threaten me with death. With all your tall talk youve only one real trump in your hand, and thats Intimidation. Well, I'm not a coward; so it's no use with me.

B. B. [*advancing upon him*]. I'll tell you what you are, sir. Youre a scoundrel.

LOUIS. Oh, I dont mind you calling me a scoundrel a bit. It's only a word: a word that you dont know the meaning of. What is a scoundrel?

B. B. You are a scoundrel, sir.

LOUIS. Just so. What is a scoundrel? I am. What am I? A scoundrel. It's just arguing in a circle. And you imagine youre a man of science!

B. B. I—I—I—I have a good mind to take you by the scruff of your neck, you infamous rascal, and give you a sound thrashing.

LOUIS. I wish you would. Youd pay me something handsome to keep it out of court afterwards. [B. B., *baffled, flings away from him with a snort.*] Have you any more civilities to address to me in my own house? I should like to get them over before my wife comes back. [*He resumes his sketching.*]

RIDGEON. My mind's made up. When the law breaks down, honest men must find a remedy for themselves. I will not lift a finger to save this reptile.

B. B. That is the word I was trying to remember. Reptile.

WALPOLE. I cant help rather liking you, Dubedat. But you certainly are a thoroughgoing specimen.

SIR PATRICK. You know our opinion of you now, at all events.

LOUIS [*patiently putting down his pencil*]. Look here. All this is no good. You dont understand. You imagine that I'm simply an ordinary criminal.

WALPOLE. Not an ordinary one, Dubedat. Do yourself justice.

LOUIS. Well, youre on the wrong track altogether. I'm not a criminal. All your moralizings have no value for me. I dont believe in morality. I'm a disciple of Bernard Shaw.

SIR PATRICK ⎱ ⎧ [*puzzled*]. Eh?
B. B.　　　 ⎰ ⎨ [*waving his hand as if the subject were now
　　　　　　　 ⎩ disposed of*]. Thats enough: I wish to hear no more.

LOUIS. Of course I havnt the ridiculous vanity to set up to be exactly a Superman; but still, it's an ideal that I strive towards just as any other man strives towards his ideal.

B. B. [*intolerant*]. Dont trouble to explain. I now understand you perfectly. Say no more, please. When a man pretends to discuss science, morals, and religion, and then avows himself a follower of a notorious and avowed anti-vaccinationist, there is nothing more to be said. [*Suddenly putting in an effusive saving clause in parentheses to Ridgeon.*] Not, my dear Ridgeon, that I believe in vaccination in the popular sense any more than you do: I neednt tell you that. But there are things that place a man socially; and anti-vaccination is one of them. [*He resumes his seat on the dais.*]

SIR PATRICK. Bernard Shaw? I never heard of him. He's a Methodist preacher, I suppose.

LOUIS [*scandalized*]. No, no. He's the most advanced man now living: he isnt anything.

SIR PATRICK. I assure you, young man, my father learnt the doctrine of deliverance from sin from John Wesley's own lips before you or Mr Shaw were born. It used to be very popular as an excuse for putting sand in sugar and water in milk. Youre a sound Methodist, my lad; only you dont know it.

LOUIS [*seriously annoyed for the first time*]. It's an intellectual insult. I dont believe theres such a thing as sin.

SIR PATRICK. Well, sir, there are people who dont believe theres such a thing as disease either. They call themselves Christian Scientists, I believe. Theyll just suit your complaint. We can do nothing for you. [*He rises.*] Good afternoon to you.

LOUIS [*running to him piteously*]. Oh dont get up, Sir Patrick. Dont go. Please dont. I didnt mean to shock you, on my word. Do sit down again. Give me another chance. Two minutes more: thats all I ask.

SIR PATRICK [*surprised by this sign of grace, and a little touched*]. Well— [*He sits down.*]—

LOUIS [*gratefully*]. Thanks awfully.

SIR PATRICK [*continuing*]. —I dont mind giving you two minutes more. But dont address yourself to me; for Ive retired from practice; and I dont pretend to be able to cure your complaint. Your life is in the hands of these gentlemen.

RIDGEON. Not in mine. My hands are full. I have no time and no means available for this case.

SIR PATRICK. What do you say, Mr Walpole?

WALPOLE. Oh, I'll take him in hand: I dont mind. I feel perfectly convinced that this is not a moral case at all: it's a physical one. Theres something abnormal about his brain. That means, probably, some morbid condition affecting the spinal cord. And that means the circulation. In short, it's clear to me that he's suffering from an obscure form of blood-poisoning, which is almost certainly due to an accumulation of ptomaines in the nuciform sac. I'll remove the sac—

LOUIS [*changing color*]. Do you mean, operate on me? Ugh! No, thank you.

WALPOLE. Never fear: you wont feel anything. Youll be under an anæsthetic, of course. And it will be extraordinarily interesting.

LOUIS. Oh, well, if it would interest you, and if it wont hurt, thats another matter. How much will you give me to let you do it?

WALPOLE [*rising indignantly*]. How much! What do you mean?

LOUIS. Well, you dont expect me to let you cut me up for nothing, do you?

WALPOLE. Will you paint my portrait for nothing?

LOUIS. No: but I'll give you the portrait when it's painted; and you can sell it afterwards for perhaps double the money. But I cant sell my nuciform sac when youve cut it out.

WALPOLE. Ridgeon: did you ever hear anything like this! [*To* LOUIS.] Well, you can keep your nuciform sac, and your tubercular lung, and your diseased brain: Ive done with you. One would think I was not conferring a favor on the fellow! [*He returns to his stool in high dudgeon.*]

SIR PATRICK. That leaves only one medical man who has not withdrawn from your case, Mr Dubedat. You have nobody left to appeal to now but Sir Ralph Bloomfield Bonington.

WALPOLE. If I were you, B. B., I shouldnt touch him with a pair of tongs. Let him take his lungs to the Brompton Hospital. They wont cure him; but theyll teach him manners.

B. B. My weakness is that I have never been able to say No, even to the most thoroughly undeserving people. Besides, I am bound to say that I dont think it is possible in medical practice to go into the question of the value of the lives we save. Just consider, Ridgeon. Let me put it to you, Paddy. Clear your mind of cant, Walpole.

WALPOLE [*indignantly*]. My mind is perfectly clear of cant.

B. B. Quite so. Well now, look at my practice. It is what I suppose you would call a fashionable practice, a smart practice, a practice among the best people. You ask me to go into the question of whether my patients are of any use either to themselves or anyone else. Well, if you apply any scientific test known to me, you will achieve a reductio ad absurdum. You will be driven to the conclusion that the majority of them would be, as my friend Mr J. M. Barrie[5] has tersely phrased it, better dead. Better dead. There are exceptions, no doubt. For instance, there is the court, an essentially social-democratic institution, supported out of public funds by the public because the public wants it and likes it. My court patients are hard-working people who give satisfaction, undoubtedly. Then I have a duke or two whose estates are probably better managed than they would be in public hands. But as to most of the rest, if I once began to argue about them, unquestionably the verdict would be, Better dead. When they actually do die, I sometimes have to offer that consolation, thinly disguised, to the family. [*Lulled by the cadences of his own voice, he becomes drowsier and drowsier.*] The fact that they spend money so extravagantly on medical attendance really would not justify me in wasting my talents—such as they are—in keeping them alive. After all, if my fees are high, I have to spend heavily. My own tastes are simple: a camp bed, a couple of rooms, a crust, a bottle of wine; and I am happy and contented. My wife's tastes are perhaps more luxurious; but even she deplores an expenditure the sole object of which is to maintain the state my patients require from their medical attendant. The—er—er—er—[*suddenly waking up*] I have lost the thread of these remarks. What was I talking about, Ridgeon?

RIDGEON. About Dubedat.

B. B. Ah yes. Precisely. Thank you. Dubedat, of course. Well, what is our friend Dubedat? A vicious and ignorant young man with a talent for drawing.

LOUIS. Thank you. Dont mind me.

B. B. But then, what are many of my patients? Vicious and ignorant young men without a talent for anything. If I were to stop to argue about their merits I should have to give up three-quarters of my practice. Therefore I have made it

---

[5] An English writer (1860–1937), principally of plays, who wrote the short story "Better Dead" in 1887.

a rule not so to argue. Now, as an honorable man, having made that rule as to paying patients, can I make an exception as to a patient who, far from being a paying patient, may more fitly be described as a borrowing patient. No. I say No. Mr Dubedat: your moral character is nothing to me. I look at you from a purely scientific point of view. To me you are simply a field of battle in which an invading army of tubercle bacilli struggles with a patriotic force of phagocytes. Having made a promise to your wife, which my principles will not allow me to break, to stimulate those phagocytes, I will stimulate them. And I take no further responsibility. [*He flings himself back in his seat exhausted.*]

SIR PATRICK. Well, Mr Dubedat, as Sir Ralph has very kindly offered to take charge of your case, and as the two minutes I promised you are up, I must ask you to excuse me. [*He rises.*]

LOUIS. Oh, certainly. Ive quite done with you. [*Rising and holding up the sketch block.*] There! While youve been talking, Ive been doing. What is there left of your moralizing? Only a little carbonic acid gas which makes the room unhealthy. What is there left of my work? That. Look at it. [RIDGEON *rises to look at it.*]

SIR PATRICK [*who has come down to him from the throne*]. You young rascal, was it drawing me you were?

LOUIS. Of course. What else?

SIR PATRICK [*takes the drawing from him and grunts approvingly*]. Thats rather good. Dont you think so, Colly?

RIDGEON. Yes. So good that I should like to have it.

SIR PATRICK. Thank you; but I should like to have it myself. What d'ye think, Walpole?

WALPOLE [*rising and coming over to look*]. No, by Jove: *I* must have this.

LOUIS. I wish I could afford to give it to you, Sir Patrick. But I'd pay five guineas sooner than part with it.

RIDGEON. Oh, for that matter, I will give you six for it.

WALPOLE. Ten.

LOUIS. I think Sir Patrick is morally entitled to it, as he sat for it. May I send it to your house, Sir Patrick, for twelve guineas?

SIR PATRICK. Twelve guineas! Not if you were President of the Royal Academy, young man. [*He gives him back the drawing decisively and turns away, taking up his hat.*]

LOUIS [*to* B. B.]. Would you like to take it at twelve, Sir Ralph?

B. B. [*coming between* LOUIS *and* WALPOLE]. Twelve guineas? Thank you: I'll take it at that. [*He takes it and presents it to* SIR PATRICK.] Accept it from me, Paddy; and may you long be spared to contemplate it.

SIR PATRICK. Thank you. [*He puts the drawing into his hat.*]

B. B. I neednt settle with you now, Mr Dubedat: my fees will come to more than that. [*He also retrieves his hat.*]

LOUIS [*indignantly*]. Well, of all the mean—[*words fail him*]! I'd let myself be shot sooner than do a thing like that. I consider youve stolen that drawing.

SIR PATRICK [*drily*]. So we've converted you to a belief in morality after all, eh?

LOUIS. Yah! [*To* WALPOLE.] I'll do another one for you, Walpole, if youll let me have the ten you promised.

WALPOLE. Very good. I'll pay on delivery.

LOUIS. Oh! What do you take me for? Have you no confidence in my honor?

WALPOLE. None whatever.

LOUIS. Oh well, of course if you feel that way, you cant help it. Before you go, Sir Patrick, let me fetch Jennifer. I know she'd like to see you, if you dont mind. [*He goes to the inner door.*] And now, before she comes in, one word. Youve all been talking here pretty freely about me—in my own house too. *I* dont mind that: I'm a man and can take care of myself. But when Jennifer comes in please remember that she's a lady, and that you are supposed to be gentlemen. [*He goes out.*]

WALPOLE. Well!!! [*He gives the situation up as indescribable, and goes for his hat.*]

RIDGEON. Damn his impudence!

B. B. I shouldnt be at all surprised to learn that he's well connected. Whenever I meet dignity and self-possession without any discoverable basis, I diagnose good family.

RIDGEON. Diagnose artistic genius, B. B. Thats what saves his self-respect.

SIR PATRICK. The world is made like that. The decent fellows are always being lectured and put out of countenance by the snobs.

B. B. [*altogether refusing to accept this*]. *I* am not out of countenance. I should like, by Jupiter, to see the man who could put me out of countenance. [JENNIFER *comes in.*] Ah, Mrs Dubedat! And how are we today?

MRS DUBEDAT [*shaking hands with him*]. Thank you all so much for coming. [*She shakes* WALPOLE'*s hand.*] Thank you, Sir Patrick. [*She shakes* SIR PATRICK'*s.*] Oh, life has been worth living since I have known you. Since Richmond I have not known a moment's fear. And it used to be nothing but fear. Wont you sit down and tell me the result of the consultation.

WALPOLE. I'll go, if you dont mind, Mrs Dubedat. I have an appointment. Before I go, let me say that I am quite agreed with my colleagues here as to the character of the case. As to the cause and the remedy, thats not my business: I'm only a surgeon; and these gentlemen are physicians and will advise you. I may have my own views: in fact I have them; and they are perfectly well known to my colleagues. If I am needed—and needed I shall be finally—they know where to find me; and I am always at your service. So for today, goodbye. [*He goes out, leaving* JENNIFER *much puzzled by his unexpected withdrawal and formal manner.*]

SIR PATRICK. I also will ask you to excuse me, Mrs Dubedat.

RIDGEON [*anxiously*]. Are you going?

SIR PATRICK. Yes: I can be of no use here; and I must be getting back. As you know, maam, I'm not in practice now; and I shall not be in charge of the case. It rests between Sir Colenso Ridgeon and Sir Ralph Bloomfield Bonington. They know my opinion. Good afternoon to you, maam. [*He bows and makes for the door.*]

MRS DUBEDAT [*detaining him*]. Theres nothing wrong, is there? You dont think Louis is worse, do you?

SIR PATRICK. No: he's not worse. Just the same as at Richmond.

MRS DUBEDAT. Oh, thank you: you frightened me. Excuse me.

SIR PATRICK. Dont mention it, maam. [*He goes out.*]

B. B. Now, Mrs Dubedat, if I am to take the patient in hand—

MRS DUBEDAT [apprehensively, with a glance at RIDGEON]. You! But I thought that Sir Colenso—

B. B. [beaming with the conviction that he is giving her a most gratifying surprise]. My dear lady, your husband shall have Me.

MRS DUBEDAT. But—

B. B. Not a word: it is a pleasure to me, for your sake. Sir Colenso Ridgeon will be in his proper place, in the bacteriological laboratory. I shall be in my proper place, at the bedside. Your husband shall be treated exactly as if he were a member of the royal family. [MRS DUBEDAT uneasy again is about to protest.] No gratitude: it would embarrass me, I assure you. Now, may I ask whether you are particularly tied to these apartments. Of course, the motor has annihilated distance; but I confess that if you were rather nearer to me, it would be a little more convenient.

MRS DUBEDAT. You see, this studio and flat are self-contained. I have suffered so much in lodgings. The servants are so frightfully dishonest.

B. B. Ah! Are they? Are they? Dear me!

MRS DUBEDAT. I was never accustomed to lock things up. And I missed so many small sums. At last a dreadful thing happened. I missed a five-pound note. It was traced to the housemaid; and she actually said Louis had given it to her. And he wouldnt let me do anything: he is so sensitive that these things drive him mad.

B. B. Ah—hm—ha—yes—say no more, Mrs Dubedat: you shall not move. If the mountain will not come to Mahomet, Mahomet must come to the mountain. Now I must be off. I will write and make an appointment. We shall begin stimulating the phagocytes on—on—probably on Tuesday next; but I will let you know. Depend on me; dont fret; eat regularly; sleep well; keep your spirits up; keep the patient cheerful; hope for the best; no tonic like a charming woman; no medicine like cheerfulness; no resource like science; goodbye, goodbye, goodbye. [Having shaken hands—she being too overwhelmed to speak—he goes out, stopping to say to RIDGEON] On Tuesday morning send me down a tube of some really stiff antitoxin. Any kind will do. Dont forget. Goodbye, Colly. [He goes out.]

RIDGEON. You look quite discouraged again. [She is almost in tears.] Whats the matter? Are you disappointed?

MRS DUBEDAT. I know I ought to be very grateful. Believe me, I am very grateful. But—but—

RIDGEON. Well?

MRS DUBEDAT. I had set my heart on your curing Louis.

RIDGEON. Well, Sir Ralph Bloomfield Bonington—

MRS DUBEDAT. Yes, I know, I know. It is a great privilege to have him. But oh, I wish it had been you. I know it's unreasonable; I cant explain; but I had such a strong instinct that you would cure him. I dont—I cant feel the same about Sir Ralph. You promised me. Why did you give Louis up?

RIDGEON. I explained to you. I cannot take another case.

MRS DUBEDAT. But at Richmond?

RIDGEON. At Richmond I thought I could make room for one more case. But my old friend Dr Blenkinsop claimed that place. His lung is attacked.

MRS DUBEDAT [attaching no importance whatever to BLENKINSOP]. Do you mean that elderly man—that rather silly--

RIDGEON [*sternly*].   I mean the gentleman that dined with us: an excellent and honest man, whose life is as valuable as anyone else's. I have arranged that I shall take his case, and that Sir Ralph Bloomfield Bonington shall take Mr Dubedat's.

MRS DUBEDAT [*turning indignantly on him*].   I see what it is. Oh! it is envious, mean, cruel. And I thought that you would be above such a thing.

RIDGEON.   What do you mean?

MRS DUBEDAT.   Oh, do you think I dont know? do you think it has never happened before? Why does everybody turn against him? Can you not forgive him for being superior to you? for being clever? for being braver? for being a great artist?

RIDGEON.   Yes: I can forgive him for all that.

MRS DUBEDAT.   Well, have you anything to say against him? I have challenged everyone who has turned against him—challenged them face to face to tell me any wrong thing he has done, any ignoble thought he has uttered. They have always confessed that they could not tell me one. I challenge you now. What do you accuse him of?

RIDGEON.   I am like all the rest. Face to face, I cannot tell you one thing against him.

MRS DUBEDAT [*not satisfied*].   But your manner is changed. And you have broken your promise to me to make room for him as your patient.

RIDGEON.   I think you are a little unreasonable. You have had the very best medical advice in London for him; and his case has been taken in hand by a leader of the profession. Surely—

MRS DUBEDAT.   Oh, it is so cruel to keep telling me that. It seems all right; and it puts me in the wrong. But I am not in the wrong. I have faith in you; and I have no faith in the others. We have seen so many doctors: I have come to know at last when they are only talking and can do nothing. It is different with you. I feel that you know. You must listen to me, doctor. [*With sudden misgiving*] Am I offending you by calling you doctor instead of remembering your title?

RIDGEON.   Nonsense. I am a doctor. But mind you dont call Walpole one.[6]

MRS DUBEDAT.   I dont care about Mr Walpole: it is you who must befriend me. Oh, will you please sit down and listen to me just for a few minutes. [*He assents with a grave inclination, and sits on the sofa. She sits on the easel chair.*] Thank you. I wont keep you long; but I must tell you the whole truth. Listen, I know Louis as nobody else in the world knows him or ever can know him. I am his wife. I know he has little faults: impatience, sensitiveness, even little selfishnesses that are too trivial for him to notice. I know that he sometimes shocks people about money because he is so utterly above it, and cant understand the value ordinary people set on it. Tell me: did he—did he borrow any money from you?

RIDGEON.   He asked me for some—once.

MRS DUBEDAT [*tears again in her eyes*].   Oh, I am so sorry—so sorry. But he will never do it again: I pledge you my word for that. He has given me his promise: here in this room just before you came; and he is incapable of breaking

6 British surgeons—of whom Walpole is one—are traditionally called "Mister" rather than "Doctor."

his word. That was his only real weakness; and now it is conquered and done with for ever.

RIDGEON.   Was that really his only weakness?

MRS DUBEDAT.   He is perhaps sometimes weak about women, because they adore him so, and are always laying traps for him. And of course when he says he doesnt believe in morality, ordinary pious people think he must be wicked. You can understand, cant you, how all this starts a great deal of gossip about him, and gets repeated until even good friends get set against him?

RIDGEON.   Yes: I understand.

MRS DUBEDAT.   Oh, if you only knew the other side of him as I do! Do you know, doctor, that if Louis dishonored himself by a really bad action, I should kill myself.

RIDGEON.   Come! dont exaggerate.

MRS DUBEDAT.   I should. You dont understand that, you east country people.

RIDGEON.   You did not see much of the world in Cornwall, did you?

MRS DUBEDAT [naïvely].   Oh yes. I saw a great deal every day of the beauty of the world—more than you ever see here in London. But I saw very few people, if that is what you mean. I was an only child.

RIDGEON.   That explains a good deal.

MRS DUBEDAT.   I had a great many dreams; but at last they all came to one dream.

RIDGEON [with half a sigh].   Yes, the usual dream.

MRS DUBEDAT [surprised].   Is it usual?

RIDGEON.   As I guess. You havnt yet told me what it was.

MRS DUBEDAT.   I didnt want to waste myself. I could do nothing myself; but I had a little property and I could help with it. I had even a little beauty: dont think me vain for knowing it. I knew that men of genius always had a terrible struggle with poverty and neglect at first. My dream was to save one of them from that, and bring some charm and happiness into his life. I prayed Heaven to send me one. I firmly believe that Louis was guided to me in answer to my prayer. He was no more like the other men I had met than the Thames Embankment is like our Cornish coasts. He saw everything that I saw, and drew it for me. He understood everything. He came to me like a child. Only fancy, doctor: he never even wanted to marry me: he never thought of the things other men think of! I had to propose it myself. Then he said he had no money. When I told him I had some, he said "Oh, all right," just like a boy. He is still like that, quite unspoiled, a man in his thoughts, a great poet and artist in his dreams, and a child in his ways. I gave him myself and all that I had that he might grow to his full height with plenty of sunshine. If I lost faith in him, it would mean the wreck and failure of my life. I should go back to Cornwall and die. I could show you the very cliff I should jump off. You must cure him: you must make him quite well again for me. I know that you can do it and that nobody else can. I implore you not to refuse what I am going to ask you to do. Take Louis yourself: and let Sir Ralph cure Dr Blenkinsop.

RIDGEON [slowly].   Mrs Dubedat: do you really believe in my knowledge and skill as you say you do?

MRS DUBEDAT.   Absolutely. I do not give my trust by halves.

RIDGEON.   I know that. Well, I am going to test you—hard. Will you believe me when I tell you that I understand what you have just told me; that I have no desire but to serve you in the most faithful friendship; and that your hero must be preserved to you.

MRS DUBEDAT. Oh forgive me. Forgive what I said. You will preserve him to me.

RIDGEON. At all hazards. [*She kisses his hand. He rises hastily.*] No: you have not heard the rest. [*She rises too.*] You must believe me when I tell you that the one chance of preserving the hero lies in Louis being in the care of Sir Ralph.

MRS DUBEDAT [*firmly*]. You say so: I have no more doubts: I believe you. Thank you.

RIDGEON. Goodbye. [*She takes his hand.*] I hope this will be a lasting friendship.

MRS DUBEDAT. It will. My friendships end only with death.

RIDGEON. Death ends everything, doesnt it? Goodbye. [*With a sigh and a look of pity at her which she does not understand, he goes.*]

ACT IV

The studio. The easel is pushed back to the wall. Cardinal Death, holding his scythe and hour-glass like a sceptre and globe, sits on the throne. On the hat-stand hang the hats of SIR PATRICK *and* BLOOMFIELD BONINGTON. WALPOLE, *just come in, is hanging up his beside them. There is a knock. He opens the door and finds* RIDGEON *there.*

WALPOLE. Hallo, Ridgeon!
[*They come into the middle of the room together, taking off their gloves.*]
RIDGEON. Whats the matter? Have you been sent for, too.
WALPOLE. We've all been sent for. Ive only just come: I havnt seen him yet. The charwoman says that old Paddy Cullen has been here with B. B. for the last half-hour. [SIR PATRICK, *with bad news in his face, enters from the inner room.*] Well: whats up?
SIR PATRICK. Go in and see. B. B. is in there with him.
[WALPOLE *goes.* RIDGEON *is about to follow him; but* SIR PATRICK *stops him with a look.*]
RIDGEON. What has happened?
SIR PATRICK. Do you remember Jane Marsh's arm?
RIDGEON. Is that whats happened?
SIR PATRICK. Thats whats happened. His lung has gone like Jane's arm. I never saw such a case. He has got through three months galloping consumption in three days.
RIDGEON. B. B. got in on the negative phase.
SIR PATRICK. Negative or positive, the lad's done for. He wont last out the afternoon. He'll go suddenly: Ive often seen it.
RIDGEON. So long as he goes before his wife finds him out, I dont care. I fully expected this.
SIR PATRICK [*drily*]. It's a little hard on a lad to be killed because his wife has too high an opinion of him. Fortunately few of us are in any danger of that.

[*Sir Ralph comes from the inner room and hastens between them, humanely concerned, but professionally elate and communicative.*]

B. B. Ah, here you are, Ridgeon. Paddy's told you, of course.

RIDGEON. Yes.

B. B. It's an enormously interesting case. You know, Colly, by Jupiter, if I didnt know as a matter of scientific fact that I'd been stimulating the phagocytes, I should say I'd been stimulating the other things. What is the explanation of it, Sir Patrick? How do you account for it, Ridgeon? Have we over-stimulated the phagocytes? Have they not only eaten up the bacilli, but attacked and destroyed the red corpuscles as well? a possibility suggested by the patient's pallor. Nay, have they finally begun to prey on the lungs themselves? Or on one another? I shall write a paper about this case.

[WALPOLE *comes back, very serious, even shocked. He comes between* B. B. *and* RIDGEON.]

WALPOLE. Whew! B. B.: youve done it this time.

B. B. What do you mean?

WALPOLE. Killed him. The worst case of neglected blood-poisoning I ever saw. It's too late now to do anything. He'd die under the anæsthetic.

B. B. [*offended*]. Killed! Really, Walpole, if your monomania were not well known, I should take such an expression very seriously.

SIR PATRICK. Come come! When youve both killed as many people as I have in my time youll feel humble enough about it. Come and look at him, Colly.

[RIDGEON *and* SIR PATRICK *go into the inner room.*]

WALPOLE. I apologize, B. B. But it's blood-poisoning.

B. B. [*recovering his irresistible good nature*]. My dear Walpole, everything is blood-poisoning. But upon my soul, I shall not use any of that stuff of Ridgeon's again. What made me so sensitive about what you said just now is that, strictly between ourselves, Ridgeon has cooked our young friend's goose.

[JENNIFER, *worried and distressed, but always gentle, comes between them from the inner room. She wears a nurse's apron.*]

MRS DUBEDAT. Sir Ralph: what am I to do? That man who insisted on seeing me, and sent in word that his business was important to Louis, is a newspaper man. A paragraph appeared in the paper this morning saying that Louis is seriously ill; and this man wants to interview him about it. How can people be so brutally callous?

WALPOLE [*moving vengefully towards the door*]. You just leave me to deal with him!

MRS DUBEDAT [*stopping him*]. But Louis insists on seeing him: he almost began to cry about it. And he says he cant bear his room any longer. He says he wants to [*She struggles with a sob.*]—to die in his studio. Sir Patrick says let him have his way: it can do no harm. What shall we do?

B. B. [*encouragingly*]. Why, follow Sir Patrick's excellent advice, of course. As he says, it can do him no harm; and it will no doubt do him good—a great deal of good. He will be much the better for it.

MRS DUBEDAT [*a little cheered*]. Will you bring the man up here, Mr Walpole, and tell him that he may see Louis, but that he mustnt exhaust him by talking? [WALPOLE *nods and goes out by the outer door.*] Sir Ralph: dont be angry with me; but Louis will die if he stays here. I must take him to Cornwall. He will recover there.

B. B. [*brightening wonderfully, as if Dubedat were already saved*]. Cornwall! The very place for him! Wonderful for the lungs. Stupid of me not to think of it before. You are his best physician after all, dear lady. An inspiration! Cornwall: of course, yes, yes, yes.

MRS DUBEDAT [*comforted and touched*]. You are so kind, Sir Ralph. But dont give me much hope or I shall cry; and Louis cant bear that.

B. B. [*gently putting his protective arm round her shoulders*]. Then let us come back to him and help to carry him in. Cornwall! of course, of course. The very thing! [*They go together into the bedroom.*]

[WALPOLE *returns with* THE NEWSPAPER MAN, *a cheerful, affable young man who is disabled for ordinary business pursuits by a congenital erroneousness which renders him incapable of describing accurately anything he sees, or understanding or reporting accurately anything he hears. As the only employment in which these defects do not matter is journalism (for a newspaper, not having to act on its descriptions and reports, but only to sell them to idly curious people, has nothing but honor to lose by inaccuracy and unveracity), he has perforce become a journalist, and has to keep up an air of high spirits through a daily struggle with his own illiteracy and the precariousness of his employment. He has a note-book, and occasionally attempts to make a note; but as he cannot write shorthand, and does not write with ease in any hand, he generally gives it up as a bad job before he succeeds in finishing a sentence.*]

THE NEWSPAPER MAN [*looking round and making indecisive attempts at notes*]. This is the studio, I suppose.

WALPOLE. Yes.

THE NEWSPAPER MAN [*wittily*]. Where he has his models, eh?

WALPOLE [*grimly irresponsive*]. No doubt.

THE NEWSPAPER MAN. Cubicle, you said it was?

WALPOLE. Yes, tubercle.

THE NEWSPAPER MAN. Which way do you spell it: is it c-u-b-i-c-a-l or c-l-e?

WALPOLE. Tubercle, man, not cubical. [*Spelling it for him.*] T-u-b-e-r-c-l-e.

THE NEWSPAPER MAN. Oh! tubercle. Some disease, I suppose. I thought he had consumption. Are you one of the family or the doctor?

WALPOLE. I'm neither one nor the other. I am Mister Cutler Walpole. Put that down. Then put down Sir Colenso Ridgeon.

THE NEWSPAPER MAN. Pigeon?

WALPOLE. Ridgeon [*contemptuously snatching his book*]. Here: youd better let me write the names down for you: youre sure to get them wrong. That comes of belonging to an illiterate profession, with no qualifications and no public register. [*He writes the particulars.*]

THE NEWSPAPER MAN. Oh, I say: you have got your knife into us, havnt you?

WALPOLE [*vindictively*]. I wish I had: I'd make a better man of you. Now attend. [*Shewing him the book.*] These are the names of the three doctors. This is the patient. This is the address. This is the name of the disease. [*He shuts the book with a snap which makes the journalist blink, and returns it to him.*] Mr Dubedat will be brought in here presently. He wants to see you because he doesnt know how bad he is. We'll allow you to wait a few minutes to humor him; but if you talk to him, out you go. He may die at any moment.

THE NEWSPAPER MAN [*interested*]. Is he as bad as that? I say: I am in luck today. Would you mind letting me photograph you? [*He produces a camera.*] Could you have a lancet or something in your hand?

WALPOLE.   Put it up. If you want my photograph you can get it in Baker Street in any of the series of celebrities.

THE NEWSPAPER MAN.   But theyll want to be paid. If you wouldnt mind [*fingering the camera*]—?

WALPOLE.   I would. Put it up, I tell you. Sit down there and be quiet.

[THE NEWSPAPER MAN *quickly sits down on the piano stool as* DUBEDAT, *in an invalid's chair, is wheeled in by* MRS DUBEDAT *and* SIR RALPH. *They place the chair between the dais and the sofa, where the easel stood before.* LOUIS *is not changed as a robust man would be; and he is not scared. His eyes look larger; and he is so weak physically that he can hardly move, lying on his cushions with complete languor; but his mind is active: it is making the most of his condition, finding voluptuousness in languor and drama in death. They are all impressed, in spite of themselves, except* RIDGEON, *who is implacable.* B. B. *is entirely sympathetic and forgiving.* RIDGEON *follows the chair with a tray of milk and stimulants.* SIR PATRICK, *who accompanies him, takes the tea-table from the corner and places it behind the chair for the tray.* B. B. *takes the easel chair and places it for* JENNIFER *at* DUBEDAT's *side, next the dais, from which the lay figure ogles the dying artist.* B. B. *then returns to* DUBEDAT's *left.* JENNIFER *sits.* WALPOLE *sits down on the edge of the dais.* RIDGEON *stands near him.*]

LOUIS [*blissfully*].   Thats happiness. To be in a studio! Happiness!

MRS DUBEDAT.   Yes, dear. Sir Patrick says you may stay here as long as you like.

LOUIS.   Jennifer.

MRS DUBEDAT.   Yes, my darling.

LOUIS.   Is the newspaper man here?

THE NEWSPAPER MAN [*glibly*].   Yes, Mr Dubedat: I'm here, at your service. I represent the press. I thought you might like to let us have a few words about—about—er—well, a few words on your illness, and your plans for the season.

LOUIS.   My plans for the season are very simple. I'm going to die.

MRS DUBEDAT [*tortured*].   Louis—dearest—

LOUIS.   My darling: I'm very weak and tired. Dont put on me the horrible strain of pretending that I dont know. Ive been lying there listening to the doctors—laughing to myself. They know. Dearest: dont cry. It makes you ugly; and I cant bear that. [*She dries her eyes and recovers herself with a proud effort.*] I want you to promise me something.

MRS DUBEDAT.   Yes, yes: you know I will. [*Imploringly.*] Only my love, my love, dont talk: it will waste your strength.

LOUIS.   No: it will only use it up. Ridgeon: give me something to keep me going for a few minutes—not one of your confounded anti-toxins, if you dont mind. I have some things to say before I go.

RIDGEON [*looking at* SIR PATRICK].   I suppose it can do no harm? [*He pours out some spirit, and is about to add soda water when* SIR PATRICK *corrects him.*]

SIR PATRICK.   In milk. Dont set him coughing.

LOUIS [*after drinking*].   Jennifer.

MRS DUBEDAT.   Yes, dear.

LOUIS.   If theres one thing I hate more than another, it's a widow. Promise me that youll never be a widow.

MRS DUBEDAT. My dear, what do you mean?

LOUIS. I want you to look beautiful. I want people to see in your eyes that you were married to me. The people in Italy used to point at Dante and say "There goes the man who has been in hell." I want them to point at you and say "There goes a woman who has been in heaven." It has been heaven, darling, hasnt it—sometimes?

MRS DUBEDAT. Oh yes, yes. Always, always.

LOUIS. If you wear black and cry, people will say "Look at that miserable woman: her husband made her miserable."

MRS DUBEDAT. No, never. You are the light and the blessing of my life. I never lived until I knew you.

LOUIS [his eyes glistening]. Then you must always wear beautiful dresses and splendid magic jewels. Think of all the wonderful pictures I shall never paint. [She wins a terrible victory over a sob.] Well, you must be transfigured with all the beauty of those pictures. Men must get such dreams from seeing you as they never could get from any daubing with paints and brushes. Painters must paint you as they never painted any mortal woman before. There must be a great tradition of beauty, a great atmosphere of wonder and romance. That is what men must always think of when they think of me. That is the sort of immortality I want. You can make that for me, Jennifer. There are lots of things you dont understand that every woman in the street understands; but you can understand that and do it as nobody else can. Promise me that immortality. Promise me you will not make a little hell of crape and crying and undertaker's horrors and withering flowers and all that vulgar rubbish.

MRS DUBEDAT. I promise. But all that is far off, dear. You are to come to Cornwall with me and get well. Sir Ralph says so.

LOUIS. Poor old B. B.!

B. B. [affected to tears, turns away and whispers to SIR PATRICK]. Poor fellow! Brain going.

LOUIS. Sir Patrick's there, isnt he?

SIR PATRICK. Yes, yes. I'm here.

LOUIS. Sit down, wont you? It's a shame to keep you standing about.

SIR PATRICK. Yes, yes. Thank you. All right.

LOUIS. Jennifer.

MRS DUBEDAT. Yes, dear.

LOUIS [with a strange look of delight]. Do you remember the burning bush?

MRS DUBEDAT. Yes, yes. Oh, my dear, how it strains my heart to remember it now!

LOUIS. Does it? It fills me with joy. Tell them about it.

MRS DUBEDAT. It was nothing—only that once in my old Cornish home we lit the first fire of the winter; and when we looked through the window we saw the flames dancing in a bush in the garden.

LOUIS. Such a color! Garnet color. Waving like silk. Liquid lovely flame flowing up through the bay leaves, and not burning them. Well, I shall be a flame like that. I'm sorry to disappoint the poor little worms; but the last of me shall be the flame in the burning bush. Whenever you see the flame, Jennifer, that will be me. Promise me that I shall be burnt.

MRS DUBEDAT. Oh, if I might be with you, Louis!

LOUIS. No: you must always be in the garden when the bush flames. You are my hold on the world: you are my immortality. Promise.

MRS DUBEDAT. I'm listening. I shall not forget. You know that I promise.

LOUIS. Well, thats about all; except that you are to hang my pictures at the one-man show. I can trust your eye. You wont let anyone else touch them.

MRS DUBEDAT. You can trust me.

LOUIS. Then theres nothing more to worry about, is there? Give me some more of that milk. I'm fearfully tired; but if I stop talking I shant begin again. [SIR RALPH *gives him a drink. He takes it and looks up quaintly.*] I say, B. B., do you think anything would stop you talking?

B. B. [*almost unmanned*]. He confuses me with you, Paddy. Poor fellow! Poor fellow!

LOUIS [*musing*]. I used to be awfully afraid of death; but now it's come I have no fear; and I'm perfectly happy. Jennifer.

MRS DUBEDAT. Yes, dear?

LOUIS. I'll tell you a secret. I used to think that our marriage was all an affectation, and that I'd break loose and run away some day. But now that I'm going to be broken loose whether I like it or not, I'm perfectly fond of you, and perfectly satisfied because I'm going to live as part of you and not as my troublesome self.

MRS DUBEDAT [*heartbroken*]. Stay with me, Louis. Oh, dont leave me, dearest.

LOUIS. Not that I'm selfish. With all my faults I dont think Ive ever been really selfish. No artist can: Art is too large for that. You will marry again, Jennifer.

MRS DUBEDAT. Oh, how can you, Louis?

LOUIS [*insisting childishly*]. Yes, because people who have found marriage happy always marry again. Ah, *I* shant be jealous. [*Slyly.*] But dont talk to the other fellow too much about me: he wont like it. [*Almost chuckling.*] *I* shall be your lover all the time; but it will be a secret from him, poor devil!

SIR PATRICK. Come! youve talked enough. Try to rest awhile.

LOUIS [*wearily*]. Yes: I'm fearfully tired; but I shall have a long rest presently. I have something to say to you fellows. Youre all there, arnt you? I'm too weak to see anything but Jennifer's bosom. That promises rest.

RIDGEON. We are all here.

LOUIS [*startled*]. That voice sounded devilish. Take care, Ridgeon: my ears hear things that other people's ears cant. Ive been thinking—thinking. I'm cleverer than you imagine.

SIR PATRICK [*whispering to* RIDGEON]. Youve got on his nerves, Colly. Slip out quietly.

RIDGEON [*apart to* SIR PATRICK]. Would you deprive the dying actor of his audience?

LOUIS [*his face lighting up faintly with mischievous glee*]. I heard that, Ridgeon. That was good. Jennifer, dear: be kind to Ridgeon always; because he was the last man who amused me.

RIDGEON [*relentless*]. Was I?

LOUIS. But it's not true. It's you who are still on the stage. I'm half way home already.

MRS DUBEDAT [to RIDGEON]. What did you say?

LOUIS [answering for him]. Nothing, dear. Only one of those little secrets that men keep among themselves. Well, all you chaps have thought pretty hard things of me, and said them.

B. B. [quite overcome]. No, no, Dubedat. Not at all.

LOUIS. Yes, you have. I know what you all think of me. Dont imagine I'm sore about it. I forgive you.

WALPOLE [involuntarily]. Well, damn me! [Ashamed.] I beg your pardon.

LOUIS. That was old Walpole, I know. Dont grieve, Walpole. I'm perfectly happy. I'm not in pain. I dont want to live. Ive escaped from myself. I'm in heaven, immortal in the heart of my beautiful Jennifer. I'm not afraid, and not ashamed. [Reflectively, puzzling it out for himself weakly.] I know that in an accidental sort of way, struggling through the unreal part of life, I havnt always been able to live up to my ideal. But in my own real world I have never done anything wrong, never denied my faith, never been untrue to myself. Ive been threatened and blackmailed and insulted and starved. But Ive played the game. Ive fought the good fight. And now it's all over, theres an indescribable peace. [He feebly holds his hands and utters his creed]: I believe in Michael Angelo, Velasquez, and Rembrandt; in the might of design, the mystery of color, the redemption of all things by Beauty everlasting, and the message of Art that has made these hands blessed. Amen. Amen. [He closes his eyes and lies still.]

MRS DUBEDAT [breathless]. Louis: are you—

[WALPOLE rises and comes quickly to see whether he is dead.]

LOUIS. Not yet, dear. Very nearly, but not yet. I should like to rest my head on your bosom; only it would tire you.

MRS DUBEDAT. No, no, no, darling: how could you tire me? [She lifts him so that he lies in her bosom.]

LOUIS. Thats good. Thats real.

MRS DUBEDAT. Dont spare me, dear. Indeed indeed you will not tire me. Lean on me with all your weight.

LOUIS [with a sudden half return of his normal strength and comfort]. Jinny Gwinny: I think I shall recover after all. [SIR PATRICK looks significantly at RIDGEON, mutely warning him that this is the end.]

MRS DUBEDAT [hopefully]. Yes, yes: you shall.

LOUIS. Because I suddenly want to sleep. Just an ordinary sleep.

MRS DUBEDAT [rocking him]. Yes, dear. Sleep. [He seems to go to sleep. WALPOLE makes another movement. She protests.] Sh-sh: please dont disturb him. [His lips move.] What did you say, dear? [In great distress.] I cant listen without moving him. [His lips move again: Walpole bends down and listens.]

WALPOLE. He wants to know is the newspaper man here.

THE NEWSPAPER MAN [excited; for he has been enjoying himself enormously]. Yes, Mr Dubedat. Here I am.

[WALPOLE raises his hand warningly to silence him. SIR RALPH sits down quietly on the sofa and frankly buries his face in his handkerchief.]

MRS DUBEDAT [with great relief]. Oh thats right, dear: dont spare me: lean with all your weight on me. Now you are really resting.

[SIR PATRICK quickly comes forward and feels Louis's pulse; then takes him by the shoulders.]

SIR PATRICK. Let me put him back on the pillow, maam. He will be better so.

MRS DUBEDAT [*piteously*]. Oh no, please, please, doctor. He is not tiring me; and he will be so hurt when he wakes if he finds I have put him away.

SIR PATRICK. He will never wake again. [*He takes the body from her and replaces it in the chair.* RIDGEON, *unmoved, lets down the back and makes a bier of it.*]

MRS DUBEDAT [*who has unexpectedly sprung to her feet, and stands dry-eyed and stately*]. Was that death?

WALPOLE. Yes.

MRS DUBEDAT [*with complete dignity*]. Will you wait for me a moment. I will come back. [*She goes out.*]

WALPOLE. Ought we to follow her? Is she in her right senses?

SIR PATRICK [*with quiet conviction*]. Yes. She's all right. Leave her alone. She'll come back.

RIDGEON [*callously*]. Let us get this thing out of the way before she comes.

B. B. [*rising, shocked*]. My dear Colly! The poor lad! He died splendidly.

SIR PATRICK. Aye! that is how the wicked die.

> For there are no bands in their death;
> But their strength is firm:
> They are not in trouble as other men.

No matter: it's not for us to judge. He's in another world now.

WALPOLE. Borrowing his first five-pound note there, probably.

RIDGEON. I said the other day that the most tragic thing in the world is a sick doctor. I was wrong. The most tragic thing in the world is a man of genius who is not also a man of honor.

[RIDGEON *and* WALPOLE *wheel the chair into the recess.*]

THE NEWSPAPER MAN [*to* SIR RALPH]. I thought it shewed a very nice feeling, his being so particular about his wife going into proper mourning for him and making her promise never to marry again.

B. B. [*impressively*]. Mrs Dubedat is not in a position to carry the interview any further. Neither are we.

SIR PATRICK. Good afternoon to you.

THE NEWSPAPER MAN. Mrs Dubedat said she was coming back.

B. B. After you have gone.

THE NEWSPAPER MAN. Do you think she would give me a few words on How It Feels to be a Widow? Rather a good title for an article, isnt it?

B. B. Young man: if you wait until Mrs Dubedat comes back, you will be able to write an article on How It Feels to be Turned Out of the House.

THE NEWSPAPER MAN [*unconvinced*]. You think she'd rather not—

B. B. [*cutting him short*]. Good day to you. [*Giving him a visiting-card.*] Mind you get my name correctly. Good day.

THE NEWSPAPER MAN. Good day. Thank you. [*Vaguely trying to read the card.*] Mr—

B. B. No, not Mister. This is your hat, I think [*giving it to him*]. Gloves? No, of course: no gloves. Good day to you. [*He edges him out at last; shuts the door on him; and returns to* SIR PATRICK *as* RIDGEON *and* WALPOLE *come back from the recess,* WALPOLE *crossing the room to the hat-stand, and* RIDGEON *coming be-*

tween SIR RALPH *and* SIR PATRICK.] Poor fellow! Poor young fellow! How well he died! I feel a better man, really.

SIR PATRICK.   When youre as old as I am, youll know that it matters very little how a man dies. What matters is, how he lives. Every fool that runs his nose against a bullet is a hero nowadays, because he dies for his country. Why dont he live for it to some purpose?

B. B.   No, please, Paddy: dont be hard on the poor lad. Not now, not now. After all, was he so bad? He had only two failings, money and women. Well, let us be honest. Tell the truth, Paddy. Dont be hypocritical, Ridgeon. Throw off the mask, Walpole. Are these two matters so well arranged at present that a disregard of the usual arrangements indicates real depravity?

WALPOLE.   I dont mind his disregarding the usual arrangements. Confound the usual arrangements! To a man of science theyre beneath contempt both as to money and women. What I mind is his disregarding everything except his own pocket and his own fancy. He didnt disregard the usual arrangements when they paid him. Did he give us his pictures for nothing? Do you suppose he'd have hesitated to blackmail me if I'd compromised myself with his wife? Not he.

SIR PATRICK.   Dont waste your time wrangling over him. A blackguard's a blackguard; an honest man's an honest man; and neither of them will ever be at a loss for a religion or a morality to prove that their ways are the right ways. It's the same with nations, the same with professions, the same all the world over and always will be.

B. B.   Ah, well, perhaps, perhaps, perhaps. Still, de mortuis nil nisi bonum.[7] He died extremely well, remarkably well. He has set us an example: let us endeavour to follow it rather than harp on the weaknesses that have perished with him. I think it is Shakespear who says that the good that most men do lives after them: the evil lies interréd with their bones. Yes: interréd with their bones. Believe me, Paddy, we are all mortal. It is the common lot, Ridgeon. Say what you will, Walpole, Nature's debt must be paid. If tis not today, twill be tomorrow.

> To-morrow and to-morrow and to-morrow
> After life's fitful fever they sleep well
> And like this insubstantial bourne from which
> No traveller returns
> Leave not a wrack behind.

[WALPOLE *is about to speak, but* B. B., *suddenly and vehemently proceeding, extinguishes him.*]

> Out, out, brief candle:
> For nothing canst thou to damnation add;
> The readiness is all.

WALPOLE [*gently; for* B. B.'s *feeling, absurdly expressed as it is, is too sincere and humane to be ridiculed*].   Yes, B. B. Death makes people go on like that. I dont know why it should; but it does. By the way, what are we going to do? Ought we to clear out; or had we better wait and see whether Mrs Dubedat will come back?

SIR PATRICK.   I think we'd better go. We can tell the charwoman what to do.
[*They take their hats and go to the door.*]

MRS DUBEDAT [*coming from the inner room wonderfully and beautifully*

---

[7] (Latin) Say nothing but what is good about the dead.

dressed, and radiant, carrying a great piece of purple silk, handsomely embroid- ered, over her arm].   I'm so sorry to have kept you waiting.

SIR PATRICK ⎤ [*amazed, all* ⎡ Dont mention it, madam.
B. B.   ⎥ *together in* ⎥ Not at all, not at all.
RIDGEON   ⎢ *a confused* ⎢ By no means.
WALPOLE   ⎦ *murmur*].   ⎣ It doesnt matter in the least.

MRS DUBEDAT [*coming to them*].   I felt that I must shake hands with his friends once before we part today. We have shared together a great privilege and a great happiness. I dont think we can ever think of ourselves as ordinary people again. We have had a wonderful experience; and that gives us a common faith, a common ideal, that nobody else can quite have. Life will always be beautiful to us: death will always be beautiful to us. May we shake hands on that?

SIR PATRICK [*shaking hands*].   Remember: all letters had better be left to your solicitor. Let him open everything and settle everything. Thats the law, you know.

MRS DUBEDAT.   Oh, thank you: I didnt know. [*Sir Patrick goes.*]

WALPOLE.   Goodbye. I blame myself: I should have insisted on operating. [*He goes.*]

B. B.   I will send the proper people: they will know what to do: you shall have no trouble. Goodbye, my dear lady. [*He goes.*]

RIDGEON.   Goodbye. [*He offers his hand.*]

MRS DUBEDAT [*drawing back with gentle majesty*].   I said his friends, Sir Colenso. [*He bows and goes.*]

[*She unfolds the great piece of silk, and goes into the recess to cover the dead.*]

ACT V

One of the smaller Bond Street Picture Galleries. The entrance is from a picture shop. Nearly in the middle of the gallery there is a writing-table, at which THE SECRETARY, *fashionably dressed, sits with his back to the entrance, correcting catalogue proofs. Some copies of a new book the on the desk, also* THE SECRETARY'*s shining hat and a couple of magnifying glasses. At the side, on his left, a little behind him, is a small door marked* PRIVATE. *Near the same side is a cushioned bench parallel to the walls, which are covered with* DUBEDAT'*s works. Two screens, also covered with drawings, stand near the corners right and left of the entrance.*
JENNIFER, *beautifully dressed and apparently very happy and prosperous, comes into the gallery through the private door.*

JENNIFER.   Have the catalogues come yet, Mr Danby?

THE SECRETARY.   Not yet.

JENNIFER.   What a shame! It's a quarter past: the private view will begin in less than half an hour.

THE SECRETARY.   I think I'd better run over to the printers to hurry them up.

JENNIFER.   Oh, if you would be so good, Mr Danby. I'll take your place while youre away.

THE SECRETARY.   If anyone should come before the time dont take any notice. The commissionaire wont let anyone through unless he knows him. We have a few people who like to come before the crowd—people who really buy; and of course we're glad to see them. Have you seen the notices in Brush and Crayon and in The Easel?

JENNIFER [*indignantly*].   Yes: most disgraceful. They write quite patronizingly, as if they were Mr Dubedat's superiors. After all the cigars and sandwiches they had from us on the press day, and all they drank, I really think it is infamous that they should write like that. I hope you have not sent them tickets for today.

THE SECRETARY.   Oh, they wont come again: theres no lunch today. The advance copies of your book have come. [*He indicates the new books.*]

JENNIFER [*pouncing on a copy, wildly excited*].   Give it to me. Oh! excuse me a moment [*she runs away with it through the private door*].

[*The Secretary takes a mirror from his drawer and smartens himself before going out.* RIDGEON *comes in.*]

RIDGEON.   Good morning. May I look round, as usual, before the doors open?

THE SECRETARY.   Certainly, Sir Colenso. I'm sorry the catalogues have not come: I'm just going to see about them. Heres my own list, if you dont mind.

RIDGEON.   Thanks. What's this? [*He takes up one of the new books.*]

THE SECRETARY.   Thats just come in. An advance copy of Mrs Dubedat's Life of her late husband.

RIDGEON [*reading the title*].   The Story of a King of Men: By His Wife. [*He looks at the portrait frontispiece.*] Ay: there he is. You knew him here, I suppose.

THE SECRETARY.   Oh, we knew him. Better than she did, Sir Colenso, in some ways, perhaps.

RIDGEON.   So did I. [*They look significantly at one another.*] I'll take a look round.

[THE SECRETARY *puts on the shining hat and goes out.* RIDGEON *begins looking at the pictures. Presently he comes back to the table for a magnifying glass, and scrutinizes a drawing very closely. He sighs; shakes his head, as if constrained to admit the extraordinary fascination and merit of the work; then marks* THE SECRETARY's *list. Proceeding with his survey, he disappears behind the screen.* JENNIFER *comes back with her book. A look round satisfies her that she is alone. She seats herself at the table and admires the memoir—her first printed book—to her heart's content.* RIDGEON *re-appears, face to the wall, scrutinizing the drawings. After using his glass again, he steps back to get a more distant view of one of the larger pictures. She hastily closes the book at the sound; looks round; recognizes him; and stares, petrified. He takes a further step back which brings him nearer to her.*]

RIDGEON [*shaking his head as before, ejaculates*].   Clever brute! [*She flushes as though he had struck her. He turns to put the glass down on the desk, and finds himself face to face with her intent gaze.*] I beg your pardon. I thought I was alone.

JENNIFER [*controlling herself, and speaking steadily and meaningly*].   I am glad we have met, Sir Colenso Ridgeon. I met Dr Blenkinsop yesterday. I congratulate you on a wonderful cure.

RIDGEON [*can find no words: makes an embarrassed gesture of assent after a moment's silence, and puts down the glass and* THE SECRETARY's *list on the table.*]

JENNIFER.   He looked the picture of health and strength and prosperity. [*She looks for a moment at the walls, contrasting* BLENKINSOP's *fortune with the artist's fate.*]

RIDGEON [*in low tones, still embarrassed*].   He has been fortunate.

JENNIFER.   Very fortunate. His life has been spared.

RIDGEON.   I mean that he has been made a Medical Officer of Health. He cured the Chairman of the Borough Council very successfully.

JENNIFER.   With your medicines?

RIDGEON.   No. I believe it was with a pound of ripe greengages.

JENNIFER [*with deep gravity*].   Funny!

RIDGEON.   Yes. Life does not cease to be funny when people die any more than it ceases to be serious when people laugh.

JENNIFER.   Dr Blenkinsop said one very strange thing to me.

RIDGEON.   What was that?

JENNIFER.   He said that private practice in medicine ought to be put down by law. When I asked him why, he said that private doctors were ignorant licensed murderers.

RIDGEON.   That is what the public doctor always thinks of the private doctor. Well, Blenkinsop ought to know. He was a private doctor long enough himself. Come! you have talked at me long enough. Talk to me. You have something to reproach me with. There is reproach in your face, in your voice: you are full of it. Out with it.

JENNIFER.   It is too late for reproaches now. When I turned and saw you just now, I wondered how you could come here coolly to look at his pictures. You answered the question. To you, he was only a clever brute.

RIDGEON [*quivering*].   Oh, dont. You know I did not know you were here.

JENNIFER [*raising her head a little with a quite gentle impulse of pride*]. You think it only mattered because I heard it. As if it could touch me, or touch him! Dont you see that what is really dreadful is that to you living things have no souls.

RIDGEON [*with a sceptical shrug*].   The soul is an organ I have not come across in the course of my anatomical work.

JENNIFER.   You know you would not dare to say such a silly thing as that to anybody but a woman whose mind you despise. If you dissected me you could not find my conscience. Do you think I have got none?

RIDGEON.   I have met people who had none.

JENNIFER.   Clever brutes? Do you know, doctor, that some of the dearest and most faithful friends I ever had were only brutes! You would have vivisected them. The dearest and greatest of all my friends had a sort of beauty and affectionateness that only animals have. I hope you may never feel what I felt when I had to put him into the hands of men who defend the torture of animals because they are only brutes.

RIDGEON.   Well, did you find us so very cruel, after all? They tell me that though you have dropped me, you stay for weeks with the Bloomfield Boningtons and the Walpoles. I think it must be true, because they never mention you to me now.

JENNIFER.   The animals in Sir Ralph's house are like spoiled children. When Mr Walpole had to take a splinter out of the mastiff's paw, I had to hold the poor dog myself; and Mr Walpole had to turn Sir Ralph out of the room.

And Mrs Walpole has to tell the gardener not to kill wasps when Mr Walpole is looking. But there are doctors who are naturally cruel; and there are others who get used to cruelty and are callous about it. They blind themselves to the souls of animals; and that blinds them to the souls of men and women. You made a dreadful mistake about Louis; but you would not have made it if you had not trained yourself to make the same mistake about dogs. You saw nothing in them but dumb brutes; and so you could see nothing in him but a clever brute.

RIDGEON [*with sudden resolution*]. I made no mistake whatever about him.

JENNIFER. Oh, doctor!

RIDGEON [*obstinately*]. I made no mistake whatever about him.

JENNIFER. Have you forgotten that he died?

RIDGEON [*with a sweep of his hand towards the pictures*]. He is not dead. He is there. [*Taking up the book.*] And there.

JENNIFER [*springing up with blazing eyes*]. Put that down. How dare you touch it?

[*Ridgeon, amazed at the fierceness of the outburst, puts it down with a deprecatory shrug. She takes it up and looks at it as if he had profaned a relic.*]

RIDGEON. I am very sorry. I see I had better go.

JENNIFER [*putting the book down*]. I beg your pardon. I—I forgot myself. But it is not yet—it is a private copy.

RIDGEON. But for me it would have been a very different book.

JENNIFER. But for you it would have been a longer one.

RIDGEON. You know then that I killed him?

JENNIFER [*suddenly moved and softened*]. Oh, doctor, if you acknowledge that—if you have confessed it to yourself—if you realize what you have done, then there is forgiveness. I trusted in your strength instinctively at first; then I thought I had mistaken callousness for strength. Can you blame me? But if it was really strength—if it was only such a mistake as we all make sometimes—it will make me so happy to be friends with you again.

RIDGEON. I tell you I made no mistake. I cured Blenkinsop: was there any mistake there?

JENNIFER. He recovered. Oh, dont be foolishly proud, doctor. Confess to a failure, and save our friendship. Remember, Sir Ralph gave Louis your medicine; and it made him worse.

RIDGEON. I cant be your friend on false pretences. Something has got me by the throat: the truth must come out. I used that medicine myself on Blenkinsop. It did not make him worse. It is a dangerous medicine: it cured Blenkinsop: it killed Louis Dubedat. When I handle it, it cures. When another man handles it, it kills,—sometimes.

JENNIFER [*naïvely: not yet taking it all in*]. Then why did you let Sir Ralph give it to Louis?

RIDGEON. I'm going to tell you. I did it because I was in love with you.

JENNIFER [*innocently surprised*]. In lo—You! an elderly man!

RIDGEON [*thunderstruck, raising his fists to heaven*]. Dubedat: thou art revenged! [*He drops his hands and collapses on the bench.*] I never thought of that. I suppose I appear to you a ridiculous old fogey.

JENNIFER. But surely—I did not mean to offend you, indeed—but you must be at least twenty years older than I am.

RIDGEON. Oh, quite. More, perhaps. In twenty years you will understand how little difference that makes.

JENNIFER. But even so, how could you think that I—his wife—could ever think of you—

RIDGEON [stopping her with a nervous waving of his fingers]. Yes, yes, yes, yes: I quite understand: you neednt rub it in.

JENNIFER. But—oh, it is only dawning on me now—I was so surprised at first—do you dare to tell me that it was to gratify a miserable jealousy that you deliberately—oh! oh! you murdered him.

RIDGEON. I think I did. It really comes to that.

> Thou shalt not kill, but needst not strive
> Officiously to keep alive.

I suppose—yes: I killed him.

JENNIFER. And you tell me that! to my face! callously! You are not afraid!

RIDGEON. I am a doctor: I have nothing to fear. It is not an indictable offence to call in B. B. Perhaps it ought to be; but it isnt.

JENNIFER. I did not mean that. I meant afraid of my taking the law into my own hands, and killing you.

RIDGEON. I am so hopelessly idiotic about you that I should not mind it a bit. You would always remember me if you did that.

JENNIFER. I shall remember you always as a little man who tried to kill a great one.

RIDGEON. Pardon me. I succeeded.

JENNIFER [with quiet conviction]. No. Doctors think they hold the keys of life and death; but it is not their will that is fulfilled. I dont believe you made any difference at all.

RIDGEON. Perhaps not. But I intended to.

JENNIFER [looking at him amazedly: not without pity]. And you tried to destroy that wonderful and beautiful life merely because you grudged him a woman whom you could never have expected to care for you!

RIDGEON. Who kissed my hands. Who believed in me. Who told me her friendship lasted until death.

JENNIFER. And whom you were betraying.

RIDGEON. No. Whom I was saving.

JENNIFER [gently]. Pray, doctor, from what?

RIDGEON. From making a terrible discovery. From having your life laid waste.

JENNIFER. How?

RIDGEON. No matter. I have saved you. I have been the best friend you ever had. You are happy. You are well. His works are an imperishable joy and pride for you.

JENNIFER. And you think that is your doing. Oh doctor, doctor! Sir Patrick is right: you do think you are a little god. How can you be so silly? You did not paint those pictures which are my imperishable joy and pride: you did not speak the words that will always be heavenly music in my ears. I listen to them now whenever I am tired or sad. That is why I am always happy.

RIDGEON. Yes, now that he is dead. Were you always happy when he was alive?

JENNIFER [*wounded*].   Oh, you are cruel, cruel. When he was alive I did not know the greatness of my blessing. I worried meanly about little things. I was unkind to him. I was unworthy of him.

RIDGEON [*laughing bitterly*].   Ha!

JENNIFER.   Dont insult me: dont blaspheme. [*She snatches up the book and presses it to her heart in a paroxysm of remorse, exclaiming.*] Oh, my King of Men!

RIDGEON.   King of Men! Oh, this is too monstrous, too grotesque. We cruel doctors have kept the secret from you faithfully; but it is like all secrets: it will not keep itself. The buried truth germinates and breaks through to the light.

JENNIFER.   What truth?

RIDGEON.   What truth! Why, that Louis Dubedat, King of Men, was the most entire and perfect scoundrel, the most miraculously mean rascal, the most callously selfish blackguard that ever made a wife miserable.

JENNIFER [*unshaken: calm and lovely*].   He made his wife the happiest woman in the world, doctor.

RIDGEON.   No: by all thats true on earth, he made his widow the happiest woman in the world; but it was I who made her a widow. And her happiness is my justification and my reward. Now you know what I did and what I thought of him. Be as angry with me as you like: at least you know me as I really am. If you ever come to care for an elderly man, you will know what you are caring for.

JENNIFER [*kind and quiet*].   I am not angry with you any more, Sir Colenso. I knew quite well that you did not like Louis: but it is not your fault: you dont understand: that is all. You never could have believed in him. It is just like your not believing in my religion: it is a sort of sixth sense that you have not got. And [*With a gentle reassuring movement towards him.*] dont think that you have shocked me so dreadfully. I know quite well what you mean by his selfishness. He sacrificed everything for his art. In a certain sense he had even to sacrifice everybody—

RIDGEON.   Everybody except himself. By keeping that back he lost the right to sacrifice you, and gave me the right to sacrifice him. Which I did.

JENNIFER [*shaking her head, pitying his error*].   He was one of the men who know what women know: that self-sacrifice is vain and cowardly.

RIDGEON.   Yes, when the sacrifice is rejected and thrown away. Not when it becomes the food of godhead.

JENNIFER.   I dont understand that. And I cant argue with you: you are clever enough to puzzle me, but not to shake me. You are so utterly, so wildly wrong; so incapable of appreciating Louis—

RIDGEON.   Oh! [*Taking up* THE SECRETARY's *list.*] I have marked five pictures as sold to me.

JENNIFER.   They will not be sold to you. Louis' creditors insisted on selling them; but this is my birthday; and they were all bought in for me this morning by my husband.

RIDGEON.   By whom?!!!

JENNIFER.   By my husband.

RIDGEON [*gabbling and stuttering*].   What husband? Whose husband? Which husband? Whom? how? what? Do you mean to say that you have married again?

JENNIFER. Do you forget that Louis disliked widows, and that people who have married happily once always marry again?

RIDGEON. Then I have committed a purely disinterested murder!

[*The Secretary returns with a pile of catalogues.*]

THE SECRETARY. Just got the first batch of catalogues in time. The doors are open.

JENNIFER [*to* RIDGEON, *politely*]. So glad you like the pictures, Sir Colenso. Good morning.

RIDGEON. Good morning. [*He goes towards the door; hesitates; turns to say something more; gives it up as a bad job; and goes.*]

COMMENTARY

Shaw called *The Doctor's Dilemma* a tragedy, but it is hard to believe that he meant the description seriously. In manner and tone the play is a comedy; this is scarcely contradicted by the fact that one of the persons in the play dies before our eyes, for Louis Dubedat's histrionic last moments make a scene that is affecting in no more than a sentimental way.

The oddity of the author's having called the play a tragedy has never engaged the kind of speculation that has long gone on about Chekhov's insistence that *Three Sisters* is a comedy. A few critics have attempted to affirm its seriousness by observing that Ridgeon undergoes a moral decline, to the point where he commits a quasi-murder; they identify this as the tragic element in the play. But although it is true that Ridgeon's moral nature deteriorates, this is hardly a tragic event; at most, it touches with a certain grimness the comedy in which it occurs. The likelihood is that Shaw had no other reason for applying the misnomer than the wish to be impudent, to amuse himself by confusing his audience.

And of course it is only if we take the play to be a comedy that we can accept the artificiality that is one of its salient features. Comedy has always claimed the right to treat probability with blithe indifference, and *The Doctor's Dilemma* takes full advantage of this ancient license. The events of the play are shameless contrivances, beginning with the terms of the "dilemma," the all too pat juxtaposition of the immoral genius and the virtuous mediocrity. Nowhere except in comedy could an eminent physician give a dinner party at which certain of the guests are co-opted to sit as a kind of investigating committee to help the host decide whether or not another of the guests deserves to receive the medical treatment that will rescue him from impending death. We are then asked to believe that the committee, once formed, cannot bring itself to disband, that three of the busiest doctors in London are so captivated by the moral situation that they find time to pursue their investigations at a meeting in Louis Dubedat's studio, and that all of them make a point of turning up at his deathbed.

But even more than by the unblushing high-handedness of its dealings with probability, the play is a comedy by its commitment to one of the oldest enterprises of the comic genre, the exhibition of the absurdity of doctors. How very old it is has been suggested by the English scholar F. M. Cornford, who traces the comic doctor through various examples of folk drama, such as the Punch and Judy shows and the medieval mummers' plays, back to the comedy of ancient Greece.[1] According to Cornford, Greek comedy had its roots in the primitive rituals of the winter solstice; the figure of the comic doctor descends from the once awesome medicine man who presided over the ceremonial representation of the death of the old year and the birth of the new. In the comedy of the Renaissance the doctor is a stock figure, mocked for his pretentiousness and pomposity. The tradition of doctor-baiting reached its climax and its classic form in the several plays in which Molière ridiculed the physicians of his day. To the traditional mockery he added an intellectual dimension by concentrating on the elaborate jargon of scholasticism by which the profession masked its invincible ignorance.

By the nineteenth century the tradition was on the wane, and now, in the popular drama of our time, no profession is accorded so much respect as that of medicine. The cinema and television seldom show the doctor as anything but virtuous and responsible, in his youth sternly dedicated to his unimpeachable profession, in his latter years endowed with a wisdom to which no layman can aspire. This change in the "image" of the doctor is connected with the advances that medicine made in the course of the nineteenth century. From our present perspective these may seem small, but they are significant because they were the result of the development of biological knowledge—medicine began to school itself in the sciences as it never had before and seemed on the point of making good the claims of its effectiveness that for so long had been empty.

It was in this period of not unjustifiable optimism, when the common opinion of the medical profession moved toward becoming what it now is, that Shaw mounted the elaborate attack, which, beginning in his youth, was to continue through the greater part of his life. *The Doctor's Dilemma* is but one of his innumerable writings on medical subjects. They have been accused of error, extravagance and perversity, in part because of their polemic style, which is often intentionally outrageous. But they are remarkably well informed, and in the main they make excellent sense.

The essence of Shaw's indictment is that the medical profession turned every new idea it acquired into authoritative doctrine and then into dogma, with the result that even its most promising discoveries became barren and often dangerous. Other of its deficiencies also contributed to his viewing it as a "conspiracy against the public," but Shaw directed his most active antagonism toward that aspect of medicine which its practitioners had come to believe was its greatest strength, its reliance on scientific research. He held that exactly when medicine based itself most confidently on science it was most likely to prove unscientific, establishing orthodoxies which stood in the way of truth. If the charge has bearing even upon the medical situation in our day, when the acceleration of research condemns received ideas to a shorter expectancy of life than they once had, in Shaw's time its cogency was still greater. A case in point is the germ theory of disease as it was then formulated. This was of obvious value, yet it served as the ground for untenable conclusions (such as that virtually all diseases are caused by germs), mistaken beliefs (such as that vaccination provided permanent immunity from smallpox and was wholly without

[1] *The Origin of Attic Comedy.*

danger), and unsalutary practices (such as Lord Lister's use of surgical antisepsis, eventually abandoned because the antiseptic interfered with the healing process).

But the scientific inadequacy of its accepted theories was not the whole of the objection that Shaw made to the state of the medical profession. He was dismayed by what he took to be its philosophical or spiritual failure. Central to his thought was the doctrine of vitalism, which holds that the life of organisms is the manifestation of a vital principle distinct from all physical and chemical forces. It was a view that led him to deny categorically the first premise of the medical practice of his day, that the human body is a mechanism and that any malfunction it may show is to be dealt with in a mechanistic way. Shaw's belief in vitalism stood in close relation to his social views, for he held that disease is best understood as a result of adverse conditions in the environment, and that health depends on comfort and beauty, which society has the duty to provide.

Even this summary account of Shaw's dealings with medicine will suggest that he must have come to the writing of his comedy of doctors in a spirit quite different from that of his predecessors in the long tradition. It is not possible to attribute any propagandistic purpose to the earlier comic writers. They mocked doctors with no intention of exciting indignation, only laughter. Even Molière, whose satire so tellingly exposes the intellectual deficiencies of medicine, does not propose that anything in particular can or should be done about the bad state of affairs. As one critic puts it, comedy for Molière was not a means but an end. Shaw often said in the most explicit way that the opposite was true of him, that he intended his art not as an end in itself but as a means to an end, the betterment of human life. He proclaimed his pre-eminent concern with ideas, and with ideas that were "constructive" and practical, and his proudest boast was that he belonged to the company of what he called the "artist-philosophers," those men who, by means of their art, addressed themselves to bringing about a change in the condition of human life. He spoke scornfully of the "pure" artists, those who did not undertake to solve life's problems but were content to represent life as it is, for what merely pleasurable interest the representation might have. Among these he includes Shakespeare, whom he lovingly scolds because "he was utterly bewildered" by life and because his "pregnant observations and demonstrations of life are not co-ordinated into any philosophy or religion."

Yet if we take *The Doctor's Dilemma* quite by itself, without reference to its author's other writings about medicine,[2] and without regard to his characterization of himself as an "artist-philosopher," the effect of the play is really not different from that of a play of Molière's. Many of the specific ideas expounded in Shaw's polemical writings find expression in *The Doctor's Dilemma*, but we feel that they are there for the sake of the comedy rather than that the comedy was written to serve them. Such conclusions as we may draw from the play are not about medicine at all; they are, rather, about "life," and do not seem different in kind from the conclusions that Molière's plays frequently yield—that Nature and common sense are good and should guide our judg-

---

[2] Notable among them is the lengthy preface which Shaw wrote for the play when it was published in 1911. The large canon of what Shaw wrote about medicine over his lifetime is fully reviewed in Roger Boxill's admirable *Shaw and the Doctors,* a Columbia University dissertation.

ment; that committing oneself to a ruling idea goes against Nature and common sense and leads to error or defeat or ridicule, or all three; that a genial flexibility of mind is a virtue, and that intellectual pride is a vice; that thinking in the terms prescribed by one's profession leads to personal and intellectual deformation; that true morality transcends moralistic judgment; that affectionate and charitable emotions are to be cherished, self-seeking motives to be condemned. Comedy has traditionally permitted us to derive just such generalizations from its laughter. They have great charm, and no doubt they serve a good purpose in disposing us to virtue, but they cannot lay claim to great intellectual originality or force. They can scarcely be "co-ordinated into any philosophy or religion"; they are not what we expect of an "artist-philosopher."

In short, *The Doctor's Dilemma,* although it advertises Shaw's ideas about medicine, does not propound them with any great didactic power. On this occasion, the "pure" artist in Shaw seems to have overcome the "artist-philosopher," and the latter cannot have put up a very determined resistance. He would appear to have been quite content to surrender into the hands of undidactic comedy all the ideas he took so seriously in his polemical writings: his doctors are menaces to the public welfare only secondarily and in a way that does not seem to matter or in some aspect other than the one in which they stand before us; we see them as on the whole rather pleasant-natured men, who are to be laughed at for comedy's usual reasons, because they are fools, or monomaniacs, or self-deceivers. And the "artist-philosopher" goes so far in conspiring in his own defeat as to make a hopelessly "pure" artist the spokesman for his cherished vitalism.

Louis Dubedat is the embodiment of an idea that had considerable interest for people at the end of the nineteenth century, as it still does—that art is not required to serve morality, that it exists for its own sake and is thus a paradigm of life itself, which is also said to exist for its own sake, for no other reason than to delight in its own energy and beauty. A corollary is that the artist is not necessarily a virtuous person, that indeed he is typically *not* virtuous and that his indifference or hostility to moral considerations is a condition of his creative power. There is no more truth in this than there was in Ruskin's assertion that only a good man can produce good art, but the new notion of the amoral artist, like the more general idea which it paralleled, served to liberate people from certain rather glum notions about art that prevailed in the Victorian age. Shaw, it may be supposed, stood in an ambivalent relation to the new conception of art and the artist. His moral temper, which he was willing to call Puritan, rejected it; yet at the same time he could respond to it affirmatively because it spoke of the energy, freedom, and beauty that life ought properly to have, and also because it outraged the merely respectable morality of the middle class, which, depressing in itself, stood in the path of ameliorating change.

As an example of the artist who stands outside the considerations of morality, Dubedat is in some ways not an altogether satisfactory creation. His infractions of the moral code are all on a small scale. Almost everything he does is touched with slyness or meanness; petty deceit is his natural medium. He can outdo the doctors themselves in conventionality: there is reason to believe that he is perfectly sincere when he mocks them for supposing that Jennifer is not married to him, for not seeing that she is "a lady" who carries "her marriage certificate in her face and in her character." He is a snob and a prig who can say of the girl he married under false pretenses that he could not stay with her long because she was "quite out of art and literature and refined living." And his stature as an artist is only little greater than as an immoralist; nothing that is said of his work leads us to believe that he is anything more than a brilliant and engaging but quite minor talent.

Dubedat's minuscule quality is in part dictated by the exigencies of comedy. If his stature were larger, if he enlisted our sympathies to a greater extent, his fate would be more moving than would have suited Shaw's purpose. As it is, his utterance of his "creed" on his deathbed creates an effect that, in its ambiguity, is quite in accord with the comic mode. When he folds his hands and affirms his belief "in Michael Angelo, Velasquez, and Rembrandt; in the might of design, the majesty of color, the redemption of all things by Beauty everlasting, and the message of Art that has made these hands blessed," the conscious pathetic eloquence of the speech is meant to mock itself, at least a little, and his subsequent question about the newspaper reporter is an obvious ironic comment on it. Yet for Shaw a creed is always momentous, especially one that speaks of redemption and a blessing, and Dubedat's death-bed avowal of faith makes the vitalistic affirmation of life that is meant to stand as the condemnation of Ridgeon and his mechanistic views.

The character of Ridgeon is puzzling almost to a fault. Upon first acquaintance we like him very much and from the description of him upon his entrance it is plain that Shaw meant that we should. The first check upon this approving opinion appears at the end of the second act, when, with the help of Sir Patrick Cullen, he is confronting his dilemma. Only for a short time is the dilemma allowed to be one of principle: whether to save the honest, decent, but not very useful doctor, Blenkinsop, or the "rotten blackguard" artist, Dubedat, "a genuine source of pretty and pleasant and good things." No sooner has the dilemma been stated in its interesting simplicity than Ridgeon introduces a complication that alters its nature: he discloses to Sir Patrick his desire to marry Dubedat's wife. This frankness we find admirable; by openly stating what he has to gain by allowing Dubedat to die, Ridgeon assures us that he is a man of wholly objective judgment. But our admiration cools when Sir Patrick says, "Perhaps she won't have you, you know," and Ridgeon answers, "I've a pretty good flair for that sort of thing. I know when a woman is interested in me. She is." There is of course no reason why Jennifer should *not* be "interested" in Ridgeon; a woman is likely to have some interested response to a man who is attractive, powerful, and drawn to her. And when, at the end of Act V, Jennifer, who is not exactly a girl, says that she had never been interested in him because he was too old—he is fifty—we may well feel that Shaw, in contriving this humiliation for Ridgeon, has made Jennifer trivial and undeveloped. Nonetheless, Ridgeon's answer to Sir Patrick, which is made "with a self-assured shake of the head," is vulgar and fatuous. The moral elevation that Ridgeon seemed about to gain by his frankness is no longer possible.

By the end of Act III, Ridgeon has become a sentimental self-deceiver, convincing himself that the motive for his decision to let Dubedat die is the noble desire to preserve Jennifer's illusions about her husband. In Act IV he speaks in a voice that Dubedat authoritatively describes as "devilish." But these manifestations of his moral decline do not carry conviction; they seem less the result of the character's inner life than of the author's manipulation.

SIX CHARACTERS
IN SEARCH
OF AN AUTHOR
A Comedy in the Making

LUIGI PIRANDELLO
1867–1936

CHARACTERS OF THE COMEDY IN THE MAKING

THE FATHER	THE SON
THE MOTHER	MADAME PACE
THE STEPDAUGHTER	THE BOY ⎱ *These two do*
	THE CHILD ⎰ *not speak*

ACTORS OF THE COMPANY

THE MANAGER	OTHER ACTORS AND ACTRESSES
LEADING LADY	PROPERTY MAN
LEADING MAN	PROMPTER
SECOND LADY LEAD	MACHINIST
L'INGÉNUE	MANAGER'S SECRETARY
JUVENILE LEAD	DOORKEEPER
	SCENE SHIFTERS

Daytime: The Stage of a Theater

ACT I

N.B. *The Comedy is without acts or scenes. The performance is interrupted once, without the curtain being lowered, when the* MANAGER *and the chief characters withdraw to arrange the scenario. A second interruption of the action takes place when, by mistake, the stage hands let the curtain down.*

The spectators will find the curtain raised and the stage as it usually is during the daytime. It will be half dark, and empty, so that from the beginning the public may have the impression of an impromptu performance.

PROMPTER's *box and a small table and chair for the* MANAGER.

Two other small tables and several chairs scattered about as during rehearsals.

The ACTORS *and* ACTRESSES *of the company enter from the back of the stage:*

First one, then another, then two together: nine or ten in all. They are about to rehearse a Pirandello play: Mixing It Up. *Some of the company move off towards their dressing rooms. The* PROMPTER *who has the "book" under his arm, is waiting for the* MANAGER *in order to begin the rehearsal.*

The ACTORS *and* ACTRESSES, *some standing, some sitting, chat and smoke. One perhaps reads a paper; another cons his part.*

Finally, the MANAGER *enters and goes to the table prepared for him. His* SECRETARY *brings him his mail, through which he glances. The* PROMPTER *takes his seat, turns on a light, and opens the "book."*

THE MANAGER [*throwing a letter down on the table*]. I can't see. [*To* PROPERTY MAN.] Let's have a little light, please!

PROPERTY MAN. Yes sir, yes, at once. [*A light comes down on to the stage.*]

THE MANAGER [*clapping his hands*]. Come along! Come along! Second act of *Mixing It Up*. [*Sits down.*]

[*The* ACTORS *and* ACTRESSES *go from the front of the stage to the wings, all except the three who are to begin the rehearsal.*]

THE PROMPTER [*reading the "book"*]. "Leo Gala's house. A curious room serving as dining-room and study."

THE MANAGER [*to* PROPERTY MAN]. Fix up the old red room.

PROPERTY MAN [*noting it down*]. Red set. All right!

THE PROMPTER [*continuing to read from the "book"*]. "Table already laid and writing desk with books and papers. Bookshelves. Exit rear to Leo's bedroom. Exit left to kitchen. Principal exit to right."

THE MANAGER [*energetically*]. Well, you understand: The principal exit over there; here the kitchen. [*Turning to* ACTOR *who is to play the part of* Socrates.] You make your entrances and exits here. [*To* PROPERTY MAN.] The baize doors at the rear, and curtains.

PROPERTY MAN [*noting it down*]. Right-o!

PROMPTER [*reading as before*]. "When the curtain rises, Leo Gala, dressed in cook's cap and apron is busy beating an egg in a cup. Philip, also dressed as a cook, is beating another egg. Guido Venanzi is seated and listening."

LEADING MAN [*to* MANAGER]. Excuse me, but must I absolutely wear a cook's cap?

THE MANAGER [*annoyed*]. I imagine so. It says so there anyway. [*Pointing to the "book."*]

LEADING MAN. But it's ridiculous!

THE MANAGER. Ridiculous? Ridiculous? Is it my fault if France won't send us any more good comedies, and we are reduced to putting on Pirandello's works, where nobody understands anything, and where the author plays the fool with us all? [*The* ACTORS *grin. The* MANAGER *goes to* LEADING MAN *and shouts.*] Yes sir, you put on the cook's cap and beat eggs. Do you suppose that with all this egg-beating business you are on an ordinary stage? Get that out of your head. You represent the shell of the eggs you are beating! [*Laughter and comments among the* ACTORS.] Silence! and listen to my explanations, please! [*To* LEADING MAN.] "The empty form of reason without the fullness of instinct, which is blind"—You stand for reason, your wife is instinct. It's a mixing up of the parts, according to which you who act your own part become the puppet of yourself. Do you understand?

LEADING MAN. I'm hanged if I do.

THE MANAGER. Neither do I. But let's get on with it. It's sure to be a glorious failure anyway. [*Confidentially.*] But I say, please face three-quarters. Otherwise, what with the abstruseness of the dialogue, and the public that won't be able to hear you, the whole thing will go to hell. Come on! come on!

PROMPTER. Pardon sir, may I get into my box? There's a bit of a draught.

THE MANAGER. Yes, yes, of course!

[*At this point, the* DOORKEEPER *has entered from the stage door and advances towards the* MANAGER's *table, taking off his braided cap. During this manœuver, the* SIX CHARACTERS *enter, and stop by the door at back of stage, so that when the* DOORKEEPER *is about to announce their coming to the* MANAGER, *they are already on the stage. A tenuous light surrounds them, almost as if irradiated by them—the faint breath of their fantastic reality.*

This light will disappear when they come forward towards the ACTORS. *They preserve, however, something of the dream lightness in which they seem almost suspended; but this does not detract from the essential reality of their forms and expressions.*

He who is known as the FATHER *is a man of about 50: hair, reddish in color, thin at the temples; he is not bald, however; thick moustaches, falling over his still fresh mouth, which often opens in an empty and uncertain smile. He is fattish, pale; with an especially wide forehead. He has blue, oval-shaped eyes, very clear and piercing. Wears light trousers and a dark jacket. He is alternately mellifluous and violent in his manner.*

The MOTHER *seems crushed and terrified as if by an intolerable weight of shame and abasement. She is dressed in modest black and wears a thick widow's veil of crêpe. When she lifts this, she reveals a wax-like face. She always keeps her eyes downcast.*

The STEPDAUGHTER *is dashing, almost impudent, beautiful. She wears mourning too, but with great elegance. She shows contempt for the timid half-frightened manner of the wretched* BOY (*14 years old, and also dressed in black*); *on the other hand, she displays a lively tenderness for her little sister, the* CHILD (*about four*), *who is dressed in white, with a black silk sash at the waist.*

The SON (*22*) *tall, severe in his attitude of contempt for the* FATHER, *supercilious and indifferent to the* MOTHER. *He looks as if he had come on the stage against his will.*]

DOORKEEPER [*cap in hand*]. Excuse me, sir . . .

THE MANAGER [*rudely*]. Eh? What is it?

DOORKEEPER [*timidly*]. These people are asking for you, sir.

THE MANAGER [*furious*]. I am rehearsing, and you know perfectly well no one's allowed to come in during rehearsals! [*Turning to the* CHARACTERS.] Who are you, please? What do you want?

THE FATHER [*coming forward a little, followed by the others who seem embarrassed*]. As a matter of fact . . . we have come here in search of an author. . . .

THE MANAGER [*half angry, half amazed*]. An author? What author?

THE FATHER. Any author, sir.

THE MANAGER. But there's no author here. We are not rehearsing a new piece.

THE STEPDAUGHTER [*vivaciously*]. So much the better, so much the better! We can be your new piece.

AN ACTOR [*coming forward from the others*]. Oh, do you hear that?

THE FATHER [*to* STEPDAUGHTER]. Yes, but if the author isn't here . . . [*to* MANAGER.] . . . unless you would be willing . . .

THE MANAGER. You are trying to be funny.

THE FATHER. No, for Heaven's sake, what are you saying? We bring you a drama, sir.

THE STEPDAUGHTER. We may be your fortune.

THE MANAGER. Will you oblige me by going away? We haven't time to waste with mad people.

THE FATHER [*mellifluously*]. Oh sir, you know well that life is full of infinite absurdities, which, strangely enough, do not even need to appear plausible, since they are true.

THE MANAGER. What the devil is he talking about?

THE FATHER. I say that to reverse the ordinary process may well be considered a madness: that is, to create credible situations, in order that they may appear true. But permit me to observe that if this be madness, it is the sole *raison d'être* of your profession, gentlemen. [*The* ACTORS *look hurt and perplexed.*]

THE MANAGER [*getting up and looking at him*]. So our profession seems to you one worthy of madmen then?

THE FATHER. Well, to make seem true that which isn't true . . . without any need . . . for a joke as it were . . . Isn't that your mission, gentlemen: to give life to fantastic characters on the stage?

THE MANAGER [*interpreting the rising anger of the* COMPANY]. But I would beg you to believe, my dear sir, that the profession of the comedian is a noble one. If today, as things go, the playwrights give us stupid comedies to play and puppets to represent instead of men, remember we are proud to have given life to immortal works here on these very boards! [*The* ACTORS, *satisfied, applaud their* MANAGER.]

THE FATHER [*interrupting furiously*]. Exactly, perfectly, to living beings more alive than those who breathe and wear clothes: being less real perhaps, but truer! I agree with you entirely. [*The* ACTORS *look at one another in amazement.*]

THE MANAGER. But what do you mean? Before, you said . . .

THE FATHER. No, excuse me, I meant it for you, sir, who were crying out that you had no time to lose with madmen, while no one better than yourself knows that nature uses the instrument of human fantasy in order to pursue her high creative purpose.

THE MANAGER. Very well—but where does all this take us?

THE FATHER. Nowhere! It is merely to show you that one is born to life in many forms, in many shapes, as tree, or as stone, as water, as butterfly, or as woman. So one may also be born a character in a play.

THE MANAGER [*with feigned comic dismay*]. So you and these other friends of yours have been born characters?

THE FATHER. Exactly, and alive as you see! [MANAGER *and* ACTORS *burst out laughing.*]

THE FATHER [*hurt*]. I am sorry you laugh, because we carry in us a drama, as you can guess from this woman here veiled in black.

THE MANAGER [*losing patience at last and almost indignant*]. Oh, chuck it! Get away please! Clear out of here! [*To* PROPERTY MAN.] For Heaven's sake, turn them out!

THE FATHER [*resisting*]. No, no, look here, we . . .

THE MANAGER [*roaring*]. We come here to work, you know.

LEADING ACTOR. One cannot let oneself be made such a fool of.

THE FATHER [*determined, coming forward*]. I marvel at your incredulity, gentlemen. Are you not accustomed to see the characters created by an author spring to life in yourselves and face each other? Just because there is no "book" [*pointing to the* PROMPTER's *box.*] which contains us, you refuse to believe . . .

THE STEPDAUGHTER [*advances towards* MANAGER, *smiling and coquettish*]. Believe me, we are really six most interesting characters, sir; side-tracked however.

THE FATHER. Yes, that is the word! [*To* MANAGER *all at once.*] In the sense, that is, that the author who created us alive no longer wished, or was no longer able, materially to put us into a work of art. And this was a real crime, sir; because he who has had the luck to be born a character can laugh even at death. He cannot die. The man, the writer, the instrument of the creation will die, but his creation does not die. And to live for ever, it does not need to have extraordinary gifts or to be able to work wonders. Who was Sancho Panza? Who was Don Abbondio? Yet they live eternally because—live germs as they were—they had the fortune to find a fecundating matrix, a fantasy which could raise and nourish them: make them live for ever!

THE MANAGER. That is quite all right. But what do you want here, all of you?

THE FATHER. We want to live.

THE MANAGER [*ironically*]. For Eternity?

THE FATHER. No, sir, only for a moment . . . in you.

AN ACTOR. Just listen to him!

LEADING LADY. They want to live, in us! . . .

JUVENILE LEAD [*pointing to the* STEPDAUGHTER]. I've no objection, as far as that one is concerned!

THE FATHER.   Look here! Look here! The comedy has to be made. [*To the* MANAGER.] But if you and your actors are willing, we can soon concert it among ourselves.

THE MANAGER [*annoyed*].   But what do you want to concert? We don't go in for concerts here. Here we play dramas and comedies!

THE FATHER.   Exactly! That is just why we have come to you.

THE MANAGER.   And where is the "book"?

THE FATHER.   It is in us! [*The* ACTORS *laugh*.] The drama is in us, and we are the drama. We are impatient to play it. Our inner passion drives us on to this.

THE STEPDAUGHTER [*disdainful, alluring, treacherous, full of impudence*]. My passion, sir! Ah, if you only knew! My passion for him! [*Points to the* FATHER *and makes a pretence of embracing him. Then she breaks out into a loud laugh.*]

THE FATHER [*angrily*].   Behave yourself! And please don't laugh in that fashion.

THE STEPDAUGHTER.   With your permission, gentlemen, I, who am a two months' orphan, will show you how I can dance and sing. [*Sings and then dances* "Prenez garde à Tchou-Tchin-Tchou."]

> Les chinois sont un peuple malin,
> De Shanghai à Pékin,
> Ils ont mis des écriteaux partout:
> Prenez garde à Tchou-Tchin-Tchou.[1]

ACTORS *and* ACTRESSES.   Bravo! Well done! Tip-top!

THE MANAGER.   Silence! This isn't a café concert, you know! [*Turning to the* FATHER *in consternation*.] Is she mad?

THE FATHER.   Mad? No, she's worse than mad.

THE STEPDAUGHTER [*to* MANAGER].   Worse? Worse? Listen! Stage this drama for us at once! Then you will see that at a certain moment I . . . when this little darling here . . . [*Takes the* CHILD *by the hand and leads her to the* MANAGER.] Isn't she a dear? [*Takes her up and kisses her.*] Darling! Darling! [*Puts her down again and adds feelingly.*] Well, when God suddenly takes this dear little child away from that poor mother there; and this imbecile here [*seizing hold of the* BOY *roughly and pushing him forward*] does the stupidest things, like the fool he is, you will see me run away. Yes, gentlemen, I shall be off. But the moment hasn't arrived yet. After what has taken place between him and me [*indicates the* FATHER *with a horrible wink*] I can't remain any longer in this society, to have to witness the anguish of this mother here for that fool . . . [*Indicates the* SON.] Look at him! Look at him! See how indifferent, how frigid he is, because he is the legitimate son. He despises me, despises him [*pointing to the* BOY], despises this baby here; because . . . we are bastards. [*Goes to the* MOTHER *and embraces her.*] And he doesn't want to recognize her as his mother —she who is the common mother of us all. He looks down upon her as if she were only the mother of us three bastards. Wretch! [*She says all this very*

[1] The Chinese are clever people,
From Shanghai to Peking,
They've put billboards everywhere:
Hearken to Tchou-Tchin-Tchou.
    (French ditty)

rapidly, excitedly. At the word "bastards" she raises her voice, and almost spits out the final "Wretch!"]

THE MOTHER [to the MANAGER, in anguish]. In the name of these two little children, I beg you . . . [She grows faint and is about to fall.] Oh God!

THE FATHER [coming forward to support her as do some of the ACTORS]. Quick a chair, a chair for this poor widow!

THE ACTORS. Is it true? Has she really fainted?

THE MANAGER. Quick, a chair! Here!

[One of the ACTORS brings a chair, the others proffer assistance. The MOTHER tries to prevent the FATHER from lifting the veil which covers her face.]

THE FATHER. Look at her! Look at her!

THE MOTHER. No, stop; stop it please!

THE FATHER [raising her veil]. Let them see you!

THE MOTHER [rising and covering her face with her hands, in desperation]. I beg you, sir, to prevent this man from carrying out his plan which is loathsome to me.

THE MANAGER [dumbfounded]. I don't understand at all. What is the situation? Is this lady your wife? [To the FATHER.]

THE FATHER. Yes, gentlemen: my wife!

THE MANAGER. But how can she be a widow if you are alive? [The ACTORS find relief for their astonishment in a loud laugh.]

THE FATHER. Don't laugh! Don't laugh like that, for Heaven's sake. Her drama lies just here in this: she has had a lover, a man who ought to be here.

THE MOTHER [with a cry]. No! No!

THE STEPDAUGHTER. Fortunately for her, he is dead. Two months ago as I said. We are in mourning, as you see.

THE FATHER. He isn't here you see, not because he is dead. He isn't here —look at her a moment and you will understand—because her drama isn't a drama of the love of two men for whom she was incapable of feeling anything except possibly a little gratitude—gratitude not for me but for the other. She isn't a woman, she is a mother, and her drama—powerful sir, I assure you—lies, as a matter of fact, all in these four children she has had by two men.

THE MOTHER. I had them? Have you got the courage to say that I wanted them? [To the COMPANY.] It was his doing. It was he who gave me that other man, who forced me to go away with him.

THE STEPDAUGHTER. It isn't true.

THE MOTHER [startled]. Not true, isn't it?

THE STEPDAUGHTER. No, it isn't true, it just isn't true.

THE MOTHER. And what can you know about it?

THE STEPDAUGHTER. It isn't true. Don't believe it. [To MANAGER] Do you know why she says so? For that fellow there. [Indicates the SON.] She tortures herself, destroys herself on account of the neglect of that son there; and she wants him to believe that if she abandoned him when he was only two years old, it was because he [indicates the FATHER] made her do so.

THE MOTHER [vigorously]. He forced me to it, and I call God to witness it. [To the MANAGER.] Ask him [indicates the FATHER] if it isn't true. Let him speak. You [to DAUGHTER] are not in a position to know anything about it.

THE STEPDAUGHTER. I know you lived in peace and happiness with my father while he lived. Can you deny it?

THE MOTHER. No, I don't deny it . . .

THE STEPDAUGHTER. He was always full of affection and kindness for you. [*To the* BOY, *angrily*.] It's true, isn't it? Tell them! Why don't you speak, you little fool?

THE MOTHER. Leave the poor boy alone. Why do you want to make me appear ungrateful, daughter? I don't want to offend your father. I have answered him that I didn't abandon my house and my son through any fault of mine, nor from any wilful passion.

THE FATHER. It is true. It was my doing.

LEADING MAN [*to the* COMPANY]. What a spectacle!

LEADING LADY. We are the audience this time.

JUVENILE LEAD. For once, in a way.

THE MANAGER [*beginning to get really interested*]. Let's hear them out. Listen!

THE SON. Oh yes, you're going to hear a fine bit now. He will talk to you of the Demon of Experiment.

THE FATHER. You are a cynical imbecile. I've told you so already a hundred times. [*To the* MANAGER.] He tries to make fun of me on account of this expression which I have found to excuse myself with.

THE SON [*with disgust*]. Yes, phrases! phrases!

THE FATHER. Phrases! Isn't everyone consoled when faced with a trouble or fact he doesn't understand, by a word, some simple word, which tells us nothing and yet calms us?

THE STEPDAUGHTER. Even in the case of remorse. In fact, especially then.

THE FATHER. Remorse? No, that isn't true. I've done more than use words to quieten the remorse in me.

THE STEPDAUGHTER. Yes, there was a bit of money too. Yes, yes, a bit of money. There were the hundred lire he was about to offer me in payment, gentlemen. . . . [*Sensation of horror among the* ACTORS.]

THE SON [*to the* STEPDAUGHTER]. This is vile.

THE STEPDAUGHTER. Vile? There they were in a pale blue envelope on a little mahogany table in the back of Madame Pace's shop. You know Madame Pace—one of those ladies who attract poor girls of good family into their ateliers, under the pretext of their selling *robes et manteaux.*[2]

THE SON. And he thinks he has bought the right to tyrannize over us all with those hundred lire he was going to pay; but which, fortunately—note this, gentlemen—he had no chance of paying.

THE STEPDAUGHTER. It was a near thing, though, you know! [*Laughs ironically*.]

THE MOTHER [*protesting*]. Shame, my daughter, shame!

THE STEPDAUGHTER. Shame indeed! This is my revenge! I am dying to live that scene. . . . The room . . . I see it . . . Here is the window with the mantles exposed, there the divan, the looking-glass, a screen, there in front of the window the little mahogany table with the blue envelope containing one hundred lire. I see it. I see it. I could take hold of it . . . But you, gentlemen, you ought to turn your backs now: I am almost nude, you know. But I don't blush: I leave that to him [*indicating the* FATHER].

[2] (French) Dresses and coats.

THE MANAGER. I don't understand this at all.

THE FATHER. Naturally enough. I would ask you, sir, to exercise your authority a little here, and let me speak before you believe all she is trying to blame me with. Let me explain.

THE STEPDAUGHTER. Ah yes, explain it in your own way.

THE FATHER. But don't you see that the whole trouble lies here. In words, words. Each one of us has within him a whole world of things, each man of us his own special world. And how can we ever come to an understanding if I put in the words I utter the sense and value of things as I see them; while you who listen to me must inevitably translate them according to the conception of things each one of you has within himself. We think we understand each other, but we never really do. Look here! This woman [*indicating the* MOTHER] takes all my pity for her as a specially ferocious form of cruelty.

THE MOTHER. But you drove me away.

THE FATHER. Do you hear her? I drove her away! She believes I really sent her away.

THE MOTHER. You know how to talk, and I don't; but, believe me, sir [*to* MANAGER], after he had married me . . . who knows why? . . . I was a poor insignificant woman . . .

THE FATHER. But, good Heaven! it was just for your humility that I married you. I loved this simplicity in you. [*He stops when he sees she makes signs to contradict him, opens his arms wide in sign of desperation, seeing how hopeless it is to make himself understood.*] You see she denies it. Her mental deafness, believe me, is phenomenal, the limit [*touches his forehead*]: deaf, deaf, mentally deaf! She has plenty of feeling. Oh yes, a good heart for the children; but the brain—deaf, to the point of desperation—!

THE STEPDAUGHTER. Yes, but ask him how his intelligence has helped us.

THE FATHER. If we could see all the evil that may spring from good, what should we do? [*At this point the* LEADING LADY *who is biting her lips with rage at seeing the* LEADING MAN *flirting with the* STEPDAUGHTER, *comes forward and says to the* MANAGER]

LEADING LADY. Excuse me, but are we going tò rehearse today?

MANAGER. Of course, of course; but let's hear them out.

JUVENILE LEAD. This is something quite new.

L'INGÉNUE. Most interesting!

LEADING LADY. Yes, for the people who like that kind of thing. [*Casts a glance at* LEADING MAN.]

THE MANAGER [*to* FATHER]. You must please explain yourself quite clearly. [*Sits down.*]

THE FATHER. Very well then: listen! I had in my service a poor man, a clerk, a secretary of mine, full of devotion, who became friends with her. [*Indicating the* MOTHER.] They understood one another, were kindred souls in fact, without, however, the least suspicion of any evil existing. They were incapable even of thinking of it.

THE STEPDAUGHTER. So he thought of it—for them!

THE FATHER. That's not true. I meant to do good to them—and to myself, I confess, at the same time. Things had come to the point that I could not say a word to either of them without their making a mute appeal, one to the other, with their eyes. I could see them silently asking each other how I was to be kept in countenance, how I was to be kept quiet. And this, believe me, was just about enough of itself to keep me in a constant rage, to exasperate me beyond measure.

THE MANAGER. And why didn't you send him away then—this secretary of yours?

THE FATHER. Precisely what I did, sir. And then I had to watch this poor woman drifting forlornly about the house like an animal without a master, like an animal one has taken in out of pity.

THE MOTHER. Ah yes! . . .

THE FATHER [*suddenly turning to the* MOTHER]. It's true about the son anyway, isn't it?

THE MOTHER. He took my son away from me first of all.

THE FATHER. But not from cruelty. I did it so that he should grow up healthy and strong by living in the country.

THE STEPDAUGHTER [*pointing to him ironically*]. As one can see.

THE FATHER [*quickly*]. Is it my fault if he has grown up like this? I sent him to a wet nurse in the country, a peasant, as *she* did not seem to me strong enough, though she is of humble origin. That was, anyway, the reason I married her. Unpleasant all this may be, but how can it be helped? My mistake possibly, but there we are! All my life I have had these confounded aspirations towards a certain moral sanity. [*At this point the* STEPDAUGHTER *bursts out into a noisy laugh.*] Oh, stop it! Stop it! I can't stand it.

THE MANAGER. Yes, please stop it, for Heaven's sake.

THE STEPDAUGHTER. But imagine moral sanity from him, if you please— the client of certain ateliers like that of Madame Pace!

THE FATHER. Fool! That is the proof that I am a man! This seeming contradiction, gentlemen, is the strongest proof that I stand here a live man before you. Why, it is just for this very incongruity in my nature that I have had to suffer what I have. I could not live by the side of that woman [*indicating the* MOTHER] any longer; but not so much for the boredom she inspired me with as for the pity I felt for her.

THE MOTHER. And so he turned me out—.

THE FATHER. —well provided for! Yes, I sent her to that man, gentlemen . . . to let her go free of me.

THE MOTHER. And to free himself.

THE FATHER. Yes, I admit it. It was also a liberation for me. But great evil has come of it. I meant well when I did it; and I did it more for her sake than mine. I swear it. [*Crosses his arms on his chest; then turns suddenly to the* MOTHER.] Did I ever lose sight of you until that other man carried you off to another town, like the angry fool he was? And on account of my pure interest in you . . . my pure interest, I repeat, that had no base motive in it . . . I watched with the tenderest concern the new family that grew up around her. She can bear witness to this. [*Points to the* STEPDAUGHTER.]

THE STEPDAUGHTER. Oh yes, that's true enough. When I was a kiddie, so so high, you know, with plaits over my shoulders and knickers longer than my skirts, I used to see him waiting outside the school for me to come out. He came to see how I was growing up.

THE FATHER. This is infamous, shameful!

THE STEPDAUGHTER. No. Why?

THE FATHER. Infamous! Infamous! [*Then excitedly to* MANAGER, *explaining.*] After she [*indicating* MOTHER] went away, my house seemed suddenly empty. She was my incubus, but she filled my house. I was like a dazed fly alone in the empty rooms. This boy here [*indicating the* SON] was educated away from home, and when he came back, he seemed to me to be no more mine. With no mother to stand between him and me, he grew up entirely for himself, on his own, apart, with no tie of intellect or affection binding him to me. And then—strange but true—I was driven, by curiosity at first and then by some tender sentiment, towards her family, which had come into being through my will. The thought of her began gradually to fill up the emptiness I felt all around me. I wanted to know if she were happy in living out the simple daily duties of life. I wanted to think of her as fortunate and happy because far away from the complicated torments of my spirit. And so, to have proof of this, I used to watch that child coming out of school.

THE STEPDAUGHTER. Yes, yes. True. He used to follow me in the street and smiled at me, waved his hand, like this. I would look at him with interest, wondering who he might be. I told my mother, who guessed at once. [*The* MOTHER *agrees with a nod.*] Then she didn't want to send me to school for some days; and when I finally went back, there he was again—looking so ridiculous—with a paper parcel in his hands. He came close to me, caressed me, and drew out a fine straw hat from the parcel, with a bouquet of flowers—all for me!

THE MANAGER. A bit discursive this, you know!

THE SON [*contemptuously*]. Literature! Literature!

THE FATHER. Literature indeed! This is life, this is passion!

THE MANAGER. It may be, but it won't act.

THE FATHER. I agree. This is only the part leading up. I don't suggest this should be staged. She [*pointing to the* STEPDAUGHTER], as you see, is no longer the flapper with plaits down her back—.

THE STEPDAUGHTER. —and the knickers showing below the skirt!

THE FATHER. The drama is coming now, sir; something new, complex, most interesting.

THE STEPDAUGHTER. As soon as my father died . . .

THE FATHER. —there was absolute misery for them. They came back here, unknown to me. Through her stupidity! [*Pointing to the* MOTHER.] It is true she can barely write her own name; but she could anyhow have got her daughter to write to me that they were in need. . . .

THE MOTHER. And how was I to divine all this sentiment in him?

THE FATHER. That is exactly your mistake, never to have guessed any of my sentiments.

THE MOTHER. After so many years apart, and all that had happened . . .

THE FATHER. Was it my fault if that fellow carried you away? It happened quite suddenly; for after he had obtained some job or other, I could find no trace of them; and so, not unnaturally, my interest in them dwindled. But the drama culminated unforeseen and violent on their return, when I was impelled by my miserable flesh that still lives . . . Ah! what misery, what wretchedness is that of the man who is alone and disdains debasing *liaisons!* Not old enough to do without women, and not young enough to go and look for one without shame. Misery? It's worse than misery; it's a horror; for no woman can any longer give him love; and when a man feels this . . . One ought to do without, you say? Yes, yes, I know. Each of us when he appears before his fellows is clothed in a certain dignity. But every man knows what unconfessable things pass within the secrecy of his own heart. One gives way to the temptation, only to rise from it again, afterwards, with a great eagerness to reestablish one's dignity, as if it were a tombstone to place on the grave of one's shame, and a monument to hide and sign the memory of our weaknesses. Everybody's in the same case. Some folks haven't the courage to say certain things, that's all!

THE STEPDAUGHTER. All appear to have the courage to do them though.

THE FATHER. Yes, but in secret. Therefore, you want more courage to say these things. Let a man but speak these things out, and folks at once label him a cynic. But it isn't true. He is like all the others, better indeed, because he isn't afraid to reveal with the light of the intelligence the red shame of human bestiality on which most men close their eyes so as not to see it. Woman—for example, look at her case! She turns tantalizing inviting glances on you. You seize her. No sooner does she feel herself in your grasp than she closes her eyes. It is the sign of her mission, the sign by which she says to man: "Blind yourself, for I am blind."

THE STEPDAUGHTER. Sometimes she can close them no more: when she no longer feels the need of hiding her shame to herself, but dry-eyed and dispassionately, sees only that of the man who has blinded himself without love. Oh, all these intellectual complications make me sick, disgust me—all his philosophy that uncovers the beast in man, and then seeks to save him, excuse him . . . I can't stand it, sir. When a man seeks to "simplify" life bestially, throwing aside every relic of humanity, every chaste aspiration, every pure feeling, all sense of ideality, duty, modesty, shame . . . then nothing is more revolting and nauseous than a certain kind of remorse—crocodiles' tears, that's what it is.

THE MANAGER. Let's come to the point. This is only discussion.

THE FATHER. Very good, sir! But a fact is like a sack which won't stand up when it is empty. In order that it may stand up, one has to put into it the reason and sentiment which have caused it to exist. I couldn't possibly know that after the death of that man, they had decided to return here, that they were in misery, and that she [*pointing to the* MOTHER] had gone to work as a modiste, and at a shop of the type of that of Madame Pace.

THE STEPDAUGHTER. A real high-class modiste, you must know, gentlemen. In appearance, she works for the leaders of the best society; but she arranges matters so that these elegant ladies serve her purpose . . . without prejudice to other ladies who are . . . well . . . only so so.

THE MOTHER. You will believe me, gentlemen, that it never entered my mind that the old hag offered me work because she had her eye on my daughter.

THE STEPDAUGHTER. Poor mamma! Do you know, sir, what that woman did when I brought her back the work my mother had finished? She would point out to me that I had torn one of my frocks, and she would give it back to my mother to mend. It was I who paid for it, always I; while this poor creature here believed she was sacrificing herself for me and these two children here, sitting up at night sewing Madame Pace's robes.

THE MANAGER. And one day you met there . . .

THE STEPDAUGHTER. Him, him. Yes, sir, an old client. There's a scene for you to play! Superb!

THE FATHER.   She, the Mother arrived just then . . .

THE STEPDAUGHTER [*treacherously*].   Almost in time!

THE FATHER [*crying out*].   No, in time! in time! Fortunately I recognized her . . . in time. And I took them back home with me to my house. You can imagine now her position and mine: she, as you see her; and I who cannot look her in the face.

THE STEPDAUGHTER.   Absurd! How can I possibly be expected—after that —to be a modest young miss, a fit person to go with his confounded aspirations for "a solid moral sanity"?

THE FATHER.   For the drama lies all in this—in the conscience that I have, that each one of us has. We believe this conscience to be a single thing, but it is many-sided. There is one for this person, and another for that. Diverse consciences. So we have this illusion of being one person for all, of having a personality that is unique in all our acts. But it isn't true. We perceive this when, tragically perhaps, in something we do, we are, as it were, suspended, caught up in the air on a kind of hook. Then we perceive that all of us was not in that act, and that it would be an atrocious injustice to judge us by that action alone, as if all our existence were summed up in that one deed. Now do you understand the perfidy of this girl? She surprised me in a place, where she ought not to have known me, just as I could not exist for her; and she now seeks to attach to me a reality such as I could never suppose I should have to assume for her in a shameful and fleeting moment of my life. I feel this above all else. And the drama, you will see, acquires a tremendous value from this point. Then there is the position of the others . . . his . . . [*Indicating the* SON.]

THE SON [*shrugging his shoulders scornfully*].   Leave me alone! I don't come into this.

THE FATHER.   What? You don't come into this?

THE SON.   I've got nothing to do with it, and don't want to have; because you know well enough I wasn't made to be mixed up in all this with the rest of you.

THE STEPDAUGHTER.   We are only vulgar folk! He is the fine gentleman. You may have noticed, Mr. Manager, that I fix him now and again with a look of scorn while he lowers his eyes—for he knows the evil he has done me.

THE SON [*scarcely looking at her*].   I?

THE STEPDAUGHTER.   You! you! I owe my life on the streets to you. Did you or did you not deny us, with your behavior, I won't say the intimacy of home, but even that mere hospitality which makes guests feel at their ease? We were intruders who had come to disturb the kingdom of your legitimacy. I should like to have you witness, Mr. Manager, certain scenes between him and me. He says I have tyrannized over everyone. But it was just his behavior which made me insist on the reason for which I had come into the house—this reason he calls "vile"—into his house, with my mother who is his mother too. And I came as mistress of the house.

THE SON.   It's easy for them to put me always in the wrong. But imagine, gentlemen, the position of a son, whose fate it is to see arrive one day at his home a young woman of impudent bearing, a young woman who inquires for his father, with whom who knows what business she has. This young man has then to witness her return bolder than ever, accompanied by that child there. He is obliged to watch her treat his father in an equivocal and confidential manner. She asks money of him in a way that lets one suppose he must give it her, *must*, do you understand, because he has every obligation to do so.

THE FATHER. But I have, as a matter of fact, this obligation. I owe it to your mother.

THE SON. How should I know? When had I ever seen or heard of her? One day there arrive with her [*indicating* STEPDAUGHTER] that lad and this baby here. I am told: "This is *your* mother too, you know." I divine from her manner [*indicating* STEPDAUGHTER *again*] why it is they have come home. I had rather not say what I feel and think about it. I shouldn't even care to confess to myself. No action can therefore be hoped for from me in this affair. Believe me, Mr. Manager, I am an "unrealized" character, dramatically speaking; and I find myself not at all at ease in their company. Leave me out of it I beg you.

THE FATHER. What? It is just because you are so that . . .

THE SON. How do you know what I am like? When did you ever bother your head about me?

THE FATHER. I admit it. I admit it. But isn't that a situation in itself? This aloofness of yours which is so cruel to me and to your mother, who returns home and sees you almost for the first time grown up, who doesn't recognize you but knows you are her son . . . [*Pointing out the* MOTHER *to the* MANAGER.] See, she's crying!

THE STEPDAUGHTER [*angrily, stamping her foot*]. Like a fool!

THE FATHER [*indicating* STEPDAUGHTER]. She can't stand him you know. [*Then referring again to the* SON.] He says he doesn't come into the affair, whereas he is really the hinge of the whole action. Look at that lad who is always clinging to his mother, frightened and humiliated. It is on account of this fellow here. Possibly his situation is the most painful of all. He feels himself a stranger more than the others. The poor little chap feels mortified, humiliated at being brought into a home out of charity as it were. [*In confidence.*] He is the image of his father. Hardly talks at all. Humble and quiet.

THE MANAGER. Oh, we'll cut him out. You've no notion what a nuisance boys are on the stage . . .

THE FATHER. He disappears soon, you know. And the baby too. She is the first to vanish from the scene. The drama consists finally in this: when that mother re-enters my house, her family born outside of it, and shall we say superimposed on the original, ends with the death of the little girl, the tragedy of the boy and the flight of the elder daughter. It cannot go on, because it is foreign to its surroundings. So after much torment, we three remain: I, the mother, that son. Then, owing to the disappearance of that extraneous family, we too find ourselves strange to one another. We find we are living in an atmosphere of mortal desolation which is the revenge, as he [*indicating* SON] scornfully said of the Demon of Experiment, that unfortunately hides in me. Thus, sir, you see when faith is lacking, it becomes impossible to create certain states of happiness, for we lack the necessary humility. Vaingloriously, we try to substitute ourselves for this faith, creating thus for the rest of the world a reality which we believe after this fashion, while, actually, it doesn't exist. For each one of us has his own reality to be respected before God, even when it is harmful to one's very self.

THE MANAGER. There is something in what you say. I assure you all this interests me very much. I begin to think there's the stuff for a drama in all this, and not a bad drama either.

THE STEPDAUGHTER [*coming forward*]. When you've got a character like me.

THE FATHER [*shutting her up, all excited to learn the decision of the* MANAGER]. You be quiet!

THE MANAGER [*reflecting, heedless of interruption*]. It's new . . . hem . . . yes . . .

THE FATHER. Absolutely new!

THE MANAGER. You've got a nerve though, I must say, to come here and fling it at me like this . . .

THE FATHER. You will understand, sir, born as we are for the stage . . .

THE MANAGER. Are you amateur actors then?

THE FATHER. No, I say born for the stage, because . . .

THE MANAGER. Oh, nonsense. You're an old hand, you know.

THE FATHER. No sir, no. We act that rôle for which we have been cast, that rôle which we are given in life. And in my own case, passion itself, as usually happens, becomes a trifle theatrical when it is exalted.

THE MANAGER. Well, well, that will do. But you see, without an author . . . I could give you the address of an author if you like.

THE FATHER. No, no. Look here! You must be the author.

THE MANAGER. I? What are you talking about?

THE FATHER. Yes, you! Why not?

THE MANAGER. Because I have never been an author: that's why.

THE FATHER. Then why not turn author now? Everybody does it. You don't want any special qualities. Your task is made much easier by the fact that we are all here alive before you . . .

THE MANAGER. It won't do.

THE FATHER. What? When you see us live our drama . . .

THE MANAGER. Yes, that's all right. But you want someone to write it.

THE FATHER. No, no. Someone to take it down, possibly, while we play it, scene by scene! It will be enough to sketch it out at first, and then try it over.

THE MANAGER. Well . . . I am almost tempted. It's a bit of an idea. One might have a shot at it.

THE FATHER. Of course. You'll see what scenes will come out of it. I can give you one, at once . . .

THE MANAGER. By Jove, it tempts me. I'd like to have a go at it. Let's try it out. Come with me to my office. [*Turning to the* ACTORS.] You are at liberty for a bit, but don't stop out of the theater for long. In a quarter of an hour, twenty minutes, all back here again! [*To the* FATHER.] We'll see what can be done. Who knows if we don't get something really extraordinary out of it?

THE FATHER. There's no doubt about it. They [*indicating the* CHARACTERS.] had better come with us too, hadn't they?

THE MANAGER. Yes, yes. Come on! come on! [*Moves away and then turning to the* ACTORS.] Be punctual, please! [MANAGER *and the* SIX CHARACTERS *cross the stage and go off. The other* ACTORS *remain, looking at one another in astonishment.*]

LEADING MAN. Is he serious? What the devil does he want to do?

JUVENILE LEAD. This is rank madness.

THIRD ACTOR. Does he expect to knock up a drama in five minutes?

JUVENILE LEAD. Like the improvisers!

LEADING LADY. If he thinks I'm going to take part in a joke like this . . .

JUVENILE LEAD. I'm out of it anyway.

FOURTH ACTOR. I should like to know who they are. [*Alludes to* CHARACTERS.]

THIRD ACTOR. What do you suppose? Madmen or rascals!

JUVENILE LEAD. And he takes them seriously!

L'INGÉNUE. Vanity! He fancies himself as an author now.

LEADING MAN. It's absolutely unheard of. If the stage has come to this . . . well I'm . . .

FIFTH ACTOR. It's rather a joke.

THIRD ACTOR. Well, we'll see what's going to happen next.

[*Thus talking, the* ACTORS *leave the stage; some going out by the little door at the back; others retiring to their dressing-rooms.*

The curtain remains up.

The action of the play is suspended for twenty minutes.]

ACT II

The stage call-bells ring to warn the company that the play is about to begin again.

THE STEPDAUGHTER *comes out of the* MANAGER's *office along with the* CHILD *and the* BOY. *As she comes out of the office, she cries:* Nonsense! Nonsense! Do it yourselves! I'm not going to mix myself up in this mess. [*Turning to the* CHILD *and coming quickly with her on to the stage.*] Come on, Rosetta, let's run!

[*The* BOY *follows them slowly, remaining a little behind and seeming perplexed.*]

THE STEPDAUGHTER [*stops, bends over the* CHILD *and takes the latter's face between her hands*]. My little darling! You're frightened, aren't you? You don't know where you are, do you? [*Pretending to reply to a question of the* CHILD.] What is the stage? It's a place, baby, you know, where people play at being serious, a place where they act comedies. We've got to act a comedy now, dead serious, you know; and you're in it also, little one. [*Embraces her, pressing the little head to her breast, and rocking the* CHILD *for a moment.*] Oh darling, darling, what a horrid comedy you've got to play! What a wretched part they've found for you! A garden . . . a fountain . . . look . . . just suppose, kiddie, it's here. Where, you say? Why, right here in the middle. It's all pretence you know. That's the trouble, my pet: it's all make-believe here. It's better to imagine it though, because if they fix it up for you, it'll only be painted cardboard, painted cardboard for the rockery, the water, the plants . . . Ah, but I think a baby like this one would sooner have a make-believe fountain than a real one, so she could play with it. What a joke it'll be for the others! But for you, alas! not quite such a joke: you who are real, baby dear, and really play by a real fountain that is big and green and beautiful, with ever so many bamboos around it that are reflected in the water, and a whole lot of little ducks swimming about . . . No, Rosetta, no, your mother doesn't bother about you on account of that wretch of a son there. I'm in the devil of a temper, and as for that lad . . . [*Seizes* BOY *by the arm to force him to take one of his hands out of his pockets.*] What have you got there? What are you hiding? [*Pulls his hand out of his pocket, looks into it and catches the glint of a revolver.*] Ah, where did you get this? [*The* BOY, *very pale in the face, looks at her, but does not answer.*] Idiot! If I'd been in your place, instead of killing myself, I'd have shot one of those two, or both of them: father and son.

[*The* FATHER *enters from the office, all excited from his work. The* MANAGER *follows him.*]

THE FATHER. Come on, come on, dear! Come here for a minute! We've arranged everything. It's all fixed up.

THE MANAGER [*also excited*]. If you please, young lady, there are one or two points to settle still. Will you come along?

THE STEPDAUGHTER [*following him towards the office*]. Ouff! what's the good, if you've arranged everything.

[*The* FATHER, MANAGER *and* STEPDAUGHTER *go back into the office again (off) for a moment. At the same time, the* SON, *followed by the* MOTHER, *comes out.*]

THE SON [*looking at the three entering office*]. Oh this is fine, fine! And to think I can't even get away!

[*The* MOTHER *attempts to look at him, but lowers her eyes immediately when he turns away from her. She then sits down. The* BOY *and the* CHILD *approach her. She casts a glance again at the* SON, *and speaks with humble tones, trying to draw him into conversation.*]

THE MOTHER. And isn't my punishment the worst of all? [*Then seeing from the* SON'S *manner that he will not bother himself about her.*] My God! Why are you so cruel? Isn't it enough for one person to support all this torment? Must you then insist on others seeing it also?

THE SON [*half to himself, meaning the* MOTHER *to hear, however*]. And they want to put it on the stage! If there was at least a reason for it! He thinks he has got at the meaning of it all. Just as if each one of us in every circumstance of life couldn't find his own explanation of it! [*Pauses.*] He complains he was discovered in a place where he ought not to have been seen, in a moment of his life which ought to have remained hidden and kept out of the reach of convention which he has to maintain for other people. And what about my case? Haven't I had to reveal what no son ought ever to reveal: how father and mother live and are man and wife for themselves quite apart from that idea of father and mother which we give them? When this idea is revealed, our life is then linked at one point only to that man and that woman; and as such it should shame them, shouldn't it?

[*The* MOTHER *hides her face in her hands. From the dressing-rooms and the little door at the back of the stage the* ACTORS *and* STAGE MANAGER *return, followed by the* PROPERTY MAN, *and the* PROMPTER. *At the same moment, the* MANAGER *comes out of his office, accompanied by the* FATHER *and the* STEPDAUGHTER.]

THE MANAGER. Come on, come on, ladies and gentlemen! Heh! you there, machinist!

MACHINIST.   Yes sir?

THE MANAGER.   Fix up the white parlor with the floral decorations. Two wings and a drop with a door will do. Hurry up!

[*The* MACHINIST *runs off at once to prepare the scene, and arranges it while the* MANAGER *talks with the* STAGE MANAGER, *the* PROPERTY MAN, *and the* PROMPTER *on matters of detail.*]

THE MANAGER [*to* PROPERTY MAN].   Just have a look, and see if there isn't a sofa or divan in the wardrobe . . .

PROPERTY MAN.   There's the green one.

THE STEPDAUGHTER.   No, no! Green won't do. It was yellow, ornamented with flowers—very large! and most comfortable!

PROPERTY MAN.   There isn't one like that.

THE MANAGER.   It doesn't matter. Use the one we've got.

THE STEPDAUGHTER.   Doesn't matter? It's most important!

THE MANAGER.   We're only trying it now. Please don't interfere. [*To* PROPERTY MAN.] See if we've got a shop window—long and narrowish.

THE STEPDAUGHTER.   And the little table! The little mahogany table for the pale blue envelope!

PROPERTY MAN [*to* MANAGER].   There's that little gilt one.

THE MANAGER.   That'll do fine.

THE FATHER.   A mirror.

THE STEPDAUGHTER.   And the screen! We must have a screen. Otherwise how can I manage?

PROPERTY MAN.   That's all right, Miss. We've got any amount of them.

THE MANAGER [*to the* STEPDAUGHTER].   We want some clothes pegs too, don't we?

THE STEPDAUGHTER.   Yes, several, several!

THE MANAGER.   See how many we've got and bring them all.

PROPERTY MAN.   All right!

[*The* PROPERTY MAN *hurries off to obey his orders. While he is putting the things in their places, the* MANAGER *talks to the* PROMPTER *and then with the* CHARACTERS *and the* ACTORS.]

THE MANAGER [*to* PROMPTER].   Take your seat. Look here: this is the outline of the scenes, act by act. [*Hands him some sheets of paper.*] And now I'm going to ask you to do something out of the ordinary.

PROMPTER.   Take it down in shorthand?

THE MANAGER [*pleasantly surprised*].   Exactly! Can you do shorthand?

PROMPTER.   Yes, a little.

MANAGER.   Good! [*Turning to a stage hand.*] Go and get some paper from my office, plenty, as much as you can find.

[*The* STAGE HAND *goes off, and soon returns with a handful of paper which he gives to the* PROMPTER.]

THE MANAGER [*to* PROMPTER].   You follow the scenes as we play them, and try to get the points down, at any rate the most important ones. [*Then addressing the* ACTORS.] Clear the stage, ladies and gentlemen! Come over here [*pointing to the Left*] and listen attentively.

LEADING LADY.   But, excuse me, we . . .

THE MANAGER [*guessing her thought*].   Don't worry! You won't have to improvise.

LEADING MAN.   What have we to do then?

THE MANAGER.   Nothing. For the moment you just watch and listen. Everybody will get his part written out afterwards. At present we're going to try the thing as best we can. They're going to act now.

THE FATHER [*as if fallen from the clouds into the confusion of the stage*]. We? What do you mean, if you please, by a rehearsal?

THE MANAGER.   A rehearsal for them. [*Points to the* ACTORS.]

THE FATHER.   But since we are the characters . . .

THE MANAGER.   All right: "characters" then, if you insist on calling yourselves such. But here, my dear sir, the characters don't act. Here the actors do the acting. The characters are there, in the "book"—[*pointing towards* PROMPTER's *box*] when there is a "book"!

THE FATHER.   I won't contradict you; but excuse me, the actors aren't the characters. They want to be, they pretend to be, don't they? Now if these gentlemen here are fortunate enough to have us alive before them . . .

THE MANAGER.   Oh this is grand! You want to come before the public yourselves then?

THE FATHER.   As we are . . .

THE MANAGER.   I can assure you it would be a magnificent spectacle!

LEADING MAN.   What's the use of us here anyway then?

THE MANAGER.   You're not going to pretend that you can act? It makes me laugh! [*The* ACTORS *laugh*.] There, you see, they are laughing at the notion. But, by the way, I must cast the parts. That won't be difficult. They cast themselves. [*To the* SECOND LADY LEAD.] You play the Mother. [*To the* FATHER.] We must find her a name.

THE FATHER.   Amalia, sir.

THE MANAGER.   But that is the real name of your wife. We don't want to call her by her real name.

THE FATHER.   Why ever not, if it is her name? . . . Still, perhaps, if that lady must . . . [*makes a slight motion of the hand to indicate the* SECOND LADY LEAD]. I see this woman here [*means the* MOTHER] as Amalia. But do as you like. [*Gets more and more confused*.] I don't know what to say to you. Already, I begin to hear my own words ring false, as if they had another sound . . .

THE MANAGER.   Don't you worry about it. It'll be our job to find the right tones. And as for her name, if you want her Amalia, Amalia it shall be; and if you don't like it, we'll find another! For the moment though, we'll call the characters in this way: [*to the* JUVENILE LEAD] You are the Son; [*to the* LEADING LADY] You naturally are the Stepdaughter . . .

THE STEPDAUGHTER [*excitedly*].   What? what? I, that woman there? [*Bursts out laughing*.]

THE MANAGER [*angry*].   What is there to laugh at?

LEADING LADY [*indignant*].   Nobody has ever dared to laugh at me. I insist on being treated with respect; otherwise I go away.

THE STEPDAUGHTER.   No, no, excuse me . . . I am not laughing at you . . .

THE MANAGER [*to* STEPDAUGHTER].   You ought to feel honored to be played by . . .

LEADING LADY [*at once, contemptuously*].   "That woman there" . . .

THE STEPDAUGHTER.   But I wasn't speaking of you, you know. I was speaking of myself—whom I can't see at all in you! That is all. I don't know . . . but . . . you . . . aren't in the least like me . . .

THE FATHER. True. Here's the point. Look here, sir, our temperaments, our souls . . .

THE MANAGER. Temperament, soul, be hanged. Do you suppose the spirit of the piece is in you? Nothing of the kind!

THE FATHER. What, haven't we our own temperaments, our own souls?

THE MANAGER. Not at all. Your soul or whatever you like to call it takes shape here. The actors give body and form to it, voice and gesture. And my actors—I may tell you—have given expression to much more lofty material than this little drama of yours, which may or may not hold up on the stage. But if it does, the merit of it, believe me, will be due to my actors.

THE FATHER. I don't dare contradict you, sir; but, believe me, it is a terrible suffering for us who are as we are, with these bodies of ours, these features to see . . .

THE MANAGER [cutting him short and out of patience]. Good heavens! The make-up will remedy all that, man, the make-up . . .

THE FATHER. Maybe. But the voice, the gestures . . .

THE MANAGER. Now, look here! On the stage, you as yourself, cannot exist. The actor here acts you, and that's an end to it!

THE FATHER. I understand. And now I think I see why our author who conceived us as we are, all alive, didn't want to put us on the stage after all. I haven't the least desire to offend your actors. Far from it! But when I think that I am to be acted by . . . I don't know by whom . . .

LEADING MAN [on his dignity]. By me, if you've no objection!

THE FATHER [humbly, mellifluously]. Honored, I assure you, sir. [Bows.] Still, I must say that try as this gentleman may, with all his good will and wonderful art, to absorb me into himself . . .

LEADING MAN. Oh chuck it! "Wonderful art!" Withdraw that, please!

THE FATHER. The performance he will give, even doing his best with make-up to look like me . . .

LEADING MAN. It will certainly be a bit difficult! [The ACTORS laugh.]

THE FATHER. Exactly! It will be difficult to act me as I really am. The effect will be rather—apart from the make-up—according as to how he supposes I am, as he senses me—if he does sense me—and not as I inside of myself feel myself to be. It seems to me then that account should be taken of this by every-one whose duty it may become to criticize us . . .

THE MANAGER. Heavens! The man's starting to think about the critics now! Let them say what they like. It's up to us to put on the play if we can. [Looking around.] Come on! come on! Is the stage set? [To the ACTORS and CHARACTERS.] Stand back—stand back! Let me see, and don't let's lose any more time! [To the STEPDAUGHTER.] Is it all right as it is now?

THE STEPDAUGHTER. Well, to tell the truth, I don't recognize the scene.

THE MANAGER. My dear lady, you can't possibly suppose that we can construct that shop of Madame Pace piece by piece here? [To the FATHER.] You said a white room with flowered wall paper, didn't you?

THE FATHER. Yes.

THE MANAGER. Well then. We've got the furniture right more or less. Bring that little table a bit further forward. [The stage hands obey the order. To

PROPERTY MAN.] You go and find an envelope, if possible, a pale blue one; and give it to that gentleman. [*Indicates the* FATHER.]

PROPERTY MAN.   An ordinary envelope?

MANAGER AND FATHER.   Yes, yes, an ordinary envelope.

PROPERTY MAN.   At once, sir. [*Exit.*]

THE MANAGER.   Ready, everyone! First scene—the Young Lady. [*The* LEADING LADY *comes forward.*] No, no, you must wait. I meant her. [*Indicating the* STEPDAUGHTER] You just watch—

THE STEPDAUGHTER [*adding at once*].   How I shall play it, how I shall live it! . . .

LEADING LADY [*offended*].   I shall live it also, you may be sure, as soon as I begin!

THE MANAGER [*with his hands to his head*].   Ladies and gentlemen, if you please! No more useless discussions! Scene I: the young lady with Madame Pace: Oh! [*Looks around as if lost.*] And this Madame Pace, where is she?

THE FATHER.   She isn't with us, sir.

THE MANAGER.   Then what the devil's to be done?

THE FATHER.   But she is alive too.

THE MANAGER.   Yes, but where is she?

THE FATHER.   One minute. Let me speak! [*Turning to the* ACTRESSES.] If these ladies would be so good as to give me their hats for a moment . . .

THE ACTRESSES [*half-surprised, half-laughing, in chorus*].   What?
Why?
Our hats?
What does he say?

THE MANAGER.   What are you going to do with the ladies' hats? [*The* ACTORS *laugh.*]

THE FATHER.   Oh nothing. I just want to put them on these pegs for a moment. And one of the ladies will be so kind as to take off her mantle . . .

THE ACTORS.   Oh, what d'you think of that?
Only the mantle?
He must be mad.

SOME ACTRESSES.   But why?
Mantles as well?

THE FATHER.   To hang them up here for a moment. Please be so kind, will you?

THE ACTRESSES [*taking off their hats, one or two also their cloaks, and going to hang them on the racks*].   After all, why not?
There you are!
This is really funny.
We've got to put them on show.

THE FATHER.   Exactly; just like that, on show.

THE MANAGER.   May we know why?

THE FATHER.   I'll tell you. Who knows if, by arranging the stage for her, she does not come here herself, attracted by the very articles of her trade? [*Inviting the* ACTORS *to look towards the exit at back of stage.*] Look! Look!

[*The door at the back of stage opens and* MADAME PACE *enters and takes a few steps forward. She is a fat, oldish woman with puffy oxygenated hair. She is rouged and powdered, dressed with a comical elegance in black silk. Round*

her waist is a long silver chain from which hangs a pair of scissors. The STEP-
DAUGHTER *runs over to her at once amid the stupor of the* ACTORS.]

THE STEPDAUGHTER [*turning towards her*].   There she is! There she is!

THE FATHER [*radiant*].   It's she! I said so, didn't I? There she is!

THE MANAGER [*conquering his surprise, and then becoming indignant*].
What sort of a trick is this?

LEADING MAN [*almost at the same time*].   What's going to happen next?

JUVENILE LEAD.   Where does *she* come from?

L'INGÉNUE.   They've been holding her in reserve, I guess.

LEADING LADY.   A vulgar trick!

THE FATHER [*dominating the protests*].   Excuse me, all of you! Why are
you so anxious to destroy in the name of a vulgar, commonplace sense of truth,
this reality which comes to birth attracted and formed by the magic of the stage
itself, which has indeed more right to live here than you, since it is much truer
than you—if you don't mind my saying so? Which is the actress among you
who is to play Madame Pace? Well, here is Madame Pace herself. And you
will allow, I fancy, that the actress who acts her will be less true than this
woman here, who is herself in person. You see my daughter recognized her and
went over to her at once. Now you're going to witness the scene.

[*But the scene between the* STEPDAUGHTER *and* MADAME PACE *has already
begun despite the protest of the* ACTORS *and the reply of the* FATHER. *It has
begun quietly, naturally, in a manner impossible for the stage. So when the*
ACTORS, *called to attention by the* FATHER, *turn round and see* MADAME PACE,
who has placed one hand under the STEPDAUGHTER's *chin to raise her head, they
observe her at first with great attention, but hearing her speak in an unintel-
ligible manner their interest begins to wane.*]

THE MANAGER.   Well? well?

LEADING MAN.   What does she say?

LEADING LADY.   One can't hear a word.

JUVENILE LEAD.   Louder! Louder please!

THE STEPDAUGHTER [*leaving* MADAME PACE, *who smiles a Sphinx-like smile,
and advancing towards the* ACTORS].   Louder? Louder? What are you talking
about? These aren't matters which can be shouted at the top of one's voice. If
I have spoken them out loud, it was to shame him and have my revenge.
[*Indicates the* FATHER.] But for Madame it's quite a different matter.

THE MANAGER.   Indeed? indeed? But here, you know, people have got to
make themselves heard, my dear. Even we who are on the stage can't hear you.
What will it be when the public's in the theater? And anyway, you can very
well speak up now among yourselves, since we shan't be present to listen to you
as we are now. You've got to pretend to be alone in a room at the back of a shop
where no one can hear you.

[*The* STEPDAUGHTER *coquettishly and with a touch of malice makes a sign
of disagreement two or three times with her finger.*]

THE MANAGER.   What do you mean by no?

THE STEPDAUGHTER [*sotto voce, mysteriously*].   There's someone who will
hear us if she [*indicating* MADAME PACE] speaks out loud.

THE MANAGER [*in consternation*].   What? Have you got someone else to
spring on us now? [*The* ACTORS *burst out laughing.*]

THE FATHER.   No, no sir. She is alluding to me. I've got to be here—there behind that door, in waiting; and Madame Pace knows it. In fact, if you will allow me, I'll go there at once, so I can be quite ready. [*Moves away.*]

THE MANAGER [*stopping him*]. No! wait! wait! We must observe the conventions of the theater. Before you are ready . . .

THE STEPDAUGHTER [*interrupting him*]. No, get on with it at once! I'm just dying, I tell you, to act this scene. If he's ready, I'm more than ready.

THE MANAGER [*shouting*]. But, my dear young lady, first of all, we must have the scene between you and this lady . . . [*Indicates* MADAME PACE.] Do you understand? . . .

THE STEPDAUGHTER. Good Heavens! She's been telling me what you know already: that mamma's work is badly done again, that the material's ruined; and that if I want her to continue to help us in our misery I must be patient . . .

MADAME PACE [*coming forward with an air of great importance*]. Yes indeed, sir, I no wanta take advantage of her, I no wanta be hard . . .

[*Note:* MADAME PACE *is supposed to talk in a jargon half Italian, half English.*]

THE MANAGER [*alarmed*]. What? What? she talks like that? [*The* ACTORS *burst out laughing again.*]

THE STEPDAUGHTER [*also laughing*]. Yes, yes, that's the way she talks, half English, half Italian! Most comical it is!

MADAME PACE. Itta seem not verra polite gentlemen laugha atta me eef I trya best speaka English.

THE MANAGER. *Diamine!*[3] Of course! Of course! Let her talk like that! Just what we want. Talk just like that, Madame, if you please! The effect will be certain. Exactly what was wanted to put a little comic relief into the crudity of the situation. Of course she talks like that! Magnificent!

THE STEPDAUGHTER. Magnificent? Certainly! When certain suggestions are made to one in language of that kind, the effect is certain, since it seems almost a joke. One feels inclined to laugh when one hears her talk about an "old signore" "who wanta talka nicely with you." Nice old signore, eh, Madame?

MADAME PACE. Not so old, my dear, not so old! And even if you no lika him, he won't make any scandal!

THE MOTHER [*jumping up amid the amazement and consternation of the* ACTORS, *who had not been noticing her. They move to restrain her*]. You old devil! You murderess!

THE STEPDAUGHTER [*running over to calm her* MOTHER]. Calm yourself, mother, calm yourself! Please don't . . .

THE FATHER [*going to her also at the same time*]. Calm yourself! Don't get excited! Sit down now!

THE MOTHER. Well then, take that woman away out of my sight!

THE STEPDAUGHTER [*to the* MANAGER]. It is impossible for my mother to remain here.

THE FATHER [*to the* MANAGER]. They can't be here together. And for this reason, you see: that woman there was not with us when we came . . . If they are on together, the whole thing is given away inevitably, as you see.

THE MANAGER. It doesn't matter. This is only a first rough sketch—just to get an idea of the various points of the scene, even confusedly . . . [*Turning*

[3] (Italian) The deuce!

to the MOTHER *and leading her to her chair.*] Come along, my dear lady, sit down now, and let's get on with the scene . . .

[*Meanwhile, the* STEPDAUGHTER, *coming forward again, turns to* MADAME PACE.]

THE STEPDAUGHTER. Come on, Madame, come on!

MADAME PACE [*offended*]. No, no, *grazie.*[4] I not do anything witha your mother present.

THE STEPDAUGHTER. Nonsense! Introduce this "old signore" who wants to talk nicely to me. [*Addressing the company imperiously.*] We've got to do this scene one way or another, haven't we? Come on! [*To* MADAME PACE.] You can go!

MADAME PACE. Ah yes! I go'way! I go'way! Certainly! [*Exit furious.*]

THE STEPDAUGHTER [*to the* FATHER]. Now you make your entry. No, you needn't go over here. Come here. Let's suppose you've already come in. Like that, yes! I'm here with bowed head, modest like. Come on! Out with your voice! Say "Good morning, Miss" in that peculiar tone, that special tone . . .

THE MANAGER. Excuse me, but are you the Manager, or am I? [*To the* FATHER, *who looks undecided and perplexed.*] Get on with it, man! Go down there to the back of the stage. You needn't go off. Then come right forward here.

[*The* FATHER *does as he is told, looking troubled and perplexed at first. But as soon as he begins to move, the reality of the action affects him, and he begins to smile and to be more natural. The* ACTORS *watch intently.*]

THE MANAGER [*sotto voce, quickly to the* PROMPTER *in his box*]. Ready! ready? Get ready to write now.

THE FATHER [*coming forward and speaking in a different tone*]. Good afternoon, Miss!

THE STEPDAUGHTER [*head bowed down slightly, with restrained disgust*]. Good afternoon!

THE FATHER [*looks under her hat which partly covers her face. Perceiving she is very young, he makes an exclamation, partly of surprise, partly of fear lest he compromise himself in a risky adventure.*] Ah . . . but . . . ah . . . I say . . . this is not the first time that you have come here, is it?

THE STEPDAUGHTER [*modestly*]. No sir.

THE FATHER. You've been here before, eh? [*Then seeing her nod agreement.*] More than once? [*Waits for her to answer, looks under her hat, smiles, and then says.*] Well then, there's no need to be so shy, is there? May I take off your hat?

THE STEPDAUGHTER [*anticipating him and with veiled disgust*]. No sir . . . I'll do it myself. [*Takes it off quickly.*]

[*The* MOTHER, *who watches the progress of the scene with the* SON *and the other two* CHILDREN, *who cling to her, is on thorns; and follows with varying expressions of sorrow, indignation, anxiety, and horror the words and actions of the other two. From time to time she hides her face in her hands and sobs.*]

THE MOTHER. Oh, my God, my God!

THE FATHER [*playing his part with a touch of gallantry*]. Give it to me! I'll put it down. [*Takes hat from her hands.*] But a dear little head like yours

[4] (Italian) Thank you (with the implication, as frequently in English, that what is offered is not really desirable).

ought to have a smarter hat. Come and help me choose one from the stock, won't you?

L'INGÉNUE [*interrupting*]. I say . . . those are our hats you know.

THE MANAGER [*furious*]. Silence! silence! Don't try and be funny, if you please . . . We're playing the scene now I'd have you notice. [*To the* STEP-DAUGHTER.] Begin again, please!

THE STEPDAUGHTER [*continuing*]. No thank you, sir.

THE FATHER. Oh, come now. Don't talk like that. You must take it. I shall be upset if you don't. There are some lovely little hats here; and then—Madame will be pleased. She expects it, anyway, you know.

THE STEPDAUGHTER. No, no! I couldn't wear it!

THE FATHER. Oh, you're thinking about what they'd say at home if they saw you come in with a new hat? My dear girl, there's always a way round these little matters, you know.

THE STEPDAUGHTER [*all keyed up*]. No, it's not that. I couldn't wear it because I am . . . as you see . . . you might have noticed . . . [*Showing her black dress.*]

THE FATHER. . . . in mourning! Of course: I beg your pardon: I'm frightfully sorry . . .

THE STEPDAUGHTER [*forcing herself to conquer her indignation and nausea*]. Stop! Stop! It's I who must thank you. There's no need for you to feel mortified or specially sorry. Don't think any more of what I've said. [*Tries to smile.*] I must forget that I am dressed so . . .

THE MANAGER [*interrupting and turning to the* PROMPTER]. Stop a minute! Stop! Don't write that down. Cut out that last bit. [*Then to the* FATHER *and the* STEPDAUGHTER.] Fine! It's going fine! [*To the* FATHER *only*.] And now you can go on as we arranged. [*To the* ACTORS.] Pretty good that scene, where he offers her the hat, eh?

THE STEPDAUGHTER. The best's coming now. Why can't we go on?

THE MANAGER. Have a little patience! [*To the* ACTORS.] Of course, it must be treated rather lightly.

LEADING MAN. Still, with a bit of go in it!

LEADING LADY. Of course! It's easy enough! [*To the* LEADING MAN.] Shall you and I try it now?

LEADING MAN. Why, yes! I'll prepare my entrance. [*Exit in order to make his entrance.*]

THE MANAGER [*to the* LEADING LADY]. See here! The scene between you and Madame Pace is finished. I'll have it written out properly after. You remain here . . . oh, where are you going?

LEADING LADY. One minute. I want to put my hat on again. [*Goes over to hat-rack and puts her hat on her head.*]

THE MANAGER. Good! You stay here with your head bowed down a bit.

THE STEPDAUGHTER. But she isn't dressed in black.

LEADING LADY. But I shall be, and much more effectively than you.

THE MANAGER [*to* STEPDAUGHTER]. Be quiet please, and watch! You'll be able to learn something. [*Clapping his hands.*] Come on! come on! Entrance, please!

[*The door at rear of stage opens, and the* LEADING MAN *enters with the lively manner of an old gallant. The rendering of the scene by the* ACTORS *from the very first words is seen to be quite a different thing, though it has not in any way the air of a parody. Naturally, the* STEPDAUGHTER *and the* FATHER, *not being able to recognize themselves in the* LEADING LADY *and the* LEADING MAN, *who deliver their words in different tones and with a different psychology, express, sometimes with smiles, sometimes with gestures, the impression they receive.*]

LEADING MAN. Good afternoon, Miss . . .

THE FATHER [*at once unable to contain himself*]. No! no!

[*The* STEPDAUGHTER *noticing the way the* LEADING MAN *enters, bursts out laughing.*]

THE MANAGER [*furious*]. Silence! And you please just stop that laughing. If we go on like this, we shall never finish.

THE STEPDAUGHTER. Forgive me, sir, but it's natural enough. This lady [*indicating* LEADING LADY] stands there still; but if she is supposed to be me, I can assure you that if I heard anyone say "Good afternoon" in that manner and in that tone, I should burst out laughing as I did.

THE FATHER. Yes, yes, the manner, the tone . . .

THE MANAGER. Nonsense! Rubbish! Stand aside and let me see the action.

LEADING MAN. If I've got to represent an old fellow who's coming into a house of an equivocal character . . .

THE MANAGER. Don't listen to them, for Heaven's sake! Do it again! It goes fine. [*Waiting for the* ACTORS *to begin again.*] Well?

LEADING MAN. Good afternoon, Miss.

LEADING LADY. Good afternoon.

LEADING MAN [*imitating the gesture of the* FATHER *when he looked under the hat, and then expressing quite clearly first satisfaction and then fear*]. Ah, but . . . I say . . . this is not the first time that you have come here, is it?

THE MANAGER. Good, but not quite so heavily. Like this. [*Acts himself.*] "This isn't the first time that you have come here" . . . [*To the* LEADING LADY.] And you say: "No, sir."

LEADING LADY. No, sir.

LEADING MAN. You've been here before, more than once.

THE MANAGER. No, no, stop! Let her nod "yes" first. "You've been here before, eh?" [*The* LEADING LADY *lifts up her head slightly and closes her eyes as though in disgust. Then she inclines her head twice.*]

THE STEPDAUGHTER [*unable to contain herself*]. Oh my God! [*Puts a hand to her mouth to prevent herself from laughing.*]

THE MANAGER [*turning round*]. What's the matter?

THE STEPDAUGHTER. Nothing, nothing!

THE MANAGER [*to* LEADING MAN]. Go on!

LEADING MAN. You've been here before, eh? Well then, there's no need to be so shy, is there? May I take off your hat?

[*The* LEADING MAN *says this last speech in such a tone and with such gestures that the* STEPDAUGHTER, *though she has her hand to her mouth, cannot keep from laughing.*]

LEADING LADY [*indignant*]. I'm not going to stop here to be made a fool of by that woman there.

LEADING MAN. Neither am I! I'm through with it!

THE MANAGER [*shouting to* STEPDAUGHTER]. Silence! for once and all, I tell you!

THE STEPDAUGHTER. Forgive me! forgive me!

THE MANAGER. You haven't any manners: that's what it is! You go too far.

THE FATHER [*endeavoring to intervene*]. Yes, it's true, but excuse her . . .

THE MANAGER. Excuse what? It's absolutely disgusting.

THE FATHER. Yes, sir, but believe me, it has such a strange effect when . . .

THE MANAGER. Strange? Why strange? Where is it strange?

THE FATHER. No, sir; I admire your actors—this gentleman here, this lady; but they are certainly not us!

THE MANAGER. I should hope not. Evidently they cannot be you, if they are actors.

THE FATHER. Just so: actors! Both of them act our parts exceedingly well. But, believe me, it produces quite a different effect on us. They want to be us, but they aren't, all the same.

THE MANAGER. What is it then anyway?

THE FATHER. Something that is . . . that is theirs—and no longer ours . . .

THE MANAGER. But naturally, inevitably. I've told you so already.

THE FATHER. Yes, I understand . . . I understand . . .

THE MANAGER. Well then, let's have no more of it! [*Turning to the* ACTORS.] We'll have the rehearsals by ourselves, afterwards, in the ordinary way. I never could stand rehearsing with the author present. He's never satisfied! [*Turning to the* FATHER *and* STEPDAUGHTER.] Come on! Let's get on with it again; and try and see if you can't keep from laughing.

THE STEPDAUGHTER. Oh, I shan't laugh any more. There's a nice little bit coming for me now: you'll see.

THE MANAGER. Well then: when she says "Don't think any more of what I've said. I must forget, etc.," you [*addressing the* FATHER] come in sharp with "I understand, I understand"; and then you ask her . . .

THE STEPDAUGHTER [*interrupting*]. What?

THE MANAGER. Why she is in mourning.

THE STEPDAUGHTER. Not at all! See here: when I told him that it was useless for me to be thinking about my wearing mourning, do you know how he answered me? "Ah well," he said, "then let's take off this little frock."

THE MANAGER. Great! Just what we want, to make a riot in the theater!

THE STEPDAUGHTER. But it's the truth!

THE MANAGER. What does that matter? Acting is our business here. Truth up to a certain point, but no further.

THE STEPDAUGHTER. What do you want to do then?

THE MANAGER. You'll see, you'll see! Leave it to me.

THE STEPDAUGHTER. No sir! What you want to do is to piece together a little romantic sentimental scene out of my disgust, out of all the reasons, each more cruel and viler than the other, why I am what I am. He is to ask me why I'm in mourning; and I'm to answer with tears in my eyes, that it is just two months since papa died. No sir, no! He's got to say to me; as he did say: "Well, let's take off this little dress at once." And I; with my two months' mourning in my heart, went there behind that screen, and with these fingers tingling with shame . . .

THE MANAGER [*running his hands through his hair*]. For Heaven's sake! What are you saying?

THE STEPDAUGHTER [*crying out excitedly*]. The truth! The truth!

THE MANAGER. It may be. I don't deny it, and I can understand all your horror; but you must surely see that you can't have this kind of thing on the stage. It won't go.

THE STEPDAUGHTER. Not possible, eh? Very well! I'm much obliged to you —but I'm off!

THE MANAGER. Now be reasonable! Don't lose your temper!

THE STEPDAUGHTER. I won't stop here! I won't! I can see you've fixed it all up with him in your office. All this talk about what is possible for the stage . . . I understand! He wants to get at his complicated "cerebral drama," to have his famous remorses and torments acted; but I want to act my part, *my part!*

THE MANAGER [*annoyed, shaking his shoulders*]. Ah! Just *your* part! But, if you will pardon me, there are other parts than yours: his [*indicating the FATHER*] and hers! [*Indicating the MOTHER.*] On the stage you can't have a character becoming too prominent and overshadowing all the others. The thing is to pack them all into a neat little framework and then act what is actable. I am aware of the fact that everyone has his own interior life which he wants very much to put forward. But the difficulty lies in this fact: to set out just so much as is necessary for the stage, taking the other characters into consideration, and at the same time hint at the unrevealed interior life of each. I am willing to admit, my dear young lady, that from your point of view it would be a fine idea if each character could tell the public all his troubles in a nice monologue or a regular one-hour lecture. [*Good-humoredly.*] You must restrain yourself, my dear, and in your own interest, too; because this fury of yours, this exaggerated disgust you show, may make a bad impression, you know. After you have confessed to me that there were others before him at Madame Pace's and more than once . . .

THE STEPDAUGHTER [*bowing her head, impressed*]. It's true. But remember those others mean him for me all the same.

THE MANAGER [*not understanding*]. What? The others? What do you mean?

THE STEPDAUGHTER. For one who has gone wrong, sir, he who was responsible for the first fault is responsible for all that follow. He is responsible for my faults, was, even before I was born. Look at him, and see if it isn't true!

THE MANAGER. Well, well! And does the weight of so much responsibility seem nothing to you? Give him a chance to act it, to get it over!

THE STEPDAUGHTER. How? How can he act all his "noble remorses" all his "moral torments," if you want to spare him the horror of being discovered one day—after he had asked her what he did ask her—in the arms of her, that already fallen woman, that child, sir, that child he used to watch come out of school? [*She is moved.*]

[*The MOTHER at this point is overcome with emotion, and breaks out into a fit of crying. All are touched. A long pause.*]

THE STEPDAUGHTER [*as soon as the MOTHER becomes a little quieter, adds resolutely and gravely*]. At present, we are unknown to the public. Tomorrow, you will act us as you wish, treating us in your own manner. But do you really want to see drama, do you want to see it flash out as it really did?

THE MANAGER.   Of course! That's just what I do want, so I can use as much of it as is possible.

THE STEPDAUGHTER.   Well then, ask that Mother there to leave us.

THE MOTHER [*changing her low plaint into a sharp cry*].   No! No! Don't permit it, sir, don't permit it!

THE MANAGER.   But it's only to try it.

THE MOTHER.   I can't bear it. I can't.

THE MANAGER.   But since it has happened already . . . I don't understand!

THE MOTHER.   It's taking place now. It happens all the time. My torment isn't a pretended one. I live and feel every minute of my torture. Those two children there—have you heard them speak? They can't speak any more. They cling to me to keep my torment actual and vivid for me. But for themselves, they do not exist, they aren't any more. And she [*indicating* STEPDAUGHTER] has run away, she has left me, and is lost. If I now see her here before me, it is only to renew for me the tortures I have suffered for her too.

THE FATHER.   The eternal moment! She [*indicating the* STEPDAUGHTER] is here to catch me, fix me, and hold me eternally in the stocks for that one fleeting and shameful moment of my life. She can't give it up! And you, sir, cannot either fairly spare me it.

THE MANAGER.   I never said I didn't want to act it. It will form, as a matter of fact, the nucleus of the whole first act right up to her surprise. [*Indicating the* MOTHER.]

THE FATHER.   Just so! This is my punishment: the passion in all of us that must culminate in her final cry.

THE STEPDAUGHTER.   I can hear it still in my ears. It's driven me mad, that cry!—You can put me on as you like; it doesn't matter. Fully dressed, if you like—provided I have at least the arm bare; because, standing like this [*she goes close to the* FATHER *and leans her head on his breast*] with my head so, and my arms round his neck, I saw a vein pulsing in my arm here; and then, as if that live vein had awakened disgust in me, I closed my eyes like this, and let my head sink on his breast. [*Turning to the* MOTHER.] Cry out, mother! Cry out! [*Buries head in the* FATHER's *breast, and with her shoulders raised as if to prevent her hearing the cry, adds in tones of intense emotion.*] Cry out as you did then!

THE MOTHER [*coming forward to separate them*]. No! My daughter, my daughter! [*And after having pulled her away from him.*] You brute! you brute! She is my daughter! Don't you see she's my daughter?

THE MANAGER [*walking backwards towards footlights*]. Fine! fine! Damned good! And then, of course—curtain!

THE FATHER [*going towards him excitedly*].   Yes, of course, because that's the way it really happened.

THE MANAGER [*convinced and pleased*].   Oh, yes, no doubt about it. Curtain here, curtain!

[*At the reiterated cry of the* MANAGER, *the* MACHINIST *lets the curtain down, leaving the* MANAGER *and the* FATHER *in front of it before the footlights.*]

THE MANAGER.   The darned idiot! I said "curtain" to show the act should end there, and he goes and lets it down in earnest. [*To the* FATHER, *while he pulls the curtain back to go on to the stage again.*] Yes, yes, it's all right. Effect certain! That's the right ending. I'll guarantee the first act at any rate.

ACT III

When the curtain goes up again, it is seen that the stage hands have shifted the bit of scenery used in the last part, and have rigged up instead at the back of the stage a drop, with some trees, and one or two wings. A portion of a fountain basin is visible. The MOTHER *is sitting on the* Right *with the two children by her side. The* SON *is on the same side, but away from the others. He seems bored, angry, and full of shame. The* FATHER *and the* STEPDAUGHTER *are also seated towards the* Right *front. On the other side (*Left*) are the* ACTORS, *much in the positions they occupied before the curtain was lowered. Only the* MANAGER *is standing up in the middle of the stage, with his hand closed over his mouth in the act of meditating.*

THE MANAGER [*shaking his shoulders after a brief pause*]. Ah yes: the second act! Leave it to me, leave it all to me as we arranged, and you'll see! It'll go fine!

THE STEPDAUGHTER. Our entry into his house [*indicates the* FATHER] in spite of him . . . [*indicates the* SON].

THE MANAGER [*out of patience*]. Leave it to me. I tell you!

THE STEPDAUGHTER. Do let it be clear, at any rate, that it is in spite of my wishes.

THE MOTHER [*from her corner, shaking her head*]. For all the good that's come of it . . .

THE STEPDAUGHTER [*turning towards her quickly*]. It doesn't matter. The more harm done us, the more remorse for him.

THE MANAGER [*impatiently*]. I understand! Good Heavens! I understand! I'm taking it into account.

THE MOTHER [*supplicatingly*]. I beg you, sir, to let it appear quite plain that for conscience' sake I did try in every way . . .

THE STEPDAUGHTER [*interrupting indignantly and continuing for the* MOTHER]. . . . to pacify me, to dissuade me from spiting him. [*To* MANAGER.] Do as she wants: satisfy her, because it is true! I enjoy it immensely. Anyhow, as you can see, the meeker she is, the more she tries to get at his heart, the more distant and aloof does he become.

THE MANAGER. Are we going to begin this second act or not?

THE STEPDAUGHTER. I'm not going to talk any more now. But I must tell you this: you can't have the whole action take place in the garden, as you suggest. It isn't possible!

THE MANAGER. Why not?

THE STEPDAUGHTER. Because he [*indicates the* SON *again*] is always shut up alone in his room. And then there's all the part of that poor dazed-looking boy there which takes place indoors.

THE MANAGER. Maybe! On the other hand, you will understand—we can't change scenes three or four times in one act.

THE LEADING MAN.   They used to once.

THE MANAGER.   Yes, when the public was up to the level of that child there.

THE LEADING LADY.   It makes the illusion easier.

THE FATHER [irritated].   The illusion! For Heaven's sake, don't say illusion. Please don't use that word, which is particularly painful for us.

THE MANAGER [astounded].   And why, if you please?

THE FATHER.   It's painful, cruel, really cruel; and you ought to understand that.

THE MANAGER.   But why? What ought we to say then? The illusion, I tell you sir, which we've got to create for the audience . . .

THE LEADING MAN.   With our acting.

THE MANAGER.   The illusion of a reality.

THE FATHER.   I understand; but you, perhaps, do not understand us. Forgive me! You see . . . here for you and your actors, the thing is only—and rightly so . . . a kind of game . . .

THE LEADING LADY [interrupting indignantly].   A game! We're not children here, if you please! We are serious actors.

THE FATHER.   I don't deny it. What I mean is the game, or play, of your art, which has to give, as the gentleman says, a perfect illusion of reality.

THE MANAGER.   Precisely——!

THE FATHER.   Now, if you consider the fact that we [indicates himself and the other five CHARACTERS], as we are, have no other reality outside of this illusion . . .

THE MANAGER [astonished, looking at his ACTORS, who are also amazed]. And what does that mean?

THE FATHER [after watching them for a moment with a wan smile].   As I say, sir, that which is a game of art for you is our sole reality. [Brief pause. He goes a step or two nearer the MANAGER and adds] But not only for us, you know, by the way. Just you think it over well. [Looks him in the eyes.] Can you tell me who you are?

THE MANAGER [perplexed, half smiling.]   What? Who am I? I am myself.

THE FATHER.   And if I were to tell you that that isn't true, because you are I? . . .

THE MANAGER.   I should say you were mad——! [The ACTORS laugh.]

THE FATHER.   You're quite right to laugh: because we are all making believe here. [To the MANAGER.] And you can therefore object that it's only for a joke that that gentleman there [indicates the LEADING MAN], who naturally is himself, has to be me, who am on the contrary myself—this thing you see here. You see I've caught you in a trap! [The ACTORS laugh.]

THE MANAGER [annoyed].   But we've had all this over once before. Do you want to begin again?

THE FATHER.   No, no! that wasn't my meaning! In fact, I should like to request you to abandon this game of art [looking at the LEADING LADY as if anticipating her] which you are accustomed to play here with your actors, and to ask you seriously once again: who are you?

THE MANAGER [astonished and irritated, turning to his ACTORS].   If this fellow here hasn't got a nerve! A man who calls himself a character comes and asks me who I am!

THE FATHER [*with dignity, but not offended*]. A character, sir, may always ask a man who he is. Because a character has really a life of his own, marked with his especial characteristics; for which reason he is always "somebody." But a man—I'm not speaking of you now—may very well be "nobody."

THE MANAGER. Yes, but you are asking these questions of me, the boss, the manager! Do you understand?

THE FATHER. But only in order to know if you, as you really are now, see yourself as you once were with all the illusions that were yours then, with all the things both inside and outside of you as they seemed to you—as they were then indeed for you. Well, sir, if you think of all those illusions that mean nothing to you now, of all those things which don't even *seem* to you to exist any more, while once they *were* for you, don't you feel that—I won't say these boards—but the very earth under your feet is sinking away from you when you reflect that in the same way this *you* as you feel it today—all this present reality of yours—is fated to seem a mere illusion to you tomorrow?

THE MANAGER [*without having understood much, but astonished by the specious argument*]. Well, well! And where does all this take us anyway?

THE FATHER. Oh, nowhere! It's only to show you that if we [*indicating the* CHARACTERS] have no other reality beyond illusion, you too must not count overmuch on your reality as you feel it today, since, like that of yesterday, it may prove an illusion for you tomorrow.

THE MANAGER [*determining to make fun of him*]. Ah, excellent! Then you'll be saying next that you, with this comedy of yours that you brought here to act, are truer and more real than I am.

THE FATHER [*with the greatest seriousness*]. But of course; without doubt!

THE MANAGER. Ah, really?

THE FATHER. Why, I thought you'd understand that from the beginning.

THE MANAGER. More real than I?

THE FATHER. If your reality can change from one day to another . . .

THE MANAGER. But everyone knows it can change. It is always changing, the same as anyone else's.

THE FATHER [*with a cry*]. No, sir, not ours! Look here! That is the very difference! Our reality doesn't change: it can't change! It can't be other than what it is, because it is already fixed for ever. It's terrible. Ours is an immutable reality which should make you shudder when you approach us if you are really conscious of the fact that your reality is a mere transitory and fleeting illusion, taking this form today and that tomorrow, according to the conditions, according to your will, your sentiments, which in turn are controlled by an intellect that shows them to you today in one manner and tomorrow . . . who knows how? . . . Illusions of reality represented in this fatuous comedy of life that never ends, nor can ever end! Because if tomorrow it were to end . . . then why, all would be finished.

THE MANAGER. Oh for God's sake, will you *at least* finish with this philosophizing and let us try and shape this comedy which you yourself have brought me here? You argue and philosophize a bit too much, my dear sir. You know you seem to me almost, almost . . . [*Stops and looks him over from head to foot.*] Ah, by the way, I think you introduced yourself to me as a—what shall . . . we say—a "character," created by an author who did not afterwards care to make a drama of his own creations.

THE FATHER. It is the simple truth, sir.

THE MANAGER. Nonsense! Cut that out, please! None of us believes it, because it isn't a thing, as you must recognize yourself, which one can believe seriously. If you want to know, it seems to me you are trying to imitate the manner of a certain author whom I heartily detest—I warn you—although I have unfortunately bound myself to put on one of his works. As a matter of fact, I was just starting to rehearse it, when you arrived. [*Turning to the* ACTORS.] And this is what we've gained—out of the frying-pan into the fire!

THE FATHER. I don't know to what author you may be alluding, but believe me I feel what I think; and I seem to be philosophizing only for those who do not think what they feel, because they blind themselves with their own sentiment. I know that for many people this self-blinding seems much more "human"; but the contrary is really true. For man never reasons so much and becomes so introspective as when he suffers; since he is anxious to get at the cause of his sufferings, to learn who has produced them, and whether it is just or unjust that he should have to bear them. On the other hand, when he is happy, he takes his happiness as it comes and doesn't analyze it, just as if happiness were his right. The animals suffer without reasoning about their sufferings. But take the case of a man who suffers and begins to reason about it. Oh no! it can't be allowed! Let him suffer like an animal, and then—ah yes, he is "human!"

THE MANAGER. Look here! Look here! You're off again, philosophizing worse than ever.

THE FATHER. Because I suffer, sir! I'm not philosophizing: I'm crying aloud the reason of my sufferings.

THE MANAGER [*makes brusque movement as he is taken with a new idea*]. I should like to know if anyone has ever heard of a character who gets right out of his part and perorates and speechifies as you do. Have you ever heard of a case? I haven't.

THE FATHER. You have never met such a case, sir, because authors, as a rule, hide the labor of their creations. When the characters are really alive before their author, the latter does nothing but follow them in their action, in their words, in the situations which they suggest to him; and he has to will them the way they will themselves—for there's trouble if he doesn't. When a character is born, he acquires at once such an independence, even of his own author, that he can be imagined by everybody even in many other situations where the author never dreamed of placing him; and so he acquires for himself a meaning which the author never thought of giving him.

THE MANAGER. Yes, yes, I know this.

THE FATHER. What is there then to marvel at in us? Imagine such a misfortune for characters as I have described to you: to be born of an author's fantasy, and be denied life by him; and then answer me if these characters left alive, and yet without life, weren't right in doing what they did do and are doing now, after they have attempted everything in their power to persuade him to give them their stage life. We've all tried him in turn, I, she [*indicating the* STEPDAUGHTER] and she [*indicating the* MOTHER].

THE STEPDAUGHTER. It's true. I too have sought to tempt him, many, many times, when he has been sitting at his writing table, feeling a bit melancholy, at the twilight hour. He would sit in his armchair too lazy to switch on the light, and all the shadows that crept into his room were full of our presence coming to tempt him. [*As if she saw herself still there by the writing table, and was annoyed by the presence of the* ACTORS.] Oh, if you would only go away, go away and leave us alone—mother here with that son of hers—I with that Child —that Boy there always alone—and then I with him—[*just hints at the* FATHER] —and then I alone, alone . . . in those shadows! [*Makes a sudden movement as if in the vision she has of herself illuminating those shadows she wanted to seize hold of herself.*]Ah! my life! my life! Oh, what scenes we proposed to him —and I tempted him more than any of the others!

THE FATHER.   Maybe. But perhaps it was your fault that he refused to give us life: because you were too insistent, too troublesome.

THE STEPDAUGHTER.   Nonsense! Didn't he make me so himself? [*Goes close to the* MANAGER *to tell him as if in confidence.*] In my opinion he abandoned us in a fit of depression, of disgust for the ordinary theater as the public knows it and likes it.

THE SON.   Exactly what it was, sir; exactly that!

THE FATHER.   Not at all! Don't believe it for a minute. Listen to me! You'll be doing quite right to modify, as you suggest, the excesses both of this girl here, who wants to do too much, and of this young man, who won't do anything at all.

THE SON.   No, nothing!

THE MANAGER.   You too get over the mark occasionally, my dear sir, if I may say so.

THE FATHER.   I? When? Where?

THE MANAGER.   Always! Continuously! Then there's this insistence of yours in trying to make us believe you are a character. And then too, you must really argue and philosophize less, you know, much less.

THE FATHER.   Well, if you want to take away from me the possibility of representing the torment of my spirit which never gives me peace, you will be suppressing me: that's all. Every true man, sir, who is a little above the level of the beasts and plants does not live for the sake of living, without knowing how to live; but he lives so as to give a meaning and a value of his own to life. For me this is *everything*. I cannot give up this, just to represent a mere fact as she [*indicating the* STEPDAUGHTER] wants. It's all very well for her, since her "vendetta" lies in the "fact." I'm not going to do it. It destroys my *raison d'être*.

THE MANAGER.   Your *raison d'être*! Oh, we're going ahead fine! First she starts off, and then you jump in. At this rate, we'll never finish.

THE FATHER.   Now, don't be offended. Have it your own way—provided, however, that within the limits of the parts you assign us each one's sacrifice isn't too great.

THE MANAGER.   You've got to understand that you can't go on arguing at your own pleasure. Drama is action, sir, action and not confounded philosophy.

THE FATHER.   All right. I'll do just as much arguing and philosophizing as everybody does when he is considering his own torments.

THE MANAGER.   If the drama permits! But for Heaven's sake, man, let's get along and come to the scene.

THE STEPDAUGHTER.   It seems to me we've got too much action with our coming into his house. [*Indicating* FATHER.] You said, before, you couldn't change the scene every five minutes.

THE MANAGER.   Of course not. What we've got to do is to combine and group up all the facts in one simultaneous, close-knit action. We can't have it as you want, with your little brother wandering like a ghost from room to room, hiding behind doors and meditating a project which—what did you say it did to him?

THE STEPDAUGHTER. Consumes him, sir, wastes him away!

THE MANAGER. Well, it may be. And then at the same time, you want the little girl there to be playing in the garden . . . one in the house, and the other in the garden: isn't that it?

THE STEPDAUGHTER. Yes, in the sun, in the sun! That is my only pleasure: to see her happy and careless in the garden after the misery and squalor of the horrible room where we all four slept together. And I had to sleep with her—I, do you understand?—with my vile contaminated body next to hers with her folding me fast in her loving little arms. In the garden, whenever she spied me, she would run to take me by the hand. She didn't care for the big flowers, only the little ones; and she loved to show me them and pet me.

THE MANAGER. Well then, we'll have it in the garden. Everything shall happen in the garden; and we'll group the other scenes there. [*Calls a stage hand.*] Here, a back-cloth with trees and something to do as a fountain basin. [*Turning around to look at the back of the stage.*] Ah, you've fixed it up. Good! [*To the* STEPDAUGHTER.] This is just to give an idea, of course. The boy, instead of hiding behind the doors, will wander about here in the garden, hiding behind the trees. But it's going to be rather difficult to find a child to do that scene with you where she shows you the flowers. [*Turning to the* YOUTH.] Come forward a little, will you please? Let's try it now! Come along! come along! [*Then seeing him come shyly forward, full of fear and looking lost.*] It's a nice business, this lad here. What's the matter with him? We'll have to give him a word or two to say. [*Goes close to him, puts a hand on his shoulders, and leads him behind one of the trees.*] Come on! come on! Let me see you a little! Hide here . . . yes, like that. Try and show your head just a little as if you were looking for someone . . . [*Goes back to observe the effect, when the* BOY *at once goes through the action.*] Excellent! fine! [*Turning to the* STEPDAUGHTER.] Suppose the little girl there were to surprise him as he looks round, and run over to him, so we could give him a word or two to say?

THE STEPDAUGHTER. It's useless to hope he will speak, as long as that fellow there is here . . . [*Indicates the* SON.] You must send him away first.

THE SON [*jumping up*]. Delighted! delighted! I don't ask for anything better. [*Begins to move away.*]

THE MANAGER [*at once stopping him*]. No! No! Where are you going? Wait a bit!

[*The* MOTHER *gets up alarmed and terrified at the thought the he is really about to go away. Instinctively she lifts her arms to prevent him, without, however, leaving her seat.*]

THE SON [*to* MANAGER *who stops him*]. I've got nothing to do with this affair. Let me go please! Let me go!

THE MANAGER. What do you mean by saying you've got nothing to do with this?

THE STEPDAUGHTER [*calmly, with irony*]. Don't bother to stop him: he won't go away.

THE FATHER. He has to act the terrible scene in the garden with his mother.

THE SON [*suddenly resolute and with dignity*]. I shall act nothing at all. I've said so from the very beginning. [*To the* MANAGER.] Let me go!

THE STEPDAUGHTER [*going over to the* MANAGER]. Allow me? [*Puts down the* MANAGER's *arm, which is restraining the* SON.] Well, go away then, if you want to! [*The* SON *looks at her with contempt and hatred. She laughs and says.*] You see, he can't, he can't go away! He is obliged to stay here, indissolubly bound to the chain. If I, who fly off when that happens which has to happen, because I can't bear him—if I am still here and support that face and expression of his, you can well imagine that he is unable to move. He has to remain here, has to stop with that nice father of his, and that mother whose only son he is. [*Turning to the* MOTHER.] Come on, mother, come along! [*Turning to the* MANAGER *to indicate her.*] You see, she was getting up to keep him back. [*To the* MOTHER, *beckoning her with her hand.*] Come on! come on! [*Then to the* MANAGER.] You can imagine how little she wants to show these actors of yours what she really feels; so eager is she to get near him that . . . There, you see? She is willing to act her part. [*And in fact, the* MOTHER *approaches him; and as soon as the* STEPDAUGHTER *has finished speaking, opens her arms to signify that she consents.*]

THE SON [*suddenly*]. No! no! I can't go away, then I'll stop here; but I repeat: I act nothing!

THE FATHER [*to the* MANAGER *excitedly*]. You can force him, sir.

THE SON. Nobody can force me.

THE FATHER. I can.

THE STEPDAUGHTER. Wait a minute, wait . . . First of all, the baby has to go to the fountain . . . [*Runs to take the* CHILD *and leads her to the fountain.*]

THE MANAGER. Yes, yes of course; that's it. Both at the same time.

[*The* SECOND LADY LEAD *and the* JUVENILE LEAD *at this point separate themselves from the group of* ACTORS. *One watches the* MOTHER *attentively; the other moves about studying the movements and manner of the* SON, *whom he will have to act.*]

THE SON [*to the* MANAGER]. What do you mean by both at the same time? It isn't right. There was no scene between me and her. [*Indicates the* MOTHER.] Ask her how it was!

THE MOTHER. Yes, it's true. I had come into his room . . .

THE SON. Into my room, do you understand? Nothing to do with the garden.

THE MANAGER. It doesn't matter. Haven't I told you we've got to group the action?

THE SON [*observing the* JUVENILE LEAD *studying him*]. What do you want?

THE JUVENILE LEAD. Nothing! I was just looking at you.

THE SON [*turning towards the* SECOND LADY LEAD]. Ah! she's at it too: to re-act her part [*indicating the* MOTHER]!

THE MANAGER. Exactly! And it seems to me that you ought to be grateful to them for their interest.

THE SON. Yes, but haven't you yet perceived that it isn't possible to live in front of a mirror which not only freezes us with the image of ourselves, but throws our likeness back at us with a horrible grimace?

THE FATHER. That is true, absolutely true. You must see that.

THE MANAGER [to the SECOND LADY LEAD and the JUVENILE LEAD]. He's right! Move away from them!

THE SON. Do as you like. I'm out of this!

THE MANAGER. Be quiet, you, will you? And let me hear your mother! [To the MOTHER.] You were saying you had entered . . .

THE MOTHER. Yes, into his room, because I couldn't stand it any longer. I went to empty my heart to him of all the anguish that tortures me . . . But as soon as he saw me come in . . .

THE SON. Nothing happened! There was no scene. I went away, that's all! I don't care for scenes!

THE MOTHER. It's true, true. That's how it was.

THE MANAGER. Well now, we've got to do this bit between you and him. It's indispensable.

THE MOTHER. I'm ready . . . when you are ready. If you could only find a chance for me to tell him what I feel here in my heart.

THE FATHER [going to SON in a great rage]. You'll do this for your mother, for your mother, do you understand?

THE SON [quite determined]. I do nothing!

THE FATHER [taking hold of him and shaking him]. For God's sake, do as I tell you! Don't you hear your mother asking you for a favor? Haven't you even got the guts to be a son?

THE SON [taking hold of the FATHER]. No! No! And for God's sake stop it, or else . . . [General agitation. The MOTHER, frightened, tries to separate them.]

THE MOTHER [pleading]. Please! please!

THE FATHER [not leaving hold of the SON]. You've got to obey, do you hear?

THE SON [almost crying from rage]. What does it mean, this madness you've got? [They separate.] Have you no decency, that you insist on showing everyone our shame? I won't do it! I won't! And I stand for the will of our author in this. He didn't want to put us on the stage, after all!

THE MANAGER. Man alive! You came here . . .

THE SON [indicating the FATHER]. He did! I didn't!

THE MANAGER. Aren't you here now?

THE SON. It was his wish, and he dragged us along with him. He's told you not only the things that did happen, but also things that have never happened at all.

THE MANAGER. Well, tell me then what did happen. You went out of your room without saying a word?

THE SON. Without a word, so as to avoid a scene!

THE MANAGER. And then what did you do?

THE SON. Nothing . . . walking in the garden . . . [Hesitates for a moment with expression of gloom.]

THE MANAGER [coming closer to him, interested by his extraordinary reserve]. Well, well . . . walking in the garden . . .

THE SON [*exasperated*]. Why on earth do you insist? It's horrible! [*The* MOTHER *trembles, sobs, and looks towards the fountain.*]

THE MANAGER [*slowly observing the glance and turning towards the* SON *with increasing apprehension*]. The baby?

THE SON. There in the fountain . . .

THE FATHER [*pointing with tender pity to the* MOTHER]. She was following him at the moment . . .

THE SON. I ran over to her; I was jumping in to drag her out when I saw something that froze my blood . . . the boy there standing stock still, with eyes like a madman's, watching his little drowned sister, in the fountain! [*The* STEPDAUGHTER *bends over the fountain to hide the* CHILD. *She sobs.*] Then . . . [*A revolver shot rings out behind the trees where the* BOY *is hidden.*]

THE MOTHER [*with a cry of terror runs over in that direction together with several of the* ACTORS *amid general confusion*]. My son! My son! [*Then amid the cries and exclamations one hears her voice.*] Help! Help!

THE MANAGER [*pushing the* ACTORS *aside while they lift up the* BOY *and carry him off*]. Is he really wounded?

SOME ACTORS. He's dead! dead!

OTHER ACTORS. No, no, it's only make believe, it's only pretence!

THE FATHER [*with a terrible cry*]. Pretence? Reality, sir, reality!

THE MANAGER. Pretence? Reality? To hell with it all! Never in my life has such a thing happened to me. I've lost a whole day over these people, a whole day!

Curtain

COMMENTARY

The essence of the theatre, as everyone is quick to understand, is illusion. The theatre sets out to induce in an audience the belief that the things and events it presents are not what they are known to be. The man on the stage who wears a crown and a purple robe and stalks with so stately a tread is a salaried actor who will go home after the performance to a light supper, a glass of beer, and bed. The audience knows this to be so but consents to accept him as "the King" and it has appropriate emotions when, in the course of the play, his "sacred" person is assaulted. Of course these emotions are not the same as would be felt by actual loyal subjects witnessing an actual attempt upon the life of their ruler, but they are consonant with the actual situation and they are often intense.

The audience comes to the performance with good will toward the theatre's designs upon it, with every intention of submitting to such illusion as the theatre can produce. The theatre, for its part, undertakes to provide the audience with adequate ground for suspending or mitigating its ordinary common-sense knowledge. The range of means by which the theatre brings about a successful illusion is wide. It includes, among other things, the distance set between the audience and the actors, scenery and lighting-effects, costume and make-up, the mimetic skill of the actors, the kind of language the actors are given to speak. The number of such devices employed varies considerably from epoch to epoch. Some cultural periods require more of them, some less. Victorian audiences would have considered inadequate the bare stage with which the Elizabethans were quite content. In our own day, the theatre is eclectic in its modes of production, which sometimes are very elaborate, sometimes so sparse as to suggest that all the theatre needs in order to bring illusion into being is to show that it wishes to do so.

Yet in the degree that the theatre is devoted to illusion, it delights in destroying it, or in seeming to destroy it. The word *illusion* comes from the Latin word meaning "to mock" (*illudere*), which in turn comes from the word meaning "to play" (*ludere*), and a favorite activity of the theatre is to play with the idea of illusion itself, to mock the very thing it most tries to create—and the audience that accepts it. Sometimes, having brought the illusion into being, it seems to suggest that it has no belief whatever in its own creation.

An amusing example of this occurs far back in the history of the theatre. The ancient Athenian drama was sacred to the god Dionysus, and the only time plays were presented was at the festival in his honor. On these occasions the priest of the god's cult presided over the performance and sat in the audience in a place of honor close to the stage. In one of the comedies of Aristophanes, *The Frogs,* the chief character is the god himself; he is represented as an arrant coward, and at one point in the action, when threatened with a beating, the comic Dionysus runs from the stage toward the audience and throws himself at the feet of the presiding priest whose protection he claims. The priest would seem to have been visibly disconcerted by this unexpected turn of events, and the Dionysus-character mocked his blushes and other signs of embarrassment.

No doubt the audience found the episode especially funny, and in a way that was different from the other comic moments in the play. The sudden destruction of the assumptions that the spectators had been making, the unexpected mingling of the world of the stage with the world of actuality, surely delighted the Athenians as similar shocks to their expectation have delighted all audiences since. Nothing that the theatre does is more engaging than its disclosing its own theatricality, its opening to question the illusion it has contrived. When Hamlet discusses the art of acting with the strolling players who have come to Elsinore there is always a little stir of new attention in the audience as it receives this reminder that the Prince of Denmark is himself an actor, and the excitement increases when, in a succeeding scene, the players act before the royal court the beginning of a crude little drama called "The Murder of Gonzago." This play-within-a-play is much less "real" than the play that contains it and it is usually acted in a stilted, unrealistic manner to emphasize the difference. But it has the effect of recalling to us that *Hamlet* is itself "merely" a play. Part of our experience of *Hamlet* becomes the awareness of the theatre itself—and of the theatre's awareness of itself.

One reason why these awarenesses—ours of the theatre and the theatre's of itself—are so engaging is that they relate to a primitive tendency to question the reality of what is commonly accepted as reality, to speculate whether life itself is not an illusion. The tendency may justly be called primitive because it is so commonly observed in children, who often have moments of thinking that all that goes on around them is but a show devised (sometimes with the purpose of putting them to a "test") by some supernal agency. This supposition of the nonreality of the actual world is of great importance in philosophic thought. Plato conceived of all that we see and know as the simulacrum of a reality that is concealed from us, and the continued interest of philosophers in the question of whether what we know is consonant with what really is made possible Alfred North Whitehead's statement that all succeeding philosophy is but "a series of footnotes to Plato." That life is a dream has often been said. Sometimes life is spoken of as a game. It is also said to be a play, and this is perhaps the most common expression of the impulse to doubt life's literal reality. Jaques' famous speech in *As You Like It,* "All the world's a stage / And all the men and women merely players," sums up an idea that has established itself in our language—we naturally speak of the "part" a person "plays" in life or in some particular situation, and of the way in which he fulfills his "rôle." Indeed the very word *person* suggests the theatre, for the original meaning of the Latin word *persona* was the mask worn by the actors of antiquity.

Of all the theatre's many celebrations of its own mysterious power, of all the challenging comparisons it makes between its own reality and that of life, Pirandello's *Six Characters in Search of an Author* is the most elaborate and brilliant. It carries the fascinating contrivance of the play-within-a-play to the point where it becomes a play-about-a-play. One might say that its *dramatis personae* are the elements of the theatre itself, all of them, as the author himself observed, in conflict with one another. The Six Characters have been "rejected" by the author, or at least he has declared himself unwilling to present their drama. The director, who despises the plays of Pirandello which he is required to put on, consents, after some resistance, to show interest in the Characters, but he finds them difficult and eventually not very satisfactory. The actors who are to play the Characters are contemptuous of them and hostile to them, an attitude which is reciprocated by the Father and the Stepdaughter, both because the actors have no drama of their own and also because they falsify the essence of the characters they play. The illusion of the theatre is wholly negated: we are permitted—forced, indeed—to see the bare stage and the shabby "properties" that are used for its contrivance. Yet of course, in spite of the civil war taking place within it, the theater realizes its familiar purpose. We of the audience do indeed believe in the reality of the Characters who are said to have been denied their existence by the author; we are fascinated and distressed by their painful situation and shocked by its outcome. The theatre as Pirandello represents it is very much like life itself, always at odds with itself, always getting in its own way, yet always pursuing and, in the end, having its way.

It is, of course, life itself that the Characters hope that the theatre will give them, and they are not concerned with distinguishing between real life and theatrical life, between life as people and life as characters. "The drama is in us and we are the drama," says the Father. "We are impatient to play it. Our inner passion drives us on to this." The Father's speech confirms—in this most un-Aristotelian play—Aristotle's idea that a drama is not the representation of a person but of an action.

Yet there is a distinction to be observed among the various ways in which the Characters think about the possibility of their realization. The Father and the Stepdaughter are fierce and explicit in their demand that they be permitted to come into existence through the acting out of their drama. Painful and shameful as their fate is, they insist upon fulfilling and demonstrating it; they may be said to love it as the means by which they attain life—they *are* their fate, they are the drama it makes. The Son, however, wants no part of the drama in which he is inextricably, although marginally, involved. It can only distress and disgust him. He is, he says, an " 'unrealized' character" and wishes to remain just that. And we, aware of the pale, thin censoriousness and self-regard that make him stand aloof from his ill-fated family, agree with his estimate of the quality of his existence, except that we take him to be personally rather than dramatically unrealized: to us he seems fully projected as the dramatic representation of an unrealized person, one whose being is in the control of his personal deficiencies. His refusal to take part in the drama as a Character is tantamount to refusing to be what in colloquial speech we call a "real person," someone whose force or courage or definiteness we necessarily perceive. Yet, for all his objection to being implicated in the drama, and despite his repugnance to the family's fate, he has had to come to the theatre as part of the family; and when, in a moment of indignation, he says that he is leaving the situation from which he is so alienated, he does not go, he cannot go. Whatever his desire may be, he is bound to the family fate and has his part in its drama; against his will, he is *in* life even though he does not occupy much space in it.

As for the Mother, she is incapable of conceiving herself as dramatic. She is wholly committed to her motherly functions and feelings and for her such ideas as "fate" and "existence," let alone "drama," have no meaning. She cannot conceive them because to do so requires a double vision that she lacks: the ability to stand off from her function and feelings and observe them. The Father, the Stepdaughter—and even, in his own dim way, the Son—have this capacity; they "see themselves" and they put a value upon what they see. But the Mother, who cannot see herself, sets no value upon herself. It is not merely that, like the Son, she objects to being in this particular drama; the very idea of drama, since it involves observation and a degree of conceptualization, is offensive to her: it belittles the actuality of life. She is, Pirandello says in his Preface to the play, realized as Nature, while the Father and the Stepdaughter (and in some degree the Son) are realized as Mind.

In the preface Pirandello speaks of "the inherent tragic conflict between life (which is always moving and changing) and 'form (which fixes it, immutable)." The conflict is not only tragic but ironic, for the "form" that Pirandello conceives of as the antagonist of "life" would seem to be brought into being by life itself for the furtherance of life. (A similar idea is central to Thomas Mann's story, "Disorder and Early Sorrow" [pages 685 ff.].) The Characters exist, they live, by reason of their fixity and immutability: the word *character* derives from the Greek word meaning to engrave, and it suggests the quality of permanence. The Father and the Stepdaughter are committed to repeat the situation that pains and shames them; they cannot move beyond it, yet it is through this compulsive reliving of the past, which denies a future in which they might move and change, that they achieve their reality of existence, their life. Realized as Mind, they are fixed by the form appropriate to Mind, their idea of themselves. The Mother, realized as Nature, is fixed by the form appropriate to Nature, her instinctual blind devotion to her maternal function of bringing life into being and preserving it.

PURGATORY

WILLIAM BUTLER YEATS

1865–1939

CHARACTERS

A BOY

AN OLD MAN

SCENE: *A ruined house and a bare tree in the background.*

BOY.   Half-door, hall door,
Hither and thither day and night,
Hill or hollow, shouldering this pack,
Hearing you talk.
   OLD MAN.   Study that house.
I think about its jokes and stories;
I try to remember what the butler
Said to a drunken gamekeeper
In mid-October, but I cannot.
If I cannot, none living can.
Where are the jokes and stories of a house,
Its threshold gone to patch a pig-sty?
   BOY.   So you have come this path before?

OLD MAN.   The moonlight falls upon the path,
The shadow of a cloud upon the house,
And that's symbolical; study that tree,
What is it like?
          BOY.   A silly old man.
     OLD MAN.   It's like—no matter what it's like.
I saw it a year ago stripped bare as now,
So I chose a better trade.
I saw it fifty years ago
Before the thunderbolt had riven it,
Green leaves, ripe leaves, leaves thick as butter,
Fat, greasy life. Stand there and look,
Because there is somebody in that house.
          [*The* BOY *puts down pack and stands in the doorway.*]
     BOY.   There's nobody here.
     OLD MAN.   There's somebody there.
     BOY.   The floor is gone, the window's gone,
And where there should be roof there's sky,
And here's a bit of an egg-shell thrown
Out of a jackdaw's nest.
     OLD MAN.   But there are some
That do not care what's gone, what's left:
The souls of Purgatory that come back
To habitations and familiar spots.
     BOY.   Your wits are out again.
     OLD MAN.   Re-live
Their transgressions, and that not once
But many times; they know at last
The consequence of those transgressions
Whether upon others or upon themselves;
Upon others, others may bring help,
For when the consequence is at an end
The dream must end; if upon themselves,
There is no help but in themselves
And in the mercy of God.
     BOY.   I have had enough!
Talk to the jackdaws, if talk you must.
     OLD MAN.   Stop! Sit there upon that stone.
That is the house where I was born.
     BOY.   The big old house that was burnt down?
     OLD MAN.   My mother that was your grand-dam owned it,
This scenery and this countryside,
Kennel and stable, horse and hound—
She had a horse at Curragh,[1] and there met
My father, a groom in the training stable,
Looked at him and married him.
Her mother never spoke to her again,

---

[1] A plain in County Kildare, Ireland.

And she did right.

    BOY.   What's right and wrong?
My grand-dad got the girl and the money.

    OLD MAN.   Looked at him and married him,
And he squandered everything she had.
She never knew the worst, because
She died in giving birth to me,
But now she knows it all, being dead.
Great people lived and died in this house;
Magistrates, colonels, members of Parliament,
Captains and Governors, and long ago
Men that had fought at Aughrim[2] and the Boyne.[3]
Some that had gone on government work
To London or to India came home to die,
Or came from London every spring
To look at the may-blossom in the park.
They had loved the trees that he cut down
To pay what he had lost at cards
Or spent on horses, drink, and women;
Had loved the house, had loved all
The intricate passages of the house,
But he killed the house; to kill a house
Where great men grew up, married, died,
I here declare a capital offense.

    BOY. My God, but you had luck! Grand clothes,
And maybe a grand horse to ride.

    OLD MAN.   That he might keep me upon his level
He never sent me to school, but some
Half-loved me for my half of her:
A gamekeeper's wife taught me to read,
A Catholic curate taught me Latin.
There were old books and books made fine
By eighteenth-century French binding, books
Modern and ancient, books by the ton.

    BOY. What education have you given me?

    OLD MAN. I gave the education that befits
A bastard that a pedlar got
Upon a tinker's daughter in a ditch.
When I had come to sixteen years old
My father burned down the house when drunk.

    BOY. But that is my age, sixteen years old,
At the Puck Fair.

    OLD MAN.   And everything was burnt;
Books, library, all were burnt.

    BOY. Is what I have heard upon the road the truth,

---

[2] In 1691, William III (William and Mary) won a decisive victory over James II for the English throne at Aughrim. The Irish forces, who fought under the Catholic James II, suffered great losses.

[3] William had earlier (1690) and less decisively defeated James at the river Boyne.

That you killed him in the burning house?

    OLD MAN.   There's nobody here but our two selves?

    BOY. Nobody, Father.

    OLD MAN.   I stuck him with a knife,

That knife that cuts my dinner now,

And after that I left him in the fire.

They dragged him out, somebody saw

The knife wound but could not be certain

Because the body was all black and charred.

Then some that were his drunken friends

Swore they would put me upon trial,

Spoke of quarrels, a threat I had made.

The gamekeeper gave me some old clothes,

I ran away, worked here and there

Till I became a pedlar on the roads,

No good trade, but good enough

Because I am my father's son,

Because of what I did or may do.

Listen to the hoof-beats! Listen, listen!

    BOY. I cannot hear a sound.

    OLD MAN.   Beat! Beat!

This night is the anniversary

Of my mother's wedding night,

Or of the night wherein I was begotten.

My father is riding from the public-house,

A whiskey-bottle under his arm.

           [*A window is lit showing a young girl.*]

Look at the window; she stands there

Listening, the servants are all in bed,

She is alone, he has stayed late

Bragging and drinking in the public-house.

    BOY. There's nothing but an empty gap in the wall.

You have made it up. No, you are mad!

You are getting madder every day.

    OLD MAN. It's louder now because he rides

Upon a graveled avenue

All grass today. The hoof-beat stops,

He has gone to the other side of the house,

Gone to the stable, put the horse up.

She has gone down to open the door.

This night she is no better than her man

And does not mind that he is half drunk,

She is mad about him. They mount the stairs.

She brings him into her own chamber.

And that is the marriage-chamber now.

The window is dimly lit again.

Do not let him touch you! It is not true

That drunken men cannot beget,

And if he touch he must beget
And you must bear his murderer,
Deaf! Both deaf! If I should throw
A stick or a stone they would not hear;
And that's a proof my wits are out.
But there's a problem: she must live
Through everything in exact detail,
Driven to it by remorse, and yet
Can she renew the sexual act
And find no pleasure in it, and if not,
If pleasure and remorse must both be there,
Which is the greater?
                              I lack schooling.
Go fetch Tertullian;[4] he and I
Will ravel all that problem out
Whilst those two lie upon the mattress
Begetting me.
                    Come back! Come back!
And so you thought to slip away,
My bag of money between your fingers,
And that I could not talk and see!
You have been rummaging in the pack.
              [*The light in the window has faded out.*]
    BOY. You never gave me my right share.
    OLD MAN. And had I given it, young as you are,
You would have spent it upon drink.
    BOY. What if I did? I had a right
To get it and spend it as I chose.
    OLD MAN. Give me that bag and no more words.
    BOY. I will not.
    OLD MAN.   I will break your fingers.
[*They struggle for the bag. In the struggle it drops, scattering the money. The*
OLD MAN *staggers but does not fall. They stand looking at each other. The win-*
          dow is lit up. A man is seen pouring whiskey into a glass.]
    BOY. What if I killed you? You killed my grand-dad.
Because you were young and he was old.
Now I am young and you are old.
    OLD MAN [*staring at window*]. Better-looking, those sixteen years——
    BOY. What are you muttering?
    OLD MAN.   Younger—and yet
She should have known he was not her kind.
    BOY. What are you saying? Out with it!
              [OLD MAN *points to window.*]
My God! The window is lit up
And somebody stands there, although

----

    [4] The first Christian theologian to write extensively in Latin. His works, which are
greatly admired for their personal, yet powerful, style, bear the stamp of his juridical training.

The floorboards are all burnt away.

    OLD MAN.   The window is lit up because my father
Has come to find a glass for his whiskey.
He leans there like some tired beast.

    BOY.   A dead, living, murdered man!

    OLD MAN.   "Then the bride-sleep fell upon Adam":
Where did I read those words?

                  And yet
There's nothing leaning in the window
But the impression upon my mother's mind;
Being dead she is alone in her remorse.

    BOY.   A body that was a bundle of old bones
Before I was born. Horrible! Horrible!

                 [*He covers his eyes.*]

    OLD MAN.   That beast there would know nothing, being nothing,
If I should kill a man under the window
He would not even turn his head.

               [*He stabs the* BOY.]
My father and my son on the same jack-knife!
That finishes—there—there—there—

       [*He stabs again and again. The window grows dark.*]
"Hush-a-bye baby, thy father's a knight,
Thy mother a lady, lovely and bright."
No, that is something that I read in a book,
And if I sing it must be to my mother,
And I lack rhyme.

    [*The stage has grown dark except where the tree stands in white light.*]
                Study that tree.
It stands there like a purified soul,
All cold, sweet, glistening light.
Dear mother, the window is dark again,
But you are in the light because,
I finished all that consequence.
I killed that lad because had he grown up
He would have struck a woman's fancy,
Begot, and passed pollution on.

I am a wretched foul old man
And therefore harmless. When I have stuck
This old jack-knife into a sod[5]
And pulled it out all bright again,
And picked up all the money that he dropped,
I'll to a distant place, and there
Tell my old jokes among new men.

         [*He cleans the knife and begin to pick up money.*]
Hoof-beats! Dear God,
How quickly it returns—beat—beat—!

[5] A piece of turf.

Her mind cannot hold up that dream.
Twice a murderer and all for nothing,
And she must animate that dead night
Not once but many times!
                    O God,
Release my mother's soul from its dream!
Mankind can do no more. Appease
The misery of the living and the remorse of the dead.

COMMENTARY

The ghost or *revenant*—the spirit of a dead person returned to the world of the living and manifesting its presence in some physical way—has its established place in modern literature. But of course it is established only as a literary convention—few people actually believe in the existence of ghosts. The author of a ghost-story takes this for granted. He himself, in all likelihood, does not believe in ghosts, and all that he counts on in the reader is a readiness to make what Coleridge called a "willing suspension of disbelief." If the reader consents to suspend his disbelief and if the author is sufficiently skilful, he can lead the reader's imagination to entertain feelings similar to those that would attend an actual experience of a ghost. Reader and author enter into an agreement, as it were, to make believe—or to *make belief*—for as long as the story lasts.

But Yeats entered into no such argument with the reader when he wrote *Purgatory*. His attitude toward the ghosts in his play is wholly the opposite of what we expect from a modern writer. When *Purgatory* was first produced—at the Abbey Theatre, Dublin, in 1939—the author was present and was called to the stage to respond to the applause of the audience. In the course of his speech he said, "I have put nothing into the play because it seemed picturesque; I have put here my own conviction about this world and the next." He meant that he believed quite literally in life after death, in the actuality of the spirits of the dead manifesting themselves as they do in the play, and in the complex conditions of the after-life that the action of the play implies. And *Purgatory* is by no means his only expression of this belief in the occult and the preternatural—from young manhood on, it stood at the very center of Yeats's intellectual and creative life. It is affirmed in many of his plays and poems and in *A Vision,* the book in which he gives a systematic account of the relation of human life to supernatural forces.

To some readers this belief will seem so bizarre that they will scarcely credit Yeats's own affirmation of it. Indeed, some critics have denied that Yeats really held the ideas he enunciated, saying that they were an elaborate fiction which he deliberately maintained because it aided his poetic imagination. I do not share this opinion. It may be that there was some ambiguity in Yeats's belief in the supernatural, or a degree of irony, but I am certain, as are most students of Yeats, that he believed what he said he believed.

A person of extremely rationalistic temper might be alienated from Yeats's play by the occultism and preternaturalism that inform it. Such a reader might say that he was perfectly willing to be entertained, or even affected, by a ghost-play if the ghosts are conceived of in the usual modern way, as a literary convention, but that, because he cannot accept the actuality of ghosts, he can take no interest in a moral situation which is based on the assumption that ghosts exist. Most people, however, will not be so absolute. While they will perceive that Yeats's literalness of belief puts a demand upon them to believe as Yeats does, and although they will no doubt refuse this demand, the knowledge that Yeats literally believed what he set forth is likely to enhance rather than diminish the effect of the play. However much we may be attracted by those elements of a work which Yeats calls "picturesque," our response to what he calls his "conviction" is bound to be graver and solider. It is one thing to suspend our disbelief in improbable or, as most of us would say, impossible circumstances. It is quite another thing, and a far more momentous one, to suspend our disbelief in what to someone else is a conviction, especially if it is a conviction about the nature of man's destiny.

My own experience with *Purgatory* may be in point. When I read the play for the first time, I supposed it to be nothing more than "picturesque." I thought that Yeats had been chiefly concerned to contrive a situation which would allow the expression of an extreme—an ultimate—rage against life and disgust with it, emotions so intense that they would lead a man to destroy not only his own father but his own son, both the root and the fruit of his life. Taking this view of the play, I regarded the ghosts as a device for telling about past events in an immediate and vivid way. So understood, the play had considerable interest for me. The spareness of its verse, the harshness of its diction, and the violence of its action commanded my attention and engaged my curiosity. But when I read Yeats's statement about the literalness of his belief in life after death and then looked into the details of his conviction, I found that the play began to exert a new and more imperative power. And perhaps it will suggest how much greater this power was if I say that although, on my first reading of the play, its conscious reminiscences of *King Lear* seemed to me rather presumptuous, as did the reference to *Oedipus Rex* which we must inevitably suppose the action implies, these allusions seemed entirely appropriate after I had understood that I was confronting Yeats's "conviction about this world and the next." I saw *Purgatory* as being, like *Oedipus Rex* and *King Lear,* a tragic confrontation of destiny, less grand than its predecessors but not less intense.

Yeats's conviction about the life after death is given systematic expression in Book III of *A Vision,* a strange work which may be described as a theory of history and a theory of personality, a detailed statement of how things happen in the world and why people are as they are. It takes for granted the existence of supernatural forces and of personal entities apart from the flesh; it represents the human soul as going through a continuous cycle of birth, death, and purification, and describes this process in detail. How Yeats came into possession of this information is explained in the introduction to the volume, which tells how certain teacher-spirits undertook to instruct him and did so over a period of years, communicating with him through Mrs. Yeats by means of automatic writing.

According to *A Vision,* the career of the soul after death is complex, but to understand *Purgatory* it is enough to know that after the soul is separated from the body at death it is not separated from its passions, its pains, and—this is of particular importance to the play—from the consequences of its actions during life. In order to achieve freedom, the soul must purge away these elements of its fleshly existence that still remain in its imagination. It accomplishes this by returning to its fleshly experiences, seeking to understand them and to disengage itself from them. The process—it has something of the aspect of a spiritual psychoanalysis—can, Yeats tells us, go on for a very long time.[1] He says that where the soul has great intensity and where the consequences of its passions have affected great numbers of people, the process of purging its passion and its experience "may last with diminishing pain and joy for centuries." But in the work of liberation, the dead can be aided by the living, who are able, Yeats says, "to assist the imaginations of the dead."

Only when we are aware of all this can we begin to understand the Old Man's motive in murdering the Boy. He kills his son in order, as he says, to finish "all that consequence."

> I killed that lad because had he grown up
> He would have struck a woman's fancy,
> Begot, and passed pollution on.

He believes that, by bringing the "consequence" to an end, he will free his mother's spirit from her sexual passion so that it will be "all cold, sweet, glistening light," and for a moment, after the murder of his son, he supposes that he has accomplished his intention.

> Dear mother, the window is dark again,
> But you are in the light because
> I finished all that consequence.

But he hears the hoofbeats of his father returning to enact yet again the moment of his conception and he knows that he is "twice a murderer and all for nothing." Inevitably we ask why he failed. And so far do we go in our willing suspension of disbelief in Yeats's conviction that we speculate about the reason in terms of Yeats' own account of the process of the spirit's liberation. We find it possible to suppose, that is, that the Old Man's act of killing the Boy is itself a "consequence," that it is charged with the passion of hatred and contempt. And how, we ask, can the Old Man believe that he has "finished all that consequence" when he himself, a chief consequence, remains? In other words, we find ourselves—to our amusement—putting rational questions on the basis of a system of belief to which we deny rationality.

[1] The Characters of *Six Characters in Search of an Author* are similarly compelled to re-enact the painful experiences that define their being, but not for the purpose of understanding them and of becoming detached from them.

GALILEO

BERTOLT BRECHT

1898–1956

It is my opinion that the earth is very noble and admirable by reason of so many and so different alterations and generations which are incessantly made therein

GALILEO GALILEI

CHARACTERS

GALILEO GALILEI

ANDREA SARTI (*two actors: boy and man*)

MRS. SARTI

LUDOVICO MARSILI

PRIULI, THE CURATOR

SAGREDO, *Galileo's friend*

VIRGINIA GALILEI

TWO SENATORS

MATTI, *an iron founder*

PHILOSOPHER (*later, Rector of the University*)

ELDERLY LADY

YOUNG LADY

FEDERZONI, *assistant to Galileo*

MATHEMATICIAN

LORD CHAMBERLAIN

FAT PRELATE

TWO SCHOLARS

TWO MONKS

INFURIATED MONK

OLD CARDINAL

ATTENDANT MONK

CHRISTOPHER CLAVIUS

LITTLE MONK

TWO SECRETARIES

CARDINAL BELLARMIN

CARDINAL BARBERINI

CARDINAL INQUISITOR

YOUNG GIRL

HER FRIEND

GIUSEPPE

STREET SINGER

HIS WIFE

REVELLER   PEASANT
A LOUD VOICE   CUSTOMS OFFICER
INFORMER   BOY
TOWN CRIER   SENATORS, OFFICIALS, PROFESSORS,
OFFICIAL   LADIES, GUESTS, CHILDREN

There are two wordless roles: THE DOGE *in Scene II and* PRINCE COSMO DI
MEDICI *in Scene IV. The ballad of Scene IX is filled out by a pantomime:
among the individuals in the pantomimic crowd are three extras (including
the* "KING OF HUNGARY"), COBBLER'S BOY, THREE CHILDREN, PEASANT WOMAN,
MONK, RICH COUPLE, DWARF, BEGGAR, *and* GIRL.

SCENE I

*In the year sixteen hundred and nine
Science' light began to shine.
At Padua City, in a modest house
Galileo Galilei set out to prove
The sun is still, the earth is on the move.*[1]

GALILEO's *scantily furnished study. Morning.* GALILEO *is washing himself.
A bare-footed boy,* ANDREA, *son of his housekeeper,* MRS. SARTI, *enters with a big
astronomical model.*

GALILEO.   Where did you get that thing?

ANDREA.   The coachman brought it.

GALILEO.   Who sent it?

ANDREA.   It said "From the Court of Naples" on the box.

GALILEO.   I don't want their stupid presents. Illuminated manuscripts, a
statue of Hercules the size of an elephant—they never send money.

ANDREA.   But isn't this an astronomical instrument, Mr. Galilei?

GALILEO.   That is an antique too. An expensive toy.

ANDREA.   What's it for?

GALILEO.   It's a map of the sky according to the wise men of ancient
Greece. Bosh! We'll try and sell it to the university. They still teach it there.

ANDREA.   How does it work, Mr. Galilei?

GALILEO.   It's complicated.

ANDREA.   I think I could understand it.

GALILEO [*interested*].   Maybe. Let's begin at the beginning. Description!

ANDREA.   There are metal rings, a lot of them.

GALILEO.   How many?

ANDREA.   Eight.

GALILEO.   Correct. And?

ANDREA.   There are words painted on the bands.

GALILEO.   What words?

ANDREA.   The names of stars.

GALILEO.   Such as?

---

[1] In the original production these initial verses were sung by a small group of choir-
boys.

ANDREA. Here is a band with the sun on it and on the inside band is the moon.

GALILEO. Those metal bands represent crystal globes, eight of them.

ANDREA. Crystal?

GALILEO. Like huge soap bubbles one inside the other and the stars are supposed to be tacked on to them. Spin the band with the sun on it. [ANDREA does.] You see the fixed ball in the middle?

ANDREA. Yes.

GALILEO. That's the earth. For two thousand years man has chosen to believe that the sun and all the host of stars revolve about him. Well. The Pope, the Cardinals, the princes, the scholars, captains, merchants, housewives, have pictured themselves squatting in the middle of an affair like that.

ANDREA. Locked up inside?

GALILEO [triumphant]. Ah!

ANDREA. It's like a cage.

GALILEO. So you sensed that. [Against the model.] I like to think the ships began it.

ANDREA. Why?

GALILEO. They used to hug the coasts and then all of a sudden they left the coasts and spread over the oceans. A new age was coming. I was on to it years ago. I was a young man, in Siena. There was a group of masons arguing. They had to raise a block of granite. It was hot. To help matters, one of them wanted to try a new arrangement of ropes. After five minutes' discussion, out went a method which had been employed for a thousand years. The millenium of faith is ended, said I, this is the millenium of doubt. And we are pulling out of that contraption. The sayings of the wise men won't wash any more. Everybody, at last, is getting nosey. I predict that in our time astronomy will become the gossip of the market place and the sons of fishwives will pack the schools.

ANDREA. You're off again, Mr. Galilei. Give me the towel. [He wipes some soap from GALILEO's back.]

GALILEO. By that time, with any luck, they will be learning that the earth rolls round the sun, and that their mothers, the captains, the scholars, the princes and the Pope are rolling with it.

ANDREA. That turning-round business is no good. I can see with my own eyes that the sun comes up in one place in the morning and goes down in a different place in the evening. It doesn't stand still, I can see it move.

GALILEO. You see nothing, all you do is gawk. Gawking is not seeing. [He puts the iron washstand in the middle of the room.] Now: that's the sun. Sit down. [ANDREA sits on a chair. GALILEO stands behind him.] Where is the sun, on your right or on your left?

ANDREA. Left.

GALILEO. And how will it get to the right?

ANDREA. By your putting it there, of course.

GALILEO. Of course? [He picks ANDREA up, chair and all, and carries him round to the other side of the washstand.] Now where is the sun?

ANDREA. On the right.

GALILEO. And did it move?

ANDREA. I did.

GALILEO. Wrong. Stupid! The chair moved.

ANDREA. But I was on it.

GALILEO. Of course. The chair is the earth, and you're sitting on it.

[MRS. SARTI, *who has come in with a glass of milk and a roll, has been watching.*]

MRS. SARTI. What are you doing with my son, Mr. Galilei?

ANDREA. Now, mother, you don't understand.

MRS. SARTI. You understand, don't you? Last night he tried to tell me that the earth goes round the sun. You'll soon have him saying that two times two is five.

GALILEO [*eating his breakfast*]. Apparently we are on the threshold of a new era, Mrs. Sarti.

MRS. SARTI. Well, I hope we can pay the milkman in this new era. A young gentleman is here to take private lessons and he is well-dressed and don't you frighten him away like you did the others. Wasting your time with Andrea! [*To* ANDREA.] How many times have I told you not to wheedle free lessons out of Mr. Galilei? [MRS. SARTI *goes.*]

GALILEO. So you thought enough of the turning-round-business to tell your mother about it.

ANDREA. Just to surprise her.

GALILEO. Andrea, I wouldn't talk about our ideas outside.

ANDREA. Why not?

GALILEO. Certain of the authorities won't like it.

ANDREA. Why not, if it's the truth?

GALILEO [*laughs*]. Because we are like the worms who are little and have dim eyes and can hardly see the stars at all, and the new astronomy is a framework of guesses or very little more—yet.

[MRS. SARTI *shows in* LUDOVICO MARSILI, *a presentable young man.*]

GALILEO. This house is like a marketplace. [*Pointing to the model.*] Move that out of the way! Put it down there!

[LUDOVICO *does.*]

LUDOVICO. Good morning, sir. My name is Ludovico Marsili.

GALILEO [*reading a letter of recommendation he has brought*]. You came by way of Holland and your family lives in the Campagna? Private lessons, thirty scudi a month.

LUDOVICO. That's all right, of course, sir.

GALILEO. What is your subject?

LUDOVICO. Horses.

GALILEO. Aha.

LUDOVICO. I don't understand science, sir.

GALILEO. Aha.

LUDOVICO. They showed me an instrument like that in Amsterdam. You'll pardon me, sir, but it didn't make sense to me at all.

GALILEO. It's out of date now.

[ANDREA *goes.*]

LUDOVICO. You'll have to be patient with me, sir. Nothing in science makes sense to me.

GALILEO. Aha.

LUDOVICO. I saw a brand new instrument in Amsterdam. A tube affair. "See things five times as large as life!" It had two lenses, one at each end, one lens bulged and the other was like that. [*Gesture.*] Any normal person would think that different lenses cancel each other out. They didn't! I just stood and looked a fool.

GALILEO.   I don't quite follow you. What does one see enlarged?

LUDOVICO.   Church steeples, pigeons, boats. Anything at a distance.

GALILEO.   Did you yourself—see things enlarged?

LUDOVICO.   Yes, sir.

GALILEO.   And the tube had two lenses? Was it like this? [*He has been making a sketch.*]

[LUDOVICO *nods.*]

GALILEO.   A recent invention?

LUDOVICO.   It must be. They only started peddling it on the streets a few days before I left Holland.

GALILEO [*starts to scribble calculations on the sketch; almost friendly*]. Why do you bother your head with science? Why don't you just breed horses?

[*Enter* MRS. SARTI. GALILEO *doesn't see her. She listens to the following.*]

LUDOVICO.   My mother is set on the idea that science is necessary nowadays for conversation.

GALILEO.   Aha. You'll find Latin or philosophy easier. [MRS. SARTI *catches his eye.*] I'll see you on Tuesday afternoon.

LUDOVICO.   I shall look forward to it, sir.

GALILEO.   Good morning. [*He goes to the window and shouts into the street.*] Andrea! Hey, Redhead, Redhead!

MRS. SARTI.   The curator of the museum is here to see you.

GALILEO.   Don't look at me like that. I took him, didn't I?

MRS. SARTI.   I caught your eye in time.

GALILEO.   Show the curator in.

[*She goes. He scribbles something on a new sheet of paper.* THE CURATOR comes in.]

CURATOR.   Good morning, Mr. Galilei.

GALILEO.   Lend me a scudo. [*He takes it and goes to the window, wrapping the coin in the paper on which he has been scribbling.*] Redhead, run to the spectacle-maker and bring me two lenses; here are the measurements. [*He throws the paper out of the window. During the following scene* GALILEO *studies his sketch of the lenses.*]

CURATOR.   Mr. Galilei, I have come to return your petition for an honorarium. Unfortunately I am unable to recommend your request.

GALILEO.   My good sir, how can I make ends meet on five hundred scudi?

CURATOR.   What about your private students?

GALILEO.   If I spend all my time with students, when am I to study? My particular science is on the threshold of important discoveries. [*He throws a manuscript on the table.*] Here are my findings on the laws of falling bodies. That should be worth 200 scudi.

CURATOR.   I am sure that any paper of yours is of infinite worth, Mr. Galilei. . . .

GALILEO.   I was limiting it to 200 scudi.

CURATOR [*cool*].   Mr. Galilei, if you want money and leisure, go to Florence.[2] I have no doubt Prince Cosmo de Medici will be glad to subsidize

---

[2] Italy in the seventeenth century was an assemblage of city-states, some of them republics and some ruled by princes.

you, but eventually you will be forbidden to think—in the name of the Inquisition. [GALILEO *says nothing*.] Now let us not make a mountain out of a molehill. You are happy here in the Republic of Venice but you need money. Well, that's human, Mr. Galilei, may I suggest a simple solution? You remember that chart you made for the army to extract cube roots without any knowledge of mathematics? Now that was practical!

GALILEO. Bosh!

CURATOR. Don't say bosh about something that astounded the Chamber of Commerce. Our city elders are businessmen. Why don't you invent something useful that will bring them a little profit?

GALILEO [*playing with the sketch of the lenses; suddenly*]. I see. Mr. Priuli, I may have something for you.

CURATOR. You don't say so.

GALILEO. It's not quite there yet, but . . .

CURATOR. You've never let me down yet, Galilei.

GALILEO. You are always an inspiration to me, Priuli.

CURATOR. You are a great man: a discontented man, but I've always said you are a great man.

GALILEO [*tartly*]. My discontent, Priuli, is for the most part with myself. I am forty-six years of age and have achieved nothing which satisfies me.

CURATOR. I won't disturb you any further.

GALILEO. Thank you. Good morning.

CURATOR. Good morning. And thank you.

[*He goes.* GALILEO *sighs.* ANDREA *returns, bringing lenses.*]

ANDREA. One scudo was not enough. I had to leave my cap with him before he'd let me take them away.

GALILEO. We'll get it back some day. Give them to me. [*He takes the lenses over to the window, holding them in the relation they would have in a telescope.*]

ANDREA. What are those for?

GALILEO. Something for the senate. With any luck, they will rake in 200 scudi. Take a look!

ANDREA. My, things look close! I can read the copper letters on the bell in the Campanile. And the washerwomen by the river, I can see their washboards!

GALILEO. Get out of the way. [*Looking through the lenses himself.*] Aha!

SCENE II

No one's virtue is complete:
Great Galileo liked to eat.
You will not resent, we hope,
The truth about his telescope.

The great arsenal of Venice, overlooking the harbor full of ships. SENATORS *and* OFFICIALS *on one side,* GALILEO, *his daughter* VIRGINIA *and his friend* SAGREDO, *on the other side. They are dressed in formal, festive clothes.* VIRGINIA *is fourteen and charming. She carries a velvet cushion on which lies a brand new telescope. Behind* GALILEO *are some* ARTISANS *from the arsenal. There are onlookers,* LUDOVICO *amongst them.*

CURATOR [*announcing*]. Senators, Artisans of the Great Arsenal of Venice; Mr. Galileo Galilei, professor of mathematics at your University of Padua.

[GALILEO *steps forward and starts to speak.*]

GALILEO. Members of the High Senate! Gentlemen: I have great pleasure, as director of this institute, in presenting for your approval and acceptance an entirely new instrument originating from this our great arsenal of the Republic of Venice. As professor of mathematics at your University of Padua, your obedient servant has always counted it his privilege to offer you such discoveries and inventions as might prove lucrative to the manufacturers and merchants of our Venetian Republic. Thus, in all humility, I tender you this, my optical tube, or telescope, constructed, I assure you, on the most scientific and Christian principles, the product of seventeen years patient research at your University of Padua.

[GALILEO *steps back. The* SENATORS *applaud.*]

SAGREDO [*aside to* GALILEO]. Now you will be able to pay your bills.

GALILEO. Yes. It will make money for them. But you realize that it is more than a money-making gadget?—I turned it on the moon last night . . .

CURATOR [*in his best chamber-of-commerce manner*]. Gentlemen: Our Republic is to be congratulated not only because this new acquisition will be one more feather in the cap of Venetian culture . . . [*Polite applause.*] . . . not only because our own Mr. Galilei has generously handed this fresh product of his teeming brain entirely over to you, allowing you to manufacture as many of these highly saleable articles as you please . . . [*Considerable applause.*] But Gentlemen of the Senate, has it occurred to you that—with the help of this remarkable new instrument—the battlefleet of the enemy will be visible to us a full two hours before we are visible to him? [*Tremendous applause.*]

GALILEO [*aside to* SAGREDO]. We have been held up three generations for lack of a thing like this. I want to go home.

SAGREDO. What about the moon?

GALILEO. Well, for one thing, it doesn't give off its own light.

CURATOR [*continuing his oration*]. And now, Your Excellency, and Members of the Senate, Mr. Galilei entreats you to accept the instrument from the hands of his charming daughter Virginia.

[*Polite applause. He beckons to* VIRGINIA, *who steps forward and presents the telescope to the* DOGE.]

CURATOR [*during this*]. Mr. Galilei gives his invention entirely into your hands, Gentlemen, enjoining you to construct as many of these instruments as you may please.

[*More applause. The* SENATORS *gather round the telescope, examining it, and looking through it.*]

GALILEO [*aside to* SAGREDO]. Do you know what the Milky Way is made of?

SAGREDO. No.

GALILEO. I do.

CURATOR [*interrupting*]. Congratulations, Mr. Galilei. Your extra five hundred scudi a year are safe.

GALILEO. Pardon? What? Of course, the five hundred scudi! Yes!

[*A prosperous man is standing beside the* CURATOR.]

CURATOR. Mr. Galilei, Mr. Matti of Florence.

MATTI. You're opening new fields, Mr. Galilei. We could do with you at Florence.

CURATOR. Now, Mr. Matti, leave something to us poor Venetians.

MATTI. It is a pity that a great republic has to seek an excuse to pay its great men their right and proper dues.

CURATOR. Even a great man has to have an incentive. [*He joins the* SENATORS *at the telescope.*]

MATTI. I am an iron founder.

GALILEO. Iron founder!

MATTI. With factories at Pisa and Florence. I wanted to talk to you about a machine you designed for a friend of mine in Padua.

GALILEO. I'll put you on to someone to copy it for you, I am not going to have the time.—How are things in Florence?

[*They wander away.*]

FIRST SENATOR [*peering*]. Extraordinary! They're having their lunch on that frigate. Lobsters! I'm hungry!

[*Laughter.*]

SECOND SENATOR. Oh, good heavens, look at her! I must tell my wife to stop bathing on the roof. When can I buy one of these things?

[*Laughter.* VIRGINIA *has spotted* LUDOVICO *among the onlookers and drags him to* GALILEO.]

VIRGINIA [*to* LUDOVICO]. Did I do it nicely?

LUDOVICO. I thought so.

VIRGINIA. Here's Ludovico to congratulate you, father.

LUDOVICO [*embarrassed*]. Congratulations, sir.

GALILEO. I improved it.

LUDOVICO. Yes, sir. I am beginning to understand science.

[GALILEO *is surrounded.*]

VIRGINIA. Isn't father a great man?

LUDOVICO. Yes.

VIRGINIA. Isn't that new thing father made pretty?

LUDOVICO. Yes, a pretty red. Where I saw it first it was covered in green.

VIRGINIA. What was?

LUDOVICO. Never mind. [*A short pause.*] Have you ever been to Holland?

[*They go. All Venice is congratulating* GALILEO, *who wants to go home.*]

SCENE III

January ten, sixteen ten:
Galileo Galilei abolishes heaven.

GALILEO's *study at Padua. It is night.* GALILEO *and* SAGREDO *at a telescope.*

SAGREDO [*softly*]. The edge of the crescent is jagged. All along the dark part, near the shiny crescent, bright particles of light keep coming up, one after the other and growing larger and merging with the bright crescent.

GALILEO. How do you explain those spots of light?

SAGREDO. It can't be true . . .

GALILEO. It *is* true: they are high mountains.

SAGREDO. On a star?

GALILEO. Yes. The shining particles are mountain peaks catching the first rays of the rising sun while the slopes of the mountains are still dark, and what you see is the sunlight moving down from the peaks into the valleys.

SAGREDO. But this gives the lie to all the astronomy that's been taught for the last two thousand years.

GALILEO. Yes. What you are seeing now has been seen by no other man beside myself.

SAGREDO. But the moon can't be an earth with mountains and valleys like our own any more than the earth can be a star.

GALILEO. The moon *is* an earth with mountains and valleys,—and the earth *is* a star. As the moon appears to us, so we appear to the moon. From the moon, the earth looks something like a crescent, sometimes like a half-globe, sometimes a full-globe, and sometimes it is not visible at all.

SAGREDO. Galileo, this is frightening.

[*An urgent knocking on the door.*]

GALILEO. I've discovered something else, something even more astonishing.

[*More knocking.* GALILEO *opens the door and the* CURATOR *comes in.*]

CURATOR. There it is—your "miraculous optical tube." Do you know that this invention he so picturesquely termed "the fruit of seventeen years research" will be on sale tomorrow for two scudi apiece at every street corner in Venice? A shipload of them has just arrived from Holland.

SAGREDO. Oh, dear!

[GALILEO *turns his back and adjusts the telescope.*]

CURATOR. When I think of the poor gentlemen of the senate who believed they were getting an invention they could monopolize for their own profit. . . . Why, when they took their first look through the glass, it was only by the merest chance that they didn't see a peddler, seven times enlarged, selling tubes exactly like it at the corner of the street.

SAGREDO. Mr. Priuli, with the help of this instrument, Mr. Galilei has made discoveries that will revolutionize our concept of the universe.

CURATOR. Mr. Galilei provided the city with a first rate water pump and the irrigation works he designed function splendidly. How was I to expect this?

GALILEO [*still at the telescope*]. Not so fast, Priuli. I may be on the track of a very large gadget. Certain of the stars appear to have regular movements. If there were a clock in the sky, it could be seen from anywhere. That might be useful for your shipowners.

CURATOR. I won't listen to you. I listened to you before, and as a reward for my friendship you have made me the laughingstock of the town. You can laugh—you got your money. But let me tell you this: you've destroyed my faith in a lot of things, Mr. Galilei. I'm disgusted with the world. That's all I have to say. [*He storms out.*]

GALILEO [*embarrassed*]. Businessmen bore me, they suffer so. Did you see the frightened look in his eyes when he caught sight of a world not created solely for the purpose of doing business?

SAGREDO. Did you know that telescopes had been made in Holland?

GALILEO. I'd heard about it. But the one I made for the Senators was twice as good as any Dutchman's. Besides, I needed the money. How can I work, with the tax collector on the doorstep? And my poor daughter will never acquire a husband unless she has a dowry, she's not too bright. And I like to buy books— all kinds of books. Why not? And what about my appetite? I don't think well unless I eat well. Can I help it if I get my best ideas over a good meal and a bottle of wine? They don't pay me as much as they pay the butcher's boy. If only I could have five years to do nothing but research! Come on. I am going to show you something else.

SAGREDO.   I don't know that I want to look again.

GALILEO.   This is one of the brighter nebulae of the Milky Way. What do you see?

SAGREDO.   But it's made up of stars—countless stars.

GALILEO.   Countless worlds.

SAGREDO [*hesitating*].   What about the theory that the earth revolves round the sun? Have you run across anything about that?

GALILEO.   No. But I noticed something on Tuesday that might prove a step towards even that. Where's Jupiter? There are four lesser stars near Jupiter. I happened on them on Monday but didn't take any particular note of their position. On Tuesday I looked again. I could have sworn they had moved. They have changed again. Tell me what you see.

SAGREDO.   I only see three.

GALILEO.   Where's the fourth? Let's get the charts and settle down to work.

[*They work and the lights dim. The lights go up again. It is near dawn.*]

GALILEO.   The only place the fourth can be is round at the back of the larger star where we cannot see it. This means there are small stars revolving around a big star. Where are the crystal shells now that the stars are supposed to be fixed to?

SAGREDO.   Jupiter can't be attached to anything: there are other stars revolving round it.

GALILEO.   There is no support in the heavens. [SAGREDO *laughs awkwardly*.] Don't stand there looking at me as if it weren't true.

SAGREDO.   I suppose it is true. I'm afraid.

GALILEO.   Why?

SAGREDO.   What do you think is going to happen to you for saying that there is another sun around which other earths revolve? And that there are only stars and no difference between earth and heaven? Where is God then?

GALILEO.   What do you mean?

SAGREDO.   God? Where is God?

GALILEO [*angrily*].   Not there! Any more than he'd be here—if creatures from the moon came down to look for him!

SAGREDO.   Then where is He?

GALILEO.   I'm not a theologian: I'm a mathematician.

SAGREDO.   You are a human being! [*Almost shouting.*] Where is God in your system of the universe?

GALILEO.   Within ourselves. Or—nowhere.

SAGREDO.   Ten years ago a man was burned at the stake for saying that.

GALILEO.   Giordano Bruno was an idiot: he spoke too soon. He would never have been condemned if he could have backed up what he said with proof.

SAGREDO [*incredulously*]. Do you really believe proof will make any difference?

GALILEO. I believe in the human race The only people that can't be reasoned with are the dead. Human beings are intelligent.

SAGREDO. Intelligent—or merely shrewd?

GALILEO. I know they call a donkey a horse when they want to sell it, and a horse a donkey when they want to buy it. But is that the whole story? Aren't they susceptible to truth as well? [*He fishes a small pebble out of his pocket.*] If anybody were to drop a stone . . . [*Drops the pebble.*] . . . and tell them that it didn't fall, do you think they would keep quiet? The evidence of your own eyes is a very seductive thing. Sooner or later everybody must succumb to it.

SAGREDO. Galileo, I am helpless when you talk.

[*A church bell has been ringing for some time, calling people to mass. Enter* VIRGINIA, *muffled up for mass, carrying a candle protected from the wind by a globe.*]

VIRGINIA. Oh, father, you promised to go to bed tonight, and it's five o'clock again.

GALILEO. Why are you up at this hour?

VIRGINIA. I'm going to mass with Mrs. Sarti. Ludovico is going too. How was the night, father?

GALILEO. Bright.

VIRGINIA. What did you find through the tube?

GALILEO. Only some little specks by the side of a star. I must draw attention to them somehow. I think I'll name them after the Prince of Florence. Why not call them the Medicean planets? By the way, we may move to Florence. I've written to His Highness, asking if he can use me as Court Mathematician.

VIRGINIA. Oh, father, we'll be at the court!

SAGREDO [*amazed*]. Galileo!

GALILEO. My dear Sagredo, I must have leisure. My only worry is that His Highness after all may not take me. I'm not accustomed to writing formal letters to great personages. Here, do you think this is the right sort of thing?

SAGREDO [*reads and quotes*]. "Whose sole desire is to reside in Your Highness' presence—the rising sun of our great age." Cosmo de Medici is a boy of nine.

GALILEO. The only way a man like me can land a good job is by crawling on his stomach. Your father, my dear, is going to take his share of the pleasures of life in exchange for all his hard work, and about time too. I have no patience, Sagredo, with a man who doesn't use his brains to fill his belly. Run along to mass now.

[VIRGINIA *goes.*]

SAGREDO. Galileo, do not go to Florence.

GALILEO. Why not?

SAGREDO. The monks are in power there.

GALILEO. Going to mass is a small price to pay for a full belly. And there are many famous scholars at the court of Florence.

SAGREDO. Court monkeys.

GALILEO. I shall enjoy taking them by the scruff of the neck and making them look through the telescope.

SAGREDO. Galileo, you are traveling the road to disaster. You are suspicious and skeptical in science, but in politics you are as naive as your daughter! How can people in power leave a man at large who tells the truth, even if it be the truth about the distant stars? Can you see the Pope scribbling a note in his diary: "10th of January, 1610, Heaven abolished?" A moment ago when you were at the telescope, I saw you tied to the stake, and when you said you believed in proof, I smelt burning flesh!

GALILEO. I am going to Florence.

[*Before the next scene a curtain with the following legend on it is lowered*]

> By setting the name of Medici in the sky, I am bestowing immortality upon the stars. I commend myself to you as your most faithful and devoted servant, whose sole desire is to reside in Your Highness' presence, the rising sun of our great age.
>
> GALILEO GALILEI

SCENE IV

GALILEO's *house at Florence. Well-appointed.* GALILEO *is demonstrating his telescope to* PRINCE COSMO DE MEDICI, *a boy of nine, accompanied by his* LORD CHAMBERLAIN, LADIES *and* GENTLEMEN *of the Court and an assortment of university* PROFESSORS. *With* GALILEO *are* ANDREA *and* FEDERZONI, *the new assistant* (*an old man*). MRS. SARTI *stands by. Before the scene opens the voice of the* PHILOSOPHER *can be heard.*

VOICE OF THE PHILOSOPHER. Quaedam miracula universi. Orbes mystice canorae, arcus crystallini, circulatio corporum coelestium. Cyclorum epicyclorumque intoxicatio, integritas tabulae chordarum et architectura elata globorum coelestium.

GALILEO. Shall we speak in everyday language? My colleague Mr. Federzoni does not understand Latin.

PHILOSOPHER. Is it necessary that he should?

GALILEO. Yes.

PHILOSOPHER. Forgive me. I thought he was your mechanic.

ANDREA. Mr. Federzoni is a mechanic and a scholar.

PHILOSOPHER. Thank you, young man. If Mr. Federzoni insists . . .

GALILEO. I insist.

PHILOSOPHER. It will not be as clear, but it's your house. Your Highness . . . [THE PRINCE *is ineffectually trying to establish contact with* ANDREA.] I was about to recall to Mr. Galilei some of the wonders of the universe as they are set down for us in the Divine Classics. [THE LADIES "*ah*."] Remind him of the "mystically musical spheres, the crystal arches, the circulation of the heavenly bodies—"

ELDERLY LADY. Perfect poise!

PHILOSOPHER. "—the intoxication of the cycles and epicycles, the integrity of the tables of chords and the enraptured architecture of the celestial globes."

ELDERLY LADY. What diction!

PHILOSOPHER. May I pose the question: Why should we go out of our way to look for things that can only strike a discord in this ineffable harmony?

[*The* LADIES *applaud.*]

FEDERZONI. Take a look through here—you'll be interested.

ANDREA. Sit down here, please.

[*The* PROFESSORS *laugh.*]

MATHEMATICIAN. Mr. Galilei, nobody doubts that your brain child—or is it your adopted brain child?—is brilliantly contrived.

GALILEO. Your Highness, one can see the four stars as large as life, you know.

[*The* PRINCE *looks to the* ELDERLY LADY *for guidance.*]

MATHEMATICIAN. Ah. But has it occurred to you that an eyeglass through which one sees such phenomena might not be a too reliable eyeglass?

GALILEO. How is that?

MATHEMATICIAN. If one could be sure you would keep your temper, Mr. Galilei, I could suggest that what one sees in the eyeglass and what is in the heavens are two entirely different things.

GALILEO [*quietly*]. You are suggesting fraud?

MATHEMATICIAN. No! How could I, in the presence of His Highness?

ELDERLY LADY. The gentlemen are just wondering if Your Highness' stars are really, really there!

[*Pause.*]

YOUNG LADY [*trying to be helpful*]. Can one see the claws on the Great Bear?

GALILEO. And everything on Taurus the Bull.

FEDERZONI. Are you going to look through it or not?

MATHEMATICIAN. With the greatest of pleasure.

[*Pause. Nobody goes near the telescope. All of a sudden the boy* ANDREA *turns and marches pale and erect past them through the whole length of the room. The* GUESTS *follow with their eyes.*]

MRS. SARTI [*as he passes her*]. What is the matter with you?

ANDREA [*shocked*]. They are wicked.

PHILOSOPHER. Your Highness, it is a delicate matter and I had no intention of bringing it up, but Mr. Galilei was about to demonstrate the impossible. His new stars would have broken the outer crystal sphere—which we know of on the authority of Aristotle. I am sorry.

MATHEMATICIAN. The last word.

FEDERZONI. He had no telescope.

MATHEMATICIAN. Quite.

GALILEO [*keeping his temper*]. "Truth is the daughter of Time, not of Authority." Gentlemen, the sum of our knowledge is pitiful. It has been my singular good fortune to find a new instrument which brings a small patch of the universe a little bit closer. It is at your disposal.

PHILOSOPHER. Where is all this leading?

GALILEO. Are we, as scholars, concerned with where the truth might lead us?

PHILOSOPHER. Mr. Galilei, the truth might lead us anywhere!

GALILEO. I can only beg you to look through my eyeglass.

MATHEMATICIAN [*wild*].   If I understand Mr. Galilei correctly, he is asking us to discard the teachings of two thousand years.

GALILEO.   For two thousand years we have been looking at the sky and didn't see the four moons of Jupiter, and there they were all the time. Why defend shaken teachings? You should be doing the shaking. [*The* PRINCE *is sleepy.*] Your Highness! My work in the Great Arsenal of Venice brought me in daily contact with sailors, carpenters, and so on. These men are unread. They depend on the evidence of their senses. But they taught me many new ways of doing things. The question is whether these gentlemen here want to be found out as fools by men who might not have had the advantages of a classical education but who are not afraid to use their eyes. I tell you that our dockyards are stirring with that same high curiosity which was the true glory of Ancient Greece.

[*Pause.*]

PHILOSOPHER.   I have no doubt Mr. Galilei's theories will arouse the enthusiasm of the dockyards.

CHAMBERLAIN.   Your Highness, I find to my amazement that this highly informative discussion has exceeded the time we had allowed for it. May I remind Your Highness that the State Ball begins in three-quarters of an hour?

[*The* COURT *bows low.*]

ELDERLY LADY.   We would really have liked to look through your eyeglass, Mr. Galilei, wouldn't we, Your Highness?

[*The* PRINCE *bows politely and is led to the door.* GALILEO *follows the* PRINCE, CHAMBERLAIN *and* LADIES *towards the exit. The* PROFESSORS *remain at the telescope.*]

GALILEO [*almost servile*].   All anybody has to do is look through the telescope, Your Highness.

[MRS. SARTI *takes a plate with candies to the* PRINCE *as he is walking out.*]

MRS. SARTI.   A piece of homemade candy, Your Highness?

ELDERLY LADY.   Not now. Thank you. It is too soon before His Highness' supper.

PHILOSOPHER.   Wouldn't I like to take that thing to pieces.

MATHEMATICIAN.   Ingenious contraption. It must be quite difficult to keep clean. [*He rubs the lens with his handkerchief and looks at the handkerchief.*]

FEDERZONI.   We did not paint the Medicean stars on the lens.

ELDERLY LADY [*to the* PRINCE, *who has whispered something to her*].   No, no, no, there is nothing the matter with your stars!

CHAMBERLAIN [*across the stage to* GALILEO].   His Highness will of course seek the opinion of the greatest living authority: Christopher Clavius, Chief Astronomer to the Papal College in Rome.

SCENE V

Things take indeed a wondrous turn
When learned men do stoop to learn.
Clavius, we are pleased to say,
Upheld Galileo Galilei.

A burst of laughter is heard and the curtains reveal a hall in the Collegium Romanum. HIGH CHURCHMEN, MONKS *and* SCHOLARS *standing about talking and laughing.* GALILEO *by himself in a corner.*

FAT PRELATE [*shaking with laughter*].   Hopeless! Hopeless! Hopeless! Will you tell me something people won't believe?

A SCHOLAR.   Yes, that you don't love your stomach!

FAT PRELATE.   They'd believe that. They only do not believe what's good for them. They doubt the devil, but fill them up with some fiddle-de-dee about the earth rolling like a marble in the gutter and they swallow it hook, line, and sinker. Sancta simplicitas!

[*He laughs until the tears run down his cheeks. The others laugh with him. A group has formed whose members boisterously begin to pretend they are standing on a rolling globe.*]

A MONK.   It's rolling fast, I'm dizzy. May I hold on to you, Professor?

[*He sways dizzily and clings to one of the scholars for support.*]

THE SCHOLAR.   Old Mother Earth's been at the bottle again. Whoa!

MONK.   Hey! Hey! We're slipping off! Help!

SECOND SCHOLAR.   Look! There's Venus! Hold me, lads. Whee!

SECOND MONK.   Don't, don't hurl us off on to the moon. There are nasty sharp mountain peaks on the moon, brethren!

VARIOUSLY.   Hold tight! Hold tight! Don't look down! Hold tight! It'll make you giddy!

FAT PRELATE.   And we cannot have giddy people in Holy Rome.

[*They rock with laughter. An* INFURIATED MONK *comes out from a large door at the rear holding a bible in his hand and pointing out a page with his finger.*]

INFURIATED MONK.   What does the bible say—"Sun, stand thou still on Gideon and thou, moon, in the valley of Ajalon."[3] Can the sun come to a standstill if it doesn't ever move? Does the bible lie?

FAT PRELATE.   How did Christopher Clavius, the greatest astronomer we have, get mixed up in an investigation of this kind?

INFURIATED MONK.   He's in there with his eye glued to that diabolical instrument.

FAT PRELATE [*to* GALILEO, *who has been playing with his pebble and has dropped it*].   Mr. Galilei, something dropped down.

GALILEO.   Monsignor, are you sure it didn't drop up?

INFURIATED MONK.   As astronomers we are aware that there are phenomena which are beyond us, but man can't expect to understand everything!

[*Enter a very old* CARDINAL *leaning on a* MONK *for support. Others move aside.*]

OLD CARDINAL.   Aren't they out yet? Can't they reach a decision on that paltry matter? Christopher Clavius ought to know his astronomy after all these years. I am informed that Mr. Galilei transfers mankind from the center of the universe to somewhere on the outskirts. Mr. Galilei is therefore an enemy of mankind and must be dealt with as such. Is it conceivable that God would trust this most precious fruit of His labor to a minor frolicking star? Would He have

---

[3] Joshua 10:12.

sent His Son to such a place? How can there be people with such twisted minds that they believe what they're told by the slave of a multiplication table?

FAT PRELATE [*quietly to* CARDINAL]. The gentleman is over there.

OLD CARDINAL. So you are the man. You know my eyes are not what they were, but I can see you bear a striking resemblance to the man we burned. What was his name?

MONK. Your Eminence must avoid excitement the doctor said . . .

OLD CARDINAL [*disregarding him*]. So you have degraded the earth despite the fact that you live by her and receive everything from her. I won't have it! I won't have it! I won't be a nobody on an inconsequential star briefly twirling hither and thither. I tread the earth, and the earth is firm beneath my feet, and there is no motion to the earth, and the earth is the center of all things, and I am the center of the earth, and the eye of the creator is upon me. About me revolve, affixed to their crystal shells, the lesser lights of the stars and the great light of the sun, created to give light upon me that God might see me—Man, God's greatest effort, the center of creation. "In the image of God created He him."[4] Immortal . . .

[*His strength fails him and he catches for the* MONK *for support.*]

MONK. You mustn't overtax your strength, Your Eminence.

[*At this moment the door at the rear opens and* CHRISTOPHER CLAVIUS *enters followed by his* ASTRONOMERS. *He strides hastily across the hall, looking neither right nor left. As he goes by we hear him say—*]

CLAVIUS. He is right.

[*Deadly silence. All turn to* GALILEO.]

OLD CARDINAL. What is it? Have they reached a decision?

[*No one speaks.*]

MONK. It is time that Your Eminence went home.

[*The hall is emptying fast. One little* MONK *who had entered with* CLAVIUS *speaks to* GALILEO.]

LITTLE MONK. Mr. Galilei, I heard Father Clavius say: "Now it's for the theologians to set the heavens right again." You have won.

[*Before the next scene a curtain with the following legend on it is lowered:*]

> . . . As these new astronomical charts enable us to determine longitudes at sea and so make it possible to reach the new continents by the shortest routes, we would beseech Your Excellency to aid us in reaching Mr. Galilei, mathematician to the Court of Florence, who is now in Rome . . .
>
> —FROM A LETTER WRITTEN BY A MEMBER OF THE GENOA CHAMBER OF COMMERCE AND NAVIGATION TO THE PAPAL LEGATION

SCENE VI

When Galileo was in Rome
A Cardinal asked him to his home
He wined and dined him as his guest
And only made one small request.

---

[4] Genesis 1:27.

CARDINAL BELLARMIN's *house in Rome. Music is heard and the chatter of many guests. Two* SECRETARIES *are at the rear of the stage at a desk.* GALILEO, *his daughter* VIRGINIA, *now 21, and* LUDOVICO MARSILI, *who has become her fiancé, are just arriving. A few* GUESTS, *standing near the entrance with masks in their hands, nudge each other and are suddenly silent.* GALILEO *looks at them.*
They applaud him politely and bow.

VIRGINIA.   O father! I'm so happy. I won't dance with anyone but you, Ludovico.

GALILEO [*to a* SECRETARY].   I was to wait here for His Eminence.

FIRST SECRETARY.   His Eminence will be with you in a few minutes.

VIRGINIA.   Do I look proper?

LUDOVICO.   You are showing some lace.

[GALILEO *puts his arms around their shoulders.*]

GALILEO [*quoting mischievously*].

Fret not, daughter, if perchance
You attract a wanton glance.
The eyes that catch a trembling lace
Will guess the heartbeat's quickened pace.
Lovely woman still may be
Careless with felicity.

VIRGINIA [*to* GALILEO].   Feel my heart.

GALILEO [*to* LUDOVICO].   It's thumping.

VIRGINIA.   I hope I always say the right thing.

LUDOVICO.   She's afraid she's going to let us down.

VIRGINIA.   Oh, I want to look beautiful.

GALILEO.   You'd better. If you don't they'll start saying all over again that the earth doesn't turn.

LUDOVICO [*laughing*].   It *doesn't* turn, sir.

[GALILEO *laughs.*]

GALILEO.   Go and enjoy yourselves. [*He speaks to one of the* SECRETARIES.] A large fête?

FIRST SECRETARY.   Two hundred and fifty guests, Mr. Galilei. We have represented here this evening most of the great families of Italy, the Orsinis, the Villanis, the Nuccolis, the Soldanieris, the Canes, the Lecchis, the Estensis, the Colombinis, the . . .

[VIRGINIA *comes running back.*]

VIRGINIA.   Oh father, I didn't tell you: you're famous.

GALILEO.   Why?

VIRGINIA.   The hairdresser in the Via Vittorio kept four other ladies waiting and took me first. [*Exit.*]

GALILEO [*at the stairway, leaning over the well*].   Rome!

[*Enter* CARDINAL BELLARMIN, *wearing the mask of a lamb, and* CARDINAL BARBERINI, *wearing the mask of a dove.*]

SECRETARIES.   Their Eminences, Cardinals Bellarmin and Barberini.

[*The* CARDINALS *lower their masks.*]

GALILEO [*to* BELLARMIN].   Your Eminence.

BELLARMIN.   Mr. Galilei, Cardinal Barberini.

GALILEO. Your Eminence.

BARBERINI. So you are the father of that lovely child!

BELLARMIN. Who is inordinately proud of being her father's daughter.

[*They laugh.*]

BARBERINI [*points his finger at* GALILEO]. "The sun riseth and setteth and returneth to its place,"[5] saith the bible. What saith Galilei?

GALILEO. Appearances are notoriously deceptive, Your Eminence. Once when I was so high, I was standing on a ship that was pulling away from the shore and I shouted, "The shore is moving!" I know now that it was the ship which was moving.

BARBERINI [*laughs*]. You can't catch that man. I tell you, Bellarmin, his moons around Jupiter are hard nuts to crack. Unfortunately for me I happened to glance at a few papers on astronomy once. It is harder to get rid of than the itch.

BELLARMIN. Let's move with the times. If it makes navigation easier for sailors to use new charts based on a new hypothesis let them have them. We only have to scotch doctrines that contradict Holy Writ.

[*He leans over the balustrade of the well and acknowledges various* GUESTS.]

BARBERINI. But Bellarmin, you haven't caught on to this fellow. The scriptures don't satisfy him. Copernicus[6] does.

GALILEO. Copernicus? "He that withholdeth corn the people shall curse him."[7] Book of Proverbs.

BARBERINI. "A prudent man concealeth knowledge."[8] Also Book of Proverbs.

GALILEO. "Where no oxen are, the stable is clean, but much increase is by the strength of the ox."[9]

BARBERINI. "He that ruleth his spirit is better than he that taketh a city."[10]

GALILEO. "But a broken spirit drieth up the bones."[11] [*Pause.*] "Doth not wisdom cry?"[12]

BARBERINI. "Can one walk on hot coals and his feet not be scorched?"[13]— Welcome to Rome, Friend Galileo. You recall the legend of our city's origin?[14] Two small boys found sustenance and refuge with a she-wolf and from that day we have paid the price for the she-wolf's milk. But the place is not bad. We have everything for your pleasure—from a scholarly dispute with Bellarmin to

---

[5] Ecclesiastes 1:5.

[6] Copernicus (1473–1543) had held that the sun was the center of the universe to which the earth belonged and that the earth revolved about it, but it remained for Galileo and other scientists of the seventeenth century to prove the Copernican theory.

[7] Proverbs 11:26.

[8] Proverbs 12:23.

[9] Proverbs 14:4.

[10] Proverbs 16:32.

[11] Proverbs 17:22.

[12] Proverbs 8:1.

[13] Proverbs 6:28.

[14] The legend relates that the twins, Romulus and Remus, were sons of Mars and the daughter of a king and that they were cast out by the usurper of their grandfather's throne. A she-wolf suckled them, and a shepherd reared them. When grown, they restored their grandfather's throne and founded the new city, Rome, for themselves. They quarreled, however, and Remus was slain by his brother.

ladies of high degree. Look at that woman flaunting herself. No? He wants a weighty discussion! All right! [*To* GALILEO.] You people speak in terms of circles and ellipses and regular velocities—simple movements that the human mind can grasp—very convenient—but suppose Almighty God had taken it into his head to make the stars move like that . . . [*He describes an irregular motion with his fingers through the air.*] . . . then where would you be?

GALILEO. My good man—the Almighty would have endowed us with brains like that . . . [*Repeats the movement.*] . . . so that we could grasp the movements . . . [*Repeats the movement.*] . . . like that. I believe in the brain.

BARBERINI. I consider the brain inadequate. He doesn't answer. He is too polite to tell me he considers *my* brain inadequate. What is one to do with him? Butter wouldn't melt in his mouth. All he wants to do is to prove that God made a few boners in astronomy. God didn't study his astronomy hard enough before he composed Holy Writ. [*To the* SECRETARIES.] Don't take anything down. This is a scientific discussion among friends.

BELLARMIN [*to* GALILEO]. Does it not appear more probable—even to you —that the Creator knows more about his work than the created?

GALILEO. In his blindness man is liable to misread not only the sky but also the bible.

BELLARMIN. The interpretation of the bible is a matter for the ministers of God. [GALILEO *remains silent.*] At last you are quiet. [*He gestures to the* SECRETARIES. *They start writing.*] Tonight the Holy Office has decided that the theory according to which the earth goes around the sun is foolish, absurd, and a heresy. I am charged, Mr. Galilei, with cautioning you to abandon these teachings. [*To the* FIRST SECRETARY.] Would you repeat that?

FIRST SECRETARY [*reading*]. "His Eminence, Cardinal Bellarmin, to the aforesaid Galilei: The Holy Office has resolved that the theory according to which the earth goes around the sun is foolish, absurd, and a heresy. I am charged, Mr. Galilei, with cautioning you to abandon these teachings."

GALILEO [*rocking on his base.*]. But the facts!

BARBERINI [*consoling*]. Your findings have been ratified by the Papal Observatory, Galilei. That should be most flattering to you . . .

BELLARMIN [*cutting in*]. The Holy Office formulated the decree without going into details.

GALILEO [*to* BARBERINI]. Do you realize, the future of all scientific research is . . .

BELLARMIN [*cutting in*]. Completely assured, Mr. Galilei. It is not given to man to know the truth: it is granted to him to seek after the truth. Science is the legitimate and beloved daughter of the Church. She must have confidence in the Church.

GALILEO [*infuriated*]. I would not try confidence by whistling her too often.

BARBERINI [*quickly*]. Be careful what you're doing—you'll be throwing out the baby with the bath water, friend Galilei. [*Serious.*] We need you more than you need us.

BELLARMIN. Well, it is time we introduced our distinguished friend to our guests. The whole country talks of him!

BARBERINI. Let us replace our masks, Bellarmin. Poor Galilei hasn't got one.

[He laughs. They take GALILEO *out.]*

FIRST SECRETARY.   Did you get his last sentence?

SECOND SECRETARY.   Yes. Do you have what he said about believing in the brain?

[Another cardinal—the INQUISITOR—*enters.]*

INQUISITOR.   Did the conference take place?

[The FIRST SECRETARY *hands him the papers and the* INQUISITOR *dismisses the* SECRETARIES. *They go. The* INQUISITOR *sits down and starts to read the transcription. Two or three* YOUNG LADIES *skitter across the stage; they see the* INQUISITOR *and curtsy as they go.]*

YOUNG GIRL.   Who was that?

HER FRIEND.   The Cardinal Inquisitor.

[They giggle and go. Enter VIRGINIA. *She curtsies as she goes. The* IN-QUISITOR *stops her.]*

INQUISITOR.   Good evening, my child. Beautiful night. May I congratulate you on your betrothal? Your young man comes from a fine family. Are you staying with us here in Rome?

VIRGINIA.   Not now, Your Eminence. I must go home to prepare for the wedding.

INQUISITOR.   Ah. You are accompanying your father to Florence. That should please him. Science must be cold comfort in a home. Your youth and warmth will keep him down to earth. It is easy to get lost up there. *[He gestures to the sky.]*

VIRGINIA.   He doesn't talk to me about the stars, Your Eminence.

INQUISITOR.   No. *[He laughs.]* They don't eat fish in the fisherman's house. I can tell you something about astronomy. My child, it seems that God has blessed our modern astronomers with imaginations. It is quite alarming! Do you know that the earth—which we old fogies supposed to be so large—has shrunk to something no bigger than a walnut, and the new universe has grown so vast that prelates—and even cardinals—look like ants. Why, God Almighty might lose sight of a Pope! I wonder if I know your Father Confessor.

VIRGINIA.   Father Christopherus, from Saint Ursula's at Florence, Your Eminence.

INQUISITOR.   My dear child, your father will need you. Not so much now perhaps, but one of these days. You are pure, and there is strength in purity. Greatness is sometimes, indeed often, too heavy a burden for those to whom God has granted it. What man is so great that he has no place in a prayer? But I am keeping you, my dear. Your fiancé will be jealous of me, and I am afraid your father will never forgive me for holding forth on astronomy. Go to your dancing and remember me to Father Christopherus.

*[*VIRGINIA *kisses his ring and runs off. The* INQUISITOR *resumes his reading.]*

SCENE VII

Galileo, feeling grim,
A young monk came to visit him.
The monk was born of common folk.
It was of science that they spoke.

Garden of the Florentine AMBASSADOR *in Rome. Distant hum of a great city.* GALILEO *and the* LITTLE MONK *of Scene V are talking.*

GALILEO. Let's hear it. That robe you're wearing gives you the right to say whatever you want to say. Let's hear it.

LITTLE MONK. I have studied physics, Mr. Galilei.

GALILEO. That might help us if it enabled you to admit that two and two are four.

LITTLE MONK. Mr. Galilei, I have spent four sleepless nights trying to reconcile the decree that I have read with the moons of Jupiter that I have seen. This morning I decided to come to see you after I had said Mass.

GALILEO. To tell me that Jupiter has no moons?

LITTLE MONK. No, I found out that I think the decree a wise decree. It has shocked me into realizing that free research has its dangers. I have had to decide to give up astronomy. However, I felt the impulse to confide in you some of the motives which have impelled even a passionate physicist to abandon his work.

GALILEO. Your motives are familiar to me.

LITTLE MONK. You mean, of course, the special powers invested in certain commissions of the Holy Office? But there is something else. I would like to talk to you about my family. I do not come from the great city. My parents are peasants in the Campagna, who know about the cultivation of the olive tree, and not much about anything else. Too often these days when I am trying to concentrate on tracking down the moons of Jupiter, I see my parents. I see them sitting by the fire with my sister, eating their curded cheese. I see the beams of the ceiling above them, which the smoke of centuries has blackened, and I can see the veins stand out on their toil-worn hands, and the little spoons in their hands. They scrape a living, and underlying their poverty there is a sort of order. There are routines. The routine of scrubbing the floors, the routine of the seasons in the olive orchard, the routine of paying taxes. The troubles that come to them are recurrent troubles. My father did not get his poor bent back all at once, but little by little, year by year, in the olive orchard; just as year after year, with unfailing regularity, childbirth has made my mother more and more sexless. They draw the strength they need to sweat with their loaded baskets up the stony paths, to bear children, even to eat, from the sight of the trees greening each year anew, from the reproachful face of the soil, which is never satisfied, and from the little church and bible texts they hear there on Sunday. They have been told that God relies upon them and that the pageant of the world has been written around them that they may be tested in the important or unimportant parts handed out to them. How could they take it, were I to tell them that they are on a lump of stone ceaselessly spinning in empty space, circling around a second-rate star? What, then, would be the use of their patience, their acceptance of misery? What comfort, then, the Holy Scriptures, which have mercifully explained their crucifixion? The Holy Scriptures would then be proved full of mistakes. No, I see them begin to look frightened. I see them slowly put their spoons down on the table. They would feel cheated. "There is no eye watching over us, after all," they would say. "We have to start out on our own, at our time of life. Nobody has planned a part for us beyond this wretched one on a worthless star. There is no meaning in our misery. Hunger is just not having eaten. It is no test of strength. Effort is just stooping and carrying. It is not a virtue." Can you understand that I read into the decree of the Holy Office a noble motherly pity and a great goodness of the soul?

GALILEO [*embarrassed*]. Hm, well at least you have found out that it is not a question of the satellites of Jupiter, but of the peasants of the Campagna! And don't try to break me down by the halo of beauty that radiates from old age. How does a pearl develop in an oyster? A jagged grain of sand makes its way into the oyster's shell and makes its life unbearable. The oyster exudes slime to cover the grain of sand and the slime eventually hardens into a pearl. The oyster nearly dies in the process. To hell with the pearl, give me the healthy oyster! And virtues are not exclusive to misery. If your parents were prosperous and happy, they might develop the virtues of happiness and prosperity. Today the virtues of exhaustion are caused by the exhausted land. For that my new water pumps could work more wonders than their ridiculous superhuman efforts. Be fruitful and multiply: for war will cut down the population, and our fields are barren! [*A pause.*] Shall I lie to your people?

LITTLE MONK. We must be silent from the highest of motives: the inward peace of less fortunate souls.

GALILEO. My dear man, as a bonus for not meddling with your parents' peace, the authorities are tendering me, on a silver platter, persecution-free, my share of the fat sweated from your parents, who, as you know, were made in God's image. Should I condone this decree, my motives might not be disinterested: easy life, no persecution and so on.

LITTLE MONK. Mr. Galilei, I am a priest.

GALILEO. You are also a physicist. How can new machinery be evolved to domesticate the river water if we physicists are forbidden to study, discuss, and pool our findings about the greatest machinery of all, the machinery of the heavenly bodies? Can I reconcile my findings on the paths of falling bodies with the current belief in the tracks of witches on broom sticks [*A pause.*] I am sorry—I shouldn't have said that.

LITTLE MONK. You don't think that the truth, if it is the truth, would make its way without us?

GALILEO. No! No! No! As much of the truth gets through as we push through. You talk about the Campagna peasants as if they were the moss on their huts. Naturally, if they don't get a move on and learn to think for themselves, the most efficient of irrigation systems cannot help them. I can see their divine patience, but where is their divine fury?

LITTLE MONK [*helpless*]. They are old!

[GALILEO *stands for a moment, beaten; he cannot meet the* LITTLE MONK's *eyes. He takes a manuscript from the table and throws it violently on the ground.*]

LITTLE MONK. What is that?

GALILEO. Here is writ what draws the ocean when it ebbs and flows. Let it lie there. Thou shalt not read. [LITTLE MONK *has picked up the manuscript.*] Already! An apple of the tree of knowledge, he can't wait, he wolfs it down. He will rot in hell for all eternity. Look at him, where are his manners?—Sometimes I think I would let them imprison me in a place a thousand feet beneath the earth where no light could reach me, if in exchange I could find out what stuff that is: "Light." The bad thing is that, when I find something, I have to boast about it like a lover or a drunkard or a traitor. That is a hopeless vice and leads to the abyss. I wonder how long I shall be content to discuss it with my dog!

LITTLE MONK [*immersed in the manuscript*].   I don't understand this sentence.

GALILEO.   I'll explain it to you. I'll explain it to you.

[*They are sitting on the floor.*]

SCENE VIII

Eight long years with tongue in cheek
Of what he knew he did not speak.
Then temptation grew too great
And Galileo challenged fate.

GALILEO's *house in Florence again.* GALILEO *is supervising his Assistants* ANDREA, FEDERZONI, *and the* LITTLE MONK, *who are about to prepare an experiment.* MRS. SARTI *and* VIRGINIA *are at a long table sewing bridal linen. There is a new telescope, larger than the old one. At the moment it is covered with a cloth.*

ANDREA [*looking up a schedule*].   Thursday. Afternoon. Floating bodies again. Ice, bowl of water, scales, and it says here an iron needle. Aristotle.

VIRGINIA.   Ludovico likes to entertain. We must take care to be neat. His mother notices every stitch. She doesn't approve of father's books.

MRS. SARTI.   That's all a thing of the past. He hasn't published a book for years.

VIRGINIA.   That's true. Oh Sarti, it's fun sewing a trousseau.

MRS. SARTI.   Virginia, I want to talk to you. You are very young, and you have no mother, and your father is putting those pieces of ice in water, and marriage is too serious a business to go into blind. Now you should go to see a real astronomer from the university and have him cast your horoscope so you know where you stand. [VIRGINIA *giggles.*] What's the matter?

VIRGINIA.   I've been already.

MRS. SARTI.   Tell Sarti.

VIRGINIA.   I have to be careful for three months now because the sun is in Capricorn, but after that I get a favorable ascendant, and I can undertake a journey if I am careful of Uranus, as I'm a Scorpion.

MRS. SARTI.   What about Ludovico?

VIRGINIA.   He's a Leo, the astronomer said. Leos are sensual. [*Giggles.*]

[*There is a knock at the door, it opens. Enter the* RECTOR OF THE UNIVERSITY, *the philosopher of Scene IV, bringing a book.*]

RECTOR [*to* VIRGINIA].   This is about the burning issue of the moment. He may want to glance over it. My faculty would appreciate his comments. No, don't disturb him now, my dear. Every minute one takes of your father's time is stolen from Italy. [*He goes.*]

VIRGINIA.   Federzoni! The rector of the university brought this.

[FEDERZONI *takes it.*]

GALILEO. What's it about?

FEDERZONI [*spelling*]. DE MACULIS IN SOLE.

ANDREA. Oh, it's on the sun spots!

[ANDREA *comes one side, and the* LITTLE MONK *the other, to look at the book.*]

ANDREA. A new one!

[FEDERZONI *resentfully puts the book into their hands and continues with the preparation of the experiment.*]

ANDREA. Listen to this dedication. [*Quotes.*] "To the greatest living authority on physics, Galileo Galilei."—I read Fabricius'[15] paper the other day. Fabricius says the spots are clusters of planets between us and the sun.

LITTLE MONK. Doubtful.

GALILEO [*noncommittal*]. Yes?

ANDREA. Paris and Prague hold that they are vapors from the sun. Federzoni doubts that.

FEDERZONI. Me? You leave me out. I said "hm," that was all. And don't discuss new things before me. I can't read the material, it's in Latin. [*He drops the scales and stands trembling with fury.*] Tell me, can I doubt anything?

[GALILEO *walks over and picks up the scales silently. Pause.*]

LITTLE MONK. There is happiness in doubting, I wonder why.

ANDREA. Aren't we going to take this up?

GALILEO. At the moment we are investigating floating bodies.

ANDREA. Mother has baskets full of letters from all over Europe asking his opinion.

FEDERZONI. The question is whether you can afford to remain silent.

GALILEO. I cannot afford to be smoked on a wood fire like a ham.

ANDREA [*surprised*]. Ah. You think the sun spots may have something to do with that again? [GALILEO *does not answer.*]

ANDREA. Well, we stick to fiddling about with bits of ice in water. That can't hurt you.

GALILEO. Correct.—Our thesis!

ANDREA. All things that are lighter than water float, and all things that are heavier sink.

GALILEO. Aristotle says—

LITTLE MONK [*reading out of a book, translating*]. "A broad and flat disk of ice, although heavier than water, still floats, because it is unable to divide the water."

GALILEO. Well. Now I push the ice below the surface. I take away the pressure of my hands. What happens?

[*Pause.*]

LITTLE MONK. It rises to the surface.

GALILEO. Correct. It seems to be able to divide the water as it's coming up, doesn't it?

LITTLE MONK. Could it be lighter than water after all?

GALILEO. Aha!

ANDREA. Then all things that are lighter than water float, and all things that are heavier sink. Q. e. d.

15 Italian anatomist and embryologist (1537–1619) who taught at Padua.

GALILEO. Not at all. Hand me that iron needle. Heavier than water? [*They all nod.*] A piece of paper. [*He places the needle on a piece of paper and floats it on the surface of the water. Pause.*] Do not be hasty with your conclusion. [*Pause.*] What happens?

FEDERZONI. The paper has sunk, the needle is floating.

VIRGINIA. What's the matter?

MRS. SARTI. Every time I hear them laugh it sends shivers down my spine. [*There is a knocking at the outer door.*]

MRS. SARTI. Who's that at the door?

[*Enter* LUDOVICO. VIRGINIA *runs to him. They embrace.* LUDOVICO *is followed by a servant with baggage.*]

MRS. SARTI. Well!

VIRGINIA. Oh! Why didn't you write that you were coming?

LUDOVICO. I decided on the spur of the moment. I was over inspecting our vineyards at Bucciole. I couldn't keep away.

GALILEO. Who's that?

LITTLE MONK. Miss Virginia's intended. What's the matter with your eyes?

GALILEO [*blinking*]. Oh yes, it's Ludovico, so it is. Well! Sarti, get a jug of that Sicilian wine, the old kind. We celebrate.

[*Everybody sits down.* MRS. SARTI *has left, followed by* LUDOVICO'S SERVANT.]

GALILEO. Well, Ludovico, old man. How are the horses?

LUDOVICO. The horses are fine.

GALILEO. Fine.

LUDOVICO. But those vineyards need a firm hand. [*To* VIRGINIA.] You look pale. Country life will suit you. Mother's planning on September.

VIRGINIA. I suppose I oughtn't, but stay here, I've got something to show you.

LUDOVICO. What?

VIRGINIA. Never mind. I won't be ten minutes. [*She runs out.*]

LUDOVICO. How's life these days, sir?

GALILEO. Dull. —How was the journey?

LUDOVICO. Dull. —Before I forget, mother sends her congratulations on your admirable tact over the latest rumblings of science.

GALILEO. Thank her from me.

LUDOVICO. Christopher Clavius had all Rome on its ears. He said he was afraid that the turning around business might crop up again on account of these spots on the sun.

ANDREA. Clavius is on the same track! [*To* LUDOVICO.] My mother's baskets are full of letters from all over Europe asking Mr. Galilei's opinion.

GALILEO. I am engaged in investigating the habits of floating bodies. Any harm in that?

[MRS. SARTI *re-enters, followed by the* SERVANT. *They bring wine and glasses on a tray.*]

GALILEO [*hands out the wine*]. What news from the Holy City, apart from the prospect of my sins?

LUDOVICO. The Holy Father is on his death bed. Hadn't you heard?

LITTLE MONK. My goodness! What about the succession?

LUDOVICO. All the talk is of Barberini.

GALILEO. Barberini?

ANDREA. Mr. Galilei knows Barberini.

LITTLE MONK. Cardinal Barberini is a mathematician.

FEDERZONI. A scientist in the chair of Peter!

[Pause.]

GALILEO [cheering up enormously]. This means change. We might live to see the day, Federzoni, when we don't have to whisper that two and two are four. [To LUDOVICO.] I like this wine. Don't you, Ludovico?

LUDOVICO. I like it.

GALILEO. I know the hill where it is grown. The slope is steep and stony, the grape almost blue. I am fond of this wine.

LUDOVICO. Yes, sir.

GALILEO. There are shadows in this wine. It is almost sweet, but just stops short.—Andrea, clear that stuff away, ice, bowl and needle.—I cherish the consolations of the flesh. I have no patience with cowards who call them weaknesses. I say there is a certain achievement in enjoying things.

[The PUPILS get up and go to the experiment table.]

LITTLE MONK. What are we to do?

FEDERZONI. He is starting on the sun.

[They begin with clearing up.]

ANDREA [singing in a low voice].

> The bible proves the earth stands still,
> The Pope, he swears with tears:
> The earth stands still. To prove it so
> He takes it by the ears.

LUDOVICO. What's the excitement?

MRS. SARTI. You're not going to start those hellish goings-on again, Mr. Galilei?

ANDREA.

> And gentlefolk, they say so too.
> Each learned doctor proves,
> (If you grease his palm): The earth stands still.
> And yet—and yet it moves.

GALILEO. Barberini is in the ascendant, so your mother is uneasy, and you're sent to investigate me. Correct me if I am wrong, Ludovico. Clavius is right: these spots on the sun interest me.

ANDREA. We might find out that the sun also revolves. How would you like that, Ludovico?

GALILEO. Do you like my wine, Ludovico?

LUDOVICO. I told you I did, sir.

GALILEO. You really like it?

LUDOVICO. I like it.

GALILEO. Tell me, Ludovico, would you consider going so far as to accept a man's wine or his daughter without insisting that he drop his profession? I have no wish to intrude, but have the moons of Jupiter affected Virginia's bottom?

MRS. SARTI.   That isn't funny, it's just vulgar. I am going for Virginia.

LUDOVICO [*keeps her back*].   Marriages in families such as mine are not arranged on a basis of sexual attraction alone.

GALILEO.   Did they keep you back from marrying my daughter for eight years because I was on probation?

LUDOVICO.   My future wife must take her place in the family pew.

GALILEO.   You mean, if the daughter of a bad man sat in your family pew, your peasants might stop paying the rent?

LUDOVICO.   In a sort of way.

GALILEO.   When I was your age, the only person I allowed to rap me on the knuckles was my girl.

LUDOVICO.   My mother was assured that you had undertaken not to get mixed up in this turning around business again, sir.

GALILEO.   We had a conservative Pope then.

MRS. SARTI.   Had! His Holiness is not dead yet!

GALILEO [*with relish*].   Pretty nearly.

MRS. SARTI.   That man will weigh a chip of ice fifty times, but when it comes to something that's convenient, he believes it blindly. "Is His Holiness dead?"—"Pretty nearly!"

LUDOVICO.   You will find, sir, if His Holiness passes away, the new Pope, whoever he turns out to be, will respect the convictions held by the solid families of the country.

GALILEO [*to* ANDREA].   That remains to be seen.—Andrea, get out the screen. We'll throw the image of the sun on our screen to save our eyes.

LITTLE MONK.   I thought you'd been working at it. Do you know when I guessed it? When you didn't recognize Mr. Marsili.

MRS. SARTI.   If my son has to go to hell for sticking to you, that's my affair, but you have no right to trample on your daughter's happiness.

LUDOVICO [*to his* SERVANT].   Giuseppe, take my baggage back to the coach, will you?

MRS. SARTI.   This will kill her. [*She runs out, still clutching the jug.*]

LUDOVICO [*politely*].   Mr. Galilei, if we Marsilis were to countenance teachings frowned on by the church, it would unsettle our peasants. Bear in mind: these poor people in their brute state get everything upside down. They are nothing but animals. They will never comprehend the finer points of astronomy. Why, two months ago a rumor went around, an apple had been found on a pear tree, and they left their work in the fields to discuss it.

GALILEO [*interested*].   Did they?

LUDOVICO.   I have seen the day when my poor mother has had to have a dog whipped before their eyes to remind them to keep their place. Oh, you may have seen the waving corn from the window of your comfortable coach. You have, no doubt, nibbled our olives, and absentmindedly eaten our cheese, but you can have no idea how much responsibility that sort of thing entails.

GALILEO.   Young man, I do not eat my cheese absentmindedly. [*To* ANDREA.] Are we ready?

ANDREA.   Yes, sir.

GALILEO [*leaves* LUDOVICO *and adjusts the mirror*].   You would not confine your whippings to dogs to remind your peasants to keep their places, would you, Marsili?

LUDOVICO [*after a pause*].   Mr. Galilei, you have a wonderful brain, it's a pity.

LITTLE MONK [*astonished*].   He threatened you.

GALILEO.   Yes. And he threatened you too. We might unsettle his peasants. Your sister, Fulganzio, who works the lever of the olive press, might laugh out loud if she heard the sun is not a gilded coat of arms but a lever too. The earth turns because the sun turns it.

ANDREA.   That could interest his steward too and even his money lender—and the seaport towns. . . .

FEDERZONI.   None of them speak Latin.

GALILEO.   I might write in plain language. The work we do is exacting. Who would go through the strain for less than the population at large!

LUDOVICO.   I see you have made your decision. It was inevitable. You will always be a slave of your passions. Excuse me to Virginia, I think it's as well I don't see her now.

GALILEO.   The dowry is at your disposal at any time.

LUDOVICO.   Good afternoon. [*He goes followed by the* SERVANT.]

ANDREA.   Exit Ludovico. To hell with all Marsilis, Villanis, Orsinis, Canes, Nuccolis, Soldanieris. . . .

FEDERZONI.   . . . who ordered the earth stand still because their castles might be shaken loose if it revolves . . .

LITTLE MONK.   . . . and who only kiss the Pope's feet as long as he uses them to trample on the people. God made the physical world, God made the human brain. God will allow physics.

ANDREA.   They will try to stop us.

GALILEO.   Thus we enter the observation of these spots on the sun in which we are interested, at our own risk, not counting on protection from a problematical new Pope . . .

ANDREA.   . . . but with great likelihood of dispelling Fabrizius' vapors, and the shadows of Paris and Prague, and of establishing the rotation of the sun . . .

GALILEO.   . . . and with *some* likelihood of establishing the rotation of the sun. My intention is not to prove that I was right but to find out *whether* I was right. "Abandon hope all ye who enter—an observation."[16] Before assuming these phenomena are spots, which would suit us, let us first set about proving that they are not—fried fish. We crawl by inches. What we find today we will wipe from the blackboard tomorrow and reject it—unless it shows up again the day after tomorrow. And if we find anything which would suit us, that thing we will eye with particular distrust. In fact, we will approach this observing of the sun with the implacable determination to prove that the earth stands still and only if hopelessly defeated in this pious undertaking can we allow ourselves to wonder if we may not have been right all the time: the earth revolves. Take the cloth off the telescope and turn it on the sun.

[*Quietly they start work. When the corruscating image of the sun is focused on the screen,* VIRGINIA *enters hurriedly, her wedding dress on, her hair disheveled,* MRS. SARTI *with her, carrying her wedding veil. The two women realize what has happened.* VIRGINIA *faints.* ANDREA, LITTLE MONK *and* GALILEO *rush to her.* FEDERZONI *continues working.*]

---

[16] In Dante's *Divine Comedy*, the inscription above the gates of Hell is "Abandon hope all ye who enter here."

SCENE IX

On April Fool's Day, thirty two,
Of science there was much ado:
People had learned from Galilei:
They used his teaching in their way.

Around the corner from the market place a STREET SINGER *and his* WIFE, *who is costumed to represent the earth in a skeleton globe made of thin bands of brass, are holding the attention of a sprinkling of representative citizens, some in masquerade who were on their way to see the carnival procession. From the market place the noise of an impatient crowd.*

BALLAD SINGER [*accompanied by his* WIFE *on the guitar*].
When the Almighty made the universe
He made the earth and then he made the sun.
Then round the earth he bade the sun to turn—
That's in the bible, Genesis, Chapter One.
And from that time all beings here below
Were in obedient circles meant to go:
    Around the pope the cardinals
    Around the cardinals the bishops
    Around the bishops the secretaries
    Around the secretaries the aldermen
    Around the aldermen the craftsmen
    Around the craftsmen the servants
    Around the servants the dogs, the chickens, and the beggars.

[*A conspicuous reveller—henceforth called the* SPINNER—*has slowly caught on and is exhibiting his idea of spinning around. He does not lose dignity, he faints with mock grace.*]

BALLAD SINGER.
Up stood the learned Galileo
Glanced briefly at the sun
And said: "Almighty God was wrong
In Genesis, Chapter One!"
    Now that was rash, my friends, it is no matter small
    For heresy will spread today like foul diseases.
    Change Holy Writ, forsooth? What will be left at all?
    Why: each of us would say and do just what he pleases!

[*Three wretched* EXTRAS, *employed by the chamber of commerce, enter. Two of them, in ragged costumes, moodily bear a litter with a mock throne. The third sits on the throne. He wears sacking, a false beard, a prop crown, he carries a prop orb and sceptre, and around his chest the inscription "*THE KING OF HUNGARY.*" The litter has a card with "No. 4" written on it. The litter bearers dump him down and listen to the* BALLAD SINGER.]

BALLAD SINGER.
Good people, what will come to pass
If Galileo's teachings spread?
No altar boy will serve the mass
No servant girl will make the bed.
    Now that is grave, my friends, it is no matter small:

For independent spirit spreads like foul diseases!
(Yet life is sweet and man is weak and after all—
How nice it is, for a little change, to do just as one pleases!)

[*The* BALLAD SINGER *takes over the guitar. His* WIFE *dances around him, illustrating the motion of the earth. A* COBBLER'S BOY *with a pair of resplendent lacquered boots hung over his shoulder has been jumping up and down in mock excitement. There are three more children, dressed as grownups among the spectators, two together and a single one with mother. The* COBBLER'S BOY *takes the three* CHILDREN *in hand, forms a chain and leads it, moving to the music, in and out among the spectators, "whipping" the chain so that the last child bumps into people. On the way past a* PEASANT WOMAN, *he steals an egg from her basket. She gestures to him to return it. As he passes her again he quietly breaks the egg over her head. The* KING OF HUNGARY *ceremoniously hands his orb to one of his bearers, marches down with mock dignity, and chastises the* COBBLER'S BOY. *The parents remove the three* CHILDREN. *The unseemliness subsides.*]

BALLAD SINGER.
The carpenters take wood and build
Their houses—not the church's pews.
And members of the cobblers' guild
Now boldly walk the streets—in shoes.
The tenant kicks the noble lord
Quite off the land he owned—like that!
The milk his wife once gave the priest
Now makes (at last!) her children fat.

    Ts, ts, ts, ts, my friends, this is no matter small
    For independent spirit spreads like foul diseases
    People must keep their place, some down and some on top!
    (Though it is nice, for a little change, to do just as one pleases!)

[*The* COBBLER'S BOY *has put on the lacquered boots he was carrying. He struts off. The* BALLAD SINGER *takes over the guitar again. His* WIFE *dances around him in increased tempo. A* MONK *has been standing near a rich* COUPLE, *who are in subdued costly clothes, without masks: shocked at the song, he now leaves. A* DWARF *in the costume of an astronomer turns his telescope on the departing* MONK, *thus drawing attention to the rich* COUPLE. *In imitation of the* COBBLER'S BOY, *the* SPINNER *forms a chain of grownups. They move to the music, in and out, and between the rich* COUPLE. *The* SPINNER *changes the* GENTLE-MAN'S *bonnet for the ragged hat of a* BEGGAR. *The* GENTLEMAN *decides to take this in good part, and a* GIRL *is emboldened to take his dagger. The* GENTLEMAN *is miffed, throws the* BEGGAR'S *hat back. The* BEGGAR *discards the* GENTLEMAN'S *bonnet and drops it on the ground. The* KING OF HUNGARY *has walked from his throne, taken an egg from the* PEASANT WOMAN, *and paid for it. He now ceremoniously breaks it over the* GENTLEMAN'S *head as he is bending down to pick up his bonnet. The* GENTLEMAN *conducts the* LADY *away from the scene. The* KING OF HUNGARY, *about to resume his throne, finds one of the* CHILDREN *sitting on it. The* GENTLEMAN *returns to retrieve his dagger. Merriment. The* BALLAD SINGER *wanders off. This is part of his routine. His* WIFE *sings to the* SPINNER.]

WIFE.
Now speaking for myself I feel

That I could also do with a change.
You know, for me . . . [*Turning to a reveller.*] . . . you have appeal
Maybe tonight we could arrange . . .

> [*The* DWARF-ASTRONOMER *has been amusing the people by focusing his
> telescope on her legs. The* BALLAD SINGER *has returned.*]

BALLAD SINGER.

No, no, no, no, no, stop, Galileo, stop!
For independent spirit spreads like foul diseases
People must keep their place, some down and some on top!
(Though it is nice, for a little change, to do just as one pleases!)

> [*The* SPECTATORS *stand embarrassed. A* GIRL *laughs loudly.*]

BALLAD SINGER [*and his* WIFE].

Good people who have trouble here below
In serving cruel lords and gentle Jesus
Who bids you turn the other cheek just so . . . [*With mimicry.*]
While they prepare to strike the second blow:
Obedience will never cure your woe
So each of you wake up and do just as he pleases!

> [*The* BALLAD SINGER *and his* WIFE *hurriedly start to try to sell pamphlets to
> the spectators.*]

BALLAD SINGER.   Read all about the earth going round the sun, two centesimi only. As proved by the great Galileo. Two centesimi only. Written by a
local scholar. Understandable to one and all. Buy one for your friends, your
children and your aunty Rosa, two centesimi only. Abbreviated but complete. Fully illustrated with pictures of the planets, including Venus, two
centesimi only.

> [*During the speech of the* BALLAD SINGER *we hear the carnival procession
> approaching followed by laughter. A* REVELLER *rushes in.*]

REVELLER.   The procession!

> [*The litter bearers speedily joggle out the* KING OF HUNGARY. *The* SPEC-
> TATORS *turn and look at the first float of the procession, which now makes its
> appearance. It bears a gigantic figure of* GALILEO, *holding in one hand an open
> bible with the pages crossed out. The other hand points to the bible, and the
> head mechanically turns from side to side as if to say "No! No!"*]

A LOUD VOICE.   Galileo the bible killer!

> [*The laughter from the market place becomes uproarious. The* MONK *comes
> flying from the market place followed by delighted* CHILDREN.]

SCENE X

*The depths are hot, the heights are chill
The streets are loud, the court is still.*

Ante-Chamber and staircase in the Medicean palace in Florence. GALILEO,
with a book under his arm, waits with his DAUGHTER *to be admitted to the
presence of the* PRINCE.

VIRGINIA. They are a long time.

GALILEO. Yes.

VIRGINIA. Who is that funny looking man? [*She indicates the* INFORMER, *who has entered casually and seated himself in the background, taking no apparent notice of* GALILEO.]

GALILEO. I don't know.

VIRGINIA. It's not the first time I have seen him around. He gives me the creeps.

GALILEO. Nonsense. We're in Florence, not among robbers in the mountains of Corsica.

VIRGINIA. Here comes the Rector.

[*The* RECTOR *comes down the stairs.*]

GALILEO. Gaffone is a bore. He attaches himself to you.

[*The* RECTOR *passes, scarcely nodding.*]

GALILEO. My eyes are bad today. Did he acknowledge us?

VIRGINIA. Barely. [*Pause.*] What's in your book? Will they say it's heretical?

GALILEO. You hang around church too much. And getting up at dawn and scurrying to mass is ruining your skin. You pray for me, don't you?

[*A* MAN *comes down the stairs.*]

VIRGINIA. Here's Mr. Matti. You designed a machine for his Iron Foundries.

MATTI. How were the squabs, Mr. Galilei? [*Low.*] My brother and I had a good laugh the other day. He picked up a racy pamphlet against the bible somewhere. It quoted you.

GALILEO. The squabs, Matti, were wonderful, thank you again. Pamphlets I know nothing about. The bible and Homer are my favorite reading.

MATTI. No necessity to be cautious with me, Mr. Galilei. I am on your side. I am not a man who knows about the motions of the stars, but you have championed the freedom to teach new things. Take that mechanical cultivator they have in Germany which you described to me. I can tell you, it will never be used in this country. The same circles that are hampering you now will forbid the physicians at Bologna to cut up corpses for research. Do you know, they have such things as money markets in Amsterdam and in London? Schools for business, too. Regular papers with news. Here we are not even free to make money. I have a stake in your career. They are against iron foundries because they say the gathering of so many workers in one place fosters immorality! If they ever try anything, Mr. Galilei, remember you have friends in all walks of life including an iron founder. Good luck to you. [*He goes.*]

GALILEO. Good man, but need he be so affectionate in public? His voice carries. They will always claim me as their spiritual leader particularly in places where it doesn't help me at all. I have written a book about the mechanics of the firmament, that is all. What they do or don't do with it is not my concern.

VIRGINIA [*loud*]. If people only knew how you disagreed with those goings-on all over the country last All Fools day.

GALILEO. Yes. Offer honey to a bear, and lose your arm if the beast is hungry.

VIRGINIA [*low*]. Did the prince ask you to come here today?

GALILEO.   I sent word I was coming. He will want the book, he has paid for it. My health hasn't been any too good lately. I may accept Sagredo's invitation to stay with him in Padua for a few weeks.

VIRGINIA.   You couldn't manage without your books.

GALILEO.   Sagredo has an excellent library.

VIRGINIA.   We haven't had this month's salary yet—

GALILEO.   Yes. [*The* CARDINAL INQUISITOR *passes down the staircase. He bows deeply in answer to* GALILEO's *bow.*] What is he doing in Florence? If they try to do anything to me, the new Pope will meet them with an iron NO. And the Prince is my pupil, he would never have me extradited.

VIRGINIA.   Psst. The Lord Chamberlain.

[*The* LORD CHAMBERLAIN *comes down the stairs.*]

LORD CHAMBERLAIN.   His Highness had hoped to find time for you, Mr. Galilei. Unfortunately, he has to leave immediately to judge the parade at the Riding Academy. On what business did you wish to see His Highness?

GALILEO.   I wanted to present my book to His Highness.

LORD CHAMBERLAIN.   How are your eyes today?

GALILEO.   So, so. With His Highness' permission, I am dedicating the book . . .

LORD CHAMBERLAIN.   Your eyes are a matter of great concern to His Highness. Could it be that you have been looking too long and too often through your marvelous tube? [*He leaves without accepting the book.*]

VIRGINIA [*greatly agitated*].   Father, I am afraid.

GALILEO.   He didn't take the book, did he? [*Low and resolute.*] Keep a straight face. We are not going home, but to the house of the lens-grinder. There is a coach and horses in his backyard. Keep your eyes to the front, don't look back at that man.

[*They start. The* LORD CHAMBERLAIN *comes back.*]

LORD CHAMBERLAIN.   Oh, Mr. Galilei, His Highness has just charged me to inform you that the Florentine Court is no longer in a position to oppose the request of the Holy Inquisition to interrogate you in Rome.

SCENE XI

The Pope

A chamber in the Vatican. The POPE, URBAN VIII—*formerly Cardinal* BARBERINI—*is giving audience to the* CARDINAL INQUISITOR. *The trampling and shuffling of many feet is heard throughout the scene from the adjoining corridors. During the scene the* POPE *is being robed for the conclave he is about to attend: at the beginning of the scene he is plainly* BARBERINI, *but as the scene proceeds he is more and more obscured by grandiose vestments.*

POPE.   No! No! No!

INQUISITOR [*referring to the owners of the shuffling feet*].   Doctors of all chairs from the universities, representatives of the special orders of the Church, representatives of the clergy as a whole who have come believing with child-like faith in the word of God as set forth in the Scriptures, who have come to hear Your Holiness confirm their faith: and Your Holiness is really going to tell them that the bible can no longer be regarded as the alphabet of truth?

POPE.   I will not set myself up against the multiplication table. No!

INQUISITOR.   Ah, that is what these people say, that it is the multiplication table. Their cry is, "The figures compel us," but where do these figures come from? Plainly they come from doubt. These men doubt everything. Can society stand on doubt and not on faith? "Thou art my master, but I doubt whether it is for the best." "This is my neighbor's house and my neighbor's wife, but why shouldn't they belong to me?" After the plague, after the new war, after the unparalleled disaster of the Reformation, your dwindling flock look to their shepherd, and now the mathematicians turn their tubes on the sky and announce to the world that you have not the best advice about the heavens either—up to now your only uncontested sphere of influence. This Galilei started meddling in machines at an early age. Now that men in ships are venturing on the great oceans—I am not against that of course—they are putting their faith in a brass-bowl they call a compass and not in Almighty God.

POPE.   This man is the greatest physicist of our time. He is the light of Italy, and not just any muddle-head.

INQUISITOR.   Would we have had to arrest him otherwise? This bad man knows what he is doing, not writing his books in Latin, but in the jargon of the market place.

POPE [occupied with the shuffling feet].   That was not in the best of taste. [A pause.] These shuffling feet are making me nervous.

INQUISITOR.   May they be more telling than my words, Your Holiness. Shall all these go from you with doubt in their hearts?

POPE.   This man has friends. What about Versailles? What about the Viennese court? They will call Holy Church a cesspool for defunct ideas. Keep your hands off him.

INQUISITOR.   In practice it will never get far. He is a man of the flesh. He would soften at once.

POPE.   He has more enjoyment in him than any man I ever saw. He loves eating and drinking and thinking. To excess. He indulges in thinking-bouts! He cannot say no to an old wine or a new thought. [Furious.] I do not want a condemnation of physical facts. I do not want to hear battle cries: Church, church, church! Reason, reason, reason! [Pause.] These shuffling feet are intolerable. Has the whole world come to my door?

INQUISITOR.   Not the whole world, Your Holiness. A select gathering of the faithful.

[Pause.]

POPE [exhausted].   It is clearly understood: he is not to be tortured. [Pause.] At the very most, he may be shown the instruments.

INQUISITOR.   That will be adequate, Your Holiness. Mr. Galilei understands machinery.

[The eyes of BARBERINI look helplessly at the CARDINAL INQUISITOR from under the completely assembled panoply of POPE URBAN VIII.]

SCENE XII

June twenty second, sixteen thirty three,
A momentous date for you and me.
Of all the days that was the one
An age of reason could have begun.

Again the garden of the Florentine AMBASSADOR *at Rome, where* GALILEO's *assistants wait the news of the trial. The* LITTLE MONK *and* FEDERZONI *are attempting to concentrate on a game of chess.* VIRGINIA *kneels in a corner, praying and counting her beads.*

LITTLE MONK.   The Pope didn't even grant him an audience.

FEDERZONI.   No more scientific discussions.

ANDREA.   The "Discorsi" will never be finished. The sum of his findings. They will kill him.

FEDERZONI [*stealing a glance at him*].   Do you really think so?

ANDREA.   He will never recant.

[*Silence.*]

LITTLE MONK.   You know when you lie awake at night how your mind fastens on to something irrelevant. Last night I kept thinking: if only they would let him take his little stone in with him, the appeal-to-reason-pebble that he always carries in his pocket.

FEDERZONI.   In the room *they'll* take him to, he won't have a pocket.

ANDREA.   But he will not recant.

LITTLE MONK.   How can they beat the truth out of a man who gave his sight in order to see?

FEDERZONI.   Maybe they can't.

[*Silence.*]

ANDREA [*speaking about* VIRGINIA].   She is praying that he will recant.

FEDERZONI.   Leave her alone. She doesn't know whether she's on her head or on her heels since they got hold of her. They brought her Father Confessor from Florence.

[*The* INFORMER *of Scene X enters.*]

INFORMER.   Mr. Galilei will be here soon. He may need a bed.

FEDERZONI.   Have they let him out?

INFORMER.   Mr. Galilei is expected to recant at five o'clock. The big bell of Saint Marcus will be rung and the complete text of his recantation publicly announced.

ANDREA.   I don't believe it.

INFORMER.   Mr. Galilei will be brought to the garden gate at the back of the house, to avoid the crowds collecting in the streets. [*He goes.*]

[*Silence.*]

ANDREA.   The moon is an earth because the light of the moon is not her own. Jupiter is a fixed star, and four moons turn around Jupiter, therefore we are not shut in by crystal shells. The sun is the pivot of our world, therefore the earth is not the center. The earth moves, spinning about the sun. And he showed us. You can't make a man unsee what he has seen.

[*Silence.*]

FEDERZONI.   Five o'clock in one minute.

[VIRGINIA *prays louder.*]

ANDREA. Listen all of you, they are murdering the truth.

[*He stops up his ears with his fingers. The two other pupils do the same.* FEDERZONI *goes over to the* LITTLE MONK, *and all of them stand absolutely still in cramped positions. Nothing happens. No bell sounds. After a silence, filled with the murmur of* VIRGINIA's *prayers,* FEDERZONI *runs to the wall to look at the clock. He turns around, his expression changed. He shakes his head. They drop their hands.*]

FEDERZONI. No. No bell. It is three minutes after.

LITTLE MONK. He hasn't.

ANDREA. He held true. It is all right, it is all right.

LITTLE MONK. He did not recant.

FEDERZONI. No.

[*They embrace each other, they are delirious with joy.*]

ANDREA. So force cannot accomplish everything. What has been seen can't be unseen. Man is constant in the face of death.

FEDERZONI. June 22, 1633: dawn of the age of reason. I wouldn't have wanted to go on living if he had recanted.

LITTLE MONK. I didn't say anything, but I was in agony. Oh, ye of little faith!

ANDREA. I was sure.

FEDERZONI. It would have turned our morning to night.

ANDREA. It would have been as if the mountain had turned to water.

LITTLE MONK [*kneeling down, crying*]. Oh God, I thank Thee.

ANDREA. Beaten humanity can lift its head. A man has stood up and said "no." [*At this moment the bell of Saint Marcus begins to toll. They stand like statues.* VIRGINIA *stands up.*]

VIRGINIA. The bell of Saint Marcus. He is not damned.

[*From the street one hears the* TOWN CRIER *reading* GALILEO's *recantation.*]

TOWN CRIER. I, Galileo Galilei, Teacher of Mathematics and Physics, do hereby publicly renounce my teaching that the earth moves. I foreswear this teaching with a sincere heart and unfeigned faith and detest and curse this and all other errors and heresies repugnant to the Holy Scriptures.

[*The lights dim; when they come up again the bell of Saint Marcus is petering out.* VIRGINIA *has gone but the* SCHOLARS *are still there waiting.*]

ANDREA [*loud*]. The mountain did turn to water.

[GALILEO *has entered quietly and unnoticed. He is changed, almost unrecognizable. He has heard* ANDREA. *He waits some seconds by the door for somebody to greet him. Nobody does. They retreat from him. He goes slowly and, because of his bad sight, uncertainly, to the front of the stage where he finds a chair, and sits down.*]

ANDREA. I can't look at him. Tell him to go away.

FEDERZONI. Steady.

ANDREA [*hysterically*]. He saved his big gut.

FEDERZONI. Get him a glass of water.

[*The* LITTLE MONK *fetches a glass of water for* ANDREA. *Nobody acknowledges the presence of* GALILEO, *who sits silently on his chair listening to the voice of the* TOWN CRIER, *now in another street.*]

ANDREA. I can walk. Just help me a bit.

[*They help him to the door.*]

ANDREA [*in the door*].   "Unhappy is the land that breeds no hero."

GALILEO.   No, Andrea: "Unhappy is the land that needs a hero."

[*Before the next scene a curtain with the following legend on it is lowered*]

> You can plainly see that if a horse were to fall from a
> height of three or four feet, it could break its bones, whereas
> a dog would not suffer injury. The same applies to a cat from
> a height of as much as eight or ten feet, to a grasshopper
> from the top of a tower, and to an ant falling down from
> the moon. Nature could not allow a horse to become as
> big as twenty horses nor a giant as big as ten men, unless
> she were to change the proportions of all its members, par-
> ticularly the bones. Thus the common assumption that great
> and small structures are equally tough is obviously wrong.
>
> —From the DISCORSI

SCENE XIII

1633–1642
Galileo Galilei remains a prisoner
of the Inquisition until his death.

A country house near Florence. A large room simply furnished. There is a huge table, a leather chair, a globe of the world on a stand, and a narrow bed. A portion of the adjoining anteroom is visible, and the front door which opens into it.

An OFFICIAL OF THE INQUISITION *sits on guard in the anteroom.*

In the large room, GALILEO *is quietly experimenting with a bent wooden rail and a small ball of wood. He is still vigorous but almost blind.*

After a while there is a knocking at the outside door. The OFFICIAL *opens it to a* PEASANT *who brings a plucked goose.* VIRGINIA *comes from the kitchen. She is past forty.*

PEASANT [*handing the goose to* VIRGINIA].   I was told to deliver this here.

VIRGINIA.   I didn't order a goose.

PEASANT.   I was told to say it's from someone who was passing through.

[VIRGINIA *takes the goose, surprised. The* OFFICIAL *takes it from her and examines it suspiciously. Then, reassured, he hands it back to her. The* PEASANT *goes.* VIRGINIA *brings the goose in to* GALILEO.]

VIRGINIA.   Somebody who was passing through sent you something.

GALILEO.   What is it?

VIRGINIA.   Can't you see it?

GALILEO.   No. [*He walks over.*] A goose. Any name?

VIRGINIA.   No.

GALILEO [*weighing the goose*].   Solid.

VIRGINIA [*cautiously*].   Will you eat the liver, if I have it cooked with a little apple?

GALILEO.   I had my dinner. Are you under orders to finish me off with food?

VIRGINIA. It's not rich. And what is wrong with your eyes again? You should be able to see it.

GALILEO. You were standing in the light.

VIRGINIA. I was not.—You haven't been writing again?

GALILEO [*sneering*]. What do you think?

[VIRGINIA *takes the goose out into the anteroom and speaks to the* OFFICIAL.]

VIRGINIA. You had better ask Monsignore Carpula to send the doctor. Father couldn't see this goose across the room.—Don't look at me like that. He has not been writing. He dictates everything to me, as you know.

OFFICIAL. Yes?

VIRGINIA. He abides by the rules. My father's repentance is sincere. I keep an eye on him. [*She hands him the goose.*] Tell the cook to fry the liver with an apple and an onion. [*She goes back into the large room.*] And you have no business to be doing that with those eyes of yours, Father.

GALILEO. You may read me some Horace.

VIRGINIA. We should go on with your weekly letter to the Archbishop. Monsignore Carpula to whom we owe so much was all smiles the other day because the Archbishop had expressed his pleasure at your collaboration.

GALILEO. Where were we?

VIRGINIA [*sits down to take his dictation*]. Paragraph four.

GALILEO. Read what you have.

VIRGINIA. "The position of the Church in the matter of the unrest at Genoa. I agree with Cardinal Spoletti in the matter of the unrest among the Venetian ropemakers . . ."

GALILEO. Yes. [*Dictates.*] I agree with Cardinal Spoletti in the matter of the unrest among the Venetian ropemakers: it is better to distribute good nourishing food in the name of charity than to pay them more for their bell-ropes. It being surely better to strengthen their faith than to encourage their acquisitiveness. St. Paul says: Charity never faileth.—How is that?

VIRGINIA. It's beautiful, Father.

GALILEO. It couldn't be taken as irony?

VIRGINIA. No. The Archbishop will like it. It's so practical.

GALILEO. I trust your judgment. Read it over slowly.

VIRGINIA. "The position of the Church in the matter of the unrest. . . ."

[*There is a knocking at the outside door.* VIRGINIA *goes into the anteroom. The* OFFICIAL *opens the door. It is* ANDREA.]

ANDREA. Good evening. I am sorry to call so late, I'm on my way to Holland. I was asked to look him up. Can I go in?

VIRGINIA. I don't know whether he will see you. You never came.

ANDREA. Ask him.

[GALILEO *recognizes the voice. He sits motionless.* VIRGINIA *comes in to* GALILEO.]

GALILEO. Is that Andrea?

VIRGINIA. Yes. [*Pause.*] I will send him away.

GALILEO. Show him in.

[VIRGINIA *shows* ANDREA *in.* VIRGINIA *sits,* ANDREA *remains standing.*]

ANDREA [*cool*]. Have you been keeping well, Mr. Galilei?

GALILEO. Sit down. What are you doing these days? What are you working on? I heard it was something about hydraulics in Milan.

ANDREA. As he knew I was passing through, Fabricius of Amsterdam asked me to visit you and inquire about your health.

[*Pause.*]

GALILEO. I am very well.

ANDREA [*formally*]. I am glad I can report you are in good health.

GALILEO. Fabricius will be glad to hear it. And you might inform him that, on account of the depth of my repentance, I live in comparative comfort.

ANDREA. Yes, we understand that the Church is more than pleased with you. Your complete acceptance has had its effect. Not one paper expounding a new thesis has made its appearance in Italy since your submission.

[*Pause.*]

GALILEO. Unfortunately there are countries not under the wing of the Church. Would you not say the erroneous condemned theories are still taught—there?

ANDREA [*relentless*]. Things are almost at a standstill.

GALILEO. Are they? [*Pause.*] Nothing from Descartes[17] in Paris?

ANDREA. Yes. On receiving the news of your recantation, he shelved his treatise on the nature of light.

GALILEO. I sometimes worry about my assistants whom I led into error. Have they benefited by my example?

ANDREA. In order to work I have to go to Holland.

GALILEO. Yes.

ANDREA. Federzoni is grinding lenses again, back in some shop.

GALILEO. He can't read the books.

ANDREA. Fulganzio, our little monk, has abandoned research and is resting in peace in the Church.

GALILEO. So. [*Pause.*] My superiors are looking forward to my spiritual recovery. I am progressing as well as can be expected.

VIRGINIA. You are doing well, Father.

GALILEO. Virginia, leave the room.

[VIRGINIA *rises uncertainly and goes out.*]

VIRGINIA [*to the* OFFICIAL]. He was his pupil, so now he is his enemy.—Help me in the kitchen.

[*She leaves the anteroom with the* OFFICIAL.]

ANDREA. May I go now, sir?

GALILEO. I do not know why you came, Sarti. To unsettle me? I have to be prudent.

ANDREA. I'll be on my way.

GALILEO. As it is, I have relapses. I completed the "Discorsi."

ANDREA. You completed what?

GALILEO. My "Discorsi."

ANDREA. How?

GALILEO. I am allowed pen and paper. My superiors are intelligent men. They know the habits of a lifetime cannot be broken abruptly. But they protect me from any unpleasant consequences: they lock my pages away as I dictate them. And I should know better than to risk my comfort. I wrote the

[17] Philosopher, mathematician, and scientist who attempted to apply mathematical methods to philosophy. He made many contributions to scientific knowledge and greatly influenced modern thought.

"Discorsi" out again during the night. The manuscript is in the globe. My vanity has up to now prevented me from destroying it. If you consider taking it, you will shoulder the entire risk. You will say it was pirated from the original in the hands of the Holy Office.

[ANDREA, *as if in a trance, has gone to the globe. He lifts the upper half and gets the book. He turns the pages as if wanting to devour them. In the background the opening sentences of the "Discorsi" appear:*

> *MY PURPOSE IS TO SET FORTH A VERY NEW*
> *SCIENCE DEALING WITH A VERY ANCIENT*
> *SUBJECT—MOTION. . . . AND I HAVE*
> *DISCOVERED BY EXPERIMENT SOME PROPERTIES*
> *OF IT WHICH ARE WORTH KNOWING. . . .*

GALILEO.   I had to employ my time somehow.
[*The text disappears.*]

ANDREA.   Two new sciences! This will be the foundation stone of a new physics.

GALILEO.   Yes. Put it under your coat.

ANDREA.   And we thought you had deserted. [*In a low voice.*] Mr. Galilei, how can I begin to express my shame. Mine has been the loudest voice against you.

GALILEO.   That would seem to have been proper. I taught you science and I decried the truth.

ANDREA.   Did you? I think not. Everything is changed!

GALILEO.   What is changed?

ANDREA.   You shielded the truth from the oppressor. Now I see! In your dealings with the Inquisition you used the same superb common sense you brought to physics.

GALILEO.   Oh!

ANDREA.   We lost our heads. With the crowd at the street corners we said: "He will die, he will never surrender!" You came back: "I surrendered but I am alive." We cried: "Your hands are stained!" You say: "Better stained than empty."

GALILEO.   "Better stained than empty."—It sounds realistic. Sounds like me.

ANDREA.   And I of all people should have known. I was twelve when you sold another man's telescope to the Venetian Senate, and saw you put it to immortal use. Your friends were baffled when you bowed to the Prince of Florence: Science gained a wider audience. You always laughed at heroics. "People who suffer bore me," you said. "Misfortunes are due mainly to miscalculations." And: "If there are obstacles, the shortest line between two points may be the crooked line."

GALILEO.   It makes a picture.

ANDREA.   And when you stooped to recant in 1633, I should have understood that you were again about your business.

GALILEO.   My business being?

ANDREA.   Science. The study of the properties of motion, mother of the machines which will themselves change the ugly face of the earth.

GALILEO.   Aha!

ANDREA. You gained time to write a book that only you could write. Had you burned at the stake in a blaze of glory they would have won.

GALILEO. They have won. And there is no such thing as a scientific work that only one man can write.

ANDREA. Then why did you recant, tell me that!

GALILEO. I recanted because I was afraid of physical pain.

ANDREA. No!

GALILEO. They showed me the instruments.

ANDREA. It was not a plan?

GALILEO. It was not.

[*Pause.*]

ANDREA. But you have contributed. Science has only one commandment: contribution. And you have contributed more than any man for a hundred years.

GALILEO. Have I? Then welcome to my gutter, dear colleague in science and brother in treason: I sold out, you are a buyer. The first sight of the book! His mouth watered and his scoldings were drowned. Blessed be our bargaining, whitewashing, deathfearing community!

ANDREA. The fear of death is human.

GALILEO. Even the Church will teach you that to be weak is not human. It is just evil.

ANDREA. The church, yes! But science is not concerned with our weaknesses.

GALILEO. No? My dear Sarti, in spite of my present convictions, I may be able to give you a few pointers as to the concerns of your chosen profession.

[*Enter* VIRGINIA *with a platter.*]

In my spare time, I happen to have gone over this case. I have spare time.—Even a man who sells wool, however good he is at buying wool cheap and selling it dear, must be concerned with the standing of the wool trade. The practice of science would seem to call for valor. She trades in knowledge, which is the product of doubt. And this new art of doubt has enchanted the public. The plight of the multitude is old as the rocks, and is believed to be basic as the rocks. But now they have learned to doubt. They snatched the telescopes out of our hands and had them trained on their tormentors: prince, official, public moralist. The mechanism of the heavens was clearer, the mechanism of their courts was still murky. The battle to measure the heavens is won by doubt; by credulity the Roman housewife's battle for milk will always be lost. Word is passed down that this is of no concern to the scientist who is told he will only release such of his findings as do not disturb the peace, that is, the peace of mind of the well-to-do. Threats and bribes fill the air. Can the scientist hold out on the numbers?—For what reason do you labor? I take it the intent of science is to ease human existence. If you give way to coercion, science can be crippled, and your new machines may simply suggest new drudgeries. Should you then, in time, discover all there is to be discovered, your progress must then become a progress away from the bulk of humanity. The gulf might even grow so wide that the sound of your cheering at some new achievement would be echoed by a universal howl of horror.—As a scientist I had an almost unique opportunity. In my day astronomy emerged into the market place. At that particular time, had one man put up a fight, it could have had wide repercussions. I have come to believe that I was never in real danger; for some years I was as strong as the authorities, and I surrendered my knowledge to the powers that be, to use it, no, not *use* it, *abuse* it, as it suits their ends. I have betrayed my profession. Any man who does what I have done must not be tolerated in the ranks of science.

[VIRGINIA, *who has stood motionless, puts the platter on the table.*]

VIRGINIA.   You are accepted in the ranks of the faithful, Father.

GALILEO [*sees her*].   Correct. [*He goes over to the table.*] I have to eat now.

VIRGINIA.   We lock up at eight.

ANDREA.   I am glad I came. [*He extends his hand.* GALILEO *ignores it and goes over to his meal.*]

GALILEO [*examining the plate; to* ANDREA].   Somebody who knows me sent me a goose. I still enjoy eating.

ANDREA.   And your opinion is now that the "new age" was an illusion?

GALILEO.   Well.—This age of ours turned out to be a whore, spattered with blood. Maybe, new ages look like blood-spattered whores. Take care of yourself.

ANDREA.   Yes. [*Unable to go.*] With reference to your evaluation of the author in question—I do not know the answer. But I cannot think that your savage analysis is the last word.

GALILEO.   Thank you, sir.

[OFFICIAL *knocks at the door.*]

VIRGINIA [*showing* ANDREA *out*].   I don't like visitors from the past, they excite him.

[*She lets him out. The* OFFICIAL *closes the iron door.* VIRGINIA *returns.*]

GALILEO [*eating*].   Did you try and think who sent the goose?

VIRGINIA.   Not Andrea.

GALILEO.   Maybe not. I gave Redhead his first lesson; when he held out his hand, I had to remind myself he is teaching now.—How is the sky tonight?

VIRGINIA [*at the window*].   Bright.

[GALILEO *continues eating.*]

SCENE XIV

The great book o'er the border went
And, good folk, that was the end.
But we hope you'll keep in mind
You and I were left behind.

Before a little Italian customs house early in the morning. ANDREA *sits upon one of his traveling trunks at the barrier and reads* GALILEO's *book. The window of a small house is still lit, and a big grotesque shadow, like an old witch and her cauldron, falls upon the house wall beyond. Barefoot* CHILDREN *in rags see it and point to the little house.*

CHILDREN [*singing*].

> One, two, three, four, five, six,
> Old Marina is a witch.
> At night, on a broomstick she sits
> And on the church steeple she spits.

CUSTOMS OFFICER [*to* ANDREA]. Why are you making this journey?

ANDREA. I am a scholar.

CUSTOMS OFFICER [*to his* CLERK]. Put down under "reason for leaving the country": Scholar. [*He points to the baggage.*] Books! Anything dangerous in these books?

ANDREA. What is dangerous?

CUSTOMS OFFICER. Religion. Politics.

ANDREA. These are nothing but mathematical formulas.

CUSTOMS OFFICER. What's that?

ANDREA. Figures.

CUSTOMS OFFICER. Oh, figures. No harm in figures. Just wait a minute, sir, we will soon have your papers stamped. *He exits with* CLERK.

[*Meanwhile, a little council of war among the* CHILDREN *has taken place.* ANDREA *quietly watches. One of the* BOYS, *pushed forward by the others, creeps up to the little house from which the shadow comes, and takes the jug of milk on the doorstep.*]

ANDREA [*quietly*]. What are you doing with that milk?

BOY [*stopping in mid-movement*]. She is a witch.

[*The other* CHILDREN *run away behind the Customs House. One of them shouts, "Run, Paolo!"*]

ANDREA. Hmm! — — And because she is a witch she mustn't have milk. Is that the idea?

BOY. Yes.

ANDREA. And how do you know she is a witch?

BOY [*points to shadow on house wall*]. Look!

ANDREA. Oh! I see.

BOY. And she rides on a broomstick at night—and she bewitches the coachman's horses. My cousin Luigi looked through the hole in the stable roof, that the snow storm made, and heard the horses coughing something terrible.

ANDREA. Oh!—How big was the hole in the stable roof?

BOY. Luigi didn't tell. Why?

ANDREA. I was asking because maybe the horses got sick because it was cold in the stable. You had better ask Luigi how big that hole is.

BOY. You are not going to say Old Marina isn't a witch, because you can't.

ANDREA. No, I can't say she isn't a witch. I haven't looked into it. A man can't know about a thing he hasn't looked into, or can he?

BOY. No!—But THAT! [*He points to the shadow.*] She is stirring hell-broth.

ANDREA. Let's see. Do you want to take a look? I can lift you up.

BOY. You lift me to the window, mister! [*He takes a sling shot out of his pocket.*] I can really bash her from there.

ANDREA. Hadn't we better make sure she is a witch before we shoot? I'll hold that.

[*The* BOY *puts the milk jug down and follows him reluctantly to the window.* ANDREA *lifts the boy up so that he can look in.*]

ANDREA. What do you see?

BOY [*slowly*]. Just an old girl cooking porridge.

ANDREA. Oh! Nothing to it then. Now look at her shadow, Paolo.

[*The* BOY *looks over his shoulder and back and compares the reality and the shadow.*]

BOY. The big thing is a soup ladle.

ANDREA. Ah! A ladle! You see, I would have taken it for a broomstick, but I haven't looked into the matter as you have, Paolo. Here is your sling.

CUSTOMS OFFICER [*returning with the* CLERK *and handing* ANDREA *his papers*]. All present and correct. Good luck, sir.

[ANDREA *goes, reading* GALILEO's *book. The* CLERK *starts to bring his baggage after him. The barrier rises.* ANDREA *passes through, still reading the book. The* BOY *kicks over the milk jug.*]

BOY [*shouting after* ANDREA]. She *is* a witch! She *is* a witch!

ANDREA. You saw with your own eyes: think it over!

[*The* BOY *joins the others. They sing.*]

> One, two, three, four, five, six,
> Old Marina is a witch.
> At night, on a broomstick she sits
> And on the church steeple she spits.

[*The* CUSTOMS OFFICERS *laugh.* ANDREA *goes.*]

COMMENTARY

Of the circumstances of Galileo's career that are set forth in Brecht's play, a great many are at variance with historical actuality. Thus, although it is true that the manuscript of *Two New Sciences* had to be smuggled out of the country to be published in Holland, this was done not by Andrea Sarti but by no less a person than Prince Mattia de' Medici. As a matter of fact, there was no Andrea Sarti in Galileo's life, and no Mrs. Sarti; they are inventions of the author. During his last years on his little farm at Arcetri, near Florence, Galileo was not attended by his daughter Virginia; she died, at the age of thirty-four, just after he entered the period of house arrest which was to end only with his death. And, indeed, Virginia never lived with her father after her early girlhood— Galileo had put his two illegitimate daughters into the convent at Arcetri when they were very young and both had become nuns. Virginia was nothing like the dull girl of the play. Remarkable both for her intelligence and her saintly disposition, she adored her father and he adored her, and despite her religious vocation, she approved of his work and followed it eagerly.

Although Galileo at Arcetri was strictly supervised by the Inquisition, he did not live in complete isolation. Many distinguished travelers came to pay him their respects; it was so much the thing to do that one of Galileo's biographers notes it as strange that Descartes failed to make a call when he was in Florence. Among the visitors were John Milton and Thomas Hobbes from England, and Gassendi, the famous mathematician, from France. In 1639 a gifted young scientist of eighteen by the name of Viviani attached himself to the old master as an affectionate disciple and close companion; this precocious youth was later to become the leading mathematician of his age. Castelli, the Benedictine monk who had long been Galileo's favorite pupil, spent considerable time with him. Torricelli, the famous physicist, took up residence on the farm for a period and worked with Galileo on his theories of mechanics. So much for Brecht's representation of Galileo as doing his last work in snatched clandestine moments. So much, too, for the idea that Galileo was held in contempt by his pupils and fellow workers for having abjured his views under pressure from the Inquisition.

It is also worth observing that the intellectual position of the Church in its condemnation of Galileo was much less assured and positive than we might guess from what the play tells us; as one scholar says, the Church acted with "dogmatic timidity," for although it condemned Galileo's views, it did not venture to assert in a formal way a contrary view. Moreover, the position of the public in regard to the condemnation is inaccurately represented; we are given no adequate indication of the regard in which Galileo was held by people of all classes, including important sections of the aristocracy and the clergy. And Galileo himself was an altogether larger person than Brecht has chosen to show, more conscious, intelligent, and brilliant, more powerful and forthright in polemic, and more complex intellectually, for there is every evidence that, although anticlerical, he found no difficulty in being a sincere and devout Catholic. Even his fault of vanity was on a larger scale than the play suggests.

To remark on Brecht's departures from historical fact does not constitute an adverse criticism of *Galileo*. It has never been thought incumbent upon the author of a historical play to conform to the way things really were; Shakespeare, for an obvious example, plays fast and loose with history. The loyalty of the dramatist is not to fact but to dramatic effectiveness and such moral truth as drama may propose, and he has always had the privilege of omitting and altering circumstances to suit his artistic and moral purpose. But in this instance the playwright's departures from accuracy might seem to entail a sacrifice of advantage. As compared with the historical truth, the play's account of Galileo's career is less rich and complex, less charged with interest than the corresponding actuality, and the characters are less engaging than the real persons upon whom they were modelled. If this is so, it is because Brecht wished it to be so. He precisely did not want his play to be rich and complex. He did not want his characters to be engaging. His theory of drama dictated otherwise.

That theory is best understood through the political passions that give rise to it. Brecht, the son of a middle-class North German family, had experienced to the full the horrors of the First World War—he had served as a surgical orderly—and the extreme social disorders of his nation after its defeat. The bitter anger and contempt that he felt were directed not only upon the powerful classes he held responsible for these evils but also upon the artistic culture of the nation they dominated. In his adverse judgment of the national culture, Brecht had in mind not only those works of art that might be condemned out of hand as manifestly sharing the moral failure of the ruling classes but even that "high" culture whose idealism was commonly understood to be opposed to the crass self-seeking of the wealthy and the powerful. Like many European artists in the period after 1918, Brecht discredited virtually the whole humanistic tradition of art on the grounds that it was essentially, or objectively, an apology for the corrupt and vulgar society out of which it had arisen.

That Brecht became committed to Communism in his youth and maintained the commitment—although sometimes uneasily—until his death, undoubtedly bears upon his theory of the stage. Yet neither the theory nor the work that exemplified it met with the approval of the Communist Party.[1] Brecht shared with the Party the belief that art must serve a social function and advance the cause of revolutionary progress. But the official position on how this is to be done is notably conservative—the Party is opposed to experiment; its doctrine of "socialist realism," which requires the writer to inculcate a "positive" morality by stimulating strong, simple emotions on behalf of what is "right" and "good," might have been formulated, save for its name, by some mediocre Victorian aesthetician—and it could not countenance Brecht's radicalism in the theatre, which went so far in controverting traditional canons as to seem to subvert the very idea of art.

Brecht set himself implacably against the element of the theatre that has always been thought its very essence: he had nothing but contempt for illusion. He poured scorn upon the devices of composition and production which induce an audience to believe that it is experiencing an actual event to which it responds empathetically, with the emotions that follow upon making an "identification" with the protagonist. Brecht sought to produce the very opposite effect; he wanted his audience to be at a distance and disengaged from what happened on the stage. He spoke of this as the *Verfremdungseffekt,* literally the estranging or alienating effect. The audience is meant to see things, not as the hero sees them, but rather as it is led to see them through the activity of its own intelligence. Its estrangement or distance from the events occurring on the stage does not keep the audience from being interested in what takes place. But it is not to be even momentarily under the illusion that it is witnessing events of real life; it is to be always conscious that what it sees is "nothing but" a play, and one on which the intelligence is invited to exercise itself, and at the moment of performance rather than later, when the emotions have quieted. Brecht avowed it as his intention not to arouse feeling but to initiate thought. The theatre, he insisted at one point in his career, is not meant for enjoyment. By this he meant not so much that the theatre must be "serious" rather than "light" and "entertaining" as that the audience must not sit passive while the performance elicits emotions that, in one way or another, flatter its self-esteem.

In order to deliver his audience from the traditional bondage of illusion and bring it into activity, Brecht rejected many of the hitherto unquestioned criteria of dramatic art. So far from trying to achieve the firm coherence of structure that is regarded as a prime dramatic virtue, he avoided it for the very reason that it is usually valued, because it is instrumental in arousing and directing the emotions of the audience. His plays do not mount to a dramatic climax but tell a story in numerous discrete episodes that are connected only loosely. So far as possible, they avoid the dramatic in favor of the narrative mode; in *Galileo,* for instance, the verses sung at the beginning of each scene to summarize the action that is to follow and the display of quotations from Galileo's works are consciously nondramatic devices. Brecht's theoretical preference for the narrative as against the dramatic mode led him to speak of his plays as examples of the "epic" theatre. He had in mind the effect produced by an ancient bard chanting a poem to the warriors gathered in some king's feasting-hall: though interested

---

[1] An important exception to the Communist resistance to Brecht is to be found in the success he achieved in the East German Republic. The theatre he founded in East Berlin is devoted chiefly to the production of his plays.

in what they hear, the listeners are not overpowered by it; they are being *told* what has happened, not asked to believe that the event is taking place before their eyes.

The word "epic" is perhaps not a wholly fortunate expression of Brecht's meaning, for it carries connotations of heroic largeness and nobility which Brecht certainly did not intend. Quite the contrary, indeed. Brecht sometimes spoke of his plays as being "non-Aristotelian," a description which referred to their settled indifference to symmetry and coherence of structure and to their avoidance of the strong feelings that would produce what Aristotle called *catharsis* or purgation, a discharge of emotion leading to a state of psychic rest. It also referred to his distrust of whatever might suggest the heroic dignity and grandeur upon which Aristotle put so strong an emphasis in his discussion of tragedy. For Aristotle, tragedy was to a very considerable extent a matter of style; the tragic style depends on the elevation of the characters in the drama as expressed not only in their moral disposition and social status but also in their deportment and manner, above all in their language. Brecht's temperament as a dramatist is defined by nothing so much as his antagonism to the heroic or tragic style. His characters show no trace of it; his language, determinedly colloquial and popular, even "low," and as far removed from the literary language as possible, denies the very credibility, let alone any possible relevance to human affairs, of an elevated style.

A dramaturgy so antagonistic to established tradition naturally calls for its own style of acting. Brecht trained his actors to give up the ideal of impersonation in which they had been reared. Just as he did not want his audience to "identify" with the characters, he did not want his actors to "be" the persons they portrayed. The Moscow Art Theatre had carried the ideal of personification to the point of extravagance; its famous director, Stanslavsky (see pages 251, 253), trained his actors to achieve an actually felt identity with the characters they played. For this method—which had, incidentally, a decisive influence on the Russian theatre and the Communist theory of the drama—Brecht had nothing but contempt. It was for him the extreme example of what he called "culinary" theatre, in which the audience sits passive while being served its meal of emotion. The actors of the "epic" theatre are required to make it plain that they are only actors. They are to speak not as though what they say had just occurred to them but as though they are reporting by quotation what the represented characters had said. And they are to indicate their consciousness of the presence of an audience and their awareness of the doctrinal intentions of the play, communicating the sense that they, like the audience, stand at a cool distance from what happens on the stage.

The theatre, it would seem, has autonomous powers which are not to be controlled by the theory of even so gifted a dramatist as Brecht. Despite his best efforts to achieve distance and estrangement, to circumvent the emotional response of his audiences by the negation of illusion, his plays, charged with the energies of his moral and political purposes, have the effect of enthralling and sometimes of deeply moving those who witness them.

Brecht's theory of the stage goes far toward explaining why *Galileo* departs from historical actuality in so many respects. Almost every manipulation of the real circumstances of Galileo's life is in the direction of making it simpler and more commonplace, by which means, we may suppose, it becomes the more readily available to the scrutiny and judgment of the audience. A Galileo who happens to have heard about a Dutch device of two lenses in a tube and who makes a little extra cash by giving the appropriated invention to the Venetian senate to manufacture and market, is, presumably, easier to judge than the real Galileo who, having contrived the notable improvements in the telescope that made it an effectual means of research, supplied carefully crafted instruments to the astronomers of Europe, the best that could be had at that time. A Galileo whose character is in part defined by his domestic arrangements, by a dull if dutiful daughter, a bustling housekeeper who tries to keep prudential considerations always to the fore, and assistants who are not notable for intellectual brilliance, is less likely to infect the audience with ideas of heroic dignity and charm than a Galileo who was loved by the remarkable person the real Virginia was, by princes and many dignitaries of the Church, and by younger colleagues whose range of scientific imagination make the invented Andrea and Federzoni look like mere laboratory technicians.

But one of Brecht's manipulations of history cannot be explained by reference to Brecht's theory of the stage. This is the representation of Galileo as having dishonored himself in not choosing death in preference to the abjuration of his beliefs. No modern scholar confirms the play on this point. One of the most authoritative students of Galileo's life, work, and times, Giorgio de Santillana, puts the matter unequivocally: "The abjuration itself is not at all the surrender and moral disgrace that self-appointed judges have made it out to be." We have seen that Galileo's colleagues and co-workers felt none of the scorn that Brecht finds appropriate to the situation. As Professor de Santillana says, Galileo's recantation "was not considered a moral degradation. It was a *social* degradation, and it was as such that it broke the old man's heart." (Galileo was seventy at the time of his trial.) But although Galileo's heart may have been broken, his spirit, Professor de Santillana goes on to say, was not. He continued his work, and in *Two New Sciences* produced his greatest achievement. In his letters his contempt for those who had condemned him was manifest. His pride was no doubt sustained by the active sympathy of the public, for, to quote Professor de Santillana yet again, "pious believers who would never have touched a Protestant tract, priests, monks, prelates even, vied with one another in buying up copies of the *Dialogue* on the black market to keep them from the hands of the Inquisitors."[2]

The "self-appointed judges" who hand down their condemnation of Galileo do so on the ground that he valued his life more than the truth. This is wholly to misconceive the situation. Everyone was aware that Galileo had really consented to abjure nothing but his right to publish the truth. For him to have sacrificed his life for this right, in the face of the Church's long-established dominion over the intellectual activity of its communicants in matters that affected belief, would have been not a moral but a political act of a kind that the assumptions of the time did not comprehend. There were, to be sure, men whose religious beliefs led them to renounce the Church and oppose its authority. Such men often suffered martyrdom for their faith. But Galileo was not put on trial for a matter of faith. He himself would have corrected us for speaking of the "beliefs" which he abjured: he did not hold the *belief* that the earth

2 Giorgio de Santillana, *The Crime of Galileo*, pp. 320–325 *passim*.

moved around the sun, he possessed the *knowledge* that this was so. It was a fact that did not require the witness of his martyrdom. He felt this the more because to him it was not so much the Church that had condemned him as a successful faction of the clergy and because he knew to what lengths of legal trickery it had had to go in order to secure his condemnation. He also knew how much weight his demonstrations carried with the learned among the higher clergy and understood the significance of the Pope's not making the issue one of dogma, and he could therefore suppose that the Church would eventually reverse itself, as in fact it did a century later.

Opinion will differ as to whether or not Brecht went beyond the legitimate privileges of the historical playwright in representing Galileo as a man who had betrayed the cause of truth. But whichever way opinion goes, it must remain a matter for curiosity why Brecht so grossly distorted the story of Galileo's life, when there were such strong reasons why he might have hesitated to do so.

For one thing, the harsh simplicity of the play's moral judgment violates Brecht's Marxist creed. Marxism is nothing if not historical, and strict in its historicity, and it is one of its essential tenets that conduct cannot be judged by absolute timeless standards but only by reference to the cultural conditions that prevail at a given historical moment. To project backward into the past the standards of the present, as Brecht does, and to condemn Galileo by the criteria of a modern social and political morality is a violation of this idea.

Then, in the light of his almost obsessive desire for an active, thinking audience, it must be wondered why Brecht leads the audience of *Galileo* so simplistically to the conclusion that the protagonist is to be condemned. In the last dialogue between Andrea Sarti and his master, Sarti proposes the idea that Galileo is blameless, for he perceives that in having refused martyrdom the old man had preserved himself to advance the great cause of science by the composition of his last work. But Galileo himself refuses this exculpation; his own condemnation of his conduct is the last word on the matter and the one that the audience is expected to accept, for it has been given no ground for a contrary view. In this instance at least, Brecht is not solicitous for the intellectual activity of his audience; on the contrary, he remorselessly holds the audience in bondage to the historical data he has chosen or invented. And he insists on this conclusion out of what must seem sheer wilfulness. Eric Bentley, who has translated many of Brecht's plays and whose sympathetic criticism has done much to establish the dramatist's reputation, is uncompromising on this score. "One cannot find," Professor Bentley says, "within the boundaries of the play itself, a full justification for the virulence of the final condemnation."[3]

The wilfulness and the virulence of the final condemnation are especially puzzling in the light of Brecht's earlier views of moral and political intransigence both in his work and in the conduct of his life. One of Brecht's characteristic moral positions is that in circumstances of oppression a man does well to check the impulse to forthright heroism and to seek to achieve his ends by cunning, concealing what he truly thinks or expressing it only obliquely, and biding his time. This was Brecht's own way of dealing with hostile authority— whoever writes about Brecht from knowledge of his life remarks on his unwillingness to expose himself to danger. ". . . He knew how to take care of

---

[3] "The Science Fiction of Bertolt Brecht," the introduction to the Grove Press edition of. *Galileo*, 1966, p. 21.

himself," Professor Bentley says and goes on to specify the occasions on which Brecht had cannily considered his safety or comfort rather than the demands of heroic idealism. Yet here he represents Galileo as virtually a villain for doing what he himself had not only previously advocated but had also, in effect, actually done. An earlier version of the play had invited the audience to a quite considerable activity of judgment by requiring it to deal with a man whose cunning in evasion deserves admiration even though his cowardice deserves contempt. But in the published version, Galileo's refusal to be heroically intransigent can wake only a saddening scorn.[4]

One is inevitably drawn to the speculation that Brecht, in changing his view of Galileo, was changing his view of his own course of conduct, that the Galileo who hates and condemns himself for his abjuration represents the author's own judgment on himself. But the personal interpretation, although it recommends itself, can have but a minor part in our understanding of the moral doctrine of the play. Nor, perhaps, is it finally to our purpose that Brecht himself has explained the revision of his judgment of Galileo by his response to the explosion of the atomic bomb, which induced him to take a more rigorous view of the responsibility of the scientist and of the intellectual in general. An author's testimony on why he wrote as he did must always be treated with respect, but it is not always as authoritative as it seems. If we ask why, in the second version of his *Galileo,* Brecht revised not only his earlier judgment on his protagonist but also the moral attitude of a lifetime, perhaps the satisfactory answer is that his protean mind, doctrinal but indifferent to the claims of doctrinal consistency, happened at this moment to be captivated by the idea of an absolute intransigent morality and the heroism it calls for.

[4] The first version of *Galileo* has not been published. Professor Bentley has read it in manuscript and I take my account of its tendency from his essay.

PART

2 FICTION

MY

KINSMAN,

MAJOR MOLINEUX

N A T H A N I E L   H A W T H O R N E

1 8 0 4 – 1 8 6 4

AFTER THE KINGS of Great Britain had assumed the right of appointing the colonial governors, the measures of the latter seldom met with the ready and generous approbation which had been paid to those of their predecessors, under the original charters. The people looked with most jealous scrutiny to the exercise of power which did not emanate from themselves, and they usually rewarded their rulers with slender gratitude for the compliances by which, in softening their instructions from beyond the sea, they had incurred the reprehension of those who gave them. The annals of Massachusetts Bay will inform us, that of six governors in the space of about forty years from the surrender of the old charter, under James II, two were imprisoned by a popular insurrection; a third, as Hutchinson[1] inclines to believe, was driven from the province by the whizzing of a musket-ball; a fourth, in the opinion of the same historian, was hastened to his grave by continual bickerings with the House of Representatives; and the remaining two, as well as their successors, till the Revolution, were favored with few and brief intervals of peaceful sway. The inferior members of the court party, in times of high political excitement, led scarcely a more desirable life. These remarks may serve

[1] Thomas Hutchinson, *The History of the Colony and Province of Massachusetts Bay,* Boston, 1764.

as a preface to the following adventures, which chanced upon a summer night, not far from a hundred years ago.[2] The reader, in order to avoid a long and dry detail of colonial affairs, is requested to dispense with an account of the train of circumstances that had caused much temporary inflammation of the popular mind.

It was near nine o'clock of a moonlight evening, when a boat crossed the ferry with a single passenger, who had obtained his conveyance at that unusual hour by the promise of an extra fare. While he stood on the landing-place, searching in either pocket for the means of fulfilling his agreement, the ferryman lifted a lantern, by the aid of which, and the newly risen moon, he took a very accurate survey of the stranger's figure. He was a youth of barely eighteen years, evidently country-bred, and now, as it should seem, upon his first visit to town. He was clad in a coarse gray coat, well worn, but in excellent repair; his under garments[3] were durably constructed of leather, and fitted tight to a pair of serviceable and well-shaped limbs; his stockings of blue yarn were the incontrovertible work of a mother or a sister; and on his head was a three-cornered hat, which in its better days had perhaps sheltered the graver brow of the lad's father. Under his left arm was a heavy cudgel formed of an oak sapling, and retaining a part of the hardened root; and his equipment was completed by a wallet, not so abundantly stocked as to incommode the vigorous shoulders on which it hung. Brown, curly hair, well-shaped features, and bright, cheerful eyes were nature's gifts, and worth all that art could have done for his adornment.

The youth, one of whose names was Robin, finally drew from his pocket the half of a little province bill of five shillings, which, in the depreciation in that sort of currency, did but satisfy the ferryman's demand, with the surplus of a sexangular piece of parchment, valued at three pence. He then walked forward into the town, with as light a step as if his day's journey had not already exceeded thirty miles, and with as eager an eye as if he were entering London city, instead of the little metropolis of a New England colony. Before Robin had proceeded far, however, it occurred to him that he knew not whither to direct his steps; so he paused, and looked up and down the narrow street, scrutinizing the small and mean wooden buildings that were scattered on either side.

"This low hovel cannot be my kinsman's dwelling," thought he, "nor yonder old house, where the moonlight enters at the broken casement; and truly I see none hereabouts that might be worthy of him. It would have been wise to inquire my way of the ferryman, and doubtless he would have gone with me, and earned a shilling from the Major for his pains. But the next man I meet will do as well."

He resumed his walk, and was glad to perceive that the street now became wider, and the houses more respectable in their appearance. He soon discerned a figure moving on moderately in advance, and hastened his steps to overtake it. As Robin drew nigh, he saw that the passenger was a man in years, with a full periwig of gray hair, a wide-skirted coat of dark cloth, and silk stockings rolled above his knees. He carried a long and polished cane, which he struck down perpendicularly before him at every step; and at regular intervals he uttered two successive hems, of a peculiarly solemn and sepulchral intonation. Having made these observations, Robin laid hold of the skirt of the old man's coat, just when

[2] The story was written in 1828 or 1829.
[3] Knee breeches.

the light from the open door and windows of a barber's shop fell upon both their figures.

"Good evening to you, honored sir," said he, making a low bow, and still retaining his hold of the skirt. "I pray you tell me whereabouts is the dwelling of my kinsman, Major Molineux."

The youth's question was uttered very loudly; and one of the barbers, whose razor was descending on a well-soaped chin, and another who was dressing a Ramillies wig,[4] left their occupations, and came to the door. The citizen, in the mean time, turned a long-favored countenance upon Robin, and answered him in a tone of excessive anger and annoyance. His two sepulchral hems, however, broke into the very centre of his rebuke, with most singular effect, like a thought of the cold grave obtruding among wrathful passions.

"Let go my garment, fellow! I tell you, I know not the man you speak of. What! I have authority, I have—hem, hem—authority; and if this be the respect you show for your betters, your feet shall be brought acquainted with the stocks by daylight, tomorrow morning!"

Robin released the old man's skirt, and hastened away, pursued by an ill-mannered roar of laughter from the barber's shop. He was at first considerably surprised by the result of his question, but, being a shrewd youth, soon thought himself able to account for the mystery.

"This is some country representative," was his conclusion, "who has never seen the inside of my kinsman's door, and lacks the breeding to answer a stranger civilly. The man is old, or verily—I might be tempted to turn back and smite him on the nose. Ah, Robin, Robin! even the barber's boys laugh at you for choosing such a guide! You will be wiser in time, friend Robin."

He now became entangled in a succession of crooked and narrow streets, which crossed each other, and meandered at no great distance from the water-side. The smell of tar was obvious to his nostrils, the masts of vessels pierced the moonlight above the tops of the buildings, and the numerous signs, which Robin paused to read, informed him that he was near the centre of business. But the streets were empty, the shops were closed, and lights were visible only in the second stories of a few dwelling-houses. At length, on the corner of a narrow lane, through which he was passing, he beheld the broad countenance of a British hero swinging before the door of an inn,[5] whence proceeded the voices of many guests. The casement of one of the lower windows was thrown back, and a very thin curtain permitted Robin to distinguish a party at supper, round a well-furnished table. The fragrance of the good cheer steamed forth into the outer air, and the youth could not fail to recollect that the last remnant of his travelling stock of provision had yielded to his morning appetite, and that noon had found and left him dinnerless.

"Oh, that a parchment three-penny might give me a right to sit down at yonder table!" said Robin, with a sigh. "But the Major will make me welcome to the best of his victuals; so I will even step boldly in, and inquire my way to his dwelling."

He entered the tavern, and was guided by the murmur of voices and the

4 A wig having a long plait behind tied with a bow at the top and the bottom.

5 An inn would often be named after a famous personage, whose picture would appear on a sign projecting from above the main entry.

fumes of tobacco to the public-room. It was a long and low apartment, with oaken walls, grown dark in the continual smoke, and a floor which was thickly sanded, but of no immaculate purity. A number of persons—the larger part of whom appeared to be mariners, or in some way connected with the sea—occupied the wooden benches, or leather-bottomed chairs, conversing on various matters, and occasionally lending their attention to some topic of general interest. Three or four little groups were draining as many bowls of punch, which the West India trade had long since made a familiar drink in the colony. Others, who had the appearance of men who lived by regular and laborious handicraft, preferred the insulated bliss of an unshared potation, and became more taciturn under its influence. Nearly all, in short, evinced a predilection for the Good Creature[6] in some of its various shapes, for this is a vice to which, as Fast Day sermons of a hundred years ago will testify, we have a long hereditary claim. The only guests to whom Robin's sympathies inclined him were two or three sheepish countrymen, who were using the inn somewhat after the fashion of a Turkish caravansary;[7] they had gotten themselves into the darkest corner of the room, and heedless of the Nicotian[8] atmosphere, were supping on the bread of their own ovens, and the bacon cured in their own chimney-smoke. But though Robin felt a sort of brotherhood with these strangers, his eyes were attracted from them to a person who stood near the door, holding whispered conversation with a group of ill-dressed associates. His features were separately striking almost to grotesqueness, and the whole face left a deep impression on the memory. The forehead bulged out into a double prominence, with a vale between; the nose came boldly forth in an irregular curve, and its bridge was of more than a finger's breadth; the eyebrows were deep and shaggy, and the eyes glowed beneath them like fire in a cave.

While Robin deliberated of whom to inquire respecting his kinsman's dwelling, he was accosted by the innkeeper, a little man in a stained white apron, who had come to pay his professional welcome to the stranger. Being in the second generation from a French Protestant, he seemed to have inherited the courtesy of his parent nation; but no variety of circumstances was ever known to change his voice from the one shrill note in which he now addressed Robin.

"From the country, I presume, sir?" said he, with a profound bow. "Beg leave to congratulate you on your arrival, and trust you intend a long stay with us. Fine town here, sir, beautiful buildings, and much that may interest a stranger. May I hope for the honor of your commands in respect to supper?"

"The man sees a family likeness! the rogue has guessed that I am related to the Major!" thought Robin, who had hitherto experienced little superfluous civility.

All eyes were now turned on the country lad, standing at the door, in his worn three-cornered hat, gray coat, leather breeches, and blue yarn stockings, leaning on an oaken cudgel, and bearing a wallet on his back.

Robin replied to the courteous innkeeper, with such an assumption of con-

[6] Applied humorously to intoxicating liquor, but originally signifying that part of God's creation which ministers to the material comfort of man. See I Timothy 4:4, "Every creature of God is good."

[7] A public building in which travelers prepare and eat the food they have brought with them.

[8] Filled with tobacco smoke (from the name of Jacques Nicot, who introduced tobacco into France in 1560).

fidence as befitted the Major's relative. "My honest friend," he said, "I shall make it a point to patronize your house on some occasion, when"—here he could not help lowering his voice—"when I may have more than a parchment three-pence in my pocket. My present business," continued he, speaking with lofty confidence, "is merely to inquire my way to the dwelling of my kinsman, Major Molineux."

There was a sudden and general movement in the room, which Robin interpreted as expressing the eagerness of each individual to become his guide. But the innkeeper turned his eyes to a written paper on the wall, which he read, or seemed to read, with occasional recurrences to the young man's figure.

"What have we here?" said he, breaking his speech into little dry fragments. "'Left the house of the subscriber, bounden servant,[9] Hezekiah Mudge,—had on, when he went away, gray coat, leather breeches, master's third-best hat. One pound currency reward to whosoever shall lodge him in any jail of the providence.' Better trudge, boy; better trudge!"

Robin had begun to draw his hand towards the lighter end of the oak cudgel, but a strange hostility in every countenance induced him to relinquish his purpose of breaking the courteous innkeeper's head. As he turned to leave the room, he encountered a sneering glance from the bold-featured personage whom he had before noticed; and no sooner was he beyond the door, than he heard a general laugh, in which the innkeeper's voice might be distinguished, like the dropping of small stones into a kettle.

"Now, is it not strange," thought Robin, with his usual shrewdness,—"is it not strange that the confession of an empty pocket should outweigh the name of my kinsman, Major Molineux? Oh, if I had one of those grinning rascals in the woods, where I and my oak sapling grew up together, I would teach him that my arm is heavy though my purse be light!"

On turning the corner of the narrow lane, Robin found himself in a spacious street, with an unbroken line of lofty houses on each side, and a steepled building at the upper end, whence the ringing of a bell announced the hour of nine. The light of the moon, and the lamps from the numerous shop-windows, discovered people promenading on the pavement, and amongst them Robin had hoped to recognize his hitherto inscrutable relative. The result of his former inquiries made him unwilling to hazard another, in a scene of such publicity, and he determined to walk slowly and silently up the street, thrusting his face close to that of every elderly gentleman, in search of the Major's lineaments. In his progress, Robin encountered many gay and gallant figures. Embroidered garments of showy colors, enormous periwigs, gold-laced hats, and silver-hilted swords glided past him and dazzled his optics. Travelled youths, imitators of the European fine gentlemen of the period, trod jauntily along, half dancing to the fashionable tunes which they hummed, and making poor Robin ashamed of his quiet and natural gait. At length, after many pauses to examine the gorgeous display of goods in the shop-windows, and after suffering some rebukes for the impertinence of his scrutiny into people's faces, the Major's kinsman found himself near the steepled building, still unsuccessful in his search. As yet, however, he had seen only one side of the thronged street; so Robin crossed, and continued the same

[9] An indentured servant, bound by contract to serve for a certain time before obtaining his freedom.

sort of inquisition down the opposite pavement, with stronger hopes than the philosopher seeking an honest man, but with no better fortune. He had arrived about midway towards the lower end, from which his course began, when he overheard the approach of some one who struck down a cane on the flag-stones at every step, uttering at regular intervals, two sepulchral hems.

"Mercy on us!" quoth Robin, recognizing the sound.

Turning a corner, which chanced to be close at his right hand, he hastened to pursue his researches in some other part of the town. His patience now was wearing low, and he seemed to feel more fatigue from his rambles since he crossed the ferry, than from his journey of several days on the other side. Hunger also pleaded loudly within him, and Robin began to balance the propriety of demanding, violently, and with lifted cudgel, the necessary guidance from the first solitary passenger whom he should meet. While a resolution to this effect was gaining strength, he entered a street of mean appearance, on either side of which a row of ill-built houses was straggling towards the harbor. The moonlight fell upon no passenger along the whole extent, but in the third domicile which Robin passed there was a half-opened door, and his keen glance detected a woman's garment within.

"My luck may be better here," said he to himself.

Accordingly, he approached the door, and beheld it shut closer as he did so; yet an open space remained, sufficing for the fair occupant to observe the stranger, without a corresponding display on her part. All that Robin could discern was a strip of scarlet petticoat, and the occasional sparkle of an eye, as if the moonbeams were trembling on some bright thing.

"Pretty mistress," for I may call her so with a good conscience, thought the shrewd youth, since I know nothing to the contrary,—"my sweet pretty mistress, will you be kind enough to tell me whereabouts I must seek the dwelling of my kinsman, Major Molineux?"

Robin's voice was plaintive and winning, and the female, seeing nothing to be shunned in the handsome country youth, thrust open the door, and came forth into the moonlight. She was a dainty little figure, with a white neck, round arms, and a slender waist, at the extremity of which her scarlet petticoat jutted out over a hoop, as if she were standing in a balloon. Moreover, her face was oval and pretty, her hair dark beneath the little cap, and her bright eyes possessed a sly freedom, which triumphed over those of Robin.

"Major Molineux dwells here," said this fair woman.

Now, her voice was the sweetest Robin had heard that night, yet he could not help doubting whether that sweet voice spoke Gospel truth. He looked up and down the mean street, and then surveyed the house before which they stood. It was a small, dark edifice of two stories, the second of which projected over the lower floor, and the front apartment had the aspect of a shop for petty commodities.

"Now, truly, I am in luck," replied Robin, cunningly, "and so indeed is my kinsman, the Major, in having so pretty a housekeeper. But I prithee trouble him to step to the door; I will deliver him a message from his friends in the country, and then go back to my lodgings at the inn."

"Nay, the Major has been abed this hour or more," said the lady of the scarlet petticoat; "and it would be to little purpose to disturb him to-night, seeing his evening draught was of the strongest. But he is a kind-hearted man, and it would be as much as my life's worth to let a kinsman of his turn away from the door. You are the good old gentleman's very picture, and I could swear that was his rainy-weather hat. Also he has garments very much resembling those leather small-clothes. But come in, I pray, for I bid you hearty welcome in his name."

So saying, the fair and hospitable dame took our hero by the hand; and the touch was light, and the force was gentleness, and though Robin read in her eyes what he did not hear in her words, yet the slender-waisted woman in the scarlet petticoat proved stronger than the athletic country youth. She had drawn his half-willing footsteps nearly to the threshold, when the opening of a door in the neighborhood startled the Major's housekeeper, and, leaving the Major's kinsman, she vanished speedily into her own domicile. A heavy yawn preceded the appearance of a man, who, like the Moonshine of Pyramus and Thisbe,[10] carried a lantern, needlessly aiding his sister luminary in the heavens. As he walked sleepily up the street, he turned his broad, dull face on Robin, and displayed a long staff, spiked at the end.

"Home, vagabond, home!" said the watchman, in accents that seemed to fall asleep as soon as they were uttered. "Home, or we'll set you in the stocks by peep of day!"

"This is the second hint of the kind," thought Robin. "I wish they would end my difficulties, by setting me there to-night."

Nevertheless, the youth felt an instinctive antipathy towards the guardian of midnight order, which at first prevented him from asking his usual question. But just when the man was about to vanish behind the corner, Robin resolved not to lose the opportunity, and shouted lustily after him,—

"I say, friend! will you guide me to the house of my kinsman, Major Molineux?"

The watchman made no reply, but turned the corner and was gone; yet Robin seemed to hear the sound of drowsy laughter stealing along the solitary street. At that moment, also, a pleasant titter saluted him from the open window above his head; he looked up, and caught the sparkle of a saucy eye; a round arm beckoned to him, and next he heard light footsteps descending the staircase within. But Robin, being of the household of a New England clergyman, was a good youth, as well as a shrewd one; so he resisted temptation, and fled away.

He now roamed desperately, and at random, through the town, almost ready to believe that a spell was on him, like that by which a wizard of his country had once kept three pursuers wandering, a whole winter night, within twenty paces of the cottage which they sought. The streets lay before him, strange and desolate, and the lights were extinguished in almost every house. Twice, however, little parties of men, among whom Robin distinguished individuals in outlandish attire, came hurrying along; but, though on both occasions, they paused to address him, such intercourse did not at all enlighten his perplexity. They did but utter a few words in some language of which Robin knew nothing, and perceiving his inability to answer, bestowed a curse upon him in plain English and hastened away. Finally, the lad determined to knock at the door of every mansion that might appear worthy to be occupied by his kinsman, trusting that perseverance would

[10] In Shakespeare's *A Midsummer-Night's Dream*, Act V, Scene 1, a man with a lantern represents the moon in a comically inept performance of the tragic love story of Pyramus and Thisbe.

overcome the fatality that had hitherto thwarted him. Firm in this resolve, he was passing beneath the walls of a church, which formed the corner of two streets, when, as he turned into the shade of its steeple, he encountered a bulky stranger, muffled in a cloak. The man was proceeding with the speed of earnest business, but Robin planted himself full before him, holding the oak cudgel with both hands across his body as a bar to further passage.

"Halt, honest man, and answer me a question," said he, very resolutely. "Tell me, this instant, whereabouts is the dwelling of my kinsman, Major Molineux!"

"Keep your tongue between your teeth, fool, and let me pass!" said a deep, gruff voice, which Robin partly remembered. "Let me pass, or I'll strike you to the earth!"

"No, no, neighbor!" cried Robin, flourishing his cudgel, and then thrusting its larger end close to the man's muffled face. "No, no, I'm not the fool you take me for, nor do you pass till I have an answer to my question. Whereabouts is the dwelling of my kinsman, Major Molineux?"

The stranger, instead of attempting to force his passage, stepped back into the moonlight, unmuffled his face, and stared full into that of Robin.

"Watch here an hour, and Major Molineux will pass by," said he.

Robin gazed with dismay and astonishment on the unprecedented physiognomy of the speaker. The forehead with its double prominence, the broad hooked nose, the shaggy eyebrows, and fiery eyes were those which he had noticed at the inn, but the man's complexion had undergone a singular, or, more properly, a twofold change. One side of the face blazed an intense red, while the other was black as midnight, the division line being in the broad bridge of the nose; and a mouth which seemed to extend from ear to ear was black or red, in contrast to the color of the cheek. The effect was as if two individual devils, a fiend of fire and a fiend of darkness, had united themselves to form this infernal visage. The stranger grinned in Robin's face, muffled his party-colored features, and was out of sight in a moment.

"Strange things we travellers see!" ejaculated Robin.

He seated himself, however, upon the steps of the church-door, resolving to wait the appointed time for his kinsman. A few moments were consumed in philosophical speculations upon the species of man who had just left him; but having settled this point shrewdly, rationally, and satisfactorily, he was compelled to look elsewhere for his amusement. And first he threw his eyes along the street. It was of more respectable appearance than most of those into which he had wandered; and the moon, creating, like the imaginative power, a beautiful strangeness in familiar objects, gave something of romance to a scene that might not have possessed it in the light of day. The irregular and often quaint architecture of the houses, some of whose roofs were broken into numerous little peaks, while others ascended, steep and narrow, into a single point, and others again were square; the pure snow-white of some of their complexions, the aged darkness of others, and the thousand sparklings, reflected from bright substances in the walls of many; these matters engaged Robin's attention for a while, and then began to grow wearisome. Next he endeavored to define the forms of distant objects, starting away, with almost ghostly indistinctness, just as his eye appeared to grasp them; and finally he took a minute survey of an edifice which stood on the opposite side of the street, directly in front of the church-door, where he was stationed. It was a large, square mansion, distinguished from its neighbors by a balcony, which rested on tall pillars, and by an elaborate Gothic window, communicating therewith.

"Perhaps this is the very house I have been seeking," thought Robin.

Then he strove to speed away the time, by listening to a murmur which swept continually along the street, yet was scarcely audible, except to an unaccustomed ear like his; it was a low, dull, dreamy sound, compounded of many noises, each of which was at too great a distance to be separately heard. Robin marvelled at this snore of a sleeping town, and marvelled more whenever its continuity was broken by now and then a distant shout, apparently loud where it originated. But altogether it was a sleep-inspiring sound, and, to shake off its drowsy influence, Robin arose, and climbed a window-frame, that he might view the interior of the church. There the moonbeams came trembling in, and fell down upon the deserted pews, and extended along the quiet aisles. A fainter yet more awful radiance was hovering around the pulpit, and one solitary ray had dared to rest upon the open page of the great Bible. Had nature, in that deep hour, become a worshipper in the house which man had builded? Or was that heavenly light the visible sanctity of the place,—visible because no earthly and impure feet were within the walls? The scene made Robin's heart shiver with a sensation of loneliness stronger than he had ever felt in the remotest depths of his native woods; so he turned away and sat down again before the door. There were graves around the church, and now an uneasy thought obtruded into Robin's breast. What if the object of his search, which had been so often and so strangely thwarted, were all the time mouldering in his shroud? What if his kinsman should glide through yonder gate, and nod and smile to him in dimly passing by?

"Oh that any breathing thing were here with me!" said Robin.

Recalling his thoughts from this uncomfortable track, he sent them over forest, hill, and stream, and attempted to imagine how that evening of ambiguity and weariness had been spent by his father's household. He pictured them assembled at the door, beneath the tree, the great old tree, which had been spared for its huge twisted trunk and venerable shade, when a thousand leafy brethren fell. There, at the going down of the summer sun, it was his father's custom to perform domestic worship, that the neighbors might come and join with him like brothers of the family, and that the wayfaring man might pause to drink at that fountain, and keep his heart pure by freshening the memory of home. Robin distinguished the seat of every individual of the little audience; he saw the good man in the midst, holding the Scriptures in the golden light that fell from the western clouds; he beheld him close the book and all rise up to pray. He heard the old thanksgivings for daily mercies, the old supplications for their continuance, to which he had so often listened in weariness, but which were now among his dear remembrances. He perceived the slight inequality of his father's voice when he came to speak of the absent one; he noted how his mother turned her face to the broad and knotted trunk; how his elder brother scorned, because the beard was rough upon his upper lip, to permit his features to be moved; how the younger sister drew down a low hanging branch before her eyes; and how the little one of all, whose sports had hitherto broken the decorum of the scene, understood the prayer for her playmate, and burst into clamorous grief. Then he saw them go in at the door; and when Robin would have entered also, the latch tinkled into its place, and he was excluded from his home.

"Am I here, or there?" cried Robin, starting; for all at once, when his thoughts had become visible and audible in a dream, the long, wide, solitary street shone out before him.

He aroused himself, and endeavored to fix his attention steadily upon the large edifice which he had surveyed before. But still his mind kept vibrating between fancy and reality; by turns, the pillars of the balcony lengthened into the tall, bare stems of pines, dwindled down to human figures, settled again into their true shape and size, and then commenced a new succession of changes. For a single moment, when he deemed himself awake, he could have sworn that a visage—one which he seemed to remember, yet could not absolutely name as his kinsman's—was looking towards him from the Gothic window. A deeper sleep wrestled with and nearly overcame him, but fled at the sound of footsteps along the opposite pavement. Robin rubbed his eyes, discerned a man passing at the foot of the balcony, and addressed him in a loud, peevish, and lamentable cry.

"Hallo, friend! must I wait here all night for my kinsman, Major Molineux?"

The sleeping echoes awoke, and answered the voice; and the passenger, barely able to discern a figure sitting in the oblique shade of the steeple, traversed the street to obtain a nearer view. He was himself a gentleman in his prime, of open, intelligent, cheerful, and altogether prepossessing countenance. Perceiving a country youth, apparently homeless and without friends, he accosted him in a tone of real kindness, which had become strange to Robin's ears.

"Well, my good lad, why are you sitting here?" inquired he. "Can I be of service to you in any way?"

"I am afraid not, sir," replied Robin, despondingly; "yet I shall take it kindly, if you'll answer me a single question. I've been searching, half the night, for one Major Molineux; now, sir, is there really such a person in these parts, or am I dreaming?"

"Major Molineux! The name is not altogether strange to me," said the gentleman, smiling. "Have you any objection to telling me the nature of your business with him?"

Then Robin briefly related that his father was a clergyman, settled on a small salary, at a long distance back in the country, and that he and Major Molineux were brothers' children. The Major, having inherited riches, and acquired civil and military rank, had visited his cousin, in great pomp, a year or two before; had manifested much interest in Robin and an elder brother, and, being childless himself, had thrown out hints respecting the future establishment of one of them in life. The elder brother was destined to succeed to the farm which his father cultivated in the interval of sacred duties; it was therefore determined that Robin should profit by his kinsman's generous intentions, especially as he seemed to be rather the favorite, and was thought to possess other necessary endowments.

"For I have the name of being a shrewd youth," observed Robin, in this part of his story.

"I doubt not you deserve it," replied his new friend, good-naturedly; "but pray proceed."

"Well, sir, being nearly eighteen years old, and well grown, as you see," continued Robin, drawing himself up to his full height, "I thought it high time to begin in the world. So my mother and sister put me in handsome trim, and my father gave me half the remnant of his last year's salary, and five days ago I started for this place, to pay the Major a visit. But, would you believe it, sir! I crossed the ferry a little after dark, and have yet found nobody that would show me the way to his dwelling; only, an hour or two since, I was told to wait here, and Major Molineux would pass by."

"Can you describe the man who told you this?" inquired the gentleman.

"Oh, he was a very ill-favored fellow, sir," replied Robin, "with two great bumps on his forehead, a hook nose, fiery eyes; and, what struck me as the strangest, his face was of two different colors. Do you happen to know such a man, sir?"

"Not intimately," answered the stranger, "but I chanced to meet him a little time previous to your stopping me. I believe you may trust his word, and that the Major will very shortly pass through this street. In the mean time, as I have a singular curiosity to witness your meeting, I will sit down here upon the steps and bear you company."

He seated himself accordingly, and soon engaged his companion in animated discourse. It was but of brief continuance, however, for a noise of shouting, which had long been remotely audible, drew so much nearer that Robin inquired its cause.

"What may be the meaning of this uproar?" asked he. "Truly, if your town be always as noisy, I shall find little sleep while I am an inhabitant."

"Why, indeed, friend Robin, there do appear to be three or four riotous fellows abroad to-night," replied the gentleman. "You must not expect all the stillness of your native woods here in our streets. But the watch will shortly be at the heels of these lads and"—

"Ay, and set them in the stocks by peep of day," interrupted Robin, recollecting his own encounter with the drowsy lantern-bearer. "But, dear sir, if I may trust my ears, an army of watchmen would never make head against such a multitude of rioters. There were at least a thousand voices went up to make that one shout."

"May not a man have several voices, Robin, as well as two complexions?" said his friend.

"Perhaps a man may; but Heaven forbid that a woman should!" responded the shrewd youth, thinking of the seductive tones of the Major's housekeeper.

The sounds of a trumpet in some neighboring street now became so evident and continual, that Robin's curiosity was strongly excited. In addition to the shouts, he heard frequent bursts from many instruments of discord, and a wild and confused laughter filled up the intervals. Robin rose from the steps, and looked wistfully towards a point whither people seemed to be hastening.

"Surely some prodigious merry-making is going on," exclaimed he. "I have laughed very little since I left home, sir, and should be sorry to lose an opportunity. Shall we step round the corner by that darkish house, and take our share of the fun?"

"Sit down again, sit down, good Robin," replied the gentleman, laying his hand on the skirt of the gray coat. "You forget that we must wait here for your kinsman; and there is reason to believe that he will pass by, in the course of a very few moments."

The near approach of the uproar had now disturbed the neighborhood; windows flew open on all sides; and many heads, in the attire of the pillow, and confused by sleep suddenly broken, were protruded to the gaze of whoever had leisure to observe them. Eager voices hailed each other from house to house, all demanding the explanation, which not a soul could give. Half-dressed men hurried towards the unknown commotion, stumbling as they went over the stone steps that thrust themselves into the narrow foot-walk. The shouts, the laughter, and the tuneless bray, the antipodes of music, came onwards with increasing din, till scattered individuals, and then denser bodies, began to appear round a corner at the distance of a hundred yards.

"Will you recognize your kinsman, if he passes in this crowd?" inquired the gentleman.

"Indeed, I can't warrant it, sir; but I'll take my stand here, and keep a bright lookout," answered Robin, descending to the outer edge of the pavement.

A mighty stream of people now emptied into the street, and came rolling slowly towards the church. A single horseman wheeled the corner in the midst of them, and close behind him came a band of fearful wind-instruments, sending forth a fresher discord now that no intervening buildings kept it from the ear. Then a redder light disturbed the moonbeams, and a dense multitude of torches shone along the street, concealing, by their glare, whatever object they illuminated. The single horseman, clad in a military dress, and bearing a drawn sword, rode onward as the leader, and, by his fierce and variegated countenance, appeared like war personified; the red of one cheek was an emblem of fire and sword; the blackness of the other betokened the mourning that attends them. In his train were wild figures in the Indian dress, and many fantastic shapes without a model, giving the whole march a visionary air, as if a dream had broken forth from some feverish brain, and were sweeping visibly through the midnight streets. A mass of people, inactive, except as applauding spectators, hemmed the procession in; and several women ran along the sidewalk, piercing the confusion of heavier sounds with their shrill voices of mirth or terror.

"The double-faced fellow has his eye upon me," muttered Robin, with an indefinite but an uncomfortable idea that he was himself to bear a part in the pageantry.

The leader turned himself in the saddle, and fixed his glance full upon the country youth, as the steed went slowly by. When Robin had freed his eyes from those fiery ones, the musicians were passing before him, and the torches were close at hand; but the unsteady brightness of the latter formed a veil which he could not penetrate. The rattling of wheels over the stones sometimes found its way to his ear, and confused traces of a human form appeared at intervals, and then melted into the vivid light. A moment more, and the leader thundered a command to halt: the trumpets vomited a horrid breath, and then held their peace; the shouts and laughter of the people died away, and there remained only a universal hum, allied to silence. Right before Robin's eyes was an uncovered cart. There the torches blazed the brightest, there the moon shone out like day, and there, in tar-and-feathery dignity, sat his kinsman, Major Molineux!

He was an elderly man, of large and majestic person, and strong, square features, betokening a steady soul; but steady as it was, his enemies had found means to shake it. His face was pale as death, and far more ghastly; the broad forehead was contracted in his agony, so that his eyebrows formed one grizzled line; his eyes were red and wild, and the foam hung white upon his quivering lip. His whole frame was agitated by a quick and continual tremor, which his pride strove to quell, even in those circumstances of overwhelming humiliation.

But perhaps the bitterest pang of all was when his eyes met those of Robin; for he evidently knew him on the instant, as the youth stood witnessing the foul disgrace of a head grown gray in honor. They stared at each other in silence, and Robin's knees shook, and his hair bristled, with a mixture of pity and terror. Soon, however, a bewildering excitement began to seize upon his mind; the preceding adventures of the night, the unexpected appearance of the crowd, the torches, the confused din and the hush that followed, the spectre of his kinsman reviled by that great multitude,—all this, and, more than all, a perception of tremendous ridicule in the whole scene, affected him with a sort of mental inebriety. At that moment a voice of sluggish merriment saluted Robin's ears; he turned instinctively, and just behind the corner of the church stood the lantern-bearer, rubbing his eyes, and drowsily enjoying the lad's amazement. Then he heard a peal of laughter like the ringing of silvery bells; a woman twitched his arm, a saucy eye met his, and he saw the lady of the scarlet petticoat. A sharp, dry cachinnation appealed to his memory, and, standing on tiptoe in the crowd, with his white apron over his head, he beheld the courteous little innkeeper. And lastly, there sailed over the heads of the multitude a great, broad laugh, broken in the midst by two sepulchral hems; thus, "Haw, haw, haw,—hem, hem,—haw, haw, haw, haw!"

The sound proceeded from the balcony of the opposite edifice, and thither Robin turned his eyes. In front of the Gothic window stood the old citizen, wrapped in a wide gown, his gray periwig exchanged for a nightcap, which was thrust back from his forehead, and his silk stockings hanging about his legs. He supported himself on his polished cane in a fit of convulsive merriment, which manifested itself on his solemn old features like a funny inscription on a tombstone. Then Robin seemed to hear the voices of the barbers, of the guests of the inn, and of all who had made sport of him that night. The contagion was spreading among the multitude, when all at once, it seized upon Robin, and he sent forth a shout of laughter that echoed through the street,—every man shook his sides, every man emptied his lungs, but Robin's shout was the loudest there. The cloud-spirits peeped from their silvery islands, as the congregated mirth went roaring up the sky! The Man in the Moon heard the far bellow. "Oho," quoth he, "the old earth is frolicsome to-night!"

When there was a momentary calm in that tempestuous sea of sound, the leader gave the sign, the procession resumed its march. On they went, like fiends that throng in mockery around some dead potentate, mighty no more, but majestic still in his agony. On they went, in counterfeited pomp, in senseless uproar, in frenzied merriment, trampling all on an old man's heart. On swept the tumult, and left a silent street behind.

"Well, Robin, are you dreaming?" inquired the gentleman, laying his hand on the youth's shoulder.

Robin started, and withdrew his arm from the stone post to which he had instinctively clung, as the living stream rolled by him. His cheek was somewhat pale, and his eye not quite as lively as in the earlier part of the evening.

"Will you be kind enough to show me the way to the ferry?" said he, after a moment's pause.

"You have, then, adopted a new subject of inquiry?" observed his companion, with a smile.

"Why, yes, sir," replied Robin, rather dryly. "Thanks to you, and to my other friends, I have at last met my kinsman, and he will scarce desire to see my face again. I begin to grow weary of a town life, sir. Will you show me the way to the ferry?"

"No, my good friend Robin,—not to-night, at least," said the gentleman. "Some few days hence, if you wish it, I will speed you on your journey. Or, if you prefer to remain with us, perhaps, as you are a shrewd youth, you may rise in the world without the help of your kinsman, Major Molineux."

COMMENTARY

The essential situation of this baffling story is simple enough, and it is familiar to us from scores of legends, myths, and fairy tales. The hero, a very young man, a youth, sets out on his travels to seek his fortune or to claim a birthright. His chief characteristic, apart from whatever bravery he may have, is his innocence of the ways of the world. He has been brought up in simple or humble circumstances, and now he enters a life far more complex than any he had ever imagined, in which intrigue and danger await him. A chief interest in all such tales is the young man's passage from adolescence into maturity. This is accomplished through acts of courage and ingenuity, although sometimes, as in the story of Parsifal, the achievement is more complicated and involves the making of certain moral and intellectual choices. The difficulties which the young man confronts suggest those trials or tests that regularly form part of the initiation rites by which primitive peoples induct the youths of the community into the status of manhood.

There can be no doubt that Robin's experience the night he comes into Boston brings his youth to an end, and that his maturity begins after he has identified himself with the wild insurrectionary crowd. But what are we to conclude about the nature of this maturity? Obviously, Robin's loss of his youth comes about through his loss of innocence. But are we to be glad or sorry about the loss? Probably glad, since Robin's innocence was largely compounded of ignorance and a foolish confidence in his "shrewdness." And yet, when he leaves his innocence behind, we cannot be certain whether it is for something good or for something bad; we cannot make out what Hawthorne wants us to think.

This ambiguity has a variety of sources. One of them is the author's apparently double attitude toward the popular insurrection. Although the opening paragraph of the story does not carry a strong charge of emotion in favor of the Colony's right to govern itself, even a neutral statement of the political situation is bound to prejudice at least American readers in favor of the insurrectionists with whom Robin eventually makes common cause. Yet when Hawthorne describes the members of the conspiracy, he does so in ways that are scarcely sympathetic, and he is at some pains to suggest that their leader is perhaps the devil himself.

We are also in considerable doubt about the moral meaning we are supposed to assign to Major Molineux, the victim of the successful machinations of this devil-leader. Major Molineux, for all that he is on the "wrong" political side, has a nobility that no member of the popular party can claim. "He was an elderly man, of large and majestic person, and strong, square features, betokening a steady soul . . ." The account of his degradation is shocking in the extreme; Robin is surely right in thinking that his kinsman could never endure to see him again after he had been witness to the dreadful humiliation of tar-and-feathers. And yet, although Hawthorne speaks of the disgrace as "foul," because it deprives the Major of all semblance of humanity, making him a ghastly object of ridicule, he represents his young hero as being warmly associated with the Major's tormentors, eventually joining in the hideous laughter of the mob at its victim's plight.

It is of course Robin's participation in the mob's laughter that makes the shocking climax of the story. At the sight of his degraded kinsman, Robin's first emotions had been "pity and terror"—the feelings which, as Aristotle tells us, are aroused by tragedy. But these "classic" emotions, as we might call them, quickly yield to a "bewildering excitement." When Robin hears the laughter of the crowd begin again, first the laughter of all the figures who represent the life of worldliness—the police officer, the harlot, the innkeeper, the substantial citizen, the barber—and then the laughter of the general mob, he joins in with an especial gusto: "every man shook his sides, every man emptied his lungs, but Robin's shout was the loudest there." Hawthorne abates nothing in his characterization of the wild mob in which the young hero, once so gentle, submerges himself. "When there was a momentary calm in that tempestuous sea of sound, the leader gave the sign, the procession resumed its march. On they went, like fiends that throng in mockery around some dead potentate, mighty no more, but majestic still in his agony. On they went, in counterfeited pomp, in senseless uproar, in frenzied merriment, trampling all on an old man's heart." The cruel and savage act in which Robin enthusiastically shares has quite transcended its political origin. It has become one of those great primitive orgies in which the king is ritually slain. Whether or not Hawthorne was aware that such rituals did once actually take place, it is scarcely possible for anyone today to read the passage without having them in mind.[1]

Has Robin, then, by his burst of laughter at his kinsman's plight, taken sides with the devil? If he has, the story speaks no word of blame of his act. Nor, indeed, does the story say a word of blame of the presumptive devil himself. The gentleman who befriends Robin seems genuinely kind, truly virtuous and wise, yet when Robin asks him about the satanic ringleader, he replies by saying nothing more than that he does not know him "intimately" and asking, "May not a man have several voices . . . as well as two complexions?" The description of this leader as he rides at the head of the procession makes him out to be fierce and terrible, but not malign or disgusting. He is clad in military dress and bears a drawn sword, and, with his face half red, half black, he is said to look like "war personified." But if he is war personified, we must recall that Major Molineux is himself a soldier and derives his dignity from his military character.

The final words which the friendly gentleman addresses to Robin condone, even approve, the youth's conduct. After urging Robin not to return home immediately, he says, ". . . If you prefer to remain with us, perhaps, as you are a

[1] See "The Killing of the Divine King," Chapter xxiv of Sir James Frazer's *The Golden Bough*. Frazer's study of early religious practices and beliefs is one of the great works of our time and to it may be traced much of the contemporary interest in primitive cultures.

shrewd youth, you may rise in the world without the help of your kinsman, Major Molineux." Possibly, of course, the gentleman is wicked despite his seeming to be a man of simple good will, and means to lead Robin into ways of corruption and cynicism. But if, as seems reasonable, we take him to be good and his speech to be sincere, then the story would seem to be saying that Robin is well rid of his kinsman, that he is the better for no longer depending on his help. This being so, the story makes the judgment that Robin's cruel deed of turning upon his kinsman in ridicule was a necessary step in his coming of age.

It is a strange idea to contemplate. Yet in what other way are we to resolve the ambiguities of the story? Freud says somewhere that every young man must learn that the reality of the world is the way the neighbors say it is, not the way his parents say it is—we have to learn, that is, that life does not conform to the idealism which the family tries to teach us. This is the lesson that Robin learns, not intellectually or abstractly, but by the experience of the expressed impulses that his gentle, virtuous upbringing did not recognize and would not countenance.

It is exactly his gentle, virtuous upbringing that he repudiates by his laughter. But actually Robin had already repudiated his rearing even before joining in the mob's mockery of his kinsman—at the moment, just before the climax, when he has his intense vision of his home and family. As the vision comes to its end, he sees all the members of the family going into the house, "and when Robin would have entered also, the latch tinkled into its place, and he was excluded from his home." We have had no hint that Robin harbors resentment at having been sent out into the world while his elder brother is kept at home in the bosom of the family, but clearly just such resentment announces itself here, and in very forthright terms. And it is now, after this vision of his virtual expulsion from the family, that he is carried away by the laughter of the crowd. Major Molineux, his father's cousin, is his father's surrogate and representative; when Robin laughs at the degradation of this man, his laughter is in effect directed at his father and at all the virtues that his father stood for and to which he had assented.

But how can Robin's conduct not be blamed? How can it be condoned, and even approved, as the story may very well be doing? Can we suppose that a man like Hawthorne, a man notable for his gentleness, is saying that the dark and evil impulses of the savage mob have some beneficent part in the young man's development? Can he be telling us that the experience of evil is necessary to the understanding and practice of good, or that what is thought bad by gentle and pious people is not really, or not wholly, bad?

The questions that press upon us cannot be answered with any assurance that we are responding with precise understanding to what the author means. Yet, however we do answer, we cannot fail to recognize our relief that Robin, having capitulated to his cruel impulse and having repudiated authority and dignity, need never again utter the phrase, "my kinsman, Major Molineux." From this time on, he will at least travel under his own name and in his own right.

BARTLEBY
THE SCRIVENER
A Story of Wall Street

HERMAN MELVILLE

1819–1891

I AM a rather elderly man. The nature of my avocations, for the last thirty years, has brought me into more than ordinary contact with what would seem an interesting and somewhat singular set of men, of whom, as yet, nothing, that I know of, has ever been written—I mean, the law-copyists, or scriveners.[1] I have known very many of them, professionally and privately, and, if I pleased, could relate divers histories, at which good-natured gentlemen might smile, and sentimental souls might weep. But I waive the biographies of all other scriveners, for a few passages in the life of Bartleby, who was a scrivener, the strangest I ever saw, or heard of. While, of other law-copyists, I might write the complete life, of Bartleby nothing of that sort can be done. I believe that no materials exist, for a full and satisfactory biography of this man. It is an irreparable loss to literature. Bartleby was one of those beings of whom nothing is ascertainable, except from the original sources, and, in his case, those are very small. What my own astonished eyes saw of Bartleby, *that* is all I know of him, except, indeed, one vague report, which will appear in the sequel.

Ere introducing the scrivener, as he first appeared to me, it is fit I make some

[1] Clerks who copied legal documents by hand before the typewriter came into general use.

mention of myself, my *employés,* my business, my chambers, and general surroundings; because some such description is indispensable to an adequate understanding of the chief character about to be presented. Imprimis: I am a man who,
from his youth upwards, has been filled with a profound conviction that the
easiest way of life is the best. Hence, though I belong to a profession proverbially
energetic and nervous, even to turbulence, at times, yet nothing of that sort have
I ever suffered to invade my peace. I am one of those unambitious lawyers who
never addresses a jury, or in any way draws down public applause; but, in the cool
tranquillity of a snug retreat, do a snug business among rich men's bonds, and
mortgages, and title-deeds. All who know me, consider me an eminently *safe*
man. The late John Jacob Astor,[2] a personage little given to poetic enthusiasm,
had no hesitation in pronouncing my first grand point to be prudence; my next,
method. I do not speak it in vanity, but simply record the fact, that I was not
unemployed in my profession by the late John Jacob Astor; a name which, I
admit, I love to repeat; for it hath a rounded and orbicular sound to it, and rings
like unto bullion. I will freely add, that I was not insensible to the late John
Jacob Astor's good opinion.

Some time prior to the period at which this little history begins, my avocations
had been largely increased. The good old office, now extinct in the State of New
York, of a Master in Chancery,[3] had been conferred upon me. It was not a very
arduous office, but very pleasantly remunerative. I seldom lose my temper; much
more seldom indulge in dangerous indignation at wrongs and outrages; but I
must be permitted to be rash here and declare, that I consider the sudden and
violent abrogation of the office of Master in Chancery, by the new Constitution,[4]
as a ———— premature act; inasmuch as I had counted upon a life-lease of the
profits, whereas I only received those of a few short years. But this is by the way.

My chambers were up stairs, at No. — Wall Street. At one end, they looked
upon the white wall of the interior of a spacious sky-light shaft, penetrating the
building from top to bottom.

This view might have been considered rather tame than otherwise, deficient
in what landscape painters call "life." But, if so, the view from the other end of
my chambers offered, at least, a contrast, if nothing more. In that direction, my
windows commanded an unobstructed view of a lofty brick wall, black by age
and everlasting shade; which wall required no spy-glass to bring out its lurking
beauties, but, for the benefit of all near-sighted spectators, was pushed up to
within ten feet of my window panes. Owing to the great height of the surrounding buildings, and my chambers being on the second floor, the interval between
this wall and mine not a little resembled a huge square cistern.

At the period just preceding the advent of Bartleby, I had two persons as
copyists in my employment, and a promising lad as an office-boy. First, Turkey;
second, Nippers; third, Ginger Nut. These may seem names, the like of which are
not usually found in the Directory. In truth, they were nicknames, mutually conferred upon each other by my three clerks, and were deemed expressive of their

[2] New York capitalist and fur merchant (1763–1848).
[3] A court of chancery has jurisdiction in equity, that is, the part of the law having to
do with the application of the dictates of conscience or the principles of natural justice to
the settlement of controversies. The fact that the teller of the tale is an officer appointed
to assist such a court is significant, in view of his subsequent treatment of Bartleby.
[4] In 1847.

respective persons or characters. Turkey was a short, pursy Englishman, of about my age—that is, somewhere not far from sixty. In the morning, one might say, his face was of a fine florid hue, but after twelve o'clock, meridian—his dinner hour—it blazed like a grate full of Christmas coals; and continued blazing—but, as it were, with a gradual wane—till six o'clock, P.M., or thereabouts; after which, I saw no more of the proprietor of the face, which, gaining its meridian with the sun, seemed to set with it, to rise, culminate, and decline the following day, with the like regularity and undiminished glory. There are many singular coincidences I have known in the course of my life, not the least among which was the fact, that, exactly when Turkey displayed his fullest beams from his red and radiant countenance, just then, too, at that critical moment, began the daily period when I considered his business capacities as seriously disturbed for the remainder of the twenty-four hours. Not that he was absolutely idle, or averse to business, then; far from it. The difficulty was, he was apt to be altogether too energetic. There was a strange, inflamed, flurried, flighty recklessness of activity about him. He would be incautious in dipping his pen into his inkstand. All his blots upon my documents were dropped there after twelve o'clock, meridian. Indeed, not only would he be reckless, and sadly given to making blots in the afternoon, but, some days, he went further, and was rather noisy. At such times, too, his face flamed with augmented blazonry, as if cannel coal had been heaped on anthracite.[5] He made an unpleasant racket with his chair; spilled his sand-box; in mending his pens, impatiently split them all to pieces, and threw them on the floor in a sudden passion; stood up, and leaned over his table, boxing his papers about in a most indecorous manner, very sad to behold in an elderly man like him. Nevertheless, as he was in many ways a most valuable person to me, and all the time before twelve o'clock meridian, was the quickest, steadiest creature, too, accomplishing a great deal of work in a style not easily to be matched—for these reasons, I was willing to overlook his eccentricities, though, indeed, occasionally, I remonstrated with him. I did this very gently, however, because, though the civilest, nay, the blandest and most reverential of men in the morning, yet, in the afternoon, he was disposed, upon provocation, to be slightly rash with his tongue—in fact, insolent. Now, valuing his morning services as I did, and resolved not to lose them— yet, at the same time, made uncomfortable by his inflamed ways after twelve o'clock—and being a man of peace, unwilling by my admonitions to call forth unseemly retorts from him, I took upon me, one Saturday noon (he was always worse on Saturdays) to hint to him, very kindly, that, perhaps, now that he was growing old, it might be well to abridge his labors; in short, he need not come to my chambers after twelve o'clock, but, dinner over, had best go home to his lodgings, and rest himself till tea-time. But no; he insisted upon his afternoon devotions. His countenance became intolerably fervid, as he oratorically assured me —gesticulating with a long ruler at the other end of the room—that if his services in the morning were useful, how indispensable, then, in the afternoon?

"With submission, sir," said Turkey, on this occasion, "I consider myself your right-hand man. In the morning I but marshal and deploy my columns; but in the afternoon I put myself at their head, and gallantly charge the foe, thus"— and he made a violent thrust with the ruler.

[5] Cannel coal burns brightly; anthracite gives off almost no flame.

"But the blots, Turkey," intimated I.

"True; but, with submission, sir, behold these hairs! I am getting old. Surely, sir, a blot or two of a warm afternoon is not to be severely urged against gray hairs. Old age—even if it blot the page—is honorable. With submission, sir, we *both* are getting old."

This appeal to my fellow-feeling was hardly to be resisted. At all events, I saw that go he would not. So, I made up my mind to let him stay, resolving, nevertheless, to see to it that, during the afternoon, he had to do with my less important papers.

Nippers, the second on my list, was a whiskered, sallow, and, upon the whole, rather piratical-looking young man, of about five-and-twenty. I always deemed him the victim of two evil powers—ambition and indigestion. The ambition was evinced by a certain impatience of the duties of a mere copyist, an unwarrantable usurpation of strictly professional affairs, such as the original drawing up of legal documents. The indigestion seemed betokened in an occasional nervous testiness and grinning irritability, causing the teeth to audibly grind together over mistakes committed in copying; unnecessary maledictions, hissed, rather than spoken, in the heat of business; and especially by a continual discontent with the height of the table where he worked. Though of a very ingenious mechanical turn, Nippers could never get this table to suit him. He put chips under it, blocks of various sorts, bits of pasteboard, and at last went so far as to attempt an exquisite adjustment, by final pieces of folded blotting-paper. But no invention would answer. If, for the sake of easing his back, he brought the table-lid at a sharp angle well up towards his chin, and wrote there like a man using the steep roof of a Dutch house for his desk, then he declared that it stopped the circulation in his arms. If now he lowered the table to his waistbands, and stooped over it in writing, then there was a sore aching in his back. In short, the truth of the matter was, Nippers knew not what he wanted. Or, if he wanted anything, it was to be rid of a scrivener's table altogether. Among the manifestations of his diseased ambition was a fondness he had for receiving visits from certain ambiguous-looking fellows in seedy coats, whom he called his clients. Indeed, I was aware that not only was he, at times, considerable of a ward-politician, but he occasionally did a little business at the Justices' courts, and was not unknown on the steps of the Tombs.[6] I have good reason to believe, however, that one individual who called upon him at my chambers, and who, with a grand air, he insisted was his client, was no other than a dun, and the alleged title-deed, a bill. But, with all his failings, and the annoyances he caused me, Nippers, like his compatriot Turkey, was a very useful man to me; wrote a neat, swift hand; and, when he chose, was not deficient in a gentlemanly sort of deportment. Added to this, he always dressed in a gentlemanly sort of way; and so, incidentally, reflected credit upon my chambers. Whereas, with respect to Turkey, I had much ado to keep him from being a reproach to me. His clothes were apt to look oily, and smell of eating-houses. He wore his pantaloons very loose and baggy in summer. His coats were execrable; his hat not to be handled. But while the hat was a thing of indifference to me, inasmuch as his natural civility and deference, as a dependent Englishman, always led him to doff it the moment he entered the room, yet his

[6] A prison in New York City.

coat was another matter. Concerning his coats, I reasoned with him; but with no effect. The truth was, I suppose, that a man with so small an income could not afford to sport such a lustrous face and a lustrous coat at one and the same time. As Nippers once observed, Turkey's money went chiefly for red ink. One winter day, I presented Turkey with a highly respectable-looking coat of my own—a padded gray coat, of a most comfortable warmth, and which buttoned straight up from the knee to the neck. I thought Turkey would appreciate the favor, and abate his rashness and obstreperousness of afternoons. But no; I verily believe that buttoning himself up in so downy and blanket-like a coat had a pernicious effect upon him—upon the same principle that too much oats are bad for horses. In fact, precisely as a rash, restive horse is said to feel his oats, so Turkey felt his coat. It made him insolent. He was a man whom prosperity harmed.

Though, concerning the self-indulgent habits of Turkey, I had my own private surmises, yet, touching Nippers, I was well persuaded that, whatever might be his faults in other respects, he was, at least, a temperate young man. But, indeed, nature herself seemed to have been his vintner, and, at his birth, charged him so thoroughly with an irritable, brandy-like disposition, that all subsequent potations were needless. When I consider how, amid the stillness of my chambers, Nippers would sometimes impatiently rise from his seat, and stooping over his table, spread his arms wide apart, seize the whole desk, and move it, and jerk it, with a grim, grinding motion on the floor, as if the table were a perverse voluntary agent, intent on thwarting and vexing him, I plainly perceive that, for Nippers, brandy-and-water were altogether superfluous.

It was fortunate for me that, owing to its peculiar cause—indigestion—the irritability and consequent nervousness of Nippers were mainly observable in the morning, while in the afternoon he was comparatively mild. So that, Turkey's paroxysms only coming on about twelve o'clock, I never had to do with their eccentricities at one time. Their fits relieved each other, like guards. When Nippers's was on, Turkey's was off; and *vice versa*. This was a good natural arrangement, under the circumstances.

Ginger Nut, the third on my list, was a lad, some twelve years old. His father was a carman, ambitious of seeing his son on the bench instead of a cart, before he died. So he sent him to my office, as student at law, errand-boy, cleaner and sweeper, at the rate of one dollar a week. He had a little desk to himself, but he did not use it much. Upon inspection, the drawer exhibited a great array of the shells of various sorts of nuts. Indeed, to this quick-witted youth, the whole noble science of the law was contained in a nut-shell. Not the least among the employments of Ginger Nut, as well as one which he discharged with the most alacrity, was his duty as cake and apple purveyor for Turkey and Nippers. Copying law-papers being proverbially a dry, husky sort of business, my two scriveners were fain to moisten their mouths very often with Spitzenbergs, to be had at the numerous stalls nigh the Custom House and Post Office. Also, they sent Ginger Nut very frequently for that peculiar cake—small, flat, round, and very spicy—after which he had been named by them. Of a cold morning, when business was but dull, Turkey would gobble up scores of these cakes, as if they were mere wafers—indeed, they sell them at the rate of six or eight for a penny—the scrape of his pen blending with the crunching of the crisp particles in his mouth. Rashest of all the fiery afternoon blunders and flurried rashnesses of Turkey, was his once moistening a ginger-cake between his lips, and clapping it on to a mortgage, for a seal. I came within an ace of dismissing him then. But he mollified me by making an oriental bow, and saying—

"With submission, sir, it was generous of me to find[7] you in stationery on my own account."

Now my original business—that of a conveyancer and title hunter, and drawer-up of recondite documents of all sorts—was considerably increased by receiving the master's office. There was now great work for scriveners. Not only must I push the clerks already with me, but I must have additional help.

In answer to my advertisement, a motionless young man one morning stood upon my office threshold, the door being open, for it was summer. I can see that figure now—pallidly neat, pitiably respectable, incurably forlorn! It was Bartleby.

After a few words touching his qualifications, I engaged him, glad to have among my corps of copyists a man of so singularly sedate an aspect, which I thought might operate beneficially upon the flighty temper of Turkey, and the fiery one of Nippers.

I should have stated before that ground-glass folding-doors divided my premises into two parts, one of which was occupied by my scriveners, the other by myself. According to my humor, I threw open these doors, or closed them. I resolved to assign Bartleby a corner by the folding-doors, but on my side of them, so as to have this quiet man within easy call, in case any trifling thing was to be done. I placed his desk close up to a small side-window in that part of the room, a window which originally had afforded a lateral view of certain grimy back-yards and bricks, but which, owing to subsequent erections, commanded at present no view at all, though it gave some light. Within three feet of the panes was a wall, and the light came down from far above, between two lofty buildings, as from a very small opening in a dome. Still further to a satisfactory arrangement, I procured a high green folding screen, which might entirely isolate Bartleby from my sight, though not remove him from my voice. And thus, in a manner, privacy and society were conjoined.

At first, Bartleby did an extraordinary quantity of writing. As if long famishing for something to copy, he seemed to gorge himself on my documents. There was no pause for digestion. He ran a day and night line, copying by sun-light and by candle-light. I should have been quite delighted with his application, had he been cheerfully industrious. But he wrote on silently, palely, mechanically.

It is, of course, an indispensable part of a scrivener's business to verify the accuracy of his copy, word by word. Where there are two or more scriveners in an office, they assist each other in this examination, one reading from the copy, the other holding the original. It is a very dull, wearisome, and lethargic affair. I can readily imagine that, to some sanguine temperaments, it would be altogether intolerable. For example, I cannot credit that the mettlesome poet, Byron, would have contentedly sat down with Bartleby to examine a law document of, say five hundred pages, closely written in a crimpy hand.

Now and then, in the haste of business, it had been my habit to assist in comparing some brief document myself, calling Turkey or Nippers for this purpose. One object I had, in placing Bartleby so handy to me behind the screen, was, to avail myself of his services on such trivial occasions. It was on the third day, I think, of his being with me, and before any necessity had arisen for having

[7] To provide or furnish.

his own writing examined, that, being much hurried to complete a small affair I had in hand, I abruptly called to Bartleby. In my haste and natural expectancy of instant compliance, I sat with my head bent over the original on my desk, and my right hand sideways, and somewhat nervously extended with the copy, so that, immediately upon emerging from his retreat, Bartleby might snatch it and proceed to business without the least delay.

In this very attitude did I sit when I called to him, rapidly stating what it was I wanted him to do—namely, to examine a small paper with me. Imagine my surprise, nay, my consternation, when, without moving from his privacy, Bartleby, in a singularly mild, firm voice, replied, "I would prefer not to."

I sat awhile in perfect silence, rallying my stunned faculties. Immediately it occurred to me that my ears had deceived me, or Bartleby had entirely misunderstood my meaning. I repeated my request in the clearest tone I could assume; but in quite as clear a one came the previous reply, "I would prefer not to."

"Prefer not to," echoed I, rising in high excitement, and crossing the room with a stride. "What do you mean? Are you moon-struck? I want you to help me compare this sheet here—take it," and I thrust it towards him.

"I would prefer not to," said he.

I looked at him steadfastly. His face was leanly composed; his gray eye dimly calm. Not a wrinkle of agitation rippled him. Had there been the least uneasiness, anger, impatience or impertinence in his manner; in other words, had there been anything ordinarily human about him, doubtless I should have violently dismissed him from the premises. But as it was, I should have as soon thought of turning my pale plaster-of-paris bust of Cicero out of doors. I stood gazing at him awhile, as he went on with his own writing, and then reseated myself at my desk. This is very strange, thought I. What had one best do? But my business hurried me. I concluded to forget the matter for the present, reserving it for my future leisure. So, calling Nippers from the other room, the paper was speedily examined.

A few days after this, Bartleby concluded four lengthy documents, being quadruplicates of a week's testimony taken before me in my High Court of Chancery. It became necessary to examine them. It was an important suit, and great accuracy was imperative. Having all things arranged, I called Turkey, Nippers and Ginger Nut, from the next room, meaning to place the four copies in the hands of my four clerks, while I should read from the original. Accordingly, Turkey, Nippers, and Ginger Nut had taken their seats in a row, each with his document in his hand, when I called to Bartleby to join this interesting group.

"Bartleby! quick, I am waiting."

I heard a slow scrape of his chair legs on the uncarpeted floor, and soon he appeared standing at the entrance of his hermitage.

"What is wanted?" said he, mildly.

"The copies, the copies," said I, hurriedly. "We are going to examine them. There"—and I held towards him the fourth quadruplicate.

"I would prefer not to," he said, and gently disappeared behind the screen.

For a few moments I was turned into a pillar of salt, standing at the head of my seated column of clerks. Recovering myself, I advanced towards the screen, and demanded the reason for such extraordinary conduct.

"*Why* do you refuse?"

"I would prefer not to."

With any other man I should have flown outright into a dreadful passion, scorned all further words, and thrust him ignominiously from my presence. But there was something about Bartleby that not only strangely disarmed me, but, in a wonderful manner, touched and disconcerted me. I began to reason with him.

"These are your own copies we are about to examine. It is labor saving to you, because one examination will answer for your four papers. It is common usage. Every copyist is bound to help examine his copy. Is it not so? Will you not speak? Answer!"

"I prefer not to," he replied in a flute-like tone. It seemed to me that, while I had been addressing him, he carefully revolved every statement that I made; fully comprehended the meaning; could not gainsay the irresistible conclusion; but, at the same time, some paramount consideration prevailed with him to reply as he did.

"You are decided, then, not to comply with my request—a request made according to common usage and common sense?"

He briefly gave me to understand, that on that point my judgment was sound. Yes: his decision was irreversible.

It is not seldom the case that, when a man is browbeaten in some unprecedented and violently unreasonable way, he begins to stagger in his own plainest faith. He begins, as it were, vaguely to surmise that, wonderful as it may be, all the justice and all the reason is on the other side. Accordingly, if any disinterested persons are present, he turns to them for some reinforcement for his own faltering mind.

"Turkey," said I, "what do you think of this? Am I not right?"

"With submission, sir," said Turkey, in his blandest tone, " I think that you are."

"Nippers," said I, "what do *you* think of it?"

"I think I should kick him out of the office."

(The reader of nice perceptions will here perceive that, it being morning, Turkey's answer is couched in polite and tranquil terms, but Nippers replies in ill-tempered ones. Or, to repeat a previous sentence, Nippers's ugly mood was on duty, and Turkey's off.)

"Ginger Nut," said I, willing to enlist the smallest suffrage in my behalf, "what do *you* think of it?"

"I think, sir, he's a little *luny*," replied Ginger Nut, with a grin.

"You hear what they say," said I, turning towards the screen, "come forth and do your duty."

But he vouchsafed no reply. I pondered a moment in sore perplexity. But once more business hurried me. I determined again to postpone the consideration of this dilemma to my future leisure. With a little trouble we made out to examine the papers without Bartleby, though at every page or two Turkey deferentially dropped his opinion, that this proceeding was quite out of the common; while Nippers, twitching in his chair with a dyspeptic nervousness, ground out, between his set teeth, occasional hissing maledictions against the stubborn oaf behind the screen. And for his (Nippers's) part, this was the first and the last time he would do another man's business without pay.

Meanwhile Bartleby sat in his hermitage, oblivious to everything but his own peculiar business there.

Some days passed, the scrivener being employed upon another lengthy work.

His late remarkable conduct led me to regard his ways narrowly. I observed that he never went to dinner; indeed, that he never went anywhere. As yet I had never, of my personal knowledge, known him to be outside of my office. He was a perpetual sentry in the corner. At about eleven o'clock though, in the morning, I noticed that Ginger Nut would advance toward the opening in Bartleby's screen, as if silently beckoned thither by a gesture invisible to me where I sat. The boy would then leave the office, jingling a few pence, and reappear with a handful of ginger-nuts, which he delivered in the hermitage, receiving two of the cakes for his trouble.

He lives, then, on ginger-nuts, thought I; never eats a dinner, properly speaking; he must be a vegetarian, then; but no; he never eats even vegetables, he eats nothing but ginger-nuts. My mind then ran on in reveries concerning the probable effects upon the human constitution of living entirely on ginger-nuts. Ginger-nuts are so called, because they contain ginger as one of their peculiar constituents, and the final flavoring one. Now, what was ginger? A hot, spicy thing. Was Bartleby hot and spicy? Not at all. Ginger, then, had no effect upon Bartleby. Probably he preferred it should have none.

Nothing so aggravates an earnest person as a passive resistance. If the individual so resisted be of a not inhumane temper, and the resisting one perfectly harmless in his passivity, then, in the better moods of the former, he will endeavor charitably to construe to his imagination what proves impossible to be solved by his judgment. Even so, for the most part, I regarded Bartleby and his ways. Poor fellow! thought I, he means no mischief; it is plain he intends no insolence; his aspect sufficiently evinces that his eccentricities are involuntary. He is useful to me. I can get along with him. If I turn him away, the chances are he will fall in with some less-indulgent employer, and then he will be rudely treated, and perhaps driven forth miserably to starve. Yes. Here I can cheaply purchase a delicious self-approval. To befriend Bartleby; to humor him in his strange willfulness, will cost me little or nothing, while I lay up in my soul what will eventually prove a sweet morsel for my conscience. But this mood was not invariable with me. The passiveness of Bartleby sometimes irritated me. I felt strangely goaded on to encounter him in new opposition—to elicit some angry spark from him answerable to my own. But, indeed, I might as well have essayed to strike fire with my knuckles against a bit of Windsor soap. But one afternoon the evil impulse in me mastered me, and the following little scene ensued:

"Bartleby," said I, "when those papers are all copied, I will compare them with you."

"I would prefer not to."

"How? Surely you do not mean to persist in that mulish vagary?"

No answer.

I threw open the folding-doors near by, and, turning upon Turkey and Nippers, exclaimed:

"Bartleby a second time says, he won't examine his papers. What do you think of it, Turkey?"

It was afternoon, be it remembered. Turkey sat glowing like a brass boiler; his bald head steaming; his hands reeling among his blotted papers.

"Think of it?" roared Turkey. "I think I'll just step behind his screen, and black his eyes for him!"

So saying, Turkey rose to his feet and threw his arms into a pugilistic position. He was hurrying away to make good his promise, when I detained him, alarmed at the effect of incautiously rousing Turkey's combativeness after dinner.

"Sit down, Turkey," said I, "and hear what Nippers has to say. What do you think of it, Nippers? Would I not be justified in immediately dismissing Bartleby?"

"Excuse me, that is for you to decide, sir. I think his conduct quite unusual, and, indeed, unjust, as regards Turkey and myself. But it may only be a passing whim."

"Ah," exclaimed I, "you have strangely changed your mind, then—you speak very gently of him now."

"All beer," cried Turkey; "gentleness is effects of beer—Nippers and I dined together to-day. You see how gentle *I* am, sir. Shall I go and black his eyes?"

"You refer to Bartleby, I suppose. No, not to-day, Turkey," I replied; "pray, put up your fists."

I closed the doors, and again advanced towards Bartleby. I felt additional incentives tempting me to my fate. I burned to be rebelled against again. I remembered that Bartleby never left the office.

"Bartleby," said I, "Ginger Nut is away; just step around to the Post Office, won't you?" (it was but a three minutes' walk) "and see if there is anything for me."

"I would prefer not to."

"You *will* not?"

"I *prefer* not."

I staggered to my desk, and sat there in a deep study. My blind inveteracy returned. Was there any other thing in which I could procure myself to be ignominiously repulsed by this lean, penniless wight?—my hired clerk? What added thing is there, perfectly reasonable, that he will be sure to refuse to do?

"Bartleby!"

No answer.

"Bartleby," in a louder tone.

No answer.

"Bartleby," I roared.

Like a very ghost, agreeably to the laws of magical invocation, at the third summons, he appeared at the entrance of his hermitage.

"Go to the next room, and tell Nippers to come to me."

"I prefer not to," he respectfully and slowly said, and mildly disappeared.

"Very good, Bartleby," said I, in a quiet sort of serenely-severe self-possessed tone, intimating the unalterable purpose of some terrible retribution very close at hand. At the moment I half intended something of the kind. But upon the whole, as it was drawing towards my dinner-hour, I thought it best to put on my hat and walk home for the day, suffering much from perplexity and distress of mind.

Shall I acknowledge it? The conclusion of this whole business was, that it soon became a fixed fact of my chambers, that a pale young scrivener, by the name of Bartleby, had a desk there; that he copied for me at the usual rate of four cents a folio (one hundred words); but he was permanently exempt from examining the work done by him, that duty being transferred to Turkey and Nippers, out of compliment, doubtless, to their superior acuteness; moreover, said Bartleby was never, on any account, to be dispatched on the most trivial errand of any sort; and that even if entreated to take upon him such a matter, it was generally understood that he would "prefer not to"—in other words, that he would refuse point-blank.

As days passed on, I became considerably reconciled to Bartleby. His steadiness, his freedom from all dissipation, his incessant industry (except when he chose to throw himself into a standing revery behind his screen), his great stillness, his unalterableness of demeanor under all circumstances, made him a valuable acquisition. One prime thing was this—*he was always there*—first in the morning, continually through the day, and the last at night. I had a singular confidence in his honesty. I felt my most precious papers perfectly safe in his hands. Sometimes, to be sure, I could not, for the very soul of me, avoid falling into sudden spasmodic passions with him. For it was exceeding difficult to bear in mind all the time those strange peculiarities, privileges, and unheard-of exemptions, forming the tacit stipulations on Bartleby's part under which he remained in my office. Now and then, in the eagerness of dispatching pressing business, I would inadvertently summon Bartleby, in a short, rapid tone, to put his finger, say, on the incipient tie of a bit of red tape with which I was about compressing some papers. Of course, from behind the screen the usual answer, "I prefer not to," was sure to come; and then, how could a human creature, with the common infirmities of our nature, refrain from bitterly exclaiming upon such perverseness—such unreasonableness? However, every added repulse of this sort which I received only tended to lessen the probability of my repeating the inadvertence.

Here it must be said, that, according to the custom of most legal gentlemen occupying chambers in densely-populated law buildings, there were several keys to my door. One was kept by a woman residing in the attic, which person weekly scrubbed and daily swept and dusted my apartments. Another was kept by Turkey for convenience sake. The third I sometimes carried in my own pocket. The fourth I knew not who had.

Now, one Sunday morning I happened to go to Trinity Church, to hear a celebrated preacher, and finding myself rather early on the ground I thought I would walk round to my chambers for a while. Luckily I had my key with me; but upon applying it to the lock, I found it resisted by something inserted from the inside. Quite surprised, I called out; when to my consternation a key was turned from within; and thrusting his lean visage at me, and holding the door ajar, the apparition of Bartleby appeared, in his shirtsleeves, and otherwise in a strangely tattered *déshabillé,* saying quietly that he was sorry, but he was deeply engaged just then, and—preferred not admitting me at present. In a brief word or two, he moreover added, that perhaps I had better walk round the block two or three times, and by that time he would probably have concluded his affairs.

Now, the utterly unsurmised appearance of Bartleby, tenanting my law-chambers of a Sunday morning, with his cadaverously gentlemanly *nonchalance,* yet withal firm and self-possessed, had such a strange effect upon me, that incontinently I slunk away from my own door, and did as desired. But not without sundry twinges of impotent rebellion against the mild effrontery of this unaccountable scrivener. Indeed, it was his wonderful mildness chiefly, which not only disarmed me, but unmanned me as it were. For I consider that one, for the time, is sort of unmanned when he tranquilly permits his hired clerk to dictate to him, and order him away from his own premises. Furthermore, I was full of uneasiness as to what Bartleby could possibly be doing in my office in his shirt sleeves, and in an otherwise dismantled condition of a Sunday morning. Was anything amiss going on? Nay, that was out of the question. It was not to be thought of for a moment that Bartleby was an immoral person. But what could he be doing there?—copying? Nay again, whatever might be his eccentricities, Bartleby was an eminently decorous person. He would be the last man to sit down to his desk in any state approaching to nudity. Besides, it was Sunday; and there was something about Bartleby that forbade the supposition that he would by any secular occupation violate the proprieties of the day.

Nevertheless, my mind was not pacified; and full of a restless curiosity, at last I returned to the door. Without hindrance I inserted my key, opened it, and entered. Bartleby was not to be seen. I looked round anxiously, peeped behind his screen; but it was very plain that he was gone. Upon more closely examining the place, I surmised that for an indefinite period Bartleby must have eaten, dressed, and slept in my office, and that too without plate, mirror, or bed. The cushioned seat of a ricketty old sofa in one corner bore the faint impress of a lean, reclining form. Rolled away under his desk, I found a blanket; under the empty grate, a blacking box and brush; on a chair, a tin basin, with soap and a ragged towel; in a newspaper a few crumbs of ginger-nuts and a morsel of cheese. Yes, thought I, it is evident enough that Bartleby has been making his home here, keeping bachelor's hall all by himself. Immediately then the thought came sweeping across me, what miserable friendlessness and loneliness are here revealed! His poverty is great; but his solitude, how horrible! Think of it. Of a Sunday, Wall Street is deserted as Petra;[8] and every night of every day it is an emptiness. This building, too, which of week-days hums with industry and life, at nightfall echoes with sheer vacancy, and all through Sunday is forlorn. And here Bartleby makes his home; sole spectator of a solitude which he has seen all populous—a sort of innocent and transformed Marius brooding among the ruins of Carthage![9]

For the first time in my life a feeling of overpowering stinging melancholy seized me. Before, I had never experienced aught but a not unpleasing sadness. The bond of a common humanity now drew me irresistibly to gloom. A fraternal melancholy! For both I and Bartleby were sons of Adam. I remembered the bright silks and sparkling faces I had seen that day, in gala trim, swan-like sailing down the Mississippi of Broadway; and I contrasted them with the pallid copyist, and thought to myself, Ah, happiness courts the light, so we deem the world is gay; but misery hides aloof, so we deem that misery there is none. These sad fancyings —chimeras, doubtless, of a sick and silly brain—led on to other and more special thoughts, concerning the eccentricities of Bartleby. Presentiments of strange discoveries hovered round me. The scrivener's pale form appeared to me laid out, among uncaring strangers, in its shivering winding-sheet.

Suddenly I was attracted by Bartleby's closed desk, the key in open sight left in the lock.

I mean no mischief, seek the gratification of no heartless curiosity, thought I; besides, the desk is mine, and its contents, too, so I will make bold to look within. Everything was methodically arranged, the papers smoothly placed. The

8 An ancient city, now in ruins, in the present state of Jordan. It had been a flourishing center of caravan routes and trade.
9 The Roman general and consul Gaius Marius (*ca.* 155–86 B.C.) is represented as brooding among the ruins of Carthage after having lost his power and having been expelled by Sulla in 88 B.C.

pigeon holes were deep, and removing the files of documents, I groped into their recesses. Presently I felt something there, and dragged it out. It was an old bandana handkerchief, heavy and knotted. I opened it, and saw it was a savings's bank.

I now recalled all the quiet mysteries which I had noted in the man. I remembered that he never spoke but to answer; that, though at intervals he had considerable time to himself, yet I had never seen him reading—no, not even a newspaper; that for long periods he would stand looking out, at his pale window behind the screen, upon the dead brick wall; I was quite sure he never visited any refectory or eating house; while his pale face clearly indicated that he never drank beer like Turkey, or tea and coffee even, like other men; that he never went anywhere in particular that I could learn; never went out for a walk, unless, indeed, that was the case at present; that he had declined telling who he was, or whence he came, or whether he had any relatives in the world; that though so thin and pale, he never complained of ill health. And more than all, I remembered a certain unconscious air of pallid—how shall I call it?—of pallid haughtiness, say, or rather an austere reserve about him, which had positively awed me into my tame compliance with his eccentricities, when I had feared to ask him to do the slightest incidental thing for me, even though I might know, from his long-continued motionlessness, that behind his screen he must be standing in one of those dead-wall reveries of his.

Revolving all these things, and coupling them with the recently discovered fact, that he made my office his constant abiding place and home, and not forgetful of his morbid moodiness; revolving all these things, a prudential feeling began to steal over me. My first emotions had been those of pure melancholy and sincerest pity; but just in proportion as the forlornness of Bartleby grew and grew to my imagination, did that same melancholy merge into fear, that pity into repulsion. So true it is, and so terrible, too, that up to a certain point the thought or sight of misery enlists our best affections; but, in certain special cases, beyond that point it does not. They err who would assert that invariably this is owing to the inherent selfishness of the human heart. It rather proceeds from a certain hopelessness of remedying excessive and organic ill. To a sensitive being, pity is not seldom pain. And when at last it is perceived that such pity cannot lead to effectual succor, common sense bids the soul be rid of it. What I saw that morning persuaded me that the scrivener was the victim of innate and incurable disorder. I might give alms to his body; but his body did not pain him; it was his soul that suffered, and his soul I could not reach.

I did not accomplish the purpose of going to Trinity Church that morning. Somehow, the things I had seen disqualified me for the time from church-going. I walked homeward, thinking what I would do with Bartleby. Finally, I resolved upon this—I would put certain calm questions to him the next morning, touching his history, etc., and if he declined to answer them openly and unreservedly (and I supposed he would prefer not), then to give him a twenty dollar bill over and above whatever I might owe him, and tell him his services were no longer required; but that if in any other way I could assist him, I would be happy to do so, especially if he desired to return to his native place, wherever that might be, I would willingly help to defray the expenses. Moreover, if, after reaching home, he found himself at any time in want of aid, a letter from him would be sure of a reply.

The next morning came.

"Bartleby," said I, gently calling to him behind his screen.

No reply.

"Bartleby," said, in a still gentler tone, "come here; I am not going to ask you to do anything you would prefer not to do—I simply wish to speak to you."

Upon this he noiselessly slid into view.

"Will you tell me, Bartleby, where you were born?"

"I would prefer not to."

"Will you tell me *anything* about yourself?"

"I would prefer not to."

"But what reasonable objection can you have to speak to me? I feel friendly towards you."

He did not look at me while I spoke, but kept his glance fixed upon my bust of Cicero, which, as I then sat, was directly behind me, some six inches above my head.

"What is your answer, Bartleby?" said I, after waiting a considerable time for a reply, during which his countenance remained immovable, only there was the faintest conceivable tremor of the white attenuated mouth.

"At present I prefer to give no answer," he said, and retired into his hermitage.

It was rather weak in me I confess, but his manner, on this occasion, nettled me. Not only did there seem to lurk in it a certain calm disdain, but his perverseness seemed ungrateful, considering the undeniable good usage and indulgence he had received from me.

Again I sat ruminating what I should do. Mortified as I was at his behavior, and resolved as I had been to dismiss him when I entered my office, nevertheless I strangely felt something superstitious knocking at my heart, and forbidding me to carry out my purpose, and denouncing me for a villain if I dared to breathe one bitter word against this forlornest of mankind. At last, familiarly drawing my chair behind his screen, I sat down and said: "Bartleby, never mind, then, about revealing your history; but let me entreat you, as a friend, to comply as far as may be with the usages of this office. Say now, you will help to examine papers to-morrow or next day: in short, say now, that in a day or two you will begin to be a little reasonable:—say so, Bartleby."

"At present I would prefer not to be a little reasonable," was his mildly cadaverous reply.

Just then the folding-doors opened, and Nippers approached. He seemed suffering from an unusually bad night's rest, induced by severer indigestion than common. He overheard those final words of Bartleby.

"*Prefer not*, eh?" gritted Nippers—"I'd *prefer* him, if I were you, sir," addressing me—"I'd *prefer* him; I'd give him preferences, the stubborn mule! What is it, sir, pray, that he *prefers* not to do now?"

Bartleby moved not a limb.

"Mr. Nippers," said I, "I'd prefer that you would withdraw for the present."

Somehow, of late, I had got into the way of involuntarily using this word "prefer" upon all sorts of not exactly suitable occasions. And I trembled to think that my contact with the scrivener had already and seriously affected me in a mental way. And what further and deeper aberration might it not yet produce?

This apprehension had not been without efficacy in determining me to summary measures.

As Nippers, looking very sour and sulky, was departing, Turkey blandly and deferentially approached.

"With submission, sir," said he, "yesterday I was thinking about Bartleby here, and I think that if he would but prefer to take a quart of good ale every day, it would do much towards mending him, and enabling him to assist in examining his papers."

"So you have got the word, too," said I, slightly excited.

"With submission, what word, sir?" asked Turkey, respectfully crowding himself into the contracted space behind the screen, and by so doing, making me jostle the scrivener. "What word, sir?"

"I would prefer to be left alone here," said Bartleby, as if offended at being mobbed in his privacy.

"*That's* the word, Turkey," said I—"*that's* it."

"Oh, *prefer?* oh yes—queer word. I never use it myself. But, sir, as I was saying, if he would but prefer—"

"Turkey," interrupted I, "you will please withdraw."

"Oh certainly, sir, if you prefer that I should."

As he opened the folding-door to retire, Nippers at his desk caught a glimpse of me, and asked whether I would prefer to have a certain paper copied on blue paper or white. He did not in the least roguishly accent the word "prefer." It was plain that it involuntarily rolled from his tongue. I thought to myself, surely I must get rid of a demented man, who already has in some degree turned the tongues, if not the heads of myself and clerks. But I thought it prudent not to break the dismission at once.

The next day I noticed that Bartleby did nothing but stand at his window in his dead-wall revery. Upon asking him why he did not write, he said that he had decided upon doing no more writing.

"Why, how now? what next?" exclaimed I, "do no more writing?"

"No more."

"And what is the reason?"

"Do you not see the reason for yourself?" he indifferently replied.

I looked steadfastly at him, and perceived that his eyes looked dull and glazed. Instantly it occurred to me, that his unexampled diligence in copying by his dim window for the first few weeks of his stay with me might have temporarily impaired his vision.

I was touched. I said something in condolence with him. I hinted that of course he did wisely in abstaining from writing for a while; and urged him to embrace that opportunity of taking wholesome exercise in the open air. This, however, he did not do. A few days after this, my other clerks being absent, and being in a great hurry to dispatch certain letters by the mail, I thought that, having nothing else earthly to do, Bartleby would surely be less inflexible than usual, and carry these letters to the post-office. But he blankly declined. So, much to my inconvenience, I went myself.

Still added days went by. Whether Bartleby's eyes improved or not, I could not say. To all appearance, I thought they did. But when I asked him if they did, he vouchsafed no answer. At all events, he would do no copying. At last, in reply to my urgings, he informed me that he had permanently given up copying.

"What!" exclaimed I; "suppose your eyes should get entirely well—better than ever before—would you not copy then?"

"I have given up copying," he answered, and slid aside.

He remained as ever, a fixture in my chamber. Nay—if that were possible—he became still more of a fixture than before. What was to be done? He would do nothing in the office; why should he stay there? In plain fact, he had now become a millstone to me, not only useless as a necklace, but afflictive to bear. Yet I was sorry for him. I speak less than truth when I say that, on his own account, he occasioned me uneasiness. If he would but have named a single relative or friend, I would instantly have written, and urged their taking the poor fellow away to some convenient retreat. But he seemed alone, absolutely alone in the universe. A bit of wreck in the mid Atlantic. At length, necessities connected with my business tyrannized over all other considerations. Decently as I could, I told Bartleby that in six days' time he must unconditionally leave the office. I warned him to take measures, in the interval, for procuring some other abode. I offered to assist him in this endeavor, if he himself would but take the first step towards a removal. "And when you finally quit me, Bartleby," added I, "I shall see that you go not away entirely unprovided. Six days from this hour, remember."

At the expiration of that period, I peeped behind the screen, and lo! Bartleby was there.

I buttoned up my coat, balanced myself; advanced slowly towards him, touched his shoulder, and said, "The time has come; you must quit this place; I am sorry for you; here is money; but you must go."

"I would prefer not," he replied, with his back still towards me.

"You *must.*"

He remained silent.

Now I had an unbounded confidence in this man's common honesty. He had frequently restored to me sixpences and shillings carelessly dropped upon the floor, for I am apt to be very reckless in such shirt-button affairs. The proceeding, then, which followed will not be deemed extraordinary.

"Bartleby," said I, "I owe you twelve dollars on account; here are thirty-two; the odd twenty are yours—Will you take it?" and I handed the bills towards him.

But he made no motion.

"I will leave them here, then," putting them under a weight on the table. Then taking my hat and cane and going to the door, I tranquilly turned and added—"After you have removed your things from these offices, Bartleby, you will of course lock the door—since every one is now gone for the day but you—and if you please, slip your key underneath the mat, so that I may have it in the morning. I shall not see you again; so good-by to you. If, hereafter, in your new place of abode, I can be of any service to you, do not fail to advise me by letter. Good-by, Bartleby, and fare you well."

But he answered not a word; like the last column of some ruined temple, he remained standing mute and solitary in the middle of the otherwise deserted room.

As I walked home in a pensive mood, my vanity got the better of my pity. I could not but highly plume myself on my masterly management in getting rid of

Bartleby. Masterly I call it, and such it must appear to any dispassionate thinker. The beauty of my procedure seemed to consist in its perfect quietness. There was no vulgar bullying, no bravado of any sort, no choleric hectoring, and striding to and fro across the apartment, jerking out vehement commands for Bartleby to bundle himself off with his beggarly traps. Nothing of the kind. Without loudly bidding Bartleby depart—as an inferior genius might have done—I *assumed* the ground that depart he must; and upon that assumption built all I had to say. The more I thought over my procedure, the more I was charmed with it. Nevertheless, next morning, upon awakening, I had my doubts—I had somehow slept off the fumes of vanity. One of the coolest and wisest hours a man has, is just after he awakes in the morning. My procedure seemed as sagacious as ever—but only in theory. How it would prove in practice—there was the rub. It was truly a beautiful thought to have assumed Bartleby's departure; but, after all, that assumption was simply my own, and none of Bartleby's. The great point was, not whether I had assumed that he would quit me, but whether he would prefer so to do. He was more a man of preferences than assumptions.

After breakfast, I walked down town, arguing the probabilities *pro* and *con*. One moment I thought it would prove a miserable failure, and Bartleby would be found all alive at my office as usual; the next moment it seemed certain that I should find his chair empty. And so I kept veering about. At the corner of Broadway and Canal Street, I saw quite an excited group of people standing in earnest conversation.

"I'll take odds he doesn't," said a voice as I passed.

"Doesn't go?—done!" said I, "put up your money."

I was instinctively putting my hand in my pocket to produce my own, when I remembered that this was an election day. The words I had overheard bore no reference to Bartleby, but to the success or non-success of some candidate for the mayoralty. In my intent frame of mind, I had, as it were, imagined that all Broadway shared in my excitement, and were debating the same question with me. I passed on, very thankful that the uproar of the street screened my momentary absent-mindedness.

As I had intended, I was earlier than usual at my office door. I stood listening for a moment. All was still. He must be gone. I tried the knob. The door was locked. Yes, my procedure had worked to a charm; he indeed must be vanished. Yet a certain melancholy mixed with this: I was almost sorry for my brilliant success. I was fumbling under the door mat for the key, which Bartleby was to have left there for me, when accidentally my knee knocked against a panel, producing a summoning sound, and in response a voice came to me from within—"Not yet; I am occupied."

It was Bartleby.

I was thunderstruck. For an instant I stood like the man who, pipe in mouth, was killed one cloudless afternoon long ago in Virginia, by summer lightning; at his own warm open window he was killed, and remained leaning out there upon the dreamy afternoon, till some one touched him, when he fell.

"Not gone!" I murmured at last. But again obeying that wondrous ascendancy which the inscrutable scrivener had over me, and from which ascendancy, for all my chafing, I could not completely escape, I slowly went down stairs and out into the street, and while walking round the block, considered what I should next do in this unheard-of perplexity. Turn the man out by an actual thrusting I could not; to drive him away by calling him hard names would not do; calling in the police was an unpleasant idea; and yet, permit him to enjoy his cadaverous triumph over me—this, too, I could not think of. What was to be done? or, if nothing could be done, was there anything further that I could *assume* in the matter? Yes, as before I had prospectively assumed that Bartleby would depart, so now I might retrospectively assume that departed he was. In the legitimate carrying out of this assumption, I might enter my office in a great hurry, and pretending not to see Bartleby at all, walk straight against him as if he were air. Such a proceeding would in a singular degree have the appearance of a home-thrust. It was hardly possible that Bartleby could withstand such an application of the doctrine of assumptions. But upon second thoughts the success of the plan seemed rather dubious. I resolved to argue the matter over with him again.

"Bartleby," said I, entering the office, with a quietly severe expression, "I am seriously displeased. I am pained, Bartleby. I had thought better of you. I had imagined you of such a gentlemanly organization, that in any delicate dilemma a slight hint would suffice—in short, an assumption. But it appears I am deceived. Why," I added, unaffectedly starting, "you have not even touched that money yet," pointing to it, just where I had left it the evening previous.

He answered nothing.

"Will you, or will you not, quit me?" I now demanded in a sudden passion, advancing close to him.

"I would prefer *not* to quit you," he replied, gently emphasizing the *not*.

"What earthly right have you to stay here? Do you pay any rent? Do you pay my taxes? Or is this property yours?"

He answered nothing.

"Are you ready to go on and write now? Are your eyes recovered? Could you copy a small paper for me this morning? or help examine a few lines? or step round to the post-office? In a word, will you do anything at all, to give a coloring to your refusal to depart the premises?"

He silently retired into his hermitage.

I was now in such a state of nervous resentment that I thought it but prudent to check myself at present from further demonstrations. Bartleby and I were alone. I remembered the tragedy of the unfortunate Adams and the still more unfortunate Colt[10] in the solitary office of the latter; and how poor Colt, being dreadfully incensed by Adams, and imprudently permitted himself to get wildly excited, was at unawares hurried into his fatal act—an act which certainly no man could possibly deplore more than the actor himself. Often it had occurred to me in my ponderings upon the subject that had that altercation taken place in the public street, or at a private residence, it would not have terminated as it did. It was the circumstance of being alone in a solitary office, up stairs, of a building entirely unhallowed by humanizing domestic associations—an uncarpeted office, doubtless, of a dusty, haggard sort of appearance—this it must have been, which greatly helped to enhance the irritable desperation of the hapless Colt.

But when this old Adam of resentment rose in me and tempted me con-

[10] A famous New York murder case of 1841. John C. Colt, brother of the firearms manufacturer, killed Samuel Adams, a printer, by hitting him an unpremeditated blow on the head during a scuffle.

cerning Bartleby, I grappled him and threw him. How? Why, simply by recalling the divine injunction: "A new commandment give I unto you, that ye
love one another." Yes, this it was that saved me. Aside from higher considerations, charity often operates as a vastly wise and prudent principle—a great
safeguard to its possessor. Men have committed murder for jealousy's sake, and
anger's sake, and hatred's sake, and selfishness' sake, and spiritual pride's sake;
but no man, that ever I heard of, ever committed a diabolical murder for sweet
charity's sake. Mere self-interest, then, if no better motive can be enlisted, should,
especially with high-tempered men, prompt all beings to charity and philan-
thropy. At any rate, upon the occasion in question, I strove to drown my exasperated feelings towards the scrivener by benevolently construing his conduct.
Poor fellow, poor fellow! thought I, he don't mean anything; and besides, he has
seen hard times, and ought to be indulged.

I endeavored, also, immediately to occupy myself, and at the same time to
comfort my despondency. I tried to fancy, that in the course of the morning, at
such time as might prove agreeable to him, Bartleby, of his own free accord,
would emerge from his hermitage and take up some decided line of march in the
direction of the door. But no. Half-past twelve o'clock came; Turkey began to
glow in the face, overturn his inkstand, and become generally obstreperous;
Nippers abated down into quietude and courtesy; Ginger Nut munched his
noon apple; and Bartleby remained standing at his window in one of his pro-
foundest dead-wall reveries. Will it be credited? Ought I to acknowledge it?
That afternoon I left the office without saying one further word to him.

Some days now passed, during which, at leisure intervals I looked a little
into "Edwards on the Will,"[11] and "Priestley on Necessity."[12] Under the circumstances, those books induced a salutary feeling. Gradually I slid into the persuasion that these troubles of mine, touching the scrivener, had been all predestinated from eternity, and Bartleby was billeted upon me for some mysterious
purpose of an allwise Providence, which it was not for a mere mortal like me
to fathom. Yes, Bartleby, stay there behind your screen, thought I; I shall per-
secute you no more; you are harmless and noiseless as any of these old chairs;
in short, I never feel so private as when I know you are here. At last I see it, I
feel it; I penetrate to the predestinated purpose of my life. I am content. Others
may have loftier parts to enact; but my mission in this world, Bartleby, is to
furnish you with office-room for such period as you may see fit to remain.

I believe that this wise and blessed frame of mind would have continued
with me, had it not been for the unsolicited and uncharitable remarks obtruded
upon me by my professional friends who visited the rooms. But thus it often is,
that the constant friction of illiberal minds wears out at last the best resolves
of the more generous. Though to be sure, when I reflected upon it, it was not
strange that people entering my office should be struck by the peculiar aspect
of the unaccountable Bartleby, and so be tempted to throw out some sinister observations concerning him. Sometimes an attorney, having business with me,
and calling at my office, and finding no one but the scrivener there, would under-

[11] In *The Freedom of the Will* the New England divine and theologian, Jonathan
Edwards (1703–1758), maintained that the human will is subject, not free.
[12] Joseph Priestley (1733–1803), an English clergyman who discovered oxygen, also
wrote on theological and philosophical problems. He spent the last years of his life in
the United States.

take to obtain some sort of precise information from him touching my whereabouts; but without heeding his idle talk, Bartleby would remain standing immovable in the middle of the room. So after contemplating him in that position for a time, the attorney would depart, no wiser than he came.

Also, when a reference was going on, and the room full of lawyers and witnesses, and business driving fast, some deeply-occupied legal gentleman present, seeing Bartleby wholly unemployed, would request him to run round to his (the legal gentleman's) office and fetch some papers for him. Thereupon, Bartleby would tranquilly decline, and yet remain idle as before. Then the lawyer would give a great stare, and turn to me. And what could I say? At last I was made aware that all through the circle of my professional acquaintance, a whisper of wonder was running round, having reference to the strange creature I kept at my office. This worried me very much. And as the idea came upon me of his possibly turning out a long-lived man, and keep occupying my chambers, and denying my authority; and perplexing my visitors; and scandalizing my professional reputation; and casting a general gloom over the premises; keeping soul and body together to the last upon his savings (for doubtless he spent but half a dime a day), and in the end perhaps outlive me, and claim possession of my office by right of his perpetual occupancy: as all these dark anticipations crowded upon me more and more, and my friends continually intruded their relentless remarks upon the apparition in my room; a great change was wrought in me. I resolved to gather all my faculties together, and forever rid me of this intolerable incubus.

Ere revolving any complicated project, however, adapted to this end, I first simply suggested to Bartleby the propriety of his permanent departure. In a calm and serious tone, I commended the idea to his careful and mature consideration. But, having taken three days to meditate upon it, he apprised me, that his original determination remained the same; in short, that he still preferred to abide with me.

What shall I do? I now said to myself, buttoning up my coat to the last button. What shall I do? what ought I to do? what does conscience say I *should* do with this man, or, rather, ghost. Rid myself of him, I must; go, he shall. But how? You will not thrust him, the poor, pale, passive mortal—you will not thrust such a helpless creature out of your door? you will not dishonor yourself by such cruelty? No, I will not, I cannot do that. Rather would I let him live and die here, and then mason up his remains in the wall. What, then, will you do? For all your coaxing, he will not budge. Bribes he leaves under your own paperweight on your table; in short, it is quite plain that he prefers to cling to you.

Then something severe, something unusual must be done. What! surely you will not have him collared by a constable, and commit his innocent pallor to the common jail? And upon what ground could you procure such a thing to be done? —a vagrant, is he? What! he a vagrant, a wanderer, who refuses to budge? It is because he will *not* be a vagrant, then, that you seek to count him *as* a vagrant. That is too absurd. No visible means of support: there I have him. Wrong again: for indubitably he *does* support himself, and that is the only unanswerable proof that any man can show of his possessing the means so to do. No more, then. Since he will not quit me, I must quit him. I will change my offices; I will move elsewhere, and give him fair notice, that if I find him on my new premises I will then proceed against him as a common trespasser.

Acting accordingly, next day I thus addressed him: "I find these chambers too far from the City Hall; the air is unwholesome. In a word, I propose to remove my offices next week, and shall no longer require your services. I tell you this now, in order that you may seek another place."

He made no reply, and nothing more was said.

On the appointed day I engaged carts and men, proceeded to my chambers, and, having but little furniture, everything was removed in a few hours. Throughout, the scrivener remained standing behind the screen, which I directed to be removed the last thing. It was withdrawn; and, being folded up like a huge folio, left him the motionless occupant of a naked room. I stood in the entry watching him a moment, while something from within me upbraided me.

I re-entered, with my hand in my pocket—and—and my heart in my mouth.

"Good-by, Bartleby; I am going—good-by, and God some way bless you; and take that," slipping something in his hand. But it dropped upon the floor, and then—strange to say—I tore myself from him whom I had so longed to be rid of.

Established in my new quarters, for a day or two I kept the door locked, and started at every footfall in the passages. When I returned to my rooms, after any little absence, I would pause at the threshold for an instant, and attentively listen, ere applying my key. But these fears were needless. Bartleby never came nigh me.

I thought all was going well, when a perturbed-looking stranger visited me, inquiring whether I was the person who had recently occupied rooms at No. — Wall Street.

Full of forebodings, I replied that I was.

"Then, sir," said the stranger, who proved a lawyer, "you are responsible for the man you left there. He refuses to do any copying; he refuses to do anything; he says he prefers not to; and he refuses to quit the premises."

"I am very sorry, sir," said I, with assumed tranquillity, but an inward tremor, "but, really, the man you allude to is nothing to me—he is no relation or apprentice of mine, that you should hold me responsible for him."

"In mercy's name, who is he?"

"I certainly cannot inform you. I know nothing about him. Formerly I employed him as a copyist; but he has done nothing for me now for some time past."

"I shall settle him, then—good morning, sir."

Several days passed, and I heard nothing more; and, though I often felt a charitable prompting to call at the place and see poor Bartleby, yet a certain squeamishness, of I know not what, withheld me.

All is over with him, by this time, thought I, at last, when, through another week, no further intelligence reached me. But, coming to my room the day after, I found several persons waiting at my door in a high state of nervous excitement.

"That's the man—here he comes," cried the foremost one, whom I recognized as the lawyer who had previously called upon me alone.

"You must take him away, sir, at once," cried a portly person among them, advancing upon me, and whom I knew to be the landlord of No. — Wall Street. "These gentlemen, my tenants, cannot stand it any longer; Mr. B———," pointing to the lawyer, "has turned him out of his room, and he now persists in haunting the building generally, sitting upon the banisters of the stairs by day, and sleeping in the entry by night. Everybody is concerned; clients are leaving the offices; some fears are entertained of a mob; something you must do, and that without delay."

Aghast at this torrent, I fell back before it, and would fain have locked myself in my new quarters. In vain I persisted that Bartleby was nothing to me—no more than to any one else. In vain—I was the last person known to have anything to do with him, and they held me to the terrible account. Fearful, then, of being exposed in the papers (as one person present obscurely threatened), I considered the matter, and, at length, said, that if the lawyer would give me a confidential interview with the scrivener, in his (the lawyer's) own room, I would, that afternoon, strive my best to rid them of the nuisance they complained of.

Going up stairs to my old haunt, there was Bartleby silently sitting upon the banister at the landing.

"What are you doing here, Bartleby?" said I.

"Sitting upon the banister," he mildly replied.

I motioned him into the lawyer's room, who then left us.

"Bartleby," said I, "are you aware that you are the cause of great tribulation to me, by persisting in occupying the entry after being dismissed from the office?"

No answer.

"Now one of two things must take place. Either you must do something, or something must be done to you. Now what sort of business would you like to engage in? Would you like to re-engage in copying for some one?"

"No; I would prefer not to make any change."

"Would you like a clerkship in a dry-goods store?"

"There is too much confinement about that. No, I would not like a clerkship; but I am not particular."

"Too much confinement," I cried, "why, you keep yourself confined all the time!"

"I would prefer not to take a clerkship," he rejoined, as if to settle that little item at once.

"How would a bar-tender's business suit you? There is no trying of the eye-sight in that."

"I would not like it at all; though, as I said before, I am not particular."

His unwonted wordiness inspirited me. I returned to the charge.

"Well, then, would you like to travel through the country collecting bills for the merchants? That would improve your health."

"No, I would prefer to be doing something else."

"How, then, would going as a companion to Europe, to entertain some young gentleman with your conversation—how would that suit you?"

"Not at all. It does not strike me that there is anything definite about that. I like to be stationary. But I am not particular."

"Stationary you shall be, then," I cried, now losing all patience, and, for the first time in all my exasperating connection with him, fairly flying into a passion. "If you do not go away from these premises before night, I shall feel bound—indeed, I *am* bound—to—to—to quit the premises myself!" I rather absurdly concluded, knowing not with what possible threat to try to frighten his immobility into compliance. Despairing of all further efforts, I was precipitately leaving him, when a final thought occurred to me—one which had not been wholly unindulged before.

"Bartleby," said I, in the kindest tone I could assume under such exciting circumstances, "will you go home with me now—not to my office, but my dwelling —and remain there till we can conclude upon some convenient arrangement for you at our leisure? Come, let us start now, right away."

"No: at present I would prefer not to make any change at all."

I answered nothing; but, effectually dodging every one by the suddenness and rapidity of my flight, rushed from the building, ran up Wall Street towards Broadway, and, jumping into the first omnibus, was soon removed from pursuit. As soon as tranquillity returned, I distinctly perceived that I had now done all that I possibly could, both in respect to the demands of the landlord and his tenants, and with regard to my own desire and sense of duty, to benefit Bartleby, and shield him from rude persecution. I now strove to be entirely care-free and quiescent; and my conscience justified me in the attempt; though, indeed, it was not so successful as I could have wished. So fearful was I of being again hunted out by the incensed landlord and his exasperated tenants, that, surrendering my business to Nippers, for a few days, I drove about the upper part of the town and through the suburbs, in my rockaway; crossed over to Jersey City and Hoboken, and paid fugitive visits to Manhattanville and Astoria. In fact, I almost lived in my rockaway for the time.

When again I entered my office, lo, a note from the landlord lay upon the desk. I opened it with trembling hands. It informed me that the writer had sent to the police, and had Bartleby removed to the Tombs as a vagrant. Moreover, since I knew more about him than any one else, he wished me to appear at that place, and make a suitable statement of the facts. These tidings had a conflicting effect upon me. At first I was indignant; but, at last, almost approved. The land-lord's energetic, summary disposition, had led him to adopt a procedure which I do not think I would have decided upon myself; and yet, as a last resort, under such peculiar circumstances, it seemed the only plan.

As I afterwards learned, the poor scrivener, when told that he must be conducted to the Tombs, offered not the slightest obstacle, but, in his pale, unmoving way, silently acquiesced.

Some of the compassionate and curious bystanders joined the party; and headed by one of the constables arm-in-arm with Bartleby, the silent procession filed its way through all the noise, and heat, and joy of the roaring thoroughfares at noon.

The same day I received the note, I went to the Tombs, or, to speak more properly, the Halls of Justice. Seeking the right officer, I stated the purpose of my call, and was informed that the individual I described was, indeed, within. I then assured the functionary that Bartleby was a perfectly honest man, and greatly to be compassionated, however unaccountably eccentric. I narrated all I knew, and closed by suggesting the idea of letting him remain in as indulgent confinement as possible, till something less harsh might be done—though, indeed, I hardly knew what. At all events, if nothing else could be decided upon, the alms-house must receive him. I then begged to have an interview.

Being under no disgraceful charge, and quite serene and harmless in all his ways, they had permitted him freely to wander about the prison, and, especially, in the inclosed grass-platted yards thereof. And so I found him there, standing all alone in the quietest of the yards, his face towards a high wall, while all around, from the narrow slits of the jail windows, I thought I saw peering out upon him the eyes of murderers and thieves.

"Bartleby!"

"I know you," he said, without looking round— "and I want nothing to say to you."

"It was not I that brought you here, Bartleby," said I, keenly pained at his implied suspicion. "And to you, this should not be so vile a place. Nothing reproachful attaches to you by being here. And see, it is not so sad a place as one might think. Look, there is the sky, and here is the grass."

"I know where I am," he replied, but would say nothing more, and so I left him.

As I entered the corridor again, a broad meat-like man, in an apron, accosted me, and, jerking his thumb over his shoulder, said— "Is that your friend?"

"Yes."

"Does he want to starve? If he does, let him live on the prison fare, that's all."

"Who are you?" asked I, not knowing what to make of such an unofficially speaking person in such a place.

"I am the grub-man. Such gentlemen as have friends here, hire me to provide them with something good to eat."

"Is this so?" said I, turning to the turnkey.

He said it was.

"Well, then," said I, slipping some silver into the grub-man's hands (for so they called him), "I want you to give particular attention to my friend there; let him have the best dinner you can get. And you must be as polite to him as possible."

"Introduce me, will you?" said the grub-man, looking at me with an expression which seemed to say he was all impatience for an opportunity to give a specimen of his breeding.

Thinking it would prove of benefit to the scrivener, I acquiesced; and, asking the grub-man his name, went up with him to Bartleby.

"Bartleby, this is a friend; you will find him very useful to you."

"Your sarvant, sir, your sarvant," said the grub-man, making a low salutation behind his apron. "Hope you find it pleasant here, sir; nice grounds—cool apartments—hope you'll stay with us some time—try to make it agreeable. What will you have for dinner to-day?"

"I prefer not to dine to-day," said Bartleby, turning away. "It would disagree with me; I am unused to dinners." So saying, he slowly moved to the other side of the inclosure, and took up a position fronting the dead-wall.

"How's this?" said the grub-man, addressing me with a stare of astonishment. "He's odd, ain't he?"

"I think he is a little deranged," said I, sadly.

"Deranged? deranged is it? Well, now, upon my word, I thought that friend of yourn was a gentleman forger; they are always pale and genteel-like, them forgers. I can't help pity 'em—can't help it, sir. Did you know Monroe Edwards?" he added, touchingly, and paused. Then, laying his hand piteously on my shoulder, sighed, "he died of consumption at Sing-Sing. So you weren't acquainted with Monroe?"

"No, I was never socially acquainted with any forgers. But I cannot stop longer. Look to my friend yonder. You will not lose by it. I will see you again."

Some few days after this, I again obtained admission to the Tombs, and went through the corridors in quest of Bartleby; but without finding him.

"I saw him coming from his cell not long ago," said a turnkey, "may be he's gone to loiter in the yards."

So I went in that direction.

"Are you looking for the silent man?" said another turnkey, passing me. "Yonder he lies—sleeping in the yard there. 'Tis not twenty minutes since I saw him lie down."

The yard was entirely quiet. It was not accessible to the common prisoners. The surrounding walls, of amazing thickness, kept off all sounds behind them. The Egyptian character of the masonry weighed upon me with its gloom. But a soft imprisoned turf grew under foot. The heart of the eternal pyramids, it seemed, wherein, by some strange magic, through the clefts, grass-seed, dropped by birds, had sprung.

Strangely huddled at the base of the wall, his knees drawn up, and lying on his side, his head touching the cold stones, I saw the wasted Bartleby. But nothing stirred. I paused; then went close up to him; stooped over, and saw that his dim eyes were open; otherwise he seemed profoundly sleeping. Something prompted me to touch him. I felt his hand, when a tingling shiver ran up my arm and down my spine to my feet.

The round face of the grub-man peered upon me now. "His dinner is ready. Won't he dine to-day, either? Or does he live without dining?"

"Lives without dining," said I, and closed the eyes.

"Eh!—He's asleep, ain't he?"

"With kings and counselors," murmured I.

There would seem little need for proceeding further in this history. Imagination will readily supply the meagre recital of poor Bartleby's interment. But, ere parting with the reader, let me say, that if this little narrative has sufficiently interested him, to awaken curiosity as to who Bartleby was, and what manner of life he led prior to the present narrator's making his acquaintance, I can only reply, that in such curiosity I fully share, but am wholly unable to gratify it. Yet here I hardly know whether I should divulge one little item of rumor, which came to my ear a few months after the scrivener's decease. Upon what basis it rested, I could never ascertain; and hence, how true it is I cannot now tell. But, inasmuch as this vague report has not been without a certain suggestive interest to me, however sad, it may prove the same with some others; and so I will briefly mention it. The report was this: that Bartleby had been a subordinate clerk in the Dead Letter Office at Washington, from which he had been suddenly removed by a change in the administration. When I think over this rumor, hardly can I express the emotions which seize me. Dead letters! does it not sound like dead men? Conceive a man by nature and misfortune prone to a pallid hopelessness, can any business seem more fitted to heighten it than that of continually handling these dead letters, and assorting them for the flames? For by the cartload they are annually burned. Sometimes from out the folded paper the pale clerk takes a ring—the finger it was meant for, perhaps, moulders in the grave; a bank-note sent in swiftest charity—he whom it would relieve, nor eats nor hungers any more; pardon for those who died despairing; hope for those who died unhoping; good tidings for those who died stifled by unrelieved calamities. On errands of life, these letters speed to death.

Ah, Bartleby! Ah, humanity!

In a letter he wrote to Hawthorne in 1851, Melville, speaking of his friend in the third person, offered him this praise: "There is the grand truth about Nathaniel Hawthorne. He says NO! in thunder; but the Devil himself cannot make him say *yes*. For all men who say *yes*, lie. . . ." Melville was referring to Hawthorne's relation to the moral order of the universe as it is conventionally imagined, but his statement, which has become famous, is often read as Melville's own call to resist the conformity that society seeks to impose. It was taken in this way by one of the notable students of Melville, Richard Chase, who quotes it at the beginning of an account of Melville's attitude toward the American life of his time and goes on to say that "although Melville was not exclusively a nay-sayer, his experiences and his reflections upon the quality of American civilization had taught him to utter the powerful 'no' he attributes to Hawthorne. He learned to say 'no' to the boundlessly optimistic commercialized creed of most Americans, with its superficial and mean conception of the possibilities of human life, its denial of all the genuinely creative or heroic capacities of man, and its fear and dislike of any but the mildest truths. Melville's 'no' finds expression in the tragic-comic tale of 'Bartleby the Scrivener.' . . ."[1]

But although this great story tells of a nay-saying of a quite ultimate kind, perhaps the first thing we notice about Bartleby's "no" is how far it is from being uttered "in thunder." And exactly its distance from thunder makes the negation as momentous as it is; the contrast between the extent of Bartleby's refusal and the minimal way in which he expresses it accounts for the story's strange force, its mythic impressiveness. Whether he is being asked to accommodate himself to the routine of his job in the law office or to the simplest requirements of life itself, Bartleby makes the same answer, " 'I prefer not to' "—the phrase is prim, genteel, rather finicking; the negative volition it expresses seems to be of a very low intensity. Melville is at pains to point up the odd inadequacy of that word *prefer* by the passage in which he tells how it was unconsciously adopted into the speech of the narrator and his office staff, and with what comic effect.

Actually, of course, the small, muted phrase that Bartleby chooses for his negation is the measure of his intransigence. A "NO! in thunder" implies that the person who utters it is involved with and has strong feelings about whatever it is that he rejects or opposes. The louder his thunder, the greater is his (and our) belief in the power, the interest, the real existence of what he negates. Bartleby's colorless formula of refusal has the opposite effect—in refusing to display articulate anger against the social order he rejects, our poor taciturn nay-sayer denies its interest and any claim it may have on his attention and reason. " 'I prefer not to' " implies that reason is not in point; the choice that is being made does not need the substantiation of reason: it is, as it were, a matter of "taste," even of whim, an act of pure volition, having reference to nothing but the nature of the agent. Or the muted minimal phrase might be read as an expression of the extremest possible arrogance—

---

[1] "Herman Melville" in *Major Writers of America*, edited by Perry Miller, Volume I, p. 880.

this Bartleby detaches himself from all human need or desire and acts at no behest other than that of his own unconditioned will.

It is possible that Melville never heard of Karl Marx, although the two men were contemporaries, but Melville's "story of Wall Street" exemplifies in a very striking way the concept of human alienation which plays an important part in Marx's early philosophical writings and has had considerable influence on later sociological thought. Alienation is the condition in which one acts as if at the behest not of one's own will but of some will other (Latin: *alius*) than one's own. For Marx its most important manifestation is in what he called "alienated labor," although he suggested that the phrase was redundant, since all labor is an alienated activity. In Latin *labor* has the meaning of pain and weariness as well as of work that causes pain and weariness, and we use the word to denote work that is in some degree enforced and that goes against the grain of human nature: a culprit is sentenced to a term of "hard labor," not of "hard work." By the same token, not all work is alienated; Marx cites the work of the artist as an example of free activity, happily willed, gratifying and dignifying those who perform it.[2]

In undertaking to explain the reason for the alienated condition of man, Marx refused to accept the idea that it is brought about by the necessities of survival. Man, he said, can meet these necessities with the consciousness of free will, with the sense that he is at one with himself; it is society that alienates man from himself. And Marx held that alienation is at its extreme in those societies which are governed by money-values. In a spirited passage, he describes the process of accumulating capital in terms of the sacrifice of the free human activities that it entails: "The less you eat, drink, and read books; the less you go to the theatre, the dance hall, the public-house; the less you think, love, theorize, sing, paint, fence, etc., and the more you *save* —the greater becomes your treasure which neither moth nor dust will devour— your *capital*. The less you *are*, the more you *have*; the less you express your own life, the greater is your *externalized* life—the greater is the store of your alienated being."[3] This describes the program for success in a money society; it was followed, we may note, in his early days by John Jacob Astor, who commands the ironized respect of the narrator of "Bartleby the Scrivener," and no doubt to some extent by the narrator himself. Those members of a money society who do not consent to submit to the program are, of course, no less alienated, and they do not have the comforting illusion of freedom that the power of money can give.

It can be said of Bartleby that he behaves quite as if he were devoting himself to capitalist accumulation. He withdraws from one free human activity after another. If "the theatre, the dance hall, the public-house" had ever been within his ken, they are now far beyond it. If there had ever been a time when he delighted to "think, love, theorize, sing, paint, fence, etc.," it

[2] Perhaps sport provides a more immediately cogent example of a free and therefore highly valued activity. Many sports require a submission to the most gruelling discipline in training and a quite painful expenditure of energy in performance. Those who engage in them take this for granted and, it would seem, even find that it contributes to the gratification they experience. If the same activity were not freely chosen but enforced, the discomforts would be felt as cruelty and degradation.

[3] Quoted by Robert Tucker in *Philosophy and Myth in Karl Marx*, Cambridge University Press, 1961, p. 138.

has long gone by. He never drinks. He eats less and less, eventually not at all. But of course nothing is further from his intention than accumulation—the self-denial he practices has been instituted in the interests of his freedom, a sad, abstract, metaphysical freedom but the only one he can aspire to. In the degree that he diminishes his self, he is the less an alienated self: his will is free, he cannot be compelled. A theory of suicide advanced by Sigmund Freud is in point here. It proposes the idea that the suicide's chief although unconscious purpose is to destroy not himself but some other person whom he has incorporated into his psychic fabric and whom he conceives to have great malign authority over him. Bartleby, by his gradual self-annihilation, annihilates the social order as it exists within himself.

An important complication is added to the story of Bartleby's fate by the character and the plight of the nameless narrator. No one could have behaved in a more forebearing and compassionate way than this good-tempered gentleman. He suffers long and is kind; he finds it hard, almost impossible, to do what common sense has long dictated he should do—have Bartleby expelled from the office by force—and he goes so far in charity as to offer to take Bartleby into his own home. Yet he feels that he has incurred guilt by eventually separating himself from Bartleby, and we think it appropriate that he should feel so, even while we sympathize with him; and in making this judgment we share his guilt. It is to him that Bartleby's only moment of anger is directed: " 'I know you,' " says Bartleby in the prison yard, " 'and I want nothing to say to you.' " The narrator is "keenly pained at his implied suspicion" that it was through his agency that Bartleby had been imprisoned, and we are pained for him, knowing the suspicion to be unfounded and unjust. Yet we know why it was uttered.

Bartleby's "I prefer not to" is spoken always in response to an order or request having to do with business utility. We may speculate about what would have happened if the narrator or one of Bartleby's fellow-copyists, alone with him in the office, had had occasion to say, "Bartleby, I feel sick and faint. Would you help me to the couch and fetch me a glass of water?" Perhaps the answer would have been given: " 'I prefer not to.' " But perhaps not.

THE

GRAND

INQUISITOR

FËDOR DOSTOEVSKI

1 8 2 1 – 1 8 8 1

Headnote

In Dostoevski's last novel, *The Brothers Karamazov*, near the end of a long theo-logical conversation which centers in the question of whether or not human suffering can be "justified," Ivan Karamazov tells his younger brother Alyosha that he has written a poem. It is not, he says, really a poem but a poem in prose, and he did not actually write it but he would like to tell it. Alyosha is eager to hear it. "My poem is called 'The Grand Inquisitor,'" Ivan says; "it is a ridiculous thing but I want to tell it to you," and proceeds to do so. Ivan is twenty-four; he has been a brilliant but rather irregular student at the university and has gained some little attention as a writer, having published "brilliant reviews of books upon various special subjects." He is preoccupied by the question he has been discussing with Alyosha; he has said that he is unable to "accept" the moral order of the universe as it is expounded by Chris-tianity, and has indicated an intention of suicide. Alyosha is four years younger than his brother. A sweet-tempered and charming young man, he has for a year been a novice in a local monastery.

*   *   *

"EVEN THIS must have a preface—that is, a literary preface," laughed Ivan, "and I am a poor hand at making one. You see, my action takes place in the sixteenth century, and at that time, as you probably learnt at school, it was customary in poetry to bring down heavenly powers on earth. Not to speak of Dante, in France, clerks, as well as the monks in the monasteries, used to give regular performances in which the Madonna, the saints, the angels, Christ, and God Himself were brought on the stage. In those days it was done in all simplicity. In Victor Hugo's 'Notre Dame de Paris' an edifying and gratuitous spectacle was provided for the people in the Hotel de Ville of Paris in the reign of Louis XI in honor of the birth of the dauphin. It was called *Le bon jugement de la très sainte et gracieuse Vierge Marie,*[1] and she appears herself on the stage and pronounces her *bon jugement.* Similar plays, chiefly from the Old Testament, were occasionally performed in Moscow too, up to the times of Peter the Great. But besides plays there were all sorts of legends and ballads scattered about the world, in which the saints and angels and all the powers of Heaven took part when required. In our monasteries the monks busied themselves with translating, copying, and even composing such poems—and even under the Tatars. There is, for instance, one such poem (of course, from the Greek), 'The Wanderings of Our Lady through Hell,' with descriptions as bold as Dante's. Our Lady visits Hell, and the Archangel Michael leads her through the torments. She sees the sinners and their punishment. There she sees among others one noteworthy set of sinners in a burning lake; some of them sink to the bottom of the lake so that they can't swim out, and 'these God forgets'—an expression of extraordinary depth and force. And so Our Lady, shocked and weeping, falls before the throne of God and begs for mercy for all in Hell—for all she has seen there, indiscriminately. Her conversation with God is immensely interesting. She beseeches Him, she will not desist, and when God points to the hands and feet of her Son, nailed to the Cross, and asks, 'How can I forgive His tormentors?' she bids all the saints, all the martyrs, all the angels and archangels to fall down with her and pray for mercy on all without distinction. It ends by her winning from God a respite of suffering every year from Good Friday till Trinity day, and the sinners at once raise a cry of thankfulness from Hell, chanting, 'Thou art just, O Lord, in this judgment.' Well, my poem would have been of that kind if it had appeared at that time. He comes on the scene in my poem, but He says nothing, only appears and passes on. Fifteen centuries have passed since He promised to come in His glory, fifteen centuries since His prophet wrote, 'Behold, I come quickly'; 'Of that day and that hour knoweth no man, neither the Son, but the Father,' as He Himself predicted on earth. But humanity awaits him with the same faith and with the same love. Oh, with greater faith, for it is fifteen centuries since man has ceased to see signs from Heaven.

> *No signs from Heaven come today*
> *To add to what the heart doth say.*

There was nothing left but faith in what the heart doth say. It is true there were many miracles in those days. There were saints who performed miraculous cures; some holy people, according to their biographies, were visited by the Queen of Heaven herself. But the devil did not slumber, and doubts were already arising among men of the truth of these miracles. And just then there appeared in the north of Germany a terrible new heresy. 'A huge star like to a torch' (that is, to a church) 'fell on the sources of the waters and they became bitter.'[2] These heretics began blasphemously denying miracles. But those who remained faithful

---

[1] (French) "The Sound Verdict of the Most Holy and Gracious Virgin Mary."
[2] Revelation 8 : 10–11.

were all the more ardent in their faith. The tears of humanity rose up to Him as before, awaited His coming, loved Him, hoped for Him, yearned to suffer and die for Him as before. And so many ages mankind had prayed with faith and fervor, 'O Lord our God, hasten Thy coming,' so many ages called upon Him, that in His infinite mercy He deigned to come down to His servants. Before that day He had come down, He had visited some holy men, martyrs and hermits, as is written in their 'Lives.' Among us, Tyutchev,[3] with absolute faith in the truth of his words, bore witness that

> *Bearing the Cross, in slavish dress,*
> *Weary and worn, the Heavenly King*
> *Our mother, Russia, came to bless,*
> *And through our land went wandering.*

And that certainly was so, I assure you.

"And behold, He deigned to appear for a moment to the people, to the tortured, suffering people, sunk in iniquity, but loving Him like children. My story is laid in Spain, in Seville, in the most terrible time of the Inquisition, when fires were lighted every day to the glory of God, and 'in the splendid *auto da fé*[4] the wicked heretics were burnt.' Oh, of course, this was not the coming in which He will appear according to His promise at the end of time in all His heavenly glory, and which will be sudden 'as lightning flashing from east to west.' No, He visited His children only for a moment, and there where the flames were crackling round the heretics. In His infinite mercy He came once more among men in that human shape in which He walked among men for three years fifteen centuries ago. He came down to the 'hot pavement' of the southern town in which on the day before almost a hundred heretics had, *ad majorem gloriam Dei*,[5] been burnt by the cardinal, the Grand Inquisitor, in a magnificent *auto da fé*, in the presence of the king, the court, the knights, the cardinals, the most charming ladies of the court, and the whole population of Seville.

"He came softly, unobserved, and yet, strange to say, every one recognized Him. That might be one of the best passages in the poem. I mean, why they recognized Him. The people are irresistibly drawn to Him, they surround Him, they flock about Him, follow Him. He moves silently in their midst with a gentle smile of infinite compassion. The sun of love burns in His heart, light and power shine from His eyes, and their radiance, shed on the people, stirs their hearts with responsive love. He holds out His hands to them, blesses them, and a healing virtue comes from contact with Him, even with His garments. An old man in the crowd, blind from childhood, cries out, 'O Lord, heal me and I shall see Thee!' and, as it were, scales fall from his eyes and the blind man sees Him. The crowd weeps and kisses the earth under His feet. Children throw flowers before Him, sing, and cry hosannah. 'It is He—it is He!' all repeat. 'It must be He, it can be no one but Him!' He stops at the steps of the Seville cathedral at the moment when the weeping mourners are bringing in a little open white coffin. In it lies a child of seven, the only daughter of a prominent citizen. The dead child lies hidden in flowers. 'He

---

[3] A lyricist (1803–1873) ranking very high in Russian literature.

[4] A burning at the stake of heretics condemned in the courts of the Spanish Inquisition (Portuguese: act of faith).

[5] (Latin) To the greater glory of God (the motto of the Jesuits).

will raise your child,' the crowd shouts to the weeping mother. The priest, coming to meet the coffin, looks perplexed, and frowns, but the mother of the dead child throws herself at His feet with a wail. 'If it is Thou, raise my child!' she cries, holding out her hands to Him. The procession halts, the coffin is laid on the steps at His feet. He looks with compassion, and His lips once more softly pronounce, 'Maiden, arise!'[6] and the maiden arises. The little girl sits up in the coffin and looks round, smiling with wide-open wondering eyes, holding a bunch of white roses they had put in her hand.

"There are cries, sobs, confusion among the people, and at that moment the cardinal himself, the Grand Inquisitor, passes by the cathedral. He is an old man, almost ninety, tall and erect, with a withered face and sunken eyes, in which there is still a gleam of light. He is not dressed in his gorgeous cardinal's robes, as he was the day before, when he was burning the enemies of the Roman Church —at that moment he was wearing his coarse, old, monk's cassock. At a distance behind him come his gloomy assistants and slaves and the 'holy guard.' He stops at the sight of the crowd and watches it from a distance. He sees everything; he sees them set the coffin down at His feet, sees the child rise up, and his face darkens. He knits his thick gray brows and his eyes gleam with a sinister fire. He holds out his finger and bids the guards take Him. And such is his power, so completely are the people cowed into submission and trembling obedience to him, that the crowd immediately make way for the guards, and in the midst of deathlike silence they lay hands on Him and lead Him away. The crowd instantly bows down to the earth, like one man, before the old inquisitor. He blesses the people in silence and passes on. The guards lead their prisoner to the close, gloomy vaulted prison in the ancient palace of the Holy Inquisition and shut Him in it. The day passes and is followed by the dark, burning 'breathless' night of Seville. The air is 'fragrant with laurel and lemon.' In the pitch darkness the iron door of the prison is suddenly opened and the Grand Inquisitor himself comes in with a light in his hand. He is alone; the door is closed at once behind him. He stands in the doorway and for a minute or two gazes into His face. At last he goes up slowly, sets the light on the table and speaks.

" 'Is it Thou? Thou?' but receiving no answer, he adds at once, 'Don't answer, be silent. What canst Thou say, indeed? I know too well what Thou wouldst say. And Thou hast no right to add anything to what Thou hadst said of old. Why, then, art Thou come to hinder us? For Thou hast come to hinder us, and Thou knowest that. But dost Thou know what will be tomorrow? I know not who Thou art and care not to know whether it is Thou or only a semblance of Him, but tomorrow I shall condemn Thee and burn Thee at the stake as the worst of heretics. And the very people who have today kissed Thy feet, tomorrow at the faintest sign from me will rush to heap up the embers of Thy fire. Knowest Thou that? Yes, maybe Thou knowest it,' he added with thoughtful penetration, never for a moment taking his eyes off the Prisoner."

"I don't quite understand, Ivan. What does it mean?" Alyosha, who had been listening in silence, said with a smile. "Is it simply a wild fantasy, or a mistake on the part of the old man—some impossible *quiproquo*?"[7]

"Take it as the last," said Ivan, laughing, "if you are so corrupted by modern

---

[6] So Jesus addressed the dead daughter of the ruler of the synagogue (see Mark 5 : 35–43).
[7] (Latin) One person taken for another.

realism and can't stand anything fantastic. If you like it to be a case of mistaken identity, let it be so. It is true," he went on, laughing, "the old man was ninety, and he might well be crazy over his set idea. He might have been struck by the appearance of the Prisoner. It might, in fact, be simply his ravings, the delusion of an old man of ninety, over-excited by the *auto da fé* of a hundred heretics the day before. But does it matter to us after all whether it was a mistake of identity or a wild fantasy? All that matters is that the old man should speak out, should speak openly of what he has thought in silence for ninety years."

"And the Prisoner too is silent? Does He look at him and not say a word?"

"That's inevitable in any case," Ivan laughed again. "The old man has told Him He hasn't the right to add anything to what He has said of old. One may say it is the most fundamental feature of Roman Catholicism, in my opinion at least. 'All has been given by Thee to the Pope,' they say, 'and all, therefore, is still in the Pope's hands, and there is no need for Thee to come now at all. Thou must not meddle for the time, at least.' That's how they speak and write too—the Jesuits, at any rate. I have read it myself in the works of their theologians. 'Hast Thou the right to reveal to us one of the mysteries of that world from which Thou hast come?' my old man asks Him, and answers the question for Him. 'No, Thou hast not; that Thou mayest not add to what has been said of old, and mayest not take from men the freedom which Thou didst exalt when Thou wast on earth. Whatsoever Thou revealest anew will encroach on men's freedom of faith; for it will be manifest as a miracle, and the freedom of their faith was dearer to Thee than anything in those days fifteen hundred years ago. Didst Thou not often say then, "I will make you free"? But now Thou hast seen these "free" men,' the old man adds suddenly, with a pensive smile. 'Yes, we've paid dearly for it,' he goes on, looking sternly at Him, 'but at last we have completed that work in Thy name. For fifteen centuries we have been wrestling with Thy freedom, but now it is ended and over for good. Dost Thou not believe that it's over for good? Thou lookest meekly at me and deignest not even to be wroth with me. But let me tell Thee that now, today, people are more persuaded than ever that they have perfect freedom, yet they have brought their freedom to us and laid it humbly at our feet. But that has been our doing. Was this what Thou didst? Was this Thy freedom?'"

"I don't understand again," Alyosha broke in. "Is he ironical, is he jesting?"

"Not a bit of it! He claims it as a merit for himself and his Church that at last they have vanquished freedom and have done so to make men happy. 'For now' (he is speaking of the Inquisition, of course) 'for the first time it has become possible to think of the happiness of men. Man was created a rebel; and how can rebels be happy? Thou wast warned,' he says to Him. 'Thou hast had no lack of admonitions and warnings, but Thou didst not listen to those warnings; Thou didst reject the only way by which men might be made happy. But fortunately, departing Thou didst hand on the work to us. Thou hast promised, Thou hast established by Thy word, Thou hast given to us the right to bind and to unbind, and now, of course, Thou canst not think of taking it away. Why, then, hast Thou come to hinder us?'"

"And what's the meaning of 'no lack of admonitions and warnings'?" asked Alyosha.

"Why, that's the chief part of what the old man must say."

"'The wise and dread spirit, the spirit of self-destruction and non-existence,' the old man goes on, 'the great spirit talked with Thee in the wilderness, and we are told in the books that he "tempted" Thee.[8] Is that so? And could anything truer be said than what he revealed to Thee in three questions and what Thou didst reject, and what in the books is called "the temptation"? And yet if there has ever been on earth a real stupendous miracle, it took place on that day, on the day of the three temptations. The statement of those three questions was itself the miracle. If it were possible to imagine simply for the sake of argument that those three questions of the dread spirit had perished utterly from the books, and that we had to restore them and to invent them anew, and to do so had gathered together all the wise men of the earth—rulers, chief priests, learned men, philosophers, poets—and had set them the task to invent three questions, such as would not only fit the occasion, but express in three words, three human phrases, the whole future history of the world and of humanity—dost Thou believe that all the wisdom of the earth united could have invented anything in depth and force equal to the three questions which were actually put to Thee then by the wise and mighty spirit in the wilderness? From those questions alone, from the miracle of their statement, we can see that we have here to do not with the fleeting human intelligence, but with the absolute and eternal. For in those three questions the whole subsequent history of mankind is, as it were, brought together into one whole, and foretold, and in them are united all the unsolved historical contradictions of human nature. At the time it could not be so clear, since the future was unknown; but now that fifteen hundred years have passed, we see that everything in those three questions was so justly divined and foretold, and has been so truly fulfilled, that nothing can be added to them or taken from them.

"'Judge Thyself who was right—Thou or he who questioned Thee then? Remember the first question; its meaning, in other words, was this: "Thou wouldst go into the world, and art going with empty hands, with some promise of freedom which men in their simplicity and their natural unruliness cannot even understand, which they fear and dread—for nothing has ever been more insupportable for a man and a human society than freedom. But seest Thou these stones in this parched and barren wilderness? Turn them into bread, and mankind will run after Thee like a flock of sheep, grateful and obedient, though for ever trembling, lest Thou withdraw Thy hand and deny them Thy bread." But Thou wouldst not deprive man of freedom and didst reject the offer, thinking, what is that freedom worth, if obedience is bought with bread? Thou didst reply that man lives not by bread alone. But dost Thou know that for the sake of that earthly bread the spirit of the earth will rise up against Thee and will strive with Thee and overcome Thee, and all will follow him, crying, "Who can compare with this beast? He has given us fire from heaven!" Dost Thou know that the ages will pass, and humanity will proclaim by the lips of their sages that there is no crime, and therefore no sin; there is only hunger? "Feed men, and then ask of them virtue!" that's what they'll write on the banner, which they will raise against Thee, and with which they will destroy Thy temple. Where Thy temple stood will rise a new building; the terrible tower of Babel will be built again, and though, like the one of old, it will not be finished, yet Thou mightest have prevented that new tower and have cut short the sufferings of men for a thousand years; for they will come

[8] The temptation of Jesus by the devil is recounted in Luke 4 : 1–13; see commentary, p. 483.

back to us after a thousand years of agony with their tower. They will seek us again, hidden underground in the catacombs, for we shall be again persecuted and tortured. They will find us and cry to us, "Feed us, for those who have promised us fire from heaven haven't given it!" And then we shall finish building their tower, for he finishes the building who feeds them. And we alone shall feed them in Thy name, declaring falsely that it is in Thy name. Oh, never, never can they feed themselves without us! No science will give them bread so long as they remain free. In the end they will lay their freedom at our feet, and say to us, "Make us your slaves, but feed us." They will understand themselves, at last, that freedom and bread enough for all are inconceivable together, for never, never will they be able to share between them! They will be convinced, too, that they can never be free, for they are weak, vicious, worthless and rebellious. Thou didst promise them the bread of Heaven, but, I repeat again, can it compare with earthly bread in the eyes of the weak, ever sinful and ignoble race of man? And if for the sake of the bread of Heaven thousands and tens of thousands shall follow Thee, what is to become of the millions and tens of thousands of millions of creatures who will not have the strength to forgo the earthly bread for the sake of the heavenly? Or dost Thou care only for the tens of thousands of the great and strong, while the millions, numerous as the sands of the sea, who are weak but love Thee, must exist only for the sake of the great and strong? No, we care for the weak too. They are sinful and rebellious, but in the end they too will become obedient. They will marvel at us and look on us as gods, because we are ready to endure the freedom which they have found so dreadful and to rule over them—so awful it will seem to them to be free. But we shall tell them that we are Thy servants and rule them in Thy name. We shall deceive them again, for we will not let Thee come to us again. That deception will be our suffering, for we shall be forced to lie.

" 'This is the significance of the first question in the wilderness, and this is what Thou hast rejected for the sake of that freedom which Thou hast exalted above everything. Yet in this question lies hid the great secret of this world. Choosing "bread," Thou wouldst have satisfied the universal and everlasting craving of humanity—to find some one to worship. So long as man remains free he strives for nothing so incessantly and so painfully as to find some one to worship. But man seeks to worship what is established beyond dispute, so that all men would agree at once to worship it. For these pitiful creatures are concerned not only to find what one or the other can worship, but to find something that all would believe in and worship; what is essential is that all may be *together* in it. This craving for community of worship is the chief misery of every man individually and of all humanity from the beginning of time. For the sake of common worship they've slain each other with the sword. They have set up gods and challenged one another, "Put away your gods and come and worship ours, or we will kill you and your gods!" And so it will be to the end of the world, even when gods disappear from the earth; they will fall down before idols just the same. Thou didst know, Thou couldst not but have known, this fundamental secret of human nature, but Thou didst reject the one infallible banner which was offered Thee to make all men bow down to Thee alone—the banner of earthly bread; and Thou hast rejected it for the sake of freedom and the bread of Heaven. Behold what Thou didst further. And all again in the name of freedom! I tell Thee that man is tormented by no greater anxiety than to find some one quickly to whom he can hand over that gift of freedom with which the ill-fated creature is born. But only one who can appease their conscience can take over their freedom. In bread there was offered Thee an invincible banner; give bread, and man will worship Thee, for nothing is more certain than bread. But if some one else gains possession of his conscience—oh! then he will cast away Thy bread and follow after him who has ensnared his conscience. In that Thou wast right. For the secret of man's being is not only to live but to have something to live for. Without a stable conception of the object of life, man would not consent to go on living, and would rather destroy himself than remain on earth, though he had bread in abundance. That is true. But what happened? Instead of taking men's freedom from them, Thou didst make it greater than ever! Didst Thou forget that man prefers peace, and even death, to freedom of choice in the knowledge of good and evil? Nothing is more seductive for man than his freedom of conscience, but nothing is a greater cause of suffering. And behold, instead of giving a firm foundation for setting the conscience of man at rest for ever, Thou didst choose all that is exceptional, vague and enigmatic; Thou didst choose what was utterly beyond the strength of men, acting as though Thou didst not love them at all—Thou who didst come to give Thy life for them! Instead of taking possession of men's freedom, Thou didst increase it, and burdened the spiritual kingdom of mankind with its sufferings for ever. Thou didst desire man's free love, that he should follow Thee freely, enticed and taken captive by Thee. In place of the rigid ancient law, man must hereafter with free heart decide for himself what is good and what is evil, having only Thy image before him as his guide. But didst Thou not know he would at last reject even Thy image and Thy truth, if he is weighed down with the fearful burden of free choice? They will cry aloud at last that the truth is not in Thee, for they could not have been left in greater confusion and suffering than Thou hast caused, laying upon them so many cares and unanswerable problems.

"'So that, in truth, Thou didst Thyself lay the foundation for the destruction of Thy kingdom, and no one is more to blame for it. Yet what was offered Thee? There are three powers, three powers alone, able to conquer and to hold captive for ever the conscience of these impotent rebels for their happiness—those forces are miracle, mystery and authority. Thou hast rejected all three and hast set the example for doing so. When the wise and dread spirit set Thee on the pinnacle of the temple and said to Thee, "If Thou wouldst know whether Thou art the Son of God then cast Thyself down, for it is written: the angels shall hold him up lest he fall and bruise himself, and Thou shalt know then whether Thou art the Son of God and shalt prove then how great is Thy faith in Thy Father." But Thou didst refuse and wouldst not cast Thyself down. Oh! of course, Thou didst proudly and well, like God; but the weak, unruly race of men, are they gods? Oh, Thou didst know then that in taking one step, in making one movement to cast Thyself down, Thou wouldst be tempting God and have lost all Thy faith in Him, and wouldst have been dashed to pieces against that earth which Thou didst come to save. And the wise spirit that tempted Thee would have rejoiced. But I ask again, are there many like Thee? And couldst Thou believe for one moment that men, too, could face such a temptation? Is the nature of men such, that they can reject miracle, and at the great moments of their life, the moments of their deepest, most agonizing spiritual difficulties, cling only to the free verdict of the heart? Oh, Thou didst know that Thy deed would be recorded in books, would be handed down to remote times and the utmost ends of the earth, and Thou didst hope that man, following Thee, would cling to God and not ask for a miracle. But Thou didst not know that when man rejects miracle he rejects God too; for man seeks not so much God as the miraculous. And as man cannot bear to be without the miraculous, he will create new miracles of his own for himself, and will worship deeds of sorcery and witchcraft, though he might be a hundred times over a rebel, heretic and infidel. Thou didst not come down from the Cross when they shouted to Thee, mocking and reviling Thee, "Come down from the cross and we will believe that Thou art He." Thou didst not come down, for again Thou wouldst not enslave man by a miracle, and didst crave faith given freely, not based on miracle. Thou didst crave for free love and not the base raptures of the slave before the might that has overawed him for ever. But Thou didst think too highly of men therein, for they are slaves, of course, though rebellious by nature. Look round and judge; fifteen centuries have passed, look upon them. Whom hast Thou raised up to Thyself? I swear, man is weaker and baser by nature than Thou hast believed him! Can he, can he do what Thou didst? By showing him so much respect, Thou didst, as it were, cease to feel for him, for Thou didst ask far too much from him—Thou who hast loved him more than Thyself! Respecting him less, Thou wouldst have asked less of him. That would have been more like love, for his burden would have been lighter. He is weak and vile. What though he is everywhere now rebelling against our power, and proud of his rebellion? It is the pride of a child and a schoolboy. They are little children rioting and barring out the teacher at school. But their childish delight will end; it will cost them dear. They will cast down temples and drench the earth with blood. But they will see at last, the foolish children, that, though they are rebels, they are impotent rebels, unable to keep up their own rebellion. Bathed in their foolish tears, they will recognize at last that He who created them rebels must have meant to mock at them. They will say this in despair, and their utterance will be a blasphemy which will make them more unhappy still, for man's nature cannot bear blasphemy, and in the end always avenges it on itself. And so unrest, confusion and unhappiness—that is the present lot of man after Thou didst bear so much for their freedom! Thy great prophet tells in vision and in image, that he saw all those who took part in the first resurrection and that there were of each tribe twelve thousand.[9] But if there were so many of them, they must have been not men but gods. They had borne Thy cross, they had endured scores of years in the barren, hungry wilderness, living upon locusts and roots—and Thou mayest indeed point with pride at those children of freedom, of free love, of free and splendid sacrifice for Thy name. But remember that they were only some thousands; and what of the rest? And how are the other weak ones to blame, because they could not endure what the strong have endured? How is the weak soul to blame that it is unable to receive such terrible gifts? Canst Thou have simply come to the elect and for the elect? But if so, it is a mystery and we cannot understand it. And if it is a mystery, we too have a right to preach a mystery, and to teach them that it's not the free judgment of their hearts, not love that matters, but a mystery which they must follow blindly, even against their conscience. So we have done. We have corrected Thy work and have founded it upon *miracle*, *mystery* and *authority*. And men rejoiced that they were again led like sheep, and that the terrible gift that had brought them such suffering, was, at last, lifted

[9] Revelation 7 : 4–8.

from their hearts. Were we right teaching them this? Speak! Did we not love mankind, so meekly acknowledging their feebleness, lovingly lightening their burden, and permitting their weak nature even sin with our sanction? Why hast Thou come now to hinder us? And why dost Thou look silently and searchingly at me with Thy mild eyes? Be angry. I don't want Thy love, for I love Thee not. And what use is it for me to hide anything from Thee? Don't I know to Whom I am speaking? All that I can say is known to Thee already. And is it for me to conceal from Thee our mystery? Perhaps it is Thy will to hear it from my lips. Listen, then. We are not working with Thee, but with *him*—that is our mystery. It's long —eight centuries—since we have been on *his* side and not on Thine. Just eight centuries ago, we took from him what Thou didst reject with scorn, that last gift he offered Thee, showing Thee all the kingdoms of the earth. We took from him Rome and the sword of Cæsar, and proclaimed ourselves sole rulers of the earth, though hitherto we have not been able to complete our work. But whose fault is that? Oh, the work is only beginning, but it has begun. It has long to await completion and the earth has yet much to suffer, but we shall triumph and shall be Caesars, and then we shall plan the universal happiness of man. But Thou mightest have taken even then the sword of Caesar. Why didst Thou reject that last gift? Hadst Thou accepted that last counsel of the mighty spirit, Thou wouldst have accomplished all that man seeks on earth—that is, some one to worship, some one to keep his conscience, and some means of uniting all in one unanimous and harmonious ant-heap, for the craving for universal unity is the third and last anguish of men. Mankind as a whole has always striven to organize a universal state. There have been many great nations with great histories, but the more highly they were developed the more unhappy they were, for they felt more acutely than other people the craving for worldwide union. The great conquerors, Timours and Ghengis-Khans, whirled like hurricanes over the face of the earth striving to subdue its people, and they too were but the unconscious expression of the same craving for universal unity. Hadst Thou taken the world and Caesar's purple,[10] Thou wouldst have founded the universal state and have given universal peace. For who can rule men if not he who holds their conscience and their bread in his hands? We have taken the sword of Caesar, and in taking it, of course, have rejected Thee and followed *him*. Oh, ages are yet to come of the confusion of free thought, of their science and cannibalism. For having begun to build their tower of Babel without us, they will end, of course, with cannibalism. But then the beast[11] will crawl to us and lick our feet and spatter them with tears of blood. And we shall sit upon the beast and raise the cup, and on it will be written, "Mystery." But then, and only then, the reign of peace and happiness will come for men. Thou art proud of Thine elect, but Thou hast only the elect, while we give rest to all. And besides, how many of those elect, those mighty ones who could become elect, have grown weary waiting for Thee, and have transferred and will transfer the powers of their spirit and the warmth of their heart to the other camp, and end by raising their *free* banner against Thee. Thou didst Thyself lift up that banner. But with us all will be happy and will no more rebel nor destroy one another as under Thy freedom. Oh, we shall persuade them that they will only become free when they renounce their freedom to us and sub-

[10] Royal purple or regal purple, used here as a symbol of absolute political power.
[11] This allusion, and also "the harlot who sits upon the beast," below, refers to Revelation 17.

mit to us. And shall we be right or shall we be lying? They will be convinced that we are right, for they will remember the horrors of slavery and confusion to which Thy freedom brought them. Freedom, free thought and science, will lead them into such straits and will bring them face to face with such marvels and insoluble mysteries, that some of them, the fierce and rebellious, will destroy themselves, others, rebellious but weak, will destroy one another, while the rest, weak and unhappy, will crawl fawning to our feet and whine to us: "Yes, you were right, you alone possess His mystery, and we come back to you, save us from ourselves!"

" 'Receiving bread from us, they will see clearly that we take the bread made by their hands from them, to give it to them, without any miracle. They will see that we do not change the stones to bread, but in truth they will be more thankful for taking it from our hands than for the bread itself! For they will remember only too well that in old days, without our help, even the bread they made turned to stones in their hands, while since they have come back to us, the very stones have turned to bread in their hands. Too, too well they know the value of complete submission! And until men know that, they will be unhappy. Who is most to blame for their not knowing it, speak? Who scattered the flock and sent it astray on unknown paths? But the flock will come together again and will submit once more, and then it will be once for all. Then we shall give them the quiet humble happiness of weak creatures such as they are by nature. Oh, we shall persuade them at last not to be proud, for Thou didst lift them up and thereby taught them to be proud. We shall show them that they are weak, that they are only pitiful children, but that childlike happiness is the sweetest of all. They will become timid and will look to us and huddle close to us in fear, as chicks to the hen. They will marvel at us and will be awe-stricken before us, and will be proud at our being so powerful and clever, that we have been able to subdue such a turbulent flock of thousands of millions. They will tremble impotently before our wrath, their minds will grow fearful, they will be quick to shed tears like women and children, but they will be just as ready at a sign from us to pass to laughter and rejoicing, to happy mirth and childish song. Yes, we shall set them to work, but in their leisure hours we shall make their life like a child's game, with children's songs and innocent dance. Oh, we shall allow them even sin, they are weak and helpless, and they will love us like children because we allow them to sin. We shall tell them that every sin will be expiated, if it is done with our permission, that we allow them to sin because we love them, and the punishment for these sins we take upon ourselves. And we shall take it upon ourselves, and they will adore us as their saviors who have taken on themselves their sins before God. And they will have no secrets from us. We shall allow or forbid them to live with their wives and mistresses, to have or not to have children—according to whether they have been obedient or disobedient—and they will submit to us gladly and cheerfully. The most painful secrets of their conscience, all, all they will bring to us, and we shall have an answer for all. And they will be glad to believe our answer, for it will save them from the great anxiety and terrible agony they endure at present in making a free decision for themselves. And all will be happy, all the millions of creatures except the hundred thousand who rule over them. For only we, we who guard the mystery, shall be unhappy. There will be thousands of millions of happy babes, and a hundred thousand sufferers who have taken upon themselves the curse of the knowledge of good and evil. Peacefully they will die, peacefully they will expire in Thy name, and beyond the grave they will find nothing but death. But we shall keep the secret, and for their happiness we shall allure them with the reward of heaven and eternity. Though if there were anything in the other world, it certainly would not be for such as they. It is prophesied that Thou wilt come again in victory, Thou wilt come with Thy chosen, the proud and strong, but we will say that they have only saved themselves, but we have saved all. We are told that the harlot who sits upon the beast, and holds in her hands the *mystery,* shall be put to shame, that the weak will rise up again, and will rend her royal purple and will strip naked her loathsome body. But then I will stand up and point out to Thee the thousand millions of happy children who have known no sin. And we who have taken their sins upon us for their happiness will stand up before Thee and say: "Judge us if Thou canst and darest." Know that I fear Thee not. Know that I too have been in the wilderness, I too have lived on roots and locusts, I too prized the freedom with which Thou hast blessed men, and I too was striving to stand among Thy elect, among the strong and powerful, thirsting "to make up the number."[12] But I awakened and would not serve madness. I turned back and joined the ranks of those *who have corrected Thy work.* I left the proud and went back to the humble, for the happiness of the humble. What I say to Thee will come to pass, and our dominion will be built up. I repeat, to-morrow Thou shalt see that obedient flock who at a sign from me will hasten to heap up the hot cinders about the pile on which I shall burn Thee for coming to hinder us. For if any one has ever deserved our fires, it is Thou. To-morrow I shall burn Thee. *Dixi.*' "[13]

Ivan stopped. He was carried away as he talked and spoke with excitement; when he had finished, he suddenly smiled.

Alyosha had listened in silence; towards the end he was greatly moved and seemed several times on the point of interrupting, but restrained himself. Now his words came with a rush.

"But . . . that's absurd!" he cried, flushing. "Your poem is in praise of Jesus, not in blame of Him—as you meant it to be. And who will believe you about freedom? Is that the way to understand it? That's not the idea of it in the Orthodox Church . . . That's Rome, and not even the whole of Rome, it's false—those are the worst of the Catholics, the Inquisitors, the Jesuits! . . . And there could not be such a fantastic creature as your Inquisitor. What are these sins of mankind they take on themselves? Who are these keepers of the mystery who have taken some curse upon themselves for the happiness of mankind? When have they been seen? We know the Jesuits, they are spoken ill of, but surely they are not what you describe? They are not that at all, not at all. . . . They are simply the Romish army for the earthly sovereignty of the world in the future, with the Pontiff of Rome for Emperor . . . that's their ideal, but there's no sort of mystery or lofty melancholy about it. . . . It's simple lust of power, of filthy earthly gain, of domination—something like a universal serfdom with them as masters—that's all they stand for. They don't even believe in God perhaps. Your suffering inquisitor is a mere fantasy."

"Stay, stay," laughed Ivan, "how hot you are! A fantasy you say, let it be so! Of course it's a fantasy. But allow me to say: do you really think that the Roman

[12] The reference is to the number of the elect, the twelve thousand of each tribe (see Revelation 14).

[13] (Latin) I have spoken.

Catholic movement of the last centuries is actually nothing but the lust of power, of filthy earthly gain? Is that Father Païssy's teaching?"[14]

"No, no, on the contrary, Father Païssy did once say something rather the same as you . . . but of course it's not the same, not a bit the same," Alyosha hastily corrected himself.

"A precious admission, in spite of your 'not a bit the same.' I ask you why your Jesuits and Inquisitors have united simply for vile material gain? Why can there not be among them one martyr oppressed by great sorrow and loving humanity? You see, only suppose that there was one such man among all those who desire nothing but filthy material gain—if there's only one like my old inquisitor, who had himself eaten roots in the desert and made frenzied efforts to subdue his flesh to make himself free and perfect. But yet all his life he loved humanity, and suddenly his eyes were opened, and he saw that it is no great moral blessedness to attain perfection and freedom, if at the same time one gains the conviction that millions of God's creatures have been created as a mockery, that they will never be capable of using their freedom, that these poor rebels can never turn into giants to complete the tower, that it was not for such geese that the great idealist dreamt his dream of harmony. Seeing all that he turned back and joined—the clever people. Surely that could have happened?"

"Joined whom, what clever people?" cried Alyosha, completely carried away. "They have no such great cleverness and no mysteries and secrets. . . . Perhaps nothing but Atheism, that's all their secret. Your inquisitor does not believe in God, that's his secret!"

"What if it is so! At last you have guessed it. It's perfectly true that that's the whole secret, but isn't that suffering, at least for a man like that, who has wasted his whole life in the desert and yet could not shake off his incurable love of humanity? In his old age he reached the clear conviction that nothing but the advice of the great dread spirit could build up any tolerable sort of life for the feeble, unruly, 'incomplete, empirical creatures created in jest.' And so, convinced of this, he sees that he must follow the counsel of the wise spirit, the dread spirit of death and destruction, and therefore accept lying and deception, and lead men consciously to death and destruction, and yet deceive them all the way so that they may not notice where they are being led, that the poor blind creatures may at least on the way think themselves happy. And note, the deception is in the name of Him in Whose ideal the old man had so fervently believed all his life long. Is not that tragic? And if only one such stood at the head of the whole army 'filled with the lust of power only for the sake of filthy gain'—would not one such be enough to make a tragedy? More than that, one such standing at the head is enough to create the actual leading idea of the Roman Church with all its armies and Jesuits, its highest idea. I tell you frankly that I firmly believe that there has always been such a man among those who stood at the head of the movement. Who knows, there may have been some such even among the Roman Popes. Who knows, perhaps the spirit of that accursed old man who loves mankind so obstinately in his own way, is to be found even now in a whole multitude of such old men, existing not by chance but by agreement, as a secret league formed long ago for the guarding of the mystery, to guard it from the weak and the unhappy, so as to make them happy. No doubt it is so, and so it must be indeed. I fancy

[14] A saintly monk who is a character in *The Brothers Karamazov*.

that even among the Masons there's something of the same mystery at the bottom, and that that's why the Catholics so detest the Masons as their rivals breaking up the unity of the idea, while it is so essential that there should be one flock and one shepherd. . . . But from the way I defend my idea I might be an author impatient of your criticism. Enough of it."

"You are perhaps a Mason yourself!" broke suddenly from Alyosha. "You don't believe in God," he added, speaking this time very sorrowfully. He fancied besides that his brother was looking at him ironically. "How does your poem end?" he asked, suddenly looking down. "Or was it the end?"

"I meant to end it like this. When the Inquisitor ceased speaking he waited some time for his Prisoner to answer him. His silence weighed down upon him. He saw that the Prisoner had listened intently all the time, looking gently in his face and evidently not wishing to reply. The old man longed for Him to say something, however bitter and terrible. But He suddenly approached the old man in silence and softly kissed him on his bloodless aged lips. That was all his answer. The old man shuddered. His lips moved. He went to the door, opened it, and said to Him: 'Go, and come no more . . . come not at all, never, never!' and he let Him out into the dark alleys of the town. The Prisoner went away."

"And the old man?"

"The kiss glows in his heart, but the old man adheres to his idea."

"And you with him, you too?" cried Alyosha, mournfully.

Ivan laughed.

"Why, it's all nonsense, Alyosha. It's only a senseless poem of a senseless student, who could never write two lines of verse. Why do you take it so seriously? Surely you don't suppose I am going straight off to the Jesuits, to join the men who are correcting His work? Good Lord, it's no business of mine."

COMMENTARY

Of "The Grand Inquisitor" it can be said almost categorically that no other work of literature has made so strong an impression on the modern consciousness or has seemed so relevant to virtually any speculation about the destiny of man. The peculiar interest it arouses is not hard to explain. With extreme boldness and simplicity Dostoevski brings into confrontation the two great concepts that preoccupy the modern mind, freedom on the one hand, happiness and security on the other. These concepts he embodies in characters of transcendent stature: the person who does all the talking in the story imposes his authority upon us not merely because he is very old, powerful, and intelligent but because he is Satan himself; and the silent person is divine. No other modern literary work has speculated on human fate in terms so grandiose.

To the reader of the present day, the knowledge that Dostoevski wrote "The Grand Inquisitor" in 1879 may come as a surprise. For the story takes for granted a form of social organization that we know nowadays from actual experience but that Dostoevski did not know, the totalitarian state. The history of the last decades can be told in terms of this kind of society, for Hitler's Third Reich, Mussolini's Fascist Italy, Soviet Russia, and China are salient examples of it. By means of its police powers the totalitarian state exercises control over the actions of its citizens; it also attempts, with a considerable degree of success, to win their acquiescence and attachment by providing (or promising) material and social benefits that will relieve them of care and anxiety. It represents itself in a paternal guise, as taking responsibility for the well-being of its people, on condition that they delegate—actually surrender—to the government their will and initiative. There are, of course, genuinely democratic states which make the welfare of their citizens a chief aim of their existence—Sweden is the example most often cited—and it may be said that, to one extent or another, the ideal of welfare plays a part in the theory of all highly developed social organizations today. But even in democratic societies, and even by people who are advocates of the view that it is the duty of governments to underwrite the security and contentment of their citizens, the fear is often expressed that such a program, if carried far enough, might seduce men into conformity and passivity, leading them to give up the freedom of individual will which we believe makes people fully human. And it is just this surrender of freedom that the Grand Inquisitor regards as a necessary condition of the peace and happiness of mankind and that he confidently expects will be brought about by the development of the all-powerful, all-providing state.

The historical prescience of "The Grand Inquisitor" is indeed remarkable, but we need not be astonished by it, as if it were visionary. It derives from Dostoevski's willingness to take seriously the social and political speculations which were current in the intellectual life of his day, and from his ability to believe that what at the moment existed only in theory and desire would eventually come to exist in fact. He had but to project his bitterly adverse interpretation of the ideals of socialism and imagine them carried out to their furthest possibility to conceive most of the characteristics of the Grand Inquisitor's state. Its remaining traits were provided by the hostility that Dostoevski, an impassioned communicant of the Greek Orthodox Church, the national church of Russia, felt toward Roman Catholicism.

There is really nothing new in the criticism that Dostoevski directs against the Church of Rome. Even his bizarre idea that Roman Catholicism is an agency of state socialism is a new and imaginative version of an old charge directed against the Roman Church—that it seeks to establish its worldly power at the cost of its allegiance to spirit and truth, that it has departed from the way of Jesus to follow the way of imperial Caesar. Any non-Catholic Christian who makes this accusation is likely to draw its terms from that episode in the life of Jesus known as the Temptation in the Wilderness, in which Jesus was offered temporal power by the devil and refused it. For having made that refusal the Jesus of Dostoevsky's story is rebuked by the Grand Inquisitor. Here is the Gospel account of the episode as given by St. Luke (4:1–13):

And Jesus being full of the Holy Ghost returned from Jordan, and was led by the Spirit into the wilderness, being forty days tempted of the devil. And in those days he did eat nothing: and when they were ended, he afterward hungered. And the devil said unto him, If thou be the Son of God, command this stone that it be made bread. And Jesus answered him, saying, It is written, That man shall not live by bread alone, but by every word of God.

And the devil, taking him up into an high mountain, shewed unto him all the kingdoms of the world in a moment of time. And the devil said unto him, All this power will I give thee, and the glory of them: for that is delivered unto me; and to whomsoever I will give it. If thou therefore wilt worship me, all shall be thine. And Jesus answered and said unto him, Get thee behind me, Satan: for it is written, Thou shalt worship the Lord thy God, and him only shalt thou serve.

And he brought him to Jerusalem, and set him on a pinnacle of the temple, and said unto him, If thou be the Son of God, cast thyself down from hence: for it is written, He shall give his angels charge over thee, to keep thee: and in their hands they shall bear thee up, lest at any time thou dash thy foot against a stone. And Jesus answering said unto him, It is said, Thou shalt not tempt the Lord thy God.

And when the devil had ended all the temptation, he departed from him for a season.

Dostoevski's use of the episode is subtle and brilliant. The story in its Gospel form, although its high significance is unmistakable, has relatively little reverberation. Jesus resists each of the temptations with no difficulty whatever, with no indication that he is really being tempted. As why should he be?—for if what Satan offers him is, as it would seem to be, for his own gratification only, this can scarcely be a temptation to a being of his divine perfection. If, however, what the devil proposes is not for the sake of Jesus himself but for the sake of mankind, then it constitutes a temptation indeed. For then Jesus knows that in refusing the powers that are offered him, the powers of material sustenance, authority, and miracle, he is condemning mankind to hardship, strife, and doubt. And he imposes this hard destiny upon men for the sake of a mere intangible thing which does not promise even eventual happiness on earth, that is to say, for the sake of freedom—the freedom to know good and evil and to choose between them, and to seek salvation. When Jesus chooses not to seek dominion over men's hearts and minds by means of worldly power exercised on behalf of human contentment but only through their freely given faith, he knows that he subjects mankind to a heavy burden, a great trial. Thus understood, the temptation that he endures is surely a real one, and his choice may well be thought difficult even for a divine being—for a divine being whose divinity expresses itself in the entireness of his love for mankind.

And once we comprehend the nature of Jesus' temptation in Dostoevski's story, we are implicated in it—we too must choose between passive security and freedom. And the choice, as we confront it in the terms that Dostoevski contrives, is by no means simple, for the Inquisitor argues his case with the force of rationality and humaneness very much on his side. In his statement, "Feed men, and then ask of them virtue," must we not see both good sense and human sympathy? Do not all enlightened people incline to believe nowadays that "there is no crime, and therefore no sin; there is only hunger," that all antisocial behavior, as we have learned to call it, is to be explained by the circumstances that forced it on the person who is condemned as a criminal or a sinner? We are readily drawn to the belief that intelligent political and social organization can obviate public and personal tensions and thus make for peace and decent behavior on the part both of nations and individuals.

In short, on intellectual and moral grounds that we understand and respond to, the Grand Inquisitor offers us what we want, what we feel we properly should have, and might well have, a social arrangement that points to the possibility of the Earthly Paradise. Why, then, do we reject it, as of course we do?

One way of answering the question is to recall two striking phrases that were coined some hundreds of years ago. Both refer to the loss of the original Paradise through Adam's eating the fruit of the Tree of Knowledge, the knowledge being that of good and evil. Adam's sin was called *"felix culpa,"* the happy sin; the fall of man in which the sin resulted was called "the fortunate fall." The reason why the sin was said to be "happy" and the fall "fortunate" was that they made the occasion for Jesus to undertake the redemption and salvation of man, bringing him to a yet nobler condition than before his loss of innocence. It is not necessary to accept the religious implications of this idea to respond to what it says about the nature of man— that man is not all he might be unless he bears the burden of his knowledge of good and evil, and the pain of choosing between them, and the consequences of making the wrong choice. The Grand Inquisitor speaks of man's surrendering his freedom in exchange for happiness, and he means exactly the freedom to know good and evil and to choose between them, even though with pain. The whole intention of his Earthly Paradise is to relieve man of the pain that freedom entails. We reject what he offers because its acceptance means the loss of the dignity of freedom.

Dostoevski, we can scarcely doubt, wishes us to go beyond this rejection; he would have us believe that with each rational step a polity takes toward material well-being its people are carried that much nearer to passivity, dependence, and spiritual extinction. He is at one with his Devil-Inquisitor in offering us only extreme courses, either a life of spiritual freedom in the "wilderness" or a life of slavery in society. The spell of his art is strong indeed, and while we are under its influence it needs an effort of mind to reflect that humanity is not in reality confronted with alternatives so unmodified and, we may say, so simple in their absoluteness.

THE

DEATH

OF

IVAN ILYCH

LEO TOLSTOI
1828–1910

I

DURING AN INTERVAL in the Melvinski trial in the large building of the Law Courts, the members and public prosecutor met in Ivan Egorovich Shebek's private room, where the conversation turned on the celebrated Krasovski case. Fëdor Vasilievich warmly maintained that it was not subject to their jurisdiction, Ivan Egorovich maintained the contrary, while Peter Ivanovich, not having entered into the discussion at the start, took no part in it but looked through the *Gazette* which had just been handed in.

"Gentlemen," he said, "Ivan Ilych has died!"

"You don't say so!"

"Here, read it yourself," replied Peter Ivanovich, handing Fëdor Vasilievich the paper still damp from the press. Surrounded by a black border were the words: "Praskovya Fëdorovna Golovina, with profound sorrow, informs relatives and friends of the demise of her beloved husband Ivan Ilych Golovin, Member of the Court of Justice, which occurred on February the 4th of this year 1882. The funeral will take place on Friday at one o'clock in the afternoon."

Ivan Ilych had been a colleague of the gentlemen present and was liked by them all. He had been ill for some weeks with an illness said to be incurable.

His post had been kept open for him, but there had been conjectures that in case of his death Alexeev might receive his appointment, and that either Vinnikov or Shtabel would succeed Alexeev. So on receiving the news of Ivan Ilych's death the first thought of each of the gentlemen in that private room was of the changes and promotions it might occasion among themselves or their acquaintances.

"I shall be sure to get Shtabel's place or Vinnikov's," thought Fëdor Vasilievich. "I was promised that long ago, and the promotion means an extra eight hundred rubles a year for me besides the allowance."

"Now I must apply for my brother-in-law's transfer from Kaluga," thought Peter Ivanovich. "My wife will be very glad, and then she won't be able to say that I never do anything for her relations."

"I thought he would never leave his bed again," said Peter Ivanovich aloud. "It's very sad."

"But what really was the matter with him?"

"The doctors couldn't say—at least they could, but each of them said something different. When last I saw him I thought he was getting better."

"And I haven't been to see him since the holidays. I always meant to go."

"Had he any property?"

"I think his wife had a little—but something quite trifling."

"We shall have to go to see her, but they live so terribly far away."

"Far away from you, you mean. Everything's far away from your place."

"You see, he never can forgive my living on the other side of the river," said Peter Ivanovich, smiling at Shebek. Then, still talking of the distances between different parts of the city, they returned to the Court.

Besides considerations as to the possible transfers and promotions likely to result from Ivan Ilych's death, the mere fact of the death of a near acquaintance aroused, as usual, in all who heard of it the complacent feeling that, "it is he who is dead and not I."

Each one thought or felt, "Well, he's dead but I'm alive!" But the more intimate of Ivan Ilych's acquaintances, his so-called friends, could not help thinking also that they would now have to fulfil the very tiresome demands of propriety by attending the funeral service and paying a visit of condolence to the widow.

Fëdor Vasilievich and Peter Ivanovich had been his nearest acquaintances. Peter Ivanovich had studied law with Ivan Ilych and had considered himself to be under obligations to him.

Having told his wife at dinner-time of Ivan Ilych's death and of his conjecture that it might be possible to get her brother transferred to their circuit, Peter Ivanovich sacrificed his usual nap, put on his evening clothes, and drove to Ivan Ilych's house.

At the entrance stood a carriage and two cabs. Leaning against the wall in the hall downstairs near the cloak-stand was a coffin-lid covered with cloth of gold, ornamented with gold cord and tassels, that had been polished up with metal powder. Two ladies in black were taking off their fur cloaks. Peter Ivanovich recognized one of them as Ivan Ilych's sister, but the other was a stranger to him. His colleague Schwartz was just coming downstairs, but on seeing Peter Ivanovich enter he stopped and winked at him, as if to say: "Ivan Ilych has made a mess of things—not like you and me."

Schwartz's face with his Piccadilly whiskers[1] and his slim figure in evening dress, had as usual an air of elegant solemnity which contrasted with the playfulness of his character and had a special piquancy here, or so it seemed to Peter Ivanovich.

Peter Ivanovich allowed the ladies to precede him and slowly followed them upstairs. Schwartz did not come down but remained where he was, and Peter Ivanovich understood that he wanted to arrange where they should play bridge that evening. The ladies went upstairs to the widow's room, and Schwartz with seriously compressed lips but a playful look in his eyes, indicated by a twist of his eyebrows the room to the right where the body lay.

Peter Ivanovich, like everyone else on such occasions, entered feeling uncertain what he would have to do. All he knew was that at such times it is always safe to cross oneself. But he was not quite sure whether one should make obeisances while doing so. He therefore adopted a middle course. On entering the room he began crossing himself and made a slight movement resembling a bow. At the same time, as far as the motion of his head and arm allowed, he surveyed the room. Two young men—apparently nephews, one of whom was a high-school pupil—were leaving the room, crossing themselves as they did so. An old woman was standing motionless, and a lady with strangely arched eyebrows was saying something to her in a whisper. A vigorous, resolute Church Reader, in a frock-coat, was reading something in a loud voice with an expression that precluded any contradiction. The butler's assistant, Gerasim, stepping lightly in front of Peter Ivanovich, was strewing something on the floor. Noticing this, Peter Ivanovich was immediately aware of a faint odour of a decomposing body.

The last time he had called on Ivan Ilych, Peter Ivanovich had seen Gerasim in the study. Ivan Ilych had been particularly fond of him and he was performing the duty of a sick nurse.

Peter Ivanovich continued to make the sign of the cross slightly inclining his head in an intermediate direction between the coffin, the Reader, and the icons on the table in a corner of the room. Afterwards, when it seemed to him that this movement of his arm in crossing himself had gone on too long, he stopped and began to look at the corpse.

The dead man lay, as dead men always lie, in a specially heavy way, his rigid limbs sunk in the soft cushions of the coffin, with the head forever bowed on the pillow. His yellow waxen brow with bald patches over his sunken temples was thrust up in the way peculiar to the dead, the protruding nose seeming to press on the upper lip. He was much changed and had grown even thinner since Peter Ivanovich had last seen him, but, as is always the case with the dead, his face was handsomer and above all more dignified than when he was alive. The expression on the face said that what was necessary had been accomplished, and accomplished rightly. Besides this there was in that expression a reproach and a warning to the living. This warning seemed to Peter Ivanovich out of place, or at least not applicable to him. He felt a certain discomfort and so he hurriedly crossed himself once more and turned and went out of the door—too hurriedly and too regardless of propriety, as he himself was aware.

Schwartz was waiting for him in the adjoining room with legs spread wide

[1] Side whiskers.

apart and both hands toying with his top-hat behind his back. The mere sight of that playful, well-groomed, and elegant figure refreshed Peter Ivanovich. He felt that Schwartz was above all these happenings and would not surrender to any depressing influences. His very look said that this incident of a church service for Ivan Ilych could not be a sufficient reason for infringing the order of the session—in other words, that it would certainly not prevent his unwrapping a new pack of cards and shuffling them that evening while a footman placed four fresh candles on the table: in fact, that there was no reason for supposing that this incident would hinder their spending the evening agreeably. Indeed he said this in a whisper as Peter Ivanovich passed him, proposing that they should meet for a game at Fëdor Vasilievich's. But apparently Peter Ivanovich was not destined to play bridge that evening. Praskovya Fëdorovna (a short, fat woman who despite all efforts to the contrary had continued to broaden steadily from her shoulders downwards and who had the same extraordinarily arched eyebrows as the lady who had been standing by the coffin), dressed all in black, her head covered with lace, came out of her own room with some other ladies, conducted them to the room where the dead body lay, and said: "The service will begin immediately. Please go in."

Schwartz, making an indefinite bow, stood still, evidently neither accepting nor declining this invitation. Praskovya Fëdorovna, recognizing Peter Ivanovich, sighed, went close up to him, took his hand, and said: "I know you were a true friend to Ivan Ilych . . ." and looked at him awaiting some suitable response. And Peter Ivanovich knew that, just as it had been the right thing to cross himself in that room, so what he had to do here was to press her hand, sigh, and say, "Believe me. . . ." So he did all this and as he did it felt that the desired result had been achieved: that both he and she were touched.

"Come with me. I want to speak to you before it begins," said the widow. "Give me your arm."

Peter Ivanovich gave her his arm and they went to the inner rooms, passing Schwartz, who winked at Peter Ivanovich compassionately.

"That does for our bridge! Don't object if we find another player. Perhaps you can cut in when you do escape," said his playful look.

Peter Ivanovich sighed still more deeply and despondently, and Praskovya Fëdorovna pressed his arm gratefully. When they reached the drawing-room, upholstered in pink cretonne and lighted by a dim lamp, they sat down at the table—she on a sofa and Peter Ivanovich on a low pouffe, the springs of which yielded spasmodically under his weight. Praskovya Fëdorovna had been on the point of warning him to take another seat, but felt that such a warning was out of keeping with her present condition and so changed her mind. As he sat down on the pouffe Peter Ivanovich recalled how Ivan Ilych had arranged this room and had consulted him regarding this pink cretonne with green leaves. The whole room was full of furniture and knick-knacks, and on her way to the sofa the lace of the widow's black shawl caught on the carved edge of the table. Peter Ivanovich rose to detach it, and the springs of the pouffe, relieved of his weight, rose also and gave him a push. The widow began detaching her shawl herself, and Peter Ivanovich again sat down, suppressing the rebellious springs of the pouffe under him. But the widow had not quite freed herself and Peter Ivanovich got up again, and again the pouffe rebelled and even creaked. When this was all over she took out a clean cambric handkerchief and began to weep.

The episode with the shawl and the struggle with the pouffe had cooled Peter Ivanovich's emotions and he sat there with a sullen look on his face. This awkward situation was interrupted by Sokolov, Ivan Ilych's butler, who came to report that the plot in the cemetery that Praskovya Fëdorovna had chosen would cost two hundred rubles. She stopped weeping and, looking at Peter Ivanovich with the air of a victim, remarked in French that it was very hard for her. Peter Ivanovich made a silent gesture signifying his full conviction that it must indeed be so.

"Please smoke," she said in a magnanimous yet crushed voice, and turned to discuss with Sokolov the price of the plot for the grave.

Peter Ivanovich while lighting his cigarette heard her inquiring very circumstantially into the prices of different plots in the cemetery and finally decide which she would take. When that was done she gave instructions about engaging the choir. Sokolov then left the room.

"I look after everything myself," she told Peter Ivanovich, shifting the albums that lay on the table; and noticing that the table was endangered by his cigarette-ash, she immediately passed him an ash-tray, saying as she did so: "I consider it an affectation to say that my grief prevents my attending to practical affairs. On the contrary, if anything can—I won't say console me, but—distract me, it is seeing to everything concerning him." She again took out her handkerchief as if preparing to cry, but suddenly, as if mastering her feeling, she shook herself and began to speak calmly. "But there is something I want to talk to you about."

Peter Ivanovich bowed, keeping control of the springs of the pouffe, which immediately began quivering under him.

"He suffered terribly the last few days."

"Did he?" said Peter Ivanovich.

"Oh, terribly! He screamed unceasingly, not for minutes but for hours. For the last three days he screamed incessantly. It was unendurable. I cannot understand how I bore it; you could hear him three rooms off. Oh, what I have suffered!"

"Is it possible that he was conscious all that time?" asked Peter Ivanovich.

"Yes," she whispered. "To the last moment. He took leave of us a quarter of an hour before he died, and asked us to take Volodya away."

The thought of the sufferings of this man he had known so intimately, first as a merry little boy, then as a school-mate, and later as a grown-up colleague, suddenly struck Peter Ivanovich with horror, despite an unpleasant consciousness of his own and this woman's dissimulation. He again saw that brow, and that nose pressing down on the lip, and felt afraid for himself.

"Three days of frightful suffering and then death! Why, that might suddenly, at any time, happen to me," he thought, and for a moment felt terrified. But—he did not himself know how—the customary reflection at once occurred to him that this had happened to Ivan Ilych and not to him, and that it should not and could not happen to him, and to think that it could would be yielding to depression which he ought not to do, as Schwartz's expression plainly showed. After which reflection Peter Ivanovich felt reassured, and began to ask with interest about the details of Ivan Ilych's death, as though death was an accident natural to Ivan Ilych but certainly not to himself.

After many details of the really dreadful physical sufferings Ivan Ilych had endured (which details he learnt only from the effect those sufferings had produced on Praskovya Fёdorovna's nerves) the widow apparently found it necessary to get to business.

"Oh, Peter Ivanovich, how hard it is! How terribly, terribly hard!" and she again began to weep.

Peter Ivanovich sighed and waited for her to finish blowing her nose. When she had done so he said, "Believe me . . ." and she again began talking and brought out what was evidently her chief concern with him—namely, to question him as to how she could obtain a grant of money from the government on the occasion of her husband's death. She made it appear that she was asking Peter Ivanovich's advice about her pension, but he soon saw that she already knew about that to the minutest detail, more even than he did himself. She knew how much could be got out of the government in consequence of her husband's death, but wanted to find out whether she could not possibly extract something more. Peter Ivanovich tried to think of some means of doing so, but after reflecting for a while and, out of propriety, condemning the government for its niggardliness, he said he thought that nothing more could be got. Then she sighed and evidently began to devise means of getting rid of her visitor. Noticing this, he put out his cigarette, rose, pressed her hand, and went out into the anteroom.

In the dining-room where the clock stood that Ivan Ilych had liked so much and had bought at an antique shop, Peter Ivanovich met a priest and a few acquaintances who had come to attend the service, and he recognized Ivan Ilych's daughter, a handsome young woman. She was in black and her slim figure appeared slimmer than ever. She had a gloomy, determined, almost angry expression, and bowed to Peter Ivanovich as though he were in some way to blame. Behind her, with the same offended look, stood a wealthy young man, an examining magistrate, whom Peter Ivanovich also knew and who was her fiancé, as he had heard. He bowed mournfully to them and was about to pass into the death-chamber, when from under the stairs appeared the figure of Ivan Ilych's schoolboy son, who was extremely like his father. He seemed a little Ivan Ilych, such as Peter Ivanovich remembered when they studied law together. His tear-stained eyes had in them the look that is seen in the eyes of boys of thirteen or fourteen who are not pure-minded. When he saw Peter Ivanovich he scowled morosely and shamefacedly. Peter Ivanovich nodded to him and entered the death-chamber. The service began: candles, groans, incense, tears, and sobs. Peter Ivanovich stood looking gloomily down at his feet. He did not look once at the dead man, did not yield to any depressing influence, and was one of the first to leave the room. There was no one in the anteroom, but Gerasim darted out of the dead man's room, rummaged with his strong hands among the fur coats to find Peter Ivanovich's and helped him on with it.

"Well, friend Gerasim," said Peter Ivanovich, so as to say something. "It's a sad affair, isn't it?"

"It's God's will. We shall all come to it some day," said Gerasim, displaying his teeth—the even, white teeth of a healthy peasant—and, like a man in the thick of urgent work, he briskly opened the front door, called the coachman, helped Peter Ivanovich into the sledge, and sprang back to the porch as if in readiness for what he had to do next.

Peter Ivanovich found the fresh air particularly pleasant after the smell of incense, the dead body, and carbolic acid.

"Where to, sir?" asked the coachman.

"It's not too late even now. . . . I'll call round on Fëdor Vasilievich."

He accordingly drove there and found them just finishing the first rubber, so that it was quite convenient for him to cut in.

II

Ivan Ilych's life had been most simple and most ordinary and therefore most terrible.

He had been a member of the Court of Justice, and died at the age of forty-five. His father had been an official who after serving in various ministries and departments in Petersburg had made the sort of career which brings men to positions from which by reason of their long service they cannot be dismissed, though they are obviously unfit to hold any responsible position, and for whom therefore posts are especially created, which though fictitious carry salaries of from six to ten thousand rubles that are not fictitious, and in receipt of which they live on to a great age.

Such was the Privy Councillor and superfluous member of various superfluous institutions, Ilya Epimovich Golovin.

He had three sons, of whom Ivan Ilych was the second. The eldest son was following in his father's footsteps only in another department, and was already approaching that stage in the service at which a similar sinecure would be reached. The third son was a failure. He had ruined his prospects in a number of positions and was now serving in the railway department. His father and brothers, and still more their wives, not merely disliked meeting him, but avoided remembering his existence unless compelled to do so. His sister had married Baron Greff, a Petersburg official of her father's type. Ivan Ilych was *le phénix de la famille*[2] as people said. He was neither as cold and formal as his elder brother nor as wild as the younger, but was a happy mean between them—an intelligent, polished, lively and agreeable man. He had studied with his younger brother at the School of Law, but the latter had failed to complete the course and was expelled when he was in the fifth class. Ivan Ilych finished the course well. Even when he was at the School of Law he was just what he remained for the rest of his life: a capable, cheerful, good-natured, and sociable man, though strict in the fulfilment of what he considered to be his duty: and he considered his duty to be what was so considered by those in authority. Neither as a boy nor as a man was he a toady, but from early youth was by nature attracted to people of high station as a fly is drawn to the light, assimilating their ways and views of life and establishing friendly relations with them. All the enthusiasms of childhood and youth passed without leaving much trace on him; he succumbed to sensuality, to vanity, and latterly among the highest classes to

---

[2] (French) The uniquely perfect member of the family (as the phoenix was supposed to be among birds, there being only one example of its species at any given time). In Tolstoi's work the upper-class Russian habit of interlarding conversation with French phrases often suggests a kind of genteel self-complacency.

liberalism, but always within limits which his instinct unfailingly indicated to him as correct.

At school he had done things which had formerly seemed to him very horrid and made him feel disgusted with himself when he did them; but when later on he saw that such actions were done by people of good position and that they did not regard them as wrong, he was able not exactly to regard them as right, but to forget about them entirely or not be at all troubled at remembering them.

Having graduated from the School of Law and qualified for the tenth rank of the civil service, and having received money from his father for his equipment, Ivan Ilych ordered himself clothes at Scharmer's, the fashionable tailor, hung a medallion inscribed *respice finem*[3] on his watch-chain, took leave of his professor and the prince who was patron of the school, had a farewell dinner with his comrades at Donon's first-class restaurant, and with his new and fashionable portmanteau, linen, clothes, shaving and other toilet appliances, and a travelling rug, all purchased at the best shops, he set off for one of the provinces where, through his father's influence, he had been attached to the Governor as an official for special service.

In the province Ivan Ilych soon arranged as easy and agreeable a position for himself as he had had at the School of Law. He performed his official tasks, made his career, and at the same time amused himself pleasantly and decorously. Occasionally he paid official visits to country districts, where he behaved with dignity both to his superiors and inferiors, and performed the duties entrusted to him, which related chiefly to the sectarians, with an exactness and incorruptible honesty of which he could not but feel proud.

In official matters, despite his youth and taste for frivolous gaiety, he was exceedingly reserved, punctilious, and even severe; but in society he was often amusing and witty, and always good-natured, correct in his manner, and *bon enfant*,[4] as the governor and his wife—with whom he was like one of the family—used to say of him.

In the province he had an affair with a lady who made advances to the elegant young lawyer, and there was also a milliner; and there were carousals with aides-de-camp who visited the district, and after-supper visits to a certain outlying street of doubtful reputation; and there was too some obsequiousness to his chief and even to his chief's wife, but all this was done with such a tone of good breeding that no hard names could be applied to it. It all came under the heading of the French saying: *"Il faut que jeunesse se passe."*[5] It was all done with clean hands, in clean linen, with French phrases, and above all among people of the best society and consequently with the approval of people of rank.

So Ivan Ilych served for five years and then came a change in his official life. The new and reformed judicial institutions were introduced, and new men were needed. Ivan Ilych became such a new man. He was offered the post of examining magistrate, and he accepted it though the post was in another

[3] (Latin) Think upon, or provide for, the end. Two meanings of *end*—immediate goals and death—should be noted.

[4] (French) Well-behaved towards his elders and superiors (literally, "good child").

[5] (French) A proverbial expression signifying that the sins of youth should be treated indulgently (literally, "youth must take its course").

province and obliged him to give up the connexions he had formed and to make new ones. His friends met to give him a send-off; they had a group-photograph taken and presented him with a silver cigarette-case, and he set off to his new post.

As examining magistrate Ivan Ilych was just as *comme il faut*[6] and decorous a man, inspiring general respect and capable of separating his official duties from his private life, as he had been when acting as an official on special service. His duties now as examining magistrate were far more interesting and attractive than before. In his former position it had been pleasant to wear an undress uniform made by Scharmer, and to pass through the crowd of petitioners and officials who were timorously awaiting an audience with the governor, and who envied him as with free and easy gait he went straight into his chief's private room to have a cup of tea and a cigarette with him. But not many people had then been directly dependent on him—only police officials and the sectarians when he went on special missions—and he liked to treat them politely, almost as comrades, as if he were letting them feel that he who had the power to crush them was treating them in this simple, friendly way. There were then but few such people. But now, as an examining magistrate, Ivan Ilych felt that everyone without exception, even the most important and self-satisfied, was in his power, and that he need only write a few words on a sheet of paper with a certain heading, and this or that important, self-satisfied person would be brought before him in the role of an accused person or a witness, and if he did not choose to allow him to sit down, would have to stand before him and answer his questions. Ivan Ilych never abused his power; he tried on the contrary to soften its expression, but the consciousness of it and of the possibility of softening its effect, supplied the chief interest and attraction of his office. In his work itself, especially in his examinations, he very soon acquired a method of eliminating all considerations irrelevant to the legal aspect of the case, and reducing even the most complicated case to a form in which it would be presented on paper only in its externals, completely excluding his personal opinion of the matter, while above all observing every prescribed formality. The work was new and Ivan Ilych was one of the first men to apply the new Code of 1864.[7]

On taking up the post of examining magistrate in a new town, he made new acquaintances and connexions, placed himself on a new footing, and assumed a somewhat different tone. He took up an attitude of rather dignified aloofness towards the provincial authorities, but picked out the best circle of legal gentlemen and wealthy gentry living in the town and assumed a tone of slight dissatisfaction with the government, of moderate liberalism, and of enlightened citizenship. At the same time, without at all altering the elegance of his toilet, he ceased shaving his chin and allowed his beard to grow as it pleased.

Ivan Ilych settled down very pleasantly in this new town. The society there, which inclined towards opposition to the Governor, was friendly, his salary was larger, and he began to play *vint* [a form of bridge], which he found added not a little to the pleasure of life, for he had a capacity for cards, played good-humouredly, and calculated rapidly and astutely, so that he usually won.

After living there for two years he met his future wife, Praskovya Fëdorovna

---

[6] (French) Proper, careful to observe the proprieties.

[7] Judicial proceedings were completely reformed after the emancipation of the serfs in 1861.

Mikhel, who was the most attractive, clever, and brilliant girl of the set in which he moved, and among other amusements and relaxations from his labours as examining magistrate, Ivan Ilych established light and playful relations with her.

While he had been an official on special service he had been accustomed to dance, but now as an examining magistrate it was exceptional for him to do so. If he danced now, he did it as if to show that though he served under the reformed order of things, and had reached the fifth official rank, yet when it came to dancing he could do it better than most people. So at the end of an evening he sometimes danced with Praskovya Fëdorovna, and it was chiefly during these dances that he captivated her. She fell in love with him. Ivan Ilych had at first no definite intention of marrying, but when the girl fell in love with him he said to himself: "Really, why shouldn't I marry?"

Praskovya Fëdorovna came of a good family, was not bad looking, and had some little property. Ivan Ilych might have aspired to a more brilliant match, but even this was good. He had his salary, and she, he hoped, would have an equal income. She was well connected, and was a sweet, pretty, and thoroughly correct young woman. To say that Ivan Ilych married because he fell in love with Praskovya Fëdorovna and found that she sympathized with his views of life would be as incorrect as to say that he married because his social circle approved of the match. He was swayed by both these considerations: the marriage gave him personal satisfaction, and at the same time it was considered the right thing by the most highly placed of his associates.

So Ivan Ilych got married.

The preparations for marriage and the beginning of married life, with its conjugal caresses, the new furniture, new crockery, and new linen, were very pleasant until his wife became pregnant—so that Ivan Ilych had begun to think that marriage would not impair the easy, agreeable, gay and always decorous character of his life, approved of by society and regarded by himself as natural, but would even improve it. But from the first months of his wife's pregnancy, something new, unpleasant, depressing, and unseemly, and from which there was no way of escape, unexpectedly showed itself.

His wife, without any reason—*de gaieté de cœur*[8] as Ivan Ilych expressed it to himself—began to disturb the pleasure and propriety of their life. She began to be jealous without any cause, expected him to devote his whole attention to her, found fault with everything, and made coarse and ill-mannered scenes.

At first Ivan Ilych hoped to escape from the unpleasantness of this state of affairs by the same easy and decorous relation to life that had served him heretofore: he tried to ignore his wife's disagreeable moods, continued to live in his usual easy and pleasant way, invited friends to his house for a game of cards, and also tried going out to his club or spending his evenings with friends. But one day his wife began upbraiding him so vigorously, using such coarse words, and continued to abuse him every time he did not fulfil her demands, so resolutely and with such evident determination not to give way till he submitted—that is, till he stayed at home and was bored just as she was—that he became alarmed. He now realized that matrimony—at any rate with Praskovya Fëdorovna—was not always conducive to the pleasures and amenities of life,

[8] (French) Out of mere wantonness.

but on the contrary often infringed both comfort and propriety, and that he must therefore entrench himself against such infringement. And Ivan Ilych began to seek for means of doing so. His official duties were the one thing that imposed upon Praskovya Fëdorovna, and by means of his official work and the duties attached to it he began struggling with his wife to secure his own independence.

With the birth of their child, the attempts to feed it and the various failures in doing so, and with the real and imaginary illnesses of mother and child, in which Ivan Ilych's sympathy was demanded but about which he understood nothing, the need of securing for himself an existence outside his family life became still more imperative.

As his wife grew more irritable and exacting and Ivan Ilych transferred the centre of gravity of his life more and more to his official work, so did he grow to like his work better and became more ambitious than before.

Very soon, within a year of his wedding, Ivan Ilych had realized that marriage, though it may add some comforts to life, is in fact a very intricate and difficult affair towards which in order to perform one's duty, that is, to lead a decorous life approved of by society, one must adopt a definite attitude just as towards one's official duties.

And Ivan Ilych evolved such an attitude towards married life. He only required of it those conveniences—dinner at home, housewife, and bed—which it could give him, and above all that propriety of external forms required by public opinion. For the rest he looked for light-hearted pleasure and propriety, and was very thankful when he found them, but if he met with antagonism and querulousness he at once retired into his separate fenced-off world of official duties, where he found satisfaction.

Ivan Ilych was esteemed a good official, and after three years was made Assistant Public Prosecutor. His new duties, their importance, the possibility of indicting and imprisoning anyone he chose, the publicity his speeches received, and the success he had in all these things, made his work still more attractive.

More children came. His wife became more and more querulous and ill-tempered, but the attitude Ivan Ilych had adopted towards his home life rendered him almost impervious to her grumbling.

After seven years' service in that town he was transferred to another province as Public Prosecutor. They moved, but were short of money and his wife did not like the place they moved to. Though the salary was higher the cost of living was greater, besides which two of their children died and family life became still more unpleasant for him.

Praskovya Fëdorovna blamed her husband for every inconvenience they encountered in their new home. Most of the conversations between husband and wife, especially as to the children's education, led to topics which recalled former disputes, and those disputes were apt to flare up again at any moment. There remained only those rare periods of amorousness which still came to them at times but did not last long. These were islets at which they anchored for a while and then again set out upon that ocean of veiled hostility which showed itself in their aloofness from one another. This aloofness might have grieved Ivan Ilych had he considered that it ought not to exist, but he now regarded the position as normal, and even made it the goal at which he aimed in family life. His aim was to free himself more and more from those unpleasantnesses and to give them a semblance of harmlessness and propriety. He attained this by spending less and less time with his family, and when obliged to be at home he tried to safeguard his position by the presence of outsiders. The chief thing however was that he had his official duties. The whole interest of his life now centred in the official world and that interest absorbed him. The consciousness of his power, being able to ruin anybody he wished to ruin, the importance, even the external dignity of his entry into court, or meetings with his subordinates, his success with superiors and inferiors, and above all his masterly handling of cases, of which he was conscious—all this gave him pleasure and filled his life, together with chats with his colleagues, dinners, and bridge. So that on the whole Ivan Ilych's life continued to flow as he considered it should do—pleasantly and properly.

So things continued for another seven years. His eldest daughter was already sixteen, another child had died, and only one son was left, a schoolboy and a subject of dissension. Ivan Ilych wanted to put him in the School of Law, but to spite him Praskovya Fëdorovna entered him at the High School. The daughter had been educated at home and had turned out well: the boy did not learn badly either.

III

So Ivan Ilych lived for seventeen years after his marriage. He was already a Public Prosecutor of long standing, and had declined several proposed transfers while awaiting a more desirable post, when an unanticipated and unpleasant occurrence quite upset the peaceful course of his life. He was expecting to be offered the post of presiding judge in a University town, but Happe somehow came to the front and obtained the appointment instead. Ivan Ilych became irritable, reproached Happe, and quarrelled both with him and with his immediate superiors—who became colder to him and again passed him over when other appointments were made.

This was in 1880, the hardest year of Ivan Ilych's life. It was then that it became evident on the one hand that his salary was insufficient for them to live on, and on the other that he had been forgotten, and not only this, but that what was for him the greatest and most cruel injustice appeared to others a quite ordinary occurrence. Even his father did not consider it his duty to help him. Ivan Ilych felt himself abandoned by everyone, and that they regarded his position with a salary of 3,500 rubles as quite normal and even fortunate. He alone knew that with the consciousness of the injustices done him, with his wife's incessant nagging, and with the debts he had contracted by living beyond his means, his position was far from normal.

In order to save money that summer he obtained leave of absence and went with his wife to live in the country at her brother's place.

In the country, without his work, he experienced *ennui* for the first time in his life, and not only *ennui* but intolerable depression, and he decided that it was impossible to go on living like that, and that it was necessary to take energetic measures.

Having passed a sleepless night pacing up and down the veranda, he decided to go to Petersburg and bestir himself, in order to punish those who had failed to appreciate him and to get transferred to another ministry.

Next day, despite many protests from his wife and her brother, he started for Petersburg with the sole object of obtaining a post with a salary of five thousand rubles a year. He was no longer bent on any particular department, or tendency, or kind of activity. All he now wanted was an appointment to another post with a salary of five thousand rubles, either in the administration, in the banks, with the railways, in one of the Empress Marya's Institutions,[9] or even in the customs—but it had to carry with it a salary of five thousand rubles and be in a ministry other than that in which they had failed to appreciate him.

And this quest of Ivan Ilych's was crowned with remarkable and unexpected success. At Kursk an acquaintance of his, F. I. Ilyin, got into the first-class carriage, sat down beside Ivan Ilych, and told him of a telegram just received by the Governor of Kursk announcing that a change was about to take place in the ministry: Peter Ivanovich was to be superseded by Ivan Seménovich.

The proposed change, apart from its significance for Russia, had a special significance for Ivan Ilych, because by bringing forward a new man, Peter Petrovich, and consequently his friend Zachar Ivanovich, it was highly favourable for Ivan Ilych, since Zachar Ivanovich was a friend and colleague of his.

In Moscow this news was confirmed, and on reaching Petersburg Ivan Ilych found Zachar Ivanovich and received a definite promise of an appointment in his former department of Justice.

A week later he telegraphed to his wife: "Zachar in Miller's place. I shall receive appointment on presentation of report."

Thanks to this change of personnel, Ivan Ilych had unexpectedly obtained an appointment in his former ministry which placed him two stages above his former colleagues besides giving him five thousand rubles salary and three thousand five hundred rubles for expenses connected with his removal. All his ill humour towards his former enemies and the whole department vanished, and Ivan Ilych was completely happy.

He returned to the country more cheerful and contented than he had been for a long time. Praskovya Fëdorovna also cheered up and a truce was arranged between them. Ivan Ilych told of how he had been fêted by everybody in Petersburg, how all those who had been his enemies were put to shame and now fawned on him, how envious they were of his appointment, and how much everybody in Petersburg had liked him.

Praskovya Fëdorovna listened to all this and appeared to believe it. She did not contradict anything, but only made plans for their life in the town to which they were going. Ivan Ilych saw with delight that these plans were his plans, that he and his wife agreed, and that, after a stumble, his life was regaining its due and natural character of pleasant lightheartedness and decorum.

Ivan Ilych had come back for a short time only, for he had to take up his new duties on the 10th of September. Moreover, he needed time to settle into the new place, to move all his belongings from the province, and to buy and

[9] These were orphanage-schools for girls.

order many additional things: in a word, to make such arrangements as he had resolved on, which were almost exactly what Praskovya Fëdorovna too had decided on.

Now that everything had happened so fortunately, and that he and his wife were at one in their aims and moreover saw so little of one another, they got on together better than they had done since the first years of marriage. Ivan Ilych had thought of taking his family away with him at once, but the insistence of his wife's brother and her sister-in-law, who had suddenly become particularly amiable and friendly to him and his family, induced him to depart alone.

So he departed, and the cheerful state of mind induced by his success and by the harmony between his wife and himself, the one intensifying the other, did not leave him. He found a delightful house, just the thing both he and his wife had dreamt of. Spacious, lofty reception rooms in the old style, a convenient and dignified study, rooms for his wife and daughter, a study for his son—it might have been specially built for them. Ivan Ilych himself superintended the arrangements, chose the wallpapers, supplemented the furniture (preferably with antiques which he considered particularly *comme il faut*), and supervised the upholstering. Everything progressed and progressed and approached the ideal he had set himself: even when things were only half completed they exceeded his expectations. He saw what a refined and elegant character, free from vulgarity, it would all have when it was ready. On falling asleep he pictured to himself how the reception-room would look. Looking at the yet unfinished drawing-room he could see the fireplace, the screen, the what-not, the little chairs dotted here and there, the dishes and plates on the walls, and the bronzes, as they would be when everything was in place. He was pleased by the thought of how his wife and daughter, who shared his taste in this matter, would be impressed by it. They were certainly not expecting as much. He had been particularly successful in finding, and buying cheaply, antiques which gave a particularly aristocratic character to the whole place. But in his letters he intentionally understated everything in order to be able to surprise them. All this so absorbed him that his new duties—though he liked his official work—interested him less than he had expected. Sometimes he even had moments of absent-mindedness during the Court Sessions, and would consider whether he should have straight or curved cornices for his curtains. He was so interested in it all that he often did things himself, rearranging the furniture, or rehanging the curtains. Once when mounting a step-ladder to show the upholsterer, who did not understand, how he wanted the hangings draped, he made a false step and slipped, but being a strong and agile man he clung on and only knocked his side against the knob of the window frame. The bruised place was painful but the pain soon passed, and he felt particularly bright and well just then. He wrote: "I feel fifteen years younger." He thought he would have everything ready by September, but it dragged on till mid-October. But the result was charming not only in his eyes but to everyone who saw it.

In reality it was just what is usually seen in the houses of people of moderate means who want to appear rich, and therefore succeed only in resembling others like themselves: there were damasks, dark wood, plants, rugs, and dull and polished bronzes—all the things people of a certain class have in order to resemble other people of that class. His house was so like the others that it would never have been noticed, but to him it all seemed to be quite exceptional. He was very happy when he met his family at the station and brought them to the newly furnished house all lit up, where a footman in a white tie opened the door into the hall decorated with plants, and when they went on into the drawing-room and the study uttering exclamations of delight. He conducted them everywhere, drank in their praises eagerly, and beamed with pleasure. At tea that evening, when Praskovya Fëdorovna among other things asked him about his fall, he laughed and showed them how he had gone flying and had frightened the upholsterer.

"It's a good thing I'm a bit of an athlete. Another man might have been killed, but I merely knocked myself, just here; it hurts when it's touched, but it's passing off already—it's only a bruise."

So they began living in their new home—in which, as always happens, when they got thoroughly settled in they found they were just one room short—and with the increased income, which as always was just a little (some five hundred rubles) too little, but it was all very nice.

Things went particularly well at first, before everything was finally arranged and while something had still to be done: this thing bought, that thing ordered, another thing moved, and something else adjusted. Though there were some disputes between husband and wife, they were both so well satisfied and had so much to do that it all passed off without any serious quarrels. When nothing was left to arrange it became rather dull and something seemed to be lacking, but they were then making acquaintances, forming habits, and life was growing fuller.

Ivan Ilych spent his mornings at the law court and came home to dinner, and at first he was generally in a good humour, though he occasionally became irritable just on account of his house. (Every spot on the tablecloth or the upholstery, and every broken window-blind string, irritated him. He had devoted so much trouble to arranging it all that every disturbance of it distressed him.) But on the whole his life ran its course as he believed life should do: easily, pleasantly, and decorously.

He got up at nine, drank his coffee, read the paper, and then put on his undress uniform and went to the law courts. There the harness in which he worked had already been stretched to fit him and he donned it without a hitch: petitioners, inquiries at the chancery, the chancery itself, and the sittings public and administrative. In all this the thing was to exclude everything fresh and vital, which always disturbs the regular course of official business, and to admit only official relations with people, and then only on official grounds. A man would come, for instance, wanting some information. Ivan Ilych, as one in whose sphere the matter did not lie, would have nothing to do with him: but if the man had some business with him in his official capacity, something that could be expressed on officially stamped paper, he would do everything, positively everything he could within the limits of such relations, and in doing so would maintain the semblance of friendly human relations, that is, would observe the courtesies of life. As soon as the official relations ended, so did everything else. Ivan Ilych possessed this capacity to separate his real life from the official side of affairs and not mix the two, in the highest degree, and by long practice and natural aptitude had brought it to such a pitch that sometimes, in the manner of a virtuoso, he would even allow himself to let the human and official relations mingle. He let himself do this just because he felt that he could at any time he chose resume the strictly official attitude again and drop the human relation. And he did it all easily, pleasantly, correctly, and even artistically. In the intervals between the sessions he smoked, drank tea, chatted a little about politics, a little about general topics, a little about cards, but most of all about official appointments. Tired, but with the feelings of a virtuoso—one of the first violins who has played his part in an orchestra with precision—he would return home to find that his wife and daughter had been out paying calls, or had a visitor, and that his son had been to school, had done his homework with his tutor, and was duly learning what is taught at High Schools. Everything was as it should be. After dinner, if they had no visitors, Ivan Ilych sometimes read a book that was being much discussed at the time, and in the evening settled down to work, that is, read official papers, compared the depositions of witnesses, and noted paragraphs of the Code applying to them. This was neither dull nor amusing. It was dull when he might have been playing bridge, but if no bridge was available it was at any rate better than doing nothing or sitting with his wife. Ivan Ilych's chief pleasure was giving little dinners to which he invited men and women of good social position, and just as his drawing-room resembled all other drawing-rooms so did his enjoyable little parties resemble all other such parties.

Once they even gave a dance. Ivan Ilych enjoyed it and everything went off well, except that it led to a violent quarrel with his wife about the cakes and sweets. Praskovya Fëdorovna had made her own plans, but Ivan Ilych insisted on getting everything from an expensive confectioner and ordered too many cakes, and the quarrel occurred because some of those cakes were left over and the confectioner's bill came to forty-five rubles. It was a great and disagreeable quarrel. Praskovya Fëdorovna called him "a fool and an imbecile," and he clutched at his head and made angry allusions to divorce.

But the dance itself had been enjoyable. The best people were there, and Ivan Ilych had danced with Princess Trufonova, a sister of the distinguished founder of the Society "Bear my Burden."

The pleasures connected with his work were pleasures of ambition; his social pleasures were those of vanity; but Ivan Ilych's greatest pleasure was playing bridge. He acknowledged that whatever disagreeable incident happened in his life, the pleasure that beamed like a ray of light above everything else was to sit down to bridge with good players, not noisy partners, and of course to four-handed bridge (with five players it was annoying to have to stand out, though one pretended not to mind), to play a clever and serious game (when the cards allowed it) and then to have supper and drink a glass of wine. After a game of bridge, especially if he had won a little (to win a large sum was unpleasant), Ivan Ilych went to bed in specially good humour.

So they lived. They formed a circle of acquaintances among the best people and were visited by people of importance and by young folk. In their views as to their acquaintances, husband, wife and daughter were entirely agreed, and tacitly and unanimously kept at arm's length and shook off the shabby friends and relations who, with much show of affection, gushed into the drawing-room with its Japanese plates on the walls. Soon these shabby friends ceased to obtrude themselves and only the best people remained in the Golovins' set.

Young men made up to Lisa, and Petrishchev, an examining magistrate and

Dmitri Ivanovich Petrishchev's son and sole heir, began to be so attentive to her that Ivan Ilych had already spoken to Praskovya Fëdorovna about it, and considered whether they should not arrange a party for them, or get up some private theatricals.

So they lived, and all went well, without change, and life flowed pleasantly.

IV

They were all in good health. It could not be called ill health if Ivan Ilych sometimes said that he had a queer taste in his mouth and felt some discomfort in his left side.

But this discomfort increased and, though not exactly painful, grew into a sense of pressure in his side accompanied by ill humour. And his irritability became worse and worse and began to mar the agreeable, easy, and correct life that had established itself in the Golovin family. Quarrels between husband and wife became more and more frequent, and soon the ease and amenity disappeared and even the decorum was barely maintained. Scenes again became frequent, and very few of those islets remained on which husband and wife could meet without an explosion. Praskovya Fëdorovna now had good reason to say that her husband's temper was trying. With characteristic exaggeration she said he had always had a dreadful temper, and that it had needed all her good nature to put up with it for twenty years. It was true that now the quarrels were started by him. His bursts of temper always came just before dinner, often just as he began to eat his soup. Sometimes he noticed that a plate or dish was chipped, or the food was not right, or his son put his elbow on the table, or his daughter's hair was not done as he liked it, and for all this he blamed Praskovya Fëdorovna. At first she retorted and said disagreeable things to him, but once or twice he fell into such a rage at the beginning of dinner that she realized it was due to some physical derangement brought on by taking food, and so she restrained herself and did not answer, but only hurried to get the dinner over. She regarded this self-restraint as highly praiseworthy. Having come to the conclusion that her husband had a dreadful temper and made her life miserable, she began to feel sorry for herself, and the more she pitied herself the more she hated her husband. She began to wish he would die; yet she did not want him to die because then his salary would cease. And this irritated her against him still more. She considered herself dreadfully unhappy just because not even his death could save her, and though she concealed her exasperation, that hidden exasperation of hers increased his irritation also.

After one scene in which Ivan Ilych had been particularly unfair and after which he had said in explanation that he certainly was irritable but that it was due to his not being well, she said that if he was ill it should be attended to, and insisted on his going to see a celebrated doctor.

He went. Everything took place as he had expected and as it always does. There was the usual waiting and the important air assumed by the doctor, with which he was so familiar (resembling that which he himself assumed in court), and the sounding and listening, and the questions which called for answers that were foregone conclusions and were evidently unnecessary, and the look of importance which implied that "if only you put yourself in our hands we will arrange everything—we know indubitably how it has to be done, always in the same way for everybody alike." It was all just as it was in the law courts. The doctor put on just the same air towards him as he himself put on towards an accused person.

The doctor said that so-and-so indicated that there was so-and-so inside the patient, but if the investigation of so-and-so did not confirm this, then he must assume that and that. If he assumed that and that, then . . . and so on. To Ivan Ilych only one question was important: was his case serious or not? But the doctor ignored that inappropriate question. From his point of view it was not the one under consideration, the real question was to decide between a floating kidney, chronic catarrh, or appendicitis. It was not a question of Ivan Ilych's life or death, but one between a floating kidney and appendicitis. And that question the doctor solved brilliantly, as it seemed to Ivan Ilych, in favour of the appendix, with the reservation that should an examination of the urine give fresh indications the matter would be reconsidered. All this was just what Ivan Ilych had himself brilliantly accomplished a thousand times in dealing with men on trial. The doctor summed up just as brilliantly, looking over his spectacles triumphantly and even gaily at the accused. From the doctor's summing up Ivan Ilych concluded that things were bad, but that for the doctor, and perhaps for everybody else, it was a matter of indifference, though for him it was bad. And this conclusion struck him painfully, arousing in him a great feeling of pity for himself and of bitterness towards the doctor's indifference to a matter of such importance.

He said nothing of this, but rose, placed the doctor's fee on the table, and remarked with a sigh: "We sick people probably often put inappropriate questions. But tell me, in general, is this complaint dangerous, or not? . . ."

The doctor looked at him sternly over his spectacles with one eye, as if to say: "Prisoner, if you will not keep to the questions put to you, I shall be obliged to have you removed from the court."

"I have already told you what I consider necessary and proper. The analysis may show something more." And the doctor bowed.

Ivan Ilych went out slowly, seated himself disconsolately in his sledge, and drove home. All the way home he was going over what the doctor had said, trying to translate those complicated, obscure, scientific phrases into plain language and find in them an answer to the question: "Is my condition bad? Is it very bad? Or is there as yet nothing much wrong?" And it seemed to him that the meaning of what the doctor had said was that it was very bad. Everything in the streets seemed depressing. The cabmen, the houses, the passers-by, and the shops, were dismal. His ache, this dull gnawing ache that never ceased for a moment, seemed to have acquired a new and more serious significance from the doctor's dubious remarks. Ivan Ilych now watched it with a new and oppressive feeling.

He reached home and began to tell his wife about it. She listened, but in the middle of his account his daughter came in with her hat on, ready to go out with her mother. She sat down reluctantly to listen to this tedious story, but could not stand it long, and her mother too did not hear him to the end.

"Well, I am very glad," she said. "Mind now to take your medicine regularly. Give me the prescription and I'll send Gerasim to the chemist's." And she went to get ready to go out.

While she was in the room Ivan Ilych had hardly taken time to breathe, but he sighed deeply when she left it.

"Well," he thought, "perhaps it isn't so bad after all."

He began taking his medicine and following the doctor's directions, which had been altered after the examination of the urine. But then it happened that there was a contradiction between the indications drawn from the examination of the urine and the symptoms that showed themselves. It turned out that what was happening differed from what the doctor had told him, and that he had either forgotten, or blundered, or hidden something from him. He could not, however, be blamed for that, and Ivan Ilych still obeyed his orders implicitly and at first derived some comfort from doing so.

From the time of his visit to the doctor, Ivan Ilych's chief occupation was the exact fulfilment of the doctor's instructions regarding hygiene and the taking of medicine, and the observation of his pain and his excretions. His chief interests came to be people's ailments and people's health. When sickness, deaths, or recoveries were mentioned in his presence, especially when the illness resembled his own, he listened with agitation which he tried to hide, asked questions, and applied what he heard to his own case.

The pain did not grow less, but Ivan Ilych made efforts to force himself to think that he was better. And he could do this so long as nothing agitated him. But as soon as he had any unpleasantness with his wife, any lack of success in his official work, or held bad cards at bridge, he was at once acutely sensible of his disease. He had formerly borne such mischances, hoping soon to adjust what was wrong, to master it and attain success, or make a grand slam. But now every mischance upset him and plunged him into despair. He would say to himself: "There now, just as I was beginning to get better and the medicine had begun to take effect, comes this accursed misfortune, or unpleasantness. . . ." And he was furious with the mishap, or with the people who were causing the unpleasantness and killing him, for he felt that this fury was killing him but could not restrain it. One would have thought that it should have been clear to him that this exasperation with circumstances and people aggravated his illness, and that he ought therefore to ignore unpleasant occurrences. But he drew the very opposite conclusion: he said that he needed peace, and he watched for everything that might disturb it and became irritable at the slightest infringement of it. His condition was rendered worse by the fact that he read medical books and consulted doctors. The progress of his disease was so gradual that he could deceive himself when comparing one day with another—the difference was so slight. But when he consulted the doctors it seemed to him that he was getting worse, and even very rapidly. Yet despite this he was continually consulting them.

That month he went to see another celebrity, who told him almost the same as the first had done but put his questions rather differently, and the interview with this celebrity only increased Ivan Ilych's doubts and fears. A friend of a friend of his, a very good doctor, diagnosed his illness again quite differently from the others, and though he predicted recovery, his questions and suppositions bewildered Ivan Ilych still more and increased his doubts. A homoeopathist diagnosed the disease in yet another way, and prescribed medicine which Ivan Ilych took secretly for a week. But after a week, not feeling any improvement and having lost confidence both in the former doctor's treatment and in this one's, he became still more despondent. One day a lady acquaintance mentioned a cure effected by a wonder-working icon. Ivan Ilych caught himself listening attentively and beginning to believe that it had occurred. This incident alarmed him. "Has my mind really weakened to such an extent?" he asked himself. "Nonsense! It's all rubbish. I mustn't give way to nervous fears but having chosen a doctor must keep strictly to his treatment. That is what I will do. Now it's all settled. I won't think about it, but will follow the treatment seriously till summer, and then we shall see. From now there must be no more of this wavering!" This was easy to say but impossible to carry out. The pain in his side oppressed him and seemed to grow worse and more incessant, while the taste in his mouth grew stranger and stranger. It seemed to him that his breath had a disgusting smell, and he was conscious of a loss of appetite and strength. There was no deceiving himself: something terrible, new, and more important than anything before in his life, was taking place within him of which he alone was aware. Those about him did not understand or would not understand it, but thought everything in the world was going on as usual. That tormented Ivan Ilych more than anything. He saw that his household, especially his wife and daughter who were in a perfect whirl of visiting, did not understand anything of it and were annoyed that he was so depressed and so exacting, as if he were to blame for it. Though they tried to disguise it he saw that he was an obstacle in their path, and that his wife had adopted a definite line in regard to his illness and kept to it regardless of anything he said or did. Her attitude was this: "You know," she would say to her friends, "Ivan Ilych can't do as other people do, and keep to the treatment prescribed for him. One day he'll take his drops and keep strictly to his diet and go to bed in good time, but the next day unless I watch him he'll suddenly forget his medicine, eat sturgeon—which is forbidden—and sit up playing cards till one o'clock in the morning."

"Oh, come, when was that?" Ivan Ilych would ask in vexation. "Only once at Peter Ivanovich's."

"And yesterday with Shebek."

"Well, even if I hadn't stayed up, this pain would have kept me awake."

"Be that as it may you'll never get well like that, but will always make us wretched."

Praskovya Fëdorovna's attitude to Ivan Ilych's illness, as she expressed it both to others and to him, was that it was his own fault and was another of the annoyances he caused her. Ivan Ilych felt that this opinion escaped her involuntarily—but that did not make it easier for him.

At the law courts too, Ivan Ilych noticed, or thought he noticed, a strange attitude towards himself. It sometimes seemed to him that people were watching him inquisitively as a man whose place might soon be vacant. Then again, his friends would suddenly begin to chaff him in a friendly way about his low spirits, as if the awful, horrible, and unheard-of thing that was going on within him, incessantly gnawing at him and irresistibly drawing him away, was a very agreeable subject for jests. Schwartz in particular irritated him by his jocularity, vivacity, and *savoir-faire,* which reminded him of what he himself had been ten years ago.

Friends came to make up a set and they sat down to cards. They dealt, bending the new cards to soften them, and he sorted the diamonds in his hand and found he had seven. His partner said "No trumps" and supported him with two diamonds. What more could be wished for? It ought to be jolly and lively. They would make a grand slam. But suddenly Ivan Ilych was conscious of that gnawing pain, that taste in his mouth, and it seemed ridiculous that in such circumstances he should be pleased to make a grand slam.

He looked at his partner Mikhail Mikhaylovich, who rapped the table with his strong hand and instead of snatching up the tricks pushed the cards courteously and indulgently towards Ivan Ilych that he might have the pleasure of gathering them up without the trouble of stretching out his hand for them. "Does he think I am too weak to stretch out my arm?" thought Ivan Ilych, and forgetting what he was doing he over-trumped his partner, missing the grand slam by three tricks. And what was most awful of all was that he saw how upset Mikhail Mikhaylovich was about it but did not himself care. And it was dreadful to realize why he did not care.

They all saw that he was suffering, and said: "We can stop if you are tired. Take a rest." Lie down? No, he was not at all tired, and he finished the rubber. All were gloomy and silent. Ivan Ilych felt that he had diffused this gloom over them and could not dispel it. They had supper and went away, and Ivan Ilych was left alone with the consciousness that his life was poisoned and was poisoning the lives of others, and that this poison did not weaken but penetrated more and more deeply into his whole being.

With this consciousness, and with physical pain besides that terror, he must go to bed, often to lie awake the greater part of the night. Next morning he had to get up again, dress, go to the law courts, speak, and write; or if he did not go out, spend at home those twenty-four hours a day each of which was a torture. And he had to live thus all alone on the brink of an abyss, with no one who understood or pitied him.

V

So one month passed and then another. Just before the New Year his brother-in-law came to town and stayed at their house. Ivan Ilych was at the law courts and Praskovya Fëdorovna had gone shopping. When Ivan Ilych came home and entered his study he found his brother-in-law there—a healthy, florid man—unpacking his portmanteau himself. He raised his head on hearing Ivan Ilych's footsteps and looked up at him for a moment without a word. That stare told Ivan Ilych everything. His brother-in-law opened his mouth to utter an exclamation of surprise but checked himself, and that action confirmed it all.

"I have changed, eh?"

"Yes, there is a change."

And after that, try as he would to get his brother-in-law to return to the subject of his looks, the latter would say nothing about it. Praskovya Fëdorovna came home and her brother went out to her. Ivan Ilych locked the door and began to examine himself in the glass, first full face, then in profile. He took up a portrait of himself taken with his wife, and compared it with what he saw in the glass. The change in him was immense. Then he bared his arms to the elbow, looked at them, drew the sleeves down again, sat down on an ottoman, and grew blacker than night.

"No, no, this won't do!" he said to himself, and jumped up, went to the table, took up some law papers and began to read them, but could not continue. He unlocked the door and went into the reception-room. The door leading to the drawing-room was shut. He approached it on tiptoe and listened.

"No, you are exaggerating!" Praskovya Fëdorovna was saying.

"Exaggerating! Don't you see it? Why, he's a dead man! Look at his eyes—there's no light in them. But what is it that is wrong with him?"

"No one knows. Nikolaevich [that was another doctor] said something, but I don't know what. And Leshchetitsky [this was the celebrated specialist] said quite the contrary . . ."

Ivan Ilych walked away, went to his own room, lay down, and began musing: "The kidney, a floating kidney." He recalled all the doctors had told him of how it detached itself and swayed about. And by an effort of imagination he tried to catch that kidney and arrest it and support it. So little was needed for this, it seemed to him. "No, I'll go to see Peter Ivanovich again." [That was the friend whose friend was a doctor.] He rang, ordered the carriage, and got ready to go.

"Where are you going, Jean?"[10] asked his wife, with a specially sad and exceptionally kind look.

This exceptionally kind look irritated him. He looked morosely at her.

"I must go to see Peter Ivanovich."

He went to see Peter Ivanovich, and together they went to see his friend, the doctor. He was in, and Ivan Ilych had a long talk with him.

Reviewing the anatomical and physiological details of what in the doctor's opinion was going on inside him, he understood it all.

There was something, a small thing, in the vermiform appendix. It might all come right. Only stimulate the energy of one organ and check the activity of another, then absorption would take place and everything would come right. He got home rather late for dinner, ate his dinner, conversed cheerfully, but could not for a long time bring himself to go back to work in his room. At last, however, he went to his study and did what was necessary, but the consciousness that he had put something aside—an important, intimate matter which he would revert to when his work was done—never left him. When he had finished his work he remembered that this intimate matter was the thought of his vermiform appendix. But he did not give himself up to it, and went to the drawing-room for tea. There were callers there, including the examining magistrate who was a desirable match for his daughter, and they were conversing, playing the piano, and singing. Ivan Ilych, as Praskovya Fëdorovna remarked, spent that evening more cheerfully than usual, but he never for a moment forgot that he had postponed the important matter of the appendix. At eleven o'clock he said good-night and went to his bedroom. Since his illness he had slept alone in a small room next to his study. He undressed and took up a novel by Zola, but instead of reading it fell into thought, and in his imagination that desired im-

[10] Praskovya Fëdorovna addresses her husband familiarly not by his Russian name but by its French equivalent.

provement in the vermiform appendix occurred. There was the absorption and evacuation and the re-establishment of normal activity. "Yes, that's it!" he said to himself. "One need only assist nature, that's all." He remembered his medicine, rose, took it, and lay down on his back watching for the beneficent action of the medicine and for it to lessen the pain. "I need only take it regularly and avoid all injurious influences. I am already feeling better, much better." He began touching his side: it was not painful to the touch. "There, I really don't feel it. It's much better already." He put out the light and turned on his side. . . . "The appendix is getting better, absorption is occurring." Suddenly he felt the old, familiar, dull, gnawing pain, stubborn and serious. There was the same familiar loathsome taste in his mouth. His heart sank and he felt dazed. "My God! My God!" he muttered. "Again, again! and it will never cease." And suddenly the matter presented itself in a quite different aspect. "Vermiform appendix! Kidney!" he said to himself. "It's not a question of appendix or kidney, but of life and . . . death. Yes, life was there and now it is going, going and I cannot stop it. Yes. Why deceive myself? Isn't it obvious to everyone but me that I'm dying, and that it's only a question of weeks, days . . . it may happen this moment. There was light and now there is darkness. I was here and now I'm going there! Where?" A chill came over him, his breathing ceased, and he felt only the throbbing of his heart.

"When I am not, what will there be? There will be nothing. Then where shall I be when I am no more? Can this be dying? No, I don't want to!" He jumped up and tried to light the candle, felt for it with trembling hands, dropped candle and candlestick on the floor, and fell back on his pillow.

"What's the use? It makes no difference," he said to himself, staring with wide-open eyes into the darkness. "Death. Yes, death. And none of them know or wish to know it, and they have no pity for me. Now they are playing." (He heard through the door the distant sound of a song and its accompaniment.) "It's all the same to them, but they will die too! Fools! I first, and they later, but it will be the same for them. And now they are merry . . . the beasts!"

Anger choked him and he was agonizingly, unbearably, miserable. "It is impossible that all men have been doomed to suffer this awful horror!" He raised himself.

"Something must be wrong. I must calm myself—must think it all over from the beginning." And he again began thinking. "Yes, the beginning of my illness: I knocked my side, but I was quite well that day and the next. It hurt a little, then rather more. I saw the doctor, then followed despondency and anguish, more doctors, and I drew nearer to the abyss. My strength grew less and I kept coming nearer and nearer, and now I have wasted away and there is no light in my eyes. I think of the appendix—but this is death! I think of mending the appendix, and all the while here is death! Can it really be death?" Again terror seized him and he gasped for breath. He leant down and began feeling for the matches, pressing with his elbow on the stand beside the bed. It was in the way and hurt him, he grew furious with it, pressed on it still harder, and upset it. Breathless and in despair he fell on his back, expecting death to come immediately.

Meanwhile the visitors were leaving. Praskovya Fëdorovna was seeing them off. She heard something fall and came in.

"What has happened?"

"Nothing. I knocked it over accidentally."

She went out and returned with a candle. He lay there panting heavily, like a man who has run a thousand yards, and stared upwards at her with a fixed look.

"What is it, Jean?"

"No . . . o . . . thing. I upset it." ("Why speak of it? She won't understand," he thought.)

And in truth she did not understand. She picked up the stand, lit his candle, and hurried away to see another visitor off. When she came back he still lay on his back, looking upwards.

"What is it? Do you feel worse?"

"Yes."

She shook her head and sat down.

"Do you know, Jean, I think we must ask Leshchetitsky to come and see you here."

This meant calling in the famous specialist, regardless of expense. He smiled malignantly and said "No." She remained a little longer and then went up to him and kissed his forehead.

While she was kissing him he hated her from the bottom of his soul and with difficulty refrained from pushing her away.

"Good-night. Please God you'll sleep."

"Yes."

VI

Ivan Ilych saw that he was dying, and he was in continual despair.

In the depth of his heart he knew he was dying, but not only was he not accustomed to the thought, he simply did not and could not grasp it.

The syllogism he had learnt from Kiezewetter's Logic: "Caius is a man, men are mortal, therefore Caius is mortal," had always seemed to him correct as applied to Caius, but certainly not as applied to himself. That Caius—man in the abstract—was mortal, was perfectly correct, but he was not Caius, not an abstract man, but a creature quite, quite separate from all others. He had been little Vanya, with a mamma and a papa, with Mitya and Volodya, with the toys, a coachman and a nurse, afterwards with Katenka and with all the joys, griefs, and delights of childhood, boyhood, and youth. What did Caius know of the smell of that striped leather ball Vanya had been so fond of? Had Caius kissed his mother's hand like that, and did the silk of her dress rustle so for Caius? Had he rioted like that at school when the pastry was bad? Had Caius been in love like that? Could Caius preside at a session as he did? "Caius really was mortal, and it was right for him to die; but for me, little Vanya, Ivan Ilych, with all my thoughts and emotions, it's altogether a different matter. It cannot be that I ought to die. That would be too terrible."

Such was his feeling.

"If I had to die like Caius, I should have known it was so. An inner voice would have told me so, but there was nothing of the sort in me and I and all my friends felt that our case was quite different from that of Caius. And now here it is!" he said to himself. "It can't be. It's impossible! But here it is. How is this? How is one to understand it?"

He could not understand it, and tried to drive this false, incorrect, morbid thought away and to replace it by other proper and healthy thoughts. But that thought, and not the thought only but the reality itself, seemed to come and confront him.

And to replace that thought he called up a succession of others, hoping to find in them some support. He tried to get back into the former current of thoughts that had once screened the thought of death from him. But strange to say, all that had formerly shut off, hidden, and destroyed, his consciousness of death, no longer had that effect. Ivan Ilych now spent most of his time in attempting to re-establish that old current. He would say to himself: "I will take up my duties again—after all I used to live by them." And banishing all doubts he would go to the law courts, enter into conversation with his colleagues, and sit carelessly as was his wont, scanning the crowd with a thoughtful look and leaning both his emaciated arms on the arms of his oak chair; bending over as usual to a colleague and drawing his papers nearer he would interchange whispers with him, and then suddenly raising his eyes and sitting erect would pronounce certain words and open the proceedings. But suddenly in the midst of those proceedings the pain in his side, regardless of the stage the proceedings had reached, would begin its own gnawing work. Ivan Ilych would turn his attention to it and try to drive the thought of it away, but without success. *It* would come and stand before him and look at him, and he would be petrified and the light would die out of his eyes, and he would again begin asking himself whether *It* alone was true. And his colleagues and subordinates would see with surprise and distress that he, the brilliant and subtle judge, was becoming confused and making mistakes. He would shake himself, try to pull himself together, manage somehow to bring the sitting to a close, and return home with the sorrowful consciousness that his judicial labours could not as formerly hide from him what he wanted them to hide, and could not deliver him from *It*. And what was worst of all was that *It* drew his attention to itself not in order to make him take some action but only that he should look at *It*, look it straight in the face: look at it and without doing anything, suffer inexpressibly.

And to save himself from this condition Ivan Ilych looked for consolations —new screens—and new screens were found and for a while seemed to save him, but then they immediately fell to pieces or rather became transparent, as if *It* penetrated them and nothing could veil *It*.

In these latter days he would go into the drawing-room he had arranged— that drawing-room where he had fallen and for the sake of which (how bitterly ridiculous it seemed) he had sacrificed his life—for he knew that his illness originated with that knock. He would enter and see that something had scratched the polished table. He would look for the cause of this and find that it was the bronze ornamentation of an album, that had got bent. He would take up the expensive album which he had lovingly arranged, and feel vexed with his daughter and her friends for their untidiness—for the album was torn here and there and some of the photographs turned upside down. He would put it carefully in order and bend the ornamentation back into position. Then it would occur to him to place all those things in another corner of the room, near the plants. He would call the footman, but his daughter or wife would come to help him. They would not agree, and his wife would contradict him, and he would dispute and grow angry. But that was all right, for then he did not think about *It. It* was invisible.

But then, when he was moving something himself, his wife would say: "Let the servants do it. You will hurt yourself again." And suddenly *It* would flash through the screen and he would see it. It was just a flash, and he hoped it would disappear, but he would involuntarily pay attention to his side. "It sits there as before, gnawing just the same!" And he could no longer forget *It*, but could distinctly see it looking at him from behind the flowers. "What is it all for?"

"It really is so! I lost my life over that curtain as I might have done when storming a fort. Is that possible? How terrible and how stupid. It can't be true! It can't, but it is."

He would go to his study, lie down, and again be alone with *It*: face to face with *It*. And nothing could be done with *It* except to look at it and shudder.

VII

How it happened it is impossible to say because it came about step by step, unnoticed, but in the third month of Ivan Ilych's illness, his wife, his daughter, his son, his acquaintances, the doctors, the servants, and above all he himself, were aware that the whole interest he had for other people was whether he would soon vacate his place, and at last release the living from the discomfort caused by his presence and be himself released from his sufferings.

He slept less and less. He was given opium and hypodermic injections of morphine, but this did not relieve him. The dull depression he experienced in a somnolent condition at first gave him a little relief, but only as something new, afterwards it became as distressing as the pain itself or even more so.

Special foods were prepared for him by the doctors' orders, but all those foods became increasingly distasteful and disgusting to him.

For his excretions also special arrangements had to be made, and this was a torment to him every time—a torment from the uncleanliness, the unseemliness, and the smell, and from knowing that another person had to take part in it.

But just through this most unpleasant matter, Ivan Ilych obtained comfort. Gerasim, the butler's young assistant, always came in to carry the things out. Gerasim was a clean, fresh peasant lad, grown stout on town food and always cheerful and bright. At first the sight of him, in his clean Russian peasant costume, engaged in that disgusting task embarrassed Ivan Ilych.

Once when he got up from the commode too weak to draw up his trousers, he dropped into a soft armchair and looked with horror at his bare, enfeebled thighs with the muscles so sharply marked on them.

Gerasim with a firm light tread, his heavy boots emitting a pleasant smell of tar and fresh winter air, came in wearing a clean Hessian apron, the sleeves of his print shirt tucked up over his strong bare young arms; and refraining from looking at his sick master out of consideration for his feelings, and restraining the joy of life that beamed from his face, he went up to the commode.

"Gerasim!" said Ivan Ilych in a weak voice.

Gerasim started, evidently afraid he might have committed some blunder, and with a rapid movement turned his fresh, kind, simple young face which just showed the first downy signs of a beard.

"Yes, sir?"

"That must be very unpleasant for you. You must forgive me. I am help-less."

"Oh, why, sir," and Gerasim's eyes beamed and he showed his glistening white teeth, "what's a little trouble? It's a case of illness with you, sir."

And his deft strong hands did their accustomed task, and he went out of the room stepping lightly. Five minutes later he as lightly returned.

Ivan Ilych was still sitting in the same position in the armchair.

"Gerasim," he said when the latter had replaced the freshly-washed utensil. "Please come here and help me." Gerasim went up to him. "Lift me up. It is hard for me to get up, and I have sent Dmitri away."

Gerasim went up to him, grasped his master with his strong arms deftly but gently, in the same way that he stepped—lifted him, supported him with one hand, and with the other drew up his trousers and would have set him down again, but Ivan Ilych asked to be led to the sofa. Gerasim, without an effort and without apparent pressure, led him, almost lifting him, to the sofa and placed him on it.

"Thank you. How easily and well you do it all!"

Gerasim smiled again and turned to leave the room. But Ivan Ilych felt his presence such a comfort that he did not want to let him go.

"One thing more, please move up that chair. No, the other one—under my feet. It is easier for me when my feet are raised."

Gerasim brought the chair, set it down gently in place, and raised Ivan Ilych's legs on to it. It seemed to Ivan Ilych that he felt better while Gerasim was holding up his legs.

"It's better when my legs are higher," he said. "Place that cushion under them."

Gerasim did so. He again lifted the legs and placed them, and again Ivan Ilych felt better while Gerasim held his legs. When he set them down Ivan Ilych fancied he felt worse.

"Gerasim," he said. "Are you busy now?"

"Not at all, sir," said Gerasim, who had learnt from the townfolk how to speak to gentlefolk.

"What have you still to do?"

"What have I to do? I've done everything except chopping the logs for tomorrow."

"Then hold my legs up a bit higher, can you?"

"Of course I can. Why not?" And Gerasim raised his master's legs higher and Ivan Ilych thought that in that position he did not feel any pain at all.

"And how about the logs?"

"Don't trouble about that, sir. There's plenty of time."

Ivan Ilych told Gerasim to sit down and hold his legs, and began to talk to him. And strange to say it seemed to him that he felt better while Gerasim held his legs up.

After that Ivan Ilych would sometimes call Gerasim and get him to hold his legs on his shoulders, and he liked talking to him. Gerasim did it all easily, willingly, simply, and with a good nature that touched Ivan Ilych. Health, strength, and vitality in other people were offensive to him, but Gerasim's strength and vitality did not mortify but soothed him.

What tormented Ivan Ilych most was the deception, the lie, which for some reason they all accepted, that he was not dying but was simply ill, and that he only need keep quiet and undergo a treatment and then something very good would result. He however knew that do what they would nothing would come of it, only still more agonizing suffering and death. This deception tortured him—their not wishing to admit what they all knew and what he knew, but wanting to lie to him concerning his terrible condition, and wishing and forcing him to participate in that lie. Those lies—lies enacted over him on the eve of his death and destined to degrade this awful, solemn act to the level of their visitings, their curtains, their sturgeon for dinner—were a terrible agony for Ivan Ilych. And strangely enough, many times when they were going through their antics over him he had been within a hairbreadth of calling out to them: "Stop lying! You know and I know that I am dying. Then at least stop lying about it!" But he had never had the spirit to do it. The awful, terrible act of his dying was, he could see, reduced by those about him to the level of a casual, unpleasant, and almost indecorous incident (as if someone entered a drawing-room diffusing an unpleasant odour) and this was done by that very decorum which he had served all his life long. He saw that no one felt for him, because no one even wished to grasp his position. Only Gerasim recognized it and pitied him. And so Ivan Ilych felt at ease only with him. He felt comforted when Gerasim supported his legs (sometimes all night long) and refused to go to bed, saying: "Don't you worry, Ivan Ilych. I'll get sleep enough later on," or when he suddenly became familiar and exclaimed: "If you weren't sick it would be another matter, but as it is, why should I grudge a little trouble?" Gerasim alone did not lie; everything showed that he alone understood the facts of the case and did not consider it necessary to disguise them, but simply felt sorry for his emaciated and enfeebled master. Once when Ivan Ilych was sending him away he even said straight out: "We shall all of us die, so why should I grudge a little trouble?"—expressing the fact that he did not think his work burdensome, because he was doing it for a dying man and hoped someone would do the same for him when his time came.

Apart from this lying, or because of it, what most tormented Ivan Ilych was that no one pitied him as he wished to be pitied. At certain moments after prolonged suffering he wished most of all (though he would have been ashamed to confess it) for someone to pity him as a sick child is pitied. He longed to be petted and comforted. He knew he was an important functionary, that he had a beard turning grey, and that therefore what he longed for was impossible, but still he longed for it. And in Gerasim's attitude towards him there was something akin to what he wished for, and so that attitude comforted him. Ivan Ilych wanted to weep, wanted to be petted and cried over, and then his colleague Shebek would come, and instead of weeping and being petted,

Ivan Ilych would assume a serious, severe, and profound air, and by force of habit would express his opinion on a decision of the Court of Cassation and would stubbornly insist on that view. This falsity around him and within him did more than anything else to poison his last days.

VIII

It was morning. He knew it was morning because Gerasim had gone, and Peter the footman had come and put out the candles, drawn back one of the curtains, and begun quietly to tidy up. Whether it was morning or evening, Friday or Sunday, made no difference, it was all just the same: the gnawing, unmitigated, agonizing pain, never ceasing for an instant, the consciousness of life inexorably waning but not yet extinguished, the approach of that ever dreaded and hateful Death which was the only reality, and always the same falsity. What were days, weeks, hours, in such a case?

"Will you have some tea, sir?"

"He wants things to be regular, and wishes the gentlefolk to drink tea in the morning," thought Ivan Ilych, and only said "No."

"Wouldn't you like to move onto the sofa, sir?"

"He wants to tidy up the room, and I'm in the way. I am uncleanliness and disorder," he thought, and said only:

"No, leave me alone."

The man went on bustling about. Ivan Ilych stretched out his hand. Peter came up, ready to help.

"What is it, sir?"

"My watch."

Peter took the watch which was close at hand and gave it to his master.

"Half-past eight. Are they up?"

"No, sir, except Vladimir Ivanich" (the son) "who has gone to school. Praskovya Fëdorovna ordered me to wake her if you asked for her. Shall I do so?"

"No, there's no need to." "Perhaps I'd better have some tea," he thought, and added aloud: "Yes, bring me some tea."

Peter went to the door, but Ivan Ilych dreaded being left alone. "How can I keep him here? Oh yes, my medicine." "Peter, give me my medicine." "Why not? Perhaps it may still do me some good." He took a spoonful and swallowed it. "No, it won't help. It's all tomfoolery, all deception," he decided as soon as he became aware of the familiar, sickly, hopeless taste. "No, I can't believe in it any longer. But the pain, why this pain? If it would only cease just for a moment!" And he moaned. Peter turned towards him. "It's all right. Go and fetch me some tea."

Peter went out. Left alone Ivan Ilych groaned not so much with pain, terrible though that was, as from mental anguish. Always and for ever the same, always these endless days and nights. If only it would come quicker! If only *what* would come quicker? Death, darkness? . . . No, no! Anything rather than death!

When Peter returned with the tea on a tray, Ivan Ilych stared at him for a time in perplexity, not realizing who and what he was. Peter was disconcerted by that look and his embarrassment brought Ivan Ilych to himself.

"Oh, tea! All right, put it down. Only help me to wash and put on a clean shirt."

And Ivan Ilych began to wash. With pauses for rest, he washed his hands and then his face, cleaned his teeth, brushed his hair, and looked in the glass. He was terrified by what he saw, especially by the limp way in which his hair clung to his pallid forehead.

While his shirt was being changed he knew that he would be still more frightened at the sight of his body, so he avoided looking at it. Finally he was ready. He drew on a dressing-gown, wrapped himself in a plaid, and sat down in the armchair to take his tea. For a moment he felt refreshed, but as soon as he began to drink the tea he was again aware of the same taste, and the pain also returned. He finished it with an effort, and then lay down stretching out his legs, and dismissed Peter.

Always the same. Now a spark of hope flashes up, then a sea of despair rages, and always pain; always pain, always despair, and always the same. When alone he had a dreadful and distressing desire to call someone, but he knew beforehand that with others present it would be still worse. "Another dose of morphine—to lose consciousness. I will tell him, the doctor, that he must think of something else. It's impossible, impossible, to go on like this."

An hour and another pass like that. But now there is a ring at the door bell. Perhaps it's the doctor? It is. He comes in fresh, hearty, plump, and cheerful, with that look on his face that seems to say: "There now, you're in a panic about something, but we'll arrange it all for you directly!" The doctor knows this expression is out of place here, but he has put it on once for all and can't take it off—like a man who has put on a frock-coat in the morning to pay a round of calls.

The doctor rubs his hands vigorously and reassuringly.

"Brr! How cold it is! There's such a sharp frost; just let me warm myself!" he says, as if it were only a matter of waiting till he was warm, and then he would put everything right.

"Well now, how are you?"

Ivan Ilych feels that the doctor would like to say: "Well, how are your affairs?" but that even he feels that this would not do, and says instead: "What sort of a night have you had?"

Ivan Ilych looks at him as much as to say: "Are you really never ashamed of lying?" But the doctor does not wish to understand this question, and Ivan Ilych says: "Just as terrible as ever. The pain never leaves me and never subsides. If only something . . ."

"Yes, you sick people are always like that. . . . There, now I think I am warm enough. Even Praskovya Fëdorovna, who is so particular, could find no fault with my temperature. Well, now I can say good-morning," and the doctor presses his patient's hand.

Then, dropping his former playfulness, he begins with a most serious face to examine the patient, feeling his pulse and taking his temperature, and then begins the sounding and auscultation.

Ivan Ilych knows quite well and definitely that all this is nonsense and pure deception, but when the doctor, getting down on his knee, leans over him, putting the ear first higher than lower, and performs various gymnastic movements over him with a significant expression on his face, Ivan Ilych submits to it all as he used to submit to the speeches of the lawyers, though he knew very well that they were all lying and why they were lying.

The doctor, kneeling on the sofa, is still sounding him when Praskovya Fëdorovna's silk dress rustles at the door and she is heard scolding Peter for not having let her know of the doctor's arrival.

She comes in, kisses her husband, and at once proceeds to prove that she has been up a long time already, and only owing to a misunderstanding failed to be there when the doctor arrived.

Ivan Ilych looks at her, scans her all over, sets against her the whiteness and plumpness and cleanness of her hands and neck, the gloss of her hair, and the sparkle of her vivacious eyes. He hates her with his whole soul. And the thrill of hatred he feels for her makes him suffer from her touch.

Her attitude towards him and his disease is still the same. Just as the doctor had adopted a certain relation to his patient which he could not abandon, so had she formed one towards him—that he was not doing something he ought to do and was himself to blame, and that she reproached him lovingly for this —and she could not now change that attitude.

"You see he doesn't listen to me and doesn't take his medicine at the proper time. And above all he lies in a position that is no doubt bad for him—with his legs up."

She described how he made Gerasim hold his legs up.

The doctor smiled with a contemptuous affability that said: "What's to be done? These sick people do have foolish fancies of that kind, but we must forgive them."

When the examination was over the doctor looked at his watch, and then Praskovya Fëdorovna announced to Ivan Ilych that it was of course as he pleased, but she had sent today for a celebrated specialist who would examine him and have a consultation with Michael Danilovich (their regular doctor).

"Please don't raise any objections. I am doing this for my own sake," she said ironically, letting it be felt that she was doing it all for his sake and only said this to leave him no right to refuse. He remained silent, knitting his brows. He felt that he was so surrounded and involved in a mesh of falsity that it was hard to unravel anything.

Everything she did for him was entirely for her own sake, and she told him she was doing for herself what she actually was doing for herself, as if that was so incredible that he must understand the opposite.

At half-past eleven the celebrated specialist arrived. Again the sounding began and the significant conversations in his presence and in another room, about the kidneys and the appendix, and the questions and answers, with such an air of importance that again, instead of the real question of life and death which now alone confronted him, the question arose of the kidney and appendix which were not behaving as they ought to and would now be attacked by Michael Danilovich and the specialist and forced to mend their ways.

The celebrated specialist took leave of him with a serious though not hopeless look, and in reply to the timid question Ivan Ilych, with eyes glistening with fear and hope, put to him as to whether there was a chance of recovery, said that he could not vouch for it but there was a possibility. The look of hope with which Ivan Ilych watched the doctor out was so pathetic that Praskovya

Fëdorovna, seeing it, even wept as she left the room to hand the doctor his fee.

The gleam of hope kindled by the doctor's encouragement did not last long. The same room, the same pictures, curtains, wall-paper, medicine bottles, were all there, and the same aching suffering body, and Ivan Ilych began to moan. They gave him a subcutaneous injection and he sank into oblivion.

It was twilight when he came to. They brought him his dinner and he swallowed some beef tea with difficulty, and then everything was the same again and night was coming on.

After dinner, at seven o'clock, Praskovya Fëdorovna came into the room in evening dress, her full bosom pushed up by her corset, and with traces of powder on her face. She had reminded him in the morning that they were going to the theatre. Sarah Bernhardt was visiting the town and they had a box, which he had insisted on their taking. Now he had forgotten about it and her toilet offended him, but he concealed his vexation when he remembered that he had himself insisted on their securing a box and going because it would be an instructive and aesthetic pleasure for the children.

Praskovya Fëdorovna came in, self-satisfied but yet with a rather guilty air. She sat down and asked how he was, but, as he saw, only for the sake of asking and not in order to learn about it, knowing that there was nothing to learn—and then went on to what she really wanted to say: that she would not on any account have gone but that the box had been taken and Helen and their daughter were going, as well as Petrishchev (the examining magistrate, their daughter's fiancé) and that it was out of the question to let them go alone; but that she would have much preferred to sit with him for a while; and he must be sure to follow the doctor's orders while she was away.

"Oh, and Fëdor Petrovich" (the fiancé) "would like to come in. May he? And Lisa?"

"All right."

Their daughter came in in full evening dress, her fresh young flesh exposed (making a show of that very flesh which in his own case caused so much suffering), strong, healthy, evidently in love, and impatient with illness, suffering, and death, because they interfered with her happiness.

Fëdor Petrovich came in too, in evening dress, his hair curled *à la Capoul*,[11] a tight stiff collar round his long sinewy neck, an enormous white shirt-front and narrow black trousers tightly stretched over his strong thighs. He had one white glove tightly drawn on, and was holding his opera hat in his hand.

Following him the schoolboy crept in unnoticed, in a new uniform, poor little fellow, and wearing gloves. Terribly dark shadows showed under his eyes, the meaning of which Ivan Ilych knew well.

His son had always seemed pathetic to him, and now it was dreadful to see the boy's frightened look of pity. It seemed to Ivan Ilych that Vasya was the only one besides Gerasim who understood and pitied him.

They all sat down and again asked how he was. A silence followed. Lisa asked her mother about the opera-glasses, and there was an altercation between mother and daughter as to who had taken them and where they had been put. This occasioned some unpleasantness.

Fëdor Petrovich inquired of Ivan Ilych whether he had ever seen Sarah

[11] A rather elaborate men's hair style named after Victor Capoul (1839–1924), a brilliant French singer.

Bernhardt. Ivan Ilych did not at first catch the question, but then replied: "No, have you seen her before?"

"Yes, in *Adrienne Lecouvreur*."[12]

Praskovya Fëdorovna mentioned some rôles in which Sarah Bernhardt was particularly good. Her daughter disagreed. Conversation sprang up as to the elegance and realism of her acting—the sort of conversation that is always repeated and is always the same.

In the midst of the conversation Fëdor Petrovich glanced at Ivan Ilych and became silent. Ivan Ilych was staring with glittering eyes straight before him, evidently indignant with them. This had to be rectified, but it was impossible to do so. The silence had to be broken, but for a time no one dared to break it and they all became afraid that the conventional deception would suddenly become obvious and the truth become plain to all. Lisa was the first to pluck up courage and break that silence, but by trying to hide what everybody was feeling, she betrayed it.

"Well, if we are going it's time to start," she said, looking at her watch, a present from her father, and with a faint and significant smile at Fëdor Petrovich relating to something known only to them. She got up with a rustle of her dress.

They all rose, said good-night, and went away.

When they had gone it seemed to Ivan Ilych that he felt better; the falsity had gone with them. But the pain remained—that same pain and that same fear that made everything monotonously alike, nothing harder and nothing easier. Everything was worse.

Again minute followed minute and hour followed hour. Everything remained the same and there was no cessation. And the inevitable end of it all became more and more terrible.

"Yes, send Gerasim here," he replied to a question Peter asked.

IX

His wife returned late at night. She came in on tiptoe, but he heard her, opened his eyes, and made haste to close them again. She wished to send Gerasim away and to sit with him herself, but he opened his eyes and said: "No, go away."

"Are you in great pain?"

"Always the same."

"Take some opium."

He agreed and took some. She went away.

Till about three in the morning he was in a state of stupefied misery. It seemed to him that he and his pain were being thrust into a narrow, deep black sack, but though they were pushed further and further in they could not be pushed to the bottom. And this, terrible enough in itself, was accompanied by suffering. He struggled but yet co-operated. And suddenly he broke through, fell, and regained consciousness. Gerasim was sitting at the foot of the bed

12 A French tragedy by Scribe and Legouvé (1849) on the death of the celebrated eighteenth-century actress named in the title. The play provided Sarah Bernhardt with one of her most famous parts.

dozing quietly, while he himself lay with his emaciated stockinged legs resting on Gerasim's shoulders; the same shaded candle was there and the same unceasing pain.

"Go away, Gerasim," he whispered.

"It's all right, sir. I'll stay a while."

"No. Go away."

He removed his legs from Gerasim's shoulders, turned sideways onto his arm, and felt sorry for himself. He only waited till Gerasim had gone into the next room and then restrained himself no longer but wept like a child. He wept on account of his helplessness, his terrible loneliness, the cruelty of man, the cruelty of God, and the absence of God.

"Why hast Thou done all this? Why hast Thou brought me here? Why, why dost Thou torment me so terribly?"

He did not expect an answer and yet wept because there was no answer and could be none. The pain again grew more acute, but he did not stir and did not call. He said to himself: "Go on! Strike me! But what is it for? What have I done to Thee? What is it for?"

Then he grew quiet and not only ceased weeping but even held his breath and became all attention. It was as though he were listening not to an audible voice but to the voice of his soul, to the current of thoughts arising within him.

"What is it you want?" was the first clear conception capable of expression in words, that he heard.

"What do you want? What do you want?" he repeated to himself.

"What do I want? To live and not to suffer," he answered.

And again he listened with such concentrated attention that even his pain did not distract him.

"To live? How?" asked his inner voice.

"Why, to live as I used to—well and pleasantly."

"As you lived before, well and pleasantly?" the voice repeated.

And in imagination he began to recall the best moments of his pleasant life. But strange to say none of those best moments of his pleasant life now seemed at all what they had then seemed—none of them except the first recollections of childhood. There, in childhood, there had been something really pleasant with which it would be possible to live if it could return. But the child who had experienced that happiness existed no longer, it was like a reminiscence of somebody else.

As soon as the period began which had produced the present Ivan Ilych, all that had then seemed joys now melted before his sight and turned into something trivial and often nasty.

And the further he departed from childhood and the nearer he came to the present the more worthless and doubtful were the joys. This began with the School of Law. A little that was really good was still found there—there was light-heartedness, friendship, and hope. But in the upper classes there had already been fewer of such good moments. Then during the first years of his official career, when he was in the service of the Governor, some pleasant moments again occurred: they were the memories of love for a woman. Then all became confused and there was still less of what was good; later on again there was still less that was good, and the further he went the less there was. His marriage, a mere accident, then the disenchantment that followed it, his wife's bad breath and the sensuality and hypocrisy: then that deadly official life and those preoccupations about money, a year of it, and two, and ten, and twenty, and always the same thing. And the longer it lasted the more deadly it became. "It is as if I had been going downhill while I imagined I was going up. And that is really what it was. I was going up in public opinion, but to the same extent life was ebbing away from me. And now it is all done and there is only death."

"Then what does it mean? Why? It can't be that life is so senseless and horrible. But if it really has been so horrible and senseless, why must I die and die in agony? There is something wrong!"

"Maybe I did not live as I ought to have done," it suddenly occurred to him. "But how could that be, when I did everything properly?" he replied, and immediately dismissed from his mind this, the sole solution of all the riddles of life and death, as something quite impossible.

"Then what do you want now? To live? Live how? Live as you lived in the law courts when the usher proclaimed 'The judge is coming!' The judge is coming, the judge!" he repeated to himself. "Here he is, the judge. But I am not guilty!" he exclaimed angrily. "What is it for?" And he ceased crying, but turning his face to the wall continued to ponder on the same question: Why, and for what purpose, is there all this horror? But however much he pondered he found no answer. And whenever the thought occurred to him, as it often did, that it all resulted from his not having lived as he ought to have done, he at once recalled the correctness of his whole life and dismissed so strange an idea.

X

Another fortnight passed. Ivan Ilych now no longer left his sofa. He would not lie in bed but lay on the sofa, facing the wall nearly all the time. He suffered ever the same unceasing agonies and in his loneliness pondered always on the same insoluble question: "What is this? Can it be that it is Death?" And the inner voice answered: "Yes, it is Death."

"Why these sufferings?" And the voice answered, "For no reason—they just are so." Beyond and besides this there was nothing.

From the very beginning of his illness, ever since he had first been to see the doctor, Ivan Ilych's life had been divided between two contrary and alternating moods: now it was despair and the expectation of this uncomprehended and terrible death, and now hope and an intently interested observation of the functioning of his organs. Now before his eyes there was only a kidney or an intestine that temporarily evaded its duty, and now only that incomprehensible and dreadful death from which it was impossible to escape.

These two states of mind had alternated from the very beginning of his illness, but the further it progressed the more doubtful and fantastic became the conception of the kidney, and the more real the sense of impending death.

He had but to call to mind what he had been three months before and what he was now, to call to mind with what regularity he had been going downhill, for every possibility of hope to be shattered.

Latterly during that loneliness in which he found himself as he lay facing the back of the sofa, a loneliness in the midst of a populous town and surrounded by numerous acquaintances and relations but that yet could not have been more complete anywhere—either at the bottom of the sea or under the earth—during that terrible loneliness Ivan Ilych had lived only in memories of the past. Pictures of his past rose before him one after another. They always began with what was nearest in time and then went back to what was the most remote—to his childhood—and rested there. If he thought of the stewed prunes that had been offered him that day, his mind went back to the raw shrivelled French plums of his childhood, their peculiar flavour and the flow of saliva when he sucked their stones, and along with the memory of that taste came a whole series of memories of those days: his nurse, his brother, and their toys. "No, I mustn't think of that. . . . It is too painful," Ivan Ilych said to himself, and brought himself back to the present—to the button on the back of the sofa and the creases in its morocco. "Morocco is expensive, but it does not wear well: there had been a quarrel about it. It was a different kind of quarrel and a different kind of morocco that time when we tore father's portfolio and were punished, and Mamma brought us some tarts. . . . " And again his thoughts dwelt on his childhood, and again it was painful and he tried to banish them and fix his mind on something else.

Then again together with that chain of memories another series passed through his mind—of how his illness had progressed and grown worse. There also the further back he looked the more life there had been. There had been more of what was good in life and more of life itself. The two merged together. "Just as the pain went on getting worse and worse, so my life grew worse and worse," he thought. "There is one bright spot there at the back, at the beginning of life, and afterwards all becomes blacker and blacker and proceeds more and more rapidly—in inverse ratio to the square of the distance from death," thought Ivan Ilych. And the example of a stone falling downwards with increasing velocity entered his mind. Life, a series of increasing sufferings, flies further and further towards its end—the most terrible suffering. "I am flying. . . ." He shuddered, shifted himself, and tried to resist, but was already aware that resistance was impossible, and again with eyes weary of gazing but unable to cease seeing what was before them, he stared at the back of the sofa and waited —awaiting that dreadful fall and shock and destruction.

"Resistance is impossible!" he said to himself. "If I could only understand what it is all for! But that too is impossible. An explanation would be possible if it could be said that I have not lived as I ought to. But it is impossible to say that," and he remembered all the legality, correctitude, and propriety of his life. "That at any rate can certainly not be admitted," he thought, and his lips smiled ironically as if someone could see that smile and be taken in by it. "There is no explanation! Agony, death . . . What for?"

XI

Another two weeks went by in this way and during that fortnight an event occurred that Ivan Ilych and his wife had desired. Petrishchev formally proposed. It happened in the evening. The next day Praskovya Fëdorovna came into her husband's room considering how best to inform him of it, but that very night there had been a fresh change for the worse in his condition. She found him still lying on the sofa but in a different position. He lay on his back, groaning and staring fixedly in front of him.

She began to remind him of his medicines, but he turned his eyes toward her with such a look that she did not finish what she was saying; so great an animosity, to her in particular, did that look express.

"For Christ's sake let me die in peace!" he said.

She would have gone away, but just then their daughter came in and went up to say good morning. He looked at her as he had done at his wife, and in reply to her inquiry about his health said dryly that he would soon free them all of himself. They were both silent and after sitting with him for a while went away.

"Is it our fault?" Lisa said to her mother. "It's as if we were to blame! I am sorry for papa, but why should we be tortured?"

The doctor came at his usual time. Ivan Ilych answered "Yes" and "No," never taking his angry eyes from him, and at last said: "You know you can do nothing for me, so leave me alone."

"We can ease your sufferings."

"You can't even do that. Let me be."

The doctor went into the drawing-room and told Praskovya Fëdorovna that the case was very serious and that the only resource left was opium to allay her husband's sufferings, which must be terrible.

It was true, as the doctor said, that Ivan Ilych's physical sufferings were terrible, but worse than the physical sufferings were his mental sufferings, which were his chief torture.

His mental sufferings were due to the fact that that night, as he looked at Gerasim's sleepy, good-natured face with its prominent cheek-bones, the question suddenly occurred to him: "What if my whole life has really been wrong?"

It occurred to him that what had appeared perfectly impossible before, namely that he had not spent his life as he should have done, might after all be true. It occurred to him that his scarcely perceptible attempts to struggle against what was considered good by the most highly placed people, those scarcely noticeable impulses which he had immediately suppressed, might have been the real thing, and all the rest false. And his professional duties and the whole arrangement of his life and of his family, and all his social and official interests, might all have been false. He tried to defend all those things to himself and suddenly felt the weakness of what he was defending. There was nothing to defend.

"But if that is so," he said to himself, "and I am leaving this life with the consciousness that I have lost all that was given me and it is impossible to rectify it—what then?"

He lay on his back and began to pass his life in review in quite a new way. In the morning when he saw first his footman, then his wife, then his daughter, and then the doctor, their every word and movement confirmed to him the awful truth that had been revealed to him during the night. In them he saw himself—all that for which he had lived—and saw clearly that it was not real at all, but a terrible and huge deception which had hidden both life and death. This consciousness intensified his physical suffering tenfold. He groaned and tossed about, and pulled at his clothing which choked and stifled him. And he hated them on that account.

He was given a large dose of opium and became unconscious, but at noon his sufferings began again. He drove everybody away and tossed from side to side.

His wife came to him and said:

"Jean, my dear, do this for me. It can't do any harm and often helps. Healthy people often do it."

He opened his eyes wide.

"What? Take communion? Why? It's unnecessary! However . . ."

She began to cry.

"Yes, do, my dear. I'll send for our priest. He is such a nice man."

"All right. Very well," he muttered.

When the priest came and heard his confession, Ivan Ilych was softened and seemed to feel a relief from his doubts and consequently from his sufferings, and for a moment there came a ray of hope. He again began to think of the vermiform appendix and the possibility of correcting it. He received the sacrament with tears in his eyes.

When they laid him down again afterwards he felt a moment's ease, and the hope that he might live awoke in him again. He began to think of the operation that had been suggested to him. "To live! I want to live!" he said to himself.

His wife came to congratulate him after his communion, and when uttering the usual conventional words she added:

"You feel better, don't you?"

Without looking at her he said "Yes."

Her dress, her figure, the expression of her face, the tone of her voice, all revealed the same thing. "This is wrong, it is not as it should be. All you have lived for and still live for is falsehood and deception, hiding life and death from you." And as soon as he admitted that thought, his hatred and his agonizing physical suffering again sprang up, and with that suffering a consciousness of the unavoidable, approaching end. And to this was added a new sensation of grinding shooting pain and a feeling of suffocation.

The expression of his face when he uttered that "yes" was dreadful. Having uttered it, he looked her straight in the eyes, turned on his face with a rapidity extraordinary in his weak state and shouted:

"Go away! Go away and leave me alone!"

XII

From that moment the screaming began that continued for three days, and was so terrible that one could not hear it through two closed doors without horror. At the moment he answered his wife he realized that he was lost, that there was no return, that the end had come, the very end, and his doubts were still unsolved and remained doubts.

"Oh! Oh! Oh!" he cried in various intonations. He had begun by screaming "I won't!" and continued screaming on the letter O.

For three whole days, during which time did not exist for him, he struggled in that black sack into which he was being thrust by an invisible, resistless force.

He struggled as a man condemned to death struggles in the hands of the executioner, knowing that he cannot save himself. And every moment he felt that
despite all his efforts he was drawing nearer and nearer to what terrified him.
He felt that his agony was due to his being thrust into that black hole and
still more to his not being able to get right into it. He was hindered from getting into it by his conviction that his life had been a good one. That very
justification of his life held him fast and prevented his moving forward, and it
caused him most torment of all.

Suddenly some force struck him in the chest and side, making it still harder
to breathe, and he fell through the hole and there at the bottom was a light.
What had happened to him was like the sensation one sometimes experiences in
a railway carriage when one thinks one is going backwards while one is really
going forwards and suddenly becomes aware of the real direction.

"Yes, it was all not the right thing," he said to himself, "but that's no
matter. It can be done. But what *is* the right thing?" he asked himself, and suddenly grew quiet.

This occurred at the end of the third day, two hours before his death. Just
then his schoolboy son had crept softly in and gone up to the bedside. The
dying man was still screaming and waving his arms. His hand fell on the boy's
head, and the boy caught it, pressed it to his lips, and began to cry.

At that very moment Ivan Ilych fell through and caught sight of the light,
and it was revealed to him that though his life had not been what it should have
been, this could still be rectified. He asked himself, "What *is* the right thing?"
and grew still, listening. Then he felt that someone was kissing his hand. He
opened his eyes, looked at his son, and felt sorry for him. His wife came up to
him and he glanced at her. She was gazing at him open-mouthed, with undried
tears on her nose and cheek and a despairing look on her face. He felt sorry for
her too.

"Yes, I am making them wretched," he thought. "They are sorry, but it
will be better for them when I die." He wished to say this but had not the
strength to utter it. "Besides, why speak? I must act," he thought. With a look at
his wife he indicated his son and said: "Take him away . . . sorry for him . . .
sorry for you too. . . ." He tried to add, "forgive me," but said "forgo" and
waved his hand, knowing that He whose understanding mattered would understand.

And suddenly it grew clear to him that what had been oppressing him and
would not leave him was dropping away at once from two sides, from ten sides,
and from all sides. He was sorry for them, he must act so as not to hurt them
and free himself from these sufferings. "How good and how simple!" he thought.
"And the pain?" he asked himself. "What has become of it? Where are you,
pain?"

He turned his attention to it.

"Yes, here it is. Well, what of it? Let the pain be."

"And death . . . where is it?"

He sought his former accustomed fear of death and did not find it. "Where
is it? What death?" There was no fear because there was no death.

In place of death there was light.

"So that's what it is!" he suddenly exclaimed aloud. "What joy!"

To him all this happened in a single instant, and the meaning of that instant did not change. For those present his agony continued for another two hours. Something rattled in his throat, his emaciated body twitched, then the gasping and rattle became less and less frequent.

"It is finished!" said someone near him.

He heard these words and repeated them in his soul.

"Death is finished," he said to himself. "It is no more!"

He drew in a breath, stopped in the midst of a sigh, stretched out, and died.

COMMENTARY

We all fear death and our imaginations balk at conceiving its actuality. We say readily enough that "all men are mortal," but like Ivan Ilych in Tolstoi's story, we say it as an abstract general proposition and each one of us finds it hard to believe that the generalization has anything to do with him in particular—with him personally, as we say. And literature tends to encourage us in our evasion. Not that literature avoids dealing with death—on the contrary, there is probably no subject to which it recurs more often. But even very great writers are likely to treat it in ways which limit its fearsomeness. The death of the hero of a tragedy, for instance, seldom seems terrible to us; we often think of it as making a moment of peace and beauty, as constituting the resolution of distressing conflicts. Literature inclines to soften death's aspect by showing it as through a veil, or by suggesting that it is sad and noble rather than terrifying, or by asking us to "accept" it as part of life.

This tendency is wholly reversed by "The Death of Ivan Ilych." Tolstoi does not try to reconcile us to the idea of our extinction and he does not mask the dreadfulness of dying. Quite the contrary—not only does he choose an instance of death that is long drawn out and hideously painful, and dwell upon its details, but he emphasizes the unmitigated aloneness of the dying man, the humiliation of his helplessness, and his abject terror at the prospect of his annihilation, as well as his bitter envy of those who still continue in existence while he is in process of becoming nothing.

Tolstoi is explicit about these aspects of death as no writer before him had ever been, and the effect is excruciating. Perhaps no work of fiction is so painful to read as this story.

Why is this vicarious torture forced upon us? We can scarcely feel that the author's purpose was purely literary, that Tolstoi chose his subject as any writer chooses a subject, because it is interesting in and for itself. We cannot doubt that his intention was other than artistic, and we conjecture that it might well be religious, for religion often tries to put us in mind of the actuality of death, not in its terrors, to be sure, but in its inevitability, seeking thus to press upon us the understanding that the life of this world is not the sum of existence, and not even its most valuable part. And the circumstances of Tolstoi's life at the time he wrote "The Death of Ivan Ilych" confirm our sense of the story's religious inspiration.

Some eight years before writing "Ivan Ilych," Tolstoi experienced a great spiritual crisis which issued in religious conversion and altered the whole course of his life. He abandoned the ways of the aristocratic class into which he had been born and undertook to live as a primitive Christian, committing himself to an extreme simplicity of life and to the service of mankind, especially the poor and the humble. He repudiated art and his own great achievements as a novelist and proposed the doctrine that artistic creation was justified only when it led men to morality and piety.

The particular nature of his crisis is most relevant to "The Death of Ivan Ilych." At the age of fifty, Tolstoi was thrown into a state of despair by his insupportably intense imagination of mortality. It was not a new problem that he confronted—even in his youth he had known periods of black depression because he felt that the inevitability of death robbed life of all meaning. In *Anna Karenina,* the great novel he had completed shortly before the onset of his crisis, Prince Levin, who closely resembles Tolstoi, cannot endure the thought that "for every man, and himself too, there was nothing but suffering, death, and oblivion." Death, he feels, makes life "the evil jest of some devil," and he must either learn to see human existence in some other way or commit suicide. Levin is able to pass beyond this terrible alternative; he overcomes his despair and accepts life for what good he may find in it. For a time it lay within Tolstoi's power to make a similar decision, but the period of calm was not of long duration; the horror of death again became unbearable and could be coped with only by the help of a religious faith.

And yet, despite this much ground for supposing that Tolstoi had an overt religious purpose in writing "The Death of Ivan Ilych," it is not easy to show that the story itself supports the hypothesis. If we search it for religious doctrine, we find none. Nor can we even discover in it any significant religious emotion. Although it is true that the conclusion, the moment of Ivan Ilych's escape from pain into peace and even into "light," is charged with feelings and described in metaphors that are part of the Christian tradition, the passage can scarcely be taken as a genuinely religious affirmation or as effectually controverting the thoughts that the dying man has had about "the cruelty of God, and the absence of God."

On the contrary, it might well seem that Tolstoi, by his representation of death, is trying to win us not to the religious life but, rather, to a full acceptance of the joys of the life of this world. From the Christian point of view, his intention might even seem to be open to the charge of paganism. It was an ancient pagan custom to seat a human skeleton at a feast as *memento mori,* a reminder of death, to urge upon the revelers the idea that life is short and that the fleeting hours must be snatched; just so does Tolstoi use Ivan Ilych's death to shock us into awareness of what it means to be alive.

And it is not the virtuous life that Tolstoi has in mind or the pious life— he means life in any actuality, any life that is really lived. Ivan Ilych is remorseful not for the sins he committed but for the pleasures he never took. "Ivan Ilych's life had been most simple and most ordinary and therefore most terrible," says Tolstoi in the famous opening sentence, and as the reader follows Ivan Ilych's career as a "successful" person, he cannot but conclude that even if the poor man's taking of pleasure had involved his sinning, his life would have been less "ordinary" and therefore less "terrible."

And this would indeed seem to be a pagan conclusion. But perhaps it is not only pagan—perhaps it is also to be understood as Christian. For without life there cannot be a spiritual life, without the capacity for joy or delight there cannot be the conception of the happiness of salvation. The first inhabitants of Hell whom Dante meets on his journey are the Neutrals or Trimmers, the people who had lived "without disgrace and without praise"—those who, as Dante says of them, "were never alive." It was thus that Ivan Ilych had lived, without disgrace and without praise, as one who was never alive. In his maturity only three things had afforded him pleasure—his official position and the power over other men that it gave him; the decoration of his pretentious and conventional home; and playing whist. He had never known the joy of loving or of being loved. He had never felt the sting of passion or the energy of impulse. He had never experienced the calm pleasure of moral satisfaction such as might come from the consciousness of having been loyal or generous. He had never admired anyone or anything; he had never been interested in anything or anyone, not even, really, in himself. He had never questioned or doubted anything, not even himself.

Indeed, he had lived without any sense that he had a self or was a self. He had assumed all the roles that respectable society had assigned to him: he had been a public official, a husband, a father. But a self he had never been, not between the time of his childhood (when there had been a little glow of pleasure and affection) and the time of his dying. Only at the point of his extinction is selfhood revealed to him. The means by which the revelation is effected are agonizing; it comes through pain and fear, through self-pity, through a hopeless childlike longing for comfort and love. Yet in his awful dissolution, Ivan Ilych is more fully a human being than he had ever been in the days of his armored unawareness of himself. And it is when he has been tortured into an awareness of his own self that he can at last, for the first time, begin to recognize the actuality of other selves, that of the young peasant Gerasim and that of his poor sad son.

THE

TREASURE

WILLIAM SOMERSET
MAUGHAM

1874–1966

RICHARD HARENGER was a happy man. Notwithstanding what the pessimists, from Ecclesiastes[1] onwards, have said, this is not so rare a thing to find in this unhappy world, but Richard Harenger knew it, and that is a very rare thing indeed. The golden mean[2] which the ancients so highly prized is out of fashion, and those who follow it must put up with polite derision from those who see no merit in self-restraint and no virtue in common-sense. Richard Harenger shrugged a polite and amused shoulder. Let others live dangerously, let others burn with a hard gemlike flame,[3] let others stake their fortunes on the turn of a card, walk the tightrope that leads to glory or the grave, or hazard their lives for a cause, a passion or an adventure. He neither envied the fame their exploits brought them nor wasted his pity on them when their efforts ended in disaster.

But it must not be inferred from this that Richard Harenger was a selfish or a callous man. He was neither. He was considerate and of a generous dis-

[1] A book of the Old Testament which takes a somber view of human life: "Vanity of vanities, saith the preacher; all is vanity."

[2] Aristotle, among other philosophers, taught that happiness was most surely attained by an avoidance of extremes.

[3] Walter Pater (1839–1894), English critic of art and literature, in the "Conclusion" of his book *The Renaissance*, urged his readers to "burn always with [a] hard gem-like flame," that is, to live intensely, presumably without great concern for the consequences.

position. He was always ready to oblige a friend, and he was sufficiently well off to be able to indulge himself in the pleasure of helping others. He had some money of his own, and he occupied in the Home Office[4] a position that brought him an adequate stipend. The work suited him. It was regular, responsible and pleasant. Every day when he left the office he went to his club to play bridge for a couple of hours, and on Saturdays and Sundays he played golf. He went abroad for his holidays, staying at good hotels, and visited churches, galleries and museums. He was a regular first-nighter. He dined out a good deal. His friends liked him. He was easy to talk to. He was well-read, knowledgeable and amusing. He was besides of a personable exterior, not remarkably handsome, but tall, slim and erect of carriage, with a lean, intelligent face; his hair was growing thin, for he was now approaching the age of fifty, but his brown eyes retained their smile and his teeth were all his own. He had from nature a good constitution, and he had always taken care of himself. There was no reason in the world why he should not be a happy man, and if there had been in him a trace of self-complacency he might have claimed that he deserved to be.

He had the good fortune even to sail safely through those perilous, unquiet straits of marriage in which so many wise and good men have made shipwreck. Married for love in the early twenties, his wife and he, after some years of almost perfect felicity, had drifted gradually apart. Neither of them wished to marry anyone else, so there was no question of divorce (which indeed Richard Harenger's situation in the government service made undesirable), but for convenience' sake, with the help of the family lawyer, they arranged a separation which left them free to lead their lives as each one wished without interference from the other. They parted with mutual expressions of respect and good will.

Richard Harenger sold his house in St. John's Wood and took a flat within convenient walking distance of Whitehall.[5] It had a sitting-room which he lined with his books, a dining room into which his Chippendale furniture just fitted, a nice-sized bedroom for himself, and beyond the kitchen a couple of maids' rooms. He brought his cook, whom he had had for many years, from St. John's Wood, but needing no longer so large a staff dismissed the rest of the servants and applied at a registry office for a house-parlourmaid. He knew exactly what he wanted, and he explained his needs to the superintendent of the agency with precision. He wanted a maid who was not too young, first because young women are flighty and secondly because, though he was of mature age and a man of principle, people would talk, the porter and the tradesmen if nobody else, and both for the sake of his own reputation and that of the young person he considered that the applicant should have reached years of discretion. Besides that he wanted a maid who could clean silver well. He had always had a fancy for old silver, and it was reasonable to demand that the forks and spoons that had been used by a woman of quality under the reign of Queen Anne should be treated with tenderness and respect. He was of a hospitable nature and liked to give at least once a week little dinners of not less than four people and not more than eight. He could trust his cook to send in a meal that his guests would

[4] The department of the British government concerned with internal affairs, roughly comparable to the U.S. Department of the Interior. A high official of the Home Office would almost surely be considered socially elite in England.

[5] A broad thoroughfare in London lined with buildings which house departments and ministries of the British government.

take pleasure in eating and he desired his parlourmaid to wait with neatness and dispatch. Then he needed a perfect valet. He dressed well, in a manner that suited his age and condition, and he liked his clothes to be properly looked after. The parlourmaid he was looking for must be able to press trousers and iron a tie, and he was very particular that his shoes should be well shone. He had small feet, and he took a great deal of trouble to have well-cut shoes. He had a large supply, and he insisted that they should be treed up the moment he took them off. Finally the flat must be kept clean and tidy. It was of course understood that any applicant for the post must be of irreproachable character, sober, honest, reliable and of a pleasing exterior. In return for this he was prepared to offer good wages, reasonable liberty and ample holidays. The superintendent listened without batting an eyelash, and telling him that she was quite sure she could suit him, sent him a string of candidates which proved that she had not paid the smallest attention to a word he said. He saw them all personally. Some were obviously inefficient, some looked fast, some were too old, others too young, some lacked the presence he thought essential; there was not one to whom he was inclined even to give a trial. He was a kindly, polite man, and he declined their services with a smile and a pleasant expression of regret. He did not lose patience. He was prepared to interview house-parlourmaids till he found one who was suitable.

Now it is a funny thing about life, if you refuse to accept anything but the best you very often get it: if you utterly decline to make do with what you can get, then somehow or other you are very likely to get what you want. It is as though Fate said, "This man's a perfect fool, he's asking for perfection," and then just out of her feminine wilfulness flung it in his lap. One day the porter of the flats said to Richard Harenger out of a blue sky:

"I hear you're lookin' for a house-parlourmaid, sir. There's someone I know lookin' for a situation as might do."

"Can you recommend her personally?"

Richard Harenger had the sound opinion that one servant's recommendation of another was worth much more than that of an employer.

"I can vouch for her respectability. She's been in some very good situations."

"I shall be coming in to dress about seven. If that's convenient to her I could see her then."

"Very good, sir. I'll see that she's told."

He had not been in more than five minutes when the cook, having answered a ring at the front door, came in and told him that the person the porter had spoken to him about had called.

"Show her in," he said.

He turned on some more lights so that he could see what the applicant looked like, and getting up, stood with his back to the fireplace. A woman came in and stood just inside the door in a respectful attitude.

"Good evening," he said. "What is your name?"

"Pritchard, sir."

"How old are you?"

"Thirty-five, sir."

"Well, that's a reasonable age."

He gave his cigarette a puff and looked at her reflectively. She was on the tall side, nearly as tall as he, but he guessed that she wore high heels. Her black dress fitted her station. She held herself well. She had good features and a rather high colour.

"Will you take off your hat?" he asked.

She did so, and he saw that she had pale brown hair. It was neatly and becomingly dressed. She looked strong and healthy. She was neither fat nor thin. In a proper uniform she would look very presentable. She was not inconveniently handsome, but she was certainly a comely, in another class of life you might almost have said a handsome, woman. He proceeded to ask her a number of questions. Her answers were satisfactory. She had left her last place for an adequate reason. She had been trained under a butler and appeared to be well acquainted with her duties. In her last place she had been head parlourmaid of three, but she did not mind undertaking the work of the flat single-handed. She had valeted a gentleman before who had sent her to a tailor's to learn how to press clothes. She was a little shy, but neither timid nor ill-at-ease. Richard asked her his questions in his amiable, leisurely way, and she answered them with modest composure. He was considerably impressed. He asked her what references she could give. They seemed extremely satisfactory.

"Now look here," he said. "I'm very much inclined to engage you. But I hate changes, I've had my cook for twelve years: if you suit me and the place suits you I hope you'll stay. I mean, I don't want you to come to me in three or four months and say that you're leaving to get married."

"There's not much fear of that, sir. I'm a widow. I don't believe marriage is much catch for anyone in my position, sir. My husband never did a stroke of work from the day I married him to the day he died, and I had to keep him. What I want now is a good home."

"I'm inclined to agree with you," he smiled. "Marriage is a very good thing, but I think it's a mistake to make a habit of it."

She very properly made no reply to this, but waited for him to announce his decision. She did not seem anxious about it. He reflected that if she was as competent as she appeared she must be well aware that she would have no difficulty in finding a place. He told her what wages he was offering, and these seemed to be satisfactory to her. He gave her the necessary information about the place, but she gave him to understand that she was already apprised of this, and he received the impression, which amused rather than disconcerted him, that she had made certain enquiries about him before applying for the situation. It showed prudence on her part and good sense.

"When would you be able to come in if I engaged you? I haven't got anybody at the moment. The cook's managing as best she can with a char, but I should like to get settled as soon as possible."

"Well, sir, I was going to give myself a week's holiday, but if it's a matter of obliging a gentleman I don't mind giving that up. I could come in tomorrow if it was convenient."

Richard Harenger gave her his attractive smile.

"I shouldn't like you to do without a holiday that I daresay you've been looking forward to. I can very well go on like this for another week. Go and have your holiday and come to me when it's over."

"Thank you very much, sir. Would it do if I came in tomorrow week?"

"Quite well."

When she left, Richard Harenger felt he had done a good day's work. It looked as though he had found exactly what he was after. He rang for the cook and told her he had engaged a house-parlourmaid at last.

"I think you'll like her, sir," she said. "She came in and 'ad a talk with me this afternoon. I could see at once she knew her duties. And she's not one of them flighty ones."

"We can but try, Mrs. Jeddy. I hope you gave me a good character."

"Well, I said you was particular, sir. I said you was a gentleman as liked things just so."

"I admit that."

"She said she didn't mind that. She said she liked a gentleman as knew what was what. She said there's no satisfaction in doing things proper if nobody notices. I expect you'll find she'll take a rare lot of pride in her work."

"That's what I want her to do. I think we might go farther and fare worse."

"Well, sir, there is that to it, of course. And the proof of the pudding's the eating. But if you ask my opinion I think she's going to be a real treasure."

And that is precisely what Pritchard turned out. No man was ever better served. The way she shone shoes was marvellous, and he set out of a fine morning for his walk to the office with a more jaunty step because you could almost see yourself reflected in them. She looked after his clothes with such attention that his colleagues began to chaff him about being the best-dressed man in the Civil Service. One day, coming home unexpectedly, he found a line of socks and handkerchiefs hung up to dry in the bathroom. He called Pritchard.

"D'you wash my socks and handkerchiefs yourself, Pritchard? I should have thought you had enough to do without that."

"They do ruin them so at the laundry, sir. I prefer to do them at home if you have no objection."

She knew exactly what he should wear on every occasion, and without asking him was aware whether she should put out a dinner jacket and a black tie in the evening or a dress coat and a white one. When he was going to a party where decorations were to be worn he found his neat little row of medals automatically affixed to the lapel of his coat. He soon ceased to choose every morning from his wardrobe the tie he wanted, for he found that she put out for him without fail the one he would have himself selected. Her taste was perfect. He supposed she read his letters, for she always knew what his movements were, and if he had forgotten at what hour he had an engagement he had no need to look in his book, for Pritchard could tell him. She knew exactly what tone to use with persons with whom she conversed on the telephone. Except with trades-men, with whom she was apt to be peremptory, she was always polite, but there was a distinct difference in her manner if she was addressing one of Mr. Har-enger's literary friends or the wife of a Cabinet Minister. She knew by instinct with whom he wished to speak and with whom he didn't. From his sitting-room he sometimes heard her with placid sincerity assuring a caller that he was out, and then she would come in and tell him that So-and-so had rung up, but she thought he wouldn't wish to be disturbed.

"Quite right, Pritchard," he smiled.

"I knew she only wanted to bother you about that concert," said Pritchard.

His friends made appointments with him through her, and she would tell him what she had done on his return in the evening.

"Mrs. Soames rang up, sir, and asked if you would lunch with her on Thursday, the eighth, but I said you were very sorry but you were lunching with Lady Versinder. Mr. Oakley rang up and asked if you'd go to a cocktail party at the Savoy next Tuesday at six. I said you would if you possibly could, but you might have to go to the dentist's."

"Quite right."

"I thought you could see when the time came, sir."

She kept the flat like a new pin. On one occasion soon after she entered his service, Richard, coming back from a holiday, took out a book from his shelves and at once noticed that it had been dusted. He rang the bell.

"I forgot to tell you, when I went away under no circumstances ever to touch my books. When books are taken out to be dusted they're never put back in the right place. I don't mind my books being dirty, but I hate not being able to find them."

"I'm very sorry, sir," said Pritchard. "I know some gentlemen are very particular and I took care to put back every book exactly where I took it from."

Richard Harenger gave his books a glance. So far as he could see, every one was in its accustomed place. He smiled.

"I apologise, Pritchard."

"They were in a muck, sir. I mean, you couldn't open one without getting your hands black with dust."

She certainly kept his silver as he had never had it kept before. He felt called upon to give her a special word of praise.

"Most of it's Queen Anne and George I, you know," he explained.

"Yes, I know, sir. When you've something good like that to look after, it's a pleasure to keep it like it should be."

"You certainly have a knack for it. I never knew a butler who kept his silver as well as you do."

"Men haven't the patience women have," she replied modestly.

As soon as he thought Pritchard had settled down in the place, he resumed the little dinners he was fond of giving once a week. He had already discovered that she knew how to wait at table, but it was with warm sense of complacency that he realised then how competently she could manage a party. She was quick, silent and watchful. A guest had hardly felt the need of something before Pritchard was at his elbow offering him what he wanted. She soon learned the tastes of his more intimate friends and remembered that one liked water instead of soda with his whisky and that another particularly fancied the knuckle end of a leg of lamb. She knew exactly how cold a hock should be not to ruin its taste and how long claret should have stood in the room to bring out its bouquet. It was a pleasure to see her pour out a bottle of burgundy in such a fashion as not to disturb the grounds. On one occasion she did not serve the wine Richard had ordered. He somewhat sharply pointed this out to her.

"I opened the bottle sir, and it was slightly corked. So I got the Chambertin, as I thought it was safer."

"Quite right, Pritchard."

Presently he left this matter entirely in her hands, for he discovered that she knew perfectly what wines his guests would like. Without orders from him she would provide the best in his cellar and his oldest brandy if she thought they were the sort of people who knew what they were drinking. She had no belief in the palate of women, and when they were of the party was apt to serve the champagne which had to be drunk before it went off.[6] She had the

---

[6] Kept too long, champagne ceases to be champagne, although it remains drinkable.

English servant's instinctive knowledge of social differences, and neither rank nor money blinded her to the fact that someone was not a gentleman, but she had favourites among his friends, and when someone she particularly liked was dining, with the air of a cat that had swallowed a canary she would pour out for him a bottle of a wine that Harenger kept for very special occasions. It amused him.

"You've got on the right side of Pritchard, old boy," he exclaimed. "There aren't many people she gives this wine to."

Pritchard became an institution. She was known very soon to be the perfect parlourmaid. People envied Harenger the possession of her as they envied nothing else that he had. She was worth her weight in gold. Her price was above rubies. Richard Harenger beamed with self-complacency when they praised her.

"Good masters make good servants," he said gaily.

One evening, when they were sitting over their port and she had left the room, they were talking about her.

"It'll be an awful blow when she leaves you."

"Why should she leave me? One or two people have tried to get her away from me, but she turned them down. She knows where she's well off."

"She'll get married one of these days."

"I don't think she's that sort."

"She's a good-looking woman."

"Yes, she has quite a decent presence."

"What are you talking about? She's a very handsome creature. In another class of life she'd be a well-known society beauty with her photograph in all the papers."

At that moment Pritchard came in with the coffee. Richard Harenger looked at her. After seeing her every day, off and on, for four years it was now, my word, how time flies, he had really forgotten what she looked like. She did not seem to have changed much since he had first seen her. She was no stouter than then, she still had the high colour, and her regular features bore the same expression which was at once intent and vacuous. The black uniform suited her. She left the room.

"She's a paragon, and there's no doubt about it."

"I know she is," answered Harenger. "She's perfection. I should be lost without her. And the strange thing is that I don't very much like her."

"Why not?"

"I think she bores me a little. You see, she has no conversation. I've often tried to talk to her. She answers when I speak to her, but that's all. In four years she's never volunteered a remark of her own. I know absolutely nothing about her. I don't know if she likes me or if she's completely indifferent to me. She's an automaton. I respect her, I appreciate her, I trust her. She has every quality in the world, and I've often wondered why it is that with all that I'm so completely indifferent to her. I think it must be that she is entirely devoid of charm."

They left it at that.

Two or three days after this, since it was Pritchard's night out and he had no engagement, Richard Harenger dined by himself at his club. A page-boy came to him and told him that they had just rung up from his flat to say that he had gone out without his keys and should they be brought along to him in a

taxi? He put his hand to his pocket. It was a fact. By a singular chance he had forgotten to replace them when he had changed into his blue serge suit before
coming out to dinner. His intention had been to play bridge, but it was an off
night at the club, and there seemed little chance of a decent game; it occurred to
him that it would be a good opportunity to see a picture that he had heard
talked about, so he sent back the message by the page that he would call for the
keys himself in half an hour.

He rang at the door of his flat, and it was opened by Pritchard. She had
the keys in her hand.

"What are you doing here, Pritchard?" he asked. "It's your night out, isn't
it?"

"Yes, sir. But I didn't care about going, so I told Mrs. Jeddy she could go
instead."

"You ought to get out when you have the chance," he said, with his usual
thoughtfulness. "It's not good for you to be cooped up here all the time."

"I get out now and then on an errand, but I haven't been out in the evening
for the last month."

"Why on earth not?"

"Well, it's not very cheerful going out by yourself, and somehow I don't
know anyone just now that I'm particularly keen on going out with."

"You ought to have a bit of fun now and then. It's good for you."

"I've got out of the habit of it somehow."

"Look here, I'm just going to the cinema. Would you like to come along
with me?"

He spoke in kindliness, on the spur of the moment, and the moment he
had said the words half regretted them.

"Yes, sir, I'd like to," said Pritchard.

"Run along then and put on a hat."

"I shan't be a minute."

She disappeared, and he went into the sitting-room and lit a cigarette. He
was a little amused at what he was doing, and pleased, too; it was nice to be
able to make someone happy with so little trouble to himself. It was characteristic of Pritchard that she had shown neither surprise nor hesitation. She kept
him waiting about five minutes, and when she came back he noticed she had
changed her dress. She wore a blue frock in what he supposed was artificial silk,
a small black hat with a blue brooch on it, and a silver fox round her neck. He
was a trifle relieved to see that she looked neither shabby nor showy. It would
never occur to anyone who happened to see them that this was a distinguished
official in the Home Office taking his housemaid to the pictures.

"I'm sorry to have kept you waiting, sir."

"It doesn't matter at all," he said graciously.

He opened the front door for her, and she went out before him. He remembered the familiar anecdote of Louis XIV and the courtier and appreciated
the fact that she had not hesitated to precede him. The cinema for which they
were bound was at no great distance from Mr. Harenger's flat, and they walked
there. He talked about the weather and the state of the roads and Adolf
Hitler. Pritchard made suitable replies. They arrived just as Mickey the Mouse
was starting, and this put them in a good humour. During the four years she
had been in his service Richard Harenger had hardly ever seen Pritchard even

smile, and now it diverted him vastly to hear her peal upon peal of joyous laughter. He enjoyed her pleasure. Then the principal attraction was thrown on the screen. It was a good picture, and they both watched it with breathless excitement. Taking his cigarette-case out to help himself, he automatically offered it to Pritchard.

"Thank you, sir," she said, taking one.

He lit it for her. Her eyes were on the screen and she was almost unconscious of his action. When the picture was finished they streamed out with the crowd into the street. They walked back towards the flat. It was a fine starry night.

"Did you like it?" he said.

"Like anything, sir. It was a real treat."

A thought occurred to him.

"By the way, did you have any supper to-night?"

"No, sir. I didn't have time."

"Aren't you starving?"

"I'll have a bit of bread and cheese when I get in and I'll make meself a cup of cocoa."

"That sounds rather grim." There was a feeling of gaiety in the air, and the people who poured past them, one way and another, seemed filled with a pleasant elation. In for a penny, in for a pound, he said to himself. "Look here, would you like to come and have a bit of supper with me somewhere?"

"If you'd like to, sir."

"Come on."

He hailed a cab. He was feeling very philanthrophic and it was not a feeling that he disliked at all. He told the driver to go to a restaurant in Oxford Street which was gay, but at which he was confident there was no chance of meeting anyone he knew. There was an orchestra and people danced. It would amuse Pritchard to see them. When they sat down a waiter came up to them.

"They've got a set supper here," he said, thinking that was what she would like. "I suggest we have that. What would you like to drink? A little white wine?"

"What I really fancy is a glass of ginger beer," she said.

Richard Harenger ordered himself a whisky and soda. She ate the supper with hearty appetite, and though Harenger was not hungry, to put her at her ease he ate too. The picture they had just seen gave them something to talk about. It was quite true what they had said the other night, Pritchard was not a bad-looking woman, and even if someone had seen them together he would not have minded. It would make rather a good story for his friends when he told them how he had taken the incomparable Pritchard to the cinema and the afterwards to supper. Pritchard was looking at the dancers with a faint smile on her lips.

"Do you like dancing?" he said.

"I used to be a rare one for it when I was a girl. I never danced much after I was married. My husband was a bit shorter than me, and somehow I never think it looks well unless the gentleman's taller, if you know what I mean. I suppose I shall be getting too old for it soon."

Richard was certainly taller than his parlourmaid. They would look all right. He was fond of dancing and he danced well. But he hesitated. He did not want to embarrass Pritchard by asking her to dance with him. It was better not to go too far perhaps. And yet what did it matter? It was a drab life she led. She was so sensible, if she thought it was a mistake he was pretty sure she would find a decent excuse.

"Would you like to take a turn, Pritchard?" he said, as the band struck up again.

"I'm terribly out of practice, sir."

"What does that matter?"

"If you don't mind, sir," she answered coolly, rising from her seat.

She was not in the least shy. She was only afraid that she would not be able to follow his step. They moved on to the floor. He found she danced very well.

"Why, you dance perfectly, Pritchard," he said.

"It's coming back to me."

Although she was a big woman, she was light on her feet and she had a natural sense of rhythm. She was very pleasant to dance with. He gave a glance at the mirrors that lined the walls and he could not help reflecting that they looked very well together. Their eyes met in the mirror; he wondered whether she was thinking that, too. They had two more dances and then Richard Harenger suggested that they should go. He paid the bill and they walked out. He noticed that she threaded her way through the crowd without a trace of self-consciousness. They got into a taxi and in ten minutes were at home.

"I'll go up the back way, sir," said Pritchard.

"There's no need to do that. Come up in the lift with me."

He took her up, giving the night-porter an icy glance, so that he should not think it strange that he came back at that somewhat late hour with his parlourmaid, and with his latch-key let her into the flat.

"Well, good-night, sir," she said, "Thank you very much. It's been a real treat for me."

"Thank *you*, Pritchard. I should have had a very dull evening by myself. I hope you've enjoyed your outing."

"That I have, sir, more than I can say."

It had been a success. Richard Harenger was satisfied with himself. It was a kindly thing for him to have done. It was a very agreeable sensation to give anyone so much real pleasure. His benevolence warmed him and for a moment he felt a great love in his heart for the whole human race.

"Good-night, Pritchard," he said, and because he felt happy and good he put his arm around her waist and kissed her on the lips.

Her lips were very soft. They lingered on his, and she returned his kiss. It was the warm, hearty embrace of a healthy woman in the prime of life. He found it very pleasant, and he held her to him a little more closely. She put her arms around his neck.

As a general rule he did not wake till Pritchard came in with his letters, but next morning he woke at half-past seven. He had a curious sensation that he did not recognise. He was accustomed to sleep with two pillows under his head, and he suddenly grew aware of the fact that he had only one. Then he remembered and with a start looked round. The other pillow was beside his own. Thank God, no sleeping head rested there, but it was plain that one had. His heart sank. He broke out into a cold sweat.

"My God, what a fool I've been!" he cried out loud.

How could he have done anything so stupid? What on earth had come over him? He was the last man to play about with servant girls. What a disgraceful thing to do! At his age and in his position. He had not heard Pritchard slip away. He must have been asleep. It wasn't even as if he'd liked her very much. She wasn't his type. And, as he had said the other night, she rather bored him. Even now he only knew her as Pritchard. He had no notion what her first name was. What madness! And what was to happen now? The position was impossible. It was obvious he couldn't keep her, and yet to send her away for what was his fault as much as hers seemed shockingly unfair. How idiotic to lose the best parlourmaid a man ever had just for an hour's folly!

"It's that damned kindness of heart of mine," he groaned.

He would never find anyone else to look after his clothes so admirably or clean the silver so well. She knew all his friends' telephone numbers, and she understood wine. But of course she must go. She must see for herself that after what happened things could never be the same. He would make her a handsome present and give her an excellent reference. At any minute she would be coming in now. Would she be arch, would she be familiar? Or would she put on airs? Perhaps even she wouldn't trouble to come in with his letters. It would be awful if he had to ring the bell and Mrs. Jeddy came in and said: Pritchard's not up yet, sir, she's having a lie in after last night.

"What a fool I've been! What a contemptible cad!"

There was a knock at the door. He was sick with anxiety.

"Come in."

Richard Harenger was a very unhappy man.

Pritchard came in as the clock struck. She wore the print dress she was in the habit of wearing during the early part of the day.

"Good morning, sir," she said.

"Good morning."

She drew the curtains and handed him his letters and the papers. Her face was impassive. She looked exactly as she always looked. Her movements had the same competent deliberation that they always had. She neither avoided Richard's glance nor sought it.

"Will you wear your grey, sir? It came back from the tailor's yesterday."

"Yes."

He pretended to read his letters, but he watched from under his eyelashes. Her back was turned to him. She took his vest and drawers and folded them over a chair. She took the studs out of the shirt he had worn the day before and studded a clean one. She put out some clean socks for him and placed them on the seat of a chair with the suspenders to match by the side. Then she put out his grey suit and attached the braces to the back buttons of the trousers. She opened his wardrobe and after a moment's reflection chose a tie to go with the suit. She collected on her arm the suit of the day before and picked up the shoes.

"Will you have breakfast now, sir, or will you have your bath first?"

"I'll have breakfast now," he said.

"Very good, sir."

With her slow quiet movements, unruffled, she left the room. Her face bore that rather serious, deferential, vacuous look it always bore. What had happened might have been a dream. Nothing in Pritchard's demeanour suggested that she had the smallest recollection of the night before. He gave a sigh of relief. It was going to be all right. She need not go, she need not go. Pritchard was the perfect parlourmaid. He knew that never by word nor gesture would she ever refer to the fact that for a moment their relations had been other than those of master and servant. Richard Harenger was a very happy man.

COMMENTARY

No reader will fail to see, and without needing to give much thought to the matter, that "The Treasure" is different in kind from all the other stories in this volume. The difference can be stated quite simply: the other stories are serious, this one is not. It does not undertake to engage our deeper feelings or to communicate anything new about the nature of human existence. It proposes to do nothing except entertain.

Among people to whom literature is important, there are various ways of responding to writing of this kind, and one of them is exemplified by an opinion expressed by the philosopher George Santayana. In his old age Santayana had a lively appetite for contemporary fiction and a considerable openness of mind toward it. But he said that he found it impossible to read Somerset Maugham. In a letter to a friend, after mentioning that someone had given him several volumes of Maugham's stories, he went on to remark that what he chiefly felt about them was "wonder at anybody wishing to write such stories." He continued: "They are not pleasing, they are simply graphic and plausible, like a bit of a dream that one might drop into in an afternoon nap. Why record it? I suppose to make money, because writing stories is a profession. . . ."

This strikes me as doing rather less than justice both to Maugham's accomplishment and to the kind of pleasure one may take in a story like "The Treasure." Maugham does not sound our depths or invite us to sound his, and quite possibly he has no depths to be sounded. Perhaps he invites us to respond to nothing save his lively if limited intelligence and his cool mastery of his craft. But if this is not a high enterprise, it is not an ignoble one, and to some it will be engaging exactly because it has no designs upon their profound and serious selves.

Another philosopher, the French theologian and aesthetician Etienne Gilson, is more lenient than Santayana in his judgment of nonserious art, and, I think, more instructive. Gilson draws a distinction between "real painting" and what he calls "picturing," and as an example of the latter he cites the pleasant amusing scenes of American life that used to appear on the covers of *The Saturday Evening Post*. These, he says, are obviously not to be evaluated by the standards we apply to the work of a Rembrandt or a Cézanne; they nevertheless have appropriate standards of their own and they evoke from us a pleasure appropriate to their intention. They are not inferior or failed examples of another and higher art, and it is mere aesthetic snobbery to judge them as if they were and to refuse what pleasure they offer.

By analogy with Gilson's "picturing," we may think of certain kinds of fiction as "storying" and judge them within their own categories. Detective and spy novels and science fiction undertake to engage our interest by virtues that are peculiar to them, and there are discriminations of an appropriate sort to be made among them—they are good or bad or mediocre according to their own canons. Some readers find it impossible to respond to their attractions, or decide that they do not have time for them—it seems a pity!—but only a priggish and captious reader will condemn them because they do not match Hawthorne or Tolstoi in moral and spiritual power.

And indeed we cannot fail to observe of "The Treasure" that, despite its refusal to be serious and to propose any greater awareness of the actualities of existence, it does after all touch upon a subject which has pertinence to our real interests. It refers to our sense of the high value of natural impulse and the absurdity of social convention. What amuses us in the story is Harenger's intense relief that his episode of sexual intimacy with his efficient parlor-maid is not going to change their established relationship and that the ordered elegance of his life is not to be threatened. We find it comical that a man whose sexual impulse was at least strong enough to overwhelm him on one occasion, and presumably in a happy way, should set more store by his narcissistic love of comfort and orderliness than by his erotic satisfaction. The pleasures of habitual comfort are not to be despised, but our partisanship with nature and impulse is quick to pass adverse judgment on a man who prefers these to the passional pleasures. Our laughter over Harenger's choice announces our option —at least for the moment—in favor of "life."

An incidental charm of "The Treasure" is its representation of a vanished mode of life which, especially to American readers, might well seem quaint, even improbable. America has never had a servant class or the kind of class system which codifies the relationship between master and servant, nor has it countenanced for men the life of elegant comfort and self-regard that is so important to Harenger. And even in England the attitudes that the story takes for granted exist nowadays only in vestigial form. At least from a strictly literary point of view it is possible to regard this as something of a loss, for the master–servant relationship was one of the best subjects of comedy.

DUCHOUX

GUY DE MAUPASSANT

1850–1893

BECAUSE the great staircase of the club was like a hot-house, Baron Mordiane came down the steps with his fur-lined overcoat open; but when the front door had closed behind him, the intense cold suddenly pierced him to the marrow, increasing his despondency. He had been losing money in the gambling rooms, besides which he had for some time been suffering from indigestion, unable any longer to eat what he fancied.

He was about to return home, when the thought of his great, bare room, his valet sleeping in the anteroom, the water singing on the gas-stove in his dressing-room, and the enormous bed, as old and gloomy as a death-bed, suddenly struck him with a chill even sharper than the frosty air.

For some years he had felt weighing on him the burden of loneliness which sometimes overwhelms old bachelors. He had been strong, active and cheerful, spending his days in sport and his evenings in amusement. Now he was growing dull, and no longer took an interest in anything. Exercise tired him, suppers and even dinners made him ill, while women bored him as much as they had once amused him.

The monotony of unvarying evenings, of the same friends met in the same place—at the club—the same card parties with their run of good and bad luck evenly balanced, the same conversation on the same topics, the same wit from the same tongues, the same jokes on the same subjects, the same scandal about the same women, all sickened him so that there were times when he thought seriously of suicide. He could no longer face this regular, aimless, and commonplace life, both frivolous and dull, and, without knowing why, he longed for peace, rest and comfort.

He did not indeed think of marrying, for he lacked the courage to face a life of depression, conjugal slavery, and that hateful coexistence of two human beings who know each other so well that every word uttered by one is anticipated by the other, and every thought, wish or opinion is immediately divined. He considered that a woman was worth attention only so long as one knew very little about her, while she was still mysterious and unfathomed, vague and perplexing. Therefore what he wanted was family life without the tyranny of family ties, in which he need spend only part of his time; and again he was haunted by the memory of his son.

For the last year he had thought of him continually, with an ever-increasing, tormenting longing to see him and make his acquaintance. The affair had taken place while he was a young man, in an atmosphere of romance and tenderness. The child had been sent to the South of France, and brought up near Marseilles, without knowing his father's name. His father had paid for his upbringing, in his infancy, in his schooldays and in the activities that followed, ending up with a substantial settlement on a suitable marriage. A trustworthy lawyer had acted as intermediary without giving away the secret.

Baron Mordiane, then, knew only that a child of his was living somewhere near Marseilles, that he was said to be intelligent and well educated, and that he had married the daughter of an architect and surveyor, whom he had succeeded in the business. He was also said to be making money.

Why should he not go and see this unknown son, without disclosing his identity—study him at first hand and see whether, in case of need, he might find a welcome refuge in his home?

He had always treated him liberally, and had made a generous settlement, which had been gratefully received. He was therefore sure of not coming into conflict with an unreasonable pride, and the idea of leaving for the South had now become an oft-recurring desire which gave him no rest. He was urged on, also, by a curious feeling of self-pity at the thought of that cheerful and comfortable home on the coast where he would find his charming, young daughter-in-law, his grandchildren ready to welcome him, and his son; all this would remind him of that brief and happy love-affair so many years ago. His only regret was his past generosity, which had assisted the young man on the road to prosperity and would prevent the father from appearing amongst them in the role of benefactor.

With these thoughts running through his mind he walked along, his head buried deep in his fur collar: his decision was quickly made. Hailing a passing cab, he drove home, and said to his valet, aroused from his sleep to open the door:

"Louis, we leave for Marseilles tomorrow evening. We shall be there perhaps a fortnight. Make all preparations for the journey."

The train sped along the sandy banks of the Rhone, over yellow plains and through sunny villages—a country with gaunt encircling mountains in the distance.

Baron Mordiane, awakened after a night in the sleeping-car, gloomily contemplated his reflection in the little mirror in his dressing-case. The crude light of the South showed up wrinkles he had never seen before, and revealed a state of decrepitude that had passed unnoticed in the shaded light of Paris flats. Looking at the corners of his eyes, the wrinkled eyelids, bald temples and forehead, he said to himself:

"Good heavens, I am worse than faded: I look worn out!"

His desire for peace suddenly increased, and for the first time in his life he was conscious of a vague longing to take his grandchildren on his knee.

He hired a carriage in Marseilles and about one o'clock in the afternoon he stopped before a dazzling white country-house typical of the South of France, standing at the end of an avenue of plane-trees. He beamed with pleasure as he went along the avenue and said to himself:

"It's damned nice."

Suddenly a youngster of about five or six rushed from behind the shrubs and stood motionless at the end of the drive, gazing round-eyed at the visitor.

Mordiane approached and said to him:

"Good afternoon, my boy!"

The youngster made no reply.

The baron then stooped and picked him up to kiss him, but so strong was the odor of garlic coming from the child that he quickly put him down again, murmuring, "Oh! he must be the gardener's son." And he went on towards the house.

On the line in front of the door, the washing was drying, shirts, napkins, towels, aprons, and sheets, while a display of socks hanging in rows on cords one above another filled the whole window, like tiers of sausages in front of a pork-butcher's shop.

The baron called out, and a servant appeared, truly Southern in her dirty and unkempt state, with wisps of hair straggling across her face. Her stained skirt still retained some of its original gaudiness, suggesting a country fair or a mountebank's costume.

"Is M. Duchoux at home?" he inquired.

"You want M. Duchoux?" the servant repeated.

"Yes."

"He is in the parlor, drawing plans."

"Tell him that M. Merlin[1] wishes to see him."

She replied in surprise, "Oh! come in, if you want him," and shouted:

"M. Duchoux, a visitor to see you!"

The baron entered a large room darkened by half-closed shutters, and received a vague impression of filth and disorder.

A short, bald-headed man, standing at an untidy table, was tracing lines on a large sheet of paper. He stopped his work and came forward.

His open waistcoat, slackened trousers and rolled-up shirt-sleeves showed how hot it was, and the muddy shoes that he was wearing pointed to recent rain.

"To whom have I the honor? . . ." he asked, with a strong Southern accent.

---

[1] The Baron intentionally chooses the name of the marvelous magician of Arthurian legend as an alias.

"I am M. Merlin. I have come to consult you about some building land."

"Ah! yes. Certainly."

And turning towards his wife, who was knitting in the darkened room, Duchoux said:

"Clear one of the chairs, Josephine."

Mordiane saw a young woman, already showing signs of age, as provincial women of twenty-five do for want of attention and regular cleanliness, in fact, of all those precautions which form part of a woman's toilet, helping to preserve her youthful appearance, her charm and beauty up to the age of fifty. A kerchief hung over her shoulders, and her hair, which was beautifully thick and black, but was twisted up in slipshod fashion, looked as though it was seldom brushed. With her roughened hands she removed a child's dress, a knife, a piece of string, an empty flower-pot and a greasy plate from a chair, and offered it to the visitor.

He sat down, and then noticed that on the table at which Duchoux had been working, in addition to his books and papers, there were two freshly cut lettuces, a basin, a hairbrush, a napkin, a revolver, and several dirty cups.

The architect saw him glance at these, and smilingly remarked, "I am sorry that the room is rather untidy; that is the children's fault," and he drew up his chair to talk to his client.

"You are looking for a piece of land around Marseilles?"

Although he was some distance away, the baron smelt the odor of garlic which people of the South exhale as flowers do their perfume.

"Was that your son I met under the plane-trees?" Mordiane inquired.

"Yes, the second."

"You have two sons, then?"

"Three, sir, one a year," replied Duchoux, with evident pride.

The baron thought that if they all had the same perfume, their nursery must be a real conservatory. He resumed: "Yes, I should like a nice piece of ground near the sea, on a secluded beach. . . ."

Then Duchoux began to explain. He had ten, twenty, fifty, a hundred and more plots of land of that kind, at all prices and to suit all tastes. The words came in a torrent as he smiled and wagged his round, bald head in his satisfaction.

Meanwhile the baron was bringing to mind a little woman, slight, fair, and rather sad, who used to say with such yearning, "My own beloved," that the very memory made his blood run hot in his veins. She had loved him passionately, madly, for three months; then becoming pregnant in the absence of her husband, who was Governor of a colony, she had fled into hiding, distracted by fear and despair, until the birth of the child whom Mordiane carried off one summer evening and whom they had never seen again.

She died of consumption three years later, in the colony where she had gone to rejoin her husband. It was their son who sat beside him now, who was saying with a metallic ring in his voice:

"As for this plot, sir, it is a unique opportunity. . . ."

And Mordiane remembered the other voice, light as a zephyr, murmuring:

"My own beloved; we will never part. . . ." The memory of the gentle, devoted look in those blue eyes came back to him as he watched the round, blue, but so vacant eyes of this ridiculous little man who was so like his mother, and yet. . . .

Yes, he looked more and more like her every minute; his intonation, his demeanor, his gestures were the same; he resembled her as a monkey resembles a man; yet he was of her blood, he had many of her little habits, though distorted, irritating and revolting. The baron was in torment, haunted suddenly by that terrible, ever-growing resemblance, which enraged, maddened, and tortured him like a nightmare, or like bitter remorse.

"When can we look at this land together?" he stammered.

"Why, tomorrow, if you like."

"Yes, tomorrow. What time?"

"At one o'clock."

"Very good."

The child he had met in the avenue appeareed in the door and cried: "Father!"

No one answered him.

Mordiane stood up trembling with an intense longing to escape. That word "father" had struck him like a bullet. That garlicky "father," that Southern "father," was addressed to him, was meant for him. Oh! how sweet had been the perfume of his beloved and bygone days!

As Duchoux was showing him out, the baron said:

"Is this house yours?"

"Yes, sir, I bought it recently, and I am proud of it. I am fortune's child, sir, and I make no secret of it; I am proud of it. I owe nothing to anyone; I am the child of my own efforts, and I owe everything to myself."

The child, who had remained on the door-step, again cried, "Father!" the voice coming from a greater distance.

Mordiane, shivering with fear, seized with panic, fled as from a great danger. "He will guess who I am," he thought of himself, "he will hug me in his arms and call me 'Father' and give me a kiss reeking of garlic."

"I shall see you tomorrow, sir."

"Tomorrow, at one o'clock."

The carriage rumbled along the white road.

"Driver, take me to the station," he shouted, while two voices seemed to ring in his ears. One of them, far away and sweet, the faint, sad voice of the dead, was saying, "My own beloved"; the other, a metallic, shrill, repellent voice, crying, "Father!" much as one shouts, "Stop him!" when a thief is in flight.

As he came into the club next evening, Count d'Etreillis said to him:

"We have not seen you for three days. Have you been ill?"

"Yes, I have not been very well. I suffer from headaches occasionally. . . ."

COMMENTARY

In violation of the chronological order in which the stories of this volume are arranged, I have put "M. Duchoux" after "The Treasure" because I think that something is to be gained by reading the stories in this sequence. I said of "The Treasure" that it was unlike all the other stories in the volume in that it was not serious, and it seems to me that it may be enlightening to try to discover why Maugham's story fails of seriousness while Maupassant's achieves it.

The comparison has cogency because the two stories address themselves to the same theme. Each is about a man of extreme self-centeredness who is drawn to another person only to retreat from the relationship because it threatens his established mode of life. In both instances, the self-regard of the man is expressed in his attachment to a certain *style* of living—Harenger in "The Treasure" and the Baron in "M. Duchoux" are committed not only to comfort but to elegance.

Yet despite this virtual identity of theme, the two stories are very dissimilar in effect. If ever an author wrote stories, as Santayana says Maugham did, "because writing stories is a profession," it was Maupassant. And "M. Duchoux" has indeed the air of having been written only to amuse. Yet we can scarcely fail to see that Maupassant's story has a weight of meaning that Maugham's cannot claim.

The difference may in some part be explained by the kind of personal relationship each story describes. We think it odd of Haranger, and funny, that after a gratifying sexual experience, he has no wish to repeat it because to do so would interfere with the fussy arrangements of his life. He supposes, no doubt correctly, that it will make an impossible situation to have a servant who is also his mistress (marriage, of course, is not in question), and he has no difficulty in deciding that it is the servant he prefers. We smile at his choice and think him rather poor-spirited for having made it. Yet of course we know that sexual connections are often made only to be broken, that an erotic episode is nothing but a fortuitous event unless strong feelings are permitted or invited to intervene. But the relation between a father and a son is of a far more exigent kind. Literature treats it much less frequently than the sexual relation in any of its forms, but whenever it does touch upon it, the effect is likely to be grave and somberly moving. In the Bible, for example, no stories approach in tragic or pathetic import those of Abraham and Isaac, of Jacob and Benjamin, of David and Absalom. Especially if the father is advanced in years, the connection that he feels with his son is unspeakably intense, for it is, we suppose, the connection with life itself, with futurity and hope.

This being the traditional and, as it were, ideal paternal feeling, our expectations suffer a comic jolt when the Baron, coming to inspect the son he has never seen, rejects him out of hand because he dislikes his appearance, manner, and style of life. The Baron is in every way a deficient father, and of course he displays an absurd effrontery in thinking that he has the right to intrude himself into his son's life at this late date, as well as a monumental stupidity in fancying that he could possibly find happiness in his son's home. Yet despite his selfishness, arrogance, and stupidity, our sympathy, such as it is, goes out to the Baron—certainly to him rather than to his son.

How is this response to be explained? The Baron's rejection of his son is a very drastic action—for a father to "disown" a son, even for weighty reasons, is, we feel, a violation of nature. Our sense of this is so strong that it extends, as in the present instance, even to a father's disowning an illegitimate son whom he is seeing for the first time. We expect that "nature" and "blood" will assert themselves, that across the gulfs of their separate lives, something in each man will respond to the other; at least that the father, who is aware of the connection, will feel it strongly when in the presence of the son. Our piety prepares us for that moving dramatic event, the scene of recognition, and of course we fail to get it. And yet, cheated of our expectations though we are, we take pleasure in the Baron's decision not to disclose the relationship. The Baron, we feel, could not do otherwise than conclude that he was not, after all, a father if it was M. Duchoux who was his son. And we experience a certain satisfaction as our instinctual pieties are checked and challenged by our skeptical intelligence, which poses the question, What is a son?

It is a question that has been asked, in a very memorable way, by William Butler Yeats in one of his finest poems, "Among School Children." As Yeats puts the question, it refers not to a father's but to a mother's idea of what a son is, but its force is the same. The poet is visiting a girls' school in an official capacity and as he stands among the little pupils, he becomes conscious of his age, of his being "a sixty-year-old smiling public man," and he asks whether this could possibly have been what his mother envisioned when she conceived him in delight, bore him in agony, and reared him in hope.

> What youthful mother, a shape upon her lap [,]
> .   .   .   .
> Would think her son, did she but see that shape
> With sixty or more winters on its head,
> A compensation for the pang of his birth,
> Or the uncertainty of his setting forth?

The implication is that the mother would have lovingly imagined the son as a baby, as a little boy, as a youth, as a young man, with the charm or beauty appropriate to each age, but that she would scarcely be entranced by the thought of him in old age.

Yeats puts the question in a high, poignant way; Maupassant puts it comically and with a touch of cynicism. What is a son? Whatever else he may be, for a parent of any imagination at all, he is not merely a person in his own right but the fulfillment, in some degree, of the right way for a man to be. Whatever he may be, it is clear what a son cannot be—a short, plump, fidgety man, who, when he talks of business, wags his round head in satisfaction, who has embraced middle age before his time, whose mind gives no sign of being able to rise above real estate deals and a sordid, garlicky domesticity. Such a man denies anyone's idea of a son—M. Duchoux himself would be dismayed by a son in his own image!

ENEMIES

ANTON CHEKHOV
1860–1904

ABOUT TEN O'CLOCK of a dark September evening the *zemstvo* doctor[1] Kirilov's only son, six-year-old Andrey, died of diphtheria. As the doctor's wife dropped on to her knees before the dead child's cot and the first paroxysm of despair took hold of her, the bell rang sharply in the hall.

When the diphtheria came all the servants were sent away from the house, that very morning. Kirilov himself went to the door, just as he was, in his shirt-sleeves with his waistcoat unbuttoned, without wiping his wet face or hands, which had been burnt with carbolic acid. It was dark in the hall, and of the person who entered could be distinguished only his middle height, a white scarf and a big, extraordinarily pale face, so pale that it seemed as though its appearance made the hall brighter. . . .

"Is the doctor in?" the visitor asked abruptly.

"I'm at home," answered Kirilov. "What do you want?"

"Oh, you're the doctor? I'm so glad!" The visitor was overjoyed and began to seek for the doctor's hand in the darkness. He found it and squeezed it hard in his own. "I'm very . . . very glad! We were introduced. . . . I am Aboguin . . . had the pleasure of meeting you this summer at Mr. Gnouchev's. I am very glad

[1] The doctor appointed for the district, or *zemstvo*.

548

to have found you at home. . . . For God's sake, don't say you won't come with me immediately. . . . My wife has been taken dangerously ill . . . I have the carriage with me. . . ."

From the visitor's voice and movements it was evident that he had been in a state of violent agitation. Exactly as though he had been frightened by a fire or a mad dog, he could hardly restrain his hurried breathing, and he spoke quickly in a trembling voice. In his speech there sounded a note of real sincerity, of childish fright. Like all men who are frightened and dazed, he spoke in short, abrupt phrases and uttered many superfluous, quite unnecessary, words.

"I was afraid I shouldn't find you at home," he continued. "While I was coming to you I suffered terribly. . . . Dress yourself and let us go, for God's sake. . . . It happened like this, Papchinsky came to me—Alexander Sieminovich, you know him. . . . We were chatting. . . . Then we sat down to tea. Suddenly my wife cries out, presses her hands to her heart, and falls back in her chair. We carried her off to her bed and . . . and I rubbed her forehead with sal-volatile, and splashed her with water. . . . She lies like a corpse. . . . I'm afraid that her heart's failed. . . . Let us go. . . . Her father too died of heart-failure."

Kirilov listened in silence as though he did not understand the Russian language.

When Aboguin once more mentioned Papchinsky and his wife's father, and once more began to seek for the doctor's hand in the darkness, the doctor shook his head and said, drawling each word listlessly:

"Excuse me, but I can't go. . . . Five minutes ago my . . . son died."

"Is that true?" Aboguin whispered, stepping back. "My God, what an awful moment to come! It's a terribly fated day . . . terribly! What a coincidence . . . and it might have been on purpose."

Aboguin took hold of the door handle and dropped his head in meditation. Evidently he was hesitating, not knowing whether to go away, or to ask the doctor once more.

"Listen," he said eagerly, seizing Kirilov by the sleeve. "I fully understand your state! God knows I'm ashamed to try to hold your attention at such a moment, but what can I do? Think yourself—who can I go to? There isn't another doctor here besides you. For heaven's sake come. I'm not asking for myself. It's not I that's ill!"

Silence began. Kirilov turned his back to Aboguin, stood still for a while and slowly went out of the hall into the drawing-room. To judge by his uncertain, machine-like movement, and by the attentiveness with which he arranged the hanging shade on the unlighted lamp in the drawing-room and consulted a thick book which lay on the table—at such a moment he had neither purpose nor desire, nor did he think of anything, and probably had already forgotten that there was a stranger standing in his hall. The gloom and the quiet of the drawing-room apparently increased his insanity. As he went from the drawing-room to his study he raised his right foot higher than he need, felt with his hands for the door-posts, and then one felt a certain perplexity in his whole figure, as though he had entered a strange house by chance, or for the first time in his life had got drunk, and now was giving himself up in bewilderment to the new sensation. A wide line of light stretched across the book-shelves on one wall of the study; this light, together with the heavy stifling smell of carbolic acid and ether came from the door ajar that led from the study into the bedroom. . . .

The doctor sank into a chair before the table; for a while he looked drowsily at the shining books, then rose, and went into the bedroom.

Here, in the bedroom dead quiet reigned. Everything, down to the last trifle, spoke eloquently of the tempest undergone, of weariness, and everything rested. The candle which stood among a close crowd of phials, boxes and jars on the stool and the big lamp on the chest of drawers brightly lit the room. On the bed, by the window, the boy lay open-eyed, with a look of wonder on his face. He did not move, but it seemed that his open eyes became darker and darker every second and sank into his skull. Having laid her hands on his body and hid her face in the folds of the bed-clothes, the mother now was on her knees before the bed. Like the boy she did not move, but how much living movement was felt in the coil of her body and in her hands! She was pressing close to the bed with her whole being, with eager vehemence, as though she were afraid to violate the quiet and comfortable pose which she had found at last for her weary body. Blankets, cloths, basins, splashes on the floor, brushes and spoons scattered everywhere, a white bottle of lime-water, the stifling heavy air itself—everything died away, and as it were plunged into quietude.

The doctor stopped by his wife, thrust his hands into his trouser pockets and bending his head on one side looked fixedly at his son. His face showed indifference; only the drops which glistened on his beard revealed that he had been lately weeping.

The repulsive terror of which we think when we speak of death was absent from the bed-room. In the pervading dumbness, in the mother's pose, in the indifference of the doctor's face was something attractive that touched the heart, the subtle and elusive beauty of human grief, which it will take men long to understand and describe, and only music, it seems, is able to express. Beauty too was felt in the stern stillness. Kirilov and his wife were silent and did not weep, as though they confessed all the poetry of their condition. As once the season of their youth passed away, so now in this boy their right to bear children had passed away, alas! for ever to eternity. The doctor is forty-four years old, already grey and looks like an old man; his faded sick wife is thirty-five. Andrey was not merely the only son but the last.

In contrast to his wife the doctor's nature belonged to those which feel the necessity of movement when their soul is in pain. After standing by his wife for about five minutes, he passed from the bed-room lifting his right foot too high, into a little room half filled with a big broad divan. From there he went to the kitchen. After wandering about the fireplace and the cook's bed, he stooped through a little door and came into the hall.

Here he saw the white scarf and the pale face again.

"At last," sighed Aboguin, seizing the door-handle. "Let us go, please."

The doctor shuddered, glanced at him and remembered.

"Listen. I've told you already that I can't go," he said, livening. "What a strange idea!"

"Doctor, I'm made of flesh and blood, too. I fully understand your condition. I sympathise with you," Aboguin said in an imploring voice, putting his hand to his scarf. "But I am not asking for myself. My wife is dying. If you had heard her cry, if you'd seen her face, you would understand my insistence! My God—and I thought that you'd gone to dress yourself. The time is precious, Doctor! Let us go, I beg of you."

"I can't come," Kirilov said after a pause, and stepped into his drawing-room. Aboguin followed him and seized him by the sleeve.

"You're in sorrow. I understand. But I'm not asking you to cure a toothache, or to give expert evidence,—but to save a human life." He went on imploring like a beggar. "This life is more than any personal grief. I ask you for courage, for a brave deed—in the name of humanity."

"Humanity cuts both ways," Kirilov said irritably. "In the name of the same humanity I ask you not to take me away. My God, what a strange idea! I can hardly stand on my feet and you frighten me with humanity. I'm not fit for anything now. I won't go for anything. With whom shall I leave my wife? No, no. . . ."

Kirilov flung out his open hands and drew back.

"And . . . and don't ask me," he continued, disturbed. "I'm sorry. . . . Under the Laws, Volume XIII., I'm obliged to go and you have the right to drag me by the neck. . . . Well, drag me, but . . . I'm not fit. . . . I'm not even able to speak. Excuse me."

"It's quite unfair to speak to me in that tone, Doctor," said Aboguin, again taking the doctor by the sleeve. "The thirteenth volume be damned! I have no right to do violence to your will. If you want to, come; if you don't, then God be with you; but it's not to your will that I apply, but to your feelings. A young woman is dying! You say your son died just now. Who could understand my terror better than you?"

Aboguin's voice trembled with agitation. His tremor and his tone were much more convincing than his words. Aboguin was sincere, but it is remarkable that every phrase he used came out stilted, soulless, inopportunely florid, and as it were insulted the atmosphere of the doctor's house and the woman who was dying. He felt it himself, and in his fear of being misunderstood he exerted himself to the utmost to make his voice soft and tender so as to convince by the sincerity of his tone at least, if not by his words. As a rule, however deep and beautiful the words they affect only the unconcerned. They cannot always satisfy those who are happy or distressed because the highest expression of happiness or distress is most often silence. Lovers understand each other best when they are silent, and a fervent passionate speech at the graveside affects only outsiders. To the widow and children it seems cold and trivial.

Kirilov stood still and was silent. When Aboguin uttered some more words on the higher vocation of a doctor, and self-sacrifice, the doctor sternly asked:

"Is it far?"

"Thirteen or fourteen versts.[2] I've got good horses, Doctor. I give you my word of honour that I'll take you there and back in an hour. Only an hour."

The last words impressed the doctor more strongly than the references to humanity or the doctor's vocation. He thought for a while and said with a sigh:

"Well, let us go!"

He went off quickly, with a step that was not sure, to his study and soon after returned in a long coat. Aboguin, delighted, danced impatiently round him, helped him on with his overcoat, and accompanied him out of the house.

Outside it was dark, but brighter than in the hall. Now in the darkness the tall stooping figure of the doctor was clearly visible with the long, narrow beard

[2] Eight or nine miles.

and the aquiline nose. Besides his pale face Aboguin's big face could now be seen and a little student cap which hardly covered the crown of his head. The scarf showed white only in front, but behind it was hid under his long hair.

"Believe me, I'm able to appreciate your magnanimity," murmured Aboguin, as he helped the doctor to a seat in the carriage. "We'll whirl away. Luke, dear man, drive as fast as you can, do!"

The coachman drove quickly. First appeared a row of bare buildings, which stood along the hospital yard. It was dark everywhere, save that at the end of the yard a bright light from someone's window broke through the garden fence, and three windows in the upper story of the separate house seemed to be paler than the air. Then the carriage drove into dense obscurity where you could smell mushroom damp, and hear the whisper of the trees. The noise of the wheels awoke the rooks who began to stir in the leaves and raised a doleful, bewildered cry as if they knew that the doctor's son was dead and Aboguin's wife ill. Then began to appear separate trees, a shrub. Sternly gleamed the pond, where big black shadows slept. The carriage rolled along over an even plain. Now the cry of the rooks was but faintly heard far away behind. Soon it became completely still.

Almost all the way Kirilov and Aboguin were silent; save that once Aboguin sighed profoundly and murmured:

"It's terrible pain. One never loves his nearest so much as when there is the risk of losing them."

And when the carriage was quietly passing through the river, Kirilov gave a sudden start, as though the dashing of the water frightened him, and he began to move impatiently.

"Let me go," he said in anguish. "I'll come to you later. I only want to send the attendant to my wife. She is all alone."

Aboguin was silent. The carriage, swaying and rattling against the stones, drove over the sandy bank and went on. Kirilov began to toss about in anguish, and glanced around. Behind the road was visible in the scant light of the stars and the willows that fringed the bank disappearing into the darkness. To the right the plain stretched smooth and boundless as heaven. On it in the distance here and there dim lights were burning, probably on the turf-pits. To the left, parallel with the road stretched a little hill, tufted with tiny shrubs, and on the hill a big half-moon stood motionless, red, slightly veiled with a mist, and surrounded with fine clouds which seemed to be gazing upon it from every side, and guarding it, lest it should disappear.

In all nature one felt something hopeless and sick. Like a fallen woman who sits alone in a dark room trying not to think of her past, the earth languished with reminiscence of spring and summer and waited in apathy for ineluctable winter. Wherever one's glance turned nature showed everywhere like a dark, cold, bottomless pit, whence neither Kirilov nor Aboguin nor the red half-moon could escape. . . .

The nearer the carriage approached the destination the more impatient did Aboguin become. He moved about, jumped up and stared over the driver's shoulder in front of him. And when at last the carriage drew up at the foot of the grand staircase, nicely covered with a striped linen awning and he looked up at the lighted windows of the first floor one could hear his breath trembling.

"If anything happens . . . I shan't survive it," he said, entering the hall with the doctor and slowly rubbing his hands in his agitation. "But I can't hear any noise. That means it's all right so far," he added, listening to the stillness. No voices or steps were heard in the hall. For all the bright illumination the whole house seemed asleep. Now the doctor and Aboguin who had been in darkness up till now could examine each other. The doctor was tall, with a stoop, slovenly dressed, and his face was plain. There was something unpleasantly sharp, ungracious, and severe in his thick Negro lips, his aquiline nose and his faded, indifferent look. His tangled hair, his sunken temples, the early grey in his long thin beard, that showed his shining chin, his pale grey complexion and the slipshod awkwardness of his manners—the hardness of it all suggested to the mind bad times undergone, an unjust lot and weariness of life and men. To look at the hard figure of the man, you could not believe that he had a wife and could weep over his child. Aboguin revealed something different. He was robust, solid and fair-haired, with a big head and large, yet soft, features, exquisitely dressed in the latest fashion. In his carriage, his tight-buttoned coat and his mane of hair you felt something noble and leonine. He walked with his head straight and his chest prominent, he spoke in a pleasant baritone, and in his manner of removing his scarf or arranging his hair there appeared a subtle, almost feminine, elegance. Even his pallor and childish fear as he glanced upwards to the staircase while taking off his coat, did not disturb his carriage or take from the satisfaction, the health and aplomb which his figure breathed.

"There's no one about, nothing I can hear," he said, walking upstairs. "No commotion. May God be good!"

He accompanied the doctor through the hall to a large salon, where a big piano showed dark and a lustre[3] hung in a white cover. Thence they both passed into a small and beautiful drawing-room, very cosy, filled with a pleasant, rosy half-darkness.

"Please sit here a moment, Doctor," said Aboguin, "I . . . I won't be a second. I'll just have a look and tell them."

Kirilov was left alone. The luxury of the drawing-room, the pleasant half-darkness, even his presence in a stranger's unfamiliar house evidently did not move him. He sat in a chair looking at his hands burnt with carbolic acid. He had no more than a glimpse of the bright red lampshade, the 'cello case, and when he looked sideways across the room to where the clock was ticking, he noticed a stuffed wolf, as solid and satisfied as Aboguin himself.

It was still. . . . Somewhere far away in the other rooms someone uttered a loud "Ah!" A glass door, probably a cupboard door, rang, and again everything was still. After five minutes had passed, Kirilov did not look at his hands any more. He raised his eyes to the door through which Aboguin had disappeared.

Aboguin was standing on the threshold, but not the same man as went out. The expression of satisfaction and subtle elegance had disappeared from him. His face and hands, the attitude of his body were distorted with a disgusting expression either of horror or of tormenting physical pain. His nose, lips, moustache, all his features were moving and as it were trying to tear themselves away from his face, but the eyes were as though laughing from pain.

Aboguin took a long heavy step into the middle of the room, stooped, moaned, and shook his fists.

"Deceived!" he cried, emphasising the syllable *cei*. "She deceived me! She's gone! She fell ill and sent me for the doctor only to run away with this fool Papchinsky. My God!"

[3] Chandelier.

Aboguin stepped heavily towards the doctor, thrust his white soft fists before his face, and went on wailing, shaking his fists the while.

"She's gone off! She's deceived me! But why this lie? My God, my God! Why this dirty, foul trick, this devilish, serpent's game? What have I done to her? She's gone off."

Tears gushed from his eyes. He turned on his heel and began to pace the drawing-room. Now in his short jacket and his fashionable narrow trousers in which his legs seemed too thin for his body, he was extraordinarily like a lion. Curiosity kindled in the doctor's impassive face. He rose and eyed Aboguin.

"Well, where's the patient?"

"The patient, the patient," cried Aboguin, laughing, weeping, and still shaking his fists. "She's not ill, but accursed. Vile—dastardly. The Devil himself couldn't have planned a fouler trick. She sent me so that she could run away with a fool, an utter clown, an Alphonse![4] My God, far better she should have died. I'll not bear it. I shall not bear it."

The doctor stood up straight. His eyes began to blink, filled with tears; his thin beard began to move with his jaw right and left.

"What's this?" he asked, looking curiously about. "My child's dead. My wife in anguish, alone in all the house. . . . I can hardly stand on my feet, I haven't slept for three nights . . . and I'm made to play in a vulgar comedy, to play the part of a stage property! I don't . . . I don't understand it!"

Aboguin opened one fist, flung a crumpled note on the floor and trod on it, as upon an insect he wished to crush.

"And I didn't see . . . didn't understand," he said through his set teeth, brandishing one fist round his head, with an expression as though someone had trod on a corn. "I didn't notice how he came to see us every day. I didn't notice that he came in a carriage to-day! What was the carriage for? And I didn't see! Innocent!"

"I don't . . . I don't understand," the doctor murmured. "What's it all mean? It's jeering at a man, laughing at a man's suffering! That's impossible. . . . I've never seen it in my life before!"

With the dull bewilderment of a man who has just begun to understand that someone has bitterly offended him, the doctor shrugged his shoulders, waved his hands and not knowing what to say or do, dropped exhausted into a chair.

"Well, she didn't love me any more. She loved another man. Very well. But why the deceit, why this foul treachery?" Aboguin spoke with tears in his voice. "Why, why? What have I done to you? Listen, Doctor," he said passionately approaching Kirilov. "You were the unwilling witness of my misfortune, and I am not going to hide the truth from you. I swear I loved this woman. I loved her with devotion, like a slave. I sacrificed everything for her. I broke with my family, I gave up the service and my music. I forgave her things I could not have forgiven my mother and sister . . . I never once gave her an angry look . . . I never gave her any cause. Why this lie, then? I do not demand love, but why this abominable deceit? If you don't love any more then speak out honestly, above all when you know what I feel about this matter. . . ."

With tears in his eyes and trembling in all his bones, Aboguin was pouring out his soul to the doctor. He spoke passionately, pressing both hands to his heart. He revealed all the family secrets without hesitation, as though he were glad that

_____

[4] A man maintained at a woman's expense.

these secrets were being torn from his heart. Had he spoken thus for an hour or two and poured out all his soul, he would surely have been easier.

Who can say whether, had the doctor listened and given him friendly sympathy, he would not, as so often happens, have been reconciled to his grief unprotesting, without turning to unprofitable follies? But it happened otherwise. While Aboguin was speaking the offended doctor changed countenance visibly. The indifference and amazement in his face gradually gave way to an expression of bitter outrage, indignation, and anger. His features became still sharper, harder, and more forbidding. When Aboguin put before his eyes the photograph of his young wife, with a pretty, but dry, inexpressive face like a nun's, and asked if it were possible to look at that face and grant that it could express a lie, the doctor suddenly started away, with flashing eyes, and said, coarsely forging out each several word:

"Why do you tell me all this? I do not want to hear! I don't want to," he cried and banged his fist upon the table. "I don't want your trivial vulgar secrets—to Hell with them. You dare not tell me such trivialities. Or do you think I have not yet been insulted enough! That I'm a lackey to whom you can give the last insult? Yes?"

Aboguin drew back from Kirilov and stared at him in surprise.

"Why did you bring me here?" the doctor went on, shaking his beard. "You marry out of high spirits, get angry out of high spirits, and make a melodrama—but where do I come in? What have I got to do with your romances? Leave me alone! Get on with your noble grabbing, parade your humane ideas, play"—the doctor gave a side-glance at the 'cello-case—"the double-bass and the trombone, stuff yourselves like capons, but don't dare to jeer at a real man! If you can't respect him, then you can at least spare him your attentions."

"What does all this mean?" Aboguin asked, blushing.

"It means that it's vile and foul to play with a man! I'm a doctor. You consider doctors and all men who work and don't reek of scent and harlotry, your footmen, your *mauvais tons*.[5] Very well, but no one gave you the right to turn a man who suffers into a property."

"How dare you say that?" Aboguin asked quietly. Again his face began to twist about, this time in visible anger.

"How dare *you* bring me here to listen to trivial rubbish, when you know that I'm in sorrow?" the doctor cried and banged his fists on the table once more. "Who gave you the right to jeer at another's grief?"

"You're mad," cried Aboguin. "You're ungenerous. I too am deeply unhappy and . . . and . . ."

"Unhappy"—the doctor gave a sneering laugh—"don't touch the word, it's got nothing to do with you. Wasters who can't get money on a bill call themselves unhappy too. A capon's unhappy, oppressed with all its superfluous fat. You worthless lot!"

"Sir, you're forgetting yourself," Aboguin gave a piercing scream. "For words like those, people are beaten. Do you understand?"

Aboguin thrust his hand into his side pocket, took out a pocket-book, found two notes and flung them on the table.

"There's your fee," he said, and his nostrils trembled. "You're paid."

"You dare not offer me money," said the doctor, and brushed the notes from the table to the floor. "You don't settle an insult with money."

[5] (French) The unrefined, those lacking the manners of the fashionable world.

Aboguin and the doctor stood face to face, heaping each other with undeserved insults. Never in their lives, even in a frenzy, had they said so much that was unjust and cruel and absurd. In both the selfishness of the unhappy is violently manifest. Unhappy men are selfish, wicked, unjust, and less able to understand each other than fools. Unhappiness does not unite people, but separates them; and just where one would imagine that people should be united by the community of grief, there is more injustice and cruelty done than among the comparatively contented.

"Send me home, please," the doctor cried, out of breath.

Aboguin rang the bell violently. Nobody came. He rang once more; then flung the bell angrily to the floor. It struck dully on the carpet and gave out a mournful sound like a death-moan. The footman appeared.

"Where have you been hiding, damn you?" The master sprang upon him with clenched fists. "Where have you been just now? Go away and tell them to send the carriage round for this gentleman, and get the brougham ready for me. Wait," he called out as the footman turned to go. "Not a single traitor remains to-morrow. Pack off all of you! I will engage new ones. . . . Rabble!"

While they waited Aboguin and the doctor were silent. Already the expression of satisfaction and the subtle elegance had returned to the former. He paced the drawing-room, shook his head elegantly and evidently was planning something. His anger was not yet cool, but he tried to make as if he did not notice his enemy. . . . The doctor stood with one hand on the edge of the table, looking at Aboguin with that deep, rather cynical, ugly contempt with which only grief and an unjust lot can look, when they see satiety and elegance before them.

A little later, when the doctor took his seat in the carriage and drove away, his eyes still glanced contemptuously. It was dark, much darker than an hour ago. The red half-moon had now disappeared behind the little hill, and the clouds which watched it lay in dark spots round the stars. The brougham with the red lamps began to rattle on the road and passed the doctor. It was Aboguin on his way to protest, to commit all manner of folly.

All the way the doctor thought not of his wife or Andrey, but only of Aboguin and those who lived in the house he just left. His thoughts were unjust, inhuman, and cruel. He passed sentence on Aboguin, his wife, Papchinsky, and all those who live in rosy semi-darkness and smell of scent. All the way he hated them, and his heart ached with his contempt for them. The conviction he formed about them would last his life long.

Time will pass and Kirilov's sorrow, but this conviction, unjust and unworthy of the human heart, will not pass, but will remain in the doctor's mind until the grave.

COMMENTARY

Whoever tries to account for the peculiar charm of Chekhov's work will sooner or later touch upon a certain personal trait of the author which is suggested by his stories and plays. If we try to give this quality a name, we may call it *modesty*. Chekhov is a writer of the very highest distinction. He set great store by art, insisted on the importance of its function in our lives, and was jealous for the status of the artist in society. But in everything he wrote he seems to be saying that he does not claim for himself the brilliant dominating powers that are often thought to be the essence of artistic genius. He was a physician, although he eventually gave up medicine for literature, and in his conception of himself as a writer there is something of the self-effacement we like to think is appropriate to a good medical practitioner, subordination of himself to the case he deals with and a gentle deference to the suffering he observes.

His modesty is to be seen not only in his manner but in his choice of subjects. Chekhov does not try to achieve the intensities of Tolstoi and Dostoevski, his great compatriots of the generation before his own. He was one of the most intelligent of men, and we may suppose that there was nothing in the Russia of his time of which he was unaware, but he did not undertake to confront the high issues of politics, religion, and morality that play so decisive a part in the work of the two pre-eminent Russian novelists; his stories and plays do not deal directly with grandiose public concerns or with transcendent intentions of good or evil. His expressed sense of the nature of human existence refers to muted passions, frustrated hopes, affronted self-esteem, the boredom and listlessness that overtake once-aspiring spirits, the dull pain of isolation and alienation. It is as if he were telling us, with characteristic compassion, that the life of man as it was lived in his time in Czarist Russia is too restricted and hampered to admit the possibility of conduct and emotions which could achieve that grandeur we call heroic.

His implicit denial of the possibility of the heroic mode does not make Chekhov unique in his time, or ours. On the contrary, it brings him into one of the most important general tendencies of literature of the past three or four centuries, the adverse questioning of the heroic mode.

In the sense in which the word is most likely to be used in the history of literature, the heroic is not in the first place a category of morality but, rather, a category of style. In everyday speech we use the word to convey the idea of courage of a striking kind and its significance does not go beyond this. But in the traditional literary conception of the heroic character, although courage is indeed an essential element, it is not in itself definitive. It was essential because a person without courage cannot possibly be a person of dignity, and what is definitive of the heroic character is his dignity. Dignity, however, is not in itself a moral quality—it is a quality of appearance, of style or manner.

Not every tradition of heroic literature in Europe was directly influenced by the requirements laid down by Aristotle for the classical hero of tragedy, but all traditions have required the hero to be a person who commands our respect by reason both of his exalted social position and the qualities of temperament that are presumed to accord with this position. He was also expected to have an appearance and manner appropriate to his princely rank and temperament. Aristotle described the heroic mode only in connection with a certain kind of poetic composition, tragedy; and he understood tragedy not merely in terms of the catastrophic fate it represented but also in terms of its style, every element of which—every detail of language, music, deportment, and costume—must suggest loftiness and grandeur. Ancient tragedy made no pretensions to what we call realism. As Aristotle said by way of definition, it shows men as nobler than they really are, by which he meant more dignified and impressive than they really are. On the stage, the tragic hero indicates his nobility by the style in which he speaks and comports himself, and it is on the stage, we must remember, that the hero really has his being. An authority on the Greek theatre, Professor Margarete Bieber, reminds us of this when she says, "The hero is an actor." And the late Robert Warshow, in a brilliant essay on "Western" movies, says much the same thing when he defines the hero of a "Western" as "a man who looks like a hero."

The literary and histrionic nature of the heroic mode does not keep it from having its effect upon actual life. Indeed, it suggests an ideal to which men may actually aspire—the qualities that engage men in poetry and on the stage do so because, in one way or another, they seem desirable in our daily lives. Dignity is of course a quality of style or manner, but it has substantial and obvious moral and social implications as well; it implies the right to respect, which an American poet has called, with a curious courage of simplicity, "the ultimate good."[1] At the same time, exactly because the heroic mode is so essentially literary and histrionic, and so much concerned to transcend the actuality of the commonplace, it is open to adverse judgment. We feel that it celebrates form above content, appearance above reality; we therefore accuse it of being false, pretentious, and highfalutin. At all times, even among the Greeks themselves, the idea of the heroic has been subject to satire and burlesque. In the sixteenth century the mockery of the heroic becomes, in fact, one of the great themes of literature. Shakespeare in *Troilus and Cressida* flatly denied the dignity of the warrior princes who were the heroes of Greek epic and tragedy. In *Henry IV* he questioned the heroic ideal even more memorably in the opposition of Hotspur and Falstaff, the former ready to sacrifice his very life for the dignity of his honor, the latter mocking honor and dignity as mere words. By the end of the century, criticism of the heroic mode was in full cry. The first great novel, Cervantes' *Don Quixote* (1605–1615), begins as a satire on the heroic idea; and it is remarkable how many of the major novelists, from Fielding in the eighteenth century to James Joyce in the twentieth, make comedy out of the contrast between life as it appears in the literature of the heroic tradition and life as it really is.

But however much the writers of the last three hundred and fifty years may burlesque the heroic ideal, their preoccupation with it suggests that its power over the human mind is still very great. If, with many of our novelists, we take intense note of the dull and trivial circumstances in which we live our daily lives, and call this "reality," we do so with a degree of resentment, under the shadow, as it were, of our sense of the heroic. The realistic novel, we might say, is haunted, if not by the presence, then by the absence, of the heroic idea.

Certainly this is true of the work of Chekhov. His best plays and stories represent the pathos of lives from which the possibility of the heroic has been removed even while the conception of it remains—in the recollection that life once promised a dignity it has since denied; in the memory that people once commanded a respect that can no longer be won either from others or from themselves.

The story "Enemies" is an especially subtle and sad and comic treatment of this omnipresent preoccupation with the heroic mode. Aboguin, the deceived husband, thrusts a photograph of his unfaithful wife at the doctor, the bereaved father, who cries out in passionate revulsion, "I don't want your trivial vulgar

[1] John Berryman, "The Statue," in *The Dispossessed.*

secrets . . ." By the contemptuous adjectives that spring to his lips, the doctor lays claim to the heroic status. Triviality and vulgarity—these are the two qualities that, above all others, constitute the negation of the heroic ideal. And the bereaved father will have none of them. He thinks of his grief as conferring dignity upon him, as giving him a spiritual status which can compete with Aboguin's superior social position. His sorrow validates his existence as what he calls "a real man," and in a passion of pride he resents the intrusion of Aboguin's less noble pain.

Up to the moment when Dr. Kirilov uses his grief to assert his dignity, both grief and dignity have been very real indeed. Stricken and silent, so worn out by sorrow that he is scarcely able to move, facing the end of all hope, almost of all life, yet grimly consenting to discharge his duty, the doctor stands before us with a kind of rigid nobility, demanding both our sympathy and our respect in the highest degree. But when he asserts his right to be thought heroic and tragic because of his suffering, when he says that he must not be involved in a "vulgar comedy" or a "melodrama," and uses his terrible loss to belittle Aboguin and gain moral advantage over him, his grief becomes less compelling and his stature as a man is diminished.

Chekhov makes it as hard as possible for us to withdraw our moral approval from Dr. Kirilov. Our sympathies on his behalf are engaged by his profession, his social circumstances, his devotion to his wife, his age, and the nature of his loss. His antagonist—one might say his competitor in grief—is clearly a person of far less seriousness, sincerity, and depth of feeling. We can scarcely fail to know that the wounded pride of Aboguin will soon heal and become a mere grievance against his faithless wife. The doctor, we are sure, will never have another son in his marriage, but Aboguin will undoubtedly acquire a new wife. But although Chekhov is quite aware of Aboguin's personal inferiority to Kirilov, it is upon the latter that the weight of his moral disapproval falls. What offends him is the doctor's bitter insistence on his superiority as a person and mourner, the fact that Kirilov puts his grief at the service of his social competitiveness.

It is often said of Chekhov that he, more than any other writer, has influenced the theory and practice of the modern short-story. This is true, yet it is worth remarking that there is one element of "Enemies" that must be called anything but modern. No writer of our day would permit himself the passages of generalization and moralizing with which the story ends. The modern theory of fiction, learned in considerable part from Chekhov himself, is that the events of a story must speak for themselves, without the help of the author's explicit comment. (Hemingway's "Hills Like White Elephants" [pages 726 ff.] is an extreme demonstration of this fictional technique.) In any course on the short story an enlightened teacher would surely instruct his students that they must not, as Chekhov does here, tell the reader about the bad effects of unhappiness upon the character, or prophesy what Dr. Kirilov's moral future will be. But I find this surrender of the artist's remoteness in favor of a direct communication with the reader refreshing as well as moving. The willingness of Chekhov to put himself on a level with the reader and to speak in his own person seems to me an instance of the charming modesty of his spirit.

THE PUPIL

HENRY JAMES

1843–1916

I

THE POOR YOUNG MAN hesitated and procrastinated: it cost him such an effort to broach the subject of terms, to speak of money to a person who spoke only of feelings and, as it were, of the aristocracy. Yet he was unwilling to take leave, treating his engagement as settled, without some more conventional glance in that direction than he could find an opening for in the manner of the large affable lady who sat there drawing a pair of soiled *gants de Suède*[1] through a fat jewelled hand and, at once pressing and gliding, repeated over and over everything but the thing he would have liked to hear. He would have liked to hear the figure of his salary; but just as he was nervously about to sound that note the little boy came back—the little boy Mrs. Moreen had sent out of the room to fetch her fan. He came back without the fan, only with the casual observation that he couldn't find it. As he dropped this cynical confession he looked straight and hard at the candidate for the honour of taking his education in hand. This personage reflected somewhat grimly that the first thing he should have to teach his little charge would be to appear to address himself to

[1] (French) Suede gloves (literally, Swedish gloves).

his mother when he spoke to her—especially not to make her such an improper answer as that.

When Mrs. Moreen bethought herself of this pretext for getting rid of their companion Pemberton supposed it was precisely to approach the delicate subject of his remuneration. But it had been only to say some things about her son that it was better a boy of eleven shouldn't catch. They were extravagantly to his advantage save when she lowered her voice to sigh, tapping her left side familiarly, "And all overclouded by *this,* you know; all at the mercy of a weakness—!" Pemberton gathered that the weakness was in the region of the heart. He had known the poor child was not robust: this was the basis on which he had been invited to treat, through an English lady, an Oxford acquaintance, then at Nice, who happened to know both his needs and those of the amiable American family looking out for something really superior in the way of a resident tutor.

The young man's impression of his prospective pupil, who had come into the room as if to see for himself the moment Pemberton was admitted, was not quite the soft solicitation the visitor had taken for granted. Morgan Moreen was somehow sickly without being "delicate," and that he looked intelligent— it is true Pemberton wouldn't have enjoyed his being stupid—only added to the suggestion that, as with his big mouth and big ears he really couldn't be called pretty, he might too utterly fail to please. Pemberton was modest, was even timid; and the chance that his small scholar would prove cleverer than himself had quite figured, to his anxiety, among the dangers of an untried experiment. He reflected, however, that these were risks one had to run when one accepted a position, as it was called, in a private family; when as yet one's university honours had, pecuniarily speaking, remained barren. At any rate when Mrs. Moreen got up as to intimate that, since it was understood he would enter upon his duties within the week she would let him off now, he succeeded, in spite of the presence of the child, in squeezing out a phrase about the rate of payment. It was not the fault of the conscious smile which seemed a reference to the lady's expensive identity, it was not the fault of this demonstration, which had, in a sort, both vagueness and point, if the allusion didn't sound rather vulgar. This was exactly because she became still more gracious to reply: "Oh I can assure you that all that will be quite regular."

Pemberton only wondered, while he took up his hat, what "all that" was to amount to—people had such different ideas. Mrs. Moreen's words, however, seemed to commit the family to a pledge definite enough to elicit from the child a strange little comment in the shape of the mocking foreign ejaculation "Oh la-la!"

Pemberton, in some confusion, glanced at him as he walked slowly to the window with his back turned, his hands in his pockets and the air in his elderly shoulders of a boy who didn't play. The young man wondered if he should be able to teach him to play, though his mother had said it would never do and that this was why school was impossible. Mrs. Moreen exhibited no discomfiture; she only continued blandly: "Mr. Moreen will be delighted to meet your wishes. As I told you, he has been called to London for a week. As soon as he comes back you shall have it out with him."

This was so frank and friendly that the young man could only reply, laughing as his hostess laughed: "Oh I don't imagine we shall have much of a battle."

"They'll give you anything you like," the boy remarked unexpectedly, returning from the window. "We don't mind what anything costs—we live awfully well."

"My darling, you're too quaint!" his mother exclaimed, putting out to caress him a practised but ineffectual hand. He slipped out of it, but looked with intelligent innocent eyes at Pemberton, who had already had time to notice that from one moment to the other his small satiric face seemed to change its time of life. At this moment it was infantine, yet it appeared also to be under the influence of curious intuitions and knowledges. Pemberton rather disliked precocity and was disappointed to find gleams of it in a disciple not yet in his teens. Nevertheless he divined on the spot that Morgan wouldn't prove a bore. He would prove on the contrary a source of agitation. This idea held the young man, in spite of a certain repulsion.

"You pompous little person! We're not extravagant!" Mrs. Moreen gaily protested, making another unsuccessful attempt to draw the boy to her side. "You must know what to expect," she went on to Pemberton.

"The less you expect the better!" her companion interposed. "But we *are* people of fashion."

"Only so far as *you* make us so!" Mrs. Moreen tenderly mocked. "Well then, on Friday—don't tell me you're superstitious—and mind you don't fail us. Then you'll see us all. I'm so sorry the girls are out. I guess you'll like the girls. And, you know, I've another son, quite different from this one."

"He tries to imitate me," Morgan said to their friend.

"He tries? Why he's twenty years old!" cried Mrs. Moreen.

"You're very witty," Pemberton remarked to the child—a proposition his mother echoed with enthusiasm, declaring Morgan's sallies to be the delight of the house.

The boy paid no heed to this; he only enquired abruptly of the visitor, who was surprised afterwards that he hadn't struck him as offensively forward: "Do you *want* very much to come?"

"Can you doubt it after such a description of what I shall hear?" Pemberton replied. Yet he didn't want to come at all; he was coming because he had to go somewhere, thanks to the collapse of his fortune at the end of a year abroad spent on the system of putting his scant patrimony into a single full wave of experience. He had had his full wave but couldn't pay the score at his inn. Moreover he had caught in the boy's eyes the glimpse of a far-off appeal.

"Well, I'll do the best I can for you," said Morgan; with which he turned away again. He passed out of one of the long windows; Pemberton saw him go and lean on the parapet of the terrace. He remained there while the young man took leave of his mother, who, on Pemberton's looking as if he expected a farewell from him, interposed with: "Leave him, leave him; he's so strange!" Pemberton supposed her to fear something he might say. "He's a genius—you'll love him," she added. "He's much the most interesting person in the family." And before he could invent some civility to oppose to this she wound up with: "But we're all good, you know!"

"He's a genius—you'll love him!" were words that recurred to our aspirant before the Friday, suggesting among many things that geniuses were not invariably loveable. However, it was all the better if there was an element that would make tutorship absorbing: he had perhaps taken too much for granted it would only disgust him. As he left the villa after his interview he looked up at the balcony and saw the child leaning over it. "We shall have great larks!" he called up.

Morgan hung fire a moment and then gaily returned: "By the time you come back I shall have thought of something witty!"

This made Pemberton say to himself: "After all he's rather nice."

II

On the Friday he saw them all, as Mrs. Moreen had promised, for her husband had come back and the girls and the other son were at home. Mr. Moreen had a white moustache, a confiding manner and, in his buttonhole, the ribbon of a foreign order—bestowed, as Pemberton eventually learned, for services. For what services he never clearly ascertained: this was a point—one of a large number—that Mr. Moreen's manner never confided. What it emphatically did confide was that he was even more a man of the world than you might first make out. Ulick, the firstborn, was in visible training for the same profession—under the disadvantage as yet, however, of a buttonhole but feebly floral and a moustache with no pretensions to type. The girls had hair and figures and manners and small fat feet, but had never been out alone. As for Mrs. Moreen Pemberton saw on a nearer view that her elegance was intermittent and her parts didn't always match. Her husband, as she had promised, met with enthusiasm Pemberton's ideas in regard to a salary. The young man had endeavoured to keep these stammerings modest, and Mr. Moreen made it no secret that *he* found them wanting in "style." He further mentioned that he aspired to be intimate with his children, to be their best friend, and that he was always looking out for them. That was what he went off for, to London and other places—to look out; and this vigilance was the theory of life, as well as the real occupation, of the whole family. They all looked out, for they were very frank on the subject of its being necessary. They desired it to be understood that they were earnest people, and also that their fortune, though quite adequate for earnest people, required the most careful administration. Mr. Moreen, as the parent bird, sought sustenance for the nest. Ulick invoked support mainly at the club, where Pemberton guessed that it was usually served on green cloth.[2] The girls used to do up their hair and their frocks themselves, and our young man felt appealed to to be glad, in regard to Morgan's education, that, though it must naturally be of the best, it didn't cost too much. After a little he *was* glad, forgetting at times his own needs in the interest inspired by the child's character and culture and the pleasure of making easy terms for him.

During the first weeks of their acquaintance Morgan had been as puzzling as a page in an unknown language—altogether different from the obvious little Anglo-Saxons who had misrepresented childhood to Pemberton. Indeed the whole mystic volume in which the boy had been amateurishly bound demanded some practice in translation. Today, after a considerable interval, there is something phantasmagoric, like a prismatic reflexion or a serial novel, in Pemberton's memory of the queerness of the Moreens. If it were not for a few tangible tokens—a lock of Morgan's hair cut by his own hand, and the half-dozen letters

[2] An allusion to gambling (gambling tables are covered in green felt).

received from him when they were disjoined—the whole episode and the figures peopling it would seem too inconsequent for anything but dreamland. Their supreme quaintness was their success—as it appeared to him for a while at the time; since he had never seen a family so brilliantly equipped for failure. Wasn't it success to have kept him so hatefully long? Wasn't it success to have drawn him in that first morning at déjeuner,[3] the Friday he came—it was enough to *make* one superstitious—so that he utterly committed himself, and this not by calculation or on a signal, but from a happy instinct which made them, like a band of gipsies, work so neatly together? They amused him as much as if they had really been a band of gipsies. He was still young and had not seen much of the world—his English years had been properly arid; therefore the reversed conventions of the Moreens—for they had *their* desperate proprieties—struck him as topsy-turvy. He had encountered nothing like them at Oxford; still less had any such note been struck to his younger American ear during the four years at Yale in which he had richly supposed himself to be reacting against a Puritan strain. The reaction of the Moreens, at any rate, went ever so much further. He had thought himself very sharp that first day in hitting them all off in his mind with the "cosmopolite" label. Later it seemed feeble and colourless—confessedly helplessly provisional.

He yet when he first applied it felt a glow of joy—for an instructor he was still empirical—rise from the apprehension that living with them would really be to see life. Their sociable strangeness was an intimation of that—their chatter of tongues, their gaiety and good humour, their infinite dawdling (they were always getting themselves up, but it took for ever, and Pemberton had once found Mr. Moreen shaving in the drawing-room), their French, their Italian and, cropping up in the foreign fluencies, their cold tough slices of American. They lived on maccaroni and coffee—they had these articles prepared in perfection—but they knew recipes for a hundred other dishes. They overflowed with music and song, were always humming and catching each other up, and had a sort of professional acquaintance with Continental cities. They talked of "good places" as if they had been pickpockets or strolling players. They had at Nice a villa, a carriage, a piano and a banjo, and they went to official parties. They were a perfect calendar of the "days" of their friends, which Pemberton knew them, when they were indisposed, to get out of bed to go to, and which made the week larger than life when Mrs. Moreen talked of them with Paula and Amy. Their initiations gave their new inmate at first an almost dazzling sense of culture. Mrs. Moreen had translated something at some former period —an author whom it made Pemberton feel *borné*[4] never to have heard of. They could imitate Venetian and sing Neapolitan, and when they wanted to say something very particular communicated with each other in an ingenious dialect of their own, an elastic spoken cipher which Pemberton at first took for some *patois*[5] of one of their countries, but which he "caught on to" as he would not have grasped provincial development of Spanish or German.

"It's the family language—Ultramoreen," Morgan explained to him drolly enough; but the boy rarely condescended to use it himself, though he dealt in colloquial Latin as if he had been a little prelate.

Among all the "days" with which Mrs. Moreen's memory was taxed she

[3] (French) Breakfast.
[4] (French) Limited, parochial.
[5] (French) Provincial dialect.

managed to squeeze in one of her own, which her friends sometimes forgot. But the house drew a frequented air from the number of fine people who were freely named there and from several mysterious men with foreign titles and English clothes whom Morgan called the Princes and who, on sofas with the girls, talked French very loud—though sometimes with some oddity of accent —as if to show they were saying nothing improper. Pemberton wondered how the Princes could ever propose in that tone and so publicly: he took for granted cynically that this was what was desired of them. Then he recognised that even for the chance of such an advantage Mrs. Moreen would never allow Paula and Amy to receive alone. These young ladies were not at all timid, but it was just the safeguards that made them so candidly free. It was a houseful of Bohemians who wanted tremendously to be Philistines.

In one respect, however, certainly, they achieved no rigour—they were wonderfully amiable and ecstatic about Morgan. It was a genuine tenderness, an artless admiration, equally strong in each. They even praised his beauty, which was small, and were as afraid of him as if they felt him of finer clay. They spoke of him as a little angel and a prodigy—they touched on his want of health with long, vague faces. Pemberton feared at first an extravagance that might make him hate the boy, but before this happened he had become extravagant himself. Later, when he had grown rather to hate the others, it was a bribe to patience for him that they were at any rate nice about Morgan, going on tiptoe if they fancied he was showing symptoms, and even giving up somebody's "day" to procure him a pleasure. Mixed with this too was the oddest wish to make him independent, as if they had felt themselves not good enough for him. They passed him over to the new member of their circle very much as if wishing to force some charity of adoption on so free an agent and get rid of their own charge. They were delighted when they saw Morgan take so to his kind playfellow, and could think of no higher praise for the young man. It was strange how they contrived to reconcile the appearance, and indeed the essential fact, of adoring the child with their eagerness to wash their hands of him. Did they want to get rid of him before he should find them out? Pemberton was finding them out month by month. The boy's fond family, however this might be, turned their backs with exaggerated delicacy, as if to avoid the reproach of interfering. Seeing in time how little he had in common with them— it was by *them* he first observed it; they proclaimed it with complete humility— his companion was moved to speculate on the mysteries of transmission, the far jumps of heredity. Where this detachment from most of the things they represented had come from was more than an observer could say—it certainly had burrowed under two or three generations.

As for Pemberton's own estimate of his pupil, it was a good while before he got the point of view, so little had he been prepared for it by the smug young barbarians to whom the tradition of tutorship, as hitherto revealed to him, had been adjusted. Morgan was scrappy and surprising, deficient in many properties supposed common to the *genus* and abounding in others that were the portion only of the supernaturally clever. One day his friend made a great stride: it cleared up the question to perceive that Morgan *was* supernaturally clever and that, though the formula was temporarily meagre, this would be the only assumption on which one could successfully deal with him. He had the general quality of a child for whom life had not been simplified by school, a kind of homebred sensibility which might have been bad for himself but was charming for others, and a whole range of refinement and perception—little musical vibrations as taking as picked-up airs—begotten by wandering about Europe at the tail of his migratory tribe. This might not have been an education to recommend in advance, but its results with so special a subject were as appreciable as the marks on a piece of fine porcelain. There was at the same time in him a small strain of stoicism, doubtless the fruit of having had to begin early to bear pain, which counted for pluck and made it of less consequence that he might have been thought at school rather a polyglot little beast. Pemberton indeed quickly found himself rejoicing that school was out of the question: in any million of boys it was probably good for all but one, and Morgan was that millionth. It would have made him comparative and superior—it might have made him really require kicking. Pemberton would try to be school himself—a bigger seminary than five hundred grazing donkeys, so that, winning no prizes, the boy would remain unconscious and irresponsible and amusing—amusing, because, though life was already intense in his childish nature, freshness still made there a strong draught for jokes. It turned out that even in the still air of Morgan's various disabilities jokes flourished greatly. He was a pale lean acute undeveloped little cosmopolite, who liked intellectual gymnastics and who also, as regards the behaviour of mankind, had noticed more things than you might suppose, but who nevertheless had his proper playroom of superstitions, where he smashed a dozen toys a day.

III

At Nice once, toward evening, as the pair rested in the open air after a walk, and looked over the sea at the pink western lights, he said suddenly to his comrade: "Do you like it, you know—being with us all in this intimate way?"

"My dear fellow, why should I stay if I didn't?"

"How do I know you'll stay? I'm almost sure you won't, very long."

"I hope you don't mean to dismiss me," said Pemberton.

Morgan debated, looking at the sunset. "I think if I did right I ought to."

"Well, I know I'm supposed to instruct you in virtue; but in that case don't do right."

"You're very young—fortunately," Morgan went on, turning to him again.

"Oh yes, compared with you!"

"Therefore it won't matter so much if you do lose a lot of time."

"That's the way to look at it," said Pemberton accommodatingly.

They were silent a minute; after which the boy asked: "Do you like my father and my mother very much?"

"Dear me, yes. Charming people."

Morgan received this with another silence; then unexpectedly, familiarly, but at the same time affectionately, he remarked: "You're a jolly old humbug!"

For a particular reason the words made our young man change colour. The boy noticed in an instant that he had turned red, whereupon he turned red himself and pupil and master exchanged a longish glance in which there was a consciousness of many more things than are usually touched upon, even tacitly, in such a relation. It produced for Pemberton an embarrassment; it raised in a shadowy form a question—this was the first glimpse of it—destined to play a singular and, as he imagined, owing to the altogether peculiar conditions, an unprecedented part in his intercourse with his little companion. Later, when he found himself talking with the youngster in a way in which few youngsters could ever have been talked with, he thought of that clumsy moment on the bench at Nice as the dawn of an understanding that had broadened. What had added to the clumsiness then was that he thought it his duty to declare to Morgan that he might abuse him, Pemberton, as much as he liked, but must never abuse his parents. To this Morgan had the easy retort that he hadn't dreamed of abusing them; which appeared to be true: it put Pemberton in the wrong.

"Then why am I a humbug for saying *I* think them charming?" the young man asked, conscious of a certain rashness.

"Well—they're not your parents."

"They love you better than anything in the world—never forget that," said Pemberton.

"Is that why you like them so much?"

"They're very kind to me," Pemberton replied evasively.

"You *are* a humbug!" laughed Morgan passing an arm into his tutor's. He leaned against him looking off at the sea again and swinging his long thin legs.

"Don't kick my shins," said Pemberton while he reflected "Hang it, I can't complain of them to the child!"

"There's another reason too," Morgan went on, keeping his legs still.

"Another reason for what?"

"Besides their not being your parents."

"I don't understand you," said Pemberton.

"Well, you will before long. All right!"

He did understand fully before long, but he made a fight even with himself before he confessed it. He thought it the oddest thing to have a struggle with the child about. He wondered he didn't hate the hope of the Moreens for bringing the struggle on. But by the time it began any such sentiment for that scion was closed to him. Morgan was a special case, and to know him was to accept him on his own odd terms. Pemberton had spent his aversion to special cases before arriving at knowledge. When at last he did arrive his quandary was great. Against every interest he had attached himself. They would have to meet things together. Before they went home that evening at Nice the boy had said, clinging to his arm:

"Well, at any rate you'll hang on to the last."

"To the last?"

"Till you're fairly beaten."

"*You* ought to be fairly beaten!" cried the young man, drawing him closer.

IV

A year after he had come to live with them Mr. and Mrs. Moreen suddenly gave up the villa at Nice. Pemberton had got used to suddenness, having seen it practised on a considerable scale during two jerky little tours—one in

Switzerland the first summer, and the other late in the winter, when they all ran down to Florence and then, at the end of ten days, liking it much less than they had intended, straggled back in mysterious depression. They had returned to Nice "for ever," as they said; but this didn't prevent their squeezing, one rainy muggy May night, into a second-class railway-carriage—you could never tell by which class they would travel—where Pemberton helped them to stow away a wonderful collection of bundles and bags. The explanation of this manœuvre was that they had determined to spend the summer "in some bracing place"; but in Paris they dropped into a small furnished apartment—a fourth floor in a third-rate avenue, where there was a smell on the staircase and the *portier*[6] was hateful—and passed the next four months in blank indigence.

The better part of this baffled sojourn was for the preceptor and his pupil, who, visiting the Invalides[7] and Notre Dame, the Conciergerie[8] and all the museums, took a hundred remunerative rambles. They learned to know their Paris, which was useful, for they came back another year for a longer stay, the general character of which in Pemberton's memory today mixes pitiably and confusedly with that of the first. He sees Morgan's shabby knickerbockers— the everlasting pair that didn't match his blouse and that as he grew longer could only grow faded. He remembers the particular holes in his three or four pair of coloured stockings.

Morgan was dear to his mother, but he never was better dressed than was absolutely necessary—partly, no doubt, by his own fault, for he was as indifferent to his appearance as a German philosopher. "My dear fellow, you *are* coming to pieces," Pemberton would say to him in sceptical remonstrance; to which the child would reply, looking at him serenely up and down: "My dear fellow, so are you! I don't want to cast you in the shade." Pemberton could have no rejoinder for this—the assertion so closely represented the fact. If however the deficiencies of his own wardrobe were a chapter by themselves he didn't like his little charge to look too poor. Later he used to say "Well, if we're poor, why, after all, shouldn't we look it?" and he consoled himself with thinking there was something rather elderly and gentlemanly in Morgan's disrepair—it differed from the untidiness of the urchin who plays and spoils his things. He could trace perfectly the degrees by which, in proportion as her little son confined himself to his tutor for society, Mrs. Moreen shrewdly forbore to renew his garments. She did nothing that didn't show, neglected him because he escaped notice, and then, as he illustrated this clever policy, discouraged at home his public appearances. Her position was logical enough—those members of her family who did show had to be showy.

During this period and several others Pemberton was quite aware of how he and his comrade might strike people; wandering languidly through the Jardin des Plantes[9] as if they had nowhere to go, sitting on the winter days in the galleries of the Louvre, so splendidly ironical to the homeless, as if for the

6 (French) Doorkeeper and janitor.

7 The *Hôtel des Invalides* was founded as a military hospital. It now contains the imposing tomb of Napoleon and a military museum.

8 The old prison of the *Palais de Justice,* chiefly notable to tourists for its use as a place of execution during the Reign of Terror.

9 A large botanical garden, containing also a museum and a small zoo.

advantage of the *calorifère*.[10] They joked about it sometimes: it was the sort of joke that was perfectly within the boy's compass. They figured themselves as part of the vast vague hand-to-mouth multitude of the enormous city and pretended they were proud of their position in it—it showed them "such a lot of life" and made them conscious of a democratic brotherhood. If Pemberton couldn't feel a sympathy in destitution with his small companion—for after all Morgan's fond parents would never have let him really suffer—the boy would at least feel it with him, so it came to the same thing. He used sometimes to wonder what people would think they were—to fancy they were looked askance at, as if it might be a suspected case of kidnapping. Morgan wouldn't be taken for a young patrician with a preceptor—he wasn't smart enough; though he might pass for his companion's sickly little brother. Now and then he had a five-franc piece, and except once, when they bought a couple of lovely neckties, one of which he made Pemberton accept, they laid it out scientifically in old books. This was sure to be a great day, always spent on the quays, in a rummage of the dusty boxes that garnish the parapets.[11] Such occasions helped them to live, for their books ran low very soon after the beginning of their acquaintance. Pemberton had a good many in England, but he was obliged to write to a friend and ask him kindly to get some fellow to give him something for them.

If they had to relinquish that summer the advantage of the bracing climate the young man couldn't but suspect this failure of the cup when at their very lips to have been the effect of a rude jostle of his own. This had represented his first blow-out, as he called it, with his patrons; his first successful attempt —though there was little other success about it—to bring them to a consideration of his impossible position. As the ostensible eve of a costly journey the moment had struck him as favourable to an earnest protest, the presentation of an ultimatum. Ridiculous as it sounded, he had never yet been able to compass an uninterrupted private interview with the elder pair or with either of them singly. They were always flanked by their elder children, and poor Pemberton usually had his own little charge at his side. He was conscious of its being a house in which the surface of one's delicacy got rather smudged; nevertheless he had preserved the bloom of his scruple against announcing to Mr. and Mrs. Moreen with publicity that he shouldn't be able to go on longer without a little money. He was still simple enough to suppose Ulick and Paula and Amy might not know that since his arrival he had only had a hundred and forty francs; and he was magnanimous enough to wish not to compromise their parents in their eyes. Mr. Moreen now listened to him, as he listened to every one and to every thing, like a man of the world, and seemed to appeal to him— though not of course too grossly—to try and be a little more of one himself. Pemberton recognised in fact the importance of the character—from the advantage it gave Mr. Moreen. He was not even confused or embarrassed, whereas the young man in his service was more so than there was any reason for. Neither was he surprised—at least any more than a gentleman had to be who freely confessed himself a little shocked—though not perhaps strictly at Pemberton.

[10] (French) Hot-air stove.
[11] The booksellers' movable stalls, set up on parapets along the Seine.

"We must go into this, mustn't we, dear?" he said to his wife. He assured his young friend that the matter should have his very best attention; and he melted into space as elusively as if, at the door, he were taking an inevitable but deprecatory precedence. When, the next moment, Pemberton found himself alone with Mrs. Moreen it was to hear her say "I see, I see"—stroking the roundness of her chin and looking as if she were only hesitating between a dozen easy remedies. If they didn't make their push Mr. Moreen could at least disappear for several days. During his absence his wife took up the subject again spontaneously, but her contribution to it was merely that she had thought all the while they were getting on so beautifully. Pemberton's reply to this revelation was that unless they immediately put down something on account he would leave them on the spot and for ever. He knew she would wonder how he would get away, and for a moment expected her to enquire. She didn't, for which he was almost grateful to her, so little was he in a position to tell.

"You won't, you *know* you won't—you're too interested," she said. "You *are* interested, you know you are, you dear kind man!" She laughed with almost condemnatory archness, as if it were a reproach—though she wouldn't insist; and flirted a soiled pocket-handkerchief at him.

Pemberton's mind was fully made up to take his step the following week. This would give him time to get an answer to a letter he had dispatched to England. If he did in the event nothing of the sort—that is if he stayed another year and then went away only for three months—it was not merely because before the answer to his letter came (most unsatisfactory when it did arrive) Mr. Moreen generously counted out to him, and again with the sacrifice to "form" of a marked man of the world, three hundred francs in elegant ringing gold. He was irritated to find that Mrs. Moreen was right, that he couldn't at the pinch bear to leave the child. This stood out clearer for the very reason that, the night of his desperate appeal to his patrons, he had seen fully for the first time where he was. Wasn't it another proof of the success with which those patrons practised their arts that they had managed to avert for so long the illuminating flash? It descended on our friend with a breadth of effect which perhaps would have struck a spectator as comical, after he had returned to his little servile room, which looked into a close court where a bare dirty opposite wall took, with the sound of shrill clatter, the reflexion of lighted back windows. He had simply given himself away to a band of adventurers. The idea, the word itself, wore a romantic horror for him—he had always lived on such safe lines. Later it assumed a more interesting, almost a soothing, sense: it pointed a moral, and Pemberton could enjoy a moral. The Moreens were adventurers not merely because they didn't pay their debts, because they lived on society, but because their whole view of life, dim and confused and instinctive, like that of clever colour-blind animals, was speculative and rapacious and mean. Oh they were "respectable," and that only made them more *immondes!*[12] The young man's analysis, while he brooded, put it at last very simply—they were adventurers because they were toadies and snobs. That was the completest account of them—it was the law of their being. Even when this truth became vivid to their ingenuous inmate he remained unconscious of how much his mind had been prepared for it by the extraordinary little boy who had now

[12] (French) Impure, morally detestable.

become such a complication in his life. Much less could he then calculate on the information he was still to owe the extraordinary little boy.

V

But it was during the ensuing time that the real problem came up—the problem of how far it was excusable to discuss the turpitude of parents with a child of twelve, of thirteen, of fourteen. Absolutely inexcusable and quite impossible it of course at first appeared; and indeed the question didn't press for some time after Pemberton had received his three hundred francs. They produced a temporary lull, a relief from the sharpest pressure. The young man frugally amended his wardrobe and even had a few francs in his pocket. He thought the Moreens looked at him as if he were almost too smart, as if they ought to take care not to spoil him. If Mr. Moreen hadn't been such a man of the world he would perhaps have spoken of the freedom of such neckties on the part of a subordinate. But Mr. Moreen was always enough a man of the world to let things pass—he had certainly shown that. It was singular how Pemberton guessed that Morgan, though saying nothing about it, knew something had happened. But three hundred francs, especially when one owed money, couldn't last for ever; and when the treasure was gone—the boy knew when it had failed —Morgan did break ground. The party had returned to Nice at the beginning of the winter, but not to the charming villa. They went to an hotel, where they stayed three months, and then moved to another establishment, explaining that they had left the first because, after waiting and waiting, they couldn't get the rooms they wanted. These apartments, the rooms they wanted, were generally very splendid; but fortunately they never *could* get them—fortunately, I mean, for Pemberton, who reflected always that if they had got them there would have been a still scanter educational fund. What Morgan said at last was said suddenly, irrelevantly, when the moment came, in the middle of a lesson, and consisted of the apparently unfeeling words: "You ought to *filer*, you know—you really ought."

Pemberton stared. He had learnt enough French slang from Morgan to know that to *filer* meant to cut sticks. "Ah my dear fellow, don't turn me off!"

Morgan pulled a Greek lexicon toward him—he used a Greek-German— to look out a word, instead of asking it of Pemberton. "You can't go on like this, you know."

"Like what, my boy?"

"You know they don't pay you up," said Morgan, blushing and turning his leaves.

"Don't pay me?" Pemberton stared again and feigned amazement. "What on earth put that into your head?"

"It has been there a long time," the boy replied rummaging his book.

Pemberton was silent, then he went on: "I say, what are you hunting for? They pay me beautifully."

"I'm hunting for the Greek for awful whopper," Morgan dropped.

"Find that rather for gross impertinence and disabuse your mind. What do I want of money?"

"Oh that's another question!"

Pemberton wavered—he was drawn in different ways. The severely correct thing would have been to tell the boy that such a matter was none of his business and bid him go on with his lines. But they were really too intimate for that; it was not the way he was in the habit of treating him; there had been no reason it should be. On the other hand Morgan had quite lighted on the truth —he really shouldn't be able to keep it up much longer; therefore why not let him know one's real motive for forsaking him? At the same time it wasn't decent to abuse to one's pupil the family of one's pupil; it was better to misrepresent than to do that. So in reply to his comrade's last exclamation he just declared, to dismiss the subject, that he had received several payments.

"I say—I say!" the boy ejaculated, laughing.

"That's all right," Pemberton insisted. "Give me your written rendering."

Morgan pushed a copybook across the table, and he began to read the page, but with something running in his head that made it no sense. Looking up after a minute or two he found the child's eyes fixed on him and felt in them something strange. Then Morgan said: "I'm not afraid of the stern reality."

"I haven't yet seen the thing you *are* afraid of—I'll do you that justice!"

This came out with a jump—it was perfectly true—and evidently gave Morgan pleasure. "I've thought of it a long time," he presently resumed.

"Well, don't think of it any more."

The boy appeared to comply, and they had a comfortable and even an amusing hour. They had a theory that they were very thorough, and yet they seemed always to be in the amusing part of lessons, the intervals between the dull dark tunnels, where there were waysides and jolly views. Yet the morning was brought to a violent end by Morgan's suddenly leaning his arms on the table, burying his head in them and bursting into tears: at which Pemberton was the more startled that, as it then came over him, it was the first time he had ever seen the boy cry and that the impression was consequently quite awful.

The next day, after much thought, he took a decision and, believing it to be just, immediately acted on it. He cornered Mr. and Mrs. Moreen again and let them know that if on the spot they didn't pay him all they owed him he wouldn't only leave their house but would tell Morgan exactly what had brought him to it.

"Oh you *haven't* told him?" cried Mrs. Moreen with a pacifying hand on her well-dressed bosom.

"Without warning you? For what do you take me?" the young man returned.

Mr. and Mrs. Moreen looked at each other; he could see that they appreciated, as tending to their security, his superstition of delicacy, and yet that there was a certain alarm in their relief. "My dear fellow," Mr. Moreen demanded, "what use *can* you have, leading the quiet life we all do, for such a lot of money?"—a question to which Pemberton made no answer, occupied as he was in noting that what passed in the mind of his patrons was something like: "Oh then, if we've felt that the child, dear little angel, has judged us and how he regards us, and we haven't been betrayed, he must have guessed—and in short it's *general!*" an inference that rather stirred up Mr. and Mrs. Moreen, as Pemberton had desired it should. At the same time, if he had supposed his threat would do something towards bringing them round, he was disappointed to find them taking for granted—how vulgar their perception *had* been!—that he had already given them away. There was a mystic uneasiness in their parental breasts, and that had been the inferior sense of it. None the less, however, his threat did touch them; for if they had escaped it was only to meet a new danger. Mr. Moreen appealed to him, on every precedent, as a man of the world; but his wife had recourse, for the first time since his domestication with them, to a fine *hauteur*, reminding him that a devoted mother, with her child, had arts that protected her against gross misrepresentation.

"I should misrepresent you grossly if I accused you of common honesty!" our friend replied; but as he closed the door behind him sharply, thinking he had not done himself much good, while Mr. Moreen lighted another cigarette, he heard his hostess shout after him more touchingly:

"Oh you do, you *do,* put the knife to one's throat!"

The next morning, very early, she came to his room. He recognised her knock, but had no hope she brought him money; as to which he was wrong, for she had fifty francs in her hand. She squeezed forward in her dressing-gown, and he received her in his own, between his bath-tub and his bed. He had been tolerably schooled by this time to the "foreign ways" of his hosts. Mrs. Moreen was ardent, and when she was ardent she didn't care what she did; so she now sat down on his bed, his clothes being on the chairs, and, in her preoccupation, forgot, as she glanced round, to be ashamed of giving him such a horrid room. What Mrs. Moreen's ardour now bore upon was the design of persuading him that in the first place she was very good-natured to bring him fifty francs, and that in the second, if he would only see it, he was really too absurd to expect to be *paid.* Wasn't he paid enough without perpetual money—wasn't he paid by the comfortable luxurious home he enjoyed with them all, without a care, an anxiety, a solitary want? Wasn't he sure of his position, and wasn't that everything to a young man like him, quite unknown, with singularly little to show, the ground of whose exorbitant pretensions it had never been easy to discover? Wasn't he paid above all by the sweet relation he had established with Morgan —quite ideal as from master to pupil—and by the simple privilege of knowing and living with so amazingly gifted a child; than whom really (and she meant literally what she said) there was no better company in Europe? Mrs. Moreen herself took to appealing to him as a man of the world; she said "Voyons, mon cher,"[13] and "My dear man, look here now"; and urged him to be reasonable, putting it before him that it was truly a chance for him. She spoke as if, according as he *should* be reasonable, he would prove himself worthy to be her son's tutor and of the extraordinary confidence they had placed in him.

After all, Pemberton reflected, it was only a difference of theory and the theory didn't matter much. They had hitherto gone on that of remunerated, as now they would go on that of gratuitous, service; but why should they have so many words about it? Mrs. Moreen at all events continued to be convincing; sitting there with her fifty francs she talked and reiterated as women reiterate, and bored and irritated him, while he leaned against the wall with his hands in the pockets of his wrapper, drawing it together round his legs and looking over the head of his visitor at the grey negations of his window. She wound up with saying: "You see I bring you a definite proposal."

13 (French) Practically the equivalent of Mrs. Moreen's following sentence in English.

"A definite proposal?"

"To make our relations regular, as it were—to put them on a comfortable footing."

"I see—it's a system," said Pemberton. "A kind of organised blackmail."

Mrs. Moreen bounded up, which was exactly what he wanted. "What do you mean by that?"

"You practise on one's fears—one's fears about the child if one should go away."

"And pray what would happen to him in that event?" she demanded with majesty.

"Why he'd be alone with *you*."

"And pray with whom *should* a child be but with those whom he loves most?"

"If you think that, why don't you dismiss me?"

"Do you pretend he loves you more than he loves *us*?" cried Mrs. Moreen.

"I think he ought to. I make sacrifices for him. Though I've heard of those *you* make I don't see them."

Mrs. Moreen stared a moment; then with emotion she grasped her inmate's hand. "*Will* you make it—the sacrifice?"

He burst out laughing. "I'll see. I'll do what I can. I'll stay a little longer. Your calculation's just—I *do* hate intensely to give him up; I'm fond of him and he thoroughly interests me, in spite of the inconvenience I suffer. You know my situation perfectly. I haven't a penny in the world and, occupied as you see me with Morgan, am unable to earn money."

Mrs. Moreen tapped her undressed arm with her folded banknote. "Can't you write articles? Can't you translate as I do?"

"I don't know about translating; it's wretchedly paid."

"I'm glad to earn what I can," said Mrs. Moreen with prodigious virtue.

"You ought to tell me who you do it for." Pemberton paused a moment, and she said nothing; so he added: "I've tried to turn off some little sketches, but the magazines won't have them—they're declined with thanks."

"You see then you're not such a phœnix,"[14] his visitor pointedly smiled— "to pretend to abilities you're sacrificing for our sake."

"I haven't time to do things properly," he ruefully went on. Then as it came over him that he was almost abjectly good-natured to give these explanations he added: "If I stay on longer it must be on one condition—that Morgan shall know distinctly on what footing I am."

Mrs. Moreen demurred. "Surely you don't want to show off to a child?"

"To show *you* off, do you mean?"

Again she cast about, but this time it was to produce a still finer flower. "And *you* talk of blackmail!"

"You can easily prevent it," said Pemberton.

"And *you* talk of practising on fears!" she bravely pushed on.

"Yes, there's no doubt I'm a great scoundrel."

His patroness met his eyes—it was clear she was in straits. Then she thrust out her money at him. "Mr. Moreen desired me to give you this on account."

"I'm much obliged to Mr. Moreen, but we *have* no account."

"You won't take it?"

[14] In the sense of one of unequalled excellence.

"That leaves me more free," said Pemberton.

"To poison my darling's mind?" groaned Mrs. Moreen.

"Oh your darling's mind—!" the young man laughed.

She fixed him a moment, and he thought she was going to break out tormentedly, pleadingly: "For God's sake, tell me what *is* in it!" But she checked this impulse—another was stronger. She pocketed the money—the crudity of the alternative was comical—and swept out of the room with the desperate concession: "You may tell him any horror you like!"

VI

A couple of days after this, during which he had failed to profit by so free a permission, he had been for a quarter of an hour walking with his charge in silence when the boy became sociable again with the remark: "I'll tell you how I know it; I know it through Zénobie."

"Zénobie? Who in the world is *she?*"

"A nurse I used to have—ever so many years ago. A charming woman. I liked her awfully, and she liked me."

"There's no accounting for tastes. What is it you know through her?"

"Why what their idea is. She went away because they didn't fork out. She did like me awfully, and she stayed two years. She told me all about it—that at last she could never get her wages. As soon as they saw how much she liked me they stopped giving her anything. They thought she'd stay for nothing—just *because,* don't you know?" And Morgan had a queer little conscious lucid look. "She did stay ever so long—as long as she could. She was only a poor girl. She used to send money to her mother. At last she couldn't afford it any longer, and went away in a fearful rage one night—I mean of course in a rage against *them.* She cried over me tremendously, she hugged me nearly to death. She told me all about it," the boy repeated. "She told me it was their idea. So I guessed, ever so long ago, that they have had the same idea with you."

"Zénobie was very sharp," said Pemberton. "And she made you so."

"Oh that wasn't Zénobie; that was nature. And experience!" Morgan laughed.

"Well, Zénobie was a part of your experience."

"Certainly I was a part of hers, poor dear!" the boy wisely sighed. "And I'm part of yours."

"A very important part. But I don't see how you know I've been treated like Zénobie."

"Do you take me for the biggest dunce you've known?" Morgan asked. "Haven't I been conscious of what we've been through together?"

"What we've been through?"

"Our privations—our dark days."

"Oh our days have been bright enough."

Morgan went on in silence for a moment. Then he said: "My dear chap, you're a hero!"

"Well, you're another!" Pemberton retorted.

"No I'm not, but I ain't a baby. I won't stand it any longer. You must get some occupation that pays. I'm ashamed, I'm ashamed!" quavered the boy with a ring of passion, like some high silver note from a small cathedral chorister, that deeply touched his friend.

"We ought to go off and live somewhere together," the young man said.

"I'll go like a shot if you'll take me."

"I'd get some work that would keep us both afloat," Pemberton continued.

"So would I. Why shouldn't *I* work? I ain't such a beastly little muff[15] as *that* comes to."

"The difficulty is that your parents wouldn't hear of it. They'd never part with you; they worship the ground you tread on. Don't you see the proof of it?" Pemberton developed. "They don't dislike me; they wish me no harm; they're very amiable people, but they're perfectly ready to expose me to any awkwardness in life for your sake."

The silence in which Morgan received his fond sophistry struck Pemberton somehow as expressive. After a moment the child repeated: "You *are* a hero!" Then he added: "They leave me with you altogether. You've all the responsibility. They put me off on you from morning till night. Why then should they object to my taking up with you completely? I'd help you."

"They're not particularly keen about my being helped, and they delight in thinking of you as *theirs*. They're tremendously proud of you."

"I'm not proud of *them*. But you know that," Morgan returned.

"Except for the little matter we speak of they're charming people," said Pemberton, not taking up the point made for his intelligence, but wondering greatly at the boy's own, and especially at this fresh reminder of something he had been conscious of from the first—the strangest thing in his friend's large little composition, a temper, a sensibility, even a private ideal, which made him as privately disown the stuff his people were made of. Morgan had in secret a small loftiness which made him acute about betrayed meanness; as well as a critical sense for the manners immediately surrounding him that was quite without precedent in a juvenile nature, especially when one noted that it had not made this nature "old-fashioned," as the word is of children—quaint or wizened or offensive. It was as if he had been a little gentleman and had paid the penalty by discovering that he was the only such person in his family. This comparison didn't make him vain, but it could make him melancholy and a trifle austere. While Pemberton guessed at these dim young things, shadows of shadows, he was partly drawn on and partly checked, as for a scruple, by the charm of attempting to sound the little cool shallows that were so quickly growing deeper. When he tried to figure to himself the morning twilight of childhood, so as to deal with it safely, he saw it was never fixed, never arrested, that ignorance, at the instant he touched it, was already flushing faintly into knowledge, that there was nothing that at a given moment you could say an intelligent child didn't know. It seemed to him that he himself knew too much to imagine Morgan's simplicity and too little to disembroil his tangle.

The boy paid no heed to his last remark; he only went on: "I'd have spoken to them about their idea, as I call it, long ago, if I hadn't been sure what they'd say."

"And what would they say?"

[15] (Colloquial) One who is awkward or stupid.

"Just what they said about what poor Zénobie told me—that it was a horrid dreadful story, that they had paid her every penny they owed her."

"Well, perhaps they had," said Pemberton.

"Perhaps they've paid you!"

"Let us pretend they have, and *n'en parlons plus*."[16]

"They accused her of lying and cheating"—Morgan stuck to historic truth. "That's why I don't want to speak to them."

"Lest they should accuse me too?" To this Morgan made no answer, and his companion, looking down at him—the boy turned away his eyes, which had filled—saw that he couldn't have trusted himself to utter. "You're right. Don't worry them," Pemberton pursued. "Except for that, they *are* charming people."

"Except for *their* lying and *their* cheating?"

"I say—I say!" cried Pemberton, imitating a little tone of the lad's which was itself an imitation.

"We must be frank, at the last; we *must* come to an understanding," said Morgan with the importance of the small boy who lets himself think he is arranging great affairs—almost playing at shipwreck or at Indians. "I know all about everything."

"I dare say your father has his reasons," Pemberton replied, but too vaguely, as he was aware.

"For lying and cheating?"

"For saving and managing and turning his means to the best account. He has plenty to do with his money. You're an expensive family."

"Yes, I'm very expensive," Morgan concurred in a manner that made his preceptor burst out laughing.

"He's saving for *you*," said Pemberton. "They think of you in everything they do."

"He might, while he's about it, save a little—" The boy paused, and his friend waited to hear what. Then Morgan brought out oddly: "A little reputation."

"Oh there's plenty of that. That's all right!"

"Enough of it for the people they know, no doubt. The people they know are awful."

"Do you mean the princes? We mustn't abuse the princes."

"Why not? They haven't married Paula—they haven't married Amy. They only clean out Ulick."

"You *do* know everything!" Pemberton declared.

"No I don't after all. I don't know what they live on, or how they live, or *why* they live! What have they got and how did they get it? Are they rich, are they poor, or have they a *modeste aisance*?[17] Why are they always chivey-ing[18] me about—living one year like ambassadors and the next like paupers? Who are they, anyway, and what are they? I've thought of all that—I've thought of a lot of things. They're so beastly worldly. That's what I hate most—oh I've *seen* it! All they care about is to make an appearance and to pass for something or

16 (French) Let's not say any more about it.
17 An income leaving them in moderately easy circumstances.
18 (British colloquialism) Chasing, harassing.

other. What the dickens do they want to pass for? What *do* they, Mr. Pemberton?"

"You pause for a reply," said Pemberton, treating the question as a joke,
yet wondering too and greatly struck with his mate's intense if imperfect vision.
"I haven't the least idea."

"And what good does it do? Haven't I seen the way people treat them—
the 'nice' people, the ones they want to know? They'll take anything from them
—they'll lie down and be trampled on. The nice ones hate that—they just
sicken them. You're the only really nice person we know."

"Are you sure? They don't lie down for me!"

"Well, you shan't lie down for them. You've got to go—that's what you've
got to do," said Morgan.

"And what will become of you?"

"Oh I'm growing up. I shall get off before long. I'll see you later."

"You had better let me finish you," Pemberton urged, lending himself to
the child's strange superiority.

Morgan stopped in their walk, looking up at him. He had to look up
much less than a couple of years before—he had grown, in his loose leanness, so
long and high. "Finish me?" he echoed.

"There are such a lot of jolly things we can do together yet. I want to turn
you out—I want you to do me credit."

Morgan continued to look at him. "To give you credit—do you mean?"

"My dear fellow, you're too clever to live."

"That's just what I'm afraid you think. No, no; it isn't fair—I can't endure
it. We'll separate next week. The sooner it's over the sooner to sleep."

"If I hear of anything—any other chance—I promise to go," Pemberton
said.

Morgan consented to consider this. "But you'll be honest," he demanded;
"you won't pretend you haven't heard?"

"I'm much more likely to pretend I have."

"But what can you hear of, this way, stuck in a hole with us? You ought
to be on the spot, to go to England—you ought to go to America."

"One would think you were *my* tutor!" said Pemberton.

Morgan walked on and after a little had begun again: "Well, now that
you know I know and that we look at the facts and keep nothing back—it's
much more comfortable, isn't it?"

"My dear boy, it's so amusing, so interesting, that it will surely be quite
impossible for me to forego such hours as these."

This made Morgan stop once more. "You *do* keep something back. Oh
you're not straight—I am!"

"How am I not straight?"

"Oh you've got your idea!"

"My idea?"

"Why that I probably shan't make old—make older—bones, and that you
can stick it out till I'm removed."

"You *are* too clever to live!" Pemberton repeated.

"I call it a mean idea," Morgan pursued. "But I shall punish you by the
way I hang on."

"Look out or I'll poison you!" Pemberton laughed.

"I'm stronger and better every year. Haven't you noticed that there hasn't been a doctor near me since you came?"

"*I'm* your doctor," said the young man, taking his arm and drawing him tenderly on again.

Morgan proceeded and after a few steps gave a sigh of mingled weariness and relief. "Ah now that we look at the facts it's all right!"

VII

They looked at the facts a good deal after this; and one of the first consequences of their doing so was that Pemberton stuck it out, in his friends parlance, for the purpose. Morgan made the facts so vivid and so droll, and at the same time so bald and so ugly, that there was fascination in talking them over with him, just as there would have been heartlessness in leaving him alone with them. Now that the pair had such perceptions in common it was useless for them to pretend they didn't judge such people; but the very judgement and the exchange of perceptions created another tie. Morgan had never been so interesting as now that he himself was made plainer by the sidelight of these confidences. What came out in it most was the small fine passion of his pride. He had plenty of that, Pemberton felt—so much that one might perhaps wisely wish for it some early bruises. He would have liked his people to have a spirit and had waked up to the sense of their perpetually eating humble-pie. His mother would consume any amount, and his father would consume even more than his mother. He had a theory that Ulick had wriggled out of an "affair" at Nice: there had once been a flurry at home, a regular panic, after which they all went to bed and took medicine, not to be accounted for on any other supposition. Morgan had a romantic imagination, fed by poetry and history, and he would have liked those who "bore his name"—as he used to say to Pemberton with the humour that made his queer delicacies manly—to carry themselves with an air. But their one idea was to get in with people who didn't want them and to take snubs as if they were honourable scars. Why people didn't want them more he didn't know—that was people's own affair; after all they weren't superficially repulsive, they were a hundred times cleverer than most of the dreary grandees, the "poor swells" they rushed about Europe to catch up with. "After all they *are* amusing—they are!" he used to pronounce with the wisdom of the ages. To which Pemberton always replied: "Amusing—the great Moreen troupe? Why they're altogether delightful; and if it weren't for the hitch that you and I (feeble performers!) make in the *ensemble* they'd carry everything before them."

What the boy couldn't get over was the fact that this particular blight seemed, in a tradition of self-respect, so undeserved and so arbitrary. No doubt people had a right to take the line they liked, but why should *his* people have liked the line of pushing and toadying and lying and cheating? What had their forefathers—all decent folk, so far as he knew—done to them, or what had *he* done to them? Who had poisoned their blood with the fifth-rate social ideal, the fixed idea of making smart acquaintances and getting into the *monde chic*,[19] especially when it was foredoomed to failure and exposure? They showed so what they were after; that was what made the people they wanted not want *them*. And never a wince for dignity, never a throb of shame at looking each other in the face, never any independence or resentment or disgust. If his father or his brother would only knock some one down once or twice a year! Clever as they were they never guessed the impression they made. They were good-natured, yes—as good-natured as Jews at the doors of clothing-shops! But was that the model one wanted one's family to follow? Morgan had dim memories of an old grandfather, the maternal, in New York, whom he had been taken across the ocean at the age of five to see: a gentleman with a high neck-cloth and a good deal of pronunciation, who wore a dress-coat in the morning, which made one wonder what he wore in the evening, and had, or was supposed to have, "property" and something to do with the Bible Society. It couldn't have been but that *he* was a good type. Pemberton himself remembered Mrs. Clancy, a widowed sister of Mr. Moreen's, who was as irritating as a moral tale and had paid a fortnight's visit to the family at Nice shortly after he came to live with them. She was "pure and refined," as Amy said over the banjo, and had the air of not knowing what they meant when they talked, and of keeping something rather important back. Pemberton judged that what she kept back was an approval of many of their ways; therefore it was to be supposed that she too was of a good type, and that Mr. and Mrs. Moreen and Ulick and Paula and Amy might easily have been of a better one if they would.

But that they wouldn't was more and more perceptible from day to day. They continued to "chivey," as Morgan called it, and in due time became aware of a variety of reasons for proceeding to Venice. They mentioned a great many of them—they were always strikingly frank and had the brightest friendly chatter, at the late foreign breakfast in especial, before the ladies had made up their faces, when they leaned their arms on the table, had something to follow the *demi-tasse*, and, in the heat of familiar discussion as to what they "really ought" to do, fell inevitably into the languages in which they could *tutoyer*.[20] Even Pemberton liked them then; he could endure even Ulick when he heard him give his little flat voice for the "sweet sea-city." That was what made him have a sneaking kindness for them—that they were so out of the workaday world and kept him so out of it. The summer had waned when, with cries of ecstasy, they all passed out on the balcony that overhung the Grand Canal.[21] The sunsets then were splendid and the Dorringtons had arrived. The Dorringtons were the only reason they hadn't talked of at breakfast; but the reasons they didn't talk of at breakfast always came out in the end. The Dorringtons on the other hand came out very little; or else when they did they stayed—as was natural—for hours, during which periods Mrs. Moreen and the girls sometimes called at their hotel (to see if they had returned) as many as three times running. The gondola was for the ladies, as in Venice too there were "days," which Mrs. Moreen knew in their order an hour after she arrived. She immediately took one herself, to which the Dorringtons never came, though on a

---

[19] Fashionable society.

[20] Languages in which a distinction between formal and informal modes of address permits a clear expression of intimacy through the choice of the familiar (informal) form (French *tutoyer:* to address by the informal pronoun *tu*, not the formal *vous*).

[21] The family has now arrived in Venice, the "sweet sea-city."

certain occasion when Pemberton and his pupil were together at Saint Mark's
—where, taking the best walks they had ever had and haunting a hundred
churches, they spent a great deal of time—they saw the old lord turn up with
Mr. Moreen and Ulick, who showed him the dim basilica as if it belonged to
them. Pemberton noted how much less, among its curiosities, Lord Dorrington
carried himself as a man of the world; wondering too whether, for such services,
his companions took a fee from him. The autumn at any rate waned, the Dorringtons departed, and Lord Verschoyle, the eldest son, had proposed neither for
Amy nor for Paula.

One sad November day, while the wind roared round the old palace and
the rain lashed the lagoon, Pemberton, for exercise and even somewhat for
warmth—the Moreens were horribly frugal about fires; it was a cause of suffering to their inmate—walked up and down the big bare *sala*[22] with his pupil.
The scagliola[23] floor was cold, the high battered casements shook in the storm,
and the stately decay of the place was unrelieved by a particle of furniture.
Pemberton's spirits were low, and it came over him that the fortune of the
Moreens was now even lower. A blast of desolation, a portent of disgrace and
disaster, seemed to draw through the comfortless hall. Mr. Moreen and Ulick
were in the Piazza, looking out for something, strolling drearily, in mackintoshes,
under the arcades; but still, in spite of mackintoshes, unmistakeable men of
the world. Paula and Amy were in bed—it might have been thought they were
staying there to keep warm. Pemberton looked askance at the boy at his side, to
see to what extent he was conscious of these dark omens. But Morgan, luckily
for him, was now mainly conscious of growing taller and stronger and indeed
of being in his fifteenth year. This fact was intensely interesting to him and
the basis of a private theory—which, however, he had imparted to his tutor—that
in a little while he should stand on his own feet. He considered that the situation would change—that in short he should be "finished," grown up, producible
in the world of affairs and ready to prove himself of sterling ability. Sharply
as he was capable at times of analysing, as he called it, his life, there were happy
hours when he remained, as he also called it—and as the name, really, of their
right ideal—"jolly" superficial; the proof of which was his fundamental assumption that he should presently go to Oxford, to Pemberton's college, and aided
and abetted by Pemberton, do the most wonderful things. It depressed the
young man to see how little in such a project he took account of ways and
means: in other connexions he mostly kept to the measure. Pemberton tried to
imagine the Moreens at Oxford and fortunately failed; yet unless they were to
adopt it as a residence there would be no *modus vivendi*[24] for Morgan. How
could he live without an allowance, and where was the allowance to come from?
He, Pemberton, might live on Morgan; but how could Morgan live on *him*?
What was to become of him anyhow? Somehow the fact that he was a big boy
now, with better prospects of health, made the question of his future more
difficult. So long as he was markedly frail the great consideration he inspired
seemed enough of an answer to it. But at the bottom of Pemberton's heart was
the recognition of his probably being strong enough to live and not yet strong
enough to struggle or to thrive. Morgan himself at any rate was in the first

[22] (Italian) The reception hall.
[23] Plasterwork imitating marble.
[24] The term has ironical force here.

flush of the rosiest consciousness of adolescence, so that the beating of the tempest seemed to him after all but the voice of life and the challenge of fate. He had on his shabby little overcoat, with the collar up, but was enjoying his walk.

It was interrupted at last by the appearance of his mother at the end of the *sala*. She beckoned him to come to her, and while Pemberton saw him, complaisant, pass down the long vista and over the damp false marble, he wondered what was in the air. Mrs. Moreen said a word to the boy and made him go into the room she had quitted. Then, having closed the door after him, she directed her steps swiftly to Pemberton. There *was* something in the air, but his wildest flight of fancy wouldn't have suggested what it proved to be. She signified that she had made a pretext to get Morgan out of the way, and then she enquired— without hesitation—if the young man could favour her with the loan of three louis. While, before bursting into a laugh, he stared at her with surprise, she declared that she was awfully pressed for the money; she was desperate for it— it would save her life.

"Dear lady, *c'est trop fort!*"[25] Pemberton laughed in the manner and with the borrowed grace of idiom that marked the best colloquial, the best anecdotic, moments of his friends themselves. "Where in the world do you suppose I should get three louis, *du train dont vous allez?*"[26]

"I thought you worked—wrote things. Don't they pay you?"

"Not a penny."

"Are you such a fool as to work for nothing?"

"You ought surely to know that."

Mrs. Moreen stared, then she coloured a little. Pemberton saw she had quite forgotten the terms—if "terms" they could be called—that he had ended by accepting from herself; they had burdened her memory as little as her conscience. "Oh yes, I see what you mean—you've been very nice about that; but why drag it in so often?" She had been perfectly urbane with him ever since the rough scene of explanation in his room the morning he made her accept *his* "terms"—the necessity of his making his case known to Morgan. She had felt no resentment after seeing there was no danger Morgan would take the matter up with her. Indeed, attributing this immunity to the good taste of his influence with the boy, she had once said to Pemberton "My dear fellow, it's an immense comfort you're a gentleman." She repeated this in substance now. "Of course you're a gentleman—that's a bother the less!" Pemberton reminded her that he had not "dragged in" anything that wasn't already in as much as his foot was in his shoe; and she also repeated her prayer that, somewhere and somehow, he would find her sixty francs. He took the liberty of hinting that if he could find them it wouldn't be to lend them to *her*—as to which he consciously did himself injustice, knowing that if he had them he would certainly put them at her disposal. He accused himself, at bottom and not unveraciously, of a fantastic, a demoralised sympathy with her. If misery made strange bedfellows it also made strange sympathies. It was moreover a part of the abasement of living with such people that one had to make vulgar retorts, quite out of one's own tradition of good manners. "Morgan, Morgan, to what pass have I come for you?" he

[25] (French) It's too bad; that is, I'm sorry.
[26] (French) The way you go on.

groaned while Mrs. Moreen floated voluminously down the *sala* again to liberate the boy, wailing as she went that everything was too odious.

Before their young friend was liberated there came a thump at the door communicating with the staircase, followed by the apparition of a dripping youth who poked in his head. Pemberton recognised him as the bearer of a telegram and recognised the telegram as addressed to himself. Morgan came back as, after glancing at the signature—that of a relative in London—he was reading the words: "Found jolly job for you, engagement to coach opulent youth on own terms. Come at once." The answer happily was paid and the messenger waited. Morgan, who had drawn near, waited too and looked hard at Pemberton; and Pemberton, after a moment, having met his look, handed him the telegram. It was really by wise looks—they knew each other so well now—that, while the telegraph-boy, in his waterproof cape, made a great puddle on the floor, the thing was settled between them. Pemberton wrote the answer with a pencil against the frescoed wall, and the messenger departed. When he had gone the young man explained himself.

"I'll make a tremendous charge; I'll earn a lot of money in a short time, and we'll live on it."

"Well, I hope the opulent youth will be a dismal dunce—he probably will," Morgan parenthesised—"and keep you a long time a-hammering of it in."

"Of course the longer he keeps me the more we shall have for our old age."

"But suppose *they* don't pay you!" Morgan awfully suggested.

"Oh there are not two such—!" but Pemberton pulled up; he had been on the point of using too invidious a term. Instead of this he said "Two such fatalities."

Morgan flushed—the tears came to his eyes. "*Dites toujours*[27] two such rascally crews!" Then in a different tone he added: "Happy opulent youth!"

"Not if he's a dismal dunce."

"Oh they're happier then. But you can't have everything, can you?" the boy smiled.

Pemberton held him fast, hands on his shoulders—he had never loved him so. "What will become of *you*, what will you do?" He thought of Mrs. Moreen, desperate for sixty francs.

"I shall become an *homme fait*."[28] And then as if he recognised all the bearings of Pemberton's allusion: "I shall get on with them better when you're not here."

"Ah don't say that—it sounds as if I set you against them!"

"You do—the sight of you. It's all right; you know what I mean. I shall be beautiful. I'll take their affairs in hand; I'll marry my sisters."

"You'll marry yourself!" joked Pemberton; as high, rather tense pleasantry would evidently be the right, or the safest, tone for their separation.

It was, however, not purely in this strain that Morgan suddenly asked: "But I say—how will you get to your jolly job? You'll have to telegraph to the opulent youth for money to come on."

Pemberton bethought himself. "They won't like that, will they?"

"Oh look out for them!"

27 (French) Say what you intended to.
28 (French) A grown-up man.

Then Pemberton brought out his remedy. "I'll go to the American Consul; I'll borrow some money of him—just for the few days, on the strength of the telegram."

Morgan was hilarious. "Show him the telegram—then collar the money and stay!"

Pemberton entered into the joke sufficiently to reply that for Morgan he was really capable of that; but the boy, growing more serious, and to prove he hadn't meant what he said, not only hurried him off to the Consulate—since he was to start that evening, as he had wired to his friend—but made sure of their affair by going with him. They splashed through the tortuous perforations and over the humpbacked bridges, and they passed through the Piazza, where they saw Mr. Moreen and Ulick go into a jeweller's shop. The Consul proved accommodating—Pemberton said it wasn't the letter, but Morgan's grand air—and on their way back they went into Saint Mark's for a hushed ten minutes. Later they took up and kept up the fun of it to the very end; and it seemed to Pemberton a part of that fun that Mrs. Moreen, who was very angry when he had announced her his intention, should charge him, grotesquely and vulgarly and in reference to the loan she had vainly endeavoured to effect, with bolting lest they should "get something out" of him. On the other hand he had to do Mr. Moreen and Ulick the justice to recognise that when on coming in *they* heard the cruel news they took it like perfect men of the world.

VIII

When he got at work with the opulent youth, who was to be taken in hand for Balliol,[29] he found himself unable to say if this aspirant had really such poor parts or if the appearance were only begotten of his own long association with an intensely living little mind. From Morgan he heard half a dozen times: the boy wrote charming young letters, a patchwork of tongues, with indulgent postscripts in the family Volapuk[30] and, in little squares and rounds and crannies of the text, the drollest illustrations—letters that he was divided between the impulse to show his present charge as a vain, a wasted incentive, and the sense of something in them that publicity would profane. The opulent youth went up in due course and failed to pass; but it seemed to add to the presumption that brilliancy was not expected of him all at once that his parents, condoning the lapse, which they good-naturedly treated as little as possible as if it were Pemberton's, should have sounded the rally again, begged the young coach to renew the siege.

The young coach was now in a position to lend Mrs. Moreen three louis, and he sent her a post-office order even for a larger amount. In return for this favour he received a frantic scribbled line from her: "Implore you to come back instantly—Morgan dreadfully ill." They were on the rebound, once more in Paris—often as Pemberton had seen them depressed he had never seen them crushed—and communication was therefore rapid. He wrote to the boy to ascer-

[29] A college of Oxford University.
[30] One of the artificially constructed international languages, combining elements from a number of tongues.

tain the state of his health, but awaited the answer in vain. He accordingly, after three days, took an abrupt leave of the opulent youth and, crossing the Channel, alighted at the small hotel, in the quarter of the Champs Elysées,[31] of which Mrs. Moreen had given him the address. A deep if dumb dissatisfaction with this lady and her companions bore him company: they couldn't be vulgarly honest, but they could live at hotels, in velvety *entresols,*[32] amid a smell of burnt pastilles, surrounded by the most expensive city in Europe. When he had left them in Venice it was with an irrepressible suspicion that something was going to happen; but the only thing that could have taken place was again their masterly retreat. "How is he? where is he?" he asked of Mrs. Moreen; but before she could speak these questions were answered by the pressure round his neck of a pair of arms, in shrunken sleeves, which still were capable of an effusive young foreign squeeze.

"Dreadfully ill—I don't see it!" the young man cried. And then to Morgan: "Why on earth didn't you relieve me? Why didn't you answer my letter?"

Mrs. Moreen declared that when she wrote he was very bad, and Pemberton learned at the same time from the boy that he had answered every letter he had received. This led to the clear inference that Pemberton's note had been kept from him so that the game to be practised should not be interfered with. Mrs. Moreen was prepared to see the fact exposed, as Pemberton saw the moment he faced her that she was prepared for a good many other things. She was prepared above all to maintain that she had acted from a sense of duty, that she was enchanted she had got him over, whatever they might say, and that it was useless of him to pretend he didn't know in all his bones that his place at such a time was with Morgan. He had taken the boy away from them and now had no right to abandon him. He had created for himself the gravest responsibilities and must at least abide by what he had done.

"Taken him away from you?" Pemberton exclaimed indignantly.

"Do it—do it for pity's sake; that's just what I want. I can't stand *this*—and such scenes. They're awful frauds—poor dears!" These words broke from Morgan, who had intermitted his embrace, in a key which made Pemberton turn quickly to him and see that he had suddenly seated himself, was breathing in great pain and was very pale.

"*Now* do you say he's not in a state, my precious pet?" shouted his mother, dropping on her knees before him with clasped hands, but touching him no more than if he had been a gilded idol. "It will pass—it's only for an instant; but don't say such dreadful things!"

"I'm all right—all right," Morgan panted to Pemberton, whom he sat looking up at with a strange smile, his hands resting on either side on the sofa.

"Now do you pretend I've been dishonest, that I've deceived?" Mrs. Moreen flashed at Pemberton as she got up.

"It isn't *he* says it, it's I!" the boy returned, apparently easier but sinking back against the wall; while his restored friend, who had sat down beside him, took his hand and bent over him.

"Darling child, one does what one can; there are so many things to consider," urged Mrs. Moreen. "It's his *place*—his only place. You see *you* think it is now."

[31] An expensive district.
[32] Mezzanine rooms.

"Take me away—take me away," Morgan went on, smiling to Pemberton with his white face.

"Where shall I take you, and how—oh *how*, my boy?" the young man stammered, thinking of the rude way in which his friends in London held that, for his convenience, with no assurance of prompt return, he had thrown them over; of the just resentment with which they would already have called in a successor, and of the scant help to finding fresh employment that resided for him in the grossness of his having failed to pass his pupil.

"Oh we'll settle that. You used to talk about it," said Morgan. "If we can only go all the rest's a detail."

"Talk about it as much as you like, but don't think you can attempt it. Mr. Moreen would never consent—it would be so *very* hand-to-mouth," Pemberton's hostess beautifully explained to him. Then to Morgan she made it clearer: "It would destroy our peace, it would break our hearts. Now that he's back it will be all the same again. You'll have your life, your work and your freedom, and we'll all be happy as we used to be. You'll bloom and grow perfectly well, and we won't have any more silly experiments, will we? They're too absurd. It's Mr. Pemberton's place—every one in his place. You in yours, your papa in his, me in mine—*n'est-ce pas, chéri*?[33] We'll all forget how foolish we've been and have lovely times."

She continued to talk and to surge vaguely about the little draped stuffy salon while Pemberton sat with the boy, whose colour gradually came back; and she mixed up her reasons, hinting that there were going to be changes, that the other children might scatter (who knew?—Paula had her ideas) and that then it might be fancied how much the poor old parent-birds would want the little nestling. Morgan looked at Pemberton, who wouldn't let him move; and Pemberton knew exactly how he felt at hearing himself called a little nestling. He admitted that he had had one or two bad days, but he protested afresh against the wrong of his mother's having made them the ground of an appeal to poor Pemberton. Poor Pemberton could laugh now, apart from the comicality of Mrs. Moreen's mustering so much philosophy for her defence—she seemed to shake it out of her agitated petticoats, which knocked over the light gilt chairs—so little did their young companion, *marked*, unmistakeably marked at the best, strike him as qualified to repudiate any advantage.

He himself was in for it at any rate. He should have Morgan on his hands again indefinitely; though indeed he saw the lad had a private theory to produce which would be intended to smooth this down. He was obliged to him for it in advance; but the suggested amendment didn't keep his heart rather from sinking, any more than it prevented him from accepting the prospect on the spot, with some confidence moreover that he should do so even better if he could have a little supper. Mrs. Moreen threw out more hints about the changes that were to be looked for, but she was such a mixture of smiles and shudders—she confessed she was very nervous—that he couldn't tell if she were in high feather or only in hysterics. If the family was really at last going to pieces why shouldn't she recognise the necessity of pitching Morgan into some sort of lifeboat? This presumption was fostered by the fact that they were established in luxurious quarters in the capital of pleasure; that was exactly where they naturally *would*

[33] (French) Isn't that right, dear?

be established in view of going to pieces. Moreover didn't she mention that Mr. Moreen and the others were enjoying themselves at the opera with Mr. Granger, and wasn't *that* also precisely where one would look for them on the eve of a smash? Pemberton gathered that Mr. Granger was a rich vacant American—a big bill with a flourishy heading and no items; so that one of Paula's "ideas" was probably that this time she hadn't missed fire—by which straight shot indeed she would have shattered the general cohesion. And if the cohesion was to crumble what would become of poor Pemberton? He felt quite enough bound up with them to figure to his alarm as a dislodged block in the edifice.

It was Morgan who eventually asked if no supper had been ordered for him; sitting with him below, later, at the dim delayed meal, in the presence of a great deal of corded green plush, a plate of ornamental biscuit and an aloofness marked on the part of the waiter. Mrs. Moreen had explained that they had been obliged to secure a room for the visitor out of the house; and Morgan's consolation—he offered it while Pemberton reflected on the nastiness of lukewarm sauces—proved to be, largely, that this circumstance would facilitate their escape. He talked of their escape—recurring to it often afterwards—as if they were making up a "boy's book" together. But he likewise expressed his sense that there was something in the air, that the Moreens couldn't keep it up much longer. In point of fact, as Pemberton was to see, they kept it up for five or six months. All the while, however, Morgan's contention was designed to cheer him. Mr. Moreen and Ulick, whom he had met the day after his return, accepted that return like perfect men of the world. If Paula and Amy treated it even with less formality an allowance was to be made for them, inasmuch as Mr. Granger hadn't come to the opera after all. He had only placed his box at their service, with a bouquet for each of the party; there was even one apiece, embittering the thought of his profusion, for Mr. Moreen and Ulick. "They're all like that," was Morgan's comment; "at the very last, just when we think we've landed them they're back in the deep sea!"

Morgan's comments in the days were more and more free; they even included a large recognition of the extraordinary tenderness with which he had been treated while Pemberton was away. Oh yes, they couldn't do enough to be nice to him, to show him they had him on their mind and make up for his loss. That was just what made the whole thing so sad and caused him to rejoice after all in Pemberton's return—he had to keep thinking of their affection less, had less sense of obligation. Pemberton laughed out at this last reason, and Morgan blushed and said "Well, dash it, you know what I mean." Pemberton knew perfectly what he meant; but there were a good many things that—dash it too!—it didn't make any clearer. This episode of his second sojourn in Paris stretched itself out wearily, with their resumed readings and wanderings and maunderings, their potterings on the quays, their hauntings of the museums, their occasional lingerings in the Palais Royal[34] when the first sharp weather came on and there was a comfort in warm emanations, before Chevet's wonderful succulent window. Morgan wanted to hear all about the opulent youth—he took an immense interest in him. Some of the details of his opulence—Pemberton could spare him none of them—evidently fed the boy's appreciation of all his friend had given up to come back to him; but in addition to the greater reci-

[34] A palace now occupied by the Council of State and the *Théâtre Français,* and containing shops.

procity established by that heroism he had always his little brooding theory, in which there was a frivolous gaiety too, that their long probation was drawing to a close. Morgan's conviction that the Moreens couldn't go on much longer kept pace with the unexpected impetus with which, from month to month, they did go on. Three weeks after Pemberton had rejoined them they went on to another hotel, a dingier one than the first; but Morgan rejoiced that his tutor had at least still not sacrificed the advantage of a room outside. He clung to the romantic utility of this when the day, or rather the night, should arrive for their escape.

For the first time, in this complicated connexion, our friend felt his collar gall him. It was, as he had said to Mrs. Moreen in Venice, *trop fort*[35]—everything was *trop fort*. He could neither really throw off his blighting burden nor find in it the benefit of a pacified conscience or of a rewarded affection. He had spent all the money accruing to him in England, and he saw his youth going and that he was getting nothing back for it. It was all very well of Morgan to count it for reparation that he should now settle on him permanently—there was an irritating flaw in such a view. He saw what the boy had in his mind; the conception that as his friend had had the generosity to come back he must show his gratitude by giving him his life. But the poor friend didn't desire the gift—what could he do with Morgan's dreadful little life? Of course at the same time that Pemberton was irritated he remembered the reason, which was very honourable to Morgan and which dwelt simply in his making one so forget that he was no more than a patched urchin. If one dealt with him on a different basis one's misadventures were one's own fault. So Pemberton waited in a queer confusion of yearning and alarm for the catastrophe which was held to hang over the house of Moreen, of which he certainly at moments felt the symptoms brush his cheek and as to which he wondered much in what form it would find its liveliest effect.

Perhaps it would take the form of sudden dispersal—a frightened *sauve qui peut*,[36] a scuttling into selfish corners. Certainly they were less elastic than of yore; they were evidently looking for something they didn't find. The Dorringtons hadn't re-appeared, the princes had scattered; wasn't that the beginning of the end? Mrs. Moreen had lost her reckoning of the famous "days"; her social calendar was blurred—it had turned its face to the wall. Pemberton suspected that the great, the cruel discomfiture had been the unspeakable behaviour of Mr. Granger, who seemed not to know what he wanted, or, what was much worse, what *they* wanted. He kept sending flowers, as if to bestrew the path of his retreat, which was never the path of a return. Flowers were all very well, but—Pemberton could complete the proposition. It was now positively conspicuous that in the long run the Moreens were a social failure; so that the young man was almost grateful the run had not been short. Mr. Moreen indeed was still occasionally able to get away on business and, what was more surprising, was likewise able to get back. Ulick had no club, but you couldn't have discovered it from his appearance, which was as much as ever that of a person looking at life from the window of such an institution; therefore Pemberton was doubly surprised at an answer he once heard him make his mother in the desperate tone of a man familiar with the worst privations. Her question Pemberton had

[35] (French) Too much to stand, too painful.
[36] (French) Everyone for himself.

not quite caught; it appeared to be an appeal for a suggestion as to whom they might get to take Amy. "Let the Devil take her!" Ulick snapped; so that Pemberton could see that they had not only lost their amiability but had ceased to believe in themselves. He could also see that if Mrs. Moreen was trying to get people to take her children she might be regarded as closing the hatches for the storm. But Morgan would be the last she would part with.

One winter afternoon—it was a Sunday—he and the boy walked far together in the Bois de Boulogne.[37] The evening was so splendid, the cold lemon-coloured sunset so clear, the stream of carriages and pedestrians so amusing and the fascination of Paris so great, that they stayed out later than usual and became aware that they should have to hurry home to arrive in time for dinner. They hurried accordingly, arm-in-arm, good humoured and hungry, agreeing that there was nothing like Paris after all and that after everything too that had come and gone they were not yet sated with innocent pleasures. When they reached the hotel they found that, though scandalously late, they were in time for all the dinner they were likely to sit down to. Confusion reigned in the apartments of the Moreens—very shabby ones this time, but the best in the house —and before the interrupted service of the table, with objects displaced almost as if there had been a scuffle and a great wine-stain from an overturned bottle, Pemberton couldn't blink the fact that there had been a scene of the last proprietary firmness. The storm had come—they were all seeking refuge. The hatches were down, Paula and Amy were invisible—they had never tried the most casual art upon Pemberton, but he felt they had enough of an eye to him not to wish to meet him as young ladies whose frocks had been confiscated— and Ulick appeared to have jumped overboard. The host and his staff, in a word, had ceased to "go on" at the pace of their guests, and the air of embarrassed detention, thanks to a pile of gaping trunks in the passage, was strangely commingled with the air of indignant withdrawal.

When Morgan took all this in—and he took it in very quickly—he coloured to the roots of his hair. He had walked from his infancy among difficulties and dangers, but he had never seen a public exposure. Pemberton noticed in a second glance at him that the tears had rushed into his eyes and that they were tears of a new and untasted bitterness. He wondered an instant, for the boy's sake, whether he might successfully pretend not to understand. Not successfully, he felt, as Mr. and Mrs. Moreen, dinnerless by their extinguished hearth, rose before him in their little dishonoured salon, casting about with glassy eyes for the nearest port in such a storm. They were not prostrate but were horribly white, and Mrs. Moreen had evidently been crying. Pemberton quickly learned however that her grief was not for the loss of her dinner, much as she usually enjoyed it, but the fruit of a blow that struck even deeper, as she made all haste to explain. He would see for himself, so far as that went, how the great change had come, the dreadful bolt had fallen, and how they would now all have to turn themselves about. Therefore cruel as it was to them to part with their darling she must look to him to carry a little further the influence he had so fortunately acquired with the boy—to induce his young charge to follow him into some modest retreat. They depended on him—that was the fact—to take their delightful child temporarily under his protection: it would leave Mr.

[37] A large park, with woods and lakes.

Moreen and herself so much more free to give the proper attention (too little, alas! had been given) to the readjustment of their affairs.

"We trust you—we feel we *can*," said Mrs. Moreen, slowly rubbing her plump white hands and looking with compunction hard at Morgan, whose chin, not to take liberties, her husband stroked with a tentative paternal forefinger.

"Oh yes—we feel that we *can*. We trust Mr. Pemberton fully, Morgan," Mr. Moreen pursued.

Pemberton wondered again if he might pretend not to understand; but everything good gave way to the intensity of Morgan's understanding. "Do you mean he may take me to live with him for ever and ever?" cried the boy. "May take me away, away anywhere he likes?"

"For ever and ever? *Comme vous-y-allez!*"[38] Mr. Moreen laughed indulgently. "For as long as Mr. Pemberton may be so good."

"We've struggled, we've suffered," his wife went on; "but you've made him so your own that we've already been through the worst of the sacrifice."

Morgan had turned away from his father—he stood looking at Pemberton with a light in his face. His sense of shame for their common humiliated state had dropped; the case had another side—the thing was to clutch at *that*. He had a moment of boyish joy, scarcely mitigated by the reflexion that with this unexpected consecration of his hope—too sudden and too violent; the turn taken was away from a *good* boy's book—the "escape" was left on their hands. The boyish joy was there an instant, and Pemberton was almost scared at the rush of gratitude and affection that broke through his first abasement. When he stammered "My dear fellow, what do you say to *that*?" how could one not say something enthusiastic? But there was more need for courage at something else that immediately followed and that made the lad sit down quickly on the nearest chair. He had turned quite livid and had raised his hand to his left side. They were all three looking at him, but Mrs. Moreen suddenly bounded forward. "Ah his darling little heart!" she broke out; and this time, on her knees before him and without respect for the idol, she caught him ardently in her arms. "You walked him too far, you hurried him too fast!" she hurled over her shoulder at Pemberton. Her son made no protest, and the next instant, still holding him, she sprang up with her face convulsed and with the terrified cry "Help, help! he's going, he's gone!" Pemberton saw with equal horror, by Morgan's own stricken face, that he was beyond their wildest recall. He pulled him half out of his mother's hands, and for a moment, while they held him together, they looked all their dismay into each other's eyes. "He couldn't stand it with his weak organ," said Pemberton—"the shock, the whole scene, the violent emotion."

"But I thought he *wanted* to go to you!" wailed Mrs. Moreen.

"I *told* you he didn't, my dear," her husband made answer. Mr. Moreen was trembling all over and was in his way as deeply affected as his wife. But after the very first he took his bereavement as a man of the world.

[38] (French) How you go on!

The pathos of Morgan Moreen's fate is twofold, that of the child and that of the genius. As a genius, Morgan is nobody's child—the great point of his curious existence is that nothing has come to him from his parents. Henry James speaks of the "mysteries of transmission" and of the "far jumps of heredity," speculating that the quality of Morgan's spirit can perhaps be traced to some unknown remote ancestor. But he really means that Morgan's quality, like all great human endowments, cannot be explained.

If the quality of Morgan's spirit does indeed amount to genius, it is not of the artistic kind. Rather, it is a genius of perception and morality—Morgan possesses the rare gift of seeing things as they really are and of judging them justly. He is thus at the opposite extreme from his family, all of whom are committed only to the appearance of things. As the boy says in one of his moments of expressed misery, "All they care about is to make an appearance and to pass for something or other." They are sunk in worldliness, hopelessly bound to the hope of acquiring social standing. Their whole view of life, we are told, is not only "rapacious and mean," but also "dim and confused and instinctive," devoid of any trace of the bright conscious intelligence that makes Morgan what he is.

In some sense Morgan is no less worldly than his family. For it is the world —the worldly world of "society," of social status and the petty scheming by which it is won—that makes the matter upon which his intelligence exercises itself. About the actualities of this world he knows far more than his family does. If we respond to him as a truly innocent person, it is not because he is ignorant of corruption, or naive about it. His innocence derives from his gift of seeing things as they are and calling them by their right names.

The word *innocence* means, literally, harmless, being without sin or guilt. But certain additional meanings attach to it, of which one is *cleanness*: in our culture, white is the emblematic color of innocence and *spotlessness* its frequent synonym. And the idea of cleanness must often occur to us in the course of reading "The Pupil," in which moral deficiency is represented by a soiled shabbiness.

The note is struck in the first paragraph of the story, for nothing could be more precisely indicative of the moral life of Morgan's family than the condition of Mrs. Moreen's gloves, those "soiled *gants de Suède*." Thereafter James misses no opportunity to remind us of the slovenliness of the Moreen mode of life. Mrs. Moreen's handkerchief is as soiled as her gloves; she thinks nothing of having an interview with Pemberton in his bedroom in the morning, wearing a dressing gown and sitting on the unmade bed; her daughters are not likely to be presentably dressed except when company is expected; her husband has been seen shaving in the drawing room.

The disorder and sordidness of the Moreen household are not indicative of any moral depravity, only of a deficient sense of reality. Mr. and Mrs. Moreen are very much at ease in talking about high ideals of moral sensibility. This, to be sure, suits their purposes of fraud, especially in their dealings with poor Pemberton, but they are not wholly insincere, or at least they are not wholly conscious of their insincerity. In some part they are themselves taken in by what they say about delicacy of conduct. And it is just this easy self-deception that defeats them in their career of deceit. For these people have no talent whatever for the way of life they have chosen. Brother Ulick fancies himself a gambler, but it is usually he who is fleeced. Paula and Amy are never able to advance their plans for advantageous marriages. And the mother who aspires to marry one of her daughters to an English lord does not have sense enough to know that this is an enterprise that requires clean gloves and handkerchiefs.

It is only Morgan who comprehends the hopelessness of the family's undertaking and it is only he who perceives what it is that makes their failure inevitable—they lack the simple self-respect that is necessary for success even in a life of fraud. Nothing pains Morgan more than his family's deficiency of pride, which, as he sees, makes them the object of the world's contempt. And it offends his intelligence, his acute sense of reality, that because they lack pride they must scheme and cheat with no possible chance of success, that concerned as they are with appearances they do not know how they themselves appear to others.

James's condemnation of the Moreen "troupe" is open and unqualified. Yet he would have had no story if he had not given us the right to feel at least a little tenderness for Morgan's family. There would have been no story, that is, if Morgan did not love them, and he would not have loved them if they had not loved him. They do not love him enough, or wisely. But they do cherish him, or some idea of him; it was they who first perceived his "genius," which they respect without understanding. Their relation to Morgan is said to be possession rather than love, yet even possession is connection of a kind, and it is not until his parents surrender possession of him that Morgan dies.

And yet it is not the Moreens whom the story seems to hold accountable for Morgan's death. The blame falls upon Pemberton. We are naturally reluctant to observe this. For one thing, all through the story our censure has been directed to the Moreens; we have been trained, as it were, to hold them responsible for everything bad. And of course we have it well in mind how admirably Pemberton has behaved for four long years. We can grant that he is a rather passive young man who cannot think of a better way to make a living than as a private tutor and who is unable to insist on his rights; inevitably this somewhat diminishes the nobility we want to attribute to his devotion to Morgan. Yet even when these deductions are made, Pemberton still seems to stand as an example of that medieval loyalty of one person to another upon which Henry James, like Joseph Conrad, set the highest moral value.

Pemberton's loyalty, however, turns out to be fatally flawed. James gives no explanation of the change that has occurred in Pemberton to make him think so bitterly of the proposal that he take charge of Morgan's life, or none beyond the tutor's sense that "his youth [was] going and that he was getting nothing back for it." The idea of Morgan's going away to live with Pemberton had not originated, we recall, either with Morgan or the Moreens but with Pemberton himself—it was he who, in the first flush of his affection for Morgan, had suggested that the two "go off and live somewhere together." It had then been only a fantasy, although not without its seriousness. But now, when Pemberton returns to the Moreens after his period in England, he has the sense that Morgan is delivering the whole of his life into his care, and he can think of the responsibility only in an ugly way. Morgan's life presents itself to him as nothing but a "burden," and a burden which is not merely heavy but "blighting." What he had once seen as so bright and precious now figures in his mind as a "dreadful little life." Morgan, recovering from his crushing humiliation over his parents' sordid ruin, is enraptured at the prospect of going off with his friend, but the tutor, once so spontaneous in his affection, cannot meet the boy's rush of joy with anything more than the awareness that a warm response was called for. "When he [Morgan] stammered, 'My dear fellow, what do you say to *that?*' how could one not say something enthusiastic?" We are told that Morgan's seizure "immediately followed" Pemberton's response to Morgan's joy with nothing more than a recognition of the obligation to be enthusiastic. Mrs. Moreen's wail, "But I thought he *wanted* to go to you!" urges it upon us that Morgan's death "followed" not merely in point of time but as an effect follows a cause—the mother seems to see that the boy would not have died if he *had* wanted to go to Pemberton. We conclude that he no longer wanted to go because he was no longer wanted.

Throughout most of the story we have accepted Pemberton as not much more than the person through whose eyes we observe events. But as the story comes to its end, we must see him as something more, a moral agent. As such he fails. Out of his love for Morgan, he had given much, four years of his life. Yet it seems to be one of the paradoxes of love that the more one gives the more one commits oneself to give. But it is also true that, as Yeats says, "Too long a sacrifice makes a stone of the heart," even too long a sacrifice made in love. If we pass an adverse judgment on Pemberton, it must be with the awareness of how very difficult love is, with the understanding that only a saint or a genius of morality would have met the demands of the situation in which this poor young man was placed. Still, we cannot avoid judging him adversely: there are occasions when, if a man is not a saint or a moral genius, he is nothing at all.

THE
SECRET SHARER

JOSEPH CONRAD
1857–1924

I

ON MY RIGHT HAND there were lines of fishing-stakes resembling a mysterious system of half-submerged bamboo fences, incomprehensible in its division of the domain of tropical fishes, and crazy of aspect as if abandoned for ever by some nomad tribe of fishermen now gone to the other end of the ocean; for there was no sign of human habitation as far as the eye could reach. To the left a group of barren islets, suggesting ruins of stone walls, towers, and blockhouses, had its foundations set in a blue sea that itself looked solid, so still and stable did it lie below my feet; even the track of light from the westering sun shone smoothly, without that animated glitter which tells of an imperceptible ripple. And when I turned my head to take a parting glance at the tug which had just left us anchored outside the bar, I saw the straight line of the flat shore joined to the stable sea, edge to edge, with a perfect and unmarked closeness, in one levelled floor half brown, half blue under the enormous dome of the sky. Corresponding in their insignificance to the islets of the sea, two small clumps of trees, one on each side of the only fault in the impeccable joint, marked the mouth of the river Meinam[1] we had just left on the first preparatory stage of our homeward journey;

[1] Flowing past Bangkok into the Gulf of Siam.

594

and, far back on the inland level, a larger and loftier mass, the grove surrounding the great Paknam pagoda, was the only thing on which the eye could rest from the vain task of exploring the monotonous sweep of the horizon. Here and there gleams as of a few scattered pieces of silver marked the windings of the great river; and on the nearest of them, just within the bar, the tug steaming right into the land became lost to my sight, hull and funnel and masts, as though the impassive earth had swallowed her up without an effort, without a tremor. My eye followed the light cloud of her smoke, now here, now there, above the plain, according to the devious curves of the stream, but always fainter and farther away, till I lost it at last behind the mitre-shaped hill of the great pagoda. And then I was left alone with my ship, anchored at the head of the Gulf of Siam.

She floated at the starting-point of a long journey, very still in an immense stillness, the shadows of her spars flung far to the eastward by the setting sun. At that moment I was alone on her decks. There was not a sound in her—and around us nothing moved, nothing lived, not a canoe on the water, not a bird in the air, not a cloud in the sky. In this breathless pause at the threshold of a long passage we seemed to be measuring our fitness for a long and arduous enterprise, the appointed task of both our existences to be carried out, far from all human eyes, with only sky and sea for spectators and for judges.

There must have been some glare in the air to interfere with one's sight, because it was only just before the sun left us that my roaming eyes made out beyond the highest ridge of the principal islet of the group something which did away with the solemnity of perfect solitude. The tide of darkness flowed on swiftly; and with tropical suddenness a swarm of stars came out above the shadowy earth, while I lingered yet, my hand resting lightly on my ship's rail as if on the shoulder of a trusted friend. But, with all that multitude of celestial bodies staring down at one, the comfort of quiet communion with her was gone for good. And there were also disturbing sounds by this time—voices, footsteps forward; the steward flitted along the maindeck, a busily ministering spirit; a hand-bell tinkled urgently under the poopdeck. . . .

I found my two officers waiting for me near the supper table, in the lighted cuddy. We sat down at once, and as I helped the chief mate, I said:

"Are you aware that there is a ship anchored inside the islands? I saw her mastheads above the ridge as the sun went down."

He raised sharply his simple face, overcharged by a terrible growth of whisker, and emitted his usual ejaculations: "Bless my soul, sir! You don't say so!"

My second mate was a round-cheeked, silent young man, grave beyond his years, I thought; but as our eyes happened to meet I detected a slight quiver on his lips. I looked down at once. It was not my part to encourage sneering on board my ship. It must be said, too, that I knew very little of my officers. In consequence of certain events of no particular significance, except to myself, I had been appointed to the command only a fortnight before. Neither did I know much of the hands forward. All these people had been together for eighteen months or so, and my position was that of the only stranger on board. I mention this because it has some bearing on what is to follow. But what I felt most was my being a stranger to the ship; and if all the truth must be told, I was somewhat of a stranger to myself. The youngest man on board (barring the second mate), and untried as yet by a position of the fullest responsibility, I was willing to take the adequacy of the others for granted. They had simply to be equal to their tasks; but I wondered how far I should turn out faithful to that ideal conception of one's own personality every man sets up for himself secretly.

Meantime the chief mate, with an almost visible effect of collaboration on the part of his round eyes and frightful whiskers, was trying to evolve a theory of the anchored ship. His dominant trait was to take all things into earnest consideration. He was of a painstaking turn of mind. As he used to say, he "liked to account to himself" for practically everything that came in his way, down to a miserable scorpion he had found in his cabin a week before. The why and the wherefore of that scorpion—how it got on board and came to select his room rather than the pantry (which was a dark place and more what a scorpion would be partial to), and how on earth it managed to drown itself in the inkwell of his writing-desk—had exercised him infinitely. The ship within the islands was much more easily accounted for; and just as we were about to rise from table he made his pronouncement. She was, he doubted not, a ship from home lately arrived. Probably she drew too much water to cross the bar except at the top of spring tides. Therefore she went into that natural harbor to wait for a few days in preference to remaining in an open roadstead.

"That's so," confirmed the second mate, suddenly, in his slightly hoarse voice. "She draws over twenty feet. She's the Liverpool ship *Sephora* with a cargo of coal. Hundred and twenty-three days from Cardiff."

We looked at him in surprise.

"The tugboat skipper told me when he came on board for your letters, sir," explained the young man. "He expects to take her up the river the day after tomorrow."

After thus overwhelming us with the extent of his information he slipped out of the cabin. The mate observed regretfully that he "could not account for that young fellow's whims." What prevented him telling us all about it at once, he wanted to know.

I detained him as he was making a move. For the last two days the crew had had plenty of hard work, and the night before they had very little sleep. I felt painfully that I—a stranger—was doing something unusual when I directed him to let all hands turn in without setting an anchor-watch. I proposed to keep on deck myself till one o'clock or thereabouts. I would get the second mate to relieve me at that hour.

"He will turn out the cook and the steward at four," I concluded, "and then give you a call. Of course at the slightest sign of any sort of wind we'll have the hands up and make a start at once."

He concealed his astonishment. "Very well, sir." Outside the cuddy he put his head in the second mate's door to inform him of my unheard-of caprice to take a five hours' anchor-watch on myself. I heard the other raise his voice incredulously—"What? The Captain himself?" Then a few more murmurs, a door closed, then another. A few moments later I went on deck.

My strangeness, which had made me sleepless, had prompted that unconventional arrangement, as if I had expected in those solitary hours of the night to get on terms with the ship of which I knew nothing, manned by men of whom I knew very little more. Fast alongside a wharf, littered like any ship in port with a tangle of unrelated things, invaded by unrelated shore people, I had hardly seen her yet properly. Now, as she lay cleared for sea, the stretch of her main-deck seemed to me very fine under the stars. Very fine, very roomy for her size, and very inviting. I descended the poop and paced the waist, my mind picturing to myself the coming passage through the Malay Archipelago, down the Indian Ocean, and up the Atlantic. All its phases were familiar enough to me, every characteristic, all the alternatives which were likely to face me on the high seas—everything! . . . except the novel responsibility of command. But I took heart from the reasonable thought that the ship was like other ships, the men like other men, and that the sea was not likely to keep any special surprises expressly for my discomfiture.

Arrived at that comforting conclusion, I bethought myself of a cigar and went below to get it. All was still down there. Everybody at the after end of the ship was sleeping profoundly. I came out again on the quarter-deck, agreeably at ease in my sleeping-suit on that warm breathless night, barefooted, a glowing cigar in my teeth, and, going forward, I was met by the profound silence of the fore end of the ship. Only as I passed the door of the forecastle I heard a deep, quiet, trustful sigh of some sleeper inside. And suddenly I rejoiced in the great security of the sea as compared with the unrest of the land, in my choice of that untempted life presenting no disquieting problems, invested with an elementary moral beauty by the absolute straightforwardness of its appeal and by the singleness of its purpose.

The riding-light in the fore-rigging burned with a clear, untroubled, as if symbolic, flame, confident and bright in the mysterious shades of the night. Passing on my way aft along the other side of the ship, I observed that the rope side-ladder, put over, no doubt, for the master of the tug when he came to fetch away our letters, had not been hauled in as it should have been. I became annoyed at this, for exactitude in small matters is the very soul of discipline. Then I reflected that I had myself peremptorily dismissed my officers from duty, and by my own act had prevented the anchor-watch being formally set and things properly attended to. I asked myself whether it was wise ever to interfere with the established routine of duties even from the kindest of motives. My action might have made me appear eccentric. Goodness only knew how that absurdly whiskered mate would "account" for my conduct, and what the whole ship thought of that informality of their new captain. I was vexed with myself.

Not from compunction certainly, but, as it were mechanically, I proceeded to get the ladder in myself. Now a side-ladder of that sort is a light affair and comes in easily, yet my vigorous tug, which should have brought it flying on board, merely recoiled upon my body in a totally unexpected jerk. What the devil! . . . I was so astounded by the immovableness of that ladder that I remained stock-still, trying to account for it to myself like that imbecile mate of mine. In the end, of course, I put my head over the rail.

The side of the ship made an opaque belt of shadow on the darkling glassy shimmer of the sea. But I saw at once something elongated and pale floating very close to the ladder. Before I could form a guess a faint flash of phosphorescent light, which seemed to issue suddenly from the naked body of a man, flickered in the sleeping water with the elusive, silent play of summer lightning in a night sky. With a gasp I saw revealed to my stare a pair of feet, the long legs, a broad livid back immersed right up to the neck in a greenish cadaverous glow. One hand, awash, clutched the bottom rung of the ladder. He was complete but for the head. A headless corpse! The cigar dropped out of my gaping mouth with a tiny plop and a short hiss quite audible in the absolute stillness of all things under heaven. At that I suppose he raised up his face, a dimly pale oval in the shadow of the ship's side. But even then I could only barely make out down there the shape of his black-haired head. However, it was enough for the horrid, frost-bound sensation which had gripped me about the chest to pass off. The moment of vain exclamations was past, too. I only climbed on the spare spar and leaned over the rail as far as I could, to bring my eyes nearer to that mystery floating alongside.

As he hung by the ladder, like a resting swimmer, the sea-lightning played about his limbs at every stir; and he appeared in it ghastly, silvery, fish-like. He remained as mute as a fish, too. He made no motion to get out of the water, either. It was inconceivable that he should not attempt to come on board, and strangely troubling to suspect that perhaps he did not want to. And my first words were prompted by just that troubled incertitude.

"What's the matter?" I asked in my ordinary tone, speaking down to the face upturned exactly under mine.

"Cramp," it answered, no louder. Then slightly anxious, "I say, no need to call any one."

"I was not going to," I said.

"Are you alone on deck?"

"Yes."

I had somehow the impression that he was on the point of letting go the ladder to swim away beyond my ken—mysterious as he came. But, for the moment, this being appearing as if he had risen from the bottom of the sea (it was certainly the nearest land to the ship) wanted only to know the time. I told him. And he, down there, tentatively:

"I suppose your captain's turned in?"

"I am sure he isn't," I said.

He seemed to struggle with himself, for I heard something like the low, bitter murmur of doubt. "What's the good?" His next words came out with a hesitating effort.

"Look here, my man. Could you call him out quietly?"

I thought the time had come to declare myself.

"I am the captain."

I heard a "By Jove!" whispered at the level of the water. The phosphorescence flashed in the swirl of the water all about his limbs, his other hand seized the ladder.

"My name's Leggatt."

The voice was calm and resolute. A good voice. The self-possession of that man had somehow induced a corresponding state in myself. It was very quietly that I remarked:

"You must be a good swimmer."

"Yes. I've been in the water practically since nine o'clock. The question for me now is whether I am to let go this ladder and go on swimming till I sink from exhaustion, or—to come on board here."

I felt this was no mere formula of desperate speech, but a real alternative in the view of a strong soul. I should have gathered from this that he was young; indeed, it is only the young who are ever confronted by such clear issues. But at the time it was pure intuition on my part. A mysterious communication was established already between us two—in the face of that silent, darkened tropical sea. I was young, too; young enough to make no comment. The man in the water began suddenly to climb up the ladder, and I hastened away from the rail to fetch some clothes.

Before entering the cabin I stood still, listening in the lobby at the foot of the stairs. A faint snore came through the closed door of the chief mate's room. The second mate's door was on the hook, but the darkness in there was absolutely soundless. He, too, was young and could sleep like a stone. Remained the steward, but he was not likely to wake up before he was called. I got a sleeping-suit out of my room and, coming back on deck, saw the naked man from the sea sitting on the main-hatch, glimmering white in the darkness, his elbows on his knees and his head in his hands. In a moment he had concealed his damp body in a sleeping-suit of the same grey-stripe pattern as the one I was wearing and followed me like my double on the poop. Together we moved right aft, barefooted, silent.

"What is it?" I asked in a deadened voice, taking the lighted lamp out of the binnacle, and raising it to his face.

"An ugly business."

He had rather regular features; a good mouth; light eyes under somewhat heavy, dark eyebrows; a smooth, square forehead; no growth on his cheeks; a small, brown moustache, and a well-shaped, round chin. His expression was concentrated, meditative, under the inspecting light of the lamp I held up to his face; such as a man thinking hard in solitude might wear. My sleeping-suit was just right for his size. A well-knit young fellow of twenty-five at most. He caught his lower lip with the edge of white, even teeth.

"Yes," I said, replacing the lamp in the binnacle. The warm, heavy tropical night closed upon his head again.

"There's a ship over there," he murmured.

"Yes, I know. The *Sephora*. Did you know of us?"

"Hadn't the slightest idea. I am the mate of her——" He paused and corrected himself. "I should say I was."

"Aha! Something wrong?"

"Yes. Very wrong indeed. I've killed a man."

"What do you mean? Just now?"

"No, on the passage. Weeks ago. Thirty-nine south. When I say a man——"

"Fit of temper," I suggested, confidently.

The shadowy, dark head, like mine, seemed to nod imperceptibly above the ghostly grey of my sleeping-suit. It was, in the night, as though I had been faced by my own reflection in the depths of a sombre and immense mirror.

"A pretty thing to have to own up to for a Conway[2] boy," murmured my double, distinctly.

"You're a Conway boy?"

"I am," he said, as if startled. Then, slowly . . . "Perhaps you too——"

It was so; but being a couple of years older I had left before he joined. After a quick interchange of dates a silence fell; and I thought suddenly of my absurd mate with his terrific whiskers and the "Bless my soul—you don't say so" type of intellect. My double gave me an inkling of his thoughts by saying: "My father's a parson in Norfolk. Do you see me before a judge and jury on

[2] A British merchant marine training ship.

that charge? For myself I can't see the necessity. There are fellows that an angel from heaven—— And I am not that. He was one of those creatures that are just simmering all the time with a silly sort of wickedness. Miserable devils that have no business to live at all. He wouldn't do his duty and wouldn't let anybody else do theirs. But what's the good of talking! You know well enough the sort of ill-conditioned snarling cur——"

He appealed to me as if our experiences had been as identical as our clothes. And I knew well enough the pestiferous danger of such a character where there are no means of legal repression. And I knew well enough also that my double there was no homicidal ruffian. I did not think of asking him for details, and he told me the story roughly in brusque, disconnected sentences. I needed no more. I saw it all going on as though I were myself inside that other sleeping-suit.

"It happened while we were setting a reefed foresail, at dusk. Reefed fore-sail! You understand the sort of weather. The only sail we had left to keep the ship running; so you may guess what it had been like for days. Anxious sort of job, that. He gave me some of his cursed insolence at the sheet. I tell you I was overdone with this terrific weather that seemed to have no end to it. Terrific, I tell you—and a deep ship. I believe the fellow himself was half crazed with funk. It was no time for gentlemanly reproof, so I turned round and felled him like an ox. He up and at me. We closed just as an awful sea made for the ship. All hands saw it coming and took to the rigging, but I had him by the throat, and went on shaking him like a rat, the men above us yelling, 'Look out! look out!'" Then a crash as if the sky had fallen on my head. They say that for over ten minutes hardly anything was to be seen of the ship—just the three masts and a bit of the forecastle head and of the poop all awash driving along in a smother of foam. It was a miracle that they found us, jammed together behind the forebits. It's clear that I meant business, because I was holding him by the throat still when they picked us up. He was black in the face. It was too much for them. It seems they rushed us aft together, gripped as we were, screaming 'Murder!' like a lot of luna-tics, and broke into the cuddy. And the ship running for her life, touch and go all the time, any minute her last in a sea fit to turn your hair grey only a-looking at it. I understand that the skipper, too, started raving like the rest of them. The man had been deprived of sleep for more than a week, and to have this sprung on him at the height of a furious gale nearly drove him out of his mind. I wonder they didn't fling me overboard after getting the carcass of their precious ship-mate out of my fingers. They had rather a job to separate us, I've been told. A sufficiently fierce story to make an old judge and a respectable jury sit up a bit. The first thing I heard when I came to myself was the maddening howling of that endless gale, and on that the voice of the old man. He was hanging on to my bunk, staring into my face out of his sou'wester.

"'Mr. Leggatt, you have killed a man. You can act no longer as chief mate of this ship.'"

His care to subdue his voice made it sound monotonous. He rested a hand on the end of the skylight to steady himself with, and all that time did not stir a limb, so far as I could see. "Nice little tale for a quiet tea-party," he concluded in the same tone.

One of my hands, too, rested on the end of the sky-light; neither did I stir a limb, so far as I knew. We stood less than a foot from each other. It occurred to me that if old "Bless my soul—you don't say so" were to put his head up the companion and catch sight of us, he would think he was seeing double, or imagine himself come upon a scene of weird witchcraft; the strange captain having a quiet confabulation by the wheel with his own grey ghost. I became very much concerned to prevent anything of the sort. I heard the other's soothing undertone.

"My father's a parson in Norfolk," it said. Evidently he had forgotten he had told me this important fact before. Truly a nice little tale.

"You had better slip down into my stateroom now," I said, moving off stealthily. My double followed my movements; our bare feet made no sound; I let him in, closed the door with care, and, after giving a call to the second mate, returned on deck for my relief.

"Not much sign of any wind yet," I remarked when he approached.

"No, sir. Not much," he assented, sleepily, in his hoarse voice, with just enough deference, no more, and barely suppressing a yawn.

"Well, that's all you have to look out for. You have got your orders."

"Yes, sir."

I paced a turn or two on the poop and saw him take up his position face forward with his elbow in the ratlines of the mizzen-rigging before I went below. The mate's faint snoring was still going on peacefully. The cuddy lamp was burning over the table on which stood a vase with flowers, a polite attention from the ship's provision merchant—the last flowers we should see for the next three months at the very least. Two bunches of bananas hung from the beam symmetrically, one on each side of the rudder-casing. Everything was as before in the ship—except that two of her captain's sleeping-suits were simultaneously in use, one motionless in the cuddy, the other keeping very still in the captain's stateroom.

It must be explained here that my cabin had the form of the capital letter L, the door being within the angle and opening into the short part of the letter. A couch was to the left, the bed-place to the right; my writing-desk and the chronometers' table faced the door. But any one opening it, unless he stepped right inside, had no view of what I call the long (or vertical) part of the letter. It contained some lockers surmounted by a bookcase; and a few clothes, a thick jacket or two, caps, oilskin coat, and such like, hung on hooks. There was at the bottom of that part a door opening into my bath-room, which could be entered also directly from the saloon. But that way was never used.

The mysterious arrival had discovered the advantage of this particular shape. Entering my room, lighted strongly by a big bulkhead lamp swung on gimbals above my writing-desk, I did not see him anywhere till he stepped out quietly from behind the coats hung in the recessed part.

"I heard somebody moving about, and went in there at once," he whispered.

I, too, spoke under my breath.

"Nobody is likely to come in here without knocking and getting permission."

He nodded. His face was thin and the sunburn faded, as though he had been ill. And no wonder. He had been, I heard presently, kept under arrest in his cabin for nearly seven weeks. But there was nothing sickly in his eyes or in his expression. He was not a bit like me, really; yet, as we stood leaning over my bed-place, whispering side by side, with our dark heads together and our backs to the door, anybody bold enough to open it stealthily would have been treated to the uncanny sight of a double captain busy talking in whispers with his other self.

"But all this doesn't tell me how you came to hang on to our side-ladder," I inquired, in the hardly audible murmurs we used, after he had told me something more of the proceedings on board the *Sephora* once the bad weather was over.

"When we sighted Java Head I had had time to think all those matters out several times over. I had six weeks of doing nothing else, and with only an hour or so every evening for a tramp on the quarter-deck."

He whispered, his arms folded on the side of my bed-place, staring through the open port. And I could imagine perfectly the manner of this thinking out—a stubborn if not a steadfast operation; something of which I should have been perfectly incapable.

"I reckoned it would be dark before we closed with the land," he continued, so low that I had to strain my hearing, near as we were to each other, shoulder touching shoulder almost. "So I asked to speak to the old man. He always seemed very sick when he came to see me—as if he could not look me in the face. You know, that foresail saved the ship. She was too deep to have run long under bare poles. And it was I that managed to set it for him. Anyway, he came. When I had him in my cabin—he stood by the door looking at me as if I had the halter round my neck already—I asked him right away to leave my cabin door unlocked at night while the ship was going through Sunda Straits. There would be the Java coast within two or three miles, off Angier Point. I wanted nothing more. I've had a prize for swimming my second year in the Conway."

"I can believe it," I breathed out.

"God only knows why they locked me in every night. To see some of their faces you'd have thought they were afraid I'd go about at night strangling people. Am I a murdering brute? Do I look it? By Jove! if I had been he wouldn't have trusted himself like that into my room. You'll say I might have chucked him aside and bolted out, there and then—it was dark already. Well, no. And for the same reason I wouldn't think of trying to smash the door. There would have been a rush to stop me at the noise, and I did not mean to get into a confounded scrimmage. Somebody else might have got killed—for I would not have broken out only to get chucked back, and I did not want any more of that work. He refused, looking more sick than ever. He was afraid of the men, and also of that old second mate of his who had been sailing with him for years—a grey-headed old humbug; and his steward, too, had been with him devil knows how long—seventeen years or more—a dogmatic sort of loafer who hated me like poison, just because I was the chief mate. No chief mate ever made more than one voyage in the *Sephora*, you know. Those two old chaps ran the ship. Devil only knows what the skipper wasn't afraid of (all his nerve went to pieces altogether in that hellish spell of bad weather we had)—of what the law would do to him—of his wife, perhaps. Oh, yes! she's on board. Though I don't think she would have meddled. She would have been only too glad to have me out of the ship in any way. The 'brand of Cain'[3] business, don't you see. That's all right. I was ready enough to go off wandering on the face of the earth—and that was price enough to pay for an Abel of that sort. Anyhow, he wouldn't listen to me. 'This thing must take its course. I represent the law here.' He was shaking like a leaf. 'So you won't?' 'No!' 'Then

[3] After killing Abel, Cain is condemned to wander the earth as a fugitive and vagabond, but the Lord puts a mark on his forehead so that no one will kill him. (See Genesis 4 : 12–15).

I hope you will be able to sleep on that,' I said, and turned my back on him. 'I wonder that *you* can,' cries he, and locks the door.

"Well, after that, I couldn't. Not very well. That was three weeks ago. We have had a slow passage through the Java Sea; drifted about Carimata for ten days. When we anchored here they thought, I suppose, it was all right. The nearest land (and that's five miles) is the ship's destination; the consul would soon set about catching me; and there would have been no object in bolting to these islets there. I don't suppose there's a drop of water on them. I don't know how it was, but to-night that steward, after bringing me my supper, went out to let me eat it, and left the door unlocked. And I ate it—all there was, too. After I had finished I strolled out on the quarter-deck. I don't know that I meant to do anything. A breath of fresh air was all I wanted, I believe. Then a sudden temptation came over me. I kicked off my slippers and was in the water before I had made up my mind fairly. Somebody heard the splash and they raised an awful hullabaloo. 'He's gone! Lower the boats! He's committed suicide! No, he's swimming.' Certainly I was swimming. It's not so easy for a swimmer like me to commit suicide by drowning. I landed on the nearest islet before the boat left the ship's side. I heard them pulling about in the dark, hailing, and so on, but after a bit they gave up. Everything quieted down and the anchorage became as still as death. I sat down on a stone and began to think. I felt certain they would start searching for me at daylight. There was no place to hide on those stony things— and if there had been, what would have been the good? But now I was clear of that ship, I was not going back. So after a while I took off all my clothes, tied them up in a bundle with a stone inside, and dropped them in the deep water on the outer side of that islet. That was suicide enough for me. Let them think what they liked, but I didn't mean to drown myself. I meant to swim till I sank— but that's not the same thing. I struck out for another of these little islands, and it was from that one that I first saw your riding-light. Something to swim for. I went on easily, and on the way I came upon a flat rock a foot or two above water. In the daytime, I dare say, you might make it out with a glass from your poop. I scrambled up on it and rested myself for a bit. Then I made another start. That last spell must have been over a mile."

His whisper was getting fainter and fainter, and all the time he stared straight out through the port-hole, in which there was not even a star to be seen. I had not interrupted him. There was something that made comment impossible in his narrative, or perhaps in himself; a sort of feeling, a quality, which I can't find a name for. And when he ceased, all I found was a futile whisper: "So you swam for our light?"

"Yes—straight for it. It was something to swim for. I couldn't see any stars low down because the coast was in the way, and I couldn't see the land, either. The water was like glass. One might have been swimming in a confounded thousand-feet deep cistern with no place for scrambling out anywhere; but what I didn't like was the notion of swimming round and round like a crazed bullock before I gave out; and as I didn't mean to go back . . . No. Do you see me being hauled back, stark naked, off one of these little islands by the scruff of the neck and fighting like a wild beast? Somebody would have got killed for certain, and I did not want any of that. So I went on. Then your ladder——"

"Why didn't you hail the ship?" I asked, a little louder.

He touched my shoulder lightly. Lazy footsteps came right over our heads and stopped. The second mate had crossed from the other side of the poop and might have been hanging over the rail, for all we knew.

"He couldn't hear us talking—could he?" My double breathed into my very ear, anxiously.

His anxiety was an answer, a sufficient answer, to the question I had put to him. An answer containing all the difficulty of that situation. I closed the port hole quietly, to make sure. A louder word might have been overheard.

"Who's that?" he whispered then.

"My second mate. But I don't know much more of the fellow than you do."

And I told him a little about myself. I had been appointed to take charge while I least expected anything of the sort, not quite a fortnight ago. I didn't know either the ship or the people. Hadn't had the time in port to look about me or size anybody up. And as to the crew, all they knew was that I was appointed to take the ship home. For the rest, I was almost as much of a stranger on board as himself, I said. And at the moment I felt it most acutely. I felt that it would take very little to make me a suspect person in the eyes of the ship's company.

He had turned about meantime; and we, the two strangers in the ship, faced each other in identical attitudes.

"Your ladder——" he murmured, after a silence. "Who'd have thought of finding a ladder hanging over at night in a ship anchored out here! I felt just then a very unpleasant faintness. After the life I've been leading for nine weeks, anybody would have got out of condition. I wasn't capable of swimming round as far as your rudder-chains. And, lo and behold! there was a ladder to get hold of. After I gripped it I said to myself, 'What's the good?' When I saw a man's head looking over I thought I would swim away presently and leave him shouting—in whatever language it was. I didn't mind being looked at. I—I liked it. And then you speaking to me so quietly—as if you had expected me—made me hold on a little longer. It had been a confounded lonely time—I don't mean while swimming. I was glad to talk a little to somebody that didn't belong to the *Sephora*. As to asking for the captain, that was a mere impulse. It could have been no use, with all the ship knowing about me and the other people pretty certain to be round here in the morning. I don't know—I wanted to be seen, to talk with somebody, before I went on. I don't know what I would have said. . . . 'Fine night, isn't it?' or something of the sort."

"Do you think they will be round here presently?" I asked with some incredulity.

"Quite likely," he said, faintly.

He looked extremely haggard all of a sudden. His head rolled on his shoulders.

"H'm. We shall see then. Meantime get into that bed," I whispered. "Want help? There."

It was a rather high bed-place with a set of drawers underneath. This amazing swimmer really needed the lift I gave him by seizing his leg. He tumbled in, rolled over on his back, and flung one arm across his eyes. And then, with his face nearly hidden, he must have looked exactly as I used to look in that bed. I gazed upon my other self for a while before drawing across carefully the two green serge curtains which ran on a brass rod. I thought for a moment of pinning them together for greater safety, but I sat down on the couch, and once there I felt unwilling to rise and hunt for a pin. I would do it in a moment. I was extremely tired, in a peculiarly intimate way, by the strain of stealthiness, by the effort of whispering and the general secrecy of this excitement. It was three o'clock by now and I had been on my feet since nine, but I was not sleepy; I could not have gone to sleep. I sat there, fagged out, looking at the curtains, trying to clear my mind of the confused sensation of being in two places at once, and greatly bothered by an exasperating knocking in my head. It was a relief to discover suddenly that it was not in my head at all, but on the outside of the door. Before I could collect myself the words "Come in" were out of my mouth, and the steward entered with a tray, bringing in my morning coffee. I had slept, after all, and I was so frightened that I shouted, "This way! I am here, steward," as though he had been miles away. He put down the tray on the table next the couch and only then said, very quietly, "I can see you are here, sir." I felt him give me a keen look, but I dared not meet his eyes just then. He must have wondered why I had drawn the curtains of my bed before going to sleep on the couch. He went out, hooking the door open as usual.

I heard the crew washing decks above me. I knew I would have been told at once if there had been any wind. Calm, I thought, and I was doubly vexed. Indeed, I felt dual more than ever. The steward reappeared suddenly in the doorway. I jumped up from the couch so quickly that he gave a start.

"What do you want here?"

"Close your port, sir—they are washing decks."

"It is closed," I said, reddening.

"Very well, sir." But he did not move from the doorway and returned my stare in an extraordinary, equivocal manner for a time. Then his eyes wavered, all his expression changed, and in a voice unusually gentle, almost coaxingly:

"May I come in to take the empty cup away, sir?"

"Of course!" I turned my back on him while he popped in and out. Then I unhooked and closed the door and even pushed the bolt. This sort of thing could not go on very long. The cabin was as hot as an oven, too. I took a peep at my double, and discovered that he had not moved, his arm was still over his eyes; but his chest heaved; his hair was wet; his chin glistened with perspiration. I reached over him and opened the port.

"I must show myself on deck," I reflected.

Of course, theoretically, I could do what I liked, with no one to say nay to me within the whole circle of the horizon; but to lock my cabin door and take the key away I did not dare. Directly I put my head out of the companion I saw the group of my two officers, the second mate barefooted, the chief mate in long india-rubber boots, near the break of the poop, and the steward half-way down the poop-ladder talking to them eagerly. He happened to catch sight of me and dived, the second ran down on the main-deck shouting some order or other, and the chief mate came to meet me, touching his cap.

There was a sort of curiosity in his eye that I did not like. I don't know whether the steward had told them that I was "queer" only, or downright drunk, but I know the man meant to have a good look at me. I watched him coming with a smile which, as he got into point-blank range, took effect and froze his very whiskers. I did not give him time to open his lips.

"Square the yards by lifts and braces before the hands go to breakfast."

It was the first particular order I had given on board that ship; and I stayed on deck to see it executed, too. I had felt the need of asserting myself without loss of time. That sneering young cub got taken down a peg or two on that occasion, and I also seized the opportunity of having a good look at the face of every fore-mast man as they filed past me to go to the after braces. At breakfast time, eating nothing myself, I presided with such frigid dignity that the two mates were only too glad to escape from the cabin as soon as decency permitted; and all the time the dual working of my mind distracted me almost to the point of insanity. I was constantly watching myself, my secret self, as dependent on my actions as my own personality, sleeping in that bed, behind that door which faced me as I sat at the head of the table. It was very much like being mad, only it was worse be-cause one was aware of it.

I had to shake him for a solid minute, but when at last he opened his eyes it was in the full possession of his senses, with an inquiring look.

"All's well so far," I whispered. "Now you must vanish into the bath-room."

He did so, as noiseless as a ghost, and then I rang for the steward, and facing him boldly, directed him to tidy up my stateroom while I was having my bath—"and be quick about it." As my tone admitted of no excuses, he said, "Yes, sir," and ran off to fetch his dust-pan and brushes. I took a bath and did most of my dressing, splashing, and whistling softly for the steward's edification, while the secret sharer of my life stood drawn up bolt upright in that little space, his face looking very sunken in daylight, his eyelids lowered under the stern, dark line of his eyebrows drawn together by a slight frown.

When I left him there to go back to my room the steward was finishing dust-ing. I sent for the mate and engaged him in some insignificant conversation. It was, as it were, trifling with the terrific character of his whiskers; but my object was to give him an opportunity for a good look at my cabin. And then I could at last shut, with a clear conscience, the door of my stateroom and get my double back into the recessed part. There was nothing else for it. He had to sit still on a small folding stool, half smothered by the heavy coats hanging there. We listened to the steward going into the bath-room out of the saloon, filling the water-bottles there, scrubbing the bath, setting things to rights, whisk, bang, clatter—out again into the saloon—turn the key—click. Such was my scheme for keeping my second self invisible. Nothing better could be contrived under the circumstances. And there we sat; I at my writing-desk ready to appear busy with some papers, he behind me out of sight of the door. It would not have been pru-dent to talk in daytime; and I could not have stood the excitement of that queer sense of whispering to myself. Now and then, glancing over my shoulder, I saw him far back there, sitting rigidly on the low stool, his bare feet close together, his arms folded, his head hanging on his breast—and perfectly still. Anybody would have taken him for me.

I was fascinated by it myself. Every moment I had to glance over my shoul-der. I was looking at him when a voice outside the door said:

"Beg pardon, sir."

"Well!" . . . I kept my eyes on him, and so when the voice outside the door announced, "There's a ship's boat coming our way, sir," I saw him give a start—the first movement he had made for hours. But he did not raise his bowed head.

"All right. Get the ladder over."

I hesitated. Should I whisper something to him? But what? His immobility seemed to have been never disturbed. What could I tell him he did not know already? . . . Finally I went on deck.

II

The skipper of the *Sephora* had a thin red whisker all round his face, and the sort of complexion that goes with hair of that colour; also the particular, rather smeary shade of blue in the eyes. He was not exactly a showy figure; his shoulders were high, his stature but middling—one leg slightly more bandy than the other. He shook hands, looking vaguely around. A spiritless tenacity was his main characteristic, I judged. I behaved with a politeness which seemed to disconcert him. Perhaps he was shy. He mumbled to me as if he were ashamed of what he was saying; gave his name (it was something like Archbold—but at this distance of years I hardly am sure), his ship's name, and a few other particulars of that sort, in the manner of a criminal making a reluctant and doleful confession. He had had terrible weather on the passage out—terrible—terrible—wife aboard, too.

By this time we were seated in the cabin and the steward brought in a tray with a bottle and glasses. "Thanks! No." Never took liquor. Would have some water, though. He drank two tumblerfuls. Terrible thirsty work. Ever since daylight had been exploring the islands round his ship.

"What was that for—fun?" I asked, with an appearance of polite interest.

"No!" He sighed. "Painful duty."

As he persisted in his mumbling and I wanted my double to hear every word, I hit upon the notion of informing him that I regretted to say I was hard of hearing.

"Such a young man, too!" he nodded, keeping his smeary blue, unintelligent eyes fastened upon me. "What was the cause of it—some disease?" he inquired, without the least sympathy and as if he thought that, if so, I'd got no more than I deserved.

"Yes; disease," I admitted in a cheerful tone which seemed to shock him. But my point was gained, because he had to raise his voice to give me his tale. It is not worth while to record that version. It was just over two months since all this had happened, and he had thought so much about it that he seemed completely muddled as to its bearings, but still immensely impressed.

"What would you think of such a thing happening on board your own ship? I've had the *Sephora* for these fifteen years. I am a well-known shipmaster."

He was densely distressed—and perhaps I should have sympathised with him if I had been able to detach my mental vision from the unsuspected sharer of my cabin as though he were my second self. There he was on the other side of the bulkhead, four or five feet from us, no more, as we sat in the saloon. I looked politely at Captain Archbold (if that was his name), but it was the other I saw, in a grey sleeping-suit, seated on a low stool, his bare feet close together, his arms folded, and every word said between us falling into the ears of his dark head bowed on his chest.

"I have been at sea now, man and boy, for seven-and-thirty years, and I've never heard of such a thing happening in an English ship. And that it should be my ship. Wife on board, too."

I was hardly listening to him.

"Don't you think," I said, "that the heavy sea which, you told me, came aboard just then might have killed the man? I have seen the sheer weight of a sea kill a man very neatly, by simply breaking his neck."

"Good God!" he uttered, impressively, fixing his smeary blue eyes on me. "The sea! No man killed by the sea ever looked like that." He seemed positively scandalised at my suggestion. And as I gazed at him, certainly not prepared for anything original on his part, he advanced his head close to mine and thrust his tongue out at me so suddenly that I couldn't help starting back.

After scoring over my calmness in this graphic way he nodded wisely. If I had seen the sight, he assured me, I would never forget it as long as I lived. The weather was too bad to give the corpse a proper sea burial. So next day at dawn they took it up on the poop, covering its face with a bit of bunting; he read a short prayer, and then, just as it was, in its oilskins and long boots, they launched it amongst those mountainous seas that seemed ready every moment to swallow up the ship herself and the terrified lives on board of her.

"That reefed foresail saved you," I threw in.

"Under God—it did," he exclaimed fervently. "It was by a special mercy, I firmly believe, that it stood some of those hurricane squalls."

"It was the setting of that sail which——" I began.

"God's own hand in it," he interrupted me. "Nothing less could have done it. I don't mind telling you that I hardly dared give the order. It seemed impossible that we could touch anything without losing it, and then our last hope would have been gone."

The terror of that gale was on him yet. I let him go on for a bit, then said, casually—as if returning to a minor subject:

"You were very anxious to give up your mate to the shore people, I believe?"

He was. To the law. His obscure tenacity on that point had in it something incomprehensible and a little awful; something, as it were, mystical, quite apart from his anxiety that he should not be suspected of "countenancing any doings of that sort." Seven-and-thirty virtuous years at sea, of which over twenty of immaculate command, and the last fifteen in the *Sephora*, seemed to have laid him under some pitiless obligation.

"And you know," he went on, groping shamefacedly amongst his feelings, "I did not engage that young fellow. His people had some interest with my owners. I was in a way forced to take him on. He looked very smart, very gentlemanly, and all that. But do you know—I never liked him, somehow. I am a plain man. You see, he wasn't exactly the sort for the chief mate of a ship like the *Sephora*."

I had become so connected in thought and impressions with the secret sharer of my cabin that I felt as if I, personally, were being given to understand that I, too, was not the sort that would have done for the chief mate of a ship like the *Sephora*. I had no doubt of it in my mind.

"Not at all the style of man. You understand," he insisted, superfluously, looking hard at me.

I smiled urbanely. He seemed at a loss for a while.

"I suppose I must report a suicide."

"Beg pardon?"

"Sui-cide! That's what I'll have to write to my owners directly I get in."

"Unless you manage to recover him before to-morrow," I assented, dispassionately. . . . "I mean, alive."

He mumbled something which I really did not catch, and I turned my ear to him in a puzzled manner. He fairly bawled:

"The land—I say, the mainland is at least seven miles off my anchorage."

"About that."

My lack of excitement, of curiosity, of surprise, of any sort of pronounced interest, began to arouse his distrust. But except for the felicitous pretense of deafness I had not tried to pretend anything. I had felt utterly incapable of playing the part of ignorance properly, and therefore was afraid to try. It is also certain that he had brought some ready-made suspicions with him, and that he viewed my politeness as a strange and unnatural phenomenon. And yet how else could I have received him? Not heartily! That was impossible for psychological reasons, which I need not state here. My only object was to keep off his inquiries. Surlily? Yes, but surliness might have provoked a point-blank question. From its novelty to him and from its nature, punctilious courtesy was the manner best calculated to restrain the man. But there was the danger of his breaking through my defense bluntly. I could not, I think, have met him by a direct lie, also for psychological (not moral) reasons. If he had only known how afraid I was of his putting my feeling of identity with the other to the test! But, strangely enough—(I thought of it only afterwards)—I believe that he was not a little disconcerted by the reverse side of that weird situation, by something in me that reminded him of the man he was seeking—suggested a mysterious similitude to the young fellow he had distrusted and disliked from the first.

However that might have been, the silence was not very prolonged. He took another oblique step.

"I reckon I had no more than a two-mile pull to your ship. Not a bit more."

"And quite enough, too, in this awful heat," I said.

Another pause full of mistrust followed. Necessity, they say, is mother of invention, but fear, too, is not barren of ingenious suggestions. And I was afraid he would ask me point-blank for news of my other self.

"Nice little saloon, isn't it?" I remarked, as if noticing for the first time the way his eyes roamed from one closed door to the other. "And very well fitted out, too. Here, for instance," I continued, reaching over the back of my seat negligently and flinging the door open, "is my bath-room."

He made an eager movement, but hardly gave it a glance. I got up, shut the door of the bath-room, and invited him to have a look round, as if I were very proud of my accommodation. He had to rise and be shown round, but he went through the business without any raptures whatever.

"And now we'll have a look at my stateroom," I declared, in a voice as loud as I dared to make it, crossing the cabin to the starboard side with purposely heavy steps.

He followed me in and gazed around. My intelligent double had vanished. I played my part.

"Very convenient—isn't it?"

"Very nice. Very comf . . ." He didn't finish and went out brusquely as if to escape from some unrighteous wiles of mine. But it was not to be. I had been too frightened not to feel vengeful; I felt I had him on the run, and I meant to keep him on the run. My polite insistence must have had something menacing in it, because he gave in suddenly. And I did not let him off a single item; mate's room, pantry, storerooms, the very sail-locker which was also under the poop—he had to look into them all. When at last I showed him out on the quarter-deck he drew a long, spiritless sigh, and mumbled dismally that he must really be going back to his ship now. I desired my mate, who had joined us, to see to the captain's boat.

The man of whiskers gave a blast on the whistle which he used to wear hanging round his neck, and yelled, "*Sephora's* away!" My double down there in my cabin must have heard, and certainly could not feel more relieved than I. Four fellows came running out from somewhere forward and went over the side, while my own men, appearing on deck too, lined the rail. I escorted my visitor to the gangway ceremoniously, and nearly overdid it. He was a tenacious beast. On the very ladder he lingered, and in that unique, guiltily conscientious manner of sticking to the point:

"I say . . . you . . . you don't think that——"

I covered his voice loudly:

"Certainly not. . . . I am delighted. Goodby."

I had an idea of what he meant to say, and just saved myself by the privilege of defective hearing. He was too shaken generally to insist, but my mate, close witness of that parting, looked mystified and his face took on a thoughtful cast. As I did not want to appear as if I wished to avoid all communication with my officers, he had the opportunity to address me.

"Seems a very nice man. His boat's crew told our chaps a very extraordinary story, if what I am told by the steward is true. I suppose you had it from the captain, sir?"

"Yes. I had a story from the captain."

"A very horrible affair—isn't it, sir?"

"It is."

"Beats all these tales we hear about murders in Yankee ships."

"I don't think it beats them. I don't think it resembles them in the least."

"Bless my soul—you don't say so! But of course I've no acquaintance whatever with American ships, not I, so I couldn't go against your knowledge. It's horrible enough for me. . . . But the queerest part is that those fellows seemed to have some idea the man was hidden aboard here. They had really. Did you ever hear of such a thing?"

"Preposterous—isn't it?"

We were walking to and fro athwart the quarterdeck. No one of the crew forward could be seen (the day was Sunday), and the mate pursued:

"There was some little dispute about it. Our chaps took offense. 'As if we would harbor a thing like that,' they said. 'Wouldn't you like to look for him in our coal-hole?' Quite a tiff. But they made it up in the end. I suppose he did drown himself. Don't you, sir?"

"I don't suppose anything."

"You have no doubt in the matter, sir?"

"None whatever."

I left him suddenly. I felt I was producing a bad impression, but with my double down there it was most trying to be on deck. And it was almost as trying to be below. Altogether a nerve-trying situation. But on the whole I felt less torn in two when I was with him. There was no one in the whole ship whom I dared take into my confidence. Since the hands had got to know his story, it would have been impossible to pass him off for any one else, and an accidental discovery was to be dreaded now more than ever. . . .

The steward being engaged in laying the table for dinner, we could talk only with our eyes when I first went down. Later in the afternoon we had a cautious try at whispering. The Sunday quietness of the ship was against us; the stillness of air and water around her was against us; the elements, the men were against us—everything was against us in our secret partnership; time itself—for this could not go on forever. The very trust in Providence was, I suppose, denied to his guilt. Shall I confess that this thought cast me down very much? And as to the chapter of accidents which counts for so much in the book of success, I could only hope that it was closed. For what favorable accident could be expected?

"Did you hear everything?" were my first words as soon as we took up our position side by side, leaning over my bed-place.

He had. And the proof of it was his earnest whisper, "The man told you he hardly dared to give the order."

I understood the reference to be to that saving foresail.

"Yes. He was afraid of it being lost in the setting."

"I assure you he never gave the order. He may think he did, but he never gave it. He stood there with me on the break of the poop after the maintopsail blew away, and whimpered about our last hope—positively whimpered about it and nothing else—and the night coming on! To hear one's skipper go on like that in such weather was enough to drive any fellow out of his mind. It worked me up into a sort of desperation. I just took it into my own hands and went away from him, boiling, and—— But what's the use telling you? *You* know! . . . Do you think that if I had not been pretty fierce with them I should have got the men to do anything? Not it! The bo's'n perhaps? Perhaps! It wasn't a heavy sea—it was a sea gone mad! I suppose the end of the world will be something like that; and a man may have the heart to see it coming once and be done with it—but to have to face it day after day—— I don't blame anybody. I was precious little better than the rest. Only—I was an officer of that old coal-wagon, anyhow——"

"I quite understand," I conveyed that sincere assurance into his ear. He was out of breath with whispering; I could hear him pant slightly. It was all very simple. The same strung-up force which had given twenty-four men a chance, at least, for their lives, had, in a sort of recoil, crushed an unworthy mutinous existence.

But I had no leisure to weigh the merits of the matter—footsteps in the saloon, a heavy knock. "There's enough wind to get under way with, sir." Here was the call of a new claim upon my thoughts and even upon my feelings.

"Turn the hands up," I cried through the door. "I'll be on deck directly."

I was going out to make the acquaintance of my ship. Before I left the cabin our eyes met—the eyes of the only two strangers on board. I pointed to the recessed part where the little camp-stool awaited him and laid my finger on my lips. He made a gesture—somewhat vague—a little mysterious, accompanied by a faint smile, as if of regret.

This is not the place to enlarge upon the sensations of a man who feels for the first time a ship move under his feet to his own independent word. In my case they were not unalloyed. I was not wholly alone with my command; for there was that stranger in my cabin. Or rather, I was not completely and wholly with her. Part of me was absent. That mental feeling of being in two places at once affected me physically as if the mood of secrecy had penetrated my very soul. Before an hour had elapsed since the ship had begun to move, having occasion to ask the mate (he stood by my side) to take a compass bearing of the Pagoda, I caught myself reaching up to his ear in whispers. I say I caught myself, but enough had escaped to startle the man. I can't describe it otherwise than by saying that he shied. A grave, preoccupied manner, as though he were in possession of some perplexing intelligence, did not leave him henceforth. A little later I moved away from the rail to look at the compass with such a stealthy gait that the helmsman noticed it—and I could not help noticing the unusual roundness of his eyes. These are trifling instances, though it's to no commander's advantage to be suspected of ludicrous eccentricities. But I was also more seriously affected. There are to a seaman certain words, gestures, that should in given conditions come as naturally, as instinctively as the winking of a menaced eye. A certain order should spring on to his lips without thinking; a certain sign should get itself made, so to speak, without reflection. But all unconscious alertness had abandoned me. I had to make an effort of will to recall myself back (from the cabin) to the conditions of the moment. I felt that I was appearing an irresolute commander to those people who were watching me more or less critically.

And, besides, there were the scares. On the second day out, for instance, coming off the deck in the afternoon (I had straw slippers on my bare feet) I stopped at the open pantry door and spoke to the steward. He was doing something there with his back to me. At the sound of my voice he nearly jumped out of his skin, as the saying is, and incidentally broke a cup.

"What on earth's the matter with you?" I asked, astonished.

He was extremely confused. "Beg your pardon, sir. I made sure you were in your cabin."

"You see I wasn't."

"No, sir. I could have sworn I had heard you moving in there not a moment ago. It's most extraordinary . . . very sorry, sir."

I passed on with an inward shudder. I was so identified with my secret double that I did not even mention the fact in those scanty, fearful whispers we exchanged. I suppose he had made some slight noise of some kind or other. It would have been miraculous if he hadn't at one time or another. And yet, haggard as he appeared, he looked always perfectly self-controlled, more than calm—almost invulnerable. On my suggestion he remained almost entirely in the bathroom, which, upon the whole, was the safest place. There could be really no shadow of an excuse for any one ever wanting to go in there, once the steward had done with it. It was a very tiny place. Sometimes he reclined on the floor, his legs bent, his head sustained on one elbow. At others I would find him on the campstool, sitting in his grey sleeping-suit and with his cropped dark hair like a patient, unmoved convict. At night I would smuggle him into my bed-place, and we would whisper together, with the regular footfalls of the officer of the watch passing and repassing over our heads. It was an infinitely miserable time. It was lucky that some tins of fine preserves were stowed in a locker in my stateroom; hard bread I could always get hold of; and so he lived on stewed chicken, paté de foie gras, asparagus, cooked oysters, sardines—on all sorts of abominable sham delicacies out of tins. My early morning coffee he always drank; and it was all I dared do for him in that respect.

Every day there was the horrible maneuvering to go through so that my room and then the bath-room should be done in the usual way. I came to hate the sight of the steward, to abhor the voice of that harmless man. I felt that it was he who would bring on the disaster of discovery. It hung like a sword over our heads.

The fourth day out, I think (we were then working down the east side of the Gulf of Siam, tack for tack, in light winds and smooth water)—the fourth day, I say, of this miserable juggling with the unavoidable, as we sat at our evening meal, that man, whose slightest movement I dreaded, after putting down the dishes ran up on deck busily. This could not be dangerous. Presently he came down again; and then it appeared that he had remembered a coat of mine which I had thrown over a rail to dry after having been wetted in a shower which had passed over the ship in the afternoon. Sitting stolidly at the head of the table I became terrified at the sight of the garment on his arm. Of course he made for my door. There was no time to lose.

"Steward," I thundered. My nerves were so shaken that I could not govern my voice and conceal my agitation. This was the sort of thing that made my terrifically whiskered mate tap his forehead with his forefinger. I had detected him using that gesture while talking on deck with a confidential air to the carpenter. It was too far to hear a word, but I had no doubt that this pantomime could only refer to the strange new captain.

"Yes, sir," the pale-faced steward turned resignedly to me. It was this maddening course of being shouted at, checked without rhyme or reason, arbitrarily chased out of my cabin, suddenly called into it, sent flying out of his pantry on incomprehensible errands, that accounted for the growing wretchedness of his expression.

"Where are you going with that coat?"

"To your room, sir."

"Is there another shower coming?"

"I'm sure I don't know, sir. Shall I go up again and see, sir?"

"No! never mind."

My object was attained, as of course my other self in there would have heard everything that passed. During this interlude my two officers never raised their eyes off their respective plates; but the lip of that confounded cub, the second mate, quivered visibly.

I expected the steward to hook my coat on and come out at once. He was very slow about it; but I dominated my nervousness sufficiently not to shout after him. Suddenly I became aware (it could be heard plainly enough) that the fellow for some reason or other was opening the door of the bath-room. It was the end. The place was literally not big enough to swing a cat in. My voice died in my throat and I went stony all over. I expected to hear a yell of surprise and terror, and made a movement, but had not the strength to get on my legs. Everything remained still. Had my second self taken the poor wretch by the throat? I don't know what I could have done next moment if I had not seen the steward come out of my room, close the door, and then stand quietly by the sideboard.

"Saved," I thought. "But, no! Lost! Gone! He was gone!"

I laid my knife and fork down and leaned back in my chair. My head swam.

After a while, when sufficiently recovered to speak in a steady voice, I instructed my mate to put the ship round at eight o'clock himself.

"I won't come on deck," I went on. "I think I'll turn in, and unless the wind shifts I don't want to be disturbed before midnight. I feel a bit seedy."

"You did look middling bad a little while ago," the chief mate remarked without showing any great concern.

They both went out, and I stared at the steward clearing the table. There was nothing to be read on that wretched man's face. But why did he avoid my eyes I asked myself. Then I thought I should like to hear the sound of his voice.

"Steward!"

"Sir!" Startled as usual.

"Where did you hang up that coat?"

"In the bath-room, sir." The usual anxious tone. "It's not quite dry yet, sir."

For some time longer I sat in the cuddy. Had my double vanished as he had come? But of his coming there was an explanation, whereas his disappearance would be inexplicable. . . . I went slowly into my dark room, shut the door, lighted the lamp, and for a time dared not turn round. When at last I did I saw him standing bolt-upright in the narrow recessed part. It would not be true to say I had a shock, but an irresistible doubt of his bodily existence flitted through my mind. Can it be, I asked myself, that he is not visible to other eyes than mine? It was like being haunted. Motionless, with a grave face, he raised his hands slightly at me in a gesture which meant clearly, "Heavens! what a narrow escape!" Narrow indeed. I think I had come creeping quietly as near insanity as any man who has not actually gone over the border. That gesture restrained me, so to speak.

The mate with the terrific whiskers was now putting the ship on the other tack. In the moment of profound silence which follows upon the hands going to their stations I heard on the poop his raised voice: "Hard alee!" and the distant shout of the order repeated on the maindeck. The sails, in that light breeze, made but a faint fluttering noise. It ceased. The ship was coming round slowly; I held my breath in the renewed stillness of expectation; one wouldn't have thought that there was a single living soul on her decks. A sudden brisk shout, "Mainsail haul!" broke the spell, and in the noisy cries and rush overhead of the men running away with the main-brace we two, down in my cabin, came together in our usual position by the bed-place.

He did not wait for my question. "I heard him fumbling here and just managed to squat myself down in the bath," he whispered to me. "The fellow only opened the door and put his arm in to hang the coat up. All the same——"

"I never thought of that," I whispered back, even more appalled than before at the closeness of the shave, and marvelling at that something unyielding in his character which was carrying him through so finely. There was no agitation in his whisper. Whoever was being driven distracted, it was not he. He was sane. And the proof of his sanity was continued when he took up the whispering again.

"It would never do for me to come to life again."

It was something that a ghost might have said. But what he was alluding to was his old captain's reluctant admission of the theory of suicide. It would obviously serve his turn—if I had understood at all the view which seemed to govern the unalterable purpose of his action.

"You must maroon me as soon as ever you can get amongst these islands off the Cambodge[4] shore," he went on.

"Maroon you! We are not living in a boy's adventure tale," I protested. His scornful whispering took me up.

"We aren't indeed! There's nothing of a boy's tale in this. But there's nothing else for it. I want no more. You don't suppose I am afraid of what can be done to me? Prison or gallows or whatever they may please. But you don't see me coming back to explain such things to an old fellow in a wig and twelve respectable tradesmen, do you? What can they know whether I am guilty or not—or of *what* I am guilty, either? That's my affair. What does the Bible say? 'Driven off the face of the earth.' Very well. I am off the face of the earth now. As I came at night so I shall go."

"Impossible!" I murmured. "You can't."

"Can't? . . . Not naked like a soul on the Day of Judgment. I shall freeze on to this sleeping-suit. The Last Day is not yet—and . . . you have understood thoroughly. Didn't you?"

I felt suddenly ashamed of myself. I may say truly that I understood—and my hesitation in letting that man swim away from my ship's side had been a mere sham sentiment, a sort of cowardice.

"It can't be done now till next night," I breathed out. "The ship is on the off-shore tack and the wind may fail us."

"As long as I know that you understand," he whispered. "But of course you do. It's a great satisfaction to have got somebody to understand. You seem to have been there on purpose." And in the same whisper, as if we two whenever we talked had to say things to each other which were not fit for the world to hear, he added, "It's very wonderful."

We remained side by side talking in our secret way—but sometimes silent or just exchanging a whispered word or two at long intervals. And as usual he stared through the port. A breath of wind came now and again into our faces. The ship might have been moored in dock, so gently and on an even keel she slipped through the water, that did not murmur even at our passage, shadowy and silent like a phantom sea.

At midnight I went on deck, and to my mate's great surprise put the ship round on the other tack. His terrible whiskers flitted round me in silent criticism. I certainly should not have done it if it had been only a question of getting out of that sleepy gulf as quickly as possible. I believe he told the second mate, who relieved him, that it was a great want of judgment. The other only yawned. That intolerable cub shuffled about so sleepily and lolled against the rails in such a slack, improper fashion that I came down on him sharply.

"Aren't you properly awake yet?"

"Yes, sir! I am awake."

"Well, then, be good enough to hold yourself as if you were. And keep a look-out. If there's any current we'll be closing with some islands before daylight."

The east side of the gulf is fringed with islands, some solitary, others in groups. On the blue background of the high coast they seem to float on silvery patches of calm water, arid and grey, or dark green and rounded like clumps of

---

[4] The French name of Cambodia. The story takes place when France controlled Indochina.

evergreen bushes, with the larger ones, a mile or two long, showing the outlines of ridges, ribs of grey rock under the dank mantle of matted leafage. Unknown to trade, to travel, almost to geography, the manner of life they harbour is an unsolved secret. There must be villages—settlements of fishermen at least—on the largest of them, and some communication with the world is probably kept up by native craft. But all that forenoon, as we headed for them, fanned along by the faintest of breezes, I saw no sign of man or canoe in the field of the telescope I kept on pointing at the scattered group.

At noon I gave no orders for a change of course, and the mate's whiskers became much concerned and seemed to be offering themselves unduly to my notice. At last I said:

"I am going to stand right in. Quite in—as far as I can take her."

The stare of extreme surprise imparted an air of ferocity also to his eyes, and he looked truly terrific for a moment.

"We're not doing well in the middle of the gulf," I continued casually. "I am going to look for the land breezes to-night."

"Bless my soul! Do you mean, sir, in the dark amongst the lot of all them islands and reefs and shoals?"

"Well—if there are any regular land breezes at all on this coast one must get close inshore to find them, mustn't one?"

"Bless my soul!" he exclaimed again under his breath. All that afternoon he wore a dreamy, contemplative appearance which in him was a mark of perplexity. After dinner I went into my stateroom as if I meant to take some rest. There we two bent our dark heads over a half-unrolled chart lying on my bed.

"There," I said. "It's got to be Koh-ring. I've been looking at it ever since sunrise. It has got two hills and a low point. It must be inhabited. And on the coast opposite there is what looks like the mouth of a biggish river—with some town, no doubt, not far up. It's the best chance for you that I can see."

"Anything. Koh-ring let it be."

He looked thoughtfully at the chart as if surveying chances and distances from a lofty height—and following with his eyes his own figure wandering on the blank land of Cochin-China,[5] and then passing off that piece of paper clean out of sight into uncharted regions. And it was as if the ship had two captains to plan her course for her. I had been so worried and restless running up and down that I had not had the patience to dress that day. I had remained in my sleeping-suit, with straw slippers and a soft floppy hat. The closeness of the heat in the gulf had been most oppressive, and the crew were used to see me wandering in that airy attire.

"She will clear the south point as she heads now," I whispered into his ear. "Goodness only knows when, though, but certainly after dark. I'll edge her in to half a mile, as far as I may be able to judge in the dark——"

"Be careful," he murmured, warningly—and I realised suddenly that all my future, the only future for which I was fit, would perhaps go irretrievably to pieces in any mishap to my first command.

I could not stop a moment longer in the room. I motioned him to get out of sight and made my way on the poop. That unplayful cub had the watch. I walked up and down for a while thinking things out, then beckoned him over.

[5] A colony of French Indochina from 1862 to 1948; now a part of South Vietnam.

"Send a couple of hands to open the two quarterdeck ports," I said, mildly. He actually had the impudence, or else so forgot himself in his wonder at such an incomprehensible order, as to repeat:

"Open the quarter-deck ports! What for, sir?"

"The only reason you need concern yourself about is because I tell you to do so. Have them opened wide and fastened properly."

He reddened and went off, but I believe made some jeering remark to the carpenter as to the sensible practice of ventilating a ship's quarter-deck. I know he popped into the mate's cabin to impart the fact to him because the whiskers came on deck, as it were by chance, and stole glances at me from below—for signs of lunacy or drunkenness, I suppose.

A little before supper, feeling more restless than ever, I rejoined, for a moment, my second self. And to find him sitting so quietly was surprising, like something against nature, inhuman.

I developed my plan in a hurried whisper.

"I shall stand in as close as I dare and then put her round. I will presently find means to smuggle you out of here into the sail-locker, which communicates with the lobby. But there is an opening, a sort of square for hauling the sails out, which gives straight on the quarter-deck and which is never closed in fine weather, so as to give air to the sails. When the ship's way is deadened in stays and all the hands are aft at the main-braces you will have a clear road to slip out and get overboard through the open quarter-deck port. I've had them both fastened up. Use a rope's end to lower yourself into the water so as to avoid a splash—you know. It could be heard and cause some beastly complication."

He kept silent for a while, then whispered, "I understand."

"I won't be there to see you go," I began with an effort. "The rest . . . I only hope I have understood, too."

"You have. From first to last"—and for the first time there seemed to be a faltering, something strained in his whisper. He caught hold of my arm, but the ringing of the supper bell made me start. He didn't, though; he only released his grip.

After supper I didn't come below again till well past eight o'clock. The faint, steady breeze was loaded with dew; and the wet, darkened sails held all there was of propelling power in it. The night, clear and starry, sparkled darkly, and the opaque, lightless patches shifting slowly against the low stars were the drifting islets. On the port bow there was a big one more distant and shadowily imposing by the great space of sky it eclipsed.

On opening the door I had a back view of my very own self looking at a chart. He had come out of the recess and was standing near the table.

"Quite dark enough," I whispered.

He stepped back and leaned against my bed with a level, quiet glance. I sat on the couch. We had nothing to say to each other. Over our heads the officer of the watch moved here and there. Then I heard him move quickly. I knew what that meant. He was making for the companion; and presently his voice was outside my door.

"We are drawing in pretty fast, sir. Land looks rather close."

"Very well," I answered. "I am coming on deck directly."

I waited till he was gone out of the cuddy, then rose. My double moved too.

The time had come to exchange our last whispers, for neither of us was ever to hear each other's natural voice.

"Look here!" I opened a drawer and took out three sovereigns. "Take this anyhow. I've got six and I'd give you the lot, only I must keep a little money to buy some fruit and vegetables for the crew from native boats as we go through Sunda Straits."

He shook his head.

"Take it," I urged him, whispering desperately. "No one can tell what——"

He smiled and slapped meaningly the only pocket of the sleeping-jacket. It was not safe, certainly. But I produced a large old silk handkerchief of mine, and tying the three pieces of gold in a corner, pressed it on him. He was touched, I suppose, because he took it at last and tied it quickly round his waist under the jacket, on his bare skin.

Our eyes met; several seconds elapsed, till, our glances still mingled, I extended my hand and turned the lamp out. Then I passed through the cuddy, leaving the door of my room wide open. . . . "Steward!"

He was still lingering in the pantry in the greatness of his zeal, giving a rub-up to a plated cruet stand the last thing before going to bed. Being careful not to wake up the mate, whose room was opposite, I spoke in an undertone.

He looked round anxiously. "Sir."

"Can you get me a little hot water from the galley?"

"I am afraid, sir, the galley fire's been out for some time now."

"Go and see."

He flew up the stairs.

"Now," I whispered, loudly, into the saloon—too loudly, perhaps, but I was afraid I couldn't make a sound. He was by my side in an instant—the double captain slipped past the stairs—through a tiny dark passage . . . a sliding door. We were in the sail-locker, scrambling on our knees over the sails. A sudden thought struck me. I saw myself wandering barefooted, bareheaded, the sun beating on my dark poll. I snatched off my floppy hat and tried hurriedly in the dark to ram it on my other self. He dodged and fended off silently. I wonder what he thought had come to me before he understood and suddenly desisted. Our hands met gropingly, lingered united in a steady, motionless clasp for a second. . . . No word was breathed by either of us when they separated.

I was standing quietly by the pantry door when the steward returned.

"Sorry, sir. Kettle barely warm. Shall I light the spirit-lamp?"

"Never mind."

I came out on deck slowly. It was now a matter of conscience to shave the land as close as possible—for now he must go overboard whenever the ship was put in stays. Must! There could be no going back for him. After a moment I walked over to leeward and my heart flew into my mouth at the nearness of the land on the bow. Under any other circumstances I would not have held on a minute longer. The second mate had followed me anxiously.

I looked on till I felt I could command my voice.

"She will weather," I said then in a quiet tone.

"Are you going to try that, sir?" he stammered out incredulously.

I took no notice of him and raised my tone just enough to be heard by the helmsman.

"Keep her good full."

"Good full, sir."

The wind fanned my cheek, the sails slept, the world was silent. The strain of watching the dark loom of the land grow bigger and denser was too much for me. I had shut my eyes—because the ship must go closer. She must! The stillness was intolerable. Were we standing still?

When I opened my eyes the second view started my heart with a thump. The black southern hill of Koh-ring seemed to hang right over the ship like a towering fragment of the everlasting night. On that enormous mass of blackness there was not a gleam to be seen, not a sound to be heard. It was gliding irresistibly towards us and yet seemed already within reach of the hand. I saw the vague figures of the watch grouped in the waist, gazing in awed silence.

"Are you going on, sir?" inquired an unsteady voice at my elbow.

I ignored it. I had to go on.

"Keep her full. Don't check her way. That won't do now," I said warningly.

"I can't see the sails very well," the helmsman answered me, in strange, quavering tones.

Was she close enough? Already she was, I won't say in the shadow of the land, but in the very blackness of it, already swallowed up as it were, gone too close to be recalled, gone from me altogether.

"Give the mate a call," I said to the young man who stood at my elbow as still as death. "And turn all hands up."

My tone had a borrowed loudness reverberated from the height of the land. Several voices cried out together: "We are all on deck, sir."

Then stillness again, with the great shadow gliding closer, towering higher, without a light, without a sound. Such a hush had fallen on the ship that she might have been a bark of the dead floating in slowly under the very gate of Erebus.[6]

"My God! Where are we?"

It was the mate moaning at my elbow. He was thunderstruck, and as it were deprived of the moral support of his whiskers. He clapped his hands and absolutely cried out, "Lost!"

"Be quiet," I said, sternly.

He lowered his tone, but I saw the shadowy gesture of his despair. "What are we doing here?"

"Looking for the land wind."

He made as if to tear his hair, and addressed me recklessly.

"She will never get out. You have done it, sir. I knew it'd end in something like this. She will never weather, and you are too close now to stay. She'll drift ashore before she's round. O my God!"

I caught his arm as he was raising it to batter his poor devoted head, and shook it violently.

"She's ashore already," he wailed, trying to tear himself away.

"Is she? . . . Keep good full there!"

"Good full, sir," cried the helmsman in a frightened, thin child-like voice.

I hadn't let go the mate's arm and went on shaking it. "Ready about, do you hear? You go forward"—shake—"and stop there"—shake—"and hold your noise"—

6 In Greek mythology, the son of Chaos and the brother of Night, hence, darkness personified.

shake—"and see these head-sheets properly overhauled"—shake, shake—shake.

And all the time I dared not look towards the land lest my heart should fail me. I released my grip at last and he ran forward as if fleeing for dear life.

I wondered what my double there in the sail-locker thought of this commotion. He was able to hear everything—and perhaps he was able to understand why, on my conscience, it had to be thus close—no less. My first order "Hard alee!" re-echoed ominously under the towering shadow of Koh-ring as if I had shouted in a mountain gorge. And then I watched the land intently. In that smooth water and light wind it was impossible to feel the ship coming-to. No! I could not feel her. And my second self was making now ready to slip out and lower himself overboard. Perhaps he was gone already . . . ?

The great black mass brooding over our very mastheads began to pivot away from the ship's side silently. And now I forgot the secret stranger ready to depart, and remembered only that I was a total stranger to the ship. I did not know her. Would she do it? How was she to be handled?

I swung the mainyard and waited helplessly. She was perhaps stopped, and her very fate hung in the balance, with the black mass of Koh-ring like the gate of the everlasting night towering over her taffrail. What would she do now? Had she way on her yet? I stepped to the side swiftly, and on the shadowy water I could see nothing except a faint phosphorescent flash revealing the glassy smoothness of the sleeping surface. It was impossible to tell—and I had not learned yet the feel of my ship. Was she moving? What I needed was something easily seen, a piece of paper, which I could throw overboard and watch. I had nothing on me. To run down for it I didn't dare. There was no time. All at once my strained, yearning stare distinguished a white object floating within a yard of the ship's side. White on the black water. A phosphorescent flash passed under it. What was that thing? . . . I recognised my own floppy hat. It must have fallen off his head . . . and he didn't bother. Now I had what I wanted—the saving mark for my eyes. But I hardly thought of my other self, now gone from the ship, to be hidden for ever from all friendly faces, to be a fugitive and a vagabond on the earth, with no brand of the curse on his sane forehead to stay a slaying hand . . . too proud to explain.

And I watched the hat—the expression of my sudden pity for his mere flesh. It had been meant to save his homeless head from the dangers of the sun. And now—behold—it was saving the ship, by serving me for a mark to help out the ignorance of my strangeness. Ha! It was drifting forward, warning me just in time that the ship had gathered sternway.

"Shift the helm," I said in a low voice to the seaman standing still like a statue.

The man's eyes glistened wildly in the binnacle light as he jumped round to the other side and spun round the wheel.

I walked to the break of the poop. On the overshadowed deck all hands stood by the forebraces waiting for my order. The stars ahead seemed to be gliding from right to left. And all was so still in the world that I heard the quiet remark, "She's round," passed in a tone of intense relief between two seamen.

"Let go and haul."

The foreyards ran round with a great noise, amidst cheery cries. And now the frightful whiskers made themselves heard giving various orders. Already the ship was drawing ahead. And I was alone with her. Nothing! no one in the world should stand now between us, throwing a shadow on the way of silent knowledge and mute affection, the perfect communion of a seaman with his first command.

Walking to the taffrail, I was in time to make out, on the very edge of a darkness thrown by a towering black mass like the very gateway of Erebus—yes, I was in time to catch an evanescent glimpse of my white hat left behind to mark the spot where the secret sharer of my cabin and of my thoughts, as though he were my second self, had lowered himself into the water to take his punishment: a free man, a proud swimmer striking out for a new destiny.

COMMENTARY

One of literature's most engaging themes is the initiation of a boy or a young man into a new stage of his development toward maturity. We have seen it strikingly handled in "My Kinsman, Major Molineux" (pages 425 ff.), and now we meet it again in "The Secret Sharer," which sustains comparison with Hawthorne's story in the subtlety and range of its psychological drama.

Some of the power of "The Secret Sharer" derives from the particular profession to which its young protagonist has devoted himself. It is a profession whose moral implications are large and manifest, for the captain of a ship exercises an authority unique in its extent, and he bears a proportionate responsibility. In the official language of maritime affairs he is called a *master*. The old-fashioned word has a double meaning. The captain is a master-mariner in the sense that once obtained when people spoke of a master-builder or a master-mason, meaning a craftsman who has been certified by his guild as knowing all that he should know of his craft or trade. A ship's captain is master of the whole art of managing a ship. Of all the ship's company, he is the man who knows most through experience and study, his knowledge having been certified by rigorous examination. (Conrad held a master's certificate in the British merchant service, and there was nothing in his life of which he was prouder.) But the captain is also master in the sense that, on the ship he commands, his word is law. The maritime code of every nation forbids his orders to be questioned, let alone disobeyed.

For any man, but especially for a man as young and as sensitive as Conrad's captain, the occasion of his taking his first command is crucial indeed. How significant is the phrase *to take command!* We say that a man is *given* the command of a ship, but the moment comes when he must *take* what he is given, when by his bearing and his conduct he must make plain his belief that he has the right to exercise the authority of his position. He does so at some cost, for by the nature and extent of his authority he is cut off from the rest of the ship's company and condemned to a lonely existence—one cannot be on familiar terms with those from whom one requires not merely cooperation but obedience, perhaps at the risk of their lives. When, in Conrad's story, the young captain says that he will stand the first watch himself, in part moved to do so by the knowledge that his officers and crew are fatigued from some days of hard work before his arrival, this unconventional behavior, his undertaking of a duty inappropriate to his status as captain, raises uneasy questions in the minds of his subordinates; far from reassuring them of his good intentions, his act leads them to wonder about his capacity to command.

Their doubts of their captain are, of course, an echo of his own doubts of himself. He is by no means easy about his new status. He is conscious of being "the youngest man on board (barring the second mate)"; it is not easy for a young man of any degree of sensitivity to assume authority over his elders, even though they may be his inferiors in intelligence and education. This natural youthful diffidence is accentuated by his readiness to make large demands upon himself. Nothing is more characteristic of him than his concern over how he will meet the test he imposes on himself—to wonder, as he says, how far he would "turn out faithful to that ideal conception of one's own personality every man sets up for himself secretly." It is surely not true that *every* man sets up for himself an ideal conception of his personality such as this young man does and, of those who do, not many have controlling images of their best selves so rigorous as the young captain's, or so grandiose. "In this breathless pause at the threshold of a long passage," he says, "we [that is, he and his ship] seemed to be measuring our fitness for a long and arduous enterprise, the appointed task of both our existences to be carried out, far from all human eyes, with only sky and sea for spectators and for judges." It is no ordinary young man, no ordinary ship's captain, who thinks of his existence as having its "appointed task," the performance of which is to be watched and judged by no mere human eyes but by, as it were, the universe itself.

A young man in this relation to an ideal is in some sense a divided being—he stands apart from himself to take his own measure; he exists both as an actual self and as the self he aspires to be. The time will come when he will, as the phrase goes, "find himself," but until then his conduct may well be checked and hampered by the division in his being. In the captain's situation his state of mind is given a literal, objective form by the disconcerting presence of Leggatt, whom he speaks of as exactly his "other self," the "secret sharer" of his existence.

The secrecy with which Leggatt's presence on the ship must be enshrouded is not an innocent one. The salient fact about Leggatt is that he is a murderer. The word may seem harsh in view of the extenuating circumstances of Leggatt's crime and the sympathy that his personality evokes. Yet the ugly word conveys the simple truth—however understandable Leggatt's act may seem to the captain and to us, it would be severely condemned in a court of law and in all probability severely punished. Are we then to conclude that when the young captain commits himself to Leggatt, taking his admired guest to be the ideal conception of his own personality, it is Leggatt's fatal violence that constitutes the ideality to which he aspires? There appears to be some ground for this conclusion in the fact that Leggatt's crime makes the single point of real difference between the captain and his hidden guest, the one element of Leggatt's being which is not already matched by the captain's. In all other respects, as their immediate sympathy with each other suggests, the two young men are virtually the same person. They are scarcely distinguishable in appearance; they share memories of *Conway,* the school ship for merchant seamen on which both had been trained, although at different times; they are of the same social class, having the same degree of social superiority not only to the members of the crew but to all the officers, including the captain of the *Sephora;* and they are alike in their high devotion to the profession they have in common. There is only the crime of one of them to make a difference between them, and it would seem to lie within the logic of the story that what constitutes Leggatt's ideality for the captain is his having killed a man who stood in the way of his effectual exercise of command.

Certainly the captain is singularly unmoved by Leggatt's act. Even before he knows about the extenuating circumstances of the killing, he is disposed to make light of it. To Leggatt's declaration, "I've killed a man," he has an explanation which comes with startling readiness—"'Fit of temper,'" he "confidently" replies. And when he hears the details of the episode, he is quick to understand that "the same strung-up force which had given twenty-four men a chance, at least, for their lives, had, in a sort of recoil, crushed an unworthy mutinous existence." As the captain well knows, this is not at all the view of the case that would be taken by the men of his crew, and of course he knows, from Leggatt's account, that it is not at all the view that was taken by the crew and the captain of Leggatt's ship: any doubt he might have on this score is dispelled by the sentiments expressed by the search party from the *Sephora*. Leggatt himself takes the killing with considerably more seriousness than the captain. He speaks of it as an "ugly business"; he remembers how tenacious had been his grip on the man's throat; he does not palter with the fact that it had been his intention to kill; he is under no illusion that the act had been a *necessity* of command: he is quite clear that it had been committed in uncontrollable rage.

Yet although Leggatt regards the incident gravely enough, he too, like the captain, understands his murderous violence as "a sort of recoil" from the terrible energy needed to enforce authority in a desperate situation; he does not take it upon his conscience. He regrets his act but has no remorse over it. He and the captain are at one in by-passing the judgment of society, both its morality and its code of law. The two young men do not think of themselves as available to judgment by standards that are merely social—they submit only to the imperatives of a transcendent law, that of "sea and sky"; their sense of duty is defined not merely by their relation to society but by their relation to the universe.

If we try to make explicit what Conrad's story communicates symbolically, we may say that the disconcerting secret that the young captain undertakes to hide from the crew in hiding Leggatt is the coercive *force* that lies concealed at the heart of all authority. Yet it is not simply because Leggatt has revealed this grim ultimate truth about what it means to command that the captain recognizes in him the ideal conception of personality to which he must be faithful. Rather, what engages the captain's loyalty to his guest is that Leggatt had risked everything in the service of his lofty view of duty. In an extreme situation he had dared to call upon the coercive force that, lying concealed in all authority, ought never be exposed; in the use of this force, his passion for duty had overreached itself by what we are asked to think of as a mishap of the emotions, with the tragic result that Leggatt is now forever barred from the exercise of command. In destroying that "unworthy mutinous existence" he had destroyed himself, or what he believes to be the best part of himself, his career as a ship's officer. The young captain's loyalty to Leggatt, his other and ideal self, takes the form of assuming a risk no less grave than Leggatt's and of the same kind. Knowing that all his future, "the only future for which [he] was fit," would in all likelihood be destroyed by any mishap to his ship, and in the face of the terrified astonishment of his officers and men, who think him quite literally insane, the captain sails dangerously close to shore to give Leggatt a chance to swim for his life. Leggatt drops over the side. The captain is at last alone and at one with himself, freed, we may say, of the guilty secret of command by his willingness to acknowledge it.

THE DEAD

JAMES JOYCE

1882–1941

LILY, THE CARETAKER'S DAUGHTER, was literally run off her feet. Hardly had she brought one gentleman into the little pantry behind the office on the ground floor and helped him off with his overcoat than the wheezy hall-door bell clanged again and she had to scamper along the bare hallway to let in another guest. It was well for her she had not to attend to the ladies also. But Miss Kate and Miss Julia had thought of that and had converted the bathroom upstairs into a ladies' dressing-room. Miss Kate and Miss Julia were there, gossiping and laughing and fussing, walking after each other to the head of the stairs, peering down over the banisters and calling down to Lily to ask her who had come.

It was always a great affair, the Misses Morkan's annual dance. Everybody who knew them came to it, members of the family, old friends of the family, the members of Julia's choir, any of Kate's pupils that were grown up enough, and even some of Mary Jane's pupils too. Never once had it fallen flat. For years and years it had gone off in splendid style, as long as anyone could remember; ever since Kate and Julia, after the death of their brother Pat, had left the house in Stoney Batter and taken Mary Jane, their only niece, to live with them in the dark, gaunt house on Usher's Island, the upper part of which they had rented from Mr. Fulham, the corn-factor on the ground floor. That was a good thirty years ago if it was a day. Mary Jane, who was then a little girl in short clothes, was now the main prop of the household, for she had the organ in Haddington Road. She had been through the Academy and gave a pupils' concert every year in the upper room of the Antient Concert Rooms. Many of her pupils belonged to the better-class families on the Kingstown and Dalkey line. Old as they were, her aunts also did their share. Julia, though she was quite grey, was still the leading soprano in Adam and Eve's, and Kate, being too feeble to go about much, gave music lessons to beginners on the old square piano in the back room. Lily, the caretaker's daughter, did housemaid's work for them. Though their life was modest, they believed in eating well; the best of everything: diamond-bone sirloins, three shilling tea and the best bottled stout. But Lily seldom made a mistake in the orders, so that she got on well with her three mistresses. They were fussy, that was all. But the only thing they would not stand was back answers.

Of course, they had good reason to be fussy on such a night. And then it was long after ten o'clock and yet there was no sign of Gabriel and his wife. Besides they were dreadfully afraid that Freddy Malins might turn up screwed. They would not wish for worlds that any of Mary Jane's pupils should see him under the influence; and when he was like that it was sometimes very hard to manage him. Freddy Malins always came late, but they wondered what could be keeping Gabriel: and that was what brought them every two minutes to the banisters to ask Lily had Gabriel or Freddy come.

"O, Mr. Conroy," said Lily to Gabriel when she opened the door for him, "Miss Kate and Miss Julia thought you were never coming. Good-night, Mrs. Conroy."

"I'll engage they did," said Gabriel, "but they forget that my wife here takes three mortal hours to dress herself."

He stood on the mat, scraping the snow from his goloshes, while Lily led his wife to the foot of the stairs and called out:

"Miss Kate, here's Mrs. Conroy."

Kate and Julia came toddling down the dark stairs at once. Both of them kissed Gabriel's wife, said she must be perished alive, and asked was Gabriel with her.

"Here I am as right as the mail, Aunt Kate! Go on up. I'll follow," called out Gabriel from the dark.

He continued scraping his feet vigorously while the three women went upstairs, laughing, to the ladies' dressing-room. A light fringe of snow lay like a cape on the shoulders of his overcoat and like toecaps on the toes of his goloshes; and, as the buttons of his overcoat slipped with a squeaking noise through the snow-stiffened frieze, a cold, fragrant air from out-of-doors escaped from crevices and folds.

"Is it snowing again, Mr. Conroy?" asked Lily.

She had preceded him into the pantry to help him off with his overcoat. Gabriel smiled at the three syllables she had given his surname and glanced at her. She was a slim, growing girl, pale in complexion and with hay-coloured hair. The gas in the pantry made her look still paler. Gabriel had known her when she was a child and used to sit on the lowest step nursing a rag doll.

"Yes, Lily," he answered, "and I think we're in for a night of it."

He looked up at the pantry ceiling, which was shaking with the stamping and shuffling of feet on the floor above, listened for a moment to the piano and then glanced at the girl, who was folding his overcoat carefully at the end of a shelf.

"Tell me, Lily," he said in a friendly tone, "do you still go to school?"

"O no, sir," she answered. "I'm done schooling this year and more."

"O, then," said Gabriel gaily, "I suppose we'll be going to your wedding one of these fine days with your young man, eh?"

The girl glanced back at him over her shoulder and said with great bitterness:

"The men that is now is only all palaver and what they can get out of you."

Gabriel coloured, as if he felt he had made a mistake and, without looking at her, kicked off his goloshes and flicked actively with his muffler at his patent-leather shoes.

He was a stout, tallish young man. The high colour of his cheeks pushed upwards even to his forehead, where it scattered itself in a few formless patches of pale red; and on his hairless face there scintillated restlessly the polished lenses and the bright gilt rims of the glasses which screened his delicate and restless eyes. His glossy black hair was parted in the middle and brushed in a long curve behind his ears where it curled slightly beneath the groove left by his hat.

When he had flicked lustre into his shoes he stood up and pulled his waistcoat down more tightly on his plump body. Then he took a coin rapidly from his pocket.

"O Lily," he said, thrusting it into her hands, "it's Christmas-time, isn't it? Just . . . here's a little. . . ."

He walked rapidly towards the door.

"O no, sir!" cried the girl, following him. "Really, sir, I wouldn't take it."

"Christmas-time! Christmas-time!" said Gabriel, almost trotting to the stairs and waving his hand to her in deprecation.

The girl, seeing that he had gained the stairs, called out after him:

"Well, thank you, sir."

He waited outside the drawing-room door until the waltz should finish, listening to the skirts that swept against it and to the shuffling of feet. He was still discomposed by the girl's bitter and sudden retort. It had cast a gloom over him which he tried to dispel by arranging his cuffs and the bows of his tie. He then took from his waistcoat pocket a little paper and glanced at the headings he had made for his speech. He was undecided about the lines from Robert Browning, for he feared they would be above the heads of his hearers. Some quotation that they would recognise from Shakespeare or from the Melodies[1] would be better. The indelicate clacking of the men's heels and the shuffling of their soles reminded him that their grade of culture differed from his. He would only make himself ridiculous by quoting poetry to them which they could not understand. They would think that he was airing his superior education. He would fail with them just as he had failed with the girl in the pantry. He had taken up a wrong tone. His whole speech was a mistake from first to last, an utter failure.

Just then his aunts and his wife came out of the ladies' dressing-room. His aunts were two small, plainly dressed old women. Aunt Julia was an inch or so the taller. Her hair, drawn low over the tops of her ears, was grey; and grey also, with darker shadows, was her large flaccid face. Though she was stout in build and

[1] The *Irish Melodies* of Thomas Moore (1779–1852).

stood erect, her slow eyes and parted lips gave her the appearance of a woman who did not know where she was or where she was going. Aunt Kate was more vivacious. Her face, healthier than her sister's, was all puckers and creases, like a shrivelled red apple, and her hair, braided in the same old-fashioned way, had not lost its ripe nut colour.

They both kissed Gabriel frankly. He was their favourite nephew, the son of their dead elder sister, Ellen, who had married T. J. Conroy of the Port and Docks.

"Gretta tells me you're not going to take a cab back to Monkstown to-night, Gabriel," said Aunt Kate.

"No," said Gabriel, turning to his wife, "we had quite enough of that last year, hadn't we? Don't you remember, Aunt Kate, what a cold Gretta got out of it? Cab windows rattling all the way, and the east wind blowing in after we passed Merrion. Very jolly it was. Gretta caught a dreadful cold."

Aunt Kate frowned severely and nodded her head at every word.

"Quite right, Gabriel, quite right," she said. "You can't be too careful."

"But as for Gretta there," said Gabriel, "she'd walk home in the snow if she were let."

Mrs. Conroy laughed.

"Don't mind him, Aunt Kate," she said. "He's really an awful bother, what with green shades for Tom's eyes at night and making him do the dumb-bells, and forcing Eva to eat the stirabout.[2] The poor child! And she simply hates the sight of it! . . . O, but you'll never guess what he makes me wear now!"

She broke out into a peal of laughter and glanced at her husband, whose admiring and happy eyes had been wandering from her dress to her face and hair. The two aunts laughed heartily, too, for Gabriel's solicitude was a standing joke with them.

"Goloshes!" said Mrs. Conroy. "That's the latest. Whenever it's wet under-foot I must put on my goloshes. To-night even, he wanted me to put them on, but I wouldn't. The next thing he'll buy me will be a diving suit."

Gabriel laughed nervously and patted his tie reassuringly, while Aunt Kate nearly doubled herself, so heartily did she enjoy the joke. The smile soon faded from Aunt Julia's face and her mirthless eyes were directed towards her nephew's face. After a pause she asked:

"And what are goloshes, Gabriel?"

"Goloshes, Julia!" exclaimed her sister. "Goodness me, don't you know what goloshes are? You wear them over your . . . over your boots, Gretta, isn't it?"

"Yes," said Mrs. Conroy. "Guttapercha[3] things. We both have a pair now. Gabriel says everyone wears them on the Continent."

"O, on the Continent," murmured Aunt Julia, nodding her head slowly.

Gabriel knitted his brows and said, as if he were slightly angered:

"It's nothing very wonderful, but Gretta thinks it very funny because she says the word reminds her of Christy Minstrels."[4]

"But tell me, Gabriel," said Aunt Kate, with brisk tact. "Of course, you've seen about the room. Gretta was saying . . ."

"O, the room is all right," replied Gabriel. "I've taken one in the Gresham."

[2] Oatmeal or other porridge.
[3] A gray to brown tough substance resembling rubber.
[4] A troupe of American Negro minstrels organized about 1860 by Edwin P. Christy.

"To be sure," said Aunt Kate, "by far the best thing to do. And the children, Gretta, you're not anxious about them?"

"O, for one night," said Mrs. Conroy. "Besides, Bessie will look after them."

"To be sure," said Aunt Kate again. "What a comfort it is to have a girl like that, one you can depend on! There's that Lily, I'm sure I don't know what has come over her lately. She's not the girl she was at all."

Gabriel was about to ask his aunt some questions on this point, but she broke off suddenly to gaze after her sister, who had wandered down the stairs and was craning her neck over the banisters.

"Now, I ask you," she said almost testily, "where is Julia going? Julia! Julia! Where are you going?"

Julia, who had gone half way down one flight, came back and announced blandly:

"Here's Freddy."

At the same moment a clapping of hands and a final flourish of the pianist told that the waltz had ended. The drawing-room door was opened from within and some couples came out. Aunt Kate drew Gabriel aside hurriedly and whispered into his ear:

"Slip down, Gabriel, like a good fellow and see if he's all right, and don't let him up if he's screwed. I'm sure he's screwed. I'm sure he is."

Gabriel went to the stairs and listened over the banisters. He could hear two persons talking in the pantry. Then he recognised Freddy Malins' laugh. He went down the stairs noisily.

"It's such a relief," said Aunt Kate to Mrs. Conroy, "that Gabriel is here. I always feel easier in my mind when he's here. . . . Julia, there's Miss Daly and Miss Power will take some refreshment. Thanks for your beautiful waltz, Miss Daly. It made lovely time."

A tall wizen-faced man, with a stiff grizzled moustache and swarthy skin, who was passing out with his partner, said:

"And may we have some refreshment, too, Miss Morkan?"

"Julia," said Aunt Kate summarily, "and here's Mr. Browne and Miss Furlong. Take them in, Julia, with Miss Daly and Miss Power."

"I'm the man for the ladies," said Mr. Browne, pursing his lips until his moustache bristled and smiling in all his wrinkles. "You know, Miss Morkan, the reason they are so fond of me is—"

He did not finish his sentence, but, seeing that Aunt Kate was out of earshot, at once led the three young ladies into the back room. The middle of the room was occupied by two square tables placed end to end, and on these Aunt Julia and the caretaker were straightening and smoothing a large cloth. On the sideboard were arrayed dishes and plates, and glasses and bundles of knives and forks and spoons. The top of the closed square piano served also as a sideboard for viands and sweets. At a smaller sideboard in one corner two young men were standing, drinking hop-bitters.

Mr. Browne led his charges thither and invited them all, in jest, to some ladies' punch, hot, strong and sweet. As they said they never took anything strong, he opened three bottles of lemonade for them. Then he asked one of the young men to move aside, and taking hold of the decanter, filled out for himself a goodly measure of whisky. The young men eyed him respectfully while he took a trial sip.

"God help me," he said, smiling, "it's the doctor's orders."

His wizened face broke into a broader smile, and the three young ladies laughed in musical echo to his pleasantry, swaying their bodies to and fro, with nervous jerks of their shoulders. The boldest said:

"O, now, Mr. Browne, I'm sure the doctor never ordered anything of the kind."

Mr. Browne took another sip of his whisky and said, with sidling mimicry:

"Well, you see, I'm like the famous Mrs. Cassidy, who is reported to have said: 'Now, Mary Grimes, if I don't take it, make me take it, for I feel I want it.'"

His hot face had leaned forward a little too confidentially and he had assumed a very low Dublin accent so that the young ladies, with one instinct, received his speech in silence. Miss Furlong, who was one of Mary Jane's pupils, asked Miss Daly what was the name of the pretty waltz she had played; and Mr. Browne, seeing that he was ignored, turned promptly to the two young men who were more appreciative.

A red-faced young woman, dressed in pansy, came into the room, excitedly clapping her hands and crying:

"Quadrilles! Quadrilles!"

Close on her heels came Aunt Kate, crying:

"Two gentlemen and three ladies, Mary Jane!"

"O, here's Mr. Bergin and Mr. Kerrigan," said Mary Jane. "Mr. Kerrigan, will you take Miss Power? Miss Furlong, may I get you a partner, Mr. Bergin. O, that'll just do now."

"Three ladies, Mary Jane," said Aunt Kate.

The two young gentlemen asked the ladies if they might have the pleasure, and Mary Jane turned to Miss Daly.

"O, Miss Daly, you're really awfully good, after playing for the last two dances, but really we're so short of ladies to-night."

"I don't mind in the least, Miss Morkan."

"But I've a nice partner for you, Mr. Bartell D'Arcy, the tenor. I'll get him to sing later on. All Dublin is raving about him."

"Lovely voice, lovely voice!" said Aunt Kate.

As the piano had twice begun the prelude to the first figure Mary Jane led her recruits quickly from the room. They had hardly gone when Aunt Julia wandered slowly into the room, looking behind her at something.

"What is the matter, Julia?" asked Aunt Kate anxiously. "Who is it?"

Julia, who was carrying in a column of table-napkins, turned to her sister and said, simply, as if the question had surprised her:

"It's only Freddy, Kate, and Gabriel with him."

In fact right behind her Gabriel could be seen piloting Freddy Malins across the landing. The latter, a young man of about forty, was of Gabriel's size and build, with very round shoulders. His face was fleshy and pallid, touched with colour only at the thick hanging lobes of his ears and at the wide wings of his nose. He had coarse features, a blunt nose, a convex and receding brow, tumid and protruded lips. His heavy-lidded eyes and the disorder of his scanty hair made him look sleepy. He was laughing heartily in a high key at a story which he had been telling Gabriel on the stairs and at the same time rubbing the knuckles of his left fist backwards and forwards into his left eye.

"Good-evening, Freddy," said Aunt Julia.

Freddy Malins bade the Misses Morkan good-evening in what seemed an offhand fashion by reason of the habitual catch in his voice and then, seeing that Mr. Browne was grinning at him from the sideboard, crossed the room on rather shaky legs and began to repeat in an undertone the story he had just told to Gabriel.

"He's not so bad, is he?" said Aunt Kate to Gabriel.

Gabriel's brows were dark but he raised them quickly and answered:

"O, no, hardly noticeable."

"Now, isn't he a terrible fellow!" she said. "And his poor mother made him take the pledge on New Year's Eve. But come on, Gabriel, into the drawing-room."

Before leaving the room with Gabriel she signalled to Mr. Browne by frowning and shaking her forefinger in warning to and fro. Mr. Browne nodded in answer and, when she had gone, said to Freddy Malins:

"Now, then, Teddy, I'm going to fill you out a good glass of lemonade just to buck you up."

Freddy Malins, who was nearing the climax of his story, waved the offer aside impatiently but Mr. Browne, having first called Freddy Malins' attention to a disarray in his dress, filled out and handed him a full glass of lemonade. Freddy Malins' left hand accepted the glass mechanically, his right hand being engaged in the mechanical readjustment of his dress. Mr. Browne, whose face was once more wrinkling with mirth, poured out for himself a glass of whisky while Freddy Malins exploded, before he had well reached the climax of his story, in a kink of high-pitched bronchitic laughter and, setting down his untasted and overflowing glass, began to rub the knuckles of his left fist backwards and forwards into his left eye, repeating words of his last phrase as well as his fit of laughter would allow him.

. . . .

Gabriel could not listen while Mary Jane was playing her Academy piece, full of runs and difficult passages, to the hushed drawing-room. He liked music but the piece she was playing had no melody for him and he doubted whether it had any melody for the other listeners, though they had begged Mary Jane to play something. Four young men, who had come from the refreshment-room to stand in the doorway at the sound of the piano, had gone away quietly in couples after a few minutes. The only persons who seemed to follow the music were Mary Jane herself, her hands racing along the key-board or lifted from it at the pauses like those of a priestess in momentary imprecation, and Aunt Kate standing at her elbow to turn the page.

Gabriel's eyes, irritated by the floor, which glittered with beeswax under the heavy chandelier, wandered to the wall above the piano. A picture of the balcony scene in *Romeo and Juliet* hung there and beside it was a picture of the two murdered princes in the Tower which Aunt Julia had worked in red, blue and brown wools when she was a girl. Probably in the school they had gone to as girls that kind of work had been taught for one year. His mother had worked for him as a birthday present a waistcoat of purple tabinet,[5] with little foxes' heads upon it, lined with brown satin and having round mulberry buttons. It was strange that his mother had had no musical talent though Aunt Kate used to call her the brains

---

[5] A watered fabric of silk and wool resembling poplin.

carrier of the Morkan family. Both she and Julia had always seemed a little proud of their serious and matronly sister. Her photograph stood before the pierglass. She held an open book on her knees and was pointing out something in it to Constantine who, dressed in a man-o'-war suit, lay at her feet. It was she who had chosen the names of her sons for she was very sensible of the dignity of family life. Thanks to her, Constantine was now senior curate in Balbriggan and, thanks to her, Gabriel himself had taken his degree in the Royal University. A shadow passed over his face as he remembered her sullen opposition to his marriage. Some slighting phrases she had used still rankled in his memory; she had once spoken of Gretta as being country cute and that was not true of Gretta at all. It was Gretta who had nursed her during all her last long illness in their house at Monkstown.

He knew that Mary Jane must be near the end of her piece for she was playing again the opening melody with runs of scales after every bar and while he waited for the end the resentment died down in his heart. The piece ended with a trill of octaves in the treble and a final deep octave in the bass. Great applause greeted Mary Jane as, blushing and rolling up her music nervously, she escaped from the room. The most vigorous clapping came from the four young men in the doorway who had gone away to the refreshment-room at the beginning of the piece but had come back when the piano had stopped.

Lancers were arranged. Gabriel found himself partnered with Miss Ivors. She was a frank-mannered talkative young lady, with a freckled face and prominent brown eyes. She did not wear a low-cut bodice and the large brooch which was fixed in the front of her collar bore on it an Irish device and motto.

When they had taken their places she said abruptly:

"I have a crow to pluck with you."

"With me?" said Gabriel.

She nodded her head gravely.

"What is it?" asked Gabriel, smiling at her solemn manner.

"Who is G. C.?" answered Miss Ivors, turning her eyes upon him.

Gabriel coloured and was about to knit his brows, as if he did not understand, when she said bluntly:

"O, innocent Amy! I have found out that you write for *The Daily Express.* Now, aren't you ashamed of yourself?"

"Why should I be ashamed of myself?" asked Gabriel, blinking his eyes and trying to smile.

"Well, I'm ashamed of you," said Miss Ivors frankly. "To say you'd write for a paper like that. I didn't think you were a West Briton."[6]

A look of perplexity appeared on Gabriel's face. It was true that he wrote a literary column every Wednesday in *The Daily Express,* for which he was paid fifteen shillings. But that did not make him a West Briton surely. The books he received for review were almost more welcome than the paltry cheque. He loved to feel the covers and turn over the pages of newly printed books. Nearly every day when his teaching in the college was ended he used to wander down the quays to the second-hand booksellers, to Hickey's on Bachelor's Walk, to Webb's or Massey's on Aston's Quay, or to O'Clohissey's in the by-street. He did not know how to meet her charge. He wanted to say that literature was above politics. But

[6] An Irishman devoted to the English interest.

they were friends of many years' standing and their careers had been parallel, first at the University and then as teachers: he could not risk a grandiose phrase with her. He continued blinking his eyes and trying to smile and murmured lamely that he saw nothing political in writing reviews of books.

When their turn to cross had come he was still perplexed and inattentive. Miss Ivors promptly took his hand in a warm grasp and said in a soft friendly tone:

"Of course, I was only joking. Come, we cross now."

When they were together again she spoke of the University question and Gabriel felt more at ease. A friend of hers had shown her his review of Browning's poems. That was how she had found out the secret: but she liked the review immensely. Then she said suddenly:

"O, Mr. Conroy, will you come for an excursion to the Aran Isles this summer? We're going to stay there a whole month. It will be splendid out in the Atlantic. You ought to come. Mr. Clancy is coming, and Mr. Kilkelly and Kathleen Kearney. It would be splendid for Gretta too if she'd come. She's from Connacht, isn't she?"

"Her people are," said Gabriel shortly.

"But you will come, won't you?" said Miss Ivors, laying her warm hand eagerly on his arm.

"The fact is," said Gabriel, "I have just arranged to go——"

"Go where?" asked Miss Ivors.

"Well, you know, every year I go for a cycling tour with some fellows and so——"

"But where?" asked Miss Ivors.

"Well, we usually go to France or Belgium or perhaps Germany," said Gabriel awkwardly.

"And why do you go to France and Belgium," said Miss Ivors, "instead of visiting your own land?"

"Well," said Gabriel, "it's partly to keep in touch with the languages and partly for a change."

"And haven't you your own language to keep in touch with—Irish?" asked Miss Ivors.

"Well," said Gabriel, "if it comes to that, you know, Irish is not my language."

Their neighbours had turned to listen to the cross-examination. Gabriel glanced right and left nervously and tried to keep his good humour under the ordeal which was making a blush invade his forehead.

"And haven't you your own land to visit," continued Miss Ivors, "that you know nothing of, your own people, and your own country?"

"O, to tell you the truth," retorted Gabriel suddenly, "I'm sick of my own country, sick of it!"

"Why?" asked Miss Ivors.

Gabriel did not answer for his retort had heated him.

"Why?" repeated Miss Ivors.

They had to go visiting together and, as he had not answered her, Miss Ivors said warmly:

"Of course, you've no answer."

Gabriel tried to cover his agitation by taking part in the dance with great energy. He avoided her eyes for he had seen a sour expression on her face. But when they met in the long chain he was surprised to feel his hand firmly pressed. She looked at him from under her brows for a moment quizzically until he smiled. Then, just as the chain was about to start again, she stood on tiptoe and whispered into his ear:

"West Briton!"

When the lancers were over Gabriel went away to a remote corner of the room where Freddy Malin's mother was sitting. She was a stout feeble old woman with white hair. Her voice had a catch in it like her son's and she stuttered slightly. She had been told that Freddy had come and that he was nearly all right. Gabriel asked her whether she had had a good crossing. She lived with her married daughter in Glasgow and came to Dublin on a visit once a year. She answered placidly that she had had a beautiful crossing and that the captain had been most attentive to her. She spoke also of the beautiful house her daughter kept in Glasgow, and of all the friends they had there. While her tongue rambled on Gabriel tried to banish from his mind all memory of the unpleasant incident with Miss Ivors. Of course the girl or woman, or whatever she was, was an enthusiast but there was a time for all things. Perhaps he ought not to have answered her like that. But she had no right to call him a West Briton before people, even in joke. She had tried to make him ridiculous before people, heckling him and staring at him with her rabbit's eyes.

He saw his wife making her way towards him through the waltzing couples. When she reached him she said into his ear:

"Gabriel, Aunt Kate wants to know won't you carve the goose as usual. Miss Daly will carve the ham and I'll do the pudding."

"All right," said Gabriel.

"She's sending in the younger ones first as soon as this waltz is over so that we'll have the table to ourselves."

"Were you dancing?" asked Gabriel.

"Of course I was. Didn't you see me? What row had you with Molly Ivors?"

"No row. Why? Did she say so?"

"Something like that. I'm trying to get that Mr. D'Arcy to sing. He's full of conceit, I think."

"There was no row," said Gabriel moodily, "only she wanted me to go for a trip to the west of Ireland and I said I wouldn't."

His wife clasped her hands excitedly and gave a little jump.

"O, do go, Gabriel," she cried. "I'd love to see Galway again."

"You can go if you like," said Gabriel coldly.

She looked at him for a moment, then turned to Mrs. Malins and said:

"There's a nice husband for you, Mrs. Malins."

While she was threading her way back across the room Mrs. Malins, without adverting to the interruption, went on to tell Gabriel what beautiful places there were in Scotland and beautiful scenery. Her son-in-law brought them every year to the lakes and they used to go fishing. Her son-in-law was a splendid fisher. One day he caught a beautiful big fish and the man in the hotel cooked it for their dinner.

Gabriel hardly heard what she said. Now that supper was coming near he began to think again about his speech and about the quotation. When he saw Freddy Malins coming across the room to visit his mother Gabriel left the chair free for him and retired into the embrasure of the window. The room had already cleared and from the back room came the clatter of plates and knives. Those who still remained in the drawing-room seemed tired of dancing and were conversing quietly in little groups. Gabriel's warm trembling fingers tapped the cold pane of the window. How cool it must be outside! How pleasant it would be to walk out alone, first along by the river and then through the park! The snow would be lying on the branches of the trees and forming a bright cap on the top of the Wellington Monument. How much more pleasant it would be there than at the supper-table!

He ran over the headings of his speech: Irish hospitality, sad memories, the Three Graces,[7] Paris,[8] the quotation from Browning. He repeated to himself a phrase he had written in his review: "One feels that one is listening to a thought-tormented music." Miss Ivors had praised the review. Was she sincere? Had she really any life of her own behind all her propagandism? There had never been any ill-feeling between them until that night. It unnerved him to think that she would be at the supper-table, looking up at him while he spoke with her critical quizzing eyes. Perhaps she would not be sorry to see him fail in his speech. An idea came into his mind and gave him courage. He would say, alluding to Aunt Kate and Aunt Julia: "Ladies and Gentlemen, the generation which is now on the wane among us may have had its faults but for my part I think it had certain qualities of hospitality, of humour, of humanity, which the new and very serious and hypereducated generation that is growing up around us seems to me to lack." Very good: that was one for Miss Ivors. What did he care that his aunts were only two ignorant old women?

A murmur in the room attracted his attention. Mr. Browne was advancing from the door, gallantly escorting Aunt Julia, who leaned upon his arm, smiling and hanging her head. An irregular musketry of applause escorted her also as far as the piano and then, as Mary Jane seated herself on the stool, and Aunt Julia, no longer smiling, half turned so as to pitch her voice fairly into the room, gradually ceased. Gabriel recognised the prelude. It was that of an old song of Aunt Julia's—*Arrayed for the Bridal*. Her voice, strong and clear in tone, attacked with great spirit the runs which embellish the air and though she sang very rapidly she did not miss even the smallest of the grace notes. To follow the voice, without looking at the singer's face, was to feel and share the excitement of swift and secure flight. Gabriel applauded loudly with all the others at the close of the song and loud applause was borne in from the invisible supper-table. It sounded so genuine that a little colour struggled into Aunt Julia's face as she bent to replace in the music-stand the old leather-bound song-book that had her initials on the cover. Freddy Malins, who had listened with his head perched sideways to hear her better, was still applauding when everyone else had ceased and talking animatedly to his mother who nodded her head gravely and slowly in acquiescence. At last, when he could clap no more, he stood up suddenly and hurried across the room to Aunt Julia whose hand he seized and held in both his hands, shaking it when words failed him or the catch in his voice proved too much for him.

"I was just telling my mother," he said, "I never heard you sing so well, never. No, I never heard your voice so good as it is to-night. Now! Would you believe

[7] In Roman mythology, goddesses who embodied beauty and charm.
[8] In Greek legend, the son of Priam, king of Troy, and through his abduction of Helen, the cause of the Trojan War.

that now? That's the truth. Upon my word and honour that's the truth. I never heard your voice sound so fresh and so . . . so clear and fresh, never."

Aunt Julia smiled broadly and murmured something about compliments as she released her hand from his grasp. Mr. Browne extended his open hand towards her and said to those who were near him in the manner of a showman introducing a prodigy to an audience:

"Miss Julia Morkan, my latest discovery!"

He was laughing very heartily at this himself when Freddy Malins turned to him and said:

"Well, Browne, if you're serious you might make a worse discovery. All I can say is I never heard her sing half so well as long as I am coming here. And that's the honest truth."

"Neither did I," said Mr. Browne. "I think her voice has greatly improved."

Aunt Julia shrugged her shoulders and said with meek pride:

"Thirty years ago I hadn't a bad voice as voices go."

"I often told Julia," said Aunt Kate emphatically, "that she was simply thrown away in that choir. But she never would be said by me."

She turned as if to appeal to the good sense of the others against a refractory child while Aunt Julia gazed in front of her, a vague smile of reminiscence playing on her face.

"No," continued Aunt Kate, "she wouldn't be said or led by anyone, slaving there in that choir night and day, night and day. Six o'clock on Christmas morning! And all for what?"

"Well, isn't it for the honour of God, Aunt Kate?" asked Mary Jane, twisting round on the piano-stool and smiling.

Aunt Kate turned fiercely on her niece and said:

"I know all about the honour of God, Mary Jane, but I think it's not at all honourable for the pope to turn out the women out of the choirs that have slaved there all their lives and put little whipper-snappers of boys over their heads. I suppose it is for the good of the Church if the pope does it. But it's not just, Mary Jane, and it's not right."

She had worked herself into a passion and would have continued in defence of her sister for it was a sore subject with her but Mary Jane, seeing that all the dancers had come back, intervened pacifically:

"Now, Aunt Kate, you're giving scandal to Mr. Browne who is of the other persuasion."

Aunt Kate turned to Mr. Browne, who was grinning at this allusion to his religion, and said hastily:

"O, I don't question the pope's being right. I'm only a stupid old woman and I wouldn't presume to do such a thing. But there's such a thing as common every-day politeness and gratitude. And if I were in Julia's place I'd tell that Father Healey straight up to his face . . ."

"And besides, Aunt Kate," said Mary Jane, "we really are all hungry and when we are hungry we are all very quarrelsome."

"And when we are thirsty we are also quarrelsome," added Mr. Browne.

"So that we had better go to supper," said Mary Jane, "and finish the discussion afterwards."

On the landing outside the drawing-room Gabriel found his wife and Mary Jane trying to persuade Miss Ivors to stay for supper. But Miss Ivors, who had put on her hat and was buttoning her cloak, would not stay. She did not feel in the least hungry and she had already overstayed her time.

"But only for ten minutes, Molly," said Mrs. Conroy. "That won't delay you."

"To take a pick itself," said Mary Jane, "after all your dancing."

"I really couldn't," said Miss Ivors.

"I am afraid you didn't enjoy yourself at all," said Mary Jane hopelessly.

"Ever so much, I assure you," said Miss Ivors, "but you really must let me run off now."

"But how can you get home?" asked Mrs. Conroy.

"O, it's only two steps up the quay."

Gabriel hesitated a moment and said:

"If you will allow me, Miss Ivors, I'll see you home if you are really obliged to go."

But Miss Ivors broke away from them.

"I won't hear of it," she cried. "For goodness' sake go in to your suppers and don't mind me. I'm quite well able to take care of myself."

"Well, you're the comical girl, Molly," said Mrs. Conroy frankly.

"*Beannacht libh*,"[9] cried Miss Ivors, with a laugh, as she ran down the staircase.

Mary Jane gazed after her, a moody puzzled expression on her face, while Mrs. Conroy leaned over the banisters to listen for the hall-door. Gabriel asked himself was he the cause of her abrupt departure. But she did not seem to be in ill humour: she had gone away laughing. He stared blankly down the staircase.

At the moment Aunt Kate came toddling out of the supper-room, almost wringing her hands in despair.

"Where is Gabriel?" she cried. "Where on earth is Gabriel? There's every-one waiting in there, stage to let, and nobody to carve the goose!"

"Here I am, Aunt Kate!" cried Gabriel, with sudden animation, "ready to carve a flock of geese, if necessary."

A fat brown goose lay at one end of the table and at the other end, on a bed of creased paper strewn with sprigs of parsley, lay a great ham, stripped of its outer skin and peppered over with crust crumbs, a neat paper frill round its shin and beside this was a round of spiced beef. Between these rival ends ran parallel lines of side-dishes: two little minsters of jelly, red and yellow; a shallow dish full of blocks of blancmange and red jam, a large green leaf-shaped dish with a stalk-shaped handle, on which lay bunches of purple raisins and peeled almonds, a companion dish on which lay a solid rectangle of Smyrna figs, a dish of custard topped with grated nutmeg, a small bowl full of chocolates and sweets wrapped in gold and silver papers and a glass vase in which stood some tall celery stalks. In the centre of the table there stood, as sentries to a fruit-stand which upheld a pyramid of oranges and American apples, two squat old-fashioned decanters of cut glass, one containing port and the other dark sherry. On the closed square piano a pudding in a huge yellow dish lay in waiting and behind it were three squads of bottles of stout and ale and minerals, drawn up according to the colours of their uniforms, the first two black, with brown and red labels, the third and smallest squad white, with transverse green sashes.

Gabriel took his seat boldly at the head of the table and, having looked to the

[9] (Irish) Blessings be with you (a form of leave-taking).

edge of the carver, plunged his fork firmly into the goose. He felt quite at ease now for he was an expert carver and liked nothing better than to find himself at the head of a well-laden table.

"Miss Furlong, what shall I send you?" he asked. "A wing or a slice of the breast?"

"Just a small slice of the breast."

"Miss Higgins, what for you?"

"O, anything at all, Mr. Conroy."

While Gabriel and Miss Daly exchanged plates of goose and plates of ham and sliced beef Lily went from guest to guest with a dish of hot floury potatoes wrapped in a white napkin. This was Mary Jane's idea and she had also suggested apple sauce for the goose but Aunt Kate had said that plain roast goose without any apple sauce had always been good enough for her and she hoped she might never eat worse. Mary Jane waited on her pupils and saw that they got the best slices and Aunt Kate and Aunt Julia opened and carried across from the piano bottles of stout and ale for the gentlemen and bottles of minerals for the ladies. There was a great deal of confusion and laughter and noise, the noise of orders and counter-orders, of knives and forks, of corks and glass-stoppers. Gabriel began to carve second helpings as soon as he had finished the first round without serving himself. Everyone protested loudly so that he compromised by taking a long draught of stout for he had found the carving hot work. Mary Jane settled down quietly to her supper but Aunt Kate and Aunt Julia were still toddling round the table, walking on each other's heels, getting in each other's way and giving each other unheeded orders. Mr. Browne begged of them to sit down and eat their suppers and so did Gabriel but they said there was time enough, so that, at last, Freddy Malins stood up and, capturing Aunt Kate, plumped her down on her chair amid general laughter.

When everyone had been well served Gabriel said, smiling:

"Now, if anyone wants a little more of what vulgar people call stuffing let him or her speak."

A chorus of voices invited him to begin his own supper and Lily came forward with three potatoes which she had reserved for him.

"Very well," said Gabriel amiably, as he took another preparatory draught, "kindly forget my existence, ladies and gentlemen, for a few minutes."

He set to his supper and took no part in the conversation with which the table covered Lily's removal of the plates. The subject of talk was the opera company which was then at the Theatre Royal. Mr. Bartell D'Arcy, the tenor, a dark-complexioned young man with a smart moustache, praised very highly the leading contralto of the company but Miss Furlong thought she had a rather vulgar style of production. Freddy Malins said there was a Negro chieftain singing in the second part of the Gaiety pantomime who had one of the finest tenor voices he had ever heard.

"Have you heard him?" he asked Mr. Bartell D'Arcy across the table.

"No," answered Mr. Bartell D'Arcy carelessly.

"Because," Freddy Malins explained, "now I'd be curious to hear your opinion of him. I think he has a grand voice."

"It takes Teddy to find out the really good things," said Mr. Browne familiarly to the table.

"And why couldn't he have a voice too?" asked Freddy Malins sharply. "Is it because he's only a black?"

Nobody answered this question and Mary Jane led the table back to the legitimate opera. One of her pupils had given her a pass for *Mignon*. Of course it was very fine, she said, but it made her think of poor Georgina Burns. Mr. Browne could go back farther still, to the old Italian companies that used to come to Dublin—Tietjens, Ilma de Murzka, Campanini, the great Trebelli, Giuglini, Ravelli, Aramburo. Those were the days, he said, when there was something like singing to be heard in Dublin. He told too of how the top gallery of the old Royal used to be packed night after night, of how one night an Italian tenor had sung five encores to *Let me like a Soldier fall*, introducing a high C every time and of how the gallery boys would sometimes in their enthusiasm unyoke the horses from the carriage of some great *prima donna* and pull her themselves through the streets to her hotel. Why did they never play the grand old operas now, he asked, *Dinorah, Lucrezia Borgia?* Because they could not get the voices to sing them: that was why.

"O, well," said Mr. Bartell D'Arcy, "I presume there are as good singers to-day as there were then."

"Where are they?" asked Mr. Browne defiantly.

"In London, Paris, Milan," said Mr. Bartell D'Arcy warmly. "I suppose Caruso, for example, is quite as good, if not better than any of the men you have mentioned."

"Maybe so," said Mr. Browne. "But I may tell you I doubt it strongly."

"O, I'd give anything to hear Caruso sing," said Mary Jane.

"For me," said Aunt Kate, who had been picking a bone, "there was only one tenor. To please me, I mean. But I suppose none of you ever heard of him."

"Who was he, Miss Morkan?" asked Mr. Bartell D'Arcy politely.

"His name," said Aunt Kate, "was Parkinson. I heard him when he was in his prime and I think he had then the purest tenor voice that was ever put into a man's throat."

"Strange," said Mr. Bartell D'Arcy. "I never even heard of him."

"Yes, yes, Miss Morkan is right," said Mr. Browne. "I remember hearing of old Parkinson but he's too far back for me."

"A beautiful, pure, sweet, mellow English tenor," said Aunt Kate with enthusiasm.

Gabriel having finished, the huge pudding was transferred to the table. The clatter of forks and spoons began again. Gabriel's wife served out spoonfuls of the pudding and passed the plates down the table. Midway down they were held up by Mary Jane, who replenished them with raspberry or orange jelly or with blancmange and jam. The pudding was of Aunt Julia's making and she received praises for it from all quarters. She herself said that it was not quite brown enough.

"Well, I hope, Miss Morkan," said Mr. Browne, "that I'm brown enough for you because, you know, I'm all brown."

All the gentlemen, except Gabriel, ate some of the pudding out of compliment to Aunt Julia. As Gabriel never ate sweets the celery had been left for him. Freddy Malins also took a stalk of celery and ate it with his pudding. He had been told that celery was a capital thing for the blood and he was just then under doctor's care. Mrs. Malins, who had been silent all through the supper, said that her son was going down to Mount Melleray in a week or so. The table then spoke of

Mount Melleray, how bracing the air was down there, how hospitable the monks were and how they never asked for a penny-piece from their guests.

"And do you mean to say," asked Mr. Browne incredulously, "that a chap can go down there and put up there as if it were a hotel and live on the fat of the land and then come away without paying anything?"

"O, most people give some donation to the monastery when they leave," said Mary Jane.

"I wish we had an institution like that in our Church," said Mr. Browne candidly.

He was astonished to hear that the monks never spoke, got up at two in the morning and slept in their coffins. He asked what they did it for.

"That's the rule of the order," said Aunt Kate firmly.

"Yes, but why?" asked Mr. Browne.

Aunt Kate repeated that it was the rule, that was all. Mr. Browne still seemed not to understand. Freddy Malins explained to him, as best he could, that the monks were trying to make up for the sins committed by all the sinners in the outside world. The explanation was not very clear for Mr. Browne grinned and said:

"I like that idea very much but wouldn't a comfortable spring bed do them as well as a coffin?"

"The coffin," said Mary Jane, "is to remind them of their last end."

As the subject had grown lugubrious it was buried in a silence of the table during which Mrs. Malins could be heard saying to her neighbour in an indistinct undertone:

"They are very good men, the monks, very pious men."

The raisins and almonds and figs and apples and oranges and chocolates and sweets were now passed about the table and Aunt Julia invited all the guests to have either port or sherry. At first Mr. Bartell D'Arcy refused to take either but one of his neighbours nudged him and whispered something to him upon which he allowed his glass to be filled. Gradually as the last glasses were being filled the conversation ceased. A pause followed, broken only by the noise of the wine and by unsettlings of chairs. The Misses Morkan, all three, looked down at the tablecloth. Someone coughed once or twice and then a few gentlemen patted the table gently as a signal for silence. The silence came and Gabriel pushed back his chair and stood up.

The patting at once grew louder in encouragement and then ceased altogether. Gabriel leaned his ten trembling fingers on the tablecloth and smiled nervously at the company. Meeting a row of upturned faces he raised his eyes to the chandelier. The piano was playing a waltz tune and he could hear the skirts sweeping against the drawing-room door. People, perhaps, were standing in the snow on the quay outside, gazing up at the lighted windows and listening to the waltz music. The air was pure there. In the distance lay the park where the trees were weighted with snow. The Wellington Monument wore a gleaming cap of snow that flashed westward over the white field of Fifteen Acres.

He began:

"Ladies and Gentlemen,

"It has fallen to my lot this evening, as in years past, to perform a very pleasing task but a task for which I am afraid my poor powers as a speaker are all too inadequate."

"No, no!" said Mr. Browne.

"But, however that may be, I can only ask you to-night to take the will for the deed and to lend me your attention for a few moments while I endeavour to express to you in words what my feelings are on this occasion.

"Ladies and Gentlemen, it is not the first time that we have gathered together under this hospitable roof, around this hospitable board. It is not the first time that we have been the recipients—or perhaps, I had better say, the victims—of the hospitality of certain good ladies."

He made a circle in the air with his arm and paused. Everyone laughed or smiled at Aunt Kate and Aunt Julia and Mary Jane who all turned crimson with pleasure. Gabriel went on more boldly:

"I feel more strongly with every recurring year that our country has no tradition which does it so much honour and which it should guard so jealously as that of its hospitality. It is a tradition that is unique as far as my experience goes (and I have visited not a few places abroad) among the modern nations. Some would say, perhaps, that with us it is rather a failing than anything to be boasted of. But granted even that, it is, to my mind, a princely failing, and one that I trust will long be cultivated among us. Of one thing, at least, I am sure. As long as this one roof shelters the good ladies aforesaid—and I wish from my heart it may do so for many and many a long year to come—the tradition of genuine warm-hearted courteous Irish hospitality, which our forefathers have handed down to us and which we in turn must hand down to our descendants, is still alive among us."

A hearty murmur of assent ran round the table. It shot through Gabriel's mind that Miss Ivors was not there and that she had gone away discourteously: and he said with confidence in himself:

"Ladies and Gentlemen,

"A new generation is growing up in our midst, a generation actuated by new ideas and new principles. It is serious and enthusiastic for these new ideas and its enthusiasm, even when it is misdirected, is, I believe, in the main sincere. But we are living in a sceptical and, if I may use the phrase, a thought-tormented age: and sometimes I fear that this new generation, educated or hypereducated as it is, will lack those qualities of humanity, of hospitality, of kindly humour which belonged to an older day. Listening tonight to the names of all those great singers of the past it seemed to me, I must confess, that we were living in a less spacious age. Those days might, without exaggeration, be called spacious days: and if they are gone beyond recall let us hope, at least, that in gatherings such as this we shall still speak of them with pride and affection, still cherish in our hearts the memory of those dead and gone great ones whose fame the world will not willingly let die."

"Hear, hear!" said Mr. Browne loudly.

"But yet," continued Gabriel, his voice falling into a softer inflection, "there are always in gatherings such as this sadder thoughts that will recur to our minds: thoughts of the past, of youth, of changes, of absent faces that we miss here tonight. Our path through life is strewn with many such sad memories: and were we to brood upon them always we could not find the heart to go on bravely with our work among the living. We have all of us living duties and living affections which claim, and rightly claim, our strenuous endeavours.

"Therefore, I will not linger on the past. I will not let any gloomy moralising intrude upon us here tonight. Here we are gathered together for a brief moment from the bustle and rush of our everyday routine. We are met here as friends, in the spirit of good-fellowship, as colleagues, also to a certain extent, in the true spirit of *camaraderie,* and as the guests of—what shall I call them?—the Three Graces of the Dublin musical world."

The table burst into applause and laughter at this allusion. Aunt Julia vainly asked each of her neighbours in turn to tell her what Gabriel had said.

"He says we are the Three Graces, Aunt Julia," said Mary Jane.

Aunt Julia did not understand but she looked up, smiling, at Gabriel, who continued in the same vein:

"Ladies and Gentlemen,

"I will not attempt to play tonight the part that Paris played on another occasion. I will not attempt to choose between them.[10] The task would be an invidious one and one beyond my poor powers. For when I view them in turn, whether it be our chief hostess herself, whose good heart, whose too good heart, has become a byword with all who know her, or her sister, who seems to be gifted with perennial youth and whose singing must have been a surprise and a revelation to us all tonight, or, last but not least, when I consider our youngest hostess, talented, cheerful, hard-working and the best of nieces, I confess, Ladies and Gentlemen, that I do not know to which of them I should award the prize."

Gabriel glanced down at his aunts and, seeing the large smile on Aunt Julia's face and the tears which had risen to Aunt Kate's eyes, hastened to his close. He raised his glass of port gallantly, while every member of the company fingered a glass expectantly, and said loudly:

"Let us toast them all three together. Let us drink to their health, wealth, long life, happiness and prosperity and may they long continue to hold the proud and self-won position which they hold in their profession and the position of honour and affection which they hold in our hearts."

All the guests stood up, glass in hand, and turning towards the three seated ladies, sang in unison, with Mr. Brown as leader:

> "For they are jolly gay fellows,
> For they are jolly gay fellows,
> For they are jolly gay fellows,
> Which nobody can deny."

Aunt Kate was making frank use of her handkerchief and even Aunt Julia seemed moved. Freddy Malins beat time with his pudding-fork and the singers turned towards one another, as if in melodious conference, while they sang with emphasis:

> "Unless he tells a lie,
> Unless he tells a lie,"

Then, turning once more towards their hostesses, they sang:

> "For they are jolly gay fellows,
> For they are jolly gay fellows,
> For they are jolly gay fellows,
> Which nobody can deny."

[10] The "judgment of Paris" involved not the Graces, but three goddesses, Hera, Aphrodite, and Athene. Paris was asked to choose the fairest.

The acclamation which followed was taken up beyond the door of the supper-room by many of the other guests and renewed time after time, Freddy Malins acting as officer with his fork on high.

The piercing morning air came into the hall where they were standing so that Aunt Kate said:

"Close the door, somebody. Mrs. Malins will get her death of cold."

"Browne is out there, Aunt Kate," said Mary Jane.

"Browne is everywhere," said Aunt Kate, lowering her voice.

Mary Jane laughed at her tone.

"Really," she said archly, "he is very attentive."

"He has been laid on here like the gas," said Aunt Kate in the same tone, "all during the Christmas."

She laughed herself this time good-humouredly and then added quickly:

"But tell him to come in, Mary Jane, and close the door. I hope to goodness he didn't hear me."

At that moment the hall-door was opened and Mr. Browne came in from the doorstep, laughing as if his heart would break. He was dressed in a long green overcoat with mock astrakhan cuffs and collar and wore on his head an oval fur cap. He pointed down the snow-covered quay from where the sound of shrill pro-longed whistling was borne in.

"Teddy will have all the cabs in Dublin out," he said.

Gabriel advanced from the little pantry behind the office, struggling into his overcoat and, looking round the hall, said:

"Gretta not down yet?"

"She's getting on her things, Gabriel," said Aunt Kate.

"Who's playing up there?" asked Gabriel.

"Nobody. They're all gone."

"O no, Aunt Kate," said Mary Jane. "Bartell D'Arcy and Miss O'Callaghan aren't gone yet."

"Someone is fooling at the piano anyhow," said Gabriel.

Mary Jane glanced at Gabriel and Mr. Browne and said with a shiver:

"It makes me feel cold to look at you two gentlemen muffled up like that. I wouldn't like to face your journey home at this hour."

"I'd like nothing better this minute," said Mr. Browne stoutly, "than a rattling fine walk in the country or a fast drive with a good spanking goer be-tween the shafts."

"We used to have a very good horse and trap at home," said Aunt Julia sadly.

"The never-to-be-forgotten Johnny," said Mary Jane, laughing.

Aunt Kate and Gabriel laughed too.

"Why, what was wonderful about Johnny?" asked Mr. Browne.

"The late lamented Patrick Morkan, our grandfather, that is," explained Gabriel, "commonly known in his later years as the old gentleman, was a glue-boiler."

"O, now, Gabriel," said Aunt Kate, laughing, "he had a starch mill."

"Well, glue or starch," said Gabriel, "the old gentleman had a horse by the name of Johnny. And Johnny used to work in the old gentleman's mill, walking round and round in order to drive the mill. That was all very well; but now comes the tragic part about Johnny. One fine day the old gentleman thought he'd like to drive out with the quality to a military review in the park."

"The Lord have mercy on his soul," said Aunt Kate compassionately.

"Amen," said Gabriel. "So the old gentleman, as I said, harnessed Johnny and put on his very best tall hat and his very best stock collar and drove out in grand style from his ancestral mansion somewhere near Back Lane, I think."

Everyone laughed, even Mrs. Malins, at Gabriel's manner and Aunt Kate said:

"O, now, Gabriel, he didn't live in Back Lane, really. Only the mill was there."

"Out from the mansion of his forefathers," continued Gabriel, "he drove with Johnny. And everything went on beautifully until Johnny came in sight of King Billy's statue: and whether he fell in love with the horse King Billy sits on or whether he thought he was back again in the mill, anyhow he began to walk round the statue."

Gabriel paced in a circle round the hall in his goloshes amid the laughter of the others.

"Round and round he went," said Gabriel, "and the old gentleman, who was a very pompous old gentleman, was highly indignant. 'Go on, sir! What do you mean, sir? Johnny! Johnny! Most extraordinary conduct! Can't understand the horse!'"

The peal of laughter which followed Gabriel's imitation of the incident was interrupted by a resounding knock at the hall door. Mary Jane ran to open it and let in Freddy Malins. Freddy Malins, with his hat well back on his head and his shoulders humped with cold, was puffing and steaming after his exertions.

"I could only get one cab," he said.

"O, we'll find another along the quay," said Gabriel.

"Yes," said Aunt Kate. "Better not keep Mrs. Malins standing in the draught."

Mrs. Malins was helped down the front steps by her son and Mr. Browne and, after many manœuvres, hoisted into the cab. Freddy Malins clambered in after her and spent a long time settling her on the seat, Mr. Browne helping him with advice. At last she was settled comfortably and Freddy Malins invited Mr. Browne into the cab. There was a good deal of confused talk, and then Mr. Browne got into the cab. The cabman settled his rug over his knees, and bent down for the address. The confusion grew greater and the cabman was directed differently by Freddy Malins and Mr. Browne, each of whom had his head out through a window of the cab. The difficulty was to know where to drop Mr. Browne along the route, and Aunt Kate, Aunt Julia and Mary Jane helped the discussion from the doorstep with cross-directions and contradictions and abundance of laughter. As for Freddy Malins he was speechless with laughter. He popped his head in and out of the window every moment to the great danger of his hat, and told his mother how the discussion was progressing, till at last Mr. Browne shouted to the bewildered cabman above the din of everybody's laughter:

"Do you know Trinity College?"

"Yes, sir," said the cabman.

"Well, drive bang up against Trinity College gates," said Mr. Browne, "and then we'll tell you where to go. You understand now?"

"Yes, sir," said the cabman.

"Make like a bird for Trinity College."

"Right, sir," said the cabman.

The horse was whipped up and the cab rattled off along the quay amid a chorus of laughter and adieus.

Gabriel had not gone to the door with the others. He was in a dark part of the hall gazing up the staircase. A woman was standing near the top of the first flight, in the shadow also. He could not see her face but he could see the terra-cotta and salmon-pink panels of her skirt which the shadow made appear black and white. It was his wife. She was leaning on the banisters, listening to something. Gabriel was surprised at her stillness and strained his ear to listen also. But he could hear little save the noise of laughter and dispute on the front steps, a few chords struck on the piano and a few notes of a man's voice singing.

He stood still in the gloom of the hall, trying to catch the air that the voice was singing and gazing up at his wife. There was grace and mystery in her attitude as if she were a symbol of something. He asked himself what is a woman standing on the stairs in the shadow, listening to distant music, a symbol of. If he were a painter he would paint her in that attitude. Her blue felt hat would show off the bronze of her hair against the darkness and the dark panels of her skirt would show off the light ones. *Distant Music* he would call the picture if he were a painter.

The hall-door was closed; and Aunt Kate, Aunt Julia and Mary Jane came down the hall, still laughing.

"Well, isn't Freddy terrible?" said Mary Jane. "He's really terrible."

Gabriel said nothing but pointed up the stairs towards where his wife was standing. Now that the hall-door was closed the voice and the piano could be heard more clearly. Gabriel held up his hand for them to be silent. The song seemed to be in the old Irish tonality and the singer seemed uncertain both of his words and of his voice. The voice, made plaintive by distance and by the singer's hoarseness, faintly illuminated the cadence of the air with words expressing grief:

> "O, the rain falls on my heavy locks
> And the dew wets my skin,
> My babe lies cold . . ."

"O," exclaimed Mary Jane. "It's Bartell D'Arcy singing and he wouldn't sing all the night. O, I'll get him to sing a song before he goes."

"O, do, Mary Jane," said Aunt Kate.

Mary Jane brushed past the others and ran to the staircase, but before she reached it the singing stopped and the piano was closed abruptly.

"O, what a pity!" she cried. "Is he coming down, Gretta?"

Gabriel heard his wife answer yes and saw her come down towards them. A few steps behind her were Mr. Bartell D'Arcy and Miss O'Callaghan.

"O, Mr. D'Arcy," cried Mary Jane, "it's downright mean of you to break off like that when we were all in raptures listening to you."

"I have been at him all the evening," said Miss O'Callaghan, "and Mrs. Conroy, too, and he told us he had a dreadful cold and couldn't sing."

"O, Mr. D'Arcy," said Aunt Kate, "now that was a great fib to tell."

"Can't you see that I'm as hoarse as a crow?" said Mr. D'Arcy roughly.

He went into the pantry hastily and put on his overcoat. The others, taken aback by his rude speech, could find nothing to say. Aunt Kate wrinkled her brows and made signs to the others to drop the subject. Mr. D'Arcy stood swathing his neck carefully and frowning.

"It's the weather," said Aunt Julia, after a pause.

"Yes, everybody has colds," said Aunt Kate readily, "everybody."

"They say," said Mary Jane, "we haven't had snow like it for thirty years; and I read this morning in the newspapers that the snow is general all over Ireland."

"I love the look of snow," said Aunt Julia sadly.

"So do I," said Miss O'Callaghan. "I think Christmas is never really Christmas unless we have the snow on the ground."

"But poor Mr. D'Arcy doesn't like the snow," said Aunt Kate, smiling.

Mr. D'Arcy came from the pantry, fully swathed and buttoned, and in a repentant tone told them the history of his cold. Everyone gave him advice and said it was a great pity and urged him to be very careful of his throat in the night air. Gabriel watched his wife, who did not join in the conversation. She was standing right under the dusty fanlight and the flame of the gas lit up the rich bronze of her hair, which he had seen her drying at the fire a few days before. She was in the same attitude and seemed unaware of the talk about her. At last she turned towards them and Gabriel saw that there was colour on her cheeks and that her eyes were shining. A sudden tide of joy went leaping out of his heart.

"Mr. D'Arcy," she said, "what is the name of that song you were singing?"

"It's called *The Lass of Aughrim*," said Mr. D'Arcy, "but I couldn't remember it properly. Why? Do you know it?"

"*The Lass of Aughrim*," she repeated. "I couldn't think of the name."

"It's a very nice air," said Mary Jane. "I'm sorry you were not in voice tonight."

"Now, Mary Jane," said Aunt Kate, "don't annoy Mr. D'Arcy. I won't have him annoyed."

Seeing that all were ready to start she shepherded them to the door, where good-night was said:

"Well, good-night, Aunt Kate, and thanks for the pleasant evening."

"Good-night, Gabriel. Good-night, Gretta!"

"Good-night, Aunt Kate, and thanks ever so much. Good-night, Aunt Julia."

"O, good-night, Gretta, I didn't see you."

"Good-night, Mr. D'Arcy. Good-night, Miss O'Callaghan."

"Good-night, Miss Morkan."

"Good-night, again."

"Good-night, all. Safe home."

"Good-night. Good-night."

The morning was still dark. A dull, yellow light brooded over the houses and the river; and the sky seemed to be descending. It was slushy underfoot; and only streaks and patches of snow lay on the roofs, on the parapets of the quay and on the area railings. The lamps were still burning redly in the murky air and, across the river, the palace of the Four Courts stood out menacingly against the heavy sky.

She was walking on before him with Mr. Bartell D'Arcy, her shoes in a brown parcel tucked under one arm and her hands holding her skirt up from the slush. She had no longer any grace of attitude, but Gabriel's eyes were still bright with happiness. The blood went bounding along his veins; and the thoughts went rioting through his brain, proud, joyful, tender, valorous.

She was walking on before him so lightly and so erect that he longed to run after her noiselessly, catch her by the shoulders and say something foolish and affectionate into her ear. She seemed to him so frail that he longed to defend her against something and then to be alone with her. Moments of their secret life together burst like stars upon his memory. A heliotrope envelope was lying beside his breakfast-cup and he was caressing it with his hand. Birds were twittering in the ivy and the sunny web of the curtain was shimmering along the floor: he could not eat for happiness. They were standing on the crowded platform and he was placing a ticket inside the warm palm of her glove. He was standing with her in the cold, looking in through a grated window at a man making bottles in a roaring furnace. It was very cold. Her face, fragrant in the cold air, was quite close to his; and suddenly he called out to the man at the furnace:

"Is the fire hot, sir?"

But the man could not hear with the noise of the furnace. It was just as well. He might have answered rudely.

A wave of yet more tender joy escaped from his heart and went coursing in warm flood along his arteries. Like the tender fire of stars moments of their life together, that no one knew of or would ever know of, broke upon and illumined his memory. He longed to recall to her those moments, to make her forget the years of their dull existence together and remember only their moments of ecstasy. For the years, he felt, had not quenched his soul or hers. Their children, his writing, her household cares had not quenched all their souls' tender fire. In one letter that he had written to her then he had said: "Why is it that words like these seem to me so dull and cold? Is it because there is no word tender enough to be your name?"

Like distant music these words that he had written years before were borne towards him from the past. He longed to be alone with her. When the others had gone away, when he and she were in the room in the hotel, then they would be alone together. He would call her softly:

"Gretta!"

Perhaps she would not hear at once: she would be undressing. Then something in his voice would strike her. She would turn and look at him. . . .

At the corner of Winetavern Street they met a cab. He was glad of its rattling noise as it saved him from conversation. She was looking out of the window and seemed tired. The others spoke only a few words, pointing out some building or street. The horse galloped along wearily under the murky morning sky, dragging his old rattling box after his heels, and Gabriel was again in a cab with her, galloping to catch the boat, galloping to their honeymoon.

As the cab drove across O'Connell Bridge Miss O'Callaghan said:

"They say you never cross O'Connell Bridge without seeing a white horse."

"I see a white man this time," said Gabriel.

"Where?" asked Mr. Bartell D'Arcy.

Gabriel pointed to the statue, on which lay patches of snow. Then he nodded familiarly to it and waved his hand.

"Good-night, Dan," he said gaily.

When the cab drew up before the hotel, Gabriel jumped out and, in spite of Mr. Bartell D'Arcy's protest, paid the driver. He gave the man a shilling over his fare. The man saluted and said:

"A prosperous New Year to you, sir."

"The same to you," said Gabriel cordially.

She leaned for a moment on his arm in getting out of the cab and while standing at the curbstone, bidding the others good-night. She leaned lightly on his arm, as lightly as when she had danced with him a few hours before. He had felt proud and happy then, happy that she was his, proud of her grace and wifely carriage. But now, after the kindling again of so many memories, the first touch of her body, musical and strange and perfumed, sent through him a keen pang of lust. Under cover of her silence he pressed her arm closely to his side; and, as they stood at the hotel door, he felt that they had escaped from their lives and duties, escaped from home and friends and run away together with wild and radiant hearts to a new adventure.

An old man was dozing in a great hooded chair in the hall. He lit a candle in the office and went before them to the stairs. They followed him in silence, their feet falling in soft thuds on the thickly carpeted stairs. She mounted the stairs behind the porter, her head bowed in the ascent, her frail shoulders curved as with a burden, her skirt tightly about her. He could have flung his arms about her hips and held her still, for his arms were trembling with desire to seize her and only the stress of his nails against the palms of his hands held the wild impulse of his body in check. The porter halted on the stairs to settle his guttering candle. They halted, too, on the steps below him. In the silence Gabriel could hear the falling of the molten wax into the tray and the thumping of his own heart against his ribs.

The porter led them along a corridor and opened a door. Then he set his unstable candle down on a toilet-table and asked at what hour they were to be called in the morning.

"Eight," said Gabriel.

The porter pointed to the tap of the electric-light and began a muttered apology, but Gabriel cut him short.

"We don't want any light. We have light enough from the street. And I say," he added, pointing to the candle, "you might remove that handsome article, like a good man."

The porter took up his candle again, but slowly, for he was surprised by such a novel idea. Then he mumbled good-night and went out. Gabriel shot the lock to.

A ghastly light from the street lamp lay in a long shaft from one window to the door. Gabriel threw his overcoat and hat on a couch and crossed the room toward the window. He looked down into the street in order that his emotion might calm a little. Then he turned and leaned against a chest of drawers with his back to the light. She had taken off her hat and cloak and was standing before a large swinging mirror, unhooking her waist. Gabriel paused for a few moments, watching her, and then said:

"Gretta!"

She turned away from the mirror slowly and walked along the shaft of light towards him. Her face looked so serious and weary that the words would not pass Gabriel's lips. No, it was not the moment yet.

"You looked tired," he said.

"I am a little," she answered.

"You don't feel ill or weak?"

"No, tired: that's all."

She went on to the window and stood there, looking out. Gabriel waited again and then fearing that diffidence was about to conquer him, he said abruptly:

"By the way, Gretta!"

"What is it?"

"You know that poor fellow Malins?" he said quickly.

"Yes. What about him?"

"Well, poor fellow, he's a decent sort of chap, after all," continued Gabriel in a false voice. "He gave me back that sovereign I lent him, and I didn't expect it, really. It's a pity he wouldn't keep away from that Browne, because he's not a bad fellow, really."

He was trembling now with annoyance. Why did she seem so abstracted? He did not know how he could begin. Was she annoyed, too, about something? If she would only turn to him or come to him of her own accord! To take her as she was would be brutal. No, he must see some ardour in her eyes first. He longed to be master of her strange mood.

"When did you lend him the pound?" she asked, after a pause.

Gabriel strove to restrain himself from breaking out into brutal language about the sottish Malins and his pound. He longed to cry to her from his soul, to crush her body against his, to overmaster her. But he said:

"Oh, at Christmas, when he opened that little Christmas-card shop in Henry Street."

He was in such a fever of rage and desire that he did not hear her come from the window. She stood before him for an instant, looking at him strangely. Then, suddenly raising herself on tiptoe and resting her hands lightly on his shoulders, she kissed him.

"You are a very generous person, Gabriel," she said.

Gabriel, trembling with delight at her sudden kiss and at the quaintness of her phrase, put his hands on her hair and began smoothing it back, scarcely touching it with his fingers. The washing had made it fine and brilliant. His heart was brimming over with happiness. Just when he was wishing for it she had come to him of her own accord. Perhaps her thoughts had been running with his. Perhaps she had felt the impetuous desire that was in him, and then the yielding mood had come upon her. Now that she had fallen to him so easily, he wondered why he had been so diffident.

He stood, holding her head between his hands. Then, slipping one arm swiftly about her body and drawing her towards him, he said softly:

"Gretta, dear, what are you thinking about?"

She did not answer nor yield wholly to his arm. He said again, softly:

"Tell me what it is, Gretta. I think I know what is the matter. Do I know?"

She did not answer at once. Then she said in an outburst of tears:

"O, I am thinking about that song, *The Lass of Aughrim*."

She broke loose from him and ran to the bed and, throwing her arms across the bed-rail, hid her face. Gabriel stood stock-still for a moment in astonishment and then followed her. As he passed in the way of the cheval-glass he caught sight of himself in full length, his broad, well-filled shirt front, the face whose expression always puzzled him when he saw it in a mirror, and his glimmering gilt-rimmed eyeglasses. He halted a few paces from her and said:

"What about the song? Why does that make you cry?"

She raised her head from her arms and dried her eyes with the back of her hand like a child. A kinder note than he had intended went into his voice.

"Why, Gretta?" he asked.

"I am thinking about a person long ago who used to sing that song."

"And who was the person long ago?" asked Gabriel, smiling.

"It was a person I used to know in Galway when I was living with my grandmother," she said.

The smile passed away from Gabriel's face. A dull anger began to gather again at the back of his mind and the dull fires of his lust began to glow angrily in his veins.

"Someone you were in love with?" he asked ironically.

"It was a young boy I used to know," she answered, "named Michael Furey. He used to sing that song, *The Lass of Aughrim*. He was very delicate."

Gabriel was silent. He did not wish her to think that he was interested in this delicate boy.

"I can see him so plainly," she said, after a moment. "Such eyes as he had: big, dark eyes! And such an expression in them—an expression!"

"O, then, you are in love with him?" said Gabriel.

"I used to go out walking with him," she said, "when I was in Galway."

A thought flew across Gabriel's mind.

"Perhaps that was why you wanted to go to Galway with that Ivors girl?" he said coldly.

She looked at him and asked in surprise:

"What for?"

Her eyes made Gabriel feel awkward. He shrugged his shoulders and said:

"How do I know? To see him, perhaps."

She looked away from him along the shaft of light towards the window in silence.

"He is dead," she said at length. "He died when he was only seventeen. Isn't it a terrible thing to die so young as that?"

"What was he?" asked Gabriel, still ironically.

"He was in the gasworks," she said.

Gabriel felt humiliated by the failure of his irony and by the evocation of this figure from the dead, a boy in the gasworks. While he had been full of memories of their secret life together, full of tenderness and joy and desire, she had been comparing him in her mind with another. A shameful consciousness of his own person assailed him. He saw himself as a ludicrous figure, acting as a pennyboy[11] for his aunts, a nervous, well-meaning sentimentalist, orating to vulgarians and idealising his own clownish lusts, the pitiable fatuous fellow he had caught a glimpse of in the mirror. Instinctively he turned his back more to the light lest she might see the shame that burned upon his forehead.

He tried to keep up his tone of cold interrogation, but his voice when he spoke was humble and indifferent.

"I suppose you were in love with this Michael Furey, Gretta," he said.

"I was great with him at that time," she said.

Her voice was veiled and sad. Gabriel, feeling now how vain it would be to try to lead her whither he had purposed, caressed one of her hands and said, also sadly:

"And what did he die of so young, Gretta? Consumption, was it?"

[11] A boy who haunts cattle markets in the hope of being employed as a drover at a penny per beast.

"I think he died for me," she answered.

A vague terror seized Gabriel at this answer, as if, at that hour when he had hoped to triumph, some impalpable and vindictive being was coming against him, gathering forces against him in its vague world. But he shook himself free of it with an effort of reason and continued to caress her hand. He did not question her again, for he felt that she would tell him of herself. Her hand was warm and moist: it did not respond to his touch, but he continued to caress it just as he had caressed her first letter to him that spring morning.

"It was in the winter," she said, "about the beginning of the winter when I was going to leave my grandmother's and come up here to the convent. And he was ill at the time in his lodgings in Galway and wouldn't be let out, and his people in Oughterard were written to. He was in decline, they said, or something like that. I never knew rightly."

She paused for a moment and sighed.

"Poor fellow," she said. "He was very fond of me and he was such a gentle boy. We used to go out together, walking, you know, Gabriel, like the way they do in the country. He was going to study singing only for his health. He had a very good voice, poor Michael Furey."

"Well; and then?" asked Gabriel.

"And then when it came to the time for me to leave Galway and come up to the convent he was much worse and I wouldn't be let see him so I wrote him a letter saying I was going up to Dublin and would be back in the summer, and hoping he would be better then."

She paused for a moment to get her voice under control, and then went on:

"Then the night before I left, I was in my grandmother's house in Nuns' Island, packing up, and I heard gravel thrown up against the window. The window was so wet I couldn't see, so I ran downstairs as I was and slipped out the back into the garden and there was the poor fellow at the end of the garden, shivering."

"And did you not tell him to go back?" asked Gabriel.

"I implored of him to go home at once and told him he would get his death in the rain. But he said he did not want to live. I can see his eyes as well as well! He was standing at the end of the wall where there was a tree."

"And did he go home?" asked Gabriel.

"Yes, he went home. And when I was only a week in the convent he died and he was buried in Oughterard, where his people came from. O, the day I heard that, that he was dead!"

She stopped, choking with sobs, and, overcome by emotion, flung herself face downward on the bed, sobbing in the quilt. Gabriel held her hand for a moment longer, irresolutely, and then, shy of intruding on her grief, let it fall gently and walked quietly to the window.

She was fast asleep.

Gabriel, leaning on his elbow, looked for a few moments unresentfully on her tangled hair and half-open mouth, listening to her deep-drawn breath. So she had had that romance in her life: a man had died for her sake. It hardly pained him now to think how poor a part he, her husband, had played in her life. He watched her while she slept, as though he and she had never lived together as man and wife. His curious eyes rested long upon her face and on her hair: and, as he thought of what she must have been then, in that time of her first girlish beauty, a strange, friendly pity for her entered his soul. He did not like to say even to himself that her face was no longer beautiful, but he knew that it was no longer the face for which Michael Furey had braved death.

Perhaps she had not told him all the story. His eyes moved to the chair over which she had thrown some of her clothes. A petticoat string dangled to the floor. One boot stood upright, its limp upper fallen down: the fellow of it lay upon its side. He wondered at his riot of emotions of an hour before. From what had it proceeded? From his aunt's supper, from his own foolish speech, from the wine and dancing, the merry-making when saying good-night in the hall, the pleasure of the walk along the river in the snow. Poor Aunt Julia! She, too, would soon be a shade with the shade of Patrick Morkan and his horse. He had caught that haggard look upon her face for a moment when she was singing *Arrayed for the Bridal*. Soon, perhaps, he would be sitting in that same drawing-room, dressed in black, his silk hat on his knees. The blinds would be drawn down and Aunt Kate would be sitting beside him, crying and blowing her nose and telling him how Julia had died. He would cast about in his mind for some words that might console her, and would find only lame and useless ones. Yes, yes: that would happen very soon.

The air of the room chilled his shoulders. He stretched himself cautiously along under the sheets and lay down beside his wife. One by one, they were all becoming shades. Better pass boldly into that other world, in the full glory of some passion, than fade and wither dismally with age. He thought of how she who lay beside him had locked in her heart for so many years that image of her lover's eyes when he had told her that he did not wish to live.

Generous tears filled Gabriel's eyes. He had never felt like that himself towards any woman, but he knew that such a feeling must be love. The tears gathered more thickly in his eyes and in the partial darkness he imagined he saw the form of a young man standing under a dripping tree. Other forms were near. His soul had approached that region where dwell the vast hosts of the dead. He was conscious of, but could not apprehend, their wayward and flickering existence. His own identity was fading out into a grey impalpable world: the solid world itself, which these dead had one time reared and lived in, was dissolving and dwindling.

A few light taps upon the pane made him turn to the window. It had begun to snow again. He watched sleepily the flakes, silver and dark, falling obliquely against the lamplight. The time had come for him to set out on his journey westward. Yes, the newspapers were right, snow was general all over Ireland. It was falling on every part of the dark central plain, on the treeless hills, falling softly upon the Bog of Allen and, farther westward, softly falling into the dark mutinous Shannon waves. It was falling, too, upon every part of the lonely churchyard on the hill where Michael Furey lay buried. It lay thickly drifted on the crooked crosses and headstones, on the spears of the little gate, on the barren thorns. His soul swooned slowly as he heard the snow falling faintly through the universe and faintly falling, like the descent of their last end, upon all the living and the dead.

COMMENTARY

" 'He died when he was only seventeen!' " says Gretta Conroy when she tells her husband about Michael Furey. " 'Isn't it a terrible thing to die so young as that?' " But no reader will give the answer that Gretta seems to expect from her husband. No reader upon whom the story has had its intended effect can fail to know that it is better to have died as Michael Furey died than to have lived after the fashion of Gabriel Conroy and all the other guests at the Christmas party. And this is the answer that Gabriel Conroy does indeed give when he lies down beside his sleeping wife. "Better pass boldly into that other world," he thinks, "in the full glory of some passion, than fade and wither dismally with age." The title of the story, we eventually understand, refers less to Michael Furey than to Gabriel Conroy, to the guests at the Christmas party, to all the people of Ireland as Conroy now perceives them. They, although still breathing, are the truly dead, and young Michael Furey, if only because he exists as he does in the minds of Gretta and Gabriel Conroy, is alive, a clearly defined personal entity, a strong energy.

"The Dead" is the last, the longest, and the most complex of the stories of James Joyce's first volume of fiction, *Dubliners*. Of this book Joyce said, "My intention was to write a chapter of the moral history of my country and I chose Dublin for the scene because the city seemed to me the centre of paralysis." What Joyce had in mind when he spoke of "paralysis" is suggested by an incident in "The Dead," Aunt Julia's singing. For a fleeting moment there is a remission of the "paralysis," for the old lady sings surprisingly well, and we are told that "to follow the voice was to feel and share the excitement of swift and secure flight." *The excitement of swift and secure flight:* here is life as the poets wish it to be, as we all at some time imagine it possibly can be. But in quoting the sentence, I have omitted a qualifying clause. The whole sentence reads: "To follow the voice, without looking at the singer's face, was to feel and share the excitement of swift and secure flight." If one did look at her face, Joyce is telling us, one saw the approach of death and the limitation of mind and spirit that marks not Aunt Julia alone but all the relatives and friends who are gathered around her. One saw the poverty of experience and passion, of gaiety, wit, intelligence—the death-in-life of a narrow, provincial existence.

Joyce writes of his own nation and city with passionate particularity. But when we consider the very high place that "The Dead" has been given in the canon of modern literature, and the admiration it has won from readers of the most diverse backgrounds, we must say that Joyce has written a chapter in the moral history not only of his own country but of the whole modern western world. Gabriel Conroy's plight, his sense that he has been overtaken by death-in-life, is shared by many in our time: it is one of the characteristics of modern society that an ever-growing number of people are not content to live by habit and routine and by the unquestioning acceptance of the circumstances into which they have been born. They believe they have the right to claim for themselves pleasure, or power, or dignity, or fullness of experience; a prerogative which in former times was exercised by relatively few people, usually members of the privileged classes, and which now seems available to many people regardless of class. Yet almost in the degree that modern man feels free to assert the personal claims which are the expression of a heightened sense of individuality, he seems to fall prey to that peculiarly modern disorder so often remarked by novelists, psychologists, and sociologists—an uncertainty about who the person is who makes the claims, a diminished sense of his personal identity.

Identity is the word that Gabriel Conroy uses when he thinks about death: he sees "his own identity . . . fading out into a grey impalpable world." And his imagination of death provides the image of his life. All through the evening his identity had been fading out into the grey impalpable world of his aunts' party. All through his youth and his early middle-age his identity had been fading out into the grey impalpable world of Dublin society.

It is sometimes said that Gabriel Conroy is what James Joyce would have been, or what he supposed he would have been, if he had not fled Dublin at the age of twenty, with no resources but his talent and his youth, risking privation for the sake of achievement and fame. And certainly the juxtaposition of the author and his character helps us understand Gabriel Conroy. Joyce was one of an old and rare species of man: he was a genius, with all the stubborn resistance and courage, all the strong sense of identity, by which, in addition to great gifts, genius is defined. Gabriel Conroy is one of a new, and very numerous, kind of man whose large demand upon life is supported neither by native gift nor moral energy. He has the knowledge of excellence but cannot achieve it for himself; he admires distinction and cannot attain it.

Poor Conroy's deficiency manifests itself most saliently and sadly in his relation to his wife. Gretta is a person of rather considerable distinction; among the guests at the party she is the only woman who possesses beauty, charm, and temperament. She is vivacious and spirited, and, as her evocation of the dead Michael Furey suggests, she has a capacity for intense feeling. To this endowment her husband responds with admiration and love, but he has the dim, implicit knowledge that he cannot match it with qualities of his own. When his wife tells him the story of her girlhood romance, his inarticulate self-knowledge is suddenly made explicit and devastating. The sharp clarity with which Michael Furey has remained in Gretta's consciousness, his embodiment of will and passion, make plain to Gabriel Conroy how fully he himself has succumbed to his aunts' impalpable grey world of habit, respectability, and mediocrity.

The literary means by which Joyce represents the world of Conroy's friends and relatives are striking in their subtlety and diversity. If Joyce has an opinion about the people who gather at the old aunts'—and we know he has—he does not express it overtly. At times he seems to subordinate his own judgment to theirs, as when he gravely tells us about the serving maid Lily that she "seldom made a mistake in the orders, so that she got on well with her three mistresses. They were fussy, that was all. But the only thing they would not stand was back answers." Now and then he seems to yield to the spirit of the party and uses a prose which, in a fatigued way, takes on something of the consciously fanciful humor of Dickens in his scenes of jollification: "On the closed square piano a pudding in a huge yellow dish lay in waiting and behind it were three squads of bottles of stout and ale and minerals, drawn up according to the colours of their uniforms, the first two black, with brown and red labels, the third and smallest squad white, with transverse green sashes." For the most part, however, the tone of the prose is neutral and a little naive, as if Joyce has no point of view of his own, or as if he were saying that he has no wish to judge, let alone to blame—for how can one blame the dead for being dead?

Nothing could be more brilliant and subtle, or humane, than Joyce's management of his own—and our—relation to Gabriel Conroy. All the details of Conroy's behavior at the party contribute to our perception of his second-rateness. But we are never invited to despise him, we are never permitted to triumph over him. Joyce spares him nothing in making us aware of his mediocrity: we know all about his nervous desire to be liked and approved, his wish to be thought superior, his fear of asserting whatever superiority he may actually have, his lack of intellectual and emotional courage, his sulky resentment when he feels slighted, his easy sentimentality. But at the same time Joyce does not obscure Conroy's genuine intention of kindness, his actual considerateness, his demand upon himself that he be large-minded and generous. And he protects Conroy from our ultimate contempt by making plain the extent of his fairly accurate self-knowledge; there is little we discern to Conroy's discredit that the unhappy man does not himself know and deplore.

But self-knowledge cannot save Conroy from being the kind of man he is, and when we try to say what that kind is, we are bound to think of his commitment to galoshes. In the British Isles, much more than in America, the wearing of galoshes and rubbers is regarded as an excessive and rather foolish caution about one's health. The fact that Conroy makes such a great thing of wearing them himself and urges them on his wife—but on the night of the party she defies him—puts him in almost too obvious contrast with Michael Furey, who had died from standing in the rain to bid his love farewell. It is Conroy's sense of his vulnerability, his uneasy feeling that almost every situation is a threat, that makes him what he is. He has no valid reason to think that the servant girl is really angry with him; when she responds to his remark about her getting married, her "great bitterness" is directed not at him but at the conditions of her life, yet Conroy feels that "he had made a mistake," that he had "failed" with her, and he is extravagantly distressed. He is equally self-conscious and timorous in his half-flirtatious dispute with Miss Ivors, feeling that the nature of their relation makes it impossible for him to "risk a grandiose phrase with her." He does indeed achieve a moment of dignity when he is moved by desire for his wife, but even here he protects himself, resolving to postpone his wooing until he is certain of being fully responded to. And when he does at last speak, it is to make an irrelevant and banal remark that quite belies his emotion.

Conroy's own last adverse judgment on himself is extreme—he sees himself as "a ludicrous figure, acting as a pennyboy for his aunts, a nervous, well-meaning sentimentalist, orating to vulgarians and idealising his own clownish lusts, the pitiable fatuous fellow he had caught a glimpse of in the mirror." This extravagance of self-contempt is not only the outcome of self-knowledge; it is also the expression of Conroy's self-pity, an emotion which we are taught to despise. But Joyce does not despise it and he does not permit us to despise it. As Conroy lies in defeat and meditation beside his sleeping wife, his evocation of the sadness of life under the dominion of death is the climax of his self-pity, yet when his commiseration with himself reaches this point of intensity, the author's own emotion is seen to be in active accord with it. This sudden identification of the author with his character is one of the most striking and effective elements of the story. Joyce feels exactly what Conroy feels about the sadness of human life, its terrible nearness to death, and the *waste* that every life is; he directs no irony upon Conroy's grief but makes Conroy's suffering his own, with no reservations whatever. At several points in the story he has clearly regarded Conroy's language, or the tone of his thoughts, as banal, or vulgar, or sentimental. But as the story approaches its conclusion, it becomes impossible for us to know whose language we are hearing, Conroy's or the author's, or to whose tone of desperate sorrow we are responding. It is as if Joyce, secure in his genius and identity, were saying that under the aspect of the imagination of death and of death-in-life there is no difference between him and the mediocre, sentimental man of whom he has been writing.

THE

HUNTER

GRACCHUS

FRANZ KAFKA

1 8 8 3 – 1 9 2 4

TWO BOYS were sitting on the harbor wall playing with dice. A man was reading a newspaper on the steps of the monument resting in the shadow of a hero who was flourishing his sword on high. A girl was filling her bucket at the fountain. A fruit-seller was lying beside his scales, staring out to sea. Through the vacant window and door openings of a café one could see two men quite at the back drinking their wine. The proprietor was sitting at a table in front and dozing, a bark was silently making for the little harbor, as if borne by invisible means over the water. A man in a blue blouse climbed ashore and drew the rope through a ring. Behind the boatman two other men in dark coats with silver buttons carried a bier, on which, beneath a great flower-patterned tasseled silk cloth, a man was apparently lying.

Nobody on the quay troubled about the newcomers; even when they lowered the bier to wait for the boatman, who was still occupied with his rope, nobody went nearer, nobody asked them a question, nobody accorded them an inquisitive glance.

The pilot was still further detained by a woman who, a child at her breast, now appeared with loosened hair on the deck of the boat. Then he advanced and indicated a yellowish two-storeyed house that rose abruptly on the left beside the sea; the bearers took up their burden and bore it to the low but grace-

656

fully pillared door. A little boy opened a window just in time to see the party vanishing into the house, then hastily shut the window again. The door too was now shut; it was of black oak, and very strongly made. A flock of doves which had been flying round the belfry alighted in the street before the house. As if their food were stored within, they assembled in front of the door. One of them flew up to the first storey and pecked at the window-pane. They were bright-hued, well-tended, beautiful birds. The woman on the boat flung grain to them in a wide sweep; they ate it up and flew across to the woman.

A man in a top hat tied with a band of crêpe now descended one of the narrow and very steep lanes that led to the harbor. He glanced round vigilantly, everything seemed to displease him, his mouth twisted at the sight of some offal in a corner. Fruit skins were lying on the steps of the monument; he swept them off in passing with his stick. He rapped at the house door, at the same time taking his top hat from his head with his black-gloved hand. The door was opened at once, and some fifty little boys appeared in two rows in the long entry-hall, and bowed to him.

The boatman descended the stairs, greeted the gentleman in black, conducted him up to the first storey, led him round the bright and elegant loggia which encircled the courtyard, and both of them entered, while the boys pressed after them at a respectful distance, a cool spacious room looking towards the back, from whose window no habitation, but only a bare, blackish grey rocky wall was to be seen. The bearers were busied in setting up and lighting several long candles at the head of the bier, yet these did not give light, but only scared away the shadows which had been immobile till then, and made them flicker over the walls. The cloth covering the bier had been thrown back. Lying on it was a man with wildly matted hair, who looked somewhat like a hunter. He lay without motion and, it seemed, without breathing, his eyes closed; yet only his trappings indicated that this man was probably dead.

The gentleman stepped up to the bier, laid his hand on the brow of the man lying upon it, then kneeled down and prayed. The boatman made a sign to the bearers to leave the room; they went out, drove away the boys who had gathered outside, and shut the door. But even that did not seem to satisfy the gentleman; he glanced at the boatman; the boatman understood, and vanished through a side door into the next room. At once the man on the bier opened his eyes, turned his face painfully towards the gentleman, and said: "Who are you?" Without any mark of surprise the gentleman rose from his kneeling posture and answered: "The Burgomaster of Riva."

The man on the bier nodded, indicated a chair with a feeble movement of his arm, and said, after the Burgomaster had accepted his invitation: "I knew that, of course, Burgomaster, but in the first moments of returning consciousness I always forget, everything goes round before my eyes, and it is best to ask about anything even if I know. You too probably know that I am the hunter Gracchus."

"Certainly," said the Burgomaster. "Your arrival was announced to me during the night. We had been asleep for a good while. Then towards midnight my wife cried: 'Salvatore'—that's my name—'look at that dove at the window.' It was really a dove, but as big as a cock. It flew over me and said in my ear: 'Tomorrow the dead hunter Gracchus is coming: receive him in the name of the city.' "

The hunter nodded and licked his lips with the tip of his tongue: "Yes, the doves flew here before me. But do you believe, Burgomaster, that I shall remain in Riva?"

"I cannot say that yet," replied the Burgomaster. "Are you dead?"

"Yes," said the hunter, "as you see. Many years ago, yes, it must be a great many years ago, I fell from a precipice in the Black Forest—that is in Germany—when I was hunting a chamois. Since then I have been dead."

"But you are alive too," said the Burgomaster.

"In a certain sense," said the hunter, "in a certain sense I am alive too. My death ship lost its way; a wrong turn of the wheel, a moment's absence of mind on the pilot's part, a longing to turn aside towards my lovely native country, I cannot tell what it was; I only know this, that I remained on earth and that ever since my ship has sailed earthly waters. So I, who asked for nothing better than to live among my mountains, travel after my death through all the lands of the earth."

"And you have no part in the other world?" asked the Burgomaster, knitting his brow.

"I am forever," replied the hunter, "on the great stair that leads up to it. On that infinitely wide and spacious stair I clamber about, sometimes up, sometimes down, sometimes on the right, sometimes on the left, always in motion. The hunter has been turned into a butterfly. Do not laugh."

"I am not laughing," said the Burgomaster in self-defense.

"That is very good of you," said the hunter. "I am always in motion. But when I make a supreme flight and see the gate actually shining before me I awaken presently on my old ship, still stranded forlornly in some earthly sea or other. The fundamental error of my one-time death grins at me as I lie in my cabin. Julia, the wife of the pilot, knocks at the door and brings me on my bier the morning drink of the land whose coasts we chance to be passing. I lie on a wooden pallet, I wear—it cannot be a pleasure to look at me—a filthy winding sheet, my hair and beard, black tinged with gray, have grown together inextricably, my limbs are covered with a great flower-patterned woman's shawl with long fringes. A sacramental candle stands at my head and lights me. On the wall opposite me is a little picture, evidently of a Bushman who is aiming his spear at me and taking cover as best he can behind a beautifully painted shield.[1] On shipboard one is often a prey to stupid imaginations, but that is the stupidest of them all. Otherwise my wooden case is quite empty. Through a hole in the side wall come in the warm airs of the southern night, and I hear the water slapping against the old boat.

"I have lain here ever since the time when, as the hunter Gracchus living in the Black Forest, I followed a chamois and fell from the precipice. Everything happened in good order. I pursued, I fell, bled to death in a ravine, died, and this ship should have conveyed me to the next world. I can still remember how gladly I stretched myself out on this pallet for the first time. Never did the mountains listen to such songs from me as these shadowy walls did then.

"I had been glad to live and I was glad to die. Before I stepped aboard, I

---

[1] The Bushmen, now a quite primitive African tribe, are believed to have produced, during a period of cultural advancement, many of the delicate and vivid paintings of animals and of humans and animals in hunting scenes that can be seen on cave walls and other protected rock surfaces throughout much of Africa. Apparently one of history's examples of cultural retrogression, the Bushmen now produce only simple utensils and primitive ornaments.

joyfully flung away my wretched load of ammunition, my knapsack, my hunting rifle that I had always been proud to carry, and I slipped into my winding sheet like a girl into her marriage dress. I lay and waited. Then came the mishap."

"A terrible fate," said the Burgomaster, raising his hand defensively. "And you bear no blame for it?"

"None," said the hunter. "I was a hunter: was there any sin in that? I followed my calling as a hunter in the Black Forest, where there were still wolves in those days. I lay in ambush, shot, hit my mark, flayed the skins from my victims: was there any sin in that? My labors were blessed. 'The great hunter of the Black Forest' was the name I was given. Was there any sin in that?"

"I am not called upon to decide that," said the Burgomaster, "But to me also there seems to be no sin in such things. But, then, whose is the guilt?"

"The boatman's," said the hunter. "Nobody will read what I say here, no one will come to help me; even if all the people were commanded to help me, every door and window would remain shut, everybody would take to bed and draw the bedclothes over his head, the whole earth would become an inn for the night. And there is sense in that, for nobody knows of me, and if anyone knew he would not know where I could be found, and if he knew where I could be found, he would not know how to deal with me, he would not know how to help me. The thought of helping me is an illness that has to be cured by taking to one's bed.

"I know that, and so I do not shout to summon help, even though at moments—when I lose control over myself, as I have done just now, for instance—I think seriously of it. But to drive out such thoughts I need only look round me and verify where I am, and—I can safely assert—have been for hundreds of years."

"Extraordinary," said the Burgomaster, "extraordinary.—And now do you think of staying here in Riva with us?"

"I think not," said the hunter with a smile, and, to excuse himself, he laid his hand on the Burgomaster's knee. "I am here, more than that I do not know, further than that I cannot go. My ship has no rudder, and it is driven by the wind that blows in the undermost regions of death."

COMMENTARY

Almost any reader of this story will say, or perhaps cry out in distraction, "What can it mean? What can this strange narrative be trying to communicate to me?" He will find himself baffled at virtually every point—he cannot tell where the story takes place, or when, or by what logic one of its events follows another. Indeed, his first desperate question might well be, "What is this story trying *to do to me?*" For, by unsettling his sense of the actual, it will have made him uneasy and apprehensive.

And yet, for all its defiance of our reason, we cannot doubt that Kafka's story does intend to say something to us. We know, even on a first puzzled reading, what *kind* of thing it is saying: something of large import, having to do with the human spirit and its fate. We recognize the sort of story it is; we identify it as a myth, a tale which explains some circumstance of human life in terms of supernatural happenings. Myths are conceived by a people in a relatively early stage of cultural development, but even when the authority of this method of explanation has been destroyed by reason and science, the interest in myth and the mythical mode of thought is strongly maintained in literature.

Some of the elements of Kafka's story remind us—perhaps by the author's intention—of certain well-known ancient myths. The dead hunter recalls Adonis, who was killed in a hunting accident. The "death ship" was surely suggested by the burial ritual of the Egyptians, who equipped their tombs with elaborate miniature ships because they believed that the departed soul traveled by water to another world. The fate of the hunter Gracchus in his "wooden case" is similar to that of the Egyptian hero-king Osiris, who was said to have been shut up in a coffer which was sealed and thrown into the Nile.

But there are striking differences between Kafka's modern myth and the ancient ones. In the story of Adonis, the beautiful young man was loved by both Aphrodite, the goddess of love, and Persephone, the goddess of death, and it was eventually his fate to spend half the year with each of the two divinities. Among the ancient peoples of Greece and Asia Minor, Adonis was the object of intense worship; in the performance of his rites, his death was wildly mourned for one day and his resurrection joyously celebrated the next. His death symbolized winter, his resurrection the rebirth of spring. The Osiris myth also tells of resurrection. Osiris, who was often identified with Adonis (in some versions of his myth he is said to have been killed by a wild boar, as Adonis was), was restored to life through the devotion of his wife Isis, and became for the Egyptians the god of both death and resurrection. But in Kafka's myth there are neither goddesses nor love, nor is there wifely devotion, and there is no resurrection. If Adonis and Osiris embody man's hope, the hunter Gracchus embodies man's despair. He can never return to the earthly region in which he delighted, and when the Burgomaster asks him, " 'And have you no part in the other world?' " his reply is conclusive—no, he can never reach it, try as he may.

Students of the history of religion regard Adonis and Osiris as prefigurations of Jesus, who, like them, died and was resurrected. And the dead hunter of Kafka's story can be thought of as a despairing Jesus who was not resurrected and who is never to be "received," either by his Father in "the other world" or by mankind in this one. In the hunter's saddest expression of his hopelessness, the whole earth is spoken of as becoming "an inn for the night," and we can scarcely fail to think of the Holy Family being turned away from the inn on its flight into Egypt. The same speech seems to propose the idea that the teachings of Jesus are to be forever rejected by the world. "Nobody will read what I say here, no one will come to help me; even if all the people were commanded to help me, every door and window would remain shut, everybody would take to bed and draw the bedclothes over his head, the whole earth would become an inn for the night. And there is sense in that, for nobody knows of me, and if anyone knew he would not know where I could be found, he would not know how to deal with me, he would not know how to help me. The thought of helping me is an illness that has to be cured by taking to one's bed."

The identification of the hunter with Jesus is neither complete nor final. It is suggested quite clearly, but it is not insisted on, nor enforced. We are free to think that the hunter is perhaps Jesus, or perhaps mankind itself, that it is the despairing voice of humanity which speaks in the hunter's awful words which close the story: " 'I am here, more than that I do not know, further than that I cannot go. My ship has no rudder, and it is driven by the wind that blows in the undermost regions of death.'" And we are by no means debarred from also supposing that in the hunter Gracchus the author is representing his sense of his own personal fate. Indeed, this becomes something more than an arbitrary— if natural—supposition when we consider the hunter's name, Gracchus. We can discern no connection between anything in the story and the two most famous bearers of the Roman name, the brothers known as the Gracchi, who defended the rights of the poor against the encroachments of the rich. But the Latin word *graculus* means jackdaw; from it comes the English word *grackle,* which is used to denote any kind of blackbird smaller than the crow, including the jackdaw. In Czech, the word for jackdaw is *kavka,* and the sign over Kafka's father's shop in Prague, the trademark of the business, was a picture of the bird. And Kafka often referred to himself as a jackdaw.[1]

Nothing in the story is more terrible than the reason for the plight of the hunter, "'My death ship lost its way; a wrong turn of the wheel, a moment's absence of mind on the pilot's part . . .'" It was a "mishap." To the Burgomaster's question "'And you bear no blame for it?'" the hunter answers decisively "'None.'"

In the Judaeo-Christian tradition, one way of explaining the pain of human existence while preserving belief in a beneficent God is to say that man's suffering is the direct consequence of his sinfulness. But the hunter, when the Burgomaster questions him about his fate, says that it has no relation to anything he has done. The death ship missed its way only through the fault of the boatman. There is of course no reason why we must believe what the hunter says. Yet we do believe it.

The hunter says nothing, and the story implies nothing, that negates the existence of divinity. Quite to the contrary, the hunter speaks of his labors as being "blessed." He refers to "the other world" with its "infinitely wide and spacious stair" and its shining gate, and this would seem to be the divine abode. The candle at the hunter's head is a "sacramental" candle, and the life of the people of the town is organized for the performance of a strictly enforced ceremonial. But if the world that Kafka describes lives under the aspect of divinity, it is not such a divinity as any known religion worships, and there would seem to be only a very tenuous connection between the divine and the human.

Certainly the belief in divinity kindles no hope or aspiration in human hearts. The life of the little port, although it encompasses the recognizable activities of mankind, seems to have been stricken by a terrible vacancy.[2] The actions

---

[1] It should be mentioned that, throughout Kafka's youth, Czechoslovakia was part of the Austrian Empire; and that Prague was a bilingual city, part of the population speaking German, part Czech. Kafka had a good command of Czech, but his mother tongue was German, he attended German schools, and he thought of himself as a German writer.

[2] Riva is an actual Italian town; it is not, however, a seaport but is situated at the head of Lake Garda in the north of Italy, bordering on Switzerland. Kafka's translators, Willa and Edwin Muir, have been most faithful to the original text and notably sensitive in their rendering of it. But in allowing us to think of the town as a seaport they have made one error of some importance. The German word *See* is used for both *lake* and *sea;* when it means *lake* it is a masculine noun and when it means *sea* it is feminine. In the German text of the story the word is used in both genders—the death-ship sails all waters, great and small. But as we see it coming to Riva, it is sailing only a rather small lake. Our awareness of this might well intensify the sense of confinement and constriction that the story generates.

of the people described in the first paragraph are curiously somnambulistic. The boys playing dice, the man reading a newspaper, the girl filling her bucket at the fountain, the men drinking in the café, all seem to participate in the life-lessness of the statue on the monument. When the death ship arrives, every-thing about the ritual of receiving it is carried out with precision; even the doves know their part, and somehow "fifty little boys" understand that they must gather to form two rows between which the Burgomaster is to walk. Yet no one attaches any emotion to the ceremony, except for the one little boy "who opened a window just in time to see the party vanishing into the house, then hastily shut the window again." The people of the town, we feel, are scarcely more alive than the passenger of the death ship. He is more distressed than they, for once he had been a famous hunter and had known delight, and now he lies in a filthy winding sheet, unshaven and unshorn; it is a curiously revolting detail of his condition that he is covered with a "great flower-patterned woman's shawl with long fringes." Yet his condition is different in degree but not in kind from that of the townsmen.

The happenings of Kafka's story are bizarre and out of the course of nature, yet we do not for that reason incline to call it a fantasy—that word suggests to us something wild and free, a liberation of the mind from the bonds of logic and actuality, whereas this story has the effect of making us feel helplessly impris-oned in the prosaic and the intractable. But if ever we have experienced the sense that life is empty and meaningless, if ever we have suffered from the feeling that our behavior is compelled, that our will is not our own, or that it has ceased to function, we can scarcely withstand· the power of Kafka's terrible imagination of man's existence.

TICKETS, PLEASE

D . H . L A W R E N C E
1 8 8 5 – 1 9 3 0

THERE IS in the Midlands[1] a single-line tramway system which boldly leaves the county town and plunges off into the black, industrial countryside, up hill and down dale, through the long, ugly villages of workmen's houses, over canals and railways, past churches perched high and nobly over the smoke and shadows, through stark, grimy, cold little market-places, tilting away in a rush past cinemas and shops down to the hollow where the collieries are, then up again, past a little rural church, under the ash trees, on in a rush to the terminus, the last little ugly place of industry, the cold little town that shivers on the edge of the wild, gloomy country beyond. There the green and creamy coloured tram-car seems to pause and purr with curious satisfaction. But in a few minutes—the clock on the turret of the Co-operative Wholesale Society's Shops gives the time—away it starts once more on the adventure. Again there are the reckless swoops downhill, bouncing the loops: again the chilly wait in the hill-top market-place: again the breathless slithering round the precipitous drop under the church: again the patient halts at the loops, waiting for the outcoming car: so on and on, for two long hours, till at last the city looms beyond the fat gas-works, the narrow factories draw near, we are in the sordid streets of the great town, once more we sidle to a stand-

[1] An industrial central section of England.

still at our terminus, abashed by the great crimson and cream-coloured city cars, but still perky, jaunty, somewhat dare-devil, green as a jaunty sprig of parsley out of a black colliery garden.

To ride on these cars is always an adventure. Since we are in war-time,[2] the drivers are men unfit for active service: cripples and hunchbacks. So they have the spirit of the devil in them. The ride becomes a steeple-chase. Hurray! we have leapt in a clear jump over the canal bridges—now for the four-lane corner. With a shriek and a trail of sparks we are clear again. To be sure, a tram often leaps the rails—but what matter! It sits in a ditch till other trams come to haul it out. It is quite common for a car, packed with one solid mass of living people, to come to a dead halt in the midst of unbroken blackness, the heart of nowhere on a dark night, and for the driver and the girl conductor to call, "All get off—car's on fire!" Instead, however, of rushing out in a panic, the passengers stolidly reply: "Get on—get on! We're not coming out. We're stopping where we are. Push on, George." So till flames actually appear.

The reason for this reluctance to dismount is that the nights are howlingly cold, black, and windswept, and a car is a haven of refuge. From village to village the miners travel, for a change of cinema, of girl, of pub. The trams are desperately packed. Who is going to risk himself in the black gulf outside, to wait perhaps an hour for another tram, then to see the forlorn notice "Depot Only," because there is something wrong! or to greet a unit of three bright cars all so tight with people that they sail past with a howl of derision. Trams that pass in the night.

This, the most dangerous tram-service in England, as the authorities themselves declare, with pride, is entirely conducted by girls, and driven by rash young men, a little crippled, or by delicate young men, who creep forward in terror. The girls are fearless young hussies. In their ugly blue uniform, skirts up to their knees, shapeless old peaked caps on their heads, they have all the sang-froid of an old non-commissioned officer. With a tram packed with howling colliers, roaring hymns downstairs and a sort of antiphony of obscenities upstairs, the lasses are perfectly at their ease. They pounce on the youths who try to evade their ticket-machine. They push off the men at the end of their distance. They are not going to be done in the eye—not they. They fear nobody—and everybody fears them.

"Hello, Annie!"

"Hello, Ted!"

"Oh, mind my corn, Miss Stone. It's my belief you've got a heart of stone, for you've trod on it again."

"You should keep it in your pocket," replies Miss Stone, and she goes sturdily upstairs in her high boots.

"Tickets, please."

She is peremptory, suspicious, and ready to hit first. She can hold her own against ten thousand. The step of that tram-car is her Thermopylæ.[3]

Therefore, there is a certain wild romance aboard these cars—and in the sturdy bosom of Annie herself. The time for soft romance is in the morning, between ten o'clock and one, when things are rather slack: that is, except market-

<hr />

[2] World War I.

[3] A narrow pass in Greece, where a handful of Spartans, under Leonidas, held off the great army of Xerxes in one of the most famous battles of the Persian Wars (480 B.C.).

day and Saturday. Thus Annie has time to look about her. Then she often hops off her car and into a shop where she has spied something, while the driver chats in the main road. There is very good feeling between the girls and the drivers. Are they not companions in peril, shipments aboard this careering vessel of a tram-car, for ever rocking on the waves of a stormy land.

Then, also, during the easy hours, the inspectors are most in evidence. For some reason, everybody employed in this tram-service is young: there are no grey heads. It would not do. Therefore the inspectors are of the right age, and one, the chief, is also good-looking. See him stand on a wet, gloomy morning, in his long oilskin, his peaked cap well down over his eyes, waiting to board a car. His face is ruddy, his small brown moustache is weathered, he has a faint impudent smile. Fairly tall and agile, even in his waterproof, he springs aboard a car and greets Annie.

"Hello! Annie! Keeping the wet out?"

"Trying to."

There are only two people in the car. Inspecting is soon over. Then for a long and impudent chat on the footboard, a good, easy, twelve-mile chat.

The inspector's name is John Thomas Raynor—always called John Thomas,[4] except sometimes, in malice, Coddy. His face sets in fury when he is addressed, from a distance, with this abbreviation. There is considerable scandal about John Thomas in half a dozen villages. He flirts with the girl conductors in the morning and walks out with them in the dark night, when they leave their tram-car at the depot. Of course, the girls quit the service frequently. Then he flirts and walks out with the newcomer: always providing she is sufficiently attractive, and that she will consent to walk. It is remarkable, however, that most of the girls are quite comely, they are all young, and this roving life aboard the car gives them a sailor's dash and recklessness. What matter how they behave when the ship is in port. Tomorrow they will be aboard again.

Annie, however, was something of a Tartar, and her sharp tongue had kept John Thomas at arm's length for many months. Perhaps, therefore, she liked him all the more: for he always came up smiling, with impudence. She watched him vanquish one girl, then another. She could tell by the movement of his mouth and eyes, when he flirted with her in the morning, that he had been walking out with this lass, or the other, the night before. A fine cock-of-the-walk he was. She could sum him up pretty well.

In this subtle antagonism they knew each other like old friends, they were as shrewd with one another almost as man and wife. But Annie had always kept him sufficiently at arm's length. Besides, she had a boy of her own.

The Statutes fair, however, came in November, at Bestwood. It happened that Annie had the Monday night off. It was a drizzling ugly night, yet she dressed herself up and went to the fair ground. She was alone, but she expected soon to find a pal of some sort.

The roundabouts were veering round and grinding out their music, the side shows were making as much commotion as possible. In the cocoanut shies[5] there were no cocoanuts, but artificial war-time substitutes, which the lads declared

---

[4] The obscene connotation (in colloquial British use) of this name is emphasized by the more definitely obscene nickname.

[5] Carnival games, in which coconuts are thrown at a target.

were fastened into the irons. There was a sad decline in brilliance and luxury. None the less, the ground was muddy as ever, there was the same crush, the press of faces lighted up by the flares and the electric lights, the same smell of naphtha[6] and a few fried potatoes, and of electricity.

Who should be the first to greet Miss Annie, on the show ground, but John Thomas. He had a black overcoat buttoned up to his chin, and a tweed cap pulled down over his brows, his face between was ruddy and smiling and handy as ever. She knew so well the way his mouth moved.

She was very glad to have a "boy." To be at the Statutes without a fellow was no fun. Instantly, like the gallant he was, he took her on the Dragons, grim-toothed, roundabout switchbacks. It was not nearly so exciting as a tram-car actually. But, then, to be seated in a shaking green dragon, uplifted above the sea of bubble faces, careering in a rickety fashion in the lower heavens, whilst John Thomas leaned over her, his cigarette in his mouth, was after all the right style. She was a plump, quick, alive little creature. So she was quite excited and happy.

John Thomas made her stay on for the next round. And therefore she could hardly for shame repulse him when he put his arm round her and drew her a little nearer to him, in a very warm and cuddly manner. Besides, he was fairly discreet, he kept his movement as hidden as possible. She looked down and saw that his red, clean hand was out of sight of the crowd. And they knew each other so well. So they warmed up to the fair.

After the dragons they went on the horses. John Thomas paid each time, so she could but be complaisant. He, of course, sat astride on the outer horse—named "Black Bess"—and she sat sideways, towards him, on the inner horse—name "Wild-fire." But of course John Thomas was not going to sit discreetly on "Black Bess," holding the brass bar. Round they spun and heaved, in the light. And round he swung on his wooden steed, flinging one leg across her mount, and perilously tipping up and down, across the space, half lying back, laughing at her. He was perfectly happy; she was afraid her hat was on one side, but she was excited.

He threw quoits on a table and won for her two large, pale-blue hat-pins. And then, hearing the noise of the cinemas, announcing another performance, they climbed the boards and went in.

Of course, during these performances pitch darkness falls from time to time, when the machine goes wrong. Then there is a wild whooping, and a loud smacking of simulated kisses. In these moments John Thomas drew Annie towards him. After all, he had a wonderfully warm, cosy way of holding a girl with his arm, he seemed to make such a nice fit. And after all, it was pleasant to be so held: so very comforting and cosy and nice. He leaned over her and she felt his breath on her hair; she knew he wanted to kiss her on the lips. And after all, he was so warm and she fitted in to him so softly. After all, she wanted him to touch her lips.

But the light sprang up; she also started electrically, and put her hat straight. He left his arm lying nonchalantly behind her. Well, it was fun, it was exciting to be at the Statutes with John Thomas.

When the cinema was over they went for a walk across the dark, damp fields. He had all the arts of love-making. He was especially good at holding a girl, when he sat with her on a stile in the black, drizzling darkness. He seemed to be holding

---

[6] Cooking and illuminating gas.

her in space, against his own warmth and gratification. And his kisses were soft and slow and searching.

So Annie walked out with John Thomas, though she kept her own boy dangling in the distance. Some of the tram-girls chose to be huffy. But there, you must take things as you find them, in this life.

There was no mistake about it, Annie liked John Thomas a good deal. She felt so rich and warm in herself wherever he was near. And John Thomas really liked Annie more than usual. The soft, melting way in which she could flow into a fellow, as if she melted into his very bones, was something rare and good. He fully appreciated this.

But with a developing acquaintance there began a developing intimacy. Annie wanted to consider him a person, a man; she wanted to take an intelligent interest in him, and to have an intelligent response. She did not want a mere nocturnal presence, which was what he was so far. And she prided herself that he could not leave her.

Here she made a mistake. John Thomas intended to remain a nocturnal presence; he had no idea of becoming an all-round individual to her. When she started to take an intelligent interest in him and his life and his character, he sheered off. He hated intelligent interest. And he knew that the only way to stop it was to avoid it. The possessive female was aroused in Annie. So he left her.

It is no use saying she was not surprised. She was at first startled, thrown out of her count. For she had been so *very* sure of holding him. For a while she was staggered, and everything became uncertain to her. Then she wept with fury, indignation, desolation, and misery. Then she had a spasm of despair. And then, when he came, still impudently, on to her car, still familiar, but letting her see by the movement of his head that he had gone away to somebody else for the time being and was enjoying pastures new, then she determined to have her own back.

She had a very shrewd idea what girls John Thomas had taken out. She went to Nora Purdy. Nora was a tall, rather pale, but well-built girl, with beautiful yellow hair. She was rather secretive.

"Hey!" said Annie, accosting her; then softly, "Who's John Thomas on with now?"

"I don't know," said Nora.

"Why tha does," said Annie, ironically lapsing into dialect. "Tha knows as well as I do."

"Well, I do, then," said Nora. "It isn't me, so don't bother."

"It's Cissy Meakin, isn't it?"

"It is, for all I know."

"Hasn't he got a face on him!" said Annie. "I don't half like his cheek. I could knock him off the footboard when he comes round at me."

"He'll get dropped-on one of these days," said Nora.

"Ay, he will when somebody makes up their mind to drop it on him. I should like to see him taken down a peg or two, shouldn't you?"

"I shouldn't mind," said Nora.

"You've got quite as much cause to as I have," said Annie. "But we'll drop on him one of these days, my girl. What? Don't you want to?"

"I don't mind," said Nora.

But as a matter of fact, Nora was much more vindictive than Annie.

One by one Annie went the round of the old flames. It so happened that Cissy Meakin left the tramway service in quite a short time. Her mother made her leave. Then John Thomas was on the qui-vive. He cast his eyes over his old flock. And his eyes lighted on Annie. He thought she would be safe now. Besides, he liked her.

She arranged to walk home with him on Sunday night. It so happened that her car would be in the depot at half-past nine: the last car would come in at ten-fifteen. So John Thomas was to wait for her there.

At the depot the girls had a little waiting-room of their own. It was quite rough, but cosy, with a fire and an oven and a mirror, and table and wooden chairs. The half dozen girls who knew John Thomas only too well had arranged to take service this Sunday afternoon. So, as the cars began to come in, early, the girls dropped into the waiting-room. And instead of hurrying off home, they sat around the fire and had a cup of tea. Outside was the darkness and lawlessness of war-time.

John Thomas came on the car after Annie, at about a quarter to ten. He poked his head easily into the girls' waiting-room.

"Prayer-meeting?" he asked.

"Ay," said Laura Sharp. "Ladies only."

"That's me!" said John Thomas. It was one of his favourite exclamations.

"Shut the door, boy," said Muriel Baggaley.

"On which side of me?" said John Thomas.

"Which tha likes," said Polly Birkin.

He had come in and closed the door behind him. The girls moved in their circle, to make a place for him near the fire. He took off his great-coat and pushed back his hat.

"Who handles the teapot?" he said.

Nora Purdy silently poured him out a cup of tea.

"Want a bit o' my bread and drippin'?" said Muriel Baggaley to him.

"Ay, give us a bit."

And he began to eat his piece of bread.

"There's no place like home, girls," he said.

They all looked at him as he uttered this piece of impudence. He seemed to be sunning himself in the presence of so many damsels.

"Especially if you're not afraid to go home in the dark," said Laura Sharp.

"Me! By myself I am."

They sat till they heard the last tram come in. In a few minutes Emma Houselay entered.

"Come on, my old duck!" cried Polly Birkin.

"It *is* perishing,"[7] said Emma, holding her fingers to the fire.

"But—I'm afraid to, go home in, the dark," sang Laura Sharp, the tune having got into her mind.

"Who're you going with tonight, John Thomas?" asked Muriel Baggaley, coolly.

"Tonight?" said John Thomas. "Oh, I'm going home by myself tonight—all on my lonely-O."

"That's me!" said Nora Purdy, using his own ejaculation.

[7] (British colloquialism) Cold.

The girls laughed shrilly.

"Me as well, Nora," said John Thomas.

"Don't know what you mean," said Laura.

"Yes, I'm toddling," said he, rising and reaching for his overcoat.

"Nay," said Polly. "We're all here waiting for you."

"We've got to be up in good time in the morning," he said in the benevolent official manner.

They all laughed.

"Nay," said Muriel. "Don't leave us all lonely, John Thomas. Take one!"

"I'll take the lot, if you like," he responded gallantly.

"That you won't, either," said Muriel. "Two's company; seven's too much of a good thing."

"Nay—take one," said Laura. "Fair and square, all above board, and say which."

"Ay," cried Annie, speaking for the first time. "Pick, John Thomas; let's hear thee."

"Nay," he said. "I'm going home quiet tonight. Feeling good, for once."

"Whereabouts?" said Annie. "Take a good un, then. But tha's got to take one of us!"

"Nay, how can I take one," he said, laughing uneasily. "I don't want to make enemies."

"You'd only make *one*," said Annie.

"The chosen *one*," added Laura.

"Oh, my! Who said girls!" exclaimed John Thomas, again turning, as if to escape. "Well—good-night."

"Nay, you've got to make your pick," said Muriel. "Turn your face to the wall and say which one touches you. Go on—we shall only just touch your back—one of us. Go on—turn your face to the wall, and don't look, and say which one touches you."

He was uneasy, mistrusting them. Yet he had not the courage to break away. They pushed him to a wall and stood him there with his face to it. Behind his back they all grimaced, tittering. He looked so comical. He looked around uneasily.

"Go on!" he cried.

"You're looking—you're looking!" they shouted.

He turned his head away. And suddenly, with a movement like a swift cat, Annie went forward and fetched him a box on the side of the head that set his cap flying, and himself staggering. He started round.

But at Annie's signal they all flew at him, slapping him, pinching him, pulling his hair, though more in fun than in spite or anger. He, however, saw red. His blue eyes flamed with strange fear as well as fury, and he butted through the girls to the door. It was locked. He wrenched at it. Roused, alert, the girls stood round and looked at him. He faced them, at bay. At that moment they were rather horrifying to him, as they stood in their short uniforms. He was distinctly afraid.

"Come on, John Thomas! Come on! Choose!" said Annie.

"What are you after? Open the door," he said.

"We sha'n't—not till you've chosen!" said Muriel.

"Chosen what?" he said.

"Chosen the one you're going to marry," she replied.

He hesitated a moment.

"Open the blasted door," he said, "and get back to your senses." He spoke with official authority.

"You've got to choose!" cried the girls.

"Come on!" cried Annie, looking him in the eye. "Come on! Come on!"

He went forward, rather vaguely. She had taken off her belt, and swinging it, she fetched him a sharp blow over the head with the buckle end. He sprang and seized her. But immediately the other girls rushed upon him, pulling and tearing and beating him. Their blood was now thoroughly up. He was their sport now. They were going to have their own back, out of him. Strange, wild creatures, they hung on him and rushed at him to bear him down. His tunic was torn right up the back, Nora had hold at the back of his collar, and was actually strangling him. Luckily the button burst. He struggled in a wild frenzy of fury and terror, almost mad terror. His tunic was simply torn off his back, his shirt-sleeves were torn away, his arms were naked. The girls rushed at him, clenched their hands on him and pulled at him: or they rushed at him and pushed him, butted him with all their might: or they struck him wild blows. He ducked and cringed and struck sideways. They became more intense.

At last he was down. They rushed on him, kneeling on him. He had neither breath nor strength to move. His face was bleeding with a long scratch, his brow was bruised.

Annie knelt on him, the other girls knelt and hung on to him. Their faces were flushed, their hair wild, their eyes were all glittering strangely. He lay at last quite still, with face averted, as an animal lies when it is defeated and at the mercy of the captor. Sometimes his eye glanced back at the wild faces of the girls. His breast rose heavily, his wrists were torn.

"Now, then, my fellow!" gasped Annie at length. "Now then—now——"

At the sound of her terrifying, cold triumph, he suddenly started to struggle as an animal might, but the girls threw themselves upon him with unnatural strength and power, forcing him down.

"Yes—now, then!" gasped Annie at length.

And there was a dead silence, in which the thud of heart-beating was to be heard. It was a suspense of pure silence in every soul.

"Now you know where you are," said Annie.

The sight of his white, bare arm maddened the girls. He lay in a kind of trance of fear and antagonism. They felt themselves filled with supernatural strength.

Suddenly Polly started to laugh—to giggle wildly—helplessly—and Emma and Muriel joined in. But Annie and Nora and Laura remained the same, tense, watchful, with gleaming eyes. He winced away from these eyes.

"Yes," said Annie, in a curious low tone, secret and deadly. "Yes! You've got it now! You know what you've done, don't you? You know what you've done."

He made no sound nor sign, but lay with bright, averted eyes, and averted, bleeding face.

"You ought to be *killed*, that's what you ought," said Annie tensely. "You ought to be *killed*." And there was a terrifying lust in her voice.

Polly was ceasing to laugh, and giving long-drawn oh-h-hs and sighs as she came to herself.

"He's got to choose," she said vaguely.

"Oh, yes, he has," said Laura, with vindictive decision.

"Do you hear—do you hear?" said Annie. And with a sharp movement that made him wince, she turned his face to her.

"Do you hear?" she repeated, shaking him.

But he was quite dumb. She fetched him a sharp slap on the face. He started, and his eyes widened. Then his face darkened with defiance, after all.

"Do you hear?" she repeated.

He only looked at her with hostile eyes.

"Speak!" she said, putting her face devilishly near his.

"What?" he said, almost overcome.

"You've got to *choose*!" she cried, as if it were some terrible menace, and as if it hurt her that she could not exact more.

"What?" he said in fear.

"Choose your girl, Coddy. You've got to choose her now. And you'll get your neck broken if you play any more of your tricks, my boy. You're settled now."

There was a pause. Again he averted his face. He was cunning in his overthrow. He did not give in to them really—no, not if they tore him to bits.

"All right, then," he said, "I choose Annie." His voice was strange and full of malice. Annie let go of him as if he had been a hot coal.

"He's chosen Annie!" said the girls in chorus.

"Me!" cried Annie. She was still kneeling, but away from him. He was still lying prostrate, with averted face. The girls grouped uneasily around.

"Me!" repeated Annie, with a terrible bitter accent.

Then she got up, drawing away from him with strange disgust and bitterness.

"I wouldn't touch him," she said.

But her face quivered with a kind of agony, she seemed as if she would fall. The other girls turned aside. He remained lying on the floor, with his torn clothes and bleeding, averted face.

"Oh, if he's chosen——" said Polly.

"I don't want him—he can choose again," said Annie, with the same rather bitter hopelessness.

"Get up," said Polly, lifting his shoulder. "Get up."

He rose slowly, a strange, ragged, dazed creature. The girls eyed him from a distance, curiously, furtively, dangerously.

"Who wants him?" cried Laura roughly.

"Nobody," they answered with contempt. Yet each one of them waited for him to look at her, hoped he would look at her. All except Annie, and something was broken in her.

He, however, kept his face closed and averted from them all. There was a silence of the end. He picked up the torn pieces of his tunic, without knowing what to do with them. The girls stood about uneasily, flushed, panting, tidying their hair and their dress unconsciously, and watching him. He looked at none of them. He espied his cap in a corner and went and picked it up. He put it on his head, and one of the girls burst into a shrill, hysteric laugh at the sight he presented. He, however, took no heed but went straight to where his overcoat hung on a peg. The girls moved away from contact with him as if he had been an electric wire. He put on his coat and buttoned it down. Then he rolled his tunic-rags into a bundle, and stood before the locked door, dumbly.

"Open the door, somebody," said Laura.

"Annie's got the key," said one.

Annie silently offered the key to the girls. Nora unlocked the door.

"Tit for tat, old man," she said. "Show yourself a man, and don't bear a grudge."

But without a word or sign he had opened the door and gone, his face closed, his head dropped.

"That'll learn him," said Laura.

"Coddy!" said Nora.

"Shut up, for God's sake!" cried Annie fiercely, as if in torture.

"Well, I'm about ready to go, Polly. Look sharp!" said Muriel.

The girls were all anxious to be off. They were tidying themselves hurriedly with mute, stupefied faces.

COMMENTARY

From the tone of its opening paragraphs it would be impossible to predict the kind of story that "Tickets, Please" turns out to be. Lawrence is unblushing in the quaint whimsicality with which he personifies the little tramcar, telling us that it seems "to pause and purr with curious satisfaction," that it is "abashed by the great crimson and cream-coloured city cars, but still perky, jaunty, somewhat dare-devil . . ." He refers to it with the coy, manipulating "we" that is deplorably used with children ("We don't spit at our little sister, do we?") or hospital patients ("We are going to have our injection now."). And with the same pronoun he contrives a companionable trio of tramcar, author, and reader, in which we are presumed to connive at the enthusiasm of his "Hurray!" and be reassured by his ". . . but what matter!" When he tells us, "Therefore, there is a certain wild romance aboard these cars—and in the sturdy bosom of Annie herself," it is as if he were cozily putting his arm around Annie's shoulder to introduce her as a really nice girl who is bound to prove a satisfactory heroine.

In short, the beginning of the story commits itself to a manner which is all too consciously "literary," all too aware of its airs and graces of style, and all too pleased with itself and its jolly intimacy with the reader. Prose of this kind, with its avowed intention of charming the reader and making him warm and comfortable, was common enough in the fiction of the Victorian period, but it has long since gone out of fashion. And it is at the furthest possible remove from the startling episode which makes the substance of the story and from the quick, spare language in which its violence is set forth: "He went forward, rather vaguely. She had taken off her belt, and swinging it, she fetched him a sharp blow over the head with the buckle end. He sprang and seized her. But immediately the other girls rushed upon him, pulling and tearing and beating him." Prose—not to say action—as direct as this puts all whimsy, coziness, and jollity to rout.

Whether or not Lawrence consciously intended a particular effect by his use of these two widely divergent styles we do not know. But once we become aware of the contrast between them, we can scarcely fail to look for meaning in it. And the meaning we are most likely to discover is social—the startling discrepancy between the way the story opens and the way it develops may be said to represent the difference between an old and a new conception of women. At the beginning of the story Annie seems ready to be the satisfactory heroine of a Victorian novel; with her sturdiness go a modesty and reserve which would once have been praised as "womanly." She disappoints this first judgment in a sufficiently remarkable way. Her conduct exemplifies the drastic revision of the notion of womanliness that was made after the First World War.

All through the nineteenth century, in the United States and in certain countries of Europe, there had been an ever-growing awareness that the status of women could no longer remain what it had traditionally been. The First World War, if only because it required many women to come out of the home and do the work of men, effected a change in the relation of the sexes which had long been in preparation and which was perhaps the most radical that history can show. Its importance was not underestimated by the fiction and drama of the time. The relations between men and women came to be thought of as a "problem" which writers undertook to "solve" or at least to state as clearly and honestly as they could. And of all writers none responded to the new sexual situation quite so intensely as D. H. Lawrence, with so much sensitivity and awareness, and with so passionate a commitment of both feeling and intelligence.

Lawrence was certainly not the first modern writer to propose the idea that between men and women there exists an intense antagonism. Nor is that idea only a modern one. Chaucer celebrated the fidelity and docility of women but he also took full notice of their desire to resist male dominance and even to gain what he called "the mastery." And the imagination of the Greeks, as their drama and legends abundantly testify, was haunted by the thought of the hostility which women might bear toward men. But the idea of the antagonism of the sexes as propounded by modern authors—Ibsen, Nietzsche, Strindberg, and Shaw may be mentioned as Lawrence's predecessors in the treatment of the subject—came to the modern consciousness as a novelty and a shock. Especially for Lawrence, it was on the sexual battlefield that the fiercest conflicts of civilization announced themselves.

But Lawrence was no less engaged by the mutual dependence of the sexes. And it is his equal recognition of both the antagonism and the reciprocal need, and of the interplay between the two, that gives his writing about love its unique air of discovery and truth. "Tickets, Please" is one of Lawrence's early stories, but it constitutes a summary statement of the emotional situation with which Lawrence was to deal throughout his career as a writer.

In their dress, in their manner of life and in their deportment, these girl-conductors of the tramline strikingly describe this century's revolution in the life of women. They are spoken of as "fearless young hussies"—they have learned to live on terms of equality, or apparent equality, with men, and to accept the manners of a rough male society. They had never, it is true, pretended to the standards of behavior that prevailed for the women of the British upper classes, which had shaped the prevailing ideal of womanliness as it was celebrated in novels. These girl-conductors had not been brought up to be *ladies*. But most of them had certainly been brought up to be "respectable." They leave respectability a long way behind when they undertake to deal with Coddy Raynor.

The maenad-like behavior of these working-class girls did have, it is worth noting, a degree of upper-class sanction. It had been validated by the conduct of many women of the very gentlest breeding, for the suffragettes, as the women who agitated for the right to vote were called, came largely from the upper classes yet did not shrink from violent means to enforce their claim to political equality with men, pouring acid into letter-boxes, destroying the putting-greens of golf courses, beating cabinet ministers over the head with umbrellas, and fighting strenuously when the police took them into custody. But the suffragettes acted out of outraged pride at the implication that women were not worthy to vote. The girls who make up the fierce little vigilance party of "Tickets, Please" are no less moved by an outrage done to their pride, but what they resent is not the political and social superiority that men insist on but the male sexual advantage.

These women need Coddy more than he needs them, and all the more because the war has created a shortage of men. They are now independent economically, but they can fulfill themselves only in marriage, while for Coddy marriage represents nothing but a surrender of freedom, a submission to whatever woman he marries, a yielding of *his* pride. From the point of view of equity, the situation is infamous and not to be borne. And yet no sooner have the girls succeeded in redressing the balance against him, at least symbolically and for the moment, than they are appalled by what they have done. They undertook to destroy this arrogant male, to humiliate him and make him ridiculous; their success makes them feel lost and miserable. For it is exactly what they resent in Coddy Raynor—his masculine pride and arrogance, his lordly independence—that constitutes his attraction as a man and draws them to him. The rough justice that the girls deal out may have its rough rationality, but the situation they confront is not to be solved by rationality. Their desires and their needs transcend justice and reason.

And here Lawrence leaves the problem. He does not try to adjudicate between the sexes but only to set forth the actuality of the relationship—and to find pleasure in it. The pleasure is quite unmistakable. As between John Thomas Raynor and Annie Stone and her embattled comrades, Lawrence does not take sides. He delights in both parties to the sexual conflict. The actual physical embroilment is grim enough, and any reader—at least any male reader—is sure to share John Thomas's fear of the enraged women he has exploited and deceived. Yet Lawrence, without at all masking the grimness, treats it as only one element of a story that is curiously tender and predominantly humorous.

The essence of both the tenderness and the humor lies in the fact that the behavior of the girls, which is so extravagantly unwomanly, reveals them, especially Annie, in the full of their female nature—and reveals them so not only to us but to themselves. The conduct that "unsexes" them, as a Victorian moralist would have put it, makes plain the intensity of their female sexuality.

THE

ROAD

FROM

COLONUS[1]

E . M . F O R S T E R

1 8 7 9 -

For no very intelligible reason, Mr. Lucas had hurried ahead of his party. He was perhaps reaching the age at which independence becomes valuable, because it is so soon to be lost. Tired of attention and consideration, he liked breaking away from the younger members, to ride by himself, and to dismount unassisted. Perhaps he also relished that more subtle pleasure of being kept waiting for lunch, and of telling the others on their arrival that it was of no consequence.

So, with childish impatience, he battered the animal's sides with his heels, and made the muleteer bang it with a thick stick and prick it with a sharp one, and jolted down the hill sides through clumps of flowering shrubs and stretches of anemones and asphodel, till he heard the sound of running water, and came in sight of the group of plane trees where they were to have their meal.

Even in England those trees would have been remarkable, so huge were they, so interlaced, so magnificently clothed in quivering green. And here in Greece they were unique, the one cool spot in that hard brilliant landscape, already scorched by the heat of an April sun. In their midst was hidden a tiny

---

[1] In Greek mythology, the blinded King Oedipus, after wandering for many years, was led by his faithful daughter, Antigone, to a grove at Colonus. There he died. See Sophocles' play, *Oedipus at Colonus*.

Khan or country inn, a frail mud building with a broad wooden balcony in which sat an old woman spinning, while a small brown pig, eating orange peel, stood beside her. On the wet earth below squatted two children, playing some primeval game with their fingers; and their mother, none too clean either, was messing with some rice inside. As Mrs. Forman would have said, it was all very Greek, and the fastidious Mr. Lucas felt thankful that they were bringing their own food with them, and should eat it in the open air.

Still, he was glad to be there—the muleteer had helped him off—and glad that Mrs. Forman was not there to forestall his opinions—glad even that he should not see Ethel for quite half an hour. Ethel was his youngest daughter, still unmarried. She was unselfish and affectionate, and it was generally understood that she was to devote her life to her father, and be the comfort of his old age. Mrs. Forman always referred to her as Antigone, and Mr. Lucas tried to settle down to the role of Oedipus, which seemed the only one that public opinion allowed him.

He had this in common with Oedipus, that he was growing old. Even to himself it had become obvious. He had lost interest in other people's affairs, and seldom attended when they spoke to him. He was fond of talking himself but often forgot what he was going to say, and even when he succeeded, it seldom seemed worth the effort. His phrases and gestures had become stiff and set, his anecdotes, once so successful, fell flat, his silence was as meaningless as his speech. Yet he had led a healthy, active life, had worked steadily, made money, educated his children. There was nothing and no one to blame: he was simply growing old.

At the present moment, here he was in Greece, and one of the dreams of his life was realized. Forty years ago he had caught the fever of Hellenism, and all his life he had felt that could he but visit that land, he would not have lived in vain. But Athens had been dusty, Delphi wet, Thermopylae flat,[2] and he had listened with amazement and cynicism to the rapturous exclamations of his companions. Greece was like England: it was a man who was growing old, and it made no difference whether that man looked at the Thames or the Eurotas.[3] It was his last hope of contradicting that logic of experience, and it was failing.

Yet Greece had done something for him, though he did not know it. It had made him discontented, and there are stirrings of life in discontent. He knew that he was not the victim of continual ill-luck. Something great was wrong, and he was pitted against no mediocre or accidental enemy. For the last month a strange desire had possessed him to die fighting.

"Greece is the land for young people," he said to himself as he stood under the plane trees, "but I will enter into it, I will possess it. Leaves shall be green again, water shall be sweet, the sky shall be blue. They were so forty years ago, and I will win them back. I do mind being old, and I will pretend no longer."

He took two steps forward, and immediately cold waters were gurgling over his ankle.

"Where does the water come from?" he asked himself. "I do not even know that." He remembered that all the hill sides were dry; yet here the road was suddenly covered with flowing streams.

---

[2] Delphi was an ancient religious center; its ruins, on a spectacular height overlooking the sea, are generally thought among the most impressive in the world. Thermopylae is the pass where three hundred Spartans fought off the whole Persian army in 480 B.C.

[3] The river on which the ancient city of Sparta stood.

He stopped still in amazement, saying: "Water out of a tree—out of a hollow tree? I never saw nor thought of that before."

For the enormous plane that leant towards the Khan was hollow—it had been burnt out for charcoal—and from its living trunk there gushed an impetuous spring, coating the bark with fern and moss, and flowing over the mule track to create fertile meadows beyond. The simple country folk had paid to beauty and mystery such tribute as they could, for in the rind of the tree a shrine was cut, holding a lamp and a little picture of the Virgin, inheritor of the Naiad's and Dryad's[4] joint abode.

"I never saw anything so marvellous before," said Mr. Lucas. "I could even step inside the trunk and see where the water comes from."

For a moment he hesitated to violate the shrine. Then he remembered with a smile his own thought—"the place shall be mine; I will enter it and possess it" —and leapt almost aggressively on to a stone within.

The water pressed up steadily and noiselessly from the hollow roots and hidden crevices of the plane, forming a wonderful amber pool ere it spilt over the lip of bark on to the earth outside. Mr. Lucas tasted it and it was sweet, and when he looked up the black funnel of the trunk he saw sky which was blue, and some leaves which were green; and he remembered, without smiling, another of his thoughts.

Others had been before him—indeed he had a curious sense of companionship. Little votive offerings to the presiding Power were fastened on to the bark— tiny arms and legs and eyes in tin, grotesque models of the brain or the heart— all tokens of some recovery of strength or wisdom or love. There was no such thing as the solitude of nature, for the sorrows and joys of humanity had pressed even into the bosom of a tree. He spread out his arms and steadied himself against the soft charred wood, and then slowly leant back, till his body was resting on the trunk behind. His eyes closed, and he had the strange feeling of one who is moving, yet at peace—the feeling of the swimmer, who, after long struggling with chopping seas, finds that after all the tide will sweep him to his goal.

So he lay motionless, conscious only of the stream below his feet, and that all things were a stream, in which he was moving.

He was aroused at last by a shock—the shock of an arrival perhaps, for when he opened his eyes, something unimagined, indefinable, had passed over all things, and made them intelligible and good.

There was meaning in the stoop of the old woman over her work, and in the quick motions of the little pig, and in her diminishing globe of wool. A young man came singing over the streams on a mule, and there was beauty in his pose and sincerity in his greeting. The sun made no accidental patterns upon the spreading roots of the trees, and there was intention in the nodding clumps of asphodel, and in the music of the water. To Mr. Lucas, who, in a brief space of time, had discovered not only Greece, but England and all the world and life, there seemed nothing ludicrous in the desire to hang within the tree another votive offering—a little model of an entire man.

"Why, here's papa, playing at being Merlin."[5]

[4] Nymphs of springs and trees, respectively.
[5] The magician of the Arthurian legends, who is supposed to have been imprisoned in a whitethorn tree.

All unnoticed they had arrived—Ethel, Mrs. Forman, Mr. Graham, and the English-speaking dragoman. Mr. Lucas peered out at them suspiciously. They had suddenly become unfamiliar, and all that they did seemed strained and coarse.

"Allow me to give you a hand," said Mr. Graham, a young man who was always polite to his elders.

Mr. Lucas felt annoyed. "Thank you, I can manage perfectly well by myself," he replied. His foot slipped as he stepped out of the tree, and went into the spring.

"Oh papa, my papa!" said Ethel, "what are you doing? Thank goodness I have got a change for you on the mule."

She tended him carefully, giving him clean socks and dry boots, and then sat him down on the rug beside the lunch basket, while she went with the others to explore the grove.

They came back in ecstasies, in which Mr. Lucas tried to join. But he found them intolerable. Their enthusiasm was superficial, commonplace, and spasmodic. They had no perception of the coherent beauty that was flowering around them. He tried at least to explain his feelings, and what he said was:

"I am altogether pleased with the appearance of this place. It impresses me very favourably. The trees are fine, remarkably fine for Greece, and there is something very poetic in the spring of clear running water. The people too seem kindly and civil. It is decidedly an attractive place."

Mrs. Forman upbraided him for his tepid praise.

"Oh, it is a place in a thousand!" she cried. "I could live and die here! I really would stop if I had not to be back at Athens! It reminds me of the Colonus of Sophocles."

"Well, *I* must stop," said Ethel. "I positively must."

"Yes, do! You and your father! Antigone and Oedipus. Of course you must stop at Colonus!"

Mr. Lucas was almost breathless with excitement. When he stood within the tree, he had believed that his happiness would be independent of locality. But these few minutes' conversation had undeceived him. He no longer trusted himself to journey through the world, for old thoughts, old wearinesses might be waiting to rejoin him as soon as he left the shade of the planes, and the music of the virgin water. To sleep in the Khan with the gracious, kind-eyed country people, to watch the bats flit about within the globe of shade, and see the moon turn the golden patterns into silver—one such night would place him beyond relapse, and confirm him for ever in the kingdom he had regained. But all his lips could say was: "I should be willing to put in a night here."

"You mean a week, papa! It would be sacrilege to put in less."

"A week then, a week," said his lips, irritated at being corrected, while his heart was leaping with joy. All through lunch he spoke to them no more, but watched the place he should know so well, and the people who would so soon be his companions and friends. The inmates of the Khan only consisted of an old woman, a middle-aged woman, a young man and two children, and to none of them had he spoken, yet he loved them as he loved everything that moved or breathed or existed beneath the benedictory shade of the planes.

"*En route!*" said the shrill voice of Mrs. Forman. "Ethel! Mr. Graham! The best of things must end."

"To-night," thought Mr. Lucas, "they will light the little lamp by the shrine. And when we all sit together on the balcony, perhaps they will tell me which offerings they put up."

"I beg your pardon, Mr. Lucas," said Graham, "but they want to fold up the rug you are sitting on."

Mr. Lucas got up, saying to himself: "Ethel shall go to bed first, and then I will try to tell them about my offering too—for it is a thing I must do. I think they will understand if I am left with them alone."

Ethel touched him on the cheek. "Papa! I've called you three times. All the mules are here."

"Mules? What mules?"

"Our mules. We're all waiting. Oh, Mr. Graham, do help my father on."

"I don't know what you're talking about, Ethel."

"My dearest papa, we must start. You know we have to get to Olympia to-night."

Mr. Lucas in pompous, confident tones replied: "I always did wish, Ethel, that you had a better head for plans. You know perfectly well that we are putting in a week here. It is your own suggestion."

Ethel was startled into impoliteness. "What a perfectly ridiculous idea. You must have known I was joking. Of course I meant I wished we could."

"Ah! if we could only do what we wished!" sighed Mrs. Forman, already seated on her mule.

"Surely," Ethel continued in calmer tones, "you didn't think I meant it."

"Most certainly I did. I have made all my plans on the supposition that we are stopping here, and it will be extremely inconvenient, indeed, impossible for me to start."

He delivered this remark with an air of great conviction, and Mrs. Forman and Mr. Graham had to turn away to hide their smiles.

"I am sorry I spoke so carelessly; it was wrong of me. But, you know, we can't break up our party, and even one night here would make us miss the boat at Patras."

Mrs. Forman, in an aside, called Mr. Graham's attention to the excellent way in which Ethel managed her father.

"I don't mind about the Patras boat. You said that we should stop here, and we are stopping."

It seemed as if the inhabitants of the Khan had divined in some mysterious way that the altercation touched them. The old woman stopped her spinning, while the young man and the two children stood behind Mr. Lucas, as if supporting him.

Neither arguments nor entreaties moved him. He said little, but he was absolutely determined, because for the first time he saw his daily life aright. What need had he to return to England? Who would miss him? His friends were dead or cold. Ethel loved him in a way, but, as was right, she had other interests. His other children he seldom saw. He had only one other relative, his sister Julia, whom he both feared and hated. It was no effort to struggle. He would be a fool as well as a coward if he stirred from the place which brought him happiness and peace.

At last Ethel, to humour him, and not disinclined to air her modern Greek, went into the Khan with the astonished dragoman to look at the rooms. The woman inside received them with loud welcomes, and the young man, when no one was looking, began to lead Mr. Lucas' mule to the stable.

"Drop it, you brigand!" shouted Graham, who always declared that foreigners could understand English if they chose. He was right, for the man obeyed, and they all stood waiting for Ethel's return.

She emerged at last, with close-gathered skirts, followed by the dragoman bearing the little pig, which he had bought at a bargain.

"My dear papa, I will do all I can for you, but stop in that Khan—no."

"Are there—fleas?" asked Mrs. Forman.

Ethel intimated that "fleas" was not the word.

"Well, I am afraid that settles it," said Mrs. Forman, "I know how particular Mr. Lucas is."

"It does not settle it," said Mr. Lucas. "Ethel, you go on. I do not want you. I don't know why I ever consulted you. I shall stop here alone."

"That is absolute nonsense," said Ethel, losing her temper. "How can you be left alone at your age? How would you get your meals or your bath? All your letters are waiting for you at Patras. You'll miss the boat. That means missing the London operas, and upsetting all your engagements for the month. And as if you could travel by yourself!"

"They might knife you," was Mr. Graham's contribution.

The Greeks said nothing; but whenever Mr. Lucas looked their way, they beckoned him towards the Khan. The children would even have drawn him by the coat, and the old woman on the balcony stopped her almost completed spinning, and fixed him with mysterious appealing eyes. As he fought, the issue assumed gigantic proportions, and he believed that he was not merely stopping because he had regained youth or seen beauty or found happiness, but because in that place and with those people a supreme event was awaiting him which would transfigure the face of the world. The moment was so tremendous that he abandoned words and arguments as useless, and rested on the strength of his mighty unrevealed allies: silent men, murmuring water, and whispering trees. For the whole place called with one voice, articulate to him, and his garrulous opponents became every minute more meaningless and absurd. Soon they would be tired and go chattering away into the sun, leaving him to the cool grove and the moonlight and the destiny he foresaw.

Mrs. Forman and the dragoman had indeed already started, amid the piercing screams of the little pig, and the struggle might have gone on indefinitely if Ethel had not called in Mr. Graham.

"Can you help me?" she whispered. "He is absolutely unmanageable."

"I'm no good at arguing—but if I could help you in any other way——" and he looked down complacently at his well-made figure.

Ethel hesitated. Then she said: "Help me in any way you can. After all, it is for his good that we do it."

"Then have his mule led up behind him."

So when Mr. Lucas thought he had gained the day, he suddenly felt himself lifted off the ground, and sat sideways on the saddle, and at the same time the mule started off at a trot. He said nothing, for he had nothing to say, and even his face showed little emotion as he felt the shade pass and heard the sound of the water cease. Mr. Graham was running at his side, hat in hand, apologizing.

"I know I had no business to do it, and I do beg your pardon awfully. But I do hope that some day you too will feel that I was—damn!"

A stone had caught him in the middle of the back. It was thrown by the little boy, who was pursuing them along the mule track. He was followed by his sister, also throwing stones.

Ethel screamed to the dragoman, who was some way ahead with Mrs. Forman, but before he could rejoin them, another adversary appeared. It was the young Greek, who had cut them off in front, and now dashed down at Mr. Lucas' bridle. Fortunately Graham was an expert boxer, and it did not take him a moment to beat down the youth's feeble defence, and to send him sprawling with a bleeding mouth into the asphodel. By this time the dragoman had arrived, the children, alarmed at the fate of their brother, had desisted, and the rescue party, if such it is to be considered, retired in disorder to the trees.

"Little devils!" said Graham, laughing with triumph. "That's the modern Greek all over. Your father meant money if he stopped, and they consider we were taking it out of their pocket."

"Oh, they are terrible—simple savages! I don't know how I shall ever thank you. You've saved my father."

"I only hope you didn't think me brutal."

"No," replied Ethel with a little sigh. "I admire strength."

Meanwhile the cavalcade reformed, and Mr. Lucas, who, as Mrs. Forman said, bore his disappointment wonderfully well, was put comfortably on to his mule. They hurried up the opposite hillside, fearful of another attack, and it was not until they had left the eventful place far behind that Ethel found an opportunity to speak to her father and ask his pardon for the way she had treated him.

"You seemed so different, dear father, and you quite frightened me. Now I feel that you are your old self again."

He did not answer, and she concluded that he was not unnaturally offended at her behavior.

By one of those curious tricks of mountain scenery, the place they had left an hour before suddenly reappeared far below them. The Khan was hidden under the green dome, but in the open there still stood three figures, and through the pure air rose up a faint cry of defiance or farewell.

Mr. Lucas stopped irresolutely, and let the reins fall from his hand.

"Come, father dear," said Ethel gently.

He obeyed, and in another moment a spur of the hill hid the dangerous scene for ever.

II

It was breakfast time, but the gas was alight, owing to the fog. Mr. Lucas was in the middle of an account of a bad night he had spent. Ethel, who was to be married in a few weeks, had her arms on the table, listening.

"First the door bell rang, then you came back from the theatre. Then the dog started, and after the dog the cat. And at three in the morning a young hooligan passed by singing. Oh yes: then there was the water gurgling in the pipe above my head."

"I think that was only the bath water running away," said Ethel, looking rather worn.

"Well, there's nothing I dislike more than running water. It's perfectly impossible to sleep in the house. I shall give it up. I shall give notice next quarter. I shall tell the landlord plainly, 'The reason I am giving up the house is this: it is perfectly impossible to sleep in it.' If he says—says—well, what has he got to say?"

"Some more toast, father?"

"Thank you, my dear." He took it, and there was an interval of peace.

But he soon recommenced. "I'm not going to submit to the practising next door as tamely as they think. I wrote and told them so—didn't I?"

"Yes," said Ethel, who had taken care that the letter should not reach. "I have seen the governess, and she has promised to arrange it differently. And Aunt Julia hates noise. It will sure to be all right."

Her aunt, being the only unattached member of the family, was coming to keep house for her father when she left him. The reference was not a happy one, and Mr. Lucas commenced a series of half articulate sighs, which was only stopped by the arrival of the post.

"Oh, what a parcel!" cried Ethel. "For me! What can it be! Greek stamps. This is most exciting!"

It proved to be some asphodel bulbs, sent by Mrs. Forman from Athens for planting in the conservatory.

"Doesn't it bring it all back! You remember the asphodels, father. And all wrapped up in Greek newspapers. I wonder if I can read them still. I used to be able to, you know."

She rattled on, hoping to conceal the laughter of the children next door—a favourite source of querulousness at breakfast time.

"Listen to me! 'A rural disaster.' Oh, I've hit on something sad. But never mind. 'Last Tuesday at Plataniste, in the province of Messenia, a shocking tragedy occurred. A large tree'—aren't I getting on well?—'blew down in the night and'—wait a minute—oh, dear! 'crushed to death the five occupants of the little Khan there, who had apparently been sitting in the balcony. The bodies of Maria Rhomaides, the aged proprietress, and of her daughter, aged forty-six, were easily recognizable, whereas that of her grandson'—oh, the rest is really too horrid; I wish I had never tried it, and what's more I feel to have heard the name Plataniste before. We didn't stop there, did we, in the spring?"

"We had lunch," said Mr. Lucas, with a faint expression of trouble on his vacant face. "Perhaps it was where the dragoman bought the pig."

"Of course," said Ethel in a nervous voice. "Where the dragoman bought the little pig. How terrible!"

"Very terrible!" said her father, whose attention was wandering to the noisy children next door. Ethel suddenly started to her feet with genuine interest.

"Good gracious!" she exclaimed. "This is an old paper. It happened not lately but in April—the night of Tuesday the eighteenth—and we—we must have been there in the afternoon."

"So we were," said Mr. Lucas. She put her hand to her heart, scarcely able to speak.

"Father, dear father, I must say it: you wanted to stop there. All those people, those poor half-savage people, tried to keep you, and they're dead. The whole place, it says, is in ruins, and even the stream has changed its course. Father, dear, if it had not been for me, and if Arthur had not helped me, you must have been killed."

Mr. Lucas waved his hand irritably. "It is not a bit of good speaking to the governess, I shall write to the landlord and say, 'The reason I am giving up the house is this: the dog barks, the children next door are intolerable, and I cannot stand the noise of running water.'"

Ethel did not check his babbling. She was aghast at the narrowness of the escape, and for a long time kept silence. At last she said: "Such marvellous deliverance does make one believe in Providence."

Mr. Lucas, who was still composing his letter to the landlord, did not reply.

COMMENTARY

In pagan days it was the custom to place on certain shrines the representation of a once-afflicted part of the body which had presumably been healed by the divinity. The practice continued in many Christian communities and it is still kept up in Greece. To Mr. Lucas in his native England the custom would no doubt have seemed the crudest of superstitions. But as he stands in the tree-shrine and sees the "tiny arms and legs and eyes in tin, grotesque models of the brain or the heart—all tokens of some recovery of strength or wisdom or love," he not only comprehends the impulse behind these votive displays but thinks that he would himself like to make just such an offering, "a little model of an entire man."

It is a long time, we gather, since Mr. Lucas has felt like an entire man. Or perhaps he has never felt so, and if he now has a sense of wholeness, it is because he has had a unique and crucial experience. Its beginning, we are told, was a sensation of peace so great that he had been almost unconscious; then he had been aroused by a shock which was "the shock of an arrival perhaps, for when he opened his eyes, something unimagined, indefinable, had passed over all things, and made them seem intelligible and good." The goodness is probably indispensable to the nature of Mr. Lucas's experience, but the crucial word here is *intelligible* and its purport is emphasized in the passage that follows. "There was meaning in the stoop of the old woman over her work, and in the quick motions of the little pig, and in her diminishing globe of wool. . . . The sun made no accidental patterns upon the spreading roots of the tree, and there was intention in the nodding clumps of asphodel, and in the music of the water."

The intelligibility of things that Mr. Lucas suddenly perceives can never yield a statement. There is no way to formulate the "meaning" of the stoop of the old woman and the motions of the little pig, or to say to what end the "intention" of the asphodels and the music of the water is directed. The sense— or, more accurately, the sensation—of a world happily available to understanding is an experience which, although it often has a quasi-mystical aspect, is not uncommon; it arises from a condition of inner harmony or peace such as Mr. Lucas has known. This sudden access of peace had not come to Mr. Lucas because of the beauty of the little hamlet, although this surely had made it the more possible. It had come to him out of his realization and acceptance of death.

Although he does not explicitly think about death, death is in his mind: it is here in this hamlet that he has had "the feeling of the swimmer, who, after long struggling with chopping seas, finds that after all the tide will sweep him to his goal." It is in this place that he wishes to end his days. The place is none other than Colonus.

Of course it is not Colonus in literal actuality. The real town, in ancient times, had been a suburb of Athens. It long ago lost its identity, having been absorbed by the city, of which it is now only an indistinguishable district, rather shabbier than others. But it had once been known for its beauty and had been loved by the great poet whose birthplace it was—Sophocles in his extreme old age made it the scene of the last play of his long career and in a lovely choral ode celebrated the holy peace of the town and its flowers, streams, and trees. In *Oedipus at Colonus* the aged hero of *Oedipus Rex* (see pages 3 ff. and the comment on the play, page 44) comes to the town on the last day of his life. Blinded by his own hand in retribution for his terrible sin of having killed his father and married his mother, although all unknowingly, and exiled by his own decree, he has wandered the earth attended only by his daughter Antigone. Sin and suffering have not subdued his spirit; the former king still reveals the pride and quick anger that had marked him in the days of his glory. What for many readers is most memorable in the play is the contrast between certain aspects of the character of Oedipus and the manner of his departure from life. His pride and anger often announce themselves in bitterness and querulousness but all these manifestations which we think unworthy of a hero are forgotten in his response to the knowledge that the hour of his death has come and in his going alone into the sacred grove to meet it. By his death Oedipus is raised to a dignity greater than he has ever had in life.

Mr. Lucas has nothing of the tragic grandeur of Oedipus, and the death that might have come to him in the hamlet could scarcely have had the high significance of the hero's passing, which was less a death than an apotheosis. Yet the moment of transcendence that comes to Mr. Lucas when he realizes and accepts his death raises him, we feel, to a dignity that makes possible the comparison of this commonplace man with Oedipus, and we respond without irony to the defeat that is summed up in one word of the story's title, the sad preposition *from*. "Death destroys a man," says Mr. Forster in his novel *Howards End*, "but the idea of death saves him"; and when Mr. Lucas is led down the road from his Colonus, we know that he has been deprived of his salvation. Had he stayed he would have died that night—"What a deliverance," says his daughter Ethel when she reads of the fall of the great tree in the storm and realizes the narrowness of her father's escape. But we, seeing Mr. Lucas in his suburban safety, given over to senile petulance about the noise of children and running water, are as little inclined to agree with this false Antigone as we are with Gretta Conroy when in Joyce's "The Dead" (see page 649) she says of Michael Furey, " 'Isn't it a terrible thing to die so young as that?' "

DISORDER

AND

EARLY

SORROW

THOMAS MANN

1875–1955

THE PRINCIPAL DISH at dinner had been croquettes made of turnip greens. So there follows a trifle,[1] concocted out of those dessert powders we use nowadays,[2] that taste like almond soap. Xaver, the youthful manservant, in his outgrown striped jacket, white woollen gloves, and yellow sandals, hands it round, and the "big folk" take this opportunity to remind their father, tactfully, that company is coming today.

The "big folk" are two, Ingrid and Bert. Ingrid is brown-eyed, eighteen, and perfectly delightful. She is on the eve of her exams, and will probably pass them, if only because she knows how to wind masters, and even headmasters, round her finger. She does not, however, mean to use her certificate once she gets it; having leanings towards the stage, on the ground of her ingratiating smile, her equally ingratiating voice, and a marked and irresistible talent for burlesque. Bert is blond and seventeen. He intends to get done with school somehow, anyhow, and fling himself into the arms of life. He will be a dancer, or a cabaret actor, possibly even a waiter—but not a waiter anywhere else save at Cairo, the night-club, whither he has once already taken flight, at five in the morning, and been brought back

---

[1] A dessert, usually made with sponge cake and custard.
[2] The period of the ruinous inflation in Germany after World War I. Mann's story appeared in 1925.

crestfallen. Bert bears a strong resemblance to the youthful manservant. Xaver Kleinsgutl, of about the same age as himself; not because he looks common—in features he is strikingly like his father, Professor Cornelius—but by reason of an approximation of types, due in its turn to far-reaching compromises in matters of dress and bearing generally. Both lads wear their heavy hair very long on top, with a cursory parting in the middle, and give their heads the same characteristic toss to throw it off the forehead. When one of them leaves the house, by the garden gate, bareheaded in all weathers, in a blouse rakishly girt with a leather strap, and sheers off bent well over with his head on one side; or else mounts his push-bike—Xaver makes free with his employers', of both sexes, or even, in acutely irresponsible mood, with the Professor's own—Dr. Cornelius from his bedroom window cannot, for the life of him, tell whether he is looking at his son or his servant. Both, he thinks, look like young moujiks.[3] And both are impassioned cigarette-smokers, though Bert has not the means to compete with Xaver, who smokes as many as thirty a day of a brand named after a popular cinema star. The big folk call their father and mother the "old folk"—not behind their backs, but as a form of address and in all affection: "Hullo, old folks," they will say; though Cornelius is only forty-seven years old and his wife eight years younger. And the Professor's parents, who lead in his household the humble and hesitant life of the really old, are on the big folk's lips the "ancients." As for the "little folk," Ellie and Snapper, who take their meals upstairs with blue-faced Ann— so-called because of her prevailing facial hue—Ellie and Snapper follow their mother's example and address their father by his first name, Abel. Unutterably comic it sounds, in its pert, confiding familiarity; particularly on the lips, in the sweet accents, of five-year-old Eleanor, who is the image of Frau Cornelius's baby pictures and whom the Professor loves above everything else in the world.

"Darling old thing," says Ingrid affably, laying her large but shapely hand on his, as he presides in proper middle-class style over the family table, with her on his left and the mother opposite: "Parent mine, may I ever so gently jog your memory, for you have probably forgotten: this is the afternoon we were to have our little jollification, our turkey-trot with eats to match. You haven't a thing to do but just bear up and not funk it; everything will be over by nine o'clock."

"Oh—ah!" says Cornelius, his face falling. "Good!" he goes on, and nods his head to show himself in harmony with the inevitable. "I only meant—is this really the day? Thursday, yes. How time flies! Well, what time are they coming?"

"Half past four they'll be dropping in, I should say," answers Ingrid, to whom her brother leaves the major rôle in all dealings with the father. Upstairs, while he is resting, he will hear scarcely anything, and from seven to eight he takes his walk. He can slip out by the terrace if he likes.

"Tut!" says Cornelius deprecatingly, as who should say: "You exaggerate." But Bert puts in: "It's the one evening in the week Wanja doesn't have to play. Any other night he'd have to leave by half past six, which would be painful for all concerned."

Wanja is Ivan Herzl, the celebrated young leading man at the Stadttheater.[4] Bert and Ingrid are on intimate terms with him, they often visit him in his dressing-room and have tea. He is an artist of the modern school, who stands on the stage in strange and, to the professor's mind, utterly affected dancing attitudes,

[3] Russian peasants.
[4] The municipal theater in Munich.

and shrieks lamentably. To a professor of history, all highly repugnant; but Bert has entirely succumbed to Herzl's influence, blackens the lower rim of his eyelids—despite painful but fruitless scenes with the father—and with youthful carelessness of the ancestral anguish declares that not only will he take Herzl for his model if he becomes a dancer, but in case he turns out to be a waiter at the Cairo he means to walk precisely thus.

Cornelius slightly raises his brows and makes his son a little bow—indicative of the unassumingness and self-abnegation that befits his age. You could not call it a mocking bow or suggestive in any special sense. Bert may refer it to himself or equally to his so talented friend.

"Who else is coming?" next inquires the master of the house. They mention various people, names all more or less familiar, from the city, from the suburban colony, from Ingrid's school. They still have some telephoning to do, they say. They have to phone Max. This is Max Hergesell, an engineering student; Ingrid utters his name in the nasal drawl which according to her is the traditional intonation of all the Hergesells. She goes on to parody it in the most abandonedly funny and lifelike way, and the parents laugh until they nearly choke over the wretched trifle. For even in these times when something funny happens people have to laugh.

From time to time the telephone bell rings in the Professor's study, and the big folk run across, knowing it is their affair. Many people had to give up their telephones the last time the price rose, but so far the Corneliuses have been able to keep theirs, just as they have kept their villa, which was built before the war, by dint of the salary Cornelius draws as professor of history—a million marks, and more or less adequate to the chances and changes of post-war life. The house is comfortable, even elegant, though sadly in need of repairs that cannot be made for lack of materials, and at present disfigured by iron stoves with long pipes. Even so, it is still the proper setting of the upper middle class, though they themselves look odd enough in it, with their worn and turned clothing and altered way of life. The children, of course, know nothing else; to them it is normal and regular, they belong by birth to the "villa proletariat." The problem of clothing troubles them not at all. They and their like have evolved a costume to fit the time, by poverty out of taste for innovation: in summer it consists of scarcely more than a belted linen smock and sandals. The middle-class parents find things rather more difficult.

The big folk's table-napkins hang over their chair-backs, they talk with their friends over the telephone. These friends are the invited guests who have rung up to accept or decline or arrange; and the conversation is carried on in the jargon of the clan, full of slang and high spirits, of which the old folk understand hardly a word. These consult together meantime about the hospitality to be offered to the impending guests. The Professor displays a middle-class ambitiousness: he wants to serve a sweet—or something that looks like a sweet—after the Italian salad and brownbread sandwiches. But Frau Cornelius says that would be going too far. The guests would not expect it, she is sure—and the big folk, returning once more to their trifle, agree with her.

The mother of the family is of the same general type as Ingrid, though not so tall. She is languid; the fantastic difficulties of the housekeeping have broken and worn her. She really ought to go and take a cure,[5] but feels incapable; the

_____
[5] A rest cure, a visit to a spa.

floor is always swaying under her feet, and everything seems upside down. She speaks of what is uppermost in her mind: the eggs, they simply must be bought today. Six thousand marks apiece they are, and just so many are to be had on this one day of the week at one single shop fifteen minutes' journey away. Whatever else they do, the big folk must go and fetch them immediately after luncheon, with Danny, their neighbour's son, who will soon be calling for them; and Xaver Kleinsgutl will don civilian garb and attend his young master and mistress. For no single household is allowed more than five eggs a week; therefore the young people will enter the shop singly, one after another, under assumed names, and thus wring twenty eggs from the shopkeeper for the Cornelius family. This enterprise is the sporting event of the week for all participants, not excepting the moujik Kleinsgutl, and most of all for Ingrid and Bert, who delight in misleading and mystifying their fellow-men and would revel in the performance even if it did not achieve one single egg. They adore impersonating fictitious characters; they love to sit in a bus and carry on long lifelike conversations in a dialect which they otherwise never speak, the most commonplace dialogue about politics and people and the price of food, while the whole bus listens open-mouthed to this incredibly ordinary prattle, though with a dark suspicion all the while that something is wrong somewhere. The conversation waxes ever more shameless, it enters into revolting detail about these people who do not exist. Ingrid can make her voice sound ever so common and twittering and shrill as she impersonates a shop-girl with an illegitimate child, said child being a son with sadistic tendencies, who lately out in the country treated a cow with such unnatural cruelty that no Christian could have borne to see it. Bert nearly explodes at her twittering, but restrains himself and displays a grisly sympathy; he and the unhappy shop-girl entering into a long, stupid, depraved, and shuddery conversation over the particular morbid cruelty involved; until an old gentleman opposite, sitting with his ticket folded between his index finger and his seal ring, can bear it no more and makes public protest against the nature of the themes these young folk are discussing with such particularity. He uses the Greek plural: "themata." Whereat Ingrid pretends to be dissolving in tears, and Bert behaves as though his wrath against the old gentleman was with difficulty being held in check and would probably burst out before long. He clenches his fists, he gnashes his teeth, he shakes from head to foot; and the unhappy old gentleman, whose intentions had been of the best, hastily leaves the bus at the next stop.

Such are the diversions of the big folk. The telephone plays a prominent part in them: they ring up any and everybody—members of government, opera singers, dignitaries of the Church—in the character of shop assistants, or perhaps as Lord or Lady Doolittle. They are only with difficulty persuaded that they have the wrong number. Once they emptied their parents' card-tray[6] and distributed its contents among the neighbours' letter-boxes, wantonly, yet not without enough impish sense of the fitness of things to make it highly upsetting. God only knowing why certain people should have called where they did.

Xaver comes in to clear away, tossing the hair out of his eyes. Now that he has taken off his gloves you can see the yellow chain-ring[7] on his left hand. And as

[6] A tray on which visitors had left calling cards.
[7] A wrist chain, something like an identification chain or charm bracelet, worn by young men of bohemian tendencies at this time. It sometimes conveyed a slight hint of effeminacy.

the Professor finishes his watery eight-thousand-mark beer and lights a cigarette, the little folk can be heard scrambling down the stair, coming, by established custom, for their after-dinner call on Father and Mother. They storm the dining-room, after a struggle with the latch clutched by both pairs of little hands at once; their clumsy small feet twinkle over the carpet, in red felt slippers with the socks falling down on them. With prattle and shoutings each makes for his own place: Snapper to Mother, to climb on her lap, boast of all he has eaten, and thump his fat little tum; Ellie to her Abel, so much hers because she is so very much his; because she consciously luxuriates in the deep tenderness—like all deep feeling, concealing a melancholy strain—with which he holds her small form embraced; in the love in his eyes as he kisses her little fairy hand or the sweet brow with its delicate tracery of tiny blue veins.

The little folk look like each other, with the strong undefined likeness of brother and sister. In clothing and haircut they are twins. Yet they are sharply distinguished after all, and quite on sex lines. It is a little Adam and a little Eve. Not only is Snapper the sturdier and more compact, he appears consciously to emphasize his four-year-old masculinity in speech, manner, and carriage, lifting his shoulders and letting the little arms hang down quite like a young American athlete, drawing down his mouth when he talks and seeking to give his voice a gruff and forthright ring. But all this masculinity is the result of effort rather than natively his. Born and brought up in these desolate, distracted times, he has been endowed by them with an unstable and hypersensitive nervous system and suffers greatly under life's disharmonies. He is prone to sudden anger and outbursts of bitter tears, stamping his feet at every trifle; for this reason he is his mother's special nursling and care. His round, round eyes are chestnut brown and already inclined to squint, so that he will need glasses in the near future. His little nose is long, the mouth small—the father's nose and mouth they are, more plainly than ever since the Professor shaved his pointed beard and goes smooth-faced. The pointed beard had become impossible—even professors must make some concession to the changing times.

But the little daughter sits on her father's knee, his Eleonorchen,[8] his little Eve, so much more gracious a little being, so much sweeter-faced than her brother—and he holds his cigarette away from her while she fingers his glasses with her dainty wee hands. The lenses are divided for reading and distance, and each day they tease her curiosity afresh.

At bottom he suspects that his wife's partiality may have a firmer basis than his own: that Snapper's refractory masculinity perhaps is solider stuff than his own little girl's more explicit charm and grace. But the heart will not be commanded, that he knows; and once and for all his heart belongs to the little one, as it has since the day she came, since the first time he saw her. Almost always when he holds her in his arms he remembers that first time: remembers the sunny room in the Women's Hospital, where Ellie first saw the light, twelve years after Bert was born. He remembers how he drew near, the mother smiling the while, and cautiously put aside the canopy of the diminutive bed that stood beside the large one. There lay the little miracle among the pillows: so well formed, so encompassed, as it were, with the harmony of sweet proportions, with little hands that even then, though so much tinier, were beautiful as now; with

___

[8] Affectionate diminutive form of Eleanor, "little Eleanor."

wide-open eyes blue as the sky and brighter than the sunshine—and almost in that very second he felt himself captured and held fast. This was love at first sight, love everlasting: a feeling unknown, unhoped for, unexpected—in so far as it could be a matter of conscious awareness; it took entire possession of him, and he understood, with joyous amazement, that this was for life.

But he understood more. He knows, does Dr. Cornelius, that there is something not quite right about this feeling, so unaware, so undreamed of, so involuntary. He has a shrewd suspicion that it is not by accident it has so utterly mastered him and bound itself up with his existence; that he had—even subconsciously—been preparing for it, or, more precisely, been prepared for it. There is, in short, something in him which at a given moment was ready to issue in such a feeling; and this something, highly extraordinary to relate, is his essence and quality as a professor of history. Dr. Cornelius, however, does not actually say this, even to himself; he merely realizes it, at odd times, and smiles a private smile. He knows that history professors do not love history because it is something that comes to pass, but only because it is something that *has* come to pass; that they hate a revolution like the present one because they feel it is lawless, incoherent, irrelevant—in a word, unhistoric; that their hearts belong to the coherent, disciplined, historic past. For the temper of timelessness, the temper of eternity—thus the scholar communes with himself when he takes his walk by the river before supper—that temper broods over the past; and it is a temper much better suited to the nervous system of a history professor than are the excesses of the present. The past is immortalized; that is to say, it is dead; and death is the root of all godliness and all abiding significance. Dr. Cornelius, walking alone in the dark, has a profound insight into this truth. It is this conservative instinct of his, his sense of the eternal, that has found in his love for his little daughter a way to save itself from the wounding inflicted by the times. For father love, and a little child on its mother's breast—are not these timeless, and thus very, very holy and beautiful? Yet Cornelius, pondering there in the dark, descries something not perfectly right and good in his love. Theoretically, in the interests of science, he admits it to himself. There is something ulterior about it, in the nature of it; that something is hostility, hostility against the history of to-day, which is still in the making and thus not history at all, in behalf of the genuine history that has already happened—that is to say, death. Yes, passing strange though all this is, yet it is true; true in a sense, that is. His devotion to this priceless little morsel of life and new growth has something to do with death, it clings to death as against life; and that is neither right nor beautiful—in a sense. Though only the most fanatical asceticism could be capable, on no other ground than such casual scientific perception, of tearing this purest and most precious of feelings out of his heart.

He holds his darling on his lap and her slim rosy legs hang down. He raises his brows as he talks to her, tenderly, with a half-teasing note of respect, and listens enchanted to her high, sweet little voice calling him Abel. He exchanges a look with the mother, who is caressing her Snapper and reading him a gentle lecture. He must be more reasonable, he must learn self-control; today again, under the manifold exasperations of life, he has given way to rage and behaved like a howling dervish. Cornelius casts a mistrustful glance at the big folk now and then, too; he thinks it not unlikely they are not unaware of those scientific preoccupations of his evening walks. If such be the case they do not show it. They stand there leaning their arms on their chair-backs and with a benevolence not untinctured with irony look on at the parental happiness.

The children's frocks are of a heavy, brick-red stuff, embroidered in modern "arty" style. They once belonged to Ingrid and Bert and are precisely alike, save that little knickers come out beneath Snapper's smock. And both have their hair bobbed. Snapper's is a streaky blond, inclined to turn dark. It is bristly and sticky and looks for all the world like a droll, badly fitting wig. But Ellie's is chestnut brown, glossy and fine as silk, as pleasing as her whole little personality. It covers her ears—and these ears are not a pair, one of them being the right size, the other distinctly too large. Her father will sometimes uncover this little abnormality and exclaim over it as though he had never noticed it before, which both makes Ellie giggle and covers her with shame. Her eyes are now golden brown, set far apart and with sweet gleams in them—such a clear and lovely look! The brows above are blond; the nose still unformed, with thick nostrils and almost circular holes; the mouth large and expressive, with a beautifully arching and mobile upper lip. When she laughs, dimples come in her cheeks and she shows her teeth like loosely strung pearls. So far she has lost but one tooth, which her father gently twisted out with his handkerchief after it had grown very wobbling. During this small operation she had paled and trembled very much. Her cheeks have the softness proper to her years, but they are not chubby; indeed, they are rather concave, due to her facial structure, with its somewhat prominent jaw. On one, close to the soft fall of her hair, is a downy freckle.

Ellie is not too well pleased with her looks—a sign that already she troubles about such things. Sadly she thinks it is best to admit it once for all, her face is "homely"; though the rest of her, "on the other hand," is not bad at all. She loves expressions like "on the other hand"; they sound choice and grown-up to her, and she likes to string them together, one after the other: "very likely," "probably," "after all." Snapper is self-critical too, though more in the moral sphere: he suffers from remorse for his attacks of rage and considers himself a tremendous sinner. He is quite certain that heaven is not for such as he; he is sure to go to "the bad place" when he dies, and no persuasions will convince him to the contrary—as that God sees the heart and gladly makes allowances. Obstinately he shakes his head, with the comic, crooked little peruke,[9] and vows there is no place for him in heaven. When he has a cold he is immediately quite choked with mucus; rattles and rumbles from top to toe if you even look at him; his temperature flies up at once and he simply puffs. Nursy is pessimistic on the score of his constitution: such fat-blooded children as he might get a stroke any minute. Once she even thought she saw the moment at hand: Snapper had been in one of his berserker rages, and in the ensuing fit of penitence stood himself in the corner with his back to the room. Suddenly Nursy noticed that his face had gone all blue, far bluer, even, than her own. She raised the alarm, crying out that the child's all too rich blood had at length brought him to his final hour; and Snapper, to his vast astonishment, found himself, so far from being rebuked for evil-doing, encompassed in tenderness and anxiety—until it turned out that his colour was not caused by apoplexy but by the distempering on the nursery wall, which had come off on his tear-wet face.

Nursy has come downstairs too, and stands by the door, sleek-haired, owl-

[9] A wig.

eyed, with her hands folded over her white apron, and a severely dignified manner born of her limited intelligence. She is very proud of the care and training
she gives her nurslings and declares that they are "enveloping wonderfully."
She has had seventeen suppurated teeth lately removed from her jaws and been
measured for a set of symmetrical yellow ones in dark rubber gums; these now
embellish her peasant face. She is obsessed with the strange conviction that these
teeth of hers are the subject of general conversation, that, as it were, the sparrows
on the housetops chatter of them. "Everybody knows I've had a false set put in,"
she will say; "there has been a great deal of foolish talk about them." She is
much given to dark hints and veiled innuendo: speaks, for instance, of a certain
Dr. Bleifuss, whom every child knows, and "there are even some in the house
who pretend to be him." All one can do with talk like this is charitably to pass it
over in silence. But she teaches the children nursery rhymes: gems like:

> "Puff, puff, here comes the train!
> Puff, puff, toot, toot,
> Away it goes again,"

Or that gastronomical jingle, so suited, in its sparseness, to the times, and yet
seemingly with a blitheness of its own:

> "Monday we begin the week,
> Tuesday there's a bone to pick.
> Wednesday we're half way through,
> Thursday what a great to-do!
> Friday we eat what fish we're able,
> Saturday we dance round the table.
> Sunday brings us pork and greens—
> Here's a feast for kings and queens!"

Also a certain four-line stanza with a romantic appeal, unutterable and un-
uttered:

> "Open the gate, open the gate
> And let the carriage drive in.
> Who is it in the carriage sits?
> A lordly sir with golden hair."

Or, finally that ballad about golden-haired Marianne who sat on a, sat on a,
sat on a stone, and combed out her, combed out her, combed out her hair; and
about blood-thirsty Rudolph, who pulled out a, pulled out a, pulled out a knife—
and his ensuing direful end. Ellie enunciates all these ballads charmingly, with
her mobile little lips, and sings them in her sweet little voice—much better than
Snapper. She does everything better than he does, and he pays her honest admiration and homage and obeys her in all things except when visited by one of
his attacks. Sometimes she teaches him, instructs him upon the birds in the
picture-book and tells him their proper names: "This is a chaffinch, Buddy, this
is a bullfinch, this is a cowfinch." He has to repeat them after her. She gives him
medical instruction too, teaches him the names of diseases, such as infammation
of the lungs, infammation of the blood, infammation of the air. If he does not pay
attention and cannot say the words after her, she stands him in the corner. Once
she even boxed his ears, but was so ashamed that she stood herself in the corner

for a long time. Yes, they are fast friends, two souls with but a single thought, and have all their adventures in common. They come home from a walk and relate as with one voice that they have seen two moollies and a teenty-weenty baby calf. They are on familiar terms with the kitchen, which consists of Xaver and the ladies Hinterhofer, two sisters once of the lower middle class who, in these evil days, are reduced to living *"au pair"*[10] as the phrase goes and officiating as cook and housemaid for their board and keep. The little ones have a feeling that Xaver and the Hinterhofers are on much the same footing with their father and mother as they are themselves. At least sometimes, when they have been scolded, they go downstairs and announce that the master and mistress are cross. But playing with the servants lacks charm compared with the joys of playing upstairs. The kitchen could never rise to the height of the games their father can invent. For instance, there is "four gentlemen taking a walk." When they play it Abel will crook his knees until he is the same height with themselves and go walking with them, hand in hand. They never get enough of this sport; they could walk round and round the dining-room a whole day on end, five gentlemen in all, counting the diminished Abel.

Then there is the thrilling cushion game. One of the children, usually Ellie, seats herself, unbeknownst to Abel, in his seat at table. Still as a mouse she awaits his coming. He draws near with his head in the air, descanting in loud, clear tones upon the surpassing comfort of his chair; and sits down on top of Ellie. "What's this, what's this?" says he. And bounces about, deaf to the smothered giggles exploding behind him. "Why have they put a cushion in my chair? And what a queer, hard, awkward-shaped cushion it is!" he goes on. "Frightfully uncomfortable to sit on!" And keeps pushing and bouncing about more and more on the astonishing cushion and clutching behind him into the rapturous giggling and squeaking, until at last he turns round, and the game ends with a magnificent climax of discovery and recognition. They might go through all this a hundred times without diminishing by an iota its power to thrill.

Today is no time for such joys. The imminent festivity disturbs the atmosphere, and besides there is work to be done, and, above all, the eggs to be got. Ellie has just time to recite "Puff, puff," and Cornelius to discover that her ears are not mates, when they are interrupted by the arrival of Danny, come to fetch Bert and Ingrid. Xaver, meantime, has exchanged his striped livery for an ordinary coat, in which he looks rather rough-and-ready, though as brisk and attractive as ever. So then Nursy and the children ascend to the upper regions, the Professor withdraws to his study to read, as always after dinner, and his wife bends her energies upon the sandwiches and salad that must be prepared. And she has another errand as well. Before the young people arrive she has to take her shopping-basket and dash into town on her bicycle, to turn into provisions a sum of money she has in hand, which she dares not keep lest it lose all value.

Cornelius reads, leaning back in his chair, with his cigar between his middle and index finger. First he reads Macaulay[11] on the origin of the English public debt at the end of the seventeenth century; then an article in a French periodical on the rapid increase in the Spanish debt towards the end of the sixteenth. Both these for his lecture on the morrow. He intends to compare the astonishing

10 (French) Without pay; working in return for room and board.
11 Thomas Babington, Baron Macaulay (1800–1859), English historian, writer, and statesman.

prosperity which accompanied the phenomenon in England with its fatal effects a hundred years earlier in Spain, and to analyse the ethical and psychological grounds of the difference in results. For that will give him a chance to refer back from the England of William III, which is the actual subject in mind, to the time of Philip II and the Counter-Reformation,[12] which is his own special field. He has already written a valuable work on this period; it is much cited and got him his professorship. While his cigar burns down and gets strong, he excogitates a few pensive sentences in a key of gentle melancholy, to be delivered before his class next day: about the practically hopeless struggle carried on by the belated Philip against the whole trend of history: against the new, the kingdom-disrupting power of the Germanic ideal of freedom and individual liberty. And about the persistent, futile struggle of the aristocracy, condemned by God and rejected of man, against the forces of progress and change. He savours his sentences; keeps on polishing them while he puts back the books he has been using; then goes upstairs for the usual pause in his day's work, the hour with drawn blinds and closed eyes, which he so imperatively needs. But today, he recalls, he will rest under disturbed conditions, amid the bustle of preparations for the feast. He smiles to find his heart giving a mild flutter at the thought. Disjointed phrases on the theme of black-clad Philip and his times mingle with a confused consciousness that they will soon be dancing down below. For five minutes or so he falls asleep.

As he lies and rests he can hear the sound of the garden gate and the repeated ringing at the bell. Each time a little pang goes through him, of excitement and suspense, at the thought that the young people have begun to fill the floor below. And each time he smiles at himself again—though even his smile is slightly nervous, is tinged with the pleasurable anticipations people always feel before a party. At half past four—it is already dark—he gets up and washes at the washstand. The basin has been out of repair for two years. It is supposed to tip, but has broken away from its socket on one side and cannot be mended because there is nobody to mend it; neither replaced because no shop can supply another. So it has to be hung up above the vent and emptied by lifting in both hands and pouring out the water. Cornelius shakes his head over this basin, as he does several times a day—whenever, in fact, he has occasion to use it. He finishes his toilet with care, standing under the ceiling light to polish his glasses till they shine. Then he goes downstairs.

On his way to the dining-room he hears the gramophone already going, and the sound of voices. He puts on a polite, society air; at his tongue's end is the phrase he means to utter: "Pray don't let me disturb you," as he passes directly into the dining-room for his tea. "Pray don't let me disturb you"—it seems to him precisely the *mot juste*; towards the guests cordial and considerate, for himself a very bulwark.

The lower floor is lighted up, all the bulbs in the chandelier are burning save one that has burned out. Cornelius pauses on a lower step and surveys the entrance hall. It looks pleasant and cosy in the bright light, with its copy of Marées[13] over the brick chimney-piece, its wainscoted walls—wainscoted in soft wood—and red-carpeted floor, where the guests stand in groups, chatting, each with his tea-cup and slice of bread-and-butter spread with anchovy paste. There

[12] The Catholic reaction to the Protestant Reformation (16th century).
[13] Hans von Marées (1837–1887), German Romantic painter.

is a festal haze, faint scents of hair and clothing and human breath come to him across the room, it is all characteristic and familiar and highly evocative. The door into the dressing-room is open, guests are still arriving.

A large group of people is rather bewildering at first sight. The Professor takes in only the general scene. He does not see Ingrid, who is standing just at the foot of the steps, in a dark silk frock with a pleated collar falling softly over the shoulders, and bare arms. She smiles up at him, nodding and showing her lovely teeth.

"Rested?" she asks, for his private ear. With a quite unwarranted start he recognizes her, and she presents some of her friends.

"May I introduce Herr Zuber?" she says. "And this is Fräulein Plaichinger."

Herr Zuber is insignificant. But Fräulein Plaichinger is a perfect Germania, blond and voluptuous, arrayed in floating draperies. She has a snub nose, and answers the Professor's salutation in the high, shrill pipe so many stout women have.

"Delighted to meet you," he says. "How nice of you to come! A classmate of Ingrid's, I suppose?"

And Herr Zuber is a golfing partner of Ingrid's. He is in business; he works in his uncle's brewery. Cornelius makes a few jokes about the thinness of the beer and professes to believe that Herr Zuber could easily do something about the quality if he would. "But pray don't let me disturb you," he goes on, and turns towards the dining-room.

"There comes Max," says Ingrid. "Max, you sweep, what do you mean by rolling up at this time of day?" For such is the way they talk to each other, offensively to an older ear; of social forms, of hospitable warmth, there is no faintest trace. They all call each other by their first names.

A young man comes up to them out of the dressing-room and makes his bow; he has an expanse of white shirt-front and a little black string tie. He is as pretty as a picture, dark, with rosy cheeks, clean-shaven of course, but with just a sketch of side-whisker. Not a ridiculous or flashy beauty, not like a gypsy fiddler, but just charming to look at, in a winning, well-bred way, with kind dark eyes. He even wears his dinner-jacket a little awkwardly.

"Please don't scold me, Cornelia," he says; "it's the idiotic lectures." And Ingrid presents him to her father as Herr Hergesell.

Well, and so this is Herr Hergesell. He knows his manners, does Herr Hergesell, and thanks the master of the house quite ingratiatingly for his invitation as they shake hands. "I certainly seem to have missed the bus," says he jocosely. "Of course I have lectures today up to four o'clock; I would have; and after that I had to go home to change." Then he talks about his pumps, with which he has just been struggling in the dressing-room.

"I brought them with me in a bag," he goes on. "Mustn't tramp all over the carpet in our brogues—it's not done. Well, I was ass enough not to fetch along a shoe-horn, and I find I simply can't get in! What a sell! They are the tightest I've ever had, the numbers don't tell you a thing, and all the leather today is just cast iron. It's not leather at all. My poor finger"—he confidingly displays a reddened digit and once more characterizes the whole thing as a "sell," and a putrid sell into the bargain. He really does talk just as Ingrid said he did, with a peculiar nasal drawl, not affectedly in the least, but merely because that is the way of all the Hergesells.

Dr. Cornelius says it is very careless of them not to keep a shoe-horn in the cloak-room and displays proper sympathy with the mangled finger. "But now you *really* must not let me disturb you any longer," he goes on. "*Auf wiedersehen!*" And he crosses the hall into the dining-room.

There are guests there too, drinking tea; the family table is pulled out. But the Professor goes at once to his own little upholstered corner with the electric light bulb above it—the nook where he usually drinks his tea. His wife is sitting there talking with Bert and two other young men, one of them Herzl, whom Cornelius knows and greets; the other a typical "Wandervogel"[14] named Möller, a youth who obviously neither owns nor cares to own the correct evening dress of the middle classes (in fact, there is no such thing any more), nor to ape the manners of a gentleman (and, in fact, there is no such thing any more either). He has a wilderness of hair, horn spectacles, and a long neck, and wears golf stockings and a belted blouse. His regular occupation, the Professor learns, is banking, but he is by way of being an amateur folk-lorist and collects folk-songs from all localities and in all languages. He sings them, too, and at Ingrid's command has brought his guitar; it is hanging in the dressing-room in an oilcloth case. Herzl, the actor, is small and slight, but he has a strong growth of black beard, as you can tell by the thick coat of powder on his cheeks. His eyes are larger than life, with a deep and melancholy glow. He has put on rouge besides the powder— those dull carmine high-lights on the cheeks can be nothing but a cosmetic. "Queer," thinks the Professor. "You would think a man would be one thing or the other—not melancholic and use face paint at the same time. It's a psychological contradiction. How can a melancholy man rouge? But here we have a perfect illustration of the abnormality of the artist soul-form. It can make possible a contradiction like this—perhaps it even consists in the contradiction. All very interesting—and no reason whatever for not being polite to him. Politeness is a primitive convention—and legitimate. . . . Do take some lemon, Herr Hofschauspieler!"[15]

Court actors and court theatres—there are no such things any more, really. But Herzl relishes the sound of the title, notwithstanding he is a revolutionary artist. This must be another contradiction inherent in his soul-form; so, at least, the Professor assumes, and he is probably right. The flattery he is guilty of is a sort of atonement for his previous hard thoughts about the rouge.

"Thank you so much—it's really too good of you, sir," says Herzl, quite embarrassed. He is so overcome that he almost stammers; only his perfect enunciation saves him. His whole bearing towards his hostess and the master of the house is exaggeratedly polite. It is almost as though he had a bad conscience in respect of his rouge; as though an inward compulsion had driven him to put it on, but now, seeing it through the Professor's eyes, he disapproves of it himself, and thinks, by an air of humility towards the whole of unrouged society, to mitigate its effect.

They drink their tea and chat: about Möller's folk-songs, about Basque folk-songs and Spanish folk-songs; from which they pass to the new production of *Don Carlos*[16] at the Stadttheater, in which Herzl plays the title-role. He talks about his

[14] (German) Literally, bird of passage: someone with no fixed status.
[15] (German) Court actor.
[16] Play by Johann Christoph Friedrich von Schiller (1759–1805).

own rendering of the part and says he hopes his conception of the character has unity. They go on to criticize the rest of the cast, the setting, and the production as a whole; and Cornelius is struck, rather painfully, to find the conversation trending towards his own special province, back to Spain and the Counter-Reformation. He has done nothing at all to give it this turn, he is perfectly innocent, and hopes it does not look as though he had sought an occasion to play the professor. He wonders, and falls silent, feeling relieved when the little folk come up to the table. Ellie and Snapper have on their blue velvet Sunday frocks; they are permitted to partake in the festivities up to bed-time. They look shy and large-eyed as they say how-do-you-do to the strangers and, under pressure, repeat their names and ages. Herr Möller does nothing but gaze at them solemnly, but Herzl is simply ravished. He rolls his eyes up to heaven and puts his hands over his mouth; he positively blesses them. It all, no doubt, comes from his heart, but he is so addicted to theatrical methods of making an impression and getting an effect that both words and behaviour ring frightfully false. And even his enthusiasm for the little folk looks too much like part of his general craving to make up for the rouge on his cheeks.

The tea-table has meanwhile emptied of guests, and dancing is going on in the hall. The children run off, the Professor prepares to retire. "Go and enjoy yourselves," he says to Möller and Herzl, who have sprung from their chairs as he rises from his. They shake hands and he withdraws into his study, his peaceful kingdom, where he lets down the blinds, turns on the desk lamp, and sits down to his work.

It is work which can be done, if necessary, under disturbed conditions: nothing but a few letters and a few notes. Of course, Cornelius's mind wanders. Vague impressions float through it: Herr Hergesell's refractory pumps, the high pipe in that plump body of the Plaichinger female. As he writes, or leans back in his chair and stares into space, his thoughts go back to Herr Möller's collection of Basque folk-songs, to Herzl's posings and humility, to "his" Carlos and the court of Philip II. There is something strange, he thinks, about conversations. They are so ductile, they will flow of their own accord in the direction of one's dominating interest. Often and often he has seen this happen. And while he is thinking, he is listening to the sounds next door—rather subdued, he finds them. He hears only voices, no sound of footsteps. The dancers do not glide or circle round the room; they merely walk about over the carpet, which does not hamper their movements in the least. Their way of holding each other is quite different and strange, and they move to the strains of the gramophone, to the weird music of the new world. He concentrates on the music and makes out that it is a jazz-band record, with various percussion instruments and the clack and clatter of castanets, which, however, are not even faintly suggestive of Spain, but merely jazz like the rest. No, not Spain. . . . His thoughts are back at their old round.

Half an hour goes by. It occurs to him it would be no more than friendly to go and contribute a box of cigarettes to the festivities next door. Too bad to ask the young people to smoke their own—though they have probably never thought of it. He goes into the empty dining-room and takes a box from his supply in the cupboard: not the best ones, nor yet the brand he himself prefers, but a certain long, thin kind he is not averse to getting rid of—after all, they are nothing but youngsters. He takes the box into the hall, holds it up with a smile, and deposits it on the mantel-shelf. After which he gives a look round and returns to his own room.

There comes a lull in dance and music. The guests stand about the room in groups or round the table at the window or are seated in a circle by the fireplace. Even the built-in stairs, with their worn velvet carpet, are crowded with young folk as in an amphitheatre: Max Hergesell is there, leaning back with one elbow on the step above and gesticulating with his free hand as he talks to the shrill, voluptuous Plaichinger. The floor of the hall is nearly empty, save just in the centre: there, directly beneath the chandelier, the two little ones in their blue velvet frocks clutch each other in an awkward embrace and twirl silently round and round, oblivious of all else. Cornelius, as he passes, strokes their hair, with a friendly word; it does not distract them from their small solemn preoccupation. But at his own door he turns to glance round and sees young Hergesell push himself off the stair by his elbow—probably because he noticed the Professor. He comes down into the arena, takes Ellie out of her brother's arms, and dances with her himself. It looks very comic, without the music, and he crouches down just as Cornelius does when he goes walking with the four gentlemen, holding the fluttered Ellie as though she were grown up and taking little "shimmying" steps. Everybody watches with huge enjoyment, the gramophone is put on again, dancing becomes general. The Professor stands and looks, with his hand on the door-knob. He nods and laughs; when he finally shuts himself into his study the mechanical smile still lingers on his lips.

Again he turns over pages by his desk lamp, takes notes, attends to a few simple matters. After a while he notices that the guests have forsaken the entrance hall for his wife's drawing-room, into which there is a door from his own study as well. He hears their voices and the sounds of a guitar being tuned. Herr Möller, it seems, is to sing—and does so. He twangs the strings of his instrument and sings in a powerful bass a ballad in a strange tongue, possibly Swedish. The Professor does not succeed in identifying it, though he listens attentively to the end, after which there is great applause. The sound is deadened by the portière that hangs over the dividing door. The young bank-clerk begins another song. Cornelius goes softly in.

It is half-dark in the drawing-room; the only light is from the shaded standard lamp, beneath which Möller sits, on the divan, with his legs crossed, picking his strings. His audience is grouped easily about; as there are not enough seats, some stand, and more, among them many young ladies, are simply sitting on the floor with their hands clasped round their knees or even with their legs stretched out before them. Hergesell sits thus, in his dinner-jacket, next the piano, with Fräulein Plaichinger beside him. Frau Cornelius is holding both children on her lap as she sits in her easy-chair opposite the singer. Snapper, the Bœotian,[17] begins to talk loud and clear in the middle of the song and has to be intimidated with hushings and finger-shakings. Never, never would Ellie allow herself to be guilty of such conduct. She sits there daintily erect and still on her mother's knee. The Professor tries to catch her eye and exchange a private signal with his little girl; but she does not see him. Neither does she seem to be looking at the singer. Her gaze is directed lower down.

[17] Dullard, clown; derived from the proverbial rusticity of the inhabitants of the ancient Greek city of Bœotia.

Möller sings the "joli tambour":[18]

"Sire, mon roi, donnez-moi votre fille—"

They are all enchanted. "How good!" Hergesell is heard to say, in the odd, nasally condescending Hergesell tone. The next one is a beggar ballad, to a tune composed by young Möller himself; it elicits a storm of applause:

"Gypsy lassie a-goin' to the fair,
Huzza!
Gypsy laddie a-goin' to be there—
Huzza, diddlety umpty dido!"

Laughter and high spirits, sheer reckless hilarity, reigns after this jovial ballad. "Frightfully good!" Hergesell comments again, as before. Follows another popular song, this time a Hungarian one; Möller sings it in its own outlandish tongue, and most effectively. The Professor applauds with ostentation. It warms his heart and does him good, this outcropping of artistic, historic, and cultural elements all amongst the shimmying. He goes up to young Möller and congratulates him, talks about the songs and their sources, and Möller promises to lend him a certain annotated book of folk-songs. Cornelius is the more cordial because all the time, as fathers do, he has been comparing the parts and achievements of this young stranger with those of his own son, and being gnawed by envy and chagrin. This young Möller, he is thinking, is a capable bank-clerk (though about Möller's capacity he knows nothing whatever) and has this special gift besides, which must have taken talent and energy to cultivate. "And here is my poor Bert, who knows nothing and can do nothing and thinks of nothing except playing the clown, without even talent for that!" He tries to be just; he tells himself that, after all, Bert has innate refinement; that probably there is a good deal more to him than there is to the successful Möller; that perhaps he has even something of the poet in him, and his dancing and table-waiting are due to mere boyish folly and the distraught times. But paternal envy and pessimism win the upper hand; when Möller begins another song, Dr. Cornelius goes back to his room.

He works as before, with divided attention, at this and that, while it gets on for seven o'clock. Then he remembers a letter he may just as well write, a short letter and not very important, but letter-writing is wonderful for the way it takes up the time, and it is almost half past when he has finished. At half past eight the Italian salad will be served; so now is the prescribed moment for the Professor to go out into the wintry darkness to post his letters and take his daily quantum of fresh air and exercise. They are dancing again, and he will have to pass through the hall to get his hat and coat; but they are used to him now, he need not stop and beg them not to be disturbed. He lays away his papers, takes up the letters he has written, and goes out. But he sees his wife sitting near the door of his room and pauses a little by her easy-chair.

She is watching the dancing. Now and then the big folk or some of their guests stop to speak to her; the party is at its height, and there are more onlookers than these two: blue-faced Ann is standing at the bottom of the stairs, in all the dignity of her limitations. She is waiting for the children, who simply cannot get their fill of these unwonted festivities, and watching over Snapper, lest his

[18] An old French folk song.

all too rich blood be churned to the danger-point by too much twirling round. And not only the nursery but the kitchen takes an interest: Xaver and the two ladies Hinterhofer are standing by the pantry door looking on with relish. Fräulein Walburga, the elder of the two sunken sisters (the culinary section—she objects to being called a cook), is a whimsical, good-natured sort, brown-eyed, wearing glasses with thick circular lenses; the nose-piece is wound with a bit of rag to keep it from pressing on her nose. Fräulein Cecilia is younger, though not so precisely young either. Her bearing is as self-assertive as usual, this being her way of sustaining her dignity as a former member of the middle class. For Fräulein Cecilia feels acutely her descent into the ranks of domestic service. She positively declines to wear a cap or other badge of servitude, and her hardest trial is on the Wednesday evening when she has to serve the dinner while Xaver has his after-noon out. She hands the dishes with averted face and elevated nose—a fallen queen; and so distressing is it to behold her degradation that one evening when the little folk happened to be at table and saw her they both with one accord burst into tears. Such anguish is unknown to young Xaver. He enjoys serving and does it with an ease born of practice as well as talent, for he was once a "piccolo."[19] But otherwise he is a thorough-paced good-for-nothing and windbag—with quite dis-tinct traits of character of his own, as his long-suffering employers are always ready to concede, but perfectly impossible and a bag of wind for all that. One must just take him as he is, they think, and not expect figs from thistles. He is the child and product of the disrupted times, a perfect specimen of his genera-tion, follower of the revolution, Bolshevist sympathizer. The Professor's name for him is the "minute-man," because he is always to be counted on in any sudden crisis, if only it address his sense of humour or love of novelty, and will display therein amazing readiness and resource. But he utterly lacks a sense of duty and can as little be trained to the performance of the daily round and common task as some kinds of dog can be taught to jump over a stick. It goes so plainly against the grain that criticism is disarmed. One becomes resigned. On grounds that appealed to him as unusual and amusing he would be ready to turn out of his bed at any hour of the night. But he simply cannot get up before eight in the morning, he cannot do it, he will not jump over the stick. Yet all day long the evidence of this free and untrammelled existence, the sound of his mouth-organ, his joyous whistle, or his raucous but expressive voice lifted in song, rises to the hearing of the world above-stairs; and the smoke of his cigarettes fills the pantry. While the Hinterhofer ladies work he stands and looks on. Of a morning while the Professor is breakfasting, he tears the leaf off the study calendar—but does not lift a finger to dust the room. Dr. Cornelius has often told him to leave the calen-dar alone, for he tends to tear off two leaves at a time and thus to add to the general confusion. But young Xaver appears to find joy in this activity, and will not be deprived of it.

Again, he is fond of children, a winning trait. He will throw himself into games with the little folk in the garden, make and mend their toys with great ingenuity, even read aloud from their books—and very droll it sounds in his thick-lipped pronunciation. With his whole soul he loves the cinema; after an evening spent there he inclines to melancholy and yearning and talking to himself. Vague hopes stir in him that some day he may make his fortune in that gay world and

[19] Apprentice waiter in a restaurant.

belong to it by rights—hopes based on his shock of hair and his physical agility and daring. He likes to climb the ash tree in the front garden, mounting branch by branch to the very top and frightening everybody to death who sees him. Once there he lights a cigarette and smokes it as he sways to and fro, keeping a look-out for a cinema director who might chance to come along and engage him.

If he changed his striped jacket for mufti, he might easily dance with the others and no one would notice the difference. For the big folk's friends are rather anomalous in their clothing: evening dress is worn by a few, but it is by no means the rule. There is quite a sprinkling of guests, both male and female, in the same general style as Möller the ballad-singer. The Professor is familiar with the circumstances of most of this young generation he is watching as he stands beside his wife's chair; he has heard them spoken of by name. They are students at the high school or at the School of Applied Art; they lead, at least the masculine portion, that precarious and scrambling existence which is purely the product of the time. There is a tall, pale, spindling youth, the son of a dentist, who lives by speculation. From all the Professor hears, he is a perfect Aladdin. He keeps a car, treats his friends to champagne suppers, and showers presents upon them on every occasion, costly little trifles in mother-of-pearl and gold. So today he has brought gifts to the young givers of the feast: for Bert a gold lead-pencil, and for Ingrid a pair of earrings of barbaric size, great gold circlets that fortunately do not have to go through the little ear-lobe, but are fastened over it by means of a clip. The big folk come laughing to their parents to display these trophies; and the parents shake their heads even while they admire—Aladdin bowing over and over from afar.

The young people appear to be absorbed in their dancing—if the performance they are carrying out with so much still concentration can be called dancing. They stride across the carpet, slowly, according to some unfathomable prescript, strangely embraced; in the newest attitude, tummy advanced and shoulders high, waggling the hips. They do not get tired, because nobody could. There is no such thing as heightened colour or heaving bosoms. Two girls may dance together or two young men—it is all the same. They move to the exotic strains of the gramophone, played with the loudest needles to procure the maximum of sound: shimmies, fox-trots, one-steps, double foxes, African shimmies, Java dances, and Creole polkas, the wild musky melodies follow one another, now furious, now languishing, a monotonous Negro programme in unfamiliar rhythm, to a clacking, clashing, and strumming orchestral accompaniment.

"What is that record?" Cornelius inquires of Ingrid, as she passes him by in the arms of the pale young speculator, with reference to the piece then playing, whose alternate languors and furies he finds comparatively pleasing and showing a certain resourcefulness in detail.

"*Prince of Pappenheim*: 'Console thee, dearest child,'" she answers, and smiles pleasantly back at him with her white teeth.

The cigarette smoke wreathes beneath the chandelier. The air is blue with a festal haze compact of sweet and thrilling ingredients that stir the blood with memories of green-sick pains and are particularly poignant to those whose youth— like the Professor's own—has been over-sensitive. . . . The little folk are still on the floor. They are allowed to stop up until eight, so great is their delight in the party. The guests have got used to their presence; in their own way, they have their place in the doings of the evening. They have separated, anyhow: Snapper revolves all alone in the middle of the carpet, in his little blue velvet smock, while Ellie is running after one of the dancing couples, trying to hold the man fast by his coat. It is Max Hergesell and Fräulein Plaichinger. They dance well, it is a pleasure to watch them. One has to admit that these mad modern dances, when the right people dance them, are not so bad after all—they have something quite taking. Young Hergesell is a capital leader, dances according to rule, yet with individuality. So it looks. With what aplomb can he walk backwards—when space permits! And he knows how to be graceful standing still in a crowd. And his partner supports him well, being unsuspectedly lithe and buoyant, as fat people often are. They look at each other, they are talking, paying no heed to Ellie, though others are smiling to see the child's persistence. Dr. Cornelius tries to catch up his little sweetheart as she passes and draw her to him. But Ellie eludes him, almost peevishly; her dear Abel is nothing to her now. She braces her little arms against his chest and turns her face away with a persecuted look. Then escapes to follow her fancy once more.

The Professor feels an involuntary twinge. Uppermost in his heart is hatred for this party, with its power to intoxicate and estrange his darling child. His love for her—that not quite disinterested, not quite unexceptionable love of his—is easily wounded. He wears a mechanical smile, but his eyes have clouded, and he stares fixedly at a point in the carpet, between the dancers' feet.

"The children ought to go to bed," he tells his wife. But she pleads for another quarter of an hour; she has promised already, and they do love it so! He smiles again and shakes his head, stands so a moment and then goes across to the cloak-room, which is full of coats and hats and scarves and overshoes. He has trouble in rummaging out his own coat, and Max Hergesell comes out of the hall, wiping his brow.

"Going out, sir?" he asks, in Hergesellian accents, dutifully helping the older man on with his coat. "Silly business this, with my pumps," he says. "They pinch like hell. The brutes are simply too tight for me, quite apart from the bad leather. They press just here on the ball of my great toe"—he stands on one foot and holds the other in his hand—"it's simply unbearable. There's nothing for it but to take them off; my brogues will have to do the business. . . . Oh, let me help you, sir."

"Thanks," says Cornelius. "Don't trouble. Get rid of your own tormentors. . . . Oh, thanks very much!" For Hergesell has gone on one knee to snap the fasteners of his snow-boots.

Once more the Professor expresses his gratitude; he is pleased and touched by so much sincere respect and youthful readiness to serve. "Go and enjoy yourself," he counsels. "Change your shoes and make up for what you have been suffering. Nobody can dance in shoes that pinch. Good-bye, I must be off to get a breath of fresh air."

"I'm going to dance with Ellie now," calls Hergesell after him. "She'll be a first-rate dancer when she grows up, and that I'll swear to."

"Think so?" Cornelius answers, already half out. "Well, you are a connoisseur, I'm sure. Don't get curvature of the spine with stooping."

He nods again and goes. "Fine lad," he thinks as he shuts the door. "Student of engineering. Knows what he's bound for, got a good clear head, and so well set up and pleasant too." And again paternal envy rises as he compares his poor Bert's status with this young man's, which he puts in the rosiest light that his son's may look the darker. Thus he sets out on his evening walk.

He goes up the avenue, crosses the bridge, and walks along the bank on the other side as far as the next bridge but one. The air is wet and cold, with a little snow now and then. He turns up his coat-collar and slips the crook of his cane over the arm behind his back. Now and then he ventilates his lungs with a long deep breath of the night air. As usual when he walks, his mind reverts to his professional preoccupations, he thinks about his lectures and the things he means to say tomorrow about Philip's struggle against the Germanic revolution, things steeped in melancholy and penetratingly just. Above all just, he thinks. For in one's dealings with the young it behooves one to display the scientific spirit, to exhibit the principles of enlightenment—not only for purposes of mental discipline, but on the human and individual side, in order not to wound them or indirectly offend their political sensibilities; particularly in these days, when there is so much tinder in the air, opinions are so frightfully split up and chaotic, and you may so easily incur attacks from one party or the other, or even give rise to scandal, by taking sides on a point of history. "And taking sides is unhistoric anyhow," so he muses. "Only justice, only impartiality is historic." And could not, properly considered, be otherwise. . . . For justice can have nothing of youthful fire and blithe, fresh, loyal conviction. It is by nature melancholy. And, being so, has secret affinity with the lost cause and the forlorn hope rather than with the fresh and blithe and loyal—perhaps this affinity is its very essence and without it it would not exist at all! . . . "And is there then no such thing as justice?" the Professor asks himself, and ponders the question so deeply that he absently posts his letters in the next box and turns round to go home. This thought of his is unsettling and disturbing to the scientific mind—but is it not after all itself scientific, psychological, conscientious, and therefore to be accepted without prejudice, no matter how upsetting? In the midst of which musings Dr. Cornelius finds himself back at his own door.

On the outer threshold stands Xaver, and seems to be looking for him.

"Herr Professor," says Xaver, tossing back his hair, "go upstairs to Ellie straight off. She's in a bad way."

"What's the matter?" asks Cornelius in alarm. "Is she ill?"

"No-o, not to say ill," answers Xaver. "She's just in a bad way and crying fit to bust her little heart. It's along o' that chap with the shirt-front that danced with her—Herr Hergesell. She couldn't be got to go upstairs peaceably, not at no price at all, and she's b'en crying bucketfuls."

"Nonsense," says the Professor, who has entered and is tossing off his things in the cloak-room. He says no more; opens the glass door and without a glance at the guests turns swiftly to the stairs. Takes them two at a time, crosses the upper hall and the small room leading into the nursery. Xaver follows at his heels, but stops at the nursery door.

A bright light still burns within, showing the gay frieze that runs all round the room, the large row of shelves heaped with a confusion of toys, the rocking-horse on his swaying platform, with red-varnished nostrils and raised hoofs. On the linoleum lie other toys—building blocks, railway trains, a little trumpet. The two white cribs stand not far apart, Ellie's in the window corner, Snapper's out in the room.

Snapper is asleep. He has said his prayers in loud, ringing tones, prompted by Nurse, and gone off at once into vehement, profound, and rosy slumber—from which a cannon-ball fired at close range could not rouse him. He lies with both fists flung back on the pillows on either side of the tousled head with its funny crooked little slumber-tossed wig.

A circle of females surrounds Ellie's bed: not only blue-faced Ann is there, but the Hinterhofer ladies too, talking to each other and to her. They make way as the Professor comes up and reveal the child sitting all pale among her pillows, sobbing and weeping more bitterly than he has ever seen her sob and weep in her life. Her lovely little hands lie on the coverlet in front of her, the nightgown with its narrow lace border has slipped down from her shoulder—such a thin, birdlike little shoulder—and the sweet head Cornelius loves so well, set on the neck like a flower on its stalk, her head is on one side, with the eyes rolled up to the corner between wall and ceiling above her head. For there she seems to en- visage the anguish of her heart and even to nod to it—either on purpose or because her head wobbles as her body is shaken with the violence of her sobs. Her eyes rain down tears. The bow-shaped lips are parted, like a little *mater dolorosa's*,[20] and from them issue long, low wails that in nothing resemble the unnecessary and exasperating shrieks of a naughty child, but rise from the deep extremity of her heart and wake in the Professor's own a sympathy that is well-nigh intolerable. He has never seen his darling so before. His feelings find immediate vent in an attack on the ladies Hinterhofer.

"What about the supper?" he asks sharply. "There must be a great deal to do. Is my wife being left to do it alone?"

For the acute sensibilities of the former middle class this is quite enough. The ladies withdraw in righteous indignation, and Xaver Kleingutl jeers at them as they pass out. Having been born to low life instead of achieving it, he never loses a chance to mock at their fallen state.

"Childie, childie," murmurs Cornelius, and sitting down by the crib enfolds the anguished Ellie in his arms. "What is the trouble with my darling?"

She bedews his face with her tears.

"Abel . . . Abel . . ." she stammers between sobs. "Why—isn't Max—my brother? Max ought to be—my brother!"

Alas, alas! What mischance is this? Is this what the party has wrought, with its fatal atmosphere? Cornelius glances helplessly up at the blue-faced Ann stand- ing there in all the dignity of her limitations with her hands before her on her apron. She purses up her mouth and makes a long face. "It's pretty young," she says, "for the female instincts to be showing up."

"Hold your tongue," snaps Cornelius, in his agony. He has this much to be thankful for, that Ellie does not turn from him now; she does not push him away as she did downstairs, but clings to him in her need, while she reiterates her absurd, bewildered prayer that Max might be her brother, or with a fresh burst of desire demands to be taken downstairs so that he can dance with her again. But Max, of course, is dancing with Fräulein Plaichinger, that behemoth who is his rightful partner and has every claim upon him; whereas Ellie—never, thinks the Professor, his heart torn with the violence of his pity, never has she looked so tiny and birdlike as now, when she nestles to him shaken with sobs and all un- aware of what is happening in her little soul. No, she does not know. She does not comprehend that her suffering is on account of Fräulein Plaichinger, fat, over- grown, and utterly within her rights in dancing with Max Hergesell, whereas

[20] (Latin) Our Lady of Sorrow: applied to the Virgin Mary mourning for Christ.

Ellie may only do it once, by way of a joke, although she is incomparably the more charming of the two. Yet it would be quite mad to reproach young Hergesell with the state of affairs or to make fantastic demands upon him. No, Ellie's suffering is without help or healing and must be covered up. Yet just as it is without understanding, so it is also without restraint—and that is what makes it so horribly painful. Xaver and blue-faced Ann do not feel this pain, it does not affect them—either because of native callousness or because they accept it as the way of nature. But the Professor's fatherly heart is quite torn by it, and by a distressful horror of this passion, so hopeless and so absurd.

Of no avail to hold forth to poor Ellie on the subject of the perfectly good little brother she already has. She only casts a distraught and scornful glance over at the other crib, where Snapper lies vehemently slumbering, and with fresh tears calls again for Max. Of no avail either the promise of a long, long walk tomorrow, all five gentlemen, round and round the dining-room table; or a dramatic description of the thrilling cushion games they will play. No, she will listen to none of all this, nor to lying down and going to sleep. She will not sleep, she will sit bolt upright and suffer. . . . But on a sudden they stop and listen, Abel and Ellie; listen to something miraculous that is coming to pass, that is approaching by strides, two strides, to the nursery door, that now overwhelmingly appears. . . .

It is Xaver's work, not a doubt of that. He has not remained by the door where he stood to gloat over the ejection of the Hinterhofers. No, he has bestirred himself, taken a notion; likewise steps to carry it out. Downstairs he has gone, twitched Herr Hergesell's sleeve, and made a thick-lipped request. So here they both are. Xaver, having done his part, remains by the door; but Max Hergesell comes up to Ellie's crib; in his dinner-jacket, with his sketchy side-whisker and charming black eyes; obviously quite pleased with his rôle of swan knight[21] and fairy prince, as one who should say: "See, here am I, now all losses are restored and sorrows end!"

Cornelius is almost as much overcome as Ellie herself.

"Just look," he says feebly, "look who's here. This is uncommonly good of you, Herr Hergesell."

"Not a bit of it," says Hergesell. "Why shouldn't I come to say good-night to my fair partner?"

And he approaches the bars of the crib, behind which Ellie sits struck mute. She smiles blissfully through her tears. A funny, high little note that is half a sigh of relief comes from her lips, then she looks dumbly up at her swan knight with her golden-brown eyes—tear-swollen though they are, so much more beautiful than the fat Plaichinger's. She does not put up her arms. Her joy, like her grief, is without understanding; but she does not do that. The lovely little hands lie quiet on the coverlet, and Max Hergesell stands with his arms leaning over the rail as on a balcony.

"And now," he says smartly, "she need not 'sit the livelong night and weep upon her bed'!"[22] He looks at the Professor to make sure he is receiving due credit

---

[21] In Richard Wagner's opera *Lohengrin* (1847) the hero arrives in a boat drawn by swans to save Elsa of Brabant.

[22] Quoted from a lyric in Chapter 13 of *Wilhelm Meister's Apprenticeship,* a novel by Johann Wolfgang von Goethe (1749–1832). The lyric expresses the plight of a man on whom the suffering and guilt implicit in living are divinely imposed without his having chosen to undergo them.

for the quotation. "Ha ha!" he laughs, "she's beginning young. 'Console thee, dearest child!' Never mind, you're all right! Just as you are you'll be wonderful! You've only got to grow up. . . . And you'll lie down and go to sleep like a good girl, now I've come to say good-night? And not cry any more, little Lorelei?"[23]

Ellie looks up at him, transfigured. One birdlike shoulder is bare; the Professor draws the lace-trimmed nighty over it. There comes into his mind a sentimental story he once read about a dying child who longs to see a clown he had once, with unforgettable ecstasy, beheld in a circus. And they bring the clown to the bedside marvellously arrayed, embroidered before and behind with silver butterflies; and the child dies happy. Max Hergesell is not embroidered, and Ellie, thank God, is not going to die, she has only been "in a bad way." But, after all, the effect is the same. Young Hergesell leans over the bars of the crib and rattles on, more for the father's ear than the child's, but Ellie does not know that—and the father's feelings towards him are a most singular mixture of thankfulness, embarrassment, and hatred.

"Good night, little Lorelei," says Hergesell, and gives her his hand through the bars. Her pretty, soft, white little hand is swallowed up in the grasp of his big, strong, red one. "Sleep well," he says, "and sweet dreams! But don't dream about me—God forbid! Not at your age—ha ha!" And then the fairy clown's visit is at an end. Cornelius accompanies him to the door. "No, no, positively, no thanks called for, don't mention it," he large-heartedly protests; and Xaver goes downstairs with him, to help serve the Italian salad.

But Dr. Cornelius returns to Ellie, who is now lying down, with her cheek pressed into her flat little pillow.

"Well, wasn't that lovely?" he says as he smooths the covers. She nods, with one last little sob. For a quarter of an hour he sits beside her and watches while she falls asleep in her turn, beside the little brother who found the right way so much earlier than she. Her silky brown hair takes the enchanting fall it always does when she sleeps; deep, deep lie the lashes over the eyes that late so abundantly poured forth their sorrow; the angelic mouth with its bowed upper lip is peacefully relaxed and a little open. Only now and then comes a belated catch in her slow breathing.

And her small hands, like pink and white flowers, lie so quietly, one on the coverlet, the other on the pillow by her face—Dr. Cornelius, gazing, feels his heart melt with tenderness as with strong wine.

"How good," he thinks, "that she breathes in oblivion with every breath she draws! That in childhood each night is a deep wide gulf between one day and the next. Tomorrow, beyond all doubt, young Hergesell will be a pale shadow, powerless to darken her little heart. Tomorrow, forgetful of all but present joy, she will walk with Abel and Snapper, all five gentlemen, round and round the table, will play the ever-thrilling cushion game."

Heaven be praised for that!

[23] Legendary siren of the Rhine, whose beauty distracted sailors from the dangers of the surrounding cliffs and rocks.

"Disorder and Early Sorrow" is written in what grammarians call the "historical present," that is to say, the present tense used to represent happenings of the past. As a literary device this has the obvious effect of making events seem immediate to our understanding and sympathy. But the historical present is usually employed with great circumspection and for a particular limited purpose, in order to make some part of a narrative more vivid than the rest. To use it for the whole of a story of considerable length is generally regarded as questionable practice. The device wears out; the reader comes to think of it as a naive trick, and whatever sympathy with the persons of the story it may at first induce is likely to deteriorate into mere condescension. But Thomas Mann is a writer who is especially sensitive to all the traditional devices of prose; he cannot be charged with committing a stylistic blunder: the historical present is entirely suited to his literary purpose.

For the story is about history itself, about the impulse of the human mind to hold the fleeting moment, to make permanent what is transient. A tense which pretends that the past is still the present is ideally appropriate to such a subject. And if Mann's extended use of the historical present does eventually give the narrative a tone of naiveté and leads us to regard the characters, especially the chief one, Professor Cornelius, with a degree of condescension, this effect is appropriate too. It suggests the hopelessness—we might almost say the childishness—of the Professor's desire to hold back the onward movement of time.

I say that "Disorder and Early Sorrow" is "about history itself" and to some readers this will perhaps seem an all too abstract description. They will protest that it makes too much of the fact that Professor Cornelius is a historian and that it gives excessive weight to the single paragraph, brilliant and moving as it is, in which he thinks about the "something not quite right" in his feeling for his little daughter, that flaw in his love which, he believes, derives from "his essence and quality as a professor of history." The story, these readers will object, is about the love of a father for his child and the pain he feels when he realizes that the love she bears toward him will one day be withdrawn to be given to some other man.

Against this objection I make no defence—or none beyond saying that the breaking, or attenuation, of the bond between parent and child is the very stuff of history. What the historian coolly investigates as happening in nations and over relatively long periods of time is but the aggregate of what is painfully experienced in every family. The unit of historical time is not the century but the generation. "One generation passeth away and another generation cometh" —this is history.

But if this is history, then I have been using the word in two separate meanings, having previously spoken of history as the expression of the impulse of the human mind to make permanent that which is transient. For this contradiction I am not responsible: it lies in the nature of the word itself, which means two quite distinct things. According to one sense of the word, history is the sum of things that happen, or at least the sum of the notable things that happen, and the emphasis is on the *happening*. In this sense, history is a flux, a ceaseless stream, although perhaps the image of a stream represents something too defined—it is rather (to use a phrase of William James's) "a blooming, buzzing confusion." According to the other sense of the word, history is the *record* of happenings, not merely the objective record (if there can be such a thing) but one that imposes order upon events and finds significance in them.

The relationship between the two meanings is in part antagonistic, just as the relation between art and life is in some measure antagonistic. The historian, like the artist, imposes order upon the chaotic flux of life and says that through his efforts life may be understood. Yet in his heart he sometimes feels that he betrays life by what he does, that when he imposes upon it a form or an idea, he negates its living actuality. As Professor Cornelius puts it, the past that the historians conceive is coherent and disciplined, which is what they mean by "historical." But life in the present is not coherent and disciplined: it becomes so only when it ceases to be life in the present, when it becomes the past and is seen as history. "The past is immortalized; that is to say, it is dead," Professor Cornelius says. And he goes on: ". . . and death is the root of all godliness and all abiding significance," by which he means that all piety, law, and morality depend upon our sense of the past, upon our reference to experiences which are no longer immediate and actual, no longer alive.

Certainly the period in which the story takes place presents the greatest possible contrast of "disorder" to the "orderliness" of the past. After the defeat of Germany in the First World War, the political system of the nation had collapsed. Germany ceased to be a monarchy and became, most uneasily, a democracy. The national economy was radically dislocated; commodities were scarce, money was progressively devalued, prices were astronomically inflated, and it was literally true that people had to carry paper currency in satchels. Both the modest savings of the prudent and the fortunes of the rich were wiped out. The devaluation of the old social modes, of traditional ideas and ideals, kept pace with the devaluation of money. Young Bert Cornelius is a typical figure of the time, with his lack of any ambition for a respectable life such as his father had lived, with his manners and admirations that are quite alien to his father's comprehension.

Yet no description of the period would be accurate that did not take into account the heady sense of possibility that it brought to many young people. Exactly because they were cut off from security and respectability, they valued whatever in life was new and adventurous. The "conservative instinct," which Professor Cornelius acknowledges as his own, was held in very low esteem. If life was chaotic, it seemed to many people to be for that very reason the more intense. Because the past could assert so little authority over life, life seemed more truly alive than ever before.

And even Professor Cornelius is aware of this new sense of excitement in his society. Or at least he is not inclined to condemn the new disorder, however much he dislikes it, for his field of historical research must inevitably suggest to him the dangers of such a judgment. Professor Cornelius is a specialist in the period of the so-called Counter-Reformation, that great expression of the conservative instinct by which sixteenth-century Catholic Europe tried to hold back the rising tide of Protestantism. He has a particular interest in a leader of this resistance to the new tendencies, Philip II of Spain, who carried on what the Professor characterizes as a "practically hopeless struggle . . . against the whole trend of history: against the new, the kingdom-disrupting power of the Germanic ideal of freedom and individual liberty." Mann could count on his

German readers to have a pretty vivid idea of this monarch and his desperate resistance to the new, for Philip's struggle is the subject of one of the classics of the German stage, Schiller's *Don Carlos*. It will be recalled that a new production of this play is discussed at the party given by Professor Cornelius' older children; one of the guests, the young actor, is to have the part of Don Carlos, the crown prince who becomes his father's antagonist by making himself the champion of the oppressed people of the conquered Netherlands. We might put it that Dr. Cornelius, historian of the Counter-Reformation, has no wish in his own life to emulate the grim, unloved, tragic king who tried to impose traditional principle and authority upon the new chaotic energies burgeoning about him.

And yet he cannot participate in these energies or give them his full assent —the "conservative instinct" of the historian, which is also the conservative instinct of the father of a family, is strong in him. He is aware of his "hostility against the history of today, which is still in the making and thus not history at all, in behalf of the genuine history that has already happened." And this stubborn preference for the past as against the present is, he perceives, the root of the "something not perfectly right and good" in his love of his little daughter. For his "devotion to this priceless little morsel of life and new growth has something to do with death, it clings to death as against life; and that is neither right nor beautiful." The accusation that Professor Cornelius directs against himself does not go as far as it might—he cannot bring himself to say what we know to be the truth, that what is not "right and beautiful" in his love of the child is the hidden wish that she never change from what she now is; that she always be beautiful in the way that she now is and in no other way; that the experience of life, with the pain and the loss of innocence it entails, shall not be hers. Ellie's sudden, uncontrollable, precocious passion for Herr Hergesell, in his dull complacency so unworthy an object of her devotion, makes it bitterly plain to her father that his wish is beyond any hope of realization, and, bitter though his feelings are, he can only be glad that this is so.

It is this ambivalence of the father, his wanting and his yet not wanting his daughter to have the experience of life, that makes the strong and complex emotion of the story. And it is the irony of the chaotic forces of life being embodied in this delicate, only momentarily awakened little girl, that makes the story's bitter charm.

DI GRASSO
A Tale of Odessa

ISAAC BABEL

1894–1939

I WAS FOURTEEN, and of the undauntable fellowship of dealers in theater tickets. My boss was a tricky customer with a permanently screwed-up eye and enormous silky handle bars; Nick Schwarz was his name. I came under his sway in that unhappy year when the Italian Opera flopped in Odessa.[1] Taking a lead from the critics on the local paper, our impresario decided not to import Anselmi and Tito Ruffo as guest artistes but to make do with a good stock company. For this he was sorely punished; he went bankrupt, and we with him. We were promised Chaliapin to straighten out our affairs, but Chaliapin wanted three thousand a performance; so instead we had the Sicilian tragedian Di Grasso with his troupe. They arrived at the hotel in peasant carts crammed with children, cats, cages in which Italian birds hopped and skipped. Casting an eye over this gypsy crew, Nick Schwarz opined:

"Children, this stuff won't sell."

When he had settled in, the tragedian made his way to the market with a bag. In the evening he arrived at the theater with another bag. Hardly fifty people had turned up. We tried selling tickets at half-price, but there were no takers.

[1] A city in the U.S.S.R.

710

That evening they staged a Sicilian folk drama, a tale as commonplace as the change from night to day and vice versa. The daughter of a rich peasant pledges her troth to a shepherd. She is faithful to him till one day there drives out from the city a young slicker in a velvet waistcoat. Passing the time of day with the new arrival, the maiden giggled in all the wrong places and fell silent when she shouldn't have. As he listened to them, the shepherd twisted his head this way and that like a startled bird. During the whole of the first act he kept flattening himself against walls, dashing off somewhere, his pants flapping, and on his return gazing wildly about.

"This stuff stinks," said Nick Schwarz in the intermission. "Only place it might go down is some dump like Kremenchug."

The intermission was designed to give the maiden time to grow ripe for betrayal. In the second act we just couldn't recognize her: she behaved insufferably, her thoughts were clearly elsewhere, and she lost no time in handing the shepherd back his ring. Thereupon he led her over to a poverty-stricken but brightly painted image of the Holy Virgin, and said in his Sicilian patois:

"Signora," said he in a low voice, turning away, "the Holy Virgin desires you to give me a hearing. To Giovanni, the fellow from the city, the Holy Virgin will grant as many women as he can cope with; but I need none save you. The Virgin Mary, our stainless intercessor, will tell you exactly the same thing if you ask Her."

The maiden stood with her back to the painted wooden image. As she listened she kept impatiently tapping her foot.

In the third act Giovanni, the city slicker, met his fate. He was having a shave at the village barber's, his powerful male legs thrust out all over the front of the stage. Beneath the Sicilian sun the pleats in his waistcoat gleamed. The scene represented a village fair. In a far corner stood the shepherd; silent he stood there amid the carefree crowd. First he hung his head; then he raised it, and beneath the weight of his attentive and burning gaze Giovanni started stirring and fidgeting in his barber chair, till pushing the barber aside he leaped to his feet. In a voice shaking with passion he demanded that the policeman should remove from the village square all persons of a gloomy and suspicious aspect. The shepherd—the part was played by Di Grasso himself—stood there lost in thought; then he gave a smile, soared into the air, sailed across the stage, plunged down on Giovanni's shoulders, and having bitten through the latter's throat, began, growling and squinting, to suck blood from the wound. Giovanni collapsed, and the curtain, falling noiselessly and full of menace, hid from us killed and killer. Waiting for no more, we dashed to the box office in Theater Lane, which was to open next day, Nick Schwarz beating the rest by a short neck. Came the dawn, and with it the *Odessa News* informed the few people who had been at the theater that they had seen the most remarkable actor of the century.

On this visit Di Grasso played *King Lear, Othello, Civil Death,* Turgenev's *The Parasite,* confirming with every word and every gesture that there is more justice in outbursts of noble passion than in all the joyless rules that run the world.

Tickets for these shows were snapped up at five times face value. Scouting round for ticket-traders, would-be purchasers found them at the inn, yelling their heads off, purple, vomiting a harmless sacrilege.

A pink and dusty sultriness was injected into Theater Lane. Shopkeepers in felt slippers bore green bottles of wine and barrels of olives out onto the pavement. In tubs outside the shops macaroni seethed in foaming water, and the steam from it melted in the distant skies. Old women in men's boots dealt in seashells and souvenirs, pursuing hesitant purchasers with loud cries. Moneyed Jews with beards parted down the middle and combed to either side would drive up to the Northern Hotel and tap discreetly on the doors of fat women with raven hair and little mustaches, Di Grasso's actresses. All were happy in Theater Lane; all, that is, save for one person. I was that person. In those days catastrophe was approaching me: at any moment my father might miss the watch I had taken without his permission and pawned to Nick Schwarz. Having had the gold turnip long enough to get used to it, and being a man who replaced tea as his morning drink by Bessarabian wine, Nick Schwarz, even with his money back, could still not bring himself to return the watch to me. Such was his character. And my father's character differed in no wise from his. Hemmed in by these two characters, I sorrowfully watched other people enjoying themselves. Nothing remained for me but to run away to Constantinople. I had made all the arrangements with the second engineer of the S.S. *Duke of Kent,* but before embarking on the deep I decided to say goodbye to Di Grasso. For the last time he was playing the shepherd who is swung aloft by an incomprehensible power. In the audience were all the Italian colony, with the bald but shapely consul at their head. There were fidgety Greeks and bearded externs with their gaze fastened fanatically upon some point invisible to all other mortals; there was the long-armed Utochkin. Nick Schwarz had even brought his missis, in a violet shawl with a fringe; a woman with all the makings of a grenadier she was, stretching right out to the steppes, and with a sleepy little crumpled face at the far end. When the curtain fell this face was drenched in tears.

"Now you see what love means," she said to Nick as they were leaving the theater.

Stomping ponderously, Madam Schwarz moved along Langeron Street; tears rolled from her fishlike eyes, and the shawl with the fringe shuddered on her obese shoulders. Dragging her mannish soles, rocking her head, she reckoned up, in a voice that made the street re-echo, the women who got on well with their husbands.

"'Ducky' they're called by their husbands; 'sweetypie' they're called . . ."

The cowed Nick walked along by his wife, quietly blowing on his silky mustaches. From force of habit I followed on behind, sobbing. During a momentary pause Madam Schwarz heard my sobs and turned around.

"See here," she said to her husband, her fisheyes agoggle, "may I not die a beautiful death if you don't give the boy his watch back!"

Nick froze, mouth agape; then came to and, giving me a vicious pinch, thrust the watch at me sideways.

"What can I expect of him," the coarse and tear-muffled voice of Madam Schwarz wailed disconsolately as it moved off into the distance, "what can I expect but beastliness today and beastliness tomorrow? I ask you, how long is a woman supposed to put up with it?"

They reached the corner and turned into Pushkin Street. I stood there clutching the watch, alone; and suddenly, with a distinctness such as I had never before experienced, I saw the columns of the Municipal Building soaring up into the heights, the gas-lit foliage of the boulevard, Pushkin's bronze head touched by the dim gleam of the moon; saw for the first time the things surrounding me as they really were: frozen in silence and ineffably beautiful.

COMMENTARY

One of the conventional ways of praising art is to associate it with the peaceful and "constructive" virtues and to put it at the furthest possible remove from violence. But artists themselves are not misled by this pious view of their enterprise. They know how often the act of creation is bound up with the aggressive impulses. And perhaps no one has made this knowledge quite so salient in his conception of art as Isaac Babel.

Babel was one of the very few writers of genius to develop under Soviet rule. For a short period after his work began to appear in the 1920's, his remarkable gifts were recognized and he enjoyed a measure of fame, but then he fell into disfavor with the regime and was accused of political crimes. Although never brought to trial, he was sent to a prison camp, where he died in 1939 or 1940.

The great—the crucial—experience of Babel's life was his service with a regiment of Cossacks in 1920 during a campaign of the terrible civil war that followed the Russian Revolution. To understand the meaning of this experience, we must know that Babel was a Jew and that no two peoples could be more completely and significantly antithetical to each other than the Jews of Eastern Europe and the Cossacks. The Jews conceived their ideal character to be intellectual, humane, and peaceable. The Cossacks were physical and violent, men of the body, the sword, and the horse. The relation between the two groups had long been extremely hostile. Each held the other in contempt, and the hatred between them was the more intense because the Czarist government of Russia had used Cossack troops in its systematic persecution of the Jews. Nothing, then, could have been more anomalous than that a Jew—and an intellectual and rather weakly Jew at that, a man "with spectacles on his nose and autumn in his heart," as Babel described himself—should ride and fight by the side of the Cossacks. It is clear from his superb stories about this experience—they were collected in a volume called *Red Cavalry*—that Babel wanted to eradicate from his temperament the quietism that had been instilled into it by his Jewish upbringing, and that it was for this reason that he undertook to share the Cossack life of physicality and violence, even of cruelty.

Babel's wish to model his behavior on that of his Cossack comrades was not easily attained. He found, as he said, that to face death was not so very hard, but that it was hard indeed to acquire what he called "the simplest of proficiencies—the ability to kill [one's] fellowmen." Much as he admired the grace and force of the Cossacks and the fierce directness with which they expressed their feelings, he could not rid himself of the pacific ideals of his Jewish heritage. But although the way of peace and the way of violence were always in conflict in his mind, it is plain that his interest was more engaged by the way of violence. It seemed to promise him a kind of liberation of spirit and his fulfilment as a man.

No less did it promise him liberation and fulfilment as a writer. Babel was intensely conscious of the problems of style, and whenever he talked about style he resorted to metaphors of physical violence. He spoke of prose as a series of military maneuvers executed by the "army of words, the army in which all kinds of weapons may be brought into play." He remarked that "there is no iron that can enter the human heart with such stupefying effect as a period placed at just the right moment." He thought that the essence of art was unexpectedness, a surprise attack upon the reader's habitual assumptions.

This conception of art as disciplined violence is the theme of what was to be the last story that Babel wrote. "Di Grasso" is composed in the intimate, colloquial, seemingly casual manner that Babel had made his own, and on first reading it may seem to be a very simple story, not much more than an anecdote. But Babel was anything but a simple man, and this story has all the subtlety and complexity that we might expect to find in a highly developed writer's apologia for his art, which in effect "Di Grasso" is.

An Italian theatrical company has come for a repertory season to Odessa, Russia's great Black Sea port, a city famous for its cosmopolitan interest in the arts of performance. The troupe's first performance begins in a most unpromising way, for the play is a dull provincial piece, the acting is ridden by cliché and convention. But then one moment brings to an end, and redeems, all the boredom—when the actor Di Grasso "gave a smile, soared into the air, sailed across the stage, plunged down on [the villain's] shoulders, and having bitten through the latter's throat, began, growling and squinting, to suck blood from the wound." Di Grasso is to go through a long repertory, and in all his performances he will "with every word and every gesture" confirm the idea that "there is more justice in outbursts of noble passion than in all the joyless rules that run the world." But although he plays Othello and King Lear, the nature of his genius is most forcibly suggested to the young protagonist of the story—whom we take to be a representation of Babel himself—not by his performance of these great rôles but by the absurd incident of physical violence in an inferior play.

What was it in that moment of melodramatic nonsense that enchanted the audience and became so memorable to the author? Certainly the sheer virtuosity of the leap is a decisive element—the actor's extraordinary ability to "soar into the air," to "sail across the stage," to do, or seem to do, what presumably cannot be done. Although the word *virtuosity* may indeed be used in praise, it may also be used with a contemptuous intention, to suggest mere technical skill, with, by implication, a paucity of spiritual or intellectual energy. Yet mere technical skill can delight us, as in the performance of jugglers, trapeze artists, and stage magicians. And an unusual degree of technical skill has the effect of enhancing or confirming the other qualities an artist may possess. Everyone who saw Nijinski perform believed him to be the greatest dancer of all time, and almost every account of his art makes reference to one extraordinary achievement— his power of levitation, his ability, like Di Grasso's, to soar into the air and sail across the stage. Those who saw him do this seem to have had an intimation of the possibility of freedom from the bondage of our human condition. It is no small idea for a leap to propose!

The naked ferocity that Di Grasso displays has an effect related to that of his astonishing leap—it, too, suggests the idea of a liberation. This, however, is a liberation not from the general human condition but from the constraints of society, from the dullness, the passivity, the acquiescence in which we live most of our lives.

But the intention of Babel's story goes beyond its celebration of the great murderous leap and its assertion that intensity, or "noble passion," is the very soul of art. Babel is concerned with the moral effect which may result from the kind of aesthetic experience he has described.

The wife of the ticket speculator would seem to be the least likely person in the world to exemplify the moral power that art can have. She is gross in manner, grotesque in appearance, and therefore she ought not, by conventional notions, be susceptible to the noble passions; and we may easily suppose that what susceptibility she does have will not last very long. Yet, if only for the moment, the great leap of Di Grasso and his display of ferocity bring to her mind ideas of love, tenderness, and generosity, and she turns upon her cadging husband in rage at his lack of all large-minded emotions. What is more, she recalls a particular instance of her husband's meanness that she will no longer put up with. Decency has become suddenly, if fleetingly, important to her—she knows that her husband has been keeping illicitly a watch that belongs to his young assistant's father; she insists that it be returned at once and she is not to be withstood.

The story might well have come to its end with this episode, but the final paragraph carries it to a further development of great charm and profundity. The young Babel—for at this point we can no longer doubt that the narrator is the author writing about himself in his youth—is freed from the anguish and fear caused by his being unable to regain possession of his father's watch, and now, all at once, he perceives the street in which he stands with "a distinctness such as [he] had never before experienced." Now, "for the first time," he sees the things around him "as they really were: frozen in silence and ineffably beautiful." His sudden unexpected relief from anxiety and wretchedness has brought about this almost mystical perception. An aesthetic experience has produced an act of moral decency; the act of moral decency becomes the cause of a transcendent experience. We can scarcely suppose that Babel was unaware of the irony implicit in the fact that the pure and peaceful contemplation described in the last paragraph of "Di Grasso" owed its existence to the violence of the actor's leap.

THE

SAILOR-BOY'S

TALE

ISAK DINESEN

1885–1962

THE BARQUE *Charlotte* was on her way from Marseille to Athens, in grey weather, on a high sea, after three days' heavy gale. A small sailor-boy, named Simon, stood on the wet, swinging deck, held on to a shroud, and looked up towards the drifting clouds, and to the upper top-gallant yard of the main-mast.

A bird, that had sought refuge upon the mast, had got her feet tangled in some loose tackle-yarn of the halliard, and high up there, struggled to get free. The boy on the deck could see her wings flapping and her head turning from side to side.

Through his own experience of life he had come to the conviction that in this world everyone must look after himself, and expect no help from others. But the mute, deadly fight kept him fascinated for more than an hour. He wondered what kind of bird it would be. These last days a number of birds had come to settle in the barque's rigging: swallows, quails, and a pair of peregrine falcons; he believed that this bird was a peregrine falcon. He remembered how, many years ago, in his own country and near his home, he had once seen a peregrine falcon quite close, sitting on a stone and flying straight up from it. Perhaps this was the same bird. He thought: "That bird is like me. Then she was there, and now she is here."

At that a fellow-feeling rose in him, a sense of common tragedy; he stood looking at the bird with his heart in his mouth. There were none of the sailors about to make fun of him; he began to think out how he might go up by the shrouds to help the falcon out. He brushed his hair back and pulled up his sleeves, gave the deck round him a great glance, and climbed up. He had to stop a couple of times in the swaying rigging.

It was indeed, he found when he got to the top of the mast, a peregrine falcon. As his head was on a level with hers, she gave up her struggle, and looked at him with a pair of angry, desperate yellow eyes. He had to take hold of her with one hand while he got his knife out, and cut off the tackle-yarn. He was scared as he looked down, but at the same time he felt that he had been ordered up by nobody, but that this was his own venture, and this gave him a proud, steadying sensation, as if the sea and the sky, the ship, the bird and himself were all one. Just as he had freed the falcon, she hacked him on the thumb, so that the blood ran, and he nearly let her go. He grew angry with her, and gave her a clout on the head, then he put her inside his jacket, and climbed down again.

When he reached the deck the mate and the cook were standing there, looking up; they roared to him to ask what he had had to do in the mast. He was so tired that the tears were in his eyes. He took the falcon out and showed her to them, and she kept still within his hands. They laughed and walked off. Simon set the falcon down, stood back and watched her. After a while he reflected that she might not be able to get up from the slippery deck, so he caught her once more, walked away with her and placed her upon a bolt of canvas. A little after she began to trim her feathers, made two or three sharp jerks forward, and then suddenly flew off. The boy could follow her flight above the troughs of the grey sea. He thought: "There flies my falcon."

When the *Charlotte* came home, Simon signed aboard another ship, and two years later he was a light hand[1] on the schooner *Hebe* lying at Bodø, high up on the coast of Norway, to buy herrings.

To the great herring-markets of Bodø ships came together from all corners of the world; here were Swedish, Finnish and Russian boats, a forest of masts, and on shore a turbulent, irregular display of life, with many languages spoken, and mighty fists. On the shore booths had been set up, and the Lapps, small, yellow people, noiseless in their movements, with watchful eyes, whom Simon had never seen before, came down to sell bead-embroidered leather-goods. It was April, the sky and the sea were so clear that it was difficult to hold one's eyes up against them—salt, infinitely wide, and filled with bird-shrieks—as if someone were incessantly whetting invisible knives, on all sides, high up in Heaven.

Simon was amazed at the lightness of these April evenings. He knew no geography, and did not assign it to the latitude, but he took it as a sign of an unwonted good-will in the Universe, a favour. Simon had been small for his age all his life, but this last winter he had grown, and had become strong of limb. That good luck, he felt, must spring from the very same source as the sweetness of the weather, from a new benevolence in the world. He had been in need of such encouragement, for he was timid by nature; now he asked for no more. The rest he felt to be his own affair. He went about slowly, and proudly.

[1] A sailor who helps make up a ship's crew which is "light handed," that is, under-manned.

One evening he was ashore with land-leave, and walked up to the booth of a small Russian trader, a Jew who sold gold watches. All the sailors knew that his watches were made from bad metal, and would not go, still they bought them, and paraded them about. Simon looked at these watches for a long time, but did not buy. The old Jew had divers goods in his shop, and amongst others a case of oranges. Simon had tasted oranges on his journeys; he bought one and took it with him. He meant to go up on a hill, from where he could see the sea, and suck it there.

As he walked on, and had got to the outskirts of the place, he saw a little girl in a blue frock, standing at the other side of a fence and looking at him. She was thirteen or fourteen years old, as slim as an eel, but with a round, clear, freckled face, and a pair of long plaits. The two looked at one another.

"Who are you looking out for?" Simon asked, to say something. The girl's face broke into an ecstatic, presumptuous smile. "For the man I am going to marry, of course," she said. Something in her countenance made the boy confident and happy; he grinned a little at her. "That will perhaps be me," he said. "Ha, ha," said the girl, "he is a few years older than you, I can tell you." "Why," said Simon, "you are not grown up yourself." The little girl shook her head solemnly. "Nay," she said, "but when I grow up I will be exceedingly beautiful, and wear brown shoes with heels, and a hat." "Will you have an orange?" asked Simon, who could give her none of the things she had named. She looked at the orange and at him. "They are very good to eat," said he. "Why do you not eat it yourself then?" she asked. "I have eaten so many already," said he, "when I was in Athens. Here I had to pay a mark for it." "What is your name?" asked she. "My name is Simon," said he. "What is yours?" "Nora," said the girl. "What do you want for your orange now, Simon?"

When he heard his name in her mouth Simon grew bold. "Will you give me a kiss for the orange?" he asked. Nora looked at him gravely for a moment. "Yes," she said, "I should not mind giving you a kiss." He grew as warm as if he had been running quickly. When she stretched out her hand for the orange he took hold of it. At that moment somebody in the house called out for her. "That is my father," said she, and tried to give him back the orange, but he would not take it. "Then come again tomorrow," she said quickly, "then I will give you a kiss." At that she slipped off. He stood and looked after her, and a little later went back to his ship.

Simon was not in the habit of making plans for the future, and now he did not know whether he would be going back to her or not.

The following evening he had to stay aboard, as the other sailors were going ashore, and he did not mind that either. He meant to sit on the deck with the ship's dog, Balthasar, and to practise upon a concertina that he had purchased some time ago. The pale evening was all round him, the sky was faintly roseate, the sea was quite calm, like milk-and-water, only in the wake of the boats going inshore it broke into streaks of vivid indigo. Simon sat and played; after a while his own music began to speak to him so strongly that he stopped, got up and looked upwards. Then he saw that the full moon was sitting high on the sky.

The sky was so light that she hardly seemed needed there; it was as if she had turned up by a caprice of her own. She was round, demure and presumptuous. At that he knew that he must go ashore, whatever it was to cost him.

But he did not know how to get away since the others had taken the yawl with them. He stood on the deck for a long time, a small lonely figure of a sailor-boy on a boat, when he caught sight of a yawl coming in from a ship farther out, and hailed her. He found that it was the Russian crew from the boat named *Anna*, going ashore. When he could make himself understood to them, they took him with them; they first asked him for money for his fare, then laughing, gave it back to him. He thought: "These people will be believing that I am going in to town, wenching." And then he felt, with some pride, that they were right, although at the same time they were infinitely wrong, and knew nothing about anything.

When they came ashore they invited him to come in and drink in their company, and he would not refuse, because they had helped him. One of the Russians was a giant, as big as a bear; he told Simon that his name was Ivan. He got drunk at once, and then fell upon the boy with a bear-like affection, pawed him, smiled and laughed into his face, made him a present of a gold watch-chain, and kissed him on both cheeks. At that Simon reflected that he also ought to give Nora a present when they met again, and as soon as he could get away from the Russians he walked up to a booth that he knew of, and bought a small blue silk handkerchief, the same colour as her eyes.

It was Saturday evening, and there were many people amongst the houses; they came in long rows, some of them singing, all keen to have some fun that night. Simon, in the midst of this rich, bawling life under the clear moon, felt his head light with the flight from the ship and the strong drinks. He crammed the handkerchief in his pocket; it was silk, which he had never touched before, a present for his girl.

He could not remember the path up to Nora's house, lost his way, and came back to where he had started. Then he grew deadly afraid that he should be too late, and began to run. In a small passage between two wooden huts he ran straight into a big man, and found that it was Ivan once more. The Russian folded his arms round him and held him. "Good! Good!" he cried in high glee, "I have found you, my little chicken. I have looked for you everywhere, and poor Ivan has wept because he lost his friend." "Let me go, Ivan," cried Simon. "Oho," said Ivan, "I shall go with you and get you what you want. My heart and my money are all yours; I have been seventeen years old myself, a little lamb of God, and I want to be so again tonight." "Let me go," cried Simon, "I am in a hurry." Ivan held him so that it hurt, and patted him with his other hand. "I feel it, I feel it," he said. "Now trust to me, my little friend. Nothing shall part you and me, I hear the others coming; we will have such a night to-gether as you will remember when you are an old grandpapa."

Suddenly he crushed the boy to him, like a bear that carries off a sheep. The odious sensation of male bodily warmth and the bulk of a man close to him made the lean boy mad. He thought of Nora waiting, like a slender ship in the dim air, and of himself, here, in the hot embrace of a hairy animal. He struck Ivan with all his might. "I shall kill you, Ivan," he cried out, "if you do not let me go." "Oh, you will be thankful to me later on," said Ivan, and began to sing. Simon fumbled in his pocket for his knife, got it opened. He could not lift his hand, but he drove the knife, furiously, in under the big man's arm. Almost immediately he felt the blood spouting out, and running down in his sleeve. Ivan stopped short in the song, let go his hold of the boy and gave two long deep grunts. The next second he tumbled down to his knees. "Poor Ivan, poor Ivan," he groaned. He fell straight on his face. At that moment Simon heard the other sailors coming along, singing, in the by-street.

He stood still for a minute, wiped his knife, and watched the blood spread into a dark pool underneath the big body. Then he ran. As he stopped for a second to choose his way, he heard the sailors behind him scream out over their dead comrade. He thought: "I must get down to the sea, where I can wash my hand." But at the same time he ran the other way. After a little while he found himself on the path that he had walked on the day before, and it seemed as familiar to him, as if he had walked it many hundred times in his life.

He slackened his pace to look round, and suddenly saw Nora standing on the other side of the fence; she was quite close to him when he caught sight of her in the moonlight. Wavering and out of breath he sank down on his knees. For a moment he could not speak. The little girl looked down at him. "Good evening, Simon," she said in her small coy voice. "I have waited for you a long time," and after a moment she added: "I have eaten your orange."

"Oh, Nora," cried the boy. "I have killed a man." She stared at him, but did not move. "Why did you kill a man?" she asked after a moment. "To get here," said Simon. "Because he tried to stop me. But he was my friend." Slowly he got on to his feet. "He loved me!" the boy cried out, and at that burst into tears. "Yes," said she slowly and thoughtfully. "Yes, because you must be here in time." "Can you hide me?" he asked. "For they are after me." "Nay," said Nora, "I cannot hide you. For my father is the parson here at Bodø, and he would be sure to hand you over to them, if he knew that you had killed a man." "Then," said Simon, "give me something to wipe my hands on." "What is the matter with your hands?" she asked, and took a little step forward. He stretched out his hands to her. "Is that your own blood?" she asked. "No," said he, "it is his." She took the step back again. "Do you hate me now?" he asked. "No, I do not hate you," said she. "But do put your hands at your back."

As he did so she came up close to him, at the other side of the fence, and clasped her arms round his neck. She pressed her young body to his, and kissed him tenderly. He felt her face, cool as the moonlight, upon his own, and when she released him, his head swam, and he did not know if the kiss had lasted a second or an hour. Nora stood up straight, her eyes wide open. "Now," she said slowly and proudly, "I promise you that I will never marry anybody, as long as I live." The boy kept standing with his hands on his back, as if she had tied them there. "And now," she said, "you must run, for they are coming." They looked at one another. "Do not forget Nora," said she. He turned and ran.

He leapt over a fence, and when he was down amongst the houses he walked. He did not know at all where to go. As he came to a house, from where music and noise streamed out, he slowly went through the door. The room was full of people; they were dancing in here. A lamp hung from the ceiling, and shone down on them, the air was thick and brown with dust rising from the floor. There were some women in the room, but many of the men danced with each other, and gravely or laughingly stamped the floor. A moment after Simon had come in the crowd withdrew to the walls to clear the floor for two sailors, who were showing a dance from their own country.

Simon thought: "Now, very soon, the men from the boat will come round to look for their comrade's murderer, and from my hands they will know that

I have done it." These five minutes during which he stood by the wall of the dancing-room, in the midst of the gay, sweating dancers, were of great significance to the boy. He himself felt it, as if during this time he grew up, and became like other people. He did not entreat his destiny, nor complain. Here he was, he had killed a man, and had kissed a girl. He did not demand any more from life, nor did life now demand more from him. He was Simon, a man like the men round him, and going to die, as all men are going to die.

He only became aware of what was going on outside him, when he saw a woman had come in, and was standing in the midst of the cleared floor, looking round her. She was short, broad old woman, in the clothes of the Lapps, and she took her stand with such majesty and fierceness as if she owned the whole place. It was obvious that most of the people knew her, and were a little afraid of her, although a few laughed; the din of the dancing-room stopped when she spoke.

"Where is my son?" she asked in a high shrill voice, like a bird's. The next moment her eyes fell on Simon himself, and she steered through the crowd, which opened up before her, stretched out her old skinny, dark hand, and took him by the elbow. "Come home with me now," she said. "You need not dance here tonight. You may be dancing a high enough dance soon."

Simon drew back, for he thought that she was drunk. But as she looked him straight in the face with her yellow eyes, it seemed to him that he had met her before, and that he might do well in listening to her. The old woman pulled him with her across the floor, and he followed her without a word. "Do not birch your boy too badly, Sunniva," one of the men in the room cried to her. "He has done no harm, he only wanted to look at the dance."

At the same moment as they came out through the door there was an alarm in the street, a flock of people came running down it, and one of them as he turned into the house, knocked against Simon, looked at him and the old woman, and ran on.

While the two walked along the street, the old woman lifted up her skirt, and put the hem of it into the boy's hand. "Wipe your hand on my skirt," she said. They had not gone far before they came to a small wooden house, and stopped; the door to it was so low that they must bend to get through it. As the Lapp-woman went in before Simon, still holding on to his arm, the boy looked up for a moment. The night had grown misty; there was a wide ring round the moon.

The old woman's room was narrow and dark, with but one small window to it; a lantern stood on the floor and lighted it up dimly. It was all filled with reindeer skins and wolf skins, and with reindeer horn, such as the Lapps use to make their carved buttons and knife-handles, and the air in here was rank and stifling. As soon as they were in, the woman turned to Simon, took hold of his head, and with her crooked fingers parted his hair and combed it down in Lapp fashion. She clapped a Lapp cap on him and stood back to glance at him. "Sit down on my stool, now," she said. "But first take out your knife." She was so commanding in voice and manner that the boy could not but choose to do as she told him; he sat down on the stool, and he could not take his eyes off her face, which was flat and brown, and as if smeared with dirt in its net of fine wrinkles. As he sat there he heard many people come along outside, and stop by the house; then someone knocked at the door, waited a moment and knocked again. The old woman stood and listened, as still as a mouse.

"Nay," said the boy and got up. "This is no good, for it is me that they are after. It will be better for you to let me go out to them." "Give me your knife," said she. When he handed it to her, she stuck it straight into her thumb, so that the blood spouted out, and she let it drip all over her skirt. "Come in, then," she cried.

The door opened, and two Russian sailors came and stood in the opening; there were more people outside. "Has anybody come in here?" they asked. "We are after a man who has killed our mate, but he has run away from us. Have you seen or heard anybody this way?" The old Lapp-woman turned upon them, and her eyes shone like gold in the lamplight. "Have I seen or heard anyone?" she cried, "I have heard you shriek murder all over the town. You frightened me, and my poor silly boy there, so that I cut my thumb as I was ripping the skin-rug that I sew. The boy is too scared to help me, and the rug is all ruined. I shall make you pay me for that. If you are looking for a murderer, come in and search my house for me, and I shall know you when we meet again." She was so furious that she danced where she stood, and jerked her head like an angry bird of prey.

The Russian came in, looked round the room, and at her and her blood-stained hand and skirt. "Do not put a curse on us now, Sunniva," he said timidly. "We know that you can do many things when you like. Here is a mark to pay you for the blood you have spilled." She stretched out her hand, and he placed a piece of money in it. She spat on it. "Then go, and there shall be no bad blood between us," said Sunniva, and shut the door after them. She stuck her thumb in her mouth, and chuckled a little.

The boy got up from his stool, stood up before her and stared into her face. He felt as if he were swaying high up in the air, with but a small hold. "Why have you helped me?" he asked her. "Do you not know?" she answered. "Have you not recognised me yet? But you will remember the peregrine falcon which was caught in the tackle-yarn of your boat, the *Charlotte,* as she sailed in the Mediterranean. That day you climbed up by the shrouds of the top-gallantmast to help her out, in a stiff wind, and with a high sea. That falcon was me. We Lapps often fly in such a manner, to see the world. When I first met you I was on my way to Africa, to see my younger sister and her children. She is a falcon too, when she chooses. By that time she was living at Takaunga, within an old ruined tower, which down there they call a minaret." She swathed a corner of her skirt round her thumb, and bit at it, "We do not forget," she said. "I hacked your thumb, when you took hold of me; it is only fair that I should cut my thumb for you tonight."

She came close to him, and gently rubbed her two brown, clawlike fingers against his forehead. "So you are a boy," she said, "who will kill a man rather than be late to meet your sweetheart? We hold together, the females of this earth. I shall mark your forehead now, so that the girls will know of that, when they look at you, and they will like you for it." She played with the boy's hair, and twisted it round her finger.

"Listen now, my little bird," said she. "My great grandson's brother-in-law is lying with his boat by the landing-place at this moment; he is to take a con-signment of skins out to a Danish boat. He will bring you back to your boat, in time, before your mate comes. The *Hebe* is sailing tomorrow morning, is it not so? But when you are aboard, give him back my cap for me." She took up his knife, wiped it in her skirt and handed it to him. "Here is your knife," she said. "You will stick it into no more men; you will not need to, for from now you will sail the seas like a faithful seaman. We have enough trouble with our sons as it is."

The bewildered boy began to stammer his thanks to her. "Wait," said she, "I shall make you a cup of coffee, to bring back your wits, while I wash your jacket." She went and rattled an old copper kettle upon the fireplace. After a while she handed him a hot, strong, black drink in a cup without a handle to it. "You have drunk with Sunniva now," she said; "you have drunk down a little wisdom, so that in the future all your thoughts shall not fall like raindrops into the salt sea."

When he had finished and set down the cup, she led him to the door and opened it for him. He was so surprised to see that it was almost clear morning. The house was so high up that the boy could see the sea from it, and a milky mist about it. He gave her his hand to say good-bye.

She stared into his face. "We do not forget," she said "And you, you knocked me on the head there, high up in the mast. I shall give you that blow back." With that she smacked him on the ear as hard as she could, so that his head swam. "Now we are quits," she said, gave him a great, mischievous, shining glance, and a little push down the doorstep, and nodded to him.

In this way the sailor-boy got back to his ship, which was to sail the next morning, and lived to tell the story.

COMMENTARY

Isak Dinesen[1] always called her stories "tales." The use of this word served notice that she intended to tell a story of a particular kind. What is a tale? Perhaps it is best defined as a narrative which counts upon a certain simplicity of acceptance from the reader or hearer, an acquiescence in the possibility of strange and unlikely events, especially marvelous ones.

In cultures which have not developed a high degree of rational thought, the marvelous is taken for granted as virtually the essence of the literary experience. This is true also of children, who have always been supposed to have a natural affinity with marvels and an appetite for them. Even the modern theory, which has established itself in some quarters, that children ought not be told fairy tales but only stories about "real life," has not been able to overcome this supposition. It has merely replaced fairy godmothers and pumpkin-coaches with infant locomotives that think, feel, and talk, and perform heroic deeds.

We cannot suppose that the child, or the adult whose culture sets less store by rational thought than ours does, accepts the marvelous in exactly the same way that he accepts the actual occurrences of daily life. Were he to do so, he would take no pleasure in the stories in which the marvelous has a part. He merely accepts it more immediately and naively than a mature person reared in

---

[1] The pseudonym of the Baroness Karen Blixen. Her mother tongue was Danish, but she wrote in English.

a culture in which rational thought is highly valued. And even such a person by no means rejects the marvelous. He has his own way of accepting it, for although he does not "believe" it, yet with no great effort he is able to make what Coleridge, in his famous phrase, called "a willing suspension of disbelief." For the purposes of literature, this does quite well enough. If anyone were to interrupt our reading of a story about ghosts, or walking corpses, or monsters from outer space in order to ask whether we believed in their actual existence, we should unhesitatingly reply that we did not, that such creatures were impossible. Yet it is likely that we should be giving this answer in circumstances which indicated just the opposite—our pulse rate would probably have gone up, our palms would be damp, and we would be experiencing some uneasiness about being alone in the house at night. We would have been interested, even absorbed, in the impossible story, to the point of resenting the interruption. We permit ourselves, that is, to respond to the unlikely beings in such a story *as if* we believed in them. The fact that we do not really believe in them but have only suspended our disbelief does not prevent their having their effect upon us.

In a culture like ours, which gives so much weight to rationality, the marvelous has a rather special place in the reading experience. In general, our literature is committed to fact and to the representation of reality. We tend to praise a literary work in the degree that we think it communicates the truth of actuality. But for that very reason, the marvelous, when it does appear, has a special value for the modern reader.[2] Coleridge suggested what this value might be when, in connection with his great poem of the marvelous, *The Rime of the Ancient Mariner,* he quoted the seventeenth-century Bishop Burnet, who said that a belief in demons—he stipulated a *judicious* belief—preserved the mind from "mean thoughts," from small and merely mundane views of life. It is often said that modern science, so far from being what science used to be called, "organized common sense," has developed only through its willingness to defy common sense and the evidence of the senses—that it is based upon an acceptance, if not of the marvelous, then at least of the unlikely, and upon conceptions which do not apply to the occurrences of daily life and which require a suspension of disbelief. Certainly for the modern reader, the element of the marvelous in literature has important moral implications: it suggests that life is not to be understood in terms only of our daily practical knowledge of it, that it is also a mystery, evoking our wonder no less than our fortitude.

"The Sailor-Boy's Tale" has in common with several other stories in this book—"Di Grasso," "The Secret Sharer," "My Kinsman, Major Molineux"— the theme of initiation, of a young man's moving forward into a new stage of growth. The attraction of this theme for writers as diverse as Babel, Conrad, Hawthorne, and Isak Dinesen indicates something of the universality of its appeal. We first encounter it in the folk-tales we read in early childhood, which tell about the youngest son of the woodcutter or the miller, who is thought to be a fool by his family but who sets out alone to make his fortune, and succeeds, showing himself to be no mere undeveloped boy but a man. As the youth goes on his journey, he encounters circumstances that try his capacities: not un-

---

[2] The commentary on W. B. Yeats's *Purgatory* (pp. 369 ff.) discusses the exceptional instance of an author who gives literal credence to beings and circumstances that most people "accept" only by suspending their disbelief, and remarks on the effect that the author's belief has on the reader.

commonly he is tested for his kindness of heart. Because he is willing to milk the cow that hasn't been milked for seven long years, or because he is courteous to the old crone whom no one will regard, some unexpected and unpredictable good befalls him. The cow and the old woman are not what they seem, they turn out to have some helpful secret to impart or some magical assistance to offer. So in "The Sailor-Boy's Tale," the peregrine hawk that young Simon frees from the rigging is a Lapland witch—the people of Lapland have always been known as the most accomplished of witches and wizards—who, when Simon is in danger, repays in kind the help he had given her.

This is the kind of marvelous event we are all familiar with from the tales of our childhood, and much of the charm of Isak Dinesen's story lies in its use of the matter of a children's tale in a story not meant for children. But all the stories of initiation included in this book, not Isak Dinesen's alone, contain an element of the marvelous. Di Grasso's leap is beyond the powers of ordinary mortals; it is virtually the action of a divine being, and it appears to have a magical effect upon those who witness it. The young captain in "The Secret Sharer" is endangered but also aided by his double, who is essentially the *Doppelgänger* of folktale, the supernatural duplication of himself that it was once thought a man might encounter, and the experience of young Robin in "My Kinsman, Major Molineux" is compounded of supernatural episodes, or so at least they seem to the young hero. Inevitably we are led to wonder if the experience of initiation is not one we naturally incline to connect with happenings of a marvelous kind. And, indeed, is it not felt to be exactly a marvel by the young person who experiences it—does he not know that, in passing from boyhood to manhood, he has been *transformed?*

HILLS

LIKE

WHITE

ELEPHANTS

ERNEST HEMINGWAY

1898–1961

THE HILLS ACROSS THE VALLEY of the Ebro were long and white. On this side there was no shade and no trees and the station was between two lines of rails in the sun. Close against the side of the station there was the warm shadow of the building and a curtain, made of strings of bamboo beads, hung across the open door into the bar, to keep out flies. The American and the girl with him sat at a table in the shade, outside the building. It was very hot and the express from Barcelona would come in forty minutes. It stopped at this junction for two minutes and went on to Madrid.

"What should we drink?" the girl asked. She had taken off her hat and put it on the table.

"It's pretty hot," the man said.

"Let's drink beer."

"Doz cervezas," the man said into the curtain.

"Big ones?" a woman asked from the doorway.

"Yes. Two big ones."

The woman brought two glasses of beer and two felt pads. She put the felt pads and the beer glasses on the table and looked at the man and the girl. The girl was looking off at the line of hills. They were white in the sun and the country was brown and dry.

"They look like white elephants," she said.

"I've never seen one," the man drank his beer.

"No, you wouldn't have."

"I might have," the man said. "Just because you say I wouldn't have doesn't prove anything."

The girl looked at the bead curtain. "They've painted something on it," she said. "What does it say?"

"Anis del Toro. It's a drink."

"Could we try it?"

The man called "Listen" through the curtain. The woman came out from the bar.

"Four reales."

"We want two Anis del Toro."

"With water?"

"Do you want it with water?"

"I don't know," the girl said. "Is it good with water?"

"It's all right."

"You want them with water?" asked the woman.

"Yes, with water."

"It tastes like licorice," the girl said and put the glass down.

"That's the way with everything."

"Yes," said the girl. "Everything tastes of licorice. Especially all the things you've waited so long for, like absinthe."

"Oh, cut it out."

"You started it," the girl said. "I was being amused. I was having a fine time."

"Well, let's try to have a fine time."

"All right. I was trying. I said the mountains looked like white elephants. Wasn't that bright?"

"That was bright."

"I wanted to try this new drink. That's all we do, isn't it—look at things and try new drinks?"

"I guess so."

The girl looked across at the hills.

"They're lovely hills," she said. "They don't really look like white elephants. I just meant the coloring of their skin through the trees."

"Should we have another drink?"

"All right."

The warm wind blew the bead curtain against the table.

"The beer's nice and cool," the man said.

"It's lovely," the girl said.

"It's really an awfully simple operation, Jig," the man said. "It's not really an operation at all."

The girl looked at the ground the table legs rested on.

"I know you wouldn't mind it, Jig. It's really not anything. It's just to let the air in."

The girl did not say anything.

"I'll go with you and I'll stay with you all the time. They just let the air in and then it's all perfectly natural."

"Then what will we do afterward?"

"We'll be fine afterward. Just like we were before."

"What makes you think so?"

"That's the only thing that bothers us. It's the only thing that's made us unhappy."

The girl looked at the bead curtain, put her hand out and took hold of two of the strings of beads.

"And you think then we'll be all right and be happy."

"I know we will. You don't have to be afraid. I've known lots of people that have done it."

"So have I," said the girl. "And afterward they were all so happy."

"Well," the man said, "if you don't want to you don't have to. I wouldn't have you do it if you didn't want to. But I know it's perfectly simple."

"And you really want to?"

"I think it's the best thing to do. But I don't want you to do it if you don't really want to."

"And if I do it you'll be happy and things will be like they were and you'll love me?"

"I love you now. You know I love you."

"I know. But if I do it, then it will be nice again if I say things are like white elephants, and you'll like it?"

"I'll love it. I love it now but I just can't think about it. You know how I get when I worry."

"If I do it you won't ever worry?"

"I won't worry about that because it's perfectly simple."

"Then I'll do it. Because I don't care about me."

"What do you mean?"

"I don't care about me."

"Well, I care about you."

"Oh, yes. But I don't care about me. And I'll do it and then everything will be fine."

"I don't want you to do it if you feel that way."

The girl stood up and walked to the end of the station. Across, on the other side, were fields of grain and trees along the banks of the Ebro. Far away, beyond the river, were mountains. The shadow of a cloud moved across the field of grain and she saw the river through the trees.

"And we could have all this," she said. "And we could have everything and every day we make it more impossible."

"What did you say?"

"I said we could have everything."

"We can have everything."

" No, we can't."

"We can have the whole world."

"No, we can't."

"We can go everywhere."

"No, we can't. It isn't ours any more."

"It's ours."

"No, it isn't. And once they take it away, you never get it back."

"But they haven't taken it away."

"We'll wait and see."

"Come on back in the shade," he said. "You mustn't feel that way."

"I don't feel any way," the girl said. "I just know things."

"I don't want you to do anything that you don't want to do——"

"Nor that isn't good for me," she said. "I know. Could we have another beer?"

"All right. But you've got to realize——"

"I realize," the girl said. "Can't we maybe stop talking?"

They sat down at the table and the girl looked across at the hills on the dry side of the valley and the man looked at her and at the table.

"You've got to realize," he said, "that I don't want you to do it if you don't want to. I'm perfectly willing to go through with it if it means anything to you."

"Doesn't it mean anything to you? We could get along."

"Of course it does. But I don't want anybody but you. I don't want any one else. And I know it's perfectly simple."

"Yes, you know it's perfectly simple."

"It's all right for you to say that, but I do know it."

"Would you do something for me now?"

"I'd do anything for you."

"Would you please please please please please please please stop talking?"

He did not say anything but looked at the bags against the wall of the station. There were labels on them from all the hotels where they had spent nights.

"But I don't want you to," he said, "I don't care anything about it."

"I'll scream," said the girl.

The woman came out through the curtains with two glasses of beer and put them down on the damp felt pads. "The train comes in five minutes," he said.

"What did she say?" asked the girl.

"That the train is coming in five minutes."

The girl smiled brightly at the woman, to thank her.

"I'd rather take the bags over to the other side of the station," the man said. She smiled at him.

"All right. Then come back and we'll finish the beer."

He picked up the two heavy bags and carried them around the station to the other tracks. He looked up the tracks but could not see the train. Coming back, he walked through the barroom, where people waiting for the train were drinking. He drank an Anis at the bar and looked at the people. They were all waiting reasonably for the train. He went out through the bead curtain. She was sitting at the table and smiled at him.

"Do you feel better?" he asked.

"I feel fine," she said. "There's nothing wrong with me. I feel fine."

COMMENTARY

Ernest Hemingway recalls that when he first began to write and his stories were being steadily refused by the magazines, they were returned "with notes of rejection that would never call them stories but always anecdotes [or] sketches." One of these early stories was "Hills Like White Elephants," and it is interesting to speculate why the magazine editors of the 1920s thought it was not really a story.

One reason may be that they thought of a story as primarily something that is *told* whereas "Hills Like White Elephants" is scarcely told at all. The author makes every effort to keep himself anonymous and out of sight; he seems to refuse to have any connection either with the reader or with the people in the episode he is presenting. The scene is set in an opening paragraph which is as brief as it can be and severely impersonal in tone; and thereafter almost everything is left to the dialogue between the man and the girl, with the author intervening only to inform us that the drinks have been served, that the man carries the bags to the other side of the station, and, on two occasions, to tell us what the girl sees when she looks at the landscape. In fact, the author is so little related to what goes on in the story that he does not even take advantage of the traditional device of describing the tones of voice in which the characters speak. He does not tell us that the girl makes a remark "bitterly" or "ironically" or that the man replies "sulkily" or "placatingly." He does not presume to know anything at all about the couple, not even their names—it is by mere accident, as it were, that we learn the girl's nickname, Jig.

Nor does he undertake to tell us anything that could be learned even from direct observation of the girl and the man. Because she is always referred to as "the girl" and he as "the man," we feel free to conclude that she is younger than he and quite young—but is she twenty or twenty-three or twenty-five? Most readers will suppose her to be attractive, partly because she seems to speak and act as if she were, but the author says not a word about her appearance. There is ground for believing that the man and the girl are married, for it is still a question between them whether or not she is to bear the child with which she is pregnant. But it may also be that they are unmarried lovers and that the question of whether or not they will have the child involves the question of their getting married.

This stubborn reticence, this refusal by Hemingway to relate himself to the characters and to say anything *about* them, must surely have led the editors to feel that "Hills Like White Elephants" lacked the degree of meaning a story is expected to have as compared to an anecdote or sketch. My use of the word *meaning* must not tempt us into an elaborate theoretical discussion of what it is that we imply when we speak of a story's having, or lacking, meaning. It will be enough to say that the meaning of a story is the *sensation* of understanding which it creates in us. It may be—it usually is—scarcely possible to say what we have understood when we laugh at a joke. A story, like a joke, is successful if it sets up in us the sensation of our having understood it.

No doubt the magazine editors who first read "Hills Like White Elephants" felt that the remoteness of the author, his refusal to comment explicitly on what he presented, implied that he was not making the expected effort to give his readers this sensation. He put before his readers a human situation of considerable potential significance, without telling them how the situation was to be resolved, or what emotions and partisanships he wanted to evoke—he seemed to be indifferent as to what meaning his story might be found to have, or whether it would be found to have any meaning at all.

Today, of course, our response to Hemingway's story is very different from that of the magazine editors of the 1920s. We are not bound by their technical preconceptions; we have become habituated to literary devices which once seemed odd and impermissible. For us there is no question but that "Hills Like White Elephants" does have point, that it really is a story. Yet we shall have responded to it in a quite appropriate way if we make this judgment only slowly, if we are at first a little baffled by it and come to see its point only after some delay, if we even believe for a while that what we have read is merely an anecdote or sketch.

Should we need a clue to where the point of the story lies, we can find it in a single word in the last of the few brief passages of narration, the paragraph which tells us that the man carries the bags to the other side of the station. "Coming back, he walked through the barroom, where people waiting for the train were drinking. He drank an Anis at the bar and looked at the people. They were all waiting reasonably for the train." Waiting *reasonably*—it is a strange adverb for the man's mind to have lighted on. (We might note that by his use of this word, Hemingway does, for an instant, betray a knowledge of the man's internal life.) Why not *quietly,* or *apathetically,* or *stolidly?* Why should he choose to remark upon the people's reasonableness, taking note of it with approval, and as if it made a bond of community between him and them? It is because he, a reasonable man, has been having a rough time reasoning with an unreasonable woman.

The quality of reasonableness is central to "Hills Like White Elephants." In his conversation with the girl, the man—once he has got over, or suppressed, his anxious irritability—takes the line of detached reasonableness. He achieves, of course, nothing better than plausibility. Hemingway has no need to supply the descriptions of his tone of voice as he urges the girl to consent to the abortion —the rhythm of his sentences, the kind of words he uses, makes plain what his tone is. You cannot say "really" and "just" (in the sense of *merely*) as often as he does without sounding insincere.

Nor do we need the girl's tones of voice labelled for us. We understand that she is referring to a desire which she does not know how to defend in words and that therefore she speaks in bitterness and irony. She wants to have the child. There is no possible way to formulate a *reason* for wanting a child. It is a gratuitous desire, quite beyond reason. This is especially true if one lives the life to which this couple has devoted itself—a life, as the girl describes it in her moment of revulsion from it, of looking at things and trying new drinks. In the terms that this life sets, it is entirely *un*reasonable to want a child. But the girl has, we may say, proclaimed her emancipation from reason when she makes her remark about the hills looking like white elephants. The hills do not really look like white elephants, as the reasonable man is quick to say. They look like white elephants only if you choose to think they do, only if you think gratuitously, and with the imagination.

It is decisive in the story that the girl's simile is what it is. Some readers will have in mind the proverbial meaning of a white elephant. In certain parts of the East, this is a sacred beast; it may not be put to work but must be kept in state at great cost. Hence we call a white elephant anything that is apparently of great value and prestige but actually a drain upon our resources of which we wish we could be rid. Quite unconsciously, the girl may be making just this judgment on the life that she and her companion have chosen. But the chief effect of the simile is to focus our attention on the landscape she observes. It has two aspects, different to the point of being contradictory. This is the first: "The girl was looking off at the line of hills. They were white in the sun and the country was brown and dry." This is the second: "The girl stood up and walked to the end of the station. Across, on the other side, were fields of grain and trees along the banks of the Ebro. Far away, beyond the river, were mountains. The shadow of a cloud moved across the field of grain and she saw the river through the trees." When she looks in one direction, she sees the landscape of sterility; when she looks in the other direction, she sees the landscape of peace and fecundity. She is aware of the symbolic meaning that the two scenes have for her, for after her second view she says, "And we could have all this. . . . And we could have everything and every day we make it more impossible." It is the sudden explicitness of her desire for peace and fullness of life that makes the man's reasonable voice ring false and hollow in her ears and that leads her to her climax of desperation, her frantic request, with its seven-times repeated "please," that the man "stop talking."

It is interesting, I think, to compare the passage in the story that begins "'We want two Anis del Toro'" with the "A Game of Chess" dialogue in T. S. Eliot's "The Waste Land" (page 927). Incommensurate as they are in artistic and moral intention and achievement, the story and the poem have much in common—the theme of sterility; the representation of the boredom and vacuity and desperateness of life; the sense of lost happiness not to be regained; the awareness of the failure of love; the parched, sun-dried, stony land used as a symbol of emotional desiccation, the water used as the symbol of refreshment and salvation. Like "The Waste Land," "Hills Like White Elephants" is to be read as a comment—impassioned and by no means detached—on the human condition in the modern Western world.

BARN

BURNING

WILLIAM FAULKNER

1897–1962

THE STORE IN WHICH the Justice of the Peace's court was sitting smelled of cheese. The boy, crouched on his nail keg at the back of the crowded room, knew he smelled cheese, and more: from where he sat he could see the ranked shelves close-packed with the solid, squat, dynamic shapes of tin cans whose labels his stomach read, not from the lettering which meant nothing to his mind but from the scarlet devils and the silver curve of fish—this, the cheese which he knew he smelled and the hermetic meat which his intestines believed he smelled coming in intermittent gusts momentary and brief between the other constant one, the smell and sense just a little of fear because mostly of despair and grief, the old fierce pull of blood. He could not see the table where the Justice sat and before which his father and his father's enemy (*our enemy* he thought in that despair; *ourn! mine and hisn both! He's my father!*) stood, but he could hear them, the two of them that is, because his father had said no word yet:

"But what proof have you, Mr. Harris?"

"I told you. The hog got into my corn. I caught it up and sent it back to him. He had no fence that would hold it. I told him so, warned him. The next time I put the hog in my pen. When he came to get it I gave him enough wire to patch up his pen. The next time I put the hog up and kept it. I rode down to his house and saw the wire I gave him still rolled on to the spool in his yard. I told him he could have the hog when he paid me a dollar pound fee. That evening a nigger came with the dollar and got the hog. He was a strange nigger. He said, 'He say to tell you wood and hay kin burn.' I said, 'What?' 'That whut he say to tell you,' the nigger said. 'Wood and hay kin burn.' That night my barn burned. I got the stock out but I lost the barn."

"Where is the nigger? Have you got him?"

"He was a strange nigger, I tell you. I don't know what became of him."

"But that's not proof. Don't you see that's not proof?"

"Get that boy up here. He knows." For a moment the boy thought too that the man meant his older brother until Harris said, "Not him. The little one. The boy," and, crouching, small for his age, small and wiry like his father, in patched and faded jeans even too small for him, with straight, uncombed, brown hair and eyes gray and wild as storm scud, he saw the men between himself and the table part and become a lane of grim faces, at the end of which he saw the Justice, a shabby, collarless, graying man in spectacles, beckoning him. He felt no floor under his bare feet; he seemed to walk beneath the palpable weight of the grim turning faces. His father, stiff in his black Sunday coat donned not for the trial but for the moving, did not even look at him. *He aims for me to lie,* he thought, again with that frantic grief and despair. *And I will have to do hit.*

"What's your name, boy?" the Justice said.

"Colonel Sartoris Snopes," the boy whispered.

"Hey?" the Justice said. "Talk louder. Colonel Sartoris? I reckon anybody named for Colonel Sartoris in this country can't help but tell the truth, can they?" The boy said nothing. *Enemy! Enemy!* he thought; for a moment he could not even see, could not see that the Justice's face was kindly nor discern that his voice was troubled when he spoke to the man named Harris: "Do you want me to question this boy?" But he could hear, and during those subsequent long seconds while there was absolutely no sound in the crowded little room save that of quiet and intent breathing it was as if he had swung outward at the end of a grape vine, over a ravine, and at the top of the swing had been caught in a prolonged instant of mesmerized gravity, weightless in time.

"No!" Harris said violently, explosively. "Damnation! Send him out of here!" Now time, the fluid world, rushed beneath him again, the voices coming to him again through the smell of cheese and sealed meat, the fear and despair and the old grief of blood:

"This case is closed. I can't find against you, Snopes, but I can give you advice. Leave this country and don't come back to it."

His father spoke for the first time, his voice cold and harsh, level, without emphasis: "I aim to. I don't figure to stay in a country among people who . . ." he said something unprintable and vile, addressed to no one.

"That'll do," the Justice said. "Take your wagon and get out of this country before dark. Case dismissed."

His father turned, and he followed the stiff black coat, the wiry figure walking a little stiffly from where a Confederate provost's man's musket ball had taken him in the heel on a stolen horse thirty years ago, followed the two backs now, since his older brother had appeared from somewhere in the crowd, no taller than the father but thicker, chewing tobacco steadily, between the two

lines of grim-faced men and out of the store and across the worn gallery and
down the sagging steps and among the dogs and half-grown boys in the mild
May dust, where as he passed a voice hissed:

"Barn burner!"

Again he could not see, whirling; there was a face in a red haze, moon-
like, bigger than the full moon, the owner of it half again his size, he leaping
in the red haze toward the face, feeling no blow, feeling no shock when his
head struck the earth, scrabbling up and leaping again, feeling no blow this
time either and tasting no blood, scrabbling up to see the other boy in full
flight and himself already leaping into pursuit as his father's hand jerked him
back, the harsh, cold voice speaking above him: "Go get in the wagon."

It stood in a grove of locusts and mulberries across the road. His two hulk-
ing sisters in their Sunday dresses and his mother and her sister in calico and
sunbonnets were already in it, sitting on and among the sorry residue of the
dozen and more movings which even the boy could remember—the battered
stove, the broken beds and chairs, the clock inlaid with mother-of-pearl, which
would not run, stopped at some fourteen minutes past two o'clock of a dead
and forgotten day and time, which had been his mother's dowry. She was crying, though when she saw him she drew her sleeve across her face and began
to descend from the wagon. "Get back," the father said.

"He's hurt. I got to get some water and wash his . . ."

"Get back in the wagon," his father said. He got in too, over the tail-gate.
His father mounted to the seat where the older brother already sat and struck
the gaunt mules two savage blows with the peeled willow, but without heat. It
was not even sadistic; it was exactly that same quality which in later years
would cause his descendants to over-run the engine before putting a motor car
into motion, striking and reining back in the same movement. The wagon
went on, the store with its quiet crowd of grimly watching men dropped behind;
a curve in the road hid it. *Forever* he thought. *Maybe he's done satisfied now,
now that he has* . . . stopping himself, not to say it aloud even to himself. His
mother's hand touched his shoulder.

"Does hit hurt?" she said.

"Naw," he said. "Hit don't hurt. Lemme be."

"Can't you wipe some of the blood off before hit dries?"

"I'll wash to-night," he said. "Lemme be, I tell you."

The wagon went on. He did not know where they were going. None of
them ever did or ever asked, because it was always somewhere, always a house
of sorts waiting for them a day or two days or even three days away. Likely his
father had already arranged to make a crop on another farm before he . . .
Again he had to stop himself. He (the father) always did. There was something
about his wolflike independence and even courage when the advantage was at
least neutral which impressed strangers, as if they got from his latent ravening
ferocity not so much a sense of dependability as a feeling that his ferocious conviction in the rightness of his own actions would be of advantage to all whose
interest lay with his.

That night they camped in a grove of oaks and beeches where a spring
ran. The nights were still cool and they had a fire against it, of a rail lifted from
a nearby fence and cut into lengths—a small fire, neat, niggard almost, a shrewd
fire; such fires were his father's habit and custom always, even in freezing

weather. Older, the boy might have remarked this and wondered why not a big one; why should not a man who had not only seen the waste and extravagance of war, but who had in his blood an inherent voracious prodigality with material not his own, have burned everything in sight? Then he might have gone a step farther and thought that that was the reason: that niggard blaze was the living fruit of nights passed during those four years in the woods hiding from all men, blue or gray, with his strings of horses (captured horses, he called them). And older still, he might have divined the true reason: that the element of fire spoke to some deep mainspring of his father's being, as the element of steel or of powder spoke to other men, as the one weapon for the preservation of integrity, else breath were not worth the breathing, and hence to be regarded with respect and used with discretion.

But he did not think this now and he had seen those same niggard blazes all his life. He merely ate his supper beside it and was already half asleep over his iron plate when his father called him, and once more he followed the stiff back, the stiff and ruthless limp, up the slope and on to the starlit road where, turning, he could see his father against the stars but without face or depth—a shape black, flat, and bloodless as though cut from tin in the iron folds of the frockcoat which had not been made for him, the voice harsh like tin and without heat like tin:

"You were fixing to tell them. You would have told him." He didn't answer. His father struck him with the flat of his hand on the side of the head, hard but without heat, exactly as he had struck the two mules at the store, exactly as he would strike either of them with any stick in order to kill a horse fly, his voice still without heat or anger: "You're getting to be a man. You got to learn. You got to learn to stick to your own blood or you ain't going to have any blood to stick to you. Do you think either of them, any man there this morning, would? Don't you know all they wanted was a chance to get at me because they knew I had them beat? Eh?" Later, twenty years later, he was to tell himself, "If I had said they wanted only truth, justice, he would have hit me again." But now he said nothing. He was not crying. He just stood there. "Answer me," his father said.

"Yes," he whispered. His father turned.

"Get on to bed. We'll be there to-morrow."

To-morrow they were there. In the early afternoon the wagon stopped before a paintless two-room house identical almost with the dozen others it had stopped before even in the boy's ten years, and again, as on the other dozen occasions, his mother and aunt got down and began to unload the wagon, although his two sisters and his father and brother had not moved.

"Likely hit ain't fitten for hawgs," one of the sisters said.

"Nevertheless, fit it will and you'll hog it and like it," his father said. "Get out of them chairs and help your Ma unload."

The two sisters got down, big, bovine, in a flutter of cheap ribbons; one of them drew from the jumbled wagon bed a battered lantern, the other a worn broom. His father handed the reins to the older son and began to climb stiffly over the wheel. "When they get unloaded, take the team to the barn and feed them." Then he said, and at first the boy thought he was still speaking to his brother: "Come with me."

"Me?" he said.

"Yes," his father said. "You."

"Abner," his mother said. His father paused and looked back—the harsh level stare beneath the shaggy, graying, irascible brows.

"I reckon I'll have a word with the man that aims to begin to-morrow owning me body and soul for the next eight months."

They went back up the road. A week ago—or before last night, that is— he would have asked where they were going, but not now. His father had struck him before last night but never before had he paused afterward to explain why; it was as if the blow and the following calm, outrageous voice still rang, reper- cussed, divulging nothing to him save the terrible handicap of being young, the light weight of his few years, just heavy enough to prevent his soaring free of the world as it seemed to be ordered but not heavy enough to keep him footed solid in it, to resist it and try to change the course of its events.

Presently he could see the grove of oaks and cedars and the other flowering trees and shrubs where the house would be, though not the house yet. They walked beside a fence massed with honeysuckle and Cherokee roses and came to a gate swinging open between two brick pillars, and now, beyond a sweep of drive, he saw the house for the first time and at that instant he forgot his father and the terror and despair both, and even when he remembered his father again (who had not stopped) the terror and despair did not return. Because, for all the twelve movings, they had sojourned until now in a poor country, a land of small farms and fields and houses, and he had never seen a house like this before. *Hit's big as a courthouse* he thought quietly, with a surge of peace and joy whose reason he could not have thought into words, being too young for that: *They are safe from him. People whose lives are a part of this peace and dignity are beyond his touch, he no more to them than a buzzing wasp: capable of stinging for a little moment but that's all; the spell of this peace and dignity rendering even the barns and stable and cribs which belong to it impervious to the puny flames he might contrive* . . . this, the peace and joy, ebbing for an instant as he looked again at the stiff black back, the stiff and implacable limp of the figure which was not dwarfed by the house, for the reason that it had never looked big anywhere and which now, again the serene columned back- drop, had more than ever that impervious quality of something cut ruthlessly from tin, depthless, as though, sidewise to the sun, it would cast no shadow. Watching him, the boy remarked the absolutely undeviating course which his father held and saw the stiff foot come squarely down in a pile of fresh drop- pings where a horse had stood in the drive and which his father could have avoided by a simple change of stride. But it ebbed only for a moment, though he could not have thought this into words either, walking on in the spell of the house, which he could even want but without envy, without sorrow, certainly never with that ravening and jealous rage which unknown to him walked in the ironlike black coat before him. *Maybe he will feel it too. Maybe it will even change him now from what maybe he couldn't help but be.*

They crossed the portico. Now he could hear his father's stiff foot as it came down on the boards with clocklike finality, a sound out of all proportion to the displacement of the body it bore and which was not dwarfed either by the white door before it, as though it had attained to a sort of vicious and raven- ing minimum not to be dwarfed by anything—the flat, wide, black hat, the formal coat of broadcloth which had once been black but which had now the friction-glazed greenish cast of the bodies of old house flies, the lifted sleeve which was too large, the lifted hand like a curled claw. The door opened so promptly that the boy knew the Negro must have been watching them all the time, an old man with neat grizzled hair, in a linen jacket, who stood barring the door with his body, saying, "Wipe yo foots, white man, fo you come in here. Major ain't home nohow."

"Get out of my way, nigger," his father said, without heat too, flinging the door back and the Negro also and entering, his hat still on his head. And now the boy saw the prints of the stiff foot on the doorjamb and saw them appear on the pale rug behind the machinelike deliberation of the foot which seemed to bear (or transmit) twice the weight which the body compassed. The Negro was shouting "Miss Lula! Miss Lula!" somewhere behind them, then the boy, deluged as though by a warm wave by a suave turn of carpeted stair and a pendant glitter of chandeliers and a mute gleam of gold frames, heard the swift feet and saw her too, a lady—perhaps he had never seen her like before either—in a gray, smooth gown with lace at the throat and an apron tied at the waist and the sleeves turned back, wiping cake or biscuit dough from her hands with a towel as she came up the hall, looking not at his father at all but at the tracks on the blond rug with an expression of incredulous amazement.

"I tried," the Negro cried. "I tole him to . . ."

"Will you please go away?" she said in a shaking voice. "Major de Spain is not at home. Will you please go away?"

His father had not spoken again. He did not speak again. He did not even look at her. He just stood stiff in the center of the rug, in his hat, the shaggy iron-gray brows twitching slightly above the pebble-colored eyes as he appeared to examine the house with brief deliberation. Then with the same deliberation he turned; the boy watched him pivot on the good leg and saw the stiff foot drag round the arc of the turning, leaving a final long and fading smear. His father never looked at it, he never once looked down at the rug. The Negro held the door. It closed behind them, upon the hysteric and indistinguishable woman-wail. His father stopped at the top of the steps and scraped his boot clean on the edge of it. At the gate he stopped again. He stood for a moment, planted stiffly on the stiff foot, looking back at the house. "Pretty and white, ain't it?" he said. "That's sweat. Nigger sweat. Maybe it ain't white enough yet to suit him. Maybe he wants to mix some white sweat with it."

Two hours later the boy was chopping wood behind the house within which his mother and aunt and the two sisters (the mother and aunt, not the two girls, he knew that; even at this distance and muffled by walls the flat loud voices of the two girls emanated an incorrigible idle inertia) were setting up the stove to prepare a meal, when he heard the hooves and saw the linen-clad man on a fine sorrel mare, whom he recognized even before he saw the rolled rug in front of the Negro youth following on a fat bay carriage horse—a suffused, angry face vanishing, still at full gallop, beyond the corner of the house where his father and brother were sitting in the two tilted chairs; and a moment later, almost before he could have put the axe down, he heard the hooves again and watched the sorrel mare go back out of the yard, already galloping again. Then his father began to shout one of the sisters' names, who presently emerged backward from the kitchen door dragging the rolled rug along the ground by one end while the other sister walked behind it.

"If you ain't going to tote, go on and set up the wash pot," the first said.

"You, Sarty!" the second shouted, "Set up the wash pot!" His father appeared at the door, framed against that shabbiness, as he had been against that other bland perfection, impervious to either, the mother's anxious face at his shoulder.

"Go on," the father said. "Pick it up." The two sisters stooped, broad, lethargic; stooping, they presented an incredible expanse of pale cloth and a flutter of tawdry ribbons.

"If I thought enough of a rug to have to git hit all the way from France I wouldn't keep hit where folks coming in would have to tromp on hit," the first said. They raised the rug.

"Abner," the mother said. "Let me do it."

"You go back and git dinner," his father said. "I'll tend to this."

From the woodpile through the rest of the afternoon the boy watched them, the rug spread flat in the dust beside the bubbling wash-pot, the two sisters stooping over it with that profound and lethargic reluctance, while the father stood over them in turn, implacable and grim, driving them though never raising his voice again. He could smell the harsh homemade lye they were using; he saw his mother come to the door once and look toward them with an expression not anxious now but very like despair; he saw his father turn, and he fell to with the axe and saw from the corner of his eye his father raise from the ground a flattish fragment of field stone and examine it and return to the pot, and this time his mother actually spoke: "Abner. Abner. Please don't. Please, Abner."

Then he was done too. It was dusk; the whippoorwills had already begun. He could smell coffee from the room where they would presently eat the cold food remaining from the mid-afternoon meal, though when he entered the house he realized they were having coffee again probably because there was a fire on the hearth, before which the rug now lay spread over the backs of the two chairs. The tracks of his father's foot were gone. Where they had been were now long, water-cloudy scoriations resembling the sporadic course of a lilliputian mowing machine.

It still hung there while they ate the cold food and then went to bed, scattered without order or claim up and down the two rooms, his mother in one bed, where his father would later lie, the older brother in the other, himself, the aunt, and the two sisters on pallets on the floor. But his father was not in bed yet. The last thing the boy remembered was the depthless, harsh silhouette of the hat and coat bending over the rug and it seemed to him that he had not even closed his eyes when the silhouette was standing over him, the fire almost dead behind it, the stiff foot prodding him awake. "Catch up the mule," his father said.

When he returned with the mule his father was standing in the black door, the rolled rug over his shoulder. "Ain't you going to ride?" he said.

"No. Give me your foot."

He bent his knee into his father's hand, the wiry, surprising power flowed smoothly, rising, he rising with it, on to the mule's bare back (they had owned a saddle once; the boy could remember it though not when or where) and with the same effortlessness his father swung the rug up in front of him. Now in the starlight they retraced the afternoon's path, up the dusty road rife with honeysuckle, through the gate and up the black tunnel of the drive to the lightless house, where he sat on the mule and felt the rough warp of the rug drag across his thighs and vanish.

"Don't you want me to help?" he whispered. His father did not answer and now he heard again that stiff foot striking the hollow portico with that wooden and clocklike deliberation, that outrageous overstatement of the weight it carried. The rug, hunched, not flung (the boy could tell that even in the darkness) from his father's shoulder struck the angle of wall and floor with a sound unbelievably loud, thunderous, then the foot again, unhurried and enormous; a light came on in the house and the boy sat, tense, breathing steadily and quietly and just a little fast, though the foot itself did not increase its beat at all, descending the steps now; now the boy could see him.

"Don't you want to ride now?" he whispered. "We kin both ride now," the light within the house altering now, flaring up and sinking. *He's coming down the stairs now*, he thought. He had already ridden the mule up beside the horse block; presently his father was up behind him and he doubled the reins over and slashed the mule across the neck, but before the animal could begin to trot the hard, thin arm came round him, the hard, knotted hand jerking the mule back to a walk.

In the first red rays of the sun they were in the lot, putting plow gear on the mules. This time the sorrel mare was in the lot before he heard it at all, the rider collarless and even bareheaded, trembling, speaking in a shaking voice as the woman in the house had done, his father merely looking up once before stooping again to the hame he was buckling, so that the man on the mare spoke to his stooping back:

"You must realize you have ruined that rug. Wasn't there anybody here, any of your women . . ." he ceased, shaking, the boy watching him, the older brother leaning now in the stable door, chewing, blinking slowly and steadily at nothing apparently. "It cost a hundred dollars. But you never had a hundred dollars. You never will. So I'm going to charge you twenty bushels of corn against your crop. I'll add it in your contract and when you come to the commissary you can sign it. That won't keep Mrs. de Spain quiet but maybe it will teach you to wipe your feet off before you enter her house again."

Then he was gone. The boy looked at his father, who still had not spoken or even looked up again, who was now adjusting the logger-head in the hame.

"Pap," he said. His father looked at him—the inscrutable face, the shaggy brows beneath which the gray eyes glinted coldly. Suddenly the boy went toward him, fast, stopping as suddenly. "You done the best you could!" he cried. "If he wanted hit done different why didn't he wait and tell you how? He won't git no twenty bushels! He won't git none! We'll gether hit and hide hit! I kin watch . . ."

"Did you put the cutter back in the straight stock like I told you?"

"No sir," he said.

"Then go do it."

That was Wednesday. During the rest of that week he worked steadily, at what was within his scope and some which was beyond it, with an industry that did not need to be driven nor even commanded twice; he had this from his mother, with the difference that some at least of what he did he liked to do, such as splitting wood with the half-size axe which his mother and aunt had earned, or saved money somehow, to present him with at Christmas. In company with the two older women (and on one afternoon, even one of the sisters), he built pens for the shoat and the cow which were a part of his father's contract with the landlord, and one afternoon, his father being absent, gone somewhere on one of the mules, he went to the field.

They were running a middle buster now, his brother holding the plow straight while he handled the reins, and walking beside the straining mule, the rich black soil shearing cool and damp against his bare ankles, he thought *Maybe this is the end of it. Maybe even that twenty bushels that seems hard to have to pay for just a rug will be a cheap price for him to stop forever and always from being what he used to be*; thinking, dreaming now, so that his brother had to speak sharply to him to mind the mule: *Maybe he even won't collect the twenty bushels. Maybe it will all add up and balance and vanish— corn, rug, fire; the terror and grief, the being pulled two ways like between two teams of horses—gone, done with for ever and ever.*

Then it was Saturday; he looked up from beneath the mule he was harnessing and saw his father in the black coat and hat. "Not that," his father said. "The wagon gear." And then, two hours later, sitting in the wagon bed behind his father and brother on the seat, the wagon accomplished a final curve, and he saw the weathered paintless store with its tattered tobacco and patent-medicine posters and the tethered wagons and saddle animals below the gallery. He mounted the gnawed steps behind his father and brother, and there again was the lane of quiet, watching faces for the three of them to walk through. He saw the man in spectacles sitting at the plank table and he did not need to be told this was a Justice of the Peace; he sent one glare of fierce, exultant, partisan defiance at the man in collar and cravat now, whom he had seen but twice before in his life, and that on a galloping horse, who now wore on his face an expression not of rage but of amazed unbelief which the boy could not have known was at the incredible circumstance of being sued by one of his own tenants, and came and stood against his father and cried at the Justice: "He ain't done it! He ain't burnt . . ."

"Go back to the wagon," his father said.

"Burnt?" the Justice said. "Do I understand this rug was burned too?"

"Does anybody here claim it was?" his father said. "Go back to the wagon." But he did not, he merely retreated to the rear of the room, crowded as that other had been, but not to sit down this time, instead, to stand pressing among the motionless bodies, listening to the voices:

"And you claim twenty bushels of corn is too high for the damage you did to the rug?"

"He brought the rug to me and said he wanted the tracks washed out of it. I washed the tracks out and took the rug back to him."

"But you didn't carry the rug back to him in the same condition it was in before you made the tracks on it."

His father did not answer, and now for perhaps half a minute there was no sound at all save that of breathing, the faint, steady suspiration of complete and intent listening.

"You decline to answer that, Mr. Snopes?" Again his father did not answer. "I'm going to find against you, Mr. Snopes. I'm going to find that you were responsible for the injury to Major de Spain's rug and hold you liable for it.

But twenty bushels of corn seems a little high for a man in your circumstances to have to pay. Major de Spain claims it cost a hundred dollars. October corn will be worth about fifty cents. I figure that if Major de Spain can stand a ninety-five dollar loss on something he paid cash for, you can stand a five-dollar loss you haven't earned yet. I hold you in damages to Major de Spain to the amount of ten bushels of corn over and above your contract with him, to be paid to him out of your crop at gathering time. Court adjourned."

It had taken no time hardly, the morning was but half begun. He thought they would return home and perhaps back to the field, since they were late, far behind all other farmers. But instead his father passed on behind the wagon, merely indicating with his hand for the older brother to follow with it, and he crossed the road toward the blacksmith shop opposite, pressing on after his father, overtaking him, speaking, whispering up at the harsh, calm face beneath the weathered hat: "He won't git no ten bushels neither. He won't git one. We'll . . ." until his father glanced for an instant down at him, the face absolutely calm, the grizzled eyebrows tangled above the cold eyes, the voice almost pleasant, almost gentle:

"You think so? Well, we'll wait till October anyway."

The matter of the wagon—the setting of a spoke or two and the tightening of the tires—did not take long either, the business of the tires accomplished by driving the wagon into the spring branch behind the shop and letting it stand there, the mules nuzzling into the water from time to time, and the boy on the seat with the idle reins, looking up the slope and through the sooty tunnel of the shed where the slow hammer rang and where his father sat on an upended cypress bolt, easily, either talking or listening, still sitting there when the boy brought the dripping wagon up out of the branch and halted it before the door.

"Take them on to the shade and hitch," his father said. He did so and returned. His father and the smith and a third man squatting on his heels inside the door were talking, about crops and animals; the boy, squatting too in the ammoniac dust and hoof-parings and scales of rust, heard his father tell a long and unhurried story out of the time before the birth of the older brother even when he had been a professional horsetrader. And then his father came up beside him where he stood before a tattered last year's circus poster on the other side of the store, gazing rapt and quiet at the scarlet horses, the incredible poisings and convolutions of tulle and tights and the painted leer of comedians, and said, "It's time to eat."

But not at home. Squatting beside his brother against the front wall, he watched his father emerge from the store and produce from a paper sack a segment of cheese and divide it carefully and deliberately into three with his pocket knife and produce crackers from the same sack. They all three squatted on the gallery and ate, slowly, without talking; then in the store again, they drank from a tin dipper tepid water smelling of the cedar bucket and of living beech trees. And still they did not go home. It was a horse lot this time, a tall rail fence upon and along which men stood and sat and out of which one by one horses were led, to be walked and trotted and then cantered back and forth along the road while the slow swapping and buying went on and the sun began to slant westward, they—the three of them—watching and listening, the older brother with his muddy eyes and his steady, inevitable tobacco, the father commenting now and then on certain of the animals, to no one in particular.

It was after sundown when they reached home. They ate supper by lamp-light, then, sitting on the doorstep, the boy watched the night fully accomplished, listening to the whippoorwills and the frogs, when he heard his mother's voice: "Abner! No! No! Oh, God. Oh, God. Abner!" and he rose, whirled, and saw the altered light through the door where a candle stub now burned in a bottle neck on the table and his father, still in the hat and coat, at once formal and burlesque as though dressed carefully for some shabby and ceremonial violence, emptying the reservoir of the lamp back into the five-gallon kerosene can from which it had been filled, while the mother tugged at his arm until he shifted the lamp to the other hand and flung her back, not savagely or viciously, just hard, into the wall, her hands flung out against the wall for balance, her mouth open and in her face the same quality of hopeless despair as had been in her voice. Then his father saw him standing in the door.

"Go to the barn and get that can of oil we were oiling the wagon with," he said. The boy did not move. Then he could speak.

"What . . ." he cried "What are you . . ."

"Go get that oil," his father said. "Go."

Then he was moving, running outside the house, toward the stable: this the old habit, the old blood which he had not been permitted to choose for himself, which had been bequeathed him willy nilly and which had run for so long (and who knew where, battening on what of outrage and savagery and lust) before it came to him. *I could keep on*, he thought. *I could run on and on and never look back, never need to see his face again. Only I can't. I can't*, the rusted can in his hand now, the liquid sploshing in it as he ran back to the house and into it, into the sound of his mother's weeping in the next room, and handed the can to his father.

"Ain't you going to even send a nigger?" he cried. "At least you sent a nigger before!"

This time his father didn't strike him. The hand came even faster than the blow had, the same hand which had set the can on the table with almost excruciating care flashing from the can toward him too quick for him to follow it, gripping him by the back of the shirt and on to tiptoe before he had seen it quit the can, the face stooping at him in breathless and frozen ferocity, the cold, dead voice speaking over him to the older brother who leaned against the table, chewing with that steady, curious, sidewise motion of cows:

"Empty the can into the big one and go on. I'll ketch up with you."

"Better tie him to the bedpost," the brother said.

"Do like I told you," the father said. Then the boy was moving, his bunched shirt and the hard, bony hand between his shoulder-blades, his toes just touching the floor, across the room and into the other one, past the sisters sitting with spread heavy thighs in the two chairs over the cold hearth, and to where his mother and aunt sat side by side on the bed, the aunt's arms about his mother's shoulders.

"Hold him," the father said. The aunt made a startled movement. "Not you," the father said. "Lennie. Take hold of him. I want to see you do it." His mother took him by the wrist. "You'll hold him better than that. If he gets loose don't you know what he is going to do? He will go up yonder." He jerked his head toward the road. "Maybe I'd better tie him."

"I'll hold him," his mother whispered.

"See you do then." Then his father was gone, the stiff foot heavy and measured upon the boards, ceasing at last.

Then he began to struggle. His mother caught him in both arms, he jerking and wrenching at them. He would be stronger in the end, he knew that. But he had no time to wait for it. "Lemme go!" he cried. "I don't want to have to hit you!"

"Let him go!" the aunt said. "If he don't go, before God, I am going up there myself!"

"Don't you see I can't?" his mother cried. "Sarty! Sarty! No! No! Help me, Lizzie!"

Then he was free. His aunt grasped at him but was too late. He whirled, running, his mother stumbled forward on to her knees behind him, crying to the nearer sister: "Catch him, Net! Catch him!" But that was too late too, the sister (the sisters were twins, born at the same time, yet either of them now gave the impression of being, encompassing as much living meat and volume and weight as any other two of the family) not yet having begun to rise from the chair, her head, face, alone merely turned, presenting to him in the flying instant an astonishing expanse of young female features untroubled by any surprise even, wearing only an expression of bovine interest. Then he was out of the room, out of the house, in the mild dust of the starlit road and the heavy rifeness of honeysuckle, the pale ribbon unspooling with terrific slowness under his running feet, reaching the gate at last and turning in, running, his heart and lungs drumming, on up the drive toward the lighted house, the lighted door. He did not knock, he burst in, sobbing for breath, incapable for the moment of speech; he saw the astonished face of the Negro in the linen jacket without knowing when the Negro had appeared.

"De Spain!" he cried, panted. "Where's . . ." then he saw the white man too emerging from a white door down the hall. "Barn!" he cried. "Barn!"

"What?" the white man said. "Barn?"

"Yes!" the boy cried. "Barn!"

"Catch him!" the white man shouted.

But it was too late this time too. The Negro grasped his shirt, but the entire sleeve, rotten with washing, carried away, and he was out that door too and in the drive again, and had actually never ceased to run even while he was screaming into the white man's face.

Behind him the white man was shouting, "My horse! Fetch my horse!" and he thought for an instant of cutting across the park and climbing the fence into the road, but he did not know the park nor how high the vine-massed fence might be and he dared not risk it. So he ran on down the drive, blood and breath roaring; presently he was in the road again though he could not see it. He could not hear either: the galloping mare was almost upon him before he heard her, and even then he held his course, as if the urgency of his wild grief and need must in a moment more find him wings, waiting until the ultimate instant to hurl himself aside and into the weed-choked roadside ditch as the horse thundered past and on, for an instant in furious silhouette against the stars, the tranquil early summer night sky which, even before the shape of the horse and rider vanished, strained abruptly and violently upward: a long, swirling roar incredible and soundless, blotting the stars, and he springing up and into the road again, running again, knowing it was too late yet still running even after he heard the shot and, an instant later, two shots, pausing now without knowing he had ceased to run, crying "Pap! Pap!", running again before he knew he had begun to run, stumbling, tripping over something and scrabbling up again without ceasing to run, looking backward over his shoulder at the glare as he got up, running on among the invisible trees, panting, sobbing, "Father! Father!"

At midnight he was sitting on the crest of a hill. He did not know it was midnight and he did not know how far he had came. But there was no glare behind him now and he sat now, his back toward what he had called home for four days anyhow, his face toward the dark woods which he would enter when breath was strong again, small, shaking steadily in the chill darkness, hugging himself into the remainder of his thin, rotten shirt, the grief and despair now no longer terror and fear but just grief and despair. *Father. My father,* he thought. "He was brave!" he cried suddenly, aloud but not loud, no more than a whisper: "He was! He was in the war! He was in Colonel Sartoris' cav'ry!" not knowing that his father had gone to that war a private in the fine old European sense, wearing no uniform, admitting the authority of and giving fidelity to no man or army or flag, going to war as Malbrouck[1] himself did: for booty—it meant nothing and less than nothing to him if it were enemy booty or his own.

The slow constellations wheeled on. It would be dawn and then sun-up after a while and he would be hungry. But that would be to-morrow and now he was only cold, and walking would cure that. His breathing was easier now and he decided to get up and go on, and then he found that he had been asleep because he knew it was almost dawn, the night almost over. He could tell that from the whippoorwills. They were everywhere now among the dark trees below him, constant and inflectioned and ceaseless, so that, as the instant for giving over to the day birds drew nearer and nearer, there was no interval at all between them. He got up. He was a little stiff, but walking would cure that too as it would the cold, and soon there would be the sun. He went on down the hill, toward the dark woods within which the liquid silver voices of the birds called unceasing—the rapid and urgent beating of the urgent and quiring heart of the late spring night. He did not look back.

COMMENTARY

A salient characteristic of William Faulkner's imagination is its preocccupation with conduct that is in the highest degree principled and magnanimous. Faulkner seems to take a special pleasure in representing men incapable of acting merely for their own advantage. Such men are Major de Spain of this story, and Colonel Sartoris, after whom the little boy Sarty has been named. They appear again and again in Faulkner's novels and stories as representatives of the ideal of personal honor. Their mode of life is established and affluent; their bearing is dignified and benign; their military titles suggest a heroic past and a continuing devotion to the lost cause of the Confederacy; and their

[1] An allusion to an old French song, *Malbrouk s'en va-t-en guerre* (Marlborough is off to the wars).

sonorous and "romantic" surnames imply their patrician connection with still further reaches of the past. The past, indeed, is more their natural habitat than the present: perhaps honor is always to be regarded as an archaic virtue.

But Faulkner's imagination is no less captivated by the opposite of large-mindedness and honor, by whatever we are to call the state of moral being that characterizes the ever-proliferating family of the Snopeses. Their very name suggests—rather too obviously, some will think—both their inferior social situation and their meanness of spirit. (It makes a nice subject for speculation why so many English words beginning with *sn* have unpleasant connotations, for example, *snake, snarl, sneak, sneer, snipe, snide, snivel, snob, snore, snout, snub.* Perhaps the only pleasant *sn* words are *snow, snood, snug,* and *snuggle!*) Of lowly origin, disadvantaged in every social and economic way, the Snopeses are determined to rise by any means at hand. They find an especial satisfaction in succeeding at the expense of others, for they are consumed by resentment of those who are better off than they, and they cherish their malice and ruthlessness as Major de Spain and Colonel Sartoris cherish their honor. In Faulkner's understanding of society and social history, the two gentlemen represent the old South with its respect for the patrician values of dignity and responsibility; the Snopes clan represents the plebeian modern spirit that asserts itself in the South of the present time, a calculating, unfeeling spirit which is not checked in its self-seeking by the sanctions of tradition. As times passes in the canon of Faulkner's work, certain members of the Snopes family acquire more and more power and prestige, and at the expense of the men of honor and magnanimity.

By every ethical, social, and personal standard Faulkner condemns and despises the Snopeses, but it is plain that they fascinate him. They appear in his novels and stories with increasing frequency, and we must suppose that he creates them and the situations in which they exercise their malice and shrewdness because he takes pleasure in doing so—as a matter of fact, he seems to take as much pleasure in their contemptibleness as in the admirable traits of Major de Spain and Colonel Sartoris. This impression, derived from the works themselves, is confirmed in an interesting way by an anecdote about the author. The occasion was a large party in New York at which Faulkner was a guest; he stood surrounded by a group of admirers and discoursed about rats (the report of the event does not make plain how the subject was introduced), speaking eloquently and at length of his respect for them, praising their indomitable power of survival, their way of taking every possible advantage, their cool intelligence in making use of mankind. Some of those who listened were distressed by this avowal of sympathy with a repellent and despised animal and undertook to defend the conventional view that rats are—rats. Others tried to make out that Faulkner was being ironic. But he gravely held his ground with the air of a man who had thought long about his subject and has all his arguments in order. It can scarcely be doubted that he was talking about the Snopeses.

He was saying pretty much what Keats said in a famous letter, making his point by reference to another rodent of unpleasant reputation, the stoat. Keats is writing about the ruthlessness and cruelty displayed in what he calls "wild nature"; as he thinks about this from the moral point of view, he is horrified, but then he is suddenly caught by a sense of how brilliant are the energies that come into play in the bitter struggle for existence. "This is what makes the Amusement of Life—to a speculative Mind. I go among the Fields and catch a glimpse of a Stoat or a field-mouse peeping out of the withered grass—the creature hath a purpose and its eyes are bright with it. I go among the buildings of a city and I see a Man hurrying along—to what? The creature hath a purpose and his eyes are bright with it." He goes on to speak of morality and love and concern for others and of how little they establish themselves in life, and then it occurs to him to wonder if life may not be justified by its sheer energy, quite without reference to morality. "May there not be superior beings [he means gods of some kind, not human beings] amused by any graceful though instinctive attitude my mind may fall into, as I am entertained by the alertness of a Stoat or the anxiety of a Deer? Though a quarrel in the Streets is a thing to be hated, the energies displayed in it are fine; the commonest Man shows a grace in his quarrel. . . ."

But Keats cannot rest in this conclusion. Energy, he says, is "the very thing in which consists poetry," and then he goes on to say that if this is so, "poetry is not so fine a thing as philosophy,—For the same reason that an eagle is not so fine a thing as a truth." Energy of itself is not enough, poetry of itself is not enough—this is a great and daring thing for a poet to say. Yet if we are speaking not about life but only about poetry, then energy is paramount: "energy is the very thing in which consists poetry." The mind of the poet is defined by what Keats calls its "gusto" rather than by its moral discriminations. "As to the poetical character itself . . . it is not itself—it has no self—it is every thing and nothing —It has no character—it enjoys light and shade; it lives in gusto be it foul or fair, high or low, rich or poor, mean or elevated—It has as much delight in conceiving an Iago [the villain of Shakespeare's *Othello*] as an Imogen [the virtuous heroine of Shakespeare's *Cymbeline*]. What shocks the virtuous philosopher, delights the Camelion Poet."

As much delight in conceiving an Iago as an Imogen: as much delight in conceiving a Snopes as a de Spain or a Sartoris. *The commonest man shows a grace in his quarrel:* the quarrel of the Snopeses with their fellow men is unending, and Faulkner does not fail to see its "grace," even though it is of a perverse kind. Again and again in "Barn Burning" he speaks of Abner Snopes's actuality of existence, the curious definiteness of his outline. It need not be thought a pleasing definiteness, "cut from tin" as it is, but it is strikingly *there.* In communicating his sense of Abner Snopes's *thereness*, Faulkner does not withhold his moral judgment, but his emphasis falls on what we might call the aesthetic aspect of the man's existence—he speaks of "that impervious quality of something cut ruthlessly from tin, depthless, as though, sidewise to the sun, it would cast no shadow." He describes Snopes's body as it confronts the traditional graciousness of Major de Spain's house as not being "dwarfed . . . , as though it had attained to a sort of vicious and ravening minimum not to be dwarfed by anything." And this harsh, metallic, impervious existence has even a kind of moral meaning and gives a kind of moral satisfaction. Like the rattle-snake on the flag of the insurgent American colonies, Abner Snopes says with his whole being, "Don't tread on me," a statement of great moral force. Faulkner is quite explicit about this curious moral power of Snopes: "There was something about his wolflike independence and even courage when the advantage was at least neutral which impressed strangers, as if they got from his latent ravening ferocity not so much a sense of dependability as a feeling that his ferocious conviction in the rightness of his own actions would be of advantage to all whose interest lay with his."

It is this quality of his father that makes the dilemma of little Sarty's life. The boy is deeply drawn to the very things that his father hates and opposes—community, justice, truth, the peace and order that are symbolized by Major de Spain's fine house. Yet apart from the habit of family loyalty and dependence, which a ten-year-old cannot easily break, there is his father's harsh power to claim his allegiance. And the reader cannot but share Sarty's division of mind. Much as he may dislike Abner Snopes, if only for his ugly trick of whipping up the mules and at the same time reining them in, he yet must feel that, as compared with Major de Spain, Snopes has much more at stake, that he is the more morally serious of the two. In this story, indeed, the magnanimous Major de Spain does not show to the best advantage. His rage over the rug that Snopes had maliciously and contemptuously soiled is of course wholly justified, yet it sinks to a kind of childishness before Abner Snopes's passion for independence, even though that is virtually an insanity. Nor can the reader escape the uncomfortable sense that Snopes has a kind of ultimate justice on his side when he says of Major de Spain's house that its whiteness is the sweat of the men, black and white, who have worked the Major's land. Harsh and unfeeling this father certainly is, yet he has the integration and definiteness which in a better man would make a paternal virtue and which in him make a paternal force.

For many readers Sarty's conflict with his father will bring to mind the filial troubles of another Southern boy, Huck Finn. For all Huck's fear of the efforts of respectable people to "sivilize" him, he likes and admires at least as much of civilization as is to be found in the amenity of a handsome and comfortable house, and he is instinctively attracted to goodness, instinctively repelled by meanness and violence; in these respects Sarty is much like him. As for Huck's father, although he has none of the metallic integration of Abner Snopes, being a ruin of a man, yet he does share Snopes's bitter hostility to society and his sense of outraged social status, and of course his brutality.

But if the situations of the two boys are similar, there is a wide difference in the way they are presented. In *Huckleberry Finn,* Mark Twain uses the established device of having his young hero tell his story in his own words and thus achieves a prose of beautiful simplicity. There is nothing that puzzles Huck's comprehension; he understands everything that he sees and endures, and he communicates it directly and lucidly. Faulkner tells Sarty's story in the third person, and the complexity of the rhetoric expresses the complexity of the boy's perceptions. Sarty, unlike Huck, sees nothing in a clear and distinct way. The world of his perception is still inchoate, not wholly formed; seen in its parts, it is puzzling. It is also a little threatening, as well it might be for a ten-year-old boy who is moving toward a decision that must seem so far beyond his years and powers, the breaking of his tie with his father and all his family, at the behest of his idea of order and beauty.

SUMMER'S
DAY

J O H N   O ' H A R A

1 9 0 5 –

THERE WERE NOT very many people at the beach when Mr. and Mrs. Attrell arrived. On this particular day, a Wednesday, possibly a little more than half the morning swimming crowd had come out of the water and gone home for lunch, some on their bicycles, some on the bus which stopped almost anywhere you asked to stop, and a still rather large number driving their cars and station wagons. The comparatively few persons who stayed at the club for lunch sat about in their bathing suits in groups of anywhere from two to seven.

Mrs. Attrell got out of the car—a shiny black 1932[1] Buick with fairly good rubber and only about thirty thousand miles on it—at the clubhouse steps and waited while Mr. Attrell parked it at the space marked "A. T. Attrell." Mr. Attrell then joined his wife, took her by the arm, and adapted his pace to her slightly shorter steps. Together they made their way to their bench. The bench, seating six, had a sign with "A. T. Attrell" on it nailed to the back, and it was placed a few feet from the boardwalk. On this day, however, it was occupied by four young persons, and so Mr. and Mrs. Attrell altered their course and went to a bench just a bit lower on the dune than their own. Mrs. Attrell placed her blue tweed bag and her book, which was in its lending-library jacket, in her lap.

1 "Summer's Day" was first published in 1942.

749

She folded her hands and looked out at the sea. Mr. Attrell seated himself on her left, with his right arm resting on the back of the bench. In this way he was not sitting too close to her, but he had only to raise his hand and he could touch her shoulder. From time to time he did this, as they both looked out at the sea.

It was a beautiful, beautiful day and some of the hungry youngsters of teen age forgot about lunch and continued to swim and splash. Among them was Bryce Cartwright, twelve, grandson of Mr. and Mrs. Attrell's friend T. K. Cartwright, whose bench they now occupied.

"Bryce," said Mr. Attrell.

"Mm-hmm," said Mrs. Attrell, nodding twice.

They filled their lungs with the wonderful air and did not speak for a little while. Then Mr. Attrell looked up the beach to his left. "Mr. O'Donnell," he said.

"Oh, yes. Mr. O'Donnell."

"Got some of his boys with him. Not all, though."

"I think the two oldest ones are at war," said Mrs. Attrell.

"Yes, I believe so. I think one's in the Army and the other's in, I *think,* the Navy."

Mr. O'Donnell was a powerfully built man who had played guard on an obscure Yale team before the last war. With him today, on parade, were his sons Gerald, Norton, Dwight, and Arthur Twining Hadley O'Donnell, who were sixteen, fourteen, twelve, and nine. Mrs. O'Donnell was at home with the baby which no one believed she was going to have until she actually had it. Mr. O'Donnell and the boys had been for a walk along the beach and now the proud father and his skinny brown sons were coming up the boardwalk on their way to lunch. A few yards away from the Cartwright bench Mr. O'Donnell began his big grin for the Attrells, looking at Mrs. Attrell, then at Mr. Attrell, then by compulsion at Mr. Attrell's hatband, that of a Yale society, which Mr. O'Donnell had nothing against, although he had not made it or any other.

"Mr. and Mrs. Attrell," he said, bowing.

"How do you do, Mr. O'Donnell?" said Mr. Attrell.

"How do you do, Mr. O'Donnell?" said Mrs. Attrell.

"You don't want to miss that ocean today, Mr. Attrell," said Mr. O'Donnell. "Magnificent." He passed on, and Mr. Attrell laughed politely. Mr. O'Donnell's greetings had, of course, done for the boys as well. They did not speak, nor did they even, like their father, slow down on their way to the bathhouse.

"He's an agreeable fellow, Henry O'Donnell," said Mr. Attrell.

"Yes, they're a nice big family," said his wife. Then she removed the rubber band which marked her page in her book and took out her spectacles. Mr. Attrell filled his pipe but made no move to light it. At that moment a vastly pregnant and pretty young woman—no one he knew—went down the boardwalk in her bathing suit. He turned to his wife, but she was already reading. He put his elbow on the back of the bench and he was about to touch his wife's shoulder again when a shadow fell across his leg.

"Hello, Mrs. Attrell, Mr. Attrell. I just came over to say hello." It was a tall young man in a white uniform with the shoulder-board stripe-and-a-half of a lieutenant junior grade.

"Why, it's Frank," said Mrs. Attrell. "How are you?"

"Why, hello," said Mr. Attrell, rising.

"Just fine," said Frank. "Please don't get up. I was on my way home and I saw your car in the parking space so I thought I'd come and say hello."

"Well, I should think so," said Mr. Attrell. "Sit down? Sit down and tell us all about yourself."

"Yes, we're using your bench. I suppose you noticed," said Mrs. Attrell.

"Father'll send you a bill for it, as you well know," said Frank. "You know Father."

They all had a good laugh on that.

"Where are you now?" said Mr. Attrell.

"I'm at a place called Quonset."

"Oh, yes," said Mrs. Attrell.

"Rhode Island," said Frank.

"Oh, I see," said Mrs. Attrell.

"Yes, I think I know where it is," said Mr. Attrell. "Then do you go on a ship?"

"I hope to. You both look extremely well," said Frank.

"Well, you know," said Mr. Attrell.

"When you get our age you have nothing much else to do," said Mrs. Attrell.

"Well, you do it beautifully. I'm sorry I've got to hurry away like this but I have some people waiting in the car, but I had to say hello. I'm going back this afternoon."

"Well, thank you for coming over. It was very nice of you. Is your wife down?" said Mrs. Attrell.

"No, she's with her family in Hyannis Port."

"Well, remember us to her when you see her," said Mrs. Attrell.

"Yes," said Mr. Attrell. They shook hands with Frank and he departed.

Mr. Attrell sat down. "Frank's a fine boy. That just shows how considerate, seeing our car. How old is Frank, about?"

"He'll be thirty-four in September," said Mrs. Attrell.

Mr. Attrell nodded slowly. "Yes, that's right," he said. He began tamping down the tobacco in his pipe. "You know, I think that water—would you mind if I had a dip?"

"No, dear, but I think you ought to do it soon, before it begins to get chilly."

"Remember we're on daylight saving, so it's an hour earlier by the sun." He stood up. "I think I'll just put on my suit and get wet, and if it's too cold I'll come right out."

"That's a good idea," she said.

In the bathhouse Mr. Attrell accepted two towels from the Negro attendant and went to his booth, which was open and marked "A. T. Attrell," to undress. From the voices there could not have been more than half a dozen persons in the men's side. At first he paid no attention to the voices, but after he had untied the double knot in his shoelaces he let the words come to him.

"And who is T. K. Cartwright?" a young voice was saying.

"He's dead," said the second young voice.

"No, he isn't," said the first young voice. "That's the old buzzard that's sitting in front of us."

"And what makes you think *he* isn't dead, he and the old biddy?"

"You're both wrong," said a third young voice. "That isn't Mr. Cartwright sitting there. That's Mr. Attrell."

"So what?" said the first young voice.

"All right, so what, if you don't want to hear about them, old Attrell and his wife. They're the local tragedy. Ask your mother; she used to come here. They had a daughter or, I don't know, maybe it was a son. Anyway, whichever it was, he or she hung himself."

"Or herself," said the first young voice.

"I think it was a girl. They came home and found her hanging in the stable. It was an unfortunate love affair. I don't see why—"

"Just a minute, there." Mr. Attrell recognized the voice of Henry O'Donnell.

"Yes, sir?" asked one young voice.

"You sound to me like a pack of goddam pansies. You oughta be over on the girls' side," said Mr. O'Donnell.

"I'd like to know what business of—" a young voice said, then there was a loud smack.

"Because I made it my business. Get dressed and get outa here," said O'Donnell. "I don't give a damn whose kids you are."

Mr. Attrell heard the deep breathing of Henry O'Donnell, who waited a moment for his command to be obeyed, then walked past Mr. Attrell's booth with his head in the other direction. Mr. Attrell sat there, many minutes probably, wondering how he could ever again face Henry O'Donnell, worrying about how he could face his wife. But then of course he realized that there was really nothing to face, really nothing.

COMMENTARY

"Summer's Day" is compounded of minute social observations and preoccupied with the feelings that arise from differences in social position. Such feelings are universally judged to be petty and even contemptible. It is nevertheless O'Hara's ultimate intention in this story to represent a situation of an elemental kind, far removed from the trifling considerations of social prestige.

The story turns on a point of actual snobbery, on Mr. Attrell's sense of social superiority to Mr. O'Donnell, on Mr. O'Donnell's sense of social inferiority to Mr. Attrell. The summer community on the New England coast to which they both belong is, as people say, "exclusive." Mr. Attrell belongs to it by natural right. Mr. O'Donnell, although he has made his way into it, has not been really, or fully, accepted; at best he is tolerated.

It is a mark of Mr. Attrell's social standing that, although he is well-to-do, even rich, he drives a car that must be near its superannuation. Mr. Attrell belongs, that is, to a social group so secure that it takes pride in refusing to exhibit the usual signs of establishment; his position does not depend upon mere wealth. The gentleness and the quiet uncombativeness—even the dullness—of his temperament lead us to suppose that in all his life Mr. Attrell has never had to fight for anything. Everything has come to him by inheritance.

Mr. O'Donnell's situation is the opposite of Mr. Attrell's. An Irish Catholic, he has had to make his social way against the resistance that has been offered to his ethnic-religious group by the old, established New England families. He has gone to Yale and this means much to him—it means too much: the author, whose origins are the same as Mr. O'Donnell's, intends us to be amused by the fact that one of Mr. O'Donnell's sons has been named Arthur Twining Hadley O'Donnell, after the man who was president of Yale in his father's time. Of the four O'Donnell boys who come to the beach with their father, three bear given names derived from families eminent in the New England Protestant tradition.

At Yale, Mr. O'Donnell had failed to achieve the social success he had hoped for. His disappointment has not diminished over the years: he still takes note of Mr. Attrell's hatband, "that of a Yale society, which Mr. O'Donnell had nothing against, although he had not made it or any other." From the fact that he is a member of the summer colony and of its beach club, we understand that Mr. O'Donnell has been financially successful, but no achievement of his mature life can overcome the uneasy memory of his college defeat. In a single telling phrase, the author suggests the extent of Mr. O'Donnell's lack of ease: "Mr. O'Donnell began his big grin for the Attrells,"—aware of his charm, he uses it with conscious contrivance. And of course Mr. O'Donnell is right to be guarded in his approach to the Attrells, who clearly think of him as a stranger and regard him with firm, if gentle, condescension.

But although social behavior and social feelings, of a kind not very creditable to anyone concerned, take up a great deal of room in "Summer's Day," we come to know that they are not being presented only for what importance they may have in themselves. A large part of their interest comes from their incongruity with the intense emotional experience that Mr. Attrell is going through. It is an experience which has nothing to do with the society to which Mr. Attrell belongs and in which he has a place so much envied by Mr. O'Donnell; it might have come to him had he been a peasant or a tribesman, a Biblical Jew or an ancient Greek. It relates to his essential humanity, to his being a man.

The terrible emotion that Mr. Attrell feels is never named in the story. We know that he and his wife have suffered a great bereavement; their daughter, their only child, has died, and, as we later learn, by her own hand. But Mr. Attrell feels something more than grief; he feels defeat and humiliation, and soon we discover what it is that gives the sore wound to his pride—his childlessness. He is ashamed because he is childless at an age when he can no longer expect to beget children in his marriage.

Summer is the children's season, the beach is the place of childhood and youth, and every incident of Mr. Attrell's short stay at the beach reminds him of his humiliation. He watches the little grandson of his friend Cartwright. He is engaged in conversation by Cartwright's courteous and attractive son. His gaze is drawn to the "vastly pregnant and pretty young woman" who passes. And by way of climax, he is greeted by Mr. O'Donnell walking among his four sons. (Mr. O'Donnell is in fact the father of seven sons: one of them is the baby whose birth has so surprised the community, for everyone had been quite sure Mrs. O'Donnell was too old for childbearing.) We have been told of Mr. Attrell that he seats himself on the bench beside his wife in such a way that he has only to raise his hand to be able to touch her on the shoulder, and that from time to time he does this, and our first impulse has been to suppose that his touch is meant to give comfort and reassurance to his wife. But this impression is at last corrected: the gesture is an effort to receive rather than give comfort and reassurance. Mr. Attrell is confronting the knowledge of his confirmed childlessness and his old age. The knowledge, only half-conscious through most of the story, is finally made explicit to him by the brutal remark of one of the gossiping adolescents he overhears in the bathhouse: "And what makes you think *he* isn't dead, he and the old biddy?"

There is, then, an extreme incongruity in "Summer's Day"—on the one hand, the preoccupation with the feelings about social status; on the other hand, Mr. Attrell's experience of the end of his procreative life. If we wonder what reason the author could have had for contriving this incongruity, this bringing together of the trifling and artificial with the grim and elemental, the answer is, of course, that the juxtaposition constitutes the drama of the story. It is that much the more bitter for Mr. Attrell that Mr. O'Donnell, whom he regards as socially his inferior, should be so well provided with sons. But there is more than this to be said about the conjunction of social triviality with elemental despair in O'Hara's story. Mr. O'Donnell's frustrated social aspiration, although it is an experience of a quite different order from Mr. Attrell's biological defeat, is not beyond comparison with it. Both men are wounded in their pride, and each of them is the measure of the other's failure. Each can make the other feel inferior and ashamed. If Mr. O'Donnell has the effect upon Mr. Attrell of making him feel less a man, Mr. Attrell has the effect upon Mr. O'Donnell of making him feel less a person.

But of course the wound to Mr. Attrell's pride is a mortal one, and it is the more terrible because it is suffered amid the conventionalities and artificialities of the social life. One of the functions of society is to induce us to have a diminished realization of the grimmer actualities of our biological lives. And these actualities break all the more drastically upon our consciousness when they are made manifest in the very circumstances that are meant to obscure them.

OF
THIS TIME,
OF
THAT PLACE

LIONEL TRILLING

1905–

It was a fine September day. By noon it would be summer again, but now it was true autumn with a touch of chill in the air. As Joseph Howe stood on the porch of the house in which he lodged, ready to leave for his first class of the year, he thought with pleasure of the long indoor days that were coming. It was a moment when he could feel glad of his profession.

On the lawn the peach tree was still in fruit and young Hilda Aiken was taking a picture of it. She held the camera tight against her chest. She wanted the sun behind her, but she did not want her own long morning shadow in the foreground. She raised the camera, but that did not help, and she lowered it, but that made things worse. She twisted her body to the left, then to the right. In the end she had to step out of the direct line of the sun. At last she snapped the shutter and wound the film with intense care.

Howe, watching her from the porch, waited for her to finish and called good morning. She turned, startled, and almost sullenly lowered her glance. In the year Howe had lived at the Aikens', Hilda had accepted him as one of her family, but since his absence of the summer she had grown shy. Then suddenly she lifted her head and smiled at him, and the humorous smile confirmed his pleasure in the day. She picked up her bookbag and set off for school.

The handsome houses on the streets to the college were not yet fully awake, but they looked very friendly. Howe went by the Bradby house where he would be a guest this evening at the first dinner party of the year. When he had gone the length of the picket fence, the whitest in town, he turned back. Along the path there was a fine row of asters and he went through the gate and picked one for his buttonhole. The Bradbys would be pleased if they happened to see him invading their lawn and the knowledge of this made him even more comfortable.

He reached the campus as the hour was striking. The students were hurrying to their classes. He himself was in no hurry. He stopped at his dim cubicle of an office and lit a cigarette. The prospect of facing his class had suddenly presented itself to him and his hands were cold; the lawful seizure of power he was about to make seemed momentous. Waiting did not help. He put out his cigarette, picked up a pad of theme paper, and went to his classroom.

As he entered, the rattle of voices ceased, and the twenty-odd freshmen settled themselves and looked at him appraisingly. Their faces seemed gross, his heart sank at their massed impassivity, but he spoke briskly.

'My name is Howe,' he said, and turned and wrote it on the blackboard. The carelessness of the scrawl confirmed his authority. He went on, 'My office is 412 Slemp Hall, and my office-hours are Monday, Wednesday and Friday from eleven-thirty to twelve-thirty.'

He wrote, 'M., W., F., 11:30–12:30.' He said, 'I'll be very glad to see any of you at that time. Or if you can't come then, you can arrange with me for some other time.'

He turned again to the blackboard and spoke over his shoulder. 'The text for the course is Jarman's *Modern Plays,* revised edition. The Co-op has it in stock.' He wrote the name, underlined 'revised edition' and waited for it to be taken down in the new notebooks.

When the bent heads were raised again he began his speech of prospectus. 'It is hard to explain—' he said, and paused as they composed themselves. 'It is hard to explain what a course like this is intended to do. We are going to try to learn something about modern literature and something about prose composition.'

As he spoke, his hands warmed and he was able to look directly at the class. Last year on the first day the faces had seemed just as cloddish, but as the term wore on they became gradually alive and quite likable. It did not seem possible that the same thing could happen again.

'I shall not lecture in this course,' he continued. 'Our work will be carried on by discussion and we will try to learn by an exchange of opinion. But you will soon recognize that my opinion is worth more than anyone else's here.'

He remained grave as he said it, but two boys understood and laughed. The rest took permission from them and laughed too. All Howe's private ironies protested the vulgarity of the joke, but the laughter made him feel benign and powerful.

When the little speech was finished, Howe picked up the pad of paper he had brought. He announced that they would write an extemporaneous theme. Its subject was traditional, 'Who I am and why I came to Dwight College.' By now the class was more at ease and it gave a ritualistic groan of protest. Then there was a stir as fountain pens were brought out and the writing-arms of the chairs were cleared, and the paper was passed about. At last, all the heads bent to work, and the room became still.

Howe sat idly at his desk. The sun shone through the tall clumsy windows. The cool of the morning was already passing. There was a scent of autumn and of varnish and the stillness of the room was deep and oddly touching. Now and then a student's head was raised and scratched in the old, elaborate students' pantomime that calls the teacher to witness honest intellectual effort.

Suddenly a tall boy stood within the frame of the open door. 'Is this,' he said, and thrust a large nose into a college catalogue, 'is this the meeting place of English 1A? The section instructed by Dr. Joseph Howe?'

He stood on the very sill of the door, as if refusing to enter until he was perfectly sure of all his rights. The class looked up from work, found him absurd and gave a low mocking cheer.

The teacher and the new student, with equal pointedness, ignored the disturbance. Howe nodded to the boy, who pushed his head forward and then jerked it back in a wide elaborate arc to clear his brow of a heavy lock of hair. He advanced into the room and halted before Howe, almost at attention. In a loud, clear voice he announced, 'I am Tertan, Ferdinand R., reporting at the direction of Head of Department Vincent.'

The heraldic formality of this statement brought forth another cheer. Howe looked at the class with a sternness he could not really feel, for there was indeed something ridiculous about this boy. Under his displeased regard the rows of heads dropped to work again. Then he touched Tertan's elbow, led him up to the desk and stood so as to shield their conversation from the class.

'We are writing an extemporaneous theme,' he said. 'The subject is, "Who I am and why I came to Dwight College."'

He stripped a few sheets from the pad and offered them to the boy. Tertan hesitated and then took the paper, but he held it only tentatively. As if with the effort of making something clear, he gulped, and a slow smile fixed itself on his face. It was at once knowing and shy.

'Professor,' he said, 'to be perfectly fair to my classmates'—he made a large gesture over the room—'and to you'—he inclined his head to Howe—'this would not be for me an extemporaneous subject.'

Howe tried to understand. 'You mean you've already thought about it—you've heard we always give the same subject? That doesn't matter.'

Again the boy ducked his head and gulped. It was the gesture of one who wishes to make a difficult explanation with perfect candor. 'Sir,' he said, and made the distinction with great care, 'the topic I did not expect, but I have given much ratiocination to the subject.'

Howe smiled and said, 'I don't think that's an unfair advantage. Just go ahead and write.'

Tertan narrowed his eyes and glanced sidewise at Howe. His strange mouth smiled. Then in quizzical acceptance, he ducked his head, threw back the heavy, dank lock, dropped into a seat with a great loose noise and began to write rapidly.

The room fell silent again and Howe resumed his idleness. When the bell rang, the students who had groaned when the task had been set now groaned again because they had not finished. Howe took up the papers, and held the class while he made the first assignment. When he dismissed it, Tertan bore down on him, his slack mouth held ready for speech.

'Some professors,' he said, 'are pedants. They are Dryasdusts.[1] However, some professors are free souls and creative spirits. Kant, Hegel and Nietzsche were

---

[1] Generic name used by Thomas Carlyle (1795–1881) in *Sartor Resartus* for a pedantic scholar; derived from the fictitious writer of prefaces to several of Scott's novels.

all professors.' With this pronouncement he paused. 'It is my opinion,' he continued, 'that you occupy the second category.'

Howe looked at the boy in surprise and said with good-natured irony, 'With Kant, Hegel and Nietzsche?'

Not only Tertan's hand and head but his whole awkward body waved away the stupidity. 'It is the kind and not the quantity of the kind,' he said sternly.

Rebuked, Howe said as simply and seriously as he could, 'It would be nice to think so.' He added, 'Of course I am not a professor.'

This was clearly a disappointment but Tertan met it. 'In the French sense,' he said with composure. 'Generically, a teacher.'

Suddenly he bowed. It was such a bow, Howe fancied, as a stage-director might teach an actor playing a medieval student who takes leave of Abelard[2]— stiff, solemn, with elbows close to the body and feet together. Then, quite as suddenly, he turned and left.

A queer fish, and as soon as Howe reached his office, he sifted through the batch of themes and drew out Tertan's. The boy had filled many sheets with his unformed headlong scrawl. 'Who am I?' he had begun. 'Here, in a mundane, not to say commercialized academe, is asked the question which from time long immemorially out of mind has accreted doubts and thoughts in the psyche of man to pester him as a nuisance. Whether in St. Augustine (or Austin as sometimes called) or Miss Bashkirtsieff or Frederic Amiel or Empedocles,[3] or in less lights of the intellect than these, this posed question has been ineluctable.'

Howe took out his pencil. He circled 'academe' and wrote 'vocab.' in the margin. He underlined 'time long immemorably out of mind' and wrote 'Diction!' But this seemed inadequate for what was wrong. He put down his pencil and read ahead to discover the principle of error in the theme. 'Today as ever, in spite of gloomy prophets of the dismal science (economics) the question is uninvalidated. Out of the starry depths of heaven hurtles this spear of query demanding to be caught on the shield of the mind ere it pierces the skull and the limbs be unstrung.'

Baffled but quite caught, Howe read on. 'Materialism, by which is meant the philosophic concept and not the moral idea, provides no aegis against the question which lies beyond the tangible (metaphysics). Existence without alloy is the question presented. Environment and heredity relegated aside, the rags and old clothes of practical life discarded, the name and the instrumentality of livelihood do not, as the prophets of the dismal science insist on in this connection, give solution to the interrogation which not from the professor merely but veritably from the cosmos is given. I think, therefore I am (cogito etc.)[4] but who am I? Tertan I am, but what is Tertan? Of this time, of that place, of some parentage, what does it matter?'

Existence without alloy: the phrase established itself. Howe put aside Tertan's paper and at random picked up another. 'I am Arthur J. Casebeer, Jr.,' he read. 'My father is Arthur J. Casebeer and my grandfather was Arthur J. Case-

[2] French scholastic philosopher and theologian (1079–1142) who was extremely popular as a teacher.

[3] St. Augustine (354–430), church father, author of *Confessions*, *City of God*, etc.; Maria Constantinowna Bashkirtsieff (1860–1884), Russian artist whose diaries were published in 1887; Henri Frédéric Amiel (1821–1881), Swiss scholar, poet, and philosopher; Empedocles (*ca.* 490–430 B.C.), Greek philosopher, poet, and statesman.

[4] *Cogito, ergo sum* (Latin, I think, therefore I am), a famous phrase of the philosopher René Descartes (1596–1650).

beer before him. My mother is Nina Wimble Casebeer. Both of them are college graduates and my father is in insurance. I was born in St. Louis eighteen years ago and we still make our residence there.'

Arthur J. Casebeer, who knew who he was, was less interesting than Tertan, but more coherent. Howe picked up Tertan's paper again. It was clear that none of the routine marginal comments, no 'sent. str.' or 'punct.' or 'vocab.' could cope with this torrential rhetoric. He read ahead, contenting himself with underscoring the errors against the time when he should have the necessary 'conference' with Tertan.

It was a busy and official day of cards and sheets, arrangements and small decisions, and it gave Howe pleasure. Even when it was time to attend the first of the weekly Convocations he felt the charm of the beginning of things when intention is still innocent and uncorrupted by effort. He sat among the young instructors on the platform, and joined in their humorous complaints at having to assist at the ceremony, but actually he got a clear satisfaction from the ritual of prayer, and prosy speech, and even from wearing his academic gown. And when the Convocation was over the pleasure continued as he crossed the campus, exchanging greetings with men he had not seen since the spring. They were people who did not yet, and perhaps never would, mean much to him, but in a year they had grown amiably to be part of his life. They were his fellow-townsmen.

The day had cooled again at sunset, and there was a bright chill in the September twilight. Howe carried his voluminous gown over his arm, he swung his doctoral hood by its purple neckpiece, and on his head he wore his mortarboard with its heavy gold tassel bobbing just over his eye. These were the weighty and absurd symbols of his new profession and they pleased him. At twenty-six Joseph Howe had discovered that he was neither so well off nor so bohemian as he had once thought. A small income, adequate when supplemented by a sizable cash legacy, was genteel poverty when the cash was all spent. And the literary life—the room at the Lafayette,[5] or the small apartment without a lease, the long summers on the Cape,[6] the long afternoons and the social evenings—began to weary him. His writing filled his mornings, and should perhaps have filled his life, yet it did not. To the amusement of his friends, and with a certain sense that he was betraying his own freedom, he had used the last of his legacy for a year at Harvard. The small but respectable reputation of his two volumes of verse had proved useful—he continued at Harvard on a fellowship and when he emerged as Doctor Howe he received an excellent appointment, with prospects, at Dwight.

He had his moments of fear when all that had ever been said of the dangers of the academic life had occurred to him. But after a year in which he had tested every possibility of corruption and seduction he was ready to rest easy. His third volume of verse, most of it written in his first years of teaching, was not only ampler but, he thought, better than its predecessors.

There was a clear hour before the Bradby dinner party, and Howe looked forward to it. But he was not to enjoy it, for lying with his mail on the hall table was a copy of this quarter's issue of *Life and Letters,* to which his landlord subscribed. Its severe cover announced that its editor, Frederic Woolley, had this

[5] Hotel that was well-known as a gathering place for intellectuals and bohemians in New York's Greenwich Village.
[6] Cape Cod.

month contributed an essay called 'Two Poets,' and Howe, picking it up, curious to see who the two poets might be, felt his own name start out at him with cabalistic power—Joseph Howe. As he continued to turn the pages his hand trembled.

Standing in the dark hall, holding the neat little magazine, Howe knew that his literary contempt for Frederic Woolley meant nothing, for he suddenly understood how he respected Woolley in the way of the world. He knew this by the trembling of his hand. And of the little world as well as the great, for although the literary groups of New York might dismiss Woolley, his name carried high authority in the academic world. At Dwight it was even a revered name, for it had been here at the college that Frederic Woolley had made the distinguished scholarly career from which he had gone on to literary journalism. In middle life he had been induced to take the editorship of *Life and Letters,* a literary monthly not widely read but heavily endowed, and in its pages he had carried on the defense of what he sometimes called the older values. He was not without wit, he had great knowledge and considerable taste, and even in the full movement of the 'new' literature he had won a certain respect for his refusal to accept it. In France, even in England, he would have been connected with a more robust tradition of conservatism, but America gave him an audience not much better than genteel. It was known in the college that to the subsidy of *Life and Letters* the Bradbys contributed a great part.

As Howe read, he saw that he was involved in nothing less than an event. When the Fifth Series of *Studies in Order and Value* came to be collected, this latest of Frederic Woolley's essays would not be merely another step in the old direction. Clearly and unmistakably, it was a turning point. All his literary life Woolley had been concerned with the relation of literature to morality, religion, and the private and delicate pieties, and he had been unalterably opposed to all that he had called 'inhuman humanitarianism.' But here, suddenly, dramatically late, he had made an about-face, turning to the public life and to the humanitarian politics he had so long despised. This was the kind of incident the histories of literature make much of. Frederic Woolley was opening for himself a new career and winning a kind of new youth. He contrasted the two poets, Thomas Wormser, who was admirable, Joseph Howe, who was almost dangerous. He spoke of the 'precious subjectivism of Howe's verse. 'In times like ours,' he wrote, 'with millions facing penury and want, one feels that the qualities of the *tour d'ivoire* are well-nigh inhuman, nearly insulting. The *tour d'ivoire* becomes the *tour d'ivresse,*[7] and it is not self-intoxicated poets that our people need.' The essay said more: 'The problem is one of meaning. I am not ignorant that the creed of the esoteric poets declares that a poem does not and should not *mean* anything, that it *is* something. But poetry is what the poet makes it, and if he is a true poet he makes what his society needs. And what is needed now is the tradition in which Mr. Wormser writes, the true tradition of poetry. The Howes do no harm, but they do no good when positive good is demanded of all responsible men. Or do the Howes indeed do no harm? Perhaps Plato would have said they do, that in some ways theirs is the Phrygian music that turns men's minds from the struggle. Certainly it is true that Thomas Wormser writes in the lucid Dorian mode[8] which sends men into battle with evil.'

[7] The ivory tower becomes the tower of intoxication, or madness.
[8] The Phrygian and Dorian modes were scales used in Greek and ecclesiastical music; the Phrygian was brisk and spirited and the Dorian, bold and grave.

It was easy to understand why Woolley had chosen to praise Thomas Wormser. The long, lilting lines of *Corn Under Willows* hymned, as Woolley put it, the struggle for wheat in the Iowa fields, and expressed the real lives of real people. But why out of the dozen more notable examples he had chosen Howe's little volume as the example of 'precious subjectivism' was hard to guess. In a way it was funny, this multiplication of himself into 'the Howes.' And yet this becoming the multiform political symbol by whose creation Frederic Woolley gave the sign of a sudden new life, this use of him as a sacrifice whose blood was necessary for the rites of rejuvenation, made him feel oddly unclean.

Nor could Howe get rid of a certain practical resentment. As a poet he had a special and respectable place in the college life. But it might be another thing to be marked as the poet of a willful and selfish obscurity.

As he walked to the Bradbys', Howe was a little tense and defensive. It seemed to him that all the world knew of the 'attack' and agreed with it. And, indeed, the Bradbys had read the essay but Professor Bradby, a kind and pretentious man, said, 'I see my old friend knocked you about a bit, my boy,' and his wife Eugenia looked at Howe with her child-like blue eyes and said, 'I shall *scold* Frederic for the untrue things he wrote about you. You aren't the least obscure.' They beamed at him. In their genial snobbery they seemed to feel that he had distinguished himself. He was the leader of Howeism. He enjoyed the dinner party as much as he had thought he would.

And in the following days, as he was more preoccupied with his duties, the incident was forgotten. His classes had ceased to be mere groups. Student after student detached himself from the mass and required or claimed a place in Howe's awareness. Of them all it was Tertan who first and most violently signaled his separate existence. A week after classes had begun Howe saw his silhouette on the frosted glass of his office door. It was motionless for a long time, perhaps stopped by the problem of whether or not to knock before entering. Howe called, 'Come in!' and Tertan entered with his shambling stride.

He stood beside the desk, silent and at attention. When Howe asked him to sit down, he responded with a gesture of head and hand, as if to say that such amenities were beside the point. Nevertheless, he did take the chair. He put his ragged, crammed briefcase between his legs. His face, which Howe now observed fully for the first time, was confusing, for it was made up of florid curves, the nose arched in the bone and voluted in the nostril, the mouth loose and soft and rather moist. Yet the face was so thin and narrow as to seem the very type of asceticism. Lashes of unusual length veiled the eyes and, indeed, it seemed as if there were a veil over the whole countenance. Before the words actually came, the face screwed itself into an attitude of preparation for them.

'You can confer with me now?' Tertan said.

'Yes, I'd be glad to. There are several things in your two themes I want to talk to you about.' Howe reached for the packet of themes on his desk and sought for Tertan's. But the boy was waving them away.

'These are done perforce,' he said. 'Under the pressure of your requirement. They are not significant; mere duties.' Again his great hand flapped vaguely to dismiss his themes. He leaned forward and gazed at his teacher.

'You are,' he said, 'a man of letters? You are a poet?' It was more declaration than question.

'I should like to think so,' Howe said.

At first Tertan accepted the answer with a show of appreciation, as though the understatement made a secret between himself and Howe. Then he chose to misunderstand. With his shrewd and disconcerting control of expression, he presented to Howe a puzzled grimace. 'What does that mean?' he said.

Howe retracted the irony. 'Yes. I am a poet.' It sounded strange to say.

'That,' Tertan said, 'is a wonder.' He corrected himself with his ducking head. 'I mean that is wonderful.'

Suddenly, he dived at the miserable briefcase between his legs, put it on his knees, and began to fumble with the catch, all intent on the difficulty it presented. Howe noted that his suit was worn thin, his shirt almost unclean. He became aware, even, of a vague and musty odor of garments worn too long in unaired rooms. Tertan conquered the lock and began to concentrate upon a search into the interior. At last he held in his hand what he was after, a torn and crumpled copy of *Life and Letters*.

'I learned it from here,' he said, holding it out.

Howe looked at him sharply, his hackles a little up. But the boy's face was not only perfectly innocent, it even shone with a conscious admiration. Apparently nothing of the import of the essay had touched him except the wonderful fact that his teacher was a 'man of letters.' Yet this seemed too stupid, and Howe, to test it, said, 'The man who wrote that doesn't think it's wonderful.'

Tertan made a moist hissing sound as he cleared his mouth of saliva. His head, oddly loose on his neck, wove a pattern of contempt in the air. 'A critic,' he said, 'who admits *prima facie* that he does not understand.' Then he said grandly, 'It is the inevitable fate.'

It was absurd, yet Howe was not only aware of the absurdity but of a tension suddenly and wonderfully relaxed. Now that the 'attack' was on the table between himself and this strange boy, and subject to the boy's funny and absolutely certain contempt, the hidden force of his feeling was revealed to him in the very moment that it vanished. All unsuspected, there had been a film over the world, a transparent but discoloring haze of danger. But he had no time to stop over the brightened aspect of things. Tertan was going on. 'I also am a man of letters. Putative.'

'You have written a good deal?' Howe meant to be no more than polite, and he was surprised at the tenderness he heard in his words.

Solemnly the boy nodded, threw back the dank lock, and sucked in a deep, anticipatory breath. 'First, a work of homiletics, which is a defense of the principles of religious optimism against the pessimism of Schopenhauer and the humanism of Nietzsche.'

'Humanism? Why do you call it humanism?'

'It is my nomenclature for making a deity of man,' Tertan replied negligently. 'Then three fictional works, novels. And numerous essays in science, combating materialism. Is it your duty to read these if I bring them to you?'

Howe answered simply, 'No, it isn't exactly my duty, but I shall be happy to read them.'

Tertan stood up and remained silent. He rested his bag on the chair. With a certain compunction—for it did not seem entirely proper that, of two men of letters, one should have the right to blue-pencil the other, to grade him or to question the quality of his 'sentence structure'—Howe reached for Tertan's papers. But before he could take them up, the boy suddenly made his bow-to-Abelard, the stiff inclination of the body with the hands seeming to emerge from the scholar's gown. Then he was gone.

But after his departure something was still left of him. The timbre of his curious sentences, the downright finality of so quaint a phrase as 'It is the inevitable fate' still rang in the air. Howe gave the warmth of his feeling to the new visitor who stood at the door announcing himself with a genteel clearing of the throat.

'Doctor Howe, I believe?' the student said. A large hand advanced into the room and grasped Howe's hand. 'Blackburn, sir, Theodore Blackburn, vice-president of the Student Council. A great pleasure, sir.'

Out of a pair of ruddy cheeks a pair of small eyes twinkled good-naturedly. The large face, the large body were not so much fat as beefy and suggested something 'typical'—monk, politician, or innkeeper.

Blackburn took the seat beside Howe's desk. 'I may have seemed to introduce myself in my public capacity, sir,' he said. 'But it is really as an individual that I came to see you. That is to say, as one of your students to be.'

He spoke with an English intonation and he went on, 'I was once an English major, sir.'

For a moment Howe was startled, for the roast-beef look of the boy and the manner of his speech gave a second's credibility to one sense of his statement. Then the collegiate meaning of the phrase asserted itself, but some perversity made Howe say what was not really in good taste even with so forward a student, 'Indeed? What regiment?'

Blackburn stared and then gave a little pouf-pouf of laughter. He waved the misapprehension away. '*Very* good, sir. It certainly is an ambiguous term.' He chuckled in appreciation of Howe's joke, then cleared his throat to put it aside. 'I look forward to taking your course in the romantic poets, sir,' he said earnestly. 'To me the romantic poets are the very crown of English literature.'

Howe made a dry sound, and the boy, catching some meaning in it, said, 'Little as I know them, of course. But even Shakespeare who is so dear to us of the Anglo-Saxon tradition is in a sense but the preparation for Shelley, Keats and Byron. And Wadsworth.'

Almost sorry for him, Howe dropped his eyes. With some embarrassment, for the boy was not actually his student, he said softly, 'Wordsworth.'

'Sir?'

'Wordsworth, not Wadsworth. You said Wadsworth.'

'Did I, sir?' Gravely he shook his head to rebuke himself for the error. 'Wordsworth, of course—slip of the tongue.' Then, quite in command again, he went on. 'I have a favor to ask of you, Doctor Howe. You see, I began my college course as an English major,'—he smiled—'as I said.'

'Yes?'

'But after my first year I shifted. I shifted to the social sciences. Sociology and government—I find them stimulating and very *real*.' He paused, out of respect for reality. 'But now I find that perhaps I have neglected the other side.'

'The other side?' Howe said.

'Imagination, fancy, culture. A well-rounded man.' He trailed off as if there were perfect understanding between them. 'And so, sir, I have decided to end my senior year with your course in the romantic poets.'

His voice was filled with an indulgence which Howe ignored as he said flatly and gravely, 'But that course isn't given until the spring term.'

'Yes, sir, and that is where the favor comes in. Would you let me take your romantic prose course? I can't take it for credit, sir, my program is full, but just for background it seems to me that I ought to take it. I do hope,' he concluded in a manly way, 'that you will consent.'

'Well, it's no great favor, Mr. Blackburn. You can come if you wish, though there's not much point in it if you don't do the reading.'

The bell rang for the hour and Howe got up.

'May I begin with this class, sir?' Blackburn's smile was candid and boyish.

Howe nodded carelessly and together, silently, they walked to the classroom down the hall. When they reached the door Howe stood back to let his student enter, but Blackburn moved adroitly behind him and grasped him by the arm to urge him over the threshold. They entered together with Blackburn's hand firmly on Howe's biceps, the student inducting the teacher into his own room. Howe felt a surge of temper rise in him and almost violently he disengaged his arm and walked to the desk, while Blackburn found a seat in the front row and smiled at him.

II

The question was, At whose door must the tragedy be laid?

All night the snow had fallen heavily and only now was abating in sparse little flurries. The windows were valanced high with white. It was very quiet; something of the quiet of the world had reached the class, and Howe found that everyone was glad to talk or listen. In the room there was a comfortable sense of pleasure in being human.

Casebeer believed that the blame for the tragedy rested with heredity. Picking up the book he read, 'The sins of the fathers are visited on their children.' This opinion was received with general favor. Nevertheless, Johnson ventured to say that the fault was all Pastor Manders'[9] because the Pastor had made Mrs. Alving go back to her husband and was always hiding the truth. To this Hibbard objected with logic enough, 'Well then, it was really all her husband's fault. He *did* all the bad things.' DeWitt, his face bright with an impatient idea, said that the fault was all society's. 'By society I don't mean upper-crust society,' he said. He looked around a little defiantly, taking in any members of the class who might be members of upper-crust society. 'Not in that sense. I mean the social unit.'

Howe nodded and said, 'Yes, of course.'

'If the society of the time had progressed far enough in science,' De Witt went on, 'then there would be no problem for Mr. Ibsen to write about. Captain Alving plays around a little, gives way to perfectly natural biological urges, and he gets a social disease, a venereal disease. If the disease is cured, no problem. Invent salvarsan and the disease is cured. The problem of heredity disappears and li'l Oswald just doesn't get paresis. No paresis, no problem—no problem, no play.'

[9] The play being discussed is *Ghosts* by Henrik Ibsen (1828–1906).

This was carrying the ark into battle, and the class looked at De Witt with respectful curiosity. It was his usual way and on the whole they were sympathetic with his struggle to prove to Howe that science was better than literature. Still, there was something in his reckless manner that alienated them a little.

'Or take birth-control, for instance,' De Witt went on. 'If Mrs. Alving had some knowledge of contraception, she wouldn't have had to have li'l Oswald at all. No li'l Oswald, no play.'

The class was suddenly quieter. In the back row Stettenhover swung his great football shoulders in a righteous sulking gesture, first to the right, then to the left. He puckered his mouth ostentatiously. Intellect was always ending up by talking dirty.

Tertan's hand went up, and Howe said, 'Mr. Tertan.' The boy shambled to his feet and began his long characteristic gulp. Howe made a motion with his fingers, as small as possible, and Tertan ducked his head and smiled in apology. He sat down. The class laughed. With more than half the term gone, Tertan had not been able to remember that one did not rise to speak. He seemed unable to carry on the life of the intellect without this mark of respect for it. To Howe the boy's habit of rising seemed to accord with the formal shabbiness of his dress. He never wore the casual sweaters and jackets of his classmates. Into the free and comfortable air of the college classroom he brought the stuffy sordid strictness of some crowded, metropolitan high school.

'Speaking from one sense,' Tertan began slowly, 'there is no blame ascribable. From the sense of determinism, who can say where the blame lies? The preordained is the preordained and it cannot be said without rebellion against the universe, a palpable absurdity.'

In the back row Stettenhover slumped suddenly in his seat, his heels held out before him, making a loud, dry, disgusted sound. His body sank until his neck rested on the back of his chair. He folded his hands across his belly and looked significantly out of the window, exasperated not only with Tertan, but with Howe, with the class, with the whole system designed to encourage this kind of thing. There was a certain insolence in the movement and Howe flushed. As Tertan continued to speak, Howe stalked casually toward the window and placed himself in the line of Stettenhover's vision. He stared at the great fellow, who pretended not to see him. There was so much power in the big body, so much contempt in the Greek-athlete face under the crisp Greek-athlete curls, that Howe felt almost physical fear. But at last Stettenhover admitted him to focus and under his disapproving gaze sat up with slow indifference. His eyebrows raised high in resignation, he began to examine his hands. Howe relaxed and turned his attention back to Tertan.

'Flux of existence,' Tertan was saying, 'produces all things, so that judgment wavers. Beyond the phenomena, what? But phenomena are adumbrated and to them we are limited.'

Howe saw it for a moment as perhaps it existed in the boy's mind—the world of shadows which are cast by a great light upon a hidden reality as in the old myth of the Cave.[10] But the little brush with Stettenhover had tired him, and he said irritably, 'But come to the point, Mr. Tertan.'

He said it so sharply that some of the class looked at him curiously. For three

[10] Parable used by Plato (*ca.* 429–347 B.C.) in the *Republic*, Book VII.

months he had gently carried Tertan through his verbosities, to the vaguely respectful surprise of the other students, who seemed to conceive that there existed between this strange classmate and their teacher some special understanding from which they were content to be excluded. Tertan looked at him mildly, and at once came brilliantly to the point. 'This is the summation of the play,' he said and took up his book and read, ' "Your poor father never found any outlet for the overmastering joy of life that was in him. And I brought no holiday into his home, either. Everything seemed to turn upon duty and I am afraid I made your poor father's home unbearable to him, Oswald." Spoken by Mrs. Alving.'

Yes that was surely the 'summation' of the play and Tertan had hit it, as he hit, deviously and eventually, the literary point of almost everything. But now, as always, he was wrapping it away from sight. 'For most mortals,' he said, 'there are only joys of biological urgings, gross and crass, such as the sensuous Captain Alving. For certain few there are the transmutations beyond these to a contemplation of the utter whole.'

Oh, the boy was mad. And suddenly the word, used in hyperbole, intended almost for the expression of exasperated admiration, became literal. Now that the word was used, it became simply apparent to Howe that Tertan was mad.

It was a monstrous word and stood like a bestial thing in the room. Yet it so completely comprehended everything that had puzzled Howe, it so arranged and explained what for three months had been perplexing him that almost at once its horror became domesticated. With this word Howe was able to understand why he had never been able to communicate to Tertan the value of a single criticism or correction of his wild, verbose themes. Their conferences had been frequent and long but had done nothing to reduce to order the splendid confusion of the boy's ideas. Yet, impossible though its expression was, Tertan's incandescent mind could always strike for a moment into some dark corner of thought.

And now it was suddenly apparent that it was not a faulty rhetoric that Howe had to contend with. With his new knowledge he looked at Tertan's face and wondered how he could have so long deceived himself. Tertan was still talking, and the class had lapsed into a kind of patient unconsciousness, a coma of respect for words which, for all that most of them knew, might be profound. Almost with a suffusion of shame, Howe believed that in some dim way the class had long ago had some intimation of Tertan's madness. He reached out as decisively as he could to seize the thread of Tertan's discourse before it should be entangled further.

'Mr. Tertan says that the blame must be put upon whoever kills the joy of living in another. We have been assuming that Captain Alving was a wholly bad man, but what if we assume that he became bad only because Mrs. Alving, when they were first married, acted toward him in the prudish way she says she did?'

It was a ticklish idea to advance to freshmen and perhaps not profitable. Not all of them were following.

'That would put the blame on Mrs. Alving herself, whom most of you admire. And she herself seems to think so.' He glanced at his watch. The hour was nearly over. 'What do you think, Mr. De Witt?'

De Witt rose to the idea; he wanted to know if society couldn't be blamed for educating Mrs. Alving's temperament in the wrong way. Casebeer was puzzled, Stettenhover continued to look at his hands until the bell rang.

Tertan, his brows louring in thought, was making as always for a private word. Howe gathered his books and papers to leave quickly. At this moment of his discovery and with the knowledge still raw, he could not engage himself with Tertan. Tertan sucked in his breath to prepare for speech and Howe made ready for the pain and confusion. But at that moment Casebeer detached himself from the group with which he had been conferring and which he seemed to represent. His constituency remained at a tactful distance. The mission involved the time of an assigned essay. Casebeer's presentation of the plea—it was based on the fresh-men's heavy duties at the fraternities during Carnival Week—cut across Tertan's preparations for speech. 'And so some of us fellows thought,' Casebeer concluded with heavy solemnity, 'that we could do a better job, give our minds to it more, if we had more time.'

Tertan regarded Casebeer with mingled curiosity and revulsion. Howe not only said that he would postpone the assignment but went on to talk about the Carnival, and even drew the waiting constituency into the conversation. He was conscious of Tertan's stern and astonished stare, then of his sudden departure.

Now that the fact was clear, Howe knew that he must act on it. His course was simple enough. He must lay the case before the Dean. Yet he hesitated. His feeling for Tertan must now, certainly, be in some way invalidated. Yet could he, because of a word, hurry to assign to official and reasonable solicitude what had been, until this moment, so various and warm? He could at least delay and, by moving slowly, lend a poor grace to the necessary, ugly act of making his report.

It was with some notion of keeping the matter in his own hands that he went to the Dean's office to look up Tertan's records. In the outer office the Dean's secretary greeted him brightly, and at his request brought him the manila folder with the small identifying photograph pasted in the corner. She laughed. 'He was looking for the birdie in the wrong place,' she said.

Howe leaned over her shoulder to look at the picture. It was as bad as all the Dean's-office photographs were, but it differed from all that Howe had ever seen. Tertan, instead of looking into the camera, as no doubt he had been bidden, had, at the moment of exposure, turned his eyes upward. His mouth, as though conscious of the trick played on the photographer, had the sly superior look that Howe knew.

The secretary was fascinated by the picture. 'What a funny boy,' she said. 'He looks like Tartuffe!'[11]

And so he did, with the absurd piety of the eyes and the conscious slyness of the mouth and the whole face bloated by the bad lens.

'Is he *like* that?' the secretary said.

'Like Tartuffe? No.'

From the photograph there was little enough comfort to be had. The records themselves gave no clue to madness, though they suggested sadness enough. Howe read of a father, Stanislaus Tertan, born in Budapest and trained in engineering in Berlin, once employed by the Hercules Chemical Corporation—this was one of the factories that dominated the sound end of the town—but now without em-ployment. He read of a mother Erminie (Youngfellow) Tertan, born in Man-chester, educated at a Normal School at Leeds, now housewife by profession. The family lived on Greenbriar Street which Howe knew as a row of once elegant homes near what was now the factory district. The old mansion had long ago

[11] The sanctimonious hypocrite in Molière's comedy *Tartuffe*, first produced in 1667.

been divided into small and primitive apartments. Of Ferdinand himself there was little to learn. He lived with his parents, had attended a Detroit high school and had transferred to the local school in his last year. His rating for intelligence, as expressed in numbers, was high, his scholastic record was remarkable, he held a college scholarship for his tuition.

Howe laid the folder on the secretary's desk. 'Did you find what you wanted to know?' she asked.

The phrases from Tertan's momentous first theme came back to him. 'Tertan I am, but what is Tertan? Of this time, of that place, of some parentage, what does it matter?'

'No, I didn't find it,' he said.

Now that he had consulted the sad, half-meaningless record he knew all the more firmly that he must not give the matter out of his own hands. He must not release Tertan to authority. Not that he anticipated from the Dean anything but the greatest kindness for Tertan. The Dean would have the experience and skill which he himself could not have. One way or another the Dean could answer the question, 'What is Tertan?' Yet this was precisely what he feared. He alone could keep alive—not forever but for a somehow important time—the question, 'What is Tertan?' He alone could keep it still a question. Some sure instinct told him that he must not surrender the question to a clean official desk in a clear official light to be dealt with, settled and closed.

He heard himself saying, 'Is the Dean busy at the moment? I'd like to see him.'

His request came thus unbidden, even forbidden, and it was one of the surprising and startling incidents of his life. Later when he reviewed the events, so disconnected in themselves, or so merely odd, of the story that unfolded for him that year, it was over this moment, on its face the least notable, that he paused longest. It was frequently to be with fear and never without a certainty of its meaning in his own knowledge of himself that he would recall this simple, routine request, and the feeling of shame and freedom it gave him as he sent everything down the official chute. In the end, of course, no matter what he did to 'protect' Tertan, he would have had to make the same request and lay the matter on the Dean's clean desk. But it would always be a landmark of his life that, at the very moment when he was rejecting the official way, he had been, without will or intention, so gladly drawn to it.

After the storm's last delicate flurry, the sun had come out. Reflected by the new snow, it filled the office with a golden light which was almost musical in the way it made all the commonplace objects of efficiency shine with a sudden sad and noble significance. And the light, now that he noticed it, made the utterance of his perverse and unwanted request even more momentous.

The secretary consulted the engagement pad. 'He'll be free any minute. Don't you want to wait in the parlor?'

She threw open the door of the large and pleasant room in which the Dean held his Committee meetings, and in which his visitors waited. It was designed with a homely elegance on the masculine side of the eighteenth-century manner. There was a small coal fire in the grate and the handsome mahogany table was strewn with books and magazines. The large windows gave on the snowy lawn, and there was such a fine width of window that the white casements and walls seemed at this moment but a continuation of the snow, the snow but an extension of casement and walls. The outdoors seemed taken in and made safe, the indoors seemed luxuriously freshened and expanded.

Howe sat down by the fire and lighted a cigarette. The room had its intended effect upon him. He felt comfortable and relaxed, yet nicely organized, some young diplomatic agent of the eighteenth century, the newly fledged Swift carrying out Sir William Temple's business.[12] The rawness of Tertan's case quite vanished. He crossed his legs and reached for a magazine.

It was that famous issue of *Life and Letters* that his idle hand had found and his blood raced as he sifted through it, and the shape of his own name, Joseph Howe, sprang out at him, still cabalistic in its power. He tossed the magazine back on the table as the door of the Dean's office opened and the Dean ushered out Theodore Blackburn.

'Ah, Joseph!' the Dean said.

Blackburn said, 'Good morning, Doctor.' Howe winced at the title and caught the flicker of amusement over the Dean's face. The Dean stood with his hand high on the door-jamb and Blackburn, still in the doorway, remained standing almost under the long arm.

Howe nodded briefly to Blackburn, snubbing his eager deference. 'Can you give me a few minutes?' he said to the Dean.

'All the time you want. Come in.' Before the two men could enter the office, Blackburn claimed their attention with a long full 'er.' As they turned to him, Blackburn said, 'Can *you* give *me* a few minutes, Doctor Howe?' His eyes sparkled at the little audacity he had committed, the slightly impudent play with hierarchy. Of the three of them Blackburn kept himself the lowest, but he reminded Howe of his subaltern relation to the Dean.

'I mean, of course,' Blackburn went on easily, 'when you've finished with the Dean.'

'I'll be in my office shortly,' Howe said, turned his back on the ready 'Thank you, sir,' and followed the Dean into the inner room.

'Energetic boy,' said the Dean. 'A bit beyond himself but very energetic. Sit down.'

The Dean lighted a cigarette, leaned back in his chair, sat easy and silent for a moment, giving Howe no signal to go ahead with business. He was a young Dean, not much beyond forty, a tall handsome man with sad, ambitious eyes. He had been a Rhodes scholar. His friends looked for great things from him, and it was generally said that he had notions of education which he was not yet ready to try to put into practice.

His relaxed silence was meant as a compliment to Howe. He smiled and said, 'What's the business, Joseph?'

'Do you know Tertan—Ferdinand Tertan, a freshman?'

The Dean's cigarette was in his mouth and his hands were clasped behind his head. He did not seem to search his memory for the name. He said, 'What about him?'

Clearly the Dean knew something, and he was waiting for Howe to tell him more. Howe moved only tentatively. Now that he was doing what he had resolved

<hr/>

[12] Jonathan Swift (1667–1745), author of *Gulliver's Travels*, worked as secretary to Sir William Temple (1628–1699), English statesman and author, during the years 1689–1692 and 1696–1699.

not to do, he felt more guilty at having been so long deceived by Tertan and more need to be loyal to his error.

'He's a strange fellow,' he ventured. He said stubbornly, 'In a strange way he's very brilliant.' He concluded, 'But very strange.'

The springs of the Dean's swivel chair creaked as he came out of his sprawl and leaned forward to Howe. 'Do you mean he's so strange that it's something you could give a name to?'

Howe looked at him stupidly. 'What do you mean?' he said.

'What's his trouble?' the Dean said more neutrally.

'He's very brilliant, in a way. I looked him up and he has a top intelligence rating. But somehow, and it's hard to explain just how, what he says is always on the edge of sense and doesn't quite make it.'

The Dean looked at him and Howe flushed up. The Dean had surely read Woolley on the subject of 'the Howes' and the *tour d'ivresse*. Was that quick glance ironical?

The Dean picked up some papers from his desk, and Howe could see that they were in Tertan's impatient scrawl. Perhaps the little gleam in the Dean's glance had come only from putting facts together.

'He sent me this yesterday,' the Dean said. 'After an interview I had with him. I haven't been able to do more than glance at it. When you said what you did, I realized there was something wrong.'

Twisting his mouth, the Dean looked over the letter. 'You seem to be involved,' he said without looking up. 'By the way, what did you give him at midterm?'

Flushing, setting his shoulders, Howe said firmly, 'I gave him A-minus.'

The Dean chuckled. 'Might be a good idea if some of our nicer boys went crazy—just a little.' He said, 'Well,' to conclude the matter and handed the papers to Howe. 'See if this is the same thing you've been finding. Then we can go into the matter again.'

Before the fire in the parlor, in the chair that Howe had been occupying, sat Blackburn. He sprang to his feet as Howe entered.

'I said my office, Mr. Blackburn.' Howe's voice was sharp. Then he was almost sorry for the rebuke, so clearly and naively did Blackburn seem to relish his stay in the parlor, close to authority.

'I'm in a bit of a hurry, sir,' he said, 'and I did want to be sure to speak to you, sir.'

He was really absurd, yet fifteen years from now he would have grown up to himself, to the assurance and mature beefiness. In banks, in consular offices, in brokerage firms, on the bench, more seriously affable, a little sterner, he would make use of his ability to be administered by his job. It was almost reassuring. Now he was exercising his too-great skill on Howe. 'I owe you an apology, sir,' he said.

Howe knew that he did, but he showed surprise.

'I mean, Doctor, after your having been so kind about letting me attend your class, I stopped coming.' He smiled in deprecation. 'Extracurricular activities take up so much of my time. I'm afraid I undertook more than I could perform.'

Howe had noticed the absence and had been a little irritated by it after Blackburn's elaborate plea. It was an absence that might be interpreted as a comment on the teacher. But there was only one way for him to answer. 'You've no need to apologize,' he said. 'It's wholly your affair.'

Blackburn beamed. 'I'm so glad you feel that way about it, sir. I was worried you might think I had stayed away because I was influenced by—' he stopped and lowered his eyes.

Astonished, Howe said, 'Influenced by what?'

'Well, by—' Blackburn hesitated and for answer pointed to the table on which lay the copy of *Life and Letters*. Without looking at it, he knew where to direct his hand. 'By the unfavorable publicity, sir.' He hurried on. 'And that brings me to another point, sir. I am secretary of Quill and Scroll, sir, the student literary society, and I wonder if you would address us. You could read your own poetry, sir, and defend your own point of view. It would be very interesting.'

It was truly amazing. Howe looked long and cruelly into Blackburn's face, trying to catch the secret of the mind that could have conceived this way of manipulating him, this way so daring and inept—but not entirely inept—with its malice so without malignity. The face did not yield its secret. Howe smiled broadly and said, 'Of course I don't think you were influenced by the unfavorable publicity.'

'I'm still going to take—regularly, for credit—your romantic poets course next term,' Blackburn said.

'Don't worry, my dear fellow, don't worry about it.'

Howe started to leave and Blackburn stopped him with, 'But about Quill, sir?'

'Suppose we wait until next term? I'll be less busy then.'

And Blackburn said, 'Very good, sir, and thank you.'

In his office the little encounter seemed less funny to Howe, was even in some indeterminate way disturbing. He made an effort to put it from his mind by turning to what was sure to disturb him more, the Tertan letter read in the new interpretation. He found what he had always found, the same florid leaps beyond fact and meaning, the same headlong certainty. But as his eye passed over the familiar scrawl it caught his own name, and for the second time that hour he felt the race of his blood.

'The Paraclete,' Tertan had written to the Dean, 'from a Greek word meaning to stand in place of, but going beyond the primitive idea to mean traditionally the helper, the one who comforts and assists, cannot without fundamental loss be jettisoned. Even if taken no longer in the supernatural sense, the concept remains deeply in the human consciousness inevitably. Humanitarianism is no reply, for not every man stands in the place of every other man for this other comrade's comfort. But certain are chosen out of the human race to be the consoler of some other. Of these, for example, is Joseph Barker Howe, Ph.D. Of intellects not the first yet of true intellect and lambent instructions, given to that which is intuitive and irrational, not to what is logical in the strict word, what is judged by him is of the heart and not the head. Here is one chosen, in that he chooses himself to stand in the place of another for comfort and consolation. To him more than another I give my gratitude, with all respect to our Dean who reads this, a noble man, but merely dedicated, not consecrated. But not in the aspect of the Paraclete only is Dr. Joseph Barker Howe established, for he must be the Paraclete to another aspect of himself, that which is driven and persecuted by the lack of understanding in the world at large, so that he in himself embodies the full history of man's tribulations and, overflowing upon others, notably the present writer, is the ultimate end.'

This was love. There was no escape from it. Try as Howe might to remember that Tertan was mad and all his emotions invalidated, he could not destroy the effect upon him of his student's stern, affectionate regard. He had betrayed not only a power of mind but a power of love. And, however firmly he held before his attention the fact of Tertan's madness, he could do nothing to banish the physical sensation of gratitude he felt. He had never thought of himself as 'driven and persecuted' and he did not now. But still he could not make meaningless his sensation of gratitude. The pitiable Tertan sternly pitied him, and comfort came from Tertan's never-to-be-comforted mind.

III

In an academic community, even an efficient one, official matters move slowly. The term drew to a close with no action in the case of Tertan, and Joseph Howe had to confront a curious problem. How should he grade his strange student, Tertan?

Tertan's final examination had been no different from all his other writing, and what did one 'give' such a student? De Witt must have his A, that was clear. Johnson would get a B. With Casebeer it was a question of a B-minus or a C-plus, and Stettenhover, who had been crammed by the team tutor to fill half a bluebook with his thin feminine scrawl, would have his C-minus which he would accept with mingled indifference and resentment. But with Tertan it was not so easy.

The boy was still in the college process and his name could not be omitted from the grade sheet. Yet what should a mind under suspicion of madness be graded? Until the medical verdict was given, it was for Howe to continue as Tertan's teacher and to keep his judgment pedagogical. Impossible to give him an F: he had not failed. B was for Johnson's stolid mediocrity. He could not be put on the edge of passing with Stettenhover, for he exactly did not pass. In energy and richness of intellect he was perhaps even De Witt's superior, and Howe toyed grimly with the notion of giving him an A, but that would lower the value of the A De Witt had won with his beautiful and clear, if still arrogant, mind. There was a notation which the Registrar recognized—Inc., for Incomplete, and in the horrible comedy of the situation, Howe considered that. But really only a mark of M for Mad would serve.

In his perplexity, Howe sought the Dean, but the Dean was out of town. In the end, he decided to maintain the A-minus he had given Tertan at mid-term. After all, there had been no falling away from that quality. He entered it on the grade sheet with something like bravado.

Academic time moves quickly. A college year is not really a year, lacking as it does three months. And it is endlessly divided into units which, at their beginning, appear larger than they are—terms, half-terms, months, weeks. And the ultimate unit, the hour, is not really an hour, lacking as it does ten minutes. And so the new term advanced rapidly, and one day the fields about the town were all brown, cleared of even the few thin patches of snow which had lingered so long.

Howe, as he lectured on the romantic poets, became conscious of Blackburn emanating wrath. Blackburn did it well, did it with enormous dignity. He did not stir in his seat, he kept his eyes fixed on Howe in perfect attention, but he abstained from using his notebook, there was no mistaking what he proposed to himself as an attitude. His elbow on the writing-wing of the chair, his chin on the curled fingers of his hand, he was the embodiment of intellectual indignation. He was thinking his own thoughts, would give no public offense, yet would claim his due, was not to be intimidated. Howe knew that he would present himself at the end of the hour.

Blackburn entered the office without invitation. He did not smile; there was no cajolery about him. Without invitation he sat down beside Howe's desk. He did not speak until he had taken the blue-book from his pocket. He said, 'What does this mean, sir?'

It was a sound and conservative student tactic. Said in the usual way it meant, 'How could you have so misunderstood me?' or 'What does this mean for my future in the course?' But there were none of the humbler tones in Blackburn's way of saying it.

Howe made the established reply, 'I think that's for you to tell me.'

Blackburn continued icy. 'I'm sure I can't, sir.'

There was a silence between them. Both dropped their eyes to the blue-book on the desk. On its cover Howe had penciled: 'F. This is very poor work.'

Howe picked up the blue-book. There was always the possibility of injustice. The teacher may be bored by the mass of papers and not wholly attentive. A phrase, even the student's handwriting, may irritate him unreasonably. 'Well,' said Howe, 'Let's go through it.'

He opened the first page. 'Now here: you write, "In *The Ancient Mariner,* Coleridge lives in and transports us to a honey-sweet world where all is rich and strange, a world of charm to which we can escape from the humdrum existence of our daily lives, the world of romance. Here, in this warm and honey-sweet land of charming dreams we can relax and enjoy ourselves." '

Howe lowered the paper and waited with a neutral look for Blackburn to speak. Blackburn returned the look boldly, did not speak, sat stolid and lofty. At last Howe said, speaking gently, 'Did you mean that, or were you just at a loss for something to say?'

'You imply that I was just "bluffing"?' The quotation marks hung palpable in the air about the word.

'I'd like to know. I'd prefer believing that you were bluffing to believing that you really thought this.'

Blackburn's eyebrows went up. From the height of a great and firm-based idea he looked at his teacher. He clasped the crags for a moment and then pounced, craftily, suavely. 'Do you mean, Doctor Howe, that there aren't two opinions possible?'

It was superbly done in its air of putting all of Howe's intellectual life into the balance. Howe remained patient and simple. 'Yes, many opinions are possible, but not this one. Whatever anyone believes of *The Ancient Mariner,* no one can in reason believe that it represents a—a honey-sweet world in which we can relax.'

'But that is what I *feel*, sir.'

This was well-done, too. Howe said, 'Look, Mr. Blackburn. Do you really relax with hunger and thirst, the heat and the sea-serpents, the dead men with staring eyes, Life in Death and the skeletons? Come now, Mr. Blackburn.'

Blackburn made no answer, and Howe pressed forward. 'Now, you say of Wordsworth, "Of peasant stock himself, he turned from the effete life of the salons and found in the peasant the hope of a flaming revolution which would sweep away all the old ideas. This is the subject of his best poems." '

Beaming at his teacher with youthful eagerness, Blackburn said, 'Yes, sir, a rebel, a bringer of light to suffering mankind. I see him as a kind of Prothemeus.'

'A kind of what?'

'Prothemeus, sir.'

"Think, Mr. Blackburn. We were talking about him only today and I mentioned his name a dozen times. You don't mean Prothemeus. You mean—' Howe waited, but there was no response.

'You mean Prometheus.'

Blackburn gave no assent, and Howe took the reins. 'You've done a bad job here, Mr. Blackburn, about as bad as could be done.' He saw Blackburn stiffen and his genial face harden again. 'It shows either a lack of preparation or a complete lack of understanding.' He saw Blackburn's face begin to go to pieces and he stopped.

'Oh, sir,' Blackburn burst out, 'I've never had a mark like this before, never anything below a B, never. A thing like this has never happened to me before.'

It must be true, it was a statement too easily verified. Could it be that other instructors accepted such flaunting nonsense? Howe wanted to end the interview. 'I'll set it down to lack of preparation,' he said. 'I know you're busy. That's not an excuse, but it's an explanation. Now, suppose you really prepare, and then take another quiz in two weeks. We'll forget this one and count the other.'

Blackburn squirmed with pleasure and gratitude. "Thank you, sir. You're really very kind, very kind.'

Howe rose to conclude the visit. 'All right, then—in two weeks.'

It was that day that the Dean imparted to Howe the conclusion of the case of Tertan. It was simple and a little anti-climatic. A physician had been called in, and had said the word, given the name.

'A classic case, he called it,' the Dean said. 'Not a doubt in the world,' he said. His eyes were full of miserable pity, and he clutched at a word. 'A classic case, a classic case.' To his aid and to Howe's there came the Parthenon and the form of the Greek drama, the Aristotelian logic, Racine and the Well-Tempered Clavichord, the blueness of the Aegean and its clear sky.[13] Classic—that is to say, without a doubt, perfect in its way, a veritable model, and, as the Dean had been told, sure to take a perfectly predictable and inevitable course to a foreknown conclusion.

It was not only pity that stood in the Dean's eyes. For a moment there was fear too. 'Terrible,' he said, 'it is simply terrible.'

Then he went on briskly. 'Naturally, we've told the boy nothing. And,

[13] The Parthenon, the most celebrated example of Doric architecture, is a temple of Athena, built in the fifth century B.C.; Jean Baptiste Racine (1639–1699) was a famous French tragic poet; the *Well-Tempered Clavichord* is a series of piano exercises by Johann Sebastian Bach (1685–1750).

naturally, we won't. His tuition's paid by his scholarship, and we'll continue him on the rolls until the end of the year. That will be kindest. After that the matter will be out of our control. We'll see, of course, that he gets into the proper hands. I'm told there will be no change, he'll go on like this, be as good as this, for four to six months. And so we'll just go along as usual.'

So Tertan continued to sit in Section 5 of English 1A, to his classmates still a figure of curiously dignified fun, symbol to most of them of the respectable but absurd intellectual life. But to his teacher he was now very different. He had not changed—he was still the greyhound casting[14] for the scent of ideas, and Howe could see that he was still the same Tertan, but he could not feel it. What he felt as he looked at the boy sitting in his accustomed place was the hard blank of a fact. The fact itself was formidable and depressing. But what Howe was chiefly aware of was that he had permitted the metamorphosis of Tertan from person to fact.

As much as possible he avoided seeing Tertan's upraised hand and eager eye. But the fact did not know of its mere factuality, it continued its existence as if it were Tertan, hand up and eye questioning, and one day it appeared in Howe's office with a document.

'Even the spirit who lives egregiously, above the herd, must have its relations with the fellowman,' Tertan declared. He laid the document on Howe's desk. It was headed 'Quill and Scroll Society of Dwight College. Application for Membership.'

'In most ways these are crass minds,' Tertan said, touching the paper. 'Yet as a whole, bound together in their common love of letters, they transcend their intellectual lacks since it is not a paradox that the whole is greater than the sum of its parts.'

'When are the elections?' Howe asked.

'They take place tomorrow.'

'I certainly hope you will be successful.'

'Thank you. Would you wish to implement that hope?' A rather dirty finger pointed to the bottom of the sheet. 'A faculty recommender is necessary,' Tertan said stiffly, and waited.

'And you wish me to recommend you?'

'It would be an honor.'

'You may use my name.'

Tertan's finger pointed again. 'It must be a written sponsorship, signed by the sponsor.' There was a large blank space on the form under the heading, 'Opinion of Faculty Sponsor.'

This was almost another thing and Howe hesitated. Yet there was nothing else to do and he took out his fountain pen. He wrote, 'Mr. Ferdinand Tertan is marked by his intense devotion to letters and by his exceptional love of all things of the mind.' To this he signed his name, which looked bold and assertive on the white page. It disturbed him, the strange affirming power of a name. With a businesslike air, Tertan whipped up the paper, folding it with decision, and put it into his pocket. He bowed and took his departure, leaving Howe with the sense of having done something oddly momentous.

And so much now seemed odd and momentous to Howe that should not

[14] Hunting term; searching for a scent or trail.

have seemed so. It was odd and momentous, he felt, when he sat with Blackburn's second quiz before him, and wrote in an excessively firm hand the grade of C-minus. The paper was a clear, an indisputable failure. He was carefully and consciously committing a cowardice. Blackburn had told the truth when he had pleaded his past record. Howe had consulted it in the Dean's office. It showed no grade lower than a B-minus. A canvass of some of Blackburn's previous instructors had brought vague attestations to the adequate powers of a student imperfectly remembered, and sometimes surprise that his abilities could be questioned at all.

As he wrote the grade, Howe told himself that his cowardice sprang from an unwillingness to have more dealings with a student he disliked. He knew it was simpler than that. He knew he feared Blackburn; that was the absurd truth. And cowardice did not solve the matter after all. Blackburn, flushed with a first success, attacked at once. The minimal passing grade had not assuaged his feelings and he sat at Howe's desk and again the blue-book lay between them. Blackburn said nothing. With an enormous impudence, he was waiting for Howe to speak and explain himself.

At last Howe said sharply and rudely, 'Well?' His throat was tense and the blood was hammering in his head. His mouth was tight with anger at himself for his disturbance.

Blackburn's glance was almost baleful. 'This is impossible, sir.'

'But there it is,' Howe answered.

'Sir?' Blackburn had not caught the meaning but his tone was still haughty.

Impatiently Howe said, 'There it is, plain as day. Are you here to complain again?'

'Indeed I am, sir.' There was surprise in Blackburn's voice that Howe should ask the question.

'I shouldn't complain if I were you. You did a thoroughly bad job on your first quiz. This one is a little, only a very little, better.' This was not true. If anything, it was worse.

'That might be a matter of opinion, sir.'

'It is a matter of opinion. Of my opinion.'

'Another opinion might be different, sir.'

'You really believe that?' Howe said.

'Yes.' The omission of the 'sir' was monumental.

'Whose, for example?'

'The Dean's, for example.' Then the fleshy jaw came forward a little. 'Or a certain literary critic's, for example.'

It was colossal and almost too much for Blackburn himself to handle. The solidity of his face almost crumpled under it. But he withstood his own audacity and went on. 'And the Dean's opinion might be guided by the knowledge that the person who gave me this mark is the man whom a famous critic, the most eminent judge of literature in this country, called a drunken man. The Dean might think twice about whether such a man is fit to teach Dwight students.'

Howe said in quiet admonition, 'Blackburn, you're mad,' meaning no more than to check the boy's extravagance.

But Blackburn paid no heed. He had another shot in the locker. 'And the Dean might be guided by the information, of which I have evidence, documentary evidence,'—he slapped his breast pocket twice—'that this same person personally recommended to the college literary society, the oldest in the country, that he personally recommended a student who is crazy, who threw the meeting into an uproar—a psychiatric case. The Dean might take that into account.'

Howe was never to learn the details of that 'uproar.' He had always to content himself with the dim but passionate picture which at that moment sprang into his mind, of Tertan standing on some abstract height and madly denouncing the multitude of Quill and Scroll who howled him down.

He sat quiet a moment and looked at Blackburn. The ferocity had entirely gone from the student's face. He sat regarding his teacher almost benevolently. He had played a good card and now, scarcely at all unfriendly, he was waiting to see the effect. Howe took up the blue-book and negligently sifted through it. He read a page, closed the book, struck out the C-minus and wrote an F.

'Now you may take the paper to the Dean,' he said. 'You may tell him that after reconsidering it, I lowered the grade.'

The gasp was audible. 'Oh, sir!' Blackburn cried. 'Please!' His face was agonized. 'It means my graduation, my livelihood, my future. Don't do this to me.'

'It's done already.'

Blackburn stood up. 'I spoke rashly, sir, hastily. I had no intention, no real intention, of seeing the Dean. It rests with you—entirely, entirely. I *hope* you will restore the first mark.'

'Take the matter to the Dean or not, just as you choose. The grade is what you deserve and it stands.'

Blackburn's head dropped. 'And will I be failed at mid-term, sir?'

'Of course.'

From deep out of Blackburn's great chest rose a cry of anguish. 'Oh, sir, if you want me to go down on my knees to you, I will, I will.'

Howe looked at him in amazement.

'I will, I will. On my knees, sir. This mustn't, mustn't happen.'

He spoke so literally, meaning so very truly that his knees and exactly his knees were involved and seeming to think that he was offering something of tangible value to his teacher, that Howe, whose head had become icy clear in the nonsensical drama, thought, 'The boy is mad,' and began to speculate fantastically whether something in himself attracted or developed aberration. He could see himself standing absurdly before the Dean and saying, 'I've found another. This time it's the vice-president of the Council, the manager of the debating team and secretary of Quill and Scroll.'

One more such discovery, he thought, and he himself would be discovered! And there, suddenly, Blackburn was on his knees with a thump, his huge thighs straining his trousers, his hand outstretched in a great gesture of supplication.

With a cry, Howe shoved back his swivel chair and it rolled away on its casters half across the little room. Blackburn knelt for a moment to nothing at all, then got to his feet.

Howe rose abruptly. He said, 'Blackburn, you will stop acting like an idiot. Dust your knees off, take your paper and get out. You've behaved like a fool and a malicious person. You have half a term to do a decent job. Keep your silly mouth shut and try to do it. Now get out.'

Blackburn's head was low. He raised it and there was a pious light in his eyes. 'Will you shake hands, sir?' he said. He thrust out his hand.

'I will not,' Howe said.

Head and hand sank together. Blackburn picked up his blue-book and walked to the door. He turned and said, 'Thank you, sir.' His back, as he departed, was heavy with tragedy and stateliness.

IV

After years of bad luck with the weather, the College had a perfect day for Commencement. It was wonderfully bright, the air so transparent, the wind so brisk that no one could resist talking about it.

As Howe set out for the campus he heard Hilda calling from the back yard. She called, 'Professor, professor,' and came running to him.

Howe said, 'What's this "professor" business?'

'Mother told me,' Hilda said. 'You've been promoted. And I want to take your picture.'

'Next year,' said Howe. 'I won't be a professor until next year. And you know better than to call anybody "professor."'

'It was just in fun,' Hilda said. She seemed disappointed.

'But you can take my picture if you want. I won't look much different next year.' Still, it was frightening. It might mean that he was to stay in this town all his life.

Hilda brightened. 'Can I take it in this?' she said, and touched the gown he carried over his arm.

Howe laughed. 'Yes, you can take it in this.'

'I'll get my things and meet you in front of Otis,' Hilda said. 'I have the background all picked out.'

On the campus the Commencement crowd was already large. It stood about in eager, nervous little family groups. As he crossed, Howe was greeted by a student, capped and gowned, glad of the chance to make an event for his parents by introducing one of his teachers. It was while Howe stood there chatting that he saw Tertan.

He had never seen anyone quite so alone, as though a circle had been woven about him to separate him from the gay crowd on the campus. Not that Tertan was not gay, he was the gayest of all. Three weeks had passed since Howe had last seen him, the weeks of examination, the lazy week before Commencement, and this was now a different Tertan. On his head he wore a panama hat, broad-brimmed and fine, of the shape associated with South American planters. He wore a suit of raw silk, luxurious, but yellowed with age and much too tight, and he sported a whangee cane.[15] He walked sedately, the hat tilted at a devastating angle, the stick coming up and down in time to his measured tread. He had, Howe guessed, outfitted himself to greet the day in the clothes of that ruined father whose existence was on record in the Dean's office. Gravely and arrogantly he surveyed the scene—in it, his whole bearing seemed to say, but not of it. With his haughty step, with his flashing eye, Tertan was coming nearer. Howe did not wish to be seen. He shifted his position slightly. When he looked again, Tertan was not in sight.

[15] Walking stick made from a plant similar to bamboo.

The chapel clock struck the quarter hour. Howe detached himself from his chat and hurried to Otis Hall at the far end of the campus. Hilda had not yet come. He went up into the high portico and, using the glass of the door for a mirror, put on his gown, adjusted the hood on his shoulders and set the mortarboard on his head. When he came down the steps, Hilda had arrived.

Nothing could have told him more forcibly that a year had passed than the development of Hilda's photographic possessions from the box camera of the previous fall. By a strap about her neck was hung a leather case, so thick and strong, so carefully stitched and so molded to its contents that it could only hold a costly camera. The appearance was deceptive, Howe knew, for he had been present at the Aikens' pre-Christmas conference about its purchase. It was only a fairly good domestic camera. Still, it looked very impressive. Hilda carried another leather case from which she drew a collapsible tripod. Decisively she extended each of its gleaming legs and set it up on the path. She removed the camera from its case and fixed it to the tripod. In its compact efficiency the camera almost had a life of its own, but Hilda treated it with easy familiarity, looked into its eye, glanced casually at its gauges. Then from a pocket she took still another leather case and drew from it a small instrument through which she looked first at Howe, who began to feel inanimate and lost, and then at the sky. She made some adjustment on the instrument, then some adjustment on the camera. She swept the scene with her eye, found a spot and pointed the camera in its direction. She walked to the spot, stood on it and beckoned to Howe. With each new leather case, with each new instrument, and with each new adjustment she had grown in ease and now she said, 'Joe, will you stand here?'

Obediently Howe stood where he was bidden. She had yet another instrument. She took out a tape-measure on a mechanical spool. Kneeling down before Howe, she put the little metal ring of the tape under the tip of his shoe. At her request, Howe pressed it with his toe. When she had measured her distance, she nodded to Howe who released the tape. At a touch, it sprang back into the spool. 'You have to be careful if you're going to get what you want,' Hilda said. 'I don't believe in all this snap-snap-snapping,' she remarked loftily. Howe nodded in agreement, although he was beginning to think Hilda's care excessive.

Now at last the moment had come. Hilda squinted into the camera, moved the tripod slightly. She stood to the side, holding the plunger of the shutter-cable. 'Ready,' she said. 'Will you relax, Joseph, please?' Howe realized that he was standing frozen. Hilda stood poised and precise as a setter, one hand holding the little cable, the other extended with curled dainty fingers like a dancer's, as if expressing to her subject the precarious delicacy of the moment. She pressed the plunger and there was the click. At once she stirred to action, got behind the camera, turned a new exposure. 'Thank you,' she said. 'Would you stand under that tree and let me do a character study with light and shade?'

The childish absurdity of the remark restored Howe's ease. He went to the little tree. The pattern the leaves made on his gown was what Hilda was after. He had just taken a satisfactory position when he heard in the unmistakable voice, 'Ah, Doctor! Having your picture taken?'

Howe gave up the pose and turned to Blackburn who stood on the walk, his hands behind his back, a little too large for his bachelor's gown. Annoyed that Blackburn should see him posing for a character study in light and shade, Howe said irritably, 'Yes, having my picture taken.'

Blackburn beamed at Hilda. 'And the little photographer?' he said. Hilda fixed her eyes on the ground and stood closer to her brilliant and aggressive camera. Blackburn, teetering on his heels, his hands behind his back, wholly prelatical and benignly patient, was not abashed at the silence. At last Howe said, 'If you'll excuse us, Mr. Blackburn, we'll go on with the picture.'

'Go right ahead, sir. I'm running along.' But he only came closer. 'Doctor Howe,' he said fervently, 'I want to tell you how glad I am that I was able to satisfy your standards at last.'

Howe was surprised at the hard, insulting brightness of his own voice, and even Hilda looked up curiously as he said, 'Nothing you have ever done has satisfied me, and nothing you could ever do would satisfy me, Blackburn.'

With a glance at Hilda, Blackburn made a gesture as if to hush Howe—as though all his former bold malice had taken for granted a kind of understanding between himself and his teacher, a secret which must not be betrayed to a third person. 'I only meant, sir,' he said, 'that I was able to pass your course after all.'

Howe said, 'You didn't pass my course. I passed you out of my course. I passed you without even reading your paper. I wanted to be sure the college would be rid of you. And when all the grades were in and I did read your paper, I saw I was right not to have read it first.'

Blackburn presented a stricken face. 'It was very bad, sir?'

But Howe had turned away. The paper had been fantastic. The paper had been, if he wished to see it so, mad. It was at this moment that the Dean came up behind Howe and caught his arm. 'Hello, Joseph,' he said. 'We'd better be getting along, it's almost late.'

He was not a familiar man, but when he saw Blackburn, who approached to greet him, he took Blackburn's arm, too. 'Hello, Theodore,' he said. Leaning forward on Howe's arm and on Blackburn's, he said, 'Hello, Hilda dear.' Hilda replied quietly, 'Hello, Uncle George.'

Still clinging to their arms, still linking Howe and Blackburn, the Dean said, 'Another year gone, Joe, and we've turned out another crop. After you've been here a few years, you'll find it reasonably upsetting—you wonder how there can be so many graduating classes while you stay the same. But of course, you don't stay the same.' Then he said, 'Well,' sharply, to dismiss the thought. He pulled Blackburn's arm and swung him around to Howe. 'Have you heard about Teddy Blackburn?' he asked. 'He has a job already, before graduation—the first man of his class to be placed.' Expectant of congratulations, Blackburn beamed at Howe. Howe remained silent.

'Isn't that good?' the Dean said. Still Howe did not answer and the Dean, puzzled and put out, turned to Hilda. 'That's a very fine-looking camera, Hilda.' She touched it with affectionate pride.

'Instruments of precision,' said a voice. 'Instruments of precision.' Of the three with joined arms, Howe was the nearest to Tertan, whose gaze took in all the scene except the smile and the nod which Howe gave him. The boy leaned on his cane. The broad-brimmed hat, canting jauntily over his eye, confused the image of his face that Howe had established, suppressed the rigid lines of the ascetic and brought out the baroque curves. It made an effect of perverse majesty.

'Instruments of precision,' said Tertan for the last time, addressing no one, making a casual comment to the universe. And it occurred to Howe that Tertan might not be referring to Hilda's equipment. The sense of the thrice-woven circle of the boy's loneliness smote him fiercely. Tertan stood in majestic jauntiness, superior to all the scene, but his isolation made Howe ache with a pity of which Tertan was more the cause than the object, so general and indiscriminate was it.

Whether in his sorrow he made some unintended movement toward Tertan which the Dean checked, or whether the suddenly tightened grip on his arm was the Dean's own sorrow and fear, he did not know. Tertan watched them in the incurious way people watch a photograph being taken, and suddenly the thought that, to the boy, it must seem that the three were posing for a picture together made Howe detach himself almost rudely from the Dean's grasp.

'I promised Hilda another picture,' he announced—needlessly, for Tertan was no longer there, he had vanished in the last sudden flux of visitors who, now that the band had struck up, were rushing nervously to find seats.

'You'd better hurry,' the Dean said. 'I'll go along, it's getting late for me.' He departed and Blackburn walked stately by his side.

Howe again took his position under the little tree which cast its shadow over his face and gown. 'Just hurry, Hilda, won't you?' he said. Hilda held the cable at arm's length, her other arm crooked and her fingers crisped. She rose on her toes and said 'Ready,' and pressed the release. 'Thank you,' she said gravely and began to dismantle her camera as he hurried off to join the procession.

COMMENTARY

It is not unheard of for an editor to include an example of his own work in an anthology he is making, but it is sufficiently unusual to call for a word of explanation. My thrusting upon the reader a story of my own will perhaps seem less immodest if I say that the idea of doing so originated not with me but with my publisher and that the argument he advanced for its propriety seemed to me to be cogent—he said that something was to be gained for the understanding of literature by a writer's setting down his thoughts about his own work, especially if he gave an account of the process by which a particular work had come into being.

One possibly instructive thing that such an account can do is to suggest the relation that exists between the actual facts of a writer's experience and the process of his imagination, particularly in the creation of character. Not all writers of fiction are concerned to create characters that seem to be "true to life." (In the present volume, for example, Hawthorne and Kafka have no such concern.) But whenever the nature of the story does call for versimilitude of character, it can usually be assumed—at least in modern literature—that the author's creation began with reference to an actual person.

An awareness of the relation between an actual person and a created character can have no part in our assessment of a work of fiction. Yet it is interesting in itself and it is useful in helping us understand the interplay between actuality and imagination. In the case of this story, I am conscious of how much I have relied on actuality in my representation of the two students. They were both in classes of mine in my early years of teaching at Columbia College, and I recall them as being very much as they appear in the story— so much so that if I were now to say what part my imagination played in the creation of the characters which derive from them, I should incline to claim for it nothing more than its having brought them together in the same story, for in actuality they had no connection with each other. But does this not do an injustice to my imagination, for surely it was at work in my acquaintance with the two actual students, in my observation of the details of their behavior, in the emotions and opinions I had about them?

The story had its origin, as may easily be supposed, in my feelings about the student who is represented under the name of Tertan. (I do not remember how I got this name for him, nor do I know if it is actually an Hungarian name or one that I made up, thinking it would pass for Hungarian. I have always pronounced it with the accent on the last syllable: Ter*tan*.) The moment at which the impulse came to me to write a story about him is not easily forgotten. Some time in the winter after he had been a member of one of my composition classes, I stood next to that unfortunate boy at the loan desk of the College Library; we were both waiting to charge out some books. I greeted him and he responded with a blank and haughty stare. I did not know whether I was being deliberately snubbed or whether his not recognizing me was the sign of some confusion of his mental processes. It seemed to me that both alternatives were possible. For some time I had known that he was suffering from a deep disturbance of the mind. How very deep it was and how much worse it had become since I had last seen him was made plain by his air of majestic self-reference. But also he had good reason to refuse to recognize me, for, by the end of the course he had taken with me, I had refused to recognize him—I had, that is, not consented to know him as he believed he deserved to be known, as he demanded to be known. Like his teacher in the story, I had at first been struck by his intellectual powers. But then, with the passage of time, it had become clear to me that no effort of instruction could possibly overcome the extravagant incoherence of his expression, both in speech and in writing, which I eventually had to understand as a symptom of an extreme mental pathology. He had discovered that I wrote for certain magazines he admired and this had led him to entertain an exaggerated respect for me. Very likely this flattered me into giving him a good deal of attention, which inevitably I diminished when I realized that he was beyond the help of teaching. He did not give me the affection that Tertan in the story gives Dr. Howe, and the respect he did show me was of a most abstract, impersonal kind, yet I had felt a bond with him. When I gave up my special efforts to improve his writing and when at last I communicated to the Dean of the College my opinion of his deranged condition, I felt, against all reason, that I had committed a great disloyalty.

Yet as I saw him standing at the loan desk I could not doubt that he was on the verge of actual insanity, that he was on the way to being beyond the reach of ordinary human feelings. The conflict between my knowledge of this fact and my unreasoning remorse at my "disloyalty" made an emotion which demanded a story. The story, as I at once conceived it, would present the sad irony of a passionate devotion to the intellectual life maintained by a person of deranged mind.

This was what the story was to present, but what was the story to *be*? I remember deciding that some other element was needed in addition to the student's plight and his teacher's emotions. To limit myself to these two elements would make a story that was merely static and linear—and merely pathetic. I did not want a pathetic story for Tertan. I thought he deserved something sterner than that. From the first, I conceived him to be an impressive figure, in some sense heroic, and he therefore made the demand on me that I come as close as I could to tragedy. For this a sense of emotional and physical space was needed, and the possibility of action and decision. I had no idea at all of how to go about getting what I wanted. Then, quite without my bidding, the image of the student who was the original of Blackburn popped up before me.

He had been in a class of mine two or three years earlier, and, as I say, his traits were quite precisely those that I have attributed to Blackburn. He had the same pompous busyness, the same impulse to manipulate his teachers, the same flaunting stupidity, the same sly malevolence together with the same readiness to collapse if strongly resisted or counterattacked. We got on very badly. He once really did threaten to use against me the influence he claimed to have with the Dean. The conference over his bad examination is more or less literally remembered, and in the course of that meeting he did, in a moment of intense supplication, offer to go down on his knees to me, although he did not actually do so. The thought occurred to me that this conduct was "insane," but the word presented itself more as a way of speaking than as a serious idea.

His sudden appearance in my mind to stand beside Tertan delighted me. It immediately helped me in several ways. Blackburn's malevolence rescued the teacher from being merely a sensitive, sympathetic, observing consciousness. By putting Howe in some danger, it made him that much more of a person; it made him someone with a fate and required that he should not only feel but act. And of course it gave added stature to Tertan by suggesting that, if Blackburn were to try to harm his teacher, Tertan must help or at least comfort him. Upon Howe I bestowed the insecurities I had felt as a new instructor, but I sought to give them greater point and justification by making Howe a poet, and a "difficult" and "controversial" poet at that. For the same reason I set the scene in a country college where the smallness and tightness of the community would make a newcomer more conscious of the judgments that were being passed on him.

But if the appearance of Blackburn delighted me, it also filled me with apprehension. There was, I thought, something beautifully appropriate in the juxtaposition of the two students—something all too appropriate! For it occurred to me that the juxtaposition might seem to express an idea which could be very easily formulated: that there are kinds of insanity that society does not accept and kinds of insanity that society does accept. This was an idea to which I could readily assent, and the story does of course lend support to its truth. But it was not what I wanted my story primarily to express. Not only would my feelings and the intention that arose from them be belied, but I felt that it would be an aesthetic misfortune if readers were able to make the formulation thus easily, for a story that can be "summed up" in such a way must prove lacking in power. If the reader can so readily make the point of a story explicit, he comes too quickly to terms with it and is able to put it out of his mind as a thing settled and done with.

But then it occurred to me that if my readers did understand the juxtaposition of the two students in this way, it would prove a great advantage. For the story would seem to them to say one thing when actually it was saying another.

I thought it likely that my readers would wish to reverse the judgment that society makes, that they would say that Blackburn's insanity (if that is what it is) should not be accepted by society, and that Tertan's insanity should be accepted. And it seemed to me that they might go one step further and conclude that Tertan, although apparently insane, was not really so. All the authority of certain moral ideas, quite generous ones, would urge them to this conclusion. For was not Tertan terribly alone, and in a socially disadvantaged position, and benevolent, and dedicated, and was he not by way of being a genius, and are not geniuses often said to be mad, although mistakenly?

I seem to have been right in my expectation. When the story was published, many readers wrote to me—and some telephoned—to say that they had been moved by it but disappointed because I had not made it sufficiently clear that Tertan was not really insane.

The truth is, I think, that they knew he was insane and did not want him to be. If the story has any power at all, it surely lies in its ability to generate resistance to the certitude that Tertan is deranged. The impulse to resist the undeniable fact comes, I suppose, from the common apprehension, conscious or unconscious, that the fabric of our reason is very delicate and always in danger. This impulse is reinforced by our modern anxiety at confronting a painful fate which cannot be accounted for in moral terms and which cannot be said to result from some fault of society.

And if I may speak further of the source of what power the story may have, I ought to mention the challenge it offers the reader to reconcile two dissimilar modes of judgment with each other. One is the judgment of morality, the other of science. Judged by morality, Tertan's behavior is sane and good, Blackburn's mad and bad. But no psychiatrist would adjudge Blackburn insane, and no psychiatrist would fail to say that Tertan must soon go to a mental hospital.

It perhaps does not need to be remarked that the story encourages the reader to take an adverse view of the judgment of science. In the classroom discussion of Ibsen's *Ghosts*, DeWitt's expressed belief that science can solve all moral problems is arrogant and shallow, forgivable only because DeWitt is so young. When I began the story with the little scene of Hilda and her camera, I did not have in mind the concluding scene in which Hilda prepares to take a picture with such scientific accuracy; but having begun the story with Hilda taking the picture, the use I might make of her and her camera was suggested to me by the little conversation about photographic distortion in the Dean's office: it gave me the opportunity to allow Tertan to resist the judgment that had been passed on him, to murmur his scornful phrase, "Instruments of precision." And in other details the story seems to take the traditional hostile attitude of literary humanism toward science. But this must not be accepted at its face value. Nothing, I fear, can reverse the diagnosis of Tertan's illness.

Perhaps I should mention that in writing the description of Tertan on Commencement Day, I had consciously in mind Coleridge's description of the daemonic poet at the end of "Kubla Khan" (page 871) and stole a few phrases from it.

THE
GUEST

ALBERT CAMUS

1913–1960

THE SCHOOLMASTER WAS WATCHING the two men climb toward him. One was on horseback, the other on foot. They had not yet tackled the abrupt rise leading to the schoolhouse built on the hillside. They were toiling onward, making slow progress in the snow, among the stones, on the vast expanse of the high, deserted plateau. From time to time the horse stumbled. Without hearing anything yet, he could see the breath issuing from the horse's nostrils. One of the men, at least, knew the region. They were following the trail although it had disappeared days ago under a layer of dirty white snow. The schoolmaster calculated that it would take them half an hour to get onto the hill. It was cold; he went back into the school to get a sweater.

He crossed the empty, frigid classroom. On the blackboard the four rivers of France,[1] drawn with four different colored chalks, had been flowing toward their estuaries for the past three days. Snow had suddenly fallen in mid-October after eight months of drought without the transition of rain, and the twenty pupils, more or less, who lived in the villages scattered over the plateau had stopped coming. With fair weather they would return. Daru now heated only the single room that was his lodging, adjoining the classroom and giving

[1] That is, the four *major* rivers: the Seine, the Loire, the Rhone, and the Marne. The story takes place in North Africa, when it was under French control.

785

also onto the plateau to the east. Like the class windows, his window looked to the south too. On that side the school was a few kilometers from the point where the plateau began to slope toward the south. In clear weather could be seen the purple mass of the mountain range where the gap opened onto the desert.

Somewhat warmed, Daru returned to the window from which he had first seen the two men. They were no longer visible. Hence they must have tackled the rise. The sky was not so dark, for the snow had stopped falling during the night. The morning had opened with a dirty light which had scarcely become brighter as the ceiling of clouds lifted. At two in the afternoon it seemed as if the day were merely beginning. But still this was better than those three days when thick snow was falling amidst unbroken darkness with little gusts of wind that rattled the double door of the classroom. Then Daru had spent long hours in his room, leaving it only to go to the shed and feed the chickens or get some coal. Fortunately the delivery truck from Tadjid, the nearest village to the north, had brought his supplies two days before the blizzard. It would return in forty-eight hours.

Besides, he had enough to resist a siege, for the little room was cluttered with bags of wheat that the administration left as a stock to distribute to those of his pupils whose families had suffered from the drought. Actually they had all been victims because they were all poor. Every day Daru would distribute a ration to the children. They had missed it, he knew, during these bad days. Possibly one of the fathers or big brothers would come this afternoon and he could supply them with grain. It was just a matter of carrying them over to the next harvest. Now shiploads of wheat were arriving from France and the worst was over. But it would be hard to forget that poverty, that army of ragged ghosts wandering in the sunlight, the plateaus burned to a cinder month after month, the earth shriveled up little by little, literally scorched, every stone bursting into dust under one's foot. The sheep had died then by thousands and even a few men, here and there, sometimes without anyone's knowing.

In contrast with such poverty, he who lived almost like a monk in his remote schoolhouse, nonetheless satisfied with the little he had and with the rough life, had felt like a lord with his whitewashed walls, his narrow couch, his unpainted shelves, his well, and his weekly provision of water and food. And suddenly this snow, without warning, without the foretaste of rain. This is the way the region was, cruel to live in, even without men—who didn't help matters either. But Daru had been born here. Everywhere else, he felt exiled.

He stepped out onto the terrace in front of the schoolhouse. The two men were now halfway up the slope. He recognized the horseman as Balducci, the old gendarme he had known for a long time. Balducci was holding on the end of a rope an Arab who was walking behind him with hands bound and head lowered. The gendarme waved a greeting to which Daru did not reply, lost as he was in contemplation of the Arab dressed in a faded blue jellaba,[2] his feet in sandals but covered with socks of heavy raw wool, his head surmounted by a narrow, short *chèche*.[3] They were approaching. Balducci was holding back his horse in order not to hurt the Arab, and the group was advancing slowly.

Within earshot, Balducci shouted: "One hour to do the three kilometers from El Ameur!" Daru did not answer. Short and square in his thick sweater,

[2] A hooded cloak worn by Arab men, especially in Morocco.
[3] A scarf worn by French troops in North Africa.

he watched them climb. Not once had the Arab raised his head. "Hello," said Daru when they got up onto the terrace. "Come in and warm up." Balducci painfully got down from his horse without letting go the rope. From under his bristling mustache he smiled at the schoolmaster. His little dark eyes, deep-set under a tanned forehead, and his mouth surrounded with wrinkles made him look attentive and studious. Daru took the bridle, led the horse to the shed, and came back to the two men, who were now waiting for him in the school. He led them into his room. "I am going to heat up the classroom," he said. "We'll be more comfortable there." When he entered the room again, Balducci was on the couch. He had undone the rope tying him to the Arab, who had squatted near the stove. His hands still bound, the *chèche* pushed back on his head, he was looking toward the window. At first Daru noticed only his huge lips, fat, smooth, almost Negroid; yet his nose was straight, his eyes were dark and full of fever. The *chèche* revealed an obstinate forehead and, under the weathered skin now rather discolored by the cold, the whole face had a restless and re-bellious look that struck Daru when the Arab, turning his face toward him, looked him straight in the eyes. "Go into the other room," said the school-master, "and I'll make you some mint tea." "Thanks," Balducci said. "What a chore! How I long for retirement." And addressing his prisoner in Arabic: "Come on, you." The Arab got up and, slowly, holding his bound wrists in front of him, went into the classroom.

With the tea, Daru brought a chair. But Balducci was already enthroned on the nearest pupil's desk and the Arab had squatted against the teacher's platform facing the stove, which stood between the desk and the window. When he held out the glass of tea to the prisoner, Daru hesitated at the sight of his bound hands. "He might perhaps be untied." "Sure," said Balducci. "That was for the trip." He started to get to his feet. But Daru, setting the glass on the floor, had knelt beside the Arab. Without saying anything, the Arab watched him with his feverish eyes. Once his hands were free, he rubbed his swollen wrists against each other, took the glass of tea, and sucked up the burning liquid in swift little sips.

"Good," said Daru. "And where are you headed?"

Balducci withdrew his mustache from the tea. "Here, son."

"Odd pupils! And you're spending the night?"

"No. I'm going back to El Ameur. And you will deliver this fellow to Tinguit. He is expected at police headquarters."

Balducci was looking at Daru with a friendly little smile.

"What's this story?" asked the schoolmaster. "Are you pulling my leg?"

"No, son. Those are the orders."

"The orders? I'm not . . ." Daru hesitated, not wanting to hurt the old Corsican. "I mean, that's not my job."

"What! What's the meaning of that? In wartime people do all kinds of jobs."

"Then I'll wait for the declaration of war!"

Balducci nodded.

"O.K. But the orders exist and they concern you too. Things are brewing, it appears. There is talk of a forthcoming revolt.[4] We are mobilized, in a way."

[4] Of the Arabs against the French.

Daru still had his obstinate look.

"Listen, son," Balducci said. "I like you and you must understand. There's only a dozen of us at El Ameur to patrol throughout the whole territory of a small department and I must get back in a hurry. I was told to hand this guy over to you and return without delay. He couldn't be kept there. His village was beginning to stir; they wanted to take him back. You must take him to Tinguit tomorrow before the day is over. Twenty kilometers shouldn't faze a husky fellow like you. After that, all will be over. You'll come back to your pupils and your comfortable life."

Behind the wall the horse could be heard snorting and pawing the earth. Daru was looking out the window. Decidedly, the weather was clearing and the light was increasing over the snowy plateau. When all the snow was melted, the sun would take over again and once more would burn the fields of stone. For days, still, the unchanging sky would shed its dry light on the solitary expanse where nothing had any connection with man.

"After all," he said, turning around toward Balducci, "what did he do?" And, before the gendarme had opened his mouth, he asked: "Does he speak French?"

"No, not a word. We had been looking for him for a month, but they were hiding him. He killed his cousin."

"Is he against us?"

"I don't think so. But you can never be sure."

"Why did he kill?"

"A family squabble, I think. One owed the other grain, it seems. It's not at all clear. In short, he killed his cousin with a billhook. You know, like a sheep, *kreezk!*"

Balducci made the gesture of drawing a blade across his throat and the Arab, his attention attracted, watched him with a sort of anxiety. Daru felt a sudden wrath against the man, against all men with their rotten spite, their tireless hates, their blood lust.

But the kettle was singing on the stove. He served Balducci more tea, hesitated, then served the Arab again, who, a second time, drank avidly. His raised arms made the jellaba fall open and the schoolmaster saw his thin, muscular chest.

"Thanks, kid," Balducci said. "And now, I'm off."

He got up and went toward the Arab, taking a small rope from his pocket.

"What are you doing?" Daru asked dryly.

Balducci, disconcerted, showed him the rope.

"Don't bother."

The old gendarme hesitated. "It's up to you. Of course, you are armed?"

"I have my shotgun."

"Where?"

"In the trunk."

"You ought to have it near your bed."

"Why? I have nothing to fear."

"You're crazy, son. If there's an uprising, no one is safe, we're all in the same boat."

"I'll defend myself. I'll have time to see them coming."

Balducci began to laugh, then suddenly the mustache covered the white teeth.

"You'll have time? O.K. That's just what I was saying. You have always been a little cracked. That's why I like you, my son was like that."

At the same time he took out his revolver and put it on the desk.

"Keep it; I don't need two weapons from here to El Ameur."

The revolver shone against the black paint of the table. When the gendarme turned toward him, the schoolmaster caught the smell of leather and horseflesh.

"Listen, Balducci," Daru said suddenly, "every bit of this disgusts me, and first of all your fellow here. But I won't hand him over. Fight, yes, if I have to. But not that."

The old gendarme stood in front of him and looked at him severely.

"You're being a fool," he said slowly. "I don't like it either. You don't get used to putting a rope on a man even after years of it, and you're even ashamed —yes, ashamed. But you can't let them have their way."

"I won't hand him over," Daru said again.

"It's an order, son, and I repeat it."

"That's right. Repeat to them what I've said to you: I won't hand him over."

Balducci made a visible effort to reflect. He looked at the Arab and at Daru. At last he decided.

"No, I won't tell them anything. If you want to drop us, go ahead; I'll not denounce you. I have an order to deliver the prisoner and I'm doing so. And now you'll just sign this paper for me."

"There's no need. I'll not deny that you left him with me."

"Don't be mean with me. I know you'll tell the truth. You're from hereabouts and you are a man. But you must sign, that's the rule."

Daru opened his drawer, took out a little square bottle of purple ink, the red wooden penholder with the "sergeant-major" pen[5] he used for making models of penmanship, and signed. The gendarme carefully folded the paper and put it into his wallet. Then he moved toward the door.

"I'll see you off," Daru said.

"No," said Balducci. "There's no use being polite. You insulted me."

He looked at the Arab, motionless in the same spot, sniffed peevishly, and turned away toward the door. "Good-by, son," he said. The door shut behind him. Balducci appeared suddenly outside the window and then disappeared. His footsteps were muffled by the snow. The horse stirred on the other side of the wall and several chickens fluttered in fright. A moment later Balducci reappeared outside the window leading the horse by the bridle. He walked toward the little rise without turning around and disappeared from sight with the horse following him. A big stone could be heard bouncing down. Daru walked back toward the prisoner, who, without stirring, never took his eyes off him. "Wait," the schoolmaster said in Arabic and went toward the bedroom. As he was going through the door, he had a second thought, went to the desk, took the revolver, and stuck it in his pocket. Then, without looking back, he went into his room.

[5] Probably a broad-edged pen.

For some time he lay on his couch watching the sky gradually close over, listening to the silence. It was this silence that had seemed painful to him during the first days here, after the war. He had requested a post in the little town at the base of the foothills separating the upper plateaus from the desert. There, rocky walls, green and black to the north, pink and lavender to the south, marked the frontier of eternal summer. He had been named to a post farther north, on the plateau itself. In the beginning, the solitude and the silence had been hard for him on these wastelands peopled only by stones. Occasionally, furrows suggested cultivation, but they had been dug to uncover a certain kind of stone good for building. The only plowing here was to harvest rocks. Elsewhere a thin layer of soil accumulated in the hollows would be scraped out to enrich paltry village gardens. This is the way it was: bare rock covered three quarters of the region. Towns sprang up, flourished, then disappeared; men came by, loved one another or fought bitterly, then died. No one in this desert, neither he nor his guest, mattered. And yet, outside this desert neither of them, Daru knew, could have really lived.

When he got up, no noise came from the classroom. He was amazed at the unmixed joy he derived from the mere thought that the Arab might have fled and that he would be alone with no decision to make. But the prisoner was there. He had merely stretched out between the stove and the desk. With eyes open, he was staring at the ceiling. In that position, his thick lips were particularly noticeable, giving him a pouting look. "Come," said Daru. The Arab got up and followed him. In the bedroom, the schoolmaster pointed to a chair near the table under the window. The Arab sat down without taking his eyes off Daru.

"Are you hungry?"

"Yes," the prisoner said.

Daru set the table for two. He took flour and oil, shaped a cake in a frying-pan, and lighted the little stove that functioned on bottled gas. While the cake was cooking, he went out to the shed to get cheese, eggs, dates, and condensed milk. When the cake was done he set it on the window sill to cool, heated some condensed milk diluted with water, and beat up the eggs into an omelette. In one of his motions he knocked against the revolver stuck in his right pocket. He set the bowl down, went into the classroom, and put the revolver in his desk drawer. When he came back to the room, night was falling. He put on the light and served the Arab. "Eat," he said. The Arab took a piece of the cake, lifted it eagerly to his mouth, and stopped short.

"And you?" he asked.

"After you. I'll eat too."

The thick lips opened slightly. The Arab hesitated, then bit into the cake determinedly.

The meal over, the Arab looked at the schoolmaster. "Are you the judge?"

"No, I'm simply keeping you until tomorrow."

"Why do you eat with me?"

"I'm hungry."

The Arab fell silent. Daru got up and went out. He brought back a folding bed from the shed, set it up between the table and the stove, perpendicular to his own bed. From a large suitcase which, upright in a corner, served as a shelf for papers, he took two blankets and arranged them on the camp bed. Then he stopped, felt useless, and sat down on his bed. There was nothing more to do or to get ready. He had to look at this man. He looked at him, therefore, trying to imagine his face bursting with rage. He couldn't do so. He could see nothing but the dark yet shining eyes and the animal mouth.

"Why did you kill him?" he asked in a voice whose hostile tone surprised him.

The Arab looked away.

"He ran away. I ran after him."

He raised his eyes to Daru again and they were full of a sort of woeful interrogation. "Now what will they do to me?"

"Are you afraid?"

He stiffened, turning his eyes away.

"Are you sorry?"

The Arab stared at him openmouthed. Obviously he did not understand. Daru's annoyance was growing. At the same time he felt awkward and self-conscious with his big body wedged between the two beds.

"Lie down there," he said impatiently. "That's your bed."

The Arab didn't move. He called to Daru:

"Tell me!"

The schoolmaster looked at him.

"Is the gendarme coming back tomorrow?"

"I don't know."

"Are you coming with us?"

"I don't know. Why?"

The prisoner got up and stretched out on top of the blankets, his feet toward the window. The light from the electric bulb shone straight into his eyes and he closed them at once.

"Why?" Daru repeated, standing beside the bed.

The Arab opened his eyes under the blinding light and looked at him, trying not to blink.

"Come with us," he said.

In the middle of the night, Daru was still not asleep. He had gone to bed after undressing completely; he generally slept naked. But when he suddenly realized that he had nothing on, he hesitated. He felt vulnerable and the temptation came to him to put his clothes back on. Then he shrugged his shoulders; after all, he wasn't a child and, if need be, he could break his adversary in two. From his bed he could observe him, lying on his back, still motionless with his eyes closed under the harsh light. When Daru turned out the light, the darkness seemed to coagulate all of a sudden. Little by little, the night came back to life in the window where the starless sky was stirring gently. The schoolmaster soon made out the body lying at his feet. The Arab still did not move, but his eyes seemed open. A faint wind was prowling around the schoolhouse. Perhaps it would drive away the clouds and the sun would reappear.

During the night the wind increased. The hens fluttered a little and then were silent. The Arab turned over on his side with his back to Daru, who thought he heard him moan. Then he listened for his guest's breathing, become heavier and more regular. He listened to that breath so close to him and mused without being able to go to sleep. In this room where he had been sleeping alone for a year, this presence bothered him. But it bothered him also by imposing on him a sort of brotherhood he knew well but refused to accept in the present circumstances. Men who share the same rooms, soldiers or prisoners, develop a strange alliance as if, having cast off their armor with their clothing, they fraternized every evening, over and above their differences, in the ancient community of dream and fatigue. But Daru shook himself; he didn't like such musings, and it was essential to sleep.

A little later, however, when the Arab stirred slightly, the schoolmaster was still not asleep. When the prisoner made a second move, he stiffened, on the alert. The Arab was lifting himself slowly on his arms with almost the motion of a sleepwalker. Seated upright in bed, he waited motionless without turning his head toward Daru, as if he were listening attentively. Daru did not stir; it had just occurred to him that the revolver was still in the drawer of his desk. It was better to act at once. Yet he continued to observe the prisoner, who, with the same slithery motion, put his feet on the ground, waited again, then began to stand up slowly. Daru was about to call out to him when the Arab began to walk, in a quite natural but extraordinarily silent way. He was heading toward the door at the end of the room that opened into the shed. He lifted the latch with precaution and went out, pushing the door behind him but without shutting it. Daru had not stirred. "He is running away," he merely thought. "Good riddance!" Yet he listened attentively. The hens were not fluttering; the guest must be on the plateau. A faint sound of water reached him, and he didn't know what it was until the Arab again stood framed in the doorway, closed the door carefully, and came back to bed without a sound. Then Daru turned his back on him and fell asleep. Still later he seemed, from the depths of his sleep, to hear furtive steps around the schoolhouse. "I'm dreaming! I'm dreaming!" he repeated to himself. And he went on sleeping.

When he awoke, the sky was clear; the loose window let in a cold, pure air. The Arab was asleep, hunched up under the blankets now, his mouth open, utterly relaxed. But when Daru shook him, he started dreadfully, staring at Daru with wild eyes as if he had never seen him and such a frightened expression that the schoolmaster stepped back. "Don't be afraid. It's me. You must eat." The Arab nodded his head and said yes. Calm had returned to his face, but his expression was vacant and listless.

The coffee was ready. They drank it seated together on the folding bed as they munched their pieces of the cake. Then Daru led the Arab under the shed and showed him the faucet where he washed. He went back into the room, folded the blankets and the bed, made his own bed and put the room in order. Then he went through the classroom and out onto the terrace. The sun was already rising in the blue sky; a soft, bright light was bathing the deserted plateau. On the ridge the snow was melting in spots. The stones were about to reappear. Crouched on the edge of the plateau, the schoolmaster looked at the deserted expanse. He thought of Balducci. He had hurt him, for he had sent him off in a way as if he didn't want to be associated with him. He could still hear the gendarme's farewell and, without knowing why, he felt strangely empty and vulnerable. At that moment, from the other side of the schoolhouse, the prisoner coughed. Daru listened to him almost despite himself and then, furious, threw a pebble that whistled through the air before sinking into the snow. That man's stupid crime revolted him, but to hand him over was contrary to honor. Merely thinking of it made him smart with humiliation. And he cursed at one and the same time his own people who had sent him this Arab and the Arab too who had dared to kill and not managed to get away. Daru got up, walked in a circle on the terrace, waited motionless, and then went back into the schoolhouse.

The Arab, leaning over the cement floor of the shed, was washing his teeth with two fingers. Daru looked at him and said: "Come." He went back into the room ahead of the prisoner. He slipped a hunting-jacket on over his sweater and put on walking-shoes. Standing, he waited until the Arab had put on his *chèche* and sandals. They went into the classroom and the schoolmaster pointed to the exit, saying: "Go ahead." The fellow didn't budge. "I'm coming," said Daru. The Arab went out. Daru went back into the room and made a package of pieces of rusk, dates, and sugar. In the classroom, before going out, he hesitated a second in front of his desk, then crossed the threshold and locked the door. "That's the way," he said. He started toward the east, followed by the prisoner. But, a short distance from the schoolhouse, he thought he heard a slight sound behind them. He retraced his steps and examined the surroundings of the house; there was no one there. The Arab watched him without seeming to understand. "Come on," said Daru.

They walked for an hour and rested beside a sharp peak of limestone. The snow was melting faster and faster and the sun was drinking up the puddles at once, rapidly cleaning the plateau, which gradually dried and vibrated like the air itself. When they resumed walking, the ground rang under their feet. From time to time a bird rent the space in front of them with a joyful cry. Daru breathed in deeply the fresh morning light. He felt a sort of rapture before the vast familiar expanse, now almost entirely yellow under its dome of blue sky. They walked an hour more, descending toward the south. They reached a level height made up of crumbly rocks. From there on, the plateau sloped down, eastward, toward a low plain where there were a few spindly trees and, to the south, toward outcroppings of rock that gave the landscape a chaotic look.

Daru surveyed the two directions. There was nothing but the sky on the horizon. Not a man could be seen. He turned toward the Arab, who was looking at him blankly. Daru held out the package to him. "Take it," he said. "There are dates, bread, and sugar. You can hold out for two days. Here are a thousand francs too." The Arab took the package and the money but kept his full hands at chest level as if he didn't know what to do with what was being given him. "Now look," the schoolmaster said as he pointed in the direction of the east, "there's the way to Tinguit. You have a two-hour walk. At Tinguit you'll find the administration and the police. They are expecting you." The Arab looked toward the east, still holding the package and the money against his chest. Daru took his elbow and turned him rather roughly toward the south. At the foot of the height on which they stood could be seen a faint path. "That's the trail across the plateau. In a day's walk from here you'll find pasturelands and the first nomads. They'll take you in and shelter you according to their law." The Arab had now turned toward Daru and a sort of panic was visible in his expression. "Listen," he said. Daru shook his head: "No, be quiet. Now I'm leaving you." He turned his back on him, took two long steps in the direction of the school, looked hesitantly at the motionless Arab, and started off again. For a few minutes he heard nothing but his own step resounding on the cold ground and did not turn his head. A moment later, however, he turned around. The Arab was still there on the edge of the hill, his arms hanging now, and he was looking at the schoolmaster. Daru felt something rise in his throat. But he swore with impatience, waved vaguely, and started off again. He had already gone some distance when he again stopped and looked. There was no longer anyone on the hill.

Daru hesitated. The sun was now rather high in the sky and was beginning to beat down on his head. The schoolmaster retraced his steps, at first somewhat uncertainly, then with decision. When he reached the little hill, he was bathed in sweat. He climbed it as fast as he could and stopped, out of breath, at the top. The rock-fields to the south stood out sharply against the blue sky, but on the plain to the east a steamy heat was already rising. And in that slight haze, Daru, with heavy heart, made out the Arab walking slowly on the road to prison.

A little later, standing before the window of the classroom, the schoolmaster was watching the clear light bathing the whole surface of the plateau, but he hardly saw it. Behind him on the blackboard, among the winding French rivers, sprawled the clumsily chalked-up words he had just read: "You handed over our brother. You will pay for this." Daru looked at the sky, the plateau, and, beyond, the invisible lands stretching all the way to the sea. In this vast landscape he had loved so much, he was alone.

COMMENTARY

A comparison of the English version of this story with its French original makes it plain that the translator has done his work with accuracy and sensitivity. He has, however, failed in an important detail—he has not translated the title of the story in a way that conveys the whole of the meaning it has in French. For this he can scarcely be blamed since there is no English word that can render the curious ambiguity of *L'Hôte*, which does indeed mean "the guest" but which also means "the host."[1]

That the one word stands for both the giver and the receiver of hospitality does not usually create uncertainty about the sense in which it is being used. If there is any possibility of confusion, the French speaker or writer will employ another word for "guest," *l'invité*, although generally the context indicates plainly enough which of the two meanings of *hôte* is intended. But as the French reader encounters the word standing alone as the title of Camus' story, he has no way of telling which of its two significations he is supposed to accept. And even when he has finished the story he will not be entirely sure whether its title refers to the host, the French schoolteacher, or to the guest, the Arab peasant who is put into the schoolteacher's custody.

The author intended this ambiguity and was sorry that the necessities of translation abolished it.[2] His regret is not hard to understand, for the single

[1] The double meaning of the French word is not so odd as it first appears. The English words *guest* and *host* both derive ultimately from an Indo-Iranian root, *ghosti-*, and at one time *host*, like its French cognate, had the two meanings.

[2] Camus expressed himself to this effect in a letter to his translator, Professor Justin O'Brien.

word in its doubleness of meaning proposes the whole import of the story. The teacher and the Arab murderer are poles apart in consciousness and culture, and when Daru is forced to accept the Arab as his prisoner, they stand in the relation to each other of enemies. But the behavior of Daru radically changes this situation. Since he is required to have the man in his charge, he must in common decency feed and bed him, and his simple acts of hospitality give rise in him to feelings of solicitude, even of concern. The Arab, for his part, begins to regard Daru as his protector. Different and separated as these men are, the same word may be used for each of them in his relation to the other: each is the other's *hôte*.

For two men to "break bread" together in the home of one of them is regarded among many peoples as making a connection between them which entails reciprocal obligations of a quite compelling kind, and among the Arab peoples the bond between host and guest has legendarily had peculiar strength. It is not, however, any conscious feeling for the traditional sanctity of the relationship that has power over Daru. Rather, it is the emotions that arise directly out of the situation in which he finds himself, his sense of the irreducible humanity he shares with his guest as they perform together the necessary acts of existence: eating, sleeping, excreting, washing. Communication between the two men must always be minimal, but the communion that develops between them is not small. Indeed, it is quite large enough, as Daru feels it, to induce him to make a considerable sacrifice. He gives the Arab the means of escape and this can scarcely fail to have serious consequences in Daru's own life, perhaps punitive transfer from his present post which he cherishes, perhaps dismissal from the colonial civil service and the loss of his livelihood.

The sacrificial act which expresses Daru's sense of the communion of hospitality is of no avail. The Arab guest, for all that he has been arrested for a crime of violence, is a poor-spirited creature, and when Daru gives him the chance to find refuge with the nomad tribes of the South, beyond the reach of French law, he is unwilling to take it. He has no confidence in the nomadic tradition of hospitality of which Daru reminds him; the French authorities, who are bound to punish him, seem less alien to him than the Arab tribes of an unknown place, and he submissively sets out to give himself up to the police.

The ambiguity of the word *hôte* is not exhausted by the meanings of "host" and "guest." In its complicated history there figures the Latin word *hostis*, which means "stranger" and also "enemy." This word developed another form, *hospes*, and another meaning, that of the stranger who is not hostile but who gives the kindness of hospitality. When Daru returns to his classroom, the message written on the blackboard by the Arab's kinsmen tells him that he who had in fact been the beneficent stranger is taken to be the hostile stranger, the enemy. This French Algerian, born to the country and loving it, had lived in at least a kind of amity among the Arabs even though they were on the verge of the revolt that eventually, after a long, cruel war, was to drive the French out of the land they had conquered and colonized. In the general hostility that is coming to prevail, Daru's act of individual humanity is misunderstood and resented, and he who had rejected the claims of his own government at the behest of natural human impulse, finds himself proscribed on all sides, wholly isolated.

Isolation of a certain kind was a condition of existence that Daru had sought and attained. We are led to infer that his experience of the Second

World War has disenchanted him with life in society and with much—yet not with all—of human nature. Indeed, "disenchanted" is too mild a word for what he feels. He speaks of himself as "disgusted" with the Arab for his crime and for sharing with "all men . . . their rotten spite, their tireless hates, their blood-lust." He is no less "disgusted" by the idea of being himself co-opted by the social agency that undertakes to control the "rotten spite." And this emotion is validated by the policeman, Balducci, who speaks of himself as being "ashamed" of his work. Daru cannot be thought of as a programmatic idealist. He seems to have no principled opposition to French imperialism and can even say that, in the event of an Arab uprising, he would be willing to fight on the French side. He feels of the land that it is as much his as the Arabs', and no doubt the more because the particular region which he inhabits makes possible the isolate moral condition he desires, the separation from all in people and society that can move him to disgust and shame. The sterility of the great plateau has for him a harsh nobility and beauty: and he loves the exigent, bitter terrain because it permits him the isolateness he has come to need. The bleakly moving ironies of the story are inescapable. Daru has learned that an instinctive impulse of compassion for a fellow-being will lead to his expulsion from the austere Eden of his solitude. A single involvement of feeling will implicate him in a future of human involvements.

THE

MAGIC

BARREL

BERNARD   MALAMUD

1 9 1 4 –

Not long ago there lived in uptown New York, in a small, almost meager room, though crowded with books, Leo Finkle, a rabbinical student in the Yeshivah University. Finkle, after six years of study, was to be ordained in June and had been advised by an acquaintance that he might find it easier to win himself a congregation if he were married. Since he had no present prospects of marriage, after two tormented days of turning it over in his mind, he called in Pinye Salzman, a marriage broker whose two-line advertisement he had read in the *Forward*.[1]

The matchmaker appeared one night out of the dark fourth-floor hallway of the graystone rooming house where Finkle lived, grasping a black, strapped portfolio that had been worn thin with use. Salzman, who had been long in the business, was of slight but dignified build, wearing an old hat, and an overcoat too short and tight for him. He smelled frankly of fish, which he loved to eat, and although he was missing a few teeth, his presence was not displeasing, because of an amiable manner curiously contrasted with mournful eyes. His voice, his lips, his wisp of beard, his bony fingers were animated, but give him a moment of repose and his mild blue eyes revealed a depth of sadness, a charac-

[1] The Jewish daily newspaper.

teristic that put Leo a little at ease although the situation, for him, was inherently tense.

He at once informed Salzman why he had asked him to come, explaining that his home was in Cleveland, and that but for his parents, who had married comparatively late in life, he was alone in the world. He had for six years devoted himself almost entirely to his studies, as a result of which, understandably, he had found himself without time for a social life and the company of young women. Therefore he thought it the better part of trial and error—of embarrassing fumbling—to call in an experienced person to advise him on these matters. He remarked in passing that the function of the marriage broker was ancient and honorable, highly approved in the Jewish community, because it made practical the necessary without hindering joy. Moreover, his own parents had been brought together by a matchmaker. They had made, if not a financially profitable marriage—since neither had possessed any worldly goods to speak of—at least a successful one in the sense of their everlasting devotion to each other. Salzman listened in embarrassed surprise, sensing a sort of apology. Later, however, he experienced a glow of pride in his work, an emotion that had left him years ago, and he heartily approved of Finkle.

The two went to their business. Leo had led Salzman to the only clear place in the room, a table near a window that overlooked the lamp-lit city. He seated himself at the matchmaker's side but facing him, attempting by an act of will to suppress the unpleasant tickle in his throat. Salzman eagerly unstrapped his portfolio and removed a loose rubber band from a thin packet of much-handled cards. As he flipped through them, a gesture and sound that physically hurt Leo, the student pretended not to see and gazed steadfastly out the window. Although it was still February, winter was on its last legs, signs of which he had for the first time in years begun to notice. He now observed the round white moon, moving high in the sky through a cloud menagerie, and watched with half-open mouth as it penetrated a huge hen, and dropped out of her like an egg laying itself. Salzman, though pretending through eyeglasses he had just slipped on, to be engaged in scanning the writing on the cards, stole occasional glances at the young man's distinguished face, noting with pleasure the long, severe scholar's nose, brown eyes heavy with learning, sensitive yet ascetic lips, and a certain, almost hollow quality of the dark cheeks. He gazed around at shelves upon shelves of books and let out a soft, contented sigh.

When Leo's eyes fell upon the cards, he counted six spread out in Salzman's hand.

"So few?" he asked in disappointment.

"You wouldn't believe me how much cards I got in my office," Salzman replied. "The drawers are already filled to the top, so I keep them now in a barrel, but is every girl good for a new rabbi?"

Leo blushed at this, regretting all he had revealed of himself in a curriculum vitae he had sent to Salzman. He had thought it best to acquaint him with his strict standards and specifications, but in having done so, felt he had told the marriage broker more than was absolutely necessary.

He hesitantly inquired, "Do you keep photographs of your clients on file?"

"First comes family, amount of dowry, also what kind promises," Salzman replied, unbuttoning his tight coat and settling himself in the chair. "After comes pictures, rabbi."

"Call me Mr. Finkle. I'm not yet a rabbi."

Salzman said he would, but instead called him doctor, which he changed to rabbi when Leo was not listening too attentively.

Salzman adjusted his horn-rimmed spectacles, gently cleared his throat and read in an eager voice the contents of the top card:

"Sophie P. Twenty-four years. Widow one year. No children. Educated high school and two years college. Father promises eight thousand dollars. Has wonderful wholesale business. Also real estate. On the mother's side comes teachers, also one actor. Well known on Second Avenue."

Leo gazed up in surprise. "Did you say a widow?"

"A widow don't mean spoiled, rabbi. She lived with her husband maybe four months. He was a sick boy she made a mistake to marry him."

"Marrying a widow has never entered my mind."

"This is because you have no experience. A widow, especially if she is young and healthy like this girl, is a wonderful person to marry. She will be thankful to you the rest of her life. Believe me, if I was looking now for a bride, I would marry a widow."

Leo reflected, then shook his head.

Salzman hunched his shoulders in an almost imperceptible gesture of disappointment. He placed the card down on the wooden table and began to read another:

"Lily H. High school teacher. Regular. Not a substitute. Has savings and new Dodge car. Lived in Paris one year. Father is successful dentist thirty-five years. Interested in professional man. Well Americanized family. Wonderful opportunity."

"I knew her personally," said Salzman. "I wish you could see this girl. She is a doll. Also very intelligent. All day you could talk to her about books and theyater and what not. She also knows current events."

"I don't believe you mentioned her age?"

"Her age?" Salzman said, raising his brows. "Her age is thirty-two years."

Leo said after a while, "I'm afraid that seems a little too old."

Salzman let out a laugh. "So how old are you, rabbi?"

"Twenty-seven."

"So what is the difference, tell me, between twenty-seven and thirty-two? My own wife is seven years older than me. So what did I suffer?—Nothing. If Rothschild's daughter wants to marry you, would you say on account her age, no?"

"Yes," Leo said dryly.

Salzman shook off the no in the yes. "Five years don't mean a thing. I give you my word that when you will live with her for one week you will forget her age. What does it mean five years—that she lived more and knows more than somebody who is younger? On this girl, God bless her, years are not wasted. Each one that it comes makes better the bargain."

"What subject does she teach in high school?"

"Languages. If you heard the way she speaks French, you will think it is music. I am in the business twenty-five years, and I recommend her with my whole heart. Believe me, I know what I'm talking, rabbi."

"What's on the next card?" Leo said abruptly.

Salzman reluctantly turned up the third card:

"Ruth K. Nineteen years. Honor student. Father offers thirteen thousand cash to the right bridegroom. He is a medical doctor. Stomach specialist with marvelous practice. Brother in law owns own garment business. Particular people."

Salzman looked as if he had read his trump card.

"Did you say nineteen?" Leo asked with interest.

"On the dot."

"Is she attractive?" He blushed. "Pretty?"

Salzman kissed his finger tips. "A little doll. On this I give you my word. Let me call the father tonight and you will see what means pretty."

But Leo was troubled. "You're sure she's that young?"

"This I am positive. The father will show you the birth certificate."

"Are you positive there isn't something wrong with her?" Leo insisted.

"Who says there is wrong?"

"I don't understand why an American girl her age should go to a marriage broker."

A smile spread over Salzman's face.

"So for the same reason you went, she comes."

Leo flushed. "I am pressed for time."

Salzman, realizing he had been tactless, quickly explained. "The father came, not her. He wants she should have the best, so he looks around himself. When we will locate the right boy he will introduce him and encourage. This makes a better marriage than if a young girl without experience takes for herself. I don't have to tell you this."

"But don't you think this young girl believes in love?" Leo spoke uneasily.

Salzman was about to guffaw but caught himself and said soberly, "Love comes with the right person, not before."

Leo parted dry lips but did not speak. Noticing that Salzman had snatched a glance at the next card, he cleverly asked, "How is her health?"

"Perfect," Salzman said, breathing with difficulty. "Of course, she is a little lame on her right foot from an auto accident that it happened to her when she was twelve years, but nobody notices on account she is so brilliant and also beautiful."

Leo got up heavily and went to the window. He felt curiously bitter and upbraided himself for having called in the marriage broker. Finally, he shook his head.

"Why not?" Salzman persisted, the pitch of his voice rising.

"Because I detest stomach specialists."

"So what do you care what is his business? After you marry her do you need him? Who says he must come every Friday night in your house?"

Ashamed of the way the talk was going, Leo dismissed Salzman, who went home with heavy, melancholy eyes.

Though he had felt only relief at the marriage broker's departure, Leo was in low spirits the next day. He explained it as arising from Salzman's failure to produce a suitable bride for him. He did not care for his type of clientele. But when Leo found himself hesitating whether to seek out another matchmaker, one more polished than Pinye, he wondered if it could be—his protestations to the contrary, and although he honored his father and mother—that he did not, in essence, care for the matchmaking institution? This thought he quickly put out of mind yet found himself still upset. All day he ran around in the woods—missed an important appointment, forgot to give out his laundry, walked out of a Broadway cafeteria without paying and had to run back with the ticket in his hand; had even not recognized his landlady in the street when she passed with a friend and courteously called out, "A good evening to you, Doctor Finkle." By nightfall, however, he had regained sufficient calm to sink his nose into a book and there found peace from his thoughts.

Almost at once there came a knock on the door. Before Leo could say enter, Salzman, commercial cupid, was standing in the room. His face was gray and meager, his expression hungry, and he looked as if he would expire on his feet. Yet the marriage broker managed, by some trick of the muscles, to display a broad smile.

"So good evening. I am invited?"

Leo nodded, disturbed to see him again, yet unwilling to ask the man to leave.

Beaming still, Salzman laid his portfolio on the table. "Rabbi, I got for you tonight good news."

"I've asked you not to call me rabbi. I'm still a student."

"Your worries are finished. I have for you a first-class bride."

"Leave me in peace concerning this subject." Leo pretended lack of interest.

"The world will dance at your wedding."

"Please, Mr. Salzman, no more."

"But first must come back my strength," Salzman said weakly. He fumbled with the portfolio straps and took out of the leather case an oily paper bag, from which he extracted a hard, seeded roll and a small, smoked white fish. With a quick motion of his hand he stripped the fish out of its skin and began ravenously to chew. "All day in a rush," he muttered.

Leo watched him eat.

"A sliced tomato you have maybe?" Salzman hesitantly inquired.

"No."

The marriage broker shut his eyes and ate. When he had finished he carefully cleaned up the crumbs and rolled up the remains of the fish, in the paper bag. His spectacled eyes roamed the room until he discovered, amid some piles of books, a one-burner gas stove. Lifting his hat he humbly asked, "A glass of tea you got, rabbi?"

Conscience-stricken, Leo rose and brewed the tea. He served it with a chunk of lemon and two cubes of lump sugar, delighting Salzman.

After he had drunk his tea, Salzman's strength and good spirits were restored.

"So tell me, rabbi," he said amiably, "you considered some more the three clients I mentioned yesterday?"

"There was no need to consider."

"Why not?"

"None of them suits me."

"What then suits you?"

Leo let it pass because he could give only a confused answer.

Without waiting for a reply, Salzman asked, "You remember this girl I talked to you—the high school teacher?"

"Age thirty-two?"

But, surprisingly, Salzman's face lit in a smile. "Age twenty-nine."

Leo shot him a look. "Reduced from thirty-two?"

"A mistake," Salzman avowed. "I talked today with the dentist. He took me to his safety deposit box and showed me the birth certificate. She was twenty-nine years last August. They made her a party in the mountains where she went for her vacation. When her father spoke to me the first time I forgot to write the age and I told you thirty-two, but now I remember this was a different client, a widow."

"The same one you told me about? I thought she was twenty-four?"

"A different. Am I responsible that the world is filled with widows?"

"No, but I'm not interested in them, nor for that matter, in school teachers."

Salzman pulled his clasped hand to his breast. Looking at the ceiling he devoutly exclaimed, "Yiddishe kinder, what can I say to somebody that he is not interested in high school teachers? So what then you are interested?"

Leo flushed but controlled himself.

"In what else will you be interested," Salzman went on, "if you not interested in this fine girl that she speaks four languages and has personally in the bank ten thousand dollars? Also her father guarantees further twelve thousand. Also she has a new car, wonderful clothes, talks on all subjects, and she will give you a first-class home and children. How near do we come in our life to paradise?"

"If she's so wonderful, why wasn't she married ten years ago?"

"Why?" said Salzman with a heavy laugh. "—Why? Because she is *partikiler*. This is why. She wants the *best*."

Leo was silent, amused at how he had entangled himself. But Salzman had aroused his interest in Lily H., and he began seriously to consider calling on her. When the marriage broker observed how intently Leo's mind was at work on the facts he had supplied, he felt certain they would soon come to an agreement.

Late Saturday afternoon, conscious of Salzman, Leo Finkle walked with Lily Hirschorn along Riverside Drive. He walked briskly and erectly, wearing with distinction the black fedora he had that morning taken with trepidation out of the dusty hat box on his closet shelf, and the heavy black Saturday coat he had thoroughly whisked clean. Leo also owned a walking stick, a present from a distant relative, but quickly put temptation aside and did not use it. Lily, petite and not unpretty, had on something signifying the approach of spring. She was au courant, animatedly, with all sorts of subjects, and he weighed her words and found her surprisingly sound—score another for Salzman, whom he uneasily sensed to be somewhere around, hiding perhaps high in a tree along the street, flashing the lady signals with a pocket mirror; or perhaps a cloven-hoofed Pan,[2] piping nuptial ditties as he danced his invisible way before them, strewing wild buds on the walk and purple grapes in their path, symbolizing fruit of a union, though there was of course still none.

Lily startled Leo by remarking, "I was thinking of Mr. Salzman, a curious figure, wouldn't you say?"

Not certain what to answer, he nodded.

[2] Greek god of pastures, forests, flocks, and herds; he is represented with the lower part of a goat and the upper part of a man.

She bravely went on, blushing, "I for one am grateful for his introducing us. Aren't you?"

He courteously replied, "I am."

"I mean," she said with a little laugh—and it was all in good taste, or at least gave the effect of being not in bad—"do you mind that we came together so?"

He was not displeased with her honesty, recognizing that she meant to set the relationship aright, and understanding that it took a certain amount of experience in life, and courage, to want to do it quite that way. One had to have some sort of past to make that kind of beginning.

He said that he did not mind. Salzman's function was traditional and honorable—valuable for what it might achieve, which, he pointed out, was frequently nothing.

Lily agreed with a sigh. They walked on for a while and she said after a long silence, again with a nervous laugh, "Would you mind if I asked you something a little bit personal? Frankly, I find the subject fascinating." Although Leo shrugged, she went on half embarrassedly, "How was it that you came to your calling? I mean was it a sudden passionate inspiration?"

Leo, after a time, slowly replied. "I was always interested in the Law."

"You saw revealed in it the presence of the Highest?"

He nodded and changed the subject. "I understand that you spent a little time in Paris, Miss Hirschorn?"

"Oh, did Mr. Salzman tell you, Rabbi Finkle?" Leo winced but she went on, "It was ages ago and almost forgotten. I remember I had to return for my sister's wedding."

And Lily would not be put off. "When," she asked in a trembly voice, "did you become enamored of God?"

He stared at her. Then it came to him that she was talking not about Leo Finkle, but of a total stranger, some mystical figure, perhaps even passionate prophet that Salzman had dreamed up for her—no relation to the living or dead. Leo trembled with rage and weakness. The trickster had obviously sold her a bill of goods, just as he had him, who'd expected to become acquainted with a young lady of twenty-nine, only to behold, the moment he laid eyes upon her strained and anxious face, a woman past thirty-five and aging rapidly. Only his self control had kept him this long in her presence.

"I am not," he said gravely, "a talented religious person," and in seeking words to go on, found himself possessed by shame and fear. "I think," he said in a strained manner, "that I came to God not because I loved Him, but because I did not."

This confession he spoke harshly because its unexpectedness shook him.

Lily wilted. Leo saw a profusion of loaves of bread go flying like ducks high over his head, not unlike the winged loaves by which he had counted himself to sleep last night. Mercifully, then, it snowed, which he would not put past Salzman's machinations.

He was infuriated with the marriage broker and swore he would throw him out of the room the minute he reappeared. But Salzman did not come that night, and when Leo's anger had subsided, an unaccountable despair grew in its place. At first he thought this was caused by his disappointment in Lily, but before long it became evident that he had involved himself with Salzman without a true knowledge of his own intent. He gradually realized—with an emptiness that seized him with six hands—that he had called in the broker to find him a bride because he was incapable of doing it himself. This terrifying insight he had derived as a result of his meeting and conversation with Lily Hirschorn. Her probing questions had somehow irritated him into revealing—to himself more than her—the true nature of his relationship to God, and from that it had come upon him, with shocking force, that apart from his parents, he had never loved anyone. Or perhaps it went the other way, that he did not love God so well as he might, because he had not loved man. It seemed to Leo that his whole life stood starkly revealed and he saw himself for the first time as he truly was— unloved and loveless. This bitter but somehow not fully unexpected revelation brought him to a point of panic, controlled only by extraordinary effort. He covered his face with his hands and cried.

The week that followed was the worst of his life. He did not eat and lost weight. His beard darkened and grew ragged. He stopped attending seminars and almost never opened a book. He seriously considered leaving the Yeshivah, although he was deeply troubled at the thought of the loss of all his years of study—saw them like pages torn from a book, strewn over the city—and at the devastating effect of this decision upon his parents. But he had lived without knowledge of himself, and never in the Five Books[3] and all the Commentaries— mea culpa[4]—had the truth been revealed to him. He did not know where to turn, and in all this desolating loneliness there was no *to whom,* although he often thought of Lily but not once could bring himself to go downstairs and make the call. He became touchy and irritable, especially with his landlady, who asked him all manner of personal questions; on the other hand, sensing his own disagreeableness, he waylaid her on the stairs and apologized abjectly, until mortified, she ran from him. Out of this, however, he drew the consolation that he was a Jew and that a Jew suffered. But gradually, as the long and terrible week drew to a close, he regained his composure and some idea of purpose in life: to go on as planned. Although he was imperfect, the ideal was not. As for his quest of a bride, the thought of continuing afflicted him with anxiety and heartburn, yet perhaps with this new knowledge of himself he would be more successful than in the past. Perhaps love would now come to him and a bride to that love. And for this sanctified seeking who needed a Salzman?

The marriage broker, a skeleton with haunted eyes, returned that very night. He looked, withal, the picture of frustrated expectancy—as if he had steadfastly waited the week at Miss Lily Hirschorn's side for a telephone call that never came.

Casually coughing, Salzman come immediately to the point: "So how did you like her?"

Leo's anger rose and he could not refrain from chiding the matchmaker: "Why did you lie to me, Salzman?"

Salzman's pale face went dead white, the world had snowed on him.

"Did you not state that she was twenty-nine?" Leo insisted.

"I give you my word—"

[3] The *Megilloth* (Song of Solomon, Ruth, Lamentations, Ecclesiastes, and Esther), used in the liturgy of the Jewish faith.
[4] (Latin) Through my fault.

"She was thirty-five, if a day. *At least* thirty-five."

"Of this don't be too sure. Her father told me—"

"Never mind. The worst of it was that you lied to her."

"How did I lie to her, tell me?"

"You told her things about me that weren't true. You made me out to be more, consequently less than I am. She had in mind a totally different person, a sort of semi-mystical Wonder Rabbi."

"All I said, you was a religious man."

"I can imagine."

Salzman sighed. "This is my weakness that I have," he confessed. "My wife says to me I shouldn't be a salesman, but when I have two fine people that they would be wonderful to be married, I am so happy that I talk too much." He smiled wanly. "This is why Salzman is a poor man."

Leo's anger left him. "Well, Salzman, I'm afraid that's all."

The marriage broker fastened hungry eyes on him.

"You don't want any more a bride?"

"I do," said Leo, "but I have decided to seek her in a different way. I am no longer interested in an arranged marriage. To be frank, I now admit the necessity of premarital love. That is, I want to be in love with the one I marry."

"Love?" said Salzman, astounded. After a moment he remarked, "For us, our love is our life, not for the ladies. In the ghetto they—"

"I know, I know," said Leo. "I've thought of it often. Love, I have said to myself, should be a by-product of living and worship rather than its own end. Yet for myself I find it necessary to establish the level of my need and fulfill it."

Salzman shrugged but answered, "Listen, rabbi, if you want love, this I can find for you also. I have such beautiful clients that you will love them the minute your eyes will see them."

Leo smiled unhappily. "I'm afraid you don't understand."

But Salzman hastily unstrapped his portfolio and withdrew a manila packet from it.

"Pictures," he said, quickly laying the envelope on the table.

Leo called after him to take the pictures away, but as if on the wings of the wind, Salzman had disappeared.

March came. Leo had returned to his regular routine. Although he felt not quite himself yet—lacked energy—he was making plans for a more active social life. Of course it would cost something, but he was an expert in cutting corners; and when there were no corners left he would make circles rounder. All the while Salzman's pictures had lain on the table, gathering dust. Occasionally as Leo sat studying, or enjoying a cup of tea, his eyes fell on the manila envelope, but he never opened it.

The days went by and no social life to speak of developed with a member of the opposite sex—it was difficult, given the circumstances of his situation. One morning Leo toiled up the stairs to his room and stared out the window at the city. Although the day was bright his view of it was dark. For some time he watched the people in the street below hurrying along and then turned with a heavy heart to his little room. On the table was the packet. With a sudden relentless gesture he tore it open. For a half-hour he stood by the table in a state of excitement, examining the photographs of the ladies Salzman had included.

Finally, with a deep sigh he put them down. There were six, of varying degrees of attractiveness, but look at them long enough and they all became Lily Hirschorn: all past their prime, all starved behind bright smiles, not a true personality in the lot. Life, despite their frantic yoohooings, had passed them by; they were pictures in a brief case that stank of fish. After a while, however, as Leo attempted to return the photographs into the envelope, he found in it another, a snapshot of the type taken by a machine for a quarter. He gazed at it a moment and let out a cry.

Her face deeply moved him. Why, he could at first not say. It gave him the impression of youth—spring flowers, yet age—a sense of having been used to the bone, wasted; this came from the eyes, which were hauntingly familiar, yet absolutely strange. He had a vivid impression that he had met her before, but try as he might he could not place her although he could almost recall her name, as if he had read it in her own handwriting. No, this couldn't be; he would have remembered her. It was not, he affirmed, that she had an extraordinary beauty—no, though her face was attractive enough; it was that *something* about her moved him. Feature for feature, even some of the ladies of the photographs could do better; but she leaped forth to his heart—had *lived*, or wanted to—more than just wanted, perhaps regretted how she had lived—had somehow deeply suffered: it could be seen in the depths of those reluctant eyes, and from the way the light enclosed and shone from her, and within her, opening realms of possibility: this was her own. Her he desired. His head ached and eyes narrowed with the intensity of his gazing, then as if an obscure fog had blown up in the mind, he experienced fear of her and was aware that he had received an impression, somehow, of evil. He shuddered, saying softly, it is thus with us all. Leo brewed some tea in a small pot and sat sipping it without sugar, to calm himself. But before he had finished drinking, again with excitement he examined the face and found it good: good for Leo Finkle. Only such a one could understand him and help him seek whatever he was seeking. She might, perhaps, love him. How she had happened to be among the discards in Salzman's barrel he could never guess, but he knew he must urgently go find her.

Leo rushed downstairs, grabbed up the Bronx telephone book, and searched for Salzman's home address. He was not listed, nor was his office. Neither was he in the Manhattan book. But Leo remembered having written down the address on a slip of paper after he had read Salzman's advertisement in the "personals" column of the *Forward*. He ran up to his room and tore through his papers, without luck. It was exasperating. Just when he needed the matchmaker he was nowhere to be found. Fortunately Leo remembered to look in his wallet. There on a card he found his name written and a Bronx address. No phone number was listed, the reason—Leo now recalled—he had originally communicated with Salzman by letter. He got on his coat, put a hat on over his skull cap and hurried to the subway station. All the way to the far end of the Bronx he sat on the edge of his seat. He was more than once tempted to take out the picture and see if the girl's face was as he remembered it, but he refrained, allowing the snapshot to remain in his inside coat pocket, content to have her so close. When the train pulled into the station he was waiting at the door and bolted out. He quickly located the street Salzman had advertised.

The building he sought was less than a block from the subway, but it was not an office building, nor even a loft, nor a store in which one could rent office space. It was a very old tenement house. Leo found Salzman's name in pencil on a soiled tag under the bell and climbed three dark flights to his apartment. When he knocked, the door was opened by a thin, asthmatic, gray-haired woman, in felt slippers.

"Yes?" she said, expecting nothing. She listened without listening. He could have sworn he had seen her, too, before but knew it was an illusion.

"Salzman—does he live here? Pinye Salzman," he said, "the matchmaker?"

She stared at him a long minute. "Of course."

He felt embarrassed. "Is he in?"

"No." Her mouth, though left open, offered nothing more.

"The matter is urgent. Can you tell me where his office is?"

"In the air." She pointed upward.

"You mean he has no office?" Leo asked.

"In his socks."

He peered into the apartment. It was sunless and dingy, one large room divided by a half-open curtain, beyond which he could see a sagging metal bed. The near side of a room was crowded with rickety chairs, old bureaus, a three-legged table, racks of cooking utensils, and all the apparatus of a kitchen. But there was no sign of Salzman or his magic barrel, probably also a figment of the imagination. An odor of frying fish made Leo weak to the knees.

"Where is he?" he insisted. "I've got to see your husband."

At length she answered, "So who knows where he is? Every time he thinks a new thought he runs to a different place. Go home, he will find you."

"Tell him Leo Finkle."

She gave no sign she had heard.

He walked downstairs, depressed.

But Salzman, breathless, stood waiting at his door.

Leo was astounded and overjoyed. "How did you get here before me?"

"I rushed."

"Come inside."

They entered. Leo fixed tea, and a sardine sandwich for Salzman. As they were drinking he reached behind him for the packet of pictures and handed them to the marriage broker.

Salzman put down his glass and said expectantly, "You found somebody you like?"

"Not among these."

The marriage broker turned away.

"Here is the one I want." Leo held forth the snapshot.

Salzman slipped on his glasses and took the picture into his trembling hand. He turned ghastly and let out a groan.

"What's the matter?" cried Leo.

"Excuse me. Was an accident this picture. She isn't for you."

Salzman frantically shoved the manila packet into his portfolio. He thrust the snapshot into his pocket and fled down the stairs.

Leo, after momentary paralysis, gave chase and cornered the marriage broker in the vestibule. The landlady made hysterical outcries but neither of them listened.

"Give me back the picture, Salzman."

"No." The pain in his eyes was terrible.

"Tell me who she is then."

"This I can't tell you. Excuse me."

He made to depart, but Leo, forgetting himself, seized the matchmaker by his tight coat and shook him frenziedly.

"Please," sighed Salzman. *"Please."*

Leo ashamedly let him go. "Tell me who she is," he begged. "It's very important for me to know."

"She is not for you. She is a wild one—wild, without shame. This is not a bride for a rabbi."

"What do you mean wild?"

"Like an animal. Like a dog. For her to be poor was a sin. This is why to me she is dead now."

"In God's name, what do you mean?"

"Her I can't introduce to you," Salzman cried.

"Why are you so excited?"

"Why, he asks," Salzman said, bursting into tears. "This is my baby, my Stella, she should burn in hell."

Leo hurried up to bed and hid under the covers. Under the covers he thought his life through. Although he soon fell asleep he could not sleep her out of his mind. He woke, beating his breast. Though he prayed to be rid of her, his prayers went unanswered. Through days of torment he endlessly struggled not to love her; fearing success, he escaped it. He then concluded to convert her to goodness, himself to God. The idea alternately nauseated and exalted him.

He perhaps did not know that he had come to a final decision until he encountered Salzman in a Broadway cafeteria. He was sitting alone at a rear table, sucking the bony remains of a fish. The marriage broker appeared haggard, and transparent to the point of vanishing.

Salzman looked up at first without recognizing him. Leo had grown a pointed beard and his eyes were weighted with wisdom.

"Salzman," he said, "love has at last come to my heart."

"Who can love from a picture?" mocked the marriage broker.

"It is not impossible."

"If you can love her, then you can love anybody. Let me show you some new clients that they just sent me their photographs. One is a little doll."

"Just her I want," Leo murmured.

"Don't be a fool, doctor. Don't bother with her."

"Put me in touch with her, Salzman," Leo said humbly. "Perhaps I can be of service."

Salzman had stopped eating and Leo understood with emotion that it was now arranged.

Leaving the cafeteria, he was, however, afflicted by a tormenting suspicion that Salzman had planned it all to happen this way.

Leo was informed by letter that she would meet him on a certain corner, and she was there one spring night, waiting under a street lamp. He appeared carrying a small bouquet of violets and rosebuds. Stella stood by the lamp post, smoking. She wore white with red shoes, which fitted his expectations, although in a troubled moment he had imagined the dress red, and only the shoes white. She waited uneasily and shyly. From afar he saw that her eyes—clearly her father's—were filled with desperate innocence. He pictured, in her, his own redemption. Violins and lit candles revolved in the sky. Leo ran forward with flowers outthrust.

Around the corner, Salzman, leaning against a wall, chanted prayers for the dead.

COMMENTARY

Much of the curious power and charm of "The Magic Barrel" is surely to be accounted for by the extraordinary visual intensity of a single paragraph, the last but one, which describes the rendezvous of Leo Finkle and Stella Salzman. The glare of the street lamp under which Stella stands, her white dress and red shoes, and also the red dress and white shoes that Leo had expected her to wear (for this too is envisioned), the bouquet of violets and rosebuds that Leo carries as he runs toward her—these elements of light and color make a scene which is pictorial rather than (in the literal sense of the word) dramatic. Nothing is *said* by the lovers, the whole meaning of the moment lies in what is *seen*. Indeed, had a single word been uttered, the effect of the strange and touching tableau would have been much diminished. In their silence, the lovers exist only in the instant of their first sight of each other, without past or future, unhampered by those inner conditions which we call personality. They transcend personality; they exist in their essence as lovers, as images of loving. And our sense of their transcendence is strengthened by those "violins and lit candles" that revolve in the sky, as if the rendezvous were taking place not in the ordinary world but in a world of emblems, of metaphors made actual.

This concluding scene is striking not only in itself but in the retroactive effect that it has upon the whole story. The anterior episodes take on new meaning when we perceive that they have issued in this moment, with its dignity of pictorial silence, its dreamlike massiveness of significance. The absurd transaction between Salzman and Leo Finkle, Salzman's elaboration of deceit, the dismal comedy of Leo's walk on Riverside Drive with Lily Hirschorn, the odd speech, habits, and manners of the characters—all these sordid or funny actualities of life are transmuted by the rapturous intensity and the almost mystical abstractness of the climactic rendezvous.

The intense pictorial quality of this last scene is of course a reminiscence of the iconography of a particular painter. Whoever knows the work of Marc Chagall will recognize in "the violins and lit candles [that] revolved in the sky" a reference to the pictures of this modern master, in which fantasy suspends the laws that govern the behavior of solid bodies, giving to familiar objects— violins and candles are among his favorites—a magical and emblematic life of their own. Married love is one of Chagall's subjects; many of his paintings represent bride and bridegroom or husband and wife in a moment of confrontation at once rapturous and fearful. Even the kind of bouquet that Leo carries is characteristic of Chagall—James Johnson Sweeney, in his book about the artist, tells us that "flowers, especially mixed bouquets of tiny blossoms," held for Chagall a peculiar interest at one period of his life; they charmed him visually and also by the sentiments they implied.

The knowledge of Malamud's direct reference to Chagall is helpful in understanding the story. For Chagall is the great celebrator of the religious culture of the Jews of Eastern Europe. It is this culture, now virtually gone, having been systematically destroyed by the Germans and Russians, that poor Salzman represents in a sad, attenuated, transplanted form, and that has put its mark on Leo, who regards it with ambivalence, and on Stella, who has rejected it. It was a culture based upon a devotion to strict religious observance, of which the highest expression was the study of God's Law contained in the Bible and in the vast body of commentary that had accumulated through the ages. Assiduity in study and distinction in learning made the ground not only of piety but of prestige—to rear a learned son or to acquire a learned son-in-law was the ambition of every family concerned with its social standing.

The American reader can comprehend something of the quality of this life by bringing to mind what he knows of the towns of Puritan New England in the seventeenth century. The two theocratic cultures were alike in the intensity of their faith, in the omnipresence of religion in daily life, in the pre-eminence given to intellectual activity both as an evidence of faith and as the source of authority and status—if one recalls the veneration given to Mr. Dimmesdale, the learned young minister of Hawthorne's *The Scarlet Letter,* one has a fair notion of how the rabbi of an orthodox Jewish community was regarded. The two societies are also alike in the harsh and difficult view they took of life, in their belief that life is to be lived under the control of the sterner virtues. Neither can properly be called ascetic, for both—and perhaps especially the Jewish—held marriage in high esteem. But in both societies devotion to the Word of God implied a considerable denigration of the charms and graces of life and a strict limitation upon the passions.

The artist who portrays a culture of this kind will in all probability be concerned with the elements of feeling that it represses or denies; his partisanship will be with the graces of life and the passions of human desire. *The Scarlet Letter* is a case in point—Hawthorne directs all our sympathy to the doomed love of Arthur Dimmesdale and Hester Prynne rather than to the Puritan godliness that chastises it. Chagall depicts with affectionate reverence the religious life he knew in his childhood in the little Russian city of Vitebsk, but his representation of love is marked not only by the joy that is natural to it but also by the joy of its liberation from the piety that had held it in check.

It is a great advantage to art to be able to assert its partisanship with passion as against piety and godliness; in the exercise of this preference the artist is necessarily dealing with a situation charged with high feelings. The passions of human desire probably gain in intensity, and they certainly gain in interest, when they meet with adversity. The love that proclaims itself in the face of strict prohibition has more significance for us than a love that is permitted and encouraged. And of the several kinds of illicitness in love, that which is prohibited by religion and called sin is likely to seem the most intense and interesting of all—it borrows something of the grandeur and absoluteness of the power that forbids it. The rapture of Leo's rendezvous with Stella is not merely that of a young man's erotic urgency. It has something of the ecstasy of religious crisis—Leo is experiencing the hope of what he calls his "redemption."

His crisis is the more portentous because he believes that his redemption will come to him through sin.

For that Stella is sinful, that she is sin itself, is the judgment passed upon her by her father's tradition. Her father curses her, although he loves her, and he mourns her as dead because she is unchaste. He speaks of her as "wild," "without shame," "like an animal," even "like a dog." And the young man, bred to the old tradition, is no less ready to recognize her sinfulness, although his image of sin is not repellent but attractive: he eagerly anticipates Stella's appearance in a red dress, red being the color of an open and shameless avowal of sexuality. Red may be the color of sin in general, as when the prophet Isaiah says, "Though your sins be scarlet, they shall be white as snow," but more commonly it represents sexual sin in particular—one of the synonyms the dictionary gives for *scarlet* is *whorish*.

The reader, of course, is not under the necessity of believing that Stella is what her father makes her out to be—possibly her sexual life is marked merely by a freedom of the kind that now morality scarcely reproves. Her dress is in fact not red but white, the virginal color; only her shoes are red. And in her eyes, we are told, there is a "desperate innocence." We see her not as Sin but as what William Blake called Experience, by which he meant the moral state of those who have known the passions and have been marked, and beautified, by the pain which that knowledge inflicts. This is the condition to which Leo Finkle aspires and which he calls his redemption. His meeting is with life itself, and the moment of the encounter achieves an ultimate rapture because of the awareness it brings him, like an illumination, that the joy and pain he had longed to embrace, and had been willing to embrace as sin, need not be condemned.

PART

3 POETRY

EDWARD

ANONYMOUS

"Why dois your brand[1] sae[2] drap wi bluid,
            Edward, Edward?
Why dois your brand sae drap wi bluid,
    And why sae sad gang[3] yee O?"
"O I hae killed my hauke[4] sae guid,   5
            Mither, mither,
O I hae killed my hauke sae guid,
    And I had nae mair bot[5] hee O."

Your haukis bluid was nevir sae reid,
            Edward, Edward,   10
Your haukis bluid was nevir sae reid,
    My deir son I tell thee O."
"O I hae killed my reid-roan steid,[6]
            Mither, mither,
O I hae killed my reid-roan steid,   15
    That erst[7] was sae fair and frie O."

"Your steid was auld, and ye hae gat mair,
            Edward, Edward,
Your steid was auld, and ye hae gat mair,
    Sum other dule[8] ye drie[9] O."   20
"O I hae killed my fadir[10] deir,
            Mither, mither,
O I hae killed my fadir deir,
    Alas, and wae is mee O!"

"And whatten penance wul ye drie for that,   25
            Edward, Edward?
And whatten penance wul ye drie, for that?
    My deir son, now tell me O."
"Ile set my feit in yonder boat,
            Mither, mither   30

---

[1] Sword.   [2] So.   [3] Go.   [4] Hawk.   [5] But.   [6] Steed.   [7] Once.   [8] Grief.   [9] Suffer.
[10] Father.

Ile set my feit in yonder boat,
　　And Ile fare ovir the sea O."

"And what wul ye doe wi your towirs and your ha,[11]
　　Edward, Edward?
And what wul ye doe wi your towirs and your ha,　　　　　　　　　　35
　　That were sae fair to see O?"
"Ile let thame stand tul they doun fa,
　　Mither, mither,
Ile let thame stand tul they doun fa,
　　For here nevir mair maun[12] I bee O."　　　　　　　　　　　　　40

"And what wul ye leive to your bairns[13] and your wife,
　　Edward, Edward?
And what wul ye leive to your bairns and your wife,
　　Whan ye gang ovir the sea O?"
"The warldis room, late them beg thrae[14] life,　　　　　　　　　　45
　　Mither, mither,
The warldis room, late them beg thrae life,
　　For thame nevir mair wul I see O."

"And what wul ye leive to your ain mither deir,
　　Edward, Edward?　　　　　　　　　　　　　　　　　　　50
And what wul ye leive to your ain mither deir?
　　My deir son, now tell me O."
"The curse of hell frae me sall ye beir,
　　Mither, mither,
The curse of hell frae me sall ye beir,　　　　　　　　　　　　　55
　　Sic[15] counseils ye gave to me O."

COMMENTARY

It is obvious that the extraordinary force of this poem depends largely on
its element of surprise. There are two occasions of surprise, both intense, but
the one that comes midway in the poem is less shocking than the one
at the end because in some measure we have been led to anticipate it. We
know that we can expect the disclosure of an especially terrible deed when, to
the mother's question about the blood on his sword and the look on his face,
the son returns the first of his two prevaricating answers, saying that he has
killed his hawk. The substance of this lie is dismaying enough—in the days
when hawking was a common sport of the nobility, there was felt to be a close

---

[11] Hall, house.　[12] Must.　[13] Children.　[14] Through.　[15] Such.

communion between the falcon and the falconer. For a man to kill his horse, as Edward then says he did, perhaps goes even further against natural feeling. And if Edward had in fact killed neither the hawk nor the horse, if the blood on his sword and the look on his face are to be explained by some other killing, we expect it to be yet more horrifying, and of course it is—Edward has killed his father. Shocking as this revelation is, we have been at least a little prepared for it. But we are wholly unprepared for the second revelation, that he has killed his father at the behest of his mother.

In the face of the enormity it sets forth, "Edward" maintains an entire imperturbability. *We* are taken aback, but the poem is not even startled. The violence of its subject does not disorder the strict formality of its pattern; its composure is never ruffled. And this decorum transfers itself to the two characters: the mother's first question, which is asked in a tone that is not especially agitated, is answered in kind by the son, and once the question-and-answer mode of dialogue is established, it is sustained up to the end of the poem, when all the accumulated restraint releases itself in the explosion of the son's last terrible answer. The son is certainly not without emotion from the beginning—he is "sad," he speaks of his father as "deir" to him and bewails the murder, and his reply to his mother's question about his life in the future is bitter. Yet his emotions can scarcely be considered sufficient to his deed, and they do not become so until his last utterance. Up to that point he has submitted to his mother's questioning with a kind of grim courtesy; when at last the curse is torn from him, it is that much the more terrible because it has been so long held back. Yet even when he does utter the curse, which reveals his mother's part in the murder, his utterance is in the strict form the poem has established. What I have called the imperturbability of the poem creates the quiet out of which the terrible surprise leaps at us.

Of a piece with the poem's manner is its objectivity of view, which is uncompromising. Just as "Edward" refuses to make any emotional response to its subject, it refuses to make any moral comment on it—it is wholly detached from what it represents. By employing the dialogue form without a single narrative phrase, it refuses to assume even such involvement as is implied by *telling* what has happened; it undertakes to do nothing more than record what two persons said to each other. We are left free to judge the persons of the dialogue as we will, or must, while the poem itself is silent.

Nor does it say anything by way of explaining the dire happening that it reports. It does not consent to tell us the "whole story." This would consist of many episodes, of which the confrontation of the mother and the son would be only the last. If the events that took place before the dialogue have a claim upon our interest, it is a claim the poem does not recognize. We shall never know what sort of man the dead husband and father was, nor why his wife wanted him dead, nor by what means she induced her son to serve her purpose.

This frustration of our curiosity is strangely pleasurable. We do not find ourselves at a loss because the antecedent events of the poem have not been given us; we willingly consent to the high-handed way in which the poem denies the past. Its actually represented time is a brief moment of the immediate present. Of the five questions and seven answers that occupy this moment of the present, four questions and their answers have to do with the future. But to the past there is no reference at all until the last line, when the past is loosed in all its retributive ferocity. It has, of course, been lying in wait all through the poem. Doubtless the force of that last line is in large part achieved by its effect upon our moral sense: the intensity of our surprise does indeed relate to our horror at the mother's wickedness. Yet it is not only, and perhaps not even chiefly, the moral enormity that so satisfyingly disturbs us: it is rather the sudden, inexorable—we might almost say vengeful—return of the past, which the poem had seemed determined to exclude from its purview.

It has been said of "Edward" that it is "one of the best of all the ballads," and it may enhance our sense of the poem to be reminded that its characteristics are not unique but are shared by many poems in the same tradition.

Ballads divide, roughly, into two categories, literary and traditional, the latter sometimes called "popular" or "folk" ballads. In the eighteenth century there developed a considerable interest in the traditional ballads—the genre, in England and Scotland, took its rise in the fifteenth century—and many poets began to write in imitation of them or under their inspiration. But none of the traditional ballads can be assigned to any known author. This is not to say that they were not first composed by individual poets—no credence is now given to the theory, so attractive to many scholars in the nineteenth century, that the ballads were communal creations, that "the people" or "the folk" made them up by some process of composition the nature of which was never explained. The ballads are "popular" in the sense that they were made for and loved by the people, that is to say, by those members of a society who do not belong to the nobility: the literature of the people is distinguished from the literature of the court. But though each ballad was composed by an individual poet, his name was not attached to it and it did not long remain peculiarly his, nor did it necessarily circulate in its original form. For the ballads were not composed in writing nor were they meant to be read. They were intended to be sung and they had their existence in the memories of the people who sang them. The tune of a ballad was more likely to stay constant than its words, which might be altered by the whim of the singer, or by his failure to recall accurately what he had learned, or by his inability to understand one or another detail, such as a custom or an idiom no longer familiar to him. As a consequence, most of the traditional ballads exist in a number of versions.[1]

What may be thought of as the hallmark of the traditional ballads, the trait common to all examples of the genre, is their way of telling a story. Usually the story concerns an act of violence; it consists of a single situation which is presented at its point of climax, as near as possible to its conclusion. The method of presentation is dramatic rather than narrative, in the sense that it proceeds largely by dialogue; descriptions of scene and the use of what might be called stage-directions are kept to a minimum and are always very simple (in "Edward" there are none). Although the action is violent, the manner in which it is recounted is restrained. No effort is made to achieve originality of diction—the ballad-maker uses simple language and relies upon phrases that are traditional, or even clichés of the tradition. Explanation of motives and comment on morality are rigorously suppressed, and the attitude is one of detachment. It will readily be seen that many of these characteristics derive from the fact that the ballads were sung.

[1] The taking down of the words of ballads from the lips of the singer began in the eighteenth century and still goes on.

In "Edward" two traditional devices of the ballad play a decisive part in the poem's dramatic effectiveness. One of these is called by scholars "incremental repetition," a parallelism of phrase and idea that is strictly maintained, often in the form of question and answer; in "Edward" the natural effectiveness of this device is pointed up by the reiteration of courteous vocatives: "Edward, Edward" and "Mither, mither." Incremental repetition often takes the form of the so-called "nuncupative testament"—*nuncupative* means oral, as distinguished from written, and the phrase refers to a series of questions and answers in which a person in an extreme and usually fatal situation is asked what, upon his death or exile, he will bequeath to each of his relatives. Characteristically the answers are bitter and ironic, and the answer to the last question is usually climactic in its fierceness.

Many of the traditional ballads came over to America and some of them are still sung in parts of the country. "Edward" is one of these, but the American version has none of the tragic import of the Scottish. The son explains the stain on his "shirt sleeve" first as the blood of his "little yellow dog," then as the blood of his "little yellow horse"; it is his brother, not his father, he has killed; the cause of the quarrel is fully explained; his mother is not implicated in the murder; he speaks of his departure not as exile but as escape, and he plans to take "Katie dear" with him "to bear [him] company."

THEY FLEE FROM ME

SIR THOMAS WYATT
1503–1542

They flee from me that sometime did me seek,
With naked foot stalking in my chamber.
I have seen them gentle, tame, and meek,
That now are wild, and do not remember
That some time they put themselves in danger   5
To take bread at my hand; and now they range,
Busily seeking with a continual change.

Thanked be fortune, it hath been otherwise
Twenty times better; but once, in special,
In thin array, after a pleasant guise,[1]   10
When her loose gown from her shoulders did fall,
And she caught me in her arms long and small.[2]
Therewith all sweetly did me kiss,
And softly said, Dear heart, how like you this?

It was no dream; I lay broad waking.   15
But all is turned, thorough[3] my gentleness,
Into a strange fashion of forsaking;
And I have leave to go of her goodness,
And she also to use newfangleness.
But since that I so kindely am served,[4]   20
I fain[5] would know what she hath deserved.

COMMENTARY

One of the things that are bound to strike us early in our acquaintance with this poem is the shift from the "they" of the first stanza to the "she" of the rest of the poem. In the first lines the poet seems to be recalling the high favor in which he stood with many women, or women in general. In the second stanza

---

[1] Looking pleasant.   [2] Thin.   [3] Through.   [4] Dealt with.   [5] Gladly, with pleasure.

he recalls one erotic occasion "in special," with a woman who is strongly particularized. And the emotions that follow upon this encounter occupy his bitter and bewildered thought in the third stanza.

Some interpretations of the poem tell us that we must not take the "they" literally, that from the beginning the poet is really talking about "she." There is an advantage in this view—if we accept it, we can suppose that the happening the poet remembers "in special" is not the first love-encounter with one mistress out of many, but one peculiarly memorable encounter out of many with the same woman; of the two possibilities, the latter is the more interesting. But if "they" is really "she," it is by no means clear why the poet pluralized and generalized his mistress. In any case, the visual effect that "they" makes in the first stanza cannot be easily obliterated—one has the delighted impression that all the women the poet may ever have made love to are present at the same time in his chamber, all "stalking" together, a little multitude of glimpsed presences, rather like a flock or herd. The adjectives used of them evoke the image of delicate and charming animals: the "naked foot" evokes their lightness of step; their graceful stealth is suggested by their "stalking." This word has more than one meaning—it can refer to the action of a hunter trying to approach an animal without being seen, heard, or scented; or it can describe a way of walking, of humans or animals, with stiff, high, measured steps, like a long-legged bird— but Wyatt probably intended the now obsolete use of the word, which means the soft, cautious tread of an animal. No doubt he wished to create the image of a little herd of light-stepping deer which, in the park of some great manor house, become tame enough to take food from human hands.

But in the conclusion of the stanza three words occur which, for Wyatt's contemporary audience, would tend to modify, even to dispel, the enchanting picture of the preceding lines. Hunting was the chief sport of the gentlemen and ladies of the sixteenth century and they were conversant with its elaborate technical vocabulary. "Range," "seek," and "change" are hunting terms, all referring to the behavior of dogs. "Range" was the word used to describe the action of dogs who rove and stray in search of game. " 'Seek!' " (or " 'Seek out!' ") was the command to a dog to begin the search, and "a seek" was a series of notes upon the hunting horn calling the hounds to begin a chase. A "change" was an animal which the hounds meet by chance and then hunt instead of the quarry. These technical meanings are certainly not exclusive of others, and of course they contradict the idea that the pleasing animals, once "gentle, tame, and meek," have become "wild"—hunting dogs and hounds, even when fierce, are not wild. Yet it is probably not an accident that Wyatt uses three words associated with the hunt. The vocabulary of the field suggests that "they" who might once have been hunted have taken on the character of hunters.

"They" were perhaps never without their predatory aspect, and certainly "she" was not. The charm of the remembered erotic scene of the second stanza lies in the mistress's boldness in seduction, her overt display of her erotic power over her lover. Her ever-remembered utterance on the occasion makes this plain, and to Wyatt's audience her way of addressing her lover, "Dear heart," would have brought the idea of a deer, a hart, the pun being then a common one, the easier to make because there was no established difference in the spelling of the two words.

The "specialness" of the episode is superbly conveyed by the first line of the last stanza, "It was no dream; I lay broad waking," of which the very sound suggests the lover's incredulity over the delight of the event at the same time that he insists on its actuality.

Wyatt's poem makes a particular appeal to modern taste because of the directness and colloquial simplicity of its diction: it avoids, as modern poetry characteristically does, any reliance on "poetical" language. Another claim upon modern admiration is the way it handles its metre. The basic pattern of the verse is iambic pentameter, a line of five feet, the foot being typically of two syllables with the stress on the second; for example, the first line of the poem, "They flée from mé that sómetime díd me séek," conforms to this pattern. But many of the succeeding lines—"Busily seeking with a continual change"; "And she me caught in her arms long and small"; "It was no dream; I lay broad waking"—clearly violate this metrical scheme. The prevailing modern supposition is that Wyatt knew exactly what he was doing, that he broke the pattern to achieve the effects he desired. But according to older opinion, Wyatt wrote as he did out of ignorance or incompetence; he was thought to have a bad ear and no control over metrics.

This opinion was established, at least by implication, within a few years after Wyatt's death, in 1557, when Tottel's famous miscellany, *Songs and Sonnets*, was published. Although Wyatt would seem to have had a considerable reputation as a poet, his poems had never been printed in his lifetime, and the *Miscellany* was his first significant publication. To judge by the large space he gave to Wyatt's poems, the editor of the volume had a general admiration of the poet. But he took rather a dim view of Wyatt's skill as a metrist, revising the poems extensively to make them suit the taste of a period which esteemed verse that was "musical" in a mellifluous way. The text of the poem that I use in this book is that of Wyatt's manuscript, except that the spelling has been modernized. Here is the revised and "corrected" version as it appeared in the *Miscellany*, with the spelling modernized:

> They flee from me, that sometime did me seek
> With naked foot stalking within my chamber.
> Once have I seen them gentle, tame, and meek,
> That now are wild, and do not once remember
> That sometime they have put themselves in danger,
> To take bread at my hand; and now they range,
> Busily seeking in continual change.
>   Thanked be fortune, it hath been otherwise
> Twenty times better; but once especial,
> In thin array, after a pleasant guise,
> When her loose gown did from her shoulders fall,
> And she me caught in her arms long and small,
> And therewithal so sweetly did me kiss,
> And softly said, "Dear heart, how like you this?"
>   It was no dream, for I lay broad awaking.
> But all is turned now, through my gentleness,
> Into a bitter fashion of forsaking;
> And I have leave to go, of her goodness,
> And she also to use newfangleness.
> But since that I unkindly so am served,
> How like you this? what hath she now deserved?

The emendations make a poem that is no doubt prettier than the original but, by that token, a poem less masculine and strong. They dispose of any questions about stress that the original version might present to us, but in doing this deprive the poem of a considerable part of its interest. When, for example, the two syllables are added to the line we have had occasion to notice and we read it as regular iambic pentameter, "It wás no dreám, for Í lay bróad awák-ing,"[1] it comes very smoothly off the tongue, but how much firmer, bolder, and more dramatic is the line as Wyatt actually wrote it. When we speak the original line aloud, our emphasis falls very decisively: once we are aware that it is not conforming to the pattern, we say, "It was nó dream," or perhaps, "It was no dréam," for either stress is possible and our freedom to choose between the two makes the phrase the more engaging. Then as we go on to the second half of the line, "I lay broad waking," our stress falls weightily on "broad" and we naturally tend to sustain the sound for a perceptible instant in order to accomplish the somewhat difficult transition to the stressed syllable that immediately follows, for in the line as Wyatt wrote it we naturally stress "waking" equally with "broad." The emended line, compared to the original, is light, easy, and relatively characterless, and the same judgment can be made on all the other editorial changes in the poem.

But aware as we may be of Wyatt's bold colloquialism and his roughness of metre, we must not leave out of account in our response to the poem the part played in it by formal strictness. The stanza that Wyatt uses is the so-called Rhyme Royal, which has a tradition going back to Chaucer and the Scottish poets; Shakespeare was later to use it for his *Rape of Lucrece*. The stanza moves with an energy that is at once vivacious and grave, and its inherent elegance makes a happy frame for the colloquial directness of the lines themselves.

There is one point at which we may regard the Tottel version with some degree of sympathy, in its revision of the last two lines of the poem. The editor's repetition of "How like you this?" would seem to express his sense that the stanza should be brought into a firmer relation with the rest of the poem, that it dissipates rather than discharges the energy that the first two stanzas have built up. Certainly the lover's plaint creates the effect of diffuseness, even of anticlimax. In fact, for many readers the meaning of these lines proves far too elusive, or, if discovered, inadequate to the earlier stanzas of the poem. It is not difficult to understand that the lover's "gentleness" should have been the cause of his mistress's indifference and infidelity. But why is the "fashion of forsaking" a "strange" one? (Although one would rather have it a "strange" than a "bitter" fashion, as in the revised version.) That the lover should have been given "leave to go" by the mistress's "goodness" is an irony which is either obscure or too simple, and it is certainly not clear why she has need of her own "goodness" to give her leave to "use newfangleness." Even if we have in mind the old meaning of "kindly"—that is, "naturally"—the irony of "But since that I so kindely am served" seems querulous (perhaps that is one reason why Tottel changes it to "unkindly") and the question about what the mistress "hath deserved" has the aspect of mere petulance.

Yet so great is the authority of what has gone before in the poem that many readers are not disposed to be severe upon the faults they find in the conclusion. Their love of the whole leads them to decide that the troubling part is not so much a failure as a puzzle.

[1] The concluding extra syllable does not make it irregular. Even a strict adherence to rule does not require only a series of five iambics to a line.

A VALEDICTION
Forbidding Mourning

JOHN DONNE
1573–1631

As virtuous men pass mildly away,
    And whisper to their souls, to go
Whilst some of their sad friends do say,
    The breath goes now, and some say, no:

So let us melt, and make no noise,   5
    No tear-floods, nor sigh-tempests move,
'Twere profanation of our joys
    To tell the laity our love.

Moving of th' earth brings harms and fears,
    Men reckon what it did and meant,   10
But trepidation of the spheres,
    Though greater far, is innocent.[1]

Dull sublunary[2] lovers' love
    (Whose soul is sense[3]) cannot admit
Absence, because it does remove   15
    Those things which elemented[4] it.

But we by a love, so much refin'd,
    That our selves know not what it is,
Inter-assurèd of the mind,
    Care less, eyes, lips, and hands to miss.   20

Our two souls therefore, which are one,
    Though I must go, endure not yet

---

[1] "Trepidation," in Ptolemaic astronomy, referred to motion of the outermost of the nine transparent spheres that comprised the universe, which caused the "innocent" or harmless variation in the occurrence of the equinox. [2] Terrestrial, and hence, inferior. [3] Sensuality. [4] Constituted.

A breach, but an expansion,
    Like gold to airy thinness beat.

If they be two, they are two so   25
    As stiff twin compasses[5] are two,
Thy soul the fix'd foot, makes no show
    To move, but doth, if th' other do.

And though it in the center sit,
    Yet when the other far doth roam,   30
It leans, and hearkens after it,
    And grows erect, as that comes home.

Such wilt thou be to me, who must
    Like th' other foot, obliquely run;
Thy firmness makes my circle just,[6]   35
    And makes me end, where I begun.

COMMENTARY

In 1912 the Oxford University Press published Professor H. J. C. Grierson's edition of the poems of John Donne, two handsomely printed volumes bound in the familiar Oxford dark-blue cloth. The first volume contained the poems, many of which had never before been printed; the second volume was devoted to notes which dealt with problems of the text and explicated the often obscure philosophical, scientific, and historical allusions. Perhaps no other work of English literary scholarship in our century is so famous or has had so much influence.

It would not be true to say that Donne had been unknown or unvalued in the nineteenth century and the first years of the twentieth. Edmund Gosse's biography in 1899 and three editions of the poetical works between 1872 and 1896 attest to a continuing awareness of the poet. But he was likely to be considered a minor figure, interesting chiefly for the vivacious idiosyncrasies of his style and for the discrepancy between the bold cynicism of his early poems and the passionate religious intensity of his later years when, after taking holy orders, he became one of the notable figures of the Church of England. Historians of literature were not disposed to study his work in any particularity and the criticism of the day scarcely took him into account. After Grierson's edition, however, Donne came to be seen as a pre-eminent figure not only of the seventeenth century but of the whole of English literature. The scholarly and critical studies of his work proliferated rapidly and are by now innumerable.

Yet Donne in his own time had been greatly admired; he had fallen into

[5] One pair of dividers.   [6] Perfect.

disesteem only in the eighteenth century. The reasons for the decline were formulated in Dr. Samuel Johnson's essay on Cowley in *The Lives of the English Poets*. In a passage that has become a *locus classicus* of English criticism, Johnson dealt with the group of seventeenth-century poets whom he called "metaphysical." He used the word, in the fashion of his time, with the intention of reproach, to characterize a kind of poetry that he considered so abstruse, fine-drawn, and far-fetched as to be quite out of accord with good sense and even nature itself. Johnson's name for the group established itself and is still in use, although without any of its former pejorative meaning.[1]

The first characteristic of the metaphysical poets remarked on by Johnson was their learning and their desire to exhibit it. They took pleasure in deriving the elements of their poems from esoteric knowledge of all kinds and, in what to Johnson seemed an extravagant desire to be original and striking, they brought together facts and ideas which he thought incongruous and therefore unnatural; they filled their poems, he said, with "enormous and disgusting hyperboles," their figures of speech were often "grossly absurd" and sometimes "indelicate." They gave precedence to ingenuity over emotion, with the result that "their courtship was void of fondness and their lamentations of sorrow. Their wish was only to say what they hoped had never been said before."

By their excessive concern with minute particularities they transgressed against a chief tenet of eighteenth-century poetic theory, which held that poetry's most impressive effects were to be gained through spacious generalizations. "Great thoughts," said Johnson, "are always general, and consist in positions not limited by exceptions, and in descriptions not descending to minuteness." Dryden, while belittling Donne as a poet, had conceded that he was to be praised for his wit, but Johnson, defining wit "as a kind of *discordia concors,* a combination of dissimilar images or discovery of occult resemblances in things apparently unlike," concluded that "of wit thus defined" Donne and his fellows "have more than enough." The versification of the metaphysical poets won as little approval from Johnson as their diction and imagery—he judged it to be wholly contrived and inept. He does not deny these poets a measure of respect, but the praise it yields is small indeed: "Yet great labor, directed by great abilities is never wholly lost: if they frequently threw away their wit upon false conceits, they likewise sometimes struck out unexpected truth; if their conceits were far-fetched, they were often worth the carriage. To write on their plan, it was at least necessary to read and think."

But early in the nineteenth century the pendulum of taste began its swing to a more favorable view of the metaphysical school, especially Donne. Coleridge anticipated modern opinion when he spoke of Donne's "force" and observed that his "most fantastic out of the way thoughts" were expressed in "the most pure and genuine mother English." Still, that a sense of Donne as odd and eccentric and not in the line of succession of the great English poets qualified Coleridge's admiration is made clear in his much-quoted lines describing Donne's poetical mode:

> With Donne, whose muse on dromedary trots,
> Wreathe iron pokers into true-love knots;
> Rhyme's sturdy cripple, fancy's maze and clue,
> Wit's forge and fire-blast, meaning's press and screw.

[1] Although Dryden had earlier said that "Donne affects the metaphysics," it was Johnson who gave currency to the adjective as a way of characterizing a mode of writing.

Later in the century, two other poets, Browning and Hopkins, both of them antagonistic to the prevailing belief that English verse was at its best when it was harmonious and "smooth," found an affinity with Donne and his dromedary-mounted muse and Rosetti and Swinburne held him in esteem especially for his love-poetry. But no poet of the nineteenth century could speak of him with Yeats's intensity of praise, an intensity that actually comes close to nonsense—writing to thank Professor Grierson for the gift of his edition, Yeats says of Donne that "he who is but a man like us all has seen God."

The new enthusiasm for Donne is explained, of course, by the confirmation he gave to an important tendency of modern poetry. A celebrated statement of what the new poets found in him was made by T. S. Eliot in his review of an anthology of the metaphysical poets that Grierson published in 1921. For Eliot the characteristic virtue of the seventeenth-century poets was their ability to "feel their thought," to experience it as if it were a sensation, "as immediately as the odor of a rose." At some point later in the century, Eliot goes on to say, there occurred a "dissociation of sensibility," and thought and feeling in poetry became separated from each other. Eliot does not refer explicitly to Johnson's objection that metaphysical poetry was excessively intellectual at the cost of feeling, but when he says of Donne that to him "a thought was an experience, it modified his sensibility," it is obviously Johnson's view which he has in mind and means to contradict. Yeats had said much the same thing in his letter to Grierson: "Your notes tell me exactly what I want to know. Poems that I could not understand or could but understand are now clear and I notice that the more precise and learned the thought the greater the beauty, the passion; the intricacies and subtleties of his imagination are the length and depths of the furrows made by his passion."

It was not only Donne's power of conjoining thought and emotion that seemed so important to the modern poets but also his taking it for granted that any of the seemingly disparate elements of experience might be brought together with interesting and significant effect. The conjunction of things and ideas not usually believed to consort with each other had seemed to Dr. Johnson to be a poetical vice, a departure from nature. The modern poets, and after them the modern critics, held it to be a poetical virtue, and exactly because it was natural, at least for poets. "When a poet's mind is perfectly equipped for its work," Eliot said, "it is constantly amalgamating disparate experience; the ordinary man's experience is chaotic, irregular, fragmentary. The latter falls in love or reads Spinoza, and these two experiences can have nothing to do with each other, or with the noise of the typewriter or the smell of cooking; in the mind of the poet these experiences are always forming wholes." This well-known passage exemplifies the tendency of modern writers to reject the belief that there are orders of experience, distinct in themselves and separate from each other, of which some are appropriate to art, others inappropriate.

Donne's versification was no less important to the new poets than the quality of his thought and feeling. What Dr. Johnson and most eighteenth-century readers heard as "rugged" verse and therefore unpleasing, what Coleridge heard as powerful but ungraceful, the trot of the dromedary, the limp of the sturdy cripple, was heard by the poets of the twentieth century as the authoritative accent of actuality. They understood—as had the readers of the seventeenth century—that Donne did not fail in an attempt to conform to the demands of a metrical system but that he wrote a kind of verse in which the rhythms of the natural speaking voice assert themselves against, and modify, the strict pattern of the metre. It is worth noting that Yeats received the gift of Grierson's edition at the point in his development when, under the influence of Ezra Pound, his verse was moving steadily away from the relatively soft and "poetic" mode of his early work to the harder, more downright and forceful versification (and diction) of his great period.

In reading "A Valediction: Forbidding Mourning" it is the voice of the poem that first engages our attention. The opening line is audacious in its avoidance of the metre that is to be established in the following lines of the stanza and maintained through the rest of the poem, although not in a strict or mechanical way; no matter how we read it, we cannot scan that opening line, and its bold freedom leads us to feel that it is saying something "actual" rather than "poetic." The succeeding lines, although controlled by metre, sustain this feeling; they sound in the ear as the utterance of a present speaker. It is in the ambience of the speaker's voice that the metaphysical elements of the poem are presented to us. The comparison between the significance of earthquakes and the "trepidation of the spheres" and the brief simile of the beaten gold, the elaborated simile of the pair of compasses, are the less likely to seem merely ingenious, or studied, or out of the way, because they are suffused with the tones of the voice that proposes them, its directness and masculine vigor, its gravity and its serious humor.

Dr. Johnson took particular notice of the compass simile, introducing his quotation of the three stanzas in which it is developed with this sentence: "To the following comparison of a man that travels and his wife that stays at home, with a pair of compasses, it may be doubted whether absurdity or ingenuity has a better claim." For Johnson the absurdity lay in the fact that compasses seemed to him to be incongruous with the emotional circumstances they were meant to represent. A pair of compasses suggests what is mechanical and unfeeling: it is metallic and stiff, and an instrument of precision employed in, and emblematic of, the sternly rational and abstract discipline of geometry; it therefore stands at the furthest remove from the emotion of love. The simile of the compasses substantiated Johnson's opinion that metaphysical poetry cannot express emotion and is "void of fondness."

Although we will perceive as readily as Dr. Johnson that there is some measure of unlikelihood in the comparison, this will not prevent our having pleasure in it. On the contrary, we will tend to be pleased exactly because we are taken aback. For us, the figure's suggestion of cold rationality and abstractness is modified by the humor with which it is developed, a humor which does not in the least diminish the direct sincerity of the utterance. Isaac Walton, in his brief life of his friend, tells us that Donne composed the poem in 1611 while he was on a diplomatic mission to France and that it was addressed to his wife Anne. The marriage was a famous one in its day, both because of the tempestuous courtship that preceded it and the unbroken tender devotion of the husband and wife. Walton mentions the circumstance in which the poem was written and the person to whom it was addressed out of his sense that the poem, for all the ingenuity of its "conceits," is a direct, personal, and fully felt communication, wholly appropriate to its occasion. With this judgment the modern reader would find it hard to disagree.

LYCIDAS[1]

JOHN MILTON
1608–1674

In This Monody the Author Bewails a Learned Friend, Unfortunately Drowned in His Passage from Chester on the Irish Seas, 1637; and, by Occasion, Foretells the Ruin of Our Corrupted Clergy, Then in Their Height.

Yet once more, O ye laurels, and once more,
Ye myrtles brown,[2] with ivy never sere,
I come to pluck your berries harsh and crude,[3]
And with forced fingers rude
Shatter your leaves before the mellowing year.　　　　　　5
Bitter constraint, and sad occasion dear[4]
Compels me to disturb your season due;
For Lycidas is dead, dead ere his prime,
Young Lycidas, and hath not left his peer.
Who would not sing for Lycidas? he knew　　　　　　10
Himself to sing, and build the lofty rhyme.
He must not float upon his watery bier
Unwept, and welter to the parching wind,
Without the meed of some melodious tear.
　　Begin, then, Sisters of the sacred well[5]　　　　　　15
That from beneath the seat of Jove doth spring;
Begin, and somewhat loudly sweep the string.
Hence with denial vain and coy excuse:
So may some gentle Muse[6]
With lucky words favour my destined urn,　　　　　　20
And as he passes turn,
And bid fair peace be to my sable[7] shroud!
For we[8] were nursed upon the self-same hill,
Fed the same flock, by fountain, shade, and rill.
　　Together both, ere the high lawns appeared　　　　　　25
Under the opening eyelids of the Morn,
We drove a-field, and both together heard

---

[1] Lycidas is the name of a shepherd in a poem by the Roman poet, Virgil. Milton's "Lycidas" was Edward King (1612–1637), a college friend who drowned in the Irish Sea. [2] Dark, dusky. [3] Unripe. Laurel, myrtle, and ivy are symbols of immortality that poets were crowned with in ancient Greece. [4] Keenly felt. [5] The Muses, Greek deities of the arts and sciences to whom all creative inspiration was attributed. [6] Here, poet, one inspired by a Muse. [7] Black. [8] Lycidas and the poet.

What time the gray-fly[9] winds[10] her sultry horn,
Battening[11] our flocks with the fresh dews of night,
Oft till the star that rose, at evening, bright 30
Toward heaven's descent had sloped his westering wheel.[12]
Meanwhile the rural ditties were not mute;
Tempered to[13] the oaten flute,
Rough Satyrs[14] danced, and Fauns[15] with cloven heel
From the glad sound would not be absent long; 35
And old Damaetas[16] loved to hear our song.

     But, oh! the heavy change, now thou art gone,
Now thou art gone and never must return!
Thee, Shepherd, thee the woods and desert caves,
With wild thyme and the gadding[17] vine o'ergrown, 40
And all their echoes, mourn.
The willows, and the hazel copses green,
Shall now no more be seen
Fanning their joyous leaves to thy soft lays.[18]
As killing as the canker[19] to the rose, 45
Or taint-worm to the weanling herds that graze,
Or frost to flowers, that their gay wardrobe wear,
When first the white-thorn blows;
Such, Lycidas, thy loss to shepherd's ear.

     Where were ye, Nymphs, when the remorseless deep 50
Closed o'er the head of your loved Lycidas?
For neither were ye playing on the steep
Where your old bards, the famous Druids,[20] lie,
Nor on the shaggy top of Mona[21] high,
Nor yet where Deva[22] spreads her wizard stream. 55
Ay me! I fondly dream
"Had ye been there"—for what could that have done?
What could the Muse herself that Orpheus bore,[23]
The Muse herself, for her enchanting son,
Whom universal nature did lament, 60
When, by the rout that made the hideous roar,
His gory visage down the stream was sent,
Down the swift Hebrus to the Lesbian shore?

     Alas! what boots it[24] with uncessant care
To tend the homely, slighted, shepherd's trade, 65
And strictly meditate the thankless Muse?
Were it not better done, as others use,

---

[9] Insect that flies with a loud humming noise.   [10] Blows.   [11] Fattening, feeding.
[12] Venus, the "evening star," appears in the western sky.   [13] In time with.   [14] In Greek
mythology, goat-men who lived in the woodlands and spent much time in amorous pursuit of the nymphs.   [15] Satyr-like beings.   [16] Name for a herdsman that, like "Lycidas,"
comes from Virgil.   [17] Spreading aimlessly.   [18] Tunes, poems.   [19] Cankerworm.
[20] Priests and poets (bards), of ancient Britain.   [21] The isle of Anglesey, off the coast of
Wales; it was a Druidic center.   [22] The river Dee, which runs through England and
Wales.   [23] Calliope, Muse of epic poetry, was the mother of Orpheus, who was torn to
pieces by drunken worshippers of Bacchus. His head floated down the Hebrus to the island
of Lesbos.   [24] Of what advantage is it?

To sport with Amaryllis in the shade,
Or with the tangles of Neaera's hair?[25]
Fame is the spur that the clear spirit doth raise   70
(That last infirmity of noble mind)
To scorn delights, and live laborious days;
But the fair guerdon[26] when we hope to find,
And think to burst out into sudden blaze,
Comes the blind Fury[27] with the abhorrèd shears,   75
And slits the thin-spun life. "But not the praise,"
Phoebus[28] replied, and touched my trembling ears:
"Fame is no plant that grows on mortal soil,
Nor in the glistering foil[29]
Set off to the world, nor in broad rumour lies,   80
But lives and spreads aloft by those pure eyes,
And perfect witness of all-judging Jove;
As he pronounces lastly on each deed,
Of such fame in heaven expect thy meed."
　　　O fountain Arethuse,[30] and thou honoured flood,   85
Smooth-sliding Mincius,[31] crowned with vocal reeds,
That strain I heard was of a higher mood.
But now my oat[32] proceeds,
And listens to the Herald of the Sea[33]
That came in Neptune's[34] plea.   90
He asked the waves, and asked the felon winds,
What hard mishap hath doomed this gentle swain?
And questioned every gust of rugged wings
That blows from off each beakèd promontory.
They knew not of his story;   95
And sage Hippotades[35] their answer brings;
That not a blast was from his dungeon strayed,
The air was calm, and on the level brine
Sleek Panope with all her sisters[36] played.
It was that fatal and perfidious bark,   100
Built in the eclipse, and rigged with curses dark,
That sunk so low that sacred head of thine.
　　　Next, Camus,[37] reverend sire, went footing slow,
His mantle hairy, and his bonnet sedge,
Inwrought with figures dim, and on the edge   105
Like to that sanguine flower[38] inscribed with woe.

---

[25] Amaryllis and Neaera are traditional names for nymphs. [26] Reward. [27] Probably Atropos, the Fate who cuts the thread of life. (Milton, perhaps intentionally, confuses the Fates and the Furies here.) [28] Apollo, god of—among other things—poetic inspiration. [29] A thin metal leaf used as a background for a precious stone to increase its brilliance. [30] The traditional fountain of pastoral verse in Sicily. The nymph Arethusa, pursued by the river-god Alpheus (see line 132), was changed into a fountain by Diana. [31] A river in Lombardy, Italy, that Virgil once lived near. [32] Pastoral song (see "oaten flute," line 33 above). [33] Triton, a merman, who here pleads the innocence of the sea in causing Lycidas' death. [34] Neptune was the Roman god of the sea. [35] Aeolus, god of the winds. [36] Water nymphs. [37] The river Cam, representing Cambridge University, where Milton and King first knew each other. [38] The hyacinth, which is said to bear markings resembling the Greek word for "alas."

"Ah! who hath reft," quoth he, "my dearest pledge?"[39]
Last came, and last did go,
The Pilot of the Galilean Lake;[40]
Two massy keys he bore of metals twain   110
(The golden opes, the iron shuts amain).
He shook his mitred locks, and stern bespake:—
"How well could I have spared for thee, young swain,
Enow of such as, for their bellies' sake,
Creep, and intrude, and climb into the fold!   115
Of other care they little reckoning make
Than how to scramble at the shearers' feast,
And shove away the worthy bidden guest.
Blind mouths! that scarce themselves know how to hold
A sheep-hook, or have learnt aught else the least   120
That to the faithful herdman's art belongs!
What recks it them? What need they? They are sped;[41]
And, when they list,[42] their lean and flashy songs
Grate on their scrannel[43] pipes of wretched straw;
The hungry sheep look up, and are not fed,   125
But, swoln with wind and the rank mist they draw,
Rot inwardly, and foul contagion spread;
Besides what the grim wolf[44] with privy paw
Daily devours apace, and nothing said.
But that two-handed engine at the door   130
Stands ready to smite once, and smite no more."[45]
    Return, Alpheus;[46] the dread voice is past
That shrunk thy streams; return, Sicilian Muse,[47]
And call the vales, and bid them hither cast
Their bells and flowerets of a thousand hues.   135
Ye valleys low, where the mild whispers use
Of shades, and wanton winds, and gushing brooks,
On whose fresh lap the swart star[48] sparely looks,
Throw hither all your quaint enamelled eyes,
That on the green turf suck the honeyed showers,   140
And purple all the ground with vernal flowers.
Bring the rathe[49] primrose that forsaken dies,
The tufted crow-toe, and pale jessamine,
The white pink, and the pansy freaked[50] with jet,
The glowing violet,   145

---

39 "Who hath taken away my dearest child?"   40 St. Peter, wearing a bishop's miter
(he was the first bishop of Rome) and carrying the keys of heaven. Edward King is
mourned as a poet, as a scholar, and now as a churchman.   41 What does it matter to
them? What do they need? They have fared well.   42 Want, desire.   43 Feeble.   44 Probably the Anglican Church.   45 That is, the corrupt clergy will be punished finally and
absolutely. What the "two-handed engine" is has been much debated. "Not less than 34
different explanations have been traced in print" (Le Comte, *A Milton Dictionary*). The
likeliest explanation is that it refers to the two-handled sword of the Archangel Michael.
46 The lover of Arethusa; they both symbolize pastoral poetry. He has fled from the "dread
voice" of St. Peter.   47 The muse of Theocritus, a poet of ancient Greece, and others who
wrote pastorals.   48 Sirius, the Dog Star. It is called "swart" because it rises in the late
summer when heat scorches and darkens vegetation.   49 Early.   50 Spotted.

The musk rose, and the well-attired woodbine,
With cowslips wan that hang the pensive head,
And every flower that sad embroidery wears;
Bid amaranthus all his beauty shed,
And daffadillies fill their cups with tears,   150
To strew the laureate hearse where Lycid lies.
For so, to interpose a little ease,
Let our frail thoughts dally with false surmise.
Ay me! whilst thee the shores and sounding seas
Wash far away, where'er thy bones are hurled;   155
Whether beyond the stormy Hebrides,
Where thou perhaps under the whelming tide
Visit'st the bottom of the monstrous[51] world;
Or whether thou, to our moist vows denied,
Sleep'st by the fable of Bellerus[52] old,   160
Where the great Vision of the guarded mount[53]
Looks toward Namancos and Bayona's hold.
Look homeward, Angel, now, and melt with ruth:
And, O ye dolphins, waft[54] the hapless youth.[55]
    Weep no more, woeful shepherds, weep no more,   165
For Lycidas, your sorrow, is not dead,
Sunk though he be beneath the watery floor.
So sinks the day-star[56] in the ocean bed,
And yet anon repairs his drooping head,
And tricks his beams, and with new-spangled ore   170
Flames in the forehead of the morning sky:
So Lycidas sunk low, but mounted high,
Through the dear might of Him that walked the waves,[57]
Where, other groves and other streams along,
With nectar pure his oozy locks he laves,   175
And hears the unexpressive[58] nuptial songs,
In the blest kingdoms meek of joy and love.
There entertain him all the Saints above,
In solemn troops, and sweet societies,
That sing, and singing in their glory move,   180
And wipe the tears for ever from his eyes.
Now, Lycidas, the shepherds weep no more;
Henceforth thou art the Genius[59] of the shore,
In thy large recompense, and shalt be good
To all that wander in that perilous flood.   185
    Thus sang the uncouth swain to the oaks and rills,
While the still morn went out with sandals grey:
He touched the tender stops of various quills,[60]

[51] Full of sea monsters.   [52] A mythical Cornish giant.   [53] Off Land's End in Corn-wall, a large rock, traditionally guarded by the archangel Michael, points towards Namancos (Nemancos) and Bayona in Spain.   [54] Bear, carry (through water or air).   [55] Dolphins rescued Arion, a semimythical poet who was attacked at sea by sailors who intended to rob him.   [56] The sun.   [57] Christ.   [58] Inexpressible.   [59] Protective spirit.   [60] Holes in different reeds, or pipes of Pan.

With eager thought warbling his Doric[61] lay:
And now the sun had stretched out all the hills,   190
And now was dropt into the western bay;
At last he rose, and twitched his mantle blue:
To-morrow to fresh woods, and pastures new.

COMMENTARY

It is often said by critics and teachers of literature that "Lycidas" is the greatest lyric poem in the English language, and very likely it is. But the word "greatest" applied to a work of art is not always serviceable; the superlative judgment can immobilize a reader's response to a work, or arouse his skeptical resistance. It may be that we are given a more enlightening introduction to the poem by a critic who held it in low esteem—so far from thinking that "Lycidas" was superlatively great, Samuel Johnson thought it a very bad poem. Without doubt Dr. Johnson was wrong in this judgment and the grounds on which he bases it are quite mistaken. But his erroneous views, stated in his characteristically bold and unequivocal fashion, make plain how the poem ought to be regarded.

The sum of Dr. Johnson's objections is that "Lycidas" is insincere. It purports to be a poem of mourning; the poet is expressing grief over the death of a friend. But can we possibly believe in the truth of his emotion? Grief, Dr. Johnson says in effect, inclines to be silent or at least to be simple in its utterance. It does not express itself so elaborately, with as much artifice as Milton uses or with such a refinement of fancy and such a proliferation of reference to ancient legend and lore. "Passion plucks no berries from myrtle or ivy," Dr. Johnson said, "nor calls upon Arethuse and Mincius, nor tells of rough *satyrs* or *fauns with cloven heels*. Where there is leisure for fiction, there is little grief."

Of the poem's elaborateness of artifice, even of artificiality, there can be no question. The poet does not speak in his own person but in the guise of a "shepherd" or "swain." That is to say, he expresses his grief, such as it is, through the literary convention known as the pastoral, so called because all the persons represented in it are shepherds (the Latin word for shepherd is *pastor*). This convention of poetry has a long history. It goes back to the Greek poet Theocritus (c. 310–250 B.C.), who, in certain of his poems, pretended that he and his poet-friends were shepherds of his native Sicily. Far removed from the sophistication and corruption of cities, the fancied shepherds of Theocritus devoted themselves to the care of their flocks and to two innocent pursuits—song and the cultivation of love and friendship. Their only ambition was to be accomplished in song; their only source of unhappiness was a lost love or the death of a friend, the latter being rather more grievous than the former and making the occasion for an *elegy*, a poem of lament. Virgil brought the pastoral convention into Roman literature with his *Eclogues,* and it was largely through his influence that it became enormously popular in the Renaissance. This popularity continued through the eighteenth century, but the mechanical way

[61] Pastoral.

in which it came to be used in much of the verse of that period justifies Dr. Johnson in speaking of the pastoral mode as "easy, vulgar, and therefore disgusting." In the nineteenth century the convention lost its vogue, but even then it was used for two great elegies, Shelley's "Adonais" and Matthew Arnold's "Thyrsis." For the poets of our time it seems to have no interest.

The fictional nature of the pastoral was never in doubt. Nobody was supposed to believe and nobody did believe that the high-minded poetic herdsmen were real, in charge of actual flocks. Yet the fiction engaged men's imagination for so long a time because it fulfilled so real a desire of mankind—it speaks of simplicity and innocence, youth and beauty, love and art. And although the poets were far from claiming actuality for their pastoral fancies, they often used the convention to criticize actual conditions of life, either explicitly as Milton does in the passage on the English clergy (lines 108–131) or by implication.

The traditional and avowedly artificial nature of the pastoral was exactly suited to the occasion which produced "Lycidas." Milton could scarcely have felt at Edward King's death the "passion" that Dr. Johnson blames him for not expressing, for King, although a college mate, had not been a close friend. He composed "Lycidas" not on spontaneous impulse but at the invitation of a group of Cambridge men who were bringing out a volume of poems to commemorate King. For Milton to have pretended to an àcute sense of personal loss would have been truly an insincerity. Yet he could not fail to respond to what we might call the general pathos of a former comrade's dying "ere his prime," and by means of the pastoral elegy he was able to do what was beautifully appropriate to the situation—he associated King's death with a long tradition in which the deaths of young men had been lamented. Ever since the dawn of literature the death of a young man has been felt to have an especial pathos— how often it is evoked in the *Iliad;* and few things in the Bible are more affecting than David's mourning for his young friend Jonathan and his young son Absolom. It is this traditional pathos that Milton evokes from the death of Edward King. Had he tried to achieve a more personal expression of feeling, we should have responded not more but less. What engages us is exactly the universality of the emotion.

The pastoral convention is also appropriate to King's commemoration in two other respects. One is the extent to which the pastoral elegy was known and cultivated by young men in the English universities of Milton's time, if only because in their study of the ancient languages they were assigned the task of composing verses in this genre. Milton's own earliest-known poems are such college exercises, and all the poets who are mentioned or referred to in "Lycidas"—Theocritus, Virgil, Ovid—were subjects of university study. And in Milton's age as in ours, the college days of a young man were thought to have something like a pastoral quality—from mature life men look back to that time as being more carefree, and to their relationships then as having been more generous, disinterested, and comradely than now: why else do college alumni return each spring to their old campuses? Our very word *alumnus* expresses what Milton means when he says that he and King were "nurs'd upon the selfsame hill," for an *alumnus* is a foster child, a nursling of *alma mater,* the fostering mother.

Dr. Johnson did not make it an item in his charge of insincerity that

Milton, mourning a young man dead, is so preoccupied with a young man alive —himself. But we cannot fail to see that this is the case. Milton begins his poem with an unabashed self-reference, to his feeling about himself as a young poet who has not yet reached the point of his development when he is ready to appear before the public. One reason he gives for overcoming his reluctance and undertaking the poem in memory of King is his hope that this will make it the more likely that someone will write to commemorate him when he dies. When he speaks about the poetic career and about poetic fame in relation to death, it is manifestly his own career and fame and his own death that he has in mind —the thought arouses him to a proud avowal of his sense of his high calling. And as the poem concludes, it is again to himself that he refers. Having discharged his duty of mourning, he turns from death and sorrow back to life and his own purposes:

> At last he rose, and twitch'd his mantle blue:
> To-morrow to fresh woods, and pastures new.

These passages have led many readers to conclude that "Lycidas" is not about Edward King at all but about John Milton. They are quite content that this should be so. They take the view that though the poem may fail in its avowed intention, it succeeds in an intention that it does not avow—they point to the fact that the most memorable and affecting parts of the poem are those in which Milton is his own subject. But in weighing this opinion we might ask whether it is ever possible to grieve for a person to whom we feel akin without grieving for ourselves, and, too, whether the intensity with which we are led to imagine our own inevitable death is not a measure of the kinship we feel with the person who has already died. Certainly nothing in "Lycidas" more strongly enforces upon us the pathos of untimely death than that it puts the poet in mind of his own death—for what he says of himself we are bound to feel of ourselves. And how better represent the sadness of death than to put it beside the poet's imagination of the fulness of life?

It must also be observed that Milton speaks of the death of Edward King and of his own imagined death and actual life in a context that does not permit our mere ordinary sense of the personal to prevail. He brings them into conjunction not only with the traditional pathos of young men dead ere their prime but also with the traditional evocations of the death of young gods, and their resurrection. No religious ceremonies of the ancient peoples were more fervently performed than those in which the death of a young male deity— Osiris, Adonis, Atys, Thammuz—was mourned and his resurrection rejoiced in. The myths of these gods and the celebration of their death and rebirth represented the cycles of the vital forces; the dying and reborn god symbolized the sun in its annual course, the processes of vegetation, the sexual and procreative energy, and sometimes, as in the case of Orpheus, poetic genius. Once we are aware of this, Milton's concern with himself takes on a larger significance. It is not himself-the-person that Milton is meditating upon but himself-the-poet: that is, he is thinking about himself in the service not of his own interests but of the interests of the "divine" power that he bears within him.

In this service Milton is properly associated with Edward King, who was also a poet—it does not matter that King was not distinguished in his art. But there was yet another aspect of the service of divine power in the fact that King was a clergyman, a priest of the Church of England, which licenses the inclusion in the elegy of St. Peter's explosion of wrath against the negligent and corrupt clergy of the time. This famous passage constitutes only a small part of the poem, but the importance that Milton gave it is made plain by his extended reference to it in the "argument." Some readers will find a bitter condemnation of clerical corruption inappropriate to an elegy, and will be jarred and dismayed by the sudden introduction of Christian personages and considerations into a poem that has been, up to this point, consistently pagan. That Milton is himself quite aware that the passage will seem incongruous to the pastoral form is indicated in the lines in which he invokes the "return" of the "Sicilian Muse," who has been scared away by St. Peter's "dread voice." But in Milton's thought ancient pagan literature and mythology and the Judaeo-Christian religion were never really at odds with each other. It is a salient characteristic of his great and enormously learned mind that Milton gave allegiance to both, and used for Christian ideas the literary forms of paganism. In the pastoral convention he found a natural conjunction of the two: we can readily see that the poetic convention has affinity with the feelings attached to the pastoral life by Biblical Judaism and, more elaborately, by Christianity. The peaceable Abel was a shepherd and so was Abraham. So was David, and a poet-shepherd at that, one of whose psalms begins, "The Lord is my Shepherd, I shall not want." It was shepherds who saw the Star of Bethlehem rise; Jesus is both the Lamb of God and the Good Shepherd. *Pastor* is the name for the priest of a parish, the congregation being his flock, and the form of a bishop's crozier is the shepherd's crook.[1]

As the poem moves toward its conclusion the mingling of pagan and Christian elements is taken wholly for granted. This conjunction of the two traditions exemplifies yet another characteristic of the poem, its inclusiveness. "Lycidas" gathers up all the world, things the most disparate in space and time and kind, and concentrates them in one place and moment, brings them to bear upon one event, the death of the poet-priest. The poem's action is, as it were, summarized in the lines about "the great Vision" of St. Michael the Angel who, from Land's End, the southernmost tip of England, looks afar to Spain but is abjured to "look homeward." So the poem looks afar to the ancient world and also turns its gaze upon contemporary England. From "the bottom of the monstrous world" it turns to heaven, and from all the waters of the world to all the flowers of all the seasons of the Earth, and from the isolation of Lycidas in death to the "sweet societies" of his resurrection and everlasting life through the agency of Christ. It plays literary games with the most solemn sub-

---

[1] The affinity between the pagan and the Christian idealizations of the pastoral life was no doubt affirmed by the common belief that Virgil's fourth *Eclogue* was a prophecy of the birth of Christ. The Christian acceptance of the pagan convention imposed one small condition which it is amusing to note: Although I have referred throughout my comment to shepherds, the herdsmen of the Greek bucolic poets herded either sheep or goats, and, indeed, Milton took the name Lycidas from a character in a poem by Theocritus who was not a shepherd but a goatherd. But Christianity separates the sheep from the goats, regarding the latter with suspicion and even aversion—in fact, it assigns the physical attributes of the goat to the Devil himself—and does not permit their presence in pastoral poetry. When Spenser in *The Shepheardes Calender* mentions a "Goteheard," his anonymous pedantic contemporary who annotated the poems explains: "By Gotes in scrypture he represented the wicked and reprobate, whose pastour also must needes be such."

jects, and juxtaposes the gravest ideas with the smallest blossoms, using their most delicate or homely names (culminating in the daffadillies, which sound like the very essence of irresponsible frivolity). And then, when it has brought all the world together, and life out of death and faith out of despair, it has its "uncouth swain," the shepherd-poet, with the jauntiness of a task fully discharged, announce that the mourning is now at an end. Life calls the poet to other work and he must answer the call.

TO HIS
COY MISTRESS

ANDREW MARVELL
1621–1678

Had we but world enough, and time,
This coyness, Lady, were no crime.
We would sit down and think which way
To walk and pass our long love's day.
Thou by the Indian Ganges' side   5
Shouldst rubies find;[1] I by the tide
Of Humber[2] would complain.[3] I would
Love you ten years before the Flood,
And you should, if you please, refuse
Till the conversion of the Jews.   10
My vegetable love should grow
Vaster than empires, and more slow;
An hundred years should go to praise
Thine eyes and on thy forehead gaze;
Two hundred to adore each breast,   15
But thirty thousand to the rest;
An age at least to every part,
And the last age should show your heart.
For, Lady, you deserve this state,
Nor would I love at lower rate.   20
      But at my back I always hear
Time's winged chariot[4] hurrying near;
And yonder all before us lie
Deserts of vast eternity.
Thy beauty shall no more be found,   25
Nor, in thy marble vault, shall sound
My echoing song; then worms shall try[5]
That long preserved virginity,
And your quaint honor turn to dust,
And into ashes all my lust: 30

[1] Most rubies now come from Burma, but they might once have been mined from
the Ganges Delta.   [2] An estuary in England. Marvell's town, Hull, is on it.   [3] Lament.
[4] Probably an allusion to the chariot driven by Helios, the sun god of ancient Greece.
[5] Subject to a severe test.

The grave's a fine and private place,
But none, I think, do there embrace.
　　Now therefore, while the youthful hue
Sits on thy skin like morning dew,
And while thy willing soul transpires　　　　　　　　　35
At every pore with instant fires,
Now let us sport us while we may,
And now, like amorous birds of prey,
Rather at once our time devour
Than languish in his slow-chapped[6] power.　　　　　40
Let us roll all our strength and all
Our sweetness up into one ball,
And tear our pleasures with rough strife
Thorough the iron gates of life:
Thus, though we cannot make our sun　　　　　　　45
Stand still, yet we will make him run.

COMMENTARY

In his essay on Andrew Marvell, T. S. Eliot remarks that Marvell's best poems, which are few in number, "must be well known from the *Golden Treasury* and the *Oxford Book of English Verse.*" Eliot regards "To His Coy Mistress" as one of the best of Marvell's poems and certainly it is quite the best known, occupying a special place not only in the awareness but in the affection of the readers of our time. And it is, to be sure, found in the *Oxford Book of English Verse.* But it does not appear, as Eliot supposed, in the *Golden Treasury,* the famous anthology of English lyrical poems which has been in print ever since it was first published in 1861. The editor of the *Golden Treasury,* F. T. Palgrave, was a man of excellent literary judgment. From among Marvell's poems he chose three very good ones for his volume. But he did not choose "To His Coy Mistress"—which tells us much about the Victorian age and the nature of taste and how it changes.

　　Its omission is particularly interesting in the light of what Palgrave tells us of the high esteem in which it was held by his close friend Tennyson, an esteem that Palgrave himself clearly shared. When the *Golden Treasury* was in the making, Palgrave often discussed the selections with Tennyson; in his account of their conversations, the only one of the poet's opinions that he records in detail is the one about "To His Coy Mistress," which, Palgrave says, Tennyson delighted to read aloud, "dwelling more than once on the magnificent hyperbole, the powerful union of pathos and humor." Yet despite the great authority his friend's judgment had for Palgrave, it did not induce him to include the poem in his collection.

　　It would seem that a poem for which two Victorian gentlemen might express great admiration in private conversation could, because of its unsuitable moral and emotional tone, be thought inappropriate for the general public. The

---

6 Slowly devouring (*chap,* "jaw").

erotic content of the poem is of a quite explicit kind, and the intentions of the lover are not what the Victorian audience would have called "honorable," for it is not marriage that his urgency proposes to the lady. He speaks openly of his "lust" and slightingly of the lady's ideas of honor and virginity. Despite his preoccupation with time and mortality, he does not promise the lady that his love, after its consummation, will endure at least until death: he is concerned only with *now*, and in the last of the three movements of the poem the word occurs three times. Victorian morality put a great value upon chastity; it did not sanction the directly erotic impulse outside of marriage nor did it permit the literary representation of the erotic even in the married state. It could only have been offended by Marvell's frank naturalism, which takes no account of moral considerations and even suggests that they are set at naught by the inexorability of time and the inevitability of death.

The "powerful union of pathos and humor" to which Tennyson responded so warmly is undoubtedly the element of the poem that chiefly engages the present-day reader. But Palgrave had reason to suppose that the Victorian audience would be made uncomfortable by this very thing. The Victorian reader was certainly not unused to a union of pathos and humor, but he—perhaps more especially she—was not likely to be at ease with an instance of the union that issued in an irony at once gay and bitter, especially when the irony touched the subject of love. The double-mindedness of irony is alien to the tradition of Victorian love poetry, which cherished a direct singleness of emotion.

The humor of the poem begins, of course, in the "magnificent hyperbole" and it is directed both to the lady herself and to the conventions of courtly love, according to which the lover dedicates himself to the beloved, who accepts his adoration but holds out no hope that his wooing will ever be successful. The lover says that the lady deserves to be wooed according to this convention, virtually *ad infinitum*, and he goes into precise detail to explain how much time might properly be given to the contemplation and praise of each of her charms, were the couple to have, as we say, all the time in the world. In this gay absurdity we hear a note of solemnity, even of fear—the reference to *so much* time, to the long procession of centuries and ages which is to culminate in "the last age" that brings the world to an end, cannot fail to be awesome. Yet the awe is only lightly suggested; as yet it yields no more than a faint undertone to the humor with which the lover teases his lady.

The teasing breaks off, however, with dramatic suddenness when the lover brusquely evokes "Time's winged chariot" and the death it is bringing. The huge leisure of the first movement is instantly dispelled. The world has been seen as a Garden of Eden through which the couple, its Adam and Eve, wander at will; now, at the sound of the hurrying chariot of Time, the garden, fertilized by its rivers, the distant exotic Ganges and the homely Humber, is transformed into the "deserts of vast eternity," which are not to be traversed and which do not accommodate the unceasing growth of a "vegetable love." Now the tone of the lover's urging becomes brutally explicit in its reference to death, for it is not death in the abstract that the lady is asked to think about but the physical decay which makes a mockery of the scruples that keep her from putting her body to what her lover thinks is its right and natural use. But his bitter, desperate evocation of death modulates to the magnificent whimsicality with which the second movement concludes:

> The grave's a fine and private place,
> But none, I think, do there embrace.

It is as if the lover, having done all he could to frighten the lady into an awareness of the human situation, would now wish to lighten the imposed weight of reality by a humor that is at least as tender as it is grim.

The poem, we readily perceive, is an argument in quite strict logical form. Each of the three movements is a step in a syllogism: 1. If we had all time at our disposal. . . . 2. But we do not. . . . 3. Therefore. . . . What the "therefore" proposes is, of course, love upon the instant. The metaphors in which the proposal is made are curious and of great intensity. In the second movement Time had been given something of a divine character, for the "winged chariot" brings to mind the sun-god, Phoebus Apollo, who, in ancient Greek myth, was represented as a charioteer coursing through the heavens. But now Time, in a vague yet powerful image, is represented as a carnivorous beast, the more dreadful because it is not swift and fierce; and the lover speaks of himself and the lady as no less predatory than their foe—they are to be "amorous birds of prey," capable of devouring Time itself by the ferocity of their love. The image of the lovers as birds of prey, which inverts the old conventional image of the amorous dove, was intended to be startling. To the modern reader the phrase "birds of prey" will perhaps have unpleasant connotations, but to Marvell's contemporaries it would have brought to mind the falcon, which, in a day when hunting with the falcon was still a sport of the aristocracy, was thought to be a particularly noble and beautiful animal.

The conjunction of "strength" and "sweetness," in itself one of the striking details of the poem, naturally proceeds from the representation of Time as a carnivorous beast. When the young Samson killed a lion, he left the carcass in a thicket and a swarm of bees hived in it; returning to the spot, Samson ate some of the honey and this made the substance of the famous riddle he put to the Philistines: "Out of the eater came forth meat, and out of the strong came forth sweetness." The Philistines, unable to puzzle out the riddle by themselves, prevailed upon Samson's wife to find out the answer and were able to say, "What is sweeter than honey? and what is stronger than a lion?"[1]

The lover's suggestion that he and the lady should "roll" all their strength and all their sweetness "into one ball" is curious, even bizarre. The figure may possibly have its source in the scarab or beetle by which the Egyptians symbolized Horus, their god of the sun. It is characteristic of the scarab that it makes a ball of dung in which it lays its eggs; this ball appears in the innumerable representations of the scarab that the Egyptians made. It was thought of as the sun that the god propelled before him.

The "iron gates of life" through which the pleasures of the lovers are to be "torn" are difficult to visualize and to explain. Tennyson thought that the iron gates might better have been iron *grates,* as suggesting more directly the difficulty of tearing the pleasures through them, but this change would have destroyed the awesomeness of the great vague trope which, for Marvell's contemporary readers, would probably have brought to mind the two gates of Hades in Virgil's *Aeneid,* one of ivory through which the false dreams come, the other of horn through which come the true dreams. That the iron gates cannot easily

[1] See the Book of Judges, Chapter 14.

be visualized in relation to the pleasures will suggest that the force of a metaphor does not depend on its visual explicitness.

Certain words of the poem should perhaps be glossed to ensure that they are understood in the sense that Marvell intended. *Coy* means reluctant and hesitant, with implications of a certain self-consciousness or insincerity, but it does not have the overtone it later acquired, of vapidity or cuteness. In our modern usage, a man's *mistress* is a woman with whom he has an established sexual relationship, but in Marvell's day the word denotes the woman to whom a man has pledged his love. The *vegetable* quality of the love that the poet imagines if the lovers had all time at their disposal does not have the pejorative meaning we might now find in it, of being wholly dull, without sentience; it refers to the power of growth and implies the vitality or livingness of the growing thing. *Quaint* did not have its modern sense of something pleasantly old-fashioned but rather of something elegantly fanciful, with a touch of what we should call affectation.

AN ESSAY
ON MAN
Epistle I

ALEXANDER POPE
1688–1744

ARGUMENT

Of the Nature and State of Man with respect to the UNIVERSE

Of *Man* in the abstract. I. That we can judge only with regard to our *own system,* being ignorant of the *relations* of systems and things. II. That Man is not to be deemed *imperfect,* but a Being suited to his *place* and *rank* in the creation, agreeable to the *general Order* of things, and conformable to *Ends* and *Relations* to him unknown. III. That it is partly upon his *ignorance* of *future* events, and partly upon the *hope* of a *future* state, that all his happiness in the present depends. IV. The *pride* of aiming at more knowledge, and pretending to more Perfection, the cause of Man's error and misery. The *impiety* of putting himself in the place of *God,* and judging of the fitness of unfitness, perfection or imperfection, justice or injustice of his dispensations. V. The *absurdity* of conceiting himself the *final cause* of the creation, or expecting that perfection in the *moral* world, which is not in the *natural.* VI. The *unreasonableness* of his complaints against *Providence,* while on the one hand he demands the Perfections of the Angels, and on the other the bodily qualifications of the Brutes; though, to possess any of the *sensitive faculties* in a higher degree, would render him miserable. VII. That throughout the whole visible world, an universal *order* and *gradation* in the sensual and mental faculties is observed, which causes a *subordination* of creature to creature, and of all creatures to Man. The gradations of *sense, instinct, thought, reflection, reason;* that Reason alone countervails all the other faculties. VIII. How much further this *order* and *subordination* of living creatures may extend, above and below us; were any part of which broken, not that part only, but the whole connected *creation* must be destroyed. IX. The *extravagance, madness,* and *pride* of such a desire. X. The consequence of all, the *absolute submission* due to Providence, both as to our *present* and *future* state.

Awake, my ST. JOHN![1] leave all meaner things
To low ambition, and the pride of Kings.
Let us (since Life can little more supply
Than just to look about us and to die)

---

[1] Henry St. John, Viscount Bolingbroke (1678–1751). His philosophical writings had some influence on Pope.

Expatiate free o'er all this scene of Man; 5
A mighty maze! but not without a plan;
A Wild, where weeds and flowers promiscuous shoot;
Or Garden, tempting with forbidden fruit.
Together let us beat this ample field,
Try what the open, what the covert yield; 10
The latent tracts, the giddy heights, explore
Of all who blindly creep, or sightless soar;
Eye Nature's walks, shoot Folly as it flies,
And catch the Manners living as they rise;
Laugh where we must, be candid where we can; 15
But vindicate the ways of God to Man.
  I. Say first, of God above, or Man below,
What can we reason, but from what we know?²
Of Man, what see we but his station here,
From which to reason, or to which refer? 20
Through worlds unnumbered though the God be known,
'Tis ours to trace him only in our own.
He, who through vast immensity can pierce,
See worlds on worlds compose one universe,
Observe how system into system runs, 25
What other planets circle other suns,
What varied Being peoples every star,
May tell why Heaven has made us as we are.
But of this frame the bearings, and the ties,
The strong connexions, nice dependencies, 30
Gradations just, has thy pervading soul
Looked through? or can a part contain the whole?
  Is the great chain,³ that draws all to agree,
And drawn supports, upheld by God, or thee?
  II. Presumptuous Man! the reason wouldst thou find, 35
Why formed so weak, so little, and so blind?
First, if thou canst, the harder reason guess,
Why formed no weaker, blinder, and no less?
Ask of thy mother earth, why oaks are made
Taller or stronger than the weeds they shade? 40
Or ask of yonder argent fields⁴ above,
Why Jove's Satellites⁵ are less than Jove?
  Of systems possible, if 'tis confest
That Wisdom infinite must form the best,
Where all must full or not coherent be, 45
And all that rises, rise in due degree;
Then, in the scale of reasoning life,⁶ 'tis plain,

---

² That is, how can we reason (about God or man) except on the basis of what we already know? ³ The "great chain of being," the conception of the structure of the universe put forth here, originated with the neoplatonist philosopher, Plotinus (third century), and was particularly influential in Europe in the seventeenth and early eighteenth centuries. ⁴ The heavens. *Argent*, silvery white. ⁵ The classical hierarchy of gods. ⁶ Life having the ability to reason.

There must be, somewhere, such a rank as Man:
And all the question (wrangle e'er so long)
Is only this, if God has placed him wrong?   50
　　　Respecting Man, whatever wrong we call,
May, must be right, as relative to all.[7]
In human works, though laboured on with pain,
A thousand movements scarce one purpose gain;
In God's, one single can its end produce;   55
Yet serves to second too some other use.
So Man, who here seems principal alone,
Perhaps acts second to some sphere unknown,
Touches some wheel, or verges to some goal;
'Tis but a part we see, and not a whole.   60
　　　When the proud steed shall know why Man restrains
His fiery course, or drives him o'er the plains;
When the dull Ox, why now he breaks the clod,[8]
Is now a victim, and now Egypt's God:
Then shall Man's pride and dulness comprehend   65
His actions', passions', being's, use and end;
Why doing, suffering, checked, impelled; and why
This hour a slave, the next a deity.
　　　Then say not Man's imperfect, Heaven in fault;
Say rather, Man's as perfect as he ought: 70
His knowledge measured to his state and place;
His time a moment, and a point his space.
It to be perfect in a certain sphere,
What matter, soon or late, or here or there?
The blest to day is as completely so,   75
As who began a thousand years ago.
　　　III.   Heaven from all creatures hides the book of Fate,
All but the page prescribed, their present state:
From brutes what men, from men what spirits know:
Or who could suffer Being here below?   80
The lamb thy riot[9] dooms to bleed today,
Had he thy Reason, would he skip and play?
Pleased to the last, he crops the flowery food,
And licks the hand just raised to shed his blood.
Oh blindness to the future! kindly given,   85
That each may fill the circle marked by Heaven:
Who sees with equal eye, as God of all,
A hero perish, or a sparrow fall,
Atoms or systems into ruin hurled,
And now a bubble burst, and now a world.   90
　　　Hope humbly then; with trembling pinions soar;
Wait the great teacher Death; and God adore.

---

[7] The entire universe.   [8] That is, pulls a plow. The ox is a victim when it is used as meat, and Egypt's principal god, Osiris, was often represented as an ox.   [9] Extravagance.

What future bliss, he gives not thee to know,
But gives that Hope to be thy blessing now.
Hope springs eternal in the human breast: 95
Man never Is, but always To be blest:
The soul, uneasy and confined from home,[10]
Rests and expatiates in a life to come.

    Lo, the poor Indian! whose untutored mind
Sees God in clouds, or hears him in the wind;   100
His soul, proud Science never taught to stray
Far as the solar walk, or milky way;
Yet simple Nature to his hope has given,
Behind the cloud-topped hill, an humbler heaven;
Some safer world in depth of woods embraced,   105
Some happier island in the watery waste,
Where slaves once more their native land behold,
No fiends torment, no Christians thirst for gold.
To Be, contents his natural desire,
He asks no Angel's wing, no Seraph's fire;[11]   110
But thinks, admitted to that equal sky,
His faithful dog shall bear him company.

    IV.   Go, wiser thou! and, in thy scale of sense,
Weigh thy Opinion against Providence;
Call imperfection what thou fanciest such,   115
Say, here he gives too little, there too much:
Destroy all creatures for thy sport or gust,[12]
Yet cry, If Man's unhappy, God's unjust;
If Man alone engross not Heaven's high care,
Alone made perfect here, immortal there: 120
Snatch from his hand the balance[13] and the rod,
Re-judge his justice, be the God of God.
In Pride, in reasoning Pride, our error lies;
All quit their sphere, and rush into the skies.
Pride still is aiming at the blest abodes,   125
Men would be Angels, Angels would be Gods.
Aspiring to be Gods, if Angels fell,
Aspiring to be Angels, Men rebel:
And who but[14] wishes to invert the laws
Of Order, sins against th' Eternal Cause.   130

    V.   Ask for what end the heavenly bodies shine,
Earth for whose use? Pride answers, " 'Tis for mine:
For me kind Nature wakes her genial[15] power,
Suckles each herb, and spreads out every flower;
Annual for me, the grape, the rose renew   135
The juice nectareous, and the balmy dew;

---

    [10] Heaven, or eternity.   [11] The seraphim are the highest order of angels, especially
distinguished by the ardor of their love.   [12] Inclination, taste.   [13] Scales.   [14] Merely,
only.   [15] Generative.

For me, the mine a thousand treasures brings;
For me, health gushes from a thousand springs;
Seas roll to waft me, suns to light me rise;
My footstool earth, my canopy the skies."   140
　　　But errs not Nature from this gracious end,
From burning suns when livid deaths[16] descend,
When earthquakes swallow, or when tempests sweep
Towns to one grave, whole nations to the deep?
"No" ('tis replied) "the first Almighty Cause   145
Acts not by partial, but by general laws;
Th' exceptions few; some change since all began:
And what created perfect?"—Why then Man?
If the great end be human Happiness,
The Nature deviates; and can Man do less?   150
As much that end a constant course requires
Of showers and sunshine, as of Man's desires;
As much eternal springs and cloudless skies,
As Men for ever temperate, calm, and wise.
If plagues or earthquakes break not Heaven's design,   155
Why then a Borgia,[17] or a Catiline?[18]
Who knows but he, whose hand the lightning forms,
Who heaves old Ocean, and who wings the storms;
Pours fierce Ambition in a Cæsar's mind,
Or turns young Ammon[19] loose to scourge mankind?   160
From pride, from pride, our very reasoning springs;
Account for moral, as for natural things:
Why charge we Heaven in those, in these acquit?
In both, to reason right is to submit.
　　　Better for Us, perhaps, it might appear   165
Were there all harmony, all virtue here;
That never air or ocean felt the wind;
That never passion discomposed the mind.
But ALL subsists by elemental strife;
And Passions are the elements of Life.   170
The general ORDER, since the whole began,
Is kept in Nature, and is kept in Man.
　　　VI.　What would this Man? Now upward will he soar,
And little less than Angel, would be more;
Now looking downwards, just as grieved appears   175
To want the strength of bulls, the fur of bears.
Made for his use all creatures if he call,
Say what their use, had he the powers of all?
Nature to these, without profusion, kind,

---

[16] Plagues.　[17] The Borgias rose to prominence in Italy during the Renaissance. Their name became a symbol of unbridled power, lust, and greed.　[18] An unscrupulous Roman who conspired to overthrow the government by force. He was exposed by Cicero.　[19] Alexander the Great, who was told by an oracle that he was the son of Ammon, an Egyptian deity.

The proper organs, proper powers assigned;   180
Each seeming want compensated of course,
Here with degrees of swiftness, there of force;[20]
All in exact proportion to the state;
Nothing to add, and nothing to abate.
Each beast, each insect, happy in its own: 185
Is Heaven unkind to Man, and Man alone?
Shall he alone, whom rational we call,
Be pleased with nothing, if not blessed with all?
        The bliss of Man (could Pride that blessing find)
Is not to act or think beyond mankind;   190
No powers of body or of soul to share,
But what his nature and his state can bear.
Why has not Man a microscopic eye?
For this plain reason, Man is not a Fly.
Say what the use, where finer optics given,   195
T' inspect a mite, not comprehend the heaven?
Or touch, if tremblingly alive all o'er,
To smart and agonize at every pore?
Or quick effluvia[21] darting through the brain,
Die of a rose in aromatic pain?   200
If nature thundered in his opening ears,
And stunned him with the music of the spheres,[22]
How would he wish that Heaven had left him still
The whispering Zephyr,[23] and the purling rill?
Who finds not Providence all good and wise,   205
Alike in what it gives, and what denies?
        VII.   Far as Creation's ample range extends,
The scale of sensual,[24] mental powers ascends:
Mark how it mounts, to Man's imperial race,
From the green myriads in the peopled grass: 210
What modes of sight betwixt each wide extreme,
The mole's dim curtain, and the lynx's beam:
Of smell, the headlong lioness between,[25]
And hound sagacious on the tainted green:[26]
Of hearing, from the life that fills the flood,[27]   215

[20] It is a certain axiom in the anatomy of creatures, that in proportion as they are
formed for strength, their swiftness is lessened; or as they are formed for swiftness, their
strength is abated (Pope's note).   [21] Exhalations affecting the sense of smell.   [22] Spheres
of ancient astronomy, according to which nine spheres of transparent material holding the
planets and stars surrounded the earth. Pythagoras thought the planets must make sounds
that corresponded to their different rates of motion and that, as all things in nature are
harmoniously made, the different sounds must harmonize.   [23] Gentle breeze.   [24] Sensory.
[25] The manner of the Lions hunting their prey in the deserts of Africa is this: At
their first going out in the nighttime they set up a loud roar, and then listen to the noise
made by the beasts in their flight, pursuing them by the ear, and not by the nostril. It is
probable the story of the jackal's hunting for the lion was occasioned by observation of
this defect of scent in that terrible animal (Pope's note).   [26] Hunting grounds imbued
with the scent of an animal.   [27] Waterlife.

To that which warbles through the vernal wood:
The spider's touch, how exquisitely fine!
Feels at each thread, and lives along the line:
In the nice bee, what sense so subtly true
From poisonous herbs extracts the healing dew? 220
How Instinct varies in the groveling swine,
Compared, half-reasoning elephant, with thine!
Twixt that, and Reason, what a nice[28] barrier,
For ever separate, yet for ever near!
Remembrance and Reflection how allied; 225
What thin partitions Sense[29] from Thought divide:
And Middle natures, how they long to join,
Yet never pass th' insuperable line!
Without this just graduation, could they be
Subjected, these to those, or all to thee? 230
The powers of all subdued by thee alone,
Is not thy Reason all these powers in one?
    VIII.   See, through this air, this ocean, and this earth,
All matter quick,[30] and bursting into birth.
Above, how high, progressive life may go! 235
Around, how wide! how deep extend below!
Vast chain of Being! which from God began,
Natures ethereal, human, angel, man,
Beast, bird, fish, insect, what no eye can see,
No glass can reach; from Infinite to thee, 240
From thee to Nothing.—On superior powers
Were we to press, inferior might on ours:
Or in the full creation leave a void,
Where, one step broken, the great scale's destroyed:
From Nature's chain whatever link you strike, 245
Tenth or ten thousandth, breaks the chain alike.
    And, if each system in gradation roll
Alike essential to th' amazing Whole,
The least confusion but in one, not all
That system only, but the Whole must fall. 250
Let Earth unbalanced from her orbit fly,
Planets and Suns run lawless through the sky;
Let ruling Angels from their spheres be hurled,
Being on Being wrecked, and world on world;
Heaven's whole foundations to their centre nod, 255
And Nature tremble to the throne of God.
All this dread ORDER break—for whom? for thee?
Vile worm!—Oh Madness! Pride! Impiety!
    IX.   What if the foot, ordained the dust to tread,
Or hand, to toil, aspired to be the head? 260
What if the head, the eye, or ear repined[31]
To serve mere engines to the ruling Mind?

   [28] Fine, fragile.   [29] Sensory perceptions.   [30] Alive.   [31] Complained, was discontented.

Just as absurd for any part to claim
To be another, in this general frame:
Just as absurd, to mourn the tasks or pains,   265
The great directing MIND of ALL ordains.

　　All are but parts of one stupendous whole,
Whose body Nature is, and God the soul;
That, changed through all, and yet in all the same;
Great in the earth, as in th' ethereal frame;   270
Warms in the sun, refreshes in the breeze,
Glows in the stars, and blossoms in the trees,
Lives through all life, extends through all extent,
Spreads undivided, operates unspent;
Breathes in our soul, informs our mortal part,   275
As full, as perfect, in a hair as heart;
As full, as perfect, in vile Man that mourns,
As the rapt Seraph that adores and burns:
To him no high, no low, no great, no small;
He fills, he bounds, connects, and equals all.   280

　　X.　Cease then, nor ORDER Imperfection name:
Our proper bliss depends on what we blame.
Know thy own point: This kind, this due degree
Of blindness, weakness, Heaven bestows on thee.
Submit.—In this, or any other sphere,   285
Secure to be as blest as thou canst bear:
Safe in the hand of one disposing Power,
Or in the natal, or the mortal hour.
All Nature is but Art, unknown to thee;
All Chance, Direction, which thou canst not see;   290
All Discord, Harmony not understood;
All partial Evil, universal Good:
And, spite of Pride, in erring Reason's spite,
One truth is clear, WHATEVER IS, IS RIGHT.

COMMENTARY

Modern critics, even those who take the greatness of Pope for granted, are likely
to use a tone of advocacy when they write about him. They are aware that the
taste of most of their readers does not readily respond to the poet whose genius
was universally acclaimed in his own time. Pope is the chief English poet of the
eighteenth century and it is he who bore the brunt of the Romanticists' repudia-
tion of the poetic standards of that age. To Wordsworth and Coleridge, he stood
for everything in poetry that they contemned. They saw him as virtually an
anti-poet, the corrupter of poetry's true essence. Only Byron among the Romanticists found it possible to admire him, and Byron's enthusiastic praise was
thought by many to be a mere perversity. The nineteenth century's antagonism
to Pope was brought to a climax and codified by Matthew Arnold in his famous
essay, "The Study of Poetry." Speaking of the importance that poetry would

have in the modern world and calling the roll of those English poets who were likely to be of the greatest spiritual value, Arnold explicitly excluded Pope and his great predecessor Dryden from the illustrious roster on the ground that they were really not poets at all. "Though they may write in verse," he said, "though they may in a certain sense be masters of the art of versification, Dryden and Pope are not classics of our poetry, they are classics of our prose."

In the early decades of the twentieth century the reputation of the two poets took a decided upward turn among serious students of literature: now no informed person would think it possible to say of either of them that he is not a classic of our poetry. The counter-revolution against nineteenth-century opinion as summed up by Arnold found its most notable agitator in T. S. Eliot, who, in his essays on Dryden, repelled "the reproach of the prosaic" that had so often been made and went on to question in a radical and telling way the whole nineteenth-century view of what was and what was not poetic.

Yet despite the thorough-going change in the estimate of Pope that has taken place among critics and scholars, it is still probably true that the great majority of readers who come to him for the first time and without critical indoctrination tend to resist him and to echo Arnold's judgment that he is not really a poet at all, that such virtues as are most salient in his work, those that Arnold identified as "regularity, uniformity, precision, and balance," are prose virtues; and perhaps they will go so far as to say that, of these virtues, not all pertain to the kind of prose that interests them most.

What probably makes the root of the difficulty is the verse form with which the genius of Pope is identified, the heroic couplet. It is likely to strike the unhabituated modern ear as limited, repetitive, and all too committed to syntax, justifying Keats's vehement charge that it was nothing but mechanical. The disaffected reader should know, however, that the better acquainted Keats became with the form, the more he admired it and admitted its influence upon his own verse.

Nothing could be simpler than the defining characteristics of the heroic couplet: two rhymed lines, each of five iambic feet, that is, feet of two syllables, the accent falling on the second. But as it came into wide use in the late seventeenth century and especially in the hands of Dryden, the simple form developed toward complexity and ever stricter demands were made upon it. It became the rule (which might, however, be broken now and then for the sake of variety) that each couplet be self-contained, its meaning complete. This tended to make for a sententious and even epigrammatic quality of utterance, which was much esteemed. Considerable attention was given to the caesura, a discernible pause in the progress of a line which is dictated not by the metre but by the natural rhythm of the language; variations in the placing of the caesura had the effect of helping the heroic couplet avoid its greatest danger, monotony. Rhetorical devices, such as parallelism and antithesis, were favored by the nature of the verse and came to be highly valued.

The chief advantage that Dryden ascribed to the heroic couplet will make it plain why the Romantic poets disliked the form and why many modern readers find it uncongenial. ". . . That benefit which I consider most in it," Dryden said, "is . . . that it bounds and circumscribes the fancy." And he goes on: "For imagination in a poet is a faculty so wild and lawless that, like an highranging spaniel, it must have clogs tied to it, lest it outrun the judgment.

The great easiness of blank verse renders the poet too luxuriant; he is tempted to say many things which might better be omitted, or at least shut up in fewer words; but when the difficulty of artful rhyming is interposed, where the poet commonly confines his sense to his couplet, and must contrive that sense into such words that the rhyme shall naturally follow them, not they the rhyme; the fancy then gives leisure to the judgment to come in. . . . That which most regulates the fancy, and gives the judgment its busiest employment, is like to bring forth the richest and clearest thoughts."

Nothing could be further from the nineteenth-century sense of how the poet should go about his work, of what poetry should be and do. And although modern poetry has in some measure responded to the influence of Dryden and Pope, there are few contemporary practitioners or theorists of poetry who would give their approval to a conception of poetry that was directed chiefly to bringing forth *thoughts,* no matter how rich and clear.

By Pope's time the advantages of the heroic couplet no longer seemed to be in need of reasoned defense; it was the accepted form for most poetic under-takings of importance.[1] If Pope ever thought of the limitations of the form, it was only as a challenge to his virtuosity. To him it was beyond doubt that the couplet in skilled hands—in hands made skilful as much by study and practice as by native endowment—was an instrument capable of producing the widest and most delightful range of effects. In an often-quoted passage of "An Essay on Criticism" he brilliantly demonstrated how various the "music" of the couplet may be and how precisely it could be related to the meaning that is being expressed. This correspondence of sense and sound, he says, is something to which the poet must give close attention—

> 'Tis not enough no harshness gives offence,
> The sound must seem an Echo to the sense:

He illustrates the precept by a couplet in which the sound of the verse is consonant with the "softness" of the action being referred to:

> Soft is the strain when Zephyr gently blows,
> And the smooth stream in smoother numbers flows.

There follows an example of a rough action expressed in a rough-sounding verse:

> But when loud surges lash the sounding shore,
> The hoarse, rough verse should like the torrent roar.

Then an example of laborious effort:

> When Ajax strives some rock's vast weight to throw,
> The line too labours, and the words move slow.

[1] But the taste of no period is monolithic and the dislike of the heroic couplet that was expressed by at least one considerable poet of the eighteenth century should be noted —Matthew Prior objected to it because it "produces too frequent an identity in the sound," moves too readily toward epigram, and is tiring to the reader.

And, in contrast to this, lightness and speed:

> Not so when swift Camilla scours the plain,
> Flies o'er the unbending corn, and skims along the main.

This famous display of virtuosity will suggest how large a part in Pope's art was played by the poet's sense that he was a performer, that it was his purpose to give pleasure to an audience whose right to judge his performance depended only upon a proper training of its faculty of judgment, its taste. The characteristic relation of later poets to their audiences will be very different: the idea of performance will come to be abhorrent to them and they will conceive it to be their purpose to serve not the pleasure of the reader but only the truth of their own feelings, which the reader is probably not competent to judge.

The poetry of exposition and argument, to which the heroic couplet so happily lends itself, has virtually no place in the modern tradition. In the eighteenth century the word "didactic" was used in a neutral descriptive sense when applied to poetry; early in the nineteenth century its meaning became opprobrious and has remained so. It means nothing more dreadful than "teaching," but, although we believe that much is to be learned from poetry, we now believe that it must not intend to instruct. To the poets of Pope's age, however, our adverse opinion of didactic poetry would have seemed arbitrary and pointless; they thought it nothing but natural that poetry should engage itself directly with ideas.[2]

But even if the modern reader should consent to give up his prejudice against didactic poetry in general, he is pretty sure to find that another barrier stands in the way of his coming to terms with "An Essay on Man." This is the poem's purpose of demonstrating that man has no justifiable complaint to make of the conditions of his life, that, if he truly comprehends the nature of the universe, he must see that his relation to it is wholly in accord with reason and be gratified that things are as they are and not otherwise.

Such a view can scarcely win assent in our day, when it has become virtually a commonplace of much of our influential literature that man's relation to the universe is so far out of accord with reason as to be absurd. Yet exactly the currency of this idea makes "An Essay on Man" of rather special interest to us, for the poem takes its impetus from the assumption that anyone who thinks about his relation to the universe will, as a first conclusion, judge it to be unreasonable to the point of absurdity. The Essay, of course, then undertakes to prove that the first conclusion is in error, but the arguments it advances in the demonstration are as desperate as they are ingenious. Where the ingenuity fails to convince us, the desperateness may yet succeed in moving us: there is something deeply affecting in the Essay's passionate defeated attempt to force the universe to be rational.

[2] But, again, the broad cultural generalization must be modified—in 1746, Joseph Warton, an important critic, protested the fashion of didactic poetry. And it should be said that in his preface to "An Essay on Man" Pope raised the question, perhaps only in a formal way, of whether he should not have treated his subject in prose, and he apologizes, again perhaps only in a formal way, for not having treated parts of his discourse "more *poetically.*" It would seem to have been the abstruseness of the subject that raised doubts that had not existed in connection with the earlier "Essay on Criticism," which was no less didactic but considerably easier.

When it is said that man's relation to the universe is not in accord with reason, what is primarily meant is that there is no discernible answer to the question of why man suffers or why there is an overplus of pain as against pleasure in human existence. That the question should be asked at all implies the belief that the universe is controlled by principles that are analogous with those more or less rational principles that man has evolved for the control of his own behavior. It is expected, that is, that the answer will be given in terms of man's own reason in its various social aspects—the reason of the father in the family, of the judge in the court of law, of the king in the city or nation. And when the question about the reason of the universe is posed in the Judaeo-Christian tradition, it takes the form of asking why the perfect Father, Judge, and King, the God who is believed to be both omnipotent and wholly beneficent, should have ordained man's suffering. The terms of the question being what they are, the answer is not hard to make—it is possible to "justify the ways of God to man," as Milton expressed his intention in writing *Paradise Lost*, by telling the story of a man's fall from innocence through his disobedience to the divine command and of God's consequent anger. The pain of human life is explained as a punishment for sin, mitigated by the permitted hope of an eventual redemption. Such rationality as is thought to inhere in the human concept of morality and justice is proposed as the controlling principle of the universe.

This answer is in many ways satisfactory so long as the imagination is disposed to accept its terms and to sustain the belief in a God who is Father, Judge, and King, and who is susceptible to the emotions that are appropriate to each of his functions. But in the eighteenth century the imagination of educated men was not so disposed. "An Essay on Man" undertakes to "vindicate the ways of God to man," and the conscious echo of Milton's line informs us that Pope wanted to connect the purpose of his poem with that of *Paradise Lost*. Yet the elements out of which Pope constructed his argument were very different from those available to Milton. The God of the Essay is not personal except insofar as wisdom and beneficence may be attributed to him. Having once ordained his universe in perfection, he does not intervene in its processes. Where Milton, in the traditional way of religion, frames his explanation of man's destiny in terms of man's own thought and feeling, showing that God's ways are essentially in accord with man's ways taken at their best, Pope vindicates God's ways by demonstrating the difference—which does not, however, imply the discontinuity—between the divine and the human. The famous conclusion, "Whatever is, is right," asserts the rationality and perfection of the universe as God has created it, a rationality and perfection of which man's suffering—so runs the terrible line of reasoning!—is a necessary element.

At no point in "An Essay on Man" is the actuality of human suffering denied. Indeed, the poem is charged throughout with an awareness of pain, as well it might be, considering how much of it its author had endured. The opening lines are explicit about the unsatisfactoriness of life, which "can little more supply / Than just to look about us and to die." It is this acceptance of the fact of suffering that gives the poem its desperate tragic force, for the essence of its position is not merely that human suffering is inevitable but that without it the universe would be less rational and perfect than in fact it is. The argument is based on a conception of a universal order in which all created things stand on a scale of perfection from the lowest to the highest. On this scale there may be no gaps; the gradation from the lowest to the highest is continuous, constituting a "vast Chain of Being." From this premise of the order of Nature two conclusions follow. (1) Man has his place or "station" in this order of perfection, above the animals and below the angels, and if he did not occupy this place, there would be a link missing in the chain of being, a circumstance which, if it were thinkable, would be a diminution of the perfection of the universal order. (2) Situated where he is on the scale, or in the chain, man must be understood to have been endowed in a way that makes all his attributes appropriate to his station; both his power and his weakness are exactly right for that place. Which is to say that, in relation to the universal order, man himself is perfect.

More than once the point is made that nothing would be gained for man's well-being if his powers were greater than they are. It is said, in fact, that the contrary is so. If, for example, man were better able to foretell the future, he would have a greater apprehension of the calamities that are destined to befall him and he would therefore be the less able to bear his existence. But such considerations, adduced for what comfort they may give, are of no more than secondary importance to the argument; its primary intention is to demonstrate that the perfection of the universal order depends upon man's suffering.

It is generally said that Pope derived his general position and the particularities by which he expounded it from his friend Lord Bolingbroke, the St. John to whom all four epistles of the Essay are addressed, but an educated man of the time could scarcely have read any philosophy without gaining knowledge of a doctrine that was fashionable and received. Yet it was not everywhere received; Dr. Johnson, for one, would have none of it. Johnson had the highest admiration for Pope as a poet and he said of "An Essay on Man" that it "affords an egregious instance of the predominance of genius, the dazzling splendour of imagery, and the seductive powers of eloquence." But the praise he gives to the poet is the measure of his scorn of the philosopher. "Never," he goes on, "was penury of knowledge and vulgarity of sentiment so happily disguised," and he proceeds to show that the doctrine of the Essay may be reduced to a series of truisms and platitudes. "Surely," he says when the demolition is complete, "a man of no very comprehensive search may venture to say that he has heard all this before. . . ." And then, his antagonism to the philosopher having been given full vent, he is free to return to his praise of the poet: ". . . But it was never till now recommended by such a blaze of embellishments, or such sweetness of melody. The vigorous contraction of thoughts, the luxuriant amplification of others, the incidental illustrations, and sometimes the dignity, sometimes the softness of the verses, enchain philosophy, suspend criticism, and oppress judgment by overpowering pleasure." The double opinion recommends itself.

TYGER! TYGER!

WILLIAM BLAKE
1757–1827

Tyger! Tyger! burning bright
In the forests of the night,
What immortal hand or eye
Could frame thy fearful symmetry?

In what distant deeps or skies   5
Burnt the fire of thine eyes?
On what wings dare he aspire?
What the hand dare seize the fire?

And what shoulder, & what art,
Could twist the sinews of thy heart?   10
And when thy heart began to beat,
What dread hand? & what dread feet?[1]

What the hammer? what the chain?
In what furnace was thy brain?
What the anvil? what dread grasp   15
Dare its deadly terrors clasp?

When the stars threw down their spears,
And water'd heaven with their tears,
Did he smile his work to see?
Did he who made the Lamb make thee?   20

Tyger! Tyger! burning bright
In the forests of the night,
What immortal hand or eye,
Dare frame thy fearful symmetry?

[1] In revising the poem, Blake deleted a line that might seem necessary to the thought. He originally wrote:

> What dread hand and what dread feet
> Could fetch it from the furnace deep?

COMMENTARY

The reader who comes to "Tyger! Tyger!" for the first time will have no trouble understanding what a Tyger is. But he will want to know why it is spelled in this, rather than in the usual, way. In Blake's time the spelling of the word was the same as now; Dr. Johnson, in his great dictionary, which set the standard of correctness for the period, noted *tyger* as an alternative form of *tiger,* but he did not expect anyone to use it. Yet Blake's error, if such it is, is perpetuated: most modern editors, when they reprint the poem, conscientiously maintain the poet's spelling. They feel that to make the Tyger into a tiger would alter the nature of the beast and of the poem that celebrates him.

One reason for this feeling lies in the circumstances of the poem's original publication. The book in which "Tyger! Tyger!" appeared, *Songs of Experience* (1794), was not printed in the common way, from type. Blake was an engraver by trade and also an artist of considerable stature, and he made the whole book himself, designing each page as an elaborate picture in which the text of the poem was part of the design and the elements of the picture wove themselves in and out of the lines of the text. He engraved the texts and the outlines of the pictures on copper plates from which he printed the pages; he then colored by hand each page of each copy of the book. It is a tendency of modern criticism and scholarship to pay heed to every detail of a poet's work, even such "mechanical" matters as punctuation and spelling; if one of the older poets wrote *speke* where we would now write *speak,* or *sovran* where we would now write *sovereign,* many editors think that the very look of the words is an essential quality of the poem and should be preserved. How much more is this idea likely to prevail when the poet presents his poems, as Blake did, as actual visual objects, to be looked at as well as read.[1]

And certainly the spelling has its effect, if only that of being curious and therefore of making the animal which the word denotes the more remarkable—a Tyger is surely more interesting than a tiger. It startles our habitual expectations, it jolts our settled imagination of the beast and prepares us to see it as we never saw it before, as Blake saw it. Then, too, the *y* is a stronger, as it is a larger, letter than *i*; it suggests a longer-held sound and therefore supports the idea of an animal even fiercer than the tiger. (Conversely, the little boy in A. A. Milne's stories calls one of his animal friends Tigger, and by the shortening of the *i* wipes out all possibility of the creature's being dangerous.)

The dominant, the single, emotion of the poem is amazement, and perhaps no poem has ever expressed an emotion so fully—it is as if the poem were amazement itself. The means by which it achieves this effect is in part very simple: in the course of twenty-four lines it asks fourteen astonished questions. Up through Stanza IV the tempo of the questions is in continuous acceleration, generating an intense excitement. At Stanza V the speed of the questions diminishes and the excited wonder modulates to meditative awe.

But not only does the tempo of the poem change at the fifth stanza; its point of reference, its very subject, alters. Up to Stanza V the poem has undertaken to define the nature of the Tyger by the nature of God—such is the beauty and strength and wildness of the Tyger that he must be thought to

---

[1] Although I would give at least a qualified assent to the principle evoked, for obvious reasons I have not followed it in choosing the texts of this volume.

have been created by God's greatest exercise of power, a power put forth against resistance and even with some risk of failure. But at the fifth stanza the Tyger is no longer defined by the nature of God; now, in the two remaining stanzas, it is God who is defined by the nature of the Tyger. The amazement first evoked by the Tyger is now directed to God, as God reveals himself through his wonderful and terrible creature. And what the poem finds most amazing about God is not his power but his audacity—not the fact that God *could* (as in the first stanza) but that he *dared* (as in the last stanza) create the Tyger!

To ask a question about the audacity of God is in itself an act of inordinate audacity. For to dare to do a thing implies the possibility of fearing to do it, and what can God conceivably fear? The very idea of God, since it implies omnipotence, denies the possibility of his fearing anything at all. And yet there is one thing which, at least in a formal sense, God may be imagined to fear—the violation of his own nature by himself. The import of the last question of the poem, "What immortal hand or eye / Dare frame thy fearful symmetry?" is that, in creating the Tyger, God has perhaps committed just such a violation, that he has contradicted the self-imposed laws of his own being.[2]

This idea is quite explicitly proposed in the fifth stanza:

> When the stars threw down their spears,
> And water'd heaven with their tears,
> Did he smile his work to see?
> Did he who made the Lamb make thee?

The scholars tell us that for Blake the stars are the symbols and agents of reason, law, and order. If this is so, we must understand that the stars threw down their spears in token of defeat and watered heaven with their tears in chagrin because they disapproved of God's having created the Tyger. It seemed to them a controversion of that very order which God himself had instituted and which he had enjoined them to enforce.

What chiefly makes it possible to think of God as being inconsistent with himself is his having created the Lamb before the Tyger. Just as "Tyger! Tyger!" is the central poem of *Songs of Experience,* so the poem called "The Lamb" is central to the volume called *Songs of Innocence,* which Blake had published five years before, in 1789. In the established symbolism of Western culture, the

---

[2] That Blake thought the distinction between *could* and *dare* to be of great importance is made plain by the way he revised the poem. In the early drafts of "Tyger! Tyger!" the first stanza was exactly the same as the last; in both stanzas the question read, "What immortal hand or eye / Dare frame thy fearful symmetry?" But as Blake worked over the poem and understood better what it was trying to say, he perceived the striking—we might say shocking—effect that would be achieved by changing the phrase in the first stanza to the neutral "Could frame," reserving *dare* as a startling climax in the last stanza. To be sure, this is not the only use of the word *dare* in the poem, for it occurs twice in Stanza II and once in Stanza IV. We might wish that it did not, that it occurred uniquely and therefore the more startlingly in the last line. Yet the word as it is used in Stanzas II and IV may be said to differ in meaning from the word as it is used in Stanza VI. The questions in Stanzas II and IV all have to do with the executive part of creation, with physical acts, with power. Who would venture to put his power to the test of undertaking to create the Tyger? The answer implied by the question is that God alone would take this risk; but because God is all-powerful, there really is no risk—the word *dare* therefore comes to mean no more than *could.* But in the last stanza *dare* refers to the conceptual part of creation, to the idea of the Tyger as conceived by the mind of God. And because this idea may possibly be thought a contradiction of God's nature, the word has its full dramatic force.

Lamb stands for harmlessness, gentleness, and defenselessness; in Christian icon-ography, it stands for Jesus—for the Jesus who said, "Resist not evil," and who offered himself as a sacrifice for mankind. In "The Lamb" it is a child who asks of the Lamb the same question that the poet, speaking in his own voice as a mature man, asks of the Tyger: *Who made you?* The little questioner is in no doubt about the answer:

> Little Lamb, I'll tell thee;
> Little Lamb, I'll tell thee:
> He is callèd by thy name,
> For he calls himself a Lamb.
> He is meek, & he is mild:
> He became a little child,
> I a child, & thou a lamb,
> We are callèd by his name.

That God, who had created the Lamb and had incarnated himself in Jesus who *is* the Lamb, should also have created the Tyger as another aspect of his being —this seems to the stars, who are the agents of divine law, to be a clear contra-diction by God of his own nature as he had declared it to them, and as the nega-tion of the terms of their commission to maintain reason and order.

The poem, however, does not substantiate the view of the matter that is held by the reasonable stars. Rather, it would seem to present the opinions of these guardians of order with considerable irony, as being limited, even stupid, as failing to comprehend the wonderful complexity of God's nature. In the opinion of the poem—although this is not made fully explicit—the Tyger is not the negation or contradiction of the Lamb. He is by no means the Anti-Christ. The Jesus who is meek and mild, who speaks of turning the other cheek, and who is symbolized by the animal commonly used in ancient sacrifices, is the Jesus most frequently represented to the religious imagination, but this does not mean that he is the only Jesus. There is also the Jesus who said, "I bring not peace but a sword," who undertook to disrupt the habitual respectable lives of men, commanding them to leave their fathers and mothers and to follow him, who questioned and denied the established Law, who—so he is represented by Dostoevski in "The Grand Inquisitor" (pages 469 ff.)—offered men a freedom too terrible for most to accept. This is the Jesus whom T. S. Eliot, in "Geron-tion," could precisely call "Christ the tiger."

When Blake brought together his *Songs of Innocence* and his *Songs of Experience* in a single volume, he called it *Songs of Innocence and Experience, Shewing the Two Contrary States of the Human Soul,* and the title makes it sufficiently plain that in Blake's view a "state" which is "contrary" to another state is not necessarily a negation of it or antagonistic to it. The contrary of Innocence is not Wickedness or Evil but Experience, which is the condition in which a human being comes to realize and exercise his vital energies and in which he knows both the joy and the sorrow that follow upon their use. Both the state of the Lamb and the state of the Tyger are appropriate to mankind; both are sanctioned by the nature of God.

But although Blake is so nearly explicit in making the Tyger stand for one of the two aspects of Christ, or one of the two states of man, his symbolic inten-tion is not limited to this alone. The Tyger, in its fierceness and beauty, can be regarded as that manifestation of the human mind which we call genius. (It is interesting to compare this representation of genius with that of Babel's story, "Di Grasso" [pages 710 ff.].) And it can be thought to stand for the ruthless ferocity of political revolution, specifically of the French Revolution, with which Blake was much preoccupied.

RESOLUTION
AND
INDEPENDENCE

WILLIAM WORDSWORTH
1770–1850

I

There was a roaring in the wind all night;
The rain came heavily and fell in floods;
But now the sun is rising calm and bright;
The birds are singing in the distant woods;
Over his own sweet voice the Stock-dove broods;   5
The Jay makes answer as the Magpie chatters;
And all the air is filled with pleasant noise of waters.

II

All things that love the sun are out of doors;
The sky rejoices in the morning's birth;
The grass is bright with rain-drops;—on the moors   10
The hare is running races in her mirth;
And with her feet she from the plashy earth
Raises a mist; that, glittering in the sun,
Runs with her all the way, wherever she doth run.

III

I was a Traveller then upon the moor;   15
I saw the hare that raced about with joy;
I heard the woods and distant waters roar;
Or heard them not, as happy as a boy:
The pleasant season did my heart employ:
My old remembrances went from me wholly;   20
And all the ways of men, so vain and melancholy.

IV

But, as it sometimes chanceth, from the might
Of joy in minds that can no further go,

As high as we have mounted in delight
In our dejection do we sink as low;   25
To me that morning did it happen so;
And fears and fancies thick upon me came;
Dim sadness—and blind thoughts, I knew not, nor could name

V

I heard the sky-lark warbling in the sky;
And I bethought me of the playful hare: 30
Even such a happy Child of earth am I;
Even as these blissful creatures do I fare;
Far from the world I walk, and from all care;
But there may come another day to me—
Solitude, pain of heart, distress, and poverty.   35

VI

My whole life I have lived in pleasant thought,
As if life's business were a summer mood;
As if all needful things would come unsought
To genial faith, still rich in genial good;
But how can He expect that others should   40
Build for him, sow for him, and at his call
Love him, who for himself will take no heed at all?

VII

I thought of Chatterton,[1] the marvellous Boy,
The sleepless Soul that perished in his pride;
Of Him[2] who walked in glory and in joy   45
Following his plough, along the mountain-side:
By our own spirits are we deified:
We Poets in our youth begin in gladness;
But thereof come in the end despondency and madness.

VIII

Now, whether it were by peculiar grace,   50
A leading from above, a something given,
Yet it befell that, in this lonely place,
When I with these untoward thoughts had striven,
Beside a pool bare to the eye of heaven
I saw a Man before me unawares: 55
The oldest man he seemed that ever wore grey hairs.

[1] Thomas Chatterton (1752–1770), a promising poet who committed suicide at the age of 17.   [2] Robert Burns (1759–1796), the Scottish poet, who had a difficult life and died early.

IX

As a huge stone is sometimes seen to lie
Couched on the bald top of an eminence;
Wonder to all who do the same espy,
By what means it could thither come, and whence;   60
So that it seems a thing endued with sense:
Like a sea-beast crawled forth, that on a shelf
Of rock or sand reposeth, there to sun itself;

X

Such seemed this Man, not all alive nor dead,
Nor all asleep—in his extreme old age: 65
His body was bent double, feet and head
Coming together in life's pilgrimage;
As if some dire constraint of pain, or rage
Of sickness felt by him in times long past,
A more than human weight upon his frame had cast.   70

XI

Himself he propped, limbs, body, and pale face,
Upon a long grey staff of shaven wood:
And, still as I drew near with gentle pace,
Upon the margin of that moorish[3] flood
Motionless as a cloud the old Man stood,   75
That heareth not the loud winds when they call;
And moveth all together, if it move at all.

XII

At length, himself unsettling, he the pond
Stirred with his staff, and fixedly did look
Upon the muddy water, which he conned,   80
As if he had been reading in a book:
And now a stranger's privilege I took;
And, drawing to his side, to him did say,
"This morning gives us promise of a glorious day."

XIII

A gentle answer did the old Man make,   85
In courteous speech which forth he slowly drew:
And him with further words I thus bespake,
"What occupation do you there pursue?
This is a lonesome place for one like you."

[3] On a moor.

Ere he replied, a flash of mild surprise   90
Broke from the stable orbs of his yet-vivid eyes.

XIV

His words came feebly, from a feeble chest,
But each in solemn order followed each,
With something of a lofty utterance drest—
Choice word and measured phrase, above the reach   95
Of ordinary men; a stately speech;
Such as grave Livers do in Scotland use,
Religious men, who give to God and man their dues.

XV

He told, that to these waters he had come
To gather leeches,[4] being old and poor: 100
Employment hazardous and wearisome!
And he had many hardships to endure:
From pond to pond he roamed, from moor to moor;
Housing, with God's good help, by choice or chance;
And in this way he gained an honest maintenance.   105

XVI

The old Man still stood talking by my side;
But now his voice to me was like a stream
Scarce heard; nor word from word could I divide;
And the whole body of the Man did seem
Like one whom I had met with in a dream;   110
Or like a man from some far region sent,
To give me human strength, by apt admonishment.

XVII

My former thoughts returned: the fear that kills;
And hope that is unwilling to be fed;
Cold, pain, and labour, and all fleshly ills;   115
And mighty Poets in their misery dead.
—Perplexed, and longing to be comforted,
My question eagerly did I renew,
"How is it that you live, and what is it you do?"

XVIII

He with a smile did then his words repeat;   120
And said that, gathering leeches, far and wide

---

[4] Bloodsucking worms formerly used by physicians to reduce what was thought to be an excess of blood.

He travelled; stirring thus about his feet
The waters of the pools where they abide.
"Once I could meet with them on every side;
But they have dwindled long by slow decay;   125
Yet still I persevere, and find them where I may."

XIX

While he was talking thus, the lonely place,
The old Man's shape, and speech—all troubled me:
In my mind's eye I seemed to see him pace
About the weary moors continually,   130
Wandering about alone and silently.
While I these thoughts within myself pursued,
He, having made a pause, the same discourse renewed.

XX

And soon with this he other matter blended,
Cheerfully uttered, with demeanour kind,   135
But stately in the main; and, when he ended,
I could have laughed myself to scorn to find
In that decrepit Man so firm a mind.
"God," said I, "be my help and stay secure;
I'll think of the Leech-gatherer on the lonely moor!"   140

COMMENTARY

Let us suppose that someone who had never read "Resolution and Independence" were to ask us what it is about and we were to comply with his request.
Would there be much likelihood of his believing that this could make the
material of one of the finest poems in the English language? I use the phrase
"what it is about" in the simple and quite natural sense in which we employ it
when we inquire about some story or play with which we have no acquaintance,
expecting to be answered with a summary account of its chief happenings. We
do not of course think we have been told much when we have been told only
this, yet we do feel we have been supplied some ground for estimating the
interest the story or play will have for us; we assume some relation between
even a scant *résumé* and the real nature of a work. And in general we are right
in this assumption. But not always, and not, surely, in the instance of "Resolution and Independence."

What is the poem about? It is about the poet's meeting with a very old
man and the beneficent effect that this encounter has upon him. On a fine
spring morning, the poet, who is a young or youngish man, is walking on the
moors. He is in a happy frame of mind, but suddenly his spirits fall, and he is
overcome by an intense anxiety about his future; he thinks about the disastrous

fates that have befallen other poets and that might befall him. As he walks on in his painful state of depression and fear, he comes across a solitary decrepit figure standing in a shallow pool. To the poet's questions about his way of life, the old man replies with simple dignity. He makes a bare living by gathering leeches; the work grows ever more difficult for him; he is quite alone in the world. He is so old that it seems scarcely possible that he should go on living; and he has, as we say, nothing to live for; yet he utters no complaint and shows no self-pity. The poet is moved to shame for having been so much distressed by the mere imagination of misfortune; he resolves to make the old leech-gatherer his example of fortitude.

If this is a fair statement of what happens in "Resolution and Independence," it is certainly reasonable to conclude that the content of the poem is rather trivial and dull. What is more, it has the unpleasing quality of moral didacticism; it seems to have the intention of teaching a lesson in simple morality, or even something more boring than that, a lesson in mental hygiene: "Do not allow your imagination to bedevil you with thoughts of personal disaster. Confront the chances of life with a firm and equal mind." What, then, are the elements of the poem that make for its great quality?

The first of these is the idea of greatness itself. The chief characteristic of the old man is his dignity. The simile by which he is first described compares him to a "huge stone," a massive boulder such as we sometimes see "couched on the bald top of an eminence," which raises in our minds the question of how it came there. If we do not think rationally of the glacier or flood that transported the boulder to its present unlikely place but suppose that it had moved of its own volition, its imagined movement is wonderful and awesome, and no less so is the movement of the old man. He leans on a staff because he is feeble, but his posture is majestic; his staff is an attribute of his majesty. The difficulty with which he moves appears as a sign not of weakness but of firmness, of a nature that is not easily moved by circumstance.

> Motionless as a cloud the old Man stood,
> That heareth not the loud winds when they call;
> And moveth all together, if it move at all.

In all cultures the quality of majesty is associated with weightiness and a degree of immobility, or at least slowness of movement—a king in a hurry seems a contradiction in terms. The ceremonial robes of the king express the idea that he has no need to be active. And the impression of the old man's kingliness is borne out by his "stately" speech and the imperious "flash" of his "yet vivid eyes."

In addition to this majesty, the old man has for the poet something like a supernatural authority. He seems "like one whom I had met with in a dream"—

> Or like a man from some far region sent,
> To give me human strength, by apt admonishment.

The "far region" suggests a divine region; to the poet the Leech-gatherer is an agent or messenger of God, an angel in disguise. This idea is sustained as the poet speculates on how it came about that he met the old man at this particular moment, when the meeting is of such momentous significance to him. He wonders if the encounter takes place "by peculiar grace, / A leading from above, a something given." These are theological terms having reference to divine intervention in the lives of individual persons.

But if the old man, despite his actual feebleness, is a figure of majesty, so, in his way, is the poet, who speaks not merely in his own person but as the representative of all poets. For him the sorrow of poets in misfortune is the sorrow of kings in misfortune—he speaks of "mighty Poets in their misery dead." The characteristic attributes of poets are not only "joy" but "pride" and "glory." They are, indeed, even greater than kings, for their divine right is from themselves: "By our own spirits are we deified."

Yet it is by their own spirits that they are cast down—no sooner has the poet made his proud boast than he confronts the tragic fate that threatens the possessors of the poetic power. His words are shocking in their explicitness:

> We Poets in our youth begin in gladness;
> But thereof come in the end despondency and madness.

The life of poets, our poet is saying, follows the course of his own feelings of that very morning: his despondency had succeeded his high spirits as if caused by them. His joy and its evanescence have their visual counterpart in the hare he described in Stanza II:

> All things that love the sun are out of doors;
> The sky rejoices in the morning's birth;
> The grass is bright with rain-drops;—on the moors
> The hare is running races in her mirth;
> And with her feet she from the plashy earth
> Raises a mist; that, glittering in the sun,
> Runs with her all the way, wherever she doth run.

Wherever she doth run—but not for as long as she runs. For the earth will dry and the mist that enhaloes her will vanish. We know from other of his poems that Wordsworth feared the loss of his poetic gift, which he associated with his youth and which he often represented in terms of some effect of light.

The poem, we can say, is organized by an opposition between what is suggested, on the one hand, by the hare racing in its luminous mist, and, on the other hand, by the "huge stone" to which the Leech-gatherer is compared— on the one hand, movement, speed, brightness, but also evanescence; on the other hand, immobility and lack of sentience, but also endurance. The poetic temperament, which is characterized by its quick responsiveness, Wordsworth associates with the quick-moving hare. To this he opposes—what? What name are we to give to the other temperament?

We are tempted to call it religious because one of the salient facts about the old Leech-gatherer is that he belongs to a Scottish religious sect. And religion may indeed, and often does, play a part in what we seek to name. But it need not. And then, even apart from the fact that there have been many religious poets, religion and poetry have too much in common to permit us to set up any simple opposition between them. What stands here in contrast to the poetic temperament is the temperament that finds its fulfilment in strictness of control, in what we have come to call "character." The nature of the poet, at least in the modern view, is defined by sensitivity and free responsiveness. These traits no doubt have their connection with morality as well as creativity, yet a strict moral training will undertake to limit them in the interests of character. This is exemplified in a striking way by the statement of the famous physician Sir William Osler, who, in one of his lectures to medical students, spoke of the physician's need for the quality which he called "imperturbability." He also called it "immobility" and "impassiveness" and even went so far as to call it "callousness." He admitted that this quality might appear to patients and their friends as hardness of heart, an indifference to the suffering of others that verged upon the inhuman, but he went on to say how disconcerted the patient and his family would be if the physician lacked this quality, for upon his ability to shut off his sensitivity depend his "firmness and courage," his ability to make difficult decisions and carry them out.

The poem, then, may be said to ask this question: Must the poet, for the sake of his survival, take to himself some measure of imperturbability, of rock-like fortitude, even at the cost of surrendering some of the sensitivity and responsiveness which constitute the essence of his poetic power? The question has an intrinsic psychological interest. But what gives it its peculiar force in the poem is the circumstance in which it is posed, the aura of tragic destiny which attends this confrontation of two modes of human self-realization.

Considered from the point of view of prosodic technique, "Resolution and Independence" is a most remarkable achievement. We begin our understanding of how the poem "works" by taking note of the punctuation, the sheer amount and weight of it: in the first three stanzas almost every line has a strong stop at its end. This has the effect of making each line a decisive and dramatic statement. The energy of one line is not continuous with that of the next; each line initiates its own movement, of which we become the more conscious as it discharges its energy upon the semi-colon, colon, or period that stops it; the effect is like that of watching breaker after breaker rising up to hurl itself upon a cliff. After the first three stanzas, the punctuation becomes lighter, although it is still decisive, and now we become aware of the stanza rather than the line as the unit of energy. Each stanza is as discrete as, at the beginning of the poem, each line had been, for the lengthened last line of the stanza acts as a full stop. The poem is thus a series of initiations of energy and of resistances to it, an equal display of movement and solidity.

Many readers are disturbed, even distressed, by the concluding couplet. And with some reason, for there is no doubt that

> "God," said I, "be my help and stay secure;
> I'll think of the Leech-gatherer on the lonely moor!"

is in all ways an anticlimax. It is emotionally insufficient and its tone is downright jaunty, so that it almost seems to dismiss the great episode which it brings to an end. The casual appeal to God seems merely conventional and a negation of the powerful if vague reference to the divine "far region." To these objections an admirer of the poem can offer no defence, except to say that, although cogent, they do not much matter.

KUBLA KHAN
OR
A VISION IN A DREAM
A Fragment

SAMUEL TAYLOR COLERIDGE

1772–1834

In Xanadu did Kubla Khan[1]
A stately pleasure-dome decree:
Where Alph, the sacred river, ran
  Through caverns measureless to man
    Down to a sunless sea.   5
So twice five miles of fertile ground
With walls and towers were girdled round:
And here were gardens bright with sinuous rills,
Where blossomed many an incense-bearing tree;
And here were forests ancient as the hills,   10
Enfolding sunny spots of greenery.

But oh! that deep romantic chasm which slanted
Down the green hill athwart[2] a cedarn cover!
A savage place! as holy and enchanted
As e'er beneath a waning moon was haunted   15
By woman wailing for her demon-lover!
And from this chasm, with ceaseless turmoil seething,
As if this earth in fast thick pants were breathing,
A mighty fountain momently[3] was forced:
Amid whose swift half-intermitted burst   20
Huge fragments vaulted like rebounding hail,
Or chaffy grain beneath the thresher's flail:
And 'mid these dancing rocks at once and ever
It flung up momently the sacred river.

---

[1] Kubla Khan was founder of the Mongol dynasty in China. His court, in reality, was at Yenching, near Peking.   [2] Across.   [3] Every moment, continuously.

Five miles meandering with a mazy motion   25
Through wood and dale the sacred river ran,
Then reached the caverns measureless to man,
And sank in tumult to a lifeless ocean:
And 'mid this tumult Kubla heard from far
Ancestral voices prophesying war!   30
    The shadow of the dome of pleasure
    Floated midway on the waves;
    Where was heard the mingled measure
    From the fountain and the caves.
It was a miracle of rare device,   35
A sunny pleasure-dome with caves of ice!

    A damsel with a dulcimer
    In a vision once I saw:
    It was an Abyssinian maid,
    And on her dulcimer she played,   40
    Singing of Mount Abora.
    Could I revive within me,
    Her symphony and song,
    To such a deep delight 'twould win me,
That with music loud and long,   45
I would build that dome in air,
That sunny dome! those caves of ice!
And all who heard should see them there,
And all should cry, Beware! Beware!
His flashing eyes, his floating hair!   50
Weave a circle round him thrice,
And close your eyes with holy dread,
For he on honey-dew hath fed,
And drunk the milk of Paradise.

COMMENTARY

Although the intrinsic qualities of "Kubla Khan" justify the admiration that has
been given to it, some part of its great fame must surely be attributed to the
prefatory note in which, upon its first publication in 1816, Coleridge told his
readers how the poem came to be composed, some eighteen years before. The
circumstances that Coleridge relates have so engaged the interest of the world
that we can scarcely think of the poem without having them in mind—they
have become virtually an element of the poem itself.

    "In the summer of the year 1797," Coleridge writes,[1] "the Author, then in
ill health, had retired to a lonely farm-house between Porlock and Linton. . . .

[1] But his memory played him false. All evidence points to the impossibility of his
having written the poem in that year. It was probably written in 1798, but 1799 and 1800
also fall within the possible range.

In consequence of a slight indisposition, an anodyne [it was opium] had been prescribed, from the effects of which he fell asleep in his chair at the moment that he was reading the following sentence, or words of the same substance, in 'Purchas's Pilgrimage': 'Here the Khan Kubla commanded a palace to be built, and a stately garden thereunto. And thus ten miles of fertile ground were enclosed with a wall.' The author continued for about three hours in a profound sleep, at least of the external senses, during which time he has the most vivid confidence, that he could not have composed less than from two to three hundred lines; if that indeed can be called composition in which all the images rose up before him as *things,* with a parallel production of the correspondent expressions, without any sensation or consciousness of effort. On awaking he appeared to himself to have a distinct recollection of the whole, and taking his pen, ink, and paper, instantly and eagerly wrote down the lines that are here preserved. At this moment he was unfortunately called out by a person on business from Porlock, and detained by him above an hour, and on his return to his room, found, to his no small surprise and mortification, that though he still retained some vague and dim recollection of the general purport of the vision, yet, with the exception of some eight or ten scattered lines and images, all the rest had passed away like the images on the surface of a stream into which a stone has been cast. . . ."

This account of how "Kubla Khan" was written was for a long time accepted without question. But the researches of an American scholar, Professor Elisabeth Schneider, have brought the literal truth of the story into serious question; they suggest that these circumstances of composition were as much the product of the poet's imagination as the poem itself. Yet in some sense the truthfulness of Coleridge's account does not matter—the important thing is that the poet believed that it was possible, if singular, to compose a poem in his sleep, without the aid of his conscious mind, without, as he puts it, "any sensation or consciousness of effort," and also that a particular virtue might be assigned to such a mode of composition.

We must not exaggerate the novelty of this proposition. Ever since literature has been the object of thoughtful curiosity, men have supposed that the composition of poetry may be other than a willed and conscious process. This has been commonly explained by the concept of "inspiration," the idea that a spirit—of the Muse or some other nonhuman being—enters the poet, takes possession of his mind, and speaks through him.[1] Plato, not in order to disparage poets but to explain them, said that they were "mad," and the idea of the poet's being "possessed," out of his own control, as an insane person is, became part of the popular conception of the poetic character—everybody in Shakespeare's audience knew what Theseus was talking about when he equated the lunatic and the poet and spoke of "the poet's eye, in a fine frenzy rolling." This notion of poetic composition persisted even into the era of rationalism; Dryden paid tribute to it in his famous couplet about the close alliance between great wit— by which he meant poetic genius—and madness.

Yet the rationalism of the late seventeenth and eighteenth centuries put its critical emphasis less upon the uncontrolled processes of composition than upon those that were conscious and reasoned, less upon the poet's inspired vision than

[1] For a superb exemplification of this idea, see Shelley's "Ode to the West Wind," pp. 886 ff.

upon his careful revision. Pope, like Dryden, admitted the primacy of inspiration, but the chief direction of both his precept and example was toward correctness, polish, and good taste. If nonrational inspiration was to be acknowledged in the composition of great poems, it was to be admired only if it submitted to the rule of good judgment, which might be defined as the codified knowledge of what will please men of good sense.

The preface to "Kubla Khan" constitutes, therefore, a radical denial of the character of the poet that had prevailed in the eighteenth century. We cannot read Pope's brilliant "Essay on Criticism" without understanding that it regards the poet as primarily a performer, and, as such, committed to pleasing an audience and submissive to the judgment of his audience's taste. This view of the poet was not supposed to diminish his dignity—his position can fairly be compared with that of a great performing musician or dancer of our own time. Pope assumes that in general the audience's taste is correct and to be relied upon in much the same way we now assume the authority of people who love music and the dance—if a performer can consistently meet the requirements of persons with a highly developed sensibility in his art, we by and large take it for granted that he is good. And as for the performer, he assumes that if he meets his own standard of what makes a good performance, he will be liked and praised; his standard of judgment and that of his audience are much the same.

But Coleridge's preface quite negates the idea of the poet as performer and of the poem as an artistic commodity offered to the audience for its approval. Indeed, "Kubla Khan" was so little a performance that it was not even finished. (Actually, of course, even though the poet calls it "a fragment," the poem is felt by most readers to be complete in the sense of being an aesthetic whole. But the preface inevitably tempts us to imagine how it would have continued if the person on business from Porlock had not paid his visit.) It is not something that the poet wrote with the intention of interesting or pleasing or edifying his audience. It came into being as if by its own necessity and by its own will—it is a fact in nature as much as in art, a psychological fact as much as a poetic fact. It would seem, that is, that the mind quite naturally makes poems, as it makes dreams, without intention, without effort, without thought, without revision or any awareness of the rules of literature.

Coleridge's preface is to be read, however, not only as a kind of manifesto on the working of the poetic mind but also as an explanation of how this particular poem is to be responded to. When it first appeared, there would still have been many readers whom it would have troubled and puzzled; they would have thought that Coleridge was not being unduly or falsely modest when he said that he was publishing it "rather as a psychological curiosity, than on the ground of any supposed *poetic* merits." Such readers were no doubt fewer than if the poem had appeared in the year of its composition, for in the intervening time other poets had begun to habituate the public to certain of its poetic qualities—its exoticism, its fantasy, its indifference to rational considerations. Yet there were still many who would have been at a loss to know what the poem was trying to "say" or "do," and for these the preface was, in effect, a guide. It suggested that "Kubla Khan" was not to be judged by the criteria which in its day were conventionally applied to poetry and that the reader was thus free to respond to it in new terms, the terms of the poem itself.

The modern reader is surely less likely to resist making this kind of response than was the reader of Coleridge's time. This is not to imply that we today are more sensitive to poetry and more intelligent about it than our forebears were, but only that the tendency of literary criticism and education has changed. In our time the poet's personal fantasy is given large license and authority. Less and less do we think it possible to ask that a poem conform to some preconception of what a poem should be; we even believe that we should have no such preconception. We tend to think that every poem suggests its own aesthetic criteria and that it should be judged by our sense of its being an authentic representation of the poet's state of feeling—so long, at least, as we have reason to suppose that this state of feeling is significant. We may even incline to the belief that the more alien from our own state of feeling a poem is, the more authentically it represents the poet's feelings and the more authority it has. For readers today it neither constitutes the failure of a poem nor a deficiency in our aesthetic perception if we are not readily able to say what the work means in all its various parts or as a whole. After all, we have never understood music in the sense of being able to explain its meaning, and nowadays we are surrounded by pictures which give us pleasure although (as the painters themselves are the first to say) we have no way to "understand" them rationally and articulately. We admit the possibility that a work of art can exist in its own right, without reference to us, like a tree, or a mountain, or an animal; it need have no relation to us except as we elect to have a relation to it, by finding interest and pleasure in it. We think of the work as a meaningful expression of its creator's mind but not, in any usual definition of the word, a communication.

"Kubla Khan" offers no literal difficulty to the reader—its statements, taken by themselves, are perfectly clear. Yet most readers, however strong their response to it, feel that they would be incapable of formulating what the poem as a whole is *really* saying. The concluding sentence of Coleridge's prefatory note may help us to become conscious of what it is that we respond to. "As a contrast to this vision," Coleridge says, "I have annexed a fragment of a very different character, describing with equal fidelity the dream of pain and disease." He is referring to his poem, "The Pains of Sleep," which describes in a very direct way the distress which opium and physical and mental ill-health introduced into his repose, the horrors of—as the poem calls them—"life-stifling fear, life-stifling shame." What "Kubla Khan" represents is indeed a contrast; it is the very opposite of whatever might be life-stifling—the vision is of life at its most intense. Life's power is announced in the decree of the great Khan, the mere utterance of which brought the "pleasure-dome" into being, by the ejaculative force of the "mighty fountain," by the passion of the "woman wailing for her demon-lover," by—finally—the great image of the poet in the transcendent strength of his magical art. Here, surely, is nothing "life-stifling." Nor does the war prophesied by the "ancestral voices" bring any fear: for the Khan, war is the very business of life. The woman who wails for her demon-lover utters her cry without any possibility of shame, and the poet envisages his dangerous strength ("Beware! Beware!") without compunction. To be sure, the meandering course of the "sacred river" comes to its end in a "sunless sea," a "lifeless ocean"; but the river is perpetual, having its source in the mighty fountain which is "momently" forced from the earth. The "caves of ice" beneath the "sunny pleasure-dome" contradict the fertility of the gardens and the forests, yet if they, like the sunless sea and the lifeless ocean, evoke the idea of death, they suggest the idea of a holy mystery rather than a denial of life; the fear or awe they generate is consonant with the sacredness of Alph, the sacred river; and when the poet says that with the power of his music he will "build" these caves of ice, he is as enraptured by this prospect as by the thought of building "that sunny dome" itself. The poem and what it implies of the nature of poetry celebrate pleasure but even more they celebrate life in its might and in its mystery of contradictions.

DON JUAN
An Episode from Canto II

GEORGE GORDON, LORD BYRON

1788–1824

Headnote

There are two things that the reader ought to know about Byron's Don Juan. The first is that his name is not pronounced in the Spanish fashion (*hwan*), but as if it were an English name spoken phonetically: Byron rimes it with "new one" and "true one." The second is that he has only the faintest connection with the Don Juan of legend. It is true that all his adventures involve love affairs of one kind or another, but he is nothing like the universal seducer of Molière's play or Mozart's opera. Indeed, he is a rather modest and virtuous young man whose love affairs either happen to him or are forced upon him by women. A native of Seville, he has been very strictly brought up by his extravagantly prudish and intellectual mother. When he is sixteen, his mother's friend, Donna Julia, "married, charming, chaste, and twenty-three," falls in love with him and he with her. Their liaison is discovered by Donna Julia's husband, a great scandal results, Donna Julia is packed off to a convent, and Juan is hustled out of the country by his mother. He takes ship at Cadiz; before his departure he has received from Julia a very touching letter of farewell and has been greatly moved by it.

*　　*　　*

1

Oh ye! who teach the ingenuous youth of nations,
　　Holland, France, England, Germany, or Spain,
I pray ye flog them upon all occasions,
　　It mends their morals, never mind the pain:
The best of mothers and of educations　　　　　　　　　　　　5
　　In Juan's case were but employ'd in vain,
Since, in a way that's rather of the oddest, he
Became divested of his native modesty.

2

Had he but been placed at a public school,
　　In the third form, or even in the fourth,[1]　　　　　　　　10

---

[1] Grade in a British secondary school. A "public school" in England is an endowed institution at which rather high fees are charged. It prepares for the public service or for the university.

His daily task had kept his fancy cool,
    At least, had he been nurtured in the north;
Spain may prove an exception to the rule,
    But then exceptions always prove its worth—
A lad of sixteen causing a divorce   15
Puzzled his tutors very much, of course.

    3

I can't say that it puzzles me at all,
    If all things be consider'd; first, there was
His lady-mother, mathematical,
    A——never mind;—his tutor, an old ass;   20
A pretty woman—(that's quite natural,
    Or else the thing had hardly come to pass)
A husband rather old, not much in unity
With his young wife—a time, and opportunity.

    4

Well—well; the world must turn upon its axis,   25
    And all mankind turn with it, heads or tails,
And live and die, make love and pay our taxes,
    And as the veering wind shifts, shift our sails;
The king commands us, and the doctor quacks us,
    The priest instructs, and so our life exhales,   30
A little breath, love, wine, ambition, fame,
Fighting, devotion, dust,—perhaps a name.

    5

I said, that Juan had been sent to Cadiz—
    A pretty town, I recollect it well—
'Tis there the mart of the colonial trade is,   35
    (Or was, before Peru learn'd to rebel,)
And such sweet girls—I mean, such graceful ladies,
    Their very walk would make your bosom swell;
I can't describe it, though so much it strike,
Nor liken it—I never saw the like: 40

    6

An Arab horse, a stately stag, a barb[2]
    New-broke, a cameleopard,[3] a gazelle,
No—none of these will do—and then their garb,
    Their veil and petticoat—Alas! to dwell
Upon such things would very near absorb   45

---

[2] A Barbary horse, one of a breed noted for speed and endurance.   [3] Giraffe.

A canto—then their feet and ankles,—well,
　Thank Heaven I've got no metaphor quite ready,
(And so, my sober Muse—come, let's be steady—

7

Chaste Muse!—well, if you must, you must)—the veil
　Thrown back a moment with the glancing hand,　　　　　50
While the o'erpowering eye, that turns you pale,
　Flashes into the heart:—All sunny land
Of love! when I forget you, may I fail
　To——say my prayers—but never was there plann'd
A dress through which the eyes give such a volley,　　　　55
Excepting the Venetian Fazzioli.[4]

8

But to our tale: the Donna Inez sent
　Her son to Cadiz only to embark;
To stay there had not answer'd her intent,
　But why?—we leave the reader in the dark—　　　　　60
'Twas for a voyage the young man was meant,
　As if a Spanish ship were Noah's ark,
To wean him from the wickedness of earth,
And send him like a dove of promise forth.[5]

9

Don Juan bade his valet pack his things　　　　　　　65
　According to direction, then received
A lecture and some money: for four springs
　He was to travel; and though Inez grieved
(As every kind of parting has its stings),
　She hoped he would improve—perhaps believed:　　　70
A letter, too, she gave (he never read it)
Of good advice—and two or three of credit.

10

In the mean time, to pass her hours away,
　Brave Inez now set up a Sunday school
For naughty children, who would rather play　　　　　75
　(Like truant rogues) the devil, or the fool;
Infants of three years old were taught that day,
　Dunces were whipt, or set upon a stool:
The great success of Juan's education
Spurr'd her to teach another generation.　　　　　　80

---

[4] A dress worn in Venice in Byron's time.　[5] After the flood, Noah repeatedly sent out a dove from the ark. When the bird failed to return, Noah knew that the land was dry and that it was safe to leave the ark (Genesis 8:8–13).

11

Juan embark'd—the ship got under way,
    The wind was fair, the water passing rough;
A devil of a sea rolls in that bay,
    As I, who've cross'd it oft, know well enough;
And, standing upon deck, the dashing spray   85
    Flies in one's face, and makes it weather-tough:
And there he stood to take, and take again,
His first—perhaps his last—farewell of Spain.

12

I can't but say it is an awkward sight
    To see one's native land receding through   90
The growing waters; it unmans one quite,
    Especially when life is rather new:
I recollect Great Britain's coast looks white,
    But almost every other country's blue,
When gazing on them, mystified by distance,   95
We enter on our nautical existence.

13

So Juan stood, bewilder'd on the deck:
    The wind sung, cordage strain'd, and sailors swore,
And the ship creak'd, the town became a speck,
    From which away so fair and fast they bore.   100
The best of remedies is a beef-steak
    Against sea-sickness; try it, sir, before
You sneer, and I assure you this is true,
For I have found it answer—so may you.

14

Don Juan stood, and, gazing from the stern,   105
    Beheld his native Spain receding far:
First partings form a lesson hard to learn,
    Even nations feel this when they go to war;
There is a sort of unexprest concern,
    A kind of shock that sets one's heart ajar: 110
At leaving even the most unpleasant people
And places, one keeps looking at the steeple.

15

But Juan had got many things to leave,
    His mother, and a mistress, and no wife,
So that he had much better cause to grieve   115
    Than many persons more advanced in life;
And if we now and then a sigh must heave

At quitting even those we quit in strife,
No doubt we weep for those the heart endears—
That is, till deeper griefs congeal our tears.   120

16

So Juan wept, as wept the captive Jews
    By Babel's waters, still remembering Sion:[6]
I'd weep,—but mine is not a weeping Muse,
    And such light griefs are not a thing to die on;
Young men should travel, if but to amuse   125
    Themselves; and the next time their servants tie on
Behind their carriages their new portmanteau,
Perhaps it may be lined with this my canto.[7]

17

And Juan wept, and much he sigh'd and thought,
    While his salt tears dropp'd into the salt sea,   130
"Sweets to the sweet";[8] (I like so much to quote;
    You must excuse this extract,—'t is where she,
The Queen of Denmark, for Ophelia brought
    Flowers to the grave;) and, sobbing often, he
Reflected on his present situation,   135
And seriously resolved on reformation.

18

"Farewell, my Spain! a long farewell!" he cried,
    "Perhaps I may revisit thee no more,
But die, as many an exiled heart hath died,
    Of its own thirst to see again thy shore: 140
Farewell, where Guadalquivir's waters glide!
    Farewell, my mother! and, since all is o'er,
Farewell, too, dearest Julia!—(here he drew
Her letter out again, and read it through.)

19

"And oh! if e'er I should forget, I swear—   145
    But that's impossible, and cannot be—
Sooner shall this blue ocean melt to air,
    Sooner shall earth resolve itself to sea,
Than I resign thine image, oh, my fair!
    Or think of anything, excepting thee;   150

[6] Zion, or Jerusalem; Babel, Babylon.   [7] A division of a long poem. A canto, or
song, was originally as much of a poem as a minstrel might recite without a break.   [8] So
says the queen, Gertrude, in *Hamlet* (Act V, Scene 1) as she scatters flowers over the grave
of Ophelia, who, after the death of her father, Polonius, loses her sanity and then drowns.

A mind diseased no remedy can physic—
(Here the ship gave a lurch, and he grew sea-sick.)

20

"Sooner shall heaven kiss earth—(here he fell sicker)
    Oh, Julia! what is every other woe?—
(For God's sake let me have a glass of liquor;   155
    Pedro, Battista, help me down below.)
Julia, my love—(you rascal, Pedro, quicker)—
    Oh, Julia!—(this curst vessel pitches so)—
Beloved Julia, hear me still beseeching!"
(Here he grew inarticulate with retching.)   160

21

He felt that chilling heaviness of heart,
    Or rather stomach, which, alas! attends,
Beyond the best apothecary's art,
    The loss of love, the treachery of friends,
Or death of those we dote on, when a part   165
    Of us dies with them as each fond hope ends:
No doubt he would have been much more pathetic,
But the sea acted as a strong emetic.

22

Love's a capricious power: I've known it hold
    Out through a fever caused by its own heat,   170
But be much puzzled by a cough and cold,
    And find a quinsy⁹ very hard to treat;
Against all noble maladies he's bold,
    But vulgar illnesses don't like to meet,
Nor that a sneeze should interrupt his sigh,   175
Nor inflammations redden his blind eye.

23

But worst of all is nausea, or a pain
    About the lower region of the bowels;
Love, who heroically breathes a vein,¹⁰
    Shrinks from the application of hot towels,   180
And purgatives are dangerous to his reign,
    Sea-sickness death: his love was perfect, how else
Could Juan's passion, while the billows roar,
Resist his stomach, ne'er at sea before?

⁹ Sore throat.   ¹⁰ Allows a vein to be lanced so as to let blood.

Don Juan is one of the celebrated books of the nineteenth century, and the odds are that it is quite the gayest. It is a very long poem, consisting of sixteen cantos ranging in length from 60 to 160 stanzas. It breaks off in the middle of a lively erotic adventure which the hero has embarked upon, brought to an end not by the poet's intention but by his death, and that it should stop rather than conclude is entirely appropriate to its nature. The poem has been called formless, and in some sense this is true—at least it can be said that Byron intended it to have no more form than is supplied by a single hero whose adventures and sexual escapades the poet follows, having first contrived them. Byron said that he planned to have Juan die on the guillotine during the French Revolution. But before reaching this grim consummation, he could have carried Juan through as many adventures as it pleased him to write. He intended that the chief interest of the poem should not be in the hero's living his life and dying his death but in the poet's writing the poem. Yet it would be wrong to think of Juan as a "mere puppet"—he is too engaging a figure to be regarded so; we come to have too much affection for his innocence and sweetness and readiness; and this is not to mention Byron's affection for him, as being—although of course not literally— a representation of his own youth. Nevertheless, Juan is not meant to create the illusion of being an autonomous person, like many characters in literature. His dependent status is announced in the poem's opening stanza:

> I want a hero: an uncommon want,
>   When every year and month sends forth a new one,
> Till, after cloying the gazettes with cant,
>   The age discovers he is not the true one:
> Of such as these I should not care to vaunt,
>   I'll therefore take our ancient friend Don Juan—
> We all have seen him in the pantomime,
> Sent to the devil somewhat ere his time.[1]

Having announced his selection of a hero, Byron goes on to tell us what his literary methods are going to be. Most epic poets, he says, start in the middle of the story—he quotes the famous phrase from Horace's *Art of Poetry*—and then, by some device, give the reader an account of what has gone before:

> Most epic poets plunge "in medias res"
>   (Horace makes this the heroic turnpike road),
> And then your hero tells, whene'er you please,
>   What went before—by way of episode,
> While seated after dinner at his ease,
>   Beside his mistress in some soft abode,
> Palace, or garden, paradise, or cavern,
> Which serves the happy couple for a tavern.

"Most epic poets"—does *Don Juan*, then, presume to think of itself as an epic poem? It does fulfill one requirement of an epic: it is very long. But what epic poem ever spoke in a voice so colloquial and casual, so downright careless,

---

[1] As I remarked in the headnote, Byron's hero has in fact very little in common with the legendary Don Juan.

so lacking in high seriousness? And what epic poem was ever at such pains to destroy all possibility of illusion, to make sure that the reader will not give the usual credence to the story he is being told? This epic poem—if that is what it is—mocks the very idea of epic poetry.

Don Juan is, in short, what we call a burlesque. The meaning of that word has been largely lost to a kind of theatrical entertainment which is devoted to rowdy humor, chiefly of a sexual kind, and to female nudity. But the modern burlesque show had its beginnings in actual burlesque—in, that is, the mockery of a serious play that was well known to the audience. Burlesque is a very old form of art—it was highly developed by the ancient Greeks—and many notable and even great works have been conceived in its spirit. Cervantes began Don Quixote as a burlesque of the elaborate prose romances of the sixteenth century. Fielding's Joseph Andrews is a burlesque of the moralism of Richardson's Pamela, and his Tom Jones teases the literary conventions of classical antiquity. Jane Austen's Northanger Abbey affectionately mocks the terror-novels of the day.

Burlesque is usually directed against a particular literary work or kind of work, with the intention of showing that it is false or foolish. But it may also be directed against the whole enterprise of literature, which it represents as an institution licensed to traduce reality. Parts of Flaubert's Bouvard and Pécuchet take this direction, as do parts of the great modern instance of burlesque, Joyce's Ulysses. And this is true also of Don Juan. The poet's ceaseless intrusion into his story, his avowed manipulation of it, his "asides," which must surely occupy more space than the narrative, his open references to himself, all enforce the idea that he is much too sensible a man to be taken in by the conventions of poetry, that he knows literature for what it really is, an elaborate game. He is perfectly willing to play the game, being the best-natured of men, but he will not pretend, or ask the reader to believe, that it is reality.

But although the episode of Juan struggling to maintain his high-minded sorrow against the assaults of the rising nausea of his seasickness is a notable example of burlesque, it quite transcends its genre. It goes beyond the mockery of a literary tradition, that of the faithful grieving lover, to raise radically subversive questions about the dignity of human nature and the autonomy of the human mind.

In any culture we are pretty sure to find two opposing views of man's nature. According to one view, man is at least potentially a being of great dignity, a spiritual being in the sense that he is not wholly or finally conditioned by material considerations. His dignity, spirituality, and freedom derive from his power and courage. In simpler societies power and courage are thought to belong almost exclusively to socially dominant figures, to the king, the warrior, and the priest. All these personages express by their mode of dress and by their bearing and manner of speech the dignity they claim for themselves. (The comments on the "kingliness" of Wordsworth's old Leech-gatherer [page 865] are relevant here—one of the tendencies of the literature of the late eighteenth and early nineteenth centuries was to assert the dignity of people not of the dominant classes.) The other view concentrates upon man as an animal creature, who provokes not respect but laughter. Contrary to a common assumption, even quite primitive peoples do not take their animal functions wholly for granted; in every culture sexuality and defecation are thought to be funny—

they are "accepted" as "natural" but they are thought to derogate from human dignity; they are always joked about. The same is true of the impulse to self-preservation: cowardice is thought to be "natural"—and funny.

Among the Greeks these two views of man's nature were expressed in two distinct literary forms. The view of man as a dignified, free, and spiritual being was represented by tragedy, with its persons of royal or noble birth, its grave and exalted language, its conscious suppression of all petty and sordid considerations. Comedy represented the view that man was bound by his animal nature; in the frankest possible way it took account of all the exigencies of animality, all the "low" conditions of human existence.

Aristotle said that tragedy showed men as better than they really are and that comedy showed men as worse than they really are. And of course he is right in suggesting that neither the bias of tragedy nor that of comedy tells the whole truth. But in defiance of Aristotle, as it were, comedy does claim truth for itself. If tragedy denies the comic view of man, it does so implicitly and silently; but comedy is quite often explicit in its opposition to tragedy—again and again it says straight out that the form and manner of tragedy are false and highfalutin. It claims reality for itself, insisting that reality is what is comprised by the "facts of life," by man's need and greed for food and drink, by his running away from danger, and by his copulation and defecation.

In general it can be said of the Greeks that they were able to hold the two views of man's nature in balance. They gave as much sanction to the subversive view of comedy as to the ideal view of tragedy. Yet at least one Greek, Plato, was distressed by man's double nature; his philosophy makes a strong commitment to the belief that man is most truly himself when he is free of the animal conditions of life. Christianity followed Plato in this—the essence of Christian morality lies in the wish to overcome the bondage of flesh. The way in which Christianity describes this bondage varies with the changes in the secular culture. The seventeenth century, for example, was a period of great intellectual achievement, and Christian thought at that time undertook to check intellectual pride by reminding man how conditioned by physical things his intellect was. It did this, we may say, in the manner of burlesque. The Christian poet John Donne took wry note of the fact that at a moment when his thoughts were fixed on God in prayer and meditation, a fly buzzing around his head could distract his attention from its great object and that no effort of will could restore his rapt concentration until the fly was silenced. And Pascal, one of the great mathematicians of all times as well as a profound psychologist of the religious emotions, based his whole sense of the religious life upon similar observations, upon the discrepancy between man's "greatness" and his "littleness," reminding us that, powerful as the human intellect is, a man is never in full control of the right exercise of his mind, which is always at the mercy of the most trivial material circumstances.

The early nineteenth century was an age that took pride not so much in intellectual as in emotional power; it looked upon love and passion as an indication of human freedom and dignity, and perhaps no one had done more to establish this idea than Byron himself. Whatever else Byron is burlesquing in *Don Juan* he is burlesquing his own early work, in which love and passion asserted themselves without regard to the facts of animal existence. He did indeed represent love and passion as meeting with opposition from the world and as ensuing often in pain and defeat, but this of course constitutes anything but a skeptical comment upon them—in literature the pain and defeat of a person who lives according to his belief in his spiritual nature are taken to be the affirmation of spirit itself. What Byron is now saying, however, is reductive enough; he is proposing that it is not by the great catastrophes that the life of spirit is brought into question but by the small ones. Man's sense of his autonomy and dignity is not limited by his tragic sufferings but by those that are traditionally thought to be comic—the cold in the head and the passing afflictions of the stomach.

ODE TO THE WEST WIND

PERCY BYSSHE SHELLEY
1792–1822

1

O wild West Wind, thou breath of Autumn's being,
Thou, from whose unseen presence the leaves dead
Are driven, like ghosts from an enchanter fleeing,

Yellow, and black, and pale, and hectic red,
Pestilence-stricken multitudes: O thou,   5
Who chariotest to their dark wintry bed

The wingèd seeds, where they lie cold and low,
Each like a corpse within its grave, until
Thine azure sister of the spring shall blow

Her clarion o'er the dreaming earth, and fill   10
(Driving sweet buds like flocks to feed in air)
With living hues and odors plain and hill:

Wild spirit, which art moving everywhere;
Destroyer and preserver;[1] hear, oh hear!

2

Thou on whose stream, 'mid the steep sky's commotion,   15
Loose clouds like earth's decaying leaves are shed,
Shook from the tangled boughs of Heaven and Ocean,

[1] The seemingly opposed powers of destruction and preservation were frequently attributed to a single god in ancient times.

Angels of rain and lightning: there are spread
On the blue surface of thine airy surge,
Like the bright hair uplifted from the head   20

Of some fierce Maenad,[2] even from the dim verge
Of the horizon to the zenith's height
The locks of the approaching storm. Thou dirge

Of the dying year, to which this closing night
Will be the dome of a vast sepulchre,   25
Vaulted with all thy congregated might

Of vapours, from whose solid atmosphere
Black rain, and fire, and hail will burst: O, hear!

3

Thou who didst waken from his summer dreams
The blue Mediterranean, where he lay,   30
Lulled by the coil of his crystalline streams,

Beside a pumice[3] isle in Baiæ's bay,[4]
And saw in sleep old palaces and towers
Quivering within the wave's intenser day,

All overgrown with azure moss and flowers   35
So sweet, the sense faints picturing them! Thou
For whose path the Atlantic's level powers

Cleave themselves into chasms, while far below
The sea-blooms and the oozy woods which wear
The sapless foliage of the ocean, know   40

Thy voice, and suddenly grow gray with fear,
And tremble and despoil themselves: O hear!

[2] In Greek mythology, mad or frenzied women who attended the god Dionysus, or
Bacchus.   [3] Obsidian.   [4] Bay of Naples. Baiae is a town on an inlet of the bay.

4

If I were a dead leaf thou mightest bear;
If I were a swift cloud to fly with thee;
A wave to pant beneath thy power, and share 45

The impulse of thy strength, only less free
Than thou, O, uncontrollable! If even
I were as in my boyhood, and could be

The comrade of thy wanderings over heaven,
As then, when to outstrip thy skiey speed 50
Scarce seemed a vision; I would ne'er have striven

As thus with thee in prayer in my sore need,
Oh! lift me as a wave, a leaf, a cloud!
I fall upon the thorns of life! I bleed!

A heavy weight of hours has chained and bowed 55
One too like thee: tameless, and swift, and proud.

5

Make me thy lyre, even as the forest is:
What if my leaves are falling like its own!
The tumult of thy mighty harmonies

Will take from both a deep, autumnal tone, 60
Sweet though in sadness. Be thou, Spirit fierce,
My spirit! Be thou me, impetuous one!

Drive my dead thoughts over the universe
Like withered leaves to quicken a new birth!
And, by the incantation of this verse, 65

Scatter, as from an unextinguished hearth
Ashes and sparks, my words among mankind!
Be through my lips to unawakened earth

The trumpet of a prophecy, O, Wind,
If Winter comes, can Spring be far behind? 70

COMMENTARY

This is a strangely primitive poem to have been written in the nineteenth century. Not that its language and form are primitive—they are anything but that. The primitive quality of the poem is found in certain of its modes of thought. To a very considerable extent the "Ode to the West Wind" deals with the world as men of early pagan cultures dealt with it.

The poet represents himself as experiencing a crisis of the spirit; he is at the point of despair, and in his extremity he invokes the aid of the autumn wind, asking that it give him its wild energy—"Be thou, Spirit fierce, / My spirit!" We know, certainly, that a wind cannot in actual fact do for a man what Shelley asks it to do for him. Nothing is more likely than that the poet's asking help of the wind should seem to be a mere conceit, a play of poetical fancy, and that we should satisfy our sense of actuality by explaining to ourselves that the wind "is of course only a symbol." Yet in fact we do not think of the West Wind as functioning in the poem in a merely symbolic way. We find ourselves believing that it really is the spiritual and moral force Shelley represents it as being, that, indeed, it is just what he calls it, a spirit, and that it might perfectly well enter a man and restore the power he has lost. We believe this because the poem believes it—the Ode is based on the primitive identification of spirit and wind, for the word *spirit* comes from the Latin *spiritus,* meaning breath, which in turn comes from *spirare* meaning "to blow." Shelley is entirely literal in making such an identification. Dispirited, he asks to be again inspirited, to have the breath of life blown into him.

And he goes about getting what he wants in primitive fashion. The people of an earlier time believed that words had power over things and over the unseen forces of the universe; poetry and magic were once closely allied, virtually interchangeable. The Ode assumes this old connection; Shelley would seem to have been conscious of his magician's role, for in line 65 he speaks of "the incantation of this verse." *Incantation,* although derived from the Latin word which means simply to sing or chant, always means the singing or chanting of magic spells. Another form of the word is, of course, enchantment.

Shelley's method of incantation or enchantment is in the orthodox tradition of magic. Each of the first three stanzas is an invocation—literally, a "calling" in the sense of "summoning"—of the spirit. All the three invocations follow the same form: each opens with an address to the Spirit; each ends with the plea—or is it a command?—"Oh, hear!"; in each the Spirit is characterized by his powers, and each characterization has two parts, the second beginning with the reiteration of the pronoun "Thou." The repetitiveness of this form is quite in keeping with the lore of magic, which gives great importance to the precise repetition of a fixed form of words. The order of the words is as important as the words themselves. A spell has to be exactly right or it will not work. (In this connection, it is interesting to note that our word *glamour,* in its sense of enchantment, comes from *grammar*—the modest art of using words correctly, according to rule, comes to be thought of as a magical power.)

The device by which the Spirit is summoned is also quite in accord with established magical practice. Primitive people believe that there is an integral connection between a person and a representation of him, and that by means of the representation it is possible to control him. One can, for instance, injure or destroy a human enemy by making a figure of him and mistreating it in appropriate ways; the spirit of a god is supposed to enter an image of him set up before his shrine. It is an analogous belief that the name of a person or god is integral with him and that, like an image, it can be used to control him. For that reason, in some societies, people keep their real names secret, and in the ancient Jewish ritual the name of God was permitted to be uttered only once a year, by the High Priest, and in great solemnity and fear. In the light of these primitive beliefs, we can see what the first three stanzas of the Ode are doing— they are making a verbal image of the Spirit; they are naming him as completely as possible by detailed description of his attributes, his power over the earth, over the sky, and over the sea. To define him is to circumscribe him. To know him is to have the power to influence his behavior.

The process of control by representation extends to the very structure of the verse in which the West Wind is described. *Terza rima* is a form which has an unusually urgent forward movement—such is the arrangement of the rimes (a b a, b c b, c d c, etc.) that scarcely have we begun one tercet than the rime-sound of the next is announced. In the three invocation stanzas this forward impulse is given the greatest possible freedom, for the sense of the line does not require the voice to pause at the end, but, on the contrary, carries it rapidly over to the next line. (In this respect the verse is at an opposite extreme from the opening of Wordsworth's "Resolution and Independence" [pages 862, 869].) And the syntax is as open and unchecked, as onward moving, as the verse.

In the first stanza the Spirit is addressed in a striking epithet—he is called "destroyer and preserver." This has led some readers to believe that the West Wind represents the continuing spirit of the French Revolution, for revolution, ideally conceived, may be said to destroy in order to preserve; it destroys the old and outworn elements of society in order to allow the new to develop. The interpretation is entirely consonant with what we know of Shelley's temperament and political beliefs and it does seem to be sustained by details of the poem. Thus, the line "Wild Spirit, which art moving everywhere" suggests that the Spirit moves not only over earth, sky, and sea, but also in the hearts, councils, and cities of men. And the identification might seem to be made virtually explicit by lines 63–69, in which the phrases "quicken a new birth," "my words among mankind," "the trumpet of a prophecy," all point to the poet's hope of a great social and political redemption.

We do well to have this possible meaning of the West Wind in mind. But we must be careful not to allow it to make the concluding part of the poem simpler, or more simply optimistic, than in fact it is. It may be the poet has been led beyond his personal despair by the thought that the autumnal destruction of what is bad in society will bring a springtime of happiness to mankind and that in this renovation his own ideas and suffering will have had some part. And this may permit him to feel that his autumnal despair, the devastation of his own life, is but a state in the process of life in general, and that he may hope for a personal renewal; he draws this hope from the analogy of the cycle of the seasons, for the death of the year is the augury of its rebirth—

> O, Wind,
> If Winter comes, can Spring be far behind?

So the poem ends. The terms of the poem, however, do not really allow us to assume that the concluding line expresses, though with pathetic interrogation, the emergence of the poet from despair to some degree of optimism. Actually they do not permit Shelley to rest in hope, for if his vision of the human fate, and of his own fate, must be in accord with everything to be inferred from the cycle of the seasons, it requires little skepticism, and no cynicism at all, to understand that if spring follows winter, so too does winter follow spring. Renovation may indeed come to society and to individual man but if we derive this hopeful thought from contemplation of the cycle of the seasons, we must recognize that the coming of spring portends the eventual autumnal decay. Perhaps it is the poet's repressed consciousness of this sad irony that accounts for the memorable poignancy of the triumphant cry at the end of the poem, in which there is almost as much despair as there is comfort.

Almost, but not quite. The cycle of the seasons must always have its import of despair, but its import of hope seems to be more insistent. Men have always celebrated the shortest day of the year as the time when the year turns and the days begin to grow longer, and we hang the baubles on our Christmas trees in token of our happy expectation of the blossoms of spring and the fruits of summer.

ODE TO A NIGHTINGALE

JOHN KEATS
1795–1821

My heart aches, and a drowsy numbness pains
 My sense, as though of hemlock[1] I had drunk,
Or emptied some dull opiate to the drains
 One minute past, and Lethe-wards[2] had sunk.
'Tis not through envy of thy happy lot,   5
 But being too happy in thine happiness—
   That thou, light wingèd Dryad[3] of the trees,
    In some melodious plot
Of beechen green, and shadows numberless,
   Singest of summer in full-throated ease.   10

O, for a draught of vintage! that hath been
 Cooled a long age in the deep-delvèd earth,
Tasting of Flora[4] and the country green,
 Dance, and Provençal song,[5] and sunburnt mirth!
O for a beaker full of the warm South,   15
 Full of the true, the blushful Hippocrene,[6]
   With beaded bubbles winking at the brim,
    And purple-stainèd mouth;
That I might drink, and leave the world unseen,
   And with thee fade away into the forest dim: 20

Fade far away, dissolve, and quite forget
 What thou among the leaves hast never known,
The weariness, the fever, and the fret
 Here, where men sit and hear each other groan;

---

[1] A poisonous potion obtained from the hemlock. [2] Lethe, in Greek mythology, was the river of oblivion from which all dead souls drank as they passed into Hades. [3] Tree nymph. [4] The Roman goddess of flowers and gardens. [5] Song of Provence, a region in the south of France noted, during the Middle Ages, for its troubadours, or lyric poets. [6] Water of the Hippocrene, the fountain of the Muses in Greek mythology; hence, poetic inspiration.

Where palsy shakes a few, sad, last gray hairs,   25
    Where youth grows pale, and specter-thin, and dies;
        Where but to think is to be full of sorrow
            And leaden-eyed despairs,
    Where Beauty cannot keep her lustrous eyes,
        Or new Love pine at them beyond tomorrow.   30

Away! away! for I will fly to thee,
    Not charioted by Bacchus and his pards,[7]
But on the viewless[8] wings of Poesy,
    Though the dull brain perplexes and retards:
Already with thee! tender is the night,   35
    And haply the Queen-Moon is on her throne,
        Clustered around by all her starry Fays;[9]
            But here there is no light,
    Save what from heaven is with the breezes blown
        Through verdurous glooms and winding mossy ways.   40

I cannot see what flowers are at my feet,
    Nor what soft incense hangs upon the boughs,
But, in embalmèd[10] darkness, guess each sweet
    Wherewith the seasonable month endows
The grass, the thicket, and the fruit-tree wild;   45
    White hawthorn, and the pastoral eglantine;
        Fast fading violets covered up in leaves;
            And mid-May's eldest child.
The coming musk-rose, full of dewy wine,
    The murmurous haunt of flies on summer eves.   50

Darkling[11] I listen; and, for many a time,
    I have been half in love with easeful Death,
Called him soft names in many a musèd rime,
    To take into the air my quiet breath;
Now more than ever seems it rich to die,   55
    To cease upon the midnight with no pain,
        While thou art pouring forth thy soul abroad
            In such an ecstasy!
Still wouldst thou sing, and I have ears in vain—
    To thy high requiem become a sod.   60

Thou wast not born for death, immortal Bird!
    No hungry generations tread thee down;

[7] Leopards or panthers. Bacchus, or Dionysus, the god of wine, is frequently represented in a chariot drawn by tigers.   [8] Invisible.   [9] Fairies.   [10] Aromatic, balmy.   [11] In the dark.

The voice I hear this passing night was heard
      In ancient days by emperor and clown:
Perhaps the self-same song that found a path   65
      Through the sad heart of Ruth, when, sick for home,
            She stood in tears amid the alien corn;[12]
                  The same that oft-times hath
      Charmed magic casements, opening on the foam
            Of perilous seas, in faery lands forlorn.   70

Forlorn! the very word is like a bell
      To toll me back from thee to my sole self,
Adieu! the fancy cannot cheat so well
      As she is famed to do, deceiving elf.
Adieu! adieu! thy plaintive anthem fades   75
      Past the near meadows, over the still stream,
            Up the hillside; and now 'tis buried deep
                  In the next valley glades:
      Was it a vision, or a waking dream?
            Fled is that music—Do I wake or sleep?   80

COMMENTARY

The nightingale, which is a species of thrush known in Europe and Asia although not in America, has haunted the imagination of poets for centuries
because of the beauty of its song and the strangeness of its nocturnal habit, for
the nightingale sings only in darkness. Actually it is the male bird that sings, and
medieval poetry conformed to this fact. But ancient Greek legend makes the
singing bird female. Keats, in the first stanza of his Ode, follows the Greek
mythological tradition; he addresses the nightingale as a dryad, a tree-nymph.
But in the rest of the poem we can have no doubt that he means us to think of
the bird as male. The song of the nightingale is of course erotic; the male bird
sings only in the mating season and this knowledge was adhered to in medieval
poetry. Keats's nightingale, however, does not sing of love. And when Keats
speaks of the bird as "happy," as singing in "full-throated ease," he quite controverts both the Greek and the medieval view that the song is sorrowful. The
Greek nightingale lamented the terrible wrongs done to her as a woman, before
her metamorphosis into a bird. The medieval nightingale was believed to sing
out of the pain of unfulfilled desire, although there was a charming fancy that
he pressed his breast against a thorn to induce the pain that he uttered so
beautifully. But it is exactly the point of Keats's poem that the nightingale sings
in spontaneous and unremitting joy.

An ode has no very exact definition in the usage of English poets, but in
general it may be said to be a poem on a lofty theme, of no prescribed length
but long enough to allow for considerable elaborateness of development. The

[12] See the Book of Ruth, Chapter 2.

subject to be dealt with must be worthy of great praise, and we expect of an ode that it will reach a high point in intensity in bestowing this praise. In Greek *ode* is the word for "song"; the Greek odes were sung. The English poets did not write their odes to be set to music but they nevertheless had the ancient practice in mind and sought to approximate a musical immediacy and passionateness.

Few odes achieve this goal as fully as the Nightingale Ode. The poem does more than celebrate the song of the bird, it emulates and rivals it. Although the mode of feeling of the poem is different from that of the song it describes, for the song is said to be happy whereas the poem is sad, the poem affects the reader much as the nightingale's song does the poet—to the point indeed, where many readers are so entranced by its lyric charm that they are content with only a limited sense of what, precisely, is being said. This is unfortunate since our delight in the Ode is bound to increase in the degree that we comprehend its complexity. The general purport of the Ode is clear enough. The poet feels the burden of mortality, not only death itself but illness and pain, the passing of youth, fatigue at the consciousness of the human condition. The nightingale's song suggests, and is, the opposite of all this; it is immortal and it is not subject to adverse circumstance. We understand, of course, that in actuality a nightingale is as surely destined for death as the poet himself. But it is not this particular bird that is the object of the poet's emotions, rather the generic nightingale, which is what it is by reason of its song—it is as if Keats were saying that the immortal and unchanging song creates new generations of actual birds to utter it.

In some degree the poem is dramatic; its action consists of the attempts which the poet makes in his imagination to achieve or approximate the existence of the nightingale. All these attempts fail. The first of them is represented in the opening stanza. The poet speaks of the painful depression of spirit—it seems to him the very threshold of death—into which he has fallen when his intense response to the nightingale's song has reached its climax. The human mind would seem not to be capable of sustaining the joy it can momentarily know; as Wordsworth says in "Resolution and Independence":

> . . . from the might
> Of joy in minds that can no further go,
> As high as we have mounted in delight
> In our dejection do we sink as low.

This cycle of feeling, from intensity or ecstasy to obliviousness or dissolution and pain, appears three more times in the course of the Ode. The second dissolution is achieved through wine. It is real wine that the poet asks for, even though the name that he gives it is not that of any known vintage but of a well-known water—the Hippocrene is the fountain of the Muses on Mount Helicon; a draft of its water was supposed to give poetic inspiration. Between the song of the nightingale and the wine which bears the name of the inspiring water there is a close association; the bird sings "of summer in full-throated ease" and the wine is said to be summer itself—the beaker that the poet longs for is to be "full of the warm South." The delight of the imagined intoxication turns out, however, to be only mediate, a step on the way to a desired extinction. This extinction, to be sure, is pleasurable, consisting as it does of fading, dissolving, forgetting, and it is meant to be redemptive, the means by which the poet frees himself from the burdens of his mortal condition. But the imagination of an ecstasy which will lead to extinction, and of an extinction which shall be an escape, ends in the vivid realization of what is being escaped—"the weariness, the fever, and the fret," all the frustrations of human existence as they are set forth in Stanza III.

In Stanza IV wine is rejected in favor of poetry as a means of escape. But the imagined flight of poetry toward the light ends in the darkness of Stanzas IV and V, which suggests the idea of liberation from the burden of life through death, as do also, perhaps, the ephemeral flowers and the short-lived May flies of the exquisite fifth stanza. It is not a new idea for the poet; he has, he says, "many a time / . . . been half in love with easeful Death"—the epithet "easeful" recalls the "full-throated ease" of the nightingale's song—and "now more than ever" he thinks of death as a "rich" experience. In some degree death is comparable to the nightingale's ecstasy: the image of Death taking "into the air my quiet breath" may not be equal in intensity to that of the nightingale "pouring [its] soul abroad" but there is a general likeness between them.

It is not uncommon for poetry to represent death as a positive and pleasurable experience. Death and dying seem naturally to associate themselves with love—the words are used to express the ultimate degree of erotic pleasure, and all great love stories end in death, as if this were the sign and validation of the lovers' passion. Even in casual speech, we express the force of a desire by the locution, "I am dying to . . ." or "I am dying for . . ." We think only of grace and charm when we speak of music "dying away," or when we see a dancer perform "The Dying Swan." This association with agreeable things indicates something of the nature of Keats's imagination of death as it is first expressed in the poem. But if the words "die" and "death" can suggest a pleasurable and even a voluptuous experience,[1] the word "dead" cannot; it is a harsh, grim word, meaning all that we can conceive of insentience. Although Keats first thinks of dying as an experience of ecstasy equivalent to the nightingale's song, his awareness of reality supervenes to tell him that dying leads to *being dead*—the fancy of the "richness" of dying yields to this brute fact, best communicated in a brutal word: he speaks of himself as becoming a "sod," a mere inanimate piece of earth such as that under which we are buried.

But it is the seventh stanza which is for many readers the most memorable part of the poem, presenting us with a curious and deeply moving paradox. The poet speaks of the long-dead persons who have heard the voice of the nightingale; it is his purpose to contrast the joyous immortality of the song with the sad evanescence of human life. We understand this intention; yet we are not wholly willing to accept the validity of the contrast that is being proposed. The sadness of Ruth amid the alien corn, the peril of the seas, the forlornness of the faery lands, so far from being incongruous with the nightingale's song, seem to us to be at one with it in beauty and immortality, and we may even suppose that they are what the song is *about*, for it can often seem that the pain of human life is the subject of our most beautiful poetic utterances. In "The Solitary Reaper," a poem that Keats would have known, Wordsworth finds the charm of the girl's song in what she is singing about:

> . . . old, unhappy, far-off things,
> And battles long ago . . .

[1] See the commentary on Whitman's "Out of the Cradle Endlessly Rocking," p. 909.

But although Keats, by the nature of his poetic imagination, may have been momentarily seduced into suggesting that human mortality and sorrow, seen through the veils of time and art, are more beautiful than painful, he cannot rest with this idea. His sense of reality once more enforces upon his imagination an admission of the actuality of the pain of human life.

It is with this in mind that Keats opens the eighth stanza with a repetition of the word "forlorn" which ends the seventh, pointing to it with the phrase, "the very word." And he describes its effect upon him in terms which suggest that whereas in the seventh stanza he had been speaking as one whose concern was only with beauty, now it is actuality that is his main concern—his affinity with the nightingale is at an end, now he must exist as a "sole self." In Stanza VII he had used the word "forlorn" for its charm, which derives from its lovely sound and from its possible connotation of a sadness that is distant and unreal. Now the full literal import of the word breaks upon him—it really means abandoned, lost, without hope, desperate[2]—and he is moved to a critical examination of himself as a poet; he speaks slightingly of one of a poet's faculties, the fancy. (We could wish he had called it almost anything but a "deceiving elf"!) Up to now the vanishing song of the nightingale had been only joyous; at this point it becomes "plaintive," as if the poet's certitude of the bird's joy were being denied. Still, at the same time it is called an "anthem," which is a song of joyful praise.

In sharp contrast with the lyricism which sustains itself through the whole poem and which is quite as apparent in the expressions of sadness or despair as in the expressions of ecstasy, the question with which the poem concludes— "Do I wake or sleep?"—shocks us with its sudden flatness and harshness of tone. That question was both explicated and answered by Shelley in "Adonais," his great elegy for Keats:

> Peace, peace! he is not dead, he doth not sleep—
> He hath awakened from the dream of life.

[2] It is possible that Keats knew that "the forlorn" was the old name for the call on the hunting-horn that brought back the hunters from the chase.

DOVER BEACH

MATTHEW ARNOLD
1822–1888

The sea is calm to-night.
The tide is full, the moon lies fair
Upon the straits; on the French coast the light
Gleams and is gone;[1] the cliffs of England stand,
Glimmering and vast, out in the tranquil bay.   5
Come to the window, sweet is the night-air!
Only, from the long line of spray
Where the sea meets the moon-blanched land,
Listen! you hear the grating roar
Of pebbles which the waves draw back, and fling,   10
At their return, up the high strand,
Begin, and cease, and then again begin,
With tremulous cadence slow, and bring
The eternal note of sadness in.

Sophocles long ago   15
Heard it on the Ægæan, and it brought
Into his mind the turbid ebb and flow
Of human misery; we
Find also in the sound a thought,
Hearing it by this distant northern sea.   20

The Sea of Faith
Was once, too, at the full, and round earth's shore
Lay like the folds of a bright girdle furled.
But now I only hear
Its melancholy, long, withdrawing roar,   25
Retreating, to the breath
Of the night-wind, down the vast edges drear
And naked shingles[2] of the world.

[1] Lights on the French coast are visible from Dover, the closest point in England (about 20 miles) to the continent. The cliffs near Dover are white and quite high.
[2] Coarse beach gravel.

Ah, love, let us be true
To one another! for the world, which seems   30
To lie before us like a land of dreams,
So various, so beautiful, so new,
Hath really neither joy, nor love, nor light,
Nor certitude, nor peace, nor help for pain;
And we are here as on a darkling plain   35
Swept with confused alarms of struggle and flight,
Where ignorant armies clash by night.

COMMENTARY

Matthew Arnold occupies a rather strange place in the community of English
poets. Few people, I think, would include him among the great poets of
England. The body of his work is not large, certainly not in comparison with
the production of other poets of the Victorian age, and of this relatively small
canon only a handful of poems are wholly successful. Yet Arnold is generally
ranked as one of the three most important poets of his time, the other two being
Tennyson and Browning. Indeed, despite his manifest faults, Arnold as a poet
makes an appeal to the reader of today which is likely to be greater than that of
either of his two imposing contemporaries.

A phrase I have just used, "Arnold as a poet," will perhaps seem odd and
need explanation. We do not speak of "Tennyson as a poet" or of "Browning as
a poet"—they were poets, we know them as nothing else. But Arnold, having
begun his literary life in poetry, gave up what we might call the professional
practice of the art at about the age of thirty. It was not possible for him to
make an adequate living by writing alone and he therefore accepted an appointment as an inspector of elementary schools; he served in this capacity until a few
years before his death. The work was fatiguing and depressing, and he could
command neither the leisure nor the emotional energy that poetry requires. He
did, however, find it possible to write prose, and, working in that medium, he
became one of the leading intellectual figures of England. He was the most
admired literary critic of his day, and, indeed, is generally accounted one of the
great critics of the world. He was a very notable theorist of politics, and his
writings on religion played an important part in the crisis of faith which so
deeply distressed many of his contemporaries. Perhaps more than any other
man of his time and nation he perceived the changes that were taking place in
the conditions of life and in the minds of men to bring into being the world we
now know—in certain respects he was, of all the intellectual figures of his
period, the most modern.

The sensitivity to the cultural circumstances of his day which Arnold
showed in his prose does much to explain his interest as a poet. Both in his early
poems, which make up the larger body of his canon, and in the infrequent
later poems, some of which are among his best, Arnold showed an awareness of
the emotional conditions of modern life which far exceeds that of any other poet
of his time. He spoke with great explicitness and directness of the alienation,

isolation, and excess of consciousness leading to doubt which are, as so much of later literature testifies, the lot of modern man. And it is plain that he speaks from an unabashedly personal experience of pain, fatigue, and thwarted hope— his poetry has for us the authority of authenticity even when it lacks a high poetic grace.

"Dover Beach," however, can scarcely be said to be lacking in grace. It is one of the handful of Arnold's wholly successful poems and among these it is pre-eminent. For many readers it is the single most memorable poem of the Victorian age. In it the authenticity that is in general the characteristic note of Arnold's poetry achieves a peculiar pathos. The diction is perfect in its lightness and simplicity. The verse, moving in a delicate crescendo of lyricism from the muted beginning to the full-voiced desperate conclusion, is superbly managed. Not the least of the elements of its success is that a poem so modest in tone and in apparent scope should contain within it such magnificent vistas of space and time.

The poem is dramatic in the sense that, although there is only one speaker, there are two characters, the speaker and the woman he addresses as his love, presumably his wife. The setting of the dramatic scene is of central importance; the American reader might not recognize what an English reader would know at once, that the couple are staying at a hotel, for Dover is one of the two English ports from which one takes ship to cross the English Channel to France. The circumstance that the couple are setting out on a journey abroad makes it all the more likely that they should be inclined to think of the world as being "so various, so beautiful, so new."

The window through which the speaker is gazing and to which he invites his companion might well bring to mind the "magic casements" of the "Ode to a Nightingale" (page 894). Like the window in Keats's poem, it opens "on the foam / Of perilous seas," and on forlorn lands, although not faery lands. It has the effect of framing the view and of emphasizing the sense of vista that plays so material a part in the poem. The immediate view—the great white chalk cliffs of Dover, the French coast twenty miles off, indicated by the momentary light, the moonlit waters of the Channel between—is in itself sufficiently impressive. But it opens out both in space and time to reach across Europe to the Aegean Sea and ancient Greece. It is worth noting that several of Arnold's poems depend for their most moving effects upon similar representations of great vistas both of geography and history and that in one of his early sonnets Arnold refers to Europe as "The Wide Prospect," deriving the phrase from a possible translation of the Greek name, and seeming to suggest that it was the essential quality of the European mind that it could encompass great reaches of space and time. Although in general Arnold's distances imply liberation and even joy, in "Dover Beach," when the imagination goes beyond the Aegean, it proceeds in darkness to the "vast edges drear / And naked shingles of the world."

The emptiness and despair of the vision bring the speaker back to the place from which his imagination had started, to the room from whose window he looks out, and he turns in despairing sadness to his companion, at that moment seemingly the only other person in the world, to offer her, and ask from her, loyalty in love. Perhaps literature does not know a love avowal and a love plea so sad as these—perhaps never before in literature has a lover given a *reason* for love, and a reason which, while asserting its necessity, denies its delight. It is believed by all lovers that love has the power not only of making the world various and beautiful and new, but also of maintaining it in variety, beauty, and novelty. But the lover of "Dover Beach" denies love's efficacy in this respect. Of all that love may be presumed to give, he asks only loyalty in a world that promises neither joy nor peace.

It is to this pass that the lover has been brought by his sense of modern life, which has seen the ebbing of the sea of faith. We assume that he means religious faith, and this assumption is borne out by other of Arnold's poems in which the diminution of religious faith is a reason for melancholy. But Arnold felt that the lessening of religious faith went hand in hand with the lessening of personal energy, vitality, and confidence, of that happy, unquestioning attachment to life which William James called "animal faith." When Arnold speaks of Sophocles hearing the roar of the pebbles on the beach under the receding wave and of its having brought "into his mind the turbid ebb and flow / Of human misery," he is almost certainly making reference to the opening of the third chorus of Sophocles' *Antigone*. Here is the passage in the translation of R. C. Jebb: "Blest are they whose days have not tasted of evil. For when a house hath once been shaken from heaven, there the curse fails nevermore, passing from life to life of the race [i.e., family]; even as, when the surge is driven over the darkness of the deep by the fierce breath of Thracian sea-winds, it rolls up the black sand from the depths, and there is a sullen roar from the wind-vexed headlands that front the blows of the storm." The chorus ostensibly speaks of the misery of the members of certain families living under a curse, and not of "human misery" in general. But the generalization can of course be made, and we may readily believe that Arnold had in mind the contrast between the passage from the third chorus to which he refers and the more famous second chorus of *Antigone*, which begins "Wonders are many, and none is more wonderful than man," and goes on to sing with joy of man's triumphs. It is the faith in man and his destiny so proudly expressed by the second chorus that has ebbed, leaving the world to bleakness.

The great grim simile with which the poem ends has attracted much attention, and efforts have been made to find the inspiration for it in Arnold's reading. The likeliest possibility is the account of the battle of Epipolae given by Thucydides in his *History of the Peloponnesian War* (Book VII, Chapters 43–44); this guess is encouraged by the circumstance that Arnold's father, Thomas Arnold, had published a well-known edition of the *History*. A striking quality of the simile is its unexpectedness. Up to this point the lovers have looked out on a world of wind and water, quite empty of people; now the scene is a plain filled with armies in strife. The suddenness of the shift reinforces the violence of the dark image of deteriorated existence.

OUT OF
THE CRADLE
ENDLESSLY
ROCKING

WALT WHITMAN
1819–1892

Out of the cradle endlessly rocking,
Out of the mocking-bird's throat, the musical shuttle,
Out of the Ninth-month midnight,
Over the sterile sands and the fields beyond, where the child leaving his bed
    wander'd alone, bareheaded, barefoot,
Down from the shower'd halo,   5
Up from the mystic play of shadows twining and twisting as if they were
    alive,
Out from the patches of briers and blackberries,
From the memories of the bird that chanted to me,
From your memories sad brother, from the fitful risings and fallings I
    heard,
From under that yellow half-moon late-risen and swollen as if with
    tears,   10
From those beginning notes of yearning and love there in the mist,
From the thousand responses of my heart never to cease,
From the myriad thence-arous'd words,
From the word stronger and more delicious than any,
From such as now they start the scene revisiting,   15
As a flock, twittering, rising, or overhead passing,
Borne hither, ere all eludes me, hurriedly,
A man, yet by these tears a little boy again,
Throwing myself on the sand, confronting the waves,
I, chanter of pains and joys, uniter of here and hereafter,   20
Taking all hints to use them, but swiftly leaping beyond them,
A reminiscence sing.

Once Paumanok,[1]
When the lilac-scent was in the air and Fifth-month grass was growing,
Up this seashore in some briers,   25
Two feather'd guests from Alabama, two together,
And their nest, and four light-green eggs spotted with brown,
And every day the he-bird to and fro near at hand,
And every day the she-bird crouch'd on her nest, silent, with bright
    eyes,
And every day I, a curious boy, never too close, never disturbing them,   30
Cautiously peering, absorbing, translating.

Shine! shine! shine!
Pour down your warmth, great sun!
While we bask, we two together.

Two together!   35
Winds blow south, or winds blow north,
Day come white, or night come black,
Home, or rivers and mountains from home,
Singing all time, minding no time,
While we two keep together.   40

Till of a sudden,
May-be kill'd, unknown to her mate,
One forenoon the she-bird crouch'd not on the nest,
Nor return'd that afternoon, nor the next,
Nor ever appear'd again.   45

And thenceforward all summer in the sound of the sea,
And at night under the full of the moon in calmer weather,
Over the hoarse surging of the sea,
Or flitting from brier to brier by day,
I saw, I heard at intervals the remaining one, the he-bird,   50
The solitary guest from Alabama.

Blow! blow blow!
Blow up sea-winds along Paumanok's shore;
I wait and I wait till you blow my mate to me.

Yes, when the stars glisten'd,   55
All night long on the prong of a moss-scallop'd stake,

---

[1] Indian name for Long Island.

Down almost amid the slapping waves,
Sat the lone singer wonderful causing tears.

He call'd on his mate,
He pour'd forth the meanings which I of all men know.   60

Yes my brother I know,
The rest might not, but I have treasur'd every note,
For more than once dimly down to the beach gliding,
Silent, avoiding the moonbeams, blending myself with the shadows,
Recalling now the obscure shapes, the echoes, the sounds and sights after their
        sorts,   65
The white arms out in the breakers tirelessly tossing,
I, with bare feet, a child, the wind wafting my hair,
Listen'd long and long.

Listen'd to keep, to sing, now translating the notes,
Following you my brother.   70

Soothe! soothe! soothe!
Close on its wave soothes the wave behind,
And again another behind, embracing and lapping, every one close,
But my love soothes not me, not me.

Low hangs the moon, it rose late,   75
It is lagging—O I think it is heavy with love, with love.

O madly the sea pushes upon the land,
With love, with love.

O night! do I not see my love fluttering out among the breakers?
What is that little black thing I see there in the white?   80

Loud! loud! loud!
Loud I call to you, my love!
High and clear I shoot my voice over the waves,
Surely you must know who is here, is here,
You must know who I am, my love.   85

Low-hanging moon!
What is that dusky spot in your brown yellow?

O it is the shape, the shape of my mate!
O moon do not keep her from me any longer.

Land! land! O land! 90
Whichever way I turn, O I think you could give me my mate back again if you
      only would,
For I am almost sure I see her dimly whichever way I look.

O rising stars!
Perhaps the one I want so much will rise, will rise with some of you.

O throat! O trembling throat! 95
Sound clearer through the atmosphere!
Pierce the woods, the earth,
Somewhere listening to catch you must be the one I want.

Shake out carols!
Solitary here, the night's carols! 100
Carols of lonesome love! death's carols!
Carols under the lagging, yellow, waning moon!
O under that moon where she droops almost down into the sea!
O reckless despairing carols.

But soft! sink low! 105
Soft! let me just murmur,
And do you wait a moment you husky-nois'd sea,
For somewhere I believe I heard my mate responding to me,
So faint, I must be still, be still to listen,
But not altogether still, for then she might not come immediately to me. 110

Hither my love!
Here I am! here!
With this just-sustain'd note I announce myself to you,
This gentle call is for you my love, for you.

Do not be decoy'd elsewhere, 115
That is the whistle of the wind, it is not my voice,
That is the fluttering, the fluttering of the spray,
Those are the shadows of leaves.

O darkness! O in vain!
O I am sick and sorrowful. 120

O brown halo in the sky near the moon, dropping upon the sea!
O troubled reflection in the sea!

O throat! O throbbing heart!
And I singing uselessly, uselessly all the night.

O past! O happy life! O songs of joy!   125
In the air, in the woods, over fields,
Loved! loved! loved! loved! loved!
But my mate no more, no more with me!
We two together no more.

The aria sinking,   130
All else continuing, the stars shining,
The winds blowing, the notes of the bird continuous echoing,
With angry moans the fierce old mother incessantly moaning,
On the sands of Paumanok's shore gray and rustling,
The yellow half-moon enlarged, sagging down, drooping, the face of the sea al-
          most touching,   135
The boy ecstatic, with his bare feet the waves, with his hair the atmosphere
          dallying,
The love in the heart long pent, now loose, now at last tumultuously bursting,
The aria's meaning, the ears, the soul, swiftly depositing,
The strange tears down the cheeks coursing,
The colloquy there, the trio, each uttering,   140
The undertone, the savage old mother incessantly crying,
To the boy's soul's questions sullenly timing, some drown'd secret hissing,
To the outsetting bard.

Demon or bard! (said the boy's soul,)
Is it indeed toward your mate you sing? or is it really to me?   145
For I, that was a child, my tongue's use sleeping, now I have heard you,
Now in a moment I know what I am for, I awake,
And already a thousand singers, a thousand songs, clearer, louder and more
          sorrowful than yours,
A thousand warbling echoes have started to life within me, never to die.

O you singer solitary, singing by yourself, projecting me,   150
O solitary me listening, never more shall I cease perpetuating you,
Never more shall I escape, never more the reverberations,
Never more the cries of unsatisfied love be absent from me,
Never again leave me to be the peaceful child I was before what there in the
          night,

By the sea under the yellow and sagging moon,   155
The messenger there arous'd, the fire, the sweet hell within,
The unknown want, the destiny of me.

O give me the clew! (it lurks in the night here somewhere,)
O if I am to have so much, let me have more!

A word then, (for I will conquer it,)   160
The word final, superior to all,
Subtle, sent up—what is it?—I listen;
Are you whispering it, and have all the time, you sea waves?
Is that it from your liquid rims and wet sands?

Whereto answering, the sea,   165
Delaying not, hurrying not,
Whisper'd me through the night, and very plainly before daybreak,
Lisp'd to me the low and delicious word death,
And again, death, death, death, death,
Hissing melodious, neither like the bird nor like my arous'd child's heart,   170
But edging near as privately for me rustling at my feet,
Creeping thence steadily up to my ears and laving me softly all over,
Death, death, death, death, death.

Which I do not forget,
But fuse the song of my dusky demon and brother,   175
That he sang to me in the moonlight on Paumanok's gray beach,
With the thousand responsive songs at random,
My own songs awaked from that hour,
And with them the key, the word up from the waves,
The word of the sweetest song and all songs,   180
That strong and delicious word which, creeping to my feet,
(Or like some old crone rocking the cradle, swathed in sweet garments, bending
    aside,)
The sea whisper'd me.

COMMENTARY

Historians of American literature often speak of Walt Whitman and Henry James as virtually symbolic representatives of two opposed tendencies in our national culture. Whitman in his lifetime undertook to make himself a symbolic figure—he wanted, both in his person and his art, to stand for all that was "democratic" in American life, by which he meant whatever was free, impulsive, and accepting; he spoke of himself as "one of the roughs," and described his poetry as "a barbaric yawp." James had no conscious wish to put himself before the world in a symbolic light, but it was almost inevitable that he should be seen in this way. He came of a patrician family and he had as strong a feeling for elegance and decorum as Whitman had for looseness and the free-and-easy. He lived his mature years away from his native land because of his liking for the complexity of English society and his strong commitment to the artistic traditions of Europe. By reason of his style of life, he has been taken—often all too simply—to stand for conservatism, propriety, and gentility; and by reason of the nature of his art he has come to be regarded as the very spirit of consciousness, control, and precision.

The extreme differences between the two men make the dramatic point of a famous anecdote which Edith Wharton relates in her autobiography. Mrs. Wharton was a close friend and great admirer of Henry James and she tells of an evening party at her country home at which, in the course of conversation, "someone spoke of Whitman, and it was a joy to me to discover that James thought him, as I did, the greatest of American poets." James, Mrs. Wharton tells us, read poetry aloud in a very beautiful way, and now the discussion led to his being asked to read from Whitman's *Leaves of Grass*, "and all that evening we sat rapt while he wandered from 'The Song of Myself' to 'When Lilacs Last in the Door-yard Bloomed' (when we read 'Lovely and soothing Death' his voice filled the hushed room like an organ adagio), and then let himself be lured on to the mysterious music of 'Out of the Cradle' reading, or rather crooning it in a mood of subdued ecstasy till the fivefold invocation to Death tolled out like the knocks in the opening bars of [Beethoven's] Fifth Symphony."

Mrs. Wharton concludes her story by saying that James's admiration of Whitman, "his immediate response to that mighty appeal, was a new proof of the way in which, above a certain level, the most divergent intelligences walk together like gods." The generalization is not true. We can be fairly certain that Whitman would not have given James's work the same respect that James gave his. And James himself, fine critic though he was, was incapable of responding to certain "divergent intelligences" of his time, Thomas Hardy, for example, or the young D. H. Lawrence. But it is greatly to his credit that, with so much that might stand in the way of his sympathy, he did respond to Whitman. What might have intervened was the erroneous belief, which prevailed at the time and is sometimes met with even now, that Whitman wrote on mere free impulse, without the consciousness and self-criticism that normally go into poetic composition. James, whose feeling for conscious artistry was almost a religion with him, was happily not deceived into any such false notion.

Whitman himself did much to foster the misconception of his poetry when he spoke of it as a "barbaric yawp" and in general insisted on his radical difference from all preceding poets. And the mistake is likely to be confirmed by wrong ideas about the kind of verse he wrote, whose very name, "free verse," is misleading. In point of fact, Whitman was a consummate craftsman. No poems were ever more carefully composed than those which James chose to read aloud that evening at Mrs. Wharton's; we know from Whitman's manuscripts how extensively they were revised and worked over.[1] Whitman's verse-form, so far

---

[1] It is a fact worth noting that even Whitman's letters, which are marked by an extreme simplicity of style, were very fully revised and recopied before they were mailed.

from being prosaic because it does not use meter and rime, is supremely musical, as James made plain by the manner in which he read it. James was a man not given to public display, yet when he read "Out of the Cradle Endlessly Rocking," he surrendered wholly to the demands it made upon him and, as Mrs. Wharton tells us, "crooned it in a mood of subdued ecstasy."

"Out of the Cradle Endlessly Rocking" is not the first poem in this volume in which the ecstatic song of a bird is involved with thoughts of death, and in which death is regarded in an ambiguous way—the similarity of this poem to Keats's "Ode to a Nightingale" (page 896) will be readily apparent. In both poems the poet makes an identification between the singing bird and himself in his character of poet. In both poems, although in different ways, death is the source not only of sorrow but also of the hope of transcendence.

Yet the more we are aware of the affinity which the two poems have with each other, the more striking their differences become. Certain of these differences arise from the fact that one is an English and the other an American poem. The birds they celebrate are nationally distinct: there are no American nightingales and no English mocking-birds. And Whitman, as if to emphasize his bird's American habitat, tells us the name of its native state, Alabama. It is almost as if he had Keats's nightingale in mind—its identification with the poetic traditions of Europe, its place in Greek mythology—and as if he were saying, "*That* is the bird of the Old World, *mine* is the bird of the New."

The very names of the birds—"nightingale" with its euphonic, remote loveliness, "mocking-bird" with its hard immediacy and explicitness—suggest a national difference in the language of the two poems. It was part of Whitman's conception of his poetic mission to write in the American mode of the English tongue, both in order to express the American temperament and to make his poetry readily accessible to American readers. To these ends, he used the vocabulary, syntax, and rhythms of colloquial speech, and what literary models he did turn to were such as Americans would know without special education, the oration and the Bible. But we must not suppose that Whitman was unique in his use of everyday speech. It is one of the recurrent concerns of poetry to seek to reduce the distance between the speech of the people and the special language that any tradition of poetry tends to evolve. Dante said that he wanted a language for his poetry that would be comprehensible to housewives; and Wordsworth undertook to purge poetry of artificiality by using "the real language of real men." And a comparison of the language of Whitman with that of Keats must proceed with caution, for Keats too was concerned to free himself from the linguistic conventions of poetry; his realization that he must no longer submit to the influence of Milton's elaborate diction made a crisis in his poetic life. To the first readers of the "Ode to a Nightingale" the diction might very well have seemed too relaxed and insufficiently "literary." Still, in the use of the common speech for poetry that yet aims at a beautiful exaltation of tone, there is no doubt that Whitman went further than Keats—further, indeed, than anyone before him had gone. The following lines will suggest how bold was his use of colloquialism and to what an exquisite effect:

> Oh night! do I not see my love fluttering out
> among the breakers?
> What is that little black thing I see there in the white?

Or again:

> Whichever way I turn, O I think you could give me my
> mate back again if you only would . . .

And quite apart from the colloquialisms of lines like these, we are aware—
an English reader would be still more aware—that their rhythm and idiom are
American rather than English. Keats said of Milton's majestic style, "It is
magnificent but it is not English." In effect, Whitman said of all English
poetry from Shakespeare down, "It is magnificent but it is not American."

In one of his essays, W. H. Auden tries to account for the differences between English and American poetry by reference to the dissimilar landscape
and climate of the two countries and their influence on temperament and feeling. Certainly nothing could be less alike than the settings of "Ode to a
Nightingale" and "Out of the Cradle Endlessly Rocking," especially the sense
of geography which each poem conveys. The topography of Keats's Ode is
comprised of glades, dells, and valleys, of enclosed, discrete places. Even the
darkness encloses. Indeed, the dominant emotion of the Ode can be described
as a response to limitation. The one great vista in the poem is that of time
rather than of space, the view back to the "ancient days" in which the nightingale's song was heard. When the poet expresses the wish to "fade far away,"
the furthest destination he can imagine is "the forest dim," which seems to be
quite near at hand and where he is again enclosed. And even the description
of the bird's flight, which carries its song out of hearing, does not propose the
idea of great distance:

> . . . thy plaintive anthem fades
> Past the near meadows, over the still stream,
> Up the hillside; and now 'tis buried deep
> In the next valley glades . . .

But the spaces of "Out of the Cradle" seem limitless—the unending stretch
of Long Island beach, the dunes behind, the sea in front, the sky unobstructed.
And we are mindful of the thousand miles the mocking-bird has flown to come
to Long Island from Alabama. There are no demarcations of place, no dells
and valleys. Nor are there any trees—lilacs somewhere, but not near the great
scene, and certainly none of the luxurious blossoms that blow in the fifth
stanza of the Ode, only briars and blackberries. Although it is true that no
human habitation is referred to in the Ode, yet the fertile landscape permits the
possibility of it, and nothing in the poem contradicts our extraneous knowledge
of the fact that Keats heard the nightingale and wrote his poem in the garden
of his pleasant house at Hampstead, near London. The scene of "Out of the
Cradle" is far less genial, and in it there is only one sign of human life, the
single stake in the water upon which the mourning bird sits, the one vertical
object in the poem, the one fixed thing upon which the eye may focus:

> All night long on the prong of a moss-scallop'd stake,
> Down almost amid the slapping waves,
> Sat the lone singer wonderful causing tears.

But even more divergent are the ways in which the two poems respond to death. Although Keats is able to conceive of death as a purging of life into pure being, and although, almost against his will, he represents mortality as the source of beauty, these are only momentary fancies. They give him no real consolation in the face of his knowledge that death is insentience and extinction. The ideas that Keats rejects are intensely affirmed by Whitman. For him passion itself arises from death, and it was his having heard and understood the mocking-bird's song of sorrow that changed him from a boy into a man—and into a poet. Nor is it passion only, but life itself, that arises from death: death is "the word" which the sea, the mother of all life, "lisps" and "hisses" and "whispers" to him in response to his plea for the "clew"; and that word, the poet says, is even "more" than the mocking-bird's song: it is the word "of the sweetest song and all songs."

We can scarcely think of these differing attitudes to death as in any way national. And yet Whitman himself thought that the celebration of the beauty of death was appropriate to America and pertinent to the health of the republic. In 1871 he published a great embittered essay, *Democratic Vistas,* in which he indicts America for its failure to fulfill its true moral and political destiny and speaks of the redemption that may yet come, in part from the good effects of an appropriate national poetry. "In the future of these States," he says, "must arise poets immenser far, and make great poems of death. The poems of life are great, but there must be poems of the purports of life, not only in itself, but beyond itself." The great poem of death, he says in sum, will check the growing American vulgarity by bringing faith and large-mindedness. "Then will man indeed confront Nature, and confront time and space . . . and take his right place, prepared for fortune and misfortune. And then that which was long wanted will be supplied, and the ship that had it not before in all her voyages, will have an anchor."

Perhaps Henry James had in his own way a not dissimilar conception of death. Mrs. Wharton tells us in her autobiography that when James suffered the first of the series of strokes that were to end his life, "in the very act of falling . . . he heard in the room a voice which was distinctly, it seemed, not his own, saying: 'So here it is at last, the distinguished thing.'"

THE LEADEN ECHO
AND
THE GOLDEN ECHO
(Maidens' song from
St. Winefred's Well[1])

G E R A R D   M A N L E Y   H O P K I N S

1 8 4 4 – 1 8 8 9

THE LEADEN ECHO

How to kéep[2]—is there ány any, is there none such, nowhere known some, bow
     or brooch or braid or brace, láce, latch or catch or key to keep
Back beauty, keep it, beauty, beauty, beauty, . . . from vanishing away?
Ó is there no frowning of these wrinkles, rankèd wrinkles deep,
Dówn? no waving off of these most mournful messengers, still messengers, sad
     and stealing messengers of grey?
No there's none, there's none, O no there's none,   5
Nor can you long be, what you now are, called fair,
Do what you may do, what, do what you may,
And wisdom is early to despair:
Be beginning; since, no, nothing can be done
To keep at bay   10
Age and age's evils, hoar hair,
Ruck[3] and wrinkle, drooping, dying, death's worst, winding sheets, tombs and
     worms and tumbling to decay;
So be beginning, be beginning to despair.
O there's none; no no no there's none:
Be beginning to despair, to despair,   15
Despair, despair, despair, despair.

---

[1] St. Winefred was murdered by her would-be ravisher, the chieftain Caradoc. The water of her well, which gushed spontaneously out of the ground after her death, is believed to have curative powers.   [2] Hopkins made a practice of indicating with accent marks which syllables were to receive the strongest stress.   [3] Crease.

Spare!⁴

There ís one, yes I have one (Hush there!);

Only not within seeing of the sun,

Not within the singeing of the strong sun,   20

Tall sun's tingeing, or treacherous the tainting of the earth's air,

Somewhere elsewhere there is ah well where! one,

Óne. Yes I cán tell such a key, I dó know such a place,

Where whatever's prized and passes of us, everything that's fresh and fast flying
        of us, seems to us sweet of us and swiftly away with, done away with,
        undone,

Undone, done with, soon done with, and yet dearly and dangerously sweet

Of us, the wimpled⁵-water-dimpled, not-by-morning-matchèd face,   26

The flower of beauty, fleece of beauty, too too apt to, ah! to fleet,

Never fleets móre, fastened with the tenderest truth

To its own best being and its loveliness of youth: it is an everlastingness of, O
        it is an all youth!

Come then, your ways and airs and looks, locks, maiden gear, gallantry and
        gaiety and grace,   30

Winning ways, airs innocent, maiden manners, sweet looks, loose locks, long
        locks, lovelocks, gaygear, going gallant, girlgrace—

Resign them, sign them, seal them, send them, motion them with breath,

And with sighs soaring, soaring síghs deliver

Them; beauty-in-the-ghost,⁶ deliver it, early now, long before death

Give beauty back, beauty, beauty, beauty, back to God, beauty's self and beauty's
        giver.   35

See; not a hair is, not an eyelash, not the least lash lost; every hair

Is, hair of the head, numbered.

Nay, what we had lighthanded left in surly⁷ the mere mould⁸

Will have waked and have waxed and have walked with the wind what while
        we slept,

This side, that side hurling a heavyheaded hundredfold   40

What while we, while we slumbered.

O then, weary then why should we tread? O why are we so haggard at the
        heart, so care-coiled, care-killed, so fagged, so fashed,⁹ so cogged,¹⁰ so
        cumbered,

When the thing we freely fórfeit is kept with fonder a care,

Fonder a care kept than we could have kept it, kept

Far with fonder a care (and we, we should have lost it) finer, fonder   45

A care kept.—Where kept? Do but tell us where kept, where.—

Yonder.—What high as that! We follow, now we follow.—Yonder, yes yonder,
        yonder,

Yonder.

---

⁴ Forbear.   ⁵ Rippled.   ⁶ Spiritual beauty.   ⁷ Sullenly.   ⁸ Earth.   ⁹ Troubled.
¹⁰ Deceived.

COMMENTARY

The poems of Gerard Manley Hopkins were first published in 1918, nearly thirty years after the poet's death, and to their early readers they seemed difficult and odd. They now stand in very high repute, but even a half century of habituation has not made them exactly easy for us. As for their oddness, this the poet himself was ready enough to concede; on one occasion he described himself as being taken aback by it. In a letter to his friend and future editor, Robert Bridges, Hopkins said that the oddness of his poems "may make them repulsive at first" and told how shocked he was when he read one of them that a friend had borrowed and sent back to him. ". . . I opened and read some lines, as one commonly reads whether prose or verse, with the eyes, so to say, only, and it struck me aghast with a kind of raw nakedness and unmitigated violence I was unprepared for. . . ." It needed a perceptible moment for Hopkins to perceive the true nature of his own poem. ". . . But take breath," he went on, "and read it with your ears, as I always wish to be read, and my verse becomes all right."

To take breath and read with the ears is what we must learn to do with any poem of Hopkins. "Read Hopkins aloud," says his latest editor, W. H. Gardner, "and you will find that his obscurity is never entirely opaque. . . ."

Hopkins was born in 1844, of a gifted family of the comfortable middle class. An excellent student, he devoted himself at Oxford to the study of Greek and Latin, in which he distinguished himself. In his Oxford days he came under the influence of John Henry Newman, later Cardinal Newman, and converted to the Roman Catholic Church in 1866; two years later he entered the Society of Jesus. The duties of that exigent order were arduous and sometimes personally uncongenial to Hopkins, but he discharged them with exemplary assiduity and still found time to speculate profoundly upon the nature of prosody, to develop his theory of English verse, and to write the poems which were to establish his posthumous fame. If the poems seemed odd in 1918, when literary experiment in England began to be the order of the day, they would have seemed far odder in the poet's lifetime, yet Hopkins might have risked publication had not the Jesuit discipline prevented it.

Many elements contribute to the radical novelty of Hopkins' style, but his chief theoretical statement, his preface to the manuscript volume of his mature poems, deals with one subject only, that of rhythm. The preface is not polemical: it says nothing adverse about the practice of other poets. But the implication of Hopkins' theory is that English verse had curtailed its strength by submitting to the rule of metre, by conforming, even though not with mechanical exactitude, to fixed line-patterns. His conception of the course that English verse should take has a considerable affinity with Wyatt's practice (see page 822), although of the two poets Hopkins is much the more radical. Hopkins would have stood in opposition to the "correct" taste that had contrived the version of "They Flee from Me" which appeared in Tottel's *Miscellany* and that would have led Victorian readers to prefer this revised version to the original. He would have defended the rightness of Wyatt's departures from the pattern of the iambic pentameter line and of all the roughnesses and irregularities by which the poet exploited the actuality of the speaking voice. But in his preface Hopkins confined himself to explaining his own practice; he did not advance the idea which he obviously held, that the established system of English verse seemed to its practitioners to be the only possible one merely because of long habit. For his own prosody, he drew upon the verse systems of Welsh and Greek poetry and upon the tradition of English alliterative verse which had prevailed before the Renaissance.

He also drew upon music, of which he was an accomplished amateur, and for the better understanding of his rhythmic effects he devised a system of marks, analogous to the directive marks on a musical score, which he placed over syllables, words, and groups of words in order to show the reader how to read the poem with his ears. But on the manuscript of "The Leaden Echo and the Golden Echo" he wrote this note: "I have marked the stronger stresses, but with the degree of the stress so perpetually varying no marking is satisfactory. Do you think all had best be left to the reader?" He seems to have answered his own question affirmatively; and any reader who deals with the poem as a singer deals with a new song, "running through" it experimentally a few times to see how the voice should proceed, may reasonably feel that he is not betraying Hopkins' trust in him.

Although rhythm is Hopkins' chief aural concern, it is by no means the only one. He uses alliteration to an extent that no poet has ever ventured; and internal rhyme; and assonance; and subtle, planned progressions and modulations of vowel sounds. The following portion of the first line of "The Leaden Echo and the Golden Echo" illustrates all these effects: ". . . is there none such, nowhere known some, bow or brooch or braid or brace, láce, latch or catch or key to keep." The elaborate devices of Hopkins' prosody are especially in evidence throughout the poem because of its avowed vocal nature. It is not a "lyric" in the sense of being a poem to be set to music for singing and therefore kept simple and modest so that the music may have its way. It is a lyric in the sense of being the whole song itself, words and music together, the vocal line and the accompaniment, both of considerable complexity and virtuosity.

But no doubt because it is so much a song, two characteristics of Hopkins' verse are not strongly apparent in this particular poem. One is the intense visuality that Hopkins usually sought after, the rendering of the specificity of beauty that he called "inscape," though we do have an example of it in the lines descriptive of beautiful girlhood:

> Come then, your ways and airs and looks, locks, maiden gear,
>   gallantry and gaiety and grace,
> Winning ways, airs innocent, maiden manners, sweet looks,
>   loose locks, long locks, lovelocks, gaygear, going gallant,
>   girlgrace—

The other is Hopkins' idiosyncratic rhetoric, which often, but not here, makes for difficult or delayed comprehension. In the passage

> Not within the singeing of the strong sun,
> Tall sun's tingeing, or treacherous the tainting of the earth's
>   air . . .

the last phrase offers only a momentary resistance—we quickly see that "treacherous the tainting" is to be understood as "the treacherous tainting." Nor are we much puzzled by the charming rhetorical idiosyncrasy of "it is an ever-lasting of, O it is an all youth!"

In common with the rest of Hopkins' poems, "The Leaden Echo and the Golden Echo" is suffused with religious feeling, which, as in many of the poems, is aroused (and colored) by the perception of beauty, frequently human beauty, and, as in this case, by the recognition of its transience. The passing of youth is of course one of poetry's oldest-established and most frequently recurrent themes; sadness or despair are the emotions which generally accompany its statement, and Hopkins, taking these to be the natural first response to transience, proposes the comfort that will be given by the resignation of youthful beauty into God's keeping. The recommendation is perhaps less a serious religious idea than a tender religious conceit; as such, it has an appealing sweetness of intention and but little power to hold grievous feelings at bay. It does, however, serve as the occasion for a peculiarly fresh and poignant celebration of the passing physical beauty for which it seeks a spiritual permanence.

"GO TELL IT" —
WHAT A MESSAGE —

EMILY DICKINSON
1830–1886

"Go tell it"—What a Message—
To whom—is specified—
Not murmur—not endearment—
But simply—we—obeyed—
Obeyed—a Lure—a Longing?   5
Oh Nature—none of this—
To Law—said sweet Thermopylae
I give my dying Kiss—

COMMENTARY

One of the tenets of modern literary criticism is that a poem is a self-contained entity, that it must be regarded as wholly independent of all considerations that are not proposed by its own elements. For example, any knowledge of the personal life of the poet, even of the circumstances that led to the writing of the poem, is considered irrelevant—it may be interesting in itself but it cannot tell us anything we need to know in order for the poem to have its right effect upon us. There are critics who go so far as to say that an interest in the personal existence of the poet interferes with our direct response to the poem.

This idea must be granted the merit of its intention. When we read "Resolution and Independence," it is not necessary to know that Wordsworth, shortly before he wrote the poem, actually did meet an old man such as he describes, or that he was soon to be married and might therefore be expected to feel anxiety over the future. For a precise response to "Ode to a Nightingale" we do not have to know that it was written not many weeks after Keats had witnessed the death of his younger brother. And if we felt it necessary to seek out such information, the poem could of course be thought by that much the less complete in itself, for in part it would then depend for its effect upon something outside itself.

But the truth is that extrinsic information, whether we wish it or not, and whether the critics in their strictness like it or not, often does impinge upon our awareness of a particular poem and become an element in our relation to it which we cannot ignore. When we read "Lycidas," we cannot dismiss from our minds the fact that the young poet who speaks so proudly of the profession of poetry and of his noble desire for fame is to become one of the world's great poets, as famous as ever he could have wished. How different our response to "Lycidas" would be if Milton had died not long after its composition! We should then not take the poem to be, among other things, the superb prelude to a triumphant career, but a vaunt which had been made pathetic and ironic by circumstance. In this instance, the mere awareness of Milton's reputation is an extraneous knowledge that inevitably plays some part in our reading of the poem, and it would be a strict critic indeed who would say that it should not.

Another kind of information which properly has its share in our response to a poem comes from our familiarity with other poems from the same pen. Anyone acquainted with the canon of Wordsworth's work knows that the poet conceived of his creative power as being dependent upon the emotions of his childhood and early youth and that he believed that the passing years would diminish it. Whoever has read even a few of Keats's poems is aware that the poet was preoccupied with the antithesis between what is eternal and "pure" and what is transient and mundane. Such awarenesses constitute some knowledge of the poets as persons, and this knowledge cannot fail to have its effect upon our way of responding to a single one of their poems, nor does there seem to be any good reason for supposing that this effect is anything but natural. It is a positive advantage in our reading of "Resolution and Independence" to know that Wordsworth's fear of losing his creative powers is not a momentary fancy but an emotion that conditioned his whole life. It can scarcely confuse our response to "Ode to a Nightingale" to know that Keats is *again* moved to a passionate consideration of the eternal and the transitory.

And in the case of Emily Dickinson's striking little poem, there is at least one personal fact about the author which it is essential we bring to our reading —that the poet is a woman. If we were not aware of this, we might well be made uncomfortable by the poem, for its tone and diction seem appropriate to a woman but not to a man, and we would surely be ill at ease if we thought a man had been the writer.

The poem is, as it were, based upon the femininity of the poet. The word femininity is never used in a neutral sense but always with the intention of praise; it connotes charm, delicacy, tenderness. These qualities are no doubt readily seen, or heard, in the poem, but they will be the more quickly perceived by the reader who has some previous acquaintance with Emily Dickinson's work and knows the extent to which the poet represents herself in the postures of femininity, as a young woman, or girl, of high sensitivity, delicate, fastidious, quick to be apprehensive yet courageous and even daring, standing in a daughterly relation to God, whom, on one occasion, with the licensed audacity of rebelliousness characteristic of her manner, she addresses as "Papa above" (page 1194). The rules of the world are laid down by masculine beings and the point of many of her poems lies, as in the present one, in the opposition of the feminine creature to the masculine authority, which usually delights her even though she addresses it in irony or protest.

There are two speakers in the poem. They are of opposite sexes and they are half a world and some twenty-five centuries apart. When Emily Dickinson wrote, she could count on a prompt appreciation of what "message" it is that begins "Go tell it . . ." Most readers of the nineteenth century knew the story of the Spartans at Thermopylae—how the huge Persian army under the great king Xerxes moved to conquer Greece; how the small Greek army took its stand at Thermopylae, where, between the precipitous mountain on the one side and the sea on the other, there was a pass so narrow that only a few soldiers could enter it abreast; how, when the Greek position was betrayed, the greater part of the Greek forces withdrew, leaving only the Spartans under their king Leonidas to hold the pass; and how the Spartans, some three hundred in number, were exterminated. Upon the spot a monument was erected which bore this inscription: "Go, stranger, and tell Sparta that here, obeying her commands, we fell." What a message indeed!

The feminine voice—and perhaps we should say the modern feminine voice—questions the basis of the Spartans' act even though the message says unmistakably what that is: obedience. The feminine mind wishes to understand the heroism as an impulse, specifically as an impulse of love. The language used is that of erotic attraction—the poet speaks of the heroic deed as having been a response to "a Lure—a Longing"; she sees it as instinctual, rising out of Nature. And across the centuries the men of Thermopylae refuse her interpretation of their act. They address her by the name of the principle she has invoked, speaking to her as if she were Nature itself, and, brushing aside the idea of their having responded to a "Lure" or a "Longing," assert that it was not Love but Law that moved them.

Yet the feminine voice is not to be silenced. In the very act of reporting how it is refuted and rebuked, it asserts itself in the peculiarly feminine epithet by which it characterizes the great event—"sweet Thermopylae," it says. And the men of Thermopylae seem suddenly to assent to the feminine understanding of their sacrifice—the salute which they send to Law is a kiss. The striking inappropriateness of applying the adjective *sweet* to the grim heroic battle is matched by the inappropriateness—almost comic—of the men of Thermopylae sending a kiss to the Law of Sparta, the most rigorous the world has known. The imperturbable soldiers have been beguiled into taking the feminine view of their action, and Law and Love are made one.

The text of " 'Go tell it'—" that I have used is the one established by Professor Thomas H. Johnson; it reproduces exactly the punctuation of the manuscript. The numerous dashes are characteristic of the poet's practice; Professor Edith Stamm has advanced the theory (in *The Saturday Review*, March 30, 1963) that they are intended to guide the voice in reading.

SAILING
TO BYZANTIUM[1]

WILLIAM BUTLER YEATS
1865–1939

That is no country for old men. The young
In one another's arms, birds in the trees,
—Those dying generations—at their song,
The salmon-falls, the mackerel-crowded seas,
Fish, flesh, or fowl, commend all summer long   5
Whatever is begotten, born, and dies.
Caught in that sensual music all neglect
Monuments of unaging intellect.

An aged man is but a paltry thing,
A tattered coat upon a stick, unless   10
Soul clap its hands and sing, and louder sing
For every tatter in its mortal dress,
Nor is there singing school but studying
Monuments of its own magnificence;
And therefore I have sailed the seas and come   15
To the holy city of Byzantium.

O sages standing in God's holy fire
As in the gold mosaic of a wall,
Come from the holy fire, perne[2] in a gyre,
And be the singing-masters of my soul.   20
Consume my heart away, sick with desire
And fastened to a dying animal
It knows not what it is; and gather me
Into the artifice of eternity.

Once out of nature I shall never take   25
My bodily form from any natural thing.
But such a form as Grecian goldsmiths make

[1] An ancient great city, the holy city of eastern Christendom.   [2] Turn, spin.

Of hammered gold and gold enamelling
To keep a drowsy Emperor awake;
Or set upon a golden bough to sing   30
To lords and ladies of Byzantium
Of what is past, or passing, or to come.[3]

COMMENTARY

One of Hans Christian Andersen's best-known stories tells of an Emperor of China in whose garden lived a small brown bird. It was a nightingale, and the beauty of its song was a chief delight of the Emperor's life. But one day the court jewelers presented their master with an artificial bird which they had contrived with great artistry and ingenuity. It was made of gold and set with gems, and by means of a clockwork mechanism it was able to sing. The Emperor was captivated by the wonderful toy and quite forgot the nightingale of flesh and blood, who, in sorrow over his neglect, flew away. Time passed, the unvarying song of the nightingale of artifice palled on the Emperor, who was now old and near death, and one day the clockwork gave out. The Emperor, lonely on his deathbed, longed for the comfort of the real nightingale's singing. He spoke his longing aloud, the bird appeared at his window and sang for him, and the Emperor died happy.

We cannot be sure that Yeats knew Andersen's story, although anyone who had been a child in a literate home in the late nineteenth century was likely to have been acquainted with it.[1] But whether he did or not, the story is pertinent to "Sailing to Byzantium" because it gives simple and memorable expression to an attitude which the poem controverts. For most people the word "artifice" and the adjective derived from it carry an adverse connotation. They imply something false; "nature" and "natural" suggest the real and true. Much of the force of "Sailing to Byzantium" derives from the heresy, as we might call it, of its preference for "artifice" as against "nature." The poet expresses the wish to be "out of nature," to be, exactly, a golden nightingale, a work of artifice.

The shock that the expression of this desire is calculated to produce is made the more intense by the reputation of the city that Yeats makes the comprehensive symbol of the non-natural or even of the anti-natural. Byzantium—later known as Constantinople, now as Istanbul—was the chief city of the Roman empire of the East. Eventually it became the administrative and cultural center of the whole Roman world in its long Christianized phase and, in its luxury and magnificence, it surpassed the city of Rome itself. Its architecture, which drew upon a highly developed engineering skill, has never lacked for admiration. But the pictures with which the churches, monasteries, and palaces were decorated fell into disrepute in Western Europe after the early days of the Renaissance. The chief ground for the unfavorable judgment was the indiffer-

[3] I have read somewhere that in the Emperor's palace at Byzantium was a tree made of gold and silver, and artificial birds that sang. (Yeats's note)

[1] His footnote to line 32 permits the conjecture that Yeats may indeed have known the story and that, for his own poetic purposes, he had unconsciously transformed the Chinese emperor into a Byzantine emperor.

ence that the Byzantine artists showed to naturalistic representation, especially of the human form. The personages in Byzantine pictures are always clothed, and their voluminous robes give no indication of the body beneath. Their postures are static, and we have the impression that although these people are accessible to certain religious emotions, they have no capacity either for worldly feelings or for physical movement. The personal inspiration of the artist is subordinated to the control of tradition and convention; his indifference to naturalistic considerations can by no means be ascribed to a deficiency of skill in representation but to a complex aesthetic, derived from an elaborate theology, which repudiated the body in favor of the soul.

To the taste of the present time, Byzantine painting makes a strong appeal. The development of modern painting has been away from naturalistic representation and we take pleasure in the very abstractness that once was thought uninteresting and even repellent. But this revision of judgment is relatively recent, and up through the early years of the twentieth century, Byzantine painting was not likely to be admired except by scholars and connoisseurs of unconventional taste. Byzantium figured in most people's minds as the very type of a formalized "lifeless" culture.

Yeats's interest in Byzantium began when he was advanced in middle age. This was far from being the first time that a past culture had seemed to him of momentous relevance to his own life—indeed, nothing is so characteristic of Yeats, from the start of his career, as his preoccupation with the quality of life of some epoch of the past. It was thus that he expressed his passionately adverse sense of the modern world, which he thought ignoble in its rationalism, materialism, and calculating self-interest. As an Irishman, he was especially inclined to ascribe the modern ignobility to England although he also directed his scorn upon his own countrymen for betraying their heritage of romantic magnanimity. Against the dull prudence of modern life, he set the irrational heroic passions of the legendary Irish past; against the vulgarity and disorder of the present he evoked the recollection of a past era closer at hand, that of the eighteenth century, when the proud elegance of an assured aristocracy and the rich intuitiveness of an uncorrupted peasantry made the conditions of a good life. Such were the historical-cultural fantasies of the young poet who believed that the culture in which he had his actual existence stood in the way of his desire for fullness of life. Advancing years made a very different past culture seem desirable—to the aging poet Byzantium spoke of immortality.

The established and scarcely debatable view of Yeats's development is that, although he was a gifted and interesting poet from his early youth, he did not become a great one until his middle age. He was nearly fifty before he began to write the poems that won him his high place in modern literature. A special interest of his later work derives from the new diction he taught himself to use: hard, downright, fierce in its directness, and, as we say, "unpoetic." It is a manner consonant with the characteristic matter of the later poems, which is an aging man's harsh resentment of an ineluctable circumstance of human life, that we grow old.

This matter, which is to be distinguished from a concern with the transience of youth or of all of life, is new not only to the poet but to poetry. Yeats may well be the first writer ever to make his own representation of himself as an aging man a chief element of his creation. The general human importance of this cannot be underestimated—it might even be said that Yeats added a whole stage of life to man's existence: by his impassioned resentment of it, he made the world know that old age may be as sentient and significant a period in a man's life as his youth. Hitherto old age had been represented wholly from the outside: the aged or aging person was made the *object* of understanding or sympathy; it is someone else, not the poet, who experiences the aging process.[2] But Yeats, perhaps because he so feared and hated his old age, refused to let it make him into a mere object; he claimed it and proclaimed it as his experience, he imposed his imagination upon it—and thus remained a subject.

It is, then, as an aging man, with the prospect of actual old age before him, that Yeats takes leave of "nature" and seeks refuge in the permanence of "artifice"—of art, not as it refers to life in its shifting cycles of joy or pain, but as it suggests fixity and timelessness. His hope is much the same as that of Professor Cornelius, the historian of Thomas Mann's "Disorder and Early Sorrow" (pages 685 ff.), who sees in the unchanging orderliness of the past a means of escaping from the pain of the living present of youthful desire. But one need not be a man of middle age, like Professor Cornelius, or a man on the threshold of old age, like Yeats, to entertain the imagination of beautiful permanence. Keats was only twenty-four when he wrote "Ode to a Nightingale" (pages 892 ff.), the theme of which is not unlike that of "Sailing to Byzantium"; his "Ode on a Grecian Urn" (page 1124) is yet closer to Yeats's poem in the complex opposition it makes between beauty in nature, with its susceptibility to mutability and deterioration, and beauty in the permanence of art.

But we cannot read the first stanza of "Sailing to Byzantium" without being made aware of the poet's ambivalence toward nature, of how deeply Yeats loves what he says he has rejected. The beings that "commend" the natural cycle of existence, the life of generation, birth, and death, win from the poet the commendation of his scarcely disguised envy. And when he imagines his existence in "artifice," as the golden bird, it is not of timeless abstractions that he tells us he will sing but of nature and time, or nature *in* time—the triad which describes the burden of his song, "what is past, or passing, or to come," echoes the triad of rejected things in the first stanza, "Whatever is begotten, born, and dies." This has to be seen as a contradiction, and a moving one. And perhaps equally moving is Yeats's choice of the form of artifice in which the poet would wish to have his existence—not a great, still monument of the soul's magnificence but a miniscule creature of gold and enamel, a little toy of a bird.

2 See, for example, the Leech-gatherer of "Resolution and Independence" (pp. 862 ff.), the greatest of Wordsworth's many representations of old men.

THE
WASTE LAND

THOMAS STEARNS ELIOT
1888–1965

*"Nam Sibyllam quidem Cumis ego ipse oculis meis
vidi in ampulla pendere, et cum illi pueri dicerent:
Σίβυλλα τί θέλεις; respondebat illa: ἀποθανεῖν θέλω."*[1]

For Ezra Pound
il miglior fabbro.[2]

I. THE BURIAL OF THE DEAD

April is the cruelest month, breeding
Lilacs out of the dead land, mixing
Memory and desire, stirring
Dull roots with spring rain.
Winter kept us warm, covering   5
Earth in forgetful snow, feeding
A little life with dried tubers.
Summer surprised us, coming over the Starnbergersee
With a shower of rain; we stopped in the colonnade,
And went on in sunlight, into the Hofgarten,   10
And drank coffee, and talked for an hour.
Bin gar keine Russin, stamm' aus Litauen, echt deutsch.[3]
And when we were children, staying at the arch-duke's,
My cousin's, he took me out on a sled,
And I was frightened. He said, Marie,   15
Marie, hold on tight. And down we went.
In the mountains, there you feel free.
I read, much of the night, and go south in the winter.

[1] For with my own eyes I saw the Sibyl of Cumae hanging in a cage, and when the boys cried to her, "Sibyl, what do you want?" she answered, "I want to die" (from Petronius' *Satyricon*). The Sibyl, a prophetic old woman, was about a thousand years old at this time.   [2] The superior artificer, maker.   [3] I'm by no means a Russian, I come from Lithuania—real German.

What are the roots that clutch, what branches grow
Out of this stony rubbish? Son of man,   20
You cannot say, or guess, for you know only
A heap of broken images, where the sun beats,
And the dead tree gives no shelter, the cricket no relief,
And the dry stone no sound of water. Only
There is shadow under this red rock   25
(Come in under the shadow of this red rock),
And I will show you something different from either
Your shadow at morning striding behind you
Or your shadow at evening rising to meet you;
I will show you fear in a handful of dust.   30

                    Frisch weht der Wind
                    Der Heimat zu
                    Mein Irisch Kind,
                    Wo weilest du?[4]

"You gave me hyacinths first a year ago;   35
"They called me the hyacinth girl."
—Yet when we came back, late, from the Hyacinth garden,
Your arms full, and your hair wet, I could not
Speak, and my eyes failed, I was neither
Living or dead, and I knew nothing,   40
Looking into the heart of light, the silence.
Oed' und leer das Meer.[5]

Madame Sosostris, famous clairvoyante,
Had a bad cold, nevertheless
Is known to be the wisest woman in Europe,   45
With a wicked pack of cards. Here, said she,
Is your card, the drowned Phoenician Sailor,
(Those are pearls that were his eyes. Look!)
Here is Belladonna, the Lady of the Rocks,
The lady of situations.   50
Here is the man with three staves, and here the Wheel
And here is the one-eyed merchant, and this card,
Which is blank, is something he carries on his back,
Which I am forbidden to see. I do not find
The Hanged Man. Fear death by water.   55
I see crowds of people, walking round in a ring.
Thank you. If you see dear Mrs. Equitone,
Tell her I bring the horoscope myself:
One must be so careful these days.

Unreal City,   60
Under the brown fog of a winter dawn,
A crowd flowed over London Bridge, so many,

    [4] A fresh wind blows toward the homeland; my Irish child, where are you lingering?
(See Eliot's note to line 31.)   [5] Wide and empty is the sea. (See Eliot's note to this line.)

I had not thought death had undone so many.
Sighs, short and infrequent, were exhaled,
And each man fixed his eyes before his feet.   65
Flowed up the hill and down King William Street,
To where Saint Mary Woolnoth kept the hours
With a dead sound on the final stroke of nine.
There I saw one I knew, and stopped him, crying: "Stetson!
"You who were with me in the ships at Mylae!   70
"That corpse you planted last year in your garden,
"Has it begun to sprout? Will it bloom this year?
"Or has the sudden frost disturbed its bed?
"Oh keep the Dog far hence, that's friend to men,
"Or with his nails he'll dig it up again!   75
"You! hypocrite lecteur!—mon semblable,—mon frère!"[6]

II. A GAME OF CHESS

The Chair she sat in, like a burnished throne,
Glowed on the marble, where the glass
Held up by standards wrought with fruited vines
From which a golden Cupidon peeped out   80
(Another hid his eyes behind his wing)
Doubled the flames of sevenbranched candelabra
Reflecting light upon the table as
The glitter of her jewels rose to meet it,
From satin cases poured in rich profusion;   85
In vials of ivory and coloured glass
Unstoppered, lurked her strange synthetic perfumes,
Unguent, powdered, or liquid—troubled, confused
And drowned the sense in odours; stirred by the air
That freshened from the window, these ascended   90
In fattening the prolonged candle-flames,
Flung their smoke into the laquearia,
Stirring the pattern on the coffered ceiling.
Huge sea-wood fed with copper
Burned green and orange, framed by the coloured stone,   95
In which sad light a carvèd dolphin swam.
Above the antique mantel was displayed
As though a window gave upon the sylvan scene
The change of Philomel, by the barbarous king
So rudely forced; yet there the nightingale   100
Filled all the desert with inviolable voice
And still she cried, and still the world pursues,
"Jug Jug" to dirty ears.
And other withered stumps of time
Were told upon the walls; staring forms   105
Leaned out, leaning, hushing the room enclosed.
Footsteps shuffled on the stair.

[6] Hypocritical reader!—my likeness,—my brother! (See Eliot's note to this line.)

Under the firelight, under the brush, her hair
Spread out in fiery points
Glowed into words, then would be savagely still.   110

"My nerves are bad to-night. Yes, bad. Stay with me.
"Speak to me. Why do you never speak. Speak.
        "What are you thinking of? What thinking? What?
"I never know what you are thinking. Think."

I think we are in rats' alley   115
Where the dead men lost their bones.

"What is that noise?"
                    The wind under the door.
"What is that noise now? What is the wind doing?"
                    Nothing again nothing.   120
                                        "Do
"You know nothing? Do you see nothing? Do you remember
"Nothing?"
        I remember
Those are pearls that were his eyes.   125
"Are you alive, or not? Is there nothing in your head?"
                                        But

O O O O that Shakespeherian Rag—
It's so elegant
So intelligent   130
"What shall I do now? What shall I do?"
"I shall rush out as I am, and walk the street
"With my hair down, so. What shall we do tomorrow?
"What shall we ever do?"
                    The hot water at ten.   135
And if it rains, a closed car at four.
And we shall play a game of chess,
Pressing lidless eyes and waiting for a knock upon the door.

When Lil's husband got demobbed, I said—
I didn't mince my words, I said to her myself,   140
HURRY UP PLEASE ITS TIME
Now Albert's coming back, make yourself a bit smart.
He'll want to know what you done with that money he gave you
To get yourself some teeth. He did, I was there.
You have them all out, Lil, and get a nice set,   145
He said, I swear, I can't bear to look at you.
And no more can't I, I said, and think of poor Albert,
He's been in the army four years, he wants a good time,
And if you don't give it him, there's others will, I said.
Oh is there, she said. Something o' that, I said.   150
Then I'll know who to thank, she said, and gave me a straight look.

HURRY UP PLEASE ITS TIME
If you don't like it you can get on with it, I said.
Others can pick and choose if you can't.
But if Albert makes off, it won't be for lack of telling.   155
You ought to be ashamed, I said, to look so antique.
(And her only thirty-one.)
I can't help it, she said, pulling a long face,
It's them pills I took, to bring it off, she said.
(She's had five already, and nearly died of young George.)   160
The chemist said it would be all right, but I've never been the same.
You *are* a proper fool, I said.
Well, if Albert won't leave you alone, there it is, I said,
What you get married for if you don't want children?
HURRY UP PLEASE ITS TIME   165
Well, that Sunday Albert was home, they had a hot gammon,
And they asked me in to dinner, to get the beauty of it hot—
HURRY UP PLEASE ITS TIME
HURRY UP PLEASE ITS TIME
Goonight Bill. Goonight Lou. Goonight May. Goonight.   170
Ta ta. Goonight. Goonight.
Good night, ladies, good night, sweet ladies, good night, good night.

III. THE FIRE SERMON

The river's tent is broken: the last fingers of leaf
Clutch and sink into the wet bank. The wind
Crosses the brown land, unheard. The nymphs are departed.   175
Sweet Thames, run softly, till I end my song.
The river bears no empty bottles, sandwich papers,
Silk handkerchiefs, cardboard boxes, cigarette ends
Or other testimony of summer nights. The nymphs are departed.
And their friends, the loitering heirs of city directors—   180
Departed, have left no addresses.
By the waters of Leman I sat down and wept   .   .   .
Sweet Thames, run softly till I end my song,
Sweet Thames, run softly, for I speak not loud or long.
But at my back in a cold blast I hear   185
The rattle of the bones, and chuckle spread from ear to ear.
A rat crept softly through the vegetation
Dragging its slimy belly on the bank
While I was fishing in the dull canal
On a winter evening behind the gashouse   190
Musing upon the king my brother's wreck
And on the king my father's death before him.
White bodies naked on the low damp ground
And bones cast in a little low dry garret,
Rattled by the rat's foot only, year to year.   195
But at my back from time to time I hear
The sound of horns and motors, which shall bring

Sweeney to Mrs. Porter in the spring.
O the moon shone bright on Mrs. Porter
And on her daughter   200
They wash their feet in soda water
Et O ces voix d'enfants, chantant dans la coupole![7]
Twit twit twit
Jug jug jug jug jug jug
So rudely forc'd.   205

Tereu

Unreal City
Under the brown fog of a winter noon
Mr. Eugenides, the Smyrna merchant
Unshaven, with a pocket full of currants   210
C.i.f. London: documents at sight,
Asked me in demotic French
To luncheon at the Cannon Street Hotel
Followed by a weekend at the Metropole.

At the violet hour, when the eyes and back   215
Turn upward from the desk, when the human engine waits
Like a taxi throbbing waiting,
I Tiresias, though blind, throbbing between two lives,
Old man with wrinkled female breasts, can see
At the violet hour, the evening hour that strives   220
Homeward, and brings the sailor home from sea,
The typist home at teatime, clears her breakfast, lights
Her stove, and lays out food in tins.
Out of the window perilously spread
Her drying combinations touched by the sun's last rays,   225
On the divan are piled (at night her bed)
Stockings, slippers, camisoles, and stays.
I Tiresias, old man with wrinkled dugs
Perceived the scene, and foretold the rest—
I too awaited the expected guest.   230
He, the young man carbuncular, arrives,
A small house agent's clerk, with one bold stare,
One of the low on whom assurance sits
As a silk hat on a Bradford millionaire.
The time is now propitious, as he guesses,   235
The meal is ended, she is bored and tired,
Endeavours to engage her in caresses
Which still are unreproved, if undesired.
Flushed and decided, he assaults at once;
Exploring hands encounter no defence;   240
His vanity requires no response,

[7] And oh these children's voices, singing in the cupola. (See Eliot's note to this line.)

And makes a welcome of indifference.
(And I Tiresias have foresuffered all
Enacted on this same divan or bed;
I who have sat by Thebes below the wall   245
And walked among the lowest of the dead.)
Bestows one final patronising kiss,
And gropes his way, finding the stairs unlit   . . .

She turns and looks a moment in the glass,
Hardly aware of her departed lover;   250
Her brain allows one half-formed thought to pass:
"Well now that's done: and I'm glad it's over."
When lovely woman stoops to folly and
Paces about her room again, alone,
She smoothes her hair with automatic hand,   255
And puts a record on the gramophone.

"This music crept by me upon the waters"
And along the Strand, up Queen Victoria Street.
O City city, I can sometimes hear
Beside a public bar in Lower Thames Street,   260
The pleasant whining of a mandoline
And a clatter and a chatter from within
Where fishmen lounge at noon: where the walls
Of Magnus Martyr hold
Inexplicable splendour of Ionian white and gold.   265

    The river sweats
    Oil and tar
    The barges drift
    With the turning tide
    Red sails   270
    Wide
    To leeward, swing on the heavy spar.
    The barges wash
    Drifting logs
    Down Greenwich reach   275
    Past the Isle of Dogs.
        Weialala leia
        Wallala leialala
    Elizabeth and Leicester
    Beating oars   280
    The stern was formed
    A gilded shell
    Red and gold
    The brisk swell
    Rippled both shores   285
    Southwest wind
    Carried down stream

The peal of bells
White towers
    Weialala leia
    Wallala leialala

"Trams and dusty trees.
Highbury bore me. Richmond and Kew
Undid me. By Richmond I raised my knees
Supine on the floor of a narrow canoe."
"My feet are at Moorgate, and my heart
Under my feet. After the event
He wept. He promised 'a new start.'
I made no comment. What should I resent?"

"On Margate Sands.
I can connect
Nothing with nothing.
The broken fingernails of dirty hands.
My people humble people who expect
Nothing."
        la la
To Carthage then I came

Burning burning burning burning
Oh Lord Thou pluckest me out
O Lord Thou pluckest

burning

IV. DEATH BY WATER

Phlebas the Phoenician, a fortnight dead,
Forgot the cry of gulls, and the deep sea swell
And the profit and loss.
             A current under sea
Picked his bones in whispers. As he rose and fell
He passed the stages of his age and youth
Entering the whirlpool.
             Gentile or Jew
O you who turn the wheel and look to windward,
Consider Phlebas, who was once handsome and tall as you.

V. WHAT THE THUNDER SAID

After the torchlight red on sweaty faces
After the frosty silence in the gardens
After the agony in stony places
The shouting and the crying
Prison and palace and reverberation

290

295

300

305

310

315

320

325

Of thunder of spring over distant mountains
He who was living is now dead
We who were living are now dying
With a little patience   330

Here is no water but only rock
Rock and no water and the sandy road
The road winding above among the mountains
Which are mountains of rock without water
If there were water we should stop and drink   335
Amongst the rock one cannot stop or think
Sweat is dry and feet are in the sand
If there were only water amongst the rock
Dead mountain mouth of carious teeth that cannot spit
Here one can neither stand nor lie nor sit   340
There is not even silence in the mountains
But dry sterile thunder without rain
There is not even solitude in the mountains
But red sullen faces sneer and snarl
From doors of mudcracked houses   345
                                    If there were water
        And no rock
        If there were rock
        And also water
        And water   350
        A spring
        A pool among the rock
        If there were the sound of water only
        Not the cicada
        And dry grass singing   355
        But sound of water over a rock
        Where the hermit-thrush sings in the pine trees
        Drip drop drip drop drop drop drop
        But there is no water

Who is the third who walks always beside you?   360
When I count, there are only you and I together
But when I look ahead up the white road
There is always another one walking beside you
Gliding wrapt in a brown mantle, hooded
I do not know whether a man or a woman   365
—But who is that on the other side of you?

What is that sound high in the air
Murmur of maternal lamentation
Who are those hooded hordes swarming
Over endless plains, stumbling in cracked earth   370
Ringed by the flat horizon only
What is the city over the mountains

Cracks and reforms and bursts in the violet air
Falling towers
Jerusalem Athens Alexandria   375
Vienna London
Unreal

A woman drew her long black hair out tight
And fiddled whisper music on those strings
And bats with baby faces in the violet light   380
Whistled, and beat their wings
And crawled head downward down a blackened wall
And upside down in air were towers
Tolling reminiscent bells, that kept the hours
And voices singing out of empty cisterns and exhausted wells.   385

In this decayed hole among the mountains
In the faint moonlight, the glass is singing
Over the tumbled graves, about the chapel
There is the empty chapel, only the wind's home.
It has no windows, and the door swings,   390
Dry bones can harm no one.
Only a cock stood on the rooftree
Co co rico co co rico
In a flash of lightning. Then a damp gust
Bringing rain   395
Ganga was sunken, and the limp leaves
Waited for rain, while the black clouds
Gathered far distant, over Himavant.
The jungle crouched, humped in silence.
Then spoke the thunder   400
DA
Datta: what have we given?
My friend, blood shaking my heart
The awful daring of a moment's surrender
Which an age of prudence can never retract   405
By this, and this only, we have existed
Which is not to be found in our obituaries
Or in memories draped by the beneficent spider
Or under seals broken by the lean solicitor
In our empty rooms   410
DA
Dayadhvam: I have heard the key
Turn in the door once and turn once only
We think of the key, each in his prison
Thinking of the key, each confirms a prison   415
Only at nightfall, aethereal rumours
Revive for a moment a broken Coriolanus
DA
Damyata: The boat responded

Gaily, to the hand expert with sail and oar 420
The sea was calm, your heart would have responded
Gaily, when invited, beating obedient
To controlling hands
              I sat upon the shore
Fishing, with the arid plain behind me 425
Shall I at least set my lands in order?
London Bridge is falling down falling down falling down
Poi s'ascose nel foco che gli affina
Quando fiam uti chelidon[8]—O swallow swallow
Le Prince d'Aquitaine à la tour abolie[9] 430
These fragments I have shored against my ruins
Why then Ile fit you. Hieronymo's mad againe.
Datta. Dayadhvam. Damyata.
              Shantih   shantih   shantih

NOTES ON "THE WASTE LAND"

[*T. S. Eliot*]

Not only the title, but the plan and a good deal of the incidental symbolism of the poem were suggested by Miss Jessie L. Weston's book on the Grail legend: *From Ritual to Romance* (Cambridge). Indeed, so deeply am I indebted, Miss Weston's book will elucidate the difficulties of the poem much better than my notes can do; and I recommend it (apart from the great interest of the book itself) to any who think much elucidation of the poem worth the trouble. To another work of anthropology I am indebted in general, one which has influenced our generation profoundly; I mean *The Golden Bough;* I have used especially the two volumes *Adonis, Attis, Osiris.* Anyone who is acquainted with these works will immediately recognise in the poem certain references to vegetation ceremonies.

I. THE BURIAL OF THE DEAD

LINE 20.   Cf. Ezekiel II, i.
23.   Cf. Ecclesiastes XII, v.
31.   V. Tristan und Isolde, I, verses 5–8.
42.   Id. III, verse 24.
46.   I am not familiar with the exact constitution of the Tarot pack of cards, from which I have obviously departed to suit my own convenience. The Hanged Man, a member of the traditional pack, fits my purpose in two ways: because he is associated in my mind with the Hanged God of Frazer, and because I associate him with the hooded figure in the passage of the disciples to Emmaus in Part V. The Phoenician Sailor and the Merchant appear later; also the "crowd of people," and Death by Water is executed in Part IV. The Man with Three Staves (an authentic member of the Tarot pack) I associate, quite arbitrarily, with the Fisher King himself.
60.   Cf. Baudelaire:

[8] Then he hid him in the flame that refines them / When shall I become as the swallow? (See Eliot's notes to lines 428 and 429.) The anonymous Latin poem from which Eliot has taken part of line 429 celebrates the spring festival in honor of Venus, goddess of love and increase.   [9] The Prince of Aquitaine at the ruined tower. (See Eliot's note to this line.)

"Fourmillante cité, cité pleine de rêves,
"Où le spectre en plein jour raccroche le passant."[10]

63.   Cf. Inferno III, 55–57:

"si lunga tratta
di gente, ch'io non avrei mai creduto
che morte tanta n'avesse disfatta."[11]

64.   Cf. Inferno IV, 25–27:

"Quivi, secondo che per ascolatare,
"non avea pianto, ma' che di sospiri,
"che l'aura eterna facevan tremare."[12]

68.   A phenomenon which I have often noticed.

74.   Cf. the Dirge in Webster's *White Devil*.

76.   V. Baudelaire, Preface to *Fleurs du Mal*.

II. A GAME OF CHESS

77.   Cf. *Antony and Cleopatra*, II ii, 1. 190.

92.   Laquearia. V. *Aeneid*, I, 726:

dependent lychni laquearibus aureis incensi, et noctem
flammis funalia vincunt.[13]

98.   Sylvan scene. V. Milton, *Paradise Lost*, IV, 140.

99.   V. Ovid, *Metamorphoses*, VI, Philomela.

100.   Cf. Part III, 1. 204.

115.   Cf. Part III, 1. 195.

118.   Cf. Webster: "Is the wind in that door still?"

126.   Cf. Part I, 1. 37, 48.

138.   Cf. the game of chess in Middleton's *Women Beware Women*.

III. THE FIRE SERMON

176.   V. Spenser, *Prothalamion*.

192.   Cf. *The Tempest*, I, ii.

196.   Cf. Marvell, *To His Coy Mistress*.

197.   Cf. Day, *Parliament of Bees*:

"When of the sudden, listening, you shall hear,
"A noise of horns and hunting, which shall bring
"Actaeon to Diana in the spring,
"Where all shall see her naked skin . . ."

199.   I do not know the origin of the ballad from which these lines are taken: it was reported to me from Sydney, Australia.

202.   V. Verlaine, *Parsifal*.

210.   The currants were quoted at a price "carriage and insurance free to London" and the Bill of Lading etc. were to be handed to the buyer upon payment of the sight draft.

218.   Tiresias, although a mere spectator and not indeed a "character," is yet the most important personage in the poem, uniting all the rest. Just as the one-eyed merchant seller of currants, melts into the Phoenician Sailor, and the latter is not wholly distinct from Ferdinand Prince of Naples, so all the women are one woman, and the two sexes met in Tiresias. What Tiresias *sees*, in fact, is the substance of the poem. The whole passage from Ovid is of great anthropological interest:

[10] Swarming city, full of dreams, where ghosts in broad daylight accost passers-by.
[11] So long a train of people, I had not ever believed that death had undone so many.
[12] Here there was no plaint that could be heard, except of sighs, which made the eternal air to tremble.   [13] Lighted lamps hang down from the fretted roof of gold, and flaming torches drive out the night.

"... Cum Iunone iocos et maior vestra profecto est
Quam, quae contingit maribus," dixisse, "voluptas."
Illa negat; placuit quae sit sententia docti
Quaerere Tiresiae: venus huic erat utraque nota.
Nam duo magnorum viridi coeuntia silva
Corpora serpentum baculi violaverat ictu
Deque viro factus, mirabile, femina septem
Egerat autumnos; octavo rursus eosdem
Vidit et "est vestrae si tanta potentia plagae,"
Dixit "ut auctoris sortem in contraria mutet,
Nunc quoque vos feriam!" percussis anguibus isdem
Forma prior rediit genetivaque venit imago.
Arbiter hic igitur sumptus de lite iocosa
Dicta Iovis firmat; gravius Saturnia iusto
Nec pro materia fertur doluisse suique
Iudicis aeterna demnavit lumina nocte,
At pater omnipotens (neque enim licet inrita cuiquam
Facta dei fecisse deo) pro lumine adempto
Scire futura dedit poenamque levavit honore.[14]

221. This may not appear as exact as Sappho's lines, but I had in mind the "long-shore" or "dory" fisherman, who returns at nightfall.

253. V. Goldsmith, the song in *The Vicar of Wakefield*.

257. V. *The Tempest*, as above.

264. The interior of St. Magnus Martyr is to my mind one of the finest among Wren's interiors. See *The Proposed Demolition of Nineteen City Churches*: (P. S. King & Son, Ltd.).

266. The Song of the (three) Thames-daughters begins here. From line 292 to 306 inclusive they speak in turn. V. *Gotterdammerung*, III, i: the Rhine-daughters.

279. V. Froude, *Elizabeth*, Vol. I, ch. iv, letter of De Quadra to Philip of Spain: "In the afternoon we were in a barge, watching the games on the river. (The queen) was alone with Lord Robert and myself on the poop, when they began to talk nonsense, and went so far that Lord Robert at last said, as I was on the spot there was no reason why they should not be married if the queen pleased."

293. Cf. *Purgatorio*, V, 133:
"Ricorditi di me, che son la Pia;
"Siena mi fe', disfecemi Maremma."[15]

307. V. St. Augustine's *Confessions*: "to Carthage then I came, where a cauldron of unholy loves sang all about mine ears."

308. The complete text of the Buddha's Fire Sermon (which corresponds in importance to the Sermon on the Mount) from which these words are taken, will be found translated in the late Henry Clarke Warren's *Buddhism in Translation* (Harvard Oriental Series). Mr. Warren was one of the great pioneers of Buddhist studies in the Occident.

[14] It chanced that Jove (as the story goes), while warmed with wine, put care aside and bandied good-humored jests with Juno in an idle hour. "I maintain," said he, "that your pleasure in love is greater than that which we [the male gods] enjoy." She held the opposite view. And so they decided to ask the judgment of the wise Tiresias. He knew both sides of love. For once, with a blow of his staff, he had outraged two huge serpents mating in the green forest; and, wonderful to relate, from man he was changed into a woman, and in that form spent seven years. In the eighth year he saw the same serpents again and said: "Since in striking you there is such magic power as to change the nature of the giver of the blow, now will I strike you once again." So saying, he struck the serpents, and his former state was restored, and he became as he had been born. He, therefore, being asked to arbitrate the playful dispute of the gods, took sides with Jove. Saturnia [Juno], they said, grieved more deeply than she should and than the issue warranted, and condemned the arbitrator to perpetual blindness. But the Almighty Father (for no god may undo what another god has done) in return for his loss of sight gave Tiresias the power to know the future, lightening the penalty by the honor" (*Metamorphoses*, III, 318–338, translated by Frank J. Miller in the Loeb Classical Library).   [15] Remember me, who am La Pia; Siena made me, Maremma unmade me.

309. From St. Augustine's *Confessions* again. The collocation of these two representatives of eastern and western asceticism, as the culmination of this part of the poem, is not an accident.

V. WHAT THE THUNDER SAID

In the first part of Part V three themes are employed: the journey to Emmaus, the approach to the Chapel Perilous (see Miss Weston's book) and the present decay of eastern Europe.

357.   This is *Turdus aonalaschkae pallasii,* the hermit-thrush which I have heard in Quebec Province. Chapman says (*Handbook of Birds of Eastern North America*) "it is most at home in secluded woodland and thickety retreats. . . . Its notes are not remarkable for variety or volume, but in purity and sweetness of tone and exquisite modulation they are unequalled." Its "water-dripping song" is justly celebrated.

360.   The following lines were stimulated by the account of one of the Antarctic expeditions (I forget which, but I think one of Shackleton's); it was related that the party of explorers, at the extremity of their strength, had the constant delusion that there was *one more member* than could actually be counted.

366–77. Cf. Hermann Hesse, *Blick ins Chaos:* "Schon ist halb Europa, schon ist zumindest der halbe Osten Europas auf dem Wege Chaos, fährt betrunken im heiligem Wahn am Abgrund entlang und singt dazu, singt betrunken und hymnisch wie Dmitri Karamasoff sang. Ueber diese Lieder lacht der Bürger beleidigt, der Heilige und Seher hört sie mit Tränen."[16]

402.   "Data, dayadhvam, damyata" (Give, sympathise, control). The fable of the meaning of the Thunder is found in the *Brihadaranyaka—Upanishad,* 5, 1. A translation is found in Deussen's *Sechzig Upanishads des Veda,* p. 489.

408.   Cf. Webster, *The White Devil,* V, vi:

> ". . . they'll remarry
> Ere the worm pierce your winding-sheet, ere the spider
> Make a thin curtain for your epitaphs."

412.   Cf. *Inferno,* XXXIII, 46:

> "ed io sentii chiavar l'uscio di sotto
> all'orribile torre."[17]

Also F. H. Bradley, *Appearance and Reality,* p. 346.
"My external sensations are no less private to myself than are my thoughts or my feelings. In either case my experience falls within my own circle, a circle closed on the outside; and, with all its elements alike, every sphere is opaque to the others which surround it. . . . In brief, regarded as an existence which appears in a soul, the whole world for each is peculiar and private to that soul."

425.   V. Weston: *From Ritual to Romance;* chapter on the Fisher King.

428.   V. *Purgatorio,* XXVI, 148.

> " 'Ara vos prec per aquella valor
> 'que vos guida al som de l'escalina,
> 'sovegna vos a temps dè ma dolor.'
> Poi s'ascose nel foco che gli affina."[18]

429.   V. *Pervigilium Veneris.* Cf. Philomela in Parts II and III.

430.   V. Gerard de Nerval, Sonnet *El Desdichado.*

432.   V. Kyd's *Spanish Tragedy.*

434.   Shantih. Repeated as here, a formal ending to an Upanishad. "The Peace which passeth understanding" is our equivalent to this word.

---

[16] Already half Europe, at least half of Eastern Europe, is on the way to chaos, driving drunken in sacred folly along the edge of the abyss and, drunken, singing hymnlike songs as Dmitri Karamazov sang. Offended by these songs the burgher laughs, while the saint and seer listen to them with tears" (translated by Agnes Eisenberger).   [17] And below I heard the outlet of the horrible tower locked up.   [18] Now I pray you that goodness that guides you to the top of the stairs, be mindful at times of my pain. Then he hid him in the fire that refines them.

COMMENTARY

"The Waste Land" is the most famous and influential English poem of our time, the most elaborate and highly wrought, and the most ambitious in its scope, for its subject is nothing less than the nature of modern life, which it represents as the ground of personal desperation. There is no question but that it is a difficult poem. As such, it has engaged the study of many scholars and critics. Their work, and the passage of time, which to some extent domesticates all that is strange and unapproachable in art, have considerably reduced the resistance which "The Waste Land" offered to our understanding when it first appeared in 1922. But it still remains difficult, it still demands a more than usual effort of comprehension. It requires a knowledge of its conventions and assumptions and a degree of familiarity with the recondite lore to which it refers.

The difficulty of the poem and the necessity of dealing with it in a rather special way were recognized by the poet himself. After its first publication, Eliot —perhaps with some irony—provided a series of notes to help set the reader on the right path. These notes appear at the end of the poem.

Yet acquaintance with "The Waste Land" is best begun, not with the confrontation of any of the poem's manifest difficulties, but rather with a response to that element of the poem which is not at all difficult to appreciate, its music. "The Waste Land" is a poem in which the voice plays a definitive part. This is not to underestimate the importance of its visual imagery, but if we can speak of the order in which our impressions of the poem are gained it is its voice—or voices—that we are soonest aware of. Our first experience of "The Waste Land" should be that of hearing it, whether by listening to a recorded reading or by saying it aloud, and quite without any special effort to discover the precise significance of what we hear.

This is not an evasion of what the poem communicates but a first happy step toward it, and the poet himself has given us ground for believing that it is the right first step to take. In one of his later critical essays, "The Social Function of Poetry," Eliot speaks of his pleasure in reading poems in a language he does not know well, so that he is more aware of the sound of the poem than of its exact meanings; and in another essay, "The Music of Poetry," he tells us that when he composes a poem what often comes first to his mind is a certain rhythm or tune which later, as it were, acquires words. The first experience of "The Waste Land" might well be likened to an experience of actual music— what we hear has meaning for us (although not in a denotative way), we know that the meaning of one passage or movement is different from that of another, we perhaps find one *more* meaningful than another, and yet we cannot say *what* the meaning is. If a particular piece of music initially seems difficult to "follow" or "understand," greater familiarity will lead us to a sense of more thorough comprehension. A reader will have much the same experience of "The Waste Land" if he merely listens to it, without questioning the intention of any one line, or figure of speech, or allusion.

This is by no means to say that close study of the poem is not profitable. The opposite is true. But studious reading should come only after one has responded to the poem in those of its elements—they are many—that are to be apprehended readily. My sense that this is so has led me to decide not to supplement the poet's own notes with explicatory footnotes such as are provided for other poems in this book. (An exception is made of phrases and passages in foreign languages, which have been translated.)

And it is well to know from the outset that even when all the details of the poem will eventually have been mastered, when the recondite references are understood, and all the subtle interrelations of the pattern are traced, the poem still will not be mastered: it will always have some measure of mystery; it will hold back from us some secret of its existence. This element of mystery or secrecy—as I have said of other poems less difficult than this—is not a negative but a positive quality of "The Waste Land" and of our response to it. The poem's continued resistance to our best efforts of comprehension is a sign of its vitality and an invitation to our continued interest.

If we are introduced to "The Waste Land" by listening to it, inevitably we are struck by the large variety of its vocal modes, its many different kinds of utterance—we hear speech that is sometimes grave and simple, sometimes lyric and tender, sometimes hysterical, sometimes toneless, sometimes querulous, sometimes awed; and the utterance may be song, or exhortation, or prayer. From whom do these various utterances come? The answer—or at least a first answer—is simple enough. The poem is largely dramatic in form, in the sense that it is not one voice that is heard but many voices, of many persons or characters, some of whom are in relation to one another. It is confusing that some of these utterances are set off by quotation marks and some are not. We are inclined to suppose that the passages that are not punctuated in this way are spoken by the poet himself. But we soon perceive that this is not possible, that of the several speakers in such passages the poet himself is only one and that although now and then he speaks in a manner which does seem to refer to his actual personal existence and emotions—as, for example, in the opening lines and in the passage about the Hyacinth garden—his voice is often merely that of a narrator or of a puppet-master introducing his characters. And at all times the voice of the poet is likely to change without warning into the voice of someone else.

And even our sense that we have now and then heard the poet speak in his own person is challenged by Eliot's note (to line 218) about Tiresias, who, we are told, "although a mere spectator and not indeed a 'character,' is yet a most important personage, uniting all the rest. . . . What Tiresias *sees*, in fact, is the whole substance of the poem." But Tiresias does not see as other men see—this most famous of the ancient Greek seers is blind. Of his legend the note tells us only the circumstances of his having for a time been transformed into a woman, and of how he came to be blind and a prophet; Eliot relies on the reader to remember his role in the *Odyssey* (Odysseus descends into Hades to consult his prophetic wisdom) and in two of Sophocles' plays, *Antigone,* which is about the burial of the dead, and *Oedipus Rex* (pages 3 ff.), in which Thebes is a land made waste, deprived of fertility of every kind. No human figure in Greek literature was regarded with as much awed respect as Tiresias, and his presence in the poem gives rise to large conceptions—of the distant past which in some form is still alive in the present; of the future which, by Tiresias' fore-knowledge, also exists in the present; of the dark powers in control of human life which are inaccessible to human reason although not to the prophetic mind. If the poem is difficult, if its matter is often inscrutable, if its order is not in accord with the expectations of the ordinary human mind, this is because its "whole substance" is contained in the mind of Tiresias.

Tiresias does not identify himself until the third section of the poem, but the theme of ancient prophecy has been announced well before that, and, in fact, before the poem actually begins—in the epigraph, which refers to the Sibyl of Cumae, one of the most famous of the ancient prophetesses. The epigraph is integral to the poem and a summary of its import. The great Sibyl hung up for show in a cage epitomizes the idea of degeneration and deterioration which informs "The Waste Land," just as the horror of her fate epitomizes its chief emotion—the dread of a life that is no life, that is a life-in-death. And no less significant is the nature of the person who tells of having seen the Sibyl in her cage. He is Trimalchio, one of the characters of Petronius' great novel of Roman life in the time of Nero, *The Satyricon*. Trimalchio is a millionaire, ignorant, ostentatious, boastful. His ascendancy in contrast to the degradation of the once great Sibyl points to another leading theme of "The Waste Land," that in modern life vulgarity has triumphed over the ancient pieties.

These pieties are religious, but of no specific creed. Eliot was later to become a devout Christian of the Anglican communion, and certain elements of "The Waste Land" make this not surprising. But at the time of writing the poem he had not made his religious decision. "The Waste Land" draws upon the traditions of Jewish, Christian, and Indian religion, especially as these faiths conceive of despair and the possibility of salvation. Christianity is indeed salient, but Buddhism is of almost equal authority, and for the climax of the poem Eliot uses a Brahmanic devotional text.[1] Even more important than the part played by the highly developed religions is that of primitive religion. Eliot makes this plain in the first and most general of his notes in which he speaks of his indebtedness to Jessie Weston's book, *From Ritual to Romance*, and to the more famous and comprehensive work of Sir James Frazer, *The Golden Bough* (see page 934).

The concerns of primitive religion were not spiritual, in our meaning of the word, but utilitarian. The purpose of ritual was to secure the good will of a deity who was in control of one or another of the material circumstances of life; the fertility of the earth, upon which human life depends, was a matter of especial religious anxiety. The highly developed religions preserve the vestiges of this concern in their language about the spiritual life—religion as we know it has much to say about hunger and thirst, about water and green pastures, about bread and wine. But what is now metaphorical was once literal. The elaborate rituals to which Miss Weston and Frazer refer had once the practical intention of insuring the success of the crops and the fecundity of the flocks and herds, and also, what is of central importance in "The Waste Land," human fertility.

To many men, from the nineteenth century on, this primitive relation of human beings to the processes of nature has come to seem increasingly desirable, in itself a source of life. They feel that the rational processes of the intellect, which have grown in authority in recent centuries, have resulted in a dryness and deadness of feeling, in a loss of the vital power of the primitive imagination.

---

[1] In his first version of the note on the word with which the poem closes, the thrice-repeated "Shantih," Eliot could write, " 'The Peace which passeth understanding' is a feeble translation of the content of this word."

Of the poems commented on in this volume, "The Waste Land" has its closest historical affinity with "Dover Beach"—what Eliot says through complex dramatic symbolism, Arnold says in a single explicit utterance. When Arnold speaks of the ebbing of the sea of faith, he has in mind not primarily faith in a doctrinal religion but "animal faith," the sense that the energies of men are continuous with and supported by the energies of the world, which are in some way divine. It is true that the conceptions of doctrinal religion are always in the offing of "The Waste Land," but Eliot too is primarily concerned with the cultural circumstances that are the cause—and the result—of man's loss of belief in his old organic relation to the world. This connection is made by the imagination rather than by the intellect and provides a basis for the ability to experience life immediately and intensely, and, as we say, with meaning.

Miss Weston's book deals with the legend of the Holy Grail, the subject of numerous medieval romances in the cycle of stories about the Arthurian knights. The Grail itself was the cup in which the blood of Christ was received at the Crucifixion; the bleeding lance that figures in the story is the weapon that wounded Christ upon the Cross. The legend tells of a Fisher King—one of the symbols of Christ is a fish—who has received a wound that will not heal, by which he has been made sexually impotent. His condition has its effect upon the land over which he rules, so that it has lost all its fertility and lies sere and waste. The cure of the King and the consequent redemption of the land depend upon the right action of a perfect knight, usually Parsifal, who, led to the Waste Land by a vision of the Grail, which is in the possession of the King, must overcome certain trials of temptation and then ask certain questions about the Grail and the Lance which he beholds carried in ceremonial procession. We can scarcely fail to see that the Christian elements of the story are combined with those that are manifestly pagan, and it is Miss Weston's theory that the story is derived from the vegetation mysteries of India, and that the Cup and the Lance were originally sexual symbols in these rituals. The Wounded King brings the story into obvious connection with the many ancient stories of young men or young gods dying, often of a wound that is sexual in nature, and of being restored to life. Such stories formed the basis of the cults which Frazer deals with in *The Golden Bough*. To these ritual myths, many of which associate the dying and resurrected god with a tree and some of which represent him as being hanged on a tree, the story of the crucified and resurrected Christ has its manifest analogy.

Although Miss Weston's speculations on the origins of the Grail cycle were so important in the conception of Eliot's poem, the specific elements of the story are by no means obvious. The Fisher King is referred to in a shadowy way in line 189, and it would seem that in Part V the long passage beginning with line 331 refers to Parsifal's journey through the Waste Land to the so-called Chapel Perilous that figures in the story (the "empty chapel" of line 389). But Parsifal himself appears only once and by rather recondite reference (see line 202 and Eliot's note on it), and there is no overt reference to the Grail or the Lance. The Waste Land itself appears chiefly as an emotional condition, especially as this is demonstrated by the failure of love which most of the characters of the poem experience and acknowledge.

The theme of sexual failure is proposed first, and rather gently, in the opening of Part I, "The Burial of the Dead," in the speech of the aristocratic

German lady who can recall the joy of her girlhood but whose maturity or middle age is exiled and solitary. The song of the sailor quoted from the first act of Wagner's *Tristan and Isolde,* fresh, gay, and impudent, suggests the love-passion which the opera represents and celebrates, but it is echoed by the deathly negation of the line from the last act of the opera, which speaks of the vacant desolate sea. The poignant words spoken by the "hyacinth girl" are addressed to a lover who does not—cannot—respond, being "neither / Living nor dead." In Part II, "A Game of Chess," the failure of love is presented dramatically, almost sensationally, first in the scene of luxurious and elegant life, then in the scene, in a pub, of lower-class life; in both instances the failure of love has led to despair and boredom. Part III, "The Fire Sermon," is largely given over to the representation of loveless love-making, and also of homosexuality. The description of the Thames on a holiday makes use of the refrain from Spenser's "Prothalamion," in which the poet celebrates his approaching marriage and the beauty of the idea of married love; its presence here is obviously ironic—it brings to mind the deterioration both of the ideal of love and of the beauty of the river which was invoked by the poet in the famous refrain of his marriage song. Also serving the purpose of irony is the reference to Elizabeth and Leicester on the royal barge, symbolic of a vanished age of energy and glory; the irony is compounded by the unfulfilled and tragic sexual relation of the two great personages. The concluding passage, a quotation from *The Confessions of St. Augustine,* refers to the saint's unregenerate days and his conversion, and by implication—in reference to "Carthage" and "burning"—to the funeral pyre of Dido, the legendary queen of Carthage who slew herself when she was deserted by Aeneas.

With Part III the direct representation of sexual defeat ends. The brief fourth part, "Death by Water," speaks perhaps not only of death but of baptism and regeneration. Throughout the poem, water figures as the life-giving element, fire as the destructive element. Phlebas, the drowned Phoenician sailor, is commemorated in a brief elegy which may be intended to bring to mind the cool, sad commemorative verses of the *Greek Anthology,* perhaps also the drowning of Lycidas and the elegist's affirmation (see page 833) that Lycidas is not dead, "Sunk though he be beneath the watery floor," for he is "mounted high, / Through the dear might of Him that walked the waves." There is also striking reference to *The Tempest* in the second and third parts of the poem; its themes of the rightful lord dispossessed and restored, of rescue from the sea, of repentance, purging, and reconciliation, are much to the poem's purpose.

The scene of Part V is an actual waste land, stony and sun-parched, and since Eliot tells us in his note that the journey of the two disciples to Emmaus is one of the themes of the beginning of this part, we may bring to the aid of our visual imagination what we know of the harsh landscape of Palestine. ". . . The third who walks always beside you," may well be the resurrected Jesus, who (as the story is told in Chapter 24 of The Gospel According to St. Luke) joined the two disciples on the road and spoke with them without being recognized until he identified himself. The "murmur of maternal lamentation" may be the mourning of Mary but more likely it refers to the prophecy of catastrophe that Jesus utters in Chapter 23 of Luke, which tells of his condemnation and crucifixion: "And there followed him a great company of people, and of women, which also bewailed and lamented him. But Jesus turning unto them said, Daughters of Jerusalem, weep not for me, but weep for yourselves and for your children. For, behold, the days are coming, in which they shall say, Blessed are the barren, and the wombs that never bare, and the paps which never gave suck. Then shall they begin to say to the mountains, Fall on us; and to the hills, Cover us." It is a vision which manifestly accords with the poet's vision of the cultural and political decay of Europe, which in his notes he documents by a quotation from Hermann Hesse.

In the Vedic text known as the *Brihadaranyaka Upanishad,* the god Pragapati speaks in the voice of the thunder, uttering three times the sound "Da," the initial syllable of the Sanskrit words *"Datta, Dayadhvam, Damyata,"* which mean, as Eliot's note tells us, "give, sympathise, control." He who has given, sympathized, and controlled may achieve regeneration, a new birth of the spirit. With the utterances of the thunder, which promises the relief and renewal of fertilizing rain, the sexual theme comes again to the fore. The lines following *Datta* and *Dayadhvam* are ambiguous, they may or may not refer to sexual conduct. But those following *Damyata* are plain enough—the control that is meant is not, as we might at first expect, self-control, but the lover's beneficent control of his beloved in the act of love. Perhaps nothing in the poem is more directly affecting than the lines that begin "The sea was calm," with its perhaps conscious reminiscence of the opening lines of Matthew Arnold's "Dover Beach" (see page 898), and that go on: "your heart would have responded / Gaily, when invited, beating obedient / To controlling hands"; the comparison of the beloved's heart to a boat well managed is consummated in the word "beating," which applies not only to the action of the heart but to the progress of a boat by tacking into the wind. The heart that would have responded gaily when invited had not been invited, and that word "gaily" emerges from the passage with a terrible pathos, suggesting how simple —how "human," as we say—is the quality of life that this elaborate poem mourns for.

The last passage of the poem, after a recapitulating reference to the Fisher King, proceeds to the conscious incoherence of a desperate mind. But even in its desperation it cannot refrain from repeating the thunder's three words of regeneration and from uttering, as a "formal ending," the word that means "The Peace which passeth understanding."

Perhaps something should be said about the quotations, direct or indirect, that figure so prominently in "The Waste Land." Some readers are offended by them and regard their presence as an affectation, even a pedantry. A sympathetic view might take them as additional "voices" that haunt the poem, or the poet's mind in his making of the poem.

NEITHER
OUT FAR
NOR IN DEEP

ROBERT FROST
1874–1963

The people along the sand
All turn and look one way.
They turn their back on the land.
They look at the sea all day.

As long as it takes to pass   5
A ship keeps raising its hull;
The wetter ground like glass
Reflects a standing gull.

The land may vary more;
But wherever the truth may be—   10
The water comes ashore,
And the people look at the sea.

They cannot look out far.
They cannot look in deep.
But when was that ever a bar   15
To any watch they keep?

COMMENTARY

The power and charm of this poem lie in the discrepancy between, on the one hand, its tone and ostensible subject, and, on the other hand, its actual subject. The tone can be described as minimal, flat, even pinched, and perhaps as fatigued. The ostensible subject, an observation of the behavior of people at the seashore, is scarcely of great consequence and might even be thought rather trifling. The actual subject is the response of mankind to the empty immensity of the universe.

The discrepancy becomes manifest in the last line of the poem. Up to that point what "the people" do by the seashore is denoted by the word "look." This is perhaps our most commonplace and neutral verb for the act of seeing. It is the verb that least *dignifies* the act, for in itself it carries no implication of purpose or of any intensity, as do, for example, such verbs as "gaze," "view," "stare," or even "see." In everyday speech it is often linked with the minimizing or depreciating word "just"—"I'm just looking," or "I'm just looking at . . ." Of course, linguistic circumstances can endow the word with one or another degree of force. Used by itself in the imperative—"Look!"—it is intense indeed. To "look for" something is very purposeful; but to "look at" something may or may not convey the idea of intention, and it may even, as I have suggested, indicate an entire lack of purpose, a mere idleness, as it seems to do in the first stanza of the poem.

Yet as the word is reiterated through the poem, it grows in meaning and force. It is used five times, and the mere repetition is somehow impressive, as if the poet were obsessed by the idea of mere looking. The first time it is used, "the people" simply "look one way"—we are not even told that they are looking *at* anything. There is a degree of intensity implied by the phrase, "They look at the sea all day," but the looking is still idle enough. By the third stanza, however, the word becomes very intense indeed. This is partly because the looking is suddenly—startlingly—associated with a very large question, "Wherever the truth may be," and partly because "the people" seem forever fixed in their looking: the last two lines of the stanza seem to say that just as it is a fact of nature that the water comes ashore and will come forever, so it is a fact of nature that "the people" look at the sea and will look forever. The last two uses of the word, in the last stanza, deny or limit the effectuality of the looking—

> They cannot look out far,
> They cannot look in deep—

but by doing so they suggest that the looking, which first seemed idle and then seemed almost a trance, was after all not without some purpose. And this suggestion is fully and forcefully confirmed in the concluding two lines:

> They cannot look out far.
> They cannot look in deep.
> But when was that ever a bar
> To any watch they keep?

The word "look" has suddenly yielded to the "watch they keep"—the minimal word is replaced, and explained, by a phrase of great dignity and richness of meaning. It implies a strong intention, and the activity of the mind as well as of the eye. And the activity of the heart as well as of the mind. It is a phrase that may suggest the idea of danger, or of hope, or of solicitude, or of loyalty. What is more, it has an archaic character; it is not a phrase that we use casually or lightly in ordinary speech, and its effect in the poem, the language of which is in general colloquial and flat, is solemn and ceremonial. The people who keep the watch are doing what soldiers do, warders of the coast, or what the shepherds at Bethlehem did. They await some significant event.

The small observation which is the poem's ostensible subject first presents itself to our minds as a speculation in psychology or aesthetics. If the land varies more than the sea and is therefore presumably more interesting, why do the people at the shore turn their backs upon the land to look at the sea? Why do the solitary objects that break the monotony of the sea—the nearing ship, the gull reflected in the wet sand—hold the attention so firmly? But the psychological or aesthetic speculation gives place to another of a more momentous kind. Partly because of the word "truth" in the third stanza, but not only because of that, we come to know that "the people" are looking, and waiting, for *something.* We are not told what they hope to descry on the vacant immensity of the sea, and they themselves seem not to know, but we do not doubt that the object of their silent expectation is of transcendent importance.

We are often told that poetry deals with the particular and the concrete, that this is its very essence. If this is so, how shall we account for the peculiar effectiveness of the word "people"? Surely it is the most general and abstract word possible, yet it has, as used here, a strange pathos. Is it because its generality proposes to us the ultimate generality of mankind: all people, all over the world, at all times ("When was that *ever* a bar . . .?")? For some readers, it will have a reminiscence of the effect of naive simplicity with which the word is used in the Bible, as, for example, "Where there is no vision, the people perish." The word imputes a kind of humility: "the people" all "look at the sea" at the behest of something instinctual or innate, not at the behest of intellectual curiosity; there is something dumb, something of the animal, in the accord with which they turn their gaze in the one direction and keep it there. This imputation of an animal-like humility before the power of instinct is anything but contemptuous; on the contrary, it is tender. And the quiet anonymity which is suggested by the phrase "the people" is matched by the unnamedness of the thing they watch for.

The poem does not affirm that what is watched for will appear. It says no more than that it is the nature of "the people" to keep watch, whether or not there is anything to appear.

MY FATHER MOVED THROUGH DOOMS OF LOVE

E. E. CUMMINGS
1894–1962

my father moved through dooms of love
through sames of am through haves of give,
singing each morning out of each night
my father moved through depths of height

this motionless forgetful where   5
turned at his glance to shining here;
that if (so timid air is firm)
under his eyes would stir and squirm

newly as from unburied which
floats the first who, his april touch   10
drove sleeping selves to swarm their fates
woke dreamers to their ghostly roots

and should some why completely weep
my father's fingers brought her sleep:
vainly no smallest voice might cry   15
for he could feel the mountains grow.

Lifting the valleys of the sea
my father moved through griefs of joy;
praising a forehead called the moon
singing desire into begin   20

joy was his song and joy so pure
a heart of star by him could steer

and pure so now and now so yes
the wrists of twilight would rejoice

keen as midsummer's keen beyond   25
conceiving mind of sun will stand,
so strictly (over utmost him
so hugely) stood my father's dream

his flesh was flesh his blood was blood:
no hungry man but wished him food;   30
No cripple wouldn't creep one mile
uphill to only see him smile.

Scorning the pomp of must and shall
my father moved through dooms of feel;
his anger was as right as rain   35
his pity was as green as grain

septembering arms of year extend
less humbly wealth to foe and friend
than he to foolish and to wise
offered immeasurable is   40

proudly and (by octobering flame
beckoned) as earth will downward climb,
so naked for immortal work
his shoulders marched against the dark

his sorrow was as true as bread: 45
no liar looked him in the head;
if every friend became his foe
he'd laugh and build a world with snow.

My father moved through theys of we,
singing each new leaf out of each tree   50
(and every child was sure that spring
danced when she heard my father sing)

then let men kill which cannot share,
let blood and flesh be mud and mire,
scheming imagine, passion willed,   55
freedom a drug that's bought and sold

giving to steal and cruel kind,
a heart to fear, to doubt a mind,
to differ a disease of same,
conform the pinnacle of am   60

though dull were all we taste as bright,
bitter all utterly things sweet,
maggoty minus and dumb death
all we inherit, all bequeath

and nothing quite so least as truth   65
—i say though hate were why men breathe—
because my father lived his soul
love is the whole and more than all

COMMENTARY

In our elementary schooling we are—or used to be—taught the "parts of speech" and how to distinguish one from another, only to discover that they all incline to be interchangeable, their nature being protean, and determined not by definition but by use. *Walk* is a verb until we take a walk, when it is a noun. *Clear* is an adjective until we clear the snow from the sidewalk, when it is a verb. *Further* is an adverb, but we further our sense of how English works when we confront the fact that nothing requires this word to be permanently adverbial. *Beyond* is a mere preposition, but we have no trouble in understanding that in The Great Beyond it arises to the substantive status of a noun.

The tendency to this kind of interchange among the parts of speech is very strong in English and seems to accelerate. But it does not make its way without resistance; we respond to some instances of it with more dubiety or surprise than we do to others. *Yonder* is an adjective—"Yonder peasant, who is he?"—or an adverb—"You can easily find out by walking yonder a way and asking him." And it can, under light duress, be made to serve as a noun; as in the Air Force song "The Wild Blue Yonder." But the phrase startles us a little; we recognize it as a more or less successful effort to manipulate the language in an interesting—a poetic—way, and as such we accept it, but it is not possible that any of us will make the same use of the word in ordinary speech. We are more startled, and likely to be pleased, when Gerard Manley Hopkins exclaims over a falcon in flight, "the achieve of, the mastery of the thing!" The phrase has much more energy and verve than if it had read "the achievement of, the mastery of the thing!" Yet there is but little chance that *achieve* will replace *achievement* in common usage.

A considerable part of the interest of E. E. Cummings' poem comes from our surprise over its use of parts of speech in ways that we are not accustomed to and are scarcely likely to adopt, although we can understand the mode of their use if we make the effort to do so. To say of the father that he moved "through sames of am" is to speak of the integrity of his being; he was always, as we say, himself. "Haves of give" recalls the statement of Jesus that "it is more blessed to give than to receive"; it says that for the father this was true in the most literal sense possible: for him to give was to have. His relationship to people is exemplified by the effect he has on three of them, a where, an if, and a why—the "motionless forgetful where" who turned at the father's glance "to shining here" is, we may suppose, a young man who, until touched into activity, had been lost in a passive self-absorption, not easily to be reached by actuality, not even his own, since that had not yet come into being. The "if (so timid . . .)" would seem to be another young man, distrustful of life and of his own powers, who under the father's vivifying influence undergoes meta-morphosis and is transformed from a nonpersonal being, a "which," into an actual personal self, a "who," like a butterfly emerging from its chrysalis. The weeping "why" of the next stanza is manifestly a woman or a girl whose being, at the moment, is defined by her bewilderment or resentment at some pain inflicted upon her.

"Most poetry," a critic has said, "is on commonplace themes, and the fresh-ness, what the poet supplies, is in the language." Cummings' theme may be said to be commonplace enough—how often have we heard the praise of in-tegrity and sincerity, how often have we been asked to be aware of the benefi-cent power of sympathy and unselfishness! Often enough, surely, to make the virtuous qualities that are praised seem as dull, abstract, and imprecise as the words that are used to denote them. But when the old words are translated in ways that startle us and that require some little effort of energy on our part to perceive the equivalence, the virtues being praised shed their commonplace-ness and shine with the freshness of invention.

Yet the novelty of Cummings' language cannot claim all the credit for the poem's engagingness, which in some part comes from the poet's conception of the best kind of goodness, that which is spontaneous, natural, and arises from and moves toward joy. The father is represented as being virtuous rather than moral or ethical, which suggest a state of being arrived at by intention and effort. His virtue is to be understood in the old sense of the word, which meant power—he has a natural power of goodness that makes its effect less through what he does than through what he is. And this power is represented as being analogous with the beneficent workings of Nature; the instances and images that Cummings finds appropriate to his father, who was a Unitarian clergyman, might serve as well for some pagan fertility god. The poet touches upon the existence of his father in each season of the cycle of the year, but he makes spring his characteristic time, his characteristic action being, in Lucretius' phrase, to bring living things into the borders of light.

In Memory of
SIGMUND FREUD[1]
(d. Sept. 1939)

W . H . A U D E N
1 9 0 7 –

(1940)

When there are so many we shall have to mourn,
When grief has been made so public, and exposed
        To the critique of a whole epoch
        The frailty of our conscience and anguish,

Of whom shall we speak? For every day they die   5
Among us, those who were doing us some good,
        And knew it was never enough but
        Hoped to improve a little by living.

Such was this doctor: still at eighty he wished
To think of our life, from whose unruliness   10
        So many plausible young futures
        With threats or flattery ask obedience.

But his wish was denied him; he closed his eyes
Upon that last picture common to us all,
        Of problems like relatives standing   15
        Puzzled and jealous about our dying.

For about him at the very end were still
Those he had studied, the nervous and the nights,

---

[1] Sigmund Freud (1856–1939) was the originator of psychoanalysis. As a Jew living in Austria, he was forced to flee the Nazis in 1938. He went to London, where he remained until he died.

And shades that still waited to enter
The bright circle of his recognition   20

Turned elsewhere with their disappointment as he
Was taken away from his old interest
            To go back to the earth in London,
            An important Jew who died in exile.

Only Hate was happy, hoping to augment   25
His practice now, and his shabby clientèle
            Who think they can be cured by killing
            And covering the gardens with ashes.

They are still alive but in a world he changed
Simply by looking back with no false regrets;   30
            All that he did was to remember
            Like the old and be honest like children.

He wasn't clever at all: he merely told
The unhappy Present to recite the Past
            Like a poetry lesson till sooner   35
            Or later it faltered at the line where

Long ago the accusations had begun,
And suddenly knew by whom it had been judged,
            How rich life had been and how silly,
            And was life-forgiven and most humble.   40

Able to approach the Future as a friend
Without a wardrobe of excuses, without
            A set mask of rectitude or an
            Embarrassing over-familiar gesture.

No wonder the ancient cultures of conceit   45
In his technique of unsettlement foresaw
            The fall of princes, the collapse of
            Their lucrative patterns of frustration.

If he succeeded, why, the Generalised Life
Would become impossible, the monolith   50
            Of State be broken and prevented
            The co-operation of avengers.

Of course they called on God: but he went his way,
Down among the Lost People like Dante, down
                    To the stinking fosse² where the injured   55
                    Lead the ugly life of the rejected.

And showed us what evil is: not as we thought
Deeds that must be punished, but our lack of faith,
                    Our dishonest mood of denial,
                    The concupiscence of the oppressor.   60

And if something of the autocratic pose,
The paternal strictness he distrusted, still
                    Clung to his utterance and features,
                    It was a protective imitation

For one who lived among enemies so long;   65
If often he was wrong and at times absurd,
                    To us he is no more a person
                    Now but a whole climate of opinion,

Under whom we conduct our differing lives:
Like weather he can only hinder or help,   70
                    The proud can still be proud but find it
                    A little harder, and the tyrant tries

To make him do but doesn't care for him much.
He quietly surrounds all our habits of growth;
                    He extends, till the tired in even   75
                    The remotest most miserable duchy

Have felt the change in their bones and are cheered,
And the child unlucky in his little State,
                    Some hearth where freedom is excluded,
                    A hive whose honey is fear and worry,   80

Feels calmer now and somehow assured of escape;
While as they lie in the grass of our neglect,
                    So many long-forgotten objects
                    Revealed by his undiscouraged shining

² Ditch. There are several malodorous ditches full of lost souls in Dante's representation of Hell, the *Inferno*.

Are returned to us and made precious again;
Games we had thought we must drop as we grew up,
      Little noises we dared not laugh at,
      Faces we made when no one was looking.

But he wishes us more than this: to be free
Is often to be lonely; he would unite   90
      The unequal moieties fractured
      By our own well-meaning sense of justice.

Would restore to the larger the wit and will
The smaller possesses but can only use
      For arid disputes, would give back to   95
      The son the mother's richness of feeling.

But he would have us remember most of all
To be enthusiastic over the night
      Not only for the sense of wonder
      It alone has to offer, but also   100

Because it needs our love: for with sad eyes
Its delectable creatures look up and beg
      Us dumbly to ask them to follow;
      They are exiles who long for the future

That lies in our power. They too would rejoice   105
If allowed to serve enlightenment like him,
      Even to bear our cry of "Judas,"
      As he did and all must bear who serve it.

One rational voice is dumb: over a grave
The household of Impulse mourns one dearly loved.   110
      Sad is Eros, builder of cities,
      And weeping anarchic Aphrodite.[3]

---

[3] Eros, the Greek god of love, was the son of Aphrodite, the goddess of beauty and love. Both are symbols of libidinous energy, but Eros is perhaps more often constructive or creative, whereas Aphrodite can be the cause of destruction.

Among the first acts of the Nazi party after it came to power in Germany in 1933 was the suppression of the teaching of psychoanalysis in the medical schools and a ceremonial burning of the works of Sigmund Freud. This was in part a response to the fact that the founder of psychoanalysis was a Jew, for one of the axioms of the Nazi ideology was that the Jews were the cause of all the misfortunes of the German people and the source of all that was bad in the Western world. It was also a response to the actual content of psychoanalysis, especially to its theory that many disorders of the personality have a sexual etiology and can be traced to the patient's experience of the family situation in early infancy.

Freud, living in Vienna, was naturally much distressed over the turn of events, but he persuaded himself that the hostility of the Nazis would not come closer home. He was, of course, mistaken—in 1938 Hitler sent his troops into Austria and united that nation with Germany under his rule. Freud was forbidden to carry on his work and he and his family lived under the threat of the concentration camp. Before the invasion actually took place, he had resisted all suggestions that he leave Vienna, and even now he was reluctant to think of leaving the city in which he had lived all but two of his eighty-two years. Eventually, however, the counsels of his friends and colleagues prevailed and he consented to emigrate, but it was only after prolonged negotiations with the Nazi officials and the payment by his friends abroad of a large sum of money in ransom that Freud was permitted to leave Austria and, with his family, was brought to England, a country which he had held in affectionate admiration since boyhood and which now received him with great honor. He settled in London, and, although much enfeebled by the illness which had made existence a torture for many years—cancer of the jaw, necessitating innumerable operations—he resumed his habits of arduous work, seeing patients and pupils and carrying forward the composition of a new book. He died a year later, three weeks after the beginning of the Second World War.

Freud had never concerned himself directly with politics but the therapeutic psychology of which he was the inventor had social and ultimately political implications of great moment. If these had ever been obscure, they became manifest upon the violent Nazi opposition to psychoanalysis and they constitute the informing theme of Auden's commemoration of Freud.

The theory of psychoanalysis is enormously complex, but at its heart is the quite simple idea that the individual human personality is formed, and in all too many instances malformed, by the interaction of the biological impulses or "drives" with the controlling authority of the family, which is continuous with the authority of society and the state. The individual in the course of his development incorporates this authority into his emotional system, in both its conscious and its unconscious parts. If the authority thus internalized is excessively strict—as it may be either because it mirrors the actual repressiveness of the parental control or because the individual for some reason imagines the external authority to be more exigent than it actually is—there will result a malfunction of the instinctual life, inhibiting the healthy development of the personality and causing great emotional pain. The malfunction begins in earliest childhood, though it may not manifest itself until a later time, and Freud's method of therapy is to lead the patient to bring into the light of consciousness the particular circumstances, actual or fancied, that may serve to explain where his emotional life went wrong, why the "internalized authority" is devoted to causing pain. As Auden's poem puts it, Freud

> . . . told
> The unhappy Present to recite the Past
> Like a poetry lesson till sooner
> Or later it faltered at the line where
>
> Long ago the accusations had begun,
> And suddenly knew by whom it had been judged . . .

"Accusations" and "judged" are the crucial words—neurotic suffering may be ascribed to the patient's having instituted in his unconscious mind a juridical process in which the prosecuting attorney accuses too fiercely, the judge condemns too readily and sentences too sternly, and the jailer carries out the imposed punishment too eagerly.

By the time the Nazis banned it in Germany and Austria, psychoanalysis had won a considerable degree of acceptance, but only against a stubborn and often bitter resistance. The physicians who criticized its theory seldom did so in a spirit of disinterested scientific objectivity; they were likely to share the moralizing fervor of the many laymen who denounced it as a threat to society. The therapeutic goal of psychoanalysis is scarcely subversive and nowadays it is even said by some to err in the direction of social conformity, for it undertakes to make it possible for the patient to live in reasonable accord not only with himself but with his society. Yet even from the little that has been said here about the basic theory of psychoanalysis, it will be plain that it is antagonistic to authoritarianism, though not to rational authority. What Auden's poem aptly speaks of as Freud's "technique of unsettlement" cannot really be said to have overtly and explicitly foreseen "the fall of princes," but it nevertheless did bring the very idea of arbitrary rule into question. It is therefore not surprising that it should have incurred the hatred of "the ancient cultures of conceit."

At the present time the judgment on psychoanalysis is divided. Many still regard it uneasily or hostilely, yet it has established itself as part of the substance of modern thought. Its influence is especially strong in the United States, where its premises and conclusions are taken for granted by many who have never read any of the works in which its theory is expounded. For many Freud is indeed

> . . . no more a person
> Now but a whole climate of opinion . . .

Writing not long after Freud's death, Auden naturally made the large public aspects of Freud's thought salient in his commemoration. With totalitarianism in the ascendant, the aspects of psychoanalysis that might well seem of first importance were those that bore upon politics, such as the opposition it offers to "the Generalised Life" and "the monolith / Of State." But the poem does not fail to take account of the effects that the technique of unsettlement may have upon the personal and private life, and not only in situations of extreme pathology, among "the Lost People," "the injured" who "Lead the ugly life of the rejected," but also among those who are not so grossly afflicted and who yet live less freely than they might, immobilizing themselves behind "a set mask of rectitude," having less courage, simplicity, and power of responsive emotion than it is within their capacity to have.

The last quatrain brilliantly expresses the paradoxical nature of Freud's thought. By ancient convention, rationality and impulse are believed to be at hopeless odds with each other. But Freud put his "rational voice" at the service of impulse, seeking its liberation. It may be questioned, however, whether the last two lines, fine as they are, represent Freud's thought with entire accuracy. It is certainly true that Freud was in avowed alliance with "Eros, builder of cities," the love that makes the family, society, and civilization. But nothing in his work affirms the beneficence of "anarchic Aphrodite," the irresistible, heedless love that we call passion.

The poem claims much for the intention of Freud's science, much for its achievement. Yet this large optimism is qualified by the tone in which it is asserted. One may hear a note of reserve in the large positive statements as though the recognition of Freud's purpose and achievement went along with the sense of how much is still to be accomplished for human happiness and with the awareness that any celebration of human advance must be of a muted kind when uttered at the beginning of a war that promises to be long and terrible. The restrained, slightly dry tone is in part an effect of the diction, which is determinedly plain. It is also, and perhaps to an even greater extent, an effect of the stanzaic form, which seems to have been consciously modelled on the so-called Alcaic strophe of Greek and Latin poetry. In this strophe the first two lines are of eleven syllables, the third of nine, the fourth of ten, and Auden conforms quite strictly to the pattern; there are only a very few quite minor departures. Unlike the Alcaic strophe, Auden's form has no set metrical pattern within the fixed number of syllables for each line, nor, indeed, any metrical pattern at all; but the rhythm of each line is controlled and made more or less homogeneous with that of its matching lines by the fixed number of syllables. One has the sense of prose that is always at the point of becoming metrical, or at least markedly cadenced, and always being prevented, falling back to its prose tone. And this effect of an energy continually checked, even if continually asserting itself, is supported by the interplay between the lengths of the lines of which the stanzas consist, the ranging first two lines with which each stanza begins, the sharply curtailed third, the fourth that a little recoups what its predecessor had lost.

FOR THE
UNION DEAD

ROBERT LOWELL
1917-

"Relinquunt Omnia Servare Rem Publicam."

The old South Boston Aquarium stands
in a Sahara of snow now. Its broken windows are boarded.
The bronze weathervane cod has lost half its scales.
The airy tanks are dry.

Once my nose crawled like a snail on the glass;   5
my hand tingled
to burst the bubbles
drifting from the noses of the cowed, compliant fish.

My hand draws back. I often sigh still
for the dark downward and vegetating kingdom   10
of the fish and reptile. One morning last March,
I pressed against the new barbed and galvanized

fence on the Boston Common. Behind their cage,
yellow dinosaur steamshovels were grunting
as they cropped up tons of mush and grass   15
to gouge their underworld garage.

Parking spaces luxuriate like civic
sandpiles in the heart of Boston.
A girdle of orange, Puritan-pumpkin colored girders
braces the tingling Statehouse,   20

shaking over the excavations, as it faces Colonel Shaw
and his bell-cheeked Negro infantry

on St. Gaudens' shaking Civil War relief,
propped by a plank splint against the garage's earthquake.

Two months after marching through Boston,   25
half the regiment was dead;
at the dedication,
William James could almost hear the bronze Negroes breathe.

Their monument sticks like a fishbone
in the city's throat.   30
Its Colonel is as lean
as a compass-needle.

He has an angry wrenlike vigilance,
a greyhound's gentle tautness;
he seems to wince at pleasure,   35
and suffocate for privacy.

He is out of bounds now. He rejoices in man's lovely,
peculiar power to choose life and die—
when he leads his black soldiers to death,
he cannot bend his back.   40

On a thousand small town New England greens,
the old white churches hold their air
of sparse, sincere rebellion; frayed flags
quilt the graveyards of the Grand Army of the Republic.

The stone statues of the abstract Union Soldier   45
grow slimmer and younger each year—
wasp-waisted, they doze over muskets
and muse through their sideburns . . .

Shaw's father wanted no monument
except the ditch,   50
where his son's body was thrown
and lost with his "niggers."

The ditch is nearer.
There are no statues for the last war here;
on Boylston Street, a commercial photograph   55
shows Hiroshima boiling

over a Mosler Safe, the "Rock of Ages"
that survived the blast. Space is nearer.
When I crouch to my television set,
the drained faces of Negro school-children rise like balloons. 60

Colonel Shaw
is riding on his bubble,
he waits
for the blessèd break.

The Aquarium is gone. Everywhere, 65
giant finned cars nose forward like fish;
a savage servility
slides by on grease.

COMMENTARY

In 1863, the third year of the Civil War, Governor Andrew of Massachusetts
commissioned a new regiment, all of whose rank and file were Negroes although
its officers were white men. The formation of the first Negro fighting unit had
been undertaken only after considerable hesitation. It was felt by many that
the war should not be exclusively a white man's war, that Negro citizens of the
North should be allowed to take part in the liberation of their race. In addition
to this principled consideration, there was the practical one that the Northern
forces were in need of more fighting men. But the antislavery sentiment of the
North was by no means unqualified and the considerable feeling against the
war and against Negroes had to be taken into account. Such Negroes as might
wish to bear arms in the fight against slavery had no military tradition, no one
knew how they would perform as soldiers, and it would be a severe blow to the
antislavery cause were they not to acquit themselves well.

The event proved that the doubts were quite groundless. Only a few
months after it had been formed, the 54th Massachusetts took part in the assault
on Fort Wagner, a Confederate stronghold on the South Carolina coast within
sight and cannon shot of Fort Sumter; it is said to have been one of the strongest
earthworks ever built. The 54th arrived on the field weary and hungry. It had
previously given a good account of itself in minor engagements and now the
field commander of the Union forces offered the regiment the honor of leading
the attack, which its Colonel accepted. It charged the terrible guns and penetrated the outer defences of the fort. Before it was withdrawn an hour later,
nearly half its men were killed within the fort or before its walls. The question
of Negro soldierliness had been answered forever. "Wagner still defies us," a
Union publicist said, "but prejudice is down." Before the end of the war 180,000
Negroes were under arms; President Lincoln said that they tipped the balance
in favor of Union victory.

At least one Confederate officer gave the 54th its due measure of praise.

"The Negroes fought gallantly," Lieutenant Iredell Jones wrote after the engagement, "and were headed by as brave a Colonel as ever lived." The Colonel was killed at the beginning of the attack. When he fell from the parapet into the fort, eleven of his men leaped after him and were cut down by the defenders. Although the Confederate burial-parties followed custom and interred the other dead Union officers in separate graves, the Colonel of the 54th was buried in a trench with his men; when, at a later time, an effort was made to recover his body from the common grave, his father forbade it—his community in death with his Negro men, intended as an indignity, could be nothing but an appropriate honor for Colonel Shaw.

Robert Gould Shaw was twenty-five years old when he died. The only son of a wealthy and distinguished Boston family, he had, as the phrase goes, everything to live for; he was later to be remembered as "the blue-eyed child of fortune upon whose youth every divinity had smiled." In 1863 he was serving as captain in the 2nd Massachusetts Regiment, having risen to the rank from private; he had seen action at Cedar Mountain and Antietam. When the 54th Massachusetts was being formed, the Governor offered him its command because of his military record, his personal character, and his accord with the strong and well-known anti-slavery commitment of his parents. Shaw hesitated to undertake the arduous responsibility of the post, in part because he doubted his abilities, in part because he loved the regiment with which he was serving. Indeed, his first decision was to refuse the Governor's invitation, but second thoughts led him to believe that it was his duty to accept; it was he whom Emerson had in mind in writing the once-familiar lines:

> When Duty whispers low, *Thou must,*
> The youth replies, *I can.*

An intelligent and enthusiastic soldier, he won the devotion of his men and trained them thoroughly, to what effect their conduct at Fort Wagner makes plain.

The death of the young Colonel was deeply felt in Boston, and a year after the end of the war a committee was formed to erect a memorial to him. "The monument," it was said, "is intended not only to mark the public gratitude to the fallen hero, who at a critical moment assumed a perilous responsibility, but also to commemorate that great event, wherein he was a leader, by which the title of colored men as citizen-soldiers was fixed beyond recall." It was not, however, until 1897 that the monument was erected on Boston Common and dedicated at exercises held on Memorial Day in the Boston Music Hall. The work of Augustus St. Gaudens, the most notable American sculptor of the period, it is a large bronze stele which depicts in high relief the 54th Massachusetts marching in column, its flags furled, a boy drummer at its head; the young Colonel on a superb charger, his sabre unsheathed, rides beside his men; a symbolic female figure in flight over the column beckons it forward with one arm and holds in the other the palms of glory and the poppies of death. The faces of the men are set in calm, stern determination; their stride is long and vigorous; Shaw on his reined-in, slow-stepping great horse is erect and inflexible; his movelessness at the center of the composition, its fixed and still point, emphasizes the forward-thrusting energy of the marching column. The virtuosity with which a wealth of naturalistic detail is executed does not diminish but rather enhances the heroic aspect of the work.

The demeanor of Robert Lowell's poem about the memorial of his kinsman is significantly unlike that of the monument itself; the salient characteristic of the poem is its air of acknowledged fatigue. The units of utterance are fragmented and small, their movement is never of a forward or an upward kind; the diction is dry and sparse. At only one moment does the voice of the poem move with something like happy energy, at the lines:

> He is out of bounds now. He rejoices in man's lovely,
> peculiar power to choose life and die—

The recollection of Shaw's dying for the liberty that alone makes mere existence into what may rightly be called "life" arouses the tone of the poem from its sad discouragement to a moment of affirmation. A moment only; the dry minimal tone returns, to continue to the end, and we must read the poem as a lament for the death of the monument itself—this memorial has lost its power of awakening memory and "sticks like a fishbone / in the city's throat."

The poem tells us that William James was present at the dedication exercises, but it does not tell us that the famous philosopher was one of the speakers of the occasion. James's sense that he "could almost hear the bronze Negroes breathe" was expressed in the course of the speech he made—in praising St. Gaudens' work he said, "There on foot go the dark outcasts, so true to nature that one can almost hear them breathing as they march." Another passage from the speech finds its way into the poem, which, when it speaks of "a thousand small town New England greens" on which stand "the stone statues of the abstract Union Soldier," echoes a sentence of James's about "the abstract soldier's-monuments . . . reared on every village green." These small particular references that the poem makes to the speech do not comprise the whole of the relation between what Lowell is saying and what James said. So artful a poet as Lowell would not be likely to have read the speech as part of his preparation for writing the poem without being aware of the difference, and the significance of the difference, between the nature of James's utterance and of his own. Of the five speeches that were made on that Memorial Day of 1897, one was called a "report" and three were called "addresses," but James had been designated the "Orator" of the exercises and his speech was listed as an "oration." He had been asked, that is, to speak of Colonel Shaw in a certain way, with elevation and eloquence, to the end of affecting and "inspiring" the audience. He met the demand handsomely, and to the fluency and freedom of James's oration, which are consonant with the qualities of St. Gaudens' relief, the minimal fragmented style of Lowell's poem stands in a contrast that was surely intended.

If the orator of 1897 could speak in a freer and more open voice than the poet of 1963, it was because he spoke from more confidence in the possibility of social virtue than the poet can feel. In his eulogy of Shaw, James first praised his military courage, but went on to call it a courage that was "common and gregarious" and to set above it "another courage," which was Shaw's best glory. "That lonely kind of courage (civic courage as we call it in times of peace) is the kind of valor to which the monuments of nations should most of all be reared, for the survival of the fittest has not bred it into the bone of human beings as it has bred military valor; and of five hundred of us who could storm a battery side by side with others, perhaps not one would be found ready to risk his worldly fortunes all alone in resisting an enthroned abuse." And as James drew to his conclusion, he said, "The republic to which Robert Shaw and a quarter of a million like him were faithful unto death is no republic that can live at ease hereafter on the interest of what they have won. Democracy is still upon trial. The civic genius of our people is its only bulwark, and neither laws nor monuments, neither battleships nor public libraries, nor great newspapers nor booming stocks; neither mechanical invention nor political adroitness, nor churches nor universities . . . can save us from degeneration if the inner mystery is lost."

The orator was not wholly without apprehension about the outcome of the trial of democracy, but he could be of good cheer, as the poet cannot be. In Lowell's view, the "mystery" is already lost. His commemoration of a memorial of the struggle to free some men from the servile condition imposed upon them ends with the perception of the "savage servility" which has become the general condition, freely chosen. Of this the symbol is the "giant finned cars"; the "underworld garage" that is being constructed for them makes the circumstance that beleaguers and shakes the monument. Memory, or faith, has so far failed that "there are no statues for the last war here," only the inglorious memorial of the "commercial photograph" of a safe that survived the atomic bombing of Hiroshima. "The drained faces of Negro school-children" belie the promise that might once have been seen in the firm gaze of Colonel Shaw's "bell-cheeked Negro infantry."

The bitter sadness over the decline of public life from a better state in a former time—it is one of poetry's ancient sadnesses—begins with the evocation of the poet's own lost past. And the Aquarium of his childhood, now dismantled and forlorn, is the source, as it were, of an extended series of associations, having chiefly to do with fish, which makes a thematic line easy to trace but hard to explain. The Aquarium's deteriorated "bronze weathervane cod" is of course immediately appropriate to the purport of the poem, for the cod is the official emblem of the Commonwealth of Massachusetts. The "cowed, compliant fish" introduce the idea of servility and point toward the "savage servility" which is associated with the "giant finned cars" that "nose forward like fish," almost explicitly sharks. But a connection between the passive and the active servility is not readily apparent. Then, although one can understand that a despondent man might sigh "for the dark downward and vegetating kingdom / of the fish and reptile" as representing the comfortable passivity of childhood, other dark and downward things in the poem cannot well be the objects of nostalgia; these include the "underworld garage" and the burial "ditch" which is said to be "nearer." And if it is reptiles that are sighed for, they are at hand in the steam-shovels, which are likened to dinosaurs. What relation the "fishbone / in the city's throat" has to the other fish-references is not plain. In an effort to understand the "bubble" upon which Colonel Shaw is said to ride, some readers will recall Jaques's speech about the seven ages of man in *As You Like It*, in which the soldier is said to seek "the bubble reputation / Even in the cannon's mouth"; this reading has the advantage of seeming to explain why the Colonel "waits / for the blessèd break"—because it would release him from his public symbolic existence to the privacy for which "he seems to . . . suffocate."[1] But the bubbles of the fish that the boy's "hand tingled / to burst" come in to make this interpretation difficult, as does the simile of the "balloons" which is used to describe the faces of the Negro school children on the television screen. In short, although a rather tight system of associations is manifest in the poem, its syntax is difficult.

The epigraph of the poem is derived from an inscription on the face of the monument, "*Reliquit Omnia Servare Rem Publicam.*" The Latin sentence, which may be translated "He left everything behind to serve the nation," is the motto of the Society of the Cincinnati, whose members are descendants of American officers of the Revolutionary War; Robert Shaw was himself a member.[2] By changing the canonical form of the sentence to make it say, "*They* left everything behind to serve the nation," Lowell has given his epigraph a reference beyond Shaw himself; it now includes the rank and file of Shaw's regiment and all the Union dead. It is possible to read the variant as an implied criticism of the choice of the inscription.

[1] In a letter to his brother Henry, William James, who had known the colonel in their youth, wrote of "poor . . . Robert Shaw," who had been "erected into a great symbol of deeper things than he ever realized himself. . . ."

[2] Cincinnatus was the legendary Roman hero, who, at a time of military crisis, was chosen to be dictator of Rome; the legend is that the emissaries of the Senate found him plowing in his fields, that he left the plow standing and returned to it sixteen days later, having defeated the enemy and resigned the dictatorship. Because membership was hereditary and confined to the descendants of officers, the Society at its inception was denounced as an aristocratic organization, a charge that has since been repeated.

PART

4 POETRY
FOR
FURTHER
READING

ANONYMOUS

A LYKE-WAKE[1] DIRGE

This ae nighte, this ae nighte,
  —*Every nighte and alle,*
Fire and fleet[2] and candle-lighte,
  And Christe receive thy saule.

When thou from hence away art past,   5
  —*Every nighte and alle,*
To Whinny-muir[3] thou com'st at last;
  And Christe receive thy saule.

If ever thou gavest hosen and shoon,[4]
  —*Every nighte and alle,*   10
Sit thee down and put them on;
  And Christe receive thy saule.

If hosen and shoon thou ne'er gav'st nane[5]
  —*Every nighte and alle,*
The whinnes sall prick thee to the bare bane;   15
  And Christe receive thy saule.

From Whinny-muir when thou may'st pass,
  —*Every nighte and alle,*
To Brig[6] o' Dread thou com'st at last;
  And Christe receive thy saule.   20

From Brig o' Dread when thou may'st pass,
  —*Every nighte and alle,*
To Purgatory fire thou com'st at last;
  And Christe receive thy saule.

---

[1] A watch kept at night over a dead body; a wake.   [2] Place where water flows.
[3] A moor where whins, or prickly shrubs, grow.   [4] Hose and shoes.   [5] None.
[6] Bridge.

If ever thou gavest meat or drink,   25
    —*Every nighte and alle*,
The fire shall never make thee shrink;
    And Christe receive thy saule.

If meat or drink thou ne'er gav'st nane,
    —*Every nighte and alle*,   30
The fire will burn thee to the bare bane;
    And Christe receive thy saule.

This ae nighte, this ae nighte,
    —*Every nighte and alle*,
Fire and fleet and candle-lighte,   35
    And Christe receive thy saule.

THE CHERRY-TREE CAROL

Joseph was an old man,
    and an old man was he,
When he wedded Mary,
    in the land of Galilee.

Joseph and Mary walked   5
    through an orchard good,
Where was cherries and berries,
    so red as any blood.

Joseph and Mary walked
    through an orchard green,   10
Where was berries and cherries,
    as thick as might be seen.

O then bespoke Mary,
    so meek and so mild:
"Pluck me one cherry, Joseph,   15
    for I am with child."

O then bespoke Joseph:
    with words most unkind:
"Let him pluck thee a cherry
    that brought thee with child."   20

O then bespoke the babe,
    within his mother's womb:
"Bow down then the tallest tree,
    for my mother to have some."

Then bowed down the highest tree   25
    unto his mother's hand;
Then she cried, "See, Joseph,
    I have cherries at command."

O then bespoke Joseph:
    "I have done Mary wrong;   30
But cheer up, my dearest,
    and be not cast down."

Then Mary plucked a cherry,
    as red as the blood,
Then Mary went home   35
    with her heavy load.

Then Mary took her babe,
    and sat him on her knee,
Saying, "My dear son, tell me
    what this world will be."   40

"O I shall be as dead, mother,
    as the stones in the wall;
O the stones in the streets, mother,
    shall mourn for me all.

"Upon Easter-day, mother,   45
    my uprising shall be;
O the sun and the moon, mother,
    shall both rise with me."

THE THREE RAVENS

1. There were three ravens sat on a tree,
    Downe a downe, hay downe, hay downe
There were three ravens sat on a tree,
    With a downe

There were three ravens sat on a tree,
They were as blacke as they might be.
    With a downe derrie, derrie, derrie, downe, downe. 5

2. The one of them said to his mate,
"Where shall we our breakfast take?"

3. "Downe in yonder greene field, 10
There lies a knight slain under his shield.

4. "His hounds they lie downe at his feete,
So well they can their master keepe.

5. "His haukes they flie so eagerly,
There's no fowle dare him come nie." 15

6. Downe there comes a fallow doe,
As great with yong as she might goe.

7. She lift up his bloudy hed,
And kist his wounds that were so red.

8. She got him up upon her backe, 20
And carried him to earthen lake.[1]

9. She buried him before the prime,[2]
She was dead herselfe ere even-song time.

10. God send every gentleman,
Such haukes, such hounds, and such a leman.[3] 25

SIR PATRICK SPENS

The king sits in Dumferling toune,
    Drinking the blude-reid wine:

---

[1] Pit in the earth.   [2] *Prime* is the old ecclesiastical name for the first hour of the day; *even-song* is the service of vespers, held in the evening.   [3] Lover.

"O whar will I get a guid sailor,
　　To sail this schip of mine?"

Up and spak an eldern knicht,   5
　　Sat at the kings richt kne:
"Sir Patrick Spens is the best sailor
　　That sails upon the se."

The king has written a braid¹ letter,
　　And signd it wi his hand,   10
And sent it to Sir Patrick Spens,
　　Was walking on the sand.

The first line that Sir Patrick red,
　　A loud lauch lauched he;
The next line that Sir Patrick red,   15
　　The teir blinded his ee.

"O wha is this has don this deid,
　　This ill deid don to me,
To send me out this time o' the yeir,
　　To sail upon the se!   20

'Mak hast, mak haste, my mirry men all,
　　Our guid schip sails the morne."
"O say na sae,² my master deir,
　　For I feir a deadlie storme.

"Late late yestreen³ I saw the new moone,   25
　　Wi the auld moone in hir arme,
And I feir, I feir, my deir master,
　　That we will cum to harme."

O our Scots nobles wer richt laith⁴
　　To weet⁵ their cork-heild schoone,⁶   30
Bot lang owre⁷ a' the play wer playd,
　　Thair hats they swam aboone.⁸

---

¹ Broad; that is, emphatic, explicit.　　² Say not so.　　³ Yesterday evening.
⁴ Right loath.　　⁵ Wet.　　⁶ Cork was not uncommonly used for the heels (and soles)
of gentlemen's shoes in the sixteenth and seventeenth centuries.　　⁷ Over; here, after.
⁸ Above; that is, on the water.

O lang, lang may their ladies sit,
    Wi thair fans into their hand,
Or eir they se Sir Patrick Spens
    Cum sailing to the land.   35

O lang, lang may the ladies stand,
    Wi thair gold kems in their hair,
Waiting for thair ain deir lords,
    For they'll se thame na mair.   40

Haf owre, half owre to Aberdour,
    It's fiftie fadom deip,
And thair lies guid Sir Patrick Spens,
    Wi the Scots lords at his feit.

MARY HAMILTON

Word's gane to the kitchen,
    And word's gane to the ha,[1]
That Marie Hamilton gangs[2] wi bairn[3]
    To the hichest[4] Stewart[5] of a'.

He's courted her in the kitchen,   5
    He's courted her in the ha,
He's courted her in the laigh[6] cellar,
    And that was warst of a'.

She's tyed it in her apron
    And she's thrown it in the sea   10
Says, "Sink ye, swim ye, bonny wee babe!
    You'l neer get mair o me."

Down then cam the auld queen,
    Goud[7] tassels tying her hair:
"O Marie, where's the bonny wee babe   15
    That I heard greet sae sair?"[8]

"There was never a babe intill[9] my room,
    As little designs to be;

---

[1] Hall.   [2] Goes.   [3] Child.   [4] Highest.   [5] Henry Stewart (1545–1567), second husband of Mary Queen of Scots.   [6] Low.   [7] Gold.   [8] Cry so sore.   [9] In.

It was but a touch o my sair side,
    Come oer my fair bodie."

"O Marie, put on your robes o black,
    Or else your robes o brown,
For ye maun gang wi me the night,
    To see fair Edinbro town."

I winna put on my robes o black,
    Nor yet my robes o brown;
But I'll put on my robes o white,
    To shine through Edinbro town."

When she gaed up the Cannogate,[10]
    She laughd loud laughters three;
But whan she cam down the Cannogate
    The tear blinded her ee.

When she gaed up the Parliament stair,
    The heel cam aff her shee;
And lang or she cam down again
    She was condemned to dee.

When she cam down the Cannogate,
    The Cannogate sae free,
Many a ladie lookd oer her window,
    Weeping for this ladie.

"Ye need nae weep for me," she says,
    "Ye need nae weep for me;
For had I not slain mine own sweet babe,
    This death I wadna dee.

"Bring me a bottle of wine," she says,
    "The best that eer ye hae,
That I may drink to my well-wishers,
    And they may drink to me.

"Here's a health to the jolly sailors,
    That sail upon the main;

20

25

30

35

40

45

50

[10] Cannongate, a section of Edinburgh.

Let them never let on to my father and mother
    But what I'm coming hame.

"Here's a health to the jolly sailors,
    That sail upon the sea;
Let them never let on to my father
       and mother
    That I cam here to dee.   55

"Oh little did my mother think,
    The day she cradled me,
What lands I was to travel through,
    What death I was to dee.   60

"Oh little did my father think,
    The day he held up me,
What lands I was to travel through,
    What death I was to dee.

"Last night I washd the queen's feet,   65
    And gently laid her down;
And a' the thanks I've gotten the nicht[11]
    To be hangd in Edinbro town!

"Last nicht there was four Maries,
    The nicht there'l be but three;   70
There was Marie Seton, and Marie Beton,
    And Marie Carmichael, and me."

WESTRON WINDE, WHEN WILL THOU BLOW

Westron winde, when will thou blow,
The smalle raine downe can raine?
Christ, if my love were in my armes,
And I in my bed againe.

    [11] This night.

JOHN SKELTON
1460?–1529

TO MISTRESS ISABEL PENNELL

By Saint Mary, my lady,
Your mammy and your daddy
Brought forth a goodly baby!

My maiden Isabel,
Reflaring rosabel,[1]   5
The fragrant camomel;
    The ruddy rosary,[2]
The sovereign rosemary,
The pretty strawberry;
    The columbine, the nept,[3]   10
The jelofer[4] well set,
The proper violet:
    Ennewèd[5] your colour
Is like the daisy flower
After the April shower;   15
    Star of the morrow gray,
The blossom on the spray,
The freshest flower of May;
    Maidenly demure,
Of womanhood the lure;[6]   20
Wherefore I make you sure
    It were an heavenly health,
It were an endless wealth,
A life for God himself,
    To hear this nightingale   25
Among the birdès smale
Warbeling in the vale,
    Dug, dug,
Jug, jug,
    Good year and good luck,   30
    With chuck, chuck, chuck, chuck!

[1] Smelling like a beautiful rose.   [2] Rose garden, rosarium.   [3] Catnip.   [4] Gilly-flower.   [5] Made new, restored.   [6] That is, the most attractive (alluring) of women.

TO MISTRESS MARGARET HUSSEY

Merry Margaret,
    As midsummer flower,
Gentle as falcon
Or hawk of the tower:
With solace and gladness,   5
Much mirth and no madness,
All good and no badness;
    So joyously,
    So maidenly,
    So womanly   10
    Her demeaning
    In every thing,
    Far, far passing
    That I can indite,
    Or suffice to write   15
Of Merry Margaret
    As midsummer flower,
Gentle as falcon
Or hawk of the tower.
    As patient and still   20
And as full of good will
As fair Isaphill,[1]
Coriander,
Sweet pomander,
Good Cassander,[2]   25
Steadfast of thought,
Well made, well wrought,
Far may be sought
Ere that ye can find
So courteous, so kind   30
As Merry Margaret,
    This midsummer flower,
Gentle as falcon
Or hawk of the tower.

[1] Hypsipyle, in Greek legend, a queen of Lemnos who, when the women of the island killed their husbands for infidelity, saved her father. Later, when the Argonauts arrived on their way to find the Golden Fleece, she and her women were so hospitable that they repopulated the island.   [2] Cassandra, who, in Greek mythology, was gifted with the power of prophecy. It was her fate that, although her predictions were always correct, no one believed her.

SIR THOMAS WYATT

1503–1542

MY GALLEY CHARGED WITH FORGETFULNESS

My galley chargèd with forgetfulness
Thorough sharp seas in winter nights doth pass
'Tween rock and rock; and eke mine enemy, alas,
That is my lord, steereth with cruelness;
And every oar a thought in readiness,   5
As though that death were light in such a case.
An endless wind doth tear the sail apace
Of forcèd sighs and trusty fearfulness.
A rain of tears, a cloud of dark disdain,
Hath done the wearied cords[1] great hinderance,   10
Wreathèd with error and eke with ignorance.
The stars be hid that led me to this pain;
Drownèd is reason that should me consort,[2]
And I remain despairing of the port.

FORGET NOT YET

Forget not yet the tried[1] intent
Of such a truth as I have meant,
My great travail so gladly spent
        Forget not yet.

Forget not yet when first began   5
The weary life ye know since whan,
The suit,[2] the service none tell can,
        Forget not yet.

Forget not yet the great assays,
The cruel wrong, the scornful ways,   10
The painful patience in denays,[3]
        Forget not yet.

[1] Ropes.   [2] Accompany.

[1] Proved.   [2] Pursuit or courting.   [3] Denials.

Forget not yet, forget not this,
How long ago hath been and is
The mind that never meant amiss,   15
      Forget not yet.

Forget not then thine own approved,
The which so long hath thee loved,
Whose steadfast faith yet never moved,
      Forget not this.   20

EDMUND SPENSER

1552?–1599

EPITHALAMION[1]

Ye learned sisters,[2] which have oftentimes
Been to me aiding, others to adorn,
Whom ye thought worthy of your graceful rhymes,
That even the greatest did not greatly scorn
To hear their names sung in your simple lays,[3]   5
But joyèd in their praise;
And when ye list[4] your own mishaps to mourn,
Which death, or love, or fortune's wreck did raise,
Your string could soon to sadder tenor turn,
And teach the woods and waters to lament   10
Your doleful dreariment:
Now lay those sorrowful complaints aside;
And, having all your heads with girlands crown'd,
Help me mine own love's praises to resound;
Ne let the same of any be envide:[5]   15
So Orpheus did for his own bride![6]
So I unto myself alone will sing;
The woods shall to me answer, and my echo ring.

[1] A nuptial song or poem in praise of the bride and bridegroom.   [2] The Muses, nine sister goddesses charged, in Greek mythology, with care of the arts and sciences.
[3] Poems.   [4] Want.   [5] That is, let no one be begrudged the ability to sing his love's praises.   [6] Orpheus, in Greek mythology the husband of Eurydice, was famed as a singer.

Early, before the world's light-giving lamp
His golden beam upon the hills doth spread, 20
Having dispers'd the night's uncheerful damp,
Do ye awake; and with fresh lustihead
Go to the bower of my belovèd love,
My truest turtle-dove,
Bid her awake; for Hymen[7] is awake, 25
And long since ready forth his mask[8] to move,
With his bright tead[9] that flames with many a flake,
And many a bachelor[10] to wait on him,
In their fresh garments trim.
Bid her awake therefore, and soon her dight,[11] 30
For lo! the wishèd day is come at last,
That shall, for all the pains and sorrows past,
Pay to her usury[12] of long delight:
And whilst she doth her dight,
Do ye to her of joy and solace sing, 35
That all the woods may answer, and your echo ring.

Bring with you all the nymphs that you can hear
Both of the rivers and the forests green,
And of the sea that neighbours to her near:
All with gay girlands goodly well beseen.[13] 40
And let them also with them bring in hand
Another gay girland,
For my fair love, of lilies and of roses,
Bound true-love wise,[14] with a blue silk riband.
And let them make great store of bridal posies, 45
And let them eke bring store of other flowers,
To deck the bridal bowers.
And let the ground whereas her foot shall tread,
For fear the stones her tender foot should wrong,
Be strewed with fragrant flowers all along, 50
And diap'red[15] like the discoloured mead.[16]
Which done, do at her chamber door await,
For she will waken straight;
The whiles do ye this song unto her sing,
The woods shall to you answer, and your echo ring. 55

Ye nymphs of Mulla,[17] which with careful heed
The silver scaly trouts do tend full well,
And greedy pikes which use[18] therein to feed

---

[7] A fictional figure associated with weddings who came to be though of as the god of marriage.   [8] Masque.   [9] Torch.   [10] A young knight.   [11] Get dressed.   [12] Interest.   [13] Very becoming (to the nymphs).   [14] Like a truelove knot.   [15] Decoratively covered.   [16] Varicolored meadow.   [17] A river.   [18] Are accustomed.

(Those trouts and pikes all others do excel);
And ye likewise, which keep the rushy lake,   60
Where none do fishes take:
Bind up the locks the which hang scatter'd light,
And in his waters,[19] which your mirror make,
Behold your faces as the crystal bright,
That when you come whereas my love doth lie,   65
No blemish she may spy.
And eke, ye lightfoot maids, which keep the deer,
That on the hoary mountain used to tower;
And the wild wolves, which seek them to devour,
With your steel darts do chase from coming near;   70
Be also present here,
To help to deck her, and to help to sing,
That all the woods may answer, and your echo ring.

Wake now, my love, awake! for it is time;
The rosy Morn long since left Tithone's bed,[20]   75
All ready to her silver coach to climb;
And Phoebus[21] gins to shew his glorious head.
Hark! how the cheerful birds do chant their lays
And carol of Love's praise.
The merry lark her matins sings aloft;   80
The thrush replies; the mavis[22] descant plays;
The ouzel[23] shrills; the ruddock[24] warbles soft;
So goodly all[25] agree, with sweet consent,
To this day's merriment.
Ah! my dear love, why do ye sleep thus long?   85
When meeter[26] were that ye should now awake,
T' await the coming of your joyous make,[27]
And hearken to the birds' love-learnèd song,
The dewy leaves among!
For they of joy and pleasance[28] to you sing,   90
That all the woods them answer, and their echo ring.

My love is now awake out of her dreams,
And her fair eyes, like stars that dimmèd were
With darksome cloud, now shew their goodly beams
More bright than Hesperus[29] his head doth rear.   95
Come now, ye damsels, daughters of delight,
Help quickly her to dight:

---

[19] The water of the "rushy lake."   [20] Eos, or Aurora, the dawn goddess ("Rosy Morn") was said to have a lover, Tithonus, whose bed she left every morning. She drove across the sky in a chariot and pair.   [21] Phoebus Apollo, who, although not the sun god, was often associated with the sun.   [22] Another thrush.   [23] Blackbird.   [24] Redbreast.   [25] All these good creatures.   [26] More appropriate.   [27] Mate.   [28] Pleasantness.   [29] The evening star.

But first come, ye fair hours,[30] which were begot
In Jove's sweet paradise of Day and Night;
Which do the seasons of the year allot,   100
And all, that ever in this world is fair,
Do make and still repair:
And ye three handmaids of the Cyprian Queen,[31]
The which do still adorn her beauty's pride,
Help to adorn my beautifullest bride: 105
And, as ye her array, still throw between
Some graces to be seen;[32]
And, as ye use to Venus, to her sing,
The whiles the woods shall answer, and your echo ring.

Now is my love all ready forth to come: 110
Let all the virgins therefore well await:
And ye fresh[33] boys, that tend upon[34] her groom,
Prepare yourselves, for he is coming straight.
Set all your things in seemly good array,
Fit for so joyful day: 115
The joyfull'st day that ever sun did see.
Fair sun! shew forth thy favourable ray,
And let thy lifeful heat not fervent be,
For fear of burning her sunshiny face,
Her beauty to disgrace.   120
O fairest Phœbus! father of the Muse!
If ever I did honour thee aright,
Or sing the thing that mote thy mind delight,
Do not thy servant's simple boon refuse;
But let this day, let this one day, be mine;   125
Let all the rest be thine.
Then I thy sovereign praises loud will sing,
That all the woods shall answer, and their echo ring.

Hark: how the minstrels gin[35] to shrill aloud
Their merry music that resounds from far,   130
The pipe, the tabor, and the trembling croud,[36]
That well agree withouten breach or jar.[37]
But, most of all, the damsels do delight
When they their timbrels smite,
And thereunto do dance and carol sweet,   135
That all the senses they do ravish quite
The whiles the boys run up and down the street,

[30] The Hours (Horai), Greek goddesses of the seasons.   [31] Aphrodite.   [32] That
is, as you dress her, be careful not to cover up all her beauty.   [33] Untainted.   [34] Serve,
attend.   [35] Begin.   [36] An ancient Celtic musical instrument of the viol class.
[37] That is, there is no break or disharmony in the music.

Crying aloud with strong confusèd noise,
As if it were one voice,
Hymen, iö Hymen, Hymen, they do shout;   140
That even to the heavens their shouting shrill
Doth reach, and all the firmament doth fill;
To which the people standing all about,
As in approvance,[38] do thereto applaud,
And loud advance her laud;[39]   145
And evermore they Hymen, Hymen sing,
That all the woods them answer, and their echo ring.

Lo! where she comes along with portly pace,
Like Phœbe,[40] from her chamber of the east,
Arising forth to run her mighty race,   150
Clad all in white, that 'seems[41] a virgin best.
So well it her beseems, that ye would ween[42]
Some angel she had been.
Her long loose yellow locks like golden wire,[43]
Sprinkled with pearl, and purling flowers atween,   155
Do like a golden mantle her attire;
And, being crownèd with a girland green,
Seem like some maiden queen.[44]
Her modest eyes, abashèd to behold
So many gazers as on her do stare,   160
Upon the lowly ground affixèd are;
Ne dare lift up her countenance too bold,
But blush to hear her praises sung so loud,
So far from being proud.
Nathless do ye still loud her praises sing,   165
That all the woods may answer, and your echo ring.

Tell me, ye merchants' daughters, did ye see
So fair a creature in your town before;
So sweet, so lovely, and so mild as she,
Adorned with beauty's grace and virtue's store?   170
Her goodly eyes like sapphires shining bright,
Her forehead ivory white,
Her cheeks like apples which the sun hath rudded,[45]
Her lips like cherries charming men to bite,
Her breast like to a bowl of cream uncrudded,[46]   175

---

[38] Approval.   [39] Sing her praises.   [40] A Titaness sometimes thought of as goddess of the moon.   [41] Becomes (*beseemes*, in the following line, is synonymous).   [42] Believe.   [43] Strings of a musical instrument.   [44] That is, her golden locks, because they are crowned with a green garland, make her seem like a maiden queen.   [45] Made ruddy. [46] Uncurdled.

Her paps like lilies budded,
Her snowy neck like to a marble tower;
And all her body like a palace fair,
Ascending up, with many a stately stair,
To honour's seat and chastity's sweet bower.   180
Why stand we still, ye virgins, in amaze,[47]
Upon her so to gaze,
Whiles ye forget your former lay to sing,
To which the woods did answer, and your echo ring?

But if ye saw that which no eyes can see,   185
The inward beauty of her lively sprite,[48]
Garnisht with heavenly gifts of high degree,
Much more then would ye wonder at that sight,
And stand astonisht like to those which read[49]
Medusa's mazeful head.[50]   190
There dwells sweet love, and constant chastity,
Unspotted faith, and comely womanhood,
Regard of honour, and mild modesty;
There virtue reigns as queen in royal throne,
And giveth laws alone,   195
The which the base affections[51] do obey,
And yield their services unto her will;
Ne thought of thing uncomely ever may
Thereto approach to tempt her mind to ill.
Had ye once seen these her celestial treasures.   200
And unrevealèd pleasures,[52]
Then would ye wonder, and her praises sing,
That all the woods should answer, and your echo ring.

Open the temple gates unto my love,
Open them wide that she may enter in,   205
And all the posts adorn as doth behove,[53]
And all the pillars deck with girlands trim,
For to receive this saint[54] with honour due,
That cometh in to you.
With trembling steps, and humble reverence,   210
She cometh in, before th' Almighty's view:
Of her ye virgins learn obedience,
Whenso ye come into those holy places,
To humble your proud faces:
Bring her up to th' high altar, that she may   215

[47] Amazement.   [48] Soul, spirit.   [49] Gazed upon.   [50] Medusa, a terrible monster in Greek mythology, had an ugly face, snakes instead of hair, and eyes that could transform people into stone.   [51] Passions, instincts.   [52] Hidden (interior) beauties.   [53] As is fitting.   [54] Note that Spenser's imagery, which has been classical pagan, here becomes Christian.

The sacred ceremonies there partake,
The which do endless matrimony make;
And let the roaring organs loudly play
The praises of the Lord in lively notes;
The whiles, with hollow throats,   220
The choristers the joyous anthem sing,
That all the woods should answer, and your echo ring.

Behold, whiles she before the altar stands,
Hearing the holy priest that to her speaks,
And blesseth her with his two happy hands,   225
How the red roses flush up in her cheeks,
And the pure snow, with goodly vermeil[55] stain
Like crimson dyed in grain:[56]
That even th' angels, which continually
About the sacred altar do remain,   230
Forget their service and about her fly,
Oft peeping in her face, that seems more fair
The more they on it stare.
But her sad eyes, still fastened on the ground,
Are governèd with goodly modesty,   235
That suffers not one look to glance awry,
Which may let in a little thought unsound.
Why blush ye, love, to give to me your hand,
The pledge of all our band![57]
Sing, ye sweet angels, Alleluia sing,   240
That all the woods may answer, and your echo ring.

Now all is done: bring home the bride again;
Bring home the triumph of our victory:
Bring home with you the glory of her gain
With joyance[58] bring her and with jollity.   245
Never had man more joyful day than this,
Whom heaven would heap with bliss.
Make feast therefore now all this livelong day;
This day for ever to me holy is.
Pour out the wine without restraint or stay,[59]   250
Pour not by cups, but by the bellyful,
Pour out to all that wull,[60]
And sprinkle all the posts and walls with wine,
That they may sweat, and drunken be withal.
Crown ye God Bacchus with a coronal,   255
And Hymen also crown with wreaths of vine;

---

[55] Vermillion.   [56] Crimson cloth dyed while the material is still raw.   [57] Bond.
[58] Joy.   [59] Check, pause.   [60] Will, want.

And let the Graces[61] dance unto[62] the rest,
For they can do it best:
The whiles the maidens do their carol sing,
To which the woods shall answer, and their echo ring.   260

Ring ye the bells, ye young men of the town,
And leave your wonted[63] labours for this day:
This day is holy; do ye write it down,
That ye for ever it remember may.
This day the sun is in his chiefest height,   265
With Barnaby the bright,[64]
From whence declining daily by degrees,
He somewhat loseth of his heat and light,
When once the Crab[65] behind his back he sees.
But for this time it ill ordainèd was,[66]   270
To choose the longest day in all the year,
And shortest night, when longest fitter were:
Yet never day so long, but late would pass.[67]
Ring ye the bells, to make it wear away,
And bonfires make all day;   275
And dance about them, and about them sing
That all the woods may answer, and your echo ring.

Ah! when will this long weary day have end,
And lend me leave to come unto my love?
How slowly do the hours their numbers spend!   280
How slowly does sad Time his feathers move![68]
Haste thee, O fairest planet,[69] to thy home,
Within the western foam:
Thy tired steeds long since have need of rest.[70]
Long though it be, at last I see it gloom,[71]   285
And the bright evening-star with golden crest
Appear out of the east.
Fair child of beauty![72] glorious lamp of love!
That all the host of heaven in ranks dost lead,
And guidest lovers through the night's sad dread,   290
How cheerfully thou lookest from above,
And seem'st to laugh atween thy twinkling light,
As joying in the sight

[61] In Roman mythology, goddesses who embodied beauty and charm.   [62] For.
[63] Usual.   [64] It is St. Barnabas' Day (Barnaby is a short form of Barnabas), June 11,
once reckoned the longest day.   [65] The constellation, Cancer.   [66] Would have been.
[67] Sooner or later it would pass.   [68] Time is pictured as a bird or fowl. The image seems
to be original with Spenser.   [69] The sun.   [70] In classical mythology, the sun was a
chariot drawn across the skies by horses under the command of a sun god.   [71] Darken,
become dusk.   [72] Hesperus, the evening star, pictured in art as a boy carrying a torch.

Of these glad many, which for joy do sing,
That all the woods them answer, and their echo ring! 295

Now cease, ye damsels, your delights forepast;[73]
Enough it is that all the day was yours:
Now day is done, and night is nighing[74] fast,
Now bring the bride into the bridal bowers.
The night is come, now soon her disarray, 300
And in her bed her lay;
Lay her in lilies and in violets,
And silken curtains over her display,[75]
And odour'd sheets, and arras coverlets,[76]
Behold how goodly[77] my fair love does lie, 305
In proud humility!
Like unto Maia,[78] whenas Jove her took
In Tempe,[79] lying on the flow'ry grass,
'Twixt sleep and wake, after she weary was,
With bathing in the Acidalian brook.[80] 310
Now it is night, ye damsels may be gone,
And leave my love alone,
And leave likewise your former lay to sing:[81]
The woods no more shall answer, nor your echo ring.

Now welcome, night! thou night so long expected, 315
That long day's labour dost at last defray,
And all my cares, which cruel Love collected,
Hast summ'd in one, and cancellèd for aye:
Spread thy broad wing over my love and me,
That no man us may see; 320
And in thy sable[82] mantle us enwrap,
From fear of peril and foul horror free.
Let no false treason seek us to entrap,
Nor any dread disquiet once annoy
The safety of our joy; 325
But let the night be calm, and quietsome,
Without tempestuous storms or sad affray:
Like as when Jove with fair Alcmena lay,
When he begot the great Tirynthian groom:[83]
Or like as when he with thyself did lie 330
And begot Majesty.[84]

---

[73] Delights of the past.   [74] Drawing near.   [75] Spread out, unfurl.   [76] Coverlets embroidered in the manner of Arras tapestry.   [77] Beautifully.   [78] Mother of Hermes by Zeus (Jove).   [79] A narrow valley in northern Thessaly.   [80] The Acidalian brook was associated with Venus, the goddess of love.   [81] That is, you may stop singing your lay now.   [82] Black.   [83] Heracles.   [84] The poet here pays his bride the compliment of attributing to Jove and her the engendering of the god or goddess, Majesty; that is, she is the creator of majesty.

And let the maids and young men cease to sing,
Ne let the woods them answer, nor their echo ring.

Let no lamenting cries, nor doleful tears,
Be heard all night within, nor yet without: 335
Ne let false whispers, breeding hidden fears,
Break gentle sleep with misconceivèd doubt.
Let no deluding dreams, nor dreadful sights,
Make sudden sad affrights;
Ne let house-fires, nor lightning's helpless[85] harms,   340
Ne let the Pouke,[86] nor other evil sprites,
Ne let mischievous witches with their charms,
Ne let hobgoblins, names whose sense we see not,
Fray[87] us with things that be not:
Let not the shriek-owl nor the stork be heard,   345
Nor the night-raven, that still deadly yells;
Nor damnèd ghosts, called up with mighty spells,
Nor grisly vultures, make us once afeard:
Ne let th' unpleasant quire of frogs still croaking
Make us to wish their choking.   350
Let none of these their dreary accents sing;
Ne let the woods them answer, nor their echo ring.

But let still silence true night-watches keep,
That sacred peace may in assurance reign,
And timely sleep, when it is time to sleep,   355
May pour his limbs forth on your pleasant plain;[88]
The whiles an hundred little wingèd loves,
Like divers-feathered[89] doves,
Shall fly and flutter round your bed,
And in the secret dark, that[90] none reproves,   360
Their pretty stealths shall work, and snares shall
    spread
To filch away sweet snatches of delight,
Concealed through covert night.
Ye sons of Venus[91] play your sports at will!
For greedy pleasure, careless of your toys,   365
Thinks more upon her paradise of joys,
Than what ye do, albeit good or ill.
All night therefore attend your merry play,
For it will soon be day:
Now none doth hinder you, that say or sing;[92]   370
Ne will the woods now answer, nor your echo ring.

[85] Unpreventable.   [86] A fancied mischievous goblin or sprite.   [87] Frighten.
[88] The plain of your pleasant body.   [89] Diversely feathered.   [90] When.   [91] "Little
wingèd loves" or Cupids.   [92] By talking or singing.

Who is the same, which[93] at my window peeps?
Or whose is that fair face that shines so bright?
Is it not Cynthia,[94] she that never sleeps,
But walks about high heaven all the night? 375
O! fairest goddess, do thou not envý
My love with me to spy:
For thou likewise didst love, though now unthought,
And for a fleece of wool, which privily
The Latmian shepherd once unto thee brought, 380
His pleasures with thee wrought.
Therefore to us be favourable now;
And sith[95] of women's labours thou hast charge,
And generation goodly dost enlarge,
Incline thy will t' effect our wishful vow, 385
And the chaste womb inform with timely seed,
That may our comfort breed:
Till which we cease our hopeful hap[96] to sing;
Ne let the woods us answer, nor our echo ring.

And thou, great Juno![97] which with awful might 390
The laws of wedlock still dost patronize;
And the religion of the faith first plight[98]
With sacred rites hast taught to solemnize;
And eke for comfort often callèd art
Of women in their smart;[99] 395
Eternally bind thou this lovely band,
And all thy blessings unto us impart.
And thou, glad Genius![100] in whose gentle hand
The bridal bower[101] and genial bed remain,
Without blemish or stain: 400
And the sweet pleasures of their love's delight
With secret aid dost succour and supply,
Till they bring forth the fruitful progeny;
Send us the timely fruit of this same night.
And thou fair Hebe![102] and thou, Hymen free! 405
Grant that it may so be.
Till which we cease your further praise to sing;
Ne any woods shall answer, nor your echo ring.

And ye high heavens, the temple of the gods,
In which a thousand torches flaming bright 410

---

[93] Who is it that.   [94] The moon. Cynthia met Endymion, a remarkably beautiful young man, at the cave of Latmos; however, it was the god Pan who won her with a "fleece of wool."   [95] Since.   [96] Prosperity, good luck.   [97] In Roman mythology, the consort of Jupiter and the protectress of marriage and of women.   [98] Pledged.   [99] Great pain; here, labor.   [100] The god that governed the generation of all living beings and also watched over them, warding off evil.   [101] Bedroom.   [102] Greek goddess of youth and spring.

Do burn, that to us wretched earthly clods
In dreadful darkness lend desirèd light;
And all ye powers which in the same remain,
More than we men can feign,
Pour out your blessing on us plenteously,   415
And happy influence upon us rain,
That we may raise a large posterity,
Which from the earth, which they may long possess
With lasting happiness,
Up to your haughty palaces may mount;   420
And, for the guerdon of their glorious merit,
May heavenly tabernacles there inherit,
Of blessèd saints for to increase the count.
So let us rest, sweet love, in hope of this,
And cease till then our timely joys to sing;   425
The woods no more us answer, nor our echo ring!

Song! made in lieu of many ornaments,
With which my love should duly have been deckt,
Which cutting off through hasty accidents,
Ye would not stay your due time to expect,[103]   430
But promis'd both[104] to recompense;
Be unto her a goody ornament,
And for short time an endless monument.

CHRISTOPHER MARLOWE
1564–1593

THE PASSIONATE SHEPHERD TO HIS LOVE

Come live with me, and be my love,
And we will all the pleasures prove[1]
That valleys, groves, hills and fields,
Woods, or steepy mountain yields.

[103] That is, you would not wait as long as you should have.   [104] That is, both the lack of ornaments and the accidents that precluded them.

[1] Experience.

And we will sit upon the rocks,
Seeing the shepherds feed their flocks,
By shallow rivers, to whose falls
Melodious birds sing madrigals.

And I will make thee beds of roses,
And a thousand fragrant posies,
A cap of flowers, and a kirtle,[2]
Embroider'd all with leaves of myrtle;

A gown made of the finest wool,
Which from our pretty lambs we pull,
Fair-linèd slippers for the cold,
With buckles of the purest gold;

A belt of straw, and ivy-buds,
With coral clasps and amber studs;
And if these pleasures may thee move,
Come live with me, and be my love.

The shepherd-swains shall dance and sing
For they delight each May morning;
If these delights thy mind may move,
Then live with me and be my love.

5

10

15

20

SIR WALTER RALEGH
1552?–1618

THE NYMPH'S REPLY

If all the world and love were young,
And truth in every shepherd's tongue,
These pretty pleasures might me move,
To live with thee, and be thy love.

[2] A long gown.

Time drives the flocks from field to fold, 5
When rivers rage, and rocks grow cold,
And Philomel[1] becometh dumb,
The rest complains of cares to come.

The flowers do fade, and wanton fields
To wayward winter reckoning yields, 10
A honey tongue, a heart of gall,
Is fancy's spring, but sorrow's fall.

Thy gowns, thy shoes, thy beds of roses,
Thy cap, thy kirtle, and thy posies,
Soon break, soon wither, soon forgotten: 15
In folly ripe, in reason rotten.

Thy belt of straw and ivy buds,
Thy coral clasps and amber studs,
All these in me no means can move,
To come to thee, and be thy love. 20

But could youth last, and love still breed,
Had joys no date, nor age no need,
Then these delights my mind might move,
To live with thee, and be thy love.

AS YOU CAME FROM THE HOLY LAND

As you came from the holy land
    Of Walsinghame[1]
Met you not with my true love
    By the way as you came?

How shall I know your true love 5
    That have met many one
As I went to the holy land
    That have come, that have gone?

She is neither white nor brown
    But as the heavens fair; 10

[1] The nightingale.

[1] Probably the present Little Walsingham, a village in Norfolk, and site of Walsingham Abbey, one of the great shrines of medieval England.

There is none hath a form so divine
    In the earth or the air.

Such an one did I meet, good Sir,
    Such an Angelic face,
Who like a queen, like a nymph, did appear,   15
    By her gait, by her grace.

She hath left me here all alone,
    All alone as unknown,
Who sometimes did me lead with her self,
    And me lov'd as her own.   20

What's the cause that she leaves you alone
    And a new way doth take,
Who lovèd you once as her own
    And her joy did you make?

I have lov'd her all my youth,   25
    But now old, as you see,
Loves likes not the falling fruit
    From the witherèd tree.

Know that love is a careless child
    And forgets promise past: 30
He is blind, he is deaf when he list[2]
    And in faith never fast.

His desire is a dureless[3] content
    And a trustless joy;
He is won with a world of despair   35
    And is lost with a toy.

Of women kind such indeed is the love
    Or the word Love abus'd
Under which many childish desires
    And conceits[4] are excus'd.   40

[2] Wants to be.   [3] Transient.   [4] Notions.

But true Love is a durable fire
    In the mind ever burning:
Never sick, never old, never dead,
    From itself never turning.

WILLIAM SHAKESPEARE
1 5 6 4 – 1 6 1 6

FULL FATHOM FIVE

Full fathom five thy father lies;
    Of his bones are coral made;
Those are pearls that were his eyes:
    Nothing of him that doth fade,
But doth suffer a sea-change   5
Into something rich and strange.
Sea-nymphs hourly ring his knell:
              Ding-dong
Hark! now I hear them—ding-dong **bell.**

TELL ME WHERE IS FANCY BRED

Tell me where is fancy bred,
Or in the heart or in the head?
How begot, how nourishèd?
    Reply, reply.

It is engender'd in the eyes,   5
With gazing fed; and fancy dies
In the cradle where it lies.
    Let us all ring fancy's knell:
    I'll begin it,—Ding, dong, bell.

O MISTRESS MINE

O mistress mine! where are you roaming?
O! stay and hear; you true love's coming,
    That can sing both high and low.
Trip no further, pretty sweeting;
Journeys end in lovers meeting,   5
    Every wise man's son doth know.

What is love? 'tis not hereafter;
Present mirth hath present laughter;
    What's to come is still unsure:
In delay there lies no plenty;   10
Then come kiss me, sweet-and-twenty,
    Youth's a stuff will not endure.

WHEN THAT I WAS AND A LITTLE TINY BOY

When that I was and a little tiny boy,
    With hey, ho, the wind and the rain;
A foolish thing was but a toy,
    For the rain it raineth every day.

But when I came to man's estate,   5
    With hey, ho, the wind and the rain;
'Gainst knaves and thieves men shut their gates,
    For the rain it raineth every day.

But when I came, alas! to wive,
    With hey, ho, the wind and the rain;   10
By swaggering could I never thrive,
    For the rain it raineth every day.

But when I came unto my beds,
    With hey, ho, the wind and the rain;
With toss-pots still had drunken heads,   15
    For the rain it raineth every day.

A great while ago the world begun,
    With hey, ho, the wind and the rain;

But that's all one, our play is done,
 And we'll strive to please you every day.   20

FEAR NO MORE

Fear no more the heat o' the sun,
 Nor the furious winter's rages;
Thou thy worldly task hast done,
 Home art gone, and ta'en thy wages:
Golden lads and girls all must,   5
As chimney-sweepers, come to dust.

Fear no more the frown o' the great;
 Thou art past thy tyrant's stroke;
Care no more to clothe and eat;
 To thee the reed is as the oak: 10
The sceptre, learning, physic,[1] must
All follow this, and come to dust.

Fear no more the lightning-flash,
 Nor the all-dreaded thunder-stone;[2]
Fear not slander, censure rash;   15
 Thou hast finish'd joy and moan:
All lovers young, all lovers must
Consign to[3] thee, and come to dust.

No exorciser harm thee!
 Nor no witchcraft charm thee!   20
Ghost unlaid[4] forbear[5] thee!
 Nothing ill come near thee!
Quiet consummation have;
And renownèd be thy grave!

SONNET 18

Shall I compare thee to a summer's day?
Thou art more lovely and more temperate:
Rough winds do shake the darling buds of May,
And summer's lease hath all too short a date:

[1] Kings, scholars, physicians.   [2] Thunderbolt.   [3] Come to terms with.   [4] A ghost that cannot lie quiet in the grave.   [5] Leave alone, shun.

Sometime too hot the eye of heaven shines,
And often is his gold complexion dimm'd;
And every fair from fair sometime declines,
By chance, or nature's changing course untrimm'd;
But thy eternal summer shall not fade,   5
Nor lose possession of that fair thou ow'st;[1]
Nor shall Death brag thou wander'st in his shade,
When in eternal lines to time thou grow'st.   10
    So long as men can breathe or eyes can see,
    So long lives this, and this gives life to thee.

SONNET 29

When in disgrace with fortune and men's eyes,
I all alone beweep my outcast state,
And trouble deaf heaven with my bootless cries,
And look upon myself and curse my fate,
Wishing me like to one more rich in hope,   5
Featur'd like him, like him with friends possess'd,
Desiring this man's art, and that man's scope,
With what I most enjoy contented least,
Yet in these thoughts myself almost despising,
Haply I think on thee, and then my state,   10
Like to the lark at break of day arising,
From sullen earth sings hymns at heaven's gate,
    For thy sweet love rememb'red such wealth brings,
    That then I scorn to change my state with kings.

SONNET 30

When to the sessions of sweet silent thought,
I summon up remembrance of things past,
I sigh the lack of many a thing I sought,
And with old woes new[1] wail my dear time's waste:
Then can I drown an eye, unus'd to flow,   5
For precious friends hid in death's dateless night,
And week afresh love's long-since cancel'd woe,
And moan th' expense[2] of many a vanish'd sight.
Then can I grieve at grievances foregone,
And heavily from woe to woe tell o'er   10

    [1] Ownest.

    [1] Newly.   [2] Loss.

The sad account of fore-bemoanèd moan,
Which I new pay as if not paid before.
　　　But if the while I think on thee, dear friend,
　　　All losses are restor'd, and sorrows end.

SONNET 33

Full many a glorious morning have I seen
Flatter the mountain-tops with sovereign[1] eye,
Kissing with golden face the meadows green;
Gilding pale streams with heavenly alchemy:
Anon permit the basest clouds to ride,　　　　　　　　　　5
With ugly rack[2] on his celestial face,
And from the forlorn world his visage hide,
Stealing unseen to west with this disgrace:
Even so my sun one early morn did shine,
With all-triumphant splendor on my brow,　　　　　　　　　10
But out, alack, he was but one hour mine;
The region cloud[3] hath mask'd him from me now.
　　　Yet him for this, my love no whit disdaineth;
　　　Suns of the world may stain,[4] when heaven's sun staineth.

SONNET 55

Not marble, nor the gilded monuments
Of princes, shall outlive this powerful rhyme,
But you shall shine more bright in these contents
Than unswept stone,[1] besmear'd with sluttish time.
When wasteful war shall statues overturn,　　　　　　　　5
And broils[2] root out the work of masonry,
Nor[3] Mars his sword,[4] nor war's quick fire shall burn
The living record of your memory.
'Gainst death and all-oblivious enmity
Shall you pace forth; your praise shall still find room,　　　10
Even in the eyes of all posterity
That wear this world out[5] to the ending doom.

---

[1] Efficacious, healing.　　[2] A group of storm clouds.　　[3] Cloud of the upper air.
[4] Be darkened.

[1] Stone unswept by the wind and thus not eroded.　　[2] Tumults. This line essentially repeats the preceding one.　　[3] Neither.　　[4] The sword of Mars, the Roman god of war.
[5] Stay with.

So till the judgment that yourself arise,
You live in this, and dwell in lovers' eyes.

SONNET 73

That time of year thou mayst in me behold,
When yellow leaves, or none, or few, do hang
Upon those boughs which shake against the cold,
Bare ruin'd choirs,[1] where late the sweet birds sang.
In me thou see'st the twilight of such day,   5
As after sunset fadeth in the west,
Which by and by black night doth take away,
Death's second self, that seals up all in rest.
In me thou see'st the glowing of such fire,
That on the ashes of his[2] youth doth lie,   10
As the death-bed whereon it must expire,
Consum'd with that which it was nourish'd by.
    This thou perceiv'st, which makes thy love more strong,
    To love that well, which thou must leave ere long.

SONNET 107

Not mine own fears, nor the prophetic soul
Of the wide world, dreaming on things to come,
Can yet the lease of my true love control,
Suppos'd as forfeit to a confin'd doom.[1]
The mortal moon hath her eclipse endur'd,   5
And the sad augurs mock their own presage;[2]
Incertainties now crown themselves assur'd,
And peace proclaims olives[3] of endless age.
Now with the drops[4] of this most balmy time,
My love looks fresh, and Death to me subscribes,[5]   10
Since, spite of him, I'll live in this poor rhyme,
While he insults[6] o'er dull and speechless tribes.
    And thou in this shalt find thy monument,
    When tyrants' crests and tombs of brass are spent.[7]

[1] Choir lofts.   [2] Its (that is, the fire's).

[1] Judgment.   [2] Prophesy.   [3] The olive, or olive branch, symbolizes peace.
[4] Dewdrops.   [5] Yields.   [6] Exalts insolently.   [7] Gone.

SONNET 129

Th' expense of spirit in a waste of shame
Is lust in action; and till action, lust
Is perjur'd,[1] murd'rous, bloody, full of blame,
Savage, extreme, rude, cruel, not to trust,[2]
Enjoy'd no sooner but[3] despisèd straight,　　　　　　　　5
Past reason hunted, and no sooner had
Past reason hated as a swallowed bait,
On purpose laid to make the taker mad:
Mad in pursuit, and in possession so,
Had,[4] having, and in quest to have, extreme,　　　　　　10
A bliss in proof,—and prov'd, a very woe;
Before, a joy propos'd; behind, a dream.
　　　All this the world well knows; yet none knows well,
　　　To shun the heaven that leads men to this hell.

THOMAS NASHE
1567–1601

SPRING

Spring, the sweet spring, is the year's pleasant king;
Then blooms each thing, then maids dance in a ring,
Cold doth not sting, the pretty birds do sing:
　　　Cuckoo, jug-jug, pu-we, to-witta-woo!

The palm and may[1] make country houses gay,　　　　　　5
Lambs frisk and play, the shepherds pipe all day,
And we hear aye[2] birds tune this merry lay:
　　　Cuckoo, jug-jug, pu-we, to-witta-woo!

The fields breathe sweet, the daisies kiss our feet,
Young lovers meet, old wives a-sunning sit,　　　　　　10

---

[1] Made false to itself.　　[2] Not to be trusted.　　[3] Than.　　[4] In the process of being experienced.

[1] A branch of the hawthorn or similar plant used for **May Day** decorations.　　[2] Continually.

In every street these tunes our ears do greet:
    Cuckoo, jug-jug, pu-we, to-witta-woo!
      Spring, the sweet spring!

IN TIME OF PESTILENCE 1593

Adieu, farewell earth's bliss,
This world uncertain is;
Fond[1] are life's lustful joys,
Death proves them all but toys,
None from his darts can fly.   5
I am sick, I must die.
    Lord, have mercy on us!

Rich men, trust not in wealth,
Gold cannot buy you health;
Physic himself[2] must fade,   10
All things to end are made.
The plague full swift goes by;
I am sick, I must die.
    Lord, have mercy on us!

Beauty is but a flower   15
Which wrinkles will devour;
Brightness falls from the air,
Queens have died young and fair,
Dust hath closed Helen's[3] eye.
I am sick, I must die.   20
    Lord, have mercy on us!

Strength stoops unto[4] the grave,
Worms feed on Hector[5] brave,
Swords may not fight with fate,
Earth still holds ope her gate.   25
Come! come! the bells do cry.
I am sick, I must die.
    Lord, have mercy on us!

Wit with his wantonness
Tasteth death's bitterness;   30

[1] Foolish or vain.   [2] The science of medicine itself.   [3] The beautiful Helen of Troy (see Homer's *Iliad*).   [4] Yields to.   [5] The bravest of the Trojan heroes in the *Iliad*.

Hell's executioner
Hath no ears for to hear
What vain art can reply.
I am sick, I must die.
    Lord, have mercy on us!   35

Haste, therefore, each degree,[6]
To welcome destiny.
Heaven is our heritage,
Earth but a player's stage;
Mount we unto the sky.   40
I am sick, I must die.
    Lord, have mercy on us!

SIR JOHN DAVIES
1569–1626

AFFLICTION

If aught can teach us aught, Affliction's looks,
    Making us look into ourselves so near,
Teach us to know ourselves beyond all books,
    Or all the learnèd schools that ever were.

This mistress lately pluck'd me by the ear,   5
    And many a golden lesson hath me taught;
Hath made my senses quick, and reason clear,
    Reform'd my will, and rectified my thought.

So do the winds and thunders cleanse the air;
    So working seas settle and purge the wine;   10
So lopp'd and prunèd trees do flourish fair;
    So doth the fire the drossy gold refine.

[6] Class of people.

Neither Minerva¹ nor the learnèd Muse,²
    Nor rules of art, nor precepts of the wise,
Could in my brain those beams of skill infuse,   15
    As but the glance of this dame's angry eyes.

She within lists³ my ranging mind hath brought,
    That now beyond myself I list not⁴ go:
Myself am centre of my circling thought,
    Only myself I study, learn, and know.   20

I know my body's of so frail a kind
    As force without, fevers within, can kill;
I know the heavenly nature of my mind,
    But 'tis corrupted both in wit and will.

I know my soul hath power to know all things,   25
    Yet is she blind and ignorant in all;
I know I am one of nature's little kings,
    Yet to the least and vilest things am thrall.

I know my life's a pain and but a span,
    I know my sense is mock'd with every thing: 30
And, to conclude, I know myself a man,
    Which is a proud, and yet a wretched thing.

BEN JONSON

1 5 7 2 – 1 6 3 7

ON MY FIRST SON

Farewell, thou child of my right hand, and joy;
    My sin was too much hope of thee, lov'd boy.
Seven years thou wert lent to me, and I thee pay,¹

---

¹ The Roman goddess of wisdom.   ² Any of nine Greek goddesses of song, poetry, arts, and sciences.   ³ Boundaries.   ⁴ Do not desire to.

¹ I pay (for thee) with thee.

Exacted by thy fate, on the just day.
O, could I lose all father, now! For why   5
    Will man lament the state he should envy?
To have so soon 'scap'd world's and flesh's rage,
    And, if no other misery, yet age!
Rest in soft peace, and, ask'd, say, Here doth lie
    Ben Jonson his[2] best piece of poetry.   10
For whose sake, henceforth, all his vows be such,
    As what he loves may never like too much.

EPITAPH ON ELIZABETH, L.H.

Would'st thou hear what man can say
In a little? Reader, stay.
Underneath this stone doth lie
As much beauty as could die:
Which in life did harbour give   5
To more virtue than doth live.
If, at all, she had a fault,
Leave it buried in this vault.
One name was Elizabeth,
Th' other, let it sleep with death: 10
Fitter, where it died, to tell,
Than that it liv'd at all. Farewell.

TO PENSHURST[1]

Thou art not, Penshurst, built to envious show,
Of touch[2] or marble; nor canst boast a row
Of polish'd pillars, or a roof of gold:
Thou hast no lantern,[3] whereof tales are told;
Or stair, or courts; but stand'st an ancient pile,[4]   5
And these grudg'd at, are reverenc'd the while.
Thou joy'st in better marks,[5] of soil, of air,
Of wood, of water: therein thou art fair.
Thou hast thy walks for health, as well as sport:
Thy Mount, to which thy Dryads[6] do resort,   10
Where Pan and Bacchus[7] their high feasts have made,

[2] Ben Jonson's.

[1] The seat of the Sidneys, the family of the poet, Sir Philip Sidney (1554–1586).
[2] Touchstone, a costly marble.   [3] A small tower on top of a dome with glazed openings
to admit light.   [4] A group of buildings.   [5] Characteristics.   [6] Wood nymphs.
[7] Pan was the Greek god of pastures and fields, and Bacchus the god of wine.

Beneath the broad beech and the chestnut shade;
That taller tree, which of a nut was set,[8]
At his great birth, where all the Muses met.[9]
There, in the writhèd bark, are cut the names   15
Of many a Sylvan, taken with his flames.[10]
And thence the ruddy satyrs oft provoke
The lighter Fauns to reach thy Lady's oak.[11]
Thy copse, too, nam'd of Gamage,[12] thou hast there,
That never fails to serve thee season'd[13] deer,   20
When thou wouldst feast, or exercise thy friends.
The lower land, that to the river bends,
Thy sheep, thy bullocks, kine, and calves do feed;
The middle grounds thy mares and horses breed.
Each bank doth yield thee conies;[14] and the tops   25
Fertile of wood, Ashore and Sidney's copse,
To crown thy open table, doth provide
The purpled pheasant, with the speckled side;
The painted partridge lies in every field,
And, for thy mess,[15] is willing to be kill'd.   30
And if the high-swoln Medway[16] fail thy dish,
Thou hast the ponds that pay thee tribute fish,
Fat agèd carps that run into thy net.
And pikes, now weary their own kind to eat,
As loth, the second draught,[17] or cast to stay,[18]   35
Officiously,[19] at first, themselves betray.
Bright eels that emulate them, leap on land,
Before the fisher, or into his hand.
Then hath thy orchard fruit, thy garden flowers,
Fresh as the air, and new as are the hours.   40
The early cherry, with the later plum,
Fig, grape, and quince, each in his time doth come;
The blushing apricot, and woolly peach
Hang on thy walls, that every child may reach.
And though thy walls be of the country stone,   45
They're rear'd with no man's ruin, no man's groan;
There's none that dwell about them wish them down;
But all come in, the farmer, and the clown,
And no one empty-handed, to salute
Thy lord, and lady, though they have no suit.[20]   50
Some bring a capon, some a rural cake,
Some nuts, some apples; some that think they make
The better cheeses, bring 'em; or else send

---

[8] Planted.   [9] The allusion is to the birth of Sir Philip Sidney.   [10] The passions inspired by Sidney's verses.   [11] There is a tradition that Sir Robert Sidney's wife, Lady Leicester, went into labor at Penshurst under an oak, which was subsequently called "my lady's oak."   [12] In this copse, Barbara Gamage, the first wife of Sir Robert Sidney, liked to feed the deer from her own hands.   [13] Matured.   [14] Rabbits.   [15] Company of persons eating together.   [16] A river bordering Penshurst Park.   [17] The act of drawing a net for fish.   [18] Wait for.   [19] Obligingly.   [20] Petition, request for favors.

By their ripe daughters, whom they would commend
This way to husbands, and whose baskets bear   55
An emblem of themselves in plum or pear.
But what can this, more than express their love,
Add to thy free provisions, far above
The need of such? whose liberal board doth flow
With all that hospitality doth know!   60
Where comes no guest but is allow'd to eat,
Without his fear, and of thy lord's own meat:
Where the same beer, and bread, and self-same wine,
That is his lordship's, shall be also mine.
And I not fain[21] to sit, as some, this day   65
At great men's tables, and yet dine away.
Here no man tells[22] my cups; nor, standing by,
A waiter doth my gluttony envý:
But gives me what I call, and lets me eat,
He knows, below, he shall find plenty of meat,   70
Thy tables hoard not up for the next day,
Nor, when I take my lodging, need I pray
For fire, or lights, or livery: all is there,
As if thou, then, wert mine, or I reign'd here:
There's nothing I can wish, for which I stay.   75
That found King James, when hunting late, this way,
With his brave son, the prince; they saw thy fires
Shine bright on every hearth, as[23] the desires
Of thy Penates[24] had been set on flame,
To entertain them; or the country came,   80
With all their zeal, to warm their welcome here.
What, great, I will not say, but, sudden cheer
Didst thou then make[25] 'em! and what praise was heap'd
On thy good lady, then! who therein reap'd
The just reward of all her housewifery;   85
To have her linen, plate, and all things nigh,
When she was far, and not a room but dress'd
As if it had expected such a guest!
These, Penshurst, are thy praise, and yet not all.
Thy lady's noble, fruitful, chaste withal.   90
His children thy great lord may call his own:
A fortune, in this age, but rarely known.
They are, and have been taught religion; thence
Their gentler spirits have suck'd innocence.
Each morn and even they are taught to pray,   95
With the whole household, and may, every day,
Read, in their virtuous parents' noble parts,[26]
The mysteries of manners, arms, and arts.

[21] Be obliged.   [22] Counts.   [23] As if.   [24] Roman household gods.   [25] Provide a feast for.   [26] Abilities.

Now, Penshurst, they that will proportion[27] thee
With other edifices, when they see   100
Those proud, ambitious heaps, and nothing else,
May say, their lords have built, but thy lord dwells.

SONG, TO CELIA

Drink to me only with thine eyes,
    And I will pledge with mine;
Or leave a kiss but in the cup,
    And I'll not look for wine.
The thirst that from the soul doth rise   5
    Doth ask a drink divine:
But might I of Jove's nectar sup,
    I would not change for thine.

I sent thee late a rosy wreath,
    Not so much honoring thee,   10
As giving it a hope that there
    It could not withered be.
But thou thereon didst only breathe,
    And sent'st it back to me:
Since when it grows, and smells, I swear,   15
    Not of itself, but thee.

THE TRIUMPH OF CHARIS

See the chariot at hand here of Love,
    Wherein my Lady rideth!
Each that draws is a swan or a dove,
    And well the car Love guideth.
As she goes, all hearts do duty   5
      Unto her beauty;
And enamor'd, do wish, so they might
      But enjoy such a sight,
That they still were to run by her side,
Through swords, through seas, whither she would ride.   10

Do but look on her eyes, they do light
    All that Love's world compriseth!

    [27] Compare.

Do but look on her hair, it is bright
　　As Love's star when it riseth!
Do but mark, her forehead's smoother   15
　　　Than words that soothe her!
And from her arched brows, such a grace
　　　Sheds itself through the face
As alone there triumphs to the life
All the gain, all the good, of the elements' strife.   20

Have you seen but a bright lily grow,
　　Before rude hands have touch'd it?
Have you mark'd but the fall o' the snow
　　Before the soil hath smutch'd it?
Have you felt the wool o' the beaver?   25
　　　Or swan's down ever?
Or have smelt o' the bud o' the briar?
　　　Or the nard[1] i' the fire?
Or have tasted the bag o' the bee?[2]
O so white! O so soft! O so sweet is she!   30

HYMN TO DIANA[1]

Queen and huntress, chaste and fair,
　　Now the sun is laid to sleep,
Seated in thy silver chair,
　　　State in wonted manner keep:
　　　Hesperus[2] entreats thy light,   5
　　　Goddess, excellently bright.

Earth, let not thy envious shade
　　Dare itself to interpose;
Cynthia's shining orb was made
　　　Heaven to clear[3] when day did close: 10
　　　Bless us then with wishèd sight,
　　　Goddess, excellently bright.

Lay thy bow of pearl apart
　　And thy crystal-shining quiver;
Give unto the flying hart   15

---

[1] An aromatic balsam.　　　[2] Honeycomb.

[1] The goddess Diana or Cynthia was associated with the moon and with hunting.
[2] The evening star.　　　[3] To make clear, illuminate.

Space to breathe, how short soever:
  Thou that mak'st a day of night,
  Goddess, excellently bright!

TO THE MEMORY OF MY BELOVED, THE AUTHOR, MR. WILLIAM SHAKESPEARE

To draw no envy,[1] Shakespeare, on thy name,
Am I thus ample[2] to thy book and fame:
While I confess thy writings to be such
As neither Man nor Muse can praise too much.
'Tis true, and all men's suffrage.[3] But these ways   5
Were not the paths I meant unto thy praise:
For silliest ignorance on these may light,
Which, when it sounds at best, but echoes right:
Or blind affection, which doth ne'er advance
The truth, but gropes, and urgeth all by chance;   10
Or crafty malice might pretend this praise,
And think to ruin, where it seem'd to praise.
These are as[4] some infamous bawd, or whore,
Should praise a matron.[5] What could hurt her more?
But thou art proof against them, and indeed   15
Above th' ill fortune of them, or the need.
I, therefore, will begin. Soul of the Age!
The applause, delight, the wonder of our stage!
My Shakespeare, rise. I will not lodge thee by
Chaucer or Spenser,[6] or bid Beaumont[7] lie   20
A little further to make thee a room:
Thou art a monument without a tomb,
And art alive still, while thy book doth live,
And we have wits to read, and praise to give.
That I not mix thee so, my brain excuses;   25
I mean with great, but disproportion'd Muses:[8]
For, if I thought my judgment were of years,
I should commit[9] thee surely with thy peers,
And tell how far thou didst our Lyly[10] outshine,

---

[1] Ill will.   [2] Generous.   [3] Opinion.   [4] As if.   [5] A dignified married woman.
[6] Edmund Spenser (1552?–1599) was a great lyric and narrative poet (see his "Epithalamion").   [7] Francis Beaumont (1584–1616) was a poet and a collaborator with John Fletcher in dramatic works. Chaucer, Spenser, and Beaumont have neighboring graves in Westminster Abbey.   [8] Here, poets; they are "disproportioned" in that they have less merit than Shakespeare.   [9] Match, compare.   [10] John Lyly (1554–1606) wrote drama and other works in prose.

Or sporting Kyd,[11] or Marlowe's[12] mighty line. 30
And though thou hadst small Latin, and less Greek,
From thence[13] to honour thee, I would not seek
For names, but call forth thund'ring Aeschylus,
Euripides and Sophocles[14] to us,
Pacuvius, Accius, him of Cordova dead,[15] 35
To life again, to hear thy buskin tread
And shake a stage; or, when thy socks were on,[16]
Leave thee alone for the comparison
Of all that insolent Greece or haughty Rome
Sent forth, or since did from their ashes come. 40
Triumph, my Britain, thou hast one to show,
To whom all scenes[17] of Europe homage owe.
He was not of an age, but for all time!
And all the Muses[18] still were in their prime
When like Apollo[19] he came forth to warm 45
Our ears, or like a Mercury[20] to charm.
Nature herself was proud of his designs,
And joy'd to wear the dressing of his lines;
Which were so richly spun, and woven so fit,
As, since,[21] she will vouchsafe[22] no other wit.[23] 50
The merry Greek, tart Aristophanes,[24]
Neat Terence, witty Plautus,[25] now not please;
But antiquated and deserted lie,
As they were not of Nature's[26] family.
Yet must I not give nature all: thy art, 55
My gentle Shakespeare, must enjoy a part.
For though the poet's matter nature be,
His art doth give the fashion. And that he
Who casts to write a living line must sweat,
(Such as thine are) and strike the second heat 60
Upon the Muses' anvil; turn the same[27]

---

[11] Thomas Kyd (1557?–1595?) was one of the best known tragic poets of his time. Very little is known of Kyd's life, but the fact that he died in debt perhaps explains the phrase "sporting Kyd." [12] Christopher Marlowe (1564–1593) was a poet and dramatist whose works are generally placed second only to Shakespeare's for the Elizabethan period. His best known play is *The Tragical History of Dr. Faustus*. [13] From the age of Latin and Greek literature. [14] Aeschylus, Euripedes, and Sophocles were the greatest of the Greek writers of tragedy. [15] Pacuvius, Accius, and Seneca ("him of Cordoba dead") were the best writers of Roman tragedy. [16] In Athenian drama, actors in tragedy wore a high, thick-soled boot (buskin) and those in comedy wore a low shoe (sock). Shakespeare's "buskin" is, thus, his tragic drama and his "sock," his comic drama. [17] Theatrical stages. [18] The Muses, in Greek mythology, were goddesses of the arts and learning. [19] Apollo was the Greek god of the sun. [20] Mercury is the Latin name of Hermes, who is best known as messenger of the gods. [21] That since then. [22] Acknowledge. [23] Genius. [24] Aristophanes was the foremost of Greek writers of comedy. [25] Terence and Plautus wrote the best comedies in Latin. [26] Nature, here, is a creative and regulative physical power conceived of as operating in the physical world and as the immediate cause of all its phenomena; it is contrasted with Art. [27] That is, the line of verse.

(And himself with it) that he thinks to frame;
Or for[28] the laurel he may gain a scorn,
For a good poet's made as well as born.
And such wert thou. Look how the father's face   65
Lives in his issue, even so the race
Of Shakespeare's mind and manners brightly shines
In his well-turnèd and true-filèd lines:
In each of which he seems to shake a lance
As[29] brandish'd at the eyes of ignorance.   70
Sweet swan of Avon![30] what a sight it were
To see thee in our waters yet[31] appear,
And make those flights upon the banks of Thames[32]
That so did take Eliza and our James![33]
But stay, I see thee in the Hemisphere   75
Advanc'd, and make[34] a constellation there.
Shine forth, thou star of Poets, and with rage,
Or influence,[35] chide, or cheer the drooping stage,
Which, since thy flight from hence, hath mourn'd like night,
And despairs[36] day, but for thy volume's light.[37]   80

JOHN DONNE
1 5 7 2 – 1 6 3 1

SONG

Go, and catch a falling star,
    Get with child a mandrake root,[1]
Tell me where all past years are,
    Or who cleft the Devil's foot,
Teach me to hear mermaids' singing,   5
Or to keep off envy's stinging,
        And find
        What wind
Serves to advance an honest mind.

[28] Instead of.   [29] As if it were.   [30] Shakespeare was born at Stratford, on the
river Avon.   [31] Again.   [32] The Thames flows through London.   [33] Elizabeth and
James were, successively, rulers of England during Shakespeare's career.   [34] Make out,
discern.   [35] Astral influence (Shakespeare is seen as the "Star of Poets").   [36] Despairs
of, has no hope for.   [37] The light that comes from thy plays (collectively).

[1] The forked root of the mandrake (mandragora) was thought to suggest the shape
of the human body.

If thou be'st born to² strange sights,
    Things invisible to see,
Ride ten thousand days and nights,
    Till age snow white hairs on thee,
Thou, when thou return'st, wilt tell me
All strange wonders that befell thee,
      And swear
      No where
Lives a woman true, and fair.

If thou find'st one, let me know,
    Such a pilgrimage were³ sweet;
Yet do not, I would not go,
Though at next door we⁴ might meet,
Though she were true, when you met her,
And last till you write your letter,
      Yet she
      Will be
False, ere I come, to two, or three.

THE INDIFFERENT

I can love both fair and brown,
Her whom abundance melts, and her whom want betrays,
Her who loves loneness best, and her who masks and plays,
Her whom the country form'd, and whom the town,
Her who believes, and her who tries,¹
Her who still weeps with spongy eyes,
And her who is dry cork and never cries;
I can love her, and her, and you and you,
I can love any, so she be not true.

Will no other vice content you?
Will it not serve your turn to do as did your mothers?
Or have you all old vices spent,² and now would find out³ others?
Or doth a fear that men are true torment you?
O, we are not, be not you so;
Let me, and do you, twenty know.

    ² Born for (seeing), prone to (see).   ³ Would be.   ⁴ The speaker and the "woman true and fair."

    ¹ Tests, examines.   ² Exhausted.   ³ Discover.

Rob me, but bind me not, and let me go.
Must I, who came to travail thorough[4] you,
Grow your fix'd subject because you are true?

Venus heard me sigh this song,
And by love's sweetest part,[5] variety, she swore   20
She heard not this till now, and that it should be so no more.
She went, examin'd, and return'd ere long,
And said, "Alas, some two or three
Poor heretics in love there be,
Which think to 'stablish dangerous constancy.   25
But I have told them, 'Since you be true,
You shall be true to them who are false to you.' "

THE GOOD-MORROW

I wonder, by my troth, what thou and I
Did till we lov'd? were we not wean'd till then?
But suck'd on country pleasures, childishly?
Or snorted we in the seven sleepers' den?[1]
'Twas so; but this,[2] all pleasures fancies be.   5
If ever any beauty I did see,
Which I desir'd, and got, 'twas but a dream of thee.

And now good-morrow to our waking souls,
Which watch not one another out of fear;
For love all love of other sights controls,   10
And makes one little room an everywhere.
Let sea-discoverers to new worlds have gone,[3]
Let maps to other, worlds on worlds have shown,
Let us possess one world, each hath one, and is one.

My face in thine eye, thine in mine appears,   15
And true plain hearts do in the faces rest;
Where can we find two better hemispheres
Without sharp north, without declining west?
Whatever dies, was not mixed equally;

---

[4] Through.   [5] Characteristic.

[1] The seven sleepers of Ephesus are seven Christian youths who, according to legend, hid in a cave to escape the persecution of the emperor Decius; they fell asleep and woke up two hundred years later.   [2] Except this love of ours.   [3] Go.

If our two loves be one, or thou and I   20
Love so alike that none do slacken,[4] none can die.

THE UNDERTAKING

I have done one braver thing
    Than all the Worthies did,
And yet a braver thence doth spring,
    Which is, to keep that hid.

It were but madness now t'impart   5
    The skill of specular[1] stone,
When he which can have learn'd the art
    To cut it, can find none.

So, if I now should utter this,
    Others (because no more   10
Such stuff to work upon there is)
    Would love but as before.

But he who loveliness within
    Hath found, all outward loathes,
For he who colour loves, and skin,   15
    Loves but their[2] oldest clothes.

If, as I have, you also do
    Virtue attir'd in woman see,
And dare love that, and say so too,
    And forget the he and she;   20

And if this love, though placèd so,
    From profane men you hide,
Which will no faith on this bestow,
    Or, if they do, deride:

Then you have done a braver thing   25
    Than all the Worthies did;

[4] Neither slackens.

[1] Mirror-like. "Specular stone" is probably an allusion to the astrologer's crystal.
[2] Women's.

And a braver thence will spring,
    Which is, to keep that hid.

HOLY SONNET VII

At the round earth's imagined corners,[1] blow
Your trumpets, angels, and arise, arise
From death, you numberless infinities
Of souls, and to your scattered bodies go;
All whom the flood did, and fire shall o'erthrow;   5
All whom war, dearth, age, agues, tyrannies,
Despair, law, chance, hath slain, and you whose eyes
Shall behold God, and never taste death's woe.
But let them sleep, Lord, and me mourn a space,
For, if above all these, my sins abound,   10
'Tis late to ask abundance of Thy grace,
When we are there; here on this lowly ground,[2]
Teach me how to repent; for that's as good
As if Thou hadst sealed my pardon, with Thy blood.

THE FUNERAL

Whoever comes to shroud me, do not harm
    Nor question much
That subtle wreath[1] of hair which crowns my arm;
The mystery, the sign you must not touch,
    For 'tis my outward soul,   5
Viceroy to that which, unto heaven being gone,
    Will leave this[2] to control,
And keep these limbs, her provinces, from dissolution.

For if the sinewy thread[3] my brain lets fall
    Through every part   10
Can tie those parts, and make me one of all,
Those hairs, which upward grew, and strength and art
    Have from a better brain,
Can better do it: except[4] she meant that I

---

[1] The "four corners" of the earth.   [2] The earth.

[1] Circlet.   [2] This soul (the circlet of hair).   [3] Spinal cord.   [4] Unless.

By this should know my pain,   15
As prisoners then[5] are manacled, when they're condemn'd to die.

Whate'er she meant by it, bury it with me,
    For since I am
Love's martyr, it might breed idolatry,
If into other hands these reliques came;   20
    As 'twas humility
To afford[6] to it all that a soul can do,
    So 'tis some bravery[7]
That since you would save none of me, I bury some of you.

THE AUTUMNAL

No Spring, nor Summer beauty hath such grace,
As I have seen in one Autumnal face.
Young Beauties force our love, and that's a rape,
This doth but counsel, yet you cannot 'scape.
If 'twere a shame to love, here 'twere no shame,   5
Affection here takes Reverence's name.
Were her first years the Golden Age; that's true,
But now she's gold oft-tried and ever new.
That was her torrid and inflaming time,
This is her tolerable tropic clime.   10
Fair eyes, who asks more heat than comes from hence,
He in a fever wishes pestilence.
Call not these wrinkles, graves; if graves they were,
They were Love's graves; for else he is no where.
Yet lies not Love dead here, but here doth sit   15
Vow'd to this trench, like an anachorite.[1]
And here, till hers, which must be his death, come,
He doth not dig a grave, but build a tomb.
Here dwells he, though he sojourn ev'rywhere
In Progress, yet his standing house is here.   20
Here, where still evening is; not noon, nor night;
Where no voluptuousness, yet all delight.
In all her words, unto all hearers fit.
You may at Revels, you at Council sit.[2]
This is love's timber, youth his underwood;   25
There he, as wine in June, enrages blood,
Which then comes seasonabliest,[3] when our taste

---

[5] For that reason.   [6] Give.   [7] Boldness.

[1] Anchorite, hermit.   [2] Revels are gay, mirthful gatherings, and councils are serious, judicial ones. The sense of the line is that her conversation is both witty and wise.
[3] Most opportunely.

And appetite to other things is past.
Xerxes'[4] strange Lydian[5] love, the Platane tree,
Was lov'd for age, none being so large as she,   30
Or else because, being young, nature did bless
Her youth with age's glory, barrenness.
If we love things long sought, Age is a thing
Which we are fifty years in compassing;[6]
If transitory things, which soon decay,   35
Age must be loveliest at the latest day.
But name not Winter-faces, whose skin's slack,
Lank as an unthrift's purse,[7] but a soul's sack;[8]
Whose eyes seek light within, for all here's[9] shade;
Whose mouths are holes, rather worn out than made;   40
Whose every tooth to a several[10] place is gone
To vex their souls at Resurrection;
Name not these living Death's-heads unto me,
For these not ancient, but antique be.
I hate extremes; yet I had rather stay   45
With tombs than cradles to wear out[11] a day.
Since such love's natural lation[12] is, may still
My love descend, and journey down the hill,
Not panting after growing beauties, so
I shall ebb out with them who homeward go.[13]   50

JOHN WEBSTER
1 5 8 0 ? – 1 6 2 5 ?

ALL THE FLOWERS OF THE SPRING

All the flowers of the spring
Meet to perfume our burying;
These have but their growing prime,
And man does flourish but his time.

---

[4] Xerxes, a king of Persia, in Lydia once found a plane (platane) tree so beautiful
that he decorated it with gold and left it in the charge of a member of his elite bodyguard.
[5] Lydia was an ancient country on the Aegean Sea.   [6] Attaining.   [7] An "unthrift" is
an unthrifty person.   [8] That is, although such skin is like a purse for an unthrift, it is
like a sack (a formidable restraint) to a soul.   [9] "Here" is outside the person with a
"Winter-face."   [10] Different.   [11] Pass.   [12] An astronomical term meaning "motion
from one place to another."   [13] Go towards death.

Survey our progress from our birth: 5
We are set, we grow, we turn to earth.
Courts adieu, and all delights,
All bewitching appetites.
Sweetest breath and clearest eye,
Like perfumes, go out and die;   10
And consequently this is done
As shadows wait upon the sun.
Vain the ambition of kings
Who seek by trophies and dead things
To leave a living name behind,   15
And weave but nets to catch the wind.

A DIRGE

Call for the robin-redbreast and the wren,
Since o'er shady groves they hover,
And with leaves and flowers do cover
The friendless bodies of unburied men.
Call unto his funeral dole[1]   5
The ant, the field-mouse, and the mole,
To rear him hillocks that shall keep him warm,
And, when gay tombs are robbed, sustain no harm;
But keep the wolf far thence, that's foe to men,
For with his nails he'll dig them up again.   10

ROBERT HERRICK
1591–1674

DELIGHT IN DISORDER

A sweet disorder in the dress
Kindles in clothes a wantonness:[1]
A lawn[2] about the shoulders thrown

[1] Lamentation.

[1] Capriciousness.   [2] A scarf of fine linen.

Into a fine distraction,[3]
An erring lace, which here and there   5
Enthralls the crimson stomacher,[4]
A cuff neglectful, and thereby
Ribbands to flow confusedly,
A winning wave, deserving note,
In the tempestuous petticoat,   10
A careless shoe-string, in whose tie
I see a wild civility,
Do more bewitch me, than when art
Is too precise in every part.

TO THE VIRGINS, TO MAKE MUCH OF TIME

Gather ye rose-buds while ye may,
    Old Time is still a-flying:
And this same flower that smiles today,
    Tomorrow will be dying.

The glorious lamp of heaven, the Sun,   5
    The higher he's a-getting,
The sooner will his race be run,
    And nearer he's to setting.

That age is best, which is the first,
    When youth and blood are warmer,   10
But being spent, the worse, and worst
    Times, still succeed the former.

Then be not coy, but use your time;
    And while ye may, go marry:
For having lost but once your prime,   15
    You may for ever tarry.

UPON JULIA'S CLOTHES

Whenas[1] in silks my Julia goes,
Then, then (methinks) how sweetly flows
That liquefaction of her clothes.

[3] Confusion.   [4] Part of a dress that is near the stomach.

[1] When.

Next, when I cast mine eyes and see
That brave² vibration each way free,   5
O how that glittering taketh me!

TO PHYLLIS,¹ TO LOVE
AND LIVE WITH HIM

Live, live with me, and thou shalt see
The pleasures I'll prepare for thee:
What sweets the country can afford
Shall bless thy bed, and bless thy board.²
The soft sweet moss shall be thy bed,   5
With crawling woodbine overspread:
By which the silver-shedding streams
Shall gently melt thee into dreams.
Thy clothing, next, shall be a gown
Made of the fleece's purest down.   10
The tongues of kids shall be thy meat;
Their milk thy drink; and thou shalt eat
The paste of filberts for thy bread
With cream of cowslips butterèd.
Thy feasting-tables shall be hills   15
With Daisies spread, and Daffodils,
Where thou shalt sit, and Red-breast by,
For meat, shall give thee melody.
I'll give thee chains and carcanets³
Of Primroses and Violets.   20
A bag and bottle thou shalt have;
That⁴ richly wrought, and this⁵ as brave,⁶
So that as either shall express
The wearer's no mean shepherdess.
At shearing-times, and yearly wakes,⁷   25
When Themilis his pastime makes,
There thou shalt be, and be the wit,
Nay more, the feast, and grace of it.
On holy-days, when virgins meet
To dance the hays⁸ with nimble feet,   30
Thou shalt come forth, and then appear
The Queen of Roses for that year,
And having danc'd, 'bove all the best,
Carry the garland from the rest.

² Handsome, splendid.

¹ A generic name for a rustic maiden.   ² Table used for meals; hence, meals.
³ Necklaces.   ⁴ The bag.   ⁵ The bottle.   ⁶ Handsome.   ⁷ Local festivals of English parishes.   ⁸ A country dance.

In wicker baskets maids shall bring   35
To thee, my dearest shepherdling,
The blushing apple, bashful pear,
And shame-fac'd plum, all simp'ring there.
Walk in the groves, and thou shalt find
The name of Phyllis in the rind   40
Of every straight, and smooth-skin tree,
Where kissing that, I'll twice kiss thee.
To thee a sheep-hook I will send,
Beprank'd[9] with ribbands, to this end,
This, this alluring hook might be   45
Less for to catch a sheep, than me.
Thou shalt have possets,[10] wassails fine,
Not made of ale, but spicèd wine,
To make thy maids and self free[11] mirth,
All sitting near the glitt'ring hearth.   50
Thou shalt have ribbands, roses, rings,
Gloves, garters, stockings, shoes, and strings
Of winning colours, that shall move
Others to lust, but me to love.
These, nay, and more, thine own shall be,   55
If thou wilt love, and live with me.

CEREMONIES FOR CANDLEMAS EVE

Down with the rosemary and bays,[1]
    Down with the mistletoe;
Instead of holly, now upraise
    The greener box,[2] for show.

The holly hitherto did sway;[3]   5
    Let box now domineer,
Until the dancing Easter Day
    Or Easter's Eve appear.

Then youthful box which now hath grace
    Your houses to renew,   10
Grown old, surrender must his place
    Unto the crispèd yew.[4]

[9] Bedecked, adorned.   [10] Drinks made of hot milk and some kind of liquor.
[11] Frank and open.

[1] Boughs of bay or laurel.   [2] Boxwood.   [3] Predominate.   [4] The yew is often associated with mourning.

When yew is out, then birch comes in,
    And many flowers beside,
Both of a fresh and fragrant kin   15
    To honour Whitsuntide.[5]

Green rushes then, and sweetest bents,[6]
    With cooler oaken boughs,
Come in for comely ornaments,
    To re-adorn the house.   20
Thus times do shift; each thing his turn does hold;
New things succeed, as former things grow old.

GEORGE HERBERT

1593–1633

THE QUIP

The merry World did on a day
With his train-bands[1] and mates agree
To meet together, where I lay,
And all in sport to jeer at me.

First, Beauty crept into a rose,   5
Which when I pluck'd not, Sir, said she,
Tell me, I pray, whose hands are those?[2]
But thou shalt answer, Lord, for me.

Then Money came, and chinking still,
What tune is this, poor man? said he: 10
I heard in music you had skill.
But thou shalt answer, Lord, for me.

[5] Whitsunday and the days immediately following. Whitsunday, the seventh Sunday after Easter, in the Christian Church is the festival of the descent of the Holy Spirit upon the Apostles.   [6] Grasslike reeds.

[1] Citizen soldiers, here suggesting comrades.   [2] "What kind of hands would not pluck the rose?"

Then came brave[3] Glory puffing by
In silks that whistled, who but he?
He scarce allow'd me half an eye.   15
But thou shalt answer, Lord, for me.

Then came quick Wit and Conversation,
And he would needs a comfort be,
And, to be short, make an oration.
But thou shalt answer, Lord, for me.   20

Yet when the hour of thy design
To answer these fine things shall come,
Speak not at large; say, I am thine;
And then they have their answer home.

THE COLLAR

I struck the board;[1] and cried, "No more.
                    I will abroad.
        What? shall I ever sigh and pine?
My lines[2] and life are free; free as the road,
        Loose as the wind, as large as store.[3]   5
                Shall I be still in suit?[4]
        Have I no harvest but a thorn
        To let me blood,[5] and not restore
                What I have lost with cordial[6] fruit?
                Sure there was wine   10
Before my sighs did dry it: there was corn
        Before my tears did drown it.
        Is the year only lost to me?
                Have I no bays[7] to crown it?
No flowers, no garlands gay? all blasted?   15
                All wasted?
        Not so, my heart: but there is fruit,
                And thou hast hands.
        Recover all thy sigh-blown age
On double pleasures; leave thy cold dispute   20

---

[3] Handsomely dressed.

[1] Table.   [2] Appointed lot in life.   [3] As large as abundance.   [4] In attendance,
in suit of (favor, reward).   [5] To bleed myself, with reference to the practice of bleeding
to cure ills.   [6] Invigorating.   [7] Honorary garland of bay, or laurel.

Of what is fit and not. Forsake thy cage,
      Thy rope of sands,
Which petty thoughts have made, and made to thee
    Good cable, to enforce and draw,
      And be thy law,   25
While thou didst wink and wouldst not see.
      Away; take heed:
      I will abroad.
Call in thy death's-head there;[8] tie up thy fears.
      He that forbears   30
    To suit[9] and serve his need,
      Deserves his load."
But as I rav'd and grew more fierce and wild
      At every word,
Methought I heard one calling, *Child!*   35
    And I replied, *My Lord.*

THE PULLEY

    When God at first made man,
Having a glass of blessings standing by,
Let us, said he, pour on him all we can:
Let the world's riches, which dispersèd lie,
    Contract into a span.[1]   5

    So strength first made a way;
Then beauty flow'd, then wisdom, honour, pleasure.
When almost all was out, God made a stay,[2]
Perceiving that alone of all his treasure
    Rest in the bottom lay.   10

    For if I should, said he,
Bestow this jewel also on my creature,
He would adore my gifts instead of me,
And rest in[3] nature, not the God of nature:
    So both[4] should losers be.   15

    Yet let him keep the rest,
But keep them with repining restlessness:

[8] "Put aside thoughts of death."   [9] To seek after, woo.

[1] A definitely limited space.   [2] A halt.   [3] Be content with.   [4] Both God and
man.

Let him be rich and weary, that at least,
If goodness lead him not, yet weariness
    May toss him to my breast.   20

THOMAS CAREW

1595–1645?

SONG

Ask me no more where Jove bestows,
When June is past, the fading rose;
For in your beauty's orient deep[1]
These flowers, as in their causes,[2] sleep.

Ask me no more whither doth stray   5
The golden atoms[3] of the day;
For, in pure love, heaven did prepare
Those powders to enrich your hair.

Ask me no more whither doth haste
The nightingale when May is past;   10
For in your sweet dividing[4] throat
She winters, and keeps warm her note.

Ask me no more where those stars light
That downwards fall in dead of night;
For in your eyes they sit, and there   15
Fixèd become as in their sphere.[5]

Ask me no more if east or west
The Phoenix builds her spicy nest;[6]

[1] Lustrous depths; the adjective "orient" was once applied to exceptionally beautiful pearls and precious stones, because they came from the East.   [2] In their seeds, or origins. [3] Sunbeams.   [4] Able to articulate sweetly, harmoniously (a technical term in music). [5] According to Ptolemaic astronomy, from which seventeenth century poetry adopted images, the stars were attached to translucent spheres that were arranged around the earth. [6] The Phoenix, a mythical bird, was supposed to build for itself a pyre of spices every five hundred years, to die in the pyre's flames, and to be reborn from the ashes.

For unto you at last she flies,
And in your fragrant bosom dies.   20

JAMES SHIRLEY
1 5 9 6 – 1 6 6 6

DIRGE

The glories of our blood and state
    Are shadows, not substantial things;
There is no armour against fate;
    Death lays his icy hand on kings:
        Scepter and crown   5
        Must tumble down,
And in the dust be equal made
With the poor crooked scythe and spade.

Some men with swords may reap the field,
    And plant fresh laurels[1] where they kill,   10
But their strong nerves at last must yield;
    They tame but one another still;
        Early or late
        They stoop to fate,
And must give up their murmuring breath   15
When they, pale captives, creep to death.

The garlands wither on your brow;
    Then boast no more your mighty deeds;
Upon Death's purple[2] altar now
    See where the victor-victim bleeds;   20
        Your heads must come
        To the cold tomb:
Only the actions of the just
Smell sweet, and blossom in their dust.

[1] Win new emblems of victory (see line 17).   [2] The color of royalty and also of blood.

EDMUND WALLER

1606–1687

GO, LOVELY ROSE

    Go, lovely Rose—
Tell her that wastes her time and me
    That now she knows,
When I resemble[1] her to thee,
How sweet and fair she seems to be.   5

    Tell her that's young,
And shuns to have her graces spied,
    That hadst thou sprung
In deserts, where no men abide,
Thou must have uncommended died.   10

    Small is the worth
Of beauty from the light retired:
    Bid her come forth,
Suffer herself to be desired,
And not blush so to be admired.   15

    Then die—that she
The common fate of all things rare
    May read in thee:
How small a part of time they share
That are so wondrous sweet and fair.   20

[1] Compare.

JOHN MILTON

1608–1674

ON THE MORNING OF CHRIST'S NATIVITY

I

This is the month, and this the happy morn,
Wherein the Son of Heav'ns eternal King,
Of wedded Maid, and Virgin Mother born,
Our great redemption from above did bring;
For so the holy sages[1] once did sing,   5
     That he our deadly forfeit should release,[2]
And with his Father work[3] us a perpetual peace.

II

That glorious form, that light unsufferable,
And that far-beaming blaze of majesty,
Wherewith he wont[4] at Heav'n's high council-table   10
To sit the midst of Trinal Unity,
He laid aside; and here with us to be,
     Forsook the courts of everlasting day,
And chose with us a darksome house of mortal clay.

III

Say, Heav'nly Muse,[5] shall not thy sacred vein   15
Afford a present to the infant God?
Hast thou no verse, no hymn, or solemn strain,
To welcome him to this his new abode,
Now while the Heav'n, by the sun's team untrod,[6]
     Hath took no print of the approaching light,   20
And all the spangled host keep watch in squadrons bright?

---

[1] Old Testament prophets.   [2] That he should release us from the penalty of death incurred because we, through Adam, forfeited eternal life.   [3] Make.   [4] Was wont or accustomed.   [5] The practice (or convention) of appealing to the Muses or to a god or goddess for inspiration and of drawing metaphors from Greek or Roman mythology was so intimately associated with poetry that Milton and others used it, often very loosely, to treat even Christian themes.   [6] Helios, the Greek sun god, every morning pulled the sun across the sky in his chariot.

IV

See how from far upon the eastern road
The star-led wizards[7] haste with odors sweet:
O run, prevent[8] them with thy humble ode,
And lay it lowly at his blessed feet;   25
Have thou the honor first thy Lord to greet,
    And join thy voice unto the angel choir,
From out his secret altar touch'd with hallow'd fire.[9]

THE HYMN

I

It was the winter wild,
While the Heav'n-born child,   30
    All meanly wrapp'd, in the rude manger lies;
Nature in awe to him
Had doff'd her gaudy trim,
    With her great Master so to sympathize:
It was no season then for her   35
To wanton with the sun, her lusty paramour.

II

Only with speeches fair
She woos the gentle air
    To hide her guilty front with innocent snow,[10]
And on her naked shame,   40
Pollute with sinful blame,
    The saintly veil of maiden white to throw,
Confounded, that her Maker's eyes
Should look so near upon her foul deformities.

III

But he her fears to cease,   45
Sent down the meek-ey'd Peace;
    She, crown'd with olive green, came softly sliding
Down through the turning sphere,[11]
His ready harbinger,
    With turtle[12] wing the amorous clouds dividing,   50

---

[7] The Wise Men.   [8] Anticipate, precede.   [9] In Isaiah 6:6–7, a burning coal from the Lord's altar had the power of purifying the mouth, or speech.   [10] Original sin is here attributed to nature as well as to man.   [11] The translucent sphere that, according to ancient astronomy, contained the stars and, like all spheres, revolved about the earth. It was another convention of poetry to see the universe in terms of ancient astronomy, which was outmoded in 1543 by the Copernican system.   [12] Turtledove; the turtledove is an emblem of meekness and conjugal affection.

And waving wide her myrtle[13] wand,
She strikes a universal peace through sea and land.

IV

No war or battle's sound
Was heard the world around:
    The idle spear and shield were high uphung;   55
The hooked chariot[14] stood
Unstain'd with hostile blood;
    The trumpet spake not to the armèd throng,
And kings sat still with awful[15] eye,
As if they surely knew their sovran Lord was by.   60

V

But peaceful was the night
Wherein the Prince of Light
    His reign of peace upon the earth began:
The winds with wonder whist,[16]
Smoothly the waters kiss'd,   65
    Whispering new joys to the mild ocëan,
Who now hath quite forgot to rave,
While birds of calm sit brooding on the charmèd wave.

VI

The stars with deep amaze[17]
Stand fix'd in steadfast gaze,   70
    Bending one way their precious influence,[18]
And will not take their flight
For all the morning light,
    Or Lucifer[19] that often warn'd them thence;
But in their glimmering orbs did glow,   75
Until their Lord himself bespake, and bid them go.

VII

And though the shady gloom
Had given day her room,[20]
    The sun himself withheld his wonted speed,
And hid his head for shame,   80
As his inferior flame
    The new-enlight'n'd world no more should need;

---

[13] An emblem of love.   [14] A war chariot from which sharp hooks or blades project.
[15] Full of awe, or reverence.   [16] Hushed.   [17] Amazement, awe.   [18] According to astrology, the stars influence the lives of human beings.   [19] The morning star, usually, but sometimes the sun. *Lucifer* means "light-bearer."   [20] That is, night ("the shady gloom") made room, by passing, for day.

He saw a greater sun appear
Than his bright throne, or burning axletree[21] could bear.

VIII

The shepherds on the lawn,[22]   85
Or ere[23] the point of dawn,
    Sat simply chatting in a rustic row;
Full little thought they then
That the mighty Pan[24]
    Was kindly come to live with them below;   90
Perhaps their loves, or else their sheep,
Was all that did their silly[25] thoughts so busy keep.

IX

When such music sweet
Their hearts and ears did greet,
    As never was by mortal finger struck,   95
Divinely warblèd voice
Answering the stringèd noise,[26]
    As all their souls in blissful rapture took:[27]
The air, such pleasure loth to lose,
With thousand echoes still prolongs each heav'nly close.[28]   100

X

Nature that heard such sound
Beneath the hollow round
    Of Cynthia's seat,[29] the airy region thrilling,
Now was almost won
To think her part was done,   105
    And that her reign had here its last fulfilling;
She knew such harmony alone
Could hold all Heav'n and Earth in happier union.

XI

At last surrounds their sight[30]
A globe of circular light,   110
    That with long beams the shame-fac'd Night array'd;
The helmèd Cherubim
And sworded Seraphim
    Are seen in glitttering ranks with wings display'd,

---

[21] Allusions to the sun god and his chariot.   [22] Pasture.   [23] Even before.
[24] Christ is here identified with the Greek god of nature. Shepherds might be supposed to
see God in nature especially.   [25] Simple, unsophisticated.   [26] Melodious sound.
[27] Captivated, charmed.   [28] Cadence.   [29] The sphere of the moon (Cynthia), which
was just outside that of the earth (Nature).   [30] Sight of them.

Harping in loud and solemn choir, 115

With unexpressive[31] notes to Heav'n's new-born Heir.

XII

Such music (as 'tis said)
Before was never made,
    But[32] when of old the sons of morning[33] sung,
While the Creator great 120
His constellations set,
    And the well-balanc'd world on hinges hung,
And cast the dark foundations deep,
And bid the welt'ring waves their oozy channel keep.

XIII

Ring out, ye crystal spheres, 125
Once bless our human ears
    (If ye have power to touch our senses so),
And let your silver chime[34]
Move in melodious time;
    And let the bass of Heaven's deep organ blow, 130
And with your ninefold[35] harmony
Make up full consort to th' angelic symphony.

XIV

For if such holy song
Enwrap our fancy long,
    Time will run back, and fetch the age of gold,[36] 135
And speckl'd[37] Vanity
Will sicken soon and die,
    And leprous sin will melt from earthly mold,
And Hell itself will pass away,
And leave her dolorous mansions to the peering day. 140

XV

Yea, Truth and Justice then
Will down return to men,
    Orb'd in a rainbow; and, like[38] glories wearing,
Mercy will sit between,

---

[31] Inexpressible.   [32] Except.   [33] The Lord asked Job, "Where were you when I laid the foundation of the earth? . . . On what were its bases sunk, or who laid its corner-stone, when the morning stars sang together, and all the sons of God shouted for joy?" (Job 38:4–7).   [34] Music.   [35] The universe contained nine spheres (see line 125).   [36] The golden age of man (rather than of Greece), before the Fall.   [37] Blemished.   [38] (The) similar.

Thron'd in celestial sheen, 145
    With radiant feet the tissued[39] clouds down steering,
And Heav'n, as at some festival,
Will open wide the gates of her high palace hall.

XVI

But wisest Fate says no,
This must not yet be so, 150
    The Babe lies yet in smiling infancy,
That on the bitter cross
Must redeem our loss:
    So both himself and us to glorify;
Yet first to those ychain'd[40] in sleep, 155
The wakeful trump of doom[41] must thunder through the deep,

XVII

With such a horrid clang
As on Mount Sinai rang
    While the red fire and smould'ring clouds outbrake:[42]
The aged Earth aghast 160
With terror of that blast,
    Shall from the surface to the center shake,
When at the world's last session
The dreadful Judge in middle air shall spread his throne.

XVIII

And then at last our bliss 165
Full and perfect is,
    But now begins; for from this happy day
Th' old Dragon[43] under ground,
In straiter limits bound,
    Not half so far casts his usurpèd sway, 170
And, wroth to see his kingdom fail,
Swinges[44] the scaly horror of his folded tail.

XIX

The oracles are dumb,[45]
No voice or hideous hum
    Runs through the archèd roof in words deceiving. 175

---

[39] Richly woven (with silver).   [40] The prefix *y* survives from an Old English form of the word.   [41] Doomsday trumpet.   [42] "On the morning of the third day there were thunders and lightnings, and a thick cloud upon the mountain, and a very loud trumpet blast, so that all the people who were in the camp trembled" (Exodus 19:16).   [43] Satan is called "the great dragon" in Revelation 12:9.   [44] Lashes.   [45] There is a legend that when Christ was born, pagan oracles could no longer prophesy.

Apollo from his shrine
Can no more divine,
    With hollow shriek the steep of Delphos[46] leaving.
No nightly trance, or breathèd spell,
Inspires the pale-ey'd priest from the prophetic cell.   180

        XX

The lonely mountains o'er,
And the resounding shore,
    A voice of weeping heard, and loud lament;
From haunted spring and dale,
Edg'd with poplar pale,   185
    The parting Genius[47] is with sighing sent;
With flow'r-inwov'n tresses torn
The nymphs in twilight shade of tangled thickets mourn.

        XXI

In consecrated earth,
And on the holy hearth,   190
    The Lars[48] and Lemures[49] moan with midnight plaint;
In urns and altars round,
A drear and dying sound
    Affrights the Flamens[50] at their service quaint;[51]
And the chill marble seems to sweat,[52]   195
While each peculiar power forgoes his wonted seat.

        XXII

Peor and Baalim[53]
Forsake their temples dim,
    With that twice-batter'd god[54] of Palestine;
And moonèd Ashtaroth,[55]   200
Heav'n's queen and mother both,
    Now sits not girt with tapers' holy shine;
The Libyc Hammon shrinks his horn,
In vain the Tyrian maids their wounded Thammuz mourn.

    [46] Delphi. Apollo, god of light and healing, was thought to speak to mortals at Delphi in cryptic messages uttered by his medium and interpreted by priests.   [47] The spirit that belongs to and guards a particular place. Milton is citing another illustration of the death of paganism.   [48] Lares (singular: *Lar*), Roman household gods.   [49] (Singular: *Lemur*), Roman spirits of the dead.   [50] A flamen is a priest devoted to serving a particular god.   [51] Strange, curious.   [52] The statue of the god seems to sweat in apprehension of the god's fate.   [53] These names and others in this and the following stanza belong to various Eastern deities of the ancient world.   [54] Dagon, whose image twice fell down before the ark of the Lord (see I Samuel 5:1–5).   [55] This goddess was sometimes associated with the moon.

XXIII

And sullen Moloch, fled,   205
Hath left in shadows dread
    His burning idol all of blackest hue;
In vain with cymbals' ring
They call the grisly king,
    In dismal dance about the furnace blue;   210
The brutish gods[56] of Nile as fast,
Isis and Orus, and the dog Anubis haste.

XXIV

Nor is Osiris seen
In Memphian[57] grove or green,
    Trampling the unshow'r'd grass[58] with lowings loud: 215
Nor can he be at rest
Within his sacred chest,[59]
    Nought but profoundest Hell can be his shroud;
In vain with timbrel'd anthems dark
The sable-stolèd[60] sorcerers bear his worship'd ark.   220

XXV

He feels from Judah's land
The dreaded Infant's hand,
    The rays of Bethlehem blind his dusky eyn;[61]
Nor all the gods beside
Longer dare abide,   225
Nor Typhon[62] huge ending in snaky twine:
Our Babe, to show his Godhead true,
Can in his swaddling bands control the damnèd crew.

XXVI

So when the sun in bed,
Curtain'd with cloudy red,   230
    Pillows his chin upon an orient[63] wave,
The flocking shadows pale
Troop to th' infernal jail;
    Each fetter'd ghost slips to his several[64] grave,

[56] The gods referred to were represented as animals or as human beings with animal parts. [57] Memphis was the capital of ancient Egypt, where Osiris, who was represented as a bull, was the chief god. [58] It seldom rains in Egypt. [59] Images of Osiris were carried in small chests or arks. [60] Black-stoled. [61] Eyes (archaic). [62] A Greek monster that was half man, half snake. [63] Luxurious (because pearls and other gems and rich fabrics were associated with the Orient). [64] Particular, own.

And the yellow-skirted Fays
Fly after the night-steeds, leaving their moon-lov'd maze.[65]

XXVII

But see, the Virgin blest
Hath laid her Babe to rest.
　　Time is our tedious song should here have ending;
Heav'n's youngest-teemèd star[66]
Hath fix'd her polish'd car,
　　Her sleeping Lord with handmaid lamp attending;
And all about the courtly stable
Bright-harness'd[67] angels sit in order serviceable.[68]

ON SHAKESPEARE

What[1] needs my Shakespeare for his honor'd bones
The labor of an age in pilèd stones,
Or that his hallow'd relics should be hid
Under a star-ypointing[2] pyramid?
Dear son of memory, great heir of fame, 5
What need'st thou such weak witness of thy name?
Thou in our wonder and astonishment
Hast built thyself a livelong[3] monument.
For whilst to th' shame of slow-endeavoring art
Thy easy numbers[4] flow, and that each heart 10
Hath from the leaves of thy unvalu'd[5] book
Those Delphic[6] lines with deep impression took,
Then thou, our fancy of itself bereaving,
Dost make us marble with too much conceiving,[7]
And so sepúlcher'd in such pomp dost lie, 15
That kings for such a tomb would wish to die.

[65] Labyrinth of paths and trees, or forest. [66] Latest born star (the star of Bethlehem). [67] Brightly armored. [68] In an order suggesting their willingness to serve.

[1] Why. [2] The prefix *y* survives from an Old English form of the word. [3] Longlasting. [4] Verses, measures. [5] Priceless, invaluable. [6] Oracular or inspired, as the priestess was who spoke for Apollo at Delphi. [7] Imagining.

L'ALLEGRO[1]

Hence, loathèd Melancholy,
    Of Cerberus[2] and blackest Midnight born,[3]
In Stygian cave[4] forlorn,
    'Mongst horrid shapes and shrieks, and sights unholy;
Find out some uncouth[5] cell,   5
    Where brooding darkness spreads his jealous wings,
And the night-raven sings;
    There, under ebon shades, and low-brow'd rocks,
As ragged as thy locks,
    In dark Cimmerian[6] desert ever dwell.   10
But come, thou goddess fair and free,
In Heav'n yclept[7] Euphrosyne,[8]
And by men, heart-easing Mirth,
Whom lovely Venus,[9] at a birth,
With two sister Graces more   15
To ivy-crownèd Bacchus[10] bore;
Or whether (as some sager sing)
The frolic wind that breathes the spring,
Zephyr[11] with Aurora[12] playing,
As he met her once a-Maying,   20
There on beds of violets blue,
And fresh-blown roses wash'd in dew,
Fill'd her with thee, a daughter fair,
So buxom,[13] blithe, and debonair.[14]
Haste thee, nymph, and bring with thee   25
Jest and youthful Jollity,
Quips and Cranks,[15] and wanton[16] Wiles,
Nods, and Becks,[17] and wreathèd Smiles,
Such as hang on Hebe's[18] cheek,
And love to live in dimple sleek;   30
Sport, that wrinkled Care derides,
And Laughter holding both his sides.
Come, and trip it as ye go
On the light fantastic toe,

---

[1] (Italian) The cheerful man.   [2] In Greek mythology, a many-headed dog with a mane and a tail of snakes that guarded the gate of Hades, the underworld, where spirits of the dead (both good and evil) were believed to go.   [3] This "myth" is of Milton's invention.   [4] Hades was surrounded by the river Styx.   [5] Unknown, unfamiliar.   [6] The Cimmerians, according to Homer, were a people "on whom the sun never looks." He placed them in a land of never-ending darkness just this side of Hades.   [7] Called, named (archaic).   [8] One of the Graces; her name means "joy."   [9] In Roman mythology, the goddess of love.   [10] The Roman god of wine and joy. Zeus, or Jove, is usually considered the father of the Graces.   [11] The west wind in classical mythology. [12] Roman goddess of the dawn. She is usually thought of as the mother of Zephyr. [13] Gracious, lively.   [14] Courteous.   [15] Twists or fanciful turns of speech; conceits. [16] Extravagant, impetuous.   [17] Bows, curtsies.   [18] Greek goddess of youth.

And in thy right hand lead with thee   35
The mountain nymph, sweet Liberty;
And if I give thee honor due,
Mirth, admit me of thy crew,
To live with her, and live with thee,
In unreprovèd[19] pleasures free: 40
To hear the lark begin his flight,
And, singing, startle the dull night,
From his watch-tow'r in the skies,
Till the dappled dawn doth rise;
Then to come in spite of sorrow,   45
And at my window bid good-morrow,
Through the sweet-briar, or the vine,
Or the twisted eglantine,[20]
While the cock, with lively din,
Scatters the rear of darkness thin,   50
And to the stack, or the barn door,
Stoutly struts his dames before;
Oft list'ning how the hounds and horn
Cheerly rouse the slumb'ring morn,
From the side of some hoar[21] hill,   55
Through the high wood echoing shrill;
Sometimes walking not unseen
By hedgerow elms, on hillocks green,
Right against[22] the eastern gate,
Where the great sun begins his state,[23]   60
Rob'd in flames, and amber light,
The clouds in thousand liveries dight;[24]
While the plowman near at hand,
Whistles o'er the furrow'd land,
And the milkmaid singeth blithe,   65
And the mower whets his scythe,
And every shepherd tells his tale[25]
Under the hawthorn in the dale.
Straight mine eye hath caught new pleasures
Whilst the landskip[26] round it measures: 70
Russet lawns and fallows[27] gray,
Where the nibbling flocks do stray;
Mountains on whose barren breast
The laboring clouds do often rest;
Meadows trim, with daisies pied,[28]   75
Shallow brooks, and rivers wide.
Towers, and battlements it sees
Bosom'd high in tufted trees,

---

[19] Innocent.   [20] Probably woodbine or honeysuckle. (Eglantine is another name for sweetbrier.)   [21] Gray, from absence of foliage.   [22] Towards.   [23] Stately procession.   [24] Dressed.   [25] Counts his sheep.   [26] Landscape.   [27] Plowed fields. [28] Parti-colored, speckled.

Where perhaps some beauty lies,
The cynosure of neighboring eyes. 80
Hard by, a cottage chimney smokes,
From betwixt two agèd oaks,
Where Corydon[29] and Thyrsis, met,
Are at their savory dinner set
Of herbs, and other country messes,[30] 85
Which the neat-handed Phillis dresses;
And then in haste her bow'r[31] she leaves,
With Thestylis to bind the sheaves;
Or, if the earlier season lead,
To the tannèd haycock in the mead. 90
Sometimes with secure[32] delight
The upland hamlets will invite,
When the merry bells ring round,
And the jocund rebecks[33] sound
To many a youth, and many a maid 95
Dancing in the checker'd shade;
And young and old come forth to play
On a sunshine holiday,
Till the livelong daylight fail;
Then to the spicy, nut-brown ale, 100
With stories told of many a feat,
How faery Mab[34] the junkets[35] eat;
She was pinch'd and pull'd, she said;
And he, by friar's lanthorn[36] led,
Tells how the drudging Goblin[37] sweat 105
To earn his cream-bowl duly set,
When in one night, ere glimpse of morn,
His shadowy flail hath thresh'd the corn
That ten day-laborers could not end;
Then lies him down the lubber[38] fiend, 110
And, stretch'd out all the chimney's length,
Basks at the fire his hairy strength;
And, crop-full,[39] out of doors he flings
Ere the first cock his matin rings.
Thus done the tales, to bed they creep, 115
By whispering winds soon lull'd asleep.
Tow'red cities please us then,
And the busy hum of men,
Where throngs of knights and barons bold,

---

[29] This and other names in the following lines are type names of shepherds and shepherdesses. [30] Dishes. [31] Cottage. [32] Confident. [33] Medieval fiddles. [34] Queen of the fairies. [35] Sweetened curds served with cream; *eat* (pronounced "ett") is the past tense. [36] Jack-o'-lantern, will-o'-the-wisp, *ignis fatuus*. [37] Hobgoblin, or Robin Goodfellow, an ugly sprite sometimes mischievous and sometimes (as here) helpful to the family. [38] Drudging. [39] With a full crop, or stomach.

In weeds[40] of peace, high triumphs[41] hold,   120
With store of ladies, whose bright eyes
Rain influence,[42] and judge the prize
Of wit, or arms, while both contend
To win her grace whom all commend.
There let Hymen[43] oft appear   125
In saffron robe, with taper clear,
And pomp, and feast, and revelry,
With masque,[44] and antique pageantry,
Such sights as youthful poets dream
On summer eves by haunted stream.   130
Then to the well-trod stage anon,
If Jonson's[45] learnèd sock[46] be on,
Or sweetest Shakespeare, Fancy's child,
Warble his native wood-notes wild.
And ever against eating cares,   135
Lap me in soft Lydian airs,[47]
Married to immortal verse,
Such as the meeting[48] soul may pierce
In notes, with many a winding bout[49]
Of linkèd sweetness long drawn out,   140
With wanton heed, and giddy cunning,[50]
The melting voice through mazes running,
Untwisting all the chains that tie
The hidden soul of harmony;
That Orpheus' self[51] may heave his head   145
From golden slumber on a bed
Of heap'd Elysian[52] flow'rs, and hear
Such strains as would have won the ear
Of Pluto, to have quite set free
His half-regain'd Eurydice.   150
These delights, if thou canst give,
Mirth, with thee, I mean to live.

---

[40] Garments.   [41] Festivities.   [42] That is, as the stars, according to astrology, influence men's lives.   [43] The god of marriage.   [44] Dramatic interlude performed by masked actors.   [45] Ben Jonson (1572–1637), English dramatist who wrote comedies in the classical tradition.   [46] In ancient Greece, the low shoe worn by comic actors, as opposed to the buskin, or raised shoe, worn for tragedy.   [47] In ancient Greece, the Lydian "mode" of music was soft and delicate.   [48] Responsive.   [49] Turn, phrase.   [50] Note the unusual adjective-noun combinations. Milton is suggesting a singer (or poet) abandoned to his art.   [51] In Greek mythology, Orpheus was a musician whose wife Eurydice, was killed by a snake. Orpheus went to the underworld, Hades, to find her. He played the lyre so well that Pluto, ruler of Hades, permitted him to take Eurydice back, provided that he did not look at her during the journey to the upper world. When nearly there, however, he no longer heard her behind him and turned to look. Eurydice returned to Hades.   [52] Delightful, from Elysium, the abode of the blessed in Greek mythology.

HOW SOON HATH TIME

How soon hath Time, the subtle thief of youth,
    Stol'n on his wing my three and twentieth year!
    My hasting days fly on with full career,[1]
    But my late spring no bud or blossom shew'th.
Perhaps my semblance might deceive the truth,   5
    That I to manhood am arriv'd so near,
    And inward ripeness doth much less appear,
    That[2] some more timely-happy spirits endu'th.[3]
Yet be it less or more, or soon or slow,
    It shall be still in strictest measure ev'n   10
    To that same lot, however mean or high,
Toward which Time leads me, and the will of Heav'n;
    All is, if I have grace to use it so,
    As ever in my great task-Master's eye.

WHEN I CONSIDER HOW MY LIGHT IS SPENT

When I consider how my light is spent
    Ere half my days, in this dark world and wide,
    And that one talent[1] which is death to hide,
    Lodg'd with me useless, though my soul more bent
To serve therewith my Maker, and present   5
    My true account, lest he returning chide,
    "Doth God exact day-labor, light denied?"
    I fondly[2] ask. But Patience, to prevent
That murmur, soon replies, "God doth not need
    Either man's work or his own gifts; who best   10
    Bear his mild yoke,[3] they serve him best; his state
Is kingly: thousands at his bidding speed,
    And post o'er land and ocean without rest:
    They also serve who only stand and wait."

[1] Speed.   [2] Refers to *manhood*.   [3] Endows.

[1] See the "Parable of the Talents," Matthew 25:14–30.   [2] Foolishly.   [3] The yoke of servitude, bondage.

SIR JOHN SUCKLING

1609–1642

WHY SO PALE AND WAN?

Why so pale and wan, fond lover?
    Prithee, why so pale?
Will, when looking well can't move her,
    Looking ill prevail?
    Prithee, why so pale?   5

Why so dull and mute, young sinner?
    Prithee, why so mute?
Will, when speaking well can't win her,
    Saying nothing do't?
    Prithee, why so mute?   10

Quit, quit for shame, this will not move:
    This cannot take her.
If of herself she will not love,
    Nothing can make her:
    The devil take her!   15

A BALLAD UPON A WEDDING

I tell thee, Dick,[1] where I have been,
Where I the rarest things have seen,
    O, things without compare!
Such sights again cannot be found
In any place on English ground,   5
    Be it at wake[2] or fair.

At Charing Cross, hard by the way
Where we (thou know'st) do sell our hay[3]
    There is a house with stairs;

[1] The names used in this poem are type names for rustics.   [2] Local annual festival of an English parish, an occasion of merrymaking.   [3] London's Charing Cross and Haymarket are near one another.

And there did I see coming down   10
Such folk as are not in our town,
    Vorty,[4] at least, in pairs.

Amongst the rest, one pest'lent fine[5]
(His beard no bigger, though, than thine)
    Walk'd on before the rest;   15
Our landlord looks like nothing to him;
The King (God bless him!), 'twould undo him
    Should he go still[6] so dress'd.

At Course-a-Park,[7] without all doubt,
He should have first been taken out   20
    By all the maids i' th' town:
Though lusty Roger there had been,
Or little George upon the Green,[8]
    Or Vincent of the Crown.[9]

But wot you what?[10] the youth was going   25
To make an end of all his wooing;
    The parson for him staid:[11]
Yet by his leave (for all his haste)
He did not so much wish all past
    (Perchance) as did the maid.   30

The maid—and thereby hangs a tale;
For such a maid no Whitson-ale[12]
    Could ever yet produce:
No grape, that's kindly[13] ripe, could be
So round, so plump, so soft as she,   35
    Nor half so full of juice.

Her finger was so small, the ring
Would not stay on, which they did bring;
    It was too wide a peck:
And to say truth (for out it must)   40
It look'd like the great collar (just)
    About our young colt's neck.

---

[4] Forty (the poem in part imitates rustic pronunciation).   [5] Fine gentleman, with the countryman's scorn of city manners.   [6] Always go about.   [7] A country game in which a girl called the name of a young man, who then chased her.   [8] A piece of grassy land, a small park (George lives near the green).   [9] Probably an inn.   [10] Do you know what?   [11] Stayed; that is, waited.   [12] A parish festival held on Whitsunday, the seventh Sunday after Easter.   [13] Naturally, completely.

Her feet beneath her petticoat,
Like little mice, stole in and out,
    As if they fear'd the light: 45
But O, she dances such a way!
No sun upon an Easter-day
    Is half so fine a sight.

He would have kiss'd her once or twice;
But she would not, she was so nice,[14]   50
    She would not do 't in sight:
And then she look'd as who should say,
'I will do what I list[15] to-day,
    And you shall do 't at night.'

Her cheeks so rare a white was on,   55
No daisy makes comparison
    (Who sees them is undone);
For streaks of red were mingled there,
Such as are on a Katherne pear[16]
    (The side that's next the sun).   60

Her lips were red; and one was thin,
Compar'd to that was next her chin
    (Some bee had stung it newly):
But, Dick, her eyes so guard her face,
I durst no more upon them gaze   65
    Than on the sun in July.

Her mouth so small, when she does speak,
Thou 'dst swear her teeth her words did break,
    That they might passage get;
But she so handled still the matter,   70
They came as good as ours, or better,
    And are not spent a whit.[17]

If wishing should be any sin,
The parson himself had guilty been
    (She look'd that day so purely[18]);   75
And, did the youth so oft the feat
At night, as some did in conceit,[19]
    It would have spoil'd him surely.

[14] Shy, reluctant.   [15] Want.   [16] Catherine pear (a small variety).   [17] That is, are not even a little deprived of force.   [18] Pure.   [19] Fancy, imagination.

Just in the nick the cook knock'd thrice,
And all the waiters in a trice[20]   80
    His summons did obey:
Each serving-man, with dish in hand,
March'd boldly up, like our train'd band,
    Presented, and away.

When all the meat was on the table,   85
What man of knife or teeth was able
    To stay to be intreated?[21]
And this the very reason was—
Before the parson could say grace,
    The company was seated.   90

The bus'ness of the kitchen's great,
For it is fit that man should eat;
    Nor was it there deni'd—
Passion o' me, how I run on!
There's that that would be thought upon   95
    (I trow[22]) besides the bride.

Now hats fly off, and youths carouse,
Healths first go round, and then the house:[23]
    The bride's came thick and thick;
And, when 'twas nam'd another's health,   100
Perhaps he made it hers by stealth;
    (And who could help it, Dick?)

O' th' sudden up they rise and dance;
Then sit again and sigh, and glance;
    Then dance again and kiss: 105
Thus several ways the time did pass,
Whilst ev'ry woman wished her place,
    And every man wished his.

By this time all were stol'n aside
To counsel and undress the bride;   110
    But that he must not know:
But yet 'twas thought he guess'd her mind,
And did not mean to stay behind
    Above an hour or so.

[20] In an instant, at once.   [21] To wait to be entreated.   [22] Trust, think.
[23] That is, healths, and then the house, are drunk to.

When in he came, Dick, there she lay
Like new-fall'n snow melting away
('Twas time, I trow, to part):
Kisses were now the only stay,
Which soon she gave, as who would say,
God b' w' ye, with all my heart.

But, just as Heav'ns would have, to cross it,
In came the bridemaids with the posset:[24]
The bridegroom eat[25] in spite;
For, had he left the women to 't,
It would have cost two hours to do 't,
Which were too much that night.

At length the candle's out; and now
All that they had not done they do:
What that is, who can tell?
But I believe it was no more
Than thou and I have done before
With Bridget and with Nell.

THE CONSTANT LOVER

Out upon it![1] I have lov'd
Three whole days together;
And am like to love three more,
If it prove fair weather.

Time shall moult away his wings,
Ere he shall discover
In the whole wide world again
Such a constant[2] lover.

But the spite on't is, no praise
Is due at all to me:
Love with me had made no stays,[3]
Had it any been but she.

[24] A drink of hot milk and ale, wine, or other liquor.   [25] This is the past tense.

[1] Phrase implying abhorrence.   [2] Faithful   [3] Standstill.

Had it any been but she,
    And that very face,
There had been at least ere this   15
    A dozen dozen in her place.

RICHARD CRASHAW
1 6 1 3 ? – 1 6 4 9

WISHES TO HIS (SUPPOSED) MISTRESS

Whoe'er she be,
That not impossible she
That shall command my heart and me;

Where'er she lie,
Lock'd up from mortal eye,   5
In shady leaves of destiny:

Till that ripe birth
Of studied fate stand forth,
And teach[1] her fair steps to our earth;

Till that divine   10
Idea take a shrine
Of crystal flesh, through which to shine;

Meet you her, my wishes,
Bespeak her to[2] my blisses,
And be ye call'd my absent kisses.   15

I wish her beauty,
That owes not all his[3] duty
To gaudy tire,[4] or glist'ring shoe-tie;

    [1] Guide.   [2] Speak to her about.   [3] Its.   [4] Attire.

Something more than
Taffeta or tissue can,[5]   20
Or rampant feather, or rich fan;

More than the spoil
Of shop, or silkworm's toil,
Or a bought blush, or a set smile;

A face that's best
By its own beauty dress'd,   25
And can alone commend[6] the rest;

A face made up
Out of no other shop
Than what nature's white hand sets ope;   30

A cheek where youth
And blood, with pen of truth
Write what the reader sweetly ru'th;[7]

A cheek where grows
More than a morning rose,   35
Which to no box his being owes;

Lips where all day
A lover's kiss may play,
Yet carry nothing[8] thence away;

Looks that oppress[9]   40
Their richest tires, but dress
And clothe their simplest nakedness.

Eyes that displace
The neighbour[10] diamond, and out-face
That sunshine by their own sweet grace;   45

Tresses that wear
Jewels but to declare
How much themselves more precious are;

    [5] Can manage.   [6] Recommend.   [7] Rueth, regards with compassion.   [8] None
, of the color or form.   [9] Overpower by contrast.   [10] Similar.

Whose native ray
Can tame the wanton day[11]   50
Of gems, that in their bright shades play—

Each ruby there,
Or pearl that dare appear,
Be its own blush, be its own tear;

A well-tam'd heart,   55
For whose more noble smart
Love may be long choosing a dart;

Eyes that bestow
Full quivers[12] on love's bow,
Yet pay less arrows than they owe;   60

Smiles that can warm
The blood, yet teach[13] a charm,
That chastity shall take no harm;

Blushes that bin[14]
The burnish of no sin,   65
Nor flames of aught too hot within;

Joys that confess
Virtue their mistress,
And have no other head to dress;

Fears, fond and flight,[15]   70
As the coy bride's, when night
First does the longing lover right;

Tears, quickly fled,
And vain, as those are shed
For a dying maidenhead;   75

Days that need borrow
No part of their good morrow
From a fore-spent night of sorrow;

11 Light.   12 Containers for arrows.   13 Cast.   14 Be, are.   15 Foolish and
fleeting.

Days that, in spite
Of darkness, by the light
Of a clear mind are day all night;   80

Nights, sweet as they,
Made short by lover's play,
Yet long by th' absence of the day;

Life that dares send   85
A challenge to his end,
And, when it comes, say, "Welcome, friend!"

Sidneian showers
Of sweet discourse,[16] whose powers
Can crown old winter's head with flowers;   90

Soft silken hours,
Open suns, shady bowers;
'Bove all, nothing within that lowers;

Whate'er delight
Can make day's forehead bright,   95
Or give down to the wings of night.

In her whole frame
Have nature all the name,[17]
Art and ornament the shame.

Her flattery,   100
Picture and poesy:
Her counsel her own virtue be.[18]

I wish her store
Of worth may leave her poor
Of wishes; and I wish—no more.   105

Now if time knows
That her[19] whose radiant brows
Weave them[20] a garland of my vows;

[16] A reference to the elegant conversations of Sir Philip Sidney's prose romance,
Arcadia (1590), which was still widely read. [17] Credit. [18] That is, no matter how
she is flattered in paintings and poems, let her accept only the judgment her own virtue
gives. [19] Person. [20] Themselves.

Her whose just bays[21]
My future hopes can raise,[22]   110
A trophy to her present praise:

Her that dares be
What these lines wish to see:
I seek no further—it is she.

'Tis she, and here   115
Lo I unclothe and clear
My wishes' cloudy character.

May she enjoy it
Whose merit dare apply it,
But modesty dares still deny it.   120

Such worth as this is
Shall fix my flying wishes,
And determine them to[23] kisses.

Let her full glory,
My fancies, fly before ye;   125
Be ye my fictions—but her story.

RICHARD LOVELACE
1 6 1 8 – 1 6 5 8

TO AMARANTHA, THAT SHE WOULD
DISHEVELE HER HAIR

Amarantha sweet and fair,
Ah, braid no more that shining hair!
As my curious hand or eye,
Hovering round thee, let it fly.

[21] Garlands of bay, or laurel, signifying excellence.   [22] That is, I hope I can in the
future create.   [23] Resolve them into.

Let it fly as unconfin'd
As its calm ravisher, the wind,
Who hath left his darling, th' East,
To wanton o'er that spicy nest.   5

Ev'ry tress must be confest,[1]
But neatly tangled at the best;   10
Like a clue of golden thread,
Most excellently ravellèd.

Do not then wind up that light
In ribbands, and o'ercloud in night
Like the sun in's early ray,   15
But shake your head, and scatter day!

TO ALTHEA, FROM PRISON[1]

When Love with unconfinèd wings
    Hovers within my gates,
And my divine Althea brings
    To whisper at the grates;[2]
When I lie tangled in her hair   5
    And fetter'd to her eye,
The gods that wanton in the air
    Know no such liberty.

When flowing cups run swiftly round,
    With no allaying Thames,[3]   10
Our careless heads with roses[4] bound,
    Our hearts with loyal flames;
When thirsty grief in wine we steep,
    When healths and draughts go free,
Fishes that tipple in the deep   15
    Know no such liberty.

When, like committed[5] linnets, I
    With shriller throat shall sing

[1] Admitted to, shown.

[1] Lovelace, a passionate supporter of the king (see stanzas 2 and 3), was imprisoned in 1642 by the Puritan Parliament when he presented them with a petition from the Loyalists of the Country of Kent.   [2] Prison bars.   [3] The Thames River; that is, water.   [4] The rose is the emblem of England, hence, a symbol of loyalty.   [5] Imprisoned, caged.

The sweetness, mercy, majesty,
    And glories of my King;
When I shall voice aloud how good
    He is, how great should be,
Enlargèd winds, that curl[6] the flood,
    Know no such liberty.

20

Stone walls do not a prison make,
    Nor iron bars a cage;
Minds innocent and quiet take
    That for an hermitage;
If I have freedom in my love,
    And in my soul am free,
Angels alone, that soar above,
    Enjoy such liberty.

25

30

TO LUCASTA, GOING TO THE WARS

Tell me not, Sweet, I am unkind,
That from the nunnery
Of thy chaste breast and quiet mind,
To war and arms I fly.

True, a new mistress now I chase,
The first foe in the field;
And with a stronger faith embrace
A sword, a horse, a shield.

5

Yet this inconstancy is such
As you too shall adore;
I could not love thee, Dear, so much,
Lov'd I not honour more.

10

THE GRASSHOPPER
To My Noble Friend, Mr. Charles Cotton

O thou that swing'st upon the waving hair
    Of some well-fillèd oaten beard,
Drunk ev'ry night with a delicious tear
    Dropp'd thee from heav'n, where now th'art reared;

[6] Push back.

The joys of earth and air are thine entire,   5
    That with thy feet and wings dost hop and fly;
And when thy poppy works thou dost retire
    To thy carv'd acorn-bed to lie.

Up with the day, the sun thou welcom'st then,
    Sport'st in the gilt-plats¹ of his beams,   10
And all these merry days mak'st merry men,
    Thyself, and melancholy streams.

But ah, the sickle! Golden ears are cropp'd;
    Ceres and Bacchus² bid good night;
Sharp frosty fingers all your flow'rs have topp'd,³   15
    And what scythes spar'd, winds shave off quite.

Poor verdant⁴ fool! and now green ice! thy joys
    Large and as lasting as thy perch of grass,
Bid us lay in 'gainst winter, rain, and poise⁵
    Their floods with an o'erflowing glass.   20

Thou best of men and friends! we will create
    A genuine summer in each other's breast;
And spite of this cold time and frozen fate
    Thaw us a warm seat to⁶ our rest.

Our sacred hearths shall burn eternally   25
    As vestal flames; the North Wind, he
Shall strike his frost-stretch'd wings, dissolve, and fly
    This Ætna⁷ in epitome.

Dropping December shall come weeping in,
    Bewail th' usurping of his reign;   30
But when in show'rs of old Greek⁸ we begin,
    Shall cry, he hath his crown again.

Night as clear Hesper⁹ shall our tapers¹⁰ whip
    From the light casements where we play,

---

¹ Braids (see line 1).   ² The goddess of agriculture and the god of wine, respectively, in Roman mythology.   ³ Picked.   ⁴ Green, inexperienced.   ⁵ Weight, worries.   ⁶ For.   ⁷ The Aetna (volcano) of "our sacred hearths."   ⁸ Old Greek wine.   ⁹ The evening star.   ¹⁰ Candles.

1053   RICHARD LOVELACE

And the dark hag[11] from her black mantle strip,   35
    And stick there everlasting day.

Thus richer than untempted kings are we,
    That asking nothing, nothing need:
Though lord of all what[12] seas embrace, yet he
    That wants himself is poor indeed.   40

ANDREW MARVELL
1 6 2 1 – 1 6 7 8

THE GARDEN

How vainly men themselves amaze[1]
To win the palm, the oak, or bays;[2]
And their incessant labours see
Crown'd from some single herb or tree,
Whose short and narrow vergèd[3] shade   5
Does prudently their toils upbraid;
While all flow'rs and all trees do close[4]
To weave the garlands of repose.

Fair Quiet, have I found thee here,
And Innocence, thy sister dear!   10
Mistaken long, I sought you then
In busy companies of men.
Your sacred plants, if here below,
Only among the plants will grow.
Society is all but rude,   15
To[5] this delicious solitude.

No white nor red[6] was ever seen
So am'rous as this lovely green.

---

[11] That is, night.   [12] That.

[1] Perplex   [2] Crowns made of these types of leaves were symbols, respectively, of fame in war, civil life, poetry.   [3] Bordered, limited.   [4] Combine, join together.   [5] In comparison to.   [6] Of a woman's skin.

Fond lovers, cruel as their flame,[7]
Cut in these trees their mistress' name.   20
Little, alas, they know, or heed,
How far these beauties hers exceed!
Fair trees, wheres'e'er your barks I wound,
No name shall but your own be found.

When we have run our passion's heat,   25
Love hither makes his best retreat.
The gods, that mortal beauty chase,
Still in a tree did end their race:
Apollo hunted Daphne so,
Only that she might laurel grow;   30
And Pan did after Syrinx speed,
Not as a nymph, but for a reed.[8]

What wond'rous life is this I lead!
Ripe apples drop about my head;
The luscious clusters of the vine   35
Upon my mouth do crush their wine;
The nectarine, and curious peach,
Into my hands themselves do reach;
Stumbling on melons, as I pass,
Ensnar'd with flow'rs, I fall on grass.   40

Meanwhile the mind, from pleasure less,
Withdraws its happiness:
The mind, that ocean where each kind
Does straight[9] its own resemblance find;
Yet it creates, transcending these,   45
Far other worlds, and other seas;
Annihilating all that's made
To a green thought in a green shade.

Here at the fountain's sliding foot,
Or at some fruit-tree's mossy root,   50
Casting the body's vest aside,
My soul into the boughs does glide:
There, like a bird, it sits, and sings,
Then whets[10] and combs its silver wings,

[7] Passion.   [8] Daphne and Syrinx, in Greek mythology, were nymphs who were
pursued by Apollo (god of light and medicine) and Pan (god of forests and flocks), respectively. Both wanted to escape and both succeeded: Daphne was changed into a laurel
and Syrinx into a reed.   [9] Immediately.   [10] Preens.

And, till prepar'd for longer flight,   55
Waves in its plumes the various light.

Such was that happy garden-state,
While man there walk'd without a mate:
After a place so pure, and sweet,
What other help could yet be meet!   60
But 'twas beyond a mortal's share
To wander solitary there:
Two paradises 'twere in one
To live in paradise alone.

How well the skilful gardner drew   65
Of flow'rs and herbs this dial new;[11]
Where, from above, the milder sun
Does through a fragrant zodiac run;
And, as it works, th' industrious bee
Computes its time as well as we.   70
How could such sweet and wholesome hours
Be reckon'd but with herbs and flow'rs!

THE MOWER AGAINST GARDENS

Luxurious[1] Man, to bring his vice in use,[2]
    Did after him the world seduce:
And from the fields the flow'rs and plants allure,
    Where Nature was most plain and pure.
He first enclos'd within the gardens square   5
    A dead and standing pool of air:
And a more luscious earth for them did knead,
    Which stupifi'd them while it fed.
The pink grew then as double as his mind;
    The nutriment did change the kind.   10
With strange perfumes he did the roses taint.
    And flow'rs themselves were taught to paint.
The tulip, white, did for complexion seek;
    And learn'd to interline its cheek:
Its onion root[3] they then so high did hold,   15
    That one was for a meadow sold.[4]

[11] The garden is planted in the form of a sundial.

[1] Lecherous.   [2] That is, to make use of his vice.   [3] The tulip bulb resembles an onion.   [4] A reference to the tulip mania in Holland in the 1630's.

Another world was search'd, through Oceans new,
  To find the Marvel of Peru.[5]
And yet these rarities might be allowed,
  To Man, that sov'reign thing and proud,   20
Had he not dealt between the bark and tree,
  Forbidden mixtures there to see.
No plant now knew the stock from which it came;
  He grafts upon the wild the tame:
That the uncertain and adult'rate fruit   25
  Might put the palate in dispute.
His green seraglio has its eunuchs too,
  Lest any tyrant him outdo.
And in the cherry he does Nature vex,
  To procreate without a sex.[6]   30
'Tis all enforc'd; the fountain and the grot;
  While the sweet fields do lie forgot:
Where willing Nature does to all dispence
  A wild and fragrant innocence:
And fauns and fairies do the meadows till,   35
  More by their presence than their skill.
Their statues polish'd by some ancient hand,
  May to adorn the gardens stand:
But howso'ere the figures do excel,
  The gods[7] themselves with us do dwell.   40

THE MOWER'S SONG

My mind was once the true survey[1]
Of all these meadows fresh and gay;
And in the greenness of the grass
Did see its hopes as in a glass;
  When *Juliana* came, and she   5
What I do to the grass, does to my thoughts and me.

But these, while I with sorrow pine,
Grew more luxuriant still and fine,
That not one blade of grass you spy'd,
But had a flower on either side;   10
  When *Juliana* came, and she
What I do to the grass, does to my thoughts and me.

[5] A flower.   [6] It has been conjectured that these lines refer to the growing of cherry trees by grafting.   [7] Powers.

[1] Comprehensive view.

Unthankful meadows, could you so
A fellowship so true forego,
And in your gaudy May-games meet,   15
While I lay trodden under feet?
When *Juliana* came, and she
What I do to the grass, does to my thoughts and me.

But what you in compassion ought,
Shall now by my revenge be wrought: 20
And flow'rs, and grass, and I and all,
Will in one common ruin fall.
For *Juliana* comes, and she
What I do to the grass, does to my thoughts and me.

And thus, ye meadows, which have been   25
Companions of my thoughts more green,
Shall now the heraldry[2] become
With which I shall adorn my tomb;
For *Juliana* comes, and she
What I do to the grass, does to my thoughts and me. 30

BERMUDAS

Where the remote Bermudas ride
In th' ocean's bosom unespy'd,
From a small boat that row'd along,
The list'ning winds receiv'd this song[1]:
    "What should we do but sing His praise,   5
That led us through the watery maze,
Unto an isle so long unknown,
And yet far kinder than our own?
Where He the huge sea-monsters wracks,
That lift the deep upon their backs.   10
He lands us on a grassy stage,
Safe from the storms, and prelate's rage.
He gave us this eternal spring,
Which here enamels everything;
And sends the fowls to us in care,   15
On daily visits through the air.
He hangs in shades the orange bright,
Like golden lamps in a green night;
And does in the pomegranates close

---

[2] Decorative insignia.

[1] Sung by the religious exiles from England who settled Bermuda in the early
seventeenth century.

Jewels more rich than Ormus[2] shows.   20
He makes the figs our mouths to meet,
And throws the melons at our feet.
But apples[3] plants of such a price,
No tree could ever bear them twice.
With cedars, chosen by His hand,   25
From Lebanon, He stores the land,
And makes the hollow seas, that roar
Proclaim[4] the ambergris on shore.
He cast (of which we rather boast)
The Gospel's pearl upon our coast   30
And in these rocks for us did frame
A temple, where to sound His name.
Oh let our voice His praise exalt,
Till it arrive at Heaven's vault,
Which thence (perhaps) rebounding, may   35
Echo beyond the Mexique Bay."
        Thus sung they, in the English boat,
An holy and a cheerful note;
And all the way, to guide their chime,
With falling oars they kept the time.   40

THE PICTURE OF LITTLE T.C. IN A PROSPECT[1] OF FLOWERS

See with what simplicity
This nymph begins her golden days!
In the green grass she loves to lie
And there with her fair aspect[2] tames
The wilder flow'rs and gives them names: 5
But only with the roses plays,
        And them does tell
What colour best becomes them, and what smell.

Who can fortell for what high cause
This darling of the gods was born?   10
Yet this is she whose chaster laws
The wanton Love shall one day fear,
And, under her command severe,
See his bow broke and ensigns[3] torn.
        Happy who can   15
Appease this virtuous enemy of man!

---

[2] Hormuz, an island of Iran that, in the twelfth and thirteenth centuries especially, was the market for the wares of India.   [3] Pineapples.   [4] Make known; that is, toss up.

[1] Scene, landscape.   [2] Countenance, face.   [3] Banners.

O then let me in time compound[4]
And parley with those conquering eyes,
Ere they have tried force to wound,
Ere, with their glancing wheels, they drive   20
In triumph over hearts that strive,
And them that yield but more despise.
   Let me be laid
Where I may see the glories from some shade.

Meantime, whilst every verdant thing   25
Itself does at thy beauty charm,
Reform the errors of the spring;
Make that the tulips may have share
Of sweetness, seeing they are fair;
And roses of their thorns disarm: 30
   But most procure
That violets may a longer age endure.

But O young beauty of the woods,
Whom Nature courts with fruit and flow'rs,
Gather the flow'rs, but spare the buds;   35
Lest Flora,[5] angry at thy crime,
To kill her infants in their prime,
Do quickly make th' example yours;
   And, ere we see,
Nip in the blossom all our hopes and thee.   40

HENRY VAUGHAN

1 6 2 2 – 1 6 9 5

THE PURSUIT

  Lord! what a busy, restless thing
    Hast thou made man?
  Each day, and hour he is on wing,
    Rests not a span;

---

[4] Compromise, come to terms.   [5] Roman goddess of flowers.

Then having lost[1] the sun, and light 5
    By clouds surpriz'd
He keeps a commerce[2] in the night
    With air disguis'd;
Hadst thou given to this active dust
    A state untir'd, 10
The lost son had not left the huske
    Nor home desir'd;[3]
That was thy secret, and it is
    Thy mercy too,
For when all fails to bring to bliss, 15
    Then, this[4] must do.
Ah! Lord! and what a purchase[5] will that be
To take us sick, that sound would not take thee?

THE RETREAT

Happy those early days! when I
Shin'd in my angel-infancy.
Before I understood this place
Appointed for my second race,
Or taught my soul to fancy aught 5
But a white, celestial thought,
When yet I had not walk'd above
A mile, or two, from my first love,
And looking back (at that short space),
Could see a glimpse of His bright face; 10
When on some gilded cloud, or flow'r,
My gazing soul would dwell an hour,
And in those weaker glories spy
Some shadows of eternity;
Before I taught my tongue to wound 15
My conscience with a sinful sound,
Or had the black art to dispense
A sev'ral sin[1] to ev'ry sense,
But felt through all this fleshly dress
Bright shoots of everlastingness. 20
    O how I long to travel back
And tread again that ancient track!
That I might once more reach that plain
Where first I left my glorious train,

---

[1] Missed, wasted.   [2] Carries on business, does his work.   [3] A reference to the story of the prodigal son (see Luke 15:16–19).   [4] Fatigue.   [5] Acquisition, gain.

[1] Several sins.

From whence th' enlightened spirit sees   25
That shady city of palm trees;
But (ah!) my soul with too much stay
Is drunk, and staggers in the way.
Some men a forward motion love,
But I by backward steps would move,   30
And when this dust falls to the urn
In that state I came return.

CHILDHOOD

I cannot reach it; and my striving eye
Dazzles at it, as at eternity.
    Were now that chronicle alive,
Those white designs which children drive,
And the thoughts of each harmless hour,   5
With their content, too, in my pow'r,
Quickly would I make my path even,
And by mere playing go to heaven.

    Why should men love
A wolf more than a lamb or dove?   10
Or choose hell-fire and brimstone streams
Before bright stars and God's own beams?
Who kisseth thorns will hurt his face,
But flowers do both refresh and grace,
And sweetly living (fie on men!)   15
Are, when dead, medicinal then.
If seeing much should make staid eyes,
And long experience should make wise,
Since all that age doth teach is ill,
Why should I not love childhood still?   20
Why, if I see a rock or shelf,
Shall I from thence cast down myself,
Or by complying with the world,
From the same precipice be hurl'd?
Those observations are but foul   25
Which make me[1] wise to lose my soul.

And yet the practice worldlings call
Business, and weighty action all,
Checking[2] the poor child for his play,
But gravely cast themselves away.   30

    [1] Say I am.   [2] Reprimanding.

Dear, harmless age! the short, swift span
Where weeping virtue parts with man;
Where love without lust dwells, and bends
What way we please, without self-ends.[3]

An age of mysteries! which he   35
Must live twice that would God's face see;
Which angels guard, and with it play,
Angels! which foul men drive away.

How do I study now, and scan
Thee more than e'er I studied man,   40
And only see through a long night
Thy edges and thy bordering light!
O for thy center and mid-day!
For sure that is the Narrow Way![4]

THE WORLD

I saw eternity the other night
Like a great ring of pure and endless light,
    All calm as it was bright,
And round beneath it, time in hours, days, years,
    Driv'n by the spheres,[1]   5
Like a vast shadow mov'd, in which the world
    And all her train were hurl'd;
The doting lover in his quaintest strain[2]
    Did there complain;[3]
Near him, his lute, his fancy, and his flights,   10
    Wit's sour delights,
With gloves and knots,[4] the silly snares of pleasure,
    Yet his dear treasure
All scatter'd lay, while he his eyes did pour
    Upon a flow'r.   15

The darksome statesman,[5] hung with weights and woe,
Like a thick midnight-fog, mov'd there so slow
    He did nor stay nor go;

---

[3] Its own ends.   [4] "Straight is the gate, and narrow is the way, which leadeth unto life" (Matthew 7:14).

[1] According to ancient astronomy, which Vaughan uses for figurative purposes, the heavens were a series of concentric, crystalline spheres arranged around the earth.   [2] Most elaborate verse.   [3] Plead his cause.   [4] Love knots.   [5] Unscrupulous politician.

Condemning thoughts, like sad eclipses, scowl
　　Upon his soul, 20
And clouds of crying witnesses without
　　Pursued him with one shout.
Yet digg'd the mole, and, lest his ways be found,
　　Work'd under ground,
Where he did clutch his prey, but one[6] did see 25
　　That policy:
Churches and altars fed him; perjuries
　　Were gnats and flies;[7]
It rained about him blood and tears, but he
　　Drank them as free.[8] 30

The fearful miser on a heap of rust
Sat pining all his life there, did scarce trust
　　His own hands with the dust,
Yet would not place one piece[9] above, but lives
　　In fear of thieves.
Thousands there were as frantic as himself, 35
　　And hugg'd each one his pelf:
The downright epicure plac'd heav'n in sense[10]
　　And scorn'd pretense
While others, slipp'd into a wide excess,[11] 40
　　Said little less;
The weaker sort slight, trivial wares enslave,
　　Who think them brave,[12]
And poor, despisèd Truth sat counting by[13]
　　Their victory. 45

Yet some, who all this while did weep and sing,
And sing, and weep, soar'd up into the ring,[14]
　　But most would use no wing.
"O fools!" said I, "thus to prefer dark night
　　Before true light, 50
To live in grots, and caves, and hate the day
　　Because it shows the way,
The way which from this dead and dark abode
　　Leads up to God,
A way where you might tread the sun, and be 55
　　More bright than he!"
But as I did their madness so discuss
　　One whisper'd thus:

---

[6] The speaker.　　[7] Plentiful and of no importance.　　[8] As freely as they ran; that is, he thrived on others' misfortunes.　　[9] Invest one coin. See St. Matthew's admonition to invest in heavenly, rather than earthly, goods (Matthew 6:19–20).　　[10] Sensual pleasures.　　[11] Deviation from moderation.　　[12] Splendid, handsome.　　[13] Observing.　　[14] See line 2 above.

JOHN DRYDEN
1 6 3 1 – 1 7 0 0

TO THE MEMORY OF MR. OLDHAM

Farewell, too little and too lately known,
Whom I began to think and call my own;
For sure our souls were near allied, and thine
Cast in the same poetic mold with mine.
One common note on either lyre did strike,[1]   5
And knaves and fools we both abhorr'd alike:
To the same goal did both our studies drive;
The last set out the soonest did arrive.[2]
Thus Nisus[3] fell upon the slippery place,
Whilst his young friend perform'd and won the race.   10
O early ripe! to thy abundant store
What could advancing age have added more?
It might (what nature never gives the young)
Have taught the numbers[4] of thy native tongue.
But satire needs not those, and wit will shine   15
Through the harsh cadence of a rugged line.
A noble error, and but seldom made,
When poets are by too much force betray'd.
Thy generous fruits, though gather'd ere their prime,
Still show'd a quickness;[5] and maturing time   20
But mellows what we write to the dull sweets[6] of rhyme.
Once more, hail, and farewell; farewell, thou young,

---

[15] In Revelation 21, the holy city of Jerusalem, the home of the twelve tribes of
the children of Israel who are to be granted eternal life, is compared to a bride, and God
to a bridegroom.

[1] Was struck.   [2] Oldham was born twenty-two years after Dryden but died before
him, at the age of thirty.   [3] In Virgil's *Aeneid*, Nisus slipped on the spot where steers
had been slain; knowing that he could not win the race, he threw himself in front of
another runner, permitting his friend Euryalus to win the race.   [4] Rhythm.   [5] Acuteness of feeling or perception, but also sharpness of speech.   [6] Sweetened wine or other
liquor.

But ah too short, Marcellus[7] of our tongue;
Thy brows with ivy and with laurels bound;
But Fate and gloomy night encompass thee around.   25

JOHN WILMOT,
EARL OF ROCHESTER
1612?–1658

UPON NOTHING

Nothing! thou elder brother ev'n to Shade,
That hadst a being e're the world was made,
And (well fixt) art alone, of ending not afraid.

E're time and place were, time and place were not,
When primitive Nothing something strait begot,   5
Then all proceeded from the great united—What?

Something, the gen'ral attribute of all,
Sever'd from thee, it's sole orginal,
Into thy boundless self must undistinguish'd fall.

Yet something did thy mighty pow'r command,   10
And from thy fruitful emptiness's hand,
Snatch'd men, beasts, birds, fire, water, air and land.

Matter, the wicked'st off-spring of thy race,
By Form assisted, flew from thy embrace,
And rebel Light obscur'd thy reverend dusky face.   15

With Form and Matter, Time and Place did join,
Body, thy foe, with these did leagues combine,[1]
To spoil thy peaceful realm, and ruine all thy line.[2]

7 Son of Augustus' sister, Octavia, whose death is predicted in the *Aeneid*.

1 Form.   2 Lineage.

But turn-coat Time assists the foe in vain,
And, brib'd by thee, destroys their short-liv'd reign,   20
And to thy hungry womb drives back thy slaves again.

Tho' mysteries are barr'd from laick eyes,
And the Divine alone, with warrant, pryes
Into thy bosom, where the truth in private lies,

Yet this of thee the wise may freely say,   25
Thou from the virtuous nothing tak'st away,
And to be part with thee the wicked wisely pray.

Great Negative, how vainly would the wise,
Enquire, define, distinguish, teach, devise?
Didst thou not stand to point[3] their dull philosophies.   30

Is, or *is not,* the two great ends of fate,
And, true or false, the subject of debate,
That perfect, or destroy, the vast designs of fate,

When they have rack'd the Politician's breast,
Within thy bosom most securely rest,   35
And, when reduc'd to thee, are least unsafe and best.

But, Nothing, why does Something still permit,
That sacred monarchs should at council sit,
With persons highly thought at best for nothing fit?

Whilst weighty Something modestly abstains,   40
From princes' coffers,[4] and from statesmen's brains,
And nothing there like stately Nothing reigns,

Nothing who dwell'st with fools in grave disguise,
For whom they rev'rend shapes, and forms devise,
Lawn sleeves, and furs, and gowns, when they like thee look wise.   45

French truth, Dutch prowess, Brittish policy,
Hibernian learning, Scotch civility,
Spaniards dispatch,[5] Danes wit, are mainly seen in thee.

[3] Sharpen, give a point to.   [4] Treasuries.   [5] Speed, expediency.

The great man's gratitude to his best friend,
Kings promises, whores vows, tow'rds thee they bend,   50
Flow swiftly into thee, and in thee ever end.

JONATHAN SWIFT
1667-1745

A DESCRIPTION OF A CITY SHOWER

In Imitation of Virgil's Georgics

    Careful observers may foretell the hour
(By sure prognostics) when to dread a show'r:
While rain depends,[1] the pensive cat gives o'er
Her frolics, and pursues her tail no more.
Returning home at night, you'll find the sink[2]   5
Strike your offended sense with double stink.
If you be wise, then go not far to dine,
You'll spend in coach-hire more than save in wine.
A coming show'r your shooting corns presage,
Old aches throb, your hollow tooth will rage.   10
Sauntring in coffee-house is Dulman seen;
He damns the climate, and complains of spleen.

    Meanwhile the South rising with dabbled[3] wings,
A sable cloud a-thwart the welkin[4] flings,
That swill'd more liquor than it could contain,   15
And like a drunkard gives it up again.
Brisk Susan whips her linen from the rope,
While the first drizzling show'r is borne aslope,[5]
Such is that sprinkling which some careless quean[6]
Flirts on you from her mop, but not so clean.   20
You fly, invoke the gods; then turning, stop
To rail; she singing, still whirls on her mop.
Not yet, the dust had shunn'd th' unequal strife,
But aided by the wind, fought still for life;

---

    [1] Impends, is imminent.   [2] Cesspool.   [3] Bedabbled, bespattered.   [4] Sky, firmament.   [5] On the incline, crosswise.   [6] Bold woman, jade, harlot.

And wafted with its foe[7] by violent gust,   25
'Twas doubtful which was rain, and which was dust.
Ah! where must needy poet seek for aid,
When dust and rain at once his coat invade;
His only coat! where dust confus'd with rain,
Roughen the nap, and leave a mingled stain.   30

    Now in contiguous drops the flood comes down,
Threat'ning with deluge this *devoted* town.
To shops in crowds the daggled[8] females fly,
Pretend to cheapen[9] goods, but nothing buy.
The Templar[10] spruce, while ev'ry spout's a-broach,[11]   35
Stays till 'tis fair, yet seems to call a coach.
The tuck'd-up sempstress walks with hasty strides,
While streams run down her oil'd umbrella's sides.
Here various kinds by various fortunes led,
Commence acquaintance underneath a shed.   40
Triumphant Tories, and desponding Whigs,
Forget their feuds, and join to save their wigs.
Box'd in a chair[12] the beau impatient sits,
While spouts run clatt'ring o'er the roof by fits;
And ever and anon with frightful din   45
The leather sounds, he trembles from within.
So when Troy chair-men bore the wooden steed,[13]
Pregnant with Greeks impatient to be freed,
(Those bully Greeks, who, as the moderns do,
Instead of paying chair-men, run them thro'.)   50
Laocoon[14] struck the outside with his spear,
And each imprison'd hero quak'd for fear.

    Now from all parts the swelling kennels[15] flow,
And bear their trophies with them as they go:
Filth of all hues and odours seem to tell   55
What street they sail'd from, by their sight and smell.
They, as each torrent drives, with rapid force
From Smithfield,[16] or St. Pulchre's shape their course,

---

[7] That is, rain, or water.   [8] Wet, rained upon.   [9] Price, bargain for.   [10] A barrister or other person who occupies rooms in the Inner or Middle Temple in London. [11] Broached, pierced.   [12] A sedan carried on poles.   [13] The Trojan horse. The Greeks, having tried for ten years to capture Troy, built a huge wooden horse, hid their best soldiers inside, and had it presented to the Trojans as an offering to Athena which, if brought inside the city, would make Troy invulnerable. The Trojans dragged the horse inside. At night the hidden Greeks left the horse and opened the city's gates to their countrymen. Troy was quickly captured.   [14] A Trojan priest who, in an attempt to dissuade Troy from accepting the Trojan horse, hurled his javelin into the hollow flank of the statue. There was a groan, but the Trojan's attention was diverted by a Greek who pretended to desert his countrymen.   [15] Gutters.   [16] This and the proper nouns that follow are the names of localities in London.

And in huge confluent[17] join at Snow-hill ridge,
Fall from the conduit prone to Holborn-bridge.   60
Sweepings from butchers' stalls, dung, guts, and blood,
Drown'd puppies, stinking sprats,[18] all drench'd in mud,
Dead cats and turnip-tops come tumbling down the flood.

STELLA'S BIRTHDAY[1]

March 13, 1726/7

This day, whate'er the Fates decree,
Shall still be kept with joy by me:
This day then, let us not be told,
That you are sick, and I grown old,
Nor think on our approaching ills,   5
And talk of spectacles and pills;
To-morrow will be time enough
To hear such mortifying stuff.
Yet, since from reason may be brought
A better and more pleasing thought,   10
Which can in spite of all decays,
Support a few remaining days:
From not the gravest of divines,[2]
Accept for once some serious lines.

        Although we now can form no more   15
Long schemes of life, as heretofore;
Yet you, while time is running fast,
Can look with joy on what is past.

        Were future happiness and pain,
A mere contrivance of the brain,   20
As atheists argue, to entice,
And fit their proselytes for vice;
(The only comfort they propose,
To have companions in their woes),
Grant this the case, yet sure 'tis hard,   25
That virtue, styled its own reward,
And by all sages understood
To be the chief of human good,

---

[17] A union of several streams.   [18] Small sea-fish.

[1] Swift maintained a long friendship with Stella, who died of the illness spoken of
here in January, 1728.   [2] Swift, a clergyman, was Dean of St. Patrick's in Dublin.

Should acting, die, nor leave behind
Some lasting pleasure in the mind,   30
Which by remembrance will assuage,
Grief, sickness, poverty, and age;
And strongly shoot a radiant dart,
To shine through life's declining part.

    Say, Stella, feel you no content,   35
Reflecting on a life well spent?
Your skilful hand employ'd to save
Despairing wretches from the grave;
And then supporting with your store,[3]
Those whom you dragg'd from death before: 40
So Providence on mortals waits,
Preserving what it first creates,
Your gen'rous boldness to defend
An innocent and absent friend;
That courage which can make you just   45
To merit humbled in the dust:
The detestation you express
For vice in all its glitt'ring dress;
That patience under tort'ring pain,
Where stubborn Stoics would complain.   50

    Must these like empty shadows pass,
Or forms reflected from a glass?
Or mere chimaeras in the mind,
That fly, and leave no marks behind?
Does not the body thrive and grow   55
By food of twenty years ago?
And, had it not been still supplied,
It must a thousand times have died.
Then, who with reason can maintain,
That no effects of food remain?   60
And, is not virtue in mankind
The nutriment that feeds the mind?
Upheld by each good action past,
And still continued by the last?
Then, who with reason can pretend,   65
That all effects of virtue end?

    Believe me Stella, when you show
That true contempt for things below,
Nor prize your life for other ends

    [3] Abundance, here, of spiritual goods.

Than merely to oblige your friends;   70
Your former actions claim their part,
And join to fortify your heart.
For Virtue in her daily race,
Like Janus,[4] bears a double face;
Looks back with joy where she has gone,   75
And therefore goes with courage on.
She at your sickly couch will wait,
And guide you to a better state.

    Oh then, whatever heav'n intends,
Take pity on your pitying friends;   80
Nor let your ills affect your mind,
To fancy they can be unkind.
Me, surely me, you ought to spare,
Who gladly would your suff'rings share;
Or give my scrap of life to you,   85
And think it far beneath your due;
You, to whose care so oft I owe,
That I'm alive to tell you so.

SAMUEL JOHNSON
1709-1784

ON THE DEATH OF DR. ROBERT LEVET

Condemn'd to hope's delusive mine,
    As on we toil from day to day,
By sudden blasts, or slow decline,
    Our social comforts drop away.

Well tried through many a varying year,   5
    See Levet to the grave descend;
Officious,[1] innocent, sincere,
    Of ev'ry friendless name the friend.

---

[4] In Roman mythology, the protector of doors and entrances. He was represented with two faces, one facing forward and the other backward.

[1] Kind, obliging.

Yet still he fills affection's eye,
    Obscurely wise, and coarsely kind; 10
Nor , letter'd arrogance, deny
    Thy praise to merit unrefin'd.

When fainting nature call'd for aid,
    And hov'ring death prepar'd the blow,
His vig'rous remedy display'd 15
    The power of art without the show.

In misery's darkest caverns known,
    His useful care was ever nigh.
Where hopeless anguish pour'd his groan,
    And lonely want retir'd to die. 20

No summons mock'd by chill delay,
    No petty gain disdain'd by pride,
The modest wants of ev'ry day
    The toil of ev'ry day supplied.

His virtues walk'd their narrow round, 25
    Nor made a pause, nor left a void;
And sure th' Eternal Master found
    The single talent well employ'd.

The busy day, the peaceful night,
    Unfelt, uncounted, glided by; 30
His frame was firm, his powers were bright,
    Tho' now his eightieth year was nigh.

Then with no throbbing fiery pain,
    No cold gradations of decay,
Death broke at once the vital chain, 35
    And freed his soul the nearest way.

THOMAS GRAY

1 7 1 6 – 1 7 7 1

ELEGY WRITTEN IN A COUNTRY CHURCHYARD

The curfew tolls the knell of parting day,
 The lowing herd wind slowly o'er the lea,
The ploughman homeward plods his weary way,
 And leaves the world to darkness and to me.

Now fades the glimmering landscape on the sight,   5
 And all the air a solemn stillness holds,
Save where the beetle wheels his droning flight,
 And drowsy tinklings lull the distant folds;

Save that from yonder ivy-mantled tow'r
 The moping owl does to the moon complain   10
Of such, as wand'ring near her secret bow'r,
 Molest her ancient solitary reign.

Beneath those rugged elms, that yew-tree's shade,
 Where heaves the turf in many a mold'ring heap,
Each in his narrow cell forever laid,   15
 The rude[1] forefathers of the hamlet sleep.

The breezy call of incense-breathing morn,
 The swallow twitt'ring from the straw-built shed,
The cock's shrill clarion, or the echoing horn,
 No more shall rouse them from their lowly bed.   20

For them no more the blazing hearth shall burn,
 Or busy housewife ply her evening care;
No children run to lisp their sire's return,
 Or climb his knees the envied kiss to share.

Oft did the harvest to their sickle yield;   25
 Their furrow oft the stubborn glebe[2] has broke;

[1] Rustic.   [2] Soil.

How jocund did they drive their team afield!
    How bow'd the woods beneath their sturdy stroke!

Let not Ambition mock their useful toil,
    Their homely joys, and destiny obscure;   30
Nor Grandeur hear with a disdainful smile
    The short and simple annals of the poor.

The boast of heraldry,[3] the pomp of pow'r,
    And all that beauty, all that wealth e'er gave,
Awaits alike th' inevitable hour: 35
    The paths of glory lead but to the grave.

Nor you, ye proud, impute to these the fault,
    If Mem'ry o'er their tomb no trophies raise,
Where through the long-drawn aisle and fretted vault
    The pealing anthem swells the note of praise.   40

Can storied urn,[4] or animated[5] bust,
    Back to its mansion call the fleeting breath?
Can Honour's voice provoke the silent dust,
    Or Flatt'ry soothe the dull cold ear of Death?

Perhaps in this neglected spot is laid   45
    Some heart once pregnant with celestial fire;
Hands that the rod of empire might have sway'd,
    Or wak'd to ecstasy the living lyre.

But Knowledge to their eyes her ample page,
    Rich with the spoils of time, did ne'er unroll;   50
Chill Penury repress'd their noble rage,
    And froze the genial current of the soul.

Full many a gem of purest ray serene,
    The dark unfathom'd caves of ocean bear;
Full many a flower is born to blush unseen,   55
    And waste its sweetness on the desert air.

[3] Recorded genealogies and their heraldic symbols; hence, noble birth.   [4] Funeral
urn engraved with scenes from a story.   [5] Lifelike.

Some village Hampden,[6] that with dauntless breast
    The little tyrant of his fields withstood;
Some mute inglorious Milton[7] here may rest,
    Some Cromwell,[8] guiltless of his country's blood.   60

Th' applause of list'ning senates to command,
    The threats of pain and ruin to despise,
To scatter plenty o'er a smiling land,
    And read their hist'ry in a nation's eyes,

Their lot forbade; nor circumscrib'd alone   65
    Their growing virtues, but their crimes confined;
Forbade to wade through slaughter to a throne,
    And shut the gates of mercy on mankind;

The struggling pangs of conscious truth to hide,
    To quench the blushes of ingenuous shame,   70
Or heap the shrine of Luxury and Pride
    With incense kindled at the Muse's flame.

Far from the madding[9] crowd's ignoble strife,
    Their sober wishes never learn'd to stray;
Along the cool sequester'd vale of life   75
    They kept the noiseless tenor of their way.

Yet ev'n these bones from insult to protect,
    Some frail memorial still erected nigh,
With uncouth rhymes and shapeless sculpture deck'd,
    Implores the passing tribute of a sigh.   80

Their name, their years, spelt by th' unletter'd Muse,
    The place of fame and elegy supply;
And many a holy text around she strews,
    That teach the rustic moralist to die.

For who, to dumb Forgetfulness a prey,   85
    This pleasing anxious being e'er resign'd,

---

[6] John Hampden (1594–1643), a Member of Parliament who resisted taxes levied by King Charles I because he thought them unjust. He was impeached but resisted arrest. [7] The poet John Milton (1608–1674).   [8] Oliver Cromwell, a Puritan military leader during the English Civil War and Lord Protector of the Commonwealth (1653–1658). [9] Wild, restless.

Left the warm precincts of the cheerful day,
    Nor cast one longing ling'ring look behind?

On some fond breast the parting soul relies,
    Some pious drops the closing eye requires;   90
Ev'n from the tomb the voice of Nature cries,
    Ev'n in our ashes live their wonted[10] fires.

For thee, who mindful of th' unhonour'd dead
    Dost in these lines their artless tale relate;
If chance, by lonely contemplation led,   95
    Some kindred spirit shall inquire thy fate,

Haply some hoary-headed[11] swain may say,
    "Oft have we seen him at the peep of dawn
Brushing with hasty steps the dews away
    To meet the sun upon the upland lawn.   100

"There at the foot of yonder nodding beech
    That wreathes its old fantastic roots so high,
His listless length at noontide would he stretch,
    And pore upon the brook that babbles by.

"Hard by yon wood, now smiling as in scorn,   105
    Mutt'ring his wayward fancies he would rove;
Now drooping, woeful-wan, like one forlorn,
    Or craz'd with care, or cross'd in hopeless love.

"One morn I miss'd him on the custom'd hill,
    Along the heath, and near his fav'rite tree;   110
Another came; nor yet beside the rill,
    Nor up the lawn, nor at the wood was he;

"The next, with dirges due, in sad array,
    Slow through the church-way path we saw him borne.
Approach and read (for thou canst read) the lay,   115
    Grav'd on the stone beneath yon agèd thorn."

THE EPITAPH

Here rests his head upon the lap of earth,
    A youth to Fortune and to Fame unknown;

[10] Customary.   [11] Gray- or white-haired.

Fair Science frown'd not on his humble birth,
   And Melancholy mark'd him for her own.   120

Large was his bounty, and his soul sincere;
   Heav'n did a recompense as largely send:
He gave to Mis'ry all he had, a tear;
   He gain'd from Heav'n ('twas all he wish'd) a friend.

No farther seek his merits to disclose,   125
   Or draw his frailties from their dread abode,
(There they alike in trembling hope repose)
   The bosom of his Father and his God.

CHRISTOPHER SMART

1722–1771

OF JEOFFRY, HIS CAT

For I will consider my Cat Jeoffry.
For he is the servant of the Living God, duly and daily
    serving him.
For at the first glance of the glory of God in the East he
    worships in his way.
For is this done by wreathing[1] his body seven times round
    with elegant quickness.
For then he leaps up to catch the musk,[2] which is the
    blessing of God upon his prayer.   5
For he rolls upon prank to work it in.[3]
For having done duty and received blessing he begins to
    consider himself.
For this he performs in ten degrees.
For first he looks upon his fore-paws to see if they are
    clean.
For secondly he kicks up behind to clear away there.   10
For thirdly he works it upon stretch with the fore-paws
    extended.

[1] Writhing.   [2] Muskrat.   [3] That is, as a prank, he rolls to digest the muskrat.

For fourthly he sharpens his paws by wood.
For fifthly he washes himself.
For sixthly he rolls upon wash.
For seventhly he fleas himself, that he may not be inter-
    rupted upon the beat.[4]   15
For eighthly he rubs himself against a post.
For ninthly he looks up for his instructions.[5]
For tenthly he goes in quest of food.
For having consider'd God and himself he will consider
    his neighbour.
For if he meets another cat he will kiss her in kindness.   20
For when he takes his prey he plays with it to give it
    chance.
For one mouse in seven escapes by his dallying.
For when his day's work is done his business more
    properly begins.
For [he] keeps the Lord's watch in the night against the
    adversary.
For he counteracts the powers of darkness by his electrical
    skin and glaring eyes.   25
For he counteracts the Devil, who is death, by brisking
    about the life.
For in his morning orisons he loves the sun and the sun
    loves him.
For he is of the tribe of Tiger.
For the Cherub Cat is a term[6] of the Angel Tiger.
For he has the subtlety and hissing of a serpent, which in
    goodness he suppresses.   30
For he will not do destruction, if he is well-fed, neither
    will he spit without provocation.
For he purrs in thankfulness, when God tells him he's a
    good Cat.
For he is an instrument for the children to learn
    benevolence upon.
For every house is incompleat without him and a blessing
    is lacking in the spirit.
For the Lord commanded Moses concerning the cats at
    the departure of the Children of Israel from Egypt.   35
For every family had one cat at least in the bag.
For the English Cats are the best in Europe.
For he is the cleanest in the use of his fore-paws of any
    quadrupede.
For the dexterity of his defence is an instance of the love
    of God to him exceedingly.
For he is the quickest to his mark of any creature.   40
For he is tenacious of his point.

[4] The territory he ranges over in pursuit of prey.   [5] That is, he sniffs the air for a
scent.   [6] Period, step in the progression.

For he is a mixture of gravity and waggery.
For he knows that God is his Saviour.
For there is nothing sweeter than his peace when at rest.
For there is nothing brisker than his life when in motion. 45
For he is of the Lord's poor and so indeed is he called
       by benevolence perpetually—Poor Jeoffry! poor
       Jeoffry! the rat has bit thy throat.
For I bless the name of the Lord Jesus that Jeoffry is
       better.
For the divine spirit comes about his body to sustain it in
       compleat cat.
For his tongue is exceeding pure so that it has in purity
       what it wants in musick.
For he is docile and can learn certain things. 50
For he can set up with gravity which is patience upon
       approbation.
For he can fetch and carry, which is patience in employ-
       ment.
For he can jump over a stick which is patience upon proof
       positive.
For he can spraggle upon waggle at the word of
       command.
For he can jump from an eminence into his master's
       bosom. 55
For he can catch the cork and toss it again.
For he is hated by the hypocrite and miser.
For the former is affraid of detection.
For the latter refuses the charge.
For he camels his back to bear the first notion of
       business. 60
For he is good to think on, if a man would express himself
       neatly.
For he made a great figure in Egypt for his signal
       services.
For he killed the Icneumon-rat[7] very pernicious by land.
For his ears are so acute that they sting again.
For from this proceeds the passing quickness of his
       attention. 65
For by stroaking of him I have found out electricity.
For I perceived God's light about him both wax and fire.
For the Electrical fire is the spiritual substance, which
       God sends from heaven to sustain the bodies both
       of man and beast.
For God has blessed him in the variety of his movements.
For, tho' he cannot fly, he is an excellent clamberer. 70
For his motions upon the face of the earth are more than
       any other quadrupede.

[7] Ichneumon, or mongoose.

For he can tread to all the measures upon the musick.
For he can swim for life.
For he can creep.

WILLIAM BLAKE
1757–1827

THE ECCHOING GREEN[1]

The Sun does arise,
And make happy the skies.
The merry bells ring
To welcome the Spring.
The skylark and thrush,   5
The birds of the bush,
Sing louder around
To the bells' cheerful sound;
While our sports shall be seen
On the Ecchoing Green.   10

Old John, with white hair,
Does laugh away care,
Sitting under the oak,
Among the old folk.
They laugh at our play,   15
And soon they all say:
Such, such were the joys,
When we all, girls and boys,
In our youth time were seen,
On the Ecchoing Green.   20

Till the little ones, weary,
No more can be merry;
The sun does descend,
And our sports have an end:
Round the laps of their mothers   25
Many sisters and brothers,

[1] The spelling of "Ecchoing" is Blake's.

Like birds in their nest,
Are ready for rest;
And sport no more seen,
On the darkening Green.   30

THE LAMB

    Little Lamb, who made thee?
    Dost thou know who made thee?
Gave thee life and bid thee feed,
By the stream and o'er the mead;
Gave thee clothing of delight,   5
Softest clothing wooly bright;
Gave thee such a tender voice,
Making all the vales rejoice?
    Little Lamb, who made thee?
    Dost thou know who made thee?   10

    Little Lamb, I'll tell thee,
    Little Lamb, I'll tell thee:
He is callèd by thy name,
For He calls Himself a Lamb:
He is meek, and He is mild;   15
He became a little child:
I a child, and thou a lamb,
We are callèd by His name.
    Little Lamb, God bless thee.
    Little Lamb, God bless thee.   20

THE CLOD AND THE PEBBLE

"Love seeketh not Itself to please,
 Nor for itself hath any care,
 But for another gives its ease,
 And builds a Heaven in Hell's despair."

So sang a little Clod of Clay   5
Trodden with the cattle's feet,
But a Pebble of the brook
Warbled out these metres meet:

"Love seeketh only Self to please,
 To bind another to its delight,
 Joys in another's loss of ease,
 And builds a Hell in Heaven's despite."[1]

A POISON TREE

I was angry with my friend:
I told my wrath, my wrath did end.
I was angry with my foe:
I told it not, my wrath did grow.

And I water'd it in fears,   5
Night and morning with my tears;
And I sunnèd it with smiles,
And with soft deceitful wiles.

And it grew both day and night,
Till it bore an apple bright.   10
And my foe beheld it shine,
And he knew that it was mine,

And into my garden stole
When the night had veil'd the pole;[1]
In the morning glad I see   15
My foe outstretch'd beneath the tree.

AH, SUN-FLOWER!

Ah, Sun-flower! weary of time,
Who countest the steps of the Sun:
Seeking after that sweet golden clime
Where the traveller's journey is done;

Where the Youth pined away with desire,   5
And the pale Virgin shrouded in snow,

[1] In spite of Heaven.

[1] Polestar or North Star.

Arise from their graves and aspire,[1]
Where my Sun-flower wishes to go.

LONDON

I wander through each charter'd[1] street,
Near where the charter'd Thames does flow,
And mark in every face I meet
Marks of weakness, marks of woe.

In every cry of every man,   5
In every infant's cry of fear,
In every voice, in every ban
The mind-forg'd manacles I hear.

How the chimney-sweeper's cry
Every black'ning church appalls,   10
And the hapless soldier's sigh
Runs in blood down palace walls.

But most through midnight streets I hear
How the youthful harlot's curse
Blasts the new-born infant's tear   15
And blights with plagues the marriage hearse.

STANZAS FROM *MILTON*

And did those feet in ancient time
Walk upon England's mountains green?
And was the holy Lamb of God
On England's pleasant pastures seen?

And did the Countenance Divine   5
Shine forth upon our clouded hills?
And was Jerusalem builded here,
Among these dark Satanic mills?

[1] Ascend.

[1] Privileged, licensed.

Bring me my bow of burning gold!
Bring me my arrows of desire!   10
Bring me my spear! O clouds, unfold!
Bring me my chariot of fire!

I will not cease from mental fight,
Nor shall my sword sleep in my hand:
Till we have built Jerusalem   15
In England's green and pleasant land.

ROBERT BURNS
1759-1796

MARY MORISON

O Mary, at thy window be!
    It is the wish'd, the trysted hour.[1]
Those smiles and glances let me see,
    That make the miser's treasure poor.
    How blythely wad I bide the stoure,[2]   5
A weary slave frae sun to sun,
    Could I the rich reward secure—
The lovely Mary Morison!

Yestreen,[3] when to the trembling string
    The dance gaed[4] thro' the lighted ha',   10
To thee my fancy took its wing,
    I sat, but neither heard or saw:
    Tho' this was fair, and that was braw,[5]
And yon the toast of a' the town,
    I sigh'd and said amang them a':—   15
"Ye are na Mary Morison!"

O Mary, canst thou wreck his peace
    Wha[6] for thy sake wad gladly die?

---

[1] The hour appointed for a tryst.   [2] Would I wait out the storm, or tumult.
[3] Yesterday evening.   [4] Went.   [5] Brave; that is, splendid, showy.   [6] Who.

Or canst thou break that heart of his
    Whase only faut is loving thee?
    If love for love thou wilt na gie,
At least be pity to me shown:
    A thought ungentle canna be
The thought o' Mary Morison.

ADDRESS TO THE UNCO GUID[1]

or The Rigidly Righteous

    My Son, these maxims make a rule,
      An' lump them ay thegither:
    The Rigid Righteous is a fool,
      The Rigid Wise anither;
    The cleanest corn that e'er was dight[2]
      May hae some pyles o' caff[3] in;
    So ne'er a fellow-creature slight
      For random fits o' daffin.[4]
        SOLOMON (Eccles. vii. 16)

O ye, wha are sae guid yoursel,
    Sae pious and sae holy,
Ye've nought to do but mark and tell
    Your neebours' fauts and folly;
Whase life is like a weel-gaun[5] mill,   5
    Supplied wi' store o' water;
The heapet happer's[6] ebbing still,
    An' still the clap[7] plays clatter!

Hear me, ye venerable core,
    As counsel for poor mortals   10
That frequent pass douce[8] Wisdom's door
    For glaikit[9] Folly's portals:
I for their thoughtless, careless sakes
    Would here propone[10] defences—
Their donsie[11] tricks, their black mistakes,   15
    Their failings and mischances.

Ye see your state wi' theirs compared,
    And shudder at the niffer;[12]

[1] Uncommon good; that is, those who profess to be strict in matters of morals and religion.   [2] Winnowed.   [3] Chaff.   [4] Fooling, frolicking.   [5] Wheel-driven. [6] Heaped hopper.   [7] Clapper (of the mill).   [8] Sober.   [9] Senseless, giddy.   [10] Propound, propose.   [11] Unfortunate.   [12] Exchange.

But cast a moment's fair regard,
    What makes the mighty differ?[13]   20
Discount what scant occasion[14] gave;
    That purity ye pride in;
And (what's aft mair than a' the lave[15])
    Your better art o' hidin.

Think, when your castigated pulse   25
    Gies now and then a wallop,
What ragings must his veins convulse,
    That still eternal gallop!
Wi' wind and tide fair i' your tail,
    Right on ye scud[16] your sea-way;   30
But in the teeth o' baith to sail,
    It makes an unco[17] lee-way.

See Social-life and Glee sit down
    All joyous and unthinking,
Till, quite transmugrify'd,[18] they're grown   35
    Debauchery and Drinking:
O, would they stay to calculate
    Th' eternal consequences,
Or—your more dreaded hell to state—
    Damnation of expenses!   40

Ye high, exalted, virtuous dames,
    Tied up in godly laces,
Before ye gie poor Frailty names,
    Suppose a change o' cases:
A dear-lov'd lad, convenience snug,   45
    A treach'rous inclination—
But, let me whisper i' your lug,[19]
    Ye're aiblins[20] nae temptation.

Then gently scan your brother man,
    Still gentler sister woman;   50
Tho' they may gang a kennin[21] wrang,
    To step aside is human:
One point must still be greatly dark,
    The moving[22] *why* they do it;

13 Difference.   14 Chance, coincidence.   15 What's often more than all the rest.
16 Sail swiftly, before the wind.   17 Strange, uncommon.   18 Transmogrified; that is, transformed, metamorphosed (humorous).   19 Ear.   20 Perhaps.   21 Just enough to be perceived; a little.   22 Reason.

And just as lamely can ye mark   55
   How far perhaps they rue it.

Who made the heart, 't is He alone
   Decidedly can try us:
He knows each chord, its various tone,
   Each spring, its various bias: 60
Then at the balance[23] let's be mute,
   We never can adjust it;
What's done we partly may compute,
   But know not what's resisted.

AULD LANG SYNE[1]

Should auld acquaintance be forgot,
   And never brought to mind?
Should auld acquaintance be forgot,
   And auld lang syne!

CHORUS

   For auld lang syne, my dear,   5
      For auld lang syne,
   We'll tak a cup o' kindness yet
      For auld lang syne!

And surely ye'll be your pint-stowp,[2]
   And surely I'll be mine,   10
And we'll tak a cup o' kindness yet
   For auld lang syne!

We twa hae run about the braes,[3]
   And pou'd[4] the gowans[5] fine,
But we've wander'd monie a weary fit[6]   15
   Sin' auld lang syne.

We twa hae paidl'd in the burn[7]
   Frae morning sun till dine,[8]

[23] Scale (of justice).

[1] Old long-since; that it, old times.   [2] Pint-stoup; tankard holding a pint (of beer or ale).   [3] Hillsides.   [4] Pulled, picked.   [5] Daisies.   [6] Spell (period of time).
[7] Stream, brook.   [8] Dinner.

But seas between us braid hae roar'd
    Sin' auld lang syne. 20

And there's a hand, my trusty fiere,[9]
    And gie's a hand o' thine,
And we'll tak a right guid-willie waught[10]
    For auld lang syne!

ROBERT BRUCE'S MARCH TO BANNOCKBURN[1]

Scots, wha hae wi' Wallace[2] bled,
Scots, wham Bruce has aften led;
Welcome to your gory bed,
    Or to victorie!

Now's the day, and now's the hour; 5
See the front o' battle lour:[3]
See approach proud Edward's pow'r—
    Chains and slaverie!

Wha will be a traitor-knave?
Wha can fill a coward's grave? 10
Wha sae base as be a slave?
    Let him turn and flee!

Wha for Scotland's king and law
Freedom's sword will strongly draw,
Freeman stand, or freeman fa'; 15
    Let him follow me!

By oppression's woes and pains!
By our sons in servile chains!
We will drain our dearest veins,
    But they shall be free! 20

[9] Fellow, friend.   [10] Good-will draught.

[1] In 1314, Robert Bruce routed the English under Edward II at Bannockburn.
[2] Sir William Wallace (1272?–1305), a Scottish patriot who devoted his life to resisting the English.   [3] Scowl; look dark and threatening.

Lay the proud usurpers low!
Tyrants fall in every foe!
Liberty's in every blow!—
　　Let us do or die!

A RED, RED ROSE

O, my luve is like a red, red rose,
　　That's newly sprung¹ in June.
O, my luve is like the melodie,
　　That's sweetly play'd in tune.

As fair art thou, my bonie² lass,
　　So deep in luve am I,
And I will luve thee still, my dear,
　　Till a' the seas gang dry.

Till a' the seas gang dry, my dear,
　　And the rocks melt wi' the sun!　　　　　　　　10
And I will luve thee still, my dear,
　　While the sands o' life shall run.

And fare thee weel, my only luve,
　　And fare thee weel a while!
And I will come again, my luve,　　　　　　　　15
　　Tho' it were ten thousand mile!

A MAN'S A MAN FOR A' THAT

Is there for honest poverty
　　That hings his head, an' a' that?
The coward slave, we pass him by,
　　We dare be poor for a' that!
For a' that, an' a' that,　　　　　　　　5
　　Our toils obscure, an' a' that,
The rank is but the guinea's stamp;¹
　　The man's the gowd² for a' that.

¹ Burst forth; bloomed.　　² Bonny.

¹ The guinea is the highest valued English coin.　　² Gold.

What though on hamely fare we dine,
    Wear hodd'n grey,[3] an' a' that?   10
Gie fools their silks, and knaves their wine,
    A man's a man for a' that.
For a' that, an' a' that,
    Their tinsel show, an' a' that,
The honest man, tho' e'er sae poor,   15
    Is king o' men for a' that.

Ye see yon birkie[4] ca'd a lord,
    Wha struts, an' stares, an' a' that;
Tho' hundreds worship at his word,
    He's but a coof[5] for a' that.   20
For a' that, an' a' that,
    His ribband, star, an' a' that.
The man o' independent mind,
    He looks an' laughs at a' that.

A prince can mak a belted knight,   25
    A marquis, duke, an' a' that;
But an honest man's aboon[6] his might,
    Guid faith, he mauna fa'[7] that!
For a' that, an' a' that,
    Their dignities, an' a' that,   30
The pith o' sense, an' pride o' worth,
    Are higher rank than a' that.

Then let us pray that come it may,
    As come it will, for a' that,
That sense and worth o'er a' the earth   35
    Shall bear the gree,[8] an' a' that!
For a' that an' a' that,
    It's comin yet, for a' that,
That man to man the world o'er,
    Shall brithers be for a' that.   40

[3] Hodden grey, a course woolen cloth worn by the peasantry.   [4] Strutting fellow.
[5] Dull fellow.   [6] Above.   [7] Cannot depreciate.   [8] Victory, prize.

WILLIAM WORDSWORTH

1770–1850

EXPOSTULATION AND REPLY

"Why, William, on that old grey stone,
    Thus for the length of half a day,
Why, William, sit you thus alone,
    And dream your time away?

"Where are your books?—that light bequeathed   5
    To Beings else forlorn and blind!
Up! up! and drink the spirit breathed
    From dead men to their kind.

"You look round on your Mother Earth,
    As if she for no purpose bore you;   10
As if you were her first-born birth,
    And none had lived before you!"

One morning thus, by Esthwaite lake,
    When life was sweet, I knew not why,
To me my good friend Matthew spake,   15
    And thus I made reply:

"The eye—it cannot choose but see;
    We cannot bid the ear be still;
Our bodies feel, where'er they be,
    Against or with our will.   20

"Nor less I deem that there are Powers
    Which of themselves our minds impress;
That we can feed this mind of ours
    In a wise passiveness.

"Think you, 'mid all this mighty sum   25
    Of things forever speaking,
That nothing of itself will come,
    But we must still be seeking?

"—Then ask not wherefore, here, alone,
    Conversing as I may,   30
I sit upon this old gray stone,
    And dream my time away."

THE TABLES TURNED

An Evening Scene on the Same Subject

Up! up! my Friend, and quit your books;
    Or surely you'll grow double:
Up! up! my Friend, and clear your looks;
    Why all this toil and trouble?

The sun, above the mountain's head,   5
    A freshening lustre mellow
Through all the long green fields has spread,
    His first sweet evening yellow.

Books! 'tis a dull and endless strife:
    Come, hear the woodland linnet,   10
How sweet his music! on my life,
    There's more of wisdom in it.

And hark! how blithe the throstle sings!
    He, too, is no mean preacher:
Come forth into the light of things,   15
    Let Nature be your Teacher.

She has a world of ready wealth,
    Our minds and hearts to bless—
Spontaneous wisdom breathed by health,
    Truth breathed by cheerfulness.   20

One impulse from a vernal wood
    May teach you more of man,
Of moral evil and of good,
    Than all the sages can.

Sweet is the lore which Nature brings;   25
    Our meddling intellect

Mis-shapes the beauteous forms of things:—
    We murder to dissect.

Enough of Science and of Art;
    Close up those barren leaves;   30
Come forth, and bring with you a heart
    That watches and receives.

SHE DWELT AMONG THE UNTRODDEN WAYS

She dwelt among the untrodden ways
    Beside the springs of Dove,
A Maid whom there were none to praise
    And very few to love:

A violet by a mossy stone   5
    Half hidden from the eye!
—Fair as a star, when only one
    Is shining in the sky.

She lived unknown, and few could know
    When Lucy ceased to be;   10
But she is in her grave, and, oh,
    The difference to me!

THERE WAS A BOY

        There was a Boy: ye knew him well, ye cliffs
And islands of Winander!—many a time
At evening, when the earliest stars began
To move along the edges of the hills,
Rising or setting, would he stand alone   5
Beneath the trees or by the glimmering lake,
And there, with fingers interwoven, both hands
Pressed closely palm to palm, and to his mouth
Uplifted, he, as through an instrument,
Blew mimic hootings to the silent owls,   10
That they might answer him; and they would shout
Across the watery vale, and shout again,
Responsive to his call, with quivering peals,

And long halloos and screams, and echoes loud,
Redoubled and redoubled, concourse wild   15
Of jocund din; and, when a lengthened pause
Of silence came and baffled his best skill,
Then sometimes, in that silence while he hung
Listening, a gentle shock of mild surprise
Has carried far into his heart the voice   20
Of mountain torrents; or the visible scene
Would enter unawares into his mind,
With all its solemn imagery, its rocks,
Its woods, and that uncertain heaven, received
Into the bosom of the steady lake.   25

     This Boy was taken from his mates, and died
In childhood, ere he was full twelve years old.
Fair is the spot, most beautiful the vale
Where he was born; the grassy churchyard hangs
Upon a slope above the village school,   30
And through that churchyard when my way has led
On summer evenings, I believe that there
A long half hour together I have stood
Mute, looking at the grave in which he lies!

NUTTING

     —It seems a day
(I speak of one from many singled out)
One of those heavenly days that cannot die;
When, in the eagerness of boyish hope,
I left our cottage-threshold, sallying forth   5
With a huge wallet o'er my shoulders slung,
A nutting-crook[1] in hand; and turned my steps
Tow'rd some far-distant wood, a Figure quaint,
Tricked out in proud disguise of cast-off weeds[2]
Which for that service had been husbanded,   10
By exhortation of my frugal Dame—
Motley accoutrement, of power to smile
At thorns, and brakes, and brambles,—and, in truth,
More ragged than need was! O'er pathless rocks,
Through beds of matted fern, and tangled thickets   15
Forcing my way, I came to one dear nook
Unvisited, where not a broken bough
Drooped with its withered leaves, ungracious sign

[1] A hooked implement for gathering nuts.   [2] Clothes.

Of devastation; but the hazels rose
Tall and erect, with tempting clusters hung,   20
A virgin scene!—A little while I stood,
Breathing with such suppression of the heart
As joy delights in; and with wise restraint
Voluptuous, fearless of a rival, eyed
The banquet;—or beneath the trees I sate   25
Among the flowers, and with the flowers I played;
A temper known to those who, after long
And weary expectation, have been blest
With sudden happiness beyond all hope.
Perhaps it was a bower beneath whose leaves   30
The violets of five seasons re-appear
And fade, unseen by any human eye;
Where fairy water-breaks³ do murmur on
For ever; and I saw the sparkling foam,
And—with my cheek on one of those green stones   35
That, fleeced with moss, under the shady trees,
Lay round me, scattered like a flock of sheep—
I heard the murmur and the murmuring sound.
In that sweet mood when pleasure loves to pay
Tribute to ease; and, of its joy secure,   40
The heart luxuriates with indifferent things,
Wasting its kindliness on stocks and stones,
And on the vacant air. Then up I rose,
And dragged to earth both branch and bough, with crash
And merciless ravage: and the shady nook   45
Of hazels, and the green and mossy bower,
Deformed and sullied, patiently gave up
Their quiet being: and unless I now
Confound my present feelings with the past,
Ere from the mutilated bower I turned   50
Exulting, rich beyond the wealth of kings,
I felt a sense of pain when I beheld
The silent trees, and saw the intruding sky.—
Then, dearest Maiden, move along these shades
In gentleness of heart; with gentle hand   55
Touch—for there is a spirit in the woods.

COMPOSED UPON WESTMINSTER BRIDGE

Earth has not anything to show more fair:
Dull would he be of soul who could pass by
A sight so touching in its majesty:

³ Broken water.

This city now doth, like a garment, wear
The beauty of the morning; silent, bare,   5
Ships, towers, domes, theatres, and temples lie
Open unto the fields, and to the sky;
All bright and glittering in the smokeless air.
Never did sun more beautifully steep
In his first splendour, valley, rock, or hill;   10
Ne'er saw I, never felt, a calm so deep!
The river glideth at his own sweet will:
Dear God! the very houses seem asleep;
And all that mighty heart is lying still!

THE WORLD IS TOO MUCH WITH US

The world is too much with us; late and soon,
Getting and spending, we lay waste our powers:
Little we see in Nature that is ours;
We have given our hearts away, a sordid boon!
This Sea that bares her bosom to the moon;   5
The winds that will be howling at all hours,
And are up-gathered now like sleeping flowers;
For this, for everything, we are out of tune;
It moves us not.—Great God! I'd rather be
A Pagan suckled in a creed outworn;   10
So might I, standing on this pleasant lea,
Have glimpses that would make me less forlorn;
Have sight of Proteus[1] rising from the sea;
Or hear old Triton blow his wreathèd horn.

SURPRISED BY JOY

Surprised by joy—impatient as the Wind
I turned to share the transport—Oh! with whom
But Thee,[1] deep buried in the silent tomb,
That spot which no vicissitude can find?
Love, faithful love, recalled thee to my mind—   5
But how could I forget thee? Through what power,
Even for the least division of an hour,

[1] Proteus, like Triton (line 14), was a sea god. Both were sons of Poseidon (or Neptune), principal god of the sea. Proteus could change his shape at will; Triton controlled the waves by blowing on a conch shell.

[1] Wordsworth's daughter Catherine.

Have I been so beguiled as to be blind
To my most grievous loss!—That thought's return
Was the worst pang that sorrow ever bore,   10
Save one, one only, when I stood forlorn,
Knowing my heart's best treasure was no more;
That neither present time, nor years unborn
Could to my sight that heavenly face restore.

THE SOLITARY REAPER

Behold her, single in the field,
Yon solitary Highland Lass!
Reaping and singing by herself;
Stop here, or gently pass!
Alone she cuts and binds the grain,   5
And sings a melancholy strain;
O listen! for the Vale profound
Is overflowing with the sound.

No Nightingale did ever chaunt
More welcome notes to weary bands   10
Of travellers in some shady haunt,
Among Arabian sands:
A voice so thrilling ne'er was heard
In springtime from the Cuckoo-bird,
Breaking the silence of the seas   15
Among the farthest Hebrides.[1]

Will no one tell me what she sings?—
Perhaps the plaintive numbers flow
For old, unhappy, far-off things,
And battles long ago: 20
Or is it some more humble lay,
Familiar matter of to-day?
Some natural sorrow, loss, or pain,
That has been, and may be again?

Whate'er the theme, the Maiden sang   25
As if her song could have no ending;
I saw her singing at her work,
And o'er the sickle bending:—

[1] Islands off the west coast of Scotland.

I listened, motionless and still;
And, as I mounted up the hill,
The music in my heart I bore,
Long after it was heard no more.

30

STEPPING WESTWARD

"What, you are stepping westward?"—"Yea."
—'T would be a *wildish* destiny,
If we, who thus together roam
In a strange Land, and far from home,
Were in this place the guests of Chance:
Yet who would stop, or fear to advance,
Though home or shelter he had none,
With such a sky to lead him on?

5

The dewy ground was dark and cold;
Behind, all gloomy to behold;
And stepping westward seemed to be
A kind of *heavenly* destiny:
I liked the greeting;[1] 't was a sound
Of something without place or bound;
And seemed to give me spiritual right
To travel through that region bright.

10

15

The voice was soft, and she who spake
Was walking by her native lake:
The salutation had to me
The very sound of courtesy:
Its power was felt; and while my eye
Was fixed upon the glowing Sky,
The echo of the voice enwrought
A human sweetness with the thought
Of travelling through the world that lay
Before me in my endless way.

20

25

[1] The greeting is in the first line of the poem.

ODE: INTIMATIONS OF IMMORTALITY FROM RECOLLECTIONS OF EARLY CHILDHOOD

The Child is father of the Man;
And I could wish my days to be
Bound each to each by natural piety.[1]

I

There was a time when meadow, grove, and stream,
The earth, and every common sight,
    To me did seem
    Apparelled in celestial light,
The glory and the freshness of a dream.   5
It is not now as it hath been of yore;—
    Turn wheresoe'er I may,
    By night or day,
The things which I have seen I now can see no more.

II

    The Rainbow comes and goes,   10
    And lovely is the Rose;
    The Moon doth with delight
Look round her when the heavens are bare;
    Waters on a starry night
    Are beautiful and fair;   15
    The sunshine is a glorious birth;
    But yet I know, where'er I go,
That there hath passed away a glory from the earth.

III

Now, while the birds thus sing a joyous song,
    And while the young lambs bound   20
    As to the tabor's sound,
To me alone there came a thought of grief:
A timely utterance gave that thought relief,
    And I again am strong:
The cataracts blow their trumpets from the steep;   25

[1] As the epigraph to the Ode, Wordsworth uses the last three lines of a poem of his own:

> My heart leaps up when I behold
>   A rainbow in the sky:
> So was it when my life began;
> So is it now I am a man;
> So be it when I shall grow old,
>   Or let me die!
> The child is father . . . [etc.]

No more shall grief of mine the season wrong;
I hear the Echoes through the mountains throng,
The Winds come to me from the fields of sleep,
      And all the earth is gay;
        Land and sea   30
     Give themselves up to jollity,
       And with the heart of May
      Doth every Beast keep holiday;—
        Thou Child of Joy,
Shout round me, let me hear thy shouts, thou happy Shepherd-boy!   35

IV

Ye blessèd Creatures, I have heard the call
Ye to each other make; I see
The heavens laugh with you in your jubilee;
My heart is at your festival,
      My head hath its coronal,   40
The fulness of your bliss, I feel—I feel it all.
     Oh, evil day! if I were sullen
     While Earth herself is adorning,
       This sweet May-morning,
     And the Children are culling   45
       On every side,
      In a thousand valleys far and wide,
      Fresh flowers; while the sun shines warm,
And the Babe leaps up on his Mother's arm:—
      I hear, I hear, with joy I hear!   50
     —But there's a Tree, of many, one,
A single Field which I have looked upon,
Both of them speak of something that is gone:
      The Pansy at my feet
      Doth the same tale repeat: 55
Whither is fled the visionary gleam?
Where is it now, the glory and the dream?

V

Our birth is but a sleep and a forgetting:
The Soul that rises with us, our life's Star,
      Hath had elsewhere its setting,   60
      And cometh from afar:
     Not in entire forgetfulness,
     And not in utter nakedness,
But trailing clouds of glory do we come
      From God, who is our home: 65
Heaven lies about us in our infancy!
Shades of the prison-house begin to close
      Upon the growing Boy,

But he beholds the light, and whence it flows
    He sees it in his joy;   70
The Youth, who daily farther from the east
    Must travel, still is Nature's Priest,
    And by the vision splendid
    Is on his way attended;
At length the Man perceives it die away,   75
And fade into the light of common day.

VI

Earth fills her lap with pleasures of her own;
Yearnings she hath in her own natural kind,
And, even with something of a Mother's mind,
    And no unworthy aim,   80
    The homely Nurse doth all she can
To make her Foster-child, her Inmate Man,
    Forget the glories he hath known,
And that imperial palace whence he came.

VII

Behold the Child among his new-born blisses,   85
A six years' Darling of a pigmy size!
See, where 'mid work of his own hand he lies,
Fretted by sallies of his mother's kisses,
With light upon him from his father's eyes!
See, at his feet, some little plan or chart,   90
Some fragment from his dream of human life,
Shaped by himself with newly-learnèd art;
    A wedding or a festival,
    A mourning or a funeral,
      And this hath now his heart,   95
    And unto this he frames his song:
      Then will he fit his tongue
To dialogues of business, love, or strife;
    But it will not be long
    Ere this be thrown aside,   100
    And with new joy and pride
The little Actor cons another part;
Filling from time to time his "humorous stage"
With all the Persons, down to palsied Age,
That Life brings with her in her equipage;   105
    As if his whole vocation
    Were endless imitation.

VIII

Thou, whose exterior semblance doth belie
    Thy Soul's immensity;

Thou best Philosopher, who yet dost keep 110
Thy heritage, thou Eye among the blind,
That, deaf and silent, read'st the eternal deep,
Haunted for ever by the eternal mind,—
      Mighty Prophet! Seer blest!
      On whom those truths do rest, 115
Which we are toiling all our lives to find,
In darkness lost, the darkness of the grave;
Thou, over whom thy Immortality
Broods like the Day, a Master o'er a Slave,
A Presence which is not to be put by; 120
Thou little Child, yet glorious in the might
Of heaven-born freedom on thy being's height,
Why with such earnest pains dost thou provoke
The years to bring the inevitable yoke,
Thus blindly with thy blessedness at strife? 125
Full soon thy Soul shall have her earthly freight,
And custom lie upon thee with a weight,
Heavy as frost, and deep almost as life!

IX

      O joy! that in our embers
      Is something that doth live, 130
      That nature yet remembers
      What was so fugitive!
The thought of our past years in me doth breed
Perpetual benediction: not indeed
For that which is most worthy to be blest; 135
Delight and liberty, the simple creed
Of Childhood, whether busy or at rest,
With new-fledged hope still fluttering in his breast:—
      Not for these I raise
      The song of thanks and praise; 140
      But for those obstinate questionings
      Of sense and outward things,
      Fallings from us, vanishings;
      Blank misgivings of a Creature
Moving about in worlds not realised, 145
High instincts, before which our mortal Nature
Did tremble like a guilty Thing surprised:
      But for those first affections,
      Those shadowy recollections,
      Which, be they what they may, 150
Are yet the fountain-light of all our day,
Are yet a master-light of all our seeing;
      Uphold us, cherish, and have power to make
Our noisy years seem moments in the being

Of the eternal Silence: truths that wake,
   To perish never;
Which neither listlessness, nor mad endeavour,
   Nor Man nor Boy,
Nor all that is at enmity with joy,
Can utterly abolish or destroy!
   Hence in a season of calm weather
   Though inland far we be,
Our souls have sight of that immortal sea
   Which brought us hither;
   Can in a moment travel thither,—
And see the Children sport upon the shore,
And hear the mighty waters rolling evermore.

155

160

165

X

Then, sing, ye Birds, sing, sing a joyous song!
   And let the young Lambs bound
   As to the tabor's sound!
We, in thought, will join your throng,
   Ye that pipe and ye that play,
   Ye that through your hearts to-day
   Feel the gladness of the May!
What though the radiance which was once so bright
Be now for ever taken from my sight,
   Though nothing can bring back the hour
Of splendour in the grass, of glory in the flower;
   We will grieve not, rather find
   Strength in what remains behind;
   In the primal sympathy
   Which having been must ever be;
   In the soothing thoughts that spring
   Out of human suffering;
   In the faith that looks through death,
In years that bring the philosophic mind.

170

175

180

185

XI

And O, ye Fountains, Meadows, Hills, and Groves,
Forbode not any severing of our loves!
Yet in my heart of hearts I feel your might;
I only have relinquished one delight
To live beneath your more habitual sway.
I love the Brooks which down their channels fret,
Even more than when I tripped lightly as they;
The innocent brightness of a new-born Day
   Is lovely yet;
The Clouds that gather round the setting sun
Do take a sober colouring from an eye

190

195

That hath kept watch o'er man's mortality;
Another race hath been, and other palms are won.
Thanks to the human heart by which we live, 200
Thanks to its tenderness, its joys, and fears,
To me the meanest flower that blows can give
Thoughts that do often lie too deep for tears.

SAMUEL TAYLOR COLERIDGE
1772–1834

FROST AT MIDNIGHT

The Frost performs its secret ministry,
Unhelped by any wind. The owlet's cry
Came loud—and hark, again! loud as before.
The inmates of my cottage, all at rest,
Have left me to that solitude, which suits 5
Abstruser musings: save that at my side
My cradled infant slumbers peacefully.

'Tis calm indeed! so calm, that it disturbs
And vexes meditation with its strange
And extreme silentness. Sea, hill, and wood, 10
This populous village! Sea, and hill, and wood,
With all the numberless goings-on of life,
Inaudible as dreams! the thin blue flame
Lies on my low-burnt fire, and quivers not;
Only that film, which fluttered on the grate, 15
Still flutters there, the sole unquiet thing.
Methinks, its motion in this hush of nature
Gives it dim sympathies with me who live,
Making it a companionable form,
Whose puny flaps and freaks the idling Spirit 20
By its own moods interprets, every where
Echo or mirror seeking of itself,
And makes a toy of Thought.
                    But O! how oft,
How oft, at school, with most believing mind,
Presageful, have I gazed upon the bars, 25

To watch that fluttering *stranger!* and as oft
With unclosed lids, already had I dreamt
Of my sweet birth-place, and the old church-tower,
Whose bells, the poor man's only music, rang
Form morn to evening, all the hot Fair-day,   30
So sweetly, that they stirred and haunted me
With a wild pleasure, falling on mine ear
Most like articulate sounds of things to come!
So gazed I, till the soothing things, I dreamt,
Lulled me to sleep, and sleep prolonged my dreams!   35
And so I brooded all the following morn,
Awed by the stern preceptor's face, mine eye
Fixed with mock study on my swimming book:
Save if the door half opened, and I snatched
A hasty glance, and still my heart leaped up,   40
For still I hoped to see the *stranger's* face,
Townsman, or aunt, or sister more beloved,
My play-mate when we both were clothed alike!

    Dear Babe, that sleepest cradled by my side,
Whose gentle breathings, heard in this deep calm,   45
Fill up the interspersed vacancies
And momentary pauses of the thought!
My babe so beautiful! it thrills my heart
With tender gladness, thus to look at thee,
And think that thou shalt learn far other lore,   50
And in far other scenes! For I was reared
In the great city, pent 'mid cloisters dim,
And saw nought lovely but the sky and stars.
But *thou,* my babe! shalt wander like a breeze
By lakes and sandy shores, beneath the crags   55
Of ancient mountain, and beneath the clouds,
Which image in their bulk both lakes and shores
And mountain crags: so shalt thou see and hear
The lovely shapes and sounds intelligible
Of that eternal language, which thy God   60
Utters, who from eternity doth teach
Himself in all, and all things in himself.
Great universal Teacher! he shall mould
Thy spirit, and by giving make it ask.

    Therefore all seasons shall be sweet to thee,   65
Whether the summer clothe the general earth
With greenness, or the redbreast sit and sing
Betwixt the tufts of snow on the bare branch
Of mossy apple-tree, while the night thatch

Smokes in the sun-thaw; whether the eave-drops[1] fall   70
Heard only in the trances[2] of the blast,
Or if the secret ministry of frost
Shall hang them up in silent icicles,
Quietly shining to the quiet Moon.

DEJECTION: AN ODE

Late, late yestreen I saw the new Moon,
With the old Moon in her arms;
And I fear, I fear, my Master dear!
We shall have a deadly storm.
        Ballad of Sir Patrick Spence.[1]

I

Well! If the Bard was weather-wise, who made
    The grand old ballad of Sir Patrick Spence,
    This night, so tranquil now, will not go hence
Unroused by winds, that ply a busier trade
Than those which mould yon cloud in lazy flakes,   5
Or the dull sobbing draft, that moans and rakes
Upon the strings of this Æolian lute,[2]
      Which better far were mute.
    For lo! the New-moon winter-bright!
    And overspread with phantom light,   10
    (With swimming phantom light o'erspread
    But rimmed and circled by a silver thread)
I see the old Moon in her lap, foretelling
    The coming-on of rain and squally blast.
And oh! that even now the gust were swelling,   15
    And the slant night-shower driving loud and fast!
Those sounds which oft have raised me, whilst they awed,
      And sent my soul abroad,
Might now perhaps their wonted[3] impulse give,
Might startle this dull pain, and make it move and live!   20

II

A grief without a pang, void, dark, and drear,
    A stifled, drowsy, unimpassioned grief,

---

[1] Drops of rainwater from the eaves.   [2] Suspensions, pauses.

[1] See "Sir Patrick Spens," p. 970.   [2] In Greek mythology, Aeolus was god of the winds. An Aeolian lute is a stringed instrument that is hung so that the wind can blow over it, producing sounds of a rather melancholy kind.   [3] Customary, usual.

Which finds no natural outlet, no relief,
                In word, or sigh, or tear—
O Lady! in this wan and heartless mood,   25
To other thoughts by yonder throstle⁴ woo'd,
        All this long eve, so balmy and serene,
Have I been gazing on the western sky,
        And its peculiar tint of yellow green:
And still I gaze—and with how blank an eye!   30
And those thin clouds above, in flakes and bars,
That give away their motion to the stars;
Those stars, that glide behind them or between,
Now sparkling, now bedimmed, but always seen:
Yon crescent Moon, as fixed as if it grew   35
In its own cloudless, starless lake of blue;
I see them all so excellently fair,
I see, not feel, how beautiful they are!

            III

            My genial spirits fail;
            And what can these avail   40
To lift the smothering weight from off my breast?
            It were a vain endeavour,
            Though I should gaze for ever
On that green light that lingers in the west:
I may not hope from outward forms to win   45
The passion and the life, whose fountains are within.

            IV

O Lady! we receive but what we give,
And in our life alone does Nature live:
Ours is her wedding garment, ours her shroud!
        And would we aught behold, of higher worth,   50
Than that inanimate cold world allowed
To the poor loveless ever-anxious crowd,
        Ah! from the soul itself must issue forth
A light, a glory, a fair luminous cloud
            Enveloping the Earth—   55
And from the soul itself must there be sent
        A sweet and potent voice, of its own birth,
Of all sweet sounds the life and element!

            V

O pure of heart! thou need'st not ask of me
What this strong music in the soul may be!   60

    ⁴ Thrush.

What, and wherein it doth exist,
This light, this glory, this fair luminous mist,
This beautiful and beauty-making power.
    Joy, virtuous Lady! Joy that ne'er was given,
Save to the pure, and in their purest hour,   65
Life, and Life's effluence, cloud at once and shower,
Joy, Lady! is the spirit and the power,
Which wedding Nature to us gives in dower
    A new Earth and new Heaven,
Undreamt of by the sensual and the proud—   70
Joy is the sweet voice, Joy the luminous cloud—
        We in ourselves rejoice!
And thence flows all that charms or ear or sight,
    All melodies the echoes of that voice,
All colours a suffusion from that light.   75

VI

There was a time when, though my path was rough,
    This joy within me dallied with distress,
And all misfortunes were but as the stuff
    Whence Fancy made me dreams of happiness:
For hope grew round me, like the twining vine,   80
And fruits, and foliage, not my own, seemed mine.
But now afflictions bow me down to earth:
Nor care I that they rob me of my mirth;
        But oh! each visitation
Suspends what nature gave me at my birth,   85
    My shaping spirit of Imagination.
For not to think of what I needs must feel,
    But to be still and patient, all I can;
And haply by abstruse research to steal
    From my own nature all the natural man—   90
    This was my sole resource, my only plan:
Till that which suits a part infects the whole,
And now is almost grown the habit of my soul.

VII

Hence, viper thoughts, that coil around my mind,
    Reality's dark dream!   95
I turn from you, and listen to the wind,
    Which long has raved unnoticed. What a scream
Of agony by torture lengthened out
That lute sent forth! Thou Wind, that rav'st without,
    Bare crag, or mountain-tairn, or blasted tree,   100
Or pine-grove whither woodman never clomb,
Or lonely house, long held the witches' home,
    Methinks were fitter instruments for thee,

Mad Lutanist! who in this month of showers,
Of dark-brown gardens, and of peeping flowers, 105
Mak'st Devils' yule, with worse than wintry song,
The blossoms, buds, and timorous leaves among.
    Thou Actor, perfect in all tragic sounds!
Thou mighty Poet, e'en to frenzy bold!
        What tell'st thou now about? 110
        'Tis of the rushing of an host in rout,
    With groans, of trampled men, with smarting wounds—
At once they groan with pain, and shudder with the cold!
But hush! there is a pause of deepest silence!
    And all that noise, as of a rushing crowd, 115
With groans, and tremulous shudderings—all is over—
    It tells another tale, with sounds less deep and loud!
        A tale of less affright,
        And tempered with delight,
As Otway's self[5] had framed the tender lay,— 120
        'Tis of a little child
        Upon a lonesome wild,
Not far from home, but she hath lost her way:
And now moans low in bitter grief and fear,
And now screams loud, and hopes to make her mother hear. 125

VIII

'Tis midnight, but small thoughts have I of sleep:
Full seldom may my friends such vigils keep!
Visit her, gentle Sleep! with wings of healing,
    And may this storm be but a mountain-birth,
May all the stars hang bright above her dwelling, 130
    Silent as though they watched the sleeping Earth!
        With light heart may she rise,
        Gay fancy, cheerful eyes,
    Joy lift her spirit, joy attune her voice;
To her may all things live, from pole to pole, 135
Their life the eddying of her living soul!
    O simple spirit, guided from above,
Dear Lady! friend devoutest of my choice,
Thus mayest thou ever, evermore rejoice.

[5] Thomas Otway (1642–1685) wrote tragedies in blank verse.

GEORGE GORDON, LORD BYRON

1788–1824

DARKNESS

I had a dream, which was not all a dream.
The bright sun was extinguish'd, and the stars
Did wander darkling in the eternal space,
Rayless, and pathless, and the icy earth
Swung blind and blackening in the moonless air;   5
Morn came and went—and came, and brought no day,
And men forgot their passions in the dread
Of this their desolation; and all hearts
Were chill'd into a selfish prayer for light:
And they did live by watchfires—and the thrones,   10
The palaces of crowned kings—the huts,
The habitations of all things which dwell,
Were burnt for beacons; cities were consumed,
And men were gather'd round their blazing homes
To look once more into each other's face;   15
Happy were those who dwelt within the eye
Of the volcanos, and their mountain-torch:
A fearful hope was all the world contain'd;
Forests were set on fire—but hour by hour
They fell and faded—and the crackling trunks   20
Extinguish'd with a crash—and all was black.
The brows of men by the despairing light
Wore an unearthly aspect, as by fits
The flashes fell upon them; some lay down
And hid their eyes and wept; and some did rest   25
Their chins upon their clenchèd hands, and smiled;
And others hurried to and fro, and fed
Their funeral piles with fuel, and look'd up
With mad disquietude on the dull sky,
The pall of a past world; and then again   30
With curses cast them down upon the dust,
And gnash'd their teeth and howl'd: the wild birds shriek'd,
And, terrified, did flutter on the ground,
And flap their useless wings; the wildest brutes
Came tame and tremulous; and vipers crawl'd   35
And twined themselves among the multitude,

Hissing, but stingless—they were slain for food;
And War, which for a moment was no more,
Did glut himself again:—a meal was bought
With blood, and each sate sullenly apart   40
Gorging himself in gloom: no love was left;
All earth was but one thought—and that was death,
Immediate and inglorious; and the pang
Of famine fed upon all entrails—men
Died, and their bones were tombless as their flesh;   45
The meagre by the meagre were devour'd,
Even dogs assail'd their masters, all save one,
And he was faithful to a corse,[1] and kept
The birds and beasts and famish'd men at bay,
Till hunger clung[2] them, or the dropping dead   50
Lured their lank jaws; himself sought out no food,
But with a piteous and perpetual moan,
And a quick desolate cry, licking the hand
Which answer'd not with a caress—he died.
The crowd was famish'd by degrees; but two   55
Of an enormous city did survive,
And they were enemies: they met beside
The dying embers of an altar-place
Where had been heap'd a mass of holy things
For an unholy usage; they raked up,   60
And shivering scraped with their cold skeleton hands
The feeble ashes, and their feeble breath
Blew for a little life, and made a flame
Which was a mockery; then they lifted up
Their eyes as it grew lighter, and beheld   65
Each other's aspects—saw, and shriek'd, and died—
Even of their mutual hideousness they died,
Unknowing who he was upon whose brow
Famine had written Fiend. The world was void,
The populous and the powerful was a lump,   70
Seasonless, herbless, treeless, manless, lifeless—
A lump of death—a chaos of hard clay.
The rivers, lakes, and ocean all stool still,
And nothing stirr'd within their silent depths;
Ships sailorless lay rotting on the sea,   75
And their masts fell down piecemeal: as they dropp'd
They slept on the abyss without a surge—
The waves were dead; the tides were in their grave,
The Moon, their mistress, had expired before;
The winds were wither'd in the stagnant air,   80
And the clouds perish'd; Darkness had no need
Of aid from them—She was the Universe.

[1] Corpse.   [2] Shriveled, parched.

SHE WALKS IN BEAUTY

She walks in beauty, like the night
    Of cloudless climes and starry skies;
And all that's best of dark and bright
    Meet in her aspect and her eyes:
Thus mellow'd to that tender light   5
    Which heaven to gaudy day denies.

One shade the more, one ray the less,
    Had half impair'd the nameless grace
Which waves in every raven tress,
    Or softly lightens o'er her face;   10
Where thoughts serenely sweet express
    How pure, how dear their dwelling-place.

And on that cheek, and o'er that brow,
    So soft, so calm, yet eloquent,
The smiles that win, the tints that glow,   15
    But tell of days in goodness spent,
A mind at peace with all below,
    A heart whose love is innocent!

WHEN WE TWO PARTED

When we two parted
    In silence and tears,
Half broken-hearted
    To sever for years,
Pale grew thy cheek and cold,   5
    Colder thy kiss;
Truly that hour foretold
    Sorrow to this.

The dew of the morning
    Sunk chill on my brow—   10
It felt like the warning
    Of what I feel now.
Thy vows are all broken,
    And light is thy fame:
I hear thy name spoken,   15
    And share in its shame.

They name thee before me,
    A knell to mine ear;
A shudder comes o'er me—
    Why wert thou so dear?   20
They know not I knew thee,
    Who knew thee too well:—
Long, long shall I rue thee,
    Too deeply to tell.

In secret we met—   25
    In silence I grieve,
That thy heart could forget,
    Thy spirit deceive.
If I should meet thee
    After long years,   30
How should I greet thee?—
    With silence and tears.

SO, WE'LL GO NO MORE A-ROVING

So, we'll go no more a-roving
    So late into the night,
Though the heart be still as loving,
    And the moon be still as bright.

For the sword outwears its sheath,   5
    And the soul wears out the breast,
And the heart must pause to breathe,
    And love itself have rest.

Though the night was made for loving,
    And the day returns too soon,   10
Yet we'll go no more a-roving
    By the light of the moon.

PERCY BYSSHE SHELLEY

1792–1822

HYMN TO INTELLECTUAL BEAUTY

The awful shadow of some unseen Power
    Floats tho' unseen among us; visiting
    This various world with as inconstant wing
As summer winds that creep from flower to flower;
Like moonbeams that behind some piny mountain shower,   5
    It visits with inconstant glance
    Each human heart and countenance;
Like hues and harmonies of evening,
    Like clouds in starlight widely spread,
    Like memory of music fled,   10
    Like aught that for its grace may be
Dear, and yet dearer for its mystery.

Spirit of BEAUTY, that dost consecrate
    With thine own hues all thou dost shine upon
    Of human thought or form, where art thou gone?   15
Why dost thou pass away and leave our state,
This dim vast vale of tears, vacant and desolate?
    Ask why the sunlight not forever
    Weaves rainbows o'er yon mountain river,
Why aught should fail and fade that once is shewn,   20
    Why fear and dream and death and birth
    Cast on the daylight of this earth
    Such gloom, why man has such a scope
For love and hate, despondency and hope?

No voice from some sublimer world hath ever   25
    To sage or poet these responses given:
    Therefore the names of Demon, Ghost, and Heaven,
Remain the records of their vain endeavour:
Frail spells, whose uttered charm might not avail to sever,
    From all we hear and all we see,
    Doubt, chance, and mutability.   30
Thy light alone, like mist o'er mountains driven,
    Or music by the night wind sent
    Through strings of some still instrument,

Or moonlight on a midnight stream,   35
Gives grace and truth to life's unquiet dream.

Love, Hope, and Self-esteem, like clouds, depart
        And come, for some uncertain moments lent.
        Man were immortal, and omnipotent,
Didst thou, unknown and awful as thou art,   40
Keep with thy glorious train firm state within his heart.
        Thou messenger of sympathies,
        That wax and wane in lovers' eyes;
Thou, that to human thought art nourishment,
        Like darkness to a dying flame!   45
        Depart not as thy shadow came:
        Depart not, lest the grave should be,
Like life and fear, a dark reality.

While yet a boy I sought for ghosts, and sped
        Through many a listening chamber, cave and ruin,   50
        And starlight wood, with fearful steps pursuing
Hopes of high talk with the departed dead.
I called on poisonous names with which our youth is fed:
        I was not heard: I saw them not:
        When musing deeply on the lot   55
Of life, at that sweet time when winds are wooing
        All vital things that wake to bring
        News of birds and blossoming,
        Sudden, thy shadow fell on me:
I shrieked, and clasped my hands in ecstacy!   60

I vowed that I would dedicate my powers
        To thee and thine: have I not kept the vow?
        With beating heart and streaming eyes, even now
I call the phantoms of a thousand hours
Each from his voiceless grave: they have in visioned bowers   65
        Of studious zeal or love's delight
        Outwatched with me the envious night:
They know that never joy illumed my brow,
        Unlinked with hope that thou wouldst free
        This world from its dark slavery,   70
        That thou, O awful LOVELINESS,
Wouldst give whate'er these words cannot express.

The day becomes more solemn and serene
        When noon is past: there is a harmony
        In autumn, and a lustre in its sky,   75

Which through the summer is not heard or seen,
As if it could not be, as if it had not been!
       Thus let thy power, which like the truth
       Of nature on my passive youth
  Descended, to my onward life supply   80
       Its calm, to one who worships thee,
       And every form containing thee,
       Whom, SPIRIT fair, thy spells did bind
To fear himself, and love all human kind.

OZYMANDIAS[1]

I met a traveller from an antique land
Who said: Two vast and trunkless legs of stone
Stand in the desert. Near them, on the sand,
Half sunk, a shattered visage lies, whose frown,
And wrinkled lip, and sneer of cold command,   5
Tell that its sculptor well those passions read
Which yet survive, stamped on these lifeless things,
The hand that mocked them and the heart that fed;
And on the pedestal these words appear:
"My name is Ozymandias, king of kings: 10
Look on my works, ye Mighty, and despair!"
Nothing beside remains. Round the decay
Of that colossal wreck, boundless and bare
The lone and level sands stretch far away.

SONNET: ENGLAND IN 1819

An old, mad, blind, despised, and dying king,—
Princes, the dregs of their dull race, who flow
Through public scorn,—mud from a muddy spring;
Rulers who neither see, nor feel, nor know,
But leech-like to their fainting country cling,   5
Till they drop, blind in blood, without a blow;
A people starved and stabbed in the untilled field,—
An army, which liberticide[1] and prey
Makes a two-edged sword to all who wield,—
Golden and sanguine laws which tempt and slay,—   10
Religion Christless, Godless—a book sealed;

    [1] Rameses II, Pharaoh of Egypt, whose statue stood at Thebes.

    [1] Destruction of liberty.

A Senate, Time's worst statute unrepealed,—
Are graves, from which a glorious Phantom may
Burst, to illumine our tempestuous day.

TO NIGHT

Swiftly walk over the western Wave,
      Spirit of Night!
Out of the misty eastern cave
Where, all the long and lone daylight,
Thou wovest dreams of joy and fear,   5
Which make thee terrible and dear,—
      Swift be thy flight!

Wrap thy form in a mantle gray,
      Star-inwrought!
Blind with thine hair the eyes of Day,   10
Kiss her until she be wearied out,
Then wander o'er city, and sea, and land,
Touching all with thine opiate wand—
      Come, long-sought!

When I arose and saw the dawn,   15
      I sighed for thee;
When light rode high, and the dew was gone,
And noon lay heavy on flower and tree,
And the weary Day turned to his rest,
Lingering like an unloved guest,   20
      I sighed for thee.

Thy brother Death came, and cried,
      Wouldst thou me?
Thy sweet child Sleep, the filmy-eyed,
Murmured like a noon-tide bee,   25
Shall I nestle near thy side?
Wouldst thou me?—And I replied,
      No, . . . not thee!

Death will come when thou art dead,
      Soon, too soon—   30
Sleep will come when thou art fled;
Of neither would I ask the boon
I asked of thee, belovèd Night—

Swift be thine approaching flight,
    Come soon, soon!   35

TO ———

Music, when soft voices die,
Vibrates in the memory—
Odours, when sweet violets sicken,
Live within the sense they quicken.

Rose leaves, when the rose is dead,   5
Are heaped for the belovèd's bed;
And so thy thoughts, when thou art gone,
Love itself shall slumber on.

CHORUS FROM *HELLAS*

The world's great age begins anew,
    The golden years return,
The earth doth like a snake renew
    Her winter weeds outworn:
Heaven smiles, and faiths and empires gleam,   5
Like wrecks of a dissolving dream.

A brighter Hellas[1] rears its mountains
    From waves serener far:
A new Peneus[2] rolls his fountains
    Against the morning-star.   10
Where fairer Tempes[3] bloom, there sleep
Young Cyclads[4] on a sunnier deep.

A loftier Argo[5] cleaves the main,
    Fraught with a later prize;

[1] Greece.   [2] A river in Thessaly, a district in Greece.   [3] *Tempe,* the name of a valley in ancient Greece, was used as a synonym for any valley noted for its cool shades, singing birds, and romantic scenery.   [4] The Cyclades, Greek islands where a very early culture flourished.   [5] Galley that carried Jason and the Argonauts in search of the Golden Fleece to return it to Greece, where it belonged. The ship was thought to be the first seagoing vessel.

Another Orpheus[6] sings again,
 And loves, and weeps, and dies.
A new Ulysses[7] leaves once more
Calypso[8] for his native shore.

O, write no more the tale of Troy,
 If earth Death's scroll must be!
Nor mix with Laian rage[9] the joy
 Which dawns upon the free:
Although a subtler Sphinx renew
Riddles of death Thebes never knew.[10]

Another Athens shall arise,
 And to remoter time
Bequeath, like sunset to the skies,
 The splendour of its prime;
And leave, if nought so bright may live,
All earth can take or heaven can give.

Saturn[11] and Love their long repose
 Shall burst, more bright and good
Than all who fell, than One[12] who rose,
 Than many unsubdued:
Not gold, not blood, their altar dowers,[13]
But votive tears and symbol flowers.

O cease! must hate and death return?
 Cease! must men kill and die?
Cease! drain not to its dregs the urn
 Of bitter prophecy.
The world is weary of the past,
O might it die or rest at last!

[6] In Greek mythology, a fabulous musician whose marriage to Eurydice ended tragically. [7] Odysseus, hero of Homer's *Odyssey,* which tells of the Trojan War and Odysseus' wanderings after it. [8] In the *Odyssey,* a nymph who detained Odysseus on an island for seven years. [9] Laius, the father of Oedipus, was known for his fierce anger. [10] Oedipus saved Thebes from destruction by answering a riddle posed by the Sphinx, a hideous monster. [11] Roman god of agriculture. [12] Christ. [13] Endowments.

JOHN KEATS

1795–1821

ON FIRST LOOKING INTO CHAPMAN'S HOMER[1]

Much have I travell'd in the realms of gold,
    And many goodly states and kingdoms seen;
    Round many western islands have I been
Which bards in fealty to Apollo[2] hold.
Oft of one wide expanse had I been told   5
    That deep-brow'd Homer ruled as his demesne;
    Yet did I never breathe its pure serene
Till I heard Chapman speak out loud and bold:
Then felt I like some watcher of the skies
    When a new planet swims into his ken;   10
Or like stout Cortez[3] when with eagle eyes
    He star'd at the Pacific—and all his men
Look'd at each other with a wild surmise—
    Silent, upon a peak in Darien.[4]

WHEN I HAVE FEARS

When I have fears that I may cease to be
    Before my pen has glean'd my teeming brain,
Before high-pilèd books, in charact'ry,
    Hold like rich garners the full-ripen'd grain;
When I behold, upon the night's starr'd face,   5
    Huge cloudy symbols of a high romance,[1]
And think that I may never live to trace
    Their shadows, with the magic hand of chance;
And when I feel, fair creature of an hour!
    That I shall never look upon thee more,   10
Never have relish in the faery power
    Of unreflecting love!—then on the shore

---

[1] George Chapman, an Elizabethan poet, translated both the *Iliad* (1611) and the *Odyssey* (1614) of Homer. [2] God of light and medicine and probably the most widely revered god of ancient Greece. [3] A mistake for Balboa. [4] Former name for Panama.

[1] Here, romantic story.

Of the wide world I stand alone, and think
Till love and fame to nothingness do sink.

BRIGHT STAR, WOULD I WERE STEADFAST AS THOU ART

Bright star! would I were steadfast as thou art—
    Not in lone splendour hung aloft the night
And watching, with eternal lids apart,
    Like nature's patient, sleepless Eremite,
The moving waters at their priestlike task   5
    Of pure ablution round earth's human shores,
Or gazing on the new soft fallen mask
    Of snow upon the mountains and the moors—
No—yet still steadfast, still unchangeable,
    Pillow'd upon my fair love's ripening breast,   10
To feel for ever its soft fall and swell,
    Awake for ever in a sweet unrest,
Still, still to hear her tender-taken breath,
And so live ever—or else swoon to death.

LA BELLE DAME SANS MERCI[1]

O what can ail thee, knight-at-arms,
    Alone and palely loitering?
The sedge has wither'd from the lake,
    And no birds sing.

O what can ail thee, knight at arms,   5
    So haggard and so woe-begone?
The squirrel's granary is full,
    And the harvest's done.

I see a lily on thy brow,
    With anguish moist and fever dew,   10
And on thy cheeks a fading rose
    Fast withereth too.

"I met a lady in the meads,
    Full beautiful—a faery's child;

[1] The title can be translated as "The Fair Lady without Pity." Keats revised this poem, but his first version, which is printed here, is generally regarded as superior.

Her hair was long, her foot was light,
    And her eyes were wild.

"I made a garland for her head,
    And bracelets too, and fragrant zone;[2]
She look'd at me as she did love,
    And made sweet moan.

"I set her on my pacing steed,
    And nothing else saw all day long,
For side-long would she bend, and sing
    A faery's song.

"She found me roots of relish sweet,
    And honey wild, and manna dew,
And sure in language strange she said—
    'I love thee true.'

"She took me to her elfin grot,[3]
    And there she wept, and sigh'd full sore,
And there I shut her wild wild eyes
    With kisses four.

"And there she lull'èd me asleep,
    And there I dream'd—Ah! woe betide!—
The latest dream I ever dream'd
    On the cold hill side.

"I saw pale kings and princes too,
    Pale warriors, death-pale were they all;
They cried—'La Belle Dame sans Merci
    Hath thee in thrall!'

"I saw their starved lips in the gloam,
    With horrid warning gapèd wide,
And I awoke, and found me here,
    On the cold hill's side.

"And this is why I sojourn here,
    Alone and palely loitering,

[2] An encircling band, belt, girdle.   [3] Fairy cave.

Though the sedge is wither'd from the lake,
    And no birds sing."

ODE ON A GRECIAN URN

Thou still unravish'd bride of quietness,
    Thou foster-child of silence and slow time,
Sylvan historian, who canst thus express
    A flowery tale more sweetly than our rhyme:
What leaf-fring'd legend haunts about thy shape   5
    Of dieties or mortals, or of both,
        In Tempe[1] or the dales of Arcady?[2]
What men or gods are these? What maidens loth?
    What mad pursuit? What struggle to escape?
        What pipes and timbrels? What wild ecstasy?   10

Heard melodies are sweet, but those unheard
    Are sweeter; therefore, ye soft pipes, play on;
Not to the sensual ear, but, more endear'd,
    Pipe to the spirit ditties of no tone:
Fair youth, beneath the trees, thou canst not leave   15
    Thy song, nor ever can those trees be bare;
        Bold lover, never, never canst thou kiss,
Though winning near the goal—yet, do not grieve;
    She cannot fade, though thou hast not thy bliss,
        Forever wilt thou love, and she be fair!   20

Ah, happy, happy boughs! that cannot shed
    Your leaves, nor ever bid the Spring adieu;
And, happy melodist, unwearièd,
    For ever piping songs for ever new;
More happy love! more happy, happy love!   25
    For ever warm and still to be enjoy'd,
        For ever panting, and for ever young;
All breathing human passion far above,
    That leaves a heart high-sorrowful and cloy'd,
        A burning forehead, and a parching tongue.   30

Who are these coming to the sacrifice?
    To what green altar, O mysterious priest,

[1] The name of a valley in Thessaly, in ancient Greece, that came to be a synonym for any beautiful rural spot.   [2] Arcadia, a region in ancient Greece that is taken as the ideal region of rural felicity.

Lead'st thou that heifer lowing at the skies,
    And all her silken flanks with garlands drest?
What little town by river or sea shore,   35
    Or mountain-built with peaceful citadel,
        Is emptied of this folk, this pious morn?
And, little town, thy streets for evermore
    Will silent be; and not a soul to tell
        Why thou art desolate, can e'er return.   40

O Attic[3] shape! Fair attitude! with brede[4]
    Of marble men and maidens overwrought,
With forest branches and the trodden weed;
    Thou, silent form, dost tease us out of thought
As doth eternity: Cold Pastoral!   45
    When old age shall this generation waste,
        Thou shalt remain, in midst of other woe
Than ours, a friend to man, to whom thou say'st,
    Beauty is truth, truth beauty,—that is all
        Ye know on earth, and all ye need to know.   50

TO AUTUMN

Season of mists and mellow fruitfulness,
    Close bosom-friend of the maturing sun;
Conspiring with him how to load and bless
    With fruit the vines that round the thatch-eaves run;
To bend with apples the moss'd cottage-trees,   5
    And fill all fruit with ripeness to the core;
        To swell the gourd, and plump the hazel shells
With a sweet kernel; to set budding more,
And still more, later flowers for the bees,
Until they think warm days will never cease,   10
        For summer has o'er-brimm'd their clammy cells.

Who hath not seen thee oft amid thy store?
    Sometimes whoever seeks abroad may find
Thee sitting careless on a granary floor,
    Thy hair soft-lifted by the winnowing wind;   15
Or on a half-reap'd furrow sound asleep,
    Drows'd with the fume of poppies, while thy hook
        Spares the next swath and all its twinèd flowers:

---

[3] Of Attica, the ancient region of which Athens was the capital. *Attic* has come to suggest simplicity, purity, and refinement.   [4] Embroidery, interweaving.

And sometimes like a gleaner thou dost keep
    Steady thy laden head across a brook;   20
  Or by a cider-press, with patient look,
       Thou watchest the last oozings hours by hours.

Where are the songs of Spring? Ay, where are they?
    Think not of them, thou hast thy music too,—
While barrèd clouds bloom the soft-dying day,   25
    And touch the stubble-plains with rosy hue;
Then in a wailful choir the small gnats mourn
    Among the river sallows,[1] borne aloft
      Or sinking as the light wind lives or dies;
And full-grown lambs loud bleat from hilly bourn,[2]   30
    Hedge-crickets sing; and now with treble soft
  The red-breast whistles from a garden-croft;
      And gathering swallows twitter in the skies.

ODE ON MELANCHOLY

No, no, go not to Lethe,[1] neither twist
    Wolf's-bane,[2] tight-rooted, for its poisonous wine;
Nor suffer thy pale forehead to be kiss'd
    By nightshade, ruby grape of Proserpine;[3]
Make not your rosary of yew-berries,   5
    Nor let the beetle, nor the death-moth[4] be
      Your mournful Psyche,[5] nor the downy owl[6]
A partner in your sorrow's mysteries;
    For shade to shade will come too drowsily,
      And drown the wakeful anguish of the soul.   10

But when the melancholy fit shall fall
    Sudden from heaven like a weeping cloud,
That fosters the droop-headed flowers all,
    And hides the green hill in an April shroud;

---

[1] Willows.   [2] Domain, land.

[1] In Greek mythology, a river in Hades whose water, if drunk, causes forgetfulness; hence, forgetfulness, oblivion.   [2] Wolf's-bane, nightshade, and Yew-berries are poisonous plants.   [3] Queen of Hades.   [4] Both the beetle and the death's-head moth have markings on the back of the thorax suggesting a human skull or death's-head.   [5] In Greek, the soul, with was recognized as the seat of the passions. It was pictorially represented as a beautiful maiden with the wings of a butterfly, and sometimes as a butterfly.   [6] The note of the owl is generally thought to be doleful.

Then glut thy sorrow on a morning rose,   15
 Or on the rainbow of the salt sand-wave,
  Or on the wealth of globèd peonies;
Or if thy mistress some rich anger shows,
 Emprison her soft hand, and let her rave,
  And feed deep, deep upon her peerless eyes. 20

She dwells with Beauty—Beauty that must die;
 And Joy, whose hand is ever at his lips
Bidding adieu; and aching Pleasure nigh,
 Turning to poison while the bee-mouth sips:
Ay, in the very temple of Delight   25
 Veil'd Melancholy has her sovran shrine,
  Though seen of none save him whose strenuous tongue
Can burst Joy's grape against his palate fine;
 His soul shall taste the sadness of her might,
  And be among her cloudy trophies hung. 30

RALPH WALDO EMERSON

1 8 0 3 – 1 8 8 2

HAMATREYA[1]

Bulkeley, Hunt, Willard, Hosmer, Meriam, Flint,
Possessed the land which rendered to their toil
Hay, corn, roots, hemp, flax, apples, wool and wood.
Each of these landlords walked amidst his farm,
Saying, " 'Tis mine, my children's and my name's. 5
How sweet the west wind sounds in my own trees!
How graceful climb those shadows on my hill!
I fancy these pure waters and the flags
Know me, as does my dog: we sympathize;
And, I affirm, my actions smack of the soil." 10

---

[1] This poem is a free rendering of a passage in the *Vishnu Purana*. The title seems to be a version of *Maitreya*, the name of the next future Buddha, to whom Emerson addresses, in his journal, some "stanzas that were chanted by Earth" on the "folly of princes" (in acquiring land).

Where are these men? Asleep beneath their grounds:
And strangers, fond² as they, their furrows plough.
Earth laughs in flowers, to see her boastful boys
Earth-proud, proud of the earth which is not theirs;
Who steer the plough, but cannot steer their feet   15
Clear of the grave.
They added ridge to valley, brook to pond,
And sighed for all that bounded their domain;
"This suits me for a pasture; that's my park;
We must have clay, lime, gravel, granite-ledge,³   20
And misty lowland, where to go for peat.
The land is well,—lies fairly to the south.
'Tis good, when you have crossed the sea and back,
To find the sitfast acres where you left them."
Ah! the hot owner sees not Death, who adds   25
Him to his land, a lump of mould the more.
Hear what the Earth says:—

EARTH-SONG

"Mine and yours;
Mine, not yours.
Earth endures;   30
Stars abide—
Shine down in the old sea;
Old are the shores;
But where are old men?
I who have seen much,   35
Such have I never seen.

"The lawyer's deed
Ran sure,
In tail,⁴
To them, and to their heirs   40
Who shall succeed,
Without fail,
Forevermore.

"Here is the land,
Shaggy with wood,   45
With its old valley,
Mound and flood.
But the heritors?—
Fled like the flood's foam.

---

² Foolish.   ³ A deposit of granite to be mined.   ⁴ In entail, or transmission as an
inalienable inheritance.

The lawyer, and the laws,
And the kingdom,
Clean swept herefrom.

"They called me theirs,
Who so controlled me;
Yet every one
Wished to stay, and is gone,
How am I theirs,
If they cannot hold me,
But I hold them?"

When I heard the Earth-song,
I was no longer brave;
My avarice cooled
Like lust in the chill of the grave.

GIVE ALL TO LOVE

Give all to love;
Obey thy heart;
Friends, kindred, days,
Estate, good-fame,
Plans, credit and the Muse,—
Nothing refuse.

'Tis a brave master;
Let it have scope:
Follow it utterly,
Hope beyond hope:
High and more high
It dives into noon,
With wing unspent,
Untold intent;
But it is a god,
Knows its own path
And the outlets of the sky.

It was never for the mean;
It requireth courage stout.
Souls above doubt,
Valor unbending,

It will reward,—
They shall return
More than they were,
And ever ascending.   25

Leave all for love;
Yet, hear me, yet,
One word more thy heart behoved,
One pulse more of firm endeavor,—
Keep thee today,   30
Tomorrow, forever,
Free as an Arab
Of thy beloved.

Cling with life to the maid;
But when the surprise,   35
First vague shadow of surmise
Flits across her bosom young,
Of a joy apart from thee,
Free be she, fancy-free;
Nor thou detain her vesture's hem,   40
Nor the palest rose she flung
From her summer diadem.

Though thou loved her as thyself,
As a self of purer clay,
Though her parting dims the day,   45
Stealing grace from all alive;
Heartily know,
When half-gods go,
The gods arrive.

BRAHMA[1]

If the red slayer thinks he slays,
    Or if the slain think he is slain,
They know not well the subtle ways
    I keep, and pass, and turn again.

Far or forgot to me is near;   5
    Shadow and sunlight are the same;

[1] The creator god of Hinduism. This poem was inspired by several passages of the *Bhagavat-Gita*.

The vanished gods to me appear;
　　And one to me are shame and fame.

They reckon ill who leave me out;
　　When me they fly, I am the wings;
I am the doubter and the doubt,
　　And I the hymn the Brahmin[2] sings.　　　　　　　　　10

The strong gods[3] pine for my abode,
　　And pine in vain the sacred Seven;[4]
But thou, meek lover of the good!
　　Find me, and turn thy back on heaven.　　　　　　　15

EDGAR ALLAN POE

1809–1849

THE VALLEY OF UNREST

Once it smiled a silent dell
Where the people did not dwell;
They had gone unto the wars,
Trusting to the mild-eyed stars,
Nightly, from their azure towers,　　　　　　　　　　5
To keep watch above the flowers,
In the midst of which all day
The red sun-light lazily lay.
Now each visitor shall confess
The sad valley's restlessness.　　　　　　　　　　　　10
Nothing there is motionless—
Nothing save the airs that brood
Over the magic solitude.
Ah, by no wind are stirred those trees
That palpitate like the chill seas　　　　　　　　　　15

[2] Member of the priestly and meditative caste of Hinduism. 　[3] Indra, god of the sky and wielder of the thunderbolt; Agni, god of fire; and Yoma, god of death and judgment. These gods eventually will be absorbed into Brahma. 　[4] Maharshis or highest saints.

Around the misty Hebrides!
Ah, by no wind those clouds are driven
That rustle through the unquiet Heaven
Uneasily, from morn till even,
Over the violets there that lie   20
In myriad types of the human eye—
Over three lilies there that wave
And weep above a nameless grave!
They wave:—from out their fragment tops
Eternal dews come down in drops.   25
They weep:—from off their delicate stems
Perennial tears descend in gems.

TO HELEN

Helen, thy beauty is to me
   Like those Nicèan[1] barks of yore,
That gently, o'er a perfumed sea,
   The weary, way-worn wanderer bore
   To his own native shore.   5

On desperate seas long wont to roam,
   Thy hyacinth hair, thy classic face,
Thy Naiad[2] airs have brought me home
   To the glory that was Greece
And the grandeur that was Rome.   10

Lo! in yon brilliant window-niche
   How statue-like I see thee stand,
   The agate lamp within thy hand!
Ah, Psyche,[3] from the regions which
   Are Holy Land!   15

ALONE

From childhood's hour I have not been
As others were—I have not seen
As others saw—I could not bring
My passions from a common spring—

---

[1] Of Nicaea, an ancient city in Asia Minor.   [2] A water nymph.   [3] The reference is to the legend of Psyche, who, beloved of Cupid, lit a lamp to see him while asleep.

From the same source I have not taken
My sorrow—I could not awaken
Hy heart to joy at the same tone—
And all I loved—*I* loved alone—
Then—in my childhood, in the dawn
Of a most stormy life—was drawn
From every depth of good and ill
The mystery which binds me still—
From the torrent, or the fountain—
From the red cliff of the mountain—
From the sun that round me rolled
In its autumn tint of gold—
From the lightning in the sky
As it pass'd me flying by—
From the thunder and the storm—
And the cloud that took the form
When the rest of Heaven was blue
Of a demon in my view.—

5

10

15

20

ALFRED, LORD TENNYSON

1809-1892

ULYSSES

It little profits that an idle king,
By this still hearth, among these barren crags,
Match'd with an agèd wife, I mete and dole[1]
Unequal laws unto a savage race,
That hoard, and sleep, and feed, and know not me.
I cannot rest from travel; I will drink
Life to the lees; all times I have enjoy'd
Greatly, have suffer'd greatly, both with those
That loved me, and alone; on shore, and when
Through scudding drifts the rainy Hyades[2]
Vext the dim sea: I am become a name;
For always roaming with a hungry heart
Much have I seen and known;—cities of men

5

10

[1] The speaker is Ulysses (Odysseus). The time is after his return to his kingdom of Ithaca from the travels described in Homer's *Odyssey*.   [2] A cluster of stars believed to cause rainy weather.

And manners, climates, councils, governments,
Myself not least, but honour'd of them all;—
And drunk delight of battle with my peers,
Far on the ringing plains of windy Troy.
I am a part of all that I have met;
Yet all experience is an arch wherethrough
Gleams that untravell'd world, whose margin fades
For ever and for ever when I move.
How dull it is to pause, to make an end,
To rust unburnish'd, not to shine in use!
As though to breathe were life! Life piled on life
Were all too little, and of one to me
Little remains; but every hour is saved
From that eternal silence, something more,
A bringer of new things; and vile it were
For some three suns to store and hoard myself,
And this grey spirit yearning in desire
To follow knowledge, like a sinking star,
Beyond the utmost bound of human thought.
    This is my son, mine own Telemachus,
To whom I leave the sceptre and the isle—
Well-loved of me, discerning to fulfil
This labour, by slow prudence to make mild
A rugged people, and through soft degrees
Subdue them to the useful and the good.
Most blameless is he, centred in the sphere
Of common duties, decent not to fail
In offices of tenderness, and pay
Meet adoration to my household gods,
When I am gone. He works his work, I mine.
    There lies the port; the vessel puffs her sail;
There gloom the dark, broad seas. My mariners,
Souls that have toil'd, and wrought, and thought with me—
That ever with a frolic welcome took
The thunder and the sunshine, and opposed
Free hearts, free foreheads—you and I are old;
Old age hath yet his honour and his toil;
Death closes all; but something ere the end,
Some work of noble note, may yet be done,
Not unbecoming men that strove with Gods.
The lights begin to twinkle from the rocks;
The long day wanes; the slow moon climbs; the deep
Moans round with many voices. Come, my friends,
'Tis not too late to seek a newer world.
Push off, and sitting well in order smite
The sounding furrows; for my purpose holds
To sail beyond the sunset, and the baths
Of all the western stars, until I die.
It may be that the gulfs will wash us down;

It may be we shall touch the Happy Isles,[3]
And see the great Achilles,[4] whom we knew.
Though much is taken, much abides; and though   65
We are not now that strength which in old days
Moved earth and heaven; that which we are, we are;—
One equal temper of heroic hearts,
Made weak by time and fate, but strong in will
To strive, to seek, to find, and not to yield.   70

THE LOTOS-EATERS[1]

"Courage!" he[2] said, and pointed toward the land,
"This mounting wave will roll us shoreward soon."
In the afternoon they came unto a land
In which it seemed always afternoon.
All round the coast the languid air did swoon,   5
Breathing like one that hath a weary dream.
Full-faced above the valley stood the moon;
And like a downward smoke, the slender stream
Along the cliff to fall and pause and fall did seem.

A land of streams; some, like a downward smoke,   10
Slow-dropping veils of thinnest lawn, did go;
And some through wavering lights and shadows broke,
Rolling a slumbrous sheet of foam below.
They saw the gleaming river seaward flow
From the inner land; far off, three mountain-tops,   15
Three silent pinnacles of aged snow,
Stood sunset-flush'd; and, dew'd with showery drops,
Up-clomb the shadowy pine above the woven copse.

The charmed sunset linger'd low adown
In the red West; through mountain clefts the dale   20
Was seen far inland, and the yellow down
Border'd with palm, and many a winding vale
And meadow, set with slender galingale;[3]
A land where all things always seemed the same!
And round about the keel with faces pale,   25

[3] Elysium, the Greek paradise for heroes.   [4] Hero of the *Iliad*, as Ulysses is of the
Odyssey. Both epics deal with the Trojan war.

[1] In Homer's *Odyssey*, the Lotophagi, or lotos-eaters, ate fruit that caused a state of
dreamy forgetfulness and loss of all desire to return home.   [2] Odysseus, or Ulysses.   [3] A
kind of sedge.

Dark faces pale against that rosy flame,
The mild-eyed melancholy Lotos-eaters came.

Branches they bore of that enchanted stem,
Laden with flower and fruit, whereof they gave
To each, but whoso did receive of them, 30
And taste, to him the gushing of the wave
Far far away did seem to mourn and rave
On alien shores; and if his fellow spake,
His voice was thin, as voices from the grave;
And deep-asleep he seem'd, yet all awake, 35
And music in his ears his beating heart did make.

They sat them down upon the yellow sand,
Between the sun and moon upon the shore;
And sweet it was to dream of Fatherland,
Of child, and wife, and slave; but evermore 40
Most weary seem'd the sea, weary the oar,
Weary the wandering fields of barren foam.
Then someone said, "We will return no more";
And all at once they sang, "Our island home
Is far beyond the wave; we will no longer roam." 45

CHORIC SONG

I

There is sweet music here that softer falls
Than petals from blown roses on the grass,
Or night-dews on still waters between walls
Of shadowy granite, in a gleaming pass;
Music that gentlier on the spirit lies, 50
Than tired eyelids upon tired eyes;
Music that brings sweet sleep down from the blissful skies.
Here are cool mosses deep,
And through the moss the ivies creep,
And in the stream the long-leaved flowers weep, 55
And from the craggy ledge the poppy hangs in sleep.

II

Why are we weigh'd upon with heaviness,
And utterly consumed with sharp distress,
While all things else have rest from weariness?
All things have rest: why should we toil alone, 60
We only toil, who are the first of things,

And make perpetual moan,
Still from one sorrow to another thrown:
Nor ever fold our wings,
And cease from wanderings,   65
Nor steep our brows in slumber's holy balm;
Nor hearken what the inner spirit sings,
"There is no joy but calm!"
Why should we only toil, the roof and crown of things?

III

Lo! in the middle of the wood,   70
The folded leaf is woo'd from out the bud
With winds upon the branch, and there
Grows green and broad, and takes no care,
Sun-steep'd at noon, and in the moon
Nightly dew-fed; and turning yellow   75
Falls, and floats adown the air.
Lo! sweeten'd with the summer light,
The full-juiced apple, waxing over-mellow,
Drops in a silent autumn night.
All its allotted length of days   80
The flower ripens in its place,
Ripens and fades, and falls, and hath no toil,
Fast-rooted in the fruitful soil.

IV

Hateful is the dark-blue sky,
Vaulted o'er the dark-blue sea.   85
Death is the end of life; ah, why
Should life all labour be?
Let us alone. Time driveth onward fast
And in a little while our lips are dumb.
Let us alone. What is it that will last?   90
All things are taken from us, and become
Portions and parcels of the dreadful Past.
Let us alone. What pleasure can we have
To war with evil? Is there any peace
In ever climbing up the climbing wave?   95
All things have rest, and ripen toward the grave
In silence—ripen, fall and cease:
Give us long rest or death, dark death, or dreamful ease.

V

How sweet it were, hearing the downward stream,
With half-shut eyes ever to seem   100

Falling asleep in a half-dream!
To dream and dream, like yonder amber light,
Which will not leave the myrrh-bush on the height;
To hear each other's whisper'd speech;
Eating the Lotos day by day,   105
To watch the crisping ripples on the beach,
And tender curving lines of creamy spray;
To lend our hearts and spirits wholly
To the influence of mild-minded melancholy;
To muse and brood and live again in memory,   110
With those old faces of our infancy
Heap'd over with a mound of grass,
Two handfuls of white dust, shut in an urn of brass!

VI

Dear is the memory of our wedded lives,
And dear the last embraces of our wives   115
And their warm tears; but all hath suffer'd change;
For surely now our household hearths are cold:
Our sons inherit us: our looks are strange:
And we should come like ghosts to trouble joy.
Or else the island princes over-bold   120
Have eat our substance, and the minstrel sings
Before them of the ten-years' war in Troy,
And our great deeds, as half-forgotten things.
Is there confusion in the little isle?
Let what is broken so remain.   125
The Gods are hard to reconcile:
'Tis hard to settle order once again.
There *is* confusion worse than death,
Trouble on trouble, pain on pain,
Long labour unto agèd breath,   130
Sore task to hearts worn out with many wars
And eyes grown dim with gazing on the pilot-stars.

VII

But, propt on beds of amaranth and moly,
How sweet (while warm airs lull us, blowing lowly)
With half-dropt eyelids still,   135
Beneath a heaven dark and holy,
To watch the long bright river drawing slowly
His waters from the purple hill—
To hear the dewy echoes calling
From cave to cave through the thick-twinèd vine—   140
To watch the emerald-colour'd water falling
Through many a wov'n acanthus-wreath divine!

Only to hear and see the far-off sparkling brine,
Only to hear were sweet, stretch'd out beneath the pine.

VIII

The Lotos blooms below the barren peak: 145
The Lotos blows by every winding creek:
All day the wind breathes low with mellower tone;
Through every hollow cave and alley lone
Round and round the spicy downs the yellow Lotos-dust is blown.
We have had enough of action, and of motion we,   150
Roll'd to starboard, roll'd to larboard, when the surge was seething free,
Where the wallowing monster spouted his foam-fountains in the sea.
Let us swear an oath, and keep it with an equal mind,
In the hollow Lotos-land to live and lie reclined
On the hills like Gods together, careless of mankind.   155
For they lie beside their nectar, and the bolts are hurl'd
Far below them in the valleys, and the clouds are lightly curl'd
Round their golden houses, girdled with the gleaming world:
Where they smile in secret, looking over wasted lands,
Blight and famine, plague and earthquake, roaring deeps and fiery
    sands,   160
Clanging fights, and flaming towns, and sinking ships, and praying
    hands.
But they smile, they find a music centred in a doleful song
Steaming up, a lamentation and an ancient tale of wrong,
Like a tale of little meaning though the words are strong;
Chanted from an ill-used race of men that cleave the soil,   165
Sow the seed, and reap the harvest with enduring toil,
Storing yearly little dues of wheat, and wine and oil;
Till they perish and they suffer—some, 'tis whisper'd—down in hell
Suffer endless anguish, others in Elysian valleys dwell,
Resting weary limbs at last on beds of asphodel.   170
Surely, surely, slumber is more sweet than toil, the shore
Than labour in the deep mid-ocean, wind and wave and oar;
Oh, rest ye, brother mariners, we will not wander more.

NOW SLEEPS THE CRIMSON PETAL

Now sleeps the crimson petal, now the white;
Nor waves the cypress in the palace walk;
Nor winks the gold fin in the porphyry font:
The fire-fly wakens: waken thou with me.

Now droops the milkwhite peacock like a ghost,   5
And like a ghost she glimmers on to me.

Now lies the Earth all Danaë[1] to the stars,
And all thy heart lies open unto me.

Now slides the silent meteor on, and leaves
A shining furrow, as thy thoughts in me.

Now folds the lily all her sweetness up,
And slips into the bosom of the lake:
So fold thyself, my dearest, thou, and slip
Into my bosom and be lost in me.

10

COME DOWN, O MAID

Come down, O maid, from yonder mountain height:
What pleasure lives in height (the shepherd sang)
In height and cold, the splendour of the hills?
But cease to move so near the Heavens, and cease
To glide a sunbeam by the blasted[1] Pine,   5
To sit a star upon the sparkling spire;
And come, for Love is of the valley, come,
For Love is of the valley, come thou down
And find him; by the happy threshold, he,
Or hand in hand with Plenty in the maize,   10
Or red with spirited purple of the vats,
Or foxlike in the vine; nor cares to walk
With Death and Morning on the silver horns,[2]
Nor wilt thou snare him in the white ravine,
Nor find him dropt upon the firths of ice,   15
That huddling slant in furrow-cloven falls
To roll the torrent out of dusky doors:
But follow; let the torrent dance thee down
To find him in the valley; let the wild
Lean-headed Eagles yelp alone, and leave   20
The monstrous ledges there to slope, and spill
Their thousand wreaths of dangling water-smoke,[3]
That like a broken purpose waste in air:
So waste not thou; but come; for all the vales
Await thee; azure pillars of the hearth   25
Arise to thee; the children call, and I
Thy shepherd pipe, and sweet is every sound,

[1] A princess who was visited by Zeus in the form of a golden shower. Tennyson's figure parallels the Earth and "thy heart" with Danaë, and the stars and "me" with Zeus.

[1] Blighted.   [2] The icy horns of mountains.   [3] Water vapor.

Sweeter thy voice, but every sound is sweet;
Myriads of rivulets hurrying through the lawn,
The moan of doves in immemorial elms,   30
And murmuring of innumerable bees.

MORTE D'ARTHUR

So all day long the noise of battle roll'd
Among the mountains by the winter sea,
Until King Arthur's table,[1] man by man,
Had fall'n in Lyonness about their lord,
King Arthur; then, because his wound was deep,   5
The bold Sir Bedivere uplifted him,
Sir Bedivere, the last of all his knights,
And bore him to a chapel nigh the field,
A broken chancel with a broken cross,
That stood on a dark strait of barren land.   10
On one side lay the ocean, and on one
Lay a great water, and the moon was full.
        Then spake King Arthur to Sir Bedivere:
"The sequel of to-day unsolders all
The goodliest fellowship of famous knights   15
Whereof this world holds record. Such a sleep
They sleep—the men I loved. I think that we
Shall never more, at any future time,
Delight our souls with talk of knightly deeds,
Walking about the gardens and the halls   20
Of Camelot, as in the days that were.
I perish by this people which I made,—
Tho' Merlin[2] sware that I should come again
To rule once more—but let what will be be,
I am so deeply smitten through the helm   25
That without help I cannot last till morn.
Thou therefore take my brand[3] Excalibur,
Which was my pride; for thou rememberest how
In those old days, one summer noon, an arm
Rose up from out the bosom of the lake,   30
Clothed in white samite, mystic, wonderful,
Holding the sword—and how I row'd across
And took it, and have worn it, like a king;
And, wheresoever I am sung or told
In aftertime, this also shall be known.   35
But now delay not; take Excalibur,

        [1] The famous "round table"; hence, the men that sat there.   [2] Magician of Arthur-
ian legend.   [3] Sword.

And fling him far into the middle mere;[4]
Watch what thou seest, and lightly[5] bring me word."
    To him replied the bold Sir Bedivere:
It is not meet, Sir King, to leave thee thus,   40
Aidless, alone, and smitten through the helm.
A little thing may harm a wounded man.
Yet I thy hest will all perform at full,
Watch what I see, and lightly bring thee word."
    So saying, from the ruin'd shrine he stept   45
And in the moon athwart[6] the place of tombs,
Where lay the mighty bones of ancient men,
Old knights, and over them the sea-wind sang
Shrill, chill, with flakes of foam. He, stepping down
By zigzag paths and juts of pointed rock,   50
Came on the shining levels of the lake.
    There drew he forth the brand Excalibur,
And o'er him drawing it, the winter moon,
Brightening the skirts of a long cloud, ran forth
And sparkled keen with frost against the hilt;   55
For all the haft twinkled with diamond sparks,
Myriads of topaz-lights and jacinth-work
Of subtlest jewellery. He gazed so long
That both his eyes were dazzled, as he stood,
This way and that dividing the swift mind,   60
In act to throw; but at the last it seem'd
Better to leave Excalibur conceal'd
There in the many-knotted water-flags,
That whistled stiff and dry about the marge.[7]
So strode he back slow to the wounded king.   65
    Then spake King Arthur to Sir Bedivere:
"Hast thou perform'd my mission which I gave?
What is it thou hast seen, or what hast heard?"
    And answer made the bold Sir Bedivere:
"I heard the ripple washing in the reeds,   70
And the wild water lapping on the crag."
    To whom replied King Arthur, faint and pale:
"Thou hast betray'd thy nature and thy name,
Not rendering true answer, as beseem'd
Thy fealty, nor like a noble knight;   75
For surer sign had follow'd, either hand,
Or voice, or else a motion of the mere.
This is a shameful thing for men to lie.
Yet now, I charge thee, quickly go again
As thou art lief and dear, and do the thing   80
I bade thee, watch, and lightly bring me word."
    Then went Sir Bedivere the second time

    [4] The middle of the mere, or lake.   [5] Quickly.   [6] Across.   [7] Margin (of the lake).

Across the ridge, and paced beside the mere,
Counting the dewy pebbles, fix'd in thought;
But when he saw the wonder of the hilt,   85
How curiously and strangely chased, he smote
His palms together, and he cried aloud:
    "And if indeed I cast the brand away,
Surely a precious thing, one worthy note,
Should thus be lost forever from the earth,   90
Which might have pleased the eyes of many men.
What good should follow this, if this were done?
What harm, undone? deep harm to disobey,
Seeing obedience is the bond of rule.
Were it well to obey then, if a king demand   95
An act unprofitable, against himself?
The king is sick, and knows not what he does.
What record or what relic of my lord
Should be to aftertime, but empty breath
And rumors of a doubt? but were this kept,   100
Stored in some treasure-house of mighty kings,
Some one might show it at a joust of arms,
Saying, 'King Arthur's sword, Excalibur,
Wrought by the lonely maiden of the lake;[8]
Nine years she wrought it, sitting in the deeps   105
Upon the hidden bases of the hills.'
So might some old man speak in the aftertime
To all the people, winning reverence;
But now much honor and much fame were lost."
    So spake he, clouded with his own conceit,[9]   110
And hid Excalibur the second time,
And so strode back slow to the wounded king.
    Then spoke King Arthur, breathing heavily:
"What is it thou hast seen, or what hast heard?"
    And answer made the bold Sir Bedivere: 115
"I heard the water lapping on the crag,
And the long ripple washing in the reeds."
    To whom replied King Arthur, much in wrath:
"Ah, miserable and unkind, untrue,
Unknightly, traitor-hearted! Woe is me!   120
Authority forgets a dying king,
Laid widow'd of the power in his eye
That bow'd the will. I see thee what thou art,
For thou, the latest-left of all my knights,
In whom should meet the offices of all,   125
Thou wouldst betray me for the precious hilt;
Either from lust of gold, or like a girl
Valuing the giddy pleasure of the eyes.
Yet, for a man may fail in duty twice,

[8] The "lady of the lake," who, according to legend, gave Arthur his miraculous sword.
[9] Thought.

And the third time may prosper, get thee hence;   130
But, if thou spare to fling Excalibur,
I will arise and slay thee with my hands."
    Then quickly rose Sir Bedivere, and ran,
And, leaping down the ridges lightly, plunged
Among the bulrush-beds, and clutch'd the sword,   135
And strongly wheel'd and threw it. The great brand
Made lightnings in the splendour of the moon,
And flashing round and round, and whirl'd in an arch,
Shot like a streamer of the northern morn,
Seen where the moving isles of winter shock   140
By night, with noises of the northern sea.
So flash'd and fell the brand Excalibur;
But ere he dipt the surface, rose an arm
Cloth'd in white samite, mystic, wonderful,
And caught him by the hilt, and brandish'd him   145
Three times, and drew him under in the mere.
And lightly went the other to the king.
    Then spoke King Arthur, drawing thicker breath:
"Now see I by thine eyes that this is done.
Speak out; what is it thou hast heard, or seen?"   150
    And answer made the bold Sir Bedivere:
"Sir King, I closed mine eyelids, lest the gems
Should blind my purpose, for I never saw,
Nor shall see, here or elsewhere, till I die,
Not tho' I live three lives of mortal men,   155
So great a miracle as yonder hilt.
Then with both hands I flung him, wheeling him;
But when I look'd again, behold an arm,
Clothed in white samite, mystic, wonderful,
That caught him by the hilt, and brandish'd him   160
Three times, and drew him under in the mere."
    And answer made King Arthur, breathing hard:
"My end draws nigh; 't is time that I were gone.
Make broad thy shoulders to receive my weight,
And bear me to the margin; yet I fear   165
My wound hath taken cold, and I shall die."
    So saying, from the pavement he half rose,
Slowly, with pain, reclining on his arm,
And looking wistfully with wide blue eyes
As in a picture. Him Sir Bedivere   170
Remorsefully regarded through his tears,
And would have spoken, but he found not words,
Then took with care, and kneeling on one knee,
O'er both his shoulders drew the languid hands,
And rising bore him through the place of tombs.   175
    But, as he walk'd, King Arthur panted hard,
Like one that feels a nightmare on his bed
When all the house is mute. So sigh'd the king,

Muttering and murmuring at his ear, "Quick, quick!
I fear it is too late, and I shall die." 180
But the other swiftly strode from ridge to ridge,
Clothed with his breath, and looking, as he walk'd,
Larger than human on the frozen hills.
He heard the deep behind him, and a cry
Before. His own thought drove him like a goad. 185
Dry clash'd his harness[10] in the icy caves
And barren chasms, and all to left and right
The bare black cliff clang'd round him, as he based
His feet on juts of slippery crag that rang
Sharp-smitten with the dint of armed heels— 190
And on a sudden, lo! the level lake,
And the long glories of the winter moon.

    Then saw they how there hove a dusky barge,
Dark as a funeral scarf from stem to stern,
Beneath them; and descending they were ware 195
That all the decks were dense with stately forms
Black-stoled, black-hooded, like a dream—by these
Three queens with crowns of gold—and from them rose
A cry that shiver'd to the tingling stars,
And, as it were one voice, an agony 200
Of lamentation, like a wind that shrills
All night in a waste land, where no one comes,
Or hath come, since the making of the world.

    Then murmur'd Arthur, "Place me in the barge,"
And to the barge they came. There those three queens 205
Put forth their hands, and took the king, and wept.
But she that rose the tallest of them all
And fairest laid his head upon her lap,
And loosed the shatter'd casque,[11] and chafed his hands,
And call'd him by his name, complaining[12] loud, 210
And dropping bitter tears against his brow
Striped with dark blood; for all his face was white
And colourless, and like the wither'd moon
Smote by the fresh beam of the springing east;
And all his greaves and cuisses[13] dash'd with drops 215
Of onset; and the light and lustrous curls—
That made his forehead like a rising sun
High from the dais-throne—were parch'd with dust;
Or, clotted into points and hanging loose,
Mix'd with the knightly growth that fringed his lips. 220
So like a shatter'd column lay the king;
Not like that Arthur who, with lance in rest,
From spur to plume a star of tournament,[14]
Shot through the lists[15] at Camelot, and charged

---

[10] Armor.   [11] Helmet.   [12] Expressing grief.   [13] Leg and thigh armor.
[14] The knightly sport of jousting or tilting with a blunted lance.   [15] Arenas.

Before the eyes of ladies and of kings.   225
      Then loudly cried the bold Sir Bedivere:
"Ah! my Lord Arthur, whither shall I go?
Where shall I hide my forehead and my eyes?
For now I see the true old times are dead,
When every morning brought a noble chance,   230
And every chance brought out a noble knight.
Such times have been not since the light that led
The holy Elders with the gift of myrrh.[16]
But now the whole ROUND TABLE is dissolved
Which was an image of the mighty world;   235
And I, the last, go forth companionless,
And the days darken round me, and the years,
Among new men, strange faces, other minds."
      And slowly answer'd Arthur from the barge:
"The old order changeth, yielding place to new,   240
And God fulfils himself in many ways,
Lest one good custom should corrupt the world.
Comfort thyself: what comfort is in me?
I have lived my life, and that which I have done
May He within himself make pure! but thou,   245
If thou shouldst never see my face again,
Pray for my soul. More things are wrought by prayer
Than this world dreams of. Wherefore, let thy voice
Rise like a fountain for me night and day.
For what are men better than sheep or goats   250
That nourish a blind life within the brain,
If, knowing God, they lift not hands of prayer
Both for themselves and those who call them friend?
For so the whole round earth is every way
Bound by gold chains about the feet of God.   255
But now farewell. I am going a long way
With these thou seest—if indeed I go—
For all my mind is clouded with a doubt—
To the island-valley of Avilion;[17]
Where falls not hail, or rain, or any snow,   260
Nor ever wind blows loudly, but it lies
Deep-meadow'd, happy, fair with orchard lawns
And bowery hollows crown'd with summer sea,
Where I will heal me of my grievous wound."
      So said he, and the barge with oar and sail   265
Moved from the brink, like some full-breasted swan
That, fluting a wild carol ere her death,
Ruffles her pure cold plume, and takes the flood
With swarthy webs. Long stood Sir Bedivere
Revolving many memories, till the hull   270

[16] The Wise Men.   [17] Avalon, the island to which Arthur was taken to die, according to legend.

Look'd one black dot against the verge of dawn,
And on the mere the wailing died away.

THE REVENGE[1]
A Ballad of the Fleet

I

At Flores in the Azores Sir Richard Grenville lay,
And a pinnace, like a flutter'd bird, came flying from far away:
"Spanish ships of war at sea! we have sighted fifty-three!"
Then sware Lord Thomas Howard: " 'Fore God I am no coward;
But I cannot meet them here, for my ships are out of gear,   5
And the half my men are sick. I must fly, but follow quick.
We are six ships of the line; can we fight with fifty-three?"

II

Then spake Sir Richard Grenville: "I know you are no coward;
You fly them for a moment to fight with them again.
But I've ninety men and more that are lying sick ashore.   10
I should count myself the coward if I left them, my Lord Howard,
To these Inquisition dogs and the devildoms of Spain."

III

So Lord Howard past away with five ships of war that day,
Till he melted like a cloud in the silent summer heaven;
But Sir Richard bore in hand all his sick men from the land   15
Very carefully and slow,
Men of Bideford in Devon,
And we laid them on the ballast down below;
For we brought them all aboard,
And they blest him in their pain, that they were not left to Spain,   20
To the thumb-screw and the stake, for the glory of the Lord.

IV

He had only a hundred seamen to work the ship and to fight,
And he sailed away from Flores till the Spaniard came in sight,
With his huge sea-castles heaving upon the weather[2] bow.
"Shall we fight or shall we fly?   25
Good Sir Richard, tell us now,
For to fight is but to die!

[1] The battle described here took place in 1591. The *Revenge* was Sir Richard Grenville's ship.   [2] Windward.

There'll be little of us left by the time this sun be set."
And Sir Richard said again: "We be all good English men.
Let us bang these dogs of Seville, the children of the devil,   30
For I never turn'd my back upon Don or devil yet."

V

Sir Richard spoke and he laugh'd, and we roar'd a hurrah, and so
The little Revenge ran on sheer into the heart of the foe,
With her hundred fighters on deck, and her ninety sick below;
For half of their fleet to the right and half to the left were seen,   35
And the little Revenge ran on through the long sea-lane between.

VI

Thousands of their soldiers look'd down from their decks and laugh'd,
Thousands of their seamen made mock at the mad little craft
Running on and on, till delay'd
By their mountain-like San Philip that, of fifteen hundred tons,   40
And up-shadowing high above us with her yawning tiers of guns,
Took the breath from our sails, and we stay'd.

VII

And while now the great San Philip hung above us like a cloud
Whence the thunderbolt will fall
Long and loud,   45
Four galleons drew away
From the Spanish fleet that day,
And two upon the larboard and two upon the starboard lay,
And the battle-thunder broke from them all.

VIII

But anon the great San Philip, she bethought herself and went,   50
Having that within her womb that had left her ill content;
And the rest they came aboard us, and they fought us hand to hand,
For a dozen times they came with their pikes and musqueteers,[3]
And a dozen times we shook 'em off as a dog that shakes his ears
When he leaps from the water to the land.   55

IX

And the sun went down, and the stars came out far over the summer sea,
But never a moment ceased the fight of the one and the fifty-three.
Ship after ship, the whole night long, their high-built galleons came,
Ship after ship, the whole night long, with her battle-thunder and flame;

[3] Musketeers.

Ship after ship, the whole night long, drew back with her dead and her
      shame.   60
For some were sunk and many were shatter'd, and so could fight us no
      more—
God of battles, was ever a battle like this in the world before?

X

For he said, "Fight on! fight on!"
Tho' his vessel was all but a wreck;
And it chanced that, when half of the short summer night was gone,   65
With a grisly wound to be drest he had left the deck,
But a bullet struck him that was dressing it suddenly dead,
And himself he was wounded again in the side and the head,
And he said, "Fight on! fight on!"

XI

And the night went down, and the sun smiled out far over the summer
      sea,   70
And the Spanish fleet with broken sides lay round us all in a ring;
But they dared not touch us again, for they fear'd that we still could sting,
So they watch'd what the end would be.
And we had not fought them in vain,
But in perilous plight were we,   75
Seeing forty of our poor hundred were slain,
And half the rest of us maim'd for life
In the crash of the cannonades and the desperate strife;
And the sick men down in the hold were most of them stark and cold,
And the pikes were all broken or bent, and the powder was all of it
      spent;   80
And the masts and the rigging were lying over the side;
But Sir Richard cried in his English pride:
"We have fought such a fight for a day and a night
As may never be fought again!
We have won great glory, my men!   85
And a day less or more
At sea or ashore,
We die—does it matter when?
Sink me the ship, Master Gunner—sink her, split her in twain!
Fall into the hands of God, not into the hands of Spain!"   90

XII

And the gunner said, "Ay, ay," but the seamen made reply:
"We have children, we have wives,
And the Lord hath spared our lives.
We will make the Spaniard promise, if we yield, to let us go;

We shall live to fight again and to strike another blow."
And the lion there lay dying, and they yielded to the foe.

XIII

And the stately Spanish men to their flagship bore him then,
Where they laid him by the mast, old Sir Richard caught at last,
And they praised him to his face with their courtly foreign grace;
But he rose upon their decks, and he cried:
"I have fought for Queen and Faith like a valiant man and true;
I have only done my duty as a man is bound to do.
With a joyful spirit I Sir Richard Grenville die!"
And he fell upon their decks, and he died.

XIV

And they stared at the dead that had been so valiant and true,
And had holden the power and glory of Spain so cheap
That he dared her with one little ship and his English few;
Was he devil or man? He was devil for aught they knew,
But they sank his body with honor down into the deep,
And they mann'd the Revenge with a swarthier alien crew,
And away she sail'd with her loss and long'd for her own;
When a wind from the lands they had ruin'd awoke from sleep,
And the water began to heave and the weather to moan,
And or ever that evening ended a great gale blew,
And a wave like the wave that is raised by an earthquake grew,
Till it smote on their hulls and their sails and their masts and their flags,
And the whole sea plunged and fell on the shot-shatter'd navy of Spain,
And the little Revenge herself went down by the island crags
To be lost evermore in the main.

EDWARD LEAR

1812–1888

THE JUMBLIES

I

They went to sea in a Sieve, they did;
    In a Sieve they went to sea:
In spite of all their friends could say,

On a winter's morn, on a stormy day,
    In a Sieve they went to sea! 5
And when the Sieve turned round and round,
And every one cried, "You'll all be drowned!"
They called aloud, "Our Sieve ain't big,
But we don't care a button! we don't care a fig!
    In a Sieve we'll go to sea!" 10
        Far and few, far and few,
            Are the lands where the Jumblies live;
        Their heads are green, and their hands are blue;
            And they went to sea in a Sieve.

II

They sailed away in a Sieve, they did, 15
    In a Sieve they sailed so fast,
With only a beautiful pea-green veil
Tied with a riband, by way of a sail,
    To a small tobacco-pipe mast;
And every one said, who saw them go, 20
"O won't they be soon upset, you know!
For the sky is dark, and the voyage is long,
And happen what may, it's extremely wrong
    In a Sieve to sail so fast!"
        Far and few, far and few, 25
            Are the lands where the Jumblies live;
        Their heads are green, and their hands are blue,
            And they went to sea in a Sieve.

III

The water it soon came in, it did,
    The water it soon came in; 30
So to keep them dry, they wrapped their feet
In a pinky paper all folded neat,
    And they fastened it down with a pin.
And they passed the night in a crockery-jar,
And each of them said, "How wise we are! 35
Though the sky be dark, and the voyage be long,
Yet we never can think we were rash or wrong,
    While round in our Sieve we spin!"
        Far and few, far and few,
            Are the lands where the Jumblies live; 40
        Their heads are green, and their hands are blue,
            And they went to sea in a Sieve.

IV

And all night long they sailed away;
    And when the sun went down,

They whistled and warbled a moony song   45
To the echoing sound of a coppery gong,
    In the shade of the mountains brown.
"O Timballo! How happy we are,
When we live in a Sieve and a crockery-jar,
And all night long in the moonlight pale,   50
We sail away with a pea-green sail,
    In the shade of the mountains brown."
        Far and few, far and few,
            Are the lands where the Jumblies live;
        Their heads are green, and their hands are blue,   55
            And they went to sea in a Sieve.

V

They sailed to the Western Sea, they did,
    To a land all covered with trees,
And they bought an Owl, and a useful Cart,
And a pound of Rice, and a Cranberry Tart,   60
    And a hive of silvery Bees.
And they bought a Pig, and some green Jackdaws,
And a lovely Monkey with lollipop paws,
And forty bottles of Ring-Bo-Ree,
    And no end of Stilton cheese.   65
        Far and few, far and few,
            Are the lands where the Jumblies live;
        Their heads are green, and their hands are blue,
            And they went to sea in a Sieve.

VI

And in twenty years they all came back,   70
    In twenty years or more,·
And every one said, "How tall they've grown!
For they've been to the Lakes, and the Torrible Zone,
    And the hills of the Chankly Bore."
And they drank their health, and gave them a feast   75
Of dumplings made of beautiful yeast;
And every one said, "If we only live,
We, too, will go to sea in a Sieve,
    To the hills of the Chankly Bore."
        Far and few, far and few,   80
            Are the lands where the Jumblies live;
        Their heads are green, and their hands are blue,
            And they went to sea in a Sieve.

ROBERT BROWNING

1812–1889

MY LAST DUCHESS

FERRARA

That's my last Duchess painted on the wall,
Looking as if she were alive. I call
That piece a wonder, now: Frà Pandolf's[1] hands
Worked busily a day, and there she stands.
Will't please you sit and look at her? I said   5
"Frà Pandolf" by design, for never read
Strangers like you that pictured countenance,
The depth and passion of its earnest glance,
But to myself they turned (since none puts by
The curtain I have drawn for you, but I)   10
And seemed as they would ask me, if they durst,
How such a glance came there; so, not the first
Are you to turn and ask thus. Sir, 'twas not
Her husband's presence only, called that spot
Of joy into the Duchess' cheek: perhaps   15
Frà Pandolf chanced to say, "Her mantle laps
Over my lady's wrist too much," or "Paint
Must never hope to reproduce the faint
Half-flush that dies along her throat": such stuff
Was courtesy, she thought, and cause enough   20
For calling up that spot of joy. She had
A heart—how shall I say?—too soon made glad,
Too easily impressed: she liked whate'er
She looked on, and her looks went everywhere.
Sir, 'twas all one! My favor at her breast,   25
The dropping of the daylight in the West,
The bough of cherries some officious fool
Broke in the orchard for her, the white mule
She rode with round the terrace—all and each
Would draw from her alike the approving speech,   30
Or blush, at least. She thanked men,—good! but thanked
Somehow—I know not how—as if she ranked
My gift of a nine-hundred-years-old name
With anybody's gift. Who'd stoop to blame
This sort of trifling? Even had you skill   35

[1] An imaginary painter.

In speech—(which I have not)—to make your will
Quite clear to such an one, and say, "Just this
Or that in you disgusts me; here you miss,
Or there exceed the mark"—and if she let
Herself be lessoned so, nor plainly set   40
Her wits to yours, forsooth, and made excuse,
—E'en then would be some stooping; and I choose
Never to stoop. Oh sir, she smiled, no doubt,
Whene'er I passed her; but who passed without
Much the same smile? This grew; I gave commands;   45
Then all smiles stopped together. There she stands
As if alive. Will't please you rise? We'll meet
The company below, then. I repeat,
The Count your master's known munificence
Is ample warrant that no just pretence   50
Of mine for dowry will be disallowed;
Though his fair daughter's self, as I avowed
At starting, is my object. Nay, we'll go
Together down, sir. Notice Neptune, though,
Taming a sea-horse, thought a rarity,   55
Which Claus of Innsbruck cast in bronze for me!

SOLILOQUY OF THE SPANISH CLOISTER

Gr-r-r—there go, my heart's abhorrence!
    Water your damned flower-pots, do!
If hate killed men, Brother Lawrence,
    God's blood, would not mine kill you!
What? your myrtle-bush wants trimming?   5
    Oh, that rose has prior claims—
Needs its leaden vase filled brimming?
    Hell dry you up with its flames!

At the meal we sit together:
    Salve tibi![1] I must hear   10
Wise talk of the kind of weather,
    Sort of season, time of year:
Not a plenteous cork-crop: scarcely
    Dare we hope oak-galls, I doubt:
What's the Latin name for 'parsley'?   15
    What's the Greek name for Swine's Snout?

Whew! We'll have our platter burnished,
    Laid with care on our own shelf!

    [1] (Latin) Hail to thee.

With a fire-new spoon we're furnished,
　　And a goblet for ourself,　　　　　　　　　　　　　　　　20
Rinsed like something sacrificial
　　Ere 'tis fit to touch our chaps—
Marked with L for our initial!
　　(He-he! There his lily snaps!)

Saint, forsooth! While brown Dolores　　　　　　　　　　25
　　Squats outside the Convent bank
With Sanchicha, telling stories,
　　Steeping tresses in the tank,[2]
Blue-black, lustrous, thick like horsehairs,
　　—Can't I see his dead eye glow,　　　　　　　　　　　30
Bright as 'twere a Barbary corsair's?
　　(That is, if he'd let it show!)

When he finishes refection,
　　Knife and fork he never lays
Cross-wise, to my recollection,　　　　　　　　　　　　35
　　As do I, in Jesu's praise.
I the Trinity illustrate,
　　Drinking watered orange-pulp—
In three sips the Arian[3] frustrate;
　　While he drains his at one gulp.　　　　　　　　　　40

Oh, those melons? If he's able
　　We're to have a feast! so nice!
One goes to the Abbot's table,
　　All of use get each a slice.
How go on your flowers? None double?　　　　　　　　45
　　Not one fruit-sort can you spy?
Strange!—And I, too, at such trouble,
　　Keep them close-nipped on the sly!

There's a great text in Galatians,[4]
　　Once you trip on it, entails　　　　　　　　　　　　50
Twenty-nine distinct damnations,
　　One sure, if another fails:
If I trip him just a-dying,
　　Sure of heaven as sure can be,

[2] Of rain water.　　[3] The Arian heresy, which maintained that Father and Son were
entirely separate beings and that Christ was a created being, inferior to the Father.
[4] Probably Galatians 3:10: For as many as are of the works of the law are under the curse:
for it is written, Cursed is every one that continueth not in all things which are written in
the book of the law to do them.

Spin him round and send him flying
    Off to hell, a Manichee?[5]

55

Or, my scrofulous French novel
    On grey paper with blunt type!
Simply glance at it, you grovel
    Hand and foot in Belial's[6] gripe:

60

If I double down its pages
    At the woeful sixteenth print,
When he gathers his greengages,
    Ope a sieve[7] and slip it in't?[7]

Or, there's Satan—one might venture
    Pledge one's soul to him, yet leave

65

Such a flaw in the endenture
    As he'd miss till, past retrieve,
Blasted lay that rose-acacia
    We're so proud of! *Hy, Zy Hine* . . .

70

'St, there's Vespers! *Plena gratiâ*
    Ave, Virgo![8] Gr-r-r—you swine!

A WOMAN'S LAST WORD

I

Let's contend no more, Love,
    Strive nor weep:
All be as before, Love,
    —Only sleep!

II

What so wild as words are?
    I and thou
In debate, as birds are,
    Hawk on bough!

5

III

See the creature stalking
    While we speak!

10

[5] A believer in the Manichean heresy, which holds that the world is composed of two irreducible opposing principles, light (or good) and darkness (or evil).   [6] Satan's.
[7] Basket used chiefly for produce.   [8] Full of grace, Hail, Virgin (usually, *Ave Maria gratia plena*).

Hush and hide the talking,
    Cheek on cheek!

IV

What so false as truth is,
    False to thee?
Where the serpent's tooth is   15
    Shun the tree—

V

Where the apple reddens
    Never pry—
Lest we lose our Edens,
    Eve and I.   20

VI

Be a god and hold me
    With a charm!
Be a man and fold me
    With thine arm!

VII

Teach me, only teach, Love.   25
    As I ought
I will speak thy speech, Love,
    Think thy thought—

VIII

Meet, if thou require it,
    Both demands,   30
Laying flesh and spirit
    In thy hands.

IX

That shall be to-morrow
    Not to-night:
I must bury sorrow   35
    Out of sight:

X

—Must a little weep, Love,
    (Foolish me!)

And so fall asleep, Love,
    Loved by thee.   40

"CHILDE ROLAND[1] TO THE DARK TOWER CAME"

(*See Edgar's song in* Lear)

I

My first thought was, he lied in every word,
    That hoary cripple, with malicious eye
    Askance to watch the working of his lie
On mine, and mouth scarce able to afford
Suppression of the glee, that pursed and scored   5
    Its edge, at one more victim gained thereby.

II

What else should he be set for, with his staff?
    What, save to waylay with his lies, ensnare
    All travellers who might find him posted there,
And ask the road? I guessed what skull-like laugh   10
Would break, what crutch 'gin write my epitaph
    For pastime in the dusty thoroughfare,

III

If at his counsel I should turn aside
    Into that ominous tract which, all agree,
    Hides the Dark Tower. Yet acquiescingly   15
I did turn as he pointed: neither pride
Nor hope rekindling at the end descried,
    So much as gladness that some end might be.

IV

For, what with my whole world-wide wandering,
    What with my search drawn out through years, my hope 20
    Dwindled into a ghost not fit to cope
With that obstreperous joy success would bring,
I hardly tried now to rebuke the spring
    My heart made, finding failure in its scope.

[1] Childe Roland, in legend, was a son of King Arthur whose sister was carried away by fairies to the castle of the king of Elfland. He rescues her. In Shakespeare's *King Lear*, Edgar, in feigned madness, sings "Child Rowland to the dark tower came" (see page 90).

V

As when a sick man very near to death   25
 Seems dead indeed, and feels begin and end
 The tears and takes the farewell of each friend,
And hears one bid the other go, draw breath
Freelier outside, ("since all is o'er," he saith,
 "And the blow fallen no grieving can amend;")   30

VI

While some discuss if near the other graves
 Be room enough for this, and when a day
 Suits best for carrying the corpse away,
With care about the banners, scarves and staves:
And still the man hears all, and only craves   35
 He may not shame such tender love and stay.

VII

Thus, I had so long suffered in this quest,
 Heard failure prophesied so oft, been writ
So many times among "The Band"—to wit,
The knights who to the Dark Tower's search addressed   40
Their steps—that just to fail as they, seemed best,
 And all the doubt was now—should I be fit?

VIII

So, quiet as despair, I turned from him,
 That hateful cripple, out of his highway
 Into the path he pointed. All the day   45
Had been a dreary one at best, and dim[2]
Was settling to its close, yet shot one grim
 Red leer to see the plain catch its estray.[3]

IX

For mark! no sooner was I fairly found
 Pledged to the plain, after a pace or two,   50
 Than, pausing to throw backward a last view
O'er the safe road, 'twas gone; grey plain all round:
Nothing but plain to the horizon's bound.
 I might go on; nought else remained to do.

X

So, on I went. I think I never saw   55
 Such starved ignoble nature; nothing throve:

[2] Twilight. [3] Stray (red glow).

For flowers—as well expect a cedar grove!
But cockle, spurge, according to their law
Might propagate their kind, with none to awe,
    You'd think; a burr had been[4] a treasure-trove.   60

XI

No! penury, inertness and grimace,
    In some strange sort, were the land's portion. "See
    Or shut your eyes," said Nature peevishly,
"It nothing skills:[5] I cannot help my case:
'Tis the Last Judgment's fire must cure this place,   65
    Calcine its clods and set my prisoners[6] free."

XII

If there pushed any ragged thistle-stalk
    Above its mates, the head was chopped; the bents[7]
    Were jealous else. What made those holes and rents
In the dock's harsh swarth leaves,[8] bruised as to balk   70
All hope of greenness? 'tis a brute must walk
    Pashing[9] their life out, with a brute's intents.

XIII

As for the grass, it grew as scant as hair
    In leprosy; thin dry blades pricked the mud
    Which underneath looked kneaded up with blood.   75
One stiff blind horse, his every bone a-stare,
Stood stupefied, however he came there:[10]
    Thrust out past service from the devil's stud![11]

XIV

Alive? he might be dead for aught I know,
    With that red gaunt and colloped[12] neck a-strain,   80
    And shut eyes underneath the rusty mane;
Seldom went such grotesqueness with such woe;
I never saw a brute I hated so;
    He must be wicked to deserve such pain.

XV

I shut my eyes and turned them on my heart.   85
    As a man calls for wine before he fights,

[4] Would have been (had it been there).   [5] It doesn't matter, makes no difference.
[6] My possessions, that is, plants that grow in the "clods" (soil).   [7] Stalks of stiff coarse
grass.   [8] The dock is a coarse weedy plant.   [9] Smashing.   [10] That is, he looked
as if he wondered however he came there.   [11] Place for keeping a group of animals,
especially horses.   [12] Having fatty folds; wrinkled.

I asked one draught of earlier, happier sights,
Ere fitly I could hope to play my part.
Think first, fight afterwards—the soldier's art:
    One taste of the old time sets all to rights.   90

XVI

Not it! I fancied Cuthbert's reddening face[13]
    Beneath its garniture of curly gold,
    Dear fellow, till I almost felt him fold
An arm in mine to fix me to the place,
That way he used. Alas, one night's disgrace!   95
    Out went my heart's new fire and left it cold.

XVII

Giles then, the soul of honour—there he stands
    Frank as ten years ago when knighted first.
    What honest man should dare (he said) he durst.
Good—but the scene shifts—faugh! what hangman hands   100
Pin to his breast a parchment? His own bands
    Read it. Poor traitor, spit upon and curst!

XVIII

Better this present than a past like that;
    Back therefore to my darkening path again!
    No sound, no sight as far as eye could strain.   105
Will the night send a howlet[14] or a bat?
I asked: when something on the dismal flat[15]
    Came to arrest my thoughts and change their train.

XIX

A sudden little river crossed my path
    As unexpected as a serpent comes.   110
    No sluggish tide congenial to the glooms;
This, as it frothed by, might have been a bath
For the fiend's glowing hoof[16]—to see the wrath
    Of its black eddy bespate[17] with flakes and spumes.

XX

So petty yet so spiteful! All along,   115
    Low scrubby alders kneeled down over it;
    Drenched willows flung them headlong in a fit

[13] Cuthbert and Giles are former companions of Roland.   [14] Owlet.   [15] Plain.
[16] The cloven hoof often attributed to Satan.   [17] Bespattered.

Of mute despair, a suicidal throng:
The river which had done them all the wrong,
   Whate'er that was, rolled by, deterred no whit.   120

XXI

Which, while I forded,—good saints, how I feared
   To set my foot upon a dead man's cheek,
   Each step, or feel the spear I thrust to seek
For hollows, tangled in his hair or beard!
—It may have been a water-rat I speared,   125
   But, ugh! it sounded like a baby's shriek.

XXII

Glad was I when I reached the other bank.
   Now for a better country. Vain presage!
   Who were the strugglers, what war did they wage,
Whose savage trample thus could pad the dank   130
Soil to a plash?[18] Toads in a poisoned tank,
   Or wild cats in a red-hot iron cage—

XXIII

The fight must so have seemed in that fell cirque.[19]
   What penned them there, with all the plain to choose?
   No foot-print leading to that horrid mews,[20]   135
None out of it. Mad brewage set to work
Their brains, no doubt, like galley-slaves the Turk
   Pits for his pastime, Christians against Jews.

XXIV

And more than that—a furlong on—why, there!
   What bad use was that engine for, that wheel,   140
   Or brake, not wheel—that harrow fit to reel
Men's bodies out like silk? with all the air
Of Tophet's tool,[21] on earth left unaware,
   Or brought to sharpen its rusty teeth of steel.

XXV

Then came a bit of stubbed ground, once a wood,   145
   Next a marsh, it would seem, and now mere earth
   Desperate and done with; (so a fool finds mirth,

---

   [18] Puddle.   [19] A theatre or arena (a "circle").   [20] Stable or collection of cages.
[21] Tophet was a place near Jerusalem where Jews were supposed to have made human
sacrifices (Jeremiah 19:4). Later the place was used to burn rubbish and, partly because
bonfires burned continually, became symbolic of the torments of hell.

Makes a thing and then mars it, till his mood
Changes and off he goes!) within a rood—[22]
    Bog, clay and rubble, sand and stark black dearth.   150

XXVI

Now blotches rankling, coloured gay and grim,
    Now patches where some leanness of the soil's
    Broke into moss or substances like boils;
Then came some palsied oak, a cleft in him
Like a distorted mouth that splits its rim   155
    Gaping at death, and dies while it recoils.

XXVII

And just as far as ever from the end!
    Nought in the distance but the evening, nought
    To point my footstep further! At the thought,
A great black bird, Apollyon's bosom-friend,[23]
Sailed past, nor beat his wide wing dragon-penned[24]   160
    That brushed my cap—perchance the guide I sought.

XXVIII

For, looking up, aware I somehow grew,
    'Spite of the dusk, the plain had given place
    All round to mountains—with such name to grace
Mere ugly heights and heaps now stolen in view.   165
How thus they had surprised me,—solve it, you!
    How to get from them was no clearer case.

XXIX

Yet half I seemed to recognize some trick
    Of mischief happened to me, God knows when—
    In a bad dream perhaps. Here ended, then,   170
Progress this way. When, in the very nick
Of giving up, one time more, came a click
    As when a trap shuts—you're inside the den!

XXX

Burningly it came on me all at once,
    This was the place! those two hills on the right,   175
    Crouched like two bulls locked horn in horn in fight;
While to the left, a tall scalped mountain . . . Dunce,

---

[22] About one-fourth of an acre.   [23] Apollyon, or "The Destroyer," according to Revelation 9:11, is the "angel of the bottomless pit."   [24] Having the feathers (pens) of a dragon.

Dotard, a-dozing at the very nonce,[25]
    After a life spent training for the sight!

XXXI

What in the midst lay but the Tower itself?   180
    The round squat turret, blind as the fool's heart,
    Built of brown stone, without a counterpart
In the whole world. The tempest's mocking elf
Points to the shipman thus the unseen shelf
    He strikes on, only when the timbers start.[26]   185

XXXII

Not see? because of night perhaps?—why, day
    Came back again for that! before it left,
    The dying sunset kindled through a cleft:
The hills, like giants at a hunting, lay,
Chin upon hand, to see the game at bay,—   190
    "Now stab and end the creature—to the heft!"

XXXIII

Not hear? when noise was everywhere! it tolled
    Increasing like a bell. Names in my ears
    Of all the lost adventurers my peers,—
How such a one was strong, and such was bold,   195
And such was fortunate, yet each of old
    Lost, lost! one moment knelled the woe of years.

XXXIV

There they stood, ranged along the hillsides, met
    To view the last of me, a living frame
    For one more picture! in a sheet of flame   200
I saw them and I knew them all. And yet
Dauntless the slug-horn[27] to my lips I set,
    And blew. *"Childe Roland to the Dark Tower came."*

[25] Occasion.   [26] Become loosened or forced out of place.   [27] Trumpet.

WALT WHITMAN

1819–1892

STARTING FROM PAUMANOK

1

Starting from fish-shape Paumanok[1] where I was born,
Well-begotten, and rais'd by a perfect mother,
After roaming many lands, lover of populous pavements,
Dweller in Mannahatta my city, or on southern savannas,
Or a soldier camp'd or carrying my knapsack and gun, or a miner in
    California,   5
Or rude in my home in Dakota's woods, my diet meat, my drink from
    the spring,
Or withdrawn to muse and meditate in some deep recess,
Far from the clank of crowds intervals passing rapt and happy,
Aware of the fresh free giver the flowing Missouri, aware of mighty
    Niagara,   10
Aware of the buffalo herds grazing the plains, the hirsute and strong-
    breasted bull,
Of earth, rocks, Fifth-month flowers experienced, stars, rain, snow, my
    amaze,
Having studied the mocking-bird's tones and the flight of the mountain-
    hawk,
And heard at dawn the unrivall'd one, the hermit thrush from the
    swamp-cedars,
Solitary, singing in the West, I strike up for a New World.   15

2

Victory, union, faith, identity, time,
The indissoluble compacts, riches, mystery,
Eternal progress, the kosmos, and the modern reports.

This then is life,
Here is what has come to the surface after so many throes and
    convulsions.   20

How curious! how real!
Underfoot the divine soil, overhead the sun.

[1] Indian name of Long Island, New York.

See revolving the globe,
The ancestor-continents away group'd together,
The present and future continents north and south, with the isthmus
     between. 25

See, vast trackless spaces,
As in a dream they change, they swiftly fill,
Countless masses debouch upon them,
They are now cover'd with the foremost people, arts, institutions, known.

See, projected through time,
For me an audience interminable. 30

With firm and regular step they wend, they never stop,
Successions of men, Americanos, a hundred millions,
One generation playing its part and passing on,
Another generation playing its part and passing on in its turn,
With faces turn'd sideways or backward towards me to listen, 35
With eyes retrospective towards me.

    3

Americanos! conquerors! marches humanitarian!
Foremost! century marches! Libertad![2] masses!
For you a programme of chants.

Chants of the prairies, 40
Chants of the long-running Mississippi, and down to the Mexican sea,
Chants of Ohio, Indiana, Illinois, Iowa, Wisconsin and Minnesota,
Chants going forth from the centre from Kansas, and thence equidistant,
Shooting in pulses of fire ceaseless to vivify all.

    4

Take my leaves[3] America, take them South and take them North, 45
Make welcome for them everywhere, for they are your own offspring,
Surround them East and West, for they would surround you,
And you precedents, connect lovingly with them, for they connect
     lovingly with you.

I conn'd old times,
I sat studying at the feet of the great masters, 50
Now if eligible O that the great masters might return and study me.

---

[2] (Spanish) Liberty.   [3] Poems; Whitman published his poetry in a volume entitled
Leaves of Grass.

In the name of these States shall I scorn the antique?
Why these are the children of the antique to justify it.

5

Dead poets, philosophs, priests,
Martyrs, artists, inventors, governments long since,   55
Language-shapers on other shores,
Nations once powerful, now reduced, withdrawn, or desolate,
I dare not proceed till I respectfully credit what you have left wafted
    hither,
I have perused it, own it is admirable, (moving awhile among it,)
Think nothing can ever be greater, nothing can ever deserve more than
    it deserves,   60
Regarding it all intently a long while, then dismissing it,
I stand in my place with my own day here.

Here lands female and male,
Here the heir-ship and heiress-ship of the world, here the flame of materials,
Here spirituality the translatress, the openly-avow'd,   65
The ever-tending, the finalè of visible forms,
The satisfier, after due long-waiting now advancing,
Yes here comes my mistress the soul.

6

The soul,
Forever and forever—longer than soil is brown and solid—longer than
    water ebbs and flows.   70

I will make the poems of materials, for I think they are to be the most
    spiritual poems,
And I will make the poems of my body and of mortality,
For I think I shall then supply myself with the poems of my soul and
    of immortality.

I will make a song for these States that no one State may under any
    circumstances be subjected to another State,
And I will make a song that there shall be comity by day and by night
    between all the States, and between any two of them,   75
And I will make a song for the ears of the President, full of weapons
    with menacing points,
And behind the weapons countless dissatisfied faces;
And a song make I of the One form'd out of all,
The fang'd and glittering One whose head is over all,
Resolute warlike One including and over all,   80
(However high the head of any else that head is over all.)

I will acknowledge contemporary lands,
I will trail the whole geography of the globe and salute courteously
    every city large and small,
And employments! I will put in my poems that with you is heroism
    upon land and sea,
And I will report all heroism from an American point of view.   85

I will sing the song of companionship,
I will show what alone must finally compact these,
I believe these are to found their own ideal of manly love, indicating
    it in me,
I will therefore let flame from me the burning fires that were threaten-
    ing to consume me,
I will lift what has too long kept down those smouldering fires,   90
I will give them complete abandonment,
I will write the evangel-poem of comrades and of love,
For who but I should understand love with all its sorrow and joy?
And who but I should be the poet of comrades?

    7

I am the credulous man of qualities, ages, races,   95
I advance from the people in their own spirit,
Here is what sings unrestricted faith.

Omnes![4] omnes! let others ignore what they may,
I make the poem of evil also, I commemorate that part also,
I am myself just as much evil as good, and my nation is—and I say
    there is in fact no evil,   100
(Or if there is I say it is just as important to you, to the land or to me,
    as any thing else.)

I too, following many and follow'd by many, inaugurate a religion, I
    descend into the arena,
(It may be I am destin'd to utter the loudest cries there, the winner's
    pealing shouts,
Who knows? they may rise from me yet, and soar above every thing.)

Each is not for its own sake,   105
I say the whole earth and all the stars in the sky are for religion's sake.

I say no man has ever yet been half devout enough,
None has ever yet adored or worship'd half enough,

    4 (Latin) All.

None has begun to think how divine he himself is, and how certain
    the future is.

I say that the real and permanent grandeur of these States must be
    their religion, 110
Otherwise there is no real and permanent grandeur;
(Nor character nor life worthy the name without religion,
Nor land nor man or woman without religion.)

      8

What are you doing young man?
Are you so earnest, so given up to literature, science, art, amours? 115
These ostensible realities, politics, points?
Your ambition or business whatever it may be?

It is well—against such I say not a word, I am their poet also,
But behold! such swiftly subside, burnt up for religion's sake,
For not all matter is fuel to heat, impalpable flame, the essential life
    of the earth, 120
Any more than such are to religion.

      9

What do you seek so pensive and silent?
What do you need camerado?[5]
Dear son do you think it is love?

Listen dear son—listen America, daughter or son, 125
It is a painful thing to love a man or woman to excess, and yet it
    satisfies, it is great,
But there is something else very great, it makes the whole coincide,
It, magnificent, beyond materials, with continuous hands sweeps and
    provides for all.

      10

Know you, solely to drop in the earth the germs of a greater religion,
The following chants each for its kind I sing. 130

My comrade!
For you to share with me two greatnesses, and a third one rising
    inclusive and more resplendent,
The greatness of Love and Democracy, and the greatness of Religion.

    [5] Camarado (Spanish), comrade, friend.

Melange mine own, the unseen and the seen, 135
Mysterious ocean where the streams empty,
Prophetic spirit of materials shifting and flickering around me,
Living beings, identities now doubtless near us in the air that we know
　　not of,
Contact daily and hourly that will not release me,
These selecting, these in hints demanded of me.

Not he with a daily kiss onward from childhood kissing me, 140
Has winded and twisted around me that which holds me to him,
Any more than I am held to the heavens and all the spiritual world,
After what they have done to me, suggesting themes.

O such themes—equalities! O divine average!
Warblings under the sun, usher'd as now, or at noon, or setting, 145
Strains musical flowing through ages, now reaching hither,
I take to your reckless and composite chords, add to them, and cheer-
　　fully pass them forward.

　　　11

As I have walk'd in Alabama my morning walk,
I have seen where the she-bird the mocking-bird sat on her nest in the
　　briers hatching her brood.

I have seen the he-bird also, 150
I have paus'd to hear him near at hand inflating his throat and joyfully
　　singing.

And while I paus'd it came to me that what he really sang for was not
　　there only,
Nor for his mate nor himself only, nor all sent back by the echoes,
But subtle, clandestine, away beyond,
A charge transmitted and gift occult for those being born. 155

　　　12

Democracy! near at hand to you a throat is now inflating itself and
　　joyfully singing.

Ma femme![6] for the brood beyond us and of us,
For those who belong here and those to come,

　　[6] (French) My wife.

I exultant to be ready for them will now shake out carols stronger and
      haughtier than have ever yet been heard upon earth.

I will make the songs of passion to give them their way, 160
And your songs outlaw'd offenders, for I scan you with kindred eyes,
      and carry you with me the same as any.

I will make the true poem of riches,
To earn for the body and the mind whatever adheres and goes forward
      and is not dropt by death;
I will effuse egotism and show it underlying all, and I will be the bard
      of personality,
And I will show of male and female that either is but the equal of the
      other, 165
And sexual organs and acts! do you concentrate in me, for I am deter-
      min'd to tell you with courageous clear voice to prove you
      illustrious,
And I will show that there is no imperfection in the present, and can
      be none in the future,
And I will show that whatever happens to anybody it may be turn'd to
      beautiful results,
And I will show that nothing can happen more beautiful than death,
And I will thread a thread through my poems that time and events are
      compact, 170
And that all the things of the universe are perfect miracles, each as
      profound as any.

I will not make poems with reference to parts,
But I will make poems, songs, thoughts, with reference to ensemble,
And I will not sing with reference to a day, but with reference to all
      days,
And I will not make a poem nor the least part of a poem but has
      reference to the soul, 175
Because having look'd at the objects of the universe, I find there is no
      one nor any particle of one but has reference to the soul.

13

Was somebody asking to see the soul?
See, your own shape and countenance, persons, substances, beasts, the
      trees, the running rivers, the rocks and sands.

All hold spiritual joys and afterwards loosen them;
How can the real body ever die and be buried? 180

Of your real body and any man's or woman's real body,
Item for item it will elude the hands of the corpse-cleaners and pass to
 fitting spheres,
Carrying what has accrued to it from the moment of birth to the
 moment of death.

Not the types set up by the printer return their impression, the meaning, the main concern,
Any more than a man's substance and life or a woman's substance and
 life return in the body and the soul,   185
Indifferently before death and after death.

Behold, the body includes and is the meaning, the main concern, and
 includes and is the soul;
Whoever you are, how superb and how divine is your body, or any part
 of it!

14

Whoever you are, to you endless announcements!

Daughter of the lands did you wait for your poet?   190
Did you wait for one with a flowing mouth and indicative hand?

Toward the male of the States, and toward the female of the States,
Exulting words, words to Democracy's lands.

Interlink'd, food-yielding lands!
Land of coal and iron! land of gold! land of cotton, sugar, rice! 195
Land of wheat, beef, pork! land of wool and hemp! land of the apple
 and the grape!
Land of the pastoral plains, the grass-fields of the world! land of those
 sweet-air'd interminable plateaus!
Land of the herd, the garden, the healthy house of adobie!
Lands where the north-west Columbia winds, and where the south-west
 Colorado winds!
Land of the eastern Chesapeake! land of the Delaware!   200
Land of Ontario, Erie, Huron, Michigan!
Land of the Old Thirteen! Massachusetts land! land of Vermont and
 Connecticut!
Land of the ocean shores! land of sierras and peaks!
Land of boatmen and sailors! fishermen's land!
Inextricable lands! the clutch'd together! the passionate ones! 205
The side by side! the elder and younger brothers! the bony-limb'd!

The great women's land! the feminine! the experienced sisters and the
    inexperienced sisters!
For breath'd land! Arctic braced! Mexican breez'd! the diverse! the
    compact!
The Pennsylvanian! the Virginian! the double Carolinian!
O all and each well-loved by me! my intrepid nations! O I at any rate
    include you all with perfect love!   210
I cannot be discharged from you! not from one any sooner than
    another!
O death, O for all that, I am yet of you unseen this hour with irre-
    pressible love,
Walking New England, a friend, a traveler,
Splashing my bare feet in the edge of the summer ripples on Pauma-
    nok's sands,
Crossing the prairies, dwelling again in Chicago, dwelling in every
    town,   215
Observing shows, births, improvements, structures, arts,
Listening to orators and oratresses in public halls,
Of and through the States as during life, each man and woman my
    neighbor,
The Louisianian, the Georgian, as near to me, and I as near to him
    and her,
The Mississippian and Arkansian yet with me, and I yet with any of
    them,   220
Yet upon the plains west of the spinal river,[7] yet in my house of adobie,
Yet returning eastward, yet in the Seaside State[8] or in Maryland,
Yet Kanadian[9] cheerily braving the winter, the snow and ice welcome
    to me,
Yet a true son either of Maine or of the Granite State,[10] or the Narra-
    gansett Bay State,[11] or the Empire State,[12]
Yet sailing to other shores to annex the same, yet welcoming every
    new brother,   225
Hereby applying these leaves to the new ones from the hour they unite
    with the old ones,
Coming among the new ones myself to be their companion and equal,
    coming personally to you now,
Enjoining you to acts, characters, spectacles, with me.

    15

With me with firm holding, yet haste, haste on.

For your life adhere to me,   230
(I may have to be persuaded many times before I consent to give my-
    self really to you, but what of that?
Must not Nature be persuaded many times?)

---

[7] The Mississippi.   [8] Probably New Jersey.   [9] Canadian.   [10] New Hamp-
shire.   [11] Rhode Island.   [12] New York.

No dainty dolce affettuoso[13] I,
Bearded, sun-burnt, gray-neck'd, forbidding, I have arrived,
To be wrestled with as I pass for the solid prizes of the universe,   235
For such I afford whoever can persevere to win them.

16

On my way a moment I pause,
Here for you! and here for America!
Still the present I raise aloft, still the future of the States I harbinge
    glad and sublime,
And for the past I pronounce what the air holds of the red aborigines.   240

The red aborigines,
Leaving natural breaths, sounds of rain and winds, calls as of birds and
    animals in the woods, syllabled to us for names,
Okonee, Koosa, Ottawa, Monongahela, Sauk, Natchez, Chattahoochee,
    Kaqueta, Oronoco,
Wabash, Miami, Saginaw, Chippewa, Oshkosh, Walla-Walla,
Leaving such to the States they melt, they depart, charging the water
    and the land with names.   245

17

Expanding and swift, henceforth,
Elements, breeds, adjustments, turbulent, quick and audacious,
A world primal again, vistas of glory incessant and branching,
A new race dominating previous ones and grander far, with new
    contests,
New politics, new literatures and religions, new inventions and arts.   250

These, my voice announcing—I will sleep no more but arise,
You oceans that have been calm within me! how I feel you, fathom-
    less, stirring, preparing unprecedented waves and storms.

18

See, steamers steaming through my poems,
See, in my poems immigrants continually coming and landing,
See, in arriere,[14] the wigwam, the trail, the hunter's hut, the flat-boat,
    the maize-leaf, the claim,[15] the rude fence, and the backwoods
    village,   255
See, on the one side the Western Sea and on the other the Eastern
    Sea, how they advance and retreat upon my poems as upon their
    own shores,

---

[13] (Italian) Gentle, mild, and loving person.   [14] (French) Behind (looking back-wards).   [15] Claimed tract of land.

See, pastures and forests in my poems—see, animals wild and tame—
    see, beyond the Kaw,[16] countless herds of buffalo feeding on
    short curly grass,
See, in my poems, cities, solid, vast, inland, with paved streets, with
    iron and stone edifices, ceaseless vehicles, and commerce,
See, the many-cylinder'd steam printing-press—see, the electric tele-
    graph stretching across the continent,
See, through Atlantica's depths[17] pulses American Europe reaching,
    pulses of Europe duly return'd,   260
See, the strong and quick locomotive as it departs, panting, blowing
    the steam-whistle,
See, ploughmen ploughing farms—see, miners digging mines—see, the
    numberless factories,
See, mechanics busy at their benches with tools—see from among
    them superior judges, philosophs, Presidents, emerge, drest in
    working dresses,
See, lounging through the shops and fields of the States, me well-
    belov'd, close-held by day and night,
Hear the loud echoes of my songs here—read the hints come at last.   265

19

O camerado close! O you and me at last, and us two only.
O a word to clear one's path ahead endlessly!
O something ecstatic and undemonstrable! O music wild!
O now I triumph—and you shall also;
O hand in hand—O wholesome pleasure—O one more desirer and
    lover!   270
O to haste firm holding—to haste, haste on with me.

WHEN LILACS LAST IN THE DOORYARD BLOOM'D

1

When lilacs last in the dooryard bloom'd,
And the great star[1] early droop'd in the western sky in the night,
I mourn'd, and yet shall mourn with ever-returning spring.

Ever-returning spring, trinity sure to me you bring,
Lilac blooming perennial and drooping star in the west,   5
And thought of him I love.

[16] The Kansas River.   [17] *Atlantica*, here, is the Atlantic Ocean.

[1] The planet Venus, or the "evening star."

2

O powerful western fallen star!
O shades of night—O moody, tearful night!
O great star disappear'd—O the black murk that hides the star!
O cruel hands that hold me powerless—O helpless soul of me!   10
O harsh surrounding cloud that will not free my soul.

3

In the dooryard fronting an old farm-house near the white-wash'd
        palings,
Stands the lilac-bush tall-growing with heart-shaped leaves of rich
        green,
With many a pointed blossom rising delicate, with the perfume strong
        I love,
With every leaf a miracle—and from this bush in the dooryard,   15
With delicate-color'd blossoms and heart-shaped leaves of rich green,
A sprig with its flower I break.

4

In the swamp in secluded recesses,
A shy and hidden bird is warbling a song.

Solitary the thrush,   20
The hermit withdrawn to himself, avoiding the settlements,
Sings by himself a song.

Song of the bleeding throat,
Death's outlet song of life, (for well dear brother I know,
If thou wast not granted to sing thou would'st surely die.)   25

5

Over the breast of the spring, the land, amid cities,
Amid lanes and through old woods, where lately the violets peep'd
        from the ground spotting the gray debris,
Amid the grass in the fields each side of the lanes, passing the endless
        grass,
Passing the yellow-spear'd wheat, every grain from its shroud in the
        dark-brown fields uprisen,
Passing the apple-tree blows of white and pink in the orchards,   30
Carrying a corpse to where it shall rest in the grave,
Night and day journeys a coffin.

6

Coffin that passes through lanes and streets,
Through day and night with the great cloud darkening the land,
With the pomp of the inloop'd flags with the cities draped in black,   35
With the show of the States themselves as of crape-veil'd women
    standing,
With processions long and winding and the flambeaus of the night,
With the countless torches lit, with the silent sea of faces and the
    unbared heads,
With the waiting depot, the arriving coffin, and the sombre faces,
With dirges through the night, with the thousand voices rising strong
    and solemn,   40
With all the mournful voices of the dirges pour'd around the coffin,
The dim-lit churches and the shuddering organs—where amid these
    you journey,
With the tolling tolling bells' perpetual clang,
Here, coffin that slowly passes,
I give you my sprig of lilac.   45

7

(Nor for you, for one alone,
Blossoms and branches green to coffins all I bring,
For fresh as the morning, thus would I chant a song for you O sane
    and sacred death.

All over bouquets of roses,
O death, I cover you over with roses and early lilies,   50
But mostly and now the lilac that blooms the first,
Copious I break, I break the sprigs from the bushes,
With loaded arms I come, pouring for you,
For you and the coffins all of you O death.)

8

O western orb sailing the heaven,   55
Now I know what you must have meant as a month since I walk'd,
As I walk'd in silence the transparent shadowy night,
As I saw you had something to tell as you bent to me night after night,
As you droop'd from the sky low down as if to my side, (while the
    other stars all look'd on,)
As we wander'd together the solemn night, (for something I know not
    what kept me from sleep,)   60
As the night advanced, and I saw on the rim of the west how full you
    were of woe,
As I stood on the rising ground in the breeze in the cool transparent
    night,

As I watch'd where you pass'd and was lost in the netherward black
    of the night,
As my soul in its trouble dissatisfied sank, as where you sad orb,
Concluded, dropt in the night, and was gone.   65

                9

Sing on there in the swamp,
O singer bashful and tender, I hear your notes, I hear your call,
I hear, I come presently, I understand you,
But a moment I linger, for the lustrous star has detain'd me,
The star my departing comrade holds and detains me.   70

                10

O how shall I warble myself for the dead one there I loved?
And how shall I deck my song for the large sweet soul that has gone?
And what shall my perfume be for the grave of him I love?

Sea-winds blown from east and west,
Blown from the Eastern sea and blown from the Western sea, till there
    on the prairies meeting,   75
These and with these and the breath of my chant,
I'll perfume the grave of him I love.

                11

O what shall I hang on the chamber walls?
And what shall the pictures be that I hang on the walls,
To adorn the burial-house of him I love?   80

Pictures of growing spring and farms and homes,
With the Fourth-month eve at sundown, and the gray smoke lucid and
    bright,
With floods of the yellow gold of the gorgeous, indolent, sinking sun,
    burning, expanding the air,
With the fresh sweet herbage under foot, and the pale green leaves of
    the trees prolific,
In the distance the flowing glaze, the breast of the river, with a wind-
    dapple here and there,   85
With ranging hills on the banks, with many a line against the sky, and
    shadows,
And the city at hand with dwellings so dense, and stacks of chimneys,
And all the scenes of life and the workshops, and the workmen home-
    ward returning.

12

Lo, body and soul—this land,
My own Manhattan with spires, and the sparkling and hurrying tides,
    and the ships,   90
The varied and ample land, the South and the North in the light,
    Ohio's shores and flashing Missouri,
And ever the far-spreading prairies cover'd with grass and corn.

Lo, the most excellent sun so calm and haughty,
The violet and purple morn with just-felt breezes,
The gentle soft-born measureless light,   95
The miracle spreading bathing all, the fulfill'd noon,
The coming eve delicious, the welcome night and the stars,
Over my cities shining all, enveloping man and land.

    13

Sing on, sing on you gray-brown bird,
Sing from the swamps, the recesses, pour your chant from the bushes,   100
Limitless out of the dusk, out of the cedars and pines.

Sing on dearest brother, warble your reedy song,
Loud human song, with voice of uttermost woe.

O liquid and free and tender!
O wild and loose to my soul—O wondrous singer!   105
You only I hear—yet the star holds me, (but will soon depart,)
Yet the lilac with mastering odor holds me.

    14

Now while I sat in the day and look'd forth,
In the close of the day with its light and the fields of spring, and the
    farmers preparing their crops,
In the large unconscious scenery of my land with its lakes and forests,   110
In the heavenly aerial beauty, (after the perturb'd winds and the
    storms,)
Under the arching heavens of the afternoon swift passing, and the
    voices of children and women,
The many-moving sea-tides, and I saw the ships how they sail'd,
And the summer approaching with richness, and the fields all busy
    with labor,
And the infinite separate houses, how they all went on, each with its
    meals and minutia of daily usages,   115
And the streets how their throbbings throbb'd, and the cities pent—lo,
    then and there,

Falling upon them all and among them all, enveloping me with the rest,
Appear'd the cloud, appear'd the long black trail,
And I knew death, its thought, and the sacred knowledge of death.

Then with the knowledge of death as walking one side of me,   120
And the thought of death close-walking the other side of me,
And I in the middle as with companions, and as holding the hands of
    companions,
I fled forth to the hiding receiving night that talks not,
Down to the shores of the water, the path by the swamp in the
    dimness,
To the solemn shadowy cedars and ghostly pines so still.   125

And the singer so shy to the rest receiv'd me,
The gray-brown bird I know receiv'd us comrades three,
And he sang the carol of death, and a verse for him I love.

From deep secluded recesses,
From the fragrant cedars and the ghostly pines so still,   130
Came the carol of the bird.

And the charm of the carol rapt me,
As I held as if by their hands my comrades in the night,
And the voice of my spirit tallied the song of the bird.

Come lovely and soothing death,   135
Undulate round the world, serenely arriving, arriving,
In the day, in the night, to all, to each,
Sooner or later delicate death.

Prais'd be the fathomless universe,
For life and joy, and for objects and knowledge curious,   140
And for love, sweet love—but praise! praise! praise!
For the sure-enwinding arms of cool-enfolding death.

Dark mother always gliding near with soft feet,
Have none chanted for thee a chant of fullest welcome?
Then I chant it for thee, I glorify thee above all,   145
I bring thee a song that when thou must indeed come, come
    unfalteringly.

Approach strong deliveress,
When it is so, when thou hast taken them I joyously sing the dead,
Lost in the loving floating ocean of thee,
Laved in the flood of thy bliss O death. 150

From me to thee glad serenades,
Dances for thee I propose saluting thee, adornments and feastings for
thee,
And the sights of the open landscape and the high-spread sky are
fitting,
And life and the fields, and the huge and thoughtful night.

The night in silence under many a star, 155
The ocean shore and the husky whispering wave whose voice I know,
And the soul turning to thee O vast and well-veil'd death,
And the body gratefully nestling close to thee.

Over the tree-tops I float thee a song,
Over the rising and sinking waves, over the myriad fields and the
prairies wide, 160
Over the dense-pack'd cities all and the teeming wharves and ways,
I float this carol with joy, with joy to thee O death.

15

To the tally of my soul,
Loud and strong kept up the gray-brown bird,
With pure deliberate notes spreading filling the night. 165

Loud in the pines and cedars dim,
Clear in the freshness moist and the swamp-perfume,
And I with my comrades there in the night.

While my sight that was bound in my eyes unclosed,
As to long panoramas of visions. 170

And I saw askant the armies,
I saw as in noiseless dreams hundreds of battle-flags,
Borne through the smoke of the battles and pierc'd with missiles I saw
them,
And carried hither and yon through the smoke, and torn and bloody,
And at last but a few shreds left on the staffs, (and all in silence,) 175
And the staffs all splinter'd and broken.

I saw battle-corpses, myriads of them,
And the white skeletons of young men, I saw them,
I saw the debris and debris of all the slain soldiers of the war,
But I saw they were not as was thought, 180
They themselves were fully at rest, they suffer'd not,
The living remain'd and suffer'd, the mother suffer'd,
And the wife and the child and the musing comrade suffer'd,
And the armies that remain'd suffer'd.

16

Passing the visions, passing the night, 185
Passing, unloosing the hold of my comrades' hands,
Passing the song of the hermit bird and the tallying song of my soul,
Victorious song, death's outlet song, yet varying ever-altering song,
As low and wailing, yet clear the notes, rising and falling, flooding the
    night,
Sadly sinking and fainting, as warning and warning, and yet again 190
    bursting with joy,
Covering the earth and filling the spread of the heaven,
As that powerful psalm in the night I heard from recesses,
Passing, I leave thee lilac with heart-shaped leaves,
I leave thee there in the door-yard, blooming, returning with spring.

I cease from my song for thee, 195
From my gaze on thee in the west, fronting the west, communing with
    thee,
O comrade lustrous with silver face in the night.

Yet each to keep and all, retrievements out of the night,
The song, the wondrous chant of the gray-brown bird,
And the tallying chant, the echo arous'd in my soul, 200
With the lustrous and drooping star with the countenance full of woe,
With the holders holding my hand nearing the call of the bird,
Comrades mine and I in the midst, and their memory ever to keep, for
    the dead I loved so well,
For the sweetest, wisest soul of all my days and lands—and this for his
    dear sake,
Lilac and star and bird twined with the chant of my soul, 205
There in the fragrant pines and the cedars dusk and dim.

MATTHEW ARNOLD

1 8 2 2 – 1 8 8 8

SHAKESPEARE

Others abide[1] our question. Thou art free.
We ask and ask: Thou smilest and art still,
Out-topping knowledge. For the loftiest hill
That to the stars uncrowns his majesty,
Planting his steadfast footsteps in the sea, 5
Making the Heaven of Heavens his dwelling-place,
Spares but the cloudy border of his base
To the foil'd searching of mortality:
And thou, who didst the stars and sunbeams know,
Self-school'd, self-scann'd,[2] self-honour'd, self-secure, 10
Didst walk on Earth unguess'd at. Better so!
All pains the immortal spirit must endure,
All weakness that impairs, all griefs that bow,
Find their sole voice in that victorious brow.

MEMORIAL VERSES
April, 1850

Goethe in Weimar sleeps,[1] and Greece,
Long since, saw Byron's struggle cease.[2]
But one such death remain'd to come;
The last poetic voice is dumb.
What shall be said o'er Wordsworth's tomb? 5

When Byron's eyes were shut in death,
We bow'd our head and held our breath.
He taught us little: but our soul
Had *felt* him like the thunder's roll.

[1] Submit to, face.　　[2] Self-examined (introspectively).

[1] Johann Wolfgang von Goethe (1749–1832), German poet and dramatist, was buried in Weimar.　　[2] The English poet, Byron, died in Greece in a battle for that country's independence.

With shivering heart the strife we saw
Of Passion with Eternal Law;
And yet with reverential awe
We watch'd the fount of fiery life
Which serv'd for that Titanic strife.

10

When Goethe's death was told, we said— 15
Sunk, then, is Europe's sagest head.
Physician of the Iron Age,
Goethe has done his pilgrimage.
He took the suffering human race,
He read each wound, each weakness clear— 20
And struck his finger on the place
And said—*Thou ailest here, and here—*
He look'd on Europe's dying hour
Of fitful dream and feverish power;
His eye plung'd down the weltering strife, 25
The turmoil of expiring life;
He said—*The end is everywhere:*
Art still has truth, take refuge there.
And he was happy, if to know
Causes of things, and far below 30
His feet to see the lurid flow
Of terror, and insane distress,
And headlong fate, be happiness.

And Wordsworth!—Ah, pale Ghosts, rejoice!
For never has such soothing voice 35
Been to your shadowy world convey'd,
Since erst, at morn, some wandering shade
Heard the clear song of Orpheus come
Through Hades,[3] and the mournful gloom.
Wordsworth has gone from us—and ye, 40
Ah, may ye feel his voice as we.
He too upon a wintry clime
Had fallen—on this iron time
Of doubts, disputes, distractions, fears.
He found us when the age had bound 45
Our souls in its benumbing round;
He spoke, and loos'd our heart in tears.
He laid us as we lay at birth
On the cool flowery lap of earth;
Smiles broke from us and we had ease, 50
The hills were round us, and the breeze
Went o'er the sun-lit fields again:

[3] In Greek mythology, Orpheus, a semi-divine musician, went to Hades in an attempt
to bring back Eurydice, his wife.

Our foreheads felt the wind and rain.
Our youth return'd: for there was shed
On spirits that had long been dead,   55
Spirits dried up and closely-furl'd,
The freshness of the early world.

    Ah, since dark days still bring to light
Man's prudence and man's fiery might,
Time may restore us in his course   60
Goethe's sage mind and Byron's force:
But where will Europe's latter hour
Again find Wordsworth's healing power?
Others will teach us how to dare,
And against fear our breast to steel: 65
Others will strengthen us to bear—
But who, ah who, will make us feel?
The cloud of mortal destiny,
Others will front it fearlessly—
But who, like him, will put it by?   70

    Keep fresh the grass upon his grave,
O Rotha![4] with thy living wave.
Sing him thy best! for few or none
Hears thy voice right, now he is gone.

TO MARGUERITE IN RETURNING A VOLUME OF THE LETTERS OF ORTIS

Yes: in the sea of life enisl'd,
With echoing straits between us thrown,
Dotting the shoreless watery wild,
We mortal millions live *alone*.
    The islands feel the enclasping flow,   5
And then their endless bounds they know.

But when the moon their hollow lights,
And they are swept by balms of spring,
And in their glens, on starry nights,
The nightingales divinely sing;   10
And lovely notes, from shore to shore,
Across the sounds and channels pour;

    [4] A river that flows past Grasmere churchyard, where Wordsworth is buried.

Oh then a longing like despair
Is to their farthest caverns sent;
For surely once, they feel, we were
Parts of a single continent.
Now round us spreads the watery plain—
Oh might our marges[1] meet again!

15

Who order'd, that their longing's fire
Should be, as soon as kindled, cool'd?
Who renders vain their deep desire?—
    A God, a God their severance rul'd;
And bade betwixt their shores to be
The unplumb'd, salt, estranging sea.

20

THE SCHOLAR GIPSY[1]

Go, for they call you, Shepherd, from the hill;
    Go, Shepherd, and untie the wattled cotes:[2]
        No longer leave thy wistful flock unfed,
Nor let thy bawling fellows rack their throats,
        Nor the cropp'd grasses shoot another head.
        But when the fields are still,
And the tired men and dogs all gone to rest,
        And only the white sheep are sometimes seen
        Cross and recross the strips of moon-blanch'd green;
        Come, Shepherd, and again renew the quest.

5

10

Here, where the reaper was at work of late,
    In this high field's dark corner, where he leaves
        His coat, his basket, and his earthen cruise,[3]

---

[1] Margins, boundaries.

[1] Arnold included the following passage from Glanvil's *Vanity of Dogmatizing* (1661), as a footnote to the title of this poem: "There was very lately a lad in the University of Oxford, who was by his poverty forced to leave his studies there; and at last to join himself to a company of vagabond gipsies. Among these extravagant people, by the insinuating subtilty of his carriage, he quickly got so much of their love and esteem as that they discovered to him their mystery. After he had been a pretty while will exercised in the trade, there chanced to ride by a couple of scholars, who had formerly been of his acquaintance. They quickly spied out their old friend among the gipsies; and he gave them an account of the necessity which drove him to that kind of life, and told them that the people he went with were not such impostors as they were taken for, but that they had a traditional kind of learning among them, and could do wonders by the power of imagination, their fancy binding that of others: that himself had learned much of their art, and when he had compassed the whole secret, he intended, he said, to leave their company, and give the world an account of what he had learned. [2] Pens made of poles interwoven with slender branches. [3] Cruse, that is, jar, pot.

And in the sun all morning binds the sheaves,
    Then here, at noon, comes back his stores to use; 15
       Here will I sit and wait,
While to my ear from uplands far away
    The bleating of the folded flocks is borne,
    With distant cries of reapers in the corn—
       All the live murmur of a summer's day. 20

Screen'd is this nook o'er the high, half-reap'd field,
    And here till sun-down, Shepherd, will I be.
       Through the thick corn the scarlet poppies peep,
    And round green roots and yellowing stalks I see
       Pale blue convolvulus in tendrils creep: 25
         And air-swept lindens yield
Their scent, and rustle down their perfum'd showers
    Of bloom on the bent grass where I am laid,
    And bower me from the August sun with shade;
       And the eye travels down to Oxford's towers: 30

And near me on the grass lies Glanvil's book—
    Come, let me read the oft-read tale again,
       The story of that Oxford scholar poor
Of pregnant parts[4] and quick inventive brain,
    Who, tir'd of knocking at Preferment's door, 35
       One summer morn forsook
His friends, and went to learn the Gipsy lore,
    And roam'd the world with that wild brotherhood,
    And came, as most men deem'd, to little good,
       But came to Oxford and his friends no more. 40

But once, years after, in the country lanes,
    Two scholars whom at college erst he knew
       Met him, and of his way of life inquir'd.
Whereat he answer'd, that the Gipsy crew,
    His mates, had arts to rule as they desir'd 45
       The workings of men's brains;
And they can bind them to what thoughts they will:
    "And I," he said, "the secret of their art,
    When fully learn'd, will to the world impart:
       But it needs heaven-sent moments for this skill." 50

This said, he left them, and return'd no more,
    But rumours hung about the country side
       That the lost Scholar long was seen to stray,

[4] Promising characteristics.

Seen by rare glimpses, pensive and tongue-tied,
   In hat of antique shape, and cloak of grey,   55
      The same the Gipsies wore.
Shepherds had met him on the Hurst[5] in spring;
   At some lone alehouse in the Berkshire moors,
   On the warm ingle[6] bench, the smock-frock'd boors[7]
      Had found him seated at their entering,   60

But, mid their drink and clatter, he would fly:
   And I myself seem half to know thy looks,
      And put the shepherds, Wanderer, on thy trace;
And boys who in lone wheatfields scare the rooks[8]
      I ask if thou hast pass'd their quiet place;   65
      Or in my boat I lie
Moor'd to the cool bank in the summer heats,
   Mid wide grass meadows which the sunshine fills,
   And watch the warm green-muffled Cumner hills,
      And wonder if thou haunt'st their shy retreats.   70

For most, I know, thou lov'st retired ground.
   Thee, at the ferry, Oxford riders blithe,
      Returning home on summer nights, have met
Crossing the stripling Thames at Bab-lock-hithe,
      Trailing in the cool stream thy fingers wet,   75
      As the slow punt swings round:
And leaning backwards in a pensive dream,
   And fostering in thy lap a heap of flowers
   Pluck'd in shy fields and distant Wychwood bowers,
      And thine eyes resting on the moonlit stream: 80

And then they land, and thou art seen no more.
   Maidens who from the distant hamlets come
      To dance around the Fyfield elm in May,
Oft through the darkening fields have seen thee roam,
      Or cross a stile into the public way.   85
      Oft thou hast given them store
Of flowers—the frail-leaf'd, white anemone—
   Dark bluebells drench'd with dews of summer eves—
   And purple orchises with spotted leaves—
      But none has words she can report of thee.   90

And, above Godstow Bridge, when hay-time's here
   In June, and many a scythe in sunshine flames,

---

[5] Bank or hillock.   [6] Fireside.   [7] Peasants, rustics.   [8] Birds resembling crows.

Men who through those wide fields of breezy grass
Where black-wing'd swallows haunt the glittering Thames,
    To bathe in the abandon'd lasher[9] pass,   95
       Have often pass'd thee near
Sitting upon the river bank o'ergrown:
   Mark'd thy outlandish garb, thy figure spare,
   Thy dark vague eyes, and soft abstracted air;
     But, when they came from bathing, thou wert gone.   100

At some lone homestead in the Cumner hills,
   Where at her open door the housewife darns,
     Thou hast been seen, or hanging on a gate
To watch the threshers in the mossy barns.
     Children who early range these slopes and late   105
       For cresses[10] from the rills,
Have known thee watching, all an April day,
   The springing pastures and the feeding kine;[11]
And mark'd thee, when the stars come out and shine,
     Through the long dewy grass move slow away.   110

In Autumn, on the skirts of Bagley wood,
   Where most the Gipsies by the turf-edg'd way
     Pitch their smok'd tents, and every bush you see
With scarlet patches tagg'd and shreds of grey,
     Above the forest ground call'd Thessaly—   115
       The blackbird picking food
Sees thee, nor stops his meal, nor fears at all;
   So often has he known thee past him stray
Rapt, twirling in thy hand a wither'd spray,
     And waiting for the spark from Heaven to fall.   120

And once, in winter, on the causeway chill
   Where home through flooded fields foot-travellers go,
     Have I not pass'd thee on the wooden bridge
Wrapt in thy cloak and battling with the snow,
     Thy face towards Hinksey and its wintry ridge?   125
       And thou hast climb'd the hill
And gain'd the white brow of the Cumner range,
   Turn'd once to watch, while thick the snowflakes fall,
   The line of festal light in Christ-Church hall—
     Then sought thy straw in some sequester'd grange.   130

[9] A pool formed by water (of the Thames) that lashes, or rushes, over an opening in a barrier.   [10] Watercress.   [11] Cattle.

But what—I dream! Two hundred years are flown
　　Since first thy story ran through Oxford halls,
　　　　And the grave Glanvil did the tale inscribe
　　That thou wert wander'd from the studious walls
　　　　To learn strange arts, and join a Gipsy tribe:　　　　135
　　　　　　And thou from earth art gone
　　Long since, and in some quiet churchyard laid;
　　Some country nook, where o'er thy unknown grave
　　Tall grasses and white flowering nettles wave—
　　　　Under a dark red-fruited yew-tree's shade.　　　　140

—No, no, thou hast not felt the lapse of hours.
　　For what wears out the life of mortal men?
　　　　'Tis that from change to change their being rolls:
　　'Tis that repeated shocks, again, again,
　　　　Exhaust the energy of strongest souls,　　　　145
　　　　　　And numb the elastic powers.
　　Till having us'd our nerves with bliss and teen,[12]
　　　　And tir'd upon a thousand schemes our wit,
　　　　To the just-pausing Genius we remit
　　　　　　Our worn-out life, and are—what we have been.　　　　150

Thou hast not liv'd, why should'st thou perish, so?
　　Thou hadst *one* aim, *one* business, *one* desire:
　　　　Else wert thou long since number'd with the dead—
　　Else hadst thou spent, like other men, thy fire.
　　　　The generations of thy peers are fled,　　　　155
　　　　　　And we ourselves shall go;
　　But thou possessest an immortal lot,
　　　　And we imagine thee exempt from age
　　　　And living as thou liv'st on Glanvil's page,
　　　　　　Because thou hadst—what we, alas, have not!　　　　160

For early didst thou leave the world, with powers
　　Fresh, undiverted to the world without,
　　　　Firm to their mark, not spent on other things;
　　Free from the sick fatigue, the languid doubt,
　　　　Which much to have tried, in much been baffled, brings.　　　　165
　　　　　　O Life unlike to ours!
　　Who fluctuate idly without term[13] or scope,
　　Of whom each strives, nor knows for what he strives,
　　And each half lives a hundred different lives;
　　　　Who wait like thee, but not, like thee, in hope.　　　　170

12 Suffering.　　　13 Limit (in time).

Thou waitest for the spark from Heaven: and we,
    Vague half-believers of our casual creeds,
       Who never deeply felt, nor clearly will'd,
    Whose insight never has borne fruit in deeds,
       Whose weak resolves never have been fulfill'd;   175
          For whom each year we see
Breeds new beginnings, disappointments new;
       Who hesitate and falter life away,
       And lose to-morrow the ground won to-day—
          Ah, do not we, Wanderer, await it too?   180

Yes, we await it, but it still delays,
    And then we suffer; and amongst us One,[14]
       Who most has suffer'd, takes dejectedly
His seat upon the intellectual throne;
       And all his store of sad experience he   185
          Lays bare of wretched days;
Tells us his misery's birth and growth and signs,
       And how the dying spark of hope was fed,
       And how the breast was sooth'd, and how the head,
          And all his hourly varied anodynes.   190

This for our wisest: and we others pine,
    And wish the long unhappy dream would end,
       And waive all claim to bliss, and try to bear,
With close-lipp'd Patience for our only friend,
       Sad Patience, too near neighbour to Despair: 195
          But none has hope like thine.
Thou through the fields and through the woods dost stray,
       Roaming the country side, a truant boy,
       Nursing thy project in unclouded joy,
          And every doubt long blown by time away.   200

O born in days when wits were fresh and clear,
    And life ran gaily as the sparkling Thames;
       Before this strange disease of modern life,
With its sick hurry, its divided aims,
       Its heads o'ertax'd, its palsied hearts, was rife—   205
          Fly hence, our contact fear!
Still fly, plunge deeper in the bowering wood!
       Averse, as Dido did with gesture stern

[14] Probably Goethe.

From her false friend's approach in Hades turn,[15]
 Wave us away, and keep thy solitude.   210

Still nursing the unconquerable hope,
 Still clutching the inviolable shade,
  With a free onward impulse brushing through,
 By night, the silver'd branches of the glade—
  Far on the forest skirts, where none pursue,   215
   On some mild pastoral slope
 Emerge, and resting on the moonlit pales,[16]
  Freshen thy flowers, as in former years,
  With dew, or listen with enchanted ears,
   From the dark dingles,[17] to the nightingales.   220

But fly our paths, our feverish contact fly!
 For strong the infection of our mental strife,
  Which, though it gives no bliss, yet spoils for rest;
 And we should win thee from thy own fair life,
  Like us distracted, and like us unblest.   225
   Soon, soon thy cheer would die,
 Thy hopes grow timorous, and unfix'd thy powers,
  And thy clear aims be cross and shifting made:
  And then thy glad perennial youth would fade,
   Fade, and grow old at last, and die like ours. 230

Then fly our greetings, fly our speech and smiles!
 —As some grave Tyrian trader, from the sea,
  Descried at sunrise an emerging prow
 Lifting the cool-hair'd creepers stealthily,
  The fringes of a southward-facing brow   235
   Among the Aegean isles;
 And saw the merry Grecian coaster come,
  Freighted with amber grapes, and Chian wine,
  Green bursting figs, and tunnies steep'd in brine;
   And knew the intruders on his ancient home, 240

The young light-hearted Masters of the waves;
 And snatch'd his rudder, and shook out more sail,

[15] Early in his long journey, Aeneas, hero of Virgil's *Aeneid*, comes to Carthage whose queen, Dido, falls in love with his and offers to share her throne with him. He is strongly tempted but, knowing he has a mission to accomplish, he refuses and leaves her. Later, he makes a trip to the underworld, and there meets Dido, who had committed suicide when Aeneas left her. He begs her forgiveness and weeps at her misfortune, but she refuses to recognize him. [16] Palings. [17] Deep dells or hollows.

And day and night held on indignantly
O'er the blue Midland waters with the gale,
   Betwixt the Syrtes and soft Sicily,   245
      To where the Atlantic raves
Outside the Western Straits, and unbent sails
   There, where down cloudy cliffs, through sheets of foam,
   Shy traffickers, the dark Iberians come;
      And on the beach undid his corded bales.[18]   250

GEORGE MEREDITH

1 8 2 8 – 1 9 0 9

LUCIFER IN STARLIGHT

On a starred night Prince Lucifer uprose.
Tired of his dark dominion swung the fiend
Above the rolling ball in cloud part screened,
Where sinners hugged their spectre of repose.
Poor prey to his hot fit of pride were those.   5
And now upon his western wing he leaned,
Nor his huge bulk o'er Afric's sands careened,
Now the black planet shadowed Arctic snows.
Soaring through wider zones that pricked his scars
With memory of the old revolt from Awe,   10
He reached a middle height, and at the stars,
Which are the brain of heaven, he looked, and sank.
Around the ancient track marched, rank on rank,
The army of unalterable law.

[18] Both Tyre and Iberia were great ancient civilizations that were conquered by
Greece, which Arnold here likens to the "strange disease of modern life" that he would
like the "scholar gypsy" to escape.

EMILY DICKINSON

1 8 3 0 – 1 8 8 6

PAPA ABOVE!

Papa above!
Regard a Mouse
O'erpowered by the Cat!
Reserve within thy kingdom
A "Mansion" for the Rat!   5

Snug in seraphic Cupboards
To nibble all the day,
While unsuspecting Cycles[1]
Wheel solemnly away!

THERE'S A CERTAIN SLANT OF LIGHT

There's a certain Slant of light,
Winter Afternoons—
That oppresses, like the Heft
Of Cathedral Tunes—

Heavenly Hurt, it gives us—   5
We can find no scar,
But internal difference,
Where the Meanings, are—

None may teach it—Any—
'Tis the Seal Despair—   10
An imperial affliction
Sent us of the Air—

When it comes, the Landscape listens—
Shadows—hold their breath—

> [1] Revolutions (of planets), ages; but there is an intentional pun on "bicycles" also.

When it goes, 'tis like the Distance 15
On the look of Death—

A CLOCK STOPPED—

A Clock stopped—
Not the Mantel's—
Geneva's farthest skill
Cant put the puppet bowing—
That just now dangled still— 5

An awe come on the Trinket!
The Figures hunched, with pain—
Then quivered out of Decimals—
Into Degreeless Noon—

It will not stir for Doctor's— 10
This Pendulum of snow—
The Shopman importunes it—
While cool—concernless No—

Nods from the Gilded pointers—
Nods from the Seconds slim— 15
Decades of Arrogance between
The Dial life—
And Him—

I TASTE A LIQUOR NEVER BREWED

I taste a liquor never brewed—
From Tankards scooped in Pearl—
Not all the Frankfort Berries
Yield such an Alcohol!

Inebriate of Air—am I— 5
And Debauchee of Dew—
Reeling—thro endless summer days—
From inns of Molten Blue—

When "Landlords" turn the drunken Bee
Out of the Foxglove's door— 10

When Butterflies—renounce their "drams"—
I shall but drink the more!

Till Seraphs swing their snowy Hats—
And Saints—to windows run—
To see the little Tippler   15
From Manzanilla come!

BECAUSE I COULD NOT STOP
FOR DEATH

Because I could not stop for Death—
He kindly stopped for me—
The Carriage held but just Ourselves—
And Immortality.

We slowly drove—He knew no haste   5
And I had put away
My labor and my leisure too,
For His Civility—

We passed the School, where Children strove
At Recess—in the Ring—   10
We passed the Fields of Gazing Grain—
We passed the Setting Sun—

Or rather—He passed Us—
The Dews drew quivering and chill—
For only Gossamer, my Gown—   15
My Tippet[1]—only Tulle—

We paused before a House that seemed
A Swelling of the Ground—
The Roof was scarcely visible—
The Cornice—in the Ground—   20

Since then—'tis Centuries—and yet
Feels shorter than the Day
I first surmised the Horses Heads
Were toward Eternity—

[1] Shoulder cape.

I'VE SEEN A DYING EYE

I've seen a Dying Eye
Run round and round a Room—
In search of Something—as it seemed—
Then Cloudier become—
And then—obscure with Fog—   5
And then—be soldered down
Without disclosing what it be
'Twere blessed to have seen—

A NARROW FELLOW IN THE GRASS

A narrow Fellow in the Grass
Occasionally rides—
You may have met Him—did you not
His notice sudden is—

The Grass divides as with a Comb—   5
A spotted shaft is seen—
And then it closes at your feet
And opens further on—

He likes a Boggy Acre—
A Floor too cool for Corn—   10
But when a Boy and Barefoot—
I more than once at Noon
Have passed I thought a Whip Lash
Unbraiding in the Sun
When stooping to secure it   15
It wrinkled, and was gone—

Several of Nature's People
I know, and they know me—
I feel for them a transport
Of cordiality—   20

But never met this Fellow
Attended, or alone
Without a tighter breathing
And Zero at the Bone—

"HEAVENLY FATHER"—TAKE TO THEE

"Heavenly Father"—take to thee
The supreme iniquity
Fashioned by thy candid Hand
In a moment contraband—
Though to trust us—seem to us   5
More respectful—"We are Dust"—
We apologize to thee
For thine own Duplicity—

'TWAS LATER WHEN THE
SUMMER WENT

'Twas later when the summer went
Than when the Cricket came—
And yet we knew that gentle Clock
Meant nought but Going Home—
'Twas sooner when the Cricket went   5
Than when the Winter came
Yet that pathetic Pendulum
Keeps esoteric Time.

ALGERNON CHARLES
SWINBURNE
1837–1909

BEFORE THE BEGINNING OF YEARS
Chorus from "Atlanta in Calydon"

Before the beginning of years
    There came to the making of man
Time, with a gift of tears;
    Grief, with a glass that ran;

Pleasure, with pain for leaven;   5
    Summer, with flowers that fell;
Remembrance fallen from heaven,
    And madness risen from hell;
Strength without hands to smite,
    Love that endures for a breath;   10
Night, the shadow of light,
    And life, the shadow of death.

And the high gods took in hand
    Fire, and the falling of tears,
And a measure of sliding sand   15
    From under the feet of the years;
And froth and drift of the sea;
    And dust of the labouring earth;
And bodies of things to be
    In the houses of death and of birth;   20
And wrought with weeping and laughter,
    And fashioned with loathing and love,
With life before and after
    And death beneath and above,
For a day and a night and a morrow,   25
    That his strength might endure for a span
With travail and heavy sorrow,
    The holy spirit of man.

From the winds of the north and the south
    They gathered as unto strife;   30
They breathed upon his mouth,
    They filled his body with life;
Eyesight and speech they wrought
    For the veils of the soul therein,
A time for labour and thought,   35
    A time to serve and to sin;
They gave him light in his ways,
    And love, and a space for delight,
And beauty and length of days,
    And night, and sleep in the night.   40
His speech is a burning fire;
    With his lips he travaileth;
In his heart is a blind desire,
    In his eyes foreknowledge of death;
He weaves, and is clothed with derision;   45
    Sows, and he shall not reap;
His life is a watch or a vision
    Between a sleep and a sleep.

WHEN THE HOUNDS OF SPRING

Chorus from "Atlanta in Calydon"

When the hounds of spring are on winter's traces,
 The mother of months in meadow or plain
Fills the shadows and windy places
 With lisp of leaves and ripple of rain;
And the brown bright nightingale amorous   5
Is half assuaged for Itylus,
For the Thracian ships and the foreign faces,
 The tongueless vigil, and all the pain.[1]

Come with bows bent and with emptying of quivers,
 Maiden most perfect,[2] lady of light,   10
With a noise of winds and many rivers,
 With a clamour of waters, and with might;
Bind on thy sandals, O thou most fleet,
Over the splendour and speed of thy feet;
For the faint east quickens, the wan west shivers,   15
 Round the feet of the day and the feet of the night.

Where shall we find her, how shall we sing to her,
 Fold our hands round her knees, and cling?
O that man's heart were as fire and could spring to her,
 Fire, or the strength of the streams that spring!   20
For the stars and the winds are unto her
As raiment, as songs of the harp-player;
For the risen stars and the fallen cling to her,
 And the southwest-wind and the west-wind sing.

For winter's rains and ruins are over,   25
 And all the season of snows and sins;
The days dividing lover and lover,
 The light that loses, the night that wins;
And time remembered is grief forgotten,
And frosts are slain and flowers begotten,   30
And in green underwood and cover
 Blossom by blossom the spring begins.

---

[1] The allusion is to the Greek legend that Procne, wife of Theseus, king of Thrace, killed her son, Itylus, to avenge herself on her husband, and subsequently became a nightingale. Theseus had married Procne's sister, telling her that Procne, whose tongue he had cut out, was dead.   [2] Artemis, Greek goddess of hunting and childbirth.

The full streams feed on flower of rushes,
　　Ripe grasses trammel a travelling foot,
The faint fresh flame of the young year flushes 　　　　　35
　　From leaf to flower and flower to fruit,
And fruit and leaf are as gold and fire,
And the oat³ is heard above the lyre,
And the hoofèd heel of a satyr crushes
　　The chestnut-husk at the chestnut-root. 　　　　　　40

And Pan by noon and Bacchus by night,⁴
　　Fleeter of foot than the fleet-foot kid,
Follows with dancing and fills with delight
　　The Maenad and the Bassarid;⁵
And soft as lips that laugh and hide 　　　　　　　　45
The laughing leaves of the trees divide,
And screen from seeing and leave in sight
　　The god pursuing, the maiden hid.

The ivy falls with the Bacchanal's hair⁶
　　Over her eyebrows hiding her eyes; 　　　　　　　50
The wild vine slipping down leaves bare
　　Her bright breast shortening into sighs;
The wild vine slips with the weight of its leaves,
But the berried ivy catches and cleaves
To the limbs that glitter, the feet that scare 　　　　　55
　　The wolf that follows, the fawn that flies.

THE GARDEN OF PROSERPINE¹

Here, where the world is quiet;
　　Here, where all trouble seems
Dead winds' and spent waves' riot
　　In doubtful dreams of dreams;
I watch the green field growing 　　　　　　　　　5
For reaping folk and sowing,
For harvest-time and mowing,
　　A sleepy world of streams.

---

³ Oaten pipe, a rustic musical instrument.　　⁴ Pan and Bacchus were frolicsome
gods of the forest and wine, respectively.　　⁵ The Maenads and Bassarids were women
who were inspired to ecstatic frenzy by worship of Dionysus.　　⁶ The Bacchanals were
similar to Maenads and Bassarids.

¹ Persephone, the goddess of Hades; Proserpine is her Latin name.

I am tired of tears and laughter,
        And men that laugh and weep,   10
Of what may come hereafter
        For men that sow to reap:
I am weary of days and hours,
Blown[2] buds of barren flowers,
Desires and dreams and powers   15
        And everything but sleep.

Here life has death for neighbour,
        And far from eye or ear
Wan waves and wet winds labour,
        Weak ships and spirits steer;   20
They drive adrift, and whither
They wot[3] not who make thither;
But no such winds blow hither,
        And no such things grow here.

No growth of moor or coppice,   25
        No heather-flower or vine,
But bloomless buds of poppies,
        Green grapes of Proserpine.
Pale beds of blowing rushes
Where no leaf blooms or blushes   30
Save this whereout she crushes
        For dead men deadly wine.

Pale, without name or number,
        In fruitless fields of corn,
They bow themselves and slumber   35
        All night till light is born;
And like a soul belated,
In hell and heaven unmated,
By cloud and mist abated
        Comes out of darkness morn.   40

Though one were strong as seven,
        He too with death shall dwell,
Nor wake with wings in heaven,
        Nor weep for pains in hell;
Though one were fair as roses,   45
His beauty clouds and closes;

        [2] Blossomed.   [3] Know.

And well though love reposes,
    In the end it is not well.

Pale, beyond porch and portal,
    Crowned with calm leaves, she stands   50
Who gathers all things mortal
    With cold immortal hands;
Her languid lips are sweeter
Than love's who fears to greet her
To men that mix and meet her   55
    From many times and lands.

She waits for each and other,
    She waits for all men born;
Forgets the earth her mother,[4]
    The life of fruits and corn;   60
And spring and seed and swallow
Take wing for her and follow
Where summer song rings hollow
    And flowers are put to scorn.

There go the loves that wither,   65
    The old loves with wearier wings;
And all dead years draw thither,
    And all disastrous things;
Dead dreams of days forsaken,
Blind buds that snows have shaken,   70
Wild leaves that winds have taken,
    Red strays of ruined springs.

We are not sure of sorrow,
    And joy was never sure;
To-day will die to-morrow;   75
    Time stoops to no man's lure;
And love, grown faint and fretful,
With lips but half regretful
Sighs, and with eyes forgetful
    Weeps that no loves endure.   80

From too much love of living,
    From hope and fear set free,

[4] Demeter, corn goddess, was the mother of Persephone; she governed all fruits of the earth.

We thank with brief thanksgiving
    Whatever gods may be
That no life lives for ever;   85
That dead men rise up never;
That even the weariest river
    Winds somewhere safe to sea.

Then star nor sun shall waken,
    Nor any change of light: 90
Nor sound of waters shaken,
    Nor any sound or sight:
Nor wintry leaves nor vernal,
Nor days nor things diurnal;
Only the sleep eternal   95
    In an eternal night.

SAPPHICS[1]

All the night sleep came not upon my eyelids,
Shed not dew, nor shook nor unclosed a feather,
Yet with lips shut close and with eyes of iron
    Stood and beheld me.

Then to me so lying awake a vision   5
Came without sleep over the seas and touched me,
Softly touched mine eyelids and lips; and I too,
    Full of the vision,

Saw the white implacable Aphrodite,
Saw the hair unbound and the feet unsandalled   10
Shine as fire of sunset on western waters;
    Saw the reluctant

Feet, the straining plumes of the doves that drew her,
Looking always, looking with necks reverted,
Back to Lesbos, back to the hills whereunder   15
    Shone Mitylene;[2]

[1] The poem is written in "Sapphic" verses, named after the Greek poetess, Sappho, who used this verse form. Sappho (born 612 B.C.), one of the most famous lyric poets of all time, was a native of Lesbos. She married and had a daughter. As a leader of young girls devoted to music, poetry, and Aphrodite (goddess of love and marriage), she often addressed poems to her followers.   [2] The principal city of Lesbos, where Sappho lived.

Heard the flying feet of the Loves behind her
Make a sudden thunder upon the waters,
As the thunder flung from the strong unclosing
    Wings of a great wind. 20

So the goddess fled from her place, with awful
Sound of feet and thunder of wings around her;
While behind a clamour of singing women
    Severed the twilight.

Ah the singing, ah the delight, the passion! 25
All the Loves wept, listening; sick with anguish,
Stood the crowned nine Muses about Apollo;[3]
    Fear was upon them,

While the tenth[4] sang wonderful things they knew not.
Ah the tenth, the Lesbian! the nine were silent, 30
None endured the sound of her song for weeping;
    Laurel by laurel,

Faded all their crowns; but about her forehead,
Round her woven tresses and ashen temples
White as dead snow, paler than grass in summer, 35
    Ravaged with kisses,

Shone a light of fire as a crown for ever.
Yea, almost the implacable Aphrodite
Paused, and almost wept; such a song was that song.
    Yea, by her name too 40

Called her, saying, "Turn to me, O my Sappho;"
Yet she turned her face from the Loves, she saw not
Tears for laughter darken immortal eyelids,
    Heard not about her

Fearful fitful wings of the doves departing, 45
Saw not how the bosom of Aphrodite
Shook with the weeping, saw not her shaken raiment,
    Saw not her hands wrung;

[3] The nine Muses were goddesses of arts and sciences. Apollo, the god of light and medicine, became the most widely worshipped Greek god.   [4] Sappho was often called the tenth muse.

Saw the Lesbians kissing across their smitten
Lutes with lips more sweet than the sound of lute-strings,   50
Mouth to mouth and hand upon hand, her chosen,
    Fairer than all men;

Only saw the beautiful lips and fingers,
Full of songs and kisses and little whispers,
Full of music; only beheld among them   55
    Soar, as a bird soars

Newly fledged, her visible song, a marvel,
Made of perfect sound and exceeding passion,
Sweetly shapen, terrible, full of thunders,
    Clothed with the wind's wings.   60

Then rejoiced she, laughing with love, and scattered
Roses, awful roses of holy blossom;
Then the Loves thronged sadly with hidden faces
    Round Aphrodite,

Then the Muses, stricken at heart, were silent;   65
Yea, the gods waxed pale; such a song was that song.
All reluctant, all with a fresh repulsion,
    Fled from before her.

All withdrew long since, and the land was barren,
Full of fruitless women and music only.   70
Now perchance, when winds are assuaged at sunset, —
    Lulled at the dewfall,

By the grey sea-side, unassuaged, unheard-of,
Unbeloved, unseen in the ebb of twilight,
Ghosts of outcast women return lamenting,   75
    Purged not in Lethe,[5]

Clothed about with flame and with tears, and singing
Songs that move the heart of the shaken heaven,
Songs that break the heart of the earth with pity,
    Hearing, to hear them.   80

[5] The river of Hades, whose waters bring forgetfulness.

THOMAS HARDY

1840–1928

THE SUBALTERNS

I

"Poor wanderer," said the leaden sky,
　　"I fain would lighten thee,
But there are laws in force on high
　　Which say it must not be."

II

—"I would not freeze thee, shorn one," cried   5
　　The North, "knew I but how
To warm my breath, to slack my stride;
　　But I am ruled as thou."

III

—"To-morrow I attack thee, wight,"
　　Said Sickness. "Yet I swear   10
I bear thy little ark no spite,
　　But am bid enter there."

IV

—"Come hither, Son," I heard Death say;
　　"I did not will a grave
Should end thy pilgrimage to-day,   15
　　But I, too, am a slave!"

V

We smiled upon each other then,
　　And life to me had less
Of that fell look it wore ere when
　　They owned their passiveness.   20

WIVES IN THE SERE[1]

I

Never a careworn wife but shows,
    If a joy suffuse her,
Something beautiful to those
    Patient to peruse her,
Some one charm the world unknows   5
    Precious to a muser,
Haply what, ere years were foes,
    Moved her mate to choose her.

II

But, be it a hint of rose
    That an instant hues her,   10
Or some early light or pose
    Wherewith thought renews her—
Seen by him at full, ere woes
    Practised to abuse her—
Sparely comes it, swiftly goes,   15
    Time again subdues her.

THE LACKING SENSE

Scene.—*A sad-coloured landscape, Waddon Vale*

I

"O Time, whence comes the Mother's moody look amid her labours,
    As of one who all unwittingly has wounded where she loves?
    Why weaves she not her world-webs to according lutes and tabors,[1]
    With nevermore this too remorseful air upon her face,
        As of angel fallen from grace?"   5

II

—"Her look is but her story: construe not its symbols keenly:
    In her wonderworks yea surely has she wounded where she loves.
The sense of ills misdealt for blisses blanks the mien most queenly,
    Self-smitings kill self-joys; and everywhere beneath the sun
        Such deeds her hands have done."   10

[1] The adjective *sere* is used as a noun; the title means "wives growing old" or "withering."

[1] Lutes and tabors in accord (with her weaving).

III

—"And how explains thy Ancient Mind her crimes upon her creatures,
    These fallings from her fair beginnings, woundings where she loves,
Into her would-be perfect motions, modes, effects, and features
    Admitting cramps, black humours, wan decay, and baleful blights,
        Distress into delights?"   15

IV

—"Ah! knowest thou not her secret yet, her vainly veiled deficience,
    Whence it comes that all unwittingly she wounds the lives she loves?
That sightless are those orbs[2] of hers?—which bar to her omniscience
    Brings those fearful unfulfilments, that red ravage through her zones[3]
        Whereat all creation groans.   20

V

"She whispers it in each pathetic strenuous slow endeavour,
    When in mothering she unwittingly sets wounds on what she loves;
Yet her primal doom pursues her, faultful, fatal is she ever;
    Though so deft and nigh to vision is her facile[4] finger-touch
        That the seers marvel much.   25

VI

"Deal, then, her groping skill no scorn, no note of malediction;
    Not long on thee will press the hand that hurts the lives it loves;
And while she plods dead-reckoning on, in darkness of affliction,
    Assist her where thy creaturely dependence can or may,
        For thou art of her clay."   30

THE DARKLING[1] THRUSH

I leant upon a coppice gate
    When Frost was spectre-gray,
And Winter's dregs made desolate
    The weakening eye of day.
The tangled bine-stems[2] scored the sky   5
    Like strings of broken lyres,
And all mankind that haunted nigh[3]
    Had sought their household fires.

---

[2] Eyes.   [3] From astronomy, the areas in which she moves.   [4] Assured, poised.

[1] In the dark.   [2] Stems of woodbine.   [3] Lived nearby.

The land's sharp features seemed to be
  The Century's corpse ouleant,[4]
His crypt the cloudy canopy,
  The wind his death-lament.
The ancient pulse of germ and birth
  Was shrunken hard and dry,
And every spirit upon earth
  Seemed fervourless as I.

At once a voice arose among
  The bleak twigs overhead
In a full-hearted evensong
  Of joy illimited;[5]
An aged thrush, frail, gaunt, and small,
  In blast-beruffled[6] plume,
Had chosen thus to fling his soul
  Upon the growing gloom.

So little cause for carolings
  Of such ecstatic sound
Was written on terrestrial things
  Afar or nigh around,
That I could think there trembled through
  His happy good-night air
Some blessed Hope, whereof he knew
  And I was unaware.

THE VOICE

Woman much missed, how you call to me, call to me,
Saying that now you are not as you were
When you had changed from the one who was all to me,
But as at first, when our day was fair.

Can it be you that I hear? Let me view you, then,
Standing as when I drew near to the town
Where you would wait for me: yes, as I knew you then,
Even to the original air-blue gown!

Or is it only the breeze, in its listlessness
Travelling across the wet mead to me here,

---

  [4] Outlined. [5] Unlimited. [6] Windblown.

You being ever dissolved to wan wistlessness,[1]
Heard no more again far or near?

Thus I; faltering forward,
Leaves around me falling,
Wind oozing thin through the thorn from norward,[2]   15
And the woman calling.

THE FIVE STUDENTS

The sparrow dips in his wheel-rut bath,
The sun grows passionate-eyed,
And boils the dew to smoke by the paddock-path;
As strenuously we stride,—
Five of us; dark He, fair He, dark She, fair She, I,   5
All beating by.

The air is shaken, the high-road hot,
Shadowless swoons the day,
The greens are sobered and cattle at rest; but not
We on our urgent way,—   10
Four of us; fair She, dark She, fair He, I, are there,
But one—elsewhere.

Autumn moulds the hard fruit mellow,
And forward still we press
Through moors, briar-meshed plantations, clay-pits yellow,   15
As in the spring hours—yes,
Three of us; fair He, fair She, I, as heretofore,
But—fallen one more.

The leaf drops: earthworms draw it in
At night-time noiselessly,   20
The fingers of birch and beech are skeleton-thin,
And yet on the beat are we,—
Two of us; fair She, I. But no more left to go
The track we know.

Icicles tag the church-aisle leads,[1]   25
The flag-rope gibbers hoarse,

[1] Inattentiveness.   [2] Northward.

[1] Sheets of lead forming the roof.

The home-bound foot-folk wrap their snow-flaked heads,
        Yet I still stalk the course—
One of us. . . . Dark and fair He, dark and fair She, gone
        The rest—anon.   30

"WHO'S IN THE NEXT ROOM?"

"Who's in the next room?—who?
        I seemed to see
Somebody in the dawning passing through,
        Unkown to me."
"Nay: you saw nought. He passed invisibly."   5

"Who's in the next room?—who?
        I seem to hear
Somebody muttering firm in a language new
        That chills the ear."
"No: you catch not his tongue who has entered there."   10

"Who's in the next room?—who?
        I seem to feel
His breath like a clammy draught, as if it drew
        From the Polar Wheel."
"No: none who breathes at all does the door conceal."   15

"Who's in the next room?—who?
        A figure wan
With a message to one in there of something due?
        Shall I know him anon?"
"Yea he; and he brought such; and you'll know him anon."   20

AFTERWARDS

When the Present has latched its postern behind my tremulous stay,
        And the May month flaps its glad green leaves like wings,
Delicate-filmed as new-spun silk, will the neighbours say,
        "He was a man who used to notice such things"?

If it be in the dusk when, like an eyelid's soundless blink,   5
        The dewfall-hawk comes crossing the shades to alight
Upon the wind-warped upland thorn, a gazer may think,
        "To him this must have been a familiar sight."

If I pass during some nocturnal blackness, mothy and warm,
    When the hedgehog travels furtively over the lawn,   10
One may say, "He strove that such innocent creatures should come to no harm,
    But he could do little for them; and now he is gone."

If, when hearing that I have been stilled at last, they stand at the door,
    Watching the full-starred heavens that winter sees,
Will this thought rise on those who will meet my face no more,   15
    "He was one who had an eye for such mysteries"?

And will any say when my bell of quittance is heard in the gloom,
    And a crossing breeze cuts a pause in its outrollings,
Till they rise again, as they were a new bell's boom,
    "He hears it not now, but used to notice such things?"   20

GERARD MANLEY HOPKINS

1844–1889

SPRING AND FALL

To a Young Child

Márgarét, are you gríeving
Over Goldengrove unleaving?
Leáves, líke the things of man, you
With your fresh thoughts care for, can you?
Áh! ás the heart grows older   5
It will come to such sights colder
By and by, nor spare a sigh
Though worlds of wanwood leafmeal[1] lie;
And yet you wíll weep and know why.
Now no matter, child, the name: 10
Sórrow's spríngs áre the same.
Nor mouth had, no nor mind, expressed
What heart heard of, ghost guessed:
It ís the blight man was born for,
It is Margaret you mourn for.   15

[1] Words Hopkins coined to suggest faded leaves fallen to the ground.

THE WINDHOVER[1]

To Christ Our Lord

I caught this morning morning's minion,[2] king-
    dom of daylight's dauphin,[3] dapple-dawn-drawn Falcon, in his riding
    Of the rolling level underneath him steady air, and striding
High there, how he rung[4] upon the rein of a wimpling[5] wing
In his ecstasy! then off, off forth on swing,   5
    As a skate's heel sweeps smooth on a bow-bend: the hurl and gliding
    Rebuffed the big wind. My heart in hiding
Stirred for a bird,—the achieve of, the mastery of the thing!

Brute beauty and valour and act, oh, air, pride, plume here
    Buckle! AND the fire that breaks from thee then, a billion   10
Times told lovelier, more dangerous, O my chevalier!

    No wonder of it: shéer plód makes plough down sillion[6]
Shine, and blue-bleak embers, ah my dear,
    Fall, gall themselves, and gash gold-vermilion.

PIED BEAUTY

Glory be to God for dappled things—
    For skies of couple-colour as a brinded cow;
        For rose-moles all in stipple upon trout that swim;
Fresh-firecoal chestnut-falls; finches' wings;
    Landscape plotted and pieced—fold,[1] fallow, and plough;   5
        And áll trádes, their gear and tackle and trim.

All things counter, original, spare, strange;
    Whatever is fickle, freckled (who knows how?)
        With swift, slow; sweet, sour; adazzle, dim;
He fathers-forth whose beauty is past change: 10
        Praise him.

---

[1] A small falcon that hovers in the air against the wind. The male is bluish gray.
[2] Darling, favorite.   [3] Prince.   [4] Coined word suggesting both *wrung* and *reined*.
[5] Rippling.   [6] A word coined from French *sillon*, furrow created by a plough.

[1] An undulation in the landscape.

CARRION COMFORT

Not, I'll not, carrion comfort, Despair, not feast on thee;
Not untwist—slack they may be—these last strands of man
In me ór, most weary, cry *I can no more*. I can;
Can something, hope, wish day come, not choose not to be.
But ah, but O thou terrible, why wouldst thou rude on me   5
Thy wring-world right foot rock? lay a lionlimb against me? scan
With darksome devouring eyes my bruisèd bones? and fan,
O in turns of tempest, me heaped there; me frantic to avoid thee and flee?

      Why? That my chaff might fly; my grain lie, sheer and clear.
Nay in all that toil, that coil, since (seems) I kissed the rod,[1]   10
Hand rather, my heart lo! lapped strength, stole joy, would laugh, chéer.
Cheer whom though? the hero whose heaven-handling flung me, fóot tród
Me? or me that fought him? O which one? is it each one? That night, that year
Of now done darkness I wretch lay wrestling with (my God!) my God.

A. E. HOUSMAN

1859–1936

LOVELIEST OF TREES

Loveliest of trees, the cherry now
Is hung with bloom along the bough,
And stands about the woodland ride
Wearing white for Eastertide.

Now, of my threescore years and ten,   5
Twenty will not come again,
And take from seventy springs a score,
It only leaves me fifty more.

And since to look at things in bloom
Fifty springs are little room,   10

[1] Willingly submitted to punishment or correction.

About the woodlands I will go
To see the cherry hung with snow.

BE STILL, MY SOUL, BE STILL

Be still, my soul, be still; the arms you bear are brittle,
    Earth and high heaven are fixt of old and founded strong.
Think rather,—call to thought, if now you grieve a little,
    The days when we had rest, O soul, for they were long.

Men loved unkindness then, but lightless in the quarry 5
    I slept and saw not; tears fell down, I did not mourn;
Sweat ran and blood sprang out and I was never sorry:
    Then it was well with me, in days ere I was born.

Now, and I muse for why and never find the reason,
    I pace the earth, and drink the air, and feel the sun. 10
Be still, be still, my soul; it is but for a season:
    Let us endure an hour and see injustice done.

Ay, look: high heaven and earth ail from the prime foundation;
    All thoughts to rive the heart are here, and all are vain:
Horror and scorn and hate and fear and indignation— 15
    Oh why did I awake? when shall I sleep again?

RUDYARD KIPLING

1865-1936

DANNY DEEVER

"What are the bugles blowin' for?" said Files-on-Parade.
"To turn you out, to turn you out," the Colour-Sergeant said.
"What makes you look so white, so white?" said Files-on-Parade.

"I'm dreadin' what I've got to watch," the Colour-Sergeant said.
  For they're hangin Danny Deaver, you can hear the Dead March
    play,   5
  The Regiment's in 'ollow square—they're hangin' him to-day:
  They've taken of his buttons off an' cut his stripes away,
  An' they're hangin' Danny Deever in the mornin'.

"What makes the rear-rank breathe so 'ard?" said Files-on-Parade.
"It's bitter cold, it's bitter cold," the Colour-Sergeant said.   10
"What makes that front-rank man fall down?" said Files-on-Parade.
"A touch o' sun, a touch o' sun," the Colour-Sergeant said.
  They are hangin' Danny Deever, they are marchin' of 'im round,
  They 'ave 'alted Danny Deever by 'is coffin on the ground;
  An' 'e'll swing in 'arf a minute for a sneakin' shootin' hound—   15
  O they're hangin' Danny Deever in the mornin'!

" 'Is cot was right-'and cot to mine," said Files-on-Parade.
" 'E's sleepin' out an' far to-night," the Colour-Sergeant said.
"I've drunk 'is beer a score o' times," said Files-on-Parade.
" 'E's drinkin' bitter beer alone," the Colour-Sergeant said.   20
  They are hangin' Danny Deever, you must mark 'im to 'is place,
  For 'e shot a comrade sleepin'—you must look 'im in the face;
  Nine 'undred of 'is county an' the Regiment's disgrace,
  While they're hangin' Danny Deever in the mornin'.

"What's that so black agin the sun?" said Files-on-Parade.   25
"It's Danny fightin' 'ard for life," the Colour-Sergeant said.
"What's that that whimpers over'ead?" said Files-on-Parade.
"It's Danny's soul that's passin' now," the Colour-Sergeant said.
  For they're done with Danny Deever, you can 'ear the quickstep play,
  The Regiment's in column, an' they're marchin' us away;   30
  Ho! the young recruits are shakin', an' they'll want their beer to-day,
  After hangin' Danny Deever in the mornin'!

RECESSIONAL

God of our fathers, known of old,
  Lord of our far-flung battle-line,
Beneath whose awful Hand we hold
  Dominion over palm and pine—
Lord God of Hosts, be with us yet,   5
Lest we forget—lest we forget!

The tumult and the shouting dies;
    The captains and the kings depart:
Still stands Thine ancient sacrifice,
    An humble and a contrite heart.   10
Lord God of Hosts, be with us yet,
Lest we forget—lest we forget!

Far-called, our navies melt away;
    On dune and headland sinks the fire:
Lo, all our pomp of yesterday   15
    Is one with Nineveh and Tyre![1]
Judge of the Nations, spare us yet,
Lest we forget—lest we forget!

If, drunk with sight of power, we loose
    Wild tongues that have not Thee in awe,   20
Such boastings as the Gentiles[2] use,
    Or lesser breeds without the Law—
Lord God of Hosts, be with us yet,
Lest we forget—lest we forget!

For heathen heart that puts her trust   25
    In reeking tube and iron shard,
All valiant dust that builds on dust,
    And guarding, calls not Thee to guard,
For frantic boast and foolish word—
Thy mercy on Thy People, Lord!   30

WILLIAM BUTLER YEATS

1865–1939

BYZANTIUM

The unpurged images of day recede;
The Emperor's drunken soldiery are abed;
Night resonance recedes, night-walkers' song

[1] Nineveh was the last capital of the ancient Assyrian Empire and Tyre, the most important city of ancient Phoenicia.   [2] Heathens, pagans, "the unchosen."

After great cathedral gong;
A starlit or a moonlit dome disdains
All that man is,
All mere complexities,
The fury and the mire of human veins.

Before me floats an image, man or shade,
Shade more than man, more image than a shade;
For Hades' bobbin bound in mummy-cloth
May unwind the winding path;
A mouth that has no moisture and no breath
Breathless mouths may summon;
I hail the superhuman;
I call it death-in-life and life-in-death.

Miracle, bird or golden handiwork,
More miracle than bird or handiwork,
Planted on the star-lit golden bough,
Can like the cocks of Hades crow,
Or, by the moon embittered, scorn aloud
In glory of changeless metal
Common bird or petal
And all complexities of mire or blood.

At midnight on the Emperor's pavement flit
Flames that no faggot feeds, nor steel has lit,
Nor storm disturbs, flames begotten of flame,
Where blood-begotten spirits come
And all complexities of fury leave,
Dying into a dance,
An agony of trance,
An agony of flame that cannot singe a sleeve.

Astraddle on the dolphin's mire and blood,
Spirit after spirit! The smithies break the flood,
The golden smithies of the Emperor!
Marbles of the dancing floor
Break bitter furies of complexity,
Those images that yet
Fresh images beget,
That dolphin-torn, that gong-tormented sea.

LEDA AND THE SWAN

A sudden blow: the great wings beating still
Above the staggering girl, her thighs caressed
By the dark webs, her nape caught in his bill,
He holds her helpless breast upon his breast.

How can those terrified vague fingers push   5
The feathered glory from her loosening thighs?
And how can body, laid in that white rush,
But feel the strange heart beating where it lies?

A shudder in the loins engenders there
The broken wall, the burning roof and tower   10
And Agamemnon dead.
                              Being so caught up,
So mastered by the brute blood of the air,
Did she put on his knowledge with his power
Before the indifferent beak could let her drop?

THE SECOND COMING

Turning and turning in the widening gyre
The falcon cannot hear the falconer;
Things fall apart; the centre cannot hold;
Mere anarchy is loosed upon the world,
The blood-dimmed tide is loosed, and everywhere   5
The ceremony of innocence is drowned;
The best lack all conviction, while the worst
Are full of passionate intensity.

Surely some revelation is at hand;
Surely the Second Coming is at hand.   10
The Second Coming! Hardly are those words out
When a vast image out of *Spiritus Mundi*
Troubles my sight: somewhere in sands of the desert
A shape with lion body and the head of a man,
A gaze blank and pitiless as the sun,   15
Is moving its slow thighs, while all about it
Reel shadows of the indignant desert birds.
The darkness drops again; but now I know
That twenty centuries of stony sleep
Were vexed to nightmare by a rocking cradle,   20

And what rough beast, its hour come round at last,
Slouches towards Bethlehem to be born?

A PRAYER FOR MY DAUGHTER

Once more the storm is howling, and half hid
Under this cradle-hood and coverlid
My child sleeps on. There is no obstacle
But Gregory's wood and one bare hill
Whereby the haystack- and roof-levelling wind,   5
Bred on the Atlantic, can be stayed;
And for an hour I have walked and prayed
Because of the great gloom that is in my mind.

I have walked and prayed for this young child an hour
And heard the sea-wind scream upon the tower,   10
And under the arches of the bridge, and scream
In the elms above the flooded stream;
Imagining in excited reverie
That the future years had come,
Dancing to a frenzied drum,   15
Out of the murderous innocence of the sea.

May she be granted beauty and yet not
Beauty to make a stranger's eye distraught,
Or hers before a looking-glass, for such,
Being made beautiful overmuch,   20
Consider beauty a sufficient end,
Lose natural kindness and maybe
The heart-revealing intimacy
That chooses right, and never find a friend.

Helen being chosen found life flat and dull   25
And later had much trouble from a fool,
While that great Queen, that rose out of the spray,
Being fatherless could have her way
Yet chose a bandy-leggèd smith for man.
It's certain that fine women eat   30
A crazy salad with their meat
Whereby the Horn of Plenty is undone.

In courtesy I'd have her chiefly learned;
Hearts are not had as a gift but hearts are earned

By those that are not entirely beautiful;   35
Yet many, that have played the fool
For beauty's very self, has charm made wise,
And many a poor man that has roved,
Loved and thought himself beloved,
From a glad kindness cannot take his eyes.   40

May she become a flourishing hidden tree
That all her thoughts may like the linnet be,
And have no business but dispensing round
Their magnanimities of sound,
Nor but in merriment begin a chase,   45
Nor but in merriment a quarrel.
O may she live like some green laurel
Rooted in one dear perpetual place.

My mind, because the minds that I have loved,
The sort of beauty that I have approved,   50
Prosper but little, has dried up of late,
Yet knows that to be choked with hate
May well be of all evil chances chief.
If there's no hatred in a mind
Assault and battery of the wind   55
Can never tear the linnet from the leaf.

An intellectual hatred is the worst,
So let her think opinions are accursed.
Have I not seen the loveliest woman born
Out of the mouth of Plenty's horn,   60
Because of her opinionated mind
Barter that horn and every good
By quiet natures understood
For an old bellows full of angry wind?

Considering that, all hatred driven hence,   65
The soul recovers radical innocence
And learns at last that it is self-delighting,
Self-appeasing, self-affrighting,
And that its own sweet will is Heaven's will;
She can, though every face should scowl   70
And every windy quarter howl
Or every bellows burst, be happy still.

And may her bridegroom bring her to a house
Where all's accustomed, ceremonious;

For arrogance and hatred are the wares   75
Peddled in the thoroughfares.
How but in custom and in ceremony
Are innocence and beauty born?
Ceremony's a name for the rich horn,
And custom for the spreading laurel tree.   80

EDWIN ARLINGTON ROBINSON

1869–1935

LUKE HAVERGAL

Go to the western gate, Luke Havergal,
There where the vines cling crimson on the wall,
And in the twilight wait for what will come.
The leaves will whisper there of her, and some,
Like flying words, will strike you as they fall;   5
But go, and if you listen she will call.
Go to the western gate, Luke Havergal—
Luke Havergal.

No, there is not a dawn in eastern skies
To rift the fiery night that's in your eyes;   10
But there, where western glooms are gathering,
The dark will end the dark, if anything:
God slays Himself with every leaf that flies,
And hell is more than half of paradise.
No, there is not a dawn in eastern skies—   15
In eastern skies.

Out of a grave I come to tell you this,
Out of a grave I come to quench the kiss
That flames upon your forehead with a glow
That blinds you to the way that you must go.   20

Yes, there is yet one way to where she is,
Bitter, but one that faith may never miss.
Out of a grave I come to tell you this—
To tell you this.

There is the western gate, Luke Havergal,   25
There are the crimson leaves upon the wall.
Go, for the winds are tearing them away—
Nor think to riddle the dead words they say,
Nor any more to feel them as they fall;
But go, and if you trust her she will call.   30
There is the western gate, Luke Havergal—
Luke Havergal.

MINIVER CHEEVY

Miniver Cheevy, child of scorn,
    Grew lean while he assailed the seasons;
He wept that he was ever born,
    And he had reasons.

Miniver loved the days of old   5
    When swords were bright and steeds were prancing.
The vision of a warrior bold
    Would set him dancing.

Miniver sighed for what was not,
    And dreamed, and rested from his labors;   10
He dreamed of Thebes and Camelot,
    And Priam's neighbors.

Miniver mourned the ripe renown
    That made so many a name so fragrant;
He mourned Romance, now on the town,   15
    And Art, a vagrant.

Miniver loved the Medici,
    Albeit he had never seen one;
He would have sinned incessantly
    Could he have been one.   20

Miniver cursed the commonplace
    And eyed a khaki suit with loathing;
He missed the mediæval grace
    Of iron clothing.

Miniver scorned the gold he sought,   25
    But sore annoyed was he without it;
Miniver thought, and thought, and thought,
    And thought about it.

Miniver Cheevy, born too late,
    Scratched his head and kept on thinking: 30
Miniver coughed, and called it fate,
    And kept on drinking.

MR. FLOOD'S PARTY

Old Eben Flood, climbing alone one night
Over the hill between the town below
And the forsaken upland hermitage
That held as much as he should ever know
On earth again of home, paused warily.   5
The road was his with not a native near;
And Eben, having leisure, said aloud,
For no man else in Tilbury Town to hear:

"Well, Mr. Flood, we have the harvest moon
Again, and we may not have many more;   10
The bird is on the wing, the poet says,
And you and I have said it here before.
Drink to the bird." He raised up to the light
The jug that he had gone so far to fill,
And answered huskily: "Well, Mr. Flood,   15
Since you propose it, I believe I will."

Alone, as if enduring to the end
A valiant armor of scarred hopes outworn,
He stood there in the middle of the road
Like Roland's ghost winding a silent horn.   20
Below him, in the town among the trees,
Where friends of other days had honored him,

A phantom salutation of the dead
Rang thinly till old Eben's eyes were dim.

Then, as a mother lays her sleeping child   25
Down tenderly, fearing it may awake,
He set the jug down slowly at his feet
With trembling care, knowing that most things break;
And only when assured that on firm earth
It stood, as the uncertain lives of men   30
Assuredly did not, he paced away,
And with his hand extended paused again:

"Well, Mr. Flood, we have not met like this
In a long time; and many a change has come
To both of us, I fear, since last it was   35
We had a drop together. Welcome home!"
Convivially returning with himself,
Again he raised the jug up to the light;
And with an acquiescent quaver said:
"Well, Mr. Flood, if you insist, I might.   40

"Only a very little, Mr. Flood—
For auld lang syne. No more, sir; that will do."
So, for the time, apparently it did,
And Eben evidently thought so too;
For soon amid the silver loneliness   45
Of night he lifted up his voice and sang,
Secure, with only two moons listening,
Until the whole harmonious landscape rang—
"For auld lang syne." The weary throat gave out,
The last word wavered; and the song being done,   50
He raised again the jug regretfully
And shook his head, and was again alone.
There was not much that was ahead of him,
And there was nothing in the town below—
Where strangers would have shut the many doors   55
That many friends had opened long ago.

WALTER DE LA MARE

1873–1956

THE LISTENERS

"Is there anybody there?" said the Traveller,
    Knocking on the moonlit door;
And his horse in the silence champed the grasses
    Of the forest's ferny floor:
And a bird flew up out of the turret,   5
    Above the Traveller's head:
And he smote upon the door again a second time;
    "Is there anybody there?" he said.
But no one descended to the Traveller;
    No head from the leaf-fringed sill   10
Leaned over and looked into his grey eyes,
    Where he stood perplexed and still.
But only a host of phantom listeners
    That dwelt in the lone house then
Stood listening in the quiet of the moonlight   15
    To that voice from the world of men:
Stood thronging the faint moonbeams on the dark stair,
    That goes down to the empty hall,
Hearkening in an air stirred and shaken
    By the lonely Traveller's call.   20
And he felt in his heart their strangeness,
    Their stillness answering his cry,
While his horse moved, cropping the dark turf,
    'Neath the starred and leafy sky;
For he suddenly smote on the door, even   25
    Louder, and lifted his head:—
"Tell them I came, and no one answered,
    That I kept my word," he said.
Never the least stir made the listeners,
    Though every word he spake   30
Fell echoing through the shadowiness of the still house
    From the one man left awake:
Ay, they heard his foot upon the stirrup,
    And the sound of iron on stone,
And how the silence surged softly backward,   35
    When the plunging hoofs were gone.

ROBERT FROST

1874–1963

HOME BURIAL

He saw her from the bottom of the stairs
Before she saw him. She was starting down,
Looking back over her shoulder at some fear.
She took a doubtful step and then undid it
To raise herself and look again. He spoke   5
Advancing toward her: 'What is it you see
From up there always—for I want to know.'
She turned and sank upon her skirts at that,
And her face changed from terrified to dull.
He said to gain time: 'What is it you see,'   10
Mounting until she cowered under him.
'I will find out now—you must tell me, dear.'
She, in her place, refused him any help
With the least stiffening of her neck and silence.
She let him look, sure that he wouldn't see,   15
Blind creature; and awhile he didn't see.
But at last he murmured, 'Oh,' and again, 'Oh.'

'What is it—what?' she said.

                                'Just that I see.'

'You don't,' she challenged. 'Tell me what it is.'

'The wonder is I didn't see at once.   20
I never noticed it from here before.
I must be wonted to it—that's the reason.
The little graveyard where my people are!
So small the window frames the whole of it.
Not so much larger than a bedroom, is it?   25
There are three stones of slate and one of marble,
Broad-shouldered little slabs there in the sunlight
On the sidehill. We haven't to mind *those*.
But I understand: it is not the stones,
But the child's mound—'

She withdrew shrinking from beneath his arm
That rested on the bannister, and slid downstairs;
And turned on him with such a daunting look,
He said twice over before he knew himself:
'Can't a man speak of his own child he's lost?'   35

'Not you! Oh, where's my hat? Oh, I don't need it!
I must get out of here. I must get air.
I don't know rightly whether any man can.'

'Amy! Don't go to someone else this time.
Listen to me. I won't come down the stairs.'   40
He sat and fixed his chin between his fists.
'There's something I should like to ask you, dear.'

'You don't know how to ask it.'

                    'Help me, then.'

Her fingers moved the latch for all reply.

'My words are nearly always an offense.   45
I don't know how to speak of anything
So as to please you. But I might be taught
I should suppose. I can't say I see how.
A man must partly give up being a man
With women-folk. We could have some arrangement   50
By which I'd bind myself to keep hands off
Anything special you're a-mind to name.
Though I don't like such things 'twixt those that love.
Two that don't love can't live together without them.
But two that do can't live together with them.'   55
She moved the latch a little. 'Don't—don't go.
Don't carry it to someone else this time.
Tell me about it if it's something human.
Let me into your grief. I'm not so much
Unlike other folks as your standing there   60
Apart would make me out. Give me my chance.
I do think, though, you overdo it a little.
What was it brought you up to think it the thing

To take your mother-loss of a first child
So inconsolably—in the face of love.
You'd think his memory might be satisfied—'   65

'There you go sneering now!'

                              'I'm not, I'm not!
You make me angry. I'll come down to you.
God, what a woman! And it's come to this,
A man can't speak of his own child that's dead.'   70

'You can't because you don't know how to speak.
If you had any feelings, you that dug
With your own hand—how could you?—his little grave;
I saw you from that very window there,
Making the gravel leap and leap in air,   75
Leap up, like that, like that, and land so lightly
And roll back down the mound beside the hole.
I thought, Who is that man? I didn't know you.
And I crept down the stairs and up the stairs
To look again, and still your spade kept lifting.   80
Then you came in. I heard your rumbling voice
Out in the kitchen, and I don't know why,
But I went near to see with my own eyes.
You could sit there with the stains on your shoes
Of the fresh earth from your own baby's grave   85
And talk about your everyday concerns.
You had stood the spade up against the wall
Outside there in the entry, for I saw it.'

'I shall laugh the worst laugh I ever laughed.
I'm cursed. God, if I don't believe I'm cursed.   90

'I can repeat the very words you were saying.
"Three foggy mornings and one rainy day
Will rot the best birch fence a man can build."
Think of it, talk like that at such a time!
What had how long it takes a birch to rot   95
To do with what was in the darkened parlor.
You *couldn't* care! The nearest friends can go
With anyone to death, comes so far short
They might as well not try to go at all.
No, from the time when one is sick to death,   100
One is alone, and he dies more alone.

Friends make pretense of following to the grave,
But before one is in it, their minds are turned
And making the best of their way back to life
And living people, and things they understand.   105
But the world's evil. I won't have grief so
If I can change it. Oh, I won't, I won't!'

'There, you have said it all and you feel better.
You won't go now. You're crying. Close the door.
The heart's gone out of it: why keep it up.   110
Amy! There's someone coming down the road!'

'You—oh, you think the talk is all. I must go—
Somewhere out of this house. How can I make you—'

'If—you—do!' She was opening the door wider.
'Where do you mean to go? First tell me that.   115
I'll follow and bring you back by force. I *will!*—'

STOPPING BY WOODS ON A SNOWY EVENING

Whose woods these are I think I know
His house is in the village though;
He will not see me stopping here
To watch his woods fill up with snow.

My little horse must think it queer   5
To stop without a farmhouse near
Between the woods and frozen lake
The darkest evening of the year.

He gives his harness bells a shake
To ask if there is some mistake.   10
The only other sound's the sweep
Of easy wind and downy flake.

The woods are lovely, dark and deep,
But I have promises to keep,

And miles to go before I sleep, 15
And miles to go before I sleep.

DESIGN

I found a dimpled spider, fat and white,
On a white heal-all, holding up a moth
Like a white piece of rigid satin cloth—
Assorted characters of death and blight
Mixed ready to begin the morning right, 5
Like the ingredients of a witches' broth—
A snow-drop spider, a flower like a froth,
And dead wings carried like a paper kite.

What had that flower to do with being white, 10
The wayside blue and innocent heal-all?
What brought the kindred spider to that height,
Then steered the white moth thither in the night?
What but design of darkness to appall?—
If design govern in a thing so small? 15

PROVIDE, PROVIDE

The witch that came (the withered hag)
To wash the steps with pail and rag,
Was once the beauty Abishag,

The picture pride of Hollywood.
Too many fall from great and good 5
For you to doubt the likelihood.

Die early and avoid the fate.
Or if predestined to die late,
Make up your mind to die in state.

Make the whole stock exchange your own! 10
If need be occupy a throne,
Where nobody can call *you* crone.

Some have relied on what they knew;
Others on being simply true.
What worked for them might work for you.   15

No memory of having starred
Atones for later disregard,
Or keeps the end from being hard.

Better to go down dignified
With boughten friendship at your side   20
Than none at all. Provide, provide!

DIRECTIVE

Back out of all this now too much for us,
Back in a time made simple by the loss
Of detail, burned, dissolved, and broken off
Like graveyard marble sculpture in the weather,
There is a house that is no more a house   5
Upon a farm that is no more a farm
And in a town that is no more a town.
The road there, if you'll let a guide direct you
Who only has at heart your getting lost,
May seem as if it should have been a quarry—   10
Great monolithic knees the former town
Long since gave up pretense of keeping covered.
And there's a story in a book about it:
Besides the wear of iron wagon wheels
The ledges show lines ruled southeast northwest,   15
The chisel work of an enormous Glacier
That braced his feet against the Arctic Pole.
You must not mind a certain coolness from him
Still said to haunt this side of Panther Mountain.
Nor need you mind the serial ordeal   20
Of being watched from forty cellar holes
As if by eye pairs out of forty firkins.
As for the woods' excitement over you
That sends light rustle rushes to their leaves,
Charge that to upstart inexperience.   25
Where were they all not twenty years ago?
They think too much of having shaded out
A few old pecker-fretted apple trees.
Make yourself up a cheering song of how
Someone's road home from work this once was,   30
Who may be just ahead of you on foot
Or creaking with a buggy load of grain.

The height of the adventure is the height
Of country where two village cultures faded
Into each other. Both of them are lost.   35
And if you're lost enough to find yourself
By now, pull in your ladder road behind you
And put a sign up CLOSED to all but me.
Then make yourself at home. The only field
Now left's no bigger than a harness gall.   40
First there's the children's house of make believe,
Some shattered dishes underneath a pine,
The playthings in the playhouse of the children.
Weep for what little things could make them glad.
Then for the house that is no more a house,   45
But only a belilaced cellar hole,
Now slowly closing like a dent in dough.
This was no playhouse but a house in earnest.
Your destination and your destiny's
A brook that was the water of the house,   50
Cold as a spring as yet so near its source,
Too lofty and original to rage.
(We know the valley streams that when aroused
Will leave their tatters hung on barb and thorn.)
I have kept hidden in the instep arch   55
Of an old cedar at the waterside
A broken drinking goblet like the Grail
Under a spell so the wrong ones can't find it,
So can't get saved, as Saint Mark says they mustn't.
(I stole the goblet from the children's playhouse.)   60
Here are your waters and your watering place.
Drink and be whole again beyond confusion.

WALLACE STEVENS

1879-1955

SUNDAY MORNING

I

Complacencies of the peignoir, and late
Coffee and oranges in a sunny chair,
And the green freedom of a cockatoo

Upon a rug mingle to dissipate
The holy hush of ancient sacrifice.   5
She dreams a little, and she feels the dark
Encroachment of that old catastrophe,
As a calm darkens among water-lights.
The pungent oranges and bright, green wings
Seem things in some procession of the dead,   10
Winding across wide water, without sound.
The day is like wide water, without sound,
Stilled for the passing of her dreaming feet
Over the seas, to silent Palestine,
Dominion of the blood and sepulchre.   15

    2

Why should she give her bounty to the dead?
What is divinity if it can come
Only in silent shadows and in dreams?
Shall she not find in comforts of the sun,
In pungent fruit and bright, green wings, or else   20
In any balm or beauty of the earth,
Things to be cherished like the thought of heaven?
Divinity must live within herself:
Passions of rain, or moods in falling snow;
Grievings in loneliness, or unsubdued   25
Elations when the forest blooms; gusty
Emotions on wet roads on autumn nights;
All pleasures and all pains, remembering
The bough of summer and the winter branch.
These are the measures destined for her soul.   30

    3

Jove in the clouds had his inhuman birth.
No mother suckled him, no sweet land gave
Large-mannered motions to his mythy mind.
He moved among us, as a muttering king,
Magnificent, would move among his hinds,   35
Until our blood, commingling, virginal,
With heaven, brought such requital to desire
The very hinds discerned it, in a star.
Shall our blood fail? Or shall it come to be
The blood of paradise? And shall the earth   40
Seem all of paradise that we shall know?
The sky will be much friendlier then than now,
A part of labor and a part of pain,
And next in glory to enduring love,
Not this dividing and indifferent blue.   45

4

She says, "I am content when wakened birds,
Before they fly, test the reality
Of misty fields, by their sweet questionings;
But when the birds are gone, and their warm fields
Return no more, where, then, is paradise?"   50
There is not any haunt of prophecy,
Nor any old chimera of the grave,
Neither the golden underground, nor isle
Melodious, where spirits gat them home,
Nor visionary south, nor cloudy palm   55
Remote on heaven's hill, that has endured
As April's green endures; or will endure
Like her remembrance of awakened birds,
Or her desire for June and evening, tipped
By the consummation of the swallow's wings.   60

5

She says, "But in contentment I still feel
The need of some imperishable bliss."
Death is the mother of beauty; hence from her,
Alone, shall come fulfilment to our dreams
And our desires. Although she strews the leaves   65
Of sure obliteration on our paths,
The path sick sorrow took, the many paths
Where triumph rang its brassy phrase, or love
Whispered a little out of tenderness,
She makes the willow shiver in the sun   70
For maidens who were wont to sit and gaze
Upon the grass, relinquished to their feet.
She causes boys to pile new plums and pears
On disregarded plate. The maidens taste
And stray impassioned in the littering leaves.   75

6

Is there no change of death in paradise?
Does ripe fruit never fall? Or do the boughs
Hang always heavy in that perfect sky,
Unchanging, yet so like our perishing earth,
With rivers like our own that seek for seas   80
They never find, the same receding shores
That never touch with inarticulate pang?
Why set the pear upon those river-banks
Or spice the shores with odors of the plum?
Alas, that they should wear our colors there,   85
The silken weavings of our afternoons,
And pick the strings of our insipid lutes!

Death is the mother of beauty, mystical,
Within whose burning bosom we devise
Our earthly mothers waiting, sleeplessly. 90

7

Supple and turbulent, a ring of men
Shall chant in orgy on a summer morn
Their boisterous devotion to the sun,
Not as a god, but as a god might be,
Naked among them, like a savage source. 95
Their chant shall be a chant of paradise,
Out of their blood, returning to the sky;
And in their chant shall enter, voice by voice,
The windy lake wherein their lord delights,
The trees, like serafin, and echoing hills, 100
That choir among themselves long afterward.
They shall know well the heavenly fellowship
Of men that perish and of summer morn.
And whence they came and whither they shall go
The dew upon their feet shall manifest. 105

8

She hears, upon that water without sound,
A voice that cries, "The tomb in Palestine
Is not the porch of spirits lingering.
It is the grave of Jesus, where he lay."
We live in an old chaos of the sun, 110
Or old dependency of day and night,
Or island solitude, unsponsored, free,
Of that wide water, inescapable.
Deer walk upon our mountains, and the quail
Whistle about us their spontaneous cries; 115
Sweet berries ripen in the wilderness;
And, in the isolation of the sky,
As evening, casual flocks of pigeons make
Ambiguous undulations as they sink,
Downward to darkness, on extended wings. 120

ANECDOTE OF THE JAR

I placed a jar in Tennessee,
And round it was, upon a hill.
It made the slovenly wilderness
Surround that hill.

The wilderness rose up to it,
And sprawled around, no longer wild.
The jar was round upon the ground
And tall and of a port in air.

It took dominion everywhere.
The jar was gray and bare.
It did not give of bird or bush,
Like nothing else in Tennessee.

PETER QUINCE AT THE CLAVIER

1

Just as my fingers on these keys
Make music, so the self-same sounds
On my spirit make a music too.

Music is feeling then, not sound;
And thus it is that what I feel,
Here in this room, desiring you,

Thinking of your blue-shadowed silk,
Is music. It is like the strain
Waked in the elders by Susanna:

Of a green evening, clear and warm,
She bathed in her still garden, while
The red-eyed elders, watching, felt

The basses of their being throb
In witching chords, and their thin blood
Pulse pizzicati of Hosanna.

2

In the green water, clear and warm,
Susanna lay.
She searched
The touch of springs,
And found
Concealed imaginings.
She sighed
For so much melody.

Upon the bank, she stood
In the cool

Of spent emotions.
She felt, among the leaves,
The dew
Of old devotions.

She walked upon the grass, 30
Still quavering.
The winds were like her maids,
On timid feet,
Fetching her woven scarves,
Yet wavering. 35

A breath upon her hand
Muted the night.
She turned—
A cymbal crashed,
And roaring horns. 40

3

Soon, with a noise like tambourines,
Came her attendant Byzantines.

They wondered why Susanna cried
Against the elders by her side:

And as they whispered, the refrain 45
Was like a willow swept by rain.

Anon their lamps' uplifted flame
Revealed Susanna and her shame.

And then the simpering Byzantines,
Fled, with a noise like tambourines. 50

4

Beauty is momentary in the mind—
The fitful tracing of a portal;
But in the flesh it is immortal.

The body dies; the body's beauty lives.
So evenings die, in their green going, 55
A wave, interminably flowing.
So gardens die, their meek breath scenting
The cowl of Winter, done repenting.
So maidens die to the auroral
Celebration of a maiden's choral. 60

Susanna's music touched the bawdy strings
Of those white elders; but, escaping,
Left only Death's ironic scraping.
Now in its immortality, it plays
On the clear viol of her memory,   65
And makes a constant sacrament of praise.

THIRTEEN WAYS OF LOOKING
AT A BLACKBIRD

I

Among twenty snowy mountains,
The only moving thing
Was the eye of the blackbird.

II

I was of three minds,
Like a tree   5
In which there are three blackbirds.

III

The blackbird whirled in the autumn winds.
It was a small part of the pantomime.

IV

A man and a woman
Are one.   10
A man and a woman and a blackbird
Are one.

V

I do not know which to prefer,
The beauty of inflections
Or the beauty of innuendos,   15
The blackbird whistling
Or just after.

VI

Icicles filled the long window
With barbaric glass.
The shadow of the blackbird   20

Crossed it, to and fro.
The mood
Traced in the shadow
An indecipherable cause.

VII

O thin men of Haddam,   25
Why do you imagine golden birds?
Do you not see how the blackbird
Walks around the feet
Of the women about you?

VIII

I know noble accents   30
And lucid, inescapable rhythms;
But I know, too,
That the blackbird is involved
In what I know.

IX

When the blackbird flew out of sight,   35
It marked the edge
Of one of many circles.

X

At the sight of blackbirds
Flying in a green light,
Even the bawds of euphony   40
Would cry out sharply.

XI

He rode over Connecticut
In a glass coach.
Once, a fear pierced him,
In that he mistook   45
The shadow of his equipage
For blackbirds.

XII

The river is moving.
The blackbird must be flying.

It was evening all afternoon.   50
It was snowing
And it was going to snow.
The blackbird sat
In the cedar-limbs.

SOLDIER, THERE IS A WAR

Soldier, there is a war between the mind
And sky, between thought and day and night. It is
For that the poet is always in the sun,

Patches the moon together in his room
To his Virgilian cadences, up down,   5
Up down. It is a war that never ends.

Yet it depends on yours. The two are one.
They are a plural, a right and left, a pair,
Two parallels that meet if only in

The meeting of their shadows or that meet   10
In a book in a barrack, a letter from Malay.
But your war ends. And after it you return

With six meats and twelve wines or else without
To walk another room . . . Monsieur and comrade,
The soldier is poor without the poet's lines,   15

His petty syllabi, the sounds that stick,
Inevitably modulating, in the blood.
And war for war, each has its gallant kind.

How simply the fictive hero becomes the real;
How gladly with proper words the soldier dies,   20
If he must, or lives on the bread of faithful speech.

D. H. LAWRENCE

1885–1930

TORTOISE SHOUT

I thought he was dumb,
I said he was dumb,
Yet I've heard him cry.

First faint scream,
Out of life's unfathomable dawn,   5
Far off, so far, like a madness, under the horizon's dawning rim,
Far, far off, far scream.

Tortoise *in extremis.*

Why were we crucified into sex?
Why were we not left rounded off, and finished in ourselves,   10
As we began,
As he certainly began, so perfectly alone?

A far, was-it-audible scream,
Or did it sound on the plasm direct?

Worse than the cry of the new-born,   15
A scream,
A yell,
A shout,
A pæan,
A death-agony,   20
A birth-cry,
A submission,
All, tiny, far away, reptile under the first dawn.

War-cry, triumph, acute-delight, death-scream reptilian,
Why was the veil torn?   25
The silken shriek of the soul's torn membrane?

The male soul's membrane
Torn with a shriek half music, half horror.

Crucifixion.
Male tortoise, cleaving behind the hovel-wall of that dense female,   30
Mounted and tense, spread-eagle, out-reaching out of the shell
In tortoise-nakedness,
Long neck, and long vulnerable limbs extruded, spread-eagle over her
          house-roof,
And the deep, secret, all-penetrating tail curved beneath her walls,
Reaching and gripping tense, more reaching anguish in uttermost
          tension   35
Till suddenly, in the spasm of coition, tupping like a jerking leap,
          and oh!
Opening its clenched face from his outstretched neck
And giving that fragile yell, that scream,
Super-audible,
From his pink, cleft, old-man's mouth,   40
Giving up the ghost,
Or screaming in Pentecost, receiving the ghost.

His scream, and his moment's subsidence,
The moment of eternal silence,
Yet unreleased, and after the moment, the sudden, startling jerk of
          coition, and at once   45
The inexpressible faint yell—
And so on, till the last plasm of my body was melted back
To the primeval rudiments of life, and the secret.

So he tups, and screams
Time after time that frail, torn scream   50
After each jerk, the longish interval,
The tortoise eternity,
Age-long, reptilian persistence,
Heart-throb, slow heart-throb, persistent for the next spasm.

I remember, when I was a boy,   55
I heard the scream of a frog, which was caught with his
          foot in the mouth of an up-starting snake;
I remember when I first heard bull-frogs break into sound in the spring;
I remember hearing a wild goose out of the throat of night
Cry loudly, beyond the lake of waters;
I remember the first time, out of a bush in the darkness, a nightingale's
          piercing cries and gurgles startled the depths of my soul;   60
I remember the scream of a rabbit as I went through a wood
          at midnight;

I remember the heifer in her heat, blorting and blorting through the
        hours, persistent and irrepressible;
I remember my first terror hearing the howl of weird, amorous cats;
I remember the scream of a terrified, injured horse, the sheet-lightning,
And running away from the sound of a woman in labour, something
        like an owl whooing,   65
And listening inwardly to the first bleat of a lamb,
The first wail of an infant,
And my mother singing to herself,
And the first tenor singing of the passionate throat of a young collier,
        who has long since drunk himself to death,
The first elements of foreign speech   70
On wild dark lips.

And more than all these,
And less than all these,
This last,
Strange, faint coition yell   75
Of the male tortoise at extremity,
Tiny from under the very edge of the farthest far-off horizon of life.

The cross,
The wheel on which our silence first is broken,
Sex, which breaks up our integrity, our single inviolability, our deep
        silence,   80
Tearing a cry from us.

Sex, which breaks us into voice, sets us calling across the deeps,
        calling, calling for the complement,
Singing, and calling, and singing again, being answered, having
        found.

Torn, to become whole again, after long seeking for what is lost,
The same cry from the tortoise as from Christ, the Osiris-cry of
        abandonment,   85
That which is whole, torn asunder,
That which is in part, finding its whole again throughout the uni-
        verse.

THE ELEPHANT IS SLOW TO MATE

The elephant, the huge old beast,
    is slow to mate;
he finds a female, they show no haste,
    they wait.

for the sympathy in their vast shy hearts
  slowly, slowly to rouse
as they loiter along the river-beds
  and drink and browse

and dash in panic through the brake
  of forest with the herd,
and sleep in massive silence, and wake
  together, without a word.

So slowly the great hot elephant hearts
  grow full of desire,
and the great beasts mate in secret at last,
  hiding their fire.

Oldest they are and the wisest of beasts
  so they know at last
how to wait for the loneliest of feasts,
  for the full repast.

They do not snatch, they do not tear;
  their massive blood
moves as the moon-tides, near, more near,
  till they touch in flood.

SNAKE

A snake came to my water-trough
On a hot, hot day, and I in pyjamas for the heat,
To drink there.

In the deep, strange-scented shade of the great dark carobtree
I came down the steps with my pitcher
And must wait, must stand and wait, for there he was at the trough
  before me.

He reached down from a fissure in the earth-wall in the gloom
And trailed his yellow-brown slackness soft-bellied down, over the
  edge of the stone trough
And rested his throat upon the stone bottom,

And where the water had dripped from the tap, in a small clearness,   10
He sipped with his straight mouth,
Softly drank through his straight gums, into his slack long body,
Silently.

Someone was before me at my water-trough,
And I, like a second comer, waiting.   15
He lifted his head from his drinking, as cattle do,
And looked at me vaguely, as drinking cattle do,
And flickered his two-forked tongue from his lips, and mused a
        moment,
And stooped and drank a little more,
Being earth-brown, earth-golden from the burning bowels of the earth   20
On the day of Sicilian July, with Etna smoking.

The voice of my education said to me
He must be killed,
For in Sicily the black, black snakes are innocent, the gold are
        venomous.

And voices in me said, If you were a man   25
You would take a stick and break him now, and finish him off.

But must I confess how I liked him,
How glad I was he had come like a guest in quiet, to drink at my
        water-trough
And depart peaceful, pacified, and thankless,
Into the burning bowels of this earth?   30

Was it cowardice, that I dared not kill him?
Was it perversity, that I longed to talk to him?
Was it humility, to feel so honoured?
I felt so honoured.

And yet those voices: 35
If you were not afraid, you would kill him!

And truly I was afraid, I was most afraid,
But even so, honoured still more
That he should seek my hospitality
From out the dark door of the secret earth.   40

He drank enough
And lifted his head, dreamily, as one who has drunken,
And flickered his tongue like a forked night on the air, so black,
Seeming to lick his lips,
And looked around like a god, unseeing, into the air,   45
And slowly turned his head,
And slowly, very slowly, as if thrice adream,
Proceeded to draw his slow length curving round
And climb again the broken bank of my wall-face.

And as he put his head into that dreadful hole,   50
And as he slowly drew up, snake-easing his shoulders, and entered
        farther,
A sort of horror, a sort of protest against his withdrawing into that
        horrid black hole,
Deliberately going into the blackness, and slowly drawing himself
        after,
Overcame me now his back was turned.

I looked round, I put down my pitcher,   55
I picked up a clumsy log
And threw it at the water-trough with a clatter.

I think it did not hit him,
But suddenly that part of him that was left behind convulsed in
        undignified haste,
Writhed like lightning, and was gone   60
Into the black hole, the earth-lipped fissure in the wall-front,
At which, in the intense still noon, I stared with fascination.

And immediately I regretted it.
I thought how paltry, how vulgar, what a mean act!
I despised myself and the voices of my accursed human education.   65

And I thought of the albatross,
And I wished he would come back, my snake.

For he seemed to me again like a king,
Like a king in exile, uncrowned in the underworld,
Now due to be crowned again.   70

And so, I missed my chance with one of the lords
Of life.

And I have something to expiate;
A pettiness.

EZRA POUND

1 8 8 5 –

A PACT

I make a pact with you, Walt Whitman—
I have detested you long enough.
I come to you as a grown child
Who has had a pig-headed father;
I am old enough now to make friends.   5
It was you that broke the new wood,
Now is a time for carving.
We have one sap and one root—
Let there be commerce between us.

ITE

Go, my songs, seek your praise from the young and from the intolerant,
    move among the lovers of perfection alone.
Seek ever to stand in the hard Sophoclean light
And take your wounds from it gladly.

LES MILLWIN

The little Millwins attend the Russian Ballet.
The mauve and greenish souls of the little Millwins
Were seen lying along the upper seats
Like so many unused boas.

The turbulent and undisciplined host of art students—   5
The rigorous deputation from "Slade"—
Was before them.

With arms exalted, with fore-arms
Crossed in great futuristic X's, the art students
Exulted, they beheld the splendours of *Cleopatra*.   10

And the little Millwins beheld these things;
With their large and anaemic eyes they looked out upon this configuration.

Let us therefore mention the fact,
For it seems to us worthy of record.

COME MY CANTILATIONS

Come my cantilations,
Let us dump our hatreds into one bunch and be done with them,
Hot sun, clear water, fresh wind,
Let me be free of pavements,
Let me be free of the printers.   5
Let come beautiful people
Wearing raw silk of good colour,
Let come the graceful speakers,
Let come the ready of wit,
Let come the gay of manner, the insolent and the exulting.   10
We speak of burnished lakes,
Of dry air, as clear as metal.

PRAYER FOR HIS LADY'S LIFE
From Propertius, Elegiae, lib. III, 26

Here let thy clemency, Persephone, hold firm,
Do thou, Pluto, bring here no greater harshness.
So many thousand beauties are gone down to Avernus,
Ye might let one remain above with us.

With you is Iope, with you the white-gleaming Tyro,   5
With you is Europa and the shameless Pasiphae,
And all the fair from Troy and all from Achaia,
From the sundered realms, of Thebes and of aged Priamus;
And all the maidens of Rome, as many as they were,
They died and the greed of your flame consumes them.   10

Here let thy clemency, Persephone, hold firm,
Do thou, Pluto, bring here no greater harshness.
So many thousand fair are gone down to Avernus,
Ye might let one remain above with us.

MARIANNE MOORE

1 8 8 7 –

POETRY

I, too, dislike it: there are things that are important beyond all this fiddle.
Reading it, however, with a perfect contempt for it, one discovers in
it after all, a place for the genuine.
      Hands that can grasp, eyes
        that can dilate, hair that can rise   5
            if it must, these things are important not because a

high-sounding interpretation can be put upon them but because they are
    useful. When they become so derivative as to become unintelligible,
    the same thing may be said for all of us, that we
        do not admire what   10
        we cannot understand: the bat
            holding on upside down or in quest of something to

eat, elephants pushing, a wild horse taking a roll, a tireless wolf under
    a tree, the immovable critic twitching his skin like a horse that
            feels a flea, the base-
    ball fan, the statistician—   15
        nor is it valid
            to discriminate "against business documents and

school-books"; all these phenomena are important. One must make a
            distinction
    however: when dragged into prominence by half poets, the result
            is not poetry,

nor till the poets among us can be
    "literalists of
       the imagination"—above
         insolence and triviality and can present

for inspection, imaginary gardens with real toads in them, shall we have
    it. In the meantime, if you demand on the one hand, 25
       the raw material of poetry in
         all its rawness and
           that which is on the other hand
              genuine, then you are interested in poetry.

ELEPHANTS

Uplifted and waved until immobilized
wistaria-like, the opposing opposed
mouse-grey twined proboscises' trunk formed by two
trunks, fights itself to a spiraled inter-nosed

deadlock of dyke-enforced massiveness. It's a 5
knock-down drag-out fight that asks no quarter? Just
a pastime, as when the trunk rains on itself
the pool it siphoned up; or when—since each must

provide his forty-pound bough dinner—he broke
the leafy branches. These templars of the Tooth, 10
these matched intensities, take master care of
master tools. One, sleeping with the calm of youth,

at full length in the half dry sun-flecked stream-bed,
rests his hunting-horn-curled trunk on shallowed stone.
The sloping hollow of the sleeper's body 15
cradles the gently breathing eminence's prone

mahout, asleep like a lifeless six-foot
frog, so feather light the elephant's stiff
ear's unconscious of the crossed feet's weight. And the
defenceless human thing sleeps as sound as if 20

incised with hard wrinkles, embossed with wide ears,
invincibly tusked, made safe by magic hairs!
As if, as if, it is all ifs; we are at
much unease. But magic's masterpiece is theirs,—

Houdini's serenity quelling his fears.
Elephant ear-witnesses-to-be of hymns
and glorias, these ministrants all grey or
grey with white on legs or trunks, are a pilgrims'

pattern of revery not reverence,—a
religious procession without any priests,
the centuries-old carefullest unrehearsed
play. Blessed by Buddha's Tooth, the obedient beasts

themselves as toothed temples blessing the street, see
the white elephant carry the cushion that
carries the casket that carries the Tooth.
Amenable to what, matched with him, are gnat

trustees, he does not step on them as the white-
canopied blue-cushioned Tooth is augustly
and slowly returned to the shrine. Though white is
the colour of worship and of mourning, he

is not here to worship and he is too wise
to mourn,—a life prisoner but reconciled.
With trunk tucked up compactly—the elephant's
sign of defeat—he resisted, but is the child

of reason now. His straight trunk seems to say: when
what we hoped for came to nothing, we revived.
As loss could not ever alter Socrates'
tranquillity, equanimity's contrived

by the elephant. With the Socrates of
animals as with Sophocles the Bee, on whose
tombstone a hive was incised, sweetness tinctures
his gravity. His held up fore-leg for use

as a stair, to be climbed or descended with
the aid of his ear, expounds the brotherhood
of creatures to man the encroacher, by the
small word with the dot, meaning know,—the verb bud.

These knowers 'arouse the feeling that they are
allied to man' and can change roles with their trustees.

Hardship makes the soldier; then teachableness
makes him the philosopher—as Socrates,   60

prudently testing the suspicious thing, knew
the wisest is he who's not sure that he knows.
Who rides on a tiger can never dismount;
asleep on an elephant, that is repose.

THOMAS STEARNS ELIOT

1888–1965

LA FIGLIA CHE PIANGE

O quam te memorem virgo . . .

Stand on the highest pavement of the stair—
Lean on a garden urn—
Weave, weave the sunlight in your hair—
Clasp your flowers to you with a pained surprise—
Fling them to the ground and turn   5
With a fugitive resentment in your eyes:
But weave, weave the sunlight in your hair.

    So I would have had him leave,
So I would have had her stand and grieve,
So he would have left   10
As the soul leaves the body torn and bruised,
As the mind deserts the body it has used.
I should find
Some way incomparably light and deft,
Some way we both should understand,   15
Simple and faithless as a smile and shake of the hand.

    She turned away, but with the autumn weather
Compelled my imagination many days,
Many days and many hours:
Her hair over her arms and her arms full of flowers.   20

And I wonder how they should have been together!
I should have lost a gesture and a pose.
Sometimes these cogitations still amaze
The troubled midnight and the noon's repose.

SWEENEY AMONG THE NIGHTINGALES

*Why Should I speak of the nightingale? The nightingale
sings of adulterous wrong.*

Apeneck Sweeney spreads his knees
Letting his arms hang down to laugh,
The zebra stripes along his jaw
Swelling to maculate giraffe.

The circles of the stormy moon   5
Slide westward to the River Plate,
Death and the Raven drift above
And Sweeney guards the hornèd gate.

Gloomy Orion and the Dog
Are veiled; and hushed the shrunken seas;   10
The person in the Spanish cape
Tries to sit on Sweeney's knees

Slips and pulls the table cloth
Overturns a coffee cup,
Reorganized upon the floor   15
She yawns and draws a stocking up;

The silent man in mocha brown
Sprawls at the window-sill and gapes;
The waiter brings in oranges,
Bananas, figs and hot-house grapes;   20

The silent vertebrate exhales,
Contracts and concentrates, withdraws;
Rachel *née* Rabinovitch
Tears at the grapes with murderous paws;

She and the lady in the cape   25
Are suspect, thought to be in league;

Therefore the man with heavy eyes
Declines the gambit, shows fatigue,

Leaves the room and reappears
Outside the window, leaning in,   30
Branches of wistaria
Circumscribe a golden grin;

The host with someone indistinct
Converses at the door apart,
The nightingales are singing near   35
The Convent of the Sacred Heart,

And sang within the bloody wood
When Agamemnon cried aloud,
And let their liquid siftings fall
To stain the stiff dishonoured shroud.   40

JOURNEY OF THE MAGI

"A cold coming we had of it,
Just the worst time of the year
For a journey, and such a long journey:
The ways deep and the weather sharp,
The very dead of winter."   5
And the camels galled, sore-footed, refractory,
Lying down in the melting snow.
There were times we regretted
The summer palaces on slopes, the terraces,
And the silken girls bringing sherbet.   10
Then the camel men cursing and grumbling
And running away, and wanting their liquor and women,
And the night-fires going out, and the lack of shelters,
And the cities hostile and the towns unfriendly
And the villages dirty and charging high prices: 15
A hard time we had of it.
At the end we preferred to travel all night,
Sleeping in snatches,
With the voices singing in our ears, saying
That this was all folly.   20

Then at dawn we came down to a temperate valley,
Wet, below the snow line, smelling of vegetation;
With a running stream and a water-mill beating the darkness,

And three trees on the low sky,
And an old white horse galloped away in the meadow.   25
Then we came to a tavern with vine-leaves over the lintel,
Six hands at an open door dicing for pieces of silver,
And feet kicking the empty wine-skins.
But there was no information, and so we continued
And arrived at evening, not a moment too soon   30
Finding the place; it was (you may say) satisfactory.

All this was a long time ago, I remember,
And I would do it again, but set down
This set down
This: were we led all that way for   35
Birth or Death? There was a Birth, certainly,
We had evidence and no doubt. I had seen birth and death,
But had thought they were different; this Birth was
Hard and bitter agony for us, like Death, our death.
We returned to our places, these Kingdoms,   40
But no longer at ease here, in the old dispensation,
With an alien people clutching their gods.
I should be glad of another death.

ANIMULA

"Issues from the hand of God, the simple soul"
To a flat world of changing lights and noise,
To light, dark, dry or damp, chilly or warm;
Moving between the legs of tables and of chairs,
Rising or falling, grasping at kisses and toys,   5
Advancing boldly, sudden to take alarm,
Retreating to the corner of arm and knee,
Eager to be reassured, taking pleasure
In the fragrant brilliance of the Christmas tree,
Pleasure in the wind, the sunlight and the sea;   10
Studies the sunlit pattern on the floor
And running stags around a silver tray;
Confounds the actual and the fanciful,
Content with playing-cards and kings and queens,
What the fairies do and what the servants say.   15
The heavy burden of the growing soul
Perplexes and offends more, day by day;
Week by week, offends and perplexes more
With the imperatives of "is and seems"
And may and may not, desire and control   20
The pain of living and the drug of dreams
Curl up the small soul in the window seat

Behind the *Encyclopædia Britannica*.
Issues from the hand of time the simple soul
Irresolute and selfish, misshapen, lame, 25
Unable to fare forward or retreat,
Fearing the warm reality, the offered good,
Denying the importunity of the blood,
Shadow of its own shadows, specter in its own gloom,
Leaving disordered papers in a dusty room; 30
Living first in the silence after the viaticum.

Pray for Guiterriez, avid of speed and power,
For Boudin, blown to pieces,
For this one who made a great fortune,
And that one who went his own way. 35
Pray for Floret, by the boarhound slain between the yew trees,
Pray for us now and at the hour of our birth.

JOHN CROWE RANSOM

1 8 8 8 –

HERE LIES A LADY

Here lies a lady of beauty and high degree.
Of chills and fever she died, of fever and chills,
The delight of her husband, her aunt, an infant of three,
And of medicos marveling sweetly on her ills.

For either she burned, and her confident eyes would blaze, 5
And her fingers fly in a manner to puzzle their heads—
What was she making? Why, nothing; she sat in a maze
Of old scraps of laces, snipped into curious shreds—

Or this would pass, and the light of her fire decline
Till she lay discouraged and cold, like a stalk white and blown, 10
And would not open her eyes, to kisses, to wine;
The sixth of these states was her last; the cold settled down.

Sweet ladies, long may ye bloom, and toughly I hope ye may thole,
But was she not lucky? In flowers and lace and mourning,
In love and great honor we bade God rest her soul   15
After six little spaces of chill, and six of burning.

BELLS FOR JOHN WHITESIDE'S DAUGHTER

There was such speed in her little body,
And such lightness in her footfall,
It is no wonder her brown study
Astonishes us all.

Her wars were bruited in our high window.   5
We looked among orchard trees and beyond,
Where she took arms against her shadow,
Or harried unto the pond

The lazy geese, like a snow cloud
Dripping their snow on the green grass,   10
Tricking and stopping, sleepy and proud,
Who cried in goose, Alas,

For the tireless heart within the little
Lady with rod that made them rise
From their noon apple-dreams, and scuttle   15
Goose-fashion under the skies!

But now go the bells, and we are ready;
In one house we are sternly stopped
To say we are vexed at her brown study,
Lying so primly propped.   20

BLUE GIRLS

Twirling your blue skirts, traveling the sward
Under the towers of your seminary,
Go listen to your teachers old and contrary
Without believing a word.

Tie the white fillets then about your lustrous hair
And think no more of what will come to pass
Than bluebirds that go walking on the grass
And chattering on the air.

Practice your beauty, blue girls, before it fail;
And I will cry with my loud lips and publish
Beauty which all our power shall never establish,
It is so frail.

For I could tell you a story which is true:
I know a lady with a terrible tongue,
Blear eyes fallen from blue,
All her perfections tarnished—and yet it is not long
Since she was lovelier than any of you.

ARCHIBALD MACLEISH

1892–

ARS POETICA

A poem should be palpable and mute
As a globed fruit

Dumb
As old medallions to the thumb

Silent as the sleeve-worn stone
Of casement ledges where the moss has grown—

A poem should be wordless
As the flight of birds

A poem should be motionless in time
As the moon climbs

Leaving, as the moon releases
Twig by twig the night-entangled trees,

Leaving, as the moon behind the winter leaves,
Memory by memory the mind—

A poem should be motionless in time   15
As the moon climbs

A poem should be equal to:
Not true

For all the history of grief
An empty doorway and a maple leaf   20

For love
The leaning grasses and two lights above the sea—

A poem should not mean
But be

THE END OF THE WORLD

Quite unexpectedly, as Vasserot
The armless ambidextrian was lighting
A match between his great and second toe,
And Ralph the lion was engaged in biting
The neck of Madame Sossman while the drum   5
Pointed, and Teeny was about to cough
In waltz-time swinging Jocko by the thumb—
Quite unexpectedly the top blew off:

And there, there overhead, there, there hung over
Those thousands of white faces, those dazed eyes,   10
There in the starless dark the poise, the hover,
There with vast wings across the cancelled skies,
There in the sudden blackness the black pall
Of nothing, nothing, nothing—nothing at all.

YOU, ANDREW MARVELL

And here face down beneath the sun,
And here upon earth's noonward height
To feel the always coming on,
The always rising of the night.

To feel creep up the curving east   5
The earthly chill of dusk and slow
Upon those under lands the vast
And ever-climbing shadow grow,

And strange at Ecbatan the trees
Take leaf by leaf the evening, strange,   10
The flooding dark about their knees,
The mountains over Persia change,

And now at Kermanshah the gate,
Dark, empty, and the withered grass,
And through the twilight now the late   15
Few travelers in the westward pass.

And Baghdad darken and the bridge
Across the silent river gone,
And through Arabia the edge
Of evening widen and steal on,   20

And deepen on Palmyra's street
The wheel rut in the ruined stone,
And Lebanon fade out and Crete
High through the clouds and overblown,

And over Sicily the air   25
Still flashing with the landward gulls,
And loom and slowly disappear
The sails above the shadowy hulls,

And Spain go under and the shore
Of Africa, the gilded sand,   30
And evening vanish and no more
The low pale light across that land,

Nor now the long light on the sea—
And here face downward in the sun
To feel how swift, how secretly,   35
The shadow of the night comes on. . . .

E. E. CUMMINGS

1 8 9 4 – 1 9 6 2

ALL IN GREEN WENT MY LOVE RIDING

All in green went my love riding
on a great horse of gold
into the silver dawn.

four lean hounds crouched low and smiling
the merry deer ran before.   5

Fleeter be they than dappled dreams
the swift sweet deer
the red rare deer.

Four red roebuck at a white water
the cruel bugle sang before.   10

Horn at hip went my love riding
riding the echo down
into the silver dawn.

four lean hounds crouched low and smiling
the level meadows ran before.   15

Softer be they than slippered sleep
the lean lithe deer
the fleet flown deer.

Four fleet does at a gold valley
the famished arrow sang before.

20

Bow at belt went my love riding
riding the mountain down
into the silver dawn.

four lean hounds crouched low and smiling
the sheer peaks ran before.

25

Paler be they than daunting death
the sleek slim deer
the tall tense deer.

Four tall stags at a green mountain
the lucky hunter sang before.

30

All in green went my love riding
on a great horse of gold
into the silver dawn.

four lean hounds crouched low and smiling
my heart fell dead before.

35

MY GIRL'S TALL WITH HARD LONG EYES

my girl's tall with hard long eyes
as she stands, with her long hard hands keeping
silence on her dress, good for sleeping
is her long hard body filled with surprise
like a white shocking wire, when she smiles   5
a hard long smile it sometimes makes
gaily go clean through me tickling aches,
and the weak noise of her eyes easily files
my impatience to an edge—my girl's tall
and taut, with thin legs just like a vine   10
that's spent all of its life on a garden-wall,
and is going to die. When we grimly go to bed
with these legs she begins to heave and twine
about me, and to kiss my face and head.

ANYONE LIVED IN A
PRETTY HOW TOWN

anyone lived in a pretty how town
(and up so floating many bells down)
spring summer autumn winter
he sang his didn't he danced his did.

Women and men (both little and small)   5
cared for anyone not at all
they sowed their isn't they reaped their same
sun moon stars rain

children guessed (but only a few
and down they forgot as up they grew   10
autumn winter spring summer)
that noone loved him more by more

when by now and tree by leaf
she laughed his joy she cried his grief
bird by snow and stir by still   15
anyone's any was all to her

someones married their everyones
laughed their cryings and did their dance
(sleep wake hope and then) they
said their nevers they slept their dream   20

stars rain sun moon
(and only the snow can begin to explain
how children are apt to forget to remember
with up so floating many bells down)

one day anyone died i guess   25
(and noone stooped to kiss his face)
busy folk buried them side by side
little by little and was by was

all by all and deep by deep
and more by more they dream their sleep   30
noone and anyone earth by april
wish by spirit and if by yes.

Women and men (both dong and ding)
summer autumn winter spring
reaped their sowing and went their came   35
sun moon stars rain

i say no world

can hold a you
shall see the not
because
and why but
(who   5
stood within his steam be-
ginning and
began to sing all
here is hands machine no

good too quick i know this   10
suit you pay
a store too
much yes what
too much o much cheap
me i work i know i say i have   15
not any
never
no vacation here

is hands is work since i am
born is good   20
but there this cheap this suit too
quick no suit there every
-thing
nothing i
say the   25
world not fit
you) he is

not (i say the world
yes any world is much
too not quite big enough to   30
hold one tiny this with
time's
more than

most how
immeasurable
anguish   35

pregnant one fearless
one good yes
completely kind
mindheart one true one generous child-   40
man
-god one eager
souldoll one
unsellable not buyable alive
one i say human being) one   45

goldberger

ROBERT GRAVES

1 8 9 5 –

WARNING TO CHILDREN

Children, if you dare to think
Of the greatness, rareness, muchness,
Fewness of this precious only
Endless world in which you say
You live, you think of things like this: 5
Blocks of slate enclosing dappled
Red and green, enclosing tawny
Yellow nets, enclosing white
And black acres of dominoes,
Where a neat brown paper parcel   10
Tempts you to untie the string.
In the parcel a small island,
On the island a large tree,
On the tree a husky fruit,
Strip the husk and pare the rind off: 15
In the kernel you will see

Blocks of slate enclosed by dappled
Red and green, enclosed by tawny
Yellow nets, enclosed by white
And black acres of dominoes, 20
Where the same brown paper parcel—
Children, leave the string untied!
For who dares undo the parcel
Finds himself at once inside it,
On the island, in the fruit, 25
Blocks of slate about his head,
Finds himself enclosed by dappled
Green and red, enclosed by yellow
Tawny nets, enclosed by black
And white acres of dominoes, 30
With the same brown paper parcel
Still untied upon his knee.
And, if he then should dare to think
Of the fewness, muchness, rareness,
Greatness of this endless only 35
Precious world in which he says
He lives—he then unties the string.

THE CLIMATE OF THOUGHT

The climate of thought has seldom been described.
It is no terror of Caucasian frost,
Nor yet that brooding Hindu heat
For which a loin-rag and a dish of rice
Suffice until the pestilent monsoon. 5
But, without winter, blood would run too thin;
Or, without summer, fires would burn too long.
In thought the seasons run concurrently.

Thought has a sea to gaze, not voyage on;
And hills, to rough the edge of the bland sky, 10
Not to be climbed in search of blander prospect;
Few birds, sufficient for such caterpillars
As are not fated to turn butterflies;
Few butterflies, sufficient for the flowers
That are the luxury of a full orchard; 15
Wind, sometimes, in the evening chimneys; rain
On the early morning roof, on sleepy sight;
Snow streaked upon the hilltop, feeding
The fond brook at the valley-head
That greens the valley and that parts the lips; 20

The sun, simple, like a country neighbour;
The moon, grand, not fanciful with clouds.

TO JUAN AT THE WINTER SOLSTICE

There is one story and one story only
That will prove worth your telling,
Whether as learned bard or gifted child;
To it all lines or lesser gauds belong
That startle with their shining   5
Such common stories as they stray into.

Is it of trees you tell, their months and virtues,
Or strange beasts that beset you,
Of birds that croak at you the Triple will?
Or of the Zodiac and how slow it turns   10
Below the Boreal Crown,
Prison of all true kings that ever reigned?

Water to water, ark again to ark,
From woman back to woman:
So each new victim treads unfalteringly   15
The never altered circuit of his fate,
Bringing twelve peers as witness
Both to his starry rise and starry fall.

Or is it of the Virgin's silver beauty,
All fish below the thighs?   20
She in her left hand bears a leafy quince;
When, with her right she crooks a finger smiling,
How may the King hold back?
Royally then he barters life for love.

Or of the undying snake from chaos hatched,   25
Whose coils contain the ocean,
Into whose chops with naked sword he springs,
Then in black water, tangled by the reeds,
Battles three days and nights,
To be spewed up beside her scalloped shore?   30

Much snow is falling, winds roar hollowly,
The owl hoots from the elder,

Fear in your heart cries to the loving-cup:
Sorrow to sorrow as the sparks fly upward.
The log groans and confesses   35
There is one story and one story only.

Dwell on her graciousness, dwell on her smiling,
Do not forget what flowers
The great boar trampled down in ivy time.
Her brow was creamy as the crested wave,   40
Her sea-blue eyes were wild
But nothing promised that is not performed.

HART CRANE
1899–1932

VOYAGES (II)

And yet this great wink of eternity,
Of rimless floods, unfettered leewardings,
Samite sheeted and processioned where
Her undinal vast belly moonward bends,
Laughing the wrapt inflections of our love;   5

Take this Sea whose diapason knells
On scrolls of silver snowy sentences,
The sceptred terror of whose sessions rends
As her demeanors motion well or ill,
All but the pieties of lovers' hands.   10

And onward, as bells off San Salvador
Salute the crocus lustres of the stars,
In these poinsettia meadows of her tides,—
Adagios of islands, O my Prodigal,
Complete the dark confessions her veins spell.   15

Mark how her turning shoulders wind the hours,
And hasten while her penniless rich palms

Pass superscription of bent foam and wave,—
Hasten, while they are true,—sleep, death, desire,
Close round one instant in one floating flower.   20

Bind us in time, O Seasons clear, and awe.
O minstrel galleons of Carib fire,
Bequeath us to no earthly shore until
Is answered in the vortex of our grave
The seal's wide spindrift gaze toward paradise.   25

AT MELVILLE'S TOMB

Often beneath the wave, wide from this ledge
The dice of drowned men's bones he saw bequeath
An embassy. Their numbers as he watched,
Beat on the dusty shore and were obscured.

And wrecks passed without sound of bells,   5
The calyx of death's bounty giving back
A scattered chapter, lived hieroglyph,
The portent wound in corridors of shells.

Then in the circuit calm of one vast coil,
Its lashings charmed and malice reconciled,   10
Frosted eyes there were that lifted altars;
And silent answers crept across the stars.

Compass, quadrant and sextant contrive
No farther tides . . . High in the azure steeps
Monody shall not wake the mariner.   15
This fabulous shadow only the sea keeps.

ALLEN TATE

1899–

THE MEDITERRANEAN

Quem das finem, rex magne, dolorum?

Where we went in the boat was a long bay
A slingshot wide, walled in by towering stone—
Peaked margin of antiquity's delay,
And we went there out of time's monotone:

Where we went in the black hull no light moved   5
But a gull white-winged along the feckless wave,
The breeze, unseen but fierce as a body loved,
That boat drove onward like a willing slave:

Where we went in the small ship the seaweed
Parted and gave to us the murmuring shore   10
And we made feast and in our secret need
Devoured the very plates Aeneas bore:

Where derelict you see through the low twilight
The green coast that you, thunder-tossed, would win,
Drop sail, and hastening to drink all night   15
Eat dish and bowl—to take that sweet land in!

Where we feasted and caroused on the sandless
Pebbles, affecting our day of piracy,
What prophecy of eaten plates could landless
Wanderers fulfil by the ancient sea?   20

We for that time might taste the famous age
Eternal here yet hidden from our eyes
When lust of power undid its stuffless rage;
They, in a wineskin, bore earth's paradise.

Let us lie down once more by the breathing side   25
Of Ocean, where our live forefathers sleep

As if the Known Sea still were a month wide—
Atlantis howls but is no longer steep!

What country shall we conquer, what fair land
Unman our conquest and locate our blood? 30
We've cracked the hemispheres with careless hand!
Now, from the Gates of Hercules we flood

Westward, westward till the barbarous brine
Whelms us to the tired world where tasseling corn,
Fat beans, grapes sweeter than muscadine 35
Rot on the vine: in that land were we born.

ODE TO THE CONFEDERATE DEAD

Row after row with strict impunity
The headstones yield their names to the element,
The wind whirrs without recollection;
In the riven troughs the splayed leaves
Pile up, of nature the casual sacrament 5
To the seasonal eternity of death,
Then driven by the fierce scrutiny
Of heaven to their business in the vast breath,
They sough the rumor of mortality.

Autumn is desolation in the plot 10
Of a thousand acres where these memories grow
From the inexhaustible bodies that are not
Dead, but feed the grass row after rich row:
Remember now the autumns that have gone—
Ambitious November with the humours of the year, 15
With a particular zeal for every slab,
Staining the uncomfortable angels that rot
On the slabs, a wing chipped here, an arm there:
The brute curiosity of an angel's stare
Turns you like them to stone, 20
Transforms the heaving air,
Till plunged to a heavier world below
You shift your sea-space blindly,
Heaving like the blind crab.

Dazed by the wind, only the wind 25
The leaves flying, plunge

You know who have waited by the wall
The twilit certainty of an animal;
Those midnight restitutions of the blood
You know—the immitigable pines, the smoky frieze   30
Of the sky, the sudden call; you know the rage—
The cold pool left by the mounting flood—
The rage of Zeno and Parmenides.
You who have waited for the angry resolution
Of those desires that should be yours tomorrow,
You know the unimportant shrift of death
And praise the vision
And praise the arrogant circumstance
Of those who fall
Rank upon rank, hurried beyond decision—   40
Here by the sagging gate, stopped by the wall.

     Seeing, seeing only the leaves
     Flying, plunge and expire

Turn your eyes to the immoderate past
Turn to the inscrutable infantry rising   45
Demons out of the earth—they will not last.
Stonewall, Stonewall, and the sunken fields of hemp,
Shiloh, Antietam, Malvern Hill, Bull Run.
Lost in that orient of the thick and fast
You will curse the setting sun.   50

     Cursing only the leaves crying
     Like an old man in a storm

You hear the shout—the crazy hemlocks point
With troubled fingers to the silence which
Smothers you, a mummy, in time.

                 The hound bitch   55
Toothless and dying, in a musty cellar
Hears the wind only.

          Now that the salt of their blood
Stiffens the saltier oblivion of the sea,
Seals the malignant purity of the flood,
What shall we, who count our days and bow   60
Our heads with a commemorial woe,

In the ribboned coats of grim felicity,
What shall we say of the bones, unclean
—Their verdurous anonymity will grow—
The ragged arms, the ragged heads and eyes 65
Lost in these acres of the insane green?
The gray lean spiders come; they come and go;
In a tangle of willows without light
The singular screech-owl's bright
Invisible lyric seeds the mind 70
With the furious murmur of their chivalry.

       We shall say only, the leaves
       Flying, plunge and expire

We shall say only, the leaves whispering
In the improbable mist of nightfall 75
That flies on multiple wing:
Night is the beginning and the end,
And in between the ends of distraction
Waits mute speculation, the patient curse
That stones the eyes, or like the jaguar leaps 80
For his own image in a jungle pool, his victim.

What shall we say who have knowledge
Carried to the heart? Shall we take the act
To the grave? Shall we, more hopeful, set up the grave
In the house? The ravenous grave?

                       Leave now 85
The turnstile and the old stone wall:
The gentle serpent, green in the mulberry bush,
Riots with his tongue through the hush—
Sentinel of the grave who counts us all!

ROBERT PENN WARREN

1905–

VARIATION: ODE TO FEAR

When the dentist adjusts his drill
And leers at the molar he's going to fill,
Murmuring softly as a mother,
"Just hold tight, it'll soon be over,"
    Timor mortis conturbat me.   5

When the surgeon whets his scalpel
And regards me like an apple,
And the tumor or the wart
Sings, "The best of friends must part,"
    Timor mortis conturbat me.   10

When flushed with morning's genial hope
I slit the crisped envelope
And read the message too oft known,
"Your account $3.00 overdrawn,"
    Timor mortis conturbat me.   15

When I wait on the railway platform
To say goodbye, and the friend's form,
Which was substantial, wavers there
Thinner than smoke upon the air,
    Timor mortis conturbat me.   20

When I think that the national debt
Will blight the children we beget,
And especially blight those of our heirs
Who have the instincts of financiers,
    Timor mortis conturbat me.   25

When I read in Charles A. Beard
That the Founding Fathers whom we revered
Were not above a cozy deal

And would skin a pig for the pig's squeal,
  Timor mortis conturbat me.   30

And read that Milton was neurotic
And Saint Joan charmingly psychotic
And Jesus in Gethsemane
Was simply sweating from T. B.,
  Timor mortis conturbat me.   35

When Focke-Wulf mounts, or Zero,
And my knees say I'm no hero
And manly marrow turns to soup
And lunch expertly loops the loop,
  Timor mortis conturbat me.   40

When in the midnight's pause I mark
The breath beside me in the dark,
And know that breath's a clock, and know
That breath's the clock that's never slow,
  Timor mortis conturbat me.   45

O thou, to whom the world unknown
With all its shadowy shapes is shown,
Whose foot makes no sound on the floor,
Who need no latchkey for the door
    (*Timor mortis conturbat me*),   50

Who gaze from out the chic dummy's gaze,
In the display window, to amaze
The yearning matron by whom you sat
At dinner last night and in her soup spat
    (*Timor mortis conturbat me*),   55

Who pinch the maiden's tenderest part
But warm no cockles of her heart,
Who snarl the horse's tail, who spill
The bucket fetched by Jack and Jill
    (*Timor mortis conturbat me*),   60

Whose sleights are slier than Houdini's
And make Puck's pranks look like a ninny's
—Though you were with me *in utero,*

Your own birthday was long ago
    (*Timor mortis conturbat me*),   65

And though you fawn and follow like Fido,
You'll find other master when I go.
For I'm not the first or last of men
And so I will try to remember when
    Timor mortis conturbat me.   70

That various men in various ages
Have dispensed with heroes and with sages,
And managed without our Constitution
Or intercession and absolution
    (*Timor mortis conturbat me*),   75

And when they walked by grove or shore
Enjoyed the scene, not metaphor,
And when they got it in the gut
Took what comfort they could from a cigarette butt
    (*Timor mortis conturbat me*),   80

And though they found the going hard
Did without Jesus or the gold standard,
Or lay alone, and reaching over
Could find no hand upon the cover
    (*Timor mortis conturbat me*).   85

So when I wake I'll pat the head
Of the beast that sleeps beside the bed,
And put on my pants and vest, and go
Down to eat my breakfast, though
    Timor mortis conturbat me.   90

BEARDED OAKS

The oaks, how subtle and marine,
Bearded, and all the layered light
Above them swims; and thus the scene,
Recessed, awaits the positive night.

So, waiting, we in the grass now lie   5
Beneath the langourous tread of light:

The grasses, kelp-like, satisfy
The nameless motions of the air.

Upon the floor of light, and time,
Unmurmuring, of polyp made,   10
We rest; we are, as light withdraws,
Twin atolls on a shelf of shade.

Ages to our construction went,
Dim architecture, hour by hour:
And violence, forgot now, lent   15
The present stillness all its power.

The storm of noon above us rolled,
Of light the fury, furious gold,
The long drag troubling us, the depth:
Dark is unrocking, unrippling, still.   20

Passion and slaughter, ruth, decay
Descend, minutely whispering down,
Silted down swaying streams, to lay
Foundation for our voicelessness.

All our debate is voiceless here,   25
As all our rage, the rage of stone;
If hope is hopeless, then fearless fear,
And history is thus undone.

Our feet once wrought the hollow street
With echo when the lamps were dead   30
At windows, once our headlight glare
Disturbed the doe that, leaping, fled.

I do not love you less that now
The caged heart makes iron stroke,
Or less that all that light once gave   35
The graduate dark should now revoke.

We live in time so little time
And we learn all so painfully,
That we may spare this hour's term
To practice for eternity.   40

STANLEY KUNITZ

1905–

FOREIGN AFFAIRS

We are two countries girded for the war,
Whisking our scouts across the pricked frontier
To ravage in each other's fields, cut lines
Along the lacework of strategic nerves,
Loot stores; while here and there,   5
In ambushes that trace a valley's curves,
Stark witness to the dangerous charge we bear,
A house ignites, a train's derailed, a bridge
Blows up sky-high, and water floods the mines.
Who first attacked? Who turned the other cheek?   10
Aggression perpetrated is as soon
Denied, and insult rubbed into the injury
By cunning agents trained in these affairs,
With whom it's touch-and-go, don't-tread-on-me,
I-dare-you-to, keep-off, and kiss-my-hand.   15
Tempers could sharpen knives, and do; we live
In states provocative
Where frowning headlines scare the coffee cream
And doomsday is the eighth day of the week.

Our exit through the slammed and final door   20
Is twenty times rehearsed, but when we face
The imminence of cataclysmic rupture,
A lesser pride goes down upon its knees.
Two countries separated by desire!—
Whose diplomats speed back and forth by plane,   25
Portmanteaus stuffed with fresh apologies
Outdated by events before they land.
Negotiations wear them out: they're driven mad
Between the protocols of tears and rapture.

Locked in our fated and contiguous selves,   30
These worlds that too much agitate each other,
Interdependencies from hip to head,
Twin principalities both slave and free,
We coexist, proclaiming Peace together.

Tell me no lies! We are divided nations 35
With malcontents by thousands in our streets,
These thousands torn by inbred revolutions.
A triumph is demanded, not moral victories
Deduced from small advances, small retreats.
Are the gods of our fathers not still daemonic? 40
On the steps of the Capitol
The outraged lion of our years roars panic,
And we suffer the guilty cowardice of the will,
Gathering its bankrupt slogans up for flight
Like gold from ruined treasuries. 45
And yet, and yet, although the murmur rises,
We are what we are, and only life surprises.

FOR THE WORD IS FLESH

O ruined father dead, long sweetly rotten
Under the dial, the time-dissolving urn,
Beware a second perishing, forgotten,
Heap fallen leaves of memory to burn
On the slippery rock, the black eroding heart, 5
Before the wedged frost splits it clean apart.

The nude hand drops no sacramental flower
Of blood among the tough upthrusting weeds.
Senior, in this commemorative hour,
What shall the quick commemorate, what deeds 10
Ephemeral, what dazzling words that flare
Like rockets from the mouth to burst in air?

Of hypochondriacs that gnawed their seasons
In search of proofs, Lessius found twenty-two
Fine arguments, Tolet gave sixty reasons 15
Why souls survive. And what are they to you?
And, father, what to me, who cannot blur
The mirrored brain with fantasies of Er,

Remembering such factual spikes as pierce
The supplicating palms, and by the sea 20
Remembering the eyes, I hear the fierce
Wild cry of Jesus on the holy tree,
Yet have of you no syllable to keep,
Only the deep rock crumbling in the deep.

Observe the wisdom of the Florentine   25
Who, feeling death upon him, scribbled fast
To make revision of a deathbed scene,
Gloating that he was accurate at last.
Let sons learn from their lipless fathers how
Man enters hell without a golden bough.   30

STANLEY BURNSHAW

1906–

HISTORICAL SONG OF THEN AND NOW

Earth early and huge,
No eye dared hope to travel
The palette of its rage

Till, late, they learned to wind
Shackles into its veins,   5
Shrank it to fit a cage.

So trust contracts to fear.
The tribes give up their feuds.
All wars are now one war.

And will you indict this breed   10
That strained against a code
Where safe-and-fed was good?

Fled from its mothering wood,
It found in its hand the thought
To light up endless day,   15

Revel with sleepless eye,
Make of itself a god,
And the veins a level sun—

Now it stumbles, dwarf in the maze
That the thinking hand had spun.   20
Blind in its blaze of stone,

Whom can this breed indict
That its sun is a blast of darkness,
That light is always night?

MODES OF BELIEF

Ever since I grew cold
In heart, I always hear
Most men that I behold
Cry like a creature caught
In tones of dying will,   5
Such as their eyelids bear
With cuneiforms of fail—

Where are the young and wild
Teeming in hope of power?
Though striving lifts the bud,   10
None can achieve the flower.
Where can the bud disperse
Within?   Must every man
Entomb a withered child?—

What early hearts can store   15
Of sweetness still endures
Fever of flood or drought,
Till groping up from within,
A self-bereaving curse
Masses in reefs of thought,   20
Burns and bites the blood—

POETRY: THE ART
In the Form of an Apostrophe to Whitman

I used to read your book and hear your words
Explode in me and blast new passageways
Deep in my brain, until its crowding rooms
Held more light than my head could balance. Now

That the tunnels all are cut, I pace the rooms 5
Looking for you, though certain I shall find
No more of you than you yourself could gather
Out of the pieces of self. The years have burned
The sharpness from the edges: I can fit
The pieces, but the mortar must be mixed 10
Out of our blending wills. Others have tried
And failed. I too shall fail if I forget
How thought can range beyond the last frontiers
That common sense has civilized with names.

Others who looked for you have made you say 15
Words you might have said if they were you:
Have lost you in their passion for a phrase.
The private man's infinitude defies
The singleness they look for when they strive
To sort your various colors to a scheme 20
Of thought-and-action. Desperate for pattern,
They make the key *Calamus* and they twist
Your other selves around the centerpiece,
Losing you in that love.

And others forge 25
A key of social thought that cracks apart
When words and actions contradict: *Walt Whitman,*
You said you love the common man! Where were you
When Parsons' friends were hanged? Were you asleep
Or writing more fine words about mechanics 30
And farmers?—How much cosier for you
To prate about democracy than live it—
You, its self-appointed poet!

Others,
Seeking you in your plangent celebrations
Of science and the holiness of flesh 35
And earth, end with a fierce *You too, Walt Whitman,*
You flinched, you stumbled, hankering for a "soul" . . .
The substances of sense too harsh too bitter
A truth for you to live by! Underneath
Your protest boils the soft romantic sickness 40
Of all the Shelley, Heines—bright lost leaders
We hoped were men. You were afraid of the dark:
You who had thundered "Science is true religion"
Sang the groveler's wooing song to Death
And God and Spirit! . . . Hide, at least, the image 45
Revealed: the gaudy chaos of a man
Reviling his own faith!

But who can dare
To arbitrate the depths of you that anger
Against your tranquil self? I am not certain:
I have seen the signposts of contradiction   50
Planted by men impotent to discern
The harmony beneath the subtle wholeness,
And in their self-defence erect confusion
On quiet entities. A poet's words
Are signatures of self—the many selves   55
Subsumed in one profounder sense that knows
An all-according truth: a single eye
Uncovering the countless constellations
Of heart and mind. Wherefore the syllables
Reach outward from the self in an embrace   60
Of multitudes. The poetries of speech
Are acts of thinking love; and I must find
The thought that grows the center of your passion.

And so I say to those who precontemn
The message of *Calamus* as the flowers   65
Of twisted love what Plato showed of truths
Uttered by poets. And I say to those
Who spit upon your social thought *"Respondez!"*
The human race is restive, on the watch
For some new era—some divine war—   70
Whose triumph will entrench a brave good-will
Among the common people everywhere—
The trodden multitudes for whom you clamored
A new and tender reverence.

But for those
Who sneer because you looked for lights beyond   75
The planes of sense, there is no final answer
If they deny the mind its birthright freedom
To range all worlds of thought and sense and vision.
Everything that can be believ'd is an image of truth—
The images refined to great and small   80
Will cluster into orbits of belief
And hold together as the planets hold
By kinship and denial, in one vaster
All encompassing circle. Let the sneerers
Proclaim your chief intent or keep their silence   85
Until its name is found.

It is not found,
The answer to your central search—"the problem,
The only one"—*adjust the individual*
Into your mass. For we have just begun

To fit the world to men, men to the world; 90
And we shall stumble till the single heart
Discovers all its selves and learns therefrom
How singleness and multitude can live
In valiant marriage. With your hungry hope
You pierced the shells of feeling, trumpeted 95
Into your country's ears, and flooded strength
Into the wavering hearts of men lonely
For courage to fulfill their need: to thrust
Their single faith against the massed-up wills
Of many. "Sing your self!" you told them. Listening, 100
They pledged the valors of the inward man.
And others turned from you with dull, deaf ears,
Afraid to listen, waiting to be taught
The trial-and-error way of rats in a maze . . .

A poem "is," some men believe. I say 105
A poem "is" when it has spread its root
Inside a listener's thought and grows a tree there
Strong enough to burst a room in the brain,
And bring its branch to blossom. Then the host
Forgets the verse and ponders on the mind 110
That made this seed of growth . . . as I forget
Your poem: as I strive to learn your mind,
Thinking that when I come to understand,
I may begin to touch serenities
You saw beneath the springs of pain that nourished 115
Your world that was beginning—dim, green world
Trembling with death-and-birth: divinest war.

W. H. AUDEN

1907-

MUSÉE DES BEAUX ARTS

About suffering they were never wrong,
The Old Masters: how well they understood
Its human position; how it takes place
While someone else is eating or opening a window or just walking
　　dully along;

How, when the aged are reverently, passionately waiting 5
For the miraculous birth, there always must be
Children who did not specially want it to happen, skating
On a pond at the edge of the wood:
They never forgot
That even the dreadful martyrdom must run its course 10
Anyhow in a corner, some untidy spot
Where the dogs go on with their doggy life and the torturer's horse
Scratches its innocent behind on a tree.

In Breughel's *Icarus*, for instance: how everything turns away
Quite leisurely from the disaster; the ploughman may 15
Have heard the splash, the forsaken cry,
But for him it was not an important failure; the sun shone
As it had to on the white legs disappearing into the green
Water; and the expensive delicate ship that must have seen
Something amazing, a boy falling out of the sky, 20
Had somewhere to get to and sailed calmly on.

IN MEMORY OF W. B. YEATS

I

He disappeared in the dead of winter:
The brooks were frozen, the airports almost deserted,
The snow disfigured the public statues;
The mercury sank in the mouth of the dying day.
O all the instruments agree 5
The day of his death was a dark cold day.

Far from his illness
The wolves ran on through the evergreen forests,
The peasant river was untempted by the fashionable quays;
By mourning tongues 10
The death of the poet was kept from his poems.

But for him it was his last afternoon as himself,
An afternoon of nurses and rumours;
The provinces of his body revolted, 15
The squares of his mind were empty,
Silence invaded the suburbs,
The current of his feeling failed: he became his admirers.

Now he is scattered among a hundred cities
And wholly given over to unfamiliar affections;
To find his happiness in another kind of wood 20

And be punished under a foreign code of conscience.
The words of a dead man
Are modified in the guts of the living.

But in the importance and noise of tomorrow
When the brokers are roaring like beasts on the floor of the Bourse,   25
And the poor have the sufferings to which they are fairly accustomed,
And each in the cell of himself is almost convinced of his freedom;
A few thousand will think of this day
As one thinks of a day when one did something slightly unusual.
O all the instruments agree   30
The day of his death was a dark cold day.

2

You were silly like us: your gift survived it all;
The parish of rich women, physical decay,
Yourself; mad Ireland hurt you into poetry.
Now Ireland has her madness and her weather still,   35
For poetry makes nothing happen: it survives
In the valley of its saying where executives
Would never want to tamper; it flows south
From ranches of isolation and the busy griefs,
Raw towns that we believe and die in; it survives,   40
A way of happening, a mouth.

3

Earth, receive an honoured guest;
William Yeats is laid to rest:
Let the Irish vessel lie
Emptied of its poetry.   45

Time that is intolerant
Of the brave and innocent,
And indifferent in a week
To a beautiful physique,

Worships language and forgives   50
Everyone by whom it lives;
Pardons cowardice, conceit,
Lays its honours at their feet.

Time that with this strange excuse
Pardoned Kipling and his views,   55
And will pardon Paul Claudel,
Pardons him for writing well.

In the nightmare of the dark
All the gods of Europe bark,

And the living nations wait,   60
Each sequestered in its hate;

Intellectual disgrace
Stares from every human face,
And the seas of pity lie
Locked and frozen in each eye.   65

Follow, poet, follow right
To the bottom of the night,
With your unconstraining voice
Still persuade us to rejoice;

With the farming of a verse   70
Make a vineyard of the curse,
Sing of human unsuccess
In a rapture of distress;

In the deserts of the heart
Let the healing fountain start,   75
In the prison of his days
Teach the free man how to praise.

THE SHIELD OF ACHILLES

She looked over his shoulder
    For vines and olive trees,
Marble well-governed cities
    And ships upon untamed seas,
But there on the shining metal   5
    His hands had put instead
An artificial wilderness
    And a sky like lead.

A plain without a feature, bare and brown,
    No blade of grass, no sign of neighbourhood,   10
Nothing to eat and nowhere to sit down,
    Yet, congregated on its blankness, stood
    An unintelligible multitude.
A million eyes, a million boots in line,
Without expression, waiting for a sign.   15

Out of the air a voice without a face
    Proved by statistics that some cause was just

In tones as dry and level as the place:
  No one was cheered and nothing was discussed;
    Column by column in a cloud of dust   20
They marched away enduring a belief
Whose logic brought them, somewhere else, to grief.

              She looked over his shoulder
                  For ritual pieties,
              White flower-garlanded heifers,   25
                  Libation and sacrifice,
              But there on shining metal
                  Where the altar should have been,
              She saw by his flickering forge-light
                  Quite another scene.   30

Barbed wire enclosed an arbitrary spot
    Where bored officials lounged (one cracked a joke)
And sentries sweated for the day was hot:
    A crowd of ordinary decent folk
    Watched from without and neither moved nor spoke   35
As three pale figures were led forth and bound
To three posts driven upright in the ground.

The mass and majesty of this world, all
    That carries weight and always weighs the same
Lay in the hands of others; they were small   40
    And could not hope for help and no help came:
    What their foes liked to do was done, their shame
Was all the worst could wish; they lost their pride
And died as men before their bodies died.

              She looked over his shoulder   45
                  For athletes at their games,
              Men and women in a dance
                  Moving their sweet limbs
              Quick, quick, to music,
                  But there on the shining shield   50
              His hands had set no dancing-floor
                  But a weed-choked field.

A ragged urchin, aimless and alone,
    Loitered about that vacancy, a bird
Flew up to safety from his well-aimed stone: 55
    That girls are raped, that two boys knife a third,
    Were axioms to him, who'd never heard

Of any world where promises were kept.
Or one could weep because another wept.

The thin-lipped armourer,   60
     Hephaestos hobbled away,
Thetis of the shining breasts
     Cried out in dismay
At what the god had wrought
     To please her son, the strong   65
Iron-hearted man-slaying Achilles
     Who would not live long.

THEODORE ROETHKE

1908–1963

FRAU BAUMAN, FRAU SCHMIDT, AND FRAU SCHWARTZE

Gone the three ancient ladies
Who creaked on the greenhouse ladders,
Reaching up white strings
To wind, to wind
The sweet-pea tendrils, the smilax,   5
Nasturtiums, the climbing
Roses, to straighten
Carnations, red
Chrysanthemums; the stiff
Stems, jointed like corn,   10
They tied and tucked,—
These nurses of nobody else.
Quicker than birds, they dipped
Up and sifted the dirt;
They sprinkled and shook;   15
They stood astride pipes,
Their skirts billowing out wide into tents,
Their hands twinkling with wet;
Like witches they flew along rows
Keeping creation at ease;   20
With a tendril for needle

They sewed up the air with a stem;
They teased out the seed that the cold kept asleep,—
All the coils, loops, and whorls.
They trellised the sun; they plotted for more than themselves.   25

I remember how they picked me up, a spindly kid,
Pinching and poking my thin ribs
Till I lay in their laps, laughing,
Weak as a whiffet;
Now, when I'm alone and cold in my bed,   30
They still hover over me,
These ancient leathery crones,
With their bandannas stiffened with sweat,
And their thorn-bitten wrists,
And their snuff-laden breath blowing lightly over me in my first sleep.   35

THE FAR FIELD

I

I dream of journeys repeatedly:
Of flying like a bat deep into a narrowing tunnel,
Of driving alone, without luggage, out a long peninsula,
The road lined with snow-laden second growth,
A fine dry snow ticking the windshield,   5
Alternate snow and sleet, no on-coming traffic,
And no lights behind, in the blurred side-mirror,
The road changing from glazed tarface to a rubble of stone,
Ending at last in a hopeless sand-rut,
Where the car stalls,   10
Churning in a snowdrift
Until the headlights darken.

II

At the field's end, in the corner missed by the mower,
Where the turf drops off into a grass-hidden culvert,
Haunt of the cat-bird, nesting-place of the field-mouse,   15
Not too far away from the ever-changing flower-dump,
Among the tin cans, tires, rusted pipes, broken machinery,—
One learned of the eternal;
And in the shrunken face of a dead rat, eaten by rain and ground-
      beetles
(I found it lying among the rubble of an old coal bin)   20
And the tom-cat, caught near the pheasant-run,
Its entrails strewn over the half-grown flowers,

Blasted to death by the night watchman.
I suffered for birds, for young rabbits caught in the mower,
My grief was not excessive.   25
For to come upon warblers in early May
Was to forget time and death:
How they filled the oriole's elm, a twittering restless cloud, all one
        morning,
And I watched and watched till my eyes blurred from the bird
        shapes,—
Cape May, Blackburnian, Cerulean,—   30
Moving, elusive as fish, fearless,
Hanging, bunched like young fruit, bending the end branches,
Still for a moment,
Then pitching away in half-flight,
Lighter than finches,   35
While the wrens bickered and sang in the half-green hedgerows,
And the flicker drummed from his dead tree in the chicken-yard.

—Or to lie naked in sand,
In the silted shallows of a slow river,
Fingering a shell,   40
Thinking:
Once I was something like this, mindless,
Or perhaps with another mind, less peculiar;
Or to sink down to the hips in a mossy quagmire;
Or, with skinny knees, to sit astride a wet log,   45
Believing:
I'll return again,
As a snake or a raucous bird,
Or, with luck, as a lion.

I learned not to fear infinity,   50
The far field, the windy cliffs of forever,
The dying of time in the white light of tomorrow,
The wheel turning away from itself,
The sprawl of the wave,
The on-coming water.   55

III

The river turns on itself,
The tree retreats into its own shadow.
I feel a weightless change, a moving forward
As of water quickening before a narrowing channel
When banks converge, and the wide river whitens;   60
Or when two rivers combine, the blue glacial torrent
And the yellowish-green from the mountainy upland,—

At first a swift rippling between rocks,
Then a long running over flat stones
Before descending to the alluvial plain,   65
To the clay banks, and the wild grapes hanging from the elmtrees,
The slightly trembling water
Dropping a fine yellow silt where the sun stays;
And the crabs bask near the edge,
The weedy edge, alive with small snakes and bloodsuckers,—   70

I have come to a still, but not a deep center,
A point outside the glittering current;
My eyes stare at the bottom of a river,
At the irregular stones, iridescent sandgrains,
My mind moves in more than one place,   75
In a country half-land, half-water.

I am renewed by death, thought of my death,
The dry scent of a dying garden in September,
The wind fanning the ash of a low fire.
What I love is near at hand,   80
Always, in earth and air.

      IV

The lost self changes,
Turning toward the sea,
A sea-shape turning around,—
An old man with his feet before the fire,   85
In robes of green, in garments of adieu.

A man faced with his own immensity
Wakes all the waves, all their loose wandering fire.
The murmur of the absolute, the why
Of being born fails on his naked ears.   90
His spirit moves like monumental wind
That gentles on a sunny blue plateau.
He is the end of things, the final man.

All finite things reveal infinitude:
The mountain with its singular bright shade   95
Like the blue shine on freshly frozen snow,
The after-light upon ice-burdened pines;
Odor of basswood on a mountain-slope,
A scent beloved of bees;
Silence of water above a sunken tree: 100

The pure serene of memory in one man,—
A ripple widening from a single stone
Winding around the waters of the world.

LIGHT LISTENED

O what could be more nice
Than her ways with a man?
She kissed me more than twice
Once we were left alone.
Who'd look when he could feel?   5
She'd more sides than a seal.

The close air faintly stirred.
Light deepened to a bell,
The love-beat of a bird.
She kept her body still   10
And watched the weather flow.
We live by what we do.

All's known, all, all around:
The shape of things to be;
A green thing loves the green   15
And loves the living ground.
The deep shade gathers night;
She changed with changing light.

We met to leave again
The time we broke from time;   20
A cold air brought its rain,
The singing of a stem.
She sang a final song;
Light listened when she sang.

DELMORE SCHWARTZ

1 9 1 3 –

IN THE NAKED BED, IN PLATO'S CAVE

In the naked bed, in Plato's cave,
Reflected headlights slowly slid the wall,
Carpenters hammered under the shaded window,
Wind troubled the window curtains all night long,
A fleet of trucks strained uphill, grinding,   5
Their freights covered, as usual.

The ceiling lightened again, the slanting diagram
Slid slowly forth.
     Hearing the milkman's chop,
His striving up the stair, the bottle's chink,
I rose from bed, lit a cigarette,   10
And walked to the window. The stony street
Displayed the stillness in which buildings stand,
The street-lamp's vigil and the horse's patience.
The winter sky's pure capital
Turned me back to bed with exhausted eyes.   15

Strangeness grew in the motionless air. The loose
Film grayed. Shaking wagons, hooves' waterfalls,
Sounded far off, increasing, louder and nearer.
A car coughed, starting. Morning, softly
Melting the air, lifted the half-covered chair   20
From underseas, kindled the looking-glass,
Distinguished the dresser and the white wall.
The bird called tentatively, whistled, called,
Bubbled and whistled, so! Perplexed, still wet
With sleep, affectionate, hungry and cold. So, so,   25
O son of man, the ignorant night, the travail
Of early morning, the mystery of beginning
Again and again,
     while History is unforgiven.

THE HEAVY BEAR

"the withness of the body" WHITEHEAD

The heavy bear who goes with me,
A manifold honey to smear his face,
Clumsy and lumbering here and there,
The central ton of every place,
The hungry beating brutish one   5
In love with candy, anger, and sleep,
Crazy factotum, dishevelling all,
Climbs the building, kicks the football,
Boxes his brother in the hate-ridden city.

Breathing at my side, that heavy animal,   10
That heavy bear who sleeps with me,
Howls in his sleep for a world of sugar,
A sweetness intimate as the water's clasp,
Howls in his sleep because the tight-rope
Trembles and shows the darkness beneath.   15
—The strutting show-off is terrified,
Dressed in his dress-suit, bulging his pants,
Trembles to think that his quivering meat
Must finally wince to nothing at all.

That inescapable animal walks with me,   20
Has followed me since the black womb held,
Moves where I move, distorting my gesture,
A caricature, a swollen shadow,
A stupid clown of the spirit's motive,
Perplexes and affronts with his own darkness,   25
The secret life of belly and bone,
Opaque, too near, my private, yet unknown,
Stretches to embrace the very dear
With whom I would walk without him near,
Touches her grossly, although a word   30
Would bare my heart and make me clear,
Stumbles, flounders, and strives to be fed
Dragging me with him in his mouthing care,
Amid the hundred million of his kind,
The scrimmage of appetite everywhere.   35

DYLAN THOMAS

1914–1953

THE FORCE THAT THROUGH THE
GREEN FUSE DRIVES THE FLOWER

The force that through the green fuse drives the flower
Drives my green age; that blasts the roots of trees
Is my destroyer.
And I am dumb to tell the crooked rose
My youth is bent by the same wintry fever.   5

The force that drives the water through the rocks
Drives my red blood; that dries the mouthing streams
Turns mine to wax.
And I am dumb to mouth unto my veins
How at the mountain spring that same mouth sucks.   10

The hand that whirls the water in the pool
Stirs the quicksand; that ropes the blowing wind
Hauls my shroud sail.
And I am dumb to tell the hanging man
How of my clay is made the hangman's lime.   15

The lips of time leech to the fountain head;
Love drips and gathers, but the fallen blood
Shall calm her sores.
And I am dumb to tell a weather's wind
How time has ticked a heaven round the stars.   20

And I am dumb to tell the lover's tomb
How at my sheet goes the same crooked worm.

FERN HILL

Now as I was young and easy under the apple boughs
About the lilting house and happy as the grass was green,

The night above the dingle starry,
　　　Time let me hail and climb
　　Golden in the heydays of his eyes,　　　　　　　　　　　　5
And honoured among wagons I was prince of the apple towns
And once below a time I lordly had the trees and leaves
　　　　Trail with daisies and barley
　　Down the rivers of the windfall light.

And as I was green and carefree, famous among the barns　　10
About the happy yard and singing as the farm was home,
　　　In the sun that is young once only,
　　　　Time let me play and be
　　Golden in the mercy of his means,
And green and golden I was huntsman and herdsman, the calves　　15
Sang to my horn, the foxes on the hills barked clear and cold,
　　　And the sabbath rang slowly
　　In the pebbles of the holy streams.

All the sun long it was running, it was lovely, the hay
Fields high as the house, the tunes from the chimneys, it was air　　20
　　　And playing, lovely and watery
　　　　And fire green as grass.
　　And nightly under the simple stars
As I rode to sleep the owls were bearing the farm away,
All the moon long I heard, blessed among the stables, the nightjars　　25
　　　Flying with the ricks, and the horses
　　　　Flashing into the dark.

And then to awake, and the farm, like a wanderer white
With the dew, come back, the cock on his shoulder: it was all
　　　Shining, it was Adam and maiden,　　　　　　　　　30
　　　　The sky gathered again
　　And the sun grew round that very day.
So it must have been after the birth of the simple light
In the first, spinning place, the spellbound horses walking warm
　　　Out of the whinnying green stable　　　　　　　　35
　　　　On to the fields of praise.

And honoured among foxes and pheasants by the gay house
Under the new made clouds and happy as the heart was long,
　　　In the sun born over and over,
　　　　I ran my heedless ways,　　　　　　　　　　　40
　　My wishes raced through the house high hay
And nothing I cared, at my sky blue trades, that time allows

In all his tuneful turning so few and such morning songs
    Before the children green and golden
        Follow him out of grace,   45

Nothing I cared, in the lamb white days, that time would take me
Up to the swallow thronged loft by the shadow of my hand,
    In the moon that is always rising,
        Nor that riding to sleep
    I should hear him fly with the high fields   50
And wake to the farm forever fled from the childless land.
Oh as I was young and easy in the mercy of his means,
        Time held me green and dying
    Though I sang in my chains like the sea.

DO NOT GO GENTLE
INTO THAT GOOD NIGHT

Do not go gentle into that good night,
Old age should burn and rave at close of day;
Rage, rage against the dying of the light.

Though wise men at their end know dark is right,
Because their words had forked no lightning they   5
Do not go gentle into that good night.

Good men, the last wave by, crying how bright
Their frail deeds might have danced in a green bay,
Rage, rage against the dying of the light.

Wild men who caught and sang the sun in flight,   10
And learn, too late, they grieved it on its way,
Do not go gentle into that good night.

Grave men, near death, who see with blinding sight
Blind eyes could blaze like meteors and be gay,
Rage, rage against the dying of the light.   15

And you, my father, there on the sad height,
Curse, bless, me now with your fierce tears, I pray.
Do not go gentle into that good night.
Rage, rage against the dying of the light.

IN MY CRAFT OR SULLEN ART

In my craft or sullen art
Exercised in the still night
When only the moon rages
And the lovers lie abed
With all their griefs in their arms,   5
I labour by singing light
Not for ambition or bread
Or the strut and trade of charms
On the ivory stages
But for the common wages   10
Of their most secret heart.
Not for the proud man apart
From the raging moon I write
On these spindrift pages
Not for the towering dead   15
With their nightingales and psalms
But for the lovers, their arms
Round the griefs of the ages,
Who pay no praise or wages
Nor heed my craft or art.   20

JOHN BERRYMAN

1914–

CONVERSATION

Whether the moorings are invisible
Or gone, we said we could not tell.
But argument held one thing sure
That none of us that night could well endure:
The ship is locked with fog, no man aboard   5
Can see what he is moving toward,
There's little food, less love, no sleep,
The sea is dark and we are told it's deep.

Where is an officer who knows this coast?
If all such men long since have faced   10

Downward, one summon. Who knows how,
With what fidelity his voice heard now
Could shout directions from the ocean's floor?
Traditional characters no more
Their learnéd simple parts rehearse,   15
But bed them down at last from the time's curse.

A broken log fell out upon the hearth,
The flaming harbinger come forth
Of holocausts that night and day
Shrivel from the mind its sovereignty.   20
We watched the embers cool; those embers brought
To one man there the failing thought
Of cities stripped of knowledge, men,
Our continent a wilderness again.

These are conclusions of the night, we said;   25
And drank, and were not satisfied.
The fire died down, smoke in the air
Took the alarming postures of our fear;
The overhead horror, in the padded room
The man who cannot tell his name,   30
The guns and enemies that face
Into this delicate and dangerous place.

DREAM SONG: 14

Life, friends, is boring. We must not say so.
After all, the sky flashes, the great sea yearns,
we ourselves flash and yearn,
and moreover my mother told me as a boy
(repeatingly) 'Ever to confess you're bored   5
means you have no

Inner Resources.' I conclude now I have no
inner resources, because I am heavy bored.
Peoples bore me,
literature bores me, especially great literature,   10
Henry bores me, with his plights & gripes
as bad as achilles,

who loves people and valiant art, which bores me.
And the tranquil hills, & gin, look like a drag

and somehow a dog 15
has taken itself & its tail considerably away
into mountains or sea or sky, leaving
behind: me, wag.

DREAM SONG: 18
A Strut for Roethke

Westward, hit a low note, for a roarer lost
across the Sound but north from Bremerton,
hit a way down note.
And never cadenza again of flowers, or cost.
Him who could really do that cleared his throat 5
& staggered on.

The bluebells, pool-shallows, saluted his over-needs,
while the clouds growled, heh-heh, & snapped, & crashed.

No stunt he'll ever unflinch once more will fail
(O lucky fellow, eh Bones?)—drifted off upstairs, 10
downstairs, somewheres.
No more daily, trying to hit the head on the nail:
thirstless: without a think in his head:
back from wherever, with it said.

Hit a high long note, for a lover found 15
needing a lower into friendlier ground
to bug among worms no more
around um jungles where ah blurt 'What for?'
Weeds, too, he favoured as   most men don't favour men.
The Garden Master's gone. 20

ROBERT LOWELL

1917–

THE QUAKER GRAVEYARD IN NANTUCKET
(*For Warren Winslow, Dead at Sea*)

Let man have dominion over the fishes of the sea and the
fowls of the air and the beasts and the whole earth, and
every creeping creature that moveth upon the earth.

I

A brackish reach of shoal off Madaket,—
The sea was still breaking violently and night
Had steamed into our North Atlantic Fleet,
When the drowned sailor clutched the drag-net. Light
Flashed from his matted head and marble feet,   5
He grappled at the net
With the coiled, hurdling muscles of his thighs:
The corpse was bloodless, a botch of reds and whites,
Its open, staring eyes
Were lustreless dead-lights   10
Or cabin-windows on a stranded hulk
Heavy with sand. We weight the body, close
Its eyes and heave it seaward whence it came,
Where the heel-headed dogfish barks its nose
On Ahab's void and forehead; and the name   15
Is blocked in yellow chalk.
Sailors, who pitch this portent at the sea
Where dreadnaughts shall confess
Its hell-bent deity,
When you are powerless   20
To sand-bag this Atlantic bulwark, faced
By the earth-shaker, green, unwearied, chaste
In his steel scales: ask for no Orphean lute
To pluck life back. The guns of the steeled fleet
Recoil and then repeat   25
The hoarse salute.

II

Whenever winds are moving and their breath
Heaves at the roped-in bulwarks of this pier,

The terns and sea-gulls tremble at your death
In these home waters. Sailor, can you hear   30
The Pequod's sea wings, beating landward, fall
Headlong and break on our Atlantic wall
Off 'Sconset, where the yawing S-boats splash
The bellbuoy, with ballooning spinnakers,
As the entangled, screeching mainsheet clears   35
The blocks: off Madaket, where lubbers lash
The heavy surf and throw their long lead squids
For blue-fish? Sea-gulls blink their heavy lids
Seaward. The winds' wings beat upon the stones,
Cousin, and scream for you and the caws rush   40
At the sea's throat and wring it in the slush
Of this old Quaker graveyard where the bones
Cry out in the long night for the hurt beast
Bobbing by Ahab's whaleboats in the East.

III

All you recovered from Poseidon died   45
With you, my cousin, and the harrowed brine
Is fruitless on the blue beard of the god,
Stretching beyond us to the castles in Spain,
Nantucket's westward haven. To Cape Cod
Guns, cradled on the tide,   50
Blast the eelgrass about a waterclock
Of bilge and backwash, roil the salt and sand
Lashing earth's scaffold, rock
Our warships in the hand
Of the great God, where time's contrition blues   55
Whatever it was these Quaker sailors lost
In the mad scramble of their lives. They died
When time was open-eyed,
Wooden and childish; only bones abide
There, in the nowhere, where their boats were tossed   60
Sky-high, where mariners had fabled news
Of IS, the whited monster. What it cost
Them is their secret. In the sperm-whale's slick
I see the Quakers drown and hear their cry:
"If God himself had not been on our side,   65
If God himself had not been on our side,
When the Atlantic rose against us, why,
Then it had swallowed us up quick."

IV

This is the end of the whaleroad and the whale
Who spewed Nantucket bones on the thrashed swell   70
And stirred the troubled waters to whirlpools

To send the Pequod packing off to hell:
This is the end of them, three-quarters fools,
Snatching at straws to sail
Seaward and seaward on the turntail whale, 75
Spouting out blood and water as it rolls,
Sick as a dog to these Atlantic shoals:
Clamavimus, O depths. Let the sea-gulls wail

For water, for the deep where the high tide
Mutters to its hurt self, mutters and ebbs. 80
Waves wallow in their wash, go out and out,
Leave only the death-rattle of the crabs,
The beach increasing, its enormous snout
Sucking the ocean's side.
This is the end of running on the waves; 85
We are poured out like water. Who will dance
The mast-lashed master of Leviathans
Up from this field of Quakers in their unstoned graves?

     V

When the whale's viscera go and the roll
Of its corruption overruns this world 90
Beyond tree-swept Nantucket and Wood's Hole
And Martha's Vineyard, Sailor, will your sword
Whistle and fall and sink into the fat?
In the great ash-pit of Jehoshaphat
The bones cry for the blood of the white whale, 95
The fat flukes arch and whack about its ears,
The death-lance churns into the sanctuary, tears
The gun-blue swingle, heaving like a flail,
And hacks the coiling life out: it works and drags
And rips the sperm-whale's midriff into rags, 100
Gobbets of blubber spill to wind and weather,
Sailor, and gulls go round the stoven timbers
Where the morning stars sing out together
And thunder shakes the white surf and dismembers
The red flag hammered in the mast-head. Hide, 105
Our steel, Jonas Messias, in Thy side.

    VI

    OUR LADY OF WALSINGHAM

There once the penitents took off their shoes
And then walked barefoot the remaining mile;
And the small trees, a stream and hedgerows file
Slowly along the munching English lane, 110
Like cows to the old shrine, until you lose
Track of your dragging pain.

The stream flows down under the druid tree,
Shiloah's whirlpools gurgle and make glad
The castle of God. Sailor, you were glad   115
And whistled Sion by that stream. But see:

Our Lady, too small for her canopy,
Sits near the altar. There's no comeliness
At all or charm in that expressionless
Face with its heavy eyelids. As before,   120
This face, for centuries a memory,
Non est species, neque decor,
Expressionless, expresses God: it goes
Past castled Sion. She knows what God knows,
Not Calvary's Cross nor crib at Bethlehem   125
Now, and the world shall come to Walsingham.

VII

The empty winds are creaking and the oak
Splatters and splatters on the cenotaph,
The boughs are trembling and a gaff
Bobs on the untimely stroke   130
Of the greased wash exploding on a shoal-bell
In the old mouth of the Atlantic. It's well;
Atlantic, you are fouled with the blue sailors,
Sea-monsters, upward angel, downward fish:
Unmarried and corroding, spare of flesh   135
Mart once of supercilious, wing'd clippers,
Atlantic, where your bell-trap guts its spoil
You could cut the brackish winds with a knife
Here in Nantucket, and cast up the time
When the Lord God formed man from the sea's slime   140
And breathed into his face the breath of life,
And blue-lung'd combers lumbered to the kill.
The Lord survives the rainbow of His will.

MR. EDWARDS AND THE SPIDER

I saw the spiders marching through the air,
Swimming from tree to tree that mildewed day
    In latter August when the hay
    Came creaking to the barn. But where
        The wind is westerly,   5
Where gnarled November makes the spiders fly
Into the apparitions of the sky,
They purpose nothing but their ease and die
Urgently beating east to sunrise and the sea;

What are we in the hands of the great God?   10
It was in vain you set up thorn and briar
   In battle array against the fire
   And treason crackling in your blood;
     For the wild thorns grow tame
And will do nothing to oppose the flame;   15
Your lacerations tell the losing game
You play against a sickness past your cure.
How will the hands be strong? How will the heart endure?

A very little thing, a little worm,
Or hourglass-blazoned spider, it is said,   20
   Can kill a tiger. Will the dead
   Hold up his mirror and affirm
     To the four winds the smell
And flash of his authority? It's well
If God who holds you to the pit of hell,   25
Much as one holds a spider, will destroy,
Baffle and dissipate your soul. As a small boy

On Windsor Marsh, I saw the spider die
When thrown into the bowels of fierce fire:
   There's no long struggle, no desire   30
   To get up on its feet and fly—
     It stretches out its feet
And dies. This is the sinner's last retreat;
Yes, and no strength exerted on the heat
Then sinews the abolished will, when sick   35
And full of burning, it will whistle on a brick.

But who can plumb the sinking of that soul?
Josiah Hawley, picture yourself cast
   Into a brick-kiln where the blast
   Fans your quick vitals to a coal—
     If measured by a glass,   40
How long would it seem burning! Let there pass
A minute, ten, ten trillion; but the blaze
Is infinite, eternal: this is death,
To die and know it. This is the Black Widow, death.   45

THE FAT MAN IN THE MIRROR
(*After Werfel*)

What's filling up the mirror? O, it is not I;
Hair-belly like a beaver's house? An old dog's eye?

The forenoon was blue
In the mad King's zoo
Nurse was swinging me so high, so high!   5

The bullies wrestled on the royal bowling green;
Hammers and sickles on their hoods of black sateen . . .
        Sulking on my swing
        The tobacco King
Sliced apples with a pen-knife for the Queen.   10

This *I*, who used to mouse about the parafined preserves,
And jammed a finger in the coffee-grinder, serves
        Time before the mirror.
        But this pursey terror . . .
Nurse, it is a person. *It is nerves.*   15

Where's the Queen-Mother waltzing like a top to staunch
The blood of Lewis, King of Faerie? Hip and haunch
        Lard the royal grotto;
        Straddling Lewis' motto,
Time, the Turk, its sickle on its paunch.   20

Nurse, Nurse, it rises on me . . . O, it starts to roll,
My apples, O, are ashes in the meerschaum bowl . . .
        If you'd only come,
        If you'd only come,
Darling, if . . . The apples that I stole,   25

While Nurse and I were swinging in the Old One's eye . . .
Only a fat man with his beaver on his eye,
        Only a fat man,
        Only a fat man
Bursts the mirror. O, it is not I!   30

JAMES DICKEY

1923-

THE FIEND

He has only to pass by a tree   moodily walking   head down
A worried accountant   not with it   and he is swarming
He is gliding up the underside light of leaves   upfloating
In a seersucker suit   passing window after window of her building.
He finds her at last, chewing gum   talking on the telephone.   5
The wind sways him softly   comfortably sighing   she must bathe
Or sleep.   She gets up, and he follows her along the branch
Into another room.   She stands there for a moment   and the teddy
    bear
On the bed feels its guts spin as she takes it by the leg and tosses
It off.   She touches one button at her throat, and rigor mortis   10
Slithers into his pockets, making everything there—keys, pen
And secret love—stand up.   He brings from those depths the knife
And flicks it open   it glints on the moon one time   carries
Through the dead walls   making a wormy static on the TV screen.
He parts the swarm of gnats that live excitedly at this perilous level   15
Parts the rarefied light high windows give out into inhabited trees
Opens his lower body to the moon.   This night the apartments are
    sinking

To ground level   burying their sleepers in the soil   burying all floors
But the one where a sullen shopgirl gets ready to take a shower,
Her hair in rigid curlers, and the rest.   When she gives up   20
Her aqua terry-cloth robe the wind quits in mid-tree   the birds
Freeze to their perches round his head   a purely human light
Comes out of a one-man oak   around her an energy field   she
    stands
Rooted   not turning to anything else   then begins to move like a
    saint
Her stressed nipples rising like things about to crawl off her   as he
    gets   25
A hold on himself.   With that clasp she changes   senses   some-
    thing

Some breath through the fragile walls   some all-seeing eye
Of God   some touch that enfolds her body   some hand come up
    out of roots

That carries her as she moves   swaying   at this rare height. She wraps
The curtain around her and streams.   The room fades.   Then coming
Forth magnificently   the window blurred from within   she moves in a cloud
Chamber   the tree in the oak currents sailing   in clear air keep-
      ing pace
With her white breathless closet—he sees her mistily part her lips
As if singing to him   come up from river-fog   almost hears her
      as if
She sang alone in a cloud   its warmed light streaming into his
      branches
Out through the gauze glass of the window.   She takes off her bath-
      ing cap
The tree with him ascending   himself and the birds all moving
In darkness together   sleep crumbling the bark in their claws.
By this time he holds in his awkward, subtle limbs the limbs

Of a hundred understanding trees.   He has learned what a plant is
      like
When it moves near a human habitation   moving closer the later it
      is
Unfurling its leaves near bedrooms   still keeping its wilderness life
Twigs covering his body with only one way out   for his eyes into
      inner light
Of a chosen window   living with them night after night   watch-
      ing
Watching with them at times their favorite TV shows   learning—
Though now and then he hears a faint sound: gunshot, bombing,
Building-fall—how to read lips: the lips of laconic cowboys
Bank robbers   old and young doctors tense-faced   gesturing savagely
In wards and corridors   like reading the lips of the dead

The lips of men interrupting the program at the wrong time
To sell you a good used car on the Night Owl Show   men silently
      reporting
The news out the window.   But the living as well, three-dimensioned,
Silent as the small gray dead, must sleep at last   must save their lives
By taking off their clothes. It is his beholding that saves them:
God help the dweller in windowless basements   the one obsessed
With drawing curtains this night. At three o'clock in the morning
He descends   a medium-sized shadow   while that one sleeps and
      turns
In her high bed in loss   as he goes limb by limb   quietly down
The trunk with one lighted side. Ground upon which he could not
      explain

30

35

40

45

50

55

His presence he walks with toes uncurled from branches, his bird-
    movements   60
Dying hard. At the sidewalk he changes   gains weight   a solid
    citizen

Once more.   At apartments there is less danger from dogs, but he has
For those a super-quiet hand   a hand to calm sparrows and rivers,
And watchdogs in half-tended bushes lie with him watching their
    women
Undress   the dog's honest eyes and the man's the same pure beast's   65
Comprehending the same essentials. Not one of these beheld would
    ever give
Him a second look   but he gives them all a first look that goes
On and on   conferring immortality while it lasts   while the sub-
    urb's leaves
Hold still enough   while whatever dog he has with him holds its
    breath
Yet seems to thick-pant   impatient as he with the indifferent men   70
Drifting in and out of the rooms   or staying on, too tired to move
Reading the sports page   dozing   plainly unworthy   for what
    women want
Dwells in bushes and trees: what they want is to look outward,

To look with the light streaming into the April limbs   to stand
    straighter
While their husbands' lips dry out   feeling that something is there   75
That could dwell in no earthly house: that in poplar trees or beneath
The warped roundabout of the clothesline   in the sordid disorder
Of communal backyards   some being is there in the shrubs
Sitting comfortably on a child's striped rubber ball filled with rainwater
Muffling his glasses with a small studious hand against a sudden   80
Flash of houselight from within   or flash from himself   a needle's
    eye
Uncontrollable   blaze of uncompromised being. Ah, the lingerie
Hung in the bathroom! The domestic motions of single girls living to-
    gether
A plump girl girding her loins against her moon-summoned blood:
In that moon he stands   the only male lit by it, covered with leaf-
    shapes.   85
He coughs, and the smallest root responds   and in his lust he is set
By the wind in motion. That movement can restore the green eyes
Of middle age   looking   renewed   through the qualified light
Not quite reaching him where he stands again on the ususal branch
Of his oldest love   his tie not loosened   a plastic shield   90
In his breast pocket full of pencils and ballpoint pens given him b
    salesmen
His hat correctly placed to shade his eyes   a natural gambler's ti

And in summer wears an eyeshade   a straw hat Caribbean style.
In some guise or other he is near them when they are weeping without
    sound
When the teen-age son has quit school   when the girl has broken
    up
With the basketball star   when the banker walks out on his wife.   95
He sees mothers counsel desperately with pulsing girls face down
On beds full of overstuffed beasts   sees men dress as women
In ante-bellum costumes with bonnets   sees doctors come, looking
    oddly
Like himself   though inside the houses   worming a medical arm   100
Up under the cringing covers   sees children put angrily to bed
Sees one told an invisible fairy story   with lips moving silently as
    his
Are also moving   the book's few pages bright. It will take years
But at last he will shed his leaves   burn his roots   give up
Invisibility   will step out   will make himself known to the one   105
He cannot see loosen her blouse   take off luxuriously   with lips
Compressed against her mouth-stain   her dress   her stockings
Her magic underwear.   To that one he will come   up frustrated
    pines
Down alleys   through window blinds   blind windows   kitchen
    doors
On summer evenings. It will be something small that sets him off: 110
Perhaps a pair of lace pants on a clothesline   gradually losing
Water to the sun   filling out in the warm light with a well-rounded
Feminine wind as he watches   having spent so many sleepless nights
Because of her   because of her hand on a shade always coming
    down
In his face   not leaving even a shadow stripped naked upon the
    brown paper   115
Waiting for her now in a green outdated car with a final declaration
Of love   pretending to read   and when she comes and takes down
Her pants, he will casually follow her in   like a door-to-door sales-
    man
The godlike movement of trees stiffening with him   the light
Of a hundred favored windows   gone wrong somewhere in his
    glasses   120
Where his knocked-off panama hat was   in his painfully vanishing
    hair.

ALLEN GINSBERG

1926–

A SUPERMARKET IN CALIFORNIA

What thoughts I have of you tonight, Walt Whitman, for I walked down the sidestreets under the trees with a headache self-conscious looking at the full moon.

In my hungry fatigue, and shopping for images, I went into the neon fruit supermarket, dreaming of your enumerations!

What peaches and what penumbras! Whole families shopping at night! Aisles full of husbands! Wives in the avocados, babies in the tomatoes!—and you, Garcia Lorca, what were you doing down by the watermelons?

I saw you, Walt Whitman, childless, lonely old grubber, poking among the meats in the refrigerator and eyeing the grocery boys.

I heard you asking questions of each: Who killed the pork chops? What price bananas? Are you my Angel?   5

I wandered in and out of the brilliant stacks of cans following you, and followed in my imagination by the store detective.

We strode down the open corridors together in our solitary fancy tasting artichokes, possessing every frozen delicacy, and never passing the cashier.

Where are we going, Walt Whitman? The doors close in an hour. Which way does your beard point tonight?

(I touch your book and dream of our odyssey in the supermarket and feel absurd.)

Will we walk all night through solitary streets? The trees add shade to shade, lights out in the houses, we'll both be lonely.   10

Will we stroll dreaming of the lost America of love past blue automobiles in driveways, home to our silent cottage?

Ah, dear father, graybeard, lonely old courage-teacher, what America did you have when Charon quit poling his ferry and you got out on a smoking bank and stood watching the boat disappear on the black waters of Lethe?

TO AUNT ROSE

Aunt Rose—now,—might I see you
with your thin face and buck tooth smile and pain
            of rheumatism—and a long black heavy shoe
            for your bony left leg

limping down the long hall in Newark on the running carpet 5
    past the black grand piano
      in the day room
        where the parties were
  and I sang Spanish loyalist songs
    in a high squeaky voice 10
      (hysterical) the committee listening
    while you limped around the room
      collected the money—
Aunt Honey, Uncle Sam, a stranger with a cloth arm
    in his pocket 15
      and huge young bald head
        of Abraham Lincoln Brigade

—your long sad face
    your tears of sexual frustration
      (what smothered sobs and bony hips 20
        under the pillows of Osborne Terrace)
—the time I stood on the toilet seat naked
    and you powdered my thighs with Calomine
      against the poison ivy—my tender
        and shamed first black curled hairs 25
what were you thinking in secret heart then
    knowing me a man already—
and I an ignorant girl of family silence on the thin pedestal
    of my legs in the bathroom—Museum of Newark.
      Aunt Rose 30
Hitler is dead, Hitler is in Eternity; Hitler is with
    Tamburlane and Emily Brontë

Though I see you walking still, a ghost on Osborne Terrace
    down the long dark hall to the front door
      limping a little with a pinched smile 35
      in what must have been a silken
        flower dress
  welcoming my father, the Poet, on his visit to Newark
    —see you arriving in the living room
      dancing on your crippled leg 40
    and clapping hands his book
      had been accepted by Liveright

Hitler is dead and Liveright's gone out of business
The Attic of the Past and *Everlasting Minute* are out of print
    Uncle Harry sold his last silk stocking 45
  Claire quit interpretive dancing school
    Buba sits a wrinkled monument in Old
      Ladies Home blinking at new babies

last time I saw you was the hospital
  pale skull protruding under ashen skin
   blue veined unconscious girl
    in an oxygen tent
  the war in Spain has ended long ago
    Aunt Rose

INDEX